E M Delafield, Collection novels
The Philistine: A Story

The War-Workers

Consequences

The Diary of a Provincial Lady

The Provincial Lady Goes Further

The Provincial Lady in America

The Provincial Lady in Russia
The Provincial Lady in Wartime

Edmée Elizabeth Monica Dashwood, (1890 –1943), commonly known as E. M. Delafield, was a prolific English author. She is best known for her largely autobiographical Diary of a Provincial Lady, which took the form of a journal of the life of an upper-middle class Englishwoman living mostly in a Devon village of the 1930s. In sequels, the Provincial Lady buys a flat in London, travels to America, attempts to find war-work during the Phoney War, and tours the Soviet Union.

In this book:

The Philistine: A Story

He was rather a stolid little boy, but they did their very best with him.

He had, of course, exactly the same treats as the other children, the same pleasures, the same privileges. His toys and presents were better than theirs, if anything, because his aunt, in her heart of hearts, knew him to be less attractive than her own Cynthia and Jeremy and Diana.

For one thing, Colin wasn't as good-looking as they were, and for another, he was less intelligent. Cynthia, at nine years old, had a vivid, original mind, and the few people—but they were people who really knew—to whom Lady Verulam showed her little poems had seen great promise in them.

Jeremy, a year younger, had thick, tight curls of brown hair all over his head, beautiful, long-lashed brown eyes, and an adorable smile. His manners were perfect. He said things—innocent, naive, irresistible things—about God, and the fairies, and how much he loved his mother.

Lady Verulam's youngest girl, Diana, was precociously intelligent too, with a delightfully extensive and grown-up vocabulary at five years old. She had straight, square-cut bobbed brown hair like Cynthia, but she was lovelier than either of the others, and her eyes were a pure, deep blue, fringed with long, curled black lashes.

All Lady Verulam's artist friends wanted to paint Diana, but only Sir Frederick Lorton, the best known portrait-painter in England, was allowed to do so. The portrait was exhibited at the Royal Academy.

Colin was the only child of Lady Verulam's widowed brother-in-law, and he had been sent home to her from India when his mother died. He had been five years old then, and now he was eight.

He was a dear little boy, and Lady Verulam felt remorsefully that he might have been a *darling* little boy if it hadn't been that Cynthia and Jeremy and Diana unconsciously set such a very high standard of charm and intelligence. Intelligence counted for so very much, in that political-artistic section of society in which the Verulams lived. Most children of wealthy parents could be made tolerably pretty, after all, and if they weren't born with brains and personality they stood little chance of individual distinction.

Not that Colin hadn't got personality.

Lady Verulam, who was President of the Cult of the Children Society, and had written a little book about child-psychology, had studied Colin on his own merits, as it were. And she quite recognized that he had character, and even imagination, of a sort, although when the children were all taken to see "Peter Pan" and told to clap their hands if they believed in fairies, he was the only one of Lady Verulam's large party who didn't clap.

"But I *don't* believe in them, really," said Colin, rather pale.

"But Tinker-Bell!" protested Jeremy, "She'd have died if we hadn't clapped!"

"And we do believe in fairies," said Cynthia firmly.

"Then it was all right for you to clap," said Colin. "There were enough of you without me."

But afterwards he was very silent for a long while and looked worried.

Lady Verulam saw that and she changed her seat in one of the intervals and came beside him.

"Do you like it, darling?"

"Oh, yes," he said, unusually emphatic. But his face hadn't grown scarlet with excitement, like little Diana's, and he wasn't delightfully, stammeringly enthusiastic, like Jeremy. Presently he asked Lady Verulam in rather a troubled way:

"I wasn't unkind or naughty, was I, not to clap for Tinker Bell?"

"Not at all," she was obliged to answer. "The children were only asked to clap if they believed in fairies."

"I don't really believe in them," Colin said apologetically. "Do you, Aunt Doreen?"

"Shall I tell you a secret?" she answered, bending her charming, smiling face down to his. "I like to *pretend* that I believe in fairies, little Colin."

Anyone of the others would have responded to her whimsical fancy—they'd have understood. But Colin only looked up at her with solemn gray eyes staring rather stupidly out of a puzzled face.

"Do you?" was all he said.

"Oh, belovedest, isn't it marvelous!" said Cynthia, her eyes shining and dancing with sheer rapture.

Well, Colin hadn't got the same capacity for enjoyment, that was all. And even if he'd had it, he wouldn't have been able to express it in words.

He was an *ordinary* child.

"He'll never suffer as much as I'm afraid my darlings will, because he'll never feel as much," said Lady Verulam to the French nursery governess, who had so many certificates of her training as a teacher, and as a student of psychology, and as a hospital nurse, that she was as expensive as a finishing-governess.

"Probably not, Lady Verulam. But I think they do one another good. Cynthia's and Jeremy's enthusiastic ways will help Colin to be less stolid in time. And in one way, of course, it's a relief that he's not as excitable as they are."

The head-nurse said the same.

Diana before a party or a pantomime was positively ill with excitement sometimes. They never dared to tell her of anything until just before it was going to happen.

But Colin never looked forward to things like that. He lived in the present.

"Such a relief," said Lady Verulam rather wistfully. She couldn't help wondering sometimes what her brother-in-law, Vivian, would think of his only child, when he came home...But Colin's mother, whom she had known well as a girl, had been rather stolid, too.

Every day the children went to play in Kensington Gardens. The little procession came out at the front door of the house in Lowndes Square, and Lady Verulam, who adored her children, watched them from the window of the dining room where she was having breakfast after her ride in the Park.

First the under-nurse and the footman, carefully lifting the smart white perambulator down the steps, then Nurse, in stiff white piqué, carrying the rose-colored silk bundle that was the four-months-old baby, and depositing him carefully among his lacey shawls and pillows, under the silk-fringed summer awning of the pram. Then Diana, adorable in a tiny, skimpy frock of palest lemon color, with lemon-colored streamers falling from her shade hat and sandals on her beautiful little slim brown feet. She was carrying a ridiculous little doll's parasol and walking by herself, just as she always did. There was a certain dainty pride about Diana that never allowed her to accept the nurse's hand. She walked by the side of the pram, erect and exquisite.

After the nursery party, Mademoiselle and the elder children came down the steps. In the gardens, they would all coalesce, but the nursery party always started first.

Lady Verulam, peeping out between the window-boxes of scarlet geraniums and white daisies and the edge of the red-striped sun blind, watched them.

Mademoiselle was neat, efficient, French-looking—from the top of her shiny black straw hat, tipped forward over her black hair, to the black patent-leather belt placed very low down on her short-sleeved black-and-white check frock, and the pointed tips of her buttoned black boots. She was drawing on black kid gloves, that came half-way up her arms.

One on each side of her, were the two little boys. They were dressed alike, in white silk shirts and silk ties, and dark knickerbockers. Neither wore a cap, and Jeremy's thick curls looked burnished in the strong July sunlight. People always turned to look at him and at those wonderful curls.

Colin's hair was quite straight, and it suited him best to have it cut very short. It was of no particular color. Both little boys held themselves very upright, but while Colin was stocky and rather short, Jeremy was tall and slim and beautifully made, like a little statue.

Then Cynthia came out of the house, quick and slender and radiating vitality in every graceful gesture. Her frock and hat were the replica of little Diana's, but instead of the minute, absurd parasol, some heavenly instinct had caused her to take from the big glass bowl in the hall a handful of great mauve sweet peas that looked like butterflies against the pale, soft folds of her frock.

4

Cynthia's strong, instinctive sense of beauty was a joy to her mother.

She seemed to dance, rather than walk, along the hot pavement, her long, slim brown legs bare to the sun. From the little vivid, glancing gesture of her hands and head, Lady Verulam knew that she was talking. She could even guess what Cynthia was talking about—the party.

They were giving a party the next day on Colin's birthday, just before going down into the country. It was, actually, three years since the Verulams had given a children's party. One thing and another had prevented it.

This was called Colin's party but, as usual, the other children were far more excited about it than he was.

Lady Verulam herself was a tiny bit excited about it because for the first time Royalty—very young Royalty—was to be her guest.

She wanted the party to be a great success.

Smiling, she turned away from the window.

Cynthia's mother had been quite right. The children were talking about the party.

"I'm looking forward to it more than I've ever looked forward to anything in all my life," said Jeremy solemnly. "I think if anything happened to prevent it now I'd die."

"Oh, no, you wouldn't," said Cynthia scornfully. "Besides, nothing *could* happen to prevent it."

They knew little of disappointments, any of them. They were not allowed to experience disappointments if their mother could possibly prevent it because they were such terribly highly strung children.

"Mademoiselle, may Diana be told about the party yet?"

"She may be told, but she isn't to know which day it is till the last minute," said Mademoiselle, who knew very well that it would be impossible to keep sharp little Diana from the infectious excitement and sense of preparation that had already begun to pervade the house.

So they were able to talk about the party freely when they joined Diana and the nurses.

Cynthia did not want to talk about anything else, and the others always followed her lead. Except sometimes Colin, who was what Nurse called "independent."

He was independent to-day, and when he grew tired of hearing Cynthia and Jeremy discuss what games they would play at the party, and Diana chatter about her new frock with the roses on it, he got up and went away and bounced his ball on the Broad Walk.

He was pleased about the party, and Aunt Doreen had allowed him to choose what the entertainment should be, and he had chosen a conjuror, and she had said that *perhaps* he would have a cable from Daddy, like last year, for his birthday—but Colin didn't feel that he could think, and talk, and plan about nothing but the party, like the others.

Mademoiselle often said that he had no imagination, and Colin felt sure that she was right. He wasn't certain that he even wanted to have an imagination, much. He knew that he was stupid, compared with Jeremy and Cynthia, but at least he didn't have crying fits—like a girl—as Jeremy occasionally had, and he didn't stammer from pure eagerness as Cynthia did when she got excited.

He did hope, very much, that there might be a cable from Daddy on his birthday, because that would be something of his very own. No one would be able to say that the others cared more than he did, because it wouldn't have anything at all to do with the others.

Feeling rather mean but not able to help it, Colin secretly wished that the others mightn't know anything at all about his cable if it did come. Then they couldn't exclaim and be excited and say things and make Colin feel—and look—stupider than ever.

On the way home he was very silent, trying to think of a plan by which he could prevent the other children from seeing his cable. Perhaps they'd be so busy getting ready for the party that they wouldn't remember about it.

When the next day came it really seemed as though it might be so.

The children flew up and down stairs, even down into the kitchen where the good-natured chef showed them the cakes, and the jellies and the pink and white creams, and dishes of colored sweets, and an amusing log made out of of chocolate with chopped-up green stuff all over it and cream inside it.

They ran into the dining room, too, and saw the long, decorated table and the rows of little gilt chairs.

"There are other chairs in the drawing-room—millions more of them, for the conjuror," said Diana.

"Let's go up there."

"Let's," said Cynthia and Jeremy.

They dashed off.

Colin was just going to follow when he looked out of the window. He had been looking out of the window at intervals all day long.

But this time a telegraph boy really was crossing the square and glancing up at the numbers. It must, surely, be Daddy's cable, and he could take it himself and open it and there'd be nobody there to say that he didn't seem to care half as much as Master Jeremy, not if it *were* his own father...

Colin, for once moving quickly, ran out to the hall and opened the front door before the boy could ring the bell.

"Is it a foreign telegram—a cable?" he asked anxiously.

"Yes, addressed Verulam."

"Then it's mine," said Colin with decision. "There isn't any answer."

He had often heard this said and felt sure it was right.

The telegraph boy, whistling, went away.

Colin retreated to the linen cupboard on the schoolroom landing which was large and light, and to which people seldom came, and sat down on the floor to decipher his birthday cable.

Regret inform you Major Vivian Verulam dangerously ill cholera will cable progress.

Colin's face slowly became pink and then the color ebbed away again and left him rather white. He sat on the floor of the linen cupboard for a long while, not moving.

If Aunt Doreen knew about the cable, the party would have to be stopped, surely. And Diana would cry herself ill, and everybody would be in a dreadful state, and what would happen to all those beautiful cakes? Probably they would be vexed with him, too, for having opened the telegram.

Colin's mind, his slowly moving, tenacious mind, had not yet begun to work on the exact meaning of "dangerously ill." For days he had heard of nothing but the party, and the party had become the alpha and omega of existence.

It was impossible that it should be stopped. "If no one knows but me," thought Colin, "it'll be all right."

He had a horrible feeling that it would be naughty to say nothing about the cable, and yet he felt that they would all blame him if he told about it and stopped the party. Nothing mattered, really, except the party. They had thought he didn't understand what a great event it was because he couldn't get excited like the others, but at least he could see how very important they all thought it.

Presently he stuffed the cable into the pocket of his breeches, rose slowly and carefully to his feet, and went into the schoolroom again.

The brilliant, successful party was over, the gilt chairs were stacked together, seat upon seat, ready to be taken away again, and the children—each one with a beautiful present—had all long since gone home.

Cynthia and Jeremy and Colin and Diana had been put to bed. Jeremy had said, "Thank you, you darling, beautiful Mummie, for such a lovely, *glittering* party."

His choice of words was always fantastic and charming.

Even Colin had hugged his aunt with unusual enthusiasm and said he'd never enjoyed any party so much.

"No wonder," said Mademoiselle to Nurse, with whom she was on friendly terms.

"That conjuror was good, wasn't he?" said Nurse. "The best in London, they say. I never saw anything like him, myself. Why, *I* couldn't have told how he got those toys into the box with the flags."

"If you please, Nurse," said the under-nurse, entering with her hands full of little garments, "I found this in Master Colin's pocket."

She put the crumpled telegram, in its torn envelope, into Nurse's hands.

Nurse put on her spectacles and read it and said, "What in the name of gracious—" and handed the telegram to Mademoiselle.

There was a knock at the door and the housemaid came in.

"If you please, Nurse, her Ladyship wishes to see you in the boudoir at once."

"Take this," said Mademoiselle, with presence of mind and gave back the telegram.

In the boudoir Lady Verulam sat with another telegram open in front of her. Her pretty face was pale and tearstained.

"Nurse, I'm afraid there's bad news from India. Master Colin—poor little boy—his father is very ill, I'm afraid. I don't quite understand, but we think—"

"I beg your pardon, my lady. Is it anything to do with this? Florence found it, opened like that, in the pocket of Master Colin's every-day pair of knickerbockers."

Lady Verulam read the cable, read it again, compared it with the one she held, and turned bewildered, almost frightened eyes upon the nurse.

"But this one must have come before the other one—the one I've got," she said. "Who opened it?"

"Master Colin must have done it, my lady. And never said a word—"

"He couldn't have understood."

"Is the news in the second telegram worse, my lady?"

"It says that Major Verulam is getting weaker and we must expect—" she chocked a little. "We didn't understand and Sir Frederick is telephoning now to Whitehall, to see if they can give us any further particulars. But I *can't* understand—"

She looked at the crumpled telegram again and again.

"This must have come hours ago—before the party. How *could* he have got hold of it?"

"The children were all over the place, my lady—up and down stairs, watching the men getting things ready. Master Colin might have got to the door and opened it just when the telegram was delivered."

"But it was addressed—oh, oh, poor little boy! It was only addressed to Verulam. He must have thought it was a cable for his birthday—I see—that's what happened—that's why he opened it."

"But, excuse me, my lady, why didn't he say anything to anybody? He's quite old enough to understand."

Nurse was respectfully indignant, but Lady Verulam was only tearful and unspeakably bewildered.

"I must go up to him—"

"I beg your pardon, my lady, he's asleep. They all are now, even Miss Diana, but Master Colin was asleep before any of them, though not being so excitable as the others."

"Then I can't wake him," said Lady Verulam irresolutely. "It would only upset him. And there may be news in the morning—one way or the other."

There was no more news in the morning, however, and Lady Verulam was obliged to send for Colin. She wasn't angry with him—even if his father hadn't been dying, it was against her principles to be angry with any child—but her gentleness met with very little response.

He didn't seem to understand that his father, whom he scarcely remembered, was very ill and might be going to die. His lack of imagination was absolute.

"But why didn't you bring the telegram to me, darling? I quite understand that you opened it by mistake, but you must have known it was important and that you ought to tell about it."

Colin began to cry.

She reasoned with him, and petted him, and even spoke severely to him, but he was sulky and frightened and would not say a word. At last, in despair, she sent him upstairs again.

Ten minutes later Cynthia came flying down to her mother's room, her lovely mop of hair disordered, her brilliant little face glowing. "Mummie, may I tell you what I think about Colin? Nurse doesn't understand—nor Mademoiselle, nor any of them—but I think I do."

"Tell me, precious," said Lady Verulam. She had great faith in the intuition of this sensitive, intelligent little daughter of hers.

Cynthia put her arms round her mother's neck and whispered earnestly.

"I think Colin opened the telegram about poor Uncle Vivian just before the party, and he did understand what it was, and he thought it would spoil the party and p'raps—p'raps put it off altogether, and that's why he wouldn't say anything. He didn't want all of us to be unhappy—he knew we were looking forward so to the party."

"My darling! What makes you think that?"

"It's what I'd have done," said Cynthia, her eyes shining. "I would, truly, Mummie, if my heart had been breaking—I'd have kept that dreadful telegram all to myself and let all the others enjoy the party and even have pretended that I was enjoying it too."

"My sweet—I believe you would. But if that was it, why didn't poor little Colin come to me as soon as the party was over?"

"Mummie, you know you were with the grown-ups who stayed after we'd gone to bed, and I'm sure he was waiting till you came to say good-night. And you never did."

"Nurse said you were all asleep—Colin must have gone quickly off to sleep, after all."

"But, Mummie," said Cynthia quickly, "he's very little, and one can't always keep awake, even if it's most important, and Colin especially, he's always such a sleepy head—"

"I know," said Lady Verulam.

She thought, although she did not say so, that Colin's insensitiveness had always been rather remarkable, and that where Cynthia might, as she had just said, have felt her heart to be "breaking," Colin was quite capable of falling asleep in mere reaction from an unwonted emotional strain.

She was touched at Cynthia's generous understanding and inclined to accept her interpretation.

"Poor little Colin!" she said softly. "It was brave and unselfish of him to want everyone else to enjoy the party first...although it was a mistake, and I still don't understand why he couldn't explain to me this morning."

"Mummie, you know Colin never can explain anything," said Cynthia reproachfully.

That was perfectly true. How clever she was! Lady Verulam kissed Cynthia in silence. In her heart of hearts she couldn't help feeling that, dreadful though it was to have been entertaining on such a scale while her brother-in-law was dying, it would have been very, very difficult to know what to do if the bad news had reached her when it should have reached her, just as the preparations for the party were being completed.

"You do understand about Colin, don't you, Mummie? Because Mademoiselle isn't being a bit nice to him, and she says he has no heart and that he didn't show the telegram because he didn't want the party to be stopped, and then afterwards he was afraid to tell."

"I'll speak to her," said Lady Verulam. Mademoiselle was always inclined to be hard on Colin. She couldn't bear what she called his *phleqme britannique*. Lady Verulam did not for a moment believe her interpretation to be the true one. She would sooner trust to Cynthia's quick sympathies.

According to Cynthia, little Colin had really been rather heroic. He must have had a dreadful weight on his little mind, all through the festivities...

Tender-hearted Lady Verulam found the tears rising into her eyes at the thought of it. She felt as though she had always been unjust to Colin, who had so little imagination, and couldn't express himself with fire and poetry and clearness like her own children. And now perhaps she had alienated him by not understanding or appreciating his self-sacrifice, and he would be less willing than ever to talk to her.

Before she saw Colin again a third cable had arrived.

Major Vivian Verulam was not going to die. He had turned the corner.

The joy and relief of the good news pervaded the house, and even Mademoiselle kissed Colin—who rubbed his cheek vigorously after the salute—and said nothing more about his having no heart. But Lady Verulam, who, like her children, was highly strung, had worked herself up on Colin's behalf, and she told Mademoiselle and Nurse as well that they had all of them misunderstood Colin, and that there were unsuspected depths of bravery and unselfishness in his childish heart.

There came, gradually, to be a feeling throughout the big household in Lowndes Square that this was so. Colin might be less wonderful than were Cynthia and Jeremy and Diana, but he, too, had

had his moment—his exalted and inspired moment.

Three months later Major Verulam came home on sick leave.

He made friends with his son—an enduring friendship. They resembled each other in many ways, and he never seemed to expect or to desire from Colin enthusiasms and demonstrations that would have been equally alien to them both.

He was, indeed, the only person who ever heard Colin's own version of his behavior on the day of the party.

"You see, Daddy, I opened the telegram because I thought it was from you, for me on my birthday, like the year before, and when I saw it said you were ill I did think it would mean stopping the party, and that would have been dreadful."

"Were you so frightfully keen about the party?"

"It wasn't so much that, but there'd have been such a lot of fuss about it, and they—all the others—had been so excited—and everything was ready—men had come all on purpose to bring the little gold chairs, Daddy, and to arrange the flowers and things—It would have been so dreadful, to stop it all."

"I see what you mean. And certainly it wouldn't have done *me* any good, as far as that went. But why didn't you tell them afterwards, old man? Aunt Doreen wouldn't have been angry with you, would she?"

"Oh, no, she's never angry."

"Well, then—"

Colin colored faintly.

"You see, Daddy, I didn't know you as well then as I do now, did I? And the party was fun, and the conjuror such a very, very clever one."

He gazed up at his father with solemn, trustful eyes.

"I quite and completely forgot all about the telegram till I woke up next morning," said Colin.

The War-Workers

I

At the Hostel for Voluntary Workers, in Questerham, Miss Vivian, Director of the Midland Supply Depôt, was under discussion that evening.

Half a dozen people, all of whom had been working for Miss Vivian ever since ten o'clock that morning, as they had worked the day before and would work again the next day, sat in the Hostel sitting-room and talked about their work and about Miss Vivian.

No one ever talked anything but "shop," either in the office or at the Hostel.

"Didn't you think Miss Vivian looked awfully tired today?"

"No wonder, after Monday night. You know the train wasn't in till past ten o'clock. I think those troop-trains tire her more than anything."

"She doesn't have to cut cake and bread-and-butter and sandwiches for two hours before the train gets in, though. I've got the usual blister today," said an anaemic-looking girl of twenty, examining her forefinger.

There was a low scoffing laugh from her neighbour.

"Miss Vivian cutting bread-and-butter! She does quite enough without that, Henderson. She had the D.G.V.O. in there yesterday afternoon for ages. I thought he was *never* going. I stood outside her door for half an hour, I should think, absolutely hung up over the whole of my work, and I knew she was fearfully busy herself."

"It's all very well for you, Miss Delmege-you're her secretary and work in her room, but *we* can't get at her unless we're sent for. I simply didn't know what to do about those surgical supplies for the Town Hospital this morning, and Miss Vivian never sent for me till past eleven o'clock. It simply wasted half my morning."

"She didn't have a minute; the telephone was going the whole time," said Miss Delmege quickly. "But yesterday, you know, when the D.G.V.O. wouldn't go, I thought she was going to be late at the station for that troop-train, and things were fairly desperate, so what d'you suppose I did?"

"Dashed into her room and got your head snapped off?" some one suggested languidly. "I shall never forget one day last week when *I* didn't know which way to *turn*, we were so busy, and I went in without being sent for, and Miss Vivian—"

"Oh yes, I remember," said Miss Delmege rapidly. She was a tall girl with eyeglasses and a superior manner. She did not remember Miss Marsh's irruption into her chief's sanctum with any particular clearness, but she was anxious to finish her own anecdote. "But as *I* was telling you," she hurried on, affecting to be unaware that Miss Marsh and her neighbour were exchanging glances, "when I saw that it was getting later every minute, and the D.G.V.O. seemed rooted to the spot, I simply went straight downstairs and rang up Miss Vivian on the telephone. Miss Cox was on telephone duty, and she was absolutely horrified. She said, 'You *don't* mean to say you're going to ring up Miss Vivian,' she said; and I said, 'Yes, I am. Yes, I am,' I said, and I did it. Miss Cox simply couldn't get over it."

Miss Delmege paused to laugh in solitary enjoyment of her story.

"'Who's there?' Miss Vivian said-you know what she's like when she's in a hurry. 'It's Miss Delmege,' I said. 'I thought you might want to know that the train will be in at eight o'clock, Miss Vivian, and it's half-past seven now.' She just said 'Thank you,' and rang off; but she must have told the D.G.V.O., because he came downstairs two minutes later. And she simply flung on her hat and dashed down into the car and to the station."

"And, after all, the train wasn't in till past ten, so she might just as well have stayed to put her hat on straight," said Miss Henderson boldly. She had a reputation for being "downright" of which she was aware, and which she strenuously sought to maintain by occasionally making small oblique sallies at Miss Vivian's expense.

"I must say it was most awfully crooked. I noticed it myself," said a pretty little giggling girl whom the others always called Tony, because her surname was Anthony. "How killing," I thought; "there's Miss Vivian with her hat on quite crooked."

"Yes, wasn't it killing?"

"Simply killing. I thought the minute I saw her: How killing to see Miss Vivian with her hat on like that!"

"She looked perfectly killing hurrying down the platform," remarked Miss Marsh, with an air of originality. "She was carrying cigarettes for the men, and her hat got crookeder every minute. I was pining to tell her."

"Go on, Marshy! She'd have had your head off. Fancy Marsh stopping Miss Vivian in the middle of a troop-train to say her hat was on crooked!"

Every one laughed.

"I should think she'd be shot at dawn," suggested Tony. "That's the official penalty for making personal remarks to your C.O., I believe."

"You know," said Miss Delmege, in the tones whose refinement was always calculated to show up the unmodulated accents of her neighbours, "one day I absolutely did tell Miss Vivian when her hat was crooked. I said right out: 'Do excuse me, Miss Vivian, but your hat isn't quite straight.' She didn't mind a *bit*."

"I suppose she knows she always looks nice anyway," said Tony easily.

"I mean she didn't mind me telling her," explained Miss Delmege. "She's most awfully human, you know, really. That's what I like about Miss Vivian. She's so frightfully human."

"Yes, she *is* human," Miss Marsh agreed. "Awfully human."

Miss Delmege raised her eyebrows.

"Of course," she said, with quiet emphasis, "working in her room, as I do, I suppose I see quite another side of her—the *human* side, you know."

There was a silence. Nobody felt disposed to encourage Miss Vivian's secretary in her all-too-frequent recapitulations of the privileges which she enjoyed.

Presently another worker came in, looking inky and harassed.

"You're late tonight, Mrs. Potter, aren't you?" Tony asked her.

"Oh yes. It's those awful Belgians, you know. Wherever I put them, they're miserable, and write and ask to be taken away. There's a family now that I settled simply beautifully at Little Quester village only a month ago, and this afternoon the mother came in to say the air doesn't suit them at all—she has a consumptive son or something—and could they be moved to the seaside at once. So I told Miss Vivian, and she said I was to get them moved directly. At once—today, you know. Of course, it was perfectly absurd—they couldn't even get packed up—and I told her so; but she said, 'Oh, settle it all by telephone'—you know her way. 'But, Miss Vivian,' I said, 'really I don't see how it can be managed. I've got a most fearful amount of work,' I said. 'Well,' she said, 'if you can't get through it, Mrs. Potter, I must simply put some one else at the head of the department who *can*.' It's too bad, you know."

Mrs. Potter sank into the only unoccupied wicker arm-chair in the room, looking very much jaded indeed.

Tony said sympathetically:

"What a shame! Miss Vivian doesn't realize what an awful lot you do, I'm perfectly certain."

"Well, considering that every letter and every bit of work in the whole office passes through Miss Vivian's hands, that's absurd," said Miss Delmege sharply. "She knows exactly what each department has to do, but, of course, she's such a quick worker herself that she can't understand any one not being able to get through the same amount."

Mrs. Potter looked far from enchanted with the proffered explanation.

"It isn't that I can't get through the work," she said resentfully. "Of course I can get through the regular work all right. But I must say, I do think she's inconsiderate over these lightning touches of hers. What on earth was the sense of making those people move tonight, I should like to know?"

"Miss Vivian never will let the work get behindhand if she can help it," exclaimed Miss Marsh; and Miss Henderson at the same instant said, rather defiantly:

"Well, of course, Miss Vivian always puts the work before everything. She never spares herself, so I don't quite see why she should spare any of us."

"The fact is," said the small, cool voice of Miss Delmege, as usual contriving to filter through every other less refined sound, "she is extraordinarily tender-hearted. She can't bear to think any one is suffering when she could possibly help them; she'll simply go miles out of her way to do something for a wounded soldier or a Belgian refugee. I see that in her correspondence so much. You know—the letters she writes about quite little things, because some one or other wants her to. She'll take *endless* trouble."

"I know she's wonderful," said Mrs. Potter, looking remorseful.

She was a middle-aged woman with light wispy hair, always untidy, and wearing a permanent expression of fluster. She had only been at the Hostel a few weeks. "Isn't it nearly supper-time?" yawned Tony. "I want to go to bed."

"Tired, Tony?"

"Yes, awfully. I was on telephone duty last night, stamping the letters, and I didn't get off till nearly eleven."

"There must have been a lot of letters," said Miss Delmege, with the hint of scepticism which she always managed to infuse into her tones when speaking of other people's work.

"About a hundred and thirty odd, but they didn't come down till very late. Miss Vivian was still signing the last lot at ten o'clock."

"She must have been very late getting out to Plessing. It's all very well for us," remarked Miss Marsh instructively; "*we* finish work at about six or seven o'clock, and then just come across the road, and here we are. But poor Miss Vivian has about an hour's drive before she gets home at all."

"She's always at the office by ten every morning, too."

"She ought to have some one to help her," sighed Miss Delmege. "Of course, I'd do anything to take some of the work off her hands, and I think she knows it. I think she knows I'd do simply anything for her; but she really wants some one who could take her place when she has to be away, and sign the letters for her, and see people. That's what she really needs."

"Thank goodness, there's the supper bell," said Tony.

They trooped downstairs.

The house was the ordinary high, narrow building of a provincial town, and held an insufficiency of rooms for the number of people domiciled there. The girls slept three or four in a room; the Superintendent had a tiny bedroom, and a slightly larger sitting-room adjoining the large room on the ground floor where they congregated in the evenings and on Sundays, and the dining-room was in the basement.

Gas flared on to the white shining American-cloth covering the long table and on the wooden kitchen chairs. The windows were set high up in the walls, and gave a view of area railings and, at certain angles, of a piece of pavement.

One or two coloured lithographs hung on the walls.

There was a hideous sound of scraping as chairs were drawn back or pulled forwards over the uncarpeted boards.

"Sit next me, duck."

"All right. Come on, Tony; get the other side of Sprouts."

Miss Delmege, aloof and superior, received no invitation to place herself beside any one, and settled herself with genteel swishings of her skirt at the foot of the table.

The Superintendent sat at the head.

She was a small, delicate-looking Irish woman with an enthusiastic manner, who had married late in life, and been left a widow within two years of her marriage. She worked very hard, and it was her constant endeavour to maintain an atmosphere of perpetual brightness in the Hostel.

It was with this end in view that she invariably changed her blouse for a slightly cleaner one at suppertime, although all the girls were in uniform, and many of them still wearing a hat. But little Mrs. Bullivant always appeared in a rather pallid example of the dyer or cleaner's art, and said hopefully: "One of these days I must make a rule that all you girls dress for dinner. We shall find ourselves growing dreadfully uncivilized, I'm afraid, if we go on like this."

The Hostel liked Mrs. Bullivant, although she was a bad manager and could never keep a servant for long. She made no secret of the fact that she could not afford to be a voluntary worker.

Every Hostel in the district, and they were numerous owing to the recently-opened Munitions Factory near Questerham, had rapidly become, as it were, fish for Miss Vivian's net. Each and all were under her control, and the rivalry between the Questerham Hostel "for Miss Vivian's *own* workers" and those reserved for the munition-makers was an embittered one.

"What has every one been doing to-day?" Mrs. Bullivant asked cheerfully.

The inquiry was readily responded to.

The angle of Miss Vivian's hat, when she had gone down to meet the troop-train, was again the subject of comment, and Miss Delmege was again reminded of the story, which she told with quiet and undiminished enjoyment, of her erstwhile daring in approaching Miss Vivian upon the subject.

"Did you really?" said Mrs. Bullivant admiringly. "Of course, it's different for you, Miss Delmege, working in her room all day. You see so much more of her than any one else does."

Every one except the complacent Miss Delmege looked reproachfully at the little Superintendent. She was incapable of snubbing any one, but the Hostel thought her encouragement of Miss Delmege unnecessary in the extreme.

Mrs. Bullivant changed the conversation rather hurriedly.

"Who is on telephone duty tonight?" she inquired.

"I am, worse luck."

"Miss Plumtree? And your head is bad again, isn't it, dear?"

"Yes," said Miss Plumtree wearily.

She was a fair, round-faced girl of five or six and twenty who suffered from frequent sick headaches. She worked for longer hours than any one else, and had a reputation for "making muddles." It was popularly supposed that Miss Vivian "had a down on her," but the Hostel liked Miss Plumtree, and affectionately called her Greengage and Gooseberry-bush.

"Greengage got another headache?" Miss Marsh asked concernedly. "I can take your duty to-night, dear, quite well."

"Thanks awfully, Marsh; it's sweet of you, but I haven't got leave to change. You know last time, when Tony took duty for me, Miss Vivian asked why I wasn't there."

"I can say you're sick."

"Oh, I'm sure she wouldn't like it," said Miss Plumtree, looking nervous and undecided.

"I think you ought to be in bed, I must say," said Mrs. Bullivant uncertainly.

"She certainly doesn't look fit to sit at that awful telephone for two and a half hours; and there are heaps of letters to-night. I can answer for the Hospital Department, anyway," sighed Miss Henderson. "Marshy, you look pretty tired yourself. I can quite well take the telephone if you like. I'm not doing anything."

"I thought you were going to the cinema."

"I don't care. I can do that another night. I'm not a bit keen on pictures, really, and it's raining hard."

"Thanks most awfully, both of you," repeated Miss Plumtree, "but I really think I'd better go myself. You know what Miss Vivian is, if she thinks one's shirking, and I'm not at all in her good books at the moment, either. There was the most ghastly muddle about those returns last month, and I sent in the averages as wrong as they could be."

"That's nothing to do with your being unfit for telephone duty tonight," said Miss Delmege, with acid sweetness. "I think I can answer for it that Miss Vivian would be the first person to say you ought to let some one else take duty for you. I'd do it myself, only I really must get some letters written tonight. One never has a minute here. But I think I can answer for Miss Vivian."

In spite of the number of times that Miss Delmege expressed herself as ready to answer for Miss Vivian, no one had ever yet failed to be moved to exasperation by her pretensions.

"On the whole, Plumtree, you may be right not to risk it," said Miss Henderson freezingly, as she rose from the table.

"I'll manage all right," declared Miss Plumtree; but her round apple-blossom face was drawn with pain, and she stumbled up the dark stairs.

In the hall there was a hurried consultation between Miss Marsh and Miss Anthony.

"I say, Tony, old Gooseberry-bush isn't fit to stir. She ought to be tucked up in her bye-byes this minute. Shall I risk it, and go instead of her, leave or no leave?"

"I should think so, yes. What have things been like today?"

13

"Oh, fairly serene. I didn't see Miss Vivian this morning, myself, but nobody seems to have had their heads snapped off. There wasn't a fearful lot of work for her, either, because Miss Delmege came in quite early."

"Delmege makes me sick, the way she goes on! As though nobody else knew anything about Miss Vivian, and she was a sort of connecting-link between her and us. Didn't you hear her tonight? 'I think I can answer for Miss Vivian,'" mimicked Tony in an exaggerated falsetto. "I should jolly well like Miss Vivian to hear her one of these days. She'd appreciate being answered for like that by her secretary—I don't think!"

"I say, Marshy, can you keep a secret?"

"Rather!"

"Well, swear not to tell, and, mind, I'm speaking absolutely unofficially. I've no business to know it officially at all, because I only saw it on a telegram I sent for the Billeting Department. Miss Delmege is going to get her nose put out of joint with Miss V. Another secretary is coming."

"She's not! D'you mean Delmege has got the sack?"

"Oh, Lord, no! It's only somebody coming to help her, because there is so much work for one secretary. She's coming from Wales, and her name is Jones."

"I seem to have heard that name before."

They both giggled explosively; then made a simultaneous dash at the hall-door as Miss Plumtree, in hat and coat, came slowly out of the sitting-room.

"No, you don't, Plumtree! You're going straight up to bed, and I'll tell Miss Vivian you were ill. It'll be all right."

"You are a brick, Marsh."

"Nonsense! You'll do as much for me some day. Goodnight, dear."

Miss Marsh hurried out, and Miss Plumtree thankfully took the felt uniform hat off her aching head.

"Get into bed," directed Tony, "and take an aspirin."

"Haven't got one left, worse luck."

"I'll see if any one else has any. I believe Mrs. Potter has."

Tony hurried into the sitting-room. Mrs. Potter had no aspirin, but she hoisted herself out of her arm-chair and said she would go round to the chemist and get some.

She went out into the rain.

Tony borrowed a rubber hot-water bottle from Miss Henderson, and a kettle from somebody else, and went upstairs to boil some water, forgetting that she was tired and had meant to go to bed after supper.

Presently little Mrs. Bullivant came upstairs with a cup of tea and the aspirin, both of which she administered to the patient.

"You'll go to sleep after that, I expect," she said consolingly.

"I'll tell the girls to get into bed quietly," Tony whispered.

Miss Plumtree shared a room with Miss Delmege and Miss Henderson.

"I never do make any noise in the room that I am aware of," said Miss Delmege coldly; but she and her room-mate both crept upstairs soon after nine o'clock, lest their entrance later should awaken the sufferer, and they undressed with the gas turned as low as it would go, and in silence.

Padding softly in dressing-slippers to the bathroom later on, for the lukewarm water which was all that they could hope to get until the solitary gas-ring should have served the turn of numerous waiting kettles, they heard Miss Marsh returning from telephone duty, bolting the hall-door, and putting up the chain.

"You're back early," whispered Miss Henderson, coming halfway downstairs in her pink flannelette dressing-gown, her scanty fair hair screwed back into a tight plait.

"Wasn't much doing. Miss Vivian got off at half-past nine. Jolly good thing, too; she's been late every night this week."

"Was it all right about your taking duty?"

"Ab-solutely. Said she was glad Miss Plumtree had gone to bed, and asked if she had anything to take for her head."

"How awfully decent of her!"

"Wasn't it? It'll buck old Greengage up, too. She always thinks Miss Vivian has a down on her."
Miss Delmege leant over the banisters and said in a subdued but very complacent undertone:
"I thought Miss Vivian would be all right. I thought I could safely answer for her."

II

Plessing was also speaking of Miss Vivian that evening.

"Where is this to end, Miss Bruce? I ask you, where is it to end?" demanded Miss Vivian's mother.

Miss Bruce knew quite well that Lady Vivian was not asking her at all, in the sense of expecting to receive from her any suggestion of a term to that which in fact appeared to be interminable, so she only made a clicking sound of sympathy with her tongue and went on rapidly stamping postcards.

"I am not unpatriotic, though I do dislike Flagdays, and I was the first person to say that Char must go and do work somewhere—nurse in a hospital if she liked, or do censor's work at the War Office. Sir Piers said 'No' at first—you know he's old-fashioned in many ways—and then he said Char wasn't strong enough, and to a certain extent I agreed with him. But I put aside all that and absolutely encouraged her, as you know, to organize this Supply Depôt. But I must say, Miss Bruce, that I never expected the thing to grow to these dimensions. Of course, it may be a very splendid work—in fact, I'm sure it is, and every one says how proud I must be of such a wonderful daughter but *is* it all absolutely necessary?"

"Oh, Lady Vivian," said the secretary reproachfully. "Why, the very War Office itself knows the value of dear Charmian's work. They are always asking her to take on fresh branches."

"That's just what I am complaining of. Why should the Midland Supply Depôt do all these odd jobs? Hospital supplies are all very well, but when it comes to meeting all the troop-trains and supplying all the bandages, and being central Depôt for sphagnum moss, and all the rest of it—all I can say is, that it's beyond a joke."

Miss Bruce took instant advantage of her employer's infelicitous final *cliché* to remark austerely:

"Certainly one would never dream of looking upon it as a *joke*, Lady Vivian. I quite feel with you about the working so fearfully hard, and keeping these strange, irregular hours, but I'm convinced that it's perfectly unavoidable—perfectly unavoidable. Charmian owns herself that no one can possibly take her place at the Depôt, even for a day."

This striking testimony to the irreplacableness of her daughter appeared to leave Lady Vivian cold.

"I dare say," she said curtly. "Of course, she's got a gift for organization, and all she's done is perfectly marvellous, but I must say I wish she'd taken up nursing or something reasonable, like anybody else, when she could have had proper holidays and kept regular hours."

Miss Bruce gave the secretarial equivalent for laughing the suggestion to scorn.

"As though nursing wasn't something that *anyone* could do! Why, any ordinary girl can work in a hospital. But I should like to know what other woman could do Charmian's work. Why, if she left, the whole organization would break down in a week."

"Well," said the goaded Lady Vivian, "the war wouldn't go on any the longer if it did, I don't suppose—any more than it's going to end twenty-four hours sooner because Char has dinner at eleven o'clock every night and spends five pounds a day on postage stamps."

Miss Bruce looked hurt, as she went on applying halfpenny stamps to the postcards that formed an increasing mountain on the writing-table in front of her.

"I suppose you're working for her now?"

"I only wish I could do more," said the secretary fervently. "She gives me these odd jobs because I'm always imploring her to let me do some of the mechanical work that any one can manage, and spare her for other things. But, of course, no one can really do anything much to help her."

"I'm sorry to hear it, since she has a staff of thirty or forty people there. Pray, are they all being paid out of Red Cross funds for doing nothing at all?" inquired Lady Vivian satirically.

"Oh, of course they all do their bit. Routine work, as Charmian calls it. But she has to superintend everything—hold the whole thing together. She looks through every letter that leaves that office, and knows the workings of every single department, and they come and ask her about every little thing."

"Yes, they do. She enjoys that."

Lady Vivian's tone held nothing more than reflectiveness, but the little secretary reddened unbecomingly, and said in a strongly protesting voice:

"Of course, it's a very big responsibility, and she knows that it all rests on her."

"Well, well," said Lady Vivian soothingly. "No one is ever a prophet in his own country, and I suppose Char is no exception. Anyhow, she has a most devoted champion in you, Miss Bruce."

"It has nothing to do with any—any personal liking, Lady Vivian, I assure you," said the secretary, her voice trembling and her colour rising yet more. "I don't say it because it's her, but quite dispassionately. I hope that even if I knew nothing of Charmian's own personal attractiveness and—and kindness, I should still be able to see how wonderful her devotion and self-sacrifice are, and admire her extraordinary capacity for work. Speaking quite impersonally, you know."

Anything less impersonal than her secretary's impassioned utterances, it seemed to Lady Vivian, would have been hard to find, and she shrugged her shoulders very slightly.

"Well, Char certainly needs a champion, for she's making herself very unpopular in the county. All these people who ran their small organizations and war charities quite comfortably for the first six or eight months of the war naturally don't like the way everything has been snatched away and affiliated to this Central Depôt—"

"Official co-ordination is absolutely—"

"Yes, yes, I know; that's Char's *cri de bataille*. But there are ways and ways of doing things, and I must say that some of the things she's said and written, to perfectly well-meaning people who've been doing their best and giving endless time and trouble to the work, seem to me tactless to a degree."

"She says herself that anyone in her position is bound to give offence sometimes."

"Position fiddlesticks!" said Miss Vivian's parent briskly. "Why can't she behave like anybody else? She might be the War Office and the Admiralty rolled into one, to hear her talk sometimes. Of course, people who've known her ever since she was a little scrap in short petticoats aren't going to stand it. Why, she won't even be thirty till next month!—though, I must say, she might be sixty from the way she talks. But then she always was like that, from the time she was five years old. It worried poor Sir Piers dreadfully when he wanted to show her how to manage her hoop, and she insisted on arguing with him about the law of gravitation instead. I suppose I ought to have smacked her then."

Miss Bruce choked, but any protest at the thought of the obviously regretted opportunity lost by Lady Vivian for the perpetration of the suggested outrage remained unuttered.

The sharp sound of the telephone-bell cut across the air.

Miss Bruce attempted to rise, but was hampered by the paraphernalia of her clerical work, and Lady Vivian said:

"Sir Piers will answer it. He is in the hall, and you know he likes telephoning, because then he can think he isn't really getting as deaf as he sometimes thinks he is."

Miss Bruce, respecting this rather complicated reason, sat down again, and Lady Vivian remarked dispassionately:

"Of course it's Char, probably to say she can't come back to dinner. You know, I specially asked her to get back early tonight because John Trevellyan is dining with us. There! what did I tell you?"

They listened to the one-sided conversation.

"Sir Piers Vivian speaking. What's that? Oh, you'll put me through to Miss Vivian. Very well; I'll hold on. That you, my dear? Your mother and I are most anxious you should be back for dinner—Trevellyan is coming.... We'll put off dinner for half an hour if that would help you.... But, my dear, he'll be very much disappointed not to see you, and it really seems a pity, when the

16

poor chap is just back ... he'll be so disappointed.... Yes, yes, I see. I'm sure it's very good of you, but couldn't they manage without you just for once?... Very well, my dear, I'll tell him.... It's really very good of you, my poor dear child...."

Lady Vivian stamped her foot noiselessly as her husband's voice reached her; but when Sir Piers had put back the receiver and come slowly into the room, she greeted him with a smile.

"Was that Char? To say she couldn't be back in time for dinner tonight, I suppose?"

Quick-tempered, sharp-tongued woman as she was, Joanna Vivian's voice was always gentle in speaking to her white-haired husband, twenty years her senior.

"The poor child seems to think she can't be spared. Very good of her, but isn't she overdoing it just a little—eh, Joanna? Aren't they working her rather too hard?"

"It's mostly her own doing, Piers. She's head of this show, you know. I suppose that's why she thinks she can't leave it."

"The whole thing would go to pieces without her," thrust in the secretary, in the sudden falsetto with which she always impressed upon Sir Piers her recollection of his increasing deafness. "She supervises the whole organization, and if she's away there isn't any one to take her place."

"But they don't want to work after six o'clock," said the old man, looking puzzled. "Ten to six—that's office hours. She oughtn't to want to be there after the place is shut up."

"Oh, there's no 'close time' for the Midland Supply Depôt," said Miss Bruce, looking superior. "They may have orders to meet a train at any hour of the day or night, and the telephone often goes on ringing till eleven or twelve o'clock, I believe. And Charmian *never* leaves till everyone else has finished work."

Sir Piers looked bewildered, and his wife said quietly:

"I'm thinking of suggesting to Char that she should sleep at the Hostel they opened last year, instead of coming back here at impossible hours every night. It really is very hard on the servants, and, besides, I don't think we shall have enough petrol this winter for it to be possible. She could always come home for week-ends, and on the whole it would be less tiring for her to be altogether in Questerham during the week."

"But is it necessary?" inquired Sir Piers piteously.

His wife shrugged her shoulders.

"If she'd been a boy she would be in the trenches now. I suppose we must let her do what she can, even though she's a girl. Other parents have to make greater sacrifices than ours, Piers."

"Yes, yes, to be sure," he assented. "And it's very good of the dear child to give up all her time as she does. But I'm sorry she can't be back for dinner tonight, Joanna—very sorry. Poor Trevellyan will be disappointed."

"Yes," said Lady Vivian, and refrained from adding, "I hope he will be."

She had once hoped that Char and John Trevellyan might marry; but Char's easy contempt for her cousin's Philistinism was only equalled by his unconcealed regret that so much prettiness should be allied to such alarming quick-wittedness.

"Miss Bruce," she said, turning to her secretary, "I hope you will dine with us tonight. Captain Trevellyan is bringing over a brother-officer and his wife, and we shall be an odd number, since there is no hope of Char."

"What's that, my dear?" said Sir Piers. "I hadn't heard that. Who is Trevellyan bringing with him?"

"Major Willoughby and his wife. She used to be Lesbia Carroll, and I knew her years ago—before she married. I shall be rather curious to see her again."

"Are they motoring?"

"Yes, in Johnnie's new car."

The dressing-gong reverberated through the hall.

"They will very likely be late," remarked Lady Vivian, "but I must go and dress at once."

She went across the long room, a tall, upright woman with a beautiful figure, obviously better-looking at fifty-two than she could ever have been as a girl. Her hair was thick and dark, with more than a sprinkling of white, and two deep vertical lines ran from the corners of her nostrils to her rather square chin. But her blue eyes were brilliant, and deeply set under a forehead that was singularly unlined.

As Joanna Trevellyan, ungainly and devoid of beauty, she had been far too outspoken to conceal her native cleverness, and had never known popularity. As the wife of Sir Piers Vivian, the only man who had ever wished to marry her, and mistress of Plessing, her wit and shrewdness became her, and as the years went on she was even accounted good-looking.

Miss Bruce, returning to her postcards after a hurried toilet, thought that Lady Vivian looked very handsome as she came down in her black-lace evening-dress with a high amethyst comb in her hair.

"Have the evening papers come?" was her first inquiry.

"I think Sir Piers had them taken upstairs."

Lady Vivian frowned quickly.

"How I wish he wouldn't do that! The casualty lists depress him so dreadfully. We must try and keep off the subject of the war at dinner, Miss Bruce, or he won't sleep all night."

Miss Bruce said nothing, but she pursed up her lips in a manner which meant that a possibly wakeful night for Sir Piers Vivian ought not to be weighed in the balance against the universal tendency to discuss the war. That the subject was never willingly embarked upon at Plessing, except by Char Vivian, seemed to her a confession of weakness.

Lady Vivian was perfectly aware of her secretary's point of view, and profoundly indifferent to it. She even took a rather malicious pleasure in saying lightly and yet very decidedly:

"John is safe enough, but I don't know what Lesbia Willoughby may choose to talk about. As a girl she had the voice of a pea-hen, and never stopped chattering. So, if you can, please head her off war-talk at dinner."

Her employer's trenchant simile as to Mrs. Willoughby's vocal powers could not but recur to Miss Bruce with a sense of its extreme appositeness when the guests entered.

Mrs. Willoughby billowed into the room. There was really no other word to describe that rapid, undulating, and yet buoyant advance. Tall as Lady Vivian was, and by no means slightly built, she seemed to Miss Bruce to be at once physically overpowered and almost eclipsed in the strident and voluminous greeting of her old acquaintance.

"My *dear* Joanna! After *all* these years ... how too, too delightful to see you so absolutely and utterly unchanged! *Dear* old days! And now we meet in the midst of all these horrors!"

The exaggeration of the look she cast round her seemed to include the drawing-room and its occupants alike in the pleasing category.

"I'm sorry you don't like my Louis XV.," said Lady Vivian flippantly, and turned to greet the rest of the party.

Her cousin John, who looked, even in khaki, a great deal less than his thirty years, smiled at her with steady blue eyes that bore a great resemblance to her own, and wrung her hand, saying, "This is very jolly, Cousin Joanna," in a pleasant, rather serious voice.

"And here," said Lesbia Willoughby piercingly—"here is my Lewis."

Her Lewis advanced, looking not unnaturally sheepish, and Trevellyan said conscientiously:

"May I introduce Major Willoughby to you? My cousin, Lady Vivian."

"You *never* told me, Joanna, that this dear thing was a cousin of yours," shrieked Lesbia reproachfully. "I think it quite disgustingly mean of you, considering that we were girls together."

"In the days when we were girls together," said Lady Vivian ruthlessly, "he wasn't born or thought of. Have they announced dinner, Miss Bruce?"

"This moment."

"Then, do let's go in at once. You must all be very hungry after such a drive."

"I *never* eat nowadays—simply never," proclaimed Mrs. Willoughby as she crossed the hall on Sir Piers's arm. "I think it most unpatriotic. We're all going to be starving quite soon, and the poor are living on simply nothing a day as it is. And one can't *bear* to touch food while our poor dear boys in the trenches and in Germany are literally starving."

Mrs. Willoughby's voice was of a very piercing quality, and she emphasized her words by rolling round a pair of enormous and over-prominent light grey eyes as she spoke. Seated at the dinner-table, she contrived to present an appearance that almost amounted to impropriety, by merely putting a large bare elbow on the table and flinging back an elaborately dressed head set on a short neck and opulent shoulders, thickly dredged with heavily scented powder. Miss Bruce, on

18

the opposite side of the table, eyed her with distrustful disapproval. It did not appear to her likely that she would be able to carry out Lady Vivian's injunction that war-talk was to be avoided.

"Isn't Char at home?" Trevellyan inquired of his hostess.

"She's at Questerham, and the car has gone in for her, but she telephoned to say that she couldn't get back till late. It's this Supply Depôt of hers; she's giving every minute of the day and night to it," said Lady Vivian, characteristically allowing no tinge of disapproval or disappointment to colour her voice.

"Is that your delightful girl?" inquired Lesbia across the table, and pronouncing the word as though it rhymed with "curl." "Isn't it too wonderful to see all these young things devoting themselves? As for me, I'm literally run off my feet in town. I'm having a holiday here—just to see something of Lewis, who's stationed in these parts indefinitely, poor dear lamb—because my doctor said I was *killing* myself—literally killing myself."

"Really?" said Lady Vivian placidly. "I hope you're going to be here for some time. Are you staying—"

"Only till I'm fit to move. That *moment*," said Lesbia impressively, "that very moment, I must simply dash back to London. My dear, I can't tell you what it's like. I never have an instant to call my own—have I, Lewis?"

"Rather not," said Lewis hastily.

He was a small, brown-faced man, who had won his D.S.O. in South Africa, and whom no doctor could now be induced to pass for service abroad.

"Perhaps some charitable organization takes up your time," suggested Sir Piers to Mrs. Willoughby. His deafness seldom permitted him to follow more than the drift of general conversation. "Now, Charmian, our daughter, has taken up a most creditable piece of work—most creditable—although, perhaps, she is a little inclined to overdo things just at present."

"No one can *possibly* overdo war-work," Mrs. Willoughby told him trenchantly. "Nothing that we women of England can do could ever be enough for the brave fathers, and husbands, and brothers, and sweethearts, who are risking their lives for us out there. Think of what the trenches are—just *hell*, as a boy said to me the other day—hell let loose!"

Sir Piers looked very much distressed, and his white head began to shake. He had only heard part of Lesbia's discourse. Trevellyan's boyishly fair face flushed scarlet. He had fought in Belgium, and in Flanders, until a bullet lodged in his knee, and now his next Medical Board might send him to France to rejoin his regiment. But it would have occurred to no one to suppose that the poignant description quoted by Mrs. Willoughby had ever emanated from Trevellyan.

From the head of the table Joanna Vivian said smoothly:

"You've made us all very curious as to your work, Lesbia. Do tell us what you do."

Mrs. Willoughby gave her high, strident laugh.

"Everything," was her modest claim. "Absolutely everything, my dear. Packing for prisoners three mornings a week, canteen work twice, and every Flag-day going. I can't tell you the *hours* I've stood outside Claridge's carrying a tray and seeing insolent wretches walk past me without buying. I've been *so* exhausted by the end of the day I've had to have an hour's massage before I could *drag* myself out to patronize some Red Cross entertainment. But, of course, my real work is the Colonial officers. Dear, sweet things! I take them *all* over London!"

"By Jove, though, do you really!" said Trevellyan admiringly.

Only a certain naïve quality of sincerity in his simplicities, Joanna reflected, saved Johnnie from appearing absolutely stupid. But, her husband excepted, she was secretly fonder and more proud of Johnnie than of any one in the world, and she did not make the mistake of supposing that his easy chivalry denoted any admiration for the screeching monologue of which Lesbia was delivering herself.

"I make a specialty of South Africans," she proclaimed to the table. "They're so delightfully rural—even more so than the dear Australians, though I have a passion for Anzacs. But I take *some* of them *some*where every day—just show them London, you know. Not one of them knows a soul in England, and of course London is a perfect marvel to them. I simply live in taxis, rushing the dear things round."

"Ah, we had a couple of Canadians here last week—very fine fellows," said Sir Piers. "Been in hospital in Questerham, both of them, and Char thought they'd enjoy a day out in the country.

She manages everything, you know—even the hospitals. The doctors all come to her for everything, I believe. She tells me that all the hospitals round about are affiliated to her office."

"Ranks as a sort of Universal Provider—what?" said Trevellyan.

"Yes; isn't it wonderful?" said Miss Bruce eagerly; and availed herself to the full of the double opportunity for obeying, even at the eleventh hour, Lady Vivian's injunctions as to the trend of the conversation, and at the same time making the utmost of her favourite topic, Char Vivian's work at the Midland Supply Depôt.

For the rest of dinner, in spite of several strenuous efforts from Lesbia Willoughby, nothing else was discussed.

III

Ten o'clock in the morning, and little Miss Anthony flew up Questerham High Street on her bicycle, conscious that her hurried choice of a winter hat had not only been highly unsatisfactory, owing to the extreme haste with which she had conducted it, but was also about to make her late in arriving at the office. She threw an anxious glance at the Post-Office clock, and redoubled her speed at the sight of it, though no amount of haste would get her to the Midland Supply Depôt Headquarters under another seven minutes.

But she sped gallantly across the tram-lines and in and out of the slow-moving stream of market-carts, and arrived breathless at the offices in Pollard Street just as Miss Vivian's small open car drew up at the door.

"Damn!" automatically muttered Tony under her breath, and seeing nothing for it but to put her bicycle into a corner and efface herself respectfully to let Miss Vivian pass.

But Miss Vivian, generally so unaware of any member of her staff as not even to exchange a "Good-morning," elected suddenly to reverse this policy.

"Good-morning," she said graciously. "We're both late today, I'm afraid."

The clerk in the hall, who drew an ominous line in her book under the last signature as the clock struck ten, laughed in a rather awestruck way and said, "Oh, Miss Vivian!"

"I think you must let Miss Anthony off today," said Char Vivian, smiling. "As I am late myself, you know."

She went slowly upstairs, just hearing an ecstatic gasp from the two girls in the hall.

She was vaguely aware that those few gracious words and tone of easy kindness had secured for her little Miss Anthony's unswerving loyalty and admiration.

Girls of that age and class *were* like that, she told herself with a slight smile.

The smile died away into an expression of weary concentration as she entered her private office.

"Good-morning, Miss Delmege. Is there much in today?"

"Good-morning, Miss Vivian," said Miss Delmege, elegantly rising from her knees, in which lowly position she had been trying to coax the small, indifferent fire to burn. "I am afraid there are a lot of letters."

Miss Vivian sighed and moved to the looking-glass to take off her hat. She also was in uniform, and wore several curly stripes of gold braid on her coat collar and cuffs to denote her exalted position.

Even when she had taken off her ugly and unbecoming felt hat and run her fingers through the thick, straight masses of reddish hair that hung over her forehead, Char Vivian contrived to look at least ten years older than her actual twenty-nine years.

She was very good-looking, with delicate aquiline features, a pale, fair skin powdered all over with tiny freckles, and beautiful deep-set brown eyes surrounded by unexpectedly dark lashes.

It was something quite indefinable in the lines round her pretty, decided mouth, and under her eyes that gave the odd impression of maturity. Her manner had always, from the age of five, been one of extreme self-security.

"Now, then, for the letters," she said, as she sat down before the great roll-top desk. Char Vivian's voice was deep and rather drawling in character, and she used it with great effect.

"Miss Delmege, did you put these heavenly lilies-of-the-valley here? You really mustn't—but they're too lovely. Thank you so much. They *do* make such a difference!"

She sniffed delicately, and Miss Delmege smiled with gratification. The lilies-of-the-valley had really cost more than she could afford, but those few words of appreciation sent her to her small table in the corner with a sense of great satisfaction.

Char tore open one envelope after another with murmured comments. She frequently affected an absence of mind denoted by fragmentary monologue.

"Transport wanted for fifty men going from the King Street Hospital today—and they want more sphagnum moss. There ought to be five hundred bags ready to go out this morning.... I wonder if they've seen to it. Inquiries—inquiries—inquiries! When are people ever going to stop asking me questions? Hospital accounts—that can go to the Finance Department.... The Stores bill—to the Commissariat. What's all this—transport for that man in Hospital? I shall have to see to that myself. Look me up the War Office letters as to Petrol regulations, Miss Delmege, will you? Belgians again; they're very difficult to satisfy, poor people. Madame Van Damm—I don't remember them—I must send for the files. Here are some more of those tiresome muddles of Mrs. Potter's. I told her all about those people on Monday. Why on earth hasn't it been arranged? Nothing is *ever* done unless one sees to it oneself. The Medical Officer of Health wants to see me. What are my appointments for today, Miss Delmege?"

"The man from the building contractors is coming at twelve, and the Matron from the Overseas Hospital at three, and then there's that Miss Jones who's coming to work here. And it's the day you generally go to the Convalescent Homes."

"I see. Ring up the Medical Officer and say I can give him a quarter of an hour at two o'clock. I can't really spare that," sighed Miss Vivian, "but I suppose I shall have to see him."

Miss Delmege knew that, whatever else her chief might depute to her, she never relinquished to any one a business interview, so she merely looked concerned and said: "I'm afraid it will be a great rush for you."

Miss Vivian gave her subtle, infrequent smile, and began the customary series of morning interviews which were supposed to settle the perplexities of each department for the day. That this supposition was not invariably correct was made manifest on this occasion by the demeanour of the unhappy Miss Plumtree, when her chief had made short work of a series of difficulties haltingly and stammeringly put before her in sentences made involved and awkward through sheer nervousness.

"Let me have those Requisition Averages by twelve o'clock, please—and I think that completes you, Miss Plumtree?" concluded Miss Vivian rapidly.

"Thank you, Miss Vivian. Is—are—do these averages include the first day of the month as well as the last?"

"Yes, of course. And remember to give the gross weight of the supplies as well as the net weight."

"And I—I divide by the number of days in each month. Yes, I see," faltered Miss Plumtree, seeing nothing at all except the brisk tapping of Miss Vivian's long, slight fingers on the blotting-paper in front of her, denoting with sufficient clearness that in her opinion the interview had reached its conclusion some moments since.

"It's for August, September, and October, isn't it?"

"Yes."

Miss Vivian's tone implied that the question was unnecessary in the extreme, as indeed it was, since Miss Plumtree had been engaged in conducting the quarterly Requisition Averages to an unsuccessful issue for the past eighteen months.

"Thank you."

Miss Plumtree faltered from the room, with the consciousness of past failures heavy upon her.

Char did not like an attitude of sycophantic dejection, and Miss Plumtree may therefore have been responsible for the very modified enthusiasm with which the next applicant's request for an afternoon off duty was received.

"It rather depends, Miss Cox," said Char, her drawl slightly emphasized. "I thought the work in that department was behindhand?"

"Not now, Miss Vivian," said the grey-haired spinster anxiously. "Mrs. Tweedale and I cleared it all up last night; I'm quite up to date."

"Well, I'm afraid there's a good deal for you here," said Char rather cruelly, handing her a bundle of papers. "However, please take your afternoon off if you want to, and if you feel that the work can be left."

"Thank you, Miss Vivian."

Miss Cox, who was meek and deferential, left the room, the pleasurable anticipation of a holiday quite gone from her tired face.

Char looked at the neatly coiled twist of Miss Delmege's sand-coloured hair.

"Was I a wet-blanket?" she inquired whimsically. "Really, the way these people are always asking for leave! I wonder what would happen if *I* took an afternoon off. How long is it since I had a holiday, Miss Delmege?"

"You've not had one since I've been here," declared her secretary, "and that's nearly a year."

"Exactly. But then I can't understand putting anything before the work, personally."

Char returned to her pile of letters and Miss Delmege went on with her writing in a glow of admiration, and resolved that, after all, she would come and work on Sunday morning, although nominally no one came to the office on Sundays except the clerks who took turns for telephone duty, and Miss Vivian herself in the afternoon.

The morning was a busy one. Telephone calls seemed incessant, and the operator downstairs was unintelligent and twice cut Miss Vivian off in the midst of an important trunk call.

"Hallo! hallo! are you there? Miss Henderson, what the *dickens* are you doing? You've cut me off again."

Char banged the receiver down impatiently with one hand, while the other continued to make rapid calculations on a large sheet of foolscap. She possessed and exercised to the full the faculty of following two or more trains of thought at the same moment.

Presently she rang her bell sharply, the customary signal that she was ready to dictate her letters.

Each department was supposed to possess its own typewriter and to make use of it, and the services of the shorthand-typist, who was amongst the few paid workers in the office, were exclusively reserved for Miss Vivian.

The work entailed was no sinecure, the more especially since Miss Collins was obdurate as to her time-limit of ten to five-thirty. But it was never difficult for Miss Vivian to commandeer volunteer typists from the departments when her enormous correspondence appeared to her to require it.

"Good-morning, Miss Vivian."

"Good-morning," said Char curtly, unsmiling. Miss Collins always gave her a sense of irritation. She was so jauntily competent, so consciously independent of the office.

Shorthand-typists could always find work in the big Questerham manufacturing works, and Miss Collins had only been secured for the Supply Depôt with difficulty. She received two pounds ten shillings a week, never worked overtime, and had every Saturday afternoon off. Miss Vivian had once, in the early days of Miss Collins, suggested that she might like to wear uniform, and had received a smiling and unqualified negative, coupled with a candid statement of Miss Collins's views as to the undesirability of combining clerical work with the exhausting activities required in meeting and feeding the troop-trains.

"I should be sorry to think that any of *my* staff would shirk the little additional work which brings them into contact with the men who have risked their lives for England," had been the freezing *finale* with which the dialogue had been brought to a close by the disgusted Miss Vivian.

Since then her stenographer had continued to frequent her presence in transparent and *décolletées* blouses, with short skirts swinging above silk-stockinged ankles and suede shoes. Even her red, fluffy curls were unnecessarily decked with half a dozen sparkling prongs. But she was very quick and intelligent, and Miss Vivian had perforce to accept her impudent prettiness and complete independence.

Char never, after the first week, made the mistake of supposing that Miss Collins would ever fall under that spell of personal magnetism to which the rest of the office was in more or less complete subjection, and she consequently wasted no smile upon her morning greeting.

"This is to the Director-General of Voluntary Organizations, and please do not use abbreviations. Kindly head the letter in full."

Miss Collins's small manicured hand ran easily over her notebook, leaving a trail of cabalistic signs behind it.

Char leant back, half-closing her eyes in a way which served to emphasize the tired shadows beneath them, and proceeded with her fluent, unhampered dictation.

She was seldom at a loss for a word, and had a positive gift for the production of rhetorical periods which never failed to impress Miss Delmege, still writing at her corner table. In spite of frequent interruptions, Char proceeded unconcernedly enough, until at the eleventh entry of a messenger she broke into an impatient exclamation:

"Miss Delmege, please deal for me!"

Miss Delmege swept forward, annihilating the unhappy bearer of the card with a look of deep reproach, as she took it from her.

"I'm afraid it's some one to see you," she faltered deprecatingly.

Char frowned and took the card impatiently, and Miss Delmege stood by looking nervous, as she invariably did when her chief appeared annoyed. Char Vivian, however, although frequently impatient, was not a passionate woman, and however much she might give rein to her tongue, seldom lost control of her temper, for the simple reason that she never lost sight of herself or of her own effect upon her surroundings.

Her face cleared as she read the card.

"Please ask Captain Trevellyan to come up here."

The messenger disappeared thankfully and Miss Delmege retreated relievedly to her corner.

Char leant back again in her capacious chair, a sheaf of papers, at which she only cast an occasional glance, before her.

She was not at all averse to being found in this attitude, which she judged to be most typical of herself and her work, and for an instant after Captain Trevellyan's booted tread had paused upon the threshold she affected unawareness of his presence and did not raise her eyes.

"... I am in receipt of your letter of even date, and would inform you in reply...."

"Oh, John! So you've come for an official inspection?"

"Since you're never to be seen any other way," he returned, laughing, and grasping her hand.

"I ought to send you away; we're in the midst of a heavy day's work."

"Don't you think you might call a—a sort of truce of God, for the moment, and tell me something about this office of yours? I'm much impressed by all I hear."

Miss Delmege, judging from her chief's smile that this suggestion was approved of, brought forward a chair, and acknowledged Captain Trevellyan's protesting thanks with a genteel bend at the waist and a small, tight smile.

The amenities of social intercourse were always strictly held in check by the limits of officialdom by Miss Vivian's staff, with the exception of the unregenerate Miss Collins, who tucked her pencil into her belt, uncrossed her knees, and rose from her chair.

"I'm afraid I'm interrupting you," said Trevellyan politely, addressing his remark to Char, but casting a quite unnecessary look at the now smiling Miss Collins.

"I've nearly finished," said Char.

"Shall I come back later?" suggested Miss Collins gaily, swinging a turquoise heart from the end of an outrageously long gold chain.

"I will ring if I want you," said Miss Vivian in tones eminently calculated to allay any assumption of indispensability on the part of her employée.

With a freezing eye she watched Miss Collins swing jauntily from the room, her red head cocked at an angle that enabled her to throw a farewell dimple in the direction of Captain Trevellyan.

"Is that one of your helpers?" was the rather infelicitously worded inquiry which John was inspired to put as Miss Collins disappeared.

"The office stenographer," said Char curtly.

23

"Why don't you have poor old Miss Bruce up here? She's longing to help you—couldn't talk about anything but this place last night."

"Dear old Brucey!" said Char, with more languor than enthusiasm in her voice. "But there are one or two reasons why it wouldn't quite do to have her in the office; we have to be desperately official here, you know. Besides, it's such a comfort to get back in the evenings to some one who doesn't look upon me as the Director of the Midland Supply Depôt! I sometimes feel I'm turning into an organization instead of a human being."

Miss Vivian, needless to say, had never felt anything of the sort, but there was something rather gallantly pathetic in the half-laughing turn of the phrase, and it sufficed for a weighty addition to Miss Delmege's treasured collections of "Glimpses into Miss Vivian's Real Self."

She received yet another such a few minutes later, when Captain Trevellyan began to urge Miss Vivian to come out with him in the new car waiting at the office door.

"Do! I'll take you anywhere you want to go, and I really do want you to see how beautifully she runs. Come and lunch somewhere?"

"I'd love it," declared Char wistfully, "but I really mustn't, Johnnie. There's so much to do."

Either the cousinly diminutive, or something unusually unofficial in Miss Vivian's regretful voice, caused the discreet Miss Delmege to rise and glide quietly from the room.

"Miss Vivian really is most awfully human," she declared to a fellow-worker whom she met upon the stairs. "What do you think I've left her doing?"

The fellow-worker leant comfortably against the wall, balancing a wire basket full of official-looking documents on her hip, and said interestedly:

"Do tell me."

"Refusing to go for a motor ride with a cousin of hers, an officer, who wants her to see his new car. And she awfully wants to go—I could see that—it's only the work that's keeping her."

"I must say she *is* splendid!"

"Yes, isn't she?"

"I think I saw the cousin, waiting downstairs about a quarter of an hour ago. Is he a Staff Officer, very tall and large, and awfully fair?"

"Yes. Rather nice-looking, isn't he?"

"Quite, and I do like them to be tall. He's got a nice voice, too. You know—I mean his voice is nice."

"Yes; he has got a nice voice, hasn't he? I noticed it myself. Of course, that awful Miss Collins made eyes at him like anything. She was taking letters when he came in."

"Rotten little minx! I wonder if he's engaged to Miss Vivian?"

"I couldn't say," primly returned Miss Delmege, with a sudden access of discretion, implying a reticence which in point of fact she was not in a position to exercise.

She did not go upstairs again until Captain Trevellyan and his motor-car had safely negotiated the corner of Pollard Street, unaccompanied by Miss Vivian.

This Miss Delmege ascertained from a ground-floor window, and then returned to her corner table, wearing an expression of compassionate admiration that Char was perfectly able to interpret.

"I'm afraid that was an interruption to our morning's work," she said kindly. "What time is it?"

"Nearly one o'clock, Miss Vivian."

"Oh, good heavens! Just bring me the Belgian files, will you? and then you'd better go to lunch."

"I can quite well go later," said Miss Delmege eagerly. "I—I thought perhaps you'd be lunching out today."

"No," drawled Char decisively; "in spite of the inducement of the new car, I shan't leave the office till I have to go to the Convalescent Homes. I'll send for some lunch when I want it."

Miss Delmege went to her own lunch with a vexed soul.

"I do wish one could get Miss Vivian to eat something," she murmured distractedly to her neighbour. "I know exactly what it'll be, you know. She'll sit there writing, writing, writing, and forget all about food, and then it'll be two o'clock, and she has to see the M.O. of Health and somebody else coming at three—and she'll have had no lunch at all."

"Doesn't she ever go out to lunch?"

"Only on slack days, and you know how often we get *them*, especially now that the work is simply increasing by leaps and bounds every day."

"Couldn't you take her some sandwiches?" asked Mrs. Bullivant from the head of the table. "I could cut some in a minute."

"Oh, no, thank you. She wouldn't like it. She hates a fuss," Miss Delmege declared decidedly.

The refusal, with its attendant tag of explanatory ingratitude, was received in matter-of-fact silence by every one.

Miss Vivian's hatred of a fuss, as interpreted by her secretary, merely redounded to her credit in the eyes of the Hostel.

They ate indifferent pressed beef and tepid milk-pudding, and those who could afford it—for the most part accompanied by those who could not afford it—supplemented the meal with coffee and cakes devoured in haste at the High Street confectioner's, and then hurried back to the office.

It was nearly three o'clock before Miss Delmege ventured to address her chief.

"I'm afraid you haven't had lunch. Do let me send for something."

Miss Vivian looked up, flushed and tired.

"Dear me, yes. It's much later than I thought. Send out one of the Scouts for a couple of buns and a piece of chocolate."

"Oh!" protested Miss Delmege, as she invariably did on receipt of this menu.

Char Vivian did not raise her eyes from the letter she was rapidly inditing, and her secretary retreated to give the order.

Miss Plumtree, counting on her fingers and looking acutely distressed, sat at a small table in the hall from whence the Scout was dispatched.

"Is that *all* she's having for lunch?" she paused in her pursuit of ever-elusive averages to inquire in awestruck tones.

"Yes, and she's been simply worked to death this morning. And it's nearly three now, and she won't get back to dinner till long after ten o'clock, probably; but she never will have more for lunch, when she's very busy, than just buns and a penny piece of chocolate. That," said Miss Delmege, with a sort of desperate admiration—"that is just Miss Vivian all over!"

IV

Char looked wearily at the clock.

The buns and chocolate hastily disposed of in the intervals of work during the afternoon had only served to spoil the successive cups of strong tea, which formed her only indulgence, brought to her at five o'clock. They were guiltless of sustaining qualities. It was not yet seven, and she never ordered the car until nine o'clock or later.

Her eyes dropped to the diminished, but still formidable, pile of papers on the table. She was excessively tired, and she knew that the papers before her could be dealt with in the morning.

But it was characteristic of Char Vivian that she did not make up her mind then and there to order the car round and arrive at Plessing in time for eight o'clock dinner and early bed, much as she needed both. To do so would have jarred with her own and her staff's conception of her self-sacrificing, untiring energy, her devotion to an immense and indispensable task, just as surely as would a trivial, easy interruption to the day's work in the shape of John Trevellyan and his new car, or an hour consecrated to fresh air and luncheon. Necessity compelled Char to work twelve hours a day some two evenings a week, in order that the amount undertaken by the Midland Supply Depôt might be duly accomplished; but on the remaining days, when work was comparatively light and over early in the evening, she did not choose to spoil the picture which she carried always in her mind's eye of the indefatigable and overtaxed Director of the Midland Supply Depôt.

So Miss Vivian applied herself wearily, once again, to her inspection of those Army Forms which were to be sent up to the London office on the morrow.

Presently the door opened and Miss Delmege came in with her hat and coat on, prepared to go.

"I thought I'd just tell you," she said hesitatingly, "that Miss Jones has come—the new clerk. Shall I take her over to the Hostel?"

Char sighed wearily.

"Oh, I suppose I'd better see her. If it isn't tonight, it will have to be tomorrow. I'd rather get it over. Send her up."

"Oh, Miss Vivian!"

"Never mind. I shan't be long."

Miss Vivian smiled resignedly.

As a matter of fact, she was rather relieved at the prospect of an interview to break the monotony of the evening. The Army Forms in question had failed to repay inspection, in the sense of presenting any glaring errors for which the Medical Officer in charge of the Hospital could have been brought sharply to book.

She unconsciously strewed the papers on the desk into a rather more elaborate confusion in front of her, and began to open the inkpot, although she had no further writing to do. The pen was poised between her fingers when Miss Delmege noiselessly opened the door, and shut it again on the entry of Miss Jones.

Char put down her pen, raised her heavy-lidded eyes, and said in her deep, effective voice:

"Good-evening, Miss—er—Jones."

She almost always hesitated and drawled for an instant before pronouncing the name of any member of her staff. The trick was purely instinctive, and indicated both her own overcharged memory and the insignificance of the unit, among many, whom she was addressing.

"How do you do?" said Miss Jones.

Her voice possessed the indefinable and quite unmistakable intonation of good-breeding, and Char instantly observed that she did not wind up her brief greeting with Miss Vivian's name.

She looked at her with an instant's surprise. Miss Jones was short and squarely built, looked about twenty-seven, and was not pretty. But she had a fine pair of grey eyes in her little colourless face, and her slim, ungloved hands, which Char immediately noticed, were unusually beautiful.

"You are from Wales, I believe?" said Char, unexpectedly even to herself. She made a point of avoiding personalities with the staff. But there appeared to be something which required explanation in Miss Jones.

"Yes. My father is the Dean of Penally. I have had some secretarial experience with him during the last five years."

Evidently Miss Jones wished to keep to the matter in hand. Char was rather amused, reflecting on the fluttered gratification which Miss Delmege or Miss Henderson would have displayed at any directing of the conversation into more personal channels.

"I see," she said, smiling a little. "Now, I wonder what you call secretarial experience?"

"My father naturally has a great deal of correspondence," returned Miss Jones, without any answering smile on her small, serious face. "I have been his only secretary for four years. Since the war he has employed some one else for most of his letters, so as to set me free for other work."

"Yes; I understood from your letter that you had been working in a hospital."

"As clerk."

"Excellent. That will be most useful experience here. You know this office controls the hospitals in Questerham and round about. I want you to work in this room with my secretary, and learn her work, so that she can use you as her second."

"I will do my best."

"I'm sure of that," said Miss Vivian, redoubling her charm of manner, and eyeing the impassive Miss Jones narrowly. "I hope you'll be happy here and like the work. You must always let me know if there's anything you don't like. I think you're billeted just across the road, at our Questerham Hostel?"

"Yes."

"I'll send some one to show you the way."

"Thank you; I know where it is. I left my luggage there before coming here."

"The new workers generally come to report to me before doing anything else," said Char, indefinably vexed at having failed to obtain the expected smile of gratitude.

"However, if you know the way I must let you go now, so as to be in time for supper. Good-night, Miss Jones."

"Good-night," responded Miss Jones placidly, and closed the door noiselessly behind her. Her movements were very quiet in spite of her solid build, and she moved lightly enough, but the Hostel perceived a certain irony, nevertheless, in the fact that Miss Jones's parents had bestowed upon her the baptismal name of Grace.

The appeal thus made to a rather elementary sense of humour resulted in Miss Jones holding the solitary privilege of being the only person in the Hostel who was almost invariably called by her Christian name. She enjoyed from the first a strange sort of popularity, nominally due to the fact that "you never knew what she was going to say next"; in reality owing to a curious quality of absolute sincerity which was best translated by her surroundings as "originality." Another manifestation of it, less easily defined, was the complete good faith which she placed in all those with whom she came into contact. Only a decided tincture of Welsh shrewdness preserved her from the absolute credulity of the simpleton.

Almost the first question put to Miss Jones was that favourite test one of the enthusiastic Tony, "And what do you think of Miss Vivian?"

"I think," said Miss Jones thoughtfully, "that she is a reincarnation of Queen Elizabeth."

There was a rather stunned silence in the Hostel sitting-room.

Reincarnation was not a word which had ever sounded there before, and it carried with it a subtle suggestion of impropriety to several listeners. Nor was any one at the moment sufficiently *au courant* with the Virgin Queen's leading characteristics to feel certain whether the comparison instituted was meant to be complimentary or insulting in the extreme.

Miss Delmege for once voiced the popular feeling by ejaculating coldly.

"That's rather a strange thing to say, surely!"

"Why? Hasn't it ever struck anybody before? I should have thought it so obvious. Why, even to look at, you know—that sandy colouring, and the way she holds her head: just as though there ought to be a ruff behind it."

"Oh, you mean to look at," said Miss Marsh, the general tension considerably relaxed as the trend of the conversation shifted from that dreaded line of abstract discussion whither the indiscreet Miss Jones had appeared, for one horrid moment, to conduct it.

"Had Queen Elizabeth got freckles? I really don't know much about her, except that they found a thousand dresses in her wardrobe when she died," said Tony, voicing, as it happened, the solitary fact concerning the Sovereign under discussion which any one present was able to remember, as outcome of each one's varying form of a solid English education.

"Her power of administration and personal magnetism, you know," explained Miss Jones.

"Oh, of course she's perfectly wonderful," Miss Delmege exclaimed, sure of her ground. "You'll see that more and more, working in her room."

Whether such increased perception was indeed the result of Miss Jones's activities in the room of the Director might remain open to question.

Char found her very quick, exceedingly accurate, and more conscientious than the quick-witted can generally boast of being. She remained entirely self-possessed under praise, blame, or indifference, and Miss Vivian was half-unconsciously irritated at this tacit assumption of an independence more significant and no less secure than that of Miss Collins the typist.

"Gracie, I wish you'd tell me what you *really* think of Miss Vivian," her room-mate demanded one night as they were undressing together.

Screens were chastely placed round each bed, and it was a matter of some surprise to Miss Marsh that her companion so frequently neglected these modest adjuncts to privacy, and often took off her stockings, or folded up even more intimate garments, under the full light, such as it was, of the gas-jet in the middle of the room.

Miss Jones was extremely orderly, and always folded her clothes with scrupulous tidiness. She rolled up a pair of black stockings with exactitude before answering.

"I think she's rather interesting."

"Good Lord, Gracie! if Delmege could only hear you! *Rather interesting!* The Director of the Sacred Supply Depôt! You really are the limit, the things you say, you know."

"Well, that's all I *do* think. She is very capable, and a fairly good organizer, but I don't think her as marvellous as you or Miss Delmege or Tony do. In fact, I think you're all rather *détraquées* about Miss Vivian."

Miss Marsh was as well aware as anybody in the Hostel that the insertion of a foreign word into a British discourse is the height of affectation and of bad form; and although she could not believe Grace to be at all an affected person, she felt it due to her own nationality to assume a very disapproving expression and to allow an interval of at least three seconds to elapse before she continued the conversation.

"Don't you *like* her?"

"I'm not sure."

"I suppose you don't know her well enough to say yet?" Miss Marsh suggested.

"Do you think that has anything to do with it? I often like people without knowing them a bit," said Grace cordially; "and certainly I quite often dislike them thoroughly, even if I've only heard them speak once, or perhaps not at all."

"Then you judge by appearances, which is a great mistake."

Miss Jones said in a thoughtful manner that she didn't think it was *that* exactly, and supposed regretfully that Miss Marsh would think she was "swanking" if she explained that she considered herself a sound and rapid judge of character.

"Oh, what a sweet camisole, dear!"

"My petticoat-bodice," said Grace matter-of-factly. "I'm glad you like it. The ribbon always takes a long time to put in, but it does look rather nice. I like mauve better than pink or blue."

There came a knock at the door.

"Come in!" called Miss Jones, bare-armed and bare-legged in the middle of the room.

"Wait a minute!" exclaimed the scandalized Miss Marsh, in the midst of a shuffling process by which her clothes were removed under the nightgown which hung round her with empty flapping sleeves.

"It's only me," said Miss Plumtree in melancholy tones, walking in. "I'm just waiting for my kettle to boil."

The gas-ring was on the landing just outside the bedroom door.

Grace looked up,

"How pretty you look with your hair down!" she said admiringly.

"Me? Rubbish!" exclaimed Miss Plumtree, colouring with astonishment and embarrassment, but with a much livelier note in her voice.

"Your hair is so nice," explained Grace, gazing at the soft brown mop of curls.

"Oh, lovely, of course."

Miss Plumtree wriggled with confusion, and had no mind to betray how much the unaffected little bit of praise had restored her spirits. But she sat down on Grace's bed in her pink cotton kimono in a distinctly more cheerful frame of mind than that in which she had entered the room.

"Are you in the blues, Gooseberry-bush?" was the sympathetic inquiry of Miss Marsh.

"Well, I am, rather. It's Miss Vivian, you know. She can be awfully down on one when she likes."

"I know; you always do seem to get on the wrong side of her. Grace will sympathize; she's just been abusing her like a pickpocket," said Miss Marsh, apparently believing herself to be speaking the truth.

Miss Jones raised her eyebrows rather protestingly, but said nothing. She supposed that in an atmosphere of adulation such as that which appeared to her to surround Miss Vivian, even such negative criticism as was implied in an absence of comment might be regarded seriously enough.

"But even if one doesn't like her *awfully* much, she has a sort of fascination, don't you think?" said Miss Plumtree eagerly. "I always feel like a—a sort of bird with a sort of snake, you know."

The modification which she wished to put into this trenchant comparison was successfully conveyed by the qualifying "sort of," an adverb distinctly in favour at the Hostel.

"I know what you mean exactly, dear," Miss Marsh assured her. "And of course she does work one fearfully hard. I sometimes think I shall have to leave."

"She works every bit as hard as we do—harder. I suppose you'll admit that, Gracie?"

"Oh yes."

"Don't go on like that," protested Miss Marsh, presumably with reference to some indefinable quality detected by her in these two simple monosyllables.

"I only meant," said Grace Jones diffidently, "that it might really be better if she didn't do quite so much. If she could have her luncheon regularly, for instance."

"My dear, she simply hasn't the time."

"She could make it."

"The work comes before everything with Miss Vivian. I mean, really it does," said Miss Plumtree solemnly.

Miss Jones finished off the end of a thick plait of dark hair with a neat blue bow, and said nothing.

"I suppose even you'll admit that, Gracie?"

Grace gave a sudden little laugh, and said in the midst of it:

"Really, I'm not sure."

"My dear girl, what on earth do you mean?"

"I think I mean that I don't feel certain Miss Vivian would work quite so hard or keep such very strenuous hours if she lived on a desert island, for instance."

The other two exchanged glances.

"Dotty, isn't she?"

"Mad as a hatter, I should imagine."

"Perhaps you'll explain what sort of war-work people *do* on desert islands?"

"That isn't what I mean, quite," Gracie explained. "My idea is that perhaps Miss Vivian does *partly* work so very hard because there are so many people looking on. If she was on a desert isle she might—find time for luncheon."

"My dear girl, you're ab-solutely raving, in my opinion," said Miss Plumtree with simple directness. "There! That's my kettle."

She dashed out of the room, as a hissing sound betrayed that her kettle had overboiled on to the gas-ring, as it invariably did.

After the rescue had been effected she looked in again and said:

"I suppose you wouldn't let me come in for some of your tea tomorrow morning, would you, dear? Ours is absolutely finished, and that ass Henderson forgot to get any more."

"Rather," said Miss Marsh cordially. "This extraordinary girl doesn't take any, so you can have the second cup."

"Thanks most awfully. I can do without most things, but I can't do without my tea. Good-night, girls."

It was an accepted fact all through the Hostel that, although one could do without most things, one could not do without one's tea.

This requirement was of an elastic nature, and might extend from early morning to a late return from meeting a troop-train at night. Grace every morning refused the urgent offer of her room-mate to "make her a cup of nice hot tea," and watched, with a sort of interested surprise, while Miss Marsh got out of bed a quarter of an hour earlier than was necessary in order to fill and boil a small kettle and make herself three and sometimes four successive cups of very strong tea. She was always willing to share this refreshment with any one, but every room in the Hostel had its own appliances for tea-making, and made daily and ample use of them.

Although Miss Jones did not drink tea, she often washed up the cup and saucer and the little teapot. Miss Marsh suffered from a chronic inability to arrive at the office punctually, although breakfast was at nine o'clock, and she had only to walk across the road. But she frequently said, in a very agitated way, as she rose from the breakfast-table:

"Excuse me. I simply must go and do my washing. It's Monday, and I've left it to the last moment."

This meant that the counting and dispatching of Miss Marsh's weekly bundle for the laundry would occupy all her energies until the desperate moment when she would look at her wrist-watch, exclaim in a mechanical sort of way, "Oh, damn! I shall never do it!" and dash out of the house and across Pollard Street as the clock struck ten.

"I'll wash the tea-things for you."

"Oh, no, dear! Why *should* you? I can quite well do them to-night."

But Grace knew that when her room-mate came in tired at seven o'clock that evening she might very likely want "a good hot cup of tea" then and there, and she accordingly took the little heap of crockery into the bathroom. Standing over the tiny basin jutting out of the wall, Miss Jones, with her sleeves carefully rolled up over a very solid pair of forearms, washed and dried each piece with orderly deliberation, and replaced them in the corner of Miss Marsh's cupboard.

"I'm afraid you'll be late. Can't I help you?"

"Thanks, dear, but I dare say I can just scramble through. What about *your* washing?"

"Oh, I did all that on Saturday night," said Grace, indicating a respectable brown-paper parcel tied up with string and with an orderly list pinned on to the outside.

"You're a marvel!" sighed Miss Marsh. "Don't wait, Gracie."

Miss Jones went downstairs and out into Pollard Street. She moved rather well, and had never been known to swing her arms as she walked. Her face was very serious. She often thought how kind it was of the others not to call her a prig, since her methodical habits and innate neatness appeared to be in such startling contrast to the standards prevailing at the Hostel. She had never been sent to school, or seen much of other girls, and the universal liking shown to her by her fellow-workers gave her almost daily a fresh sense of pleased surprise.

Arrived at the office, she signed her name at the door, and proceeded upstairs to Miss Vivian's room.

Miss Vivian came in, chilled from her motor drive and with that rather pinky tinge on her aquiline nose which generally forecasted a troubled morning. The observant Miss Jones regarded this law very matter-of-factly as an example of cause and effect. She felt sure that Miss Vivian only felt at her best when conscious of looking her best, and hoped very much that the winter would not be a very cold one. It was obvious that Miss Vivian suffered from defective circulation, which her sedentary existence had not improved.

But it was Miss Delmege who solicitously suggested fetching a foot-warmer from the Supplies Department, and who placed it tenderly at the disposal of Miss Vivian.

After that the atmosphere lightened, and it was with comparative equanimity that Miss Vivian received the announcement that a lady had called and desired to see her.

"Please send up her name and her business on a slip of paper, and you can tell the clerk in the outer hall that I won't have those slipshod messages sent up," was the reception of the emissary.

"Yes, Miss Vivian."

Miss Delmege gathered up a sheaf of papers from her table and glided from the room. Grace, whose powers of mental detachment permitted her to concentrate on whatever she was doing without regard to her surroundings, went on with her work.

The interviews conducted by Miss Vivian seldom interested her in the least.

That this one was, however, destined to become an exception, struck her forcibly when the sudden sound of a piercing feminine voice on the stairs came rapidly nearer.

"... as for my name on a slip of paper, I never heard such nonsensical red-tape in my life. Why, Char's mother and I were girls together!"

Although every one in the office was aware that Miss Vivian's baptismal name was Charmian, and that this was invariably shortened by her acquaintances to Char, it came as a shock even to the imperturbable Miss Jones to hear this more or less sacred monosyllable ringing up the stairs to Miss Vivian's very table.

"Who on earth—" began Char indignantly, when the door flew open before her caller, who exclaimed shrilly and affectionately on the threshold:

"My dear child, you can't possibly know who I am, but my name is Willoughby, and when I was Lesbia Carroll your mother and I were girls together. I had to come in and take a peep at you!"

There was a sort of rustling pounce, and Grace became aware that the outraged Miss Vivian had been audibly and overpoweringly kissed in the presence of a giggling Scout and of her own junior secretary.

V

Mrs. Willoughby, in Miss Vivian's private office, reversed all rules of official precedent.

"Sit down again, my dear child—sit down!" she cried cordially, at the same time establishing herself close to the table. "I hear you're doing wonderful work for all these dear people—Belgians and the dear Tommies and every one—and I felt I simply *had* to come in and hear all about it. Also, I want to propound a tiny little scheme of my own which I think will appeal to you. Or have you heard about it already from that precious boy John, with whom, I may tell you, I'm simply *madly* in love? I'm always threatening to elope with him!"

"I'm afraid," said Char, disregarding her visitor's pleasantry, "that I can really hardly undertake anything more. We are very much understaffed as it is, and the War Office is always—"

"I can turn the *whole* War Office round my little finger, my dear," declared Mrs. Willoughby. "There's the dearest lad there, a sort of under-secretary, who's absolutely devoted to me, and tells me all sorts of official tit-bits before any one else hears a word about them. I can get anything I want through him, so you needn't worry about the War Office. In fact, to tell you rather a shocking little secret, I can get what I want out of most of these big official places—just a little tiny manipulation of the wires, you know. [*Cherchez la femme*—though I oughtn't to say such things to a girl like you, ought I?"]

Char looked at Mrs. Willoughby's large, heavily powdered face, at her enormous top-heavy hat and over-ample figure, and said nothing.

But no silence, however subtly charged with uncomplimentary meanings, could stem Mrs. Willoughby's piercing eloquence.

"This is what I want to do, and I'm told at the camp here that it would be simply invaluable. I want to get up a Canteen for the troops here, and for all those dear things on leave."

"There are several Y.M.C.A. Huts already."

"My dear! I know it. But I want to do this all on my little own, and have quite different rules and regulations. My Lewis, who's been in the Army for over fifteen years, poor angel, tells me that they all—from the Colonel downwards—think it would be the greatest boon on earth, to have a *lady* at the head of things, you know."

"My time is too much taken up; it would be quite out of the question," said Char simply.

"Darling child! *Do* you suppose I meant you—a ridiculously young thing like you? Of course, it would have to be a married woman, with a certain regimental position, so to speak. And my Lewis is second in command, as you know, so that naturally his wife.... You see, the Colonel's wife is an absolute dear, but an invalid—more or less, and no more *savoir faire* than a kitten. A perfect little provincial, between ourselves. Whereas, of course, I know this sort of job inside out and upside down—literally, my dear. The *hours* I've toiled in town!"

"But I'm afraid in that case you oughtn't to leave—"

"I must! I'm compelled to! It's *too* cruel, but the doctor simply won't answer for the consequences if I go back to London in my present state. But work I *must*. One would go quite, quite mad if one wasn't working—thinking about it all, you know."

"Major Willoughby is—er—in England, isn't he?"

"Thank God, yes!" exclaimed Lesbia, with a fervour that would have startled her husband considerably. "My heart bleeds for these poor wives and mothers. I simply thank God upon my knees that I have no son! When one thinks of it all—England's life-blood—"

Char did not share her mother's objection to eloquence expended upon the subject of the war, but she cut crisply enough into this *exaltée* outpouring.

"One is extremely thankful to do what little one can," she said, half-unconsciously throwing an appraising glance at the files and papers that were littered in profusion all over the table.

"Indeed one is!" cried Lesbia, just as fervently as before. "Work is the only thing. My dear, this war is killing me—simply killing me!"

Miss Vivian was not apparently prompted to any expression of regret at the announcement.

"As I said to Lewis the other day, I must work or go quite mad. And now this Canteen scheme seems to be calling out to me, and go I must. We've got a building—that big hall just at the bottom of the street here—and I'm insisting upon having a regular opening day—so much better to start these things with a flourish, you know—and the regimental band, and hoisting the Union Jack, and everything. And what I want you to do is this."

Lesbia paused at last to take breath, and Char immediately said:

"I'm afraid I'm so fearfully busy today that I haven't one moment, but if you'd like my secretary to—"

"Not your secretary, but your *entire* staff, and your attractive self. I want you *all* down there to help!"

"Quite impossible," said Char. "I wonder, Mrs. Willoughby, if you have any idea of the scale on which this Depôt is run?"

"*Every* idea," declared Lesbia recklessly. "I'm told everywhere that all the girls in Questerham are helping you, and that's exactly why I've come. I want girls to make my Canteen attractive—all the prettiest ones you have."

"I'm afraid my staff was not selected with a view to—er—personal attractions," said Miss Vivian, in a voice which would have created havoc amongst her staff in its ironical chilliness.

"Nonsense, my dear Char! I met the sweetest thing on the stairs—a perfect gem of a creature with Titian-coloured hair. Not in that hideous uniform, either."

Miss Vivian could not but recognize the description of her typist.

"I don't quite understand," she said. "Do you want helpers on your opening day, or regularly?"

"Quite regularly—from five to eleven or thereabouts every evening. I shall be there myself, of course, to supervise the whole thing, and I've got half a dozen dear things to help me: but what I want is *girls*, who'll run about and play barmaid and wash up, you know."

"Couldn't my mother spare Miss Bruce sometimes?"

"*Is* Miss Bruce a young and lively girl?" inquired Mrs. Willoughby, not without reason. "Besides, I need dozens of them."

"Yes, I see," said Char languidly. She was tired of Mrs. Willoughby, and it was with positive relief that she heard her telephone-bell ring sharply.

There was a certain satisfaction in leaning back in her chair and calling, "Miss—er—Jones!"

Miss Jones moved quietly to answer the insistent bell.

"I'm afraid this rather breaks into our consultation," said Char, deftly making her opportunity, "but may I write to you and let you know what I can manage?"

"I shall pop in again and commandeer all these delightful young creatures of yours. I'm marvellous at recruiting, my dear; every man I met out of khaki I always attacked in the early days. White feathers, you know, and everything of that sort. I had no mercy on them. One lad I absolutely dragged by main force to the recruiting office, though he said he couldn't leave his wife and babies. But, as I told him, I'd had to let my Lewis go—he was on the East Coast then—and was *proud* to do my bit for England. I dare say the wretch got out of it afterwards, because they wouldn't let me come in with him while he was actually being sworn, or whatever it is. Such red-tape!"

Char paid small attention to these reminiscences of Lesbia's past activities.

"What is it, Miss Jones?"

"The D.G.V.O. is here."

"The Director-General of Voluntary Organizations," said Miss Vivian, carelessly tossing off the imposing syllables, with the corner of her eye, as it were, fixed upon Mrs. Willoughby. "In that case, I'm afraid I must ask you to forgive me."

"I must fly," said Lesbia in a sudden shriek, ignoring her dismissal with great skill. "Some of those boys from the camp are lunching with me, and they'll never forgive me if I'm late."

"Ask the Director-General of Voluntary Organizations to come up, Miss Jones," drawled Char. "And show Mrs. Willoughby the way downstairs."

"Good-bye, you sweet thing!" cried Lesbia gaily, agitating a tightly gloved white-kid hand. "I shall pop in again in a day or two, and you must let me help you. I adore Belgians—positively adore them, and can do anything I like with them."

Mrs. Willoughby's enthusiasm was still audible during her rustling progress down the stairs.

Char paid full attention to her interview with the opportunely arrived Director-General of Voluntary Organizations, because she wished him to think her a most official and business-like woman, entirely capable of accomplishing all that she had undertaken; but when the dignitary had departed she gave serious consideration to the scheme so lightly propounded by Mrs. Willoughby.

The visit of this enthusiast had ruffled her more than she would have owned to herself, and it was almost instinctively that she strove to readjust the disturbed balance of her own sense of competence and self-devotion by waving aside all Miss Delmege's proposals of lunch.

"I'm afraid I haven't got time for anything of that sort today. I've had a most interrupted morning. No, Miss Delmege, thank you, not even a bun. You'd better go to your own lunch now."

"I'm not in any hurry, Miss Vivian."

"It's one o'clock," Miss Vivian pointed out, quite aware that her secretary would now seek her cold mutton and milk-pudding with an absolute sense of guilt, as of one indulging in a Sybaritic orgy while her chief held aloof in austere abstention.

Miss Delmege, in fact, looked very unhappy, and said in low tones to her colleague at the other end of the room: "Miss Jones, if you care to go to lunch first, I'll take my time off between two and half-past instead, at the second table."

The second table for lunch was never a popular institution, the mutton and the milk-pudding having lost what charms they ever possessed, and, moreover, the time allowed being abridged by almost half an hour. Miss Delmege, in virtue of her seniority and of her own excessive sense of superiority, always arranged that Grace should take the second luncheon-hour, and Miss Jones looked surprised.

"Do you mind, because really I don't care when I go?"

"I'd *rather* you went first," repeated Miss Delmege unhappily.

"Thank you very much. I'm very hungry, and if you really don't mind, I shall be delighted to go now," said Grace cheerfully, in an undertone that nevertheless penetrated to Miss Vivian's annoyed perceptions.

It was evident that Miss Jones had no qualms as to enjoying a substantial lunch, however long her over-worked employer might elect to fast, and the conviction was perhaps responsible for the sharpness with which Char exclaimed: "For Heaven's sake don't chatter in the corner like that! You're driving me perfectly mad—a day when one simply doesn't know which way to *turn*."

Miss Delmege sank into her chair, looking more overwhelmed than ever, and Grace said gently, "I'm sorry, Miss Vivian," disregarding or not understanding Miss Delmege's signal that apologies were out of place in Miss Vivian's office.

Char drew pen and ink towards her, purely *pour la forme*, and began to make mechanical designs on the blotting-paper, while her mind turned over and over the question of Mrs. Willoughby's proposed canteen.

Char thought that her staff's time was fully employed already, as indeed it was, and had no wish to arouse any possible accusation of overworking. At the same time, she had hitherto succeeded in taking over the management of almost every war organization in Questerham and the district, and was by no means minded to allow a new Canteen, on a large scale, to spring into life under no better auspices than those of Mrs. Willoughby.

If she allowed her staff to go down to the Canteen in instalments, Char decided it would have to be definitely understood that the organization of the Canteen was entirely in the hands of the Midland Supply Depôt. She surmised shrewdly that such details of practical requirements as a boiler, tea-urns, kitchen utensils, and the like, had not yet crossed the sanguine line of vision of Mrs. Willoughby. It would be easy enough for Char to assume command when she alone could supply all such needs at a minimum of expenditure and trouble. The staff, she decided, should be sent down in shifts of five or six at a time, five nights a week.

Then, Char reflected considerately, no one could have more than one night in the week, whereas she herself would always put in an appearance, even if only for a few minutes. It would encourage her staff, and would also show Mrs. Willoughby quite plainly the sort of position held by the Director of the Midland Supply Depôt.

That afternoon she sent for Miss Collins and dictated a short letter to Mrs. Willoughby, in which she declared, in the third person singular, that the Director of the Midland Supply Depôt had considered the proposed scheme for the opening of a Canteen in Pollard Street, and was prepared to help with the practical management of it. She would also supply six voluntary workers between the hours of 7 and 11 P.M. for every night in the week, Saturday excepted. As she took down these official statements, Miss Collins's light eyebrows mounted almost into the roots of her red hair with surprise and disapproval.

Char, being observant, saw these symptoms of astonishment, as she was meant to do, but few thoughts were further from her mind than that of consulting the views of her stenographer on any subject. She even took a certain amount of satisfaction in dictating a rather imperiously worded document, which informed each department in the office that those workers who lived in Questerham would be required to report for duty one night a week for emergency work (7 to 11 P.M.) at the new Canteen which would shortly be opened in Pollard Street under the direction of Miss Vivian and Mrs. Willoughby. Followed a list of names, with a corresponding day of the week attached to each group of six.

"Cut a stencil and roll off six copies for each department and two or three extra ones for filing," commanded Miss Vivian. "You can add at the end: '(Signed) Director of the Midland Supply Depôt.'"

"Yes, Miss Vivian."

Miss Collins went away with her eyebrows still erect.

The new field of enterprise was loudly discussed by the staff, as they took the usual half-hour's break in the afternoon at tea-time.

"Isn't Miss Vivian wonderful?" said Tony excitedly. "She'd take on *anything*, I do believe."

"And make a success of it, too!"

"Yes, rather."

Hardly any one grumbled at the extra four hours of hard work coming at the end of the day, and there was a general feeling of disapproval when Mrs. Bullivant at the Hostel said timidly: "If you're to be down there at seven, it'll be rather difficult to arrange about supper. Cook won't like having to get a meal ready for half-past six, and, besides, you'll be so hungry by eleven o'clock."

"I'm afraid we can't think of that, Mrs. Bullivant," observed Miss Delmege severely. "Not when we remember that Miss Vivian practically *never* gets her supper till long after ten every night, and she doesn't get much lunch, either. In fact, sometimes she simply won't touch anything at all in the middle of the day."

And Mrs. Bullivant looked very much rebuked, and said that she must see what she could do.

"Anyhow, it won't be just yet awhile," she exclaimed with Irish optimism.

"Things move very quickly with Miss Vivian."

"I think they mean the Canteen to open some time in December," said Grace. "That's not so very far off."

"Time does fly," sighed Miss Plumtree, wishing that the Monthly Averages were divided from one another by a longer space of time.

"Never mind, Sunday is all the nearer."

Sunday was the day most looked forward to by the whole Hostel, although an element of uncertainty was added to the enjoyment of it by the knowledge that the arrival of a troop-train might bring orders to any or every member of the staff to report for duty at the station at half an hour's notice.

One or two of the girls were able to go out of Questerham home, or to their friends, for the week-end, but the majority remained in the Hostel. Mrs. Bullivant tried to make the day "bright and homey" at the cost of pathetic exertions to herself, for Sunday was her hardest day of work.

A certain *laissez-aller* marked the day from its earliest beginnings.

Almost every one came down to breakfast in bedroom slippers, even though fully dressed.

"A girl here—before you came, Gracie," Miss Marsh told her room-mate, "used to come down in a kimono and sort of boudoir-cap arrangement. But I must say nobody liked it—just like a greasy foreigner, she was. All the sleeves loose, you know, so that you could see right up her arms. Myself, I don't call that awfully nice—not at the breakfast-table."

"It would be very cold to do that now," said Grace, shivering. She disliked the cold very much, and the Hostel was not warmed.

"Yes, wouldn't it? It's a comfort to get into one's own clothes again and out of uniform, isn't it, dear? That's what I like about Sundays—dainty clothes again," said Miss Marsh, fiercely pulling a comb backwards through her hair so as to make it look fluffy.

"I like you in uniform, though," said Miss Jones, who had received several shocks on first beholding the Sunday garbs known to the Hostel as "plain clothes."

"Very sweet of you to say that, dear. You always look nice yourself, only your plain clothes are too like your uniform—just a white blouse and dark skirt you wear, isn't it?"

"I'm afraid it's all I've got," said Grace apologetically; and Miss Marsh at once thought that perhaps poor little Gracie couldn't afford many things, and said warmly:

"But white blouses are awfully nice, dear, and *crêpe de Chine* always looks so *good*."

Then she thrust her stockinged feet into her red slippers and shuffled across the room. "How lucky you are! You never have to back-comb your hair, do you?"

"I never do back-comb it, because it's so bad for it," said Grace seriously. She had a book open on the dressing-table in front of her, but was characteristically quite as much interested in Miss Marsh's conversation as in her own reading.

"'Daniel Deronda'?" said Miss Marsh, looking over her. "Never heard of him. How fond you are of reading, Gracie! I love it myself, but I don't ever have time for it here."

The plea being one which never fails to rouse the scorn of every book-lover, Grace remained silent. Her solitary extravagance was the maximum subscription to the Questerham library.

"There's the bell," said Miss Marsh; "I must come up and make my bed afterwards. Thank goodness, there's no hurry today."

They went down together, Miss Marsh's heelless slippers clapping behind her on every step.

In the sitting-room after breakfast the girls clustered round the tiny smoking fire.

"It's going to rain all day. How beastly!" said Tony. "Who's going to church?"

"I shall probably go to evensong," remarked Miss Delmege, upon which several people at once decided that they would risk the weather and go to the eleven o'clock service.

There was only one church in Questerham which the Hostel thought it fashionable to attend.

The day was spent in more or less desultory lounging over the fire. Miss Delmege wrote a number of letters and Tony darned stockings. Grace Jones read "Daniel Deronda" to herself.

Lunch was protracted, and Mrs. Bullivant, to mark the day, exerted herself and made some rather smoked coffee, which she brought to the sitting-room triumphantly.

"Isn't there going to be any music this afternoon?" she inquired.

Every one declared that music was the very thing for such an afternoon, but no one appeared very willing to provide it.

"Do sing, somebody," implored Miss Henderson. "Plumtree?"

Miss Plumtree had a beautiful deep voice, utterly untrained and consequently unspoilt. She stood up willingly enough and sang all the songs that she was asked for. The taste of the Hostel was definite in songs. "A Perfect Day" and "The Rosary" were listened to in the absolute silence of appreciation, and then some one asked for a selection from the latest musical comedy.

Grace played Miss Plumtree's accompaniments, and loved listening to her soft, deep tones. She tried to make her sing "Three Fishers," but Miss Plumtree said no: it was too sad for a Sunday afternoon, and it was some one else's turn.

Musical talent in the Hostel was limited, and the only other owner of a voice was Miss Delmege, the possessor of a high, thin soprano, which, she often explained, had been the subject of much attention on the part of "a really first-rate man in Clifton."

It might remain open to question whether the energies of the really first-rate man could not have been turned into channels more advantageous than that of developing Miss Delmege's attenuated thread of voice. Whatever the original organ might have been, it was now educated into a refined squeak, overweighted with affectations which to Miss Delmege represented the art of production. She sang various improvident love-songs in which Love—high F, attained to by a species of upwards slide on E and E sharp—was all, When eventide should fall—slight tremolo and a giving out of breath rather before the accompanist had struck the final chord.

"You should take the *finale* rather more *à tempo*, dear," said the singer, in a professional way which finally vindicated the first-rateness of the man at Clifton.

Every one thanked Miss Delmege very much, and said that was a sweetly pretty song; and then Grace Jones played the piano while Tony and Miss Henderson made toast for tea and put the largest and least burnt pieces aside for her. Tea, with the aid of conversation and the making of innumerable pieces of toast over the least smoky parts of the fire, could almost be prolonged till supper-time.

"I must say, I do enjoy doing nothing," said Miss Henderson, voicing the general sentiment at the end of the day of rest.

"Poor Mrs. Potter is on the telephone. How cold she'll be, sitting there all the evening!"

"I hope she saw to Miss Vivian's fire," said Miss Delmege solicitously. "I particularly reminded her to build up a good fire in Miss Vivian's room. She does feel the cold so."

"Perhaps she didn't come this afternoon," said Grace. "There was nothing left over in her basket last night."

"Oh, she always comes," Miss Delmege said quickly and rather resentfully. "I've never known her miss a Sunday yet. Besides, I know she was there today. I saw the light in her window as I came back from church."

"I do believe," said Tony in a stage whisper, "that Delmege goes to evening church on purpose to look up at the light in Miss Vivian's window as she comes back."

But the joke was received silently, as being in but indifferent taste, and verging on irreverence almost equally as regarded church and the Director of the Midland Supply Depôt.

VI

The new Canteen in Pollard Street was opened before Christmas.

Lesbia Willoughby, in an immense overall of light blue-and-white check, stood behind a long buffet and demanded stridently whether she wasn't too exactly like a barmaid for words, and Char's consignment of helpers worked for the most part briskly and efficiently, only the unfortunate Miss Plumtree upsetting a mug of scalding tea over herself at the precise moment when Miss Vivian, trim and workmanlike in her dark uniform, entered the big hall and stood watching the scene with her arrogant, observant gaze. She did not ask Miss Plumtree whether her hand was scalded, but neither did she rebuke her very evident clumsiness. She moved slowly and imperially through the thick tobacco-laden atmosphere, speaking to several of the men, and silently observing the demeanour of her staff.

The following week she issued an office circular in which the precise direction which the activity of each worker was to take was inexorably laid down.

Miss Plumtree was banished *à perpetuité* to the pantry, to wash up at full speed over a sink. She worked at the Canteen on Mondays, always the busiest evening. In the same shift were Mrs. Potter and Miss Henderson, to each of whom was appointed the care of an urn, Grace Jones, Miss Delmege, and Miss Marsh. Miss Delmege stood behind the buffet, which position, she said, seemed very strange to her from being so like a counter in a shop, and the other two took orders at the various small tables in the hall, and hurried to and fro with laden trays.

No one would have dreamed of disputing this arbitrary disposal of energies, but it struck Grace as extremely unfortunate that Miss Marsh and Miss Delmege should select their first Monday together at the Canteen for the form of unpleasantness known as "words." Miss Jones became the medium by which alone either would address the other.

"I'm sorry, dear, but Delmege has really got on my nerves lately, and you can tell her I said so if you like. When it comes to suggesting that I don't do sufficient work, there's simply nothing more to be said. You heard her the other night saying some people were so lucky they could always get off early when they liked. Just because I'd cleared up by six o'clock, for once in a way!"

"But she didn't say she meant you," urged Miss Jones, who was far too sympathetic not to take any grievance confided to her at the teller's own valuation, and foresaw besides an extremely awkward evening at the Canteen.

"Some people aren't straightforward enough to say what they mean right out, but that doesn't prevent others from seeing the point of the sort of remarks they pass," declared Miss Marsh cryptically.

"If she told you she really hadn't meant anything personal, wouldn't it be all right?"

But Grace did not make the suggestion very hopefully, and her room-mate merely repeated gloomily that Delmege had really got on her nerves lately, and though she did not think herself one to bear malice, yet there were limits to all things.

Grace's success with Miss Delmege on their way down the street at seven o'clock that evening, was even less apparent.

"It's all very well, dear, but I've always been *most* sensitive. I can't help it. I know it's very silly, but there it is. As a tiny tot, mother always used to say of me, 'That child Vera is so sensitive, she can't bear a sharp word.' I know it's very silly to be thin-skinned, and causes one a great deal of suffering as one goes through life, but it's the way I'm made. I always was so."

This complacent monologue lasted almost to the bottom of Pollard Street, when Grace interrupted desperately: "Do make it up with her before we start this job. It's so much nicer to be all cheerful together when we've got a hard evening in front of us."

"I'm quite willing to be friendly, when Miss Marsh speaks to me first. At the present moment, dear, as you know, she's behaving very strangely indeed, and doesn't speak to me at all. Of course, I don't mind either way—in fact, it only amuses me—but I don't mind telling you, Gracie, that I think her whole way of carrying on is most strange altogether."

Grace felt a desperate certainty that affairs were indeed past remedy when Miss Delmege had to resort so freely to her favourite adjective "strange" to describe the manners and conduct of Miss Marsh.

She entered the hall rather dejectedly. It was very tiring to hurry about with heavy trays at the end of a long day's work, and the atmosphere seemed thicker than ever tonight and the noise greater. Grace hung up her coat and hat, and hastily made room on the already overcrowded peg for Miss Marsh's belongings, as she heard Miss Delmege say gently "*Excuse* me," and deliberately appropriate to her own use the peg selected by her neighbour.

"Did you see that?" demanded Miss Marsh excitedly. "Isn't that Delmege all over? After this, Gracie, I shall simply not speak to her till she apologizes. Simply ignore her. Believe me, dear, it's the only way. I shall behave as though Delmege didn't exist."

This threat was hardly carried out to the letter. No one could have failed to see a poignant consciousness of Miss Delmege's existence in the elaborate blindness and deafness which assailed Miss Marsh when within her neighbourhood.

Miss Delmege adopted a still more trying policy, and addressed acid remarks in a small, penetrating voice to her surroundings.

"I must say the state of *some* trays is like nothing on earth!" she said to Grace, when Miss Marsh had spilt a cup of cocoa over her tray-cloth and brought it back to the counter for a fresh supply. "How the poor men stand it! I must say I do like things to be *dainty* myself. Give me a meal daintily served and I don't care what it is! All depends what one's been used to, I suppose."

"I should be awfully obliged, Gracie, if you could get hold of a clean tray-cloth for me," said Miss Marsh furiously. "There doesn't seem to be anybody not-what-I-call-*capable* here."

Grace looked appealingly at Miss Delmege, but the pince-nez were directed towards the roof, and Miss Delmege's elegantly curved fingers were engaged in swiftly unloading a tray of clean plates.

"A clean cloth for this tray, please," said Gracie rapidly. "There's been a spill."

Miss Delmege, appearing quite capable of seeing through the back of her head, still kept her back turned to the infuriated Miss Marsh, and said coldly: "How very messy, dear! But I'm sure you're not responsible for that. Some people are so strange; their fingers seem to be all thumbs."

"I can't stand here all night, Gracie!" exclaimed Miss Marsh, recklessly tipping all the dirty crockery from the tray on to the counter. "You wouldn't let me have your cloth, I suppose, would you, dear?" At the same time she skilfully disproved her own supposition by rapidly possessing herself of Grace's clean tray-cloth.

"Of all the coolness! Here, dear; I'll give you another one. What's your order?"

"Cup of tea, sausage and mashed, roll of bread."

Miss Delmege gave the short mirthless snigger with which she always acclaimed such orders, so as to make it clear that she did not take anything so vulgar as a sausage and mashed potatoes seriously, and further exclaimed, "They are quaint, aren't they?" as she telephoned through to the kitchen.

"Miss Jones," said Char's cool voice behind her, "I've been watching you for the last five minutes. Kindly ask for what you want a little more quickly. You seem to forget that the man is waiting for his supper."

She waited while the order was being rapidly executed from the kitchen, watching the two girls. Miss Delmege coloured faintly, and moved about restlessly under the scrutiny of which she was obviously conscious, but Grace's small, pale face had not altered, and she stood by the counter waiting for her tray, gazing quite interestedly at a small group of new arrivals.

Mrs. Willoughby stood at the door, eagerly ushering in visitors whom she had obviously invited to survey the scene of her activities.

"This is my little job—plenty of the dear fellows here tonight, you see. Aren't they dears, and don't they look too delightfully at home for words? I must fly back to my barmaid's job now; you'll see me behind the counter in another minute, Joanna. I find I have the most wonderful talent for *chaff*—the men love it so, you know. Do come in, John—you're my chief asset here tonight; the men will simply love your Military Cross. I want you to come round and tell one or two of my special pets exactly how you won it."

Only the secret pressure of his Cousin Joanna's hand on his arm and the mirthful gleam in her blue eyes prevented Captain Trevellyan, with his Military Cross, from taking an instant departure.

Lady Vivian raised her *lorgnette*. "Where's Char?"

"Much too busy on her high official horse even to see me," cried Lesbia with a sort of jovial spite. "Now, Joanna, I insist upon your getting into an overall at once, and helping me. I'll commandeer one."

Grace Jones went past them with her laden tray, and Mrs. Willoughby grasped her arm.

"I want you to find me an overall for this lady before you stir another *step*," she shrieked emphatically.

"Nonsense, Lesbia!" interposed Lady Vivian brusquely. "I don't suppose there is such a thing to spare, and, besides, I don't want one."

She wore the plainest of dark coats and skirts and a soft silk shirt. Grace looked at her with composed admiration and a sense of gratitude. She did not wish to be further delayed with the heavy tray on her hands.

"There's my dear Lance-Corporal!" exclaimed Lesbia, and hurled herself in the direction of a burly form which appeared strongly impelled to seek cover behind the piano as she advanced.

Captain Trevellyan gently took the tray from Miss Jones.

"Where shall I take it?"

"Thank you very much," said Grace thankfully, dropping her aching arms. "That table over there, right at the end, if you will. It's very kind of you."

She turned to Lady Vivian rather apologetically. "I'm afraid I ought not to have let him do that, but we're rather behindhand tonight. Are you come to help?"

She supposed that this tall, curiously attractive new-comer was the wife of one of the officers from the camp.

"Yes, if you'll tell me what to do."

"If you'd carry trays? One of our workers is—is *impeded* tonight," said Grace, conscientiously selecting a euphemism for the peculiar handicap under which Miss Marsh was labouring.

For the next two hours Lady Vivian worked vigorously, in spite of a protest from John, who took the view of feminine weakness peculiar to unusually strong men.

"These trays are too heavy for any woman to carry! It's monstrous! I shall tell Char so."

"By all means tell her. I certainly think it's very bad for these girls, and at the end of a long day's work, too. But as for me, you know I'm as strong as a horse, Johnnie, and I enjoy the exercise. It warms me!"

Her face was glowing and her step elastic. John realized, not for the first time, that Sir Piers's slow, rambling walks round the grounds and still slower evening games of billiards formed the major part of his Cousin Joanna's physical activities. He stood watching her thoughtfully.

Char stopped in his immediate vicinity, and gave a couple of orders in her slow, despotic drawl. She rather wanted Johnnie to see how promptly and unquestioningly they were received.

Johnnie, however, appeared to have his thoughts elsewhere, and Char rather vexedly followed his gaze.

"How I wish my mother wouldn't do this sort of thing!" she said under her breath. "It's most tiring for her, and besides—"

"Besides?" inquired Trevellyan, always courteous, but never of the quickest at catching an inflection.

"I'm afraid I think it *infra dig*. Darting about with all these girls, when she's capable of such very different sort of work—if only she'd do it!"

"My dear Char, what on earth do you want her to do?" demanded Trevellyan, to whom it came as a shock that any one who was privileged to live near Joanna should think her anything but perfect.

"She is an extremely capable woman of business; why shouldn't she take up some big work for the Government? They are crying out for educated women."

"She couldn't possibly leave your father alone at Plessing."

"She could do a certain amount of work at home even without that. The truth is, Johnnie, that neither she nor my father have *realized* there's a war on at all. They've no sons out there in the trenches, and it hasn't hit them materially; they've not felt it in any single, smallest way. I shouldn't say it to any one but you, but there are times at Plessing when I could go *mad*. To hear my father talk on and on about whether some tree on the estate needs cutting or not, just as though on the other side of a little strip of sea—"

She broke off with a shudder that was not altogether histrionic.

"And mother—she wouldn't even knit socks, because it interfered with his billiards in the evenings! I don't understand her, Johnnie. She must *know* what it all means, yet it's all shoved away in the background. Brucey tells me that she's under standing orders not to discuss the news in the papers at breakfast, and mother won't have a single war-book in the house—not even a war-novel, if she can help it. It's as though they were deliberately trying to blind themselves. I *can't* understand it."

Trevellyan did not feel sure that he understood it, either, but, unlike Char, there was in his mind no shadow of criticism for that which he did not understand. The limitation, Trevellyan always felt, was entirely his.

But he was able to look sympathetically also at Char's vexed bewilderment.

"You're not at Plessing very much, nowadays, yourself."

"No. I don't think I could bear it, Johnnie. Of course they say I'm doing too much, but, after all, I'm of an age to decide that for myself, and to my mind there's simply no choice in the matter. Thank Heaven one *can* work!"

"Your undertaking is a colossal thing, in its way. It's wonderful of you, Char!"

She looked pleased.

"It's running well at present. Of course, I know what a tiny part of the whole it is really, but—"

She broke off quickly as Lady Vivian joined them.

"Who is the little dark-haired girl I've been working with, Char? The one at that table...."

"Oh, a Miss—er—Jones," said Char languidly.

"You never told me you had any one of her sort here. I want to ask her out to Plessing. Couldn't we take her back in the car tonight?"

"My dear mother!" Char opened her eyes in an expression of exaggerated horror. "One of my staff?"

"Well?" queried Lady Vivian coolly, stripping off her borrowed overall.

"Quite out of the question. You don't in the least realize the official footing on which I have to keep those women."

"I should have thought you needn't be any the less official for showing some friendliness to a girl who's come all the way from Wales to help you."

"She's my under-secretary, mother."

"What! sub-scrub to the genteel Miss Delmege? She's got ten times her brains, and is a lady into the bargain."

It infuriated Char that her mother's cool, tacit refusal to acknowledge the infallibility of the Director of the Midland Supply Depôt could always make her feel like a little girl again.

She rallied all her most official mannerisms together.

"It's quite impossible for me to differentiate between the various members of the staff, or to make any unofficial advances to any of them."

"Very well, my dear. As, thank Heaven, I'm not a member of your staff, I can remain as unofficial as I please, and have nice little Miss Jones out to see me."

"Mother," said Char in an agony, "it's simply *impossible*. The girl would never know her place in the office again; and think of all the cackling there'd be at the Questerham Hostel about my asking any one out to Plessing. Johnnie, do tell her it's out of the question."

Trevellyan looked at Joanna with a laugh in his blue eyes. He realized, as Char would never realize, that her assumption of officialdom always provoked her mother to the utterance of ironical threats which she had never the slightest intention of fulfilling.

She shrugged her shoulders slightly at her daughter's vehemence, and crossed over to where Grace Jones was putting on her coat and hat again.

"Good-night. I hope you're not as tired as you look," she said with a sort of abrupt graciousness.

"Oh no, thank you. It's been an extra busy night. It was so kind of you to help."

"I wish I could come again," said Lady Vivian rather wistfully, "but I don't know that I shall be able to."

Lesbia Willoughby, dashing past them at full speed, found time to fling a piercing rebuke over her shoulder.

"There's *always* a will where there's a way, Joanna. Look at me!"

Neither of them took advantage of the invitation, and Joanna said irrelevantly: "I should like you to come and see me, if you will, but I know you're at work all day. I must try and find you next time I come into Questerham."

"Thank you very much," said Grace in a pleased voice. "I should like that very much indeed. Good-night."

"Good-night," repeated Joanna, and went back to where her daughter, with a rather indignant demeanour, was waiting for her.

"Well?" asked Char, rather sullenly.

Lady Vivian, who almost invariably became flippant when her daughter was most in earnest, said provokingly: "Well, my dear, I've made arrangements for all sorts of unofficial rendezvous. You may see Miss Delmege at Plessing yet."

"Miss Delmege is a very good worker," said Char icily. "She's very much in earnest, always ready to stay overtime and finish up anything important."

"I'm sure Miss Jones is good at her job, too," said Trevellyan, supposing himself to be tactful.

"Fairly good. Not extraordinarily quick-witted, though, and much too sure of herself. I can't help thinking it's rather a pity to distinguish her from the others, mother; she's probably only too ready to take airs as it is, if she's of rather a different class."

"Fiddlesticks!" declared Lady Vivian briskly. "Put on your coat, Char, and come along. I can't keep the car waiting any longer. Rather a different class indeed! What has that to do with it? The girl's most attractive—an original type, too."

"Of course, if mother has taken one of her sudden violent fancies to this Jones child, I may as well make up my mind to hear nothing else, morning, noon, or night," Char muttered to John Trevellyan, who replied with matter-of-fact common sense that Char wasn't at Plessing for more than an hour or two on any single day, let alone morning, noon, and night.

"Char," said Lady Vivian from the car, "if you don't come now I shall leave you to spend the night at the Questerham Hostel, where you'll lose all your prestige with the staff, and have to eat and sleep just like an ordinary human being."

The Director of the Midland Supply Depôt got into her parent's motor in silence, and with a movement that might have been fairly described as a flounce.

The members of the staff walked up the street towards the Hostel.

"Who was the lady in black who helped with the trays?" asked Grace. "She was so nice."

"My dear, didn't you know? That was Miss Vivian's *mother*!"

"Oh, was it?" said Grace placidly. "I didn't know that. Miss Vivian isn't very like her, is she?"

"No. Of course, Miss Vivian's far better looking. I'm not saying it because it's her," added Miss Delmege with great distinctness, for the benefit of Miss Marsh and Mrs. Potter, walking behind, from one of whom a sound of contemptuous mirth had proceeded faintly. "It's simply a fact. Miss Vivian is far better looking than Lady Vivian ever was. Takes after her father—Sir Piers Vivian he is, you know."

Miss Delmege had only once been afforded a view of the back of Sir Piers Vivian's white head in church, but she made the assertion with her usual air of genteel omniscience.

At the Hostel Mrs. Bullivant was waiting for them. It was past eleven o'clock, and the fire had gone out soon after eight; but in spite of cold and weariness, Mrs. Bullivant was unconquerably bright.

"Come along; I'll have some nice hot tea for you in a moment. The kettle is on the gas-ring. I *am* sorry the fire's out, but it smoked so badly all the evening I thought I'd better leave it alone. Sit down; I'm sure you're all tired."

"Simply dead," exclaimed Miss Marsh. "So are you, aren't you, Plumtree, after all those awful plates and dishes—I must say your washing-up job is the worst of the lot."

"I'm going to bed. I can't keep on my feet another minute, tea or no tea. If I don't drag myself upstairs now I never shall. It's fatal to sit down; one can't get up again."

"That's right," assented Miss Marsh. "I'll bring up your tea when I come, dear."

"Angel, thanks awfully. Good-night, ladies and gentlemen."

Miss Plumtree left the sitting-room with this languidly facetious valediction.

"That girl *does* look tired. I hope she gets into bed quickly," observed Mrs. Potter, pulling off her hat and exposing a rakishly *décoiffé* tangle of wispy hair.

"Not she—she'll dawdle for ages," prophesied Miss Marsh. "Still, it's something if she gets into her dressing-gown and bedroom slippers, out of her corsets, you know."

Miss Delmege put down her cup of tea.

"Rather a strange subject we seem to be on for mealtime, don't we?" she remarked detachedly to Grace.

"Meal-time?" exclaimed Miss Henderson derisively.

"That's what I said, dear, and I'm in the habit of meaning what I say, as far as I know."

"I really don't know how you can call it meal-time when we're not even at table. Besides, if we were, there's nothing *in* what Marsh said—absolutely nothing at all."

"Oh, of course, some people see harm in anything," burst out Miss Marsh, very red. "The harm is in their own minds, is what I say, otherwise they wouldn't see any."

"That's right," agreed Miss Henderson, but below her breath.

Miss Delmege turned with dignity to her other neighbour.

"I may be peculiar, but that's how I feel about it. I imagine that you, as a married woman, will agree with me, Mrs. Potter?"

Mrs. Potter did not agree with her at all, but something in the appeal, some subtle hint of the dignity of Mrs. Potter's position amongst so many virgins, caused her to temporize feebly.

"Really, Miss Delmege, you mustn't ask me. I—I quite see with you—but at the same time— there wasn't anything in what Miss Marsh said, now, was there? I mean, really. Simply corsets, you know."

Nearly every one had by this time forgotten exactly what Miss Marsh *had* said, and only retained a general impression of licentiousness in conversation.

"We're all girls together," exclaimed Miss Marsh furiously.

"Gentlemen in the room would be a very different thing," Miss Henderson supported her.

"I'll take a second cup, Mrs. Bullivant, if you please," said Miss Delmege with dignity.

"There!" exclaimed Miss Henderson.

Miss Marsh had suddenly begun to cry.

Mrs. Bullivant hastily poured out more tea, and said uncertainly: "Come, come!"

"There's no call for any one to cry, that I can see," observed Miss Delmege, still detached, but in a tone of uneasiness.

"The fact is, I'm not myself today," sobbed Miss Marsh.

"What is it?" said Gracie sympathetically. She slipped a friendly hand into her room-mate's.

"I had a letter which upset me this morning. A great friend of mine, who's been wounded—a boy I know most awfully well."

"Why didn't you tell me, dear?" asked Miss Henderson. "I didn't even know you had a boy out there."

"Oh, not a *feawncy*—only a chum," said Miss Marsh, still sniffing.

"Is he bad, dear?"

"A flesh-wound in the arm, and something about trench feet."

"That's a nice slow thing, and they'll send him to England to get well," prophesied Grace.

Miss Delmege rose from her seat.

"I'm sorry you've been feeling upset," she said to Miss Marsh. "It seems rather strange you didn't say anything sooner, but I'm sorry about it."

"Thank you," Miss Marsh replied with a gulp. "If I've been rather sharp in my manner today, I hope you won't think I meant anything. This has rather upset me."

Miss Delmege bowed slightly, and Grace, fearing an anticlimax, begged Miss Marsh to come up to bed.

The final amende was made next morning, when Miss Delmege, in a buff-coloured drapery known as "my fawn*peignwaw*," came to the door and asked for admittance.

Grace opened the door, and Miss Delmege said, in a voice even more distinct than usual: "I know Miss Marsh was tired last night, dear, so I've brought her a cup of our early tea."

VII

"Mother, are you coming to the Canteen again tomorrow? You remember what a rush it was last Monday, and it'll be just as bad again."

"No, Char, I am *not*," was the unvarnished reply of Lady Vivian.

Char compressed her lips and sighed. She would have been almost as much disappointed as surprised if her mother had suddenly expressed an intention of appearing regularly at the Canteen, but she knew that Miss Bruce was looking at her with an admiring and compassionate gaze.

Sir Piers, who substituted chess for billiards on Sunday evenings because he thought it due to the servants to show that the Lord's Day was respected at Plessing, looked up uneasily.

"You're not going out again tomorrow, eh, my dear? I missed our game sadly the other night."

"No, it's all right; I'm not going again."

Joanna never raised her voice very much, but Sir Piers always heard what she said. It made Char wonder sometimes, half irritably and half ashamedly, whether he could not have heard other people, had he wanted to. The overstrain from which she herself was quite unconsciously suffering made her nervously impatient of the old man's increasing slowness of perception.

"And where has Char been all this afternoon? I never see you about the house now," Sir Piers said, half maunderingly, half with a sort of bewilderment that was daily increasing in his view of small outward events.

"I've been at my work," said Char, raising her voice, partly as a vent to her own feelings. "I go into the office on Sunday afternoons always, and a very good thing I do, too. They were making a fearful muddle of some telegrams yesterday."

"Telegrams? You can't send telegrams on a Sunday, child; they aren't delivered. I don't like you to go to this place on Sundays, either. Joanna, my dear, we mustn't allow her to do that."

Char cast up her eyes in a sort of desperation, and went into the further half of the drawing-room, where Miss Bruce sat, just hearing her mother say gently: "Look, Piers, I shall take your castle."

"Brucey," said Char, "I think they'll drive me mad. I know my work is nothing, really—such a tiny, infinitesimal part of a great whole—but if I could only get a *little* sympathy. It does seem so extraordinary, when one has been working all day, giving one's whole self to it all, and then to come back to this sort of atmosphere!"

Miss Bruce was perhaps the only person with whom Char was absolutely unreserved. In younger days Miss Bruce had been her adoring governess, and the old relations still existed between them. Char knew that Miss Bruce had always thought Lady Vivian's management of her only child terribly injudicious, and that in the prolonged antagonism between herself and her mother Miss Bruce's silent loyalty had always ranged itself on Char's side.

"It's very hard on you, my dear," she sighed. "But I have been afraid lately—have you noticed, I wonder?"

"What?"

"Sir Piers seems to me to be failing; he is so much deafer, so much more dependent on Lady Vivian."

"He's always *that*," said Char. "I think it's only the beginning of the winter, Brucey. He always feels the cold weather."

But a very little while later Miss Bruce's view received unexpected corroboration.

Three Sundays later, when the weather had grown colder than ever, and Char was, as usual, spending the afternoon and evening at the Depôt, Mrs. Willoughby paid a call at Plessing.

She was followed into the room, with almost equal unwillingness, by her husband and a small, immensely stout Pekinese dog, with bulging eyes and a quick, incessant bark that only Mrs. Willoughby's voice could dominate.

"Darling Joanna!" she shrieked. "Puffles, wicked, wicked boy, be quiet! Isn't this an invasion? But my Lewis did so want—I shall smack 'oo if 'oo isn't quiet directly. *Do* you mind this little brown boy, who goes*everywhere* with his mammy? I knew you'd love him if you saw him—but *such* a noise! Lewis, tell this naughty Puff his mother can't hear herself speak."

"Down, sir!" said Lewis, in tones which might have quelled a mastiff with hydrophobia.

Puff waddled for refuge to his mistress, who immediately gathered him on to her lap as she sank on to the sofa.

"Did 'oo daddy speak in a big rough voice, and frighten the poor little manikin?" she inquired solicitously. "Isn't he *rather* twee, Joanna?"

"I've not seen it before," said Joanna, in tones more civil than enthusiastic.

"It!" screamed Lesbia. "She calls 'oo *it*, my Puffles! as though he wasn't the sweetest little brown boy in the whole world. It! You've hurt his little feelings too dreadfully, my dear—look at him sulking!"

Puff had composed himself into a sort of dribbling torpor.

"That dog doesn't get enough exercise," said Major Willoughby suddenly, fixing his eyes upon his hostess.

"Surely it—he—is too small to require a great deal," said Lady Vivian languidly. Lap-dogs bored her very much indeed, and she turned away her eyes after taking one rather disgusted look at the recumbent Puff through her eyeglasses.

"Train up a dog in the way it should go. Now, this little fellah—you'd hardly believe it, Lady Vivian, if I were to tell you the difference in him after he's had a good run over the Common."

"Lewis!" cried Lesbia, opening her eyes to an incredible extent, as was her wont whenever she wished to emphasize her words. "I *can't* have you boring people about Puff. Lewis is a perfect slave to Puffles, and tries to hide it by calling him 'the dog' and talking about his training."

Lewis looked self-conscious, and immediately said: "Not at all; not at all. But the dog is an intelligent little brute. Now, I'll tell you what happened the other day."

Major Willoughby gave various instances of Puff's discrimination, and Lesbia kissed the top of Puff's somnolent head and exclaimed shrilly at intervals that "it was too, too bad to pay the little treasure so many compliments; it would turn his little fluffy head, it would."

Lady Vivian reflected that she might certainly absolve herself from the charge of contributing to this catastrophe. The language of compliment had seldom been further from her lips; but in any case her visitors left her little of the trouble of sustaining conversation.

It was evident that Puff was a recent acquisition in the Willoughby *ménage*.

"Where's your dear girl?" Lesbia presently inquired fondly of her hostess.

"In Questerham, at the Depôt."

"Now, Joanna, I'm going to be perfectly candid. You won't mind, I know—after all, you and I were girls together. What Char needs, my dear, is *flogging*."

Lady Vivian was conscious of distinct relief at the thought that her secretary did not happen to be within earshot of this startling expression of opinion.

"You are certainly being perfectly candid, Lesbia," she said dryly. "What has poor Char been doing to require flogging, may I ask?"

"You ask me that, Joanna! Lewis, hark at her!"

Lewis, thus appealed to, looked very uncomfortable, and said in a non-committal manner: "H'm, yes, yes. Hi! Puff!—good dog, sir!" thus rousing the Pekinese to a fresh outburst of ear-piercing barks.

When this had at length been quelled by the blandishments of Lesbia and the words of command repeatedly given in a martial tone by her husband, Lady Vivian repeated her inquiry, and Mrs. Willoughby replied forcibly: "My dear, nothing but flogging would ever bring her to her senses. The way she's treating you and poor dear Sir Piers! He's looking iller and older every day, and tells me himself that he never sees her now; it's too piteous to hear him, dear old thing. It would wring tears from a stone—wouldn't it, Lewis?"

"Down, sir, down, I say!" was the reply of Major Willoughby, addressed to the investigating Puff.

"Oh, naughty boy, leave the screen alone. Now, come here to mother, then. What was I telling you, Joanna? Oh, about that girl of yours. War-work is all very well, my dear, but to *my* mind home-ties are absolutely sacred, and more than ever before in such a time as this, when we may all be swept away by some ghastly air-raid in a night. It's simply a time when homes should *cling* together. I always tell my Lewis it's a time when we should *cling* more than ever before—don't I, Lewis?"

Lewis looked at Puff with a compelling eye, but Puff was again quiescent, and gave him no opening.

Lady Vivian said, very briskly indeed: "Char is not at all a clinging person, Lesbia, and neither am I. We can each stand very comfortably on our own feet, and I'm proud of the work she's doing in Questerham. Now, do let me give you some tea."

"Joanna, I know perfectly well you're snubbing me and telling me to mind my own business, but Lewis can tell you that I'm perfectly impervious. I *always* say exactly what I want to say, and if you won't listen to me, I shall talk to your good man. I can hear him coming."

The entrance of Sir Piers Vivian was the signal for a frantic uproar from Puff, who hurled a shrill defiance at him from the hearth-rug, which he so exactly matched in colour as to be indistinguishable from it.

"Bless me, Joanna, what's all this?" inquired the astonished Sir Piers, looking all round him in search of the monster from which so much noise could proceed.

He failed to perceive it, and stumbled heavily over the hearth-rug.

There was a howl from Puff; Lesbia cried, "Oh, my little manikin, is 'oo deaded?" Major Willoughby exclaimed in agonized tones to his host, "By Jove! the dog got in your way, sir, I'm afraid;" and to Puff, "Get out of the light, sir; what are you doing there?" and Lady Vivian gave a sudden irrepressible peal of laughter.

So that Lesbia, taking her departure half an hour later, remarked conclusively to her Lewis that the strain of this dreadful war was making poor dear Joanna Vivian positively hysterical.

She repeated the same alarming statement for Char's benefit next time she saw her at the Canteen. "I shouldn't say it, my dear child, but that your darling mother and I were girls together, and it's simply breaking my heart to see how broken up your father is, and no one to take any of the strain of it off *her*."

Mrs. Willoughby spoke in her usual penetrating accents, and without any regard for the fact that at least three members of Miss Vivian's staff were well within earshot.

"No one can be keener than I am about doing one's bit for this ghastly war, but I do think, dear, that your place just now is at home—at least part of each day. You won't mind an old friend's speaking quite, quite plainly, I know."

Char minded so much that she was white with annoyance.

"I can't discuss it here," she said, in a voice even lower than usual, in rebukeful contrast to Lesbia's screeching tones. "I should be only too thankful if I could get my place satisfactorily filled here, but at present it's perfectly impossible for me to leave even for an hour or two. I very often don't get time even for lunch nowadays."

"Simply because you enjoy making a martyr of yourself!" said Mrs. Willoughby spitefully.

Char, dropping her eyelids in a manner that gave her a look of incredible insolence, moved away without replying.

For the next week she worked harder than ever, multiplying letters and incessant interviews, and depriving herself daily of an extra hour's sleep in the morning by starting for the Depôt earlier than usual, so as to cope with the press of business. It was her justification to herself for Mrs. Willoughby's crude accusations and the unspoken reproach in Sir Piers's feeble bewilderment at her activities.

Miss Plumtree fell ill with influenza, and Char took over her work, and arranged with infinite trouble to herself that Miss Plumtree should go to a small convalescent home in the country, because the doctor said she needed change of air. She was to incur no expense, Char told her, very kindly, and even remembered to order a cab for her at the country station. Miss Plumtree, owning that she could never have afforded a journey to her home in Devonshire, cried tears of mingled weakness and gratitude, and told the Hostel all that Miss Vivian had done.

Everybody said it was exactly like Miss Vivian, and that she really was too wonderful.

Then the demon of influenza began its yearly depredations. One member of the staff after another went down with it, was obliged to plead illness and go to bed at the Hostel, and inevitably pass on the complaint to her room-mate.

"I'm afraid Mrs. Potter won't be coming today," Miss Delmege announced deprecatingly to her chief, who struck the table with her hand and exclaimed despairingly:

"Of course! just because there's more to be done than ever! Influenza, I suppose?"

"I'm afraid it is."

"That's five of them down with it now—or is it six? I don't know *what* to do."

"It does seem strange," was the helpless rejoinder of Miss Vivian's secretary.

Char thought the adjective inadequate to a degree. She abated not one jot of all that she had undertaken, and accomplished the work of six people.

Miss Delmege several times ventured to exclaim, with a sort of respectful despair, that Miss Vivian would kill herself, and Char knew that the rest of the staff was saying much the same thing behind her back. At Plessing Miss Bruce remonstrated admiringly, and exclaimed every day how tired Char was looking, throwing at the same time a rather resentful glance upon Lady Vivian.

But Joanna remained quite unperceiving of the dark lines deepening daily beneath her daughter's heavy eyes.

She was entirely absorbed in Sir Piers, becoming daily more dependent upon her.

The day came, when the influenza epidemic was at its height in Questerham, when Miss Bruce exclaimed in tones of scarcely suppressed indignation as Char came downstairs after the usual hasty breakfast which she had in her own room: "My dear, you're not fit to go. Really you're not; you ought to be in bed this moment. Do, do let me telephone and say you can't come today. Indeed, it isn't right. You look as though you hadn't slept all night."

"I haven't, much," said Char hoarsely. "I have a cold, that's all."

"Miss Vivian was coughing half the night," thrust in her maid, hovering in the hall laden with wraps.

"You mustn't go!" cried Miss Bruce distractedly.

"You really aren't fit, Miss."

Lady Vivian appeared at the head of the stairs.

"What's all this?"

"Oh, Lady Vivian," cried the secretary, "do look at her! She ought to be in bed."

Char said: "Nonsense!" impatiently, but she gave her mother an opportunity for seeing that her face was white and drawn, with heavily ringed eyes and feverish lips.

"You've got influenza, Char."

"I dare say," said Char in tones of indifference. "It would be very odd if I'd escaped, since half the office is down with it. But I can't afford to give in."

"It would surely be truer economy to take a day off now than to risk a real breakdown later on," was the time-worn argument urged by Miss Bruce.

Char smiled with pale decision.

"Let me pass, Brucey. I really mean it."

"Lady Vivian!" wailed the secretary.

Joanna shrugged her shoulders. She, too, looked weary.

"Be reasonable, Char."

"It's of no use, mother. I shouldn't dream of giving in while there's work to be done."

Miss Bruce gave a sort of groan of mingled admiration and despair at this heroic statement. Char slipped her arms into the fur coat that her maid was holding out for her.

Lady Vivian stood at the top of the stairs looking at her with an air of detached consideration, and left Miss Bruce to make those hurried dispositions of foot-warmer, fur rug, and little bottles of sulphate and quinine which, the secretary resentfully felt, a more maternal woman would have taken upon herself.

But Lady Vivian's omissions were not destined to provide the only one, or even the most severe, of the shocks received by Miss Bruce's sensibilities that morning.

As Char extended her hand for the last of Miss Bruce's offerings, a small green bottle of highly pungent smelling salts, Lady Vivian's incisive tones came levelly from above.

"You'd better stay the night at Questerham, Char. It will be very cold driving back after dark."

"Oh no, mother. Besides, I don't know where I could go. I hate the hotel, and one can't inflict an influenza cold on other people."

"You can go to your Hostel. Surely there's a spare bed?"

The ghost of a smile flickered upon Lady Vivian's face, as though in mischievous anticipation of Char's refusal.

"It's quite out of the question. The Hostel is for my staff, and it would be very unsuitable for me, as Director of the Midland Supply Depôt, to go there too."

"Bless me! are they as exclusive as all that?" exclaimed Joanna flippantly. "Well, do as you like, but if you come back here, you're not to go near your father, with a cold like that."

Miss Bruce, almost before she knew it, found herself exchanging a glance of indignation with Char's maid, but she was conscious enough of her own dignity to look away again in a great hurry.

"You will certainly want to go straight to bed when you come in," she said to Char, pointedly enough. "We will have everything ready and a nice fire in your room."

"Thank you, Brucey."

Char bestowed her rare smile upon the little agitated secretary, and moved across the hall.

She felt very ill, with violent pains in her head and back, and shivered intermittently.

Leaning back in her heavy coat, under the fur rug, Char closed her eyes. She reflected on the dismay with which Miss. Delmege would greet her, and wondered rather grimly whether any further members of her staff would have succumbed to the prevailing illness. She knew that only a will of iron could surmount such physical ills as she was herself enduring, and dreaded the moment when she must rouse herself from her present torpid discomfort to the necessity of moving and speaking.

As she got out of the car, Char reeled and almost fell, in an intolerable spasm of giddiness, and her progress up the stairs was only made possible by the remnant of strength which allowed her to grasp the baluster and lean her full weight upon it as she dragged herself into her office.

She was, however, met with no wail of condolence from the genteel accents of Miss Delmege.

Grace Jones, composedly solid and healthy-looking, said placidly: "Good-morning. I'm sorry to say that Miss Delmege is in bed with influenza."

"In bed!"

"She had a very restless night and has a temperature this morning."

"She was all right yesterday."

"She had a sore throat, you know," remarked Grace, "but she didn't at all want to give in, and is very much distressed."

Char raised her heavy eyes.

"You all seem to me to collapse like a pack of cards, one after another. I think *my* bed would prove a bed of thorns while there's so much work to do, and so few people to do it. In fact, I can't imagine wanting to go there."

She made an infinitesimal pause, shaken by one of those violent, involuntary, shivering fits. Miss Jones gazed at her chief.

"I think I can manage Miss Delmege's work," she observed gently.

"Oh, I shall have to go through most of it myself, of course," was the ungrateful retort of the suffering Miss Vivian.

The day appeared to her interminable. The air was damp and raw; and although Miss Jones piled coal upon the fire, it refused to blaze up, and only smouldered in a sullen heap, with a small curling column of yellow smoke at the top. A traction-engine ground and screamed and pounded its way up and down under the window, and each time it passed directly in front of the house the floor and walls of Char's room shook slightly, with a vibration that made her feel sick and giddy.

There were no interviews, but letters and telephone messages poured in incessantly, and at about twelve o'clock a telegram marked "Priority" was brought her. With a sinking sense of utter dismay, Char tore it open.

"A rest-station for a troop-train at five o'clock this afternoon. Eight hundred. Miss Jones, please let the Commissariat Department know at once. The staff should be at the station by three. I'll make out the list at once, and you can take it round the office."

By four o'clock a fine cold rain was falling, and Char's voice had nearly gone.

As she hurried down to her car, which was to take her to the station, she heard an incautiously raised voice: "She does look so ill! Of course it's flu, and I should think this rest-station will just about finish her off."

"Not she! I do believe she'd stick it out if she were dying. No lunch today, either, only a cup of Bovril, which I simply had to force her to take."

Char recognized the voice of Miss Henderson, who had received her order for lunch in place of Miss Delmege, and had ventured to suggest the Bovril in tones of the utmost deference.

She smiled slightly.

The troop-train was late.

"Of course!" muttered Char, pacing up and down the sheltered platform with the fur collar of her motoring coat turned up, and her hands deep in its wide pockets.

In the waiting-rooms, given over to the workers for the time being, the staff was active.

Sandwiches were cut, and heavy trays and urns carried out in readiness, while orderlies from the hospitals put up light trestle tables at intervals along the platform.

Char paused, turned the handle of the waiting-room door, and stood for a moment on the threshold.

Every one was talking. Trays piled with cut and stacked sandwiches were ranged all round the room; tin mugs, again on trays, stood in groups of twelve; and the final spoonfuls of sugar were being scooped from a tin biscuit-box into the waiting bowl on each tray. Even the cake was already cut, sliced up on innumerable plates.

They had been working hard, and had more work to come, yet they all looked gay and amused, and were talking and laughing as though they did not know the meaning of fatigue. And Char was feeling so ill that she could hardly stand.

Suddenly some one caught sight of her, there was a sort of murmur, "Miss Vivian!" and in one moment self-consciousness invaded the room. Those who were sitting down stood up, trying to look at ease; little Miss Anthony, who had been manipulating the bread-cutting machine with great success all the afternoon, at once cut her finger with it, and some one else suddenly dropped a mug with a reverberating clatter.

"Miss Cox!"

She sprang forward nervously.

"Yes, Miss Vivian?"

"How many sandwiches have you got ready?"

"Sixteen hundred, Miss Vivian. That'll be two for each man, and they're very large."

"Cut another hundred, for reserve."

"Yes, Miss Vivian."

They began to work again, this time speaking almost in whispers.

Char turned away.

Her personality, as usual, had had its effect.

Nearly twenty minutes later the station-master came up to her on the platform.

"She'll be in directly now, Miss Vivian. Just signalled."

Char wheeled smartly back to the waiting-room and gave the word of command.

Within five minutes the urns and trays were all in place on the tables, and each worker was at her appointed stand. Char had indicated beforehand, as she always did, the exact duties of each one.

"That's a smart bit of work," the station-master remarked admiringly.

"Ah, well, you see, I've been at the job some time now," said Miss Vivian, pleased. She never pretended to look upon her staff as anything but a collection of pawns, to be placed or disposed of by a master hand.

And it was part of that strength of personality that lay at the back of all her powers of organization, which had given the majority of her staff exactly the same impression as her own of their relative positions with regard to the Director of the Midland Supply Depôt.

VIII

Char moved up and down the length of the train.

She never carried any of the laden trays herself, but she saw to it that no man missed his mug of steaming tea and supply of sandwiches and cake, and she exerted all the affability and charm of which she held the secret, in talking to the soldiers. The packets of cigarettes with which she was always laden added to her popularity, and when the train steamed slowly out of the station again the men raised a cheer.

"Three cheers for Miss Vivian!"

Her name had passed like lightning from one carriage to another.

"Hooray-ay."

They hung out of the window, waving their caps, and Char stood at the end of the platform, heedless of the rain now pouring down on her, and waved until the train was out of sight.

"Start washing up and packing the things at once."

"Yes, Miss Vivian."

The waiting-room was already seething and full of steam from the zinc pans of boiling water into which mugs and knives were being flung with deafening clatter.

"Here, chuck me a dry cloth! Mine's wringing."

"Oh, look out, dear! You're splashing your uniform like anything."

"I've got such a lot of work waiting for me when I get back to the office."

"Poor fellows, they did look bad! Did you see one chap, quite a young fellow, too, with his poor leg and all...."

Char turned away impatiently.

Thank Heaven, there was nothing further for her to do at the station.

The work at the office would be heavy enough, but at least she had not to stand amongst that noisy crew of workers round the big packing-cases and wash-tubs, each one screaming so as to make herself heard above the splashing water and clattered crockery.

It did not occur to her, as the car took her swiftly back to the office, also to be thankful that neither had she to walk back, as they had, in the streaming rain and cold of the dark evening.

She swallowed one of Miss Bruce's quinine tablets with her hot tea, but was unable to eat anything, and sat over her letters with throbbing temples and a temperature that she felt to be rising rapidly. She pored over each simplest sentence again and again, unable to attach any meaning to the words dancing before her aching, swimming eyes.

Soon after half-past six Grace Jones came back from the station, her pale face glowing from the wind and rain, unabated vigour in her movements.

"Have you only just got back?"

"I had some tea downstairs. I've been in about ten minutes."

Char raised her eyebrows with an expression that would have caused Miss Delmege ostentatiously to refrain from tea every day for a week, had it been directed towards herself.

But Miss Jones only said tranquilly: "Is there anything that I can do for you?"

"No. Yes. You can answer that telephone."

The bell had suddenly sounded, and Char felt no strength to exert the swollen, aching muscles of her throat.

Grace took up the receiver.

"They want to speak to you from Plessing."

Char checked an exclamation of impatience. If only Brucey wouldn't *fuss* so! She might know by this time that it was of no use.

"Please say that I can't take a private call from here. Ask if it's on business."

She waited impatiently.

"It's not on business—it's important. Lady Vivian is speaking."

Char almost snatched the receiver.

"What is it?" she asked curtly.

"Is that you, Char?" came over the wires.

"Miss Vivian speaking," returned Char officially, for the benefit of Miss Jones.

"Your father is ill. He has had a very slight stroke, and I want you to bring out Dr. Prince in the car."

"How bad is he? Have you had any one?"

"Yes. Dr. Clark came up from the village, but he suggested sending for Dr. Prince at once. He is unconscious, of course, and there isn't any immediate danger; he may get over it altogether, but—this is the first minute I've had—I am going back to him now. Come as soon as you can, Char, and bring the doctor. I can't get him on the telephone, but you must get hold of him somehow."

"Yes—yes. Is there anything else?"

"Nothing now, my dear. By great good luck John is here, and most helpful. He carried your father upstairs. Only don't delay, will you?"

"No. I'll come at once. Good-bye."

"Good-bye."

Char replaced the receiver, feeling dazed.

Involuntarily her first sensation was one of injury that any one should be more ill than she was herself, and able to excite so much stir.

The next moment she regained possession of herself.

"Miss Jones, ring up the garage and tell them to send my car round immediately. Sir Piers Vivian has been taken ill, and I am going out to Plessing at once. Tell them to hurry."

Grace obeyed, and Char began feverishly to make order amongst the pile of papers on her table.

"I'm leaving a lot undone," she muttered, "but I suppose I shall be here tomorrow morning. I must be."

Ten minutes later the car was at the door.

"Miss Jones, see that all *these* go tonight," Char rapidly instructed her secretary. "The letters I haven't been able to sign must be held over till tomorrow. By the way, didn't the—er—your Hostel Superintendent say that she wanted an appointment with me this evening?"

"Mrs. Bullivant? Yes. She was coming at eight."

"Then, please tell her what's happened, and say that I will arrange to see her some time tomorrow. That's all, I think."

"I hope Sir Piers Vivian will be better by the time you get back."

"I hope so. Thank you. Good-night, Miss Jones."

Char hurried downstairs, hoping that the tone of her voice had put Miss Jones into her proper place again. She did not encourage personal amenities between herself and her staff.

It was nearly nine o'clock before she got to Plessing. It had taken a long while to find Dr. Prince, and the chauffeur drove with maddening precautions through a thick wet mist along the sodden, slippery roads.

"A broken leg or two would delay us worse," said the doctor philosophically.

He was a bearded, hard-working man, with a reputation that extended beyond the Midlands.

After finding out from Char that she knew little or nothing of her father's state of health, he asked her with a quick look: "And yourself, Miss Charmian? You look rather washed out."

Char gave a short, hoarse cough, semi-involuntary, at this unflattering description.

"I'm afraid I'm in the midst of an influenza attack. My staff have all been down with it, more or less. However, I can't afford to give way to that sort of thing now; there's far too much work to be done."

"You ought to take six months' holiday," said the doctor decidedly, and relapsed into silence.

Char wondered if he were meditating an appeal to her. It must outrage his professional instincts to see any one looking as she did still upon her feet. The doctor, however, who had been up since two o'clock that morning, was merely trying to snatch some sleep.

He had known Char Vivian all her life, and had no thought whatever of wasting appeals upon her.

At Plessing, Trevellyan met them in the hall.

"Good-evening, Char," he greeted her. "Sir Piers is much the same. Not conscious. Will you go up, doctor? They'll have some dinner ready by the time you come down. I'm afraid you've had a cold drive."

"Freezing," answered Char, with a violent shiver.

"Better go to bed," said the doctor, without looking at her, as he went upstairs.

Char, still in her fur coat, hung over the fire.

"Tell me what's happened, Johnnie."

"Cousin Joanna says that he was very restless and low-spirited last night—talked about the war, you know, and this last air-raid. And when he came down this morning he suddenly turned giddy and fell across the hall sofa. Luckily it wasn't on the floor. Cousin Joanna was with him, and they got him flat on the sofa, and sent for Clark. I got here about the same time as he did, by pure chance—came over for a day's shooting, you know—and between us we carried him upstairs. By Jove! he's no light weight for a man of his years, either."

"What does Dr. Clark think?"

"That he'll probably recover consciousness in a day or two. But even then—don't be frightened, Char; it's only what generally happens in these cases—his—his words probably won't come quite right, you know. He may speak, but not quite normally."

Char smiled a little at her cousin's look of anxious solicitude for the effect of his surmises upon her.

"I'm not without hospital experience, you know," she said gently. "It's the left side of the brain, then? Is his right side paralyzed?"

"I'm afraid so—arm and hand, you know. We shall see what Prince says."

There was a pause, and Char said hoarsely: "I wonder if I ought to go up?"

"Is that you, Miss Vivian?" came the voice of Miss Bruce from the stairs.

Char turned and went slowly up to her.

Trevellyan did not see her again that evening, and Miss Bruce told him later, with rather a reproachful look, that poor Miss Vivian was not fit to be up.

"It was a shock to her, I'm afraid."

"Yes—oh yes; but she really was dreadfully ill when she went out this morning. She ought never, never to have been allowed to leave the house."

"You don't mean to say she's going to be ill too?" exclaimed Trevellyan in tones of dismay.

He was thinking that Joanna had enough anxiety as it was; but Miss Bruce attributed his tones entirely to concern on behalf of her adored Miss Vivian, and looked at him more amiably.

"I'm afraid it's influenza, but a couple of days in bed will make all the difference, and now that, of course, there's no question of her leaving the house, she'll be able to take care of herself for once."

"There she is," said Captain Trevellyan, and strode across the hall to meet his Cousin Joanna and the doctor.

Miss Bruce waited to hear Dr. Prince's verdict, and then went quietly up to Char's room, with offers of service that aroused the unconcealed wrath of Char's devoted maid.

"I don't want anything," Miss Vivian declared wearily. "As soon as I know whether I may see father, I can go to bed—or go up to him, as the case may be. But I suppose my mother means to come down to me some time?"

There was more than a hint of resentment in her wearied voice.

"Shall I tell her ladyship you're here, miss?" asked the maid gently.

"She knows it," said Char shortly. "I brought Dr. Prince."

The zealous Miss Bruce slipped silently from the room and down into the hall again.

Lady Vivian, oblivious of her daughter's claims, was discussing Dr. Prince's verdict in lowered tones with Captain Trevellyan.

Miss Bruce felt a sort of melancholy triumph in beholding this justification for Char's obvious sense of injury.

"Miss Vivian is in her room, and waiting for you most anxiously," she said reproachfully. "She thought you were still with Sir Piers. She won't go to bed until she knows whether she may see him."

"Poor child, it wouldn't do her any good to see him," said Joanna. "There's no sign of returning consciousness yet, though Dr. Prince thinks he may come to himself almost any time, and then everything depends upon his being kept absolutely quiet. But I'll go up to Char."

She went upstairs, but came down again much sooner than Miss Bruce approved.

"I've told her to go to bed," she placidly informed the secretary. "She can't do anything, and she looks very tired."

"She is far from well, I'm afraid," stiffly remarked Miss Bruce.

"Well, I leave her to you, Miss Bruce. I know you'll take the most devoted care of her. Let her sleep as long as she can in the morning."

"Cousin Joanna, is there anything I can do?" asked Trevellyan wistfully.

"I don't think so, Johnnie. You'll come round tomorrow?"

She was smiling at him quite naturally.

"The first thing. You're sure there's nothing I can do tonight—sit up with him, or anything?"

"My maid and I are going to do it between us. We shall have a nurse down from London by midday tomorrow, I hope."

"Let me sit up instead of you."

She smiled again.

"Certainly not. I'm only going to take the first half of the night—much the easiest. Then I shall probably go to sleep, unless there's any change, when, of course, they'll fetch me. But Dr. Prince doesn't think there will be yet, and I shall take all the rest I can. I'm much more likely to be wanted at night later on."

Miss Bruce went upstairs again, much more nearly disposed to wonder at such reasonableness than to admire it.

Her ideals were early Victorian ones, and although she knew that she could not hope for hysterics from Lady Vivian, she would have much preferred at least to hear her declare that sleep would be utterly impossible to her, and that she should spend the night hovering between her unconscious husband and her prostrate daughter.

But Lady Vivian went to bed at half-past twelve, and did not even insist upon merely lying down in her dressing-gown, nor did she reappear in Sir Piers's room until eight o'clock on the following morning.

There had been no change during the night.

Char slept heavily until ten o'clock, then woke and rang her bell rather indignantly.

Miss Bruce, who had been hovering about anxiously since seven that morning, appeared instantly at the door.

"There is no change whatever, my dear. Now, do, do lie down again and keep warm. There is nothing that you can do."

Char complied rather sullenly. She was still feeling ill, and violently resented her own involuntary physical relief at this enforced inaction.

"What on earth will happen at the office?" she muttered. "Have you told them that I'm not coming?"

"I telephoned myself," said Miss Bruce proudly.

"What did you say?"

"That you were in bed yourself with influenza, and quite unfit to move; and also that we are in great anxiety about Sir Piers."

"That's the only reason I can't go in to Questerham as usual," said Char coldly. "It was quite unnecessary to mention my having influenza, Brucey. That would never constitute a reason for my staying away from my work."

Miss Bruce looked very much crestfallen.

"You'd better telephone again, please, a little later on, with a message from me. Say that I must be rung up without fail when my secretary has gone through the letters, and I'll come to the telephone and speak to her myself."

"The draughty hall!" moaned Miss Bruce, but she dared not offer any further remonstrance.

Char's conversation on the telephone with Miss Jones was a lengthy one, and Miss Bruce, wandering in the background in search of imaginary currents of air, listened to her concluding observations with almost ludicrous dismay. "The departments must carry on as usual, of course, but don't hesitate to ring me up in any emergency. And no letters had better leave the office tonight—in fact, they can't, since there'll be nobody to sign them. What's that?... No, certainly not. How on earth could I depute such a responsibility to any one in the office. I shall have made some arrangement by tomorrow. Sir Piers may remain in this state indefinitely, and I can't have the whole of the work held up in this way.... That's all. Remember, nothing is to leave the office for the present. You can ring me up and report on the day's work at seven o'clock this evening. Good-bye."

As Char replaced the receiver, her mother entered the hall. They had already exchanged a few words earlier in the morning, and Lady Vivian only remarked dispassionately: "I thought you were in bed. By the way, Char, I'm sorry, but we shall have to have the telephone disconnected. The house *must* be kept quiet, and that bell can be heard quite plainly from upstairs. We can ring other people up, but they won't be able to get at us. Did you want to talk to your office?"

"I *must*," said Char. "Things are absolutely hung up there; no one who can even sign a letter."

"Why not? Have they all got writer's cramp all of a sudden?"

Char, never very graciously disposed towards her parent's many small leers at her official dignity, thought this one particularly ill-timed, and received it by a silence which said as much.

Lady Vivian looked at her, and said rather penitently: "Well, well, I mustn't keep you here when you ought to be in bed. My dear child, do you mean to say you're wearing nothing but your dressing-gown under that coat? Do go upstairs again."

"I want to speak to you, mother."

"I'll come up in five minutes. I'm going to give an order to the stables."

Lady Vivian walked briskly down the drive, her uncovered head thrown back to catch the chilly gleams of winter sunlight.

There were dark lines under her blue eyes, but the voice in which she gave her orders was full and serene as usual, even when she answered the chauffeur's respectful inquiries by the news that Sir Piers still remained unconscious.

Five minutes later Lady Vivian's secretary had the gratification of seeing her enter Char's bedroom and establish herself on a chair at the sufferer's bedside.

That afternoon Miss Bruce received a further satisfaction when Lady Vivian sought her in consultation.

"It's about Char, Miss Bruce. She's fretting herself into fiddlestrings about that office of hers. She thinks all the work is more or less held up while she's not there to see to it. And yet she may be kept here indefinitely. It's quite possible that Sir Piers may ask for her when he comes to himself again, so there can be no question of her going in to Questerham at present, even if she were fit for it, which she most decidedly isn't."

"*That* consideration by itself would never keep her from her work," said Miss Bruce loyally.

Lady Vivian waived the point.

"Well, as she won't do the only sensible thing, and transfer her authority to some responsible member of the staff, she'd better have one of them out here every day to go through the work with her and take back the instructions. The car is bound to be going in at least once a day."

"It won't be the rest for Charmian that one had hoped," said the secretary dismally.

"But it will be better for her to do a little work than just to sit and worry about her father and the office—though, upon my word," said Lady Vivian warmly, "I think she's a great deal more anxious about the Depôt than about his illness."

Miss Bruce, not inconceivably, thought so too, but she was very much shocked at hearing such an idea put into words, and said firmly: "Then, would you like me to write to Questerham and tell Miss Vivian's secretary that it has been arranged for her to come out here daily for the present?"

"Dear me, you're as bad as Char, Miss Bruce. Anybody would think they were all machines, to be dragged about without any will of their own. No, no! Ring up the office and get hold of the secretary, and give her a polite message, asking if she can manage it, if we send her in and out in the car."

Miss Bruce obeyed, and triumphantly told her employer that evening that all was arranged, and Miss Jones would come to Plessing on the following morning to receive Miss Vivian's directions.

"Miss Jones? You don't mean to say that the genteel Delmege has abdicated in favour of Miss Jones? What a piece of luck for us!" cried Lady Vivian.

"Miss Delmege is in bed with influenza."

"Excellent!" said Joanna callously. "I shall be delighted to see Miss Jones. I wanted to ask her here, but Char nearly had a fit at the idea. She'll certainly think I've done it out of *malice prepense*, as it is. She's got a most pigheaded prejudice against that nice Miss Jones."

"Lady Vivian!"

Lady Vivian laughed.

"You'll have to break it to her, Miss Bruce, that it's Miss Jones who is coming. And don't let her think I did it on purpose!"

"I am sure she would never think anything of the sort."

"Perhaps not. But Char does get very odd ideas into her head, when she thinks there's any risk of *lèse-majesté* to her Directorship. I must say," observed Joanna thoughtfully, preparing to go upstairs for her night watch, "I often wish that when Char was younger I'd smacked some of the nonsense out—"

But before this well-worn aspiration of Miss Vivian's parent, Miss Bruce took her indignant departure.

IX

"Rather strange, isn't it?" said Miss Delmege in tones of weak despondency. "If it hadn't been for this wretched flu, *I* should have been going out to Plessing every day with the work, I suppose, as Gracie is doing now."

"Yes, I suppose you would," agreed Miss Henderson blankly.

She sat on the foot of the bed, which was surrounded by a perfect wilderness of screens.

Miss Delmege reclined against two pillows, screwed against her back at an uncomfortable-looking angle. The room was not warmed, and the invalid wore a small flannel dressing-jacket, rather soiled and very much crumpled, a loosely knitted woolly jersey of dingy appearance and an ugly mustard colour, and over everything else an old quilted pink dressing-gown, with a cotton-wool-like substance bursting from the cuffs and elbows. Her hair was pinned up carelessly, and her expression was a much dejected one.

Miss Henderson was knitting in a spasmodic way, and stopping every now and then to blow her nose violently. She had several times during the afternoon ejaculated vehemently that a cold wasn't flu, she was thankful to say.

"It's probably the beginning of it, though," Miss Delmege replied pessimistically.

"You're hipped, Delmege, that's what you are—regularly hipped. Now, don't you think it would do you good to come downstairs for tea? There's a fire in the sitting-room."

"Well, I don't mind if I do. It'll seem quite peculiar to be downstairs again. Fancy, I've been up here five whole days! And I'm really not a person to give way, as a rule. At least, not so far as I know, I'm not."

"It's nearly four now. Look here, I'll put a kettle on, and you can have some hot water."

"Thanks, dear," said Miss Delmege graciously, "but don't bother. My hot-water bottle is still quite warm. I can use that."

"All right, then, I'll leave you. Ta-ta! You'll find me in the sitting-room. Sure you don't want any help?"

"No, thanks. I shall be quite all right. I only hope you won't be in bed yourself tomorrow, dear."

"No fear!" defiantly said Miss Henderson, at the same time sneezing loudly.

She went away before Miss Delmege had time to utter any further prognostications.

In the sitting-room she busied herself in pushing a creaking wicker arm-chair close to the fire—which for once was a roaring one, owing to the now convalescent Mrs. Potter, who had been crouching over it with a novel all day—lit the gas, and turned it up until it flared upwards with a steady, hissing noise; said "Excuse me; do you mind?" to Mrs. Potter; shut down the small crack of open window, and drew the curtains.

"Delmege is coming down, and we'd better have the room warm," she explained. "She's just out of bed."

By the time Miss Delmege, now wearing her mustard-coloured jersey over a thick stuff dress, had tottered downstairs, the room was indeed warm.

"Now, this," said Mrs. Bullivant cheerfully, when she came in to see how many of her charges wanted tea—"now this is what I call really cosy."

She looked ill, and very tired, herself. The general servant had given notice because of the number of trays that she had been required to carry upstairs of late, and had left the day before, and the cook was disobliging and would do nothing beyond her own immediate duties. Mrs. Bullivant was very much afraid of her, and did most of the work herself.

She had written to the Depôt in accordance with the official Hostel regulations, stating that a servant was required there for general housework; but no answer had come authorizing her to engage one, and Miss Marsh had explained to her that in Miss Vivian's absence such trifling questions must naturally expect to be overlooked or set aside for the time being. So little Mrs. Bullivant staggered up from the basement bearing a tray that seemed very large and heavy, and put it on the table in the sitting-room, very close to the fire, with a triumphant gasp.

"There! and it's a beautiful fire for toast. None of the munition girls are coming in for tea, are they?"

"Hope not," said Miss Henderson briefly. "I *ought* to be at the office now. I said I'd be back at five, but I shouldn't have had the afternoon off at all if Miss Vivian had been there."

Miss Delmege drew herself up. "Miss Vivian never refuses a reasonable amount of leave, that I'm aware of," she said stiffly.

"Oh, I mean we're slacker without her. There's less to do, that's all."

"Well, Grace Jones will be back presently, and I suppose she'll have work for all of us, as usual. I wonder how Miss Vivian is," said Mrs. Potter.

"And her father."

"Grace will be able to tell us," said Miss Delmege, not without a tinge of acrimony in her voice.

"It does seem so quaint, her going to and from Plessing in Miss Vivian's car, like this, every day. It somehow makes me howl with laughter."

She gave a faint, embittered snigger, and Miss Henderson and Mrs. Potter exchanged glances.

"I hear the car now," said Mrs. Bullivant. "She'll be cold. I'll get another cup, and give her some tea before she goes over to the office. I do hope she's got Miss Vivian's authority for me to find a new servant."

They heard her outside in the hall, making inquiry, and Grace's voice answering in tones of congratulation.

"Yes, it's quite all right. I asked Miss Vivian most particularly, and told her what a lot of work there was, and she said, Get some one as soon as you could. I came here before going to the office so as to tell you at once."

"Well, that *was* nice of you, dear, and now you shall have a nice cup of hot tea before you go out again. Just a minute."

"I'll fetch it, Mrs. Bullivant. Don't you bother."

"It's all right, dear, only a cup and saucer wanted; the rest is all ready."

In a few minutes Grace came into the sitting-room carefully carrying the cup and saucer.

When she saw Miss Delmege she said in a pleased way: "Oh, I'm so glad you're better. Miss Vivian asked after you. She was up herself this afternoon, and looking much better."

"And how's her father?"

"They are much happier about him since he recovered consciousness. He can talk almost quite well, and Dr. Prince is quite satisfied about him. And they've got a nurse at last. You know, they couldn't get one for love or money; none of the London places had any to spare."

"I should have thought they could get one from one of the Questerham hospitals."

"I think Lady Vivian meant to, if everything else failed, but Miss Vivian didn't think it a very good plan; she was afraid the hospitals couldn't spare any one, I suppose, and, anyhow, most of the people there are only V.A.D.'s."

"And is there any hope of seeing her back at the office?" asked Mrs. Potter, rather faintly.

"I don't know," replied Grace thoughtfully. "You see, poor Sir Piers may remain at this stage indefinitely, or may have another stroke any time. They don't really know...."

"And Miss Vivian goes on with the work just the same!" ejaculated Miss Henderson. "She really is a marvel."

"I'm sure she'd come to the office if it wasn't for poor Lady Vivian," said Miss Delmege. "But I know her mother depends on her altogether. I don't suppose she could leave her, not as things are now."

Miss Delmege's assumption of an intimate and superior knowledge of the *ménage* at Plessing was received in silence. Miss Henderson, indeed, glancing sharply at Grace, saw the merest quiver of surprise pass across her face at the assertion; but reflected charitably that, after all, Delmege had had a pretty sharp go of flu, and probably wasn't feeling up to the mark yet. Her mis-statements, however irritating, had better be left unchallenged.

"Do you ever see anything of Lady Vivian when you're at Plessing?" Miss Delmege inquired benevolently of Grace, but the benevolence faded from her expression when Miss Jones replied, with more enthusiasm than usual in her voice, that she always had lunch with Lady Vivian, and sometimes went round the garden with her before going up to Miss Vivian's room for the afternoon's work.

"Dear me! I shouldn't have thought she'd have much time for going round the garden. But she's not thoroughgoing, like Miss Vivian is, of course. It's quite a different sort of nature, I fancy. Strange, too, being mother and daughter."

Miss Henderson decided rapidly within herself that, influenza or no, Delmege was making herself unbearable.

"You're getting tired with sitting up, aren't you, dear?" she inquired crisply.

There was a moment's silence, and then Miss Delmege said in pinched accents: "Who is it you're referring to, dear? Me, by any chance?"

Grace knew the state of tension to which those aloof and refined tones were the prelude, and exclaimed hurriedly that she must go.

She did not want to hear Miss Henderson and Miss Delmege having "words," or to listen while Miss Delmege talked with genteel familiarity of Sir Piers and Lady Vivian.

Pulling on her thick uniform coat, she went out, and slowly crossed the street.

She was thinking of Lady Vivian, who had roused in her an enthusiasm which she could never feel for Char, and who had talked to her so frankly and warmly, as though to a contemporary, that afternoon in the garden at Plessing. For all her quality of matter-of-factness, there was a certain humble-mindedness about Miss Jones, which made it a matter of surprise to her when she found herself on the borders of friendship with the woman whom she thought so courageous and so lovable.

She hoped that Miss Vivian would require her to go out to Plessing every day for a long while; then reflected that the privilege rightly belonged to Miss Delmege, who would certainly avail herself of it at the earliest possible moment.

She knew, and calmly accepted, that Miss Delmege's services would certainly be preferred to her own by the Director of the Midland Supply Depôt; but she did not think that Lady Vivian proffered her liking or her confidence lightly, and felt a certain placid security that their unofficial intercourse would somehow or other continue. Then, with characteristic thoroughness, she dismissed the question from her mind and went into the office and to her work.

That evening Grace went to the Canteen. Only Miss Marsh, Miss Anthony, and Miss Henderson accompanied her.

"We shall have to work like blacks to make up for the absentees," groaned Tony.

"Never mind; it isn't quite so cold tonight. Isn't the moon nice?"

"Lovely. Just the night for Zeppelins."

Miss Henderson spoke from the pessimism of approaching influenza, but it happened that she was right. The first air raid over Questerham took place that night.

The work was rapidly lessening towards eleven o'clock, when Captain Trevellyan came into the hall. He stood for an instant gazing round him reflectively, then said to Grace: "Who is in command here?"

"Mrs. Willoughby, when Miss Vivian isn't here."

"I see, thank you."

Looking very doubtful, he sought Lesbia, who was preparing to discard her overall and to take her departure with the Pekinese.

"Johnnie! How *too* sweet of you to turn up just in time to see me home! My Lewis hates my going back alone in the dark; we've very nearly quarrelled over it already."

"The fact is," said Trevellyan, wondering if Mrs. Willoughby were the sort of person to have hysterics, "that there's been a telephone warning to say an air-raid is on, just over Staningham. They're heading this way, so we may hear a gun or two, you know; some of our machines are in pursuit."

He gazed anxiously at Lesbia, whom he characteristically supposed to be about either to burst into tears or to threaten a fainting fit.

The ideas of Captain Trevellyan were perhaps not much more advanced than those of Lady Vivian's secretary.

But Mrs. Willoughby discounted his solicitude, at least on one score, in a moment.

"Zepps!" she screamed excitedly. "How too thrilling! Can I possibly get on to the roof, I wonder? I've never seen one yet."

"Stop!" said the astonished Trevellyan. "You don't realize. They'll be over here in a few minutes, and our machines may be firing at them, besides the guns on the hill; there'll be shrapnel falling."

Mrs. Willoughby tore off her overall and snatched up Puff.

"I must, must see it all!" she declared wildly. "Have you got a pair of field-glasses?"

Trevellyan restrained her forcibly from dashing to the door.

"Mrs. Willoughby, we've got to consider that there are a number of people here, and that they are all in a certain amount of danger—not so much from bombs, though goodness knows they may very well drop one, but from our own shrapnel. Is there a basement?"

"You can't send us to the cellar? My dear boy, I, for one, refuse to go. We're not children, and we're not afraid. We're Englishwomen!"

On this superb sentiment Mrs. Willoughby swept into the middle of the hall and announced in penetrating accents that a Zepp raid was on, and had any one got a pair of field-glasses?

There was a momentary outbreak of exclamations all around, and then Captain Trevellyan raised his voice: "Please keep away from the windows. There may be broken glass about."

"Is it dangerous? What are we to do?" gasped Tony, next him. She was rather white.

At the same moment the very distant but unmistakable reverberation of guns became audible.

Trevellyan took instant advantage of the sudden cessation of sound in the room.

"If there is a basement, it would be as well for everybody to go down there, please—just for precaution's sake. And then I'm going to put out these lights." His hand was on the nearest gas-jet as he spoke.

"Nothing will induce me to *stir* while there's any danger. I can answer for every woman here!" cried Lesbia, with a gesture of noble defiance.

Grace Jones came into the middle of the room.

"Hadn't we better obey orders?" she asked gently. "There is a basement beyond the kitchen."

She held out her hand to Miss Anthony, and they went through the door into the kitchen.

After an instant's hesitation, the other women followed. Trevellyan saw that they had lit a candle, and in a moment he heard them beginning to talk quietly amongst themselves.

A few soldiers in the hall had congregated together, and were talking and laughing. The others made a dash for the door as the firing grew louder, and simultaneously exclaimed: "Here they are!"

The sound of the huge machines far overhead was unmistakable. They could see the shrapnel bursting, and the guns on the hill boomed heavily and intermittently.

"Look!" shrieked Lesbia, almost hurling herself out of the door. "They've got one of them! I can see it blazing!"

Far away, a red spot began to glow, then suddenly revealed the cigar-shaped form in flames, dropping downwards.

"They've got it!" echoed Trevellyan. "Look! it's coming down. Miles away, by this time. I wonder how many of ours are giving chase."

The air was full of whirring, buzzing wings, and very far away a red light in the sky seemed to tell of fire.

Occasional sparks and flashes told of the bursting of shrapnel, but the sounds were dying away rapidly.

"It's over, and, by Jove, we've got him!" shouted Trevellyan, dashing back into the kitchen. Every one was talking at once, Mrs. Willoughby's voice dominating the rest.

"I saw the whole thing *too* perfectly! At *least* five of the brutes, and two, if not three, of them in flames! I saw them with my own eyes!" she proclaimed, with more spirit than exactitude. "And where are those poor creatures hiding like rats in the cellar?"

"The noise was awful!" said Tony, shuddering. "It felt as though it were right over our heads. But," she added valiantly, "I do wish we'd seen it all!"

Trevellyan turned to her apologetically. "I'm so sorry. But I really couldn't help it. They sent me down on purpose to see that this place was warned. It was really perfectly splendid of you to go down like that and miss all the fun."

"I was very frightened," she told him honestly, "though I do *awfully* wish I'd seen it. They must have had a splendid view from the Hostel at the top of the street."

"There was a splendid view from *here*," said Lesbia cuttingly. "*I* saw everything there was to be seen."

Trevellyan was looking for Miss Jones.

"Thank you so much for giving them the lead you did," he said to her gratefully. "It was very good of you. I felt such a brute for asking you to do it; but there really is danger, you know, especially from the windows, if shrapnel shatters the glass."

"Oh yes, I know. I wonder," said Grace thoughtfully, "whether they heard it much at Plessing."

"I know. I was thinking of that all the time. Not that she'd be nervous, you know, except on his account."

"It would be dreadful for Sir Piers. Oh, I do hope they didn't hear much of it," said Grace.

One of the men approached her. "If you please, Sister, could you come down into the kitching 'alf a minute?"

Grace went.

Trevellyan watched them all disperse, and escorted Mrs. Willoughby to her tram, wondering if he ought not to see her home.

But Lesbia refused all escort, declaring gallantly that *she* did not know the meaning of fear, and, anyway, Puffles would protect his missus from any more dreadful, wicked Zepps.

He left her entertaining her tram conductress with a spirited account of all that she had seen, and much that she had not seen, of the raid.

As he turned down Pollard Street again, a soldier with his hand bound up lurched out of the open door of the deserted Canteen.

"Is there any one in there to shut the place up?" Trevellyan asked him.

"One of the ladies is still in there, sir. Beg pardon, sir; she's a bit upset like."

Trevellyan thought of little Miss Anthony, who had owned, with a white face, how much the sound of the guns had frightened her.

He went into the hall. It was dark, but there was a light in the kitchen.

"Who's there?" said John.

"I am. It's all right," replied an enfeebled voice; and he went into the kitchen.

Grace Jones was half leaning and half sitting against the sink, her small face haggard, her hands clutching the only support within reach, the wooden top of a roller-towel.

"I'm afraid you're ill," exclaimed Trevellyan, looking desperately round him for a chair.

"It's all right; please don't wait."

"But it's over now. They brought the brute down. It's miles away by this time."

He multiplied his reassurances.

"No, no; it's not that," gasped Miss Jones, looking whiter than ever.

"There were certainly no casualties over here. We should have seen signs of fire somewhere if they'd dropped a bomb."

"It's *not* that!" Grace told him desperately.

Trevellyan gazed at her helplessly, and repeated in an obtuse manner: "It's all over now—absolutely safe."

Grace gazed back at him with a wan smile.

"Would you mind going?" she asked him feebly. "I shall be all right in a minute. It's very tiresome, but the sight of—of blood always upsets me like this, and that man had cut his finger rather badly, and I had to do it up. It's only—that."

She put her hands up to her damp forehead as though the effort of speech had brought back the sensation of nausea.

"You're going to faint!" exclaimed Trevellyan. "Let me get some water for you."

"No, I'm not. *Oh, do go*!"

"I can't leave you like this," protested the bewildered John.

Grace staggered to her feet, and stood holding on to the edge of the sink.

"I'm afraid—I'm only going to be sick," she said with difficulty.

Ten minutes later they locked up the Canteen and went up Pollard Street.

"You see, it had nothing to do with the raid," Grace told him gently. "It was just that poor man bleeding. I've always been like that; it's the only way I'm delicate, because I'm never ill, and I don't ever have nerves. But it is very tiresome. That's why I couldn't go and work in a hospital. I did clerical work in the hospital at home for a little while, but it wasn't any good."

"Bad luck!"

"It is, rather. I hate anybody's knowing about it; that's why I said I'd stay behind and lock up. I knew it was going to happen, and I didn't want any one to be there."

"I'm sorry. I thought it was the raid that had upset you, and that you might be going to faint."

"Nothing so romantic," said Miss Jones regretfully.

But her regrets were as nothing to those of the Hostel when they learnt what had happened.

It was impossible to conceal it from them, since the window of the ground-floor bedroom had been open, and Mrs. Potter and Miss Marsh, leaning from it, and listening eagerly, had heard every word of Captain Trevellyan's final discourse to Miss Jones, and her repeated assurances of being now completely restored.

They flew into the hall to meet her.

"Gracie dear, what *has* happened to you? Tony was in such a state when she found you hadn't come in with her and the others."

"Was it that beastly raid upset you?"

Grace once more repudiated the raid with as much energy as she could muster.

"You look as white as a sheet, dear! Come into the sitting-room."

Every one was in the sitting-room, including those first back from the Canteen, and the pseudo-invalids who, having been in bed when the raid began, felt that only tea could enable them to face the night, and had hurried down in search of it.

"Oh, Gracie, there you are! I was just going back to see what had become of you," said Tony.

"Miss Vivian's cousin brought her home!" giggled Mrs. Potter. "You know, the Staff Officer one. She's been awfully upset, poor Grace! Turned quite faint, didn't you, dear?"

"But you were so brave!" cried Tony, aghast. "You were all right all the time the raid was on. You didn't mind a bit!"

"Came over you afterwards, I expect, didn't it?" said Miss Delmege kindly. "It's often the case. I'm always perfectly cool myself when anything happens—I was tonight—but I generally suffer for it afterwards. Reaction, I suppose. When I came downstairs after it was all over I was simply shaking, wasn't I, Mrs. Bullivant?"

"Now, it's a funny thing," remarked Miss Henderson, without giving any one time to dwell upon Miss Delmege's personal reminiscences—"it's a funny thing, but I simply didn't feel the least bit of fear. Not for myself, you know. I just thought, well, I hope mother doesn't see any of this—she's got a bit of a heart, you know—but I didn't seem to feel a bit as though I was in any kind of danger myself. Not a bit."

"Now, just sit down, child, and drink up this tea," said Mrs. Bullivant to Grace. "You've not a scrap of colour in your face."

"I'm really all right now, thank you very much," Grace told her as she took the tea gratefully. "And it wasn't anything to do with the raid."

Everybody looked rather disappointed.

"Aren't you well, then, dear? I do hope it isn't another case of influenza."

"I bet I know!" suddenly cried Tony. "It was doing up that man's hand upset you, wasn't it? He cut himself somehow in the excitement and was bleeding like a fountain, poor fellow! I thought you looked rather squeamish while you were doing it, poor thing! but I never thought of its bowling you over like this. Are you one of those people who faint at the sight of blood?"

"I didn't faint," said Grace mildly.

"Jolly near it, I expect, judging by your face now," said Tony critically. "Poor old dear!"

"Did Miss Vivian's cousin come back to find you?" asked Miss Delmege sharply.

"He came into the kitchen while I was still there, and afterwards he helped me to lock up."

"Afterwards?"

A tinge of colour crept into Miss Jones's face.

"I'm afraid you won't think I rose to the occasion *at all*," she said deprecatingly. "It always does make me rather ill to see blood, though I know it's idiotic, and it was the soldier's hand, not the air-raid a bit, I didn't mind that at all."

"What happened? Were you hysterical?" demanded Miss Delmege, with an inexplicable touch of umbrage in her refined little voice.

"Certainly not," said Grace emphatically. "If you really want to know, I was just sick over the sink."

Miss Jones's damaging revelation horrified the Hostel, no less than the crude manner of its avowal.

"Well," said Miss Henderson, "you really are the limit, Gracie—and a bit over."

"Poor child!" said Mrs. Bullivant kindly. "How dreadful for you! Miss Vivian's cousin and all, too! But, still, it was better than an absolute stranger, perhaps."

"I don't see how you're ever going to face him again, though—really I don't," giggled Tony.

"Poor man! so awful for him, too," minced Miss Delmege. "He must have been too uncomfortable for words."

"Not he," Miss Marsh told her with sudden defiance. "He brought poor Gracie home, and delighted to have the chance. Come on, Gracie, let's go to bed. You look done for."

She had grown very fond of her room-mate, in spite of all that she regretfully looked upon as an absence of propriety in her conduct; and when they were outside the sitting-room door, she said, without troubling to lower her voice: "Don't you mind their nonsense, dear. You couldn't help it, and *that* Delmege has only got the pip because she hadn't the chance of being brought home by Miss Vivian's cousin herself."

And when they got upstairs she "turned down" Gracie's bed for her, and put her kettle on to the gas-ring, and brought her an extra hot-water bottle.

"There! Good-night, dear, and don't you worry. I think it was splendid of you to tell the truth. Lots of girls would have fibbed, and said they'd fainted, or something highfaluting of that nature. I should myself."

"Thank you so much. You *are* nice to me," said Grace warmly. She did not look upon the affair herself as being more than a merely unfortunate incident, but she knew that Miss Marsh regarded it as an overwhelming scandal, and was proffering consolation accordingly.

Miss Marsh bent over the bed and tucked her in. "I'll turn out the gas, and you must go straight to sleep. It's frightfully late. And look here, Gracie, when we're alone together up here, I'd like you to call me Dora, if you will. It's my name, you know."

X

"That settles it," said Char. "If this sort of thing is going to happen, I *must* be there. With no definite organization, there might be a panic next time an air-raid takes place. According to Mrs. Willoughby, every one made a dash for the basement, as it was. Women are such fools when one leaves them to themselves!"

It was part of Char's policy always to disparage her own sex. It threw into greater relief the contrast which she knew to exist between herself and the majority of women-workers.

She was speaking to Miss Bruce, but, rather to her annoyance, Lady Vivian came into the room in time to overhear her.

"Surely the basement was the most sensible place to dash for?" she inquired, never able to resist an opportunity of attacking her offspring's arrogantly expressed opinions. "As for your being there, in my opinion, it's a very good thing you weren't. You'd only have drilled the poor things out of their senses, which would have taken up more valuable space in the basement."

"I should not have been in the basement," returned Char superbly.

"Then you might have been blown into bits, my dear, unless, as Director of the Midland Supply Depôt, all enemy aircraft has orders to respect your person?"

Joanna was jeering quite good-humouredly, as she generally did, and even Miss Bruce saw some exaggeration in the white, tense silence with which Char received these indifferent pleasantries.

"I hear the car," said the secretary, anxious to create a diversion.

"Miss Jones. Mother, I'm going through the work with her in here this morning. There's no fire in the morning-room."

"Very well, Char. You won't disturb me in the least."

"I thought you were going to sit with father."

"Not yet. Besides, I want to see Miss Jones."

Char sighed patiently. At Plessing only the faithful Miss Bruce gave her work that consideration to which she had become accustomed at the office. She was finding Plessing almost intolerable. There were no interviews, the telephone-bell was not allowed to ring, no one urged her not to neglect the substantial meals which were served for her with the greatest regularity, and Miss Jones daily assured her, with perfect placidity, that the whole work at the office was progressing with complete success without her.

The Director of the Midland Supply Depôt was completely shorn of her glory.

And what was she doing, Char indignantly asked herself, while the organization which she had practically made was thus abandoned to its own resources?

Nothing.

She paid a purely perfunctory visit, morning and evening, to Sir Piers, who hardly ever heard what she said to him, and had the rest of the day at her own disposal. She had no share in the work of nursing, which was divided between Lady Vivian and the professional nurse who had come from London, and when she rather indignantly demanded of Dr. Prince whether he did not think that he had better utilize her hospital experience at Plessing, the doctor merely replied dryly: "Hospital experience, as you call it, acquired on paper only, won't help you much here, or anybody else either. Nurse Williams can do all that's necessary, and Sir Piers doesn't want any one but Lady Vivian when he's awake."

"That's perfectly true," said Char sharply, "and that's why I can't help thinking it's rather waste of time for an able-bodied woman with a certain amount of brains to remain here unoccupied when there is so much to be done elsewhere."

"You can take your mother for a walk every day. She is wise enough to take an hour's exercise every afternoon, and Miss Bruce can't be much of a companion. Besides," maliciously added the doctor, who had suffered considerably under the Central Depôt's arbitrary interference with his Hospital work, "it'll do you a lot of good to keep quiet for six months or so. You've been suffering from overstrain, whether you know it or not, and your work will be all the better for some relaxation. I assure you, we haven't had a wrong enclosure sent us from the office since you left."

Dr. Prince walked off very triumphantly after this parting gibe.

"Serve her right!" he thought to himself. "Conceited monkey! Perhaps I shall get station transport for my cases properly put through now, without her interference. Hospital experience, indeed!"

"Of course," said Char to Miss Bruce, "a country doctor is naturally jealous of the R.A.M.C. men who've come to the fore. He's never forgiven me for getting his Hospital run on a proper military basis."

"I'm sure he really admires your splendid work, dear, as anybody must, but he's known you ever since you were tiny, so I suppose he allows himself a certain amount of freedom."

Char supposed so too, sombrely enough, and prepared herself to extract from Miss Jones an account of panic at the Canteen on the occasion of the air-raid which should justify her in returning to her post, even in the eyes of Dr. Prince.

Needless to say, Miss Jones was unsatisfactory.

"Oh no; there wasn't any sort of panic at all. Captain Trevellyan was there, and asked us to go to the basement, and we just went."

"John tells me that they were perfectly splendid, all of them, and that you set the first example," said Joanna cordially.

"The whole thing didn't last ten minutes," Grace told them. "We heard all the noise, but didn't see anything. The men did, of course. They saw the Zeppelin come down in the far distance. But by the time we came out there was nothing. It was all over."

"What a shame!" exclaimed Joanna.

"I must institute a proper drill for air-raid alarms," said Char, unsmiling. "That sort of haphazard *sauve qui peut* is most unofficial. I shall see about it directly I get back."

Joanna put up her lorgnon and looked at her daughter.

She did not speak, but something in her expression made Char exclaim very decisively: "I can't desert my post at a time like this. Everybody must see that unless I had any extremely definite call elsewhere, my place is at the Depôt. The work is suffering horribly from this piecemeal fashion of doing things."

She indicated Grace and her sheaf of bulging envelopes with a gesture of condemnation.

Lady Vivian glanced from her daughter's set face to Grace Jones, whose eyes were cast down. Then she left the room without speaking.

Char looked at her secretary, and said, very slowly and stiffly: "I shall probably be back at the office tomorrow or Monday, Miss Jones. You may tell the staff. Sir Piers's condition is not likely to alter at present, and, in any case, the work comes before any personal considerations at a time like this."

There was silence.

"Miss Jones!" said Char sharply.

Miss Jones lifted her great grey eyes and looked straight at the Director of the Midland Supply Depôt.

She was not at all an eloquent person, but perceptions much less acute than those of Char Vivian could have felt the intense, almost violent hostility with which the atmosphere vibrated.

Then Grace dropped her eyes and said gently and coldly, in a tone as remote as it was impersonal: "Yes, Miss Vivian."

The encounter had been a wordless one, and, indeed, Char knew that she would never have allowed it to become anything else. The relative positions of the Director of the Midland Supply Depôt and one of her staff were far too clearly defined in her mind for that. But it left in her a sort of cold, still anger, as well as an invincible determination.

That night Trevellyan dined at Plessing.

Lady Vivian did not come downstairs until dinner was over and they were in the drawing-room. Then she took out some needlework. Sir Piers had always liked to see her pretty hands working at what he generically called "embroidery."

She sat down under the big standard lamp.

Disquiet was in the air, and Char knew that only the unperceptive Trevellyan was unaware of an impending crisis. Miss Bruce fidgeted with the fire-irons, dropped them, and apologized. As though a spell had been broken, Joanna looked up and spoke.

"Char, I don't know if you realize that there can be no question of your returning to the office tomorrow—or at all, for the present."

The attack had opened.

Char was glad of it, although a flare of resentment passed through her mind that her mother should have sought a cowardly protection from a possible scene in the presence of John Trevellyan.

"Why not?" she added quietly. "My father is no worse?"

"He is exactly the same. But I am not going to risk any shock or vexation to him. He asked me this afternoon if you were at home, and was glad when I said yes. You know he never liked your doing this excessive amount of work."

"He never forbade it."

"He is not likely to forbid it. When has he ever forbidden you anything? But he thinks that your place now is at home—which it very obviously is."

"To do what?" asked Char, with rising bitterness, which she did not try to keep out of her voice. "Does he ever ask for me? Am I of the slightest use?"

"He sees you every day, and he might ask for you at any time. He wishes you to remain at home for the present."

"It's not fair, it's not reasonable. I do *nothing* here. I am of no use. It's not as though he really wanted me. It's simply because you—and he—won't be reminded of the war—of the ghastly horrors going on all round us—won't think of the war, or let it be mentioned. You want to shirk it all—"

"Don't, Char!" said John suddenly. "Don't say things you'll be sorry for afterwards."

"No. I shall not be sorry for speaking the truth. *You* know it's true, Johnnie."

"True!" said Joanna. "What if it is true? Do you suppose that if I can give him one little hour's comfort by ignoring the war, and keeping every thought of it away from him, I wouldn't do so at any cost? The war isn't your responsibility or mine—your father is."

She rose, and paced rapidly up and down the length of the room. Char had never seen her mother give way to such impetuous agitation before. She eyed her coldly, but strove to speak gently.

"Mother, if it was anything else I'd give in. But I *am* doing work in Questerham—real, absolutely necessary work—and here—why, I'm not even justifying my existence."

"You're working here. You do a lot every day, going through all those letters and things with Miss Jones," Trevellyan pointed out.

Joanna threw him a quick glance of gratitude.

"Work here, Char, as much as you like," she exclaimed eagerly. "You can have any one you please out here—so long as they don't make a noise," she added hastily.

The expression was infelicitous.

"You talk as though I were a child, and wanted to have other children out here to play with me. Good heavens, mother I do you realize that my work is *for the nation*, neither more nor less?"

"If I don't, it's not for want of being told," said her mother with sudden dryness.

"It's easy to say that sort of thing, to accuse me of self-complacency in the tiny little part I contribute to an enormous whole."

"It's not that, Char!" cried Joanna hastily. "I don't care if you have megalomania in its acutest form"—Miss Bruce bounded irrepressibly on her chair—"but I will *not* have your father distressed. That's my one and only concern. Johnnie, help me to make her understand."

"I do understand, mother," said Char. "You would sacrifice everything to the personal question—women always do. But I can't see it like that. The broader issue lies there, under my very eyes, and I can't shirk it."

"Johnnie!" said Joanna despairingly. "Tell her that she's blinding herself."

"Can't you give it up, Char?" he asked her gently. "You can do work here, you know, and let some one else carry on at Questerham."

"Yes, yes, a deputy. Some one who'll be under your orders," breathed Miss Bruce eagerly.

She cordially wished her contribution to the discussion unuttered, however, when it evoked from Johnnie the inspired suggestion: "Miss Jones! Make her your deputy, Char, and the whole thing will go like a house on fire."

Joanna, still pacing the room, gave a quick, short laugh, which made Trevellyan look at her in wondering surprise, and Char in sudden anger.

"May I suggest—" Miss Bruce began timidly, and paused.

"Anything!" said Joanna brusquely.

"Couldn't Dr. Prince tell us whether there is any reason—anything to fear—any danger," faltered Miss Bruce, becoming terribly involved.

Trevellyan came to her rescue.

"You mean whether there is likely to be any immediate change, for worse or for better, in Sir Piers's condition?"

"Of course I couldn't go if my father was in immediate danger," quoth Char impatiently. "But he's not. We've already been told so. He may go on in this state for months and months. And at the end of a telephone! Why, I could be sent for and be back here within an hour."

"I'm not discussing the question from that point of view at all," Joanna told her. "The point is not that you should be at hand in case of any crisis, but simply that he should not be vexed. Your insensate hours of work at the Depôt vex him."

The words sounded oddly trivial, but no one doubted that Joanna was angry, angrier than they had, any of them, ever seen her.

"Look here, Cousin Joanna, can't we settle this later on? There can be no need to arrange it tonight," said John. "Suppose we let the Doctor give the casting vote, as Miss Bruce suggested?"

He felt pretty sure that no vote of Dr. Prince's would ever be exercised in favour of Char's immediate return to the Midland Supply Depôt.

"Dr. Prince is coming here tonight," said Lady Vivian. "He ought to be here any minute now, if it's after nine."

"Ten past," said Miss Bruce, glancing at the clock.

"Neither he nor any one else can convince me that I ought to remain in idleness when every worker in England is needed," said Char.

"My dear Char, you can't run any risks with Sir Piers in his present condition," said John unexpectedly. "That's what we want Dr. Prince to tell us—whether there is any danger to him if you persist in going against his wishes."

Something of condemnation, such as Char had never yet heard in her easy-going cousin's voice, silenced her. She felt bitterly that every one was against her, no one understood.

Then Miss Bruce's hand came out timidly and patted her on the shoulder. Dear old Brucey! Char recognized her fidelity in a sudden spasm of most unwonted gratitude. Brucey at least knew that a real struggle was in progress between Char's sense of patriotism and the pain that it naturally gave her to resist the wishes of the parents whose point of view she could not share.

For the first time since she was a child, Char felt moved to one of her rare demonstrations of affection towards the faithful Miss Bruce. She smiled at her, pain and gratitude mingling in her gaze, and let her hand lie for a moment on the little secretary's.

Trevellyan leant against the chimney-piece, his hands in his pockets, and looked at Joanna with inarticulate, uncomprehending loyalty and admiration in his gaze.

She was pacing up and down the long room with a sort of restrained impatience, the folds of her black dress sweeping round her tall figure as she moved. In the silence, broken only by the rustling of Joanna's gown, the approach of Dr. Prince's small, old-fashioned motor-car was plainly audible.

Miss Bruce gave one timid look at Lady Vivian, then got up and went to the door.

They heard her speak to the servant in the hall, and then she came back again and took up her place close to Char.

"Did you ask him to come in here?"

"Yes, Lady Vivian. At least, I told them to show him in here."

Joanna resumed her restless pacing.

Then the drawing-room door opened and closed again upon the doctor, entering with the stooping gait of a hard-worked, tired man at the end of the day.

"Good-evening, Dr. Prince," said Joanna abruptly. "Will you give us the benefit of your advice?"

"On whose account?" demanded the doctor, glancing sharply from one to another of the group.

"It's just this," said Char's cool, incisive tones. "My mother wishes to persuade me that my father is not in a fit state for me to take up my work at Questerham again. That I ought to remain here, doing practically nothing, while there's work crying out to be done."

"Sir Piers is in no immediate danger," said the doctor slowly. "In fact, there is every reason to hope that he is getting better. Otherwise, I suppose, you would hardly contemplate leaving home."

"But she's not suggesting leaving home!" cried Miss Bruce. "It's only a case of going backwards and forwards every day."

The doctor shrugged his shoulders and glanced at Lady Vivian.

"Sir Piers doesn't wish it," said Joanna curtly. "Surely that's reason enough. It distressed him very much, even before he was ill, that she should go and do this office work."

"I see. Yes. The ideas of the present day are not very easily assimilated by our generation," said the doctor gently.

He had often thought himself that Miss Vivian of Plessing had better have worked with her needle or amongst the poor, as had done the great ladies of his own generation, instead of in a Questerham office. But he had also been rather ashamed of his thoughts, and would not for the world have had them guessed by his pushing, good-natured wife, who was proud to let her two daughters help at the Depôt.

"We live in abnormal times," Char said. "I'm not doing the work for my own pleasure, but because the need for workers is desperate. I *can* do the job I've undertaken, and so far as I can see, there is no adequate reason, unless my father gets very much worse, for me to desert it."

"It's not," said Miss Bruce judicially, "as though any one could take her place at the Depôt."

"For the matter of that," Trevellyan remarked, with unexpected logic, "it's not as though any one could take her place here."

"But that's just it!" cried Char. "I don't do anything at all here. Dr. Prince, you know perfectly well that I don't; we spoke of it the other day. Can you conscientiously tell me that my absence during the day is going to make the slightest difference to my father's case?"

"No. Speaking professionally, I can't," said the doctor.

Joanna stopped in her walking and looked at him, but it was evident that the doctor had not finished. He cleared his throat and faced Char.

"*But* if you're trying, which you obviously are, to bamboozle me into justifying you in taking your own way, Miss Charmian, then I'll tell you something else. It's not the work you want to get back to, young lady; it's the excitement, and the official position, and the right it gives you to interfere with people who knew how to run a hospital and everything connected with it some twenty years or so before you came into the world. That's what you want. I can't tell you, as a matter of medical opinion, that it will bring on a second stroke, if you vex and disappoint your good father by monkeying about in a becoming uniform and a bit of gold braid on an office stool while he desires you to stay at home; but I can and I do tell you that you're playing as heartless a trick as any I ever saw, making patriotism the excuse for bullying a lot of women who work themselves to death for you because you're of a better class, and have more personality than themselves, and pretending to yourself that it's the work you're after, when it's just because you want to get somewhere where you'll be in the limelight all the time."

There was perfect silence, while the doctor took out a large handkerchief and wiped his forehead.

At last Joanna said dryly: "Well, I don't know that I should have said it myself, but upon my word, Char, I believe you've got the case in a nutshell."

"No!" cried Miss Bruce. "It's unjust!"

Char looked at her, white and smiling.

"Yes, it's unjust enough," she said slowly. "But, as my mother has just implied, it is her own opinion, apparently, as well as Dr. Prince's."

"No! no!" cried Joanna quickly, moving towards her daughter. "Not altogether, Char. Only I can't have your father vexed—indeed, I can't."

"You are making it very hard for me. But my choice is made. I cannot, and will not, let a personal consideration come before the work."

"You mean to go back?"

"On Monday—the day after tomorrow."

For a moment Char looked at them, superbly alone. Then she moved towards the door. Miss Bruce, looking half frightened and half admiring, crept after her, and Joanna made a sudden movement that caused Trevellyan to put out his hand towards her.

"No, I'm not going to touch her. But if you go, Char, you'll stay in Questerham. I won't have you coming back and disturbing the house and waking him at all hours. I won't have you here at all, unless he asks for you."

Char made a gesture of acquiescence, and went without a word from the room.

"Oh!" cried Joanna, her blue eyes dark and her voice shaking, but unconquerably colloquial in the midst of her pain and anger. "Oh, why in Heaven's name didn't I whip Char when she was younger?"

XI

"Enter Edith Elizabeth Plumtree, restored to health and happiness. Loud cheers from the spectators."

"Hurrah! How nice to see you back, dear! You look a different girl."

"I feel it," declared Miss Plumtree, exchanging vigorous handshakes with everybody.

"What with her being in plain clothes, and having gone up about a stone in weight," said Tony, "I simply didn't know her at the station. Gracie and I tore down on our bicycles to meet her, and thought of commandeering two orderlies and a stretcher to bring her up from the station. Instead of which she's so much stronger than we are that she pushed both bikes up the hill without turning a hair, while Gracie and I panted in the rear!"

"Doesn't she look well?" cried Grace. "I've never seen her look so well—and isn't it becoming?"

Everybody laughed. Personal remarks of any but a markedly facetious order were known by the Hostel to be indelicate; but it was generally conceded that Gracie Jones was so nice it didn't matter what she said, since she probably couldn't help being unlike other people.

Miss Delmege eyed Miss Plumtree's fair round face and plump figure with approval.

"I like that costume," she observed critically. "New, isn't it, dear?"

"No, dyed. It's my last year's grey."

"You don't mean to say it's turned that sweet saxe? Well, you *have* done well with it! I must commence seeing about my own winter costume, I suppose. I'd been thinking of mole or nigger."

Miss Delmege possessed an almost technical vocabulary of descriptive adjectives which she applied prodigally and exclusively to matters of wardrobe.

She proceeded to elaborate her favourite theme, although unable to command a better audience than Grace, since every one else immediately became more absorbed than ever in Miss Plumtree.

"Of course, blue's my colour, you know, being fair. Not sky, I don't mean, but royal or navy. But, then, one sees so many of those shades about, and I do like something distinctive."

"You should get some patterns."

"I have done already. You must help me to choose, Gracie. There's a shade of elephant that I rather liked; it would look nice with my cream blouse, I thought."

"Yes, *very*," Grace agreed cordially, and perhaps not without a hope that this would now close the discussion.

"Then there's the style." Miss Delmege pursued her reflective way. "I thought of a pleat down the centre, being tall, you see; I always think one must be tall to carry things off. Unless, of course," she added hastily, "one has a really perfect figure, like Miss Vivian."

Miss Plumtree turned round.

"How *is* Miss Vivian? Didn't some one tell me she was back at the office? I suppose her father's better."

"Very much the same," Miss Delmege told her sadly. "Of course, it's perfectly wonderful of her to—"

"Oh," said Miss Marsh maliciously, "if you want news about Plessing, Greengage, you must ask Gracie. She's been out there every day in the car, so as to go through the letters with Miss Vivian."

"I say! Really?"

"Yes, rather. She had lunch with Miss Vivian's mother nearly every day."

"I rather envied her the motor ride," said Miss Delmege languidly, with the implication that no other consideration could have moved her to jealousy for a moment. "But, as a matter of fact, I couldn't manage to go myself—laid up with this wretched flu, you know. I simply wasn't fit to stir. Of course, Miss Vivian knew that; she was awfully sweet about it. But, then, I always say, the attractive thing about her *is* that she's so desperately human, when once you get to know her."

"And is she back at the office?" inquired Miss Plumtree, turning a deaf ear to these descriptive touches.

"Comes back tomorrow morning, Monday. Some one from Plessing rang up yesterday afternoon when I was on telephone duty and said so."

"That would be Lady Vivian's secretary, Miss Bruce."

"Yes," said Miss Delmege reflectively. "She's been with them for years, and is perfectly devoted to Miss Vivian. She's too sweet about her—Miss Vivian, I mean. I've heard her telephoning sometimes; she calls her Brucey."

"Frightfully human!" was Tony's enthusiastic comment.

"Yes, isn't it?"

A moment's thoughtful silence was consecrated to the consideration of Miss Vivian's humanity, and then Miss Plumtree was escorted upstairs to take off her hat.

"Really, that girl looks a different creature!" Mrs. Potter exclaimed.

"Doesn't she? She ought to be most awfully grateful to Miss Vivian. You know Miss Vivian arranged the whole thing? With all she's got to think of, too! But that's Miss Vivian all over. Never lets slip a chance of doing a kindness. I've seen her go out of her way...."

But Miss Delmege's anecdote was not fated to meet with attention.

Mrs. Bullivant walked into the sitting-room looking awestruck.

"Girls, who do you think is coming to sleep here tomorrow night?"

"There isn't *room* for any one else, is there?" mildly inquired Mrs. Potter, who slept in a bedroom which contained four beds.

"We shall have to manage somehow. I've just had a note—Miss Vivian is coming here."

"She isn't!"

There was a chorus of astonishment; then Miss Delmege's attenuated little tones contrived, as usual, to make themselves audible: "Well, I'm not altogether surprised, do you know? I'd rather suspected something of the kind. Plessing has to be kept quiet on account of Sir Piers; and she's been ill herself, and isn't fit to come backwards and forwards in this cold. I thought something of the kind would be arranged, and I had a very shrewd suspicion as to what it would be."

It need not be added that nobody made the faintest pretence of believing in this prescience.

"Well, I'm blessed!" said Miss Henderson emphatically. "Where is she going to sleep? There isn't a single room in the house, is there?"

"She must have my room," said Mrs. Bullivant simply. "I think I can make it nice and bright for her before tomorrow night. It'll just need fresh curtains and a bit of carpet or two, and I thought you'd let me have the looking-glass out of your room, Miss Jones dear. Mine is such a cracked old thing."

"Yes, of course. But where are you going to sleep yourself, Mrs. Bullivant?"

"That's another thing, dear. Your room is absolutely the only one where there's an inch of space for a spare bed. Would you and Miss Marsh mind very much...?"

"No," said Miss Marsh emphatically, "of course not. But wouldn't it be more comfortable for you to have a bed in your own sitting-room? There'd just be room behind the door, I think."

"Ah, yes, dear; but, then, I must have somewhere for Miss Vivian's meals. I can't send her down to the basement for supper very well, can I?"

"Hardly!" exclaimed Miss Delmege, with a slight, superior laugh at so outrageous a suggestion.

"I'm sure I hope she'll be fairly comfortable. It's only for a few nights, till she's made other arrangements."

"I can tell you one thing," Miss Delmege remarked authoritatively. "The one thing Miss Vivian hates is a *fuss*. I happen to know that. She'll simply want everything to go on as usual, and to be let alone."

"That's all very well, but it's easier said than done!" even the gentle Mrs. Bullivant was constrained to exclaim. "It'll mean an upset for the whole house, with extra meals and everything. I mean, dear, one really can't help seeing that it will. I don't know what cook and Mrs. Smith will say, I'm sure."

"Considering that it's Miss Vivian who pays them their wages, they won't say much, unless they want to be dismissed," Miss Delmege retorted.

Mrs. Bullivant went away looking very much harassed.

"Do let's help her to turn out of her rooms!" exclaimed Grace. "It'll be much easier for her to do it tonight, with us to help her, than tomorrow, when she's sure to be busy all day."

"Good egg! Come on, girls!" cried Tony.

Miss Marsh and Miss Plumtree responded to the summons. They helped Mrs. Bullivant to take her crumpled blouses and limp black skirts from behind the torn curtain where they were huddled against the wall; and Grace mended the curtain while Tony and Miss Plumtree put away the clothes in a big cardboard dress-box, where Mrs. Bullivant said they would do very well for the time being.

"What about that stain on the wall where the damp came through so badly?" Miss Marsh asked doubtfully.

"Pin up a copy of an Army Council Instruction as a delicate attention. Then she can learn it by heart while she gets up in the morning," was Tony's facetious suggestion.

"Put up a map of the Midlands, with a red-ink line round every affiliated depôt."

"Don't be silly, girls! You're so foolish I can't help laughing at you," declared Mrs. Bullivant.

"No; but I think we might put up a picture or something. Now, I wonder what we've got."

"There are Kitchener and Lord Roberts in the sitting-room," suggested Miss Marsh. "I'll fetch them up."

She ran down, and came back triumphantly with the large framed photogravures. It was found that Lord Roberts would successfully mask the stain on the wall, and Miss Plumtree and Mrs. Bullivant made themselves very dusty by clambering on to chairs and affixing a nail, hammered in with the heel of Miss Plumtree's shoe, from which the picture was finally suspended.

"It looks quite nice and bright, doesn't it?" Mrs. Bullivant asked them. "Not like Plessing, perhaps—but, then, Miss Vivian won't expect that. Now, is there anything else up here?"

"We might put in a kettle," Grace said. "I'm sure she won't have one of her own." So Grace's own kettle, which was a pretty little brass one, was left upon the washing-stand, and Miss Marsh said that Gracie and she would share hers. They went downstairs congratulating one another upon their forethought, and upon the renovated appearance of the tiny bedroom.

Just before supper Miss Delmege, coming upstairs with a graceful, bending gait indicative of still recent convalescence, encountered Grace.

"You've made the rooms look quite sweet, dear, and Miss Vivian is sure to appreciate it. She's one of those people who always notices little things."

Grace was tired, and had run up and down stairs a number of times, for the most part with her hands and arms full.

"I wanted to help Mrs. Bullivant, that was all," she said curtly.

"There's no call to get annoyed, dear!" exclaimed Miss Delmege, amazed.

Grace looked up penitently.

"I know there isn't. I don't know why I sounded so cross. I think perhaps I'm a little tired of the sound of Miss Vivian's name, that's all."

"Well! Of all the peculiar things to say! Upon my word, dear," said Miss Delmege scathingly, "if I didn't know you so intimately, I should sometimes consider your manner downright strange!"

This conviction remained with Miss Delmege. She went into the sitting-room to await the supper-bell, which Mrs. Bullivant generally rang some quarter of an hour after the appointed time, and remarked in a detached voice: "Poor Grace Jones seems rather upset tonight. What I should almost call sort of on edge. I suppose she doesn't like the idea of having to go back to the ordinary office routine tomorrow, after going in and out from Plessing in the way she has done."

"I didn't notice anything wrong with her, I must say!" exclaimed Miss Marsh, who was both fond of Grace and anxious to miss no opportunity for contradicting Miss Delmege.

"No, dear? Well, perhaps you wouldn't. There's none so blind as those that won't see, and we all know that love is blind," was the gentle response of Miss Delmege, as she sank into the chair nearest the fire.

Miss Marsh could think of no better retort than "I'm sure I don't know what you mean by that, Delmege, and I shouldn't think you did yourself, either."

"There's the bell," said Tony.

They trooped down to the basement, and every one said how nice it was to see old Plumtree back in her place again, and Mrs. Bullivant triumphantly announced that there would be sausages, because Miss Plumtree liked them, to celebrate her return.

"Not two for me, really, please," Miss Delmege protested elegantly, and manipulated the extreme ends of her knife and fork with the merest tips of her exclusively curved fingers, as a protest against the great enthusiasm displayed by several of her neighbours.

On the same principle, when the sausages were followed by a loaf of bread and a pot of marmalade, Miss Delmege cut up her bread into small, accurately shaped dice, and said, "Pass the preserve if you will, please, dear," between two very small sips at her cup of cocoa. She sat at the foot of the table, and the chairs on either side of her generally remained vacant. Grace came down late, and apologized. One might be, and almost inevitably was, late on week-days, owing to the exigencies of the office, but Sunday supper was something of a ritual.

"So nice and homelike, all sitting down together with no one in a hurry," Mrs. Bullivant always said. But she smiled a welcome at Grace.

"I've kept your supper nice and hot, dear," she said, uncovering a plate next to her own. "Come and sit down here, won't you? You look tired tonight."

Miss Delmege shot a triumphant glance at Miss Marsh, who pretended not to see it, and did not fail to observe that tired or not, Grace made her usual excellent supper.

"I wonder if any one has any cigs?" Tony suggested wistfully.

"Yes," said Grace promptly. "Luckily, I have a whole box."

"Oh, you angel! How lovely! I do hate Sundays without a cigarette. Somehow, on other evenings there never seems to be time to smoke, or else one's too tired and goes straight to bed."

In the sitting-room Grace produced her box of cigarettes.

It was almost a matter of course at the Hostel that such things should be treated as belonging more to the community than to the individual.

"Thanks awfully, Gracie."

"Really? Are you sure? Well, then, thanks so much, if I may—just one."

"Delmege? Oh, you don't smoke, though, do you?"

"No, thank you. I dare say I seem old-fashioned, but it's the way mother brought us all up from children, and I must say I always feel that smoking is—well, rather unwomanly, you know."

In the face of this commentary Miss Marsh struck a match, and passed it round the room.

The atmosphere became clouded.

"You know," Grace said rather mischievously to Miss Delmege, "that Miss Vivian smokes?"

"She doesn't!"

"Indeed she does. Didn't you know that? Why, I've often noticed the smell of tobacco when she hangs up her coat in the office. It's unmistakable."

"That might mean anything!" hastily exclaimed Miss Delmege. "Tobacco does *cling* so. Very likely it hangs all round the house at Plessing, you know, with a man in the house and people always coming and going, probably."

"You forget that Gracie knows all about Plessing," cried Miss Marsh instantly. "Of course, *she's* seen Miss Vivian at home."

"And does she really smoke?" asked Tony.

"Yes, she does. Quite a lot, I think."

"Ah, well, that's different, isn't it?" Miss Delmege's serenity remained quite unimpaired. "One can understand her requiring it. I believe it really is supposed to be soothing, isn't it? Of course, working as she does, her nerves probably require it. What I mean to say is, she probably requires it for her nerves."

"I dare say. I wonder where she'll smoke here?"

"In Mrs. Bullivant's sitting-room, I suppose. Not that she'll be here much, I don't suppose. Only just for her meals, you know, and then to go straight to bed when she gets in."

"I do hope that her sleeping in Questerham isn't going to serve her as an excuse for working later than ever!" exclaimed Miss Delmege, in the tones of proprietary concern with which she always spoke of Miss Vivian's strenuous habits.

"Yes, I see what you mean," Mrs. Potter agreed. "With her car waiting, she simply had to come away sooner or later."

"Exactly; and she's always so considerate for her chauffeur, and every one. I really do think that I've never seen any one—and I'm not saying it because it *is* Miss Vivian, but speaking quite impersonally—any one who went out of her way, as she does, to think of other people."

"Look at what she did for me—even ordered a cab each way for me!" cried Miss Plumtree, very simply.

"That," said Miss Delmege gently, "is just Miss Vivian all over."

Miss Marsh bounced up from her chair, rudely severing the acquiescent silence that followed on this well-worn *cliché*.

"I'm going up to get my knitting. I simply must get those socks done for Christmas. I suppose no one will be shocked at my knitting on Sunday?"

"Gracious, no! Especially when it's for the Army. When's he coming on leave, Marshie?"

"Oh, goodness knows! The poor boy's in hospital out there. Can I fetch anything for any one while I'm upstairs?"

"My work-basket, if you wouldn't mind," said Grace.

"I say," asked Mrs. Potter, as the door slammed behind Miss Marsh, "*is* she engaged?"

"Oh no. She has heaps of pals, you know," Miss Henderson explained. "She's that sort of girl, I fancy. Haven't you noticed all the letters she gets with the field postmark? It isn't always the same boy, either, because there are quite three different handwritings. And her brothers are both in the Navy, so it isn't *them*."

"Well," said Miss Delmege, with the little air of originality so seldom justified by her utterances, "they say there's safety in numbers."

"Here's your basket, Gracie," said Miss Marsh, reappearing breathless. "How extraordinarily tidy you are! I always know exactly where to find your things—that is, if mine aren't all over them!"

"What are you going to make, Gracie?"

"Only put some ribbon in my things. The washing was back last night, instead of tomorrow morning, which will be such a saving of time during the week. I wish it always came on Saturday," said Grace, serenely drawing out a small folded pile of linen from her capacious and orderly basket.

Every one looked rather awestruck.

"Do you put in ribbon every week?"

"Isn't it marvellous of her?" Miss Marsh inquired proudly, gazing at her room-mate. "She has such nice things, too."

Grace uncarded a length of ribbon, and began to thread it through the lace of the garment known to the Hostel as a camisole.

"I can't say I take the trouble myself. *My* things go to the wash as they are, ribbon and all. The colour has to take its chances," said Miss Plumtree.

"Are we going to have any music tonight?" inquired Miss Delmege, with a sudden effect of primness.

The suggestion was received without enthusiasm.

"Then," Miss Delmege said, with a glance at Grace, who had completed the adornment of her camisole, and was proceeding to unfold yet further garments, "I think I shall go to bed."

"Do, dear," Mrs. Bullivant told her kindly. "I hope any one will go early who's tired."

Miss Delmege smiled cryptically.

"Well," she said gently, "underwear in the sitting-room, you know!"

"Oh dear!" cried Grace in tones of dismay. "Is that really why she's gone upstairs?"

"No loss, either," Miss Marsh declared stoutly.

"But it's only my petticoat bodice."

"I suppose she didn't know what might be coming next."

Grace, guiltily conscious of that which might quite well have been coming next but for this timely reminder, hastily completed her work and put it away again.

She leant back in the wicker chair, unconsciously adjusting her weight with due regard to its habit of creaking, and gazed into the red embers of the dying fire.

Her mind was quite abstracted, and she was unaware of the spasmodic conversation carried on all round her.

Her thoughts were at Plessing.

How could Miss Vivian be coming to stay at the Hostel when her father was so ill, and Lady Vivian alone at Plessing? Grace remembered the expression on Joanna's face when her daughter had said that she could no longer stay away from the office at Questerham.

She supposed that a consent had been extorted from her by Char, unless, indeed, Miss Vivian had not deemed even that formality to be necessary. Grace wondered, with unusual despondency, when or if she should see Lady Vivian again. She felt quite certain now that never again would any pretext induce Char to let her return to Plessing, and was not without a suspicion that she might be made to feel, in her secretarial work, that the Plessing days had not been a success in the eyes of Miss Vivian.

"Never mind; it was quite worth it," thought Grace, and it was characteristic of her that the idea of seeking work elsewhere than with the Director of the Midland Supply Depôt never occurred to her.

"A penny for your thoughts, Gracie."

"Oh, they're not worth it, Mrs. Potter. They weren't very far away."

"Perhaps they were just where mine have been all the evening—with poor Miss Vivian. She'll be feeling it tonight, poor dear, knowing she's got to leave tomorrow, and Sir Piers so ill. I *do* think she's wonderful."

"I must say, so do I," Miss Henderson said thoughtfully. "When she used always to refuse me the afternoon off, or any sort of leave, and say that she couldn't understand putting anything before the work, I used to resent it sometimes, I must own. But, really, she's lived up to it herself so splendidly that one can't ever say another word."

"Isn't Sir Piers *any* better?" asked Miss Plumtree pityingly.

"Not a bit, I think. But he's not exactly in immediate danger, either. Only the house has to be kept quiet, so I suppose she can't come backwards and forwards like she used, and it's a choice between her leaving home or giving up the work altogether."

"Well, I *do* think it's splendid of her!"

"Because, of course," Tony said, "nobody could take her place here. And I suppose she can't help knowing that. It will seem extraordinary having her in the Hostel, won't it?"

"It won't really be comfortable for her after Plessing, I'm afraid. I wish I could think of some better arrangement...." murmured Mrs. Bullivant to herself.

"Oh, Mrs. Bullivant!" cried Grace Jones. "You couldn't do more than give up your own bedroom and your own sitting-room to her?"

Then, because the heretical words "And that's more than she deserves," were trembling on her tongue, Grace went upstairs to bed.

Her sense of loyalty to her chief did not allow her to throw any doubt on the glory of her return to work under such circumstances.

Moreover, the Hostel's point of view on the subject was as adamantine as it was universal.

XII

The next morning Char came back to the office. She found her table loaded with violets and a blazing fire on the hearth. Miss Delmege greeted her with an air of admiring wonder, suffused by a tinge of respectful pity, and ventured to hope that Sir Piers Vivian was better.

No one else was sufficiently daring to approach so personal a topic, but little Miss Anthony, blushing brightly, turned round at the door just as she was leaving the room with her work, and said stammeringly that it was so nice to see Miss Vivian back in the office again.

Char smiled.

She was still looking ill, and she knew that her departure from Plessing had been a severe strain on her barely recovered strength. The effort of giving her attention to the arrears of work which required it taxed all her powers of determination.

"Is this all the back work, Miss Delmege?"

"Yes, I think so, Miss Vivian."

"There are several things here which ought to have been brought to me."

"I suppose Miss Jones didn't know."

"But she ought to have known. It was most annoying having to leave so much to her. She hasn't the necessary experience for one thing, and is far too fond of acting on her own initiative."

It gave Char a curious satisfaction to say this in the cool and judicial tones of complete impartiality.

"I shall have a fearful amount to do with these back numbers. Bring me the Hospital files, and the Belgian file, and W.O. letters—and—yes, let me see—Colonial Officers. That will do for the moment; and send for Miss Collins, please."

The stenographer entered the room with her most *dégagé* swing, and seated herself opposite to Char, her pad poised upon her crossed knees.

"Good-morning, Miss Vivian," she said gaily. "Nice to see you back again. I hope you've quite got over the influenza?"

"Thank you," said Char icily. "Please take down a letter to the O.C. London General Hospital."

She dictated rapidly, but Miss Collins's shorthand was never at a loss, and at the end of forty minutes she still appeared tireless and quite unruffled.

"That will do, for the moment."

Miss Collins uncrossed her knees, and looked up.

"I shall be wanting ten days' leave, Miss Vivian," was her unprecedented remark.

The scratching of Miss Delmege's pen paused for a moment, and, although she did not turn round, a tremor agitated her neat, erect back.

Char looked at her unabashed typist.

"There will be no Christmas leave," she said curtly, taking the resolution on the instant.

"I expect I shall want it before Christmas—about the end of this week. The fact is—"

"I'm sorry, but it's quite out of the question. Naturally, one rule applies to the whole staff, and I shall not expect any one to be absent from duty except on Christmas Day itself, which will be treated as a Sunday. As for ten days, the suggestion is absurd, Miss Collins. I consider that you've practically had ten days' holiday during my absence—and more."

"I've been here every day as usual, and cut any number of stencils, and rolled them off," Miss Collins cried indignantly.

"I'm glad to hear it. Why do you want leave now?"

Miss Collins giggled, tried to look coy, and at last said in triumphant tones, which strove to sound matter-of-fact: "I'm going to be married."

There was silence. Char was drawing a design absently on her blotting-pad.

"My friend is getting leave at the end of next week, and we've settled to be married before he goes out again. He's an Australian boy."

"Of course, that slightly alters the case," Char said at last, stiffly. "Do you wish to go on working here just the same?"

"Oh, yes, Miss Vivian. What I feel is, that with him out there, I simply must be doing my bit at home. It'll take my mind off, too, like, and as he says—"

Char interrupted her ruthlessly.

"In the circumstances, Miss Collins, you can take eight days' leave at the end of this week. But I may tell you that you have chosen a most inconvenient moment, with the Christmas rush coming on and a great deal of back work to be done."

Her manner was a dismissal.

Miss Collins left the room.

"Miss Delmege, do you think that we could find some one to replace Miss Collins?"

"For the time—or permanently?"

"While she's away, I meant. It would be difficult to get any one permanently in her place, I'm afraid. Besides, she's an extremely good stenographer, and I can't afford to have one who'll make mistakes."

Char paused, and her feminine curiosity conquered official aloofness. "Did you know that she was engaged to be married?"

"I've seen her wearing a ring, but, naturally, I never come across her except officially," was the haughty response of her secretary.

But however detached she might proclaim herself to be, Miss Delmege did not keep the news of Miss Collins's wedding to herself. In less than twenty-four hours it was known all over the office. It was perhaps fortunate that the Director of the Midland Supply Depôt did not know the number of departments in her office that interspersed the day's work with discussions as to what Miss Collins would wear as a wedding-dress. The interest of it almost eclipsed the sensation of Char's own installation at the Hostel.

She arrived there at nine o'clock that night. It would have been possible for her to leave the office a good deal earlier, but she was aware that the members of her staff would not expect any deviation from her usual iron rule, and were probably telling one another at that moment how wonderful it was to think that Miss Vivian should never have her dinner before half-past nine at night.

Char, tired and oddly apprehensive, was inclined to think it rather wonderful herself. The door of the Hostel stood open to the street, as usual, but since the air-raid over Questerham all lights had been carefully shaded, and only the faintest glimmer of a rather dismal green light appeared to welcome Char as she rang the bell.

She thought that the hall looked narrow and dingy, and a large box took up an inconvenient amount of space at the foot of the stairs. Then it occurred to her, with an unpleasant sense of recognition, that the box was her own.

"Is that Miss Vivian?" came a voice through the gloom. "Won't you come in?"

Char came in, gingerly enough. Then a match was struck, and Mrs. Bullivant anxiously held up a lighted candle to guide her footsteps.

"Just down the step, Miss Vivian, and I've got supper all ready for you in my sitting-room. I thought you'd like it best there. Our dining-room is in the basement, you know."

"Thank you; this will do very well."

Char looked round the tiny room rather wonderingly. Preparations for a meal stood on a table that was obviously a writing-table pushed against the wall and covered with a white cloth.

"It'll be ready in one minute, Miss Vivian," repeated the Hostel Superintendent nervously. "I'll just go and tell the cook. I expect you must be hungry, and would rather have supper first, and then go to your room. And I'm very sorry, but we've had to leave your trunk downstairs. The stairs are rather too narrow, and the maids thought they couldn't manage it."

Mrs. Bullivant went away, as though supposing that the last word had been said upon the subject of the trunk.

Char thought otherwise.

In a few minutes Mrs. Bullivant came back with a tray, on which stood a cup of cocoa, another one of soup, and a plate with two pieces of bread. "I thought you'd like soup, as it's such a cold night," she said triumphantly. "Now, you must tell me if you have any special likes and dislikes, won't you? I do so hope you'll be fairly comfortable here, Miss Vivian. I can't tell you how very much it's impressed all the girls, your coming here like this, for the sake of the work. I'm afraid it won't be as comfortable as Plessing."

The same fear was also taking very definite possession of Char's mind.

She pulled up a low cane-seated chair to the table and began the soup and bread. The cocoa, already poured out, must, it was evident, be allowed to get cool until the arrival of a next course. This proved to be a dish of scrambled eggs, and was followed by one large baked apple.

Char felt thankful that she had refused her maid's solicitations to come with her. Preston confronted by such a meal, either for herself or for Miss Vivian, was quite unthinkable.

Char thought of Plessing and the dinner that had awaited her there every evening, with Miss Bruce hovering anxiously round the other end of the table, with something like homesickness.

Then she derided herself, half laughing. What did food matter, after all?

But she decided that Miss Delmege must be told to find her rooms in Questerham as soon as possible. Then Preston could join her.

This last thought was prompted by Char's strong disinclination to unpack, a duty which she realized now would, for the first time, devolve upon herself.

It would not be facilitated by the prominent position given to her trunk in the hall of the Hostel.

"Mrs. Bullivant," said Char, when the Superintendent returned, "my trunk must be taken up to my room, please."

Her tone was unmistakably, and quite intentionally, that of the Director of the Midland Supply Depôt issuing instructions to a member of her staff.

"Yes, Miss Vivian," automatically replied the little Superintendent, and added desperately: "But I'm afraid that cook and Mrs. Smith won't do it—not if they've once said they won't."

Char raised her eyebrows.

"If the servants don't obey your orders they must leave," she said. "But isn't there any one else?"

"Perhaps two of the girls—" Mrs. Bullivant hesitated, and then left the room.

Char heard her open the door of the next room, which she knew must be the sitting-room, and a babel of voices immediately became audible.

She waited, rather annoyed.

Mrs. Bullivant came out into the hall, followed by quite a large group.

"This is it. Look, dears, can you manage it? Miss Henderson, dear, you're tall."

"Oh, yes. It's only up one flight, and it isn't a very large box—only an awkward shape. Will some one give me a hand?"

Miss Plumtree, who was sturdy, came to assist, and between them, with a great deal of straining and pulling, and many anxious ejaculations from the door-way of the sitting-room, they slowly lifted the box.

"Don't hurt yourself, now!" cried Mrs. Bullivant. "Get it from underneath, Henderson!"

"Mind the paint on the wall!"

"Mind the banisters!"

"Oh, mind what you're doing, Greengage!"

Similar helpful ejaculations resounded, as the two girls carried the box up the first flight of narrow stairs.

Just as they reached the top step, Char heard the small, clear voice of her secretary, standing in the hall.

"Can you manage, or shall I help you?"

There was a general laugh, echoed from above, as Miss Henderson's voice came briefly down to them: "Thanks, Delmege; just like you, dear, but we happen to have finished."

They all laughed again.

Char, through the half-open door, saw Miss Delmege tossing her fair head. "I'm afraid I don't quite see the point of the joke," she observed acidly.

"Now go in to the fire again, all of you," Mrs. Bullivant exclaimed. "Miss Vivian will hear you if you chatter like this in the hall. I'll tell her the box is safely upstairs."

When she returned to impart the information, Char had shut the door of her little room again.

"Wouldn't you like to come upstairs, Miss Vivian?" the Superintendent asked her timidly. "They've managed to get your box up all right, and I expect you'll be wanting to unpack."

Char wanted nothing less, but she realized that the unwelcome task must of necessity precede her night's rest, and went upstairs with Mrs. Bullivant.

The bedroom seemed to her very tiny, and, indeed, what space there was, her box and dressing-bag mainly occupied. It was also exceedingly cold.

When Mrs. Bullivant had wished her good-night, with a certain wistful air of expecting an enthusiasm which Char felt quite unable to display, she slipped on her fur coat and began to tug at the strap of her trunk.

The process of unpacking at least succeeded in warming her. But there was hardly any room to put away even the limited number of belongings that she had brought, and Char told herself rather indignantly that Mrs. Bullivant seemed to be a most incompetent manager, and might at least have provided her employer with a respectably sized bedroom in her own Hostel.

Towards ten o'clock she heard the sitting-room door opened, and a general whispering and rustling proclaimed that several people were coming upstairs. Char did not, however, at once realize the full significance of the fact that her own room adjoined the bathroom. A thin but incessant stream of conversation began, punctuated by the loud hissing of a kettle which had overboiled upon the gas-ring.

"How's the water tonight?"

"Fair to middling. I don't know who is having baths, but there won't be enough water for more than two."

"It's only tepid as it is."

"I am hungry," proclaimed a plaintive voice in incautiously raised tones.

"H'sh-sh! You'll disturb Miss Vivian. Why are you hungry at this hour, Tony?"

"Well, we didn't have anything frightfully substantial for supper, did we? and I had to go after the scrambled eggs, because I was on telephone duty. So I didn't even have any pudding."

"Oh, poor kid! Couldn't Mrs. Bullivant have got you something?"

"I didn't like to ask her; she's so worried tonight, what with Miss Vivian's coming and everything. Besides"—Tony's voice sounded very serious—"there never *is* anything, you know. Only tomorrow's breakfast."

"Hasn't any one got some biscuits?"

"I'll go down to the kitchen and find some milk for you," said the peculiarly distinct tones of Grace Jones. "I know where it's kept."

"Oh, why should you bother?"

"It isn't at all a bother. You must be starving."

Char heard Miss Jones going downstairs again, and then a triumphant voice proclaimed: "*I* know who has some biscuits! Plumtree. She brought them back from her holiday. I'll go and ask her."

"Come on!"

Evidently Tony and Miss Marsh felt an equal certainty that Miss Plumtree's biscuits could be looked upon as community goods.

There was a silence, before a voice from the next story cried urgently down the stairs: "I say, is my kettle boiling? I put it on the gas-ring ages ago, as I went upstairs. Will some one have a look?"

"It boiled over some time ago," Miss Delmege proclaimed very distinctly. "I took it off for you."

"Thanks very much. I'll come."

There was a hasty descent, evidently in bedroom slippers, and then a long whispered colloquy of which Miss Vivian heard only her own name. Evidently Miss Delmege, at least, had not forgotten the proximity of her chief. Char several times heard her "H'sh!" her companions in a sibilant and penetrating whisper.

"You can't want to wash brushes at this hour!"

"My dear, I simply must. Just let me have the basin half a minute; I've got the water all ready."

"This your kettle?"

"Yes, dear, thank you."

"Oh, Mrs. Potter, have you actually got some ammonia in that water? I wish you'd let me do my brushes with yours."

"Of course, Miss Marsh. There's plenty of room."

"Well, good-night, girls," from Miss Delmege. "It may seem strange to you, me going to bed before ten o'clock, but it's the life. One gets tired, somehow."

"Good-nights" resounded, and one door banged after another.

There was splashing in the bathroom for a little while, and then silence.

Char realized with dismay that she had no hot water, and that the brass kettle on her washing-stand was empty. After reflection, she filled it from the jug, and decided that she must go to the bathroom where the gas-ring was.

She would not have been averse to being seen by her mother just then. War-work under these conditions could not be mistaken for anything but the grim reality that it was.

Lady Vivian, however, not being present, Char performed her domestic labours unobserved, and went shivering to her bed.

She wondered if any one would call her in the morning. This, however, proved not to be necessary.

The walls were thin and the stairs only carpeted with oilcloth, and before seven o'clock Char was startled out of sleep by a prolonged whirring sound overhead, which she only identified as that of an alarm-clock, when footsteps hastily crossed the floor above, and it ceased abruptly.

"Who on earth wants to get up at this hour, when they none of them start work before half-past nine!" she reflected rather disgustedly.

But she remembered that Mrs. Bullivant's duties as Superintendent might include the supervision of Mrs. Smith's arrival every morning and the preparation of breakfast, when a step stole past her door, and the reflection of a lighted candle was flung for a moment on the wall.

Conversations in the bathroom were much briefer in the morning than at night. Evidently every one was too cold, or in too much of a hurry, to talk, although there were sounds of coming and going from half-past seven onwards.

Char went to the bathroom herself at eight o'clock, selecting a moment when it appeared to be empty. She went behind the curtains that screened off the bath from the rest of the room, and found the water very cold.

"Very bad management somewhere," she reflected austerely, and wondered why it should be difficult to provide boiling water by eight o'clock in the morning.

She felt chilled, and not at all rested.

In the little sitting-room downstairs she found a rapidly cooling plate of bacon, uncovered, but solicitously placed on the floor close to the gas-fire, and some large, irregular slices of toast. Marmalade stood in a potted meat jar.

It cannot be denied that Miss Vivian flung an agonized thought to the memory of the admirably furnished breakfast-tray provided for her each morning by the agency of the invaluable Preston at Plessing.

Still very cold, and feeling utterly disinclined for the day's work, Char donned her fur coat over her uniform and went out.

She was not unconscious of the likelihood that her exit from the Hostel might be observed from the windows, and reflected that it would be incumbent on her for the present to take advantage of her new quarters by starting for the office at least an hour earlier than any one else.

But again she found here inconveniences which she had not taken into consideration. The fire in her office was not yet lit, and the charwoman who had charge of keeping the building in order greeted her with frank dismay.

"Your room isn't done yet, miss."

Miss Vivian, exasperated, and colder than ever, set her lips together in a line of endurance.

"You can leave it for today, and in future I wish it to be ready for me by nine o'clock. Please light the fire at once."

The stage of lighting the fire, however, was further off than she realized, and she was obliged to sit huddled in her fur coat, opening letters with mottled, shaking hands that were turning rapidly purple, while the charwoman made an excruciating raking sound at the grate, put up an elaborate and exceedingly deliberate erection of coal, sticks, and newspaper, and finally applied to it a match which resulted in a little pale, cold flame which did not seem to Char productive of any warmth whatever.

She sat at her table and wrote:

"DEAREST BRUCEY,

"Will you send me every woollen garment I have in the world, please? Preston will find them. The cold here is quite appalling, and, of course, one feels the absence of proper heating arrangements at the Hostel terribly. It is, however, naturally much more convenient for me to be able to give more time to the work, which is fearfully heavy after my absence, and will probably increase every day now. I am writing from the office, having been able to get in very early. It might not be a bad plan, later on, to put in a couple of hours' work before breakfast, but please don't let the suggestion dismay you! I shall move into rooms as soon as my secretary can find some, and probably send for Preston. She could be quite useful to me in several ways.

"There is a mountain of papers on my table, all waiting to be dealt with, so I can't go on writing; but I know how much you wanted to hear if the Hostel had proved at all possible. Don't worry, dear old Brucey, as I really can manage perfectly well for the present, in spite of the bitter cold and poor Mrs. Bullivant's hopeless bad management. She had not even arranged for my box to be taken upstairs; and as for hot water, decently served meals, or proper waiting, they are simply unknown quantities. I dare say I shall have to make one or two drastic changes. You won't forget to ring me up if there is any change in father's condition, of course. I could come out at once. This anxiety underlying all one's work is heart-breaking, but I *know* that I was right to decide as I did, and stick to my post.

"Yours as ever,

"CH. VIVIAN.

"P.S.—Do as you like about reading this letter to my mother."

It was fairly certain in what direction Miss Bruce's "liking" would take her on the point, and it was not without satisfaction that Char felt the certainty of her voluntarily embraced hardships becoming known at Plessing.

Her letter to Miss Bruce somehow restored to her that sense of her own adequacy which physical conditions of discomfort, against which she had felt unable to react, had almost destroyed.

When Miss Jones came to work, a few minutes earlier than usual, she noted, with a regret that was not altogether impersonal, the cold, bluish aspect of her employer's complexion, and wondered if she dared infringe on Miss Delmege's cherished privilege of producing a foot-warmer.

But she was not aware that her own excellent circulation, quite unmistakably displayed in her face and in an unusually white pair of capable hands, formed a distinct addition to the sum of calamities that had befallen Miss Vivian.

XIII

"Char, I've come to warn you," portentously said Captain Trevellyan a week later, entering the Canteen one evening.

"That's very kind of you. Is it another air-raid?"

"No; besides, you're all quite *blasées* about them now. Miss Jones, single-handed, could cope with—"

"What did you want to warn me about?" interrupted Char, with more abruptness than apprehension in her voice.

"A rescue-party. Miss Bruce is so much upset about you, because she thinks the Hostel is killing you, that she's arranged a crusade to deliver you."

"Miss Bruce means very well, but surely she knows by this time that I don't admit of interference with my work. What does she want to do?"

"You'll see in a minute. I can hear the rescue-party at the door now, I think. They were close behind me."

Char swung round abruptly, and was engulfed in a furry embrace on the instant.

"My dear, pathetic martyr of a child! I've come to take you out of this at once. I hear you've been through the most unspeakable time at that Hostel!"

Char disengaged herself from Mrs. Willoughby's clasp, and endeavoured to silence the intolerable yapping sound that was going on apparently beneath her feet.

"That's Puffles—wicked little boy, be quiet. He *would* come with me, though I told him that all good little boys went to bye-bye at this hour; but he can't bear me out of his sight, you know. Isn't that too quaint? Quiet, Puff! He understands every single word that's said to him, you know. 'Oo clever, clever little man, aren't 'oo? Everything except talk, 'oo can."

"Come, come; he makes a pretty good shot at that, doesn't he?" Trevellyan said dryly.

"Johnnie, go away and find my precious Lance-Corporal for me. He'll never forgive me if I don't go and talk to him; but you've such a crowd here tonight I can't see any one. Besides, I want to talk to this dear thing. Can't we *sit*, Char? My dear, never stand when you can possibly sit. That's been my rule *all* my life, and so I've kept my figure. Not that I'm as slim as you are; but, then, it simply wouldn't be decent if I were, at my age. My Lewis always says that my figure is exactly right, but I dare say he's biassed. Now, dear, what about *you*?"

"We are particularly busy," Char said pointedly, "and I haven't a moment to call my own. I've only looked in here tonight just to see that everything's in order. Then I must go back to the office."

"Quite unnecessary, I'm perfectly certain. And your looking in here is all nonsense, dear. They all know the work perfectly, and do it far better by themselves than when you're just pottering about, getting in the way. If you put on an overall, and really turned into a perfect barmaid, as I do, it would be different, but just to stand and look on helps nobody, and tires you for nothing. You don't mind my speaking like this? But I know your dearest mother's girl couldn't mind anything, from *me*!"

Lesbia possessed herself of Char's unresponsive fingers and squeezed them affectionately.

"Now I want to have a real heart-to-heart chat," she proclaimed, lightly but penetratingly.

Char flung a glance round the hall.

One of the men was strumming on the piano, and a group gathered round him was singing and humming, all together, "When Irish eyes are smiling."

The atmosphere was thick with tobacco-smoke, and the demands upon the tea-urns heavier even than usual. Char saw Mrs. Potter, untidier than ever, handing steaming cups across her buffet with incredible rapidity. The noise of clattered crockery was unceasing. But Mrs. Willoughby's voice dominated all these sounds.

"I've heard the whole story from your beloved mother, ridiculously monosyllabic though she always is, and, of course, from that poor, good creature, Miss Bruce, who is miserable about you. She says that your letters are *too* heartrending—about the misery of that wretched Hostel, I mean. No food, no baths, no fires—and in this weather, too! So, my dear child, you're simply coming straight home with me tonight, to stay until we can find decent rooms for you, or persuade you to give up all this nonsense and go back to Plessing."

"Thank you; but I couldn't dream—"

"Lewis will be *delighted*. I've explained the whole thing to him, and he's quite overjoyed."

It was impossible, remembering Major Willoughby's unalterable gloom of demeanour, not to suppose that Lesbia's optimism might be overstating the case, but Char only gave a fleeting thought to this consideration.

"It's more than kind of you, but I'm afraid that poor Miss Bruce may be over-anxious—"

"Not another word, Char. Can't we send some one to put your things together at once?"

"Really, I'm most grateful, but I can't accept," said Char decisively. "It's quite true that my secretary hasn't found rooms for me yet, but meanwhile the Hostel does perfectly well, and I'm glad of the opportunity for being so near my work. I couldn't dream of moving."

She began cordially to wish that she had not sought to relieve her feelings by those letters to Miss Bruce, from which the little secretary would appear to have quoted so freely, and to have derived so much food for anxiety.

"Dearest girl, listen to me!" Lesbia exclaimed, raising her voice more than ever above the increasing din and clatter all round them. "I've been talking the whole thing over with your mother, and she's more than willing that I should have you. You needn't trouble about that for a *moment*. Poor dear Joanna was simply too sweet about it for words. 'I know you'll be a mother to my girl for me,' she said."

Lesbia gazed at Char with the air of one who believes absolutely in the pathos she exploits, and Char was forced to the conclusion that she actually imagined herself to be quoting correctly. For her own part, she attached not the slightest value to Mrs. Willoughby's flights of fancy.

Nevertheless, she was vexed and uneasy. Why could not people leave her alone? It was all very well for Miss Bruce to appreciate the stress of circumstances under which Char pursued her work, but the voluble importunity of Mrs. Willoughby was as unwelcome as it was unescapable. Char looked round her, in search of a possible channel into which to direct Lesbia's attention.

"Isn't that your Lance-Corporal?" she rather basely inquired.

"Where?" shrieked Lesbia. "You know, I'm quite, quite blind!"

This was a fiction frequently indulged in by Mrs. Willoughby, whose eye could safely be trusted to pierce the densest crowd when convenient to herself.

"*I* see him, just come in. Now, I suppose he'll make a bee-line straight for my little corner. Dear thing, he always does! It's too wonderful to hear him describe all that goes on *out there*, you know. He was out right at the very beginning, all through Mons and the Marne and Ypres and everything. They say the men don't like talking about it; but I've had, I suppose, more experience than any woman in London, what with one thing and another, and they always talk to me. The dear fellows in the hospital I visit simply yarn by the hour—they *love* it—and it's too enthralling for words. They're so sweetly quaint. One dear fellow always talked about a place he called *Wipers*, and it was simply ages before I realized that he meant *Ypres*! Wasn't that too priceless?"

On this highly original anecdote Mrs. Willoughby hurried away, struggling into her blue-and-white overall as she went.

Char saw her reach the side of the Lance-Corporal and break into voluble greetings, punctuated by hysterical protests from the Pekinese, wedged firmly under her arm.

"Well?" said Trevellyan's voice behind her.

"Well! Nothing will induce me to go and stay there, with that wretched little beast making its hideous noise all day and all night."

They both laughed.

"Seriously, Johnnie, I wish you'd tell Brucey that she really has exceeded her privileges. I can't have plans of that sort made over my head, as she should have known. What on earth possessed her?"

"Your letter worried her. She thought that the Hostel sounded so uncomfortable."

"So it is. But, after all," said Char, torn between a desire to show John how very much she was enduring in a good cause, and at the same time how little she heeded such external conditions, "after all the work is what really matters. It's for the sake of the work I put up with what poor Brucey thinks are hardships."

"But are they really necessary?"

"What do you mean?" said Char, displeased. "It certainly isn't possible for a house built like the Hostel to be either as roomy or as convenient as Plessing is. A certain amount of discomfort is practically unavoidable."

"Dear me! that's very hard on all of you. Don't the others find it trying? They have to be there all the time, don't they?"

"What others?" was the freezing inquiry of the Director of the Midland Supply Depôt.

Trevellyan looked at her in surprise, and replied quite simply: "The other workers, of course."

"Oh, I really don't know. I naturally never see anything of them, except at the office; but, of course—well, I suppose they're used to very much that sort of thing at home."

"Surely not. I was really thinking," Trevellyan remarked with some superfluity, "of Miss Jones."

"You and my mother appear to find some recondite quality in Miss Jones which I'm unable to discover!" exclaimed Char, laughing a little. "Of course she's a lady, but really, as far as work goes—which is, of course, all that matters just now—I've had a great many clerks who can be of far more use than she can. It was a mistake having her out to Plessing that time."

She spoke in a reflective tone that had a conclusive quality in it, but the tactless Trevellyan ignored the hint of finality and inquired matter-of-factly: "Why?"

"Because it may make the silly girl imagine that she's on a sort of superior foothold. You know how idiotic some of them are about—well, about me—as Director of the Supply Depôt, I mean. They can't look upon me as a human being at all."

"But you don't seem to want them to, Char. If you can live in the same house with them all and yet never see them except at the office, it's no wonder they don't look upon you as a human being."

He spoke so quietly that it was only after a moment she realized the condemnation that lay behind his words.

It hurt her more than she would have supposed possible. Like most complex organisms, she had an unreasoned craving for the approval of the very simple, and she had always thought that Johnnie, easy-going and uncritical, would accept her judgment as necessarily wider and more subtle than his own.

"I see," she said, very low. "You accept me and my work only at my mother's valuation."

"Well, no, Char. It isn't only that."

John's voice held a certain regret, but no retractation.

"It isn't only that evening at Plessing—though you know very well that I didn't see that question of your leaving home as you did—but every time I see you, you say or do something that makes me understand what Dr. Prince meant that evening."

"Thank you," said Char, low and bitterly.

"Perhaps I haven't any business to say anything about it at all. Only," said Trevellyan, with his habitual extraordinarily ill-inspired candour, "you know how much I care about Cousin Joanna."

"So much that it blinds you to any point of view but hers, apparently. Don't you really think that there was anything to be said for me, John? I don't altogether enjoy giving up my whole life to this office work, you know, under conditions of great difficulty and discomfort, and with the additional pain of knowing how hopelessly misunderstood my motives are. What has my father said about my leaving Plessing?"

"I don't think Cousin Joanna has told him. You see, he's one of the people who would misunderstand your motives, too, isn't he? And it would upset him so much."

"It's only in theory. He doesn't really want me in the least. It's simply that he hasn't moved with the times, doesn't understand the necessity that has arisen for women's work."

"Yes, that's quite true," Trevellyan said, but there was no sound of concession in his voice.

"My mother has given in to that all the time. You know she has. I believe that if it had been possible she wouldn't have let him know there was a war at all. It's—it's like helping an ostrich to bury its head in the sand."

"Don't you see," Trevellyan said, with a curious effect of reluctance, as though aware that she would not see, after all, "that all that is because she cares so much?"

"I'm afraid I don't. To me, the larger issue must always come first. It's England at stake, John, and our own petty little personal problems don't seem to count any longer."

"I suppose," he acquiesced, "that the difference between your point of view and hers is just that. She thinks that the personal problem still counts, you see."

"And you, of all people, can agree to that?"

"It's not quite the same thing for me, is it? War is my profession, so to speak. There are no other claims, so I need not balance values. It's just plain-sailing—for me. And for most other men, I suppose."

"Do you mean that all the women who have been giving time and trouble to serious work, all the munition-makers, the nurses, the Government workers, ought to go home again because of the old plea that home is a woman's sphere?"

"No, I don't, and you know I don't. But I think that the question of degree enters into it, and that where some women can very well afford to give their whole time and strength, others—can't."

"I see. Then it's simply a matter of counting the cost, and if it comes too dear, hide behind the fact of being a woman!" said Char mockingly.

It was always easy to defeat Johnnie verbally.

He looked bewildered, and said: "You're too clever for me, Char, as you always were. I can't pretend to argue with you. And I do admire the work you're doing, more than I can say. Everybody says it's wonderful."

He looked at her wistfully, and Char felt glad that the conversation should end on a note that, on his part, was almost pleading.

She rose, smiling a little.

"It's all right, Johnnie. And you'll soothe Plessing for me, won't you?"

But Captain Trevellyan, also rising, shook his head and looked very uncompromising.

"Cousin Joanna is wonderful, but she looks very tired," he remarked, and moved away as the sound of Puffles's bark heralded Lesbia Willoughby's return.

Char, also moving out of reach as rapidly as possible, saw him making his way towards the corner where Grace Jones was wiping plates as fast as they were handed to her, steaming and dripping, from the zinc wash-tub.

She felt annoyed and almost uneasy, and thought to herself: "He can't be seriously attracted by her. Why, she isn't even pretty, as one or two of them are."

Attracted or not, Captain Trevellyan remained in conversation with Miss Jones for the rest of the evening. Char had not even the satisfaction of seeing her neglect her work, and forthwith rebuking her, for her exceedingly pretty hands never stopped their rapid, efficient moving.

Char decided that she owed it to the uniform to inform her cousin that members of her staff, when engaged in the performance of their duty, must not enter into unofficial conversations.

She reserved this shaft, however, for later on, not wishing Trevellyan to discover the immediate workings of the law of cause and effect.

Her energies for the time being were fully engaged in avoiding the hospitable advances of Mrs. Willoughby.

"Well, my dear, sweet child," said Lesbia acrimoniously, "you are behaving like an absolute little fool (I know you won't mind your mother's greatest friend being perfectly candid with you), and I assure you that you'll regret it bitterly. As my Lewis said to me quite the other day, that girl is simply ruining her chances. Whom does she ever see, shut up with a pack of women all day and every day? Now, with us, you'd at least have civilized meals, with half the regiment always dropping in. The boys in Lewis's regiment always *did* come to me, from the days when he was only a Captain—young things always cling to me."

"Thank you," said Char, "but I'm afraid I shouldn't be very good company. By the time I've finished work, and interviewed all the various officials and dignitaries that I'm unfortunately obliged to see on nine days out of ten, I have not very much conversation left to entertain youths from the barracks."

Mrs. Willoughby made no pretence at failing to perceive the motive inspiring these utterances.

"Yes, dear, you may drag in those moss-grown and mouldering old officials as much as you please to show me that it isn't only a pack of women, but I'm not in the least impressed. Unfortunate old dotards put into khaki which is much too tight for them, and probably thinking what a pity it is that a pretty girl should talk so much nonsense! I met Dr. Prince the other day, and I can assure you that he doesn't in the least enjoy your interference with his Hospital."

"Probably not. I've had it put on to a proper military basis, and all these country practitioners resent anything done by the R.A.M.C."

"Nothing to do with the R.A.M.C., darling," retorted Lesbia piercingly. "Don't be childish! All that *he* resents—and I perfectly sympathize with him—is being shown his business by a chit who, as he says himself, probably would never have come into the world alive at all without his help."

Char left the honours of the last word with the outspoken Mrs. Willoughby, having, indeed, no reply ready to fit the occasion.

"Well, good-night, Char, and if you like to eat humble pie and come to me at any time, Lewis and I will be perfectly delighted. I've always longed to have a girl of my own, as I told Joanna, and I understand *all* young things. Don't I, my Puffles? Now I must take 'oo home, precious one, so come along. Oh! mustn't bark—naughty, naughty!"

Char turned her back on Mrs. Willoughby and the utterly unsilenced Puff, and left the Canteen.

She had meant to return to the office again, but had stayed longer than usual at the Canteen, and decided to go back to the Hostel instead. Certainly, it was uncomfortable there, and as the piercing weather continued, she found the lack of comfort ever more trying. But to return nightly to Mrs. Willoughby and Puff! She dismissed the thought with a shudder.

Besides, there were her mother and Trevellyan and Miss Bruce to convince that she was in earnest about her work, and would undergo discomfort and privation in order to carry it on successfully. Even Dr. Prince, Char reflected with some bitterness, might admit that she was prepared to make sacrifices in the attainment of her goal.

There was also the Hostel. Char knew from Mrs. Bullivant, and less directly from Miss Delmege, that her staff felt a wondering admiration and compassion at her courage in having left home and a father who was ill for the sake of patriotic work. She knew, by the sort of uncanny intuition that is generally the possession of the ultra-subtle, that when her gaze from time to time became abstracted over her work, or her attitude of set concentration relaxed for an occasional moment, Miss Delmege thought pityingly of the anxiety which must underlie all Miss Vivian's close and capable attention to the many details of her gigantic task. Miss Delmege thought her "wonderful," undoubtedly. Char told herself, with a slight smile, that she did not deserve her secretary's blind idealisms of her, but at the same time she was subconsciously aware of a certain resentment that the idealism should be so utterly unshared by Miss Delmege's understudy, the matter-of-fact, eminently undazzled Miss Jones.

Char went into the Hostel still thinking of Miss Jones. The hall was quite dark, but the sitting-room door was open, and as she went upstairs Char glanced in, hearing the sound of voices. There was a circle gathered close round the fire, and for a moment she did not recognize the central figure, seated on the floor and drying a cloud of brown hair at the blaze. Then she saw that it was Miss Plumtree, and noted with surprise that the girl, with her hair on her shoulders and her round, flushed face, was very pretty.

"Perhaps Johnnie was right, and I really don't look upon them as human beings," she thought, rather amused.

Some obscure instinct of testing herself caused her suddenly to turn and enter the sitting-room.

There was a sudden, startled silence as she stopped in the doorway, and then, almost simultaneously, the members of the staff rose to their feet.

"Oh, don't move," Char said affably.

There was an awkward pause, and then Miss Plumtree, giggling, exclaimed: "Oh, my hair! I've been washing it, Miss Vivian."

"You're all late tonight, aren't you? I fancy I generally hear you come upstairs earlier than this."

"I do hope we don't disturb you, Miss Vivian," Miss Delmege said, in a concerned voice. "I'm so often afraid that you must hear the water going in the bathroom, and all that sort of thing."

"It doesn't matter."

There was another silence. Nobody had sat down again. Miss Plumtree had clutched at her hair with both hands and was shoving it behind her ears as though in a desperate attempt to convince Miss Vivian that it was not really loose on her shoulders.

Miss Delmege put her head on one side, and gazed at Miss Vivian with a rather concerned expression of attention.

"Well, I'm afraid I'm disturbing you."

"Oh, no, Miss Vivian," they chorused politely.

"Good-night."

"Good-night, Miss Vivian."

The relaxation of a strain was quite unmistakable in this last chorusing.

81

"Idiots!" ejaculated Miss Vivian to herself as she went to her own room. She heard voices and laughter break out again as she went up the stairs.

Obviously it was not possible to attempt any unofficial footing with her staff, even had she herself desired such a thing. To them she was Miss Vivian, a being in supreme authority, in whose presence naturalness became impossible and utterly undesirable.

John knew nothing about it.

On this summing up, Char went to bed.

Twice she heard conversations on the stairs, in which the astounding fact that "Miss Vivian came into the sitting room, and there was Plumtree with her hair down, actually *down*, my dear," was repeated, and received with incredulous ejaculations or commiserating giggles. Finally, the workers from the Canteen came in, groped their way up in the dark, and were met on the landing by the hissing, sibilant whisper peculiar to Miss Delmege.

"H'sh, girls! Don't make a noise. Miss Vivian has practically told me that she can hear you in the bathroom every night. It really is too bad, you know, when she simply needs every minute's rest she can get."

"Well, so do we. Let me get past, dear." Miss Marsh's tones spoke eloquently of the tartness induced by fatigue.

"*Must* you go to the bathroom tonight?"

"Of course we must. What an idea! How am I to get my kettle boiled? I'm simply pining for a cup of tea; the work was awful tonight."

"Was Miss Vivian at the Canteen?"

"Just for a bit; talking to that cousin of hers—the Staff Officer one, you know."

"I know. She came into the sitting-room when she got in, and what *do* you think? Plumtree had been washing her hair, and it was all down her back!"

"Gracious! And Miss Vivian came in?"

"Came in, and there was Plumtree with her hair down her back!"

"What *did* she do?"

"Nothing. There was nothing *to* do, you know; there she simply was, with her hair actually down her back!"

"I say, Gracie, do you hear that? Plumtree really has no luck. Miss Vivian came into the sitting-room tonight just when she'd been washing her hair, and had it actually down her back."

Char listened rather curiously to hear how Miss Jones would receive this climax. Her voice came distinctly, with a little amusement in it, and the usual quality of sympathetic interest which she apparently always accorded to any one's crisis.

"Well, I hope she didn't mind. She has such pretty hair."

"That's hardly the point, is it?" said Miss Delmege reprovingly. "It looked rather funny, after all, for Miss Vivian coming in like that, to see her with her hair absolutely down her back."

"Even if it was funny," said Grace literally, "I dare say Miss Vivian didn't notice it. I never think she has much sense of humour. Good-night."

XIV

"Good-morning, Miss Vivian."

"Good-morning, Miss Collins. Please take a letter to—"

The stenographer giggled and tossed her red head: "Mrs. Baker-Bridges, if you please!"

Char looked at her typist blankly for an instant, and then recovered herself, unsmiling.

"Yes. This letter is to the Town Hall Hospital, and I wish you'd remember, Miss Collins, to—"

"I haven't got used to it meself yet," Mrs. Baker-Bridges said coyly. "A double name, too, so I suppose it's harder to remember."

"Will you make me three copies of this, please?"

"Yes, Miss Vivian."

82

Char dictated her letter very briskly, and avoided the use of her stenographer's name, not wishing to submit to further correction. It did not add to her complacency, during the busy days before Christmas, when her instructions were received with an affronted giggle and "Mrs. Baker-Bridges, *please*, Miss Vivian!"

Char was in rooms now, with the devoted Preston in attendance and occasional visits from Miss Bruce. She was working very hard, and the Christmas festivities indulged in by the Questerham Hospitals frequently required her presence as guest of honour.

Char still retained a vivid recollection of finding herself next to Dr. Prince on one of these occasions, both of them required to join in a rousing chorus of which the refrain was

"All jolly comrades we!"

And the look which the doctor, singing lustily, had turned upon her, held a humorousness that Char felt no disposition to reflect in her own gaze. She was quite aware that neither of them had forgotten the doctor's peroration delivered on the night of her decision to leave Plessing, and the recollection of it still, almost unconsciously, coloured all her official dealings with him.

It was therefore with surprise that she received an announcement from Miss Jones one evening: "Dr. Prince is downstairs and wants to see you for a moment."

"At this hour? Quite impossible! It's nearly seven, and I have innumerable letters to sign."

Grace hesitated, and then said, very gently: "I think he's just come from Plessing."

Char glanced at her sharply.

"Ask him to come up, then."

Sudden apprehension had taken possession of her, and increased at the sight of the doctor's kind bearded face, with its lines of fatigue and anxiety.

"What is it, Dr. Prince?"

"Could you spare me a few moments?"

"Certainly. Miss Jones, will you—"

Char, glancing round, saw with a slight feeling of annoyance that Miss Jones had not waited to be dismissed. Char did not relish being perpetually disconcerted by the independence of her junior secretary.

"A nice girl, that," said the doctor benevolently.

Char looked utterly unresponsive, and supposed rather indignantly to herself that Dr. Prince had not come to the office at the end of a long day's work merely in order to tell her that Miss Jones was a nice girl.

Something of the supposition was so evident in her manner that the doctor added hastily: "But I mustn't take up your time. Only I've just come from Plessing, and Lady Vivian asked me herself to come in here for a moment and—and tell you—ask you, you know—just suggest—only throw it out as a suggestion, since no doubt you've thought of it for yourself—"

The doctor fell into a fine confusion, and looked imploringly at Char.

"Is my father worse?"

"No. I didn't mean to frighten you, Miss Vivian; I'm so sorry. He's not worse, though, as you know, he's not gaining ground as we'd hoped, and of course he's not getting any younger. But the fact is, that he's set his heart on your being home for Christmas."

Char drew her brows together.

"Of course, I can arrange to spend a couple of nights there if he wishes it. But my mother laid great emphasis on the fact that she did not wish there to be any going backwards and forwards between the office and Plessing, as you doubtless remember."

"My dear young lady, where Sir Piers's wishes are concerned, she has no will but his. You don't need *me* to tell you that."

"Of course," said Char musingly, "he has old-fashioned ideas as to one's spending Christmas at home."

"Yes," said the doctor, "that's it. That was our generation, though I'm twenty years younger than your father, Miss Vivian. But early Victorians I suppose you'd call us both. He can't understand your not being at home, all together, for Christmas-time. We can't disguise from ourselves that his mind is a little—a very little—clouded, and he doesn't rightly understand your absence."

"I can't go over that ground again," Char told him frigidly. "I was in an exceedingly painful position, and had to choose between my home and what I conceived to be my duty. As you know, I put my country's need before any personal question just now."

"Yes, yes," said the doctor, obviously determined to stifle recollections of his Hospital in its pre-Vivian days. "I—I see your point, you know. But Sir Piers hears very little of the war nowadays, and I don't think he connects your absence with that now."

"What does he suppose, then?" Char asked sharply.

"Miss Vivian, his mind is clouded. We can't deny that his mind is clouded. I believe," said the doctor pitifully, "that he just thinks you are away because Plessing is so dull and quiet. Lady Vivian promised him that you were coming back for Christmas, and it pleased him."

"It is most unjust to me that the facts have not been explained to him."

"But you remember," the doctor reminded her gently, "that they *were* explained to him before he got ill. And he wanted you to stay at home, you know."

Char was silent.

"Well," said the doctor at length, "Lady Vivian suggested that I should drive you out on Christmas Eve. I shall be going to Plessing then—next Thursday."

"Thank you; but I'd better hire something if they can't send the car from home. I may not get away till late. Troop-trains are pouring in, and there is a great deal to be done. There are the Hospital festivities to be considered."

The doctor repressed an inclination to say that he knew all about the Hospital festivities, and instead answered that he quite understood, but could arrange to call for Miss Vivian at any hour convenient to her.

"I will let you know, if I may."

Char, nothing if not self-possessed, rose to her feet, and it became obvious that the interview was over.

"Good-night, Dr. Prince."

The dismissed doctor hurried downstairs, muttering to himself, after his fashion when vexed and disconcerted.

At the foot of the stairs he overtook Grace Jones with her hat and coat on. She looked up at him with her ready, pleased smile.

"Good-night, doctor. I'm so glad you found Miss Vivian disengaged."

"Conceited monkey—" began Dr. Prince, almost automatically, then hastily recollected himself and said: "Yes, yes. Are you off duty now?"

"Just. I've got to go down to the station and see about a case of anti-tetanic serum for one of the hospitals, which is due by the 7.50 train, but I can take it up there to-morrow. You know how precious it is, and we daren't trust the orderlies with it since Coles had that smash."

"To be sure. Well, I'll drive you down in my car to get it, if you like, and then I can take it up to the Hospital. I've got to go there again tonight."

"Oh, thank you."

The doctor liked the pleased gratitude in Grace's voice.

"I want so much to know how Sir Piers Vivian is," she said presently.

The doctor shook his head.

"A question of time, you know, when there's been a stroke—at that age. He doesn't rally very much, either. And the brain, Miss Jones, is clouded. We can't deny that it's clouded."

"Oh, poor Lady Vivian!"

"She knows it as well as I do. Doesn't let on, you know, but she's never been deluded from the first. And there she is all day, in the room, you know, except just when he's sleeping, reading to him, and talking quite cheerfully and trying to get him to take a pleasure in some little thing or other. I've never seen her break down, and we doctors see that sort of thing when other people don't sometimes. But she's been under a strain for a long while now—oh, before he got ill—and yet she carries on somehow. Ah, breeding is a wonderful thing, Miss Jones. There have been Vivians at Plessing for more generations than I can count, and *she* was a Trevellyan. They're from these parts, too, though it's a West Country name. I may be an old snob, Miss Jones, but I was brought up to reverence those whom God Almighty had set in high places, and the Vivians of Plessing have always stood to me for the highest in the land. A pity there isn't a son there!"

"Yes."

"There are cousins, of course. Sir Piers has a brother with children. But one would have liked the direct line—and for *her* to leave Plessing, it seems hard. If there'd only been a boy!"

"He would be fighting now," Grace reminded him.

"To be sure, and so many only sons have gone. If Miss Charmian there had been a boy, though! I tell you frankly," said the doctor, in an outburst, "that I don't understand her. She and I have had ructions in our time, Miss Jones, and I've known her ever since she came into the world. And now, when it comes to a Hospital Return—!"

The doctor nearly swerved his car into a market wagon, apologized to Grace, and said candidly: "I really hardly know what I'm at when I get on to the subject. Army Form 01864A in duplicate indeed! And as for the Nomenclature of Diseases that we hear so much about nowadays, I rather fancy that I was at home there some twenty years before Miss Charmian's little typewritten pamphlets on the subject were issued. Telling me that conjunctivitis is a disease of the eye, and what V.D.H. stands for! War Office instructions, indeed!"

Grace laughed discreetly, and after an instant the doctor laughed too.

"Well, well, well, we're all working in a great cause," he conceded, "and I suppose she does wonders. They all tell me so. Perhaps it seems a little hard to those of us who've been trying to conquer pain and disease for a number of years to be put under military discipline by an impudent monk—H'm, h'm, h'm! by a young lady in a uniform striped with gold like a zebra! But she's certainly untiring in her work; so are you all. This must be quite a new style of thing to you, Miss Jones?"

"I was in a hospital for a little while at the beginning of the war, but I can only do clerical work."

"But nothing before the war, eh?"

"Oh, no. I just helped my father at home."

"I thought so," said the doctor, with an odd sound of unmistakable satisfaction in his voice. He was glad that this nice little girl who listened with such interest while he talked, and so evidently admired Sir Piers and Lady Vivian of Plessing, should have lived at home before the war and not gone dashing out in search of an independent livelihood.

"Lady Vivian asks after you very often," he told her. "You saw her every day for a time, didn't you?"

"Yes, while Miss Vivian was at Plessing. I should like to see her again. Will you give her my love?" said Grace.

"Yes, indeed I will. She's lonely out there, I often think, though young Trevellyan comes out when he can. Nice boy that, but they'll be sending him out again directly, I suppose. Now, then, Miss Jones, here's the station."

Grace despatched her business at the parcels office as quickly as possible, and came back with the neat wooden case carefully labelled all over.

"Put it there; it'll be quite safe. I wish I could take you back to Pollard Street, but they're expecting me at the Hospital and I must get on. Shall you be all right?"

"Oh, yes, and thank you so much. The walk will warm me, and it isn't far. Good-night, doctor."

"Good-night," responded the doctor cordially as the car started down the hill towards the Hospital.

He wondered whether Char would accept his offer to drive her out to Plessing on Christmas Eve, and reflected rather ruefully that, if so, it would certainly be a late and cold transit. But, at all events, his mission would have succeeded.

He triumphantly told Lady Vivian next day that Char was coming to Plessing on Christmas Eve.

"I put the case diplomatically, you know—just used a little tact, and she never made any difficulty at all. Delighted to come, if you ask me," said the doctor.

"Thank you so much, Dr. Prince. I've told Sir Piers that she's coming, and he's so pleased. Don't let her start too late; it's so bitterly cold and the roads are very bad. I can't send the car in for her, as you know; since the chauffeur was called up, I've no one to drive it. But if you're kind enough to bring her—"

"I'll bring her fast enough, if she'll let me," said the doctor. "Anyhow, she shall come, which is the point. She said at once that she'd come."

"Yes," said Joanna dryly. "You won't expect me to be enthusiastic at such condescension, will you?"

The doctor looked at her with concern evident in his shrewd, kindly gaze.

He had known Joanna Vivian ever since she had come to Plessing as a bride, and had never heard that note of bitterness in her voice before. He told himself sadly that the long strain of Sir Piers's illness was telling on her at last, in spite of her splendid physique. In his heart the doctor did not believe that the strain would last much longer.

"I wish you had some one here to keep you company," he said awkwardly. "Even Miss Bruce was better than no one."

"She's only with Char for a few days. She'll soon be back, probably tomorrow. And meanwhile I had an offer of companionship only this morning. Do you know Mrs. Willoughby?"

"Good Lord, yes!" said the doctor, and they both laughed.

"I should *really* like Char's Miss Jones to come out to me for a few days," said Joanna, rather wistfully. "She and I understand one another very well, and she's such a restful person."

"A thoroughly nice girl, and most intelligent," warmly remarked the doctor, reflecting how sympathetic Miss Jones had shown herself to be over the question of Medical Boards. "Why shouldn't I bring her out with Miss Charmian on Thursday night?"

"I only wish you would, but I don't want to throw Char into a fit."

"I'll chance that," said the doctor grimly. "She'd only tell me that fits are a disease of the nervous system, and should be shown as N.S. on all Hospital returns."

He told himself that if Lady Vivian wanted to see Miss Jones it was preposterous that she should not be allowed to have her out to Plessing. Diplomacy, the doctor reflected, could arrange the whole thing.

Believing himself to be the possessor of this attribute, Dr. Prince, on the morning before Christmas Eve, rang up the office of the Midland Supply Depôt on the telephone.

"Can I speak to Miss Vivian, if you please?"

"Who is it?" inquired an attenuated voice at the other end.

"The Officer Commanding Questerham V.A. Hospital," firmly replied the doctor.

If Miss Vivian wanted officialness, she should have it.

"Can I give a message for you?"

"I'm afraid I must speak to Miss Vivian herself."

"One moment, please."

The doctor waited, and presently the voice said: "I've put you through to Miss Vivian."

"Hallo!" exclaimed a weary tone. "Miss Vivian speaking."

"Good-evening," said the doctor briskly. "What time am I to call for you tomorrow afternoon?"

"Oh, is that you, Dr. Prince? But you really mustn't trouble to call for me; I can hire something."

"Not on Christmas Eve."

"Perhaps not. Well, let me see. Unless anything unforeseen occurs I think I could get away by eight."

"That will do splendidly," ruefully said the doctor, aware of sacrificing truth to diplomacy. "I suppose your office work will go on without you just the same?"

There was a pause, which the doctor interpreted as an astounded one.

"The office will treat Christmas Day as a Sunday. It will probably be necessary for me to come in during the afternoon, as I do on Sundays, but only for a few hours."

The doctor gathered himself together for a Machiavellian effort.

"Why not leave that very intelligent little secretary of yours, Miss Jones, to take your place?"

"A junior clerk? Out of the question. But I needn't trouble you with those details, of course. As a matter of fact, no one will be here on Christmas Day except the telephone clerk."

"I strongly advise you to leave Miss Jones in charge, if I may be permitted to suggest it."

"Miss Jones," said Char, very distinctly, "has none of the experience necessary for a position of responsibility, and I should not dream of entrusting her with one. She will have nothing whatever to do with the office during my absence."

The triumph of diplomacy was complete.

"In that case," said the doctor in a great hurry, "your mother need have no scruple as to inviting her out to Plessing for Christmas. I know she wants to—in fact, I'm charged with the invitation—but it seemed incredible that you should be able to spare her from her work. But I mustn't keep you. Good-night, Miss Vivian. At eight tomorrow I'll come for you both. Good-bye."

The triumphant doctor put back the receiver.

"Hoist with her own petard!" he muttered to himself in great satisfaction.

That afternoon he found time to call on Miss Bruce, on the verge of departure from Char's lodgings, and triumphantly charged her with a message for Lady Vivian.

"Tell her that I've arranged the whole thing, and Miss Jones is coming out tomorrow evening in the car to spend Christmas."

"At Plessing? But why?" asked the astonished Miss Bruce.

"Because Lady Vivian wants her," said the doctor stoutly. "She's taken a fancy to her, and I'm sure I don't wonder. A charming girl!"

"I had an idea that Miss Vivian never thought her very efficient," doubtfully remarked Miss Bruce.

"There are a great many people whom she doesn't think efficient, although they've been at their job more years than she's been out of long clothes; but in this case it serves our turn very well. She'll be out of that confounded office for a couple of days."

"Does Miss Vivian know this?"

"Dear me, yes," said the doctor glibly. "I talked it all over with her on the telephone this morning. That's quite all right. Now, Miss Bruce, supposing you let me give you a lift to the station? It's going to snow again."

Miss Bruce accepted gratefully, and the doctor felt slightly ashamed of his own strategy for avoiding any possible conversation between her and Char on the subject of Miss Jones's visit to Plessing.

Diplomacy was not an easy career.

Nothing now remained, however, but to tell Miss Jones of her invitation and to insure her acceptance of it.

The indefatigable doctor stopped his car at the door of the Hostel soon after half-past seven that evening.

"Would Miss Jones be good enough to speak to me for a moment?" he inquired, when Mrs. Bullivant came to the door.

"I'm sorry, but I think she's out. Some of the girls have gone to the theatre tonight. Is it a message from Miss Vivian?" the Superintendent asked anxiously.

"Not exactly," was the evasion exacted by diplomacy.

"Shall I give her any message when she gets back?"

"Yes, yes; that might be best," eagerly said the doctor, conscious of cowardice. "Would you tell her that Lady Vivian—and—and Miss Vivian—are both expecting her at Plessing tomorrow evening, to spend a couple of days? Lady Vivian particularly wants to see her again, and it will be good for her to have some one to cheer her up. Tell Miss Jones that it's all been arranged, and I'll call for her at the office tomorrow evening at eight o'clock and drive her out. I've got to go out there in any case, and the last train goes at four, so they must go by road."

"Well, I'm sure that will be delightful for her!" exclaimed the unsuspecting Mrs. Bullivant. "How very kind of Miss Vivian!"

"Yes. It's Lady Vivian, of course, who really suggested the idea, one day when I happened to mention Miss Jones. She likes her very much, and, of course, it's lonely for her now. I'm glad this should have been thought of," said the doctor, with a great effect of detachment. "Well, I mustn't keep you at the door in this cold. It's freezing tonight again, unless I'm much mistaken. Good-night."

"Good-night, doctor. I won't forget the message. I'm delighted that Gracie should have such a treat."

The doctor, as he drove away, was delighted too, with himself and with the success of his manoeuvres. He thought that Lady Vivian would be very glad to see the girl for whom she evidently felt such a sense of comradeship, and he, like Mrs. Bullivant, was glad of the pleasure for Grace; but, most of all, the doctor felt a guilty satisfaction in the knowledge of having successfully outwitted the Director of the Midland Supply Depôt.

XV

"Tell Miss Vivian that we can't wait; we must start at once. The sleet has been falling, and the roads will be impossible in less than an hour. I don't know how the car will do it as it is."

Dr. Prince was harassed but determined.

Miss Marsh reluctantly took this message upstairs. She had already had occasion to observe during the course of the evening that Miss Vivian was in no frame of mind to welcome interruptions.

"I'm not ready."

"No, Miss Vivian."

Miss Marsh stood unhappily in the doorway.

"What the *dickens* are you standing there for?" cried Miss Vivian in exasperated tones.

Miss Marsh was standing there from her own intimate conviction of being placed between the devil and the deep sea, and her extreme reluctance to confront the impatient doctor with Miss Vivian's unsatisfactory reply. To her great relief, she found Grace in conversation with him.

"Well, is she coming?"

"The moment she can, Dr. Prince. She really won't be long now," was Miss Marsh's liberal interpretation of her chief's message.

"The thaw isn't going to wait for her," said the doctor grimly. "It's begun already, and after three weeks' frost we shall have the roads like a sheet of glass."

"I think I hear the telephone," said Miss Marsh, hastening away, thankful of the opportunity to escape before the doctor should request her to return with his further commands to Miss Vivian.

But presently Char came downstairs in her fur coat and heavy motoring veil, carrying a huge sheaf of papers and a small bag.

"I'm sorry you've been kept waiting. I was afraid that, as I told you, I might not be able to start punctually."

"It's this confounded change in the weather," said the doctor disconsolately. "How could one guess that it would choose tonight to begin to rain after three weeks' black frost? However, I dare say it won't have thawed yet. Come along. At any rate, it won't be quite so cold."

The little car standing at the door was a very small two-seater, with a tiny raised seat at the back.

"Where will you sit, Miss Vivian, with me in front or on the back seat?" inquired the doctor unconcernedly. "Have either of you any preference?"

"I think I'd better come in front," said the Director of the Midland Supply Depôt, very coldly. She took no notice of Miss Jones.

It was very dark, and a thin, cold rain had begun to fall. The doctor groaned, and drove out of Questerham as rapidly as he dared. On the high road it was already terribly slippery. After the car had twice skidded badly, the doctor said resignedly: "Well, we must make up our minds to crawl. Lady Vivian will guess what's delayed us. I hope you had dinner before starting?"

"Yes, thank you," replied Grace serenely.

"Naturally, I haven't been able to leave the office, but then I never have dinner till about nine o'clock," Char said. "I've almost forgotten what it is to keep civilized hours."

"Then, all I can say is, that you'll be extremely hungry before we get to Plessing," was the doctor's only reply to this display of patriotism.

The car crawled along slowly. About four miles out of the town the doctor ventured slightly to increase speed. "Otherwise we shall never get up this hill," he prophesied.

"It's better here, I think," said Char.

"I think it is. Now for it."

The pace of the little car increased for about a hundred yards. Then there was a long grinding jar and a violent swerve.

"Confound her! she's in the ditch!" cried the doctor. "Are you all right there, Miss Jones?"

"Yes," gasped the shaken Grace, clinging to her perch.

"Get out," the doctor commanded Miss Vivian, in tones that suggested his complete oblivion of their respective positions as regarded official dignity. Char obeyed gingerly, and stood grasping the door of the car.

"Take care; it's like a sheet of ice."

The doctor slid and staggered round to the front of his car, the two front wheels of which were deeply sunken in the snow and slush of the ditch. He made a disconsolate examination by the light of the lamps.

"Stuck as tight as wax. Now, what the deuce are we to do?"

"Can't we move her? asked Grace.

"Not much chance of it, but we might as well try."

Grace got down, and they strained at the car, but without any success.

"No use," said the doctor briefly. "I think you two had better stay here while I get back to Questerham—we're nearer Questerham than Plessing, I fancy—and bring something out. Though, good heavens! I'd forgotten it's Christmas Eve. What on earth shall I get?"

"I can authorize you to call up one of the ambulance cars."

"That's an idea. I'm sorrier than I can say to leave you on the roadside like this," said the doctor distractedly. "Put the rug round you both, and if anything comes past, get a lift. The car will be all right. I defy the most determined thief to make her move an inch. H'm! I must take one of these lamps, and I'll make as much haste as this confounded sheet of ice will allow."

"Wait!" cried Grace. "I can hear something coming, I think."

They stood and listened. The hoot of a very distant motor-horn came to them distinctly.

"Coming towards us," was the doctor's verdict. "With any luck it'll take you both back to Questerham. It's your best chance of getting to bed tonight. Miss Vivian, you're shivering. Confound it all, it's enough to give you both pneumonia, hanging about on a night like this! What an old fool I've been!"

"It couldn't be helped, could it?" said Grace. "There were no trains running after four o'clock, and we couldn't guess the weather would change so. And it isn't nearly so cold as it has been."

"Have a cigarette?" said the doctor suddenly, lighting his own pipe. "It'll help you to keep warm."

"Smoking in uniform is entirely out of order, but for this once—thank you," said Miss Vivian, with a slight laugh.

The sound of a motor-bicycle became unmistakable, and the doctor advanced cautiously into the middle of the road.

"Ahoy, there! Could you stop half a minute? We've had a spill. Two ladies here."

"Is that Dr. Prince?" came a voice that made Char exclaim: "It's John Trevellyan!"

The motor-bicycle, with its small side-car, drew up beside them.

"Have you had a telephone message?" said John.

"From Plessing? No. What's happened?" said the doctor sharply.

The two men exchanged a look.

Char came forward.

"You'd better tell me," she said in her slow, deep drawl.

"Cousin Joanna telephoned just before eight o'clock, but you must have started," John said gently. "She wanted to ask Dr. Prince to make as much haste as possible—and you."

"My father?"

"I'm afraid it's another stroke, my dear."

The doctor asked a few rapid professional questions, and Grace came and stood near Char Vivian.

"When you didn't come," said John, "Miss Bruce got anxious, and felt sure there'd been a spill. Cousin Joanna was upstairs, with him; I don't think she realized. So I brought the only thing I could get hold of. You can ride a motor-bike, doctor?"

"Of course I can. But we can't leave two young ladies planted in a ditch, with that confounded machine of mine," said the doctor, his distress finding vent in irritability.

"There's the side-car," said Grace. "Miss Vivian must go with you, doctor."

"Can't we get your machine out of the ditch?" John suggested.

"Not unless you're a Hercules," said the doctor crossly. He began to examine the motor-bicycle.

"I can manage this all right, though no machine on earth will do anything but crawl on such a road. Miss Vivian, that will be our best plan."

"Yes," said Char, very quietly. "And, Johnnie, can you look after Miss—er—Jones, and take her back to Questerham?"

"Get in, Char," said Trevellyan. "I shall certainly look after Miss Jones, and bring her out to Plessing somehow or other. Your mother wants her. Send anything you can to meet us, doctor."

"Right; but I'm afraid we can't count on meeting anything tonight, of all nights. Miss Jones, I'm so sorry. All right there?"

The motor-bicycle, with a push from Trevellyan, jolted slowly away along the slippery road, and John and Miss Jones stood facing one another by the indifferent light of the motor-lamps.

Grace looked at him with her direct, gentle gaze. "Please tell me whether you really meant that," she said. "Does Lady Vivian want me at Plessing just the same?"

"Yes," he answered, with equal directness. "She said so. She told me to bring you. She said she wanted you."

Grace drew a long breath, then said: "We shall have to walk, sha'n't we?"

"I'm afraid so—at least part of the way. Unless you'd rather stay in the car, and keep as warm as you can, while I go on to Questerham and try to get hold of something that will take us both out? I'm going back there, of course. Which shall we do, Miss Jones?"

"Walk, I think. It's only about five miles, and I doubt if you could get anything tonight to go out all the way to Plessing."

"I think we can go across the fields, if you don't mind rough walking. It saves nearly a mile, and the only advantage of keeping to the road would be the chance of meeting something, which I think most unlikely. Miss Jones, you're splendid. Do you mind very much?"

"Not now that I know Lady Vivian really wants me," said Grace shyly.

Trevellyan unhooked one of the lamps.

"Shall I carry the other one?"

"It will make your hands very cold, and I think one will be enough. Have you anything that you must take?"

"My bag; it isn't heavy."

"Right. Then give it to me, and you take the lamp, if you will." Grace obeyed without any of the protestations which might have appeared suitable, and they started very cautiously down the road.

"Keep to the side," said Trevellyan; "it's not very bad there. I'm afraid you'll never get warm at this rate, but a broken leg would be awkward."

"Tell me what happened at Plessing."

He told her that Sir Piers had suddenly had a second stroke that afternoon, and was again lying unconscious. Lady Vivian had come down and spoken with Trevellyan for a few minutes, and assured him that the trained nurse would not allow her to relinquish hope.

"But it all depends upon what one means by hope," said Trevellyan. "One can hardly bear to think of his lying there day after day, unable to understand or to make himself understood—and as for *her*—"

"She is very brave," said Grace.

There was a silence, and each was thinking of Joanna.

Presently Trevellyan spoke again.

"We shall turn off in a minute and take the short cut. Are you very cold?"

"Pretty cold, but I'm glad I had dinner before starting. Did you?"

"No, worse luck! I started from Plessing at half-past eight, and the servants were in such a fuss. I'm fearfully hungry," said Trevellyan candidly.

"Well, wait a minute."

Grace stood still and put the lamp on the ground while she felt in her coat-pocket.

"I thought so. I've a packet of chocolate. Will you take it?"

"Thank you," said Trevellyan seriously; "it's very kind of you. Let's both have some."

Grace divided the little packet scrupulously, and they stood and ate it with their backs to the hedge, the bag and the lamp on the ground in front of them.

"Christmas Eve!" said Grace. "Isn't it extraordinary?"

"Where were you last Christmas?" he asked.

"In the hospital, near my home. We were decorating the wards for Christmas, and all stayed there very late. There was a convoy in, too, I remember; the nurses stayed on long after we'd all gone home. I was only a clerk, you know."

"I remember. You told me that when you—on the night of the air-raid," said the tactful Trevellyan, with a very evident recollection of the unfortunate disability which debarred Miss Jones from the nursing profession.

Grace laughed.

"Exactly. It is so idiotic and provoking, and, as a matter of absolute fact, it was because I always got ill at anything of that sort that they couldn't let me go on at the hospital any more—my father and stepmother, I mean."

"I didn't know you had a stepmother."

"I've had her about four years," Grace informed him.

"Do you like her?" Trevellyan asked bluntly.

"Very much indeed. She's only a few years older than I am, and she lets me call her Marjory. She's so nice and pretty and merry."

It was evident that Miss Jones was not a person to make capital out of circumstances.

When they started again, Trevellyan said gently: "You'd better take my arm, if you will. It's heavy going along this field."

It was, and an incessant sound of splashing told Grace that she was almost in the ditch.

"I think I can manage," she said breathlessly. "I'm afraid of the light going out, and it's easier to hold in both hands."

Trevellyan said nothing, but presently Grace felt him take hold of the lamp.

"You *must* let me," he said quietly. "You'll want all your strength, for we're going uphill now, and the ground's very rough."

They trudged up a steep incline, Grace with both cold hands deep in her pockets and her head bent against the wet driving mist that seemed to encompass them. Her feet were like ice, and she had long since given up trying to avoid the puddles and small snowy patches that lay so plentifully on the way. Twice she stumbled heavily.

"We're just at the top," said Trevellyan encouragingly. "You're perfectly splendid, Miss Jones, and I feel such a brute for not taking better care of you. Cousin Joanna will be very much distressed; but, you see, I know she wants you."

"I'm very glad," said Grace simply. "I never admired any one so much as I do her."

"Nor I. She's been so ripping to me always. Even when I was a big clumsy schoolboy, with nowhere to go to for the holidays, she'd have me out to Plessing, and make me feel that she cared about having me there. She wrote to me all the time I was in India—I don't think she ever missed a mail—and all the time I was in Flanders last year. Some day," said Johnnie, rather shyly, "I'd like to show you her letters to me. No one has ever seen them. But I've always felt that you knew what she really is—more than other people do."

"Thank you," said Grace.

John seemed satisfied with something in the tone of the brief reply, and they went on in silence till he raised the flickering lamp.

"Wait a moment. There ought to be a fence here, and it may be barbed wire. Take care."

Grace was thankful to stand still, her aching legs still trembling beneath her from the ascent. John held up the lamp and made a cautious examination.

"There ought to be an opening—here we are."

He waved the lamp in triumph; the light gave a final flicker and expired.

There was a dead silence from both, Grace speechless from dismay and fatigue, and Trevellyan from his inability to express his feelings in the normal manner in the presence of Miss Jones.

"Have you any matches?" she asked at last.

"Yes. I'm sorrier than I can say, but I'm very much afraid that the wretched thing has given out. Why on earth the doctor can't get proper electric lamps for his rotten car—"

John fumbled despairingly amongst his matches, made various unsuccessful attempts, and at last apologized again to Grace, and said that it never rained but it poured. They must go on in the dark.

"Very well. Only let's avoid the barbed wire."

"Miss Jones, I *can't* tell you what I think of you. Any one else would be perfectly frantic."

"But I'm never frantic," said Grace, rather regretfully. "I often wish I was like the people in books who feel things so desperately. Maggie Tulliver, for instance. It's so uninteresting always to be quite calm."

"Always?"

"Well," said Grace, "practically always."

"It's an invaluable quality just at present, but perhaps one of these days—"

"I'm so sorry, but I think my skirt has caught in the barbed wire."

Trevellyan released her skirt in silence.

"Now, then, if we get through the gate here, the next field takes us on to the road again, and with any luck they'll have got to Plessing and sent something back to pick us up."

Trevellyan, who knew his ground and appeared able to see in the dark, pushed at the creaking wooden gate, and Grace passed through it, feeling her feet sink into an icy bog of mud and water.

"I'm afraid I can't see much. You see, I don't know the way at all."

"I know; it makes all the difference. Look here, will you let me take your hand? I know every inch of the way."

Grace put out her small gloved hand and said very sedately: "Thank you; I think that will be the best way."

They went on steadily after that, speaking very little, and Grace stumbling from time to time. Once John asked her: "Are you very tired? This is rotten for you."

"I don't mind," said Grace shyly.

After a long pause, Trevellyan said cryptically: "Neither do I."

On this assurance they reached the high road, and Grace said gently, withdrawing her hand: "I can manage now, thank you."

"It *can't* be long now before something meets us. I don't know what they can send; but if it's only a farm cart, it will be better than nothing."

"Luckily I'm a very good walker. I don't think that poor Miss Vivian could ever have got out to Plessing unless we'd met you with that motor-bicycle. She dislikes walking, and is not used to it."

"I wouldn't have had this walk with Char," said Trevellyan fervently, "for any money you could offer me. She's a splendid companion, of course, on her own ground, but for this sort of thing— it's only two people in a million, Miss Jones, who could do it without hating one another for ever afterwards."

"We must be very remarkable, then, for I don't think it's going to have that effect," said Grace, laughing.

"As far as I'm concerned," said Trevellyan slowly, "it's exactly the opposite. You won't want me to tell you about it now, but perhaps some day soon you'll let me—Grace."

Miss Jones walked along the muddy, slushy edge of the road with her mind in a tumult. She felt quite unable to make any reply. But Captain Trevellyan, always matter-of-fact, did not appear to expect one. He presently remarked that it was getting colder again. Was Miss Jones very wet?

"Rather wet, but the worst half must be over by now. I wonder what news we shall find when we arrive. Do you know, I can't help being selfishly thankful to be going there. It's been so hard never hearing anything about her, and knowing all the time that she was in such anxiety."

"Doesn't Char tell you?"

"No; but I don't think I asked her. She likes us to be official, you know."

"I never heard such inhuman nonsense in my life!" exclaimed Trevellyan in tones of most unwonted violence.

They both laughed, and the next minute Grace said, "Listen!"

They both heard wheels.

"It's the dog-cart. I thought so. It was the only thing left, and I suppose they've got hold of a boy to drive it. Thank goodness! Miss Jones," said Trevellyan for the fourth time, "I can't tell you what I think of you; you've been simply wonderful."

"Don't! Of course I haven't."

Grace's voice was more agitated than accorded with her previous declaration of imperturbability, and something in the few shaky words caused John to put out his hand and grasp hers for a moment, while he hailed the cart.

"Here we are! Did Miss Vivian send you?"

"Her ladyship, sir. Couldn't come any faster, sir; the roads are so bad."

"They are. How is Sir Piers?"

"The same, sir—still unconscious. Dr. Prince don't anticipate no immediate change, sir, but he's staying the night."

"Good! He's telephoned to Questerham, I suppose. Now, Miss Jones, let me help you. Boy, you'd better get on to the back seat; your inches are better suited to it than mine," said John firmly. He put the rug round Grace, and she sank thankfully on to the small seat of the dog-cart.

They hardly spoke while he drove cautiously along the remaining mile of high road and up the long avenue to Plessing.

Even when John helped her down at the hall door he only said: "I shall see you tomorrow. I shall never forget this Christmas Eve."

"Nor I," said Grace.

In the hall Miss Bruce greeted them with subdued exclamations.

"*How* tired you must be, and half frozen! Sir Piers is just the same; the doctor is still upstairs. He and Charmian got here two hours ago or more, and told us what had happened. There wasn't anything to send for you but the little cart. Poor dear Charmian! such a home-coming for her! She's wonderful, of course—never given way for an instant."

"Where is she?"

"Upstairs. I've sent to tell her and Lady Vivian that you've arrived at last."

"And, Miss Bruce, we *should* like some food if it can be managed without too much trouble."

"Of course, of course. Miss Jones, your room is ready. Wouldn't you like to change your wet shoes at once?"

Miss Bruce spoke with an odd mixture of doubt and compassion, as she looked at Grace warming her frozen hands at the hall fire. It was evident that she did not feel certain whether Miss Jones was to be regarded as a friend of Lady Vivian's, whom Captain Trevellyan had judged necessary to bring to Plessing at all costs, for Joanna's sake, or as Char's junior secretary, thrusting herself upon her chief's family at a particularly inopportune moment. But the question was solved a few instants later, when Joanna Vivian herself, coming downstairs in her black tea-gown, exclaimed softly: "You've brought her, Johnnie! Well done! No; there's no change yet. I want you to see Dr. Prince." Then she took Grace's hands in hers and said: "Thank you, my dear, for coming to me."

XVI

"Well, I couldn't have believed it—Christmas morning and all!"

"What, Mrs. Bullivant?"

"This letter from the office, dear."

Little Mrs. Bullivant's face was scarlet, and her voice shaking.

"But what is it?"

"Miss Vivian has dismissed me. This was evidently written two days ago, and has been delayed in the post. She simply says that she has come to the conclusion that I find the Hostel rather too much for me and is making other arrangements at the New Year. Oh, my dear!"

Mrs. Bullivant dissolved into tears, and Tony, aghast, picked up the small trebly-folded sheet of crested paper that had fallen from its square envelope.

"Written by herself, too, not typed! Oh, I *am* sorry! But doesn't she give any reason?"

"Not any. But I suppose she wasn't comfortable when she stayed here last month. She said one or two little things at the time—the hot water, you know, and the gas giving such a poor light, and then the servants. But I never knew she was thinking of this."

"I must say, I think she might have given you a reason, or asked you to go and see her at the office," said Tony, her allegiance to Miss Vivian shaken at the sight of the little Superintendent in tears.

Every one liked Mrs. Bullivant at the Hostel, and when Tony told the others that she was to be dismissed there was a general outcry.

"But why? What a shame!"

"She always works so hard, and she's so nice to every one. It's too bad of Miss Vivian."

"It does seem very unlike her to be so inconsiderate!" Mrs. Potter exclaimed.

"I can't believe there isn't some satisfactory explanation. It's too unlike Miss Vivian."

Miss Delmege was caustically reminded by Miss Marsh that no explanation could really be satisfactory from the point of view of Mrs. Bullivant.

"Couldn't we all send round a petition, and sign it? Do let's. We can put it on her table for when she gets back tomorrow or next day."

Miss Plumtree's suggestion was acclaimed, and she and Miss Marsh spent most of the morning in composing a petition that should combine sufficiently official wording with appealing arguments in Mrs. Bullivant's favour.

"Shall we wait till Gracie gets back before fastening it up, so as to make her sign it too?"

"Why?" said Miss Delmege sharply. "Several of the others are away, too, for the week-end, and we can't wait for every one to get back."

"Well," provokingly said Miss Marsh, "as she's Miss Vivian's own secretary, one naturally looks upon her as being important. Besides, look at the way they've had her out to stay; she's a sort of special person, isn't she?"

Every one knew that Miss Marsh was "getting a rise out of Delmege," always a favourite form of amusement, and there was a general giggle when Miss Delmege said in a very aloof manner: "If you ask me, I think Miss Vivian thinks it just as strange as any one else that Gracie should be asked out there now, with Sir Piers still so ill. But Lady Vivian is quite well known to be a most eccentric person."

"I shouldn't be a bit surprised if Miss Vivian's Staff Officer cousin had got her asked. I think he admires Gracie."

"Go on, Marshie! Why, he's never seen anything of her, has he?—except, perhaps, at the Canteen."

"There was that night, you know," Miss Marsh reminded them.

"What night?"

"Why, when there was the air-raid, and he brought her back here afterwards. Don't you remember?"

"Well!" Miss Delmege exclaimed, "I must say that I should have thought—"

"I'm sure I've read somewhere that those four words '*I should have thought*' are responsible for more quarrels than any others in the language."

Miss Delmege disregarded Tony and her literary allusions.

"I should have thought that after the strange way Grace Jones behaved that night, the less said about it the better. It's not the kind of thing one cares to dwell upon."

"I must say," Miss Henderson agreed, "that it would have been more likely to put him off than to make him admire her. At least, so far as my experience of human nature goes."

"Well, just sign this, will you, girls?"

They all hung over Miss Plumtree's shoulder, and read the petition.

Miss Vivian's secretary put her signature down first on the list, as by rights, and decorated her "Vera M. Delmege" with an elegant flourish.

"I must say I do like what I call a characteristic signature," she remarked, hastening back to appropriate the wicker arm-chair nearest the fire.

The others cowered round, in twos and threes, gazing disconsolately at the driving hail and stormy clouds of the grey world outside.

94

"Rather a wretched Christmas, isn't it? I do think we might have had a week's leave, really," said Miss Henderson, shivering.

"Miss Vivian isn't taking that herself," Miss Delmege at once reminded her. "And those who live near enough have been given the week-end, after all."

"I might just have managed it if I hadn't been on telephone duty. But she wouldn't let me change with any one else. I suppose I must go over there now and release Miss Cox," said Tony, rising reluctantly to her feet.

"Well, take the petition, dear, and leave it on Miss Vivian's table, will you? Then she'll find it when she comes. I dare say she'll be in this afternoon. Poor Mrs. Bullivant!"

They talked of Mrs. Bullivant in a subdued way at intervals during the day. The little Superintendent remained in her own room.

"Oh, isn't it wretched?" groaned Miss Marsh for the hundredth time. "I declare I'd welcome a troop-train; it would give us something to do, and make a break."

But Miss Anthony returned from the office at four o'clock with an awed face and a piece of news.

"Girls, what *do* you think? It's too awful—poor Miss Vivian's father is dead. He died this morning, after a second stroke yesterday. Isn't it dreadful?"

Every one exclaimed, and echoed Miss Anthony's "dreadful!" with entire sincerity, although the announcement of Sir Piers Vivian's death had given them food for thought and conversation for the rest of the evening.

"How did you hear, Tony?"

"Gracie Jones telephoned. My dears, they've had every sort of adventure. Dr. Prince's car broke down last night, or something, and a messenger met them from Plessing to say Sir Piers had had another stroke, and Miss Vivian and the doctor were to come at once. And he never recovered consciousness, and died this morning early. Isn't it dreadful?"

"Oh, poor Miss Vivian! Did Gracie say anything about her?"

"Only that she was being very brave. Of course, that's just what she would be."

"I suppose Gracie's coming back here tonight? Rather awful for her, poor girl, to be there just now."

"That's the extraordinary thing," said Tony with great animation. "She's actually been asked to stay on."

"She hasn't!"

"She has, really. I asked her what she was doing, and she said nothing much, but that Lady Vivian wanted her to stay."

"Well, I suppose she thinks she'll be of some use to Miss Vivian, but it seems rather queer, in a way, doesn't it? I mean her not knowing them, except officially, so to speak."

"Has any one told Mrs. Bullivant?" Miss Delmege inquired.

But official intimation came to Mrs. Bullivant. A car stopped outside the door, and Dr. Prince, looking tired and haggard, asked to speak to her. He brought a note from Miss Jones, and offered to take a small suit-case out to Plessing for her, if Mrs. Bullivant would get her things together.

"But, doctor, she isn't going to stay there *now*, surely?"

"She'll stay there just exactly as long as I can persuade her to," said the doctor grimly.

Mrs. Bullivant looked thoroughly bewildered, but she gazed at the doctor's tired face, and said gently: "Come into the sitting-room while I get her things packed. There's a nice fire, and the girls have got tea in there. Do come in."

"Well," the doctor yielded.

His own home was two miles out of Questerham, and his wife would not be best pleased at his having spent Christmas Eve and Christmas morning away, and might say that he must not return to Plessing that night. The doctor fully intended to do so, but he felt far too weary for argument.

The sitting-room fire was blazing, and the Hostel community greeted him eagerly, and begged him to take the strongest arm-chair. They were glad of a guest on Christmas Day, and they wanted to hear news of Plessing.

Tony brought him a cup of tea, and Miss Plumtree shyly offered him buttered toast.

"Well, well, this is very good of you all. They're expecting me up at my Hospital, I believe, and I shall have to look in there later, I suppose, but I somehow didn't feel in tune for the festivities just at the moment. It's a sad business at Plessing, though one knew it had to come."

"How is Miss Vivian?"

"Only saw her for a moment," said the doctor briefly. "She arrived in time to see him, poor girl, but he never recovered consciousness. It's a melancholy thought for her that she wouldn't do as the poor old man begged her during the last few weeks he had to live. It wouldn't have cost her so very much to give up her position here, and it wouldn't have been for long, after all."

"But did Sir Piers want her to?" asked Tony, round-eyed.

"It made him unhappy, you see," the doctor said, almost as though apologizing for a weakness which he felt himself to share. "His generation and mine, you know, didn't look upon these things in the same light, and though he was proud of her war-work at first, later on, when his mind became clouded, he couldn't understand her always being away, and it made him unhappy. Lady Vivian tried to explain it to him as far as possible, but he couldn't understand. He didn't realize all she was doing, and he wanted her to stay at home, especially after he got ill. I fancy myself that he knew pretty well how things were—he didn't expect to get well."

"But Miss Vivian didn't know; she couldn't have known," said Miss Henderson quickly.

The doctor shrugged his shoulders.

"We've heard a lot about 'hospital experience' and the rest of it," he said curtly. "It doesn't take much science to know that an old man of seventy odd who has had a stroke stands a very good chance of having another one sooner or later—and probably sooner. *I* don't know why she couldn't have given in to him and made his last months on earth peaceful ones. It would have spared poor Lady Vivian something, too."

"But I thought that Lady Vivian did all the nursing herself?"

"Nothing of the sort!" declared the doctor vehemently. "She followed my orders and had a trained nurse, like a sensible woman. But she was with him herself whenever he wanted her, which was practically all day and half the night, and for ever having to try and explain to him, poor thing, why Miss Charmian was away. She's been wonderfully brave all along, but it isn't very difficult to understand why she feels bitter about it all now. In all the years I've known them both," said the doctor emotionally, "she's never had one thought apart from him. She was a young woman of about five-and-twenty, I suppose, when she first came to Plessing, and he was twenty years her senior, and always fussing about her, though God forgive me for saying so now. She was as fine a horsewoman as ever I saw, a perfect figure and a beautiful seat, but she gave up hunting because it made him nervous about her. She buried herself down here, and was just as gay as a lark, because she knew it was pleasing him that they should live at Plessing and only go up to town once in a blue moon. I don't believe she's ever had a thought beyond making him happy and keeping worry away from him."

"Oh, poor Lady Vivian!" cried Miss Plumtree. "What will she do now?"

"I don't know, indeed. It's simply the destruction of her whole world. But she's most wonderfully plucky, and I don't believe it's in her to give way. Miss Jones is doing more for her than any one just now. They understand one another very well, and the mere fact of having some one to talk to who isn't one of the family is a great help. Steadies everybody, you know. That nice lad, Captain Trevellyan, will be there a good deal, but he tells me that he has to go before his Board on Tuesday, and that will mean France again to a certainty. Poor Lady Vivian was dreading that—but more for Sir Piers's sake than for her own. She didn't want to have to tell him the boy had gone back to fight. Just the same with everything; she looked at it all from one angle, how it was going to affect *him*. That's why I can't help hoping that after a time she'll take up things from another point of view, so to speak—a less personal one. She's so full of energy, and there's so much to be done now."

"Lady Vivian came in once or twice to the Canteen, before Sir Piers got ill, and she said she liked the work there. Perhaps she'll take up some war-work later on," suggested Mrs. Potter.

"I hope so—I hope so very much. Miss Jones is inclined to think so, I fancy."

"Miss Vivian herself would be the best person to provide her mother with war-work, surely," said Miss Delmege between closely-folded lips.

"Well, well, I don't know that one could altogether expect that. You see, when all's said and done, her war-work was a source of great distress and vexation to Sir Piers, and Lady Vivian can't quite forget that. But perhaps," said the doctor, looking rather anxiously at the circle of absorbed faces in the firelight, "I'm an old gossip to be talking so freely. But the Vivians of Plessing—well, it's rather like the Royal Family to us ordinary folk, isn't it? That's what I always feel. And I know that you'll want me to tell Miss Vivian how much you all feel for her."

But it was only Miss Delmege who said rather elaborately: "If you will, do, please, Dr. Prince."

The others mostly looked concerned and bewildered, and Miss Plumtree exclaimed with soft abruptness: "Oh, but it's Lady Vivian—after what you've told us. It's so dreadful to think of! What a good thing she likes Gracie Jones so much! I'm glad she's got her out there."

"So am I," said the doctor heartily.

"I've got her things here," Mrs. Bullivant said in the doorway.

"I'll take them when I go out after dinner. I promised Miss Jones to come back and see if Lady Vivian is all right, and, to tell you the truth, I doubt if I could keep away. I've been there so much just lately, and then last night—"

"Was she with him when he died?"

"Yes. So was Miss Vivian. It's overset her altogether, poor thing, I believe; but I haven't seen her since early this morning. That little companion, Miss Bruce, is with her all the time. Well, poor child, one's very sorry for her, though she made a great mistake when she took her own way in spite of all their pleading, and I'm afraid she'll find it hard to forgive herself now."

"Do you mean," said little Miss Anthony, who looked rather dazed, "that when she came back to the office after she'd had influenza, and when he'd had the first stroke, that Miss Vivian _knew_ her father and mother wanted her to stay at home?"

"Well," said Miss Delmege, very much flushed, and her voice pitched higher than usual, "it was just what she's always said herself. Miss Vivian puts the work before everything."

"I don't know how to believe it," Mrs. Potter said.

The doctor misunderstood her.

"Perhaps it was that. She's done very fine work, and never spared herself any more than she's spared others. And maybe there was something in being boss of the whole show, and in hearing you all say how wonderful she was—human nature's a poor thing, after all."

The doctor shook his head and went out again to his little car.

In the sitting-room the members of Miss Vivian's staff looked at one another.

"Girls," said Miss Marsh slowly, "do you remember Gracie's once saying, ages ago, when she first came, that she wondered if Miss Vivian would do as much work if she were on a desert island? Well, after what Dr. Prince has been telling us, I'm rather inclined to think she was right. Miss Vivian can't be as wonderful as she wants us to think she is."

"It would be _too_ heartless. I can't believe it of her," said Mrs. Potter again, but she spoke very doubtfully.

"She must have thought that she owed her first duty to the work, and not to her own home. But I'm sorry for her now."

"So am I. She'll make it up to her mother by staying with her now, I suppose."

"If Lady Vivian wants her. But _I_ should imagine she'd hate the sight of her, almost."

"Tony!"

"Well," Miss Anthony asseverated, almost in tears, "I mean it. I think it's the most dreadful thing I've ever heard of, and the most unkind. And to think how we've all been admiring her for coming to live here, and for going on with the work in spite of being anxious and unhappy about her father! Why, she can't have cared a bit!"

"But she _was_ splendid, in a sort of way," Miss Henderson said, bewildered. "Look how she's worked, and never spared herself, or given herself any rest, not even proper times off for meals. She can't have liked all that."

"I suppose," said Miss Marsh grimly, "that she liked thinking how splendid she was being, and how splendid everybody thought her. It would have been much duller for her to stay at home and do nothing, just because her father asked her to."

There was silence. To hear Miss Vivian reduced by criticism and analysis to the level of an ordinary human being seemed to revolutionize the whole mental outlook of the Hostel.

When Mrs. Bullivant came into the sitting-room, she looked strangely at the disturbed faces. "Dr. Prince seems to have upset you all," she said at last.

"Did you hear what he was saying about Miss Vivian, though?"

"Some of it. He asked me in the hall just now whether he'd been indiscreet. I had to say that I was afraid we'd none of us quite realized before how very much her personal influence had been counting with us in the work."

"That's quite true," said Tony dejectedly, "and I don't believe I shall ever feel the same again. Why should we all work ourselves to death for any one like that?"

"Oh, my dear," said the Superintendent, sinking into a chair, "I'm afraid that's just the weak point in women's work. So much of it is done from the *personal* point of view. We can't keep personalities out of it."

"If you ask me, that's just what Miss Vivian has been doing. I mean, bringing her own powers of personal fascination to bear all the time."

Mrs. Bullivant sighed.

"It's the work one ought to think of, not the individual. Anyway, *my* work here is over, I'm afraid."

"There you are!" cried Miss Plumtree. "You have to leave work you care about, just because she was uncomfortable at this Hostel. Talk about personal points-of-view!"

"Well, I've been personal long enough," declared Tony. "I shall chuck the office and go to munitions. *They're* impersonal enough!"

She let the door bang behind her.

"Poor old Tony! She'll go to the other extreme now, and think everything Miss Vivian does is hopeless. I must say, it's a bit of a disillusionment."

Miss Delmege stood up, gulped two or three times, and at last said, rapidly and nervously: "I don't at all agree with you. We've no business to sit in judgment on her like this, and I for one shall always believe there's some satisfactory explanation to the whole thing. I'm not saying it in the least because it's Miss Vivian, but *quite* impartially."

"Of course," said Miss Marsh, under her breath.

"Look at the way she works and all—it *is* perfectly wonderful; and Dr. Prince probably doesn't really know anything about what Sir Piers wanted. He's always been more or less on the defensive with Miss Vivian, just because she had to get his Hospital under proper control. It's all prejudice and disloyalty. And all I can say is, that as long as there's work to be done for Miss Vivian, I'm ready to do it, single-handed if necessary, if all the rest of you choose to desert her, and I shouldn't have the least hesitation in repeating all I've said to her face."

Miss Delmege's peroration left her rather shrill-voiced and breathless, but her pose on the hearth-rug, chin uplifted and one slim foot slightly thrust forward, was heroic in the extreme.

No one believed for a moment in her defiant assertion that she was prepared to launch her rhetorical declaration at Miss Vivian in person; but it was left to her old enemy, Miss Marsh, to remark with an unpleasant matter-of-factness: "There's no need to get so excited, Delmege. There'll be no call for you to do the work single-handed, either. I should be sorry for Miss Vivian if you tried it on, in fact. We're all fairly patriotic, I hope, whatever we may think of Miss Vivian, and, as Mrs. Bullivant says, doing the work is the point, not the person we're working for."

"That's right," agreed Miss Henderson. "It's for the war, after all."

"Otherwise," said Miss Marsh, with an icy look at Miss Delmege, "I'm bound to say that after what we've just heard of Miss Vivian I should be very much inclined to chuck working for her straight away."

"Don't discuss it any more, girls. It won't do any good," Mrs. Bullivant declared. "You must just try and think more of the work and less of Miss Vivian. Now, I've got a treat for your supper, as it's Christmas night, and I must go and see after it. Do, some one, go and get Tony downstairs again. She can't really have meant to go to bed at this hour. She was just upset, poor child, but she'll feel better when the lamp is lit and it's all looking homely and bright."

The Superintendent hurried away.

"Isn't she ripping?" asked Miss Henderson. "Come on, Greengage, and let's fish out Tony."

"Yes, do let's try and all cheer up," begged Mrs. Potter. "It *has* been a depressing Christmas Day. How would it be to *change* for supper? It would please Mrs. Bullivant."

"All right, let's."

The girls hurried upstairs to hunt for clean blouses and small pieces of jewellery, and Miss Delmege was left alone, still standing in her attitude of defiance before the sitting-room fire.

XVII

"Is there any more apple-pudding?"

"Yes, my lady."

"Then I will have some," said Lady Vivian, not at all unaware of the pained expression which Miss Bruce had unconsciously assumed. The unquenchable laugh still danced in her deeply-circled blue eyes as she gazed across the luncheon-table at Grace.

"Do have some more pudding, Grace. I know you never get enough to eat at your Hostel."

Miss Bruce put down her fork with a look of resignation. The excellent appetite displayed by Lady Vivian seemed to her extraordinary enough on the part of one widowed only a week ago, but that of the still-visiting Miss Jones amounted to a scandal.

In Miss Bruce's opinion, Miss Jones should have removed herself from Plessing a week ago, in spite of the strong predilection evinced by Lady Vivian for her society. It was not decent, Miss Bruce thought, to shun one's own daughter and take so many and such lengthy walks in company of a comparative stranger of less than half one's own age.

"Un-natural, I call it," said Miss Bruce, shaking her head.

Char shrugged her shoulders.

"What does it matter? I'm glad she should take an interest in any one or anything, though I can't understand such a friendship for that trivial little girl myself. But one thing is certain enough: I shall have to ask her to resign. It would be quite impossible, since my mother has chosen to treat her as one of the family, to keep her on at the office when I go back there. Though perhaps I ought to say—if I go back there."

"Oh, my dear Charmian, why? Surely there can be no reason now—less than ever, I mean to say—why you should not take up that splendid work at the Supply Depôt again. Why, the whole thing hinges on you."

"I know," said Char dejectedly. "But there's my mother to consider. I really don't see how I'm to leave her all alone here, and I don't know if she'll care to come into Questerham with me."

Char had hardly seen her mother since Sir Piers's funeral, three days ago. Lady Vivian had refused to display any form of prostration, had discussed every necessary item of business with John Trevellyan and Dr. Prince, and when not engaged in answering innumerable letters and telegrams of condolences, had taken Grace Jones for long walks with her across the snowy fields.

"But," Char said to Miss Bruce, "we shall have to discuss business sooner or later. For all I know, we may have to leave Plessing. It was to be my mother's for her life, I believe, but she may choose to let Uncle Charles come into it at once. He has a large family of children, after all. His being in Salonika now makes it all so much more complicated."

"I dare say there will be no change just at present. Everything will be so unsettled until this dreadful war is over," Miss Bruce soothed her vaguely.

But she, too, thought that it would be necessary for Lady Vivian soon to give her daughter some outline of her future plans.

On New Year's Day, rising from the helping of apple-pudding which she had left unfinished as a protest, Miss Bruce after lunch said firmly to Lady Vivian: "You will want to talk to Charmian this afternoon, I feel sure. There is a fire in the library, so perhaps—"

She looked meaningly at Miss Jones, who, instead of making at least a pretence of at once following her out of the room, gazed imperturbably at Lady Vivian.

"Char," inquired Joanna mildly, "do you want to talk to me?"

"We'd better come to an understanding, hadn't we, mother? You see, I haven't the vaguest idea of your plans."

"But why should you have any, my dear? They won't interfere with your work at Questerham. If you want to know about Plessing, I can tell you in two words. Your Uncle Charles doesn't want any change made until after the war, so that I can either let it or go on living in it, as I please."

Decorum took Miss Bruce as far as the door of the dining-room, but was not strong enough to put her outside it while Grace Jones still remained, with no apparent consciousness of indiscretion, sitting unmoved in her place, and in full hearing of this discussion, which every tradition would restrict to a family one.

Even Char said: "Hadn't we better come to the library?"

Joanna rose.

"I'm going there now, for the very good reason that Lesbia Willoughby is to be shown in there in half an hour's time. I shall have to see her some time, and I may as well get it over."

"Mother, must you? Why not say that you're not seeing any one?"

"My dear," said Joanna dryly, "I've already answered two telegrams and three letters and several telephone messages in which she offered to come to me, and I think that nothing but word of mouth will have any effect upon her. But I'll talk to you this evening, if there's anything you want to know. John is dining here to tell us the result of his Medical Board."

Joanna left the room, with her decisive, unhurried step, and Char, ignoring Grace, said to Miss Bruce: "I have a lot of letters, sent on from the office. Perhaps you'd be kind enough to give me a little help this afternoon?"

"Certainly, Charmian."

Miss Bruce was gratified; but when Char had walked away without so much as glancing at Grace, she could not help saying to her, with a sort of flustered kindness: "I hope you'll find some way of amusing yourself, Miss Jones."

She had loyally adopted Char's prejudice, but was too kind-hearted not to try furtively to make up for it.

Miss Jones, however, was not destined to spend a solitary afternoon. Mrs. Willoughby was driven to Plessing by Captain Trevellyan in his car; and although Miss Bruce, casting sidelong glances from the window of Char's boudoir, where she was busily taking notes from her dictation, distinctly saw him enter the house, she felt certain that he proceeded no further than the hall, where Grace sat reading by the fire.

Mrs. Willoughby went at once to the library, where she enfolded the resigned Joanna in a prolonged embrace.

"My poor, poor dear! Words can *never* tell you how I've felt for you—how much I've longed to be with you!"

But despite the inadequacy of words, Mrs. Willoughby had a shrill torrent of them at her command, with which she deluged Lady Vivian for some time.

"Poor Lesbia!" Lady Vivian remarked afterwards to Grace; "she enjoyed herself so much that I really couldn't grudge it to her!"

"He was so much, much older than you, dear, that it must almost feel like losing a father, and I know that that unfortunate girl of yours isn't very much comfort. She must be racked with remorse. Now, do tell me, Joanna, would you like me to take her off your hands for six months? Let her come back to London with me next week, and get her married off before it's too late."

"Too late?"

"Well, Joanna, she must be thirty, and, mark my words, whatever people may say about there being no men left, *things are happening every day.* Half the mothers in London are getting their girls off now, what with officers back on leave and officers in hospitals, and those dear Colonials. Girls who never had a look in before the war can do anything they like in the way of nursing, or leading the blind about, or working in some of those departments where the over-age men are. Char is just the sort of creature to prefer a man old enough to be her grandfa—"

Mrs. Willoughby's jaw dropped, and she made a repentant snatch at Joanna's hand.

"Forgive me, darling! *How* idiotic to say such a thing to you, of all people! But if you'll give me your girl, I'll undertake to find chances for her. She'll be very good-looking when she doesn't look so sulky and take such airs, and one could make capital of all the patriotic work she's been doing down here. And I *always* think it's rather an asset than otherwise to be in mourning, especially in these days. Black suits her, too, with that sandy colouring. Does she choose her own clothes, Joanna?"

"She does, Lesbia, and has chosen them ever since she was out of long clothes, as far as I remember. But—"

"Joanna, you've been culpably weak, and of course that poor, dear old man had simply no idea of discipline. But I can put the whole thing right for you in six weeks, when the dear girl comes to me."

"It's no use, Lesbia," said Joanna, half laughing. "It's very kind of you, but Char wouldn't hear of it and really at thirty I can't coerce her—besides, there's her work here."

"My dear, you don't mean to say that you're going to allow that to go on?"

"To begin with, I couldn't prevent it. To go on with, I think it perfectly right that Char should do what she can in the way of war-work. There wouldn't be the slightest object in her giving it up now."

"But Sir Piers—the memory of his wishes—*his* memory!" almost shrieked Mrs. Willoughby.

"His memory will survive it, Lesbia. Besides, as long as he was himself, you know, he didn't mind her doing war-work. He quite understood the necessity, and was proud of her."

"But, my dear, wrong-headed creature, when she so deliberately and heartlessly went against his wishes at the last?"

"Well," said Joanna placidly, "she won't be doing that now, so she can go on working with a clear conscience."

"Joanna," said Mrs. Willoughby, with an air of discovery, "upon my word, I don't understand you."

Nevertheless, she devoted the major half of the afternoon to the object of her perplexity.

"One word, dearest, I must say," she declared at the end of an hour that, to Joanna's thinking, held already more than a sufficiency of words. "Have you considered what is happening to that delightful lad?"

"Never," said Joanna unhesitatingly. "And who on earth are you talking about, Lesbia?"

"That precious creature, Johnnie. Too guileless for words, my dear; but if there's one thing I do understand, inside out and upside down, it's men. I should have made a *perfect* mother—young things adore me. Look at my sweet Puffles! But I'm *miserable* about John, who really has a perfect passion for me, dear lad. Lewis always says that all the boys of his regiment go through it, just like measles."

Joanna, who had heard this quotation before, ruthlessly disregarded it.

"What is happening to John?"

"My dear, do you mean to tell me you haven't seen it? But of course you haven't, at such a time. What a brute I am! Forgive me, Joanna, but you seem so *utterly* unlike a widow. I can hardly realize it. But, of course, that little secretary creature—she's had her eye on him all along."

"I suppose, Lesbia, that you don't mean my poor old Bruce, who's been with me almost ever since John was born?"

Lesbia uttered a screech between laughter and reproach.

"What an absurdity! Of course I mean the little Canteen girl—Jones, or whatever her name is. My dear, will you believe me when I tell you that when that poor innocent boy drove us up here just now and followed me into the hall, there she was, actually waiting to pounce upon him, sitting over the fire?"

"I can believe you quite easily," said Joanna, "all but the pouncing. We none of us knew that John was going to drive you over, so she couldn't have been waiting."

"Blind, reckless one!" cried Lesbia excitedly. "I can only tell you that ever since those evenings at the Canteen I've seen what was coming. Do you suppose that a young man wipes up dripping wet mugs for nothing? Besides, Joanna, look at the air-raid! Of course, my poor dear, I know that just at that time you were thinking of something altogether different, but *I* was there, if you remember."

"I remember hearing about it," Joanna admitted, with a vivid recollection of Mrs. Willoughby's spirited behaviour on the occasion in question having been described in unflattering terms by Captain Trevellyan.

"My dear, after we'd all dispersed and the whole thing was over, that wretched girl lured him back into the basement, under pretext of fainting or something, and pretended to have hysterics on account of the fright she'd had. And I assure you that she hadn't seen anything at all of the raid, because she was the very first person to make a bolt for downstairs. In fact," said Mrs. Willoughby modestly, "really, for one moment there might have been a panic, if I hadn't *dashed* into the middle of the hall and called out that we were all Englishwomen and not afraid of anything. And *after* all that, the miserable girl goes and faints away in his hands!"

"I did hear something about it—in fact, she told me herself, but it wasn't nearly as dramatic as that, Lesbia. And his coming back and finding her was pure chance. I think it was the last thing she wanted."

Mrs. Willoughby opened her eyes to their widest extent, flung back her head, and exclaimed emphatically: "You will have no one in this world, Joanna, no one but yourself, to blame if the very worst happens. Mark my words, that uninteresting little creature, without a feature to bless herself with, is going to make poor guileless Johnnie ask her to marry him."

Joanna had some opinion of Mrs. Willoughby's shrewdness, if none of her discretion, and this prognostication gave her a sense of comfort which she had had no slightest expectation of deriving from the visit of condolence. It even enabled her to thank Lesbia with sufficient cordiality for coming, as she at last escorted her into the hall.

"When we shall meet again, dearest, I am utterly unable to declare," was a valediction which added considerably to her relief at parting. "My Lewis won't let me stay down here any longer, now that I'm fairly fit again. He's too sweet and self-sacrificing for words, poor lamb! 'Go back to London where there are a thousand jobs and undertakings *crying out for you*,' he says. I really can't bear to leave him, and the dear regiment, and my beloved Canteen, let alone you, whom I've always looked upon as the oldest, dearest of links with my girlhood. But, of course, my poor committees must be getting into the most ghastly muddles, and I know that all my officer protégés are in despair. They write me the most heartrending letters."

Lesbia shrouded herself in sables, wound a motor-veil round and round her head, and cast a piercing glance round the hall.

"What did I tell you, Joanna?"

"You told me that John was here with Miss Jones, but I don't see either of them. Is he going to drive you back?"

"So he pretended, my dear, but I can't answer for what she—"

Trevellyan came into the hall and greeted Lady Vivian.

"I've not kept you waiting, Mrs. Willoughby, I hope? I went to bring the car round."

"Where is Grace?" asked Lady Vivian, not without malice.

"Just come in and gone upstairs. We've been looking at your turnips," said John seriously. "A very fine crop, Cousin Joanna."

"We shall all be *living* on turnips quite soon," Lesbia declared with acerbity. "Good-bye, my poor dear Joanna, and do think over all I've been saying to you. Remember that a telegram would bring me at any hour, for as long as you please, and I'll take your girl off your hands whenever you like. I could make her *quite* useful in some of my war-work."

Joanna turned away from the door, thankful to reflect that neither her daughter nor Miss Bruce had been present to hear this monstrous assertion.

As she crossed the hall, Grace came downstairs. Lady Vivian smiled at her.

"You've a knack of appearing just when I want you. I've just seen Lesbia Willoughby off, since she mercifully refused to stay to tea. Has the second post come?"

"Yes. I've got a letter that I rather wanted to talk to you about, from Miss Marsh at the Hostel."

Joanna sat down, her hands lying idly folded in her lap, while Grace read aloud:

"DEAR GRACIE,

"You'll think it extraordinary, me writing to you like this, but we really do miss you here, especially in our room, and the whole place has been upside down since you went away. This is because poor Mrs. Bullivant has actually got the sack, if you can believe such a thing, for no reason on earth that any one can discover. She had a slip from Miss V. dated two days before Christmas—but it only reached her on Christmas Day—telling her that other arrangements would be made at the New Year. Of course, we're all fearfully sick, as you'll guess, and Mrs. Bullivant has been simply howling about it ever since, though she's as quiet as ever and never lets on. But she looks rotten, and Tony can hear her crying in her own room at nights. You can imagine what a jolly Christmas we've all had! The point of bothering you with all this, however, is that perhaps you can find out what she's expected to do. It's all very well to say, 'Clear out at the New Year,' but Miss Vivian's being away, and in such trouble and all, makes it all jolly awkward. We sent a petition signed by all of us to ask if Mrs. Bullivant could be kept on; but of course there's been no answer, and she simply doesn't in the least know what to do. Do you think it would be all right if she just hung on till Miss V. gets back? Perhaps then she'll have read the petition and made up her mind to let her stay on as Superintendent. Of course, that's what we all hope, and, in fact, some of the girls are so sick about it that I shouldn't be surprised if some resignations were sent in. We've been hearing something that's made us all sit up *re* Miss V. and—"

"That's all about Mrs. Bullivant," said Grace hastily.

"Nonsense!" cried Joanna vigorously; "you've stopped at the most amusing bit. Unless it's marked private, for goodness' sake go on, and tell me what this scandal can be. I'm quite relieved to hear that Char's past holds *anything* exciting."

Grace began to laugh.

"It isn't marked private, and there really isn't much to read."

"—and there'll be a good deal less said in future about how wonderful she is. Did you know that her father and mother, after he first got ill, simply *begged* her to stay at home, for his sake, and she absolutely wouldn't? Work is all very well, but I must say that seems jolly callous, and one can't help wondering whether it really was the work she was after, or just the excitement and the honour and glory of her position. I know you never—"

Grace stopped again, and Lady Vivian said: "She knows you never liked her—well, go on."

"—and most of the rest of us are feeling rather off the 'personal influence' stunt just at the moment. Delmege, of course, takes a high line and goes in for loyalty, etc., etc.—in fact, won't speak to any of us at present. But, as I say, that's her loss and not ours.

"Now, dear old thing, I'm going to leave off, as you're probably sick of my scrawl by this time, and it's high time I was off to my bed. Try and find out if there's any chance of Mrs. B.'s being allowed to carry on for the present, and send me a line if you've time.

"Every one sends all sorts of love, and we shall all be most awfully glad to see you turn up again. This place is more putrid than ever without you, and with all this fuss going on about Miss Vivian; but I dare say it'll all turn out for the best if it makes us a bit keener about the work for its own sake, and not for hers. After all, there *is* a war on!"

"Yours with best love,

"DORA MARSH."

"Dora Marsh seems to me to be an uncommonly sensible girl," observed Lady Vivian thoughtfully.

She gazed into the fire in silence for a few moments before adding: "I wonder who's been talking to them about Char? The only person I can think of is Dr. Prince. I know he felt very strongly about it, and I don't altogether wonder, though it may seem rather hard on her to have her reputation for infallibility destroyed at last."

"I think," said Grace, "that there would have been some feeling at the Hostel, in any case, at Mrs. Bullivant's dismissal. She's been so kind and nice to us all, and worked so hard always, and, of course, every one knows that the loss of the position is serious for her. She's very poor, and she has no home of her own to go to."

"Of course, it's unthinkable. Char *must* have some reason for dismissing her. I shall insist upon being told what it is!" cried Joanna.

There was more animation in her manner than Grace had seen there for some time, and she was quite ready to follow her upstairs in immediate search of Char.

The Director of the Midland Supply Depôt was at her writing-table, leaning back in the familiar attitude that invariably recalled to Grace old-fashioned engravings of an Eastern potentate, her eyes half closed, her slim fingers tapping upon the table in front of her, and her slow, deep voice drawling in fluent dictation.

Miss Bruce, far from possessing the skill of Mrs. Baker-Bridges, sat agitatedly scribbling on various odd half-sheets of paper. Further notes lay strewn all over the table and on the floor beside her chair.

She looked up with shamefaced but unmistakable relief at the interruption.

"Have you been victimized all the afternoon?" inquired Joanna kindly, but with her usual unfortunate choice of expression.

"Oh, no, no!" said Miss Bruce, almost with horror. "But Charmian must be tired. She's been working without a moment's rest, and it really does give one some sort of idea of all that she must do at the office every day."

Char rewarded her with a melancholy smile.

"At the office there are the telegrams, and the telephone messages, and endless interviews to deal with as well. I don't think I ever get a consecutive hour's time there to deal with the correspondence without interruption. Now, all these letters which you see here could—"

Joanna interrupted the Director of the Midland Supply Depôt without ceremony.

"I want you to tell me, Char, why you want that nice little Superintendent of yours to leave the Hostel. The staff there is in despair."

Char suddenly sat upright.

"That is a purely official matter, and it's disgraceful that there should have been gossip about it already."

"But why have you dismissed her?"

"Because she is quite inadequate to fill the post of Hostel Superintendent. I was there myself, and I never was in a worse-managed or more uncomfortable establishment in my life."

"I can quite believe it, my dear, but I'm inclined to think—and Grace, who knows more about it than I do, agrees with me—that she's never had a fair chance of running it properly."

"I don't propose to discuss the matter with my secretary, mother."

"But why not talk it over like ordinary human beings, Char?" said Lady Vivian, reverting to all her old half-impatient, half-humorous outspokenness. "I've no patience with you. What in the name of fortune is the sense of vexing and distressing everybody, when by a little decent management the whole thing could be put on to a proper basis? Grace, you've lived in that Hostel. If the Superintendent had a freer hand, couldn't it be made more comfortable?"

"Yes, especially with any one as hard-working and anxious to make things nice as Mrs. Bullivant. She may not be a very good manager, but, indeed," said Grace pleadingly, "things have been very much against her. If she could engage the sort of servants that she needs, and if there were fewer people in the Hostel, so as to give more room, and better arrangements made about the hot water and the food, it could be very nice."

"You are all in that Hostel for the purpose of war-work, Miss Jones, and I should have thought that with that end in view a few minor discomforts could have been overlooked. When one thinks of our men in the trenches—"

"However much you may have thought of them, Char, it didn't prevent your going into rooms before you'd been at the Hostel a fortnight," Joanna interrupted briskly. "Those girls are just as much flesh and blood as you are yourself, whether you own to it or not. But I can tell you one thing, and that is that they're beginning to find it out for themselves."

"To find out what?" said the Director of the Midland Supply Depôt, vexed to the extent of for once speaking shortly and in monosyllables.

Joanna shrugged her shoulders, and Grace said emphatically:

"Mrs. Bullivant is very popular, you know, and the staff can't understand her getting such a summary dismissal. After all, it's very serious for her, apart from everything else, because she's got to live."

"To which, I suppose, Char would like to reply, 'Je n'en vois pas la nécessité,'" quoted Lady Vivian, with her irrepressible laugh. "But it really won't do, Char. You're dealing with human beings, and you'll have to make up your mind to it."

"I am dealing," said Char magnificently, "with an organization."

"Even so, my dear, it's made up of human beings. But as it's tea-time and I'm extremely hungry," said Lady Vivian, with a side-glance at Miss Bruce, "we'd better postpone discussion until this evening. I don't know whether you feel human enough to leave your papers and eat bread and jam with the rest of us, but I dare say that Grace and Miss Bruce won't give you away to the staff if you do."

The outraged Miss Vivian left the last word to the ribald spirit apparently animating her parent.

XVIII

Captain Trevellyan's Medical Board had passed him fit for active service again, and he made matter-of-fact announcement of his approaching return to France in the course of that evening.

"Do you know when, Johnnie?"

"Next draft that goes, I suppose. I rejoin the battalion the day after tomorrow, and it might be any day after that."

Exclamations were left to Miss Bruce. Grace and Joanna received the news almost in silence, and Char remained monosyllabic.

"Will you smoke in the library, John?" said Joanna as she rose from the dining-table. "We'll have coffee there. We can also talk business, Char, if you want to."

"Then, shall I—?" said Miss Bruce, looking at Grace and feeling strongly inclined to say "Shall we—?"

Joanna laid her hand on the little secretary's shoulder. "Of course not, Miss Bruce. You know we count you as one of the family."

In the library a certain tenseness of atmosphere prevailed, until Joanna had finally dismissed the coffee equipage, and leant back in a great leather arm-chair under the lamp.

John, next her, had taken up his favourite position on the hearthrug, and was smoking in meditative silence, his eyes now and then seeking Grace, whose head was bent over a piece of needlework.

Char, presumably from force of habit, had seated herself at the writing-table, and Miss Bruce took a low chair beside her, gazing dumbly from her to Lady Vivian and back again, as though a divided loyalty harassed her thoughts.

Char broke the silence.

"Mother, you spoke about letting this place this afternoon. Is that what you mean to do?"

"No. I only said that it was in my power to let it, but as a matter of fact, since your Uncle Charles has no wish to make any change until the war is over, he and I have agreed that it had better be made use of. He is quite willing that I should do whatever seems best and most necessary."

Miss Bruce uttered an exclamation.

"Red Cross work, do you mean?"

Char made a movement to check her, as though unwilling to let any display of surprise greet Joanna's announcement.

"Of course," she said slowly, "I could find a hundred uses for a place like Plessing, from turning it into a hospital onwards. The idea had naturally occurred to me before, but as, I must say, mother, you've always discouraged any form of patriotic sacrifice by every means in your power, and done everything possible to ignore the very fact of there being a war, it never struck me that you would consent to such a plan."

John looked up.

"It isn't a question of consent, Char. The scheme is Cousin Joanna's, not any one else's."

"As I am—as I have been placed—in the position of Director of the Midland Supply Depôt, John," Char said quietly, "the voluntary organizations here, of whatever kind, come under my jurisdiction, and I must say—"

"Char," interrupted her mother, "you may say anything you please, but you'll never persuade any of us that you and I could work together comfortably, and I haven't any intention of trying the experiment. I shall offer this place as a convalescent home to be attached to the Military Hospital at Staffield. That will put it altogether outside the jurisdiction of your office."

"It's too far from the station."

"Not with a couple of cars and Government petrol," said John.

"The doctors here are overworked as it is."

"A convalescent home does not need the same amount of medical attendance as a hospital, and Dr. Prince is perfectly willing to undertake whatever is necessary."

"But you'll want a staff, and at least two trained nurses in the house."

"I have no doubt that they can be obtained. Char, I don't want to vex you and make you feel that I'm acting in opposition to all your own schemes," spoke Joanna impetuously, "but really and truly it wouldn't answer if I tried to run things on your lines. I must do something, and it seems a shame not to use Plessing. But I *had* thought of another plan, though I know Johnnie doesn't approve of it."

"No, I don't," said John stoutly.

Char had coloured deeply and her mouth was set. She spoke as though with difficulty.

"What is it?"

"Tell her, Grace. You thought of it," said Lady Vivian.

"To make Plessing the Hostel for your staff. Lady Vivian would give them their board and lodging, and superintend herself. You see, it would make an enormous difference if the present Hostel, which is much too small, were free. You could make it into an extension of the office, which is badly needed. The chief drawback, of course, is the distance, but we should have to come in by the 9 o'clock train every morning, and either bicycle back or come out by the 6.30 train. They're putting it on again next month. You see, the days will be getting longer very soon, and we've all the spring and summer in front of us."

"I don't think it's practicable," Trevellyan said.

"Nor I," echoed Miss Bruce, watching the thunder-cloud on Char's forehead.

"I thought Char might prefer it," said Joanna simply. "You would keep your own rooms, my dear, of course, and it would be very much more comfortable for all of you than the present arrangement. As to the difficulty of getting in and out, there's no reason why we shouldn't see what could be done about driving one way. I don't know if the petrol ought to be used, but there are plenty of farm-horses, and we could hire a wagonette, or something of that sort."

"And what about the nights when we're all kept late, or a troop-train comes in, and the Canteen work, which is never over before eleven or half-past?"

"You must give it up," Lady Vivian informed her placidly. "People can't work half the night as well as all day, and I've always thought that you had no business to ask it of your staff. That Canteen work is very heavy, and utterly unfit for girls who've been all day in an office. It isn't as if there weren't others to undertake it. Lesbia Willoughby says that the ladies of the regiment are quite ready to divide it amongst themselves—in fact, they've rather resented having it so completely taken out of their hands."

"Mother, you had better understand me once and for all. Nothing will induce me to give up any single item of all that I've undertaken."

"But, Char, why?" inquired Captain Trevellyan mildly. "Is it the work you care about, or just the fact of doing it yourself?"

Dead silence followed the inquiry.

At last Char said, without attempting to answer it: "The Hostel suggestion is quite impossible, mother. Even if it were not for the practical objections, such as the distance from the work, I could not accept. My staff has been put into perfectly suitable quarters, and I should not dream of moving them. But as it has become more and more evident that Miss Jones is dissatisfied there—" She paused, and looked at Grace.

Trevellyan made a sudden brusque gesture, but Grace said quickly: "I am afraid that I had better ask you to accept my resignation, Miss Vivian."

Char made no pretence at surprise, and simply bent her head in acquiescence.

Grace folded up her work and stood up. Trevellyan opened the door for her, and, with one look at Joanna, passed out of the room after her.

Miss Bruce gasped, as at a sudden illumination. But it was Joanna who exclaimed roundly: "Well, Char, you've put your foot into it with a vengeance! Unless I'm very much mistaken, John will be in no hurry to forgive you."

"Mother! why will you always obscure every issue of what is, after all, national work, by some wretched personal question?"

"Because, Char, I'm dealing with human beings, and not with machines."

"Oh, Lady Vivian!" cried Miss Bruce irrepressibly. "Forgive me, but you speak as though she— she wasn't *adored* by her staff. Look how they all admire her!"

"Yes, and she takes advantage of it to work them very much too hard, and also to use her personal influence to obtain a sort of blind loyalty and perfectly unreasoning admiration that is bad for the work, and bad for the staff, and bad for her! However, Char, I don't mind telling you that I think a good deal of that nonsense is coming to an end. Your staff has not been at all impressed by your abominable treatment of that poor little Superintendent, and they've also found out that you insisted on going off to Questerham against your father's express wishes, and then posed as a martyr to patriotism."

"Oh, Lady Vivian!" groaned the secretary.

"Yes, I know I'm losing my temper, but I always did and always shall think that Char behaved in the most heartless and disgraceful fashion. It wasn't I who told her staff about it, or Grace Jones either, but I'm heartily grateful to whoever did. The work that we hear so much about may get a chance of being attended to on its own merits now, in a reasonable manner, instead of being overdone to a senseless degree, simply because 'Miss Vivian is so wonderful!'"

Joanna went to the door.

"Think it over, Char, and if you like to behave like a reasonable being, we'll talk over the Hostel scheme. Otherwise, John thinks there's no doubt of this place being accepted as a convalescent home. But you'll have to make up your mind, in that case, to see it being mismanaged by mere military authorities."

Joanna did not bang the door behind her, but she shut it with considerable briskness, and left the appalled Miss Bruce to assist Char's decision.

The Director of the Midland Supply Depôt sat in an attitude of the most unwonted dejection, her elbows on the writing-table and her head in her hands. Miss Bruce hardly ventured to breathe in the heavy stillness that pervaded the room.

At last Char raised her head and looked at her. "Oh, Brucey," she said piteously, "they're all very difficult to deal with!"

The note of appeal, which Miss Bruce had not heard from Char since her earliest childhood, moved the little secretary to great emotion.

"Charmian, my poor dear child, it's very hard on you, after all you've been through already. I know that dear Lady Vivian has never altogether understood; and then her feelings about the war—so different—only, of course, now she needn't consider—circumstances altered—reaction—"

Miss Bruce floundered into a tangle of words, and ventured to put out her hand timidly, although aware of how much Char disliked demonstrations of affection.

It affected her with a profound sense of how far Miss Vivian must be reduced when she found her tentative hand received with a long, nervous pressure.

"Oh, what can I do? What can I say? Couldn't you make up your mind to this Hostel scheme, which would at least keep you at home?"

"I'm not thinking of myself—though, of course, it's quite true that if Plessing becomes a convalescent home, under military ruling, I can't go on living here. Nothing would induce me to remain in a place where I had no official standing. My mother doesn't seem to consider that she's practically forcing me to go on living, under most uncomfortable conditions, in Questerham. Not," added Char hastily, recollecting herself, "that I should dream of putting any personal consideration before the work, or of letting my own comfort interfere with it in any way."

"I know, I know! It's wonderful, the way you've never thought of yourself for a moment," cried Miss Bruce in all sincerity. "Even to your meals, for I know too well that half the time you never have any proper lunch at all, and your dinner at all hours. But I'm so dreadfully afraid of your breaking down."

"Not while there's work to be done, Brucey. But this winter has been appalling, with one thing and another—father, and then all the difficulties here, and half the staff getting laid up with influenza before Christmas. They're few enough, as it is, for all they have to do, and now I suppose half of them will resign."

"Impossible!"

"Not at all impossible, with Miss Jones making mischief and talking all over the place about my private affairs, and then resigning in that absurd way. No doubt that will be made into a grievance, too."

"I thought," began Miss Bruce, and then hesitated, but Char looked so impatient that she went on rather desperately—"I thought that you meant to send her away in any case?"

"Certainly I did. You must see, Brucey, how utterly out of the question it would be to have one member of the staff a sort of privileged person, who'd been out here to stay, when none of the others have so much as set foot in the place, and talking about my relations as though they were intimate friends of hers. It would be quite impossible."

If Miss Bruce saw the impossibility in question less clearly than did Char, she said nothing.

"No, Brucey, it's no good. I've set my hand to the plough, and there must be no looking back. I shall have to make up my mind to Questerham."

"But the discomfort!" wailed Miss Bruce.

"It may convince my mother that there is more than mere self-will and love of notoriety in my work. To me, Brucey, it seems almost laughable that any one should attribute my work to that sort of motive, but, you see, she has never understood me."

"Never!" said Miss Bruce with entire conviction.

"The wrench will be leaving you, dear old Brucey," Char said affectionately.

"Charmian," said the little secretary solemnly, "I can't do it. I can't face letting you go alone to those horrible lodgings, and only Preston to see to your comfort. I don't wish to say a word against Preston, and I know how devoted she is to you, but there are things that she can't be expected to think of. If you leave Plessing, you must take me with you."

An emotion such as had never shaken Miss Vivian out of her self-possession before, moved her suddenly now.

"Do you really mean that, Brucey? Would you leave my mother, and the work which she would certainly find for you here, and come and look after me in Questerham? I do know that I'm difficult sometimes, and—and I can't promise you always to come in punctually to dinner, but it would make all the difference in the world to have you there."

Miss Bruce's allegiance to Char dated from many years back, and needed no strengthening—was, indeed, beyond it; but henceforward, come what might, she would never forget that Miss Vivian had said that it made all the difference in the world to have her there.

"I will come whenever you like, and wherever you go, and I will look after you as much as you'll let me," she said tearfully.

There was a silence before Char remarked practically: "You'll have to arrange it with my mother, Brucey. I don't want her to think that you're deserting her for me."

It was difficult to see how Lady Vivian could possibly think anything else, but the uplifted Miss Bruce knew no qualms of spirit.

"I'll tell her myself, my dear, and I know she'll understand. She'll be only too glad that you should have somebody with you. Indeed, she does care, very, very much, if you'll let me say so; but all that's passed has—"

"I know, I know! It all makes it the more impossible for me to stay here with her and at the same time try to carry on the work."

"Then you won't consider the idea of making this place into a hostel?"

"I've already said that it's out of the question."

Quite evidently, the Director of the Midland Supply Depôt was herself again.

She rose, and was meekly followed by Miss Bruce into the hall, where sat Lady Vivian and Captain Trevellyan.

"Mother, I'm going to bed," said Char calmly. "With regard to your scheme of making this place into a hostel, by the way, I'm afraid it wouldn't answer. I'm most grateful to you, but as Director of the Midland Supply Depôt, I must refuse the offer."

Joanna shrugged her shoulders.

"Then, my dear, as Director of the Midland Supply Depôt, I'm afraid you must go on living uncomfortably in rooms, since I suppose you won't want to stay here when the place is full of convalescent soldiers."

"Not in the circumstances," said Char gravely.

Miss Bruce advanced valiantly.

"I have told Miss Vivian that I'm quite sure that you—you will see your way to letting me go and be of what use I can to her in Questerham, Lady Vivian."

"Leave Plessing?"

Lady Vivian's voice held surprise only, but the unfortunate Miss Bruce was again obliged to struggle with divided feelings. She gazed miserably round, but Captain Trevellyan returned her look with one of unmistakable reproach, and Char was fixing her eyes persistently upon the fire. And then reassurance came to her from Joanna's voice, unusually gentle.

"I'm very glad, dear Miss Bruce. I shall like to feel that some one is looking after Char who has known her all her life, and cared for her as you have. And you won't be far away, so that I shan't feel I've lost sight of you. You must come out and see me struggling with my convalescents."

She stretched out her left hand, and Miss Bruce, answering her smile only with a convulsive pressure and a sort of sob compounded of mingled relief, gratitude, and compunction, hurried upstairs with her handkerchief undisguisedly held to her eyes.

"Poor Miss Bruce! We shall make an exchange, Char," said her mother, "for I'm hoping that Grace will stay here and help me."

"In what capacity?"

"Any capacity she likes."

"I hope," said Char, in tones which held more of doubt than of hopefulness, "that you will find her more accurate than I have. Good-night."

She went upstairs in her turn, feeling oddly tired and with a disquieting sense of finality. Her way and her mother's had parted, and although Char knew little regret for a separation which had long held them apart in all but physical nearness, she felt to the full the disturbing element introduced by a definitely spoken renunciation.

She would return to her work on the morrow, and make the move from Plessing as speedily as might be. But even in thinking of her work Char felt, that evening, no solace, for the recollection of her mother's words as to the frame of mind in which the staff might receive her left her strangely bereft of her usual armour of self-confidence.

In the hall, Trevellyan asked Joanna rather wistfully: "Do you mind very much?"

"Exchanging Miss Bruce for Grace? Do you think I shall lose by it?"

They both laughed a little, and then Trevellyan, looking into the fire, observed: "I'm glad you're going to have her. I shall like thinking that she's working with you here."

"I'm glad, Johnnie."

There was the ghost of a flicker in Joanna's voice.

"She'll be a comfort to you."

"Yes, indeed she will. The difference of age hasn't prevented our being friends."

"And—and you'll look after her?"

"I hope so. At all events, I shan't allow her to do any nursing of wounded, since we know the unfortunate effect that the sight of blood has upon her."

Joanna was laughing outright now.

"Oh, did she tell you?"

"Yes."

"I think *that* was the first time she and I ever had any real conversation."

"Was it? It was rather talented of you, in the circumstances."

"Cousin Joanna."

"Yes, John."

Captain Trevellyan bent a yet more ardent scrutiny upon the fire.

"It seems the wrong time to say anything about it, but you always understand, and she and I could neither of us bear that you shouldn't know it at once. I couldn't go away without telling you. Not," said Johnnie, suddenly turning round and facing her, "that anything is settled, you know."

"Except the only thing that matters," said Joanna softly.

"One thing that makes us both care so much," he said diffidently, "is that we both care so much for you."

She gave him both hands, regally, and he stooped and kissed them as he might have a queen's.

Presently she said: "I'm so glad, dear Johnnie. Nothing in the world could make me happier."

It was past eleven o'clock before John left her, and his final inquiry, standing at the hall door, made her laugh outright.

"You don't think any one will guess, do you? She doesn't want anything said till her father knows, and unluckily I can't get down to Wales and see him now. There won't be time. But you didn't guess till I told you, did you?"

"My dear Johnnie," said Joanna, with a singular absence of any emotion but her habitual kindly satire in her voice, "you really remind me very much sometimes of an ostrich!"

XIX

Grace Jones went back to the Hostel soon after the New Year in order to pack up and to make her farewells before going for a month's holiday to her home in Wales.

"And then Plessing!" said Miss Marsh in an awed voice.

"And then Plessing," Grace assented. "Lady Vivian hopes that it will be properly started by that time as a convalescent home."

She looked across the sitting-room to where Mrs. Bullivant was sitting, with a smile that held inquiry and congratulation.

"Fancy!" ejaculated Mrs. Bullivant, with a sort of timorous pleasure, "Lady Vivian actually thought of me, and suggested my taking over the work of quarter-mistress there. You know, looking after the stores and all that sort of thing. I must say, it's very good of her, and I shall like working there—and Gracie as secretary and all, too. It'll be quite like old times."

"I hate changes," observed Miss Henderson gloomily.

"This place will be extraordinary, with you gone, Mrs. Bullivant, and Gracie, and probably Tony and Plumtree as well."

"Tony isn't leaving, is she?" cried Grace.

"Yes, she is. Sent in her resignation two days ago. The fact is, she was altogether upset by that fuss we had about Miss Vivian the other day, and so she's decided that she wants a change. And Greengage says she won't stay without her. They always did hang together, you know."

"I don't altogether wonder at poor old Plumtree," Mrs. Potter observed thoughtfully. "Miss Vivian has always had a down on her, hasn't she? But she and Tony will be a loss to the Hostel, and so will you, dear."

"I don't like leaving a *bit*," Grace declared; "you've all been so nice to me, and I've been very happy here."

It was undeniable, however, that happiness was not destined to be the prevailing characteristic of Miss Jones's last day in the office.

Miss Vivian, seated at her paper-strewn table with all the old arrogance, if not actually with an additional touch of it to counteract the humanizing effect of the crêpe mourning band on her left arm, ignored her junior secretary as far as possible, but inspected her work with a closeness of attention that almost argued a desire to find it defective.

"You can hand over your work to Miss Delmege, Miss—er—Jones. She will take it over on Monday next."

"Yes, Miss Vivian."

"And bring me your files."

Char ran over the papers in the old way, with the murmured running commentary that denoted her utter unconsciousness of all but the task in hand, and at the same time made the extensive area covered by her official correspondence fully evident to the perceptions of whoever might be in the room with her.

"Papers relating to that man Farmer's pension—those must go up today. That contract for the milk—send it up to the Commissariat Department, and I should like to know why they haven't sent me down the balance-sheets for the month. Nothing is ever properly checked, it seems to me, unless I do it myself, though Heaven only knows when I'm to find time for it. I've got to go through the accounts today, some time or other.... What's this? One of the nurses from the Town Hospital wants to see me, and calmly writes to say so! I never heard such unofficial nonsense in my life, as though I had time to give personal interviews to every wretched little V.A.D. who chooses to ask for them! Miss Delmege!"

"Yes, Miss Vivian?"

"Take this letter and answer it in the third person. Make it quite clear that any application of that sort is entirely out of order. If she wants to speak to any one, she can go to Matron; and if it's necessary, Matron can write to me about it."

Miss Delmege took the letter, and mentally framed to herself the sentences in which she would later on make it clear to Gracie Jones that Miss Vivian's manner never really meant anything, and that her summary dismissal of any such appeal was only the necessary concomitant to official authority. It had become increasingly clear to Miss Delmege that Gracie was somehow, by the very reticence of her unspoken judgments, at the bottom of the extraordinary prejudice with which so many members of the staff now viewed the arbitrary ways of Miss Vivian.

The clear, rapid undertones continued:

"Boiler at the Hospital burst; they should have reported it sooner, but I'll send an order to the shop people. Another list for transfer! Dr. Prince transfers his men without rhyme or reason—all cases of myalgia and trench feet, too. I shall have to write and tell him to reconsider half of them, before I should dream of letting them leave.

"What's all that?—case for massage, case for Shepherd's Bush, five transfers for convalescent homes.... Send me up the Transport Officer. Miss Delmege, what are my appointments for today?"

"The new Superintendent for the Hostel is coming for an interview at two o'clock, and Dr. Prince rang up to say that he would come in for a moment at three."

Char raised her eyebrows.

"If I happen to be engaged or busy, he will have to wait. Is that all?"

"Yes, Miss Vivian."

"Thank Heaven!" piously ejaculated Char, entirely *pour la forme*, since the interviews which cut into her day's work afforded her the only relief she obtained from its monotonous strain.

"Then I'll get through these letters at once. Send those to Mrs. Potter; and, Miss Delmege, you can take these—the rest are for the Clothing Department. Miss Jones, kindly deal with these files.... Send for Miss Coll—Mrs. Baker-Bridges, to take down some letters at once."

Miss Delmege looked rather disturbed, and remained standing at Char's elbow without speaking. Miss Vivian, as was customary with her when wishing to display absorption in her work, continued to turn over the papers on the table without raising her eyes.

At last she looked up and said sharply:

"What is it, Miss Delmege? You fidget me very much by standing there in that unmeaning way. Do you want anything?"

Miss Delmege cleared her throat nervously. Too well did she know the peculiar note of crisp asperity now sounding in her chief's voice.

"I'm afraid the stenographer isn't here today."

"And why on earth not?"

"She isn't well."

"I've had no application for sick leave."

"She only telephoned this morning to say that she didn't feel able to come today."

Char, with the calculated show of temper with which she greeted any departures from discipline, struck the table with her hand, and made the unfortunate Miss Delmege jump.

"I think you've all lost your heads completely while I've been away. Is this office under military discipline or is it not?"

The question being purely rhetorical, Miss Delmege attempted no reply to it, and merely drooped the more dejectedly over her sheaf of letters.

"You can tell Miss Collins that unless she can apply for sick leave in the proper manner, and with a medical certificate to say that she is unfit for duty, she may consider herself dismissed."

Miss Delmege, only too thankful to feel that the Director's wrath was not aimed at herself, hastened to the telephone to deliver the ultimatum. She returned scarlet, and with an air of outraged modesty that made Grace look at her in mild astonishment. Miss Jones's curiosity, however, only received satisfaction that afternoon, at the close of Dr. Prince's interview with Miss Vivian, when he casually remarked: "By the way, that pretty little red-haired typist of yours, the one who got married the other day, paid me a call yesterday."

"Then, perhaps, you can inform me why she thought proper to remain away from duty without leave today."

"Oh, you'll have her back tomorrow—for a time, anyway."

Grace saw Miss Delmege make a hurried plunge into a small stationery cupboard, where she appeared to be searching for something elaborately concealed.

"I can't have that sort of playing fast and loose with the work," Char said icily. "If Miss Collins—"

"Mrs. Baker-Bridges," the doctor corrected her cheerfully.

"If my stenographer can't attend to her work regularly, she is of very little use to me."

"She's probably going to be of more use to the nation, let me tell you, than all the rest of you put together," said Dr. Prince.

Miss Delmege's agony of mind reached its culmination, and she let drop an armful of heavy ledgers with a clatter which effectually covered any further indelicate precision of utterance of which the doctor might have been guilty.

By the time that Grace had extinguished her own laughter in the cupboard, and had assisted Miss Delmege to pick up her books, the Doctor had slammed the door behind him, with a disregard for Miss Vivian's presence which might perhaps be accounted for by the searching cross-examination to which she had just subjected his proposed Medical Board cases.

"A doctor's profession, I suppose," Miss Delmege said to Grace in tones of outraged delicacy as they left the office together, "destroys the finer feelings altogether. I'm not prudish, so far as I know, but really, after what passed in the office today—"

"I wish you'd tell me what Mrs. Baker-Bridges said to you over the telephone."

Miss Delmege coloured and tossed her head.

"Some people don't seem to mind *what* they say. I never did like her, but I certainly didn't think she had a coarse mind."

"And has she?"

"Well, I wouldn't say it to any one but you, dear, and I know you won't repeat any of it, but she was actually so pleased and proud at the mere idea that she said she couldn't keep it to herself, though she isn't even in the least certain."

The virtuous horror expressed in Miss Delmege's whole person at such deplorable outspokenness was so excessive that Grace dared not make any reply for fear of producing an anti-climax.

That evening, Grace's last at Questerham Hostel, her room-mate became disconsolate.

"I don't know what I shall do without you, Gracie, and this room will be simply awful. You've always been such a dear about my being so untidy and everything, and put up with all of it, and done such heaps of little things. I shall never forget how you washed up the cups and tea-things after our morning tea, dear, never."

"But I was only too pleased," protested Grace. "You've done a lot for me, if it comes to that. Look how often you've boiled your kettle for me, and had everything ready on nights when I came back late. I shall miss you very much, but don't forget that if ever you're in Wales you're coming to stay with us."

"I say, do you really mean that?"

"Of course I do."

"You are a brick, Gracie. The thing I like about you," said Miss Marsh instructively, "is that you don't put on any frills."

"Well, why should I?"

"Oh, I don't know—staying at Plessing, and knowing Miss Vivian's people, and so on. There are others I could name," Miss Marsh said viciously, "who take airs for a good deal less—in fact, for nothing at all, that any one but themselves can see."

Miss Jones knew from much previous experience the subject denoted by that particular edge in her room-mate's voice.

"Are you worried?" she asked sympathetically, selecting a euphemism at random.

"My dear, I've got an awful fear that Delmege means to move into this room when you're gone. You'll see if she doesn't get round the new Superintendent. She's always resented being put in with two others, and that room of theirs will always be a three-bedded one."

"But Tony and Miss Plumtree are both leaving."

"Not yet, and, anyway, two others will be put in instead. Mark my words," said Miss Marsh tragically, "that'll be the next thing. Delmege and me stuck in here *tête-à-tête*, as they say."

"I do hope not."

"I shall resign, that's all. Simply resign. *And* give my reasons. I shall say to Miss Vivian right out, when she asks me why I want to leave—"

"But she never does ask why any one wants to leave. Besides, you know you wouldn't leave for such a ridiculous reason as that."

"Well, perhaps I wouldn't! After all, I should be sorry to think I couldn't get the better of Delmege, when all's said and done. I've a very good mind to tell her quite plainly that if she's got her eye on that corner bed she'll have to come to an understanding with me first, both as to the use of the screen and who's to make tea in the morning and turn the gas out at night. I've heard tales about Delmege's trick of getting into bed in a hurry and leaving everybody else to do the work. And she and I have had words before now."

"I know you have," said Grace. "Perhaps that may prevent her from wanting to come here."

Miss Marsh looked gloomy, and then bounded up as a tap sounded on the door.

"What did I tell you? I'll take any bet you like that's Delmege nosing round now. I know the way she swishes her petticoat—such swank, wearing a silk one under uniform! Well, I'm not going to interfere with her."

Miss Marsh bounced behind her screen.

"Come in," Grace called.

"Say I'm undressing," Miss Marsh issued a whispered command.

Miss Delmege stepped elegantly into the room, her favourite "fawn" *peignoir* chastely gathered round her.

"You alone, dear?"

"No, she isn't. I'm undressing," said a sharp voice behind the screen.

Miss Delmege ignored the voice, and laid a patronizingly affectionate hand upon Grace's shoulder.

"What thick hair you have, dear! Quite a work brushing it, I should think. Now, mine is so long that it's never had time to get really thick, though I know you wouldn't guess it to look at it, but that's the way it grows. As a child I used to have a perfect mass. Mother always used to say about me, 'That child Vera's strength has all gone into her hair, every bit of it.' It used to make her quite anxious, to see me without a bit of colour in my face and this great mass of hair."

"What made it all fall out, Delmege?" came incisively from behind the screen.

Miss Delmege tossed the long attenuated plait of straight fair hair which hung artlessly over one shoulder, and simulated deafness.

"I just looked in as it's your last night here," she told Grace. "We shall miss you, I'm sure. Tell me, dear, have you any idea who is coming into this room in your place?"

"Not any," hastily said Grace, as Miss Marsh's boot was dropped on the floor with a clatter that argued a certain degree of energy in removing it. "I suppose it will be arranged by the new Superintendent."

"It might be kinder," said Miss Delmege thoughtfully, "to have all that sort of thing in order before she arrives. She'll have plenty to do without changes of bedroom. But of course this *is* a room for two, there's no doubt about it. I've sometimes thought of a move myself, and this might be a good opportunity—"

The second boot was violently sent to rejoin its fellow.

"Strange, the noise that goes on in here, isn't it, with only the pair of you, too. I wonder it doesn't disturb you; but perhaps you're used to it?"

"If you don't like noise, Delmege, don't come in here," exclaimed the still invisible Miss Marsh. "I never could bear creeping about without a sound, like a cat, myself."

"I dare say not," Miss Delmege returned, with a certain spurious assumption of extreme gentleness in her little refined enunciation. "But I hope we all know what give and take is in sharing a room—especially in war-time."

"There's more take than give about some of us, by all accounts, especially in the matter of kettles and early tea," was the retort of Miss Marsh, spoken with asperity.

Miss Delmege turned to Grace.

"Well, dear, as I don't propose to have words either now or at any other hour, I shall say good-night. Do you mean to say you manage with only one screen?"

"Quite well. Besides, there are two round the other bed."

"I dare say that's very necessary," said Miss Delmege pointedly, as she moved to the door. "Good-night, dear."

"Good-night," said Grace, not without thankfulness.

"Good-night," repeated Miss Delmege to the screen. "When I'm in here, I shall certainly insist upon having an extra screen. I can't imagine how anybody can manage with one only. And each will keep to her own side of the room, too, instead of leaving her things all over the other's. What I call untidy, some of these arrangements are. But, of course, it's all what one's been used to, isn't it?"

Leaving no time for a reply to this favourite inquiry, Miss Delmege shut the door gently behind her.

Grace, proceeding to bed under the flow of eloquence directed at her from behind Miss Marsh's screen, conjectured that the bedroom would know no lack of spirited conversation between its inmates in the future.

The next morning Miss Marsh asked her at breakfast: "Shall you go and say good-bye to Miss Vivian?"

"I don't think it's necessary, is it?" Grace said hesitatingly.

"I can easily find out for you, dear, if she can see you for a moment," Miss Delmege kindly volunteered.

The opinion of the Hostel instantly veered round to an irrevocable certainty that a farewell to Miss Vivian was not necessary.

"After all, she'd only say she was too busy to see you."

"Or say she couldn't conscientiously recommend you for clerical work, as she did to poor Plumtree when she gave in her resignation the other day."

"After Plumtree has toiled over those beastly averages for the best part of two years!"

It was evident that the temper of the staff, for one reason or another, was undergoing a very thorough reaction indeed.

Only Miss Delmege remarked firmly: "I know nothing about Plumtree's work, I'm sure, but if there's one thing Miss Vivian is, it's just. Quite impartially speaking, one can't help seeing that, and especially being, as I am, in the position of her secretary. As I always say, I get at the human side of her."

"*In*human, I call it," muttered Tony, Miss Plumtree's chief ally.

"Wherever a recommendation is possible, Miss Vivian always gives it," inflexibly replied Miss Delmege. "I can answer for that."

Few things received less consideration in the Hostel than Miss Delmege in process of answering for the Director of the Midland Supply Depôt, and Miss Marsh, Tony, and Miss Henderson dashed simultaneously into discussion of a project for seeing Grace off at the station.

"We can get off at lunch-time, and your train goes at 1.30, doesn't it, Gracie?"

"Yes, and I'd love you to come; only what about your lunch?"

114

But every one said that didn't matter at all, and that, of course, dear old Gracie must have a proper send-off.

"How nice they all are to me!" thought Grace, and recklessly purchased a supply of cigarettes, which she left with Mrs. Bullivant, for the consolation of the Hostel during many Sunday afternoons to come.

"We shall meet at Plessing," the little Superintendent said, kissing her affectionately, "and it will be a great pleasure to work with you, Miss Jones dear, and you must tell me all Lady Vivian likes, you know, and how we can help her most."

"You'll like working for her very much," Grace prophesied confidently. "Good-bye, dear Mrs. Bullivant, and thank you for all your kindness to me."

She ran down the steps and would not look back, conscious of emotion.

At the station the members of the staff were to appear when possible. But as Grace crossed Pollard Street, glancing involuntarily at the familiar office door, Miss Delmege, with a most unusual disregard for propriety, emerged hastily, hatless and with her neat coils of hair ruffled in the wind.

"Good-bye, dear. It's sad to lose you, but I'm sure I hope you'll like your new job. I must say, it's been a pleasure to work with you."

"Oh, I'm so glad! How kind of you!"

"It's not every one I could say it to," Miss Delmege observed, with great truth. "But there's never been the least little difficulty, has there? We shall all miss you, and I must say I could wish that some others I could name were leaving in your place."

Grace knew too well the nameless being alluded to, however feebly disguised by the use of the plural. "Couldn't you get away to the station?" she asked hastily.

"Well, dear, I would, but really, with so many others there—to tell you the truth, *that* Miss Marsh is beginning to get on my nerves a bit. Besides, you see, if I went off early, Miss Vivian might think it rather strange."

On this unanswerable reason, Grace took a cordial farewell of Miss Vivian's unalterably loyal remaining secretary.

At the station Tony and Mrs. Potter hailed her eagerly. "We got down early, but the others are coming. There's an awful crowd, dear; better hurry."

Grace, in obedience to their urgings, purchased her ticket, while Mrs. Potter looked after the luggage and Tony took possession for her of a corner seat facing the engine.

"Here you are, and remember," said Mrs. Potter earnestly, "that you can get a cup of nice hot tea at the Junction. There'll be plenty of time; I found out on purpose."

"Thank you very much," said Grace gratefully. She stood at the window, and presently Tony and Mrs. Potter were joined by several other members of the staff, all hurried, but eager to take an affectionate farewell of Gracie.

"Marsh ought to be here—can't think why she isn't. She was tearing about like mad so as to get off in time," said Miss Plumtree.

"That girl will come into heaven late," Miss Henderson prophesied, and looked gratified when her neighbour emitted a faint, shocked exclamation.

"Give her my love if she's too late, and say I'm so very sorry," said Grace.

"You'll be off in a minute now."

"Mind you come back next month all right. We'll come down and meet you."

"I should like that so much. I shall look out on this very platform for you all."

"Oh, Gracie! shall we any of us ever see this awful platform without thinking of those troop-trains and the ghastly weight of the trays?"

"Never!" said Grace with entire conviction.

"There's the whistle—you're off now."

"And here's Marsh—she'll just do it. Look at her!"

Grace hung out of the window, and saw the ever tardy Miss Marsh hastening up the crowded platform, making free use of her elbows.

"I started too late—that wretched Delmege pretended I was wanted—so sorry, Gracie dear. Mind you write."

"Yes, yes. And please do all write to me when you have time, and tell me all your news. And we'll meet again next month, as soon as I get back."

The train was moving now, and only the panting and energetic Miss Marsh hastened along beside it, her hand on the carriage window.

"Good-bye, good-luck. I shall miss you dreadfully in our room. Don't be surprised if you hear that Delmege and I have had words together; that girl simply gets on my nerves."

"Stand back there, please."

"Good-bye, Gracie!"

"Good-bye."

Grace stood at the window and waved to the little group until the blue uniforms were lost to sight and only the flutter of Tony's handkerchief was still visible.

The Hostel days were over, but she would remember them always with a smile for the small hardships that had been tempered by so much kindness and merriment, and with a faithful recollection of the good companionship that work and the comradeship of workers ever had brought her.

To John Trevellyan in the trenches, Grace wrote something of her thoughts two days later, amid much else.

"I'm so glad I went to Questerham, apart from everything else, for the experience. The Hostel life was sometimes uncomfortable, but it was always amusing; and when all was said and done, everybody was ready to do anything or everything for any one else. I can't believe I was only there such a little while, for more happened to me there, and I got into realer touch with more people, than ever before.

"And now the New Year is only just beginning, and there have been so many changes and happenings already. I wonder so much what else it is going to bring to all of us who were together in Questerham."

XX

To Grace Jones herself the New Year, speeding on its way until it was new no longer, brought much work in the convalescent home at Plessing, the glad realization of Joanna Vivian's need of her, and innumerable unstamped letters bearing the field postmark. The quality of Miss Jones's peculiar philosophy was much tested as the months went by, but it was characteristic of her to be much heartened and rejoiced by an announcement confided to her soon after her return by Miss Marsh.

"The boy I was such pals with has been sent back on sick leave, and they're not sending him out again. And if you'll believe me, dear, I've been persuaded into saying *yes*. He wants it to be quite soon, and really I don't mind if it is; the Hostel is quite changed nowadays, and not nearly as jolly as it was, now the new Superintendent makes us all so comfortable. Besides, I don't mind telling you between ourselves, Gracie, that I can't help fancying me going off like that and coming back with a wedding-ring and all will be rather a knock in the eye for our old friend Delmege."

If this kindly prognostication was verified, Miss Delmege gave no sign of it, beyond introducing several additional shades of superiority into the manner of her congratulations.

"Strange, isn't it?" she observed with a small and tight smile, "to see the way some people put all sorts of personal considerations first and the work afterwards! Personally, I agree with Miss Vivian on the subject."

In agreement with Miss Vivian, on that as on all else, Miss Delmege continued to find solace. The promotion of Miss Bruce to Grace Jones's vacant place in Miss Vivian's office was a source of disquiet to her for some time, but the bond of a common admiration at last asserted itself, and found expression in their united efforts to persuade Miss Vivian to her lunch every day. There was also infinite consolation to Miss Delmege in her assertions, frequently heard at the Hostel, that nowhere was the human side of the Director of the Midland Supply Depôt so touchingly and unmistakably shown as in the occasional unofficial lapses which led her to address her secretary as "Brucey."

The Hostel saw rapid changes when Tony and Miss Plumtree had both become munition-workers, and Miss Bullivant had gone to Plessing. The war-workers became the victims of a series of new superintendents, each of whom found insuperable difficulty in accommodating herself to the arbitrary ruling of Miss Vivian, and either departed summarily or received a curt dismissal. Finally, an energetic Scotswoman established herself at the Hostel and, as Miss Vivian had become exceedingly weary of the quest, remained there unchallenged. She was a better manager than little Mrs. Bullivant, and made drastic reformations in many directions, several of which were ungratefully received by the older members of the community.

"For I must say," Mrs. Potter told Miss Henderson, "it was a good deal more sociable in the old days, when we made toast for tea over the sitting-room fire on Sunday afternoons, and Dr. Prince dropped in and told us all the news."

It was Tony and Miss Plumtree who dropped in now, and did their best to bridge the gulf that had yawned so long between the munition-workers' Hostel and that sacred to Miss Vivian's clerical staff.

"It's all very well," Miss Plumtree instructively remarked as she lounged in holland overalls and a pair of baggy but entirely unmistakable garments from which Miss Delmege kept her eyes studiously averted. "It's all very well, but working at munitions gives one a bit of an idea as to what one's working for. You people may think it's all Miss Vivian's personality, etc., etc., but I can tell you that's a jolly small part of the whole show."

The independence of Miss Plumtree's manner, as well as a new and strange slanginess developed both by her and by little Miss Anthony, was noted by their old companions without enthusiasm.

"After all," Tony chimed in patronizingly, "you really have the best of it. Troop-trains simply aren't in it with our work. Standing all day long, and shifts of twelve hours at a time—and if you turn green, that little reptile of a Welfare Superintendent pouring water all over you and telling you that there's nothing the matter."

A shade of reminiscence, almost of regret, passed over her face.

"At all events, Miss Vivian never did that—and she was pretty to look at. Every one is hideous at the works—especially Jawbones."

"And who," Mrs. Potter distantly inquired, "is Jawbones?"

Her tone implied that there were nick-names *and* nicknames, and that those in use amongst the *habituées* of the munitions-factory would meet with little or no admiration from the refined inhabitants of the Hostel.

"That's what we call the Superintendent," Tony said airily.

Miss Delmege, her lips drawn into an extremely thin line, uttered her solitary contribution to the conversation, before retiring with marked aloofness to the bedroom where she hoped to defeat her old antagonist, Miss Marsh, by annexing all three screens and the largest kettle of hot water.

"I must say, it does seem to me that a happy medium might be found between doing your war work entirely for the sake of whoever's at the head of it, and calling your superintendent '*Jawbones*.'"

The conclusion was so irrefutable, that even the new-born independence acquired by the munition-makers could produce no adequate reply.

It might even be inferred from the unusual thoughtfulness with which the holland-clad enthusiasts took their departure, that neither was devoid of an occasional pang at the memory of the old days of blind obedience and enthusiastic loyalty to the ideal which Char Vivian, with all her autocratic charm and occasional flashes of kindness, still represented.

As Dr. Prince had said, "the Vivians of Plessing stood for the highest in the land."

The doctor seldom came to the Hostel now, for time had brought him more work than ever, and he spared himself none of it. Only at Plessing could he sometimes be persuaded to spend half an hour in talking to Grace or Lady Vivian after his medical inspection was over.

"A wonderful work you're doing here," he told Joanna with satisfaction. "I wish all our great houses could be turned to such good use—and all our lady-workers too," added the doctor with some significance. "When all's said and done, nursing is women's work and no one else's, and the ruling of hospital discipline and the disposal of cases for Medical Boards, or anything else, ought to be left to the Medical Officer. That's *my* opinion, right or wrong, and will be till my dying day."

To Joanna Vivian, presiding over the altered establishment at Plessing, time brought many outlets for the unquenchable spirit of energy that would always possess her. She brought gaiety to her work, and laughter that was as unofficial as her inveterate habit of referring all questions of discipline to Dr. Prince, and the management of each individual branch to the helper in charge of it. Joanna's staff was not a large one, and each member of it had her own special and peculiar interest in the work given into her hands.

It was in vain that Lesbia Willoughby, from London, wrote impassioned accounts to her poor dear Joanna of the many activities in which her days and nights appeared to fly past. "Wounded Colonials, blinded officers, Flag-days, hospitals, canteens, Red Cross entertainments—I have my finger in every single war-pie that's going, and I can't tell you how too utterly *twee* some of the dear fellows are with whom I get into touch. If you'll only trust that sulky girl of yours to me for six months, I could do wonders for her, and probably get her off your hands altogether. After all, dear, we can never forget that you and I were girls together, can we?"

"Lesbia never means to forget it, that's clear enough," was the sole comment of Lady Vivian.

She did not go through the form of transferring Mrs. Willoughby's invitation to her daughter. It gradually became evident that the Director of the Midland Supply Depôt would accord but little of her fully occupied time to a convalescent home not supplied from her own depôt, and as Joanna said to Grace, with her habitual slight shrug: "It may be just as well, my dear. I'm not Miss Bruce, and Char and I haven't the same way of looking at things. She vexed and disappointed her father, and no amount of eloquence about her high and mighty motives will ever make me altogether forget it. I shall never be able to hear her talk about her position as Director of the Midland Supply Depôt without thinking what a fool I was not to smack her well when she was a child."

Thus Joanna, half laughing, but with the eternal loneliness that all John's steadfast loyalty and Grace's loving companionship would never altogether assuage still underlying the dauntless youthfulness in her blue eyes.

For Trevellyan the months succeeded one another, strangely monotonous. In company with a hundred thousand others "somewhere in France," he moved between the mud and noise and blood in the trenches, and the eternal dreary billets where letters from home and the need of sleep were the only considerations. But to his Grace in England Johnnie wrote cheerily, of hope and good courage, and peace dawning on a far horizon, and of the prospect of ten days' leave.

To Char Vivian, Director of the Midland Supply Depôt, the advancing year, imperceptibly enough, brought certain solutions and enlightenments.

The personal fascination that she could exert when she willed would always secure for her a following of blindly devoted adherents, but her influence was not always strong enough to retain their admiration. Insensibly, Char modified a little of her arbitrariness.

"They put so much else before the work," she said helplessly to Miss Bruce.

But Char's perceptions were never lacking in acumen, and she became more and more aware of the truth of Joanna's prognostication that the work of the Supply Depôt would be done for its own sake, and for that of the cause in whose name it existed. And it was perhaps that awareness which brought to her a gradual realization of motives in her own self-devotion hitherto unacknowledged to herself.

The Director of the Midland Supply Depôt might sit day after day and hour after hour at her paper-strewn table, issuing orders and receiving the official interviews and communications that so clearly indicated the high responsibility of her position, but Char Vivian grew to exercise a certain discretion in the matter of her return to the meals and rest so anxiously watched over by Miss Bruce, whose adoring loyalty was hers beyond any possibility of shaking.

In those occasional unofficial concessions to her imploring solitude might, after all, be numbered the most creditable achievements of Miss Vivian.

Consequences

Book I

I

The Game of Consequences

The firelight flickered on the nursery wall, and the children sat round the table, learning the new game which the nursery-maid said they would like ever so, directly they understood it.

"I understand it already," said Alex, the eldest, tossing her head proudly. "Look, Barbara, you fold the piece of paper like this, and then give it to Cedric, because he's next to you, and I give mine to you, and Emily gives hers to me. That's right, isn't it, Emily?"

"Quite right, Miss Alex; what a clever girl, to be sure. Here, Master Baby, you can play with me. You're too little to do it all by yourself."

"He isn't Baby any more. We've got to call him Archie now. The new little sister is Baby," said Alex dictatorially.

She liked always to be the one to give information, and Emily had only been with them a little while. The children's own nurse would have told her to mind her own business, or to wait till she was asked, before teaching her grandmother, but Emily said complacently:

"To be sure, Miss Alex! and such a big boy as Master Archie is, too. Now you all write down a name of a gentleman."

"What gentleman?" asked Cedric judicially. He was a little boy of eight, with serious grey eyes and a good deal of dignity.

"Why, any gentleman. Some one you all know."

"I know, I know."

Alex, always the most easily excited of them all, scribbled on her piece of paper and began to bounce up and down on her chair.

"Hurry up, Barbara. You're so slow."

"I don't know who to put."

Alex began to whisper, and Barbara at once said:

"Nurse doesn't allow us to whisper. It's bad manners."

"You horrid little prig!"

Alex was furious. Barbara's priggishness always put her into a temper, because she felt it, unconsciously, to be a reflection on her own infallibility as the eldest.

"Miss Barbara," said Emily angrily, "it's not for you to say what Nurse allows or doesn't allow; *I'm* looking after you now. The idea, indeed!"

Barbara's pale, pointed little face grew very red, but she did not cry, as Alex, in spite of her twelve years, would almost certainly have cried at such a snub.

She set her mouth vindictively and shot a very angry look at Alex out of her blue eyes. Then she wrote something on the slip of paper, shielding it with her hand so that her sister could not read it.

Cedric was printing in large capitals, easily legible, but no one was interested in what Cedric wrote.

There was a good deal of whispering between Emily and little Archie, and then the papers were folded up once more and passed round the table again.

"But when do we see what we've written?" asked Alex impatiently.

"Not till the end of the game, then we read them out. That's where the fun comes in," said Emily. It was a long while before the papers were done, and most of the children found it very difficult to decide what *he* said to *her*, what she replied, and what the world said. But at last even Barbara, always lag-last, folded her slip, very grimy and thumb-marked, and put it with the others into Emily's apron.

"Now then," giggled the nursery-maid, "pull one out, Master Archie, and I'll see what it says." Archie snatched at a paper, and they opened it.

"Listen!" said Emily.

"The Queen met Master Archie—whoever of you put the Queen?"

"Cedric!" cried the other children.

Cedric's loyalty to his Sovereign was a by-word in the nursery.

"Well, the Queen met Master Archie in the Park. She said to him, 'No,' and he answered her, 'You dirty little boy, go 'ome and wash your face.' Well, if that didn't ought to be the other way round!"

"I wish it was me she'd met in the Park," said Cedric sombrely. "I might have gone back to Buckingham Palace with her and—"

"Go on, Emily, go on!" cried Alex impatiently. "Don't listen to Cedric. What comes next?"

"The consequences was—whatever's here?" said Emily, pretending an inability to decipher her own writing.

"Well, I never! The consequences was, a wedding-ring. Whoever went and thought of that now? And the world said—"

The nursery door opened, and Alex shrieked, "Oh, finish it—quick!"

She knew instinctively that it was Nurse, and that Nurse would be certain to disapprove of the new game.

"Don't you make that noise, Alex," said Nurse sharply. "You'll disturb the baby with your screaming."

For a moment Alex wondered if the game was to be allowed to proceed, but Barbara, well known to be Nurse's favourite, must needs say to her in an amiable little voice, such as she never used to her brothers and sister:

"Emily's been teaching us such a funny new game, Nurse. Come and play with us."

"I've no time to play, as you very well know, with all your clothes wanting looking over the way they do," Nurse told her complacently. "What's the game?"

Alex kicked Barbara under the table, but without much hope, and at the same moment Cedric remarked very distinctly:

"It is called Consequences, and Archie met the Queen in the Park. I wish it had been me instead."

"Well!" exclaimed Nurse. "That's the way you do when my back's turned, Miss Emily, teaching them such vulgar, nonsensical games as that. Never did I hear—now give me those papers this minute."

She did not wait to be given anything, but snatched the little slips out of Emily's apron and threw them on to the fire.

"I'm not going to have no Consequences in *my* nursery, and don't you believe it!" remarked Nurse.

But omnipotent though Nurse was, in the eyes of the Clare children, she could not altogether compass this feat.

There were consequences of all sorts.

Cedric, who was obstinate, and Barbara, also obstinate and rather sly as well, continued to play at the new game in corners by themselves, refusing to admit Alex to their society because she told them that they were playing it all wrong. She knew that they were not playing it as Emily had taught them, and was prepared to set them right, although she felt uncertain, in the depths of her heart, as to whether she herself could remember it all. But at least she knew more than Barbara, who was silly and a copy-cat, or than Cedric, who had concentrated on the possibilities the game presented to him of a hypothetical encounter between himself and his Sovereign. The game for Cedric consisted in the ever-lengthening conversation which took place under the heading of what he said to her and what she replied. When Her Majesty proceeded, under Cedric's laborious pencil, to invite him to drive her in her own carriage-and-pair, to Buckingham Palace, Alex said scornfully that Cedric was a silly little boy, and of course the Queen wouldn't say *that*. To which Cedric turned a perfectly deaf ear, and continued slowly to evolve amenities eminently satisfactory to his admiration for Her Majesty. Alex went away, shrugging her shoulders, but secretly she knew that Cedric's indifference had got the better of her. However much she might laugh, with the other children, or sometimes, even, in a superior way, with the grown-ups, when the children went into the drawing-room, at Cedric's slowness, and his curious fashion of harping upon one idea at a time, Alex was sub-consciously aware of Cedric as a force, and one which could, ultimately, always defeat her own diffused, unbalanced energies. If any one laughed at Alex, or despised one of her many enthusiasms, she would quickly grow ashamed of it, and try to pretend that she had never really been in earnest. In the same way, she would affect qualities and instincts which did not belong to her, with the hope of attracting, and of gaining affection.

But Cedric went his own way, as genuinely undisturbed by Nurse's scoldings and hustlings as by his elder sister's mockery, which had its origin in her secret longing to prove to herself, in spite of her own inmost convictions, that she was the dominant spirit in her little world.

It always made her angry when Cedric left her gibes unanswered, not from a desire to provoke her further, but simply from his complete absorption in the matter in hand, and his utter indifference to Alex's comments.

"Don't you hear what I say?" Alex asked sharply.

"No," said Cedric baldly. "I'm not listening. Don't interrupt me, Alex."

"You're playing it all wrong—you and Barbara. Two silly little babies," she cried angrily and incoherently. "And it's a stupid, vulgar game. Nurse said so."

Although Alex had been the most enthusiastic of them all when Emily had first taught her the game, she had at once begun to think it vulgar when Nurse condemned it.

She would have nothing more to do with "Consequences." It was quite likely that in a few days Barbara would get into one of her priggish, perverse moods, and in a fit of temper with Cedric go and tell Nurse that he was still indulging in the forbidden pastime. Alex thought she might as well be out of it.

She was in trouble often enough in the nursery. Nurse always took Barbara's part against her, and accused her of being violent and over-bearing, and then Lady Isabel, the children's mother, would send for her to her room while she dressed for dinner, and say complainingly:

"Alex, why do you quarrel so with the others? I shall send you to school, if you can't be happy with Barbara at home."

"Oh, don't send me to school, mummy."

"Not if you're good."

"I will be good, really, I will."

"Very well, my child. Now ring for Hawkins, or I shall be late."

"May I stay and watch you put on your diamond things, mummy? Do let me."

And Lady Isabel always laughed, and let her stay, so that Alex eventually went back to the nursery with an elated sense of having been very good, and accorded privileges which never fell to the lot of self-righteous Barbara.

She knew she was her mother's favourite, because she was the eldest, and was often sent for to the drawing-room when there were people there. Barbara, of course, was too ugly to go much to the drawing-room. Alex would toss her own mane of silky brown curls, and draw herself up conceitedly, as she thought of Barbara's pale face, and thin, attenuated ringlets. Besides, Lady Isabel had said that Barbara really mustn't come down again when "people" were there until her second teeth had put in their tardy appearance. Even Cedric, though acclaimed as "quaint" and "solemn" by his mother's friends, was too apt to make disconcerting comments on their sparkling conversation, and would return to the nursery in disgrace. Alex' only rival for downstairs' favour was little Archie, who was only four, and at present a very pretty little boy. But he was too small for Alex ever to feel jealous of him. The new baby, christened with pomp in the big Catholic Church at the end of the Square, Pamela Isabel, was, so far, a neglible quantity in the nursery world.

She slept in the little room called the inner nursery, most of the day, and was only with the others when they were taken into the Park or to play in the square garden. Then Emily pushed the big pram that contained the slumbering Pamela, and Nurse grasped the hands of Barbara and Archie and dragged them over the crossings.

121

Cedric, by Nurse's express orders, always walked just in front of her with Alex, and unwillingly submitted to having his hand held by his sister.

"Not that I trust Alex for common sense," Nurse was careful to explain, "not a yard, but so long as they're together I can keep an eye on both and see they don't get under no hansom's feet. That boy's spectacles are too downright uncanny for me to let him cross the road alone."

For Cedric was obliged to wear a large pair of round spectacles, without which he could only see things that were very close to his eyes. He even had another, different, pair for reading, which seemed to Alex an exaggerated precaution, likely to increase Cedric's sense of his own importance.

"Well," said Cedric. "You have a plate, and I haven't."

Alex's plate was an instrument of torture designed to push back two prominent front teeth. It not only hurt her and kept her awake at night, but was very disfiguring besides, and she passionately envied Barbara, who at nine years old still had only gaps where her front teeth should have been.

"Of course," Alex would sometimes declare grandly, repeating what she had heard Lady Isabel say, "Barbara is dreadfully backward. She's such a baby for her age. *I'm* very old for my age."

But she only said this in the drawing-room, where it would provoke kindly laughter or perhaps interested comment. In the nursery, Nurse never suffered any airs and graces, as she called them, and would pounce on Alex and shake her at the least hint of any such nonsense.

"Just you wait till you're sent to a good strict school, my lady, and see what you'll get then," she told her threateningly.

"I'm not going to school. Mummy said I shouldn't go if I was good."

"We shall see what we shall see. Children as think themselves everybody at home, gets whipped when they go to school," Nurse told her severely.

Alex was used to these prognostications. They did not alarm her very much, because she did not think that she would be sent to school. She knew instinctively that her father disapproved of ordinary girls' schools, and that her mother disliked convents, and indeed most things that had to do with religion.

Alex supposed that this was because Lady Isabel was a Protestant! She thought that it was much the nicest religion to belong to, on the whole, since it evidently imposed no obligations in the nature of church-going, and she often wondered why her mother had let all her children be Catholics, instead of Protestants like herself. It certainly couldn't be because father cared which church the children went to, or whether they went at all.

The only person in the house who did seem to care was Nurse, who took Alex and Barbara and Cedric to High Mass at the Oratory every Sunday, where there was a front bench reserved for them, with little cards in brass frames planted at intervals along the ledge in front of them, bearing the name of Sir Francis Clare.

Nurse put Barbara on one side of her and Alex on the other, and Cedric on the outside, and was very particular about their kneeling down and standing up at the right moment, and keeping the prayer-books open in front of them. Alex and Barbara each had a *Garden of the Soul*, but Cedric was only allowed *Holy Childhood* which had pictures and anecdotes illustrative of Vice and Virtue at the end.

Alex knew all the anecdotes by heart, and preferred her own grown-up-looking book with its small, close print. She had long since discovered that the one matter over which Nurse could be hoodwinked was print, and that she might quite safely indulge herself in the perusal of the pages devoted to the Sacrament of Holy Matrimony, or to a mysterious ceremony called Churching after Child-birth, during the many dull portions of the long service.

The only part of Church that held possibilities was when the little bell rang at the Elevation, and every one bent his or her head as far down as it would go over the bench. Alex always looked up surreptitiously, then, to see if by any chance a miracle was taking place, or to watch Cedric's invariable manoeuvre of hanging on to the ledge by his teeth and hands and trying to raise his feet from the floor at the same time.

Nurse was always piously bent double, her face hidden in her cotton gloves, breathing stertorously with Barbara on the other side devotedly imitating her, even to the production of strange sounds through her own tightly-compressed lips.

After that, Alex always knew that the end of Church was near, and that as soon as the priest had taken up his little square headgear and faced the congregation for the last time, Nurse would begin to poke her violently, as a sign that she was to get up and to make Cedric pick up his cap and his gloves.

Then came the genuflection as they filed out between the benches, and Nurse was always very particular that this should be done properly, frequently pressing a heavy hand on Alex's shoulder until her knee bumped painfully against the stone floor. The final ceremony connected with the children's religion took place at the door, when Cedric had to make his way through rustling skirts and an occasional pair of black trousers to the big stone basin of holy water. Into this, standing on tiptoe with immense difficulty, he plunged as much of his hand as was necessary to satisfy the sharp inspection of Nurse when he returned, proffering dripping fingers to her and to his sisters.

The last perfunctory sign of the cross made then, the worst of Sunday, in Alex's opinion, was over.

Roast beef and Yorkshire pudding for dinner was pleasant. Mademoiselle did not come in the afternoon, and Nurse generally went out and left Emily in charge. In the summer she took the children to sit in the Square garden—the Park on Sundays was not allowed—and in the winter they always walked as far as the Albert Memorial, for which Cedric entertained a great admiration.

Sunday was Lady Isabel's At Home day and the children, except during the season, always went down to the drawing-room after tea, Alex and Barbara in pale, rose-coloured frocks with innumerable frills at throat and wrists, and a small pad fastened under each skirt so that it might stand well out at the back. Cedric, like most other little boys of his age and standing, was forced to wear a Lord Fauntleroy suit, from which his cropped bullet head and spectacles emerged incongruously.

The half-hour in the drawing-room was not enjoyed by the others as it was by Alex, especially if there were many visitors. She would lean against Lady Isabel confidently, and hear people say how like she was to her mother, which always delighted her. Her mother looked so pretty, sitting on the sofa with her fringe beautifully curled and a lovely dress that was half a teagown, the tight bodice coming down into a sharp point in front and behind, and the skirt falling into long folds, with a train sweeping the ground, and huge loops and bows of soft ribbon draping it cross-wise.

Barbara was incurably shy, and poked her head when she was spoken to, but very few people took as much notice of her as of talkative Alex or pretty little Archie, who was all blue ribbons and fearless smiles. And before very long Lady Isabel was sure to say:

"Now, you'd better run back to the nursery, hadn't you, darlings? or Nurse will be comin' down in search of you. I've got the most invaluable old dragon for them," she generally added to her friends. "She's been with us since Alex was a baby, and rules the whole house."

"Oh, don't send them away!" one of the visiting ladies would exclaim politely. "*Such* darlings!"

"Oh, but I must! Their father won't *hear* of my spoilin' them. Now run along, infants."

Cedric and Barbara were only too ready to obey, though it was understood that Lady Isabel's "run along" only meant a very ceremonious departure from the room, Barbara taking little Archie by the hand and leading him to the door, where they both dropped the obeisance considered "picturesque," and Cedric making an unwilling progress to execute his carefully practised bow before each one of the ladies scattered about the big room.

If Alex, however, was enjoying herself, and getting the notice that her soul loved, she always said in a pleading whisper, loud enough to be heard by two or three people besides her mother:

"Oh, do let me stay with you a little longer, mummy. Don't send me upstairs yet!"

"How sweet! Do let her stay, dear Lady Isabel."

"You mustn't encourage me to spoil her. She ought to go up with the others."

"Just for this once, mummy."

"Well, just for this once, perhaps. After all," said Lady Isabel apologetically, "she *is* the eldest. She'll be comin' out before I know where I am!"

And Alex would enjoy the privilege of being the eldest, and sit beside her mother, listening to the conversation, and sometimes joining in with remarks that she thought might be acclaimed as amusing or original, or even merely precocious. No wonder that the nursery greeted her return with disdain. Even Emily called her "drawing-room child," and by her contempt brought Alex' ready tears of mortified vanity to the surface. But it was much worse on the rare Sunday afternoons when Nurse was in, when she would greatly resent the slight to Barbara if she was sent up from the drawing-room before her sister.

"Working on your mamma to spoil you like that, just because you're a couple of years older!" Nurse would say, pulling the comb fiercely through Alex' hair as she went to bed.

"I'm three whole years older."

"Don't you contradict me like that, Alex. I'm not going to have any showing-off up here, I can tell you. You can keep those airs and graces for your mamma's friends in the drawing-room."

Alex generally went to bed in tears.

If Nurse had not been scolding her, then Barbara had been quarrelling with her. They always quarrelled whenever Barbara ventured to differ from Alex and take up an attitude of her own, or still more when Barbara and Cedric made an alliance together and excluded Alex's autocratic ruling of their games.

"But it is for your good," she would tell them passionately. "I want to show you a better way. It'll be much more fun if you do it my way—you'll see."

But they did not want to see.

Their obstinacy always brought to Alex the same sense of incredulous, resentful fury. How *could* they not want to be shown the best way of doing things, when she knew it and they didn't? And, of course, she always did know it. Was she not the eldest?

It was not till Alex was almost thirteen that her belief in her own infallibility as eldest received a rude shock.

She nearly killed Barbara.

It was the first week of August, and Sir Francis and Lady Isabel had gone to Scotland. The children were going to the sea with Nurse on the following day, and took advantage of her state of excitement over the packing, and the emptiness of the downstair rooms, to play at circus on the stairs. Emily only said, "Now don't go hurting yourselves, whatever you do, or there'll be no seaside tomorrow," and then went back to amuse Pamela, who was crying and restless from the heat.

"I'll tell you what!" said Alex. "We'll have tight-rope dancing. I'm tired of learned pigs and things like that—" This last impersonation having been perseveringly rendered by Cedric with much shuffling and snorting over a pack of cards.

"Give me the skipping-rope, Barbara."

"Why?" said Barbara, whining.

"Because I say so," replied her sister, stamping her foot. "I've got an idea."

"It's my skipping-rope."

"But if you don't give it to me we can't have the tight-rope dancing," said Alex in despair.

"I don't care. Why should you do tight-rope dancing with my skipping-rope?"

"You shall do it first—you shall do it all yourself, if you'll only let me show you," Alex cried in an agony of impatience.

On this inducement Barbara slowly parted with her skipping-rope, and let Alex knot it hastily and insecurely to the newel post on the first landing above the hall.

"Now just get up on to the post, Barbara, and I'll hold the other end of the rope like this, and you'll see—"

"But I can't, I should fall off."

"Don't be such a little muff; I'll hold you on."

"No, no—I'm frightened. Let Cedric do it."

"No," said Cedric. "I'm being a learned pig." He went down the short flight of stairs and sat firmly down upon the tiled floor with the pack of cards out-spread before him.

"Now come on, Barbara," Alex commanded her; "I'll hold you."

Between hoisting and pulling and Barbara's own dread of disobeying her, Alex got her sister into a kneeling position on the broad flat top of the newel post.

"Now stand up, and then I'll hold out the rope. You'll be the famous tight-rope dancer crossing the Falls of Niagara."

"Alex, I'm frightened."

"What of, silly? If you did fall it's only a little way on to the stairs, and I'll catch you. Besides, you'll feel much safer when you're standing up."

Barbara, facing the stairs, and with her back to the alarming void between her perch and the hall-floor, rose trembling to her feet.

"You look splendid," said Alex. "Now then!" She jerked at the rope, and at the same instant Barbara screamed and tried to clutch at her.

Alex caught hold of her sister's ankles, felt Barbara's weight slip suddenly, and screamed aloud as a shriek and crash that seemed simultaneous proclaimed Barbara's fall backwards into the hall. Cedric and Barbara in a confused struggling heap on the floor—doors opening upstairs and in the basement—the flying feet of the servants—all was an agonized nightmare to Alex until Barbara, limp and inert on Nurse's lap, suddenly began to scream and cry, calling out, "My back! my back!"

They hushed her at last, and Nurse carried her into the boudoir, which was the nearest room, and laid her down on the broad sofa. Then Alex became aware of a monotonous sound that had struck on her ear without penetrating to her senses ever since the accident happened.

"My spectacles are broken. You've broken my spectacles," reiterated a lamentable voice.

"You horrid, heartless little boy, Cedric! When poor Barbara—" Sobs choked her.

"I like that!" said Cedric. "When it was all you that made her fall at all—and break my spectacles."

"What's that?" said Nurse, miraculously reappearing. "All you, was it? I might have known it, you mischievous wicked child. Tell me what happened, this minute."

But Alex was screaming and writhing on the floor, feeling as though she must die of such misery, and it was Cedric who gave the assembled household a judicial version of the accident.

The doctor came and telegrams were sent to Scotland, which brought back Lady Isabel, white-faced and tearful, and Sir Francis, very stern and monosyllabic.

"Father, my spectacles are broken," cried Cedric earnestly, running to meet them, but they did not seem to hear him.

"Where is she, Nurse?" said Lady Isabel.

"In the boudoir, my lady, and better, thank Heaven. The doctor says her back'll get right again in time."

Alex, hanging shaking over the balustrade, saw that Nurse was making faces as though she were crying. But when she came upstairs, after a long time spent with Lady Isabel in the boudoir, and saw Alex, her face was quite hard again, and she gave her a push and said, "It's no use crying those crocodile tears now. You should have thought of that before trying to kill Barbara the way you did."

"I didn't, I didn't," sobbed Alex.

But nobody paid any attention to her.

Good-natured Emily was sent away, because Nurse said she wasn't fit to be trusted, and Cook, who was Emily's aunt, and very angry about it all, told Alex that it was all her fault if poor Emily never got another place at all. Everything was Alex' fault.

There was no going to the seaside, even after Barbara was pronounced better. But Lady Isabel, who, Nurse said, had been given a dreadful shock by Alex' wickedness, was going into the country, and would take Archie and the baby with her, if they could get a new nursery-maid at once.

"And me and Cedric?" asked Alex, trembling.

"Cedric doesn't give me no trouble, as you very well know, and he'll stay here and help me amuse poor little Barbara, as has always got on with him so nicely."

"Shall I stay and play with Barbara too?"

"She's a long way from playing yet," Nurse returned grimly. "And I should think the sight of you would throw her into a fit, after what's passed."

"But what will happen to me, Nurse?" sobbed Alex.

"Your Papa will talk to you," said Nurse.

Such a thing had never happened to any of the children before, but Alex, trembling and sick from crying, found herself confronting Sir Francis in the dining-room.

"I am going to send you to school, Alex," he told her. "How old are you?"

"Twelve."

"Then I hope," said Sir Francis gravely, "that you are old enough to understand what a terrible thing it is to be sent from home in disgrace for such a reason. I am told that you have the deplorable reputation of originating quarrels with your brothers and sister, who, but for you, would lead the normal existence of happily-circumstanced children."

Alex was terrified. She could not answer these terrible imputations, and began to cry convulsively.

"I see," said Sir Francis, "that you are sensible of the appalling lengths to which this tendency has led you. Even now, I can scarcely believe it—a harmless, gentle child like your little sister, who, I am assured, has never done you wilful injury in her life—that you should deliberately endanger her life and her reason in such a fashion."

He paused, as though he were waiting for Alex to speak, but she could not say anything.

"If your repentance is sincere, as I willingly assume it to be, your future behaviour must be such as to lead us all, particularly your poor little sister, to forget this terrible beginning."

"Will Barbara get well?"

"By the great mercy of Heaven, and owing to her extreme youth, we are assured by the doctor that a year or two will entirely correct the injury to the spine. Had it been otherwise, Alex—" Sir Francis looked at his daughter in silence.

"When thanking Heaven for the mercy which has preserved your sister's life," he said gently, "I hope you will reflect seriously upon redeeming this action by your future conduct."

"Oh, I'm sorry—oh, shall you ever forgive me?" gasped Alex, amongst her sobs.

"I do forgive you, my child, as does your mother, and as I am convinced that little Barbara will do. But I cannot, nor would I if I could, avert from you the consequence of your own act," said her father.

Barbara did forgive Alex, in a little, plaintive, superior voice, as she lay very white and straight in bed. She was to stay quite flat on her back for at least a year, the doctor said, and she need do no lessons, and later she would be taken out in a long flat carriage that could be pushed from behind, then she would be able to walk again, and her back would be quite straight.

"If she'd been a hunchback, we might have played circus again, and I could have been the learned pig," said Cedric reflectively.

Alex went to school at the end of September.

And that was her first practical experience of the game of Consequences, as played by the freakish hand of fate.

II
School

Alex' schooldays were marked by a series of emotional episodes.

In her scale of values, only the personal element counted for anything. She was intelligent and industrious at her classes when she wished to gain the approbation of an attractive class-mistress, and idle and inattentive when she wanted to please the pretty girl with yellow hair, who sat next her and read a story-book under cover of a French grammar.

Alex did not read; she wanted to make the yellow-haired girl look at her and smile at her. She thought Queenie Torrance beautiful, though her beauty did not strike Alex until after she had fallen a helpless victim to one of those violent, irrational attractions for one of her own sex, that are apt to assail feminine adolescence.

"I hope that you will find some nice little companions at Liège," Sir Francis had gravely told his daughter in valediction, "but remember that exclusive friendships are not to be desired. Friendly with all, familiar with none," said Sir Francis, voicing the ideal of his class and of his period.

As well tell a stream not to flow downhill. Nothing but the most exclusive and inordinate of attachments lay within the scope of Alex' emotional capacities. She was incapable alike of asking or of bestowing in moderation.

Theoretically she would tell herself that she would give all, trust, confidence, love, friendship, and ask for nothing in return. Practically she suffered tortures of jealousy if the loved one addressed a word or smile to any but herself, and cried herself to sleep night after night in the certainty of loving infinitely more than she was loved.

The material side of her life as a *pensionnaire* at the Liège convent made very little impression upon her, excepting in relation to the emotional aspect, of which she was never unaware.

To the end of her days, the clean, pungent smell of a certain polish used upon the immense spaces of bare *parquet ciré* all over the building, would serve to recall the vivid presentment of the tall Belgian *postulante* whose duty it was to apply it with a huge mop, and whom, from a distance only to be appreciated by those who know the immensity of the gulf that in the convent world separates the novice from the pupils, Alex had worshipped blindly.

And the acrid, yet not unpleasant taste of *confiture* thinly spread over thick slices of brown bread, would remind her with equal vividness of the daily three o'clock interval for *goûter*, with Queenie Torrance pacing beside her in the garden quadrangle, one hand of each rolled into her black-stuff apron to try and keep warm, and the other grasping the enormous double *tartine* that formed the afternoon's refection.

Even the slight, steady sound of hissing escaping from a gas jet of which the flame is turned as high as it will go, stood to Alex for the noisy evening recreation, spent in the enforced and detested amusement of *la ronde*, when her only preoccupation was to place herself by the object of her adoration, for the grasp of her hand in its regulation cotton glove, as the circle of girls moved drearily round and round singing perfunctorily.

The tuneless tune of those *rondes* remained with Alex long after the words had lost the savour of irony with which novelty had once invested them.

"Quelle	*horrible*	*attente*
D'être		*postulante....*
Quel		*supplice*
D'être	*une*	*novice*
Ah!	*quel* *comble*	*d'horreur*

Devenir soeur de choeur...."

Alex' symbols were not romantic ones, but there was no romance in the life of the Liège convent, save what she brought to it herself. Even the memory of the great square *verger*, in the middle of gravelled alleys, brought to her mind for sole token of summer, only her horror of the immense pale-red slugs that crawled slowly and interminably out and across the paths in the eternal rains of the Belgian climate. Nothing mattered but people.

And of all the people in the world, only those whom one loved.

Thus Alex' sweeping, unformulated conviction, holding in it all the misapplication of an essential force, squandered for lack of a sense of proportion.

She despised herself secretly, both for her intense craving for affection and for her prodigality in bestowing it. She was like a child endeavouring to pour a great pailful of water into a very little cup.

Waste and disaster were the inevitable results.

The real love of Alex' young enthusiasm, fair-haired Queenie Torrance, was preceded by her inarticulate, unreasoned adoration for the Belgian *postulante*. But the Belgian *postulante* was never visible, save at a distance, so that even Alex' unreasonable affections found nothing to feed upon.

There was a French girl, much older than herself, for whom Alex then conceived an enthusiasm. Marie-Angèle smiled on her and encouraged the infatuation of the curiously un-English little English girl. But she gave her nothing in return. Alex knew it, and recklessly spent all her weekly pocket-money on flowers and sweets for Marie-Angèle, thinking that the gifts would touch her and awaken in her an affection that it was not her nature to bestow, least of all on an ardent and ungainly child, six years her junior. Alex shed many tears for Marie-Angèle, and years later read some words that suddenly and swiftly recalled the girl who passed in and out of her life in less than a year.

*"I   love   you   for   your   few   caresses,
I love you for my many tears"*

The lines, indeed, were curiously typical of the one-sided relations into which Alex entered so rashly and so inevitably throughout her schooldays.

She was fifteen, and had been nearly three years at Liège, when Queenie Torrance came. She was Alex' senior by a year, and the only other English girl in the school at that time. Alex was told to look after her, and went to the task with a certain naïve eagerness, that she always brought to bear upon any personal equation. In an hour, she was secretly combating an enraptured certainty, of which she felt nevertheless ashamed, that she had found at last the ideal object on whom to expend the vehement powers of affection for which she was always seeking an outlet.

Queenie was slight, very fair, with a full, serious oval face, innocent grey eyes set very far apart, and the high, rounded forehead and small, full-lipped mouth, of a type much in vogue in England at the time of the Regency. This was the more marked by the thick flaxen hair which fell back from her face, and over her shoulders into natural heavy ringlets. She was not very pretty, although she was often thought so, but she was charged with a certain animal magnetism, almost inseparable from her type. Half the girls in the school adored her. Queenie, already attractive to men, and sent to the convent in Belgium in reality on that account, nominally for a year's finishing before her début in London society, was for the most part scornful of these girlish admirers, but Alex she admitted to her friendship.

She was precociously aware that intimacy with Lady Isabel Clare's daughter was likely to accrue to her own advantage later on in London.

The genius for sympathy which led Alex to innumerable small sacrifices and tender smoothings of difficulties for her idol, Queenie at first received with a graceful gratitude which yet held in it something of suspicion, as though she wondered what return would presently be exacted of her.

But it became obvious that Alex expected nothing, and received with eager thankfulness the slightest recognition of her devotion.

Queenie despised her, but was lavish of gentle thanks and caressing exclamations. Hers was not a nature ever to make the mistake of killing the goose that laid the golden eggs.

Finding to her concealed astonishment that Alex only asked toleration, or at the most acceptance of her ardent devotion, and was transported at the slightest occasional token of affection in return, Queenie stinted her of neither. It would have seemed to her the most irrational folly to discourage a love, however one-sided, that found its expression in tireless sympathy, endless championship, and unlimited material gifts and help of any or every description. Alex did all that she could of Queenie's lessons, made her bed and mended her clothes for her whenever she could do so undetected by the authorities, spent her pocket-money on gratifying Queenie's shameless and inordinate passion for sweet things, and once or twice told lies badly and unsuccessfully, to shield Queenie from the effects of her own laziness and constant evasion of regulations.

Alex had been taught, in common with every other child of her upbringing and nationality, that to tell a lie was the worst crime to which a self-respecting human being can stoop. She also believed that a person who has told a lie is a liar, and that all liars go to Hell. Yet by some utterly illogical perversity of which she was hardly even aware, it did not shock or very much distress her, to find that Queenie Torrance told lies, and told them, moreover, with an air of quiet and convincing candour that placed them in a very different category to Alex' own halting, improbable fibs, delivered with a scarlet face and a manifest air of hunting for further corroboration as she spoke.

In the extraordinary scale of moral values unconsciously held by Alex, there were apparently no abstract standards of right and wrong. Where she loved, though she might, against her own will see defects, she was incapable of condemning.

Queenie took a curious, detached interest in coldly gratifying her vanity, by seeking to test the lengths of extravagance to which Alex' admiration would go.

"Supposing I quarrelled with every one here, and they all sent me to Coventry—whose part would you take?"

"Yours, of course."

"But if I were in the wrong?"

"That wouldn't make any difference. In fact, you'd need it more if you were in the wrong."

"I don't see that!" Queenie exclaimed. "If I were in the wrong I should have deserved it."

"But that would make it all the worse for you. It's always the people who are in the wrong who need most to have their part taken," Alex explained confusedly, yet voicing an intimate conviction.

"I don't think you have much idea of justice, Alex," said Queenie drily.

The conversation made Alex very miserable. It was characteristic of her want of logic that while she reproached herself secretly for her own impiety in setting the objects of her affection far above what she conceived to be the abstract standard of right and wrong, yet she never questioned but that any love bestowed upon herself would be measured out in direct proportion to her merits.

And despairingly did Alex sometimes review the smallness of her deserts.

She was disobedient, untruthful, quarrelsome, irreligious. It seemed to Alex that there was no fault to which she could not lay claim. Her lack of elementary religious teaching put her at a disadvantage in the convent atmosphere, and made its frequent religious services and instructions so tedious to her, that she was in constant disgrace for her weary, inattentive attitudes, not unjustly designated as irreverent, in the chapel.

She was not at all popular with the nuns. The "influence" which her class-mistress wielded over so many of the pupils, or the "interest" which the English Assistant Superior would so willingly have extended to her youthful compatriot were alike without effect upon Alex. She was not drawn to any of these holy, black-clad women, to one or other of whom almost all her French and Belgian and American contemporaries devoted a rather stereotyped enthusiasm.

Had the vagrant fancy of Alex lighted upon any one of the elder nuns charged with the direction of the school, the attraction would have been discreetly permitted, if not admittedly sanctioned, by the authorities. It would almost inevitably have led Alex to an awakening of religious sensibilities and the desirability of this result would have outweighed, even if it did not absolutely obscure in the eyes of the nuns, the excessive danger of obtaining such a result by such means.

But the stars in their courses had designed that Alex should regard the Mesdames Marie Baptiste and Marie Evangeliste of her convent days with indifference, and devote her ardent temperament and precocious sensibilities to the worship of Queenie Torrance.

The enthusiasm was smiled upon by no one, and thereby became the more inflamed.

"Je n'aime pas ces amitiés particulières," said the class-mistress of Queenie Torrance severely, to which Miss Torrance replied with polite distress that she was powerless in the matter. It made her ridiculous, she disliked the constant infringement of rules to which Alex' pursuit exposed her, but—one could not be unkind. She did not know why Alex Clare showed her especial affection—she herself had done nothing to encourage these indiscreet displays. Of course, it was pleasant to be liked, but one wished only to do right about it. Queenie mingled candour with perplexity, and succeeded in convincing every one with perfect completeness of her entire innocence of anything but a too potent attraction.

"Ce n'est donc même pas une amitié? C'est Alex qui vous recherche malgré vous!" exclaimed the class-mistress.

Under this aspect the question soon presented itself alike to the *pensionnat* and its authorities, rendering Alex ridiculous. In a system of *surveillance* which admitted of no loophole for open defiance or outspoken rebuke, Alex' evasions of that law of detachment which is the primary one in convent legislation, became the mark of every blue-ribboned *enfant de Marie* who wished to obtain a reputation for zeal by reporting the defection of a companion to her class-mistress.

It was always Alex who was reported. Queenie never sought opportunities to snatch a hurried colloquy during recreation, or manoeuvred to obtain Alex as companion at *la ronde*, or when they played games in the garden. She never infringed one of the strictest rules of the establishment, by giving presents unpermitted, or purchasing forbidden sweets and chocolate to be given away at the afternoon *goûter*.

Queenie accepted the presents, wrote tiny notes to Alex and skilfully gave them to her unperceived, and cut Alex to the heart by telling her sometimes that she made it very hard for one to try and be good and keep all the rules and perhaps get one's blue ribbon next term.

These speeches were to Queenie's credit, and made Alex cry and worship her more admiringly than ever, but they did not tend to lower the transparent, doglike devotion with which Alex would gaze at Queenie's bent profile in the chapel, utterly unconscious of the scandal which her manifest idolatry was creating for the severe nun in the carved stall opposite. She was scolded, placed under strict observation, and every obstacle placed in the way of her exchanging any word with Queenie, until she grew to see herself as a martyr to an affection which every fresh prohibition increased almost to frenzy.

One day she was made the victim of a form of rebuke much dreaded by the *pensionnaires*. A monthly convocation of the school and mistresses, officially known as *la réclame du mois*, and nicknamed by the children "the Last Judgment," was held in the *Grande Salle* downstairs, with the Superior making her state entry after the children had been decorously seated in rows at the end of the long room, and all the other nuns who had anything to do with the school had placed themselves gravely and with folded hands against the walls.

They all stood when the Superior came in, followed by the First Mistress, carrying a sheaf of notes and a great book, which each pupil firmly believed to be devoted principally to the record of her own progress through the school.

Then the Superior, with inclined head and low, distinct voice, spoke a few words of prayer, and settled herself in the large chair behind which the nuns clustered in orderly rows.

The children sat down at the signal given, and listened, at first with smiles as the record of the baby class were read aloud and each mite stood up in her place for all the universe to gaze at her, while the analysis of her month's work, mental and moral, sounded with appalling distinctness through the silence.

"Bébée de Lalonde! première en catéchisme, première en géographie ... calcul, beaucoup mieux ... elle y met beaucoup de bonne volonté!"

"A la bonne heure!"

The Superior is smiling, every one is smiling, Bébée de Lalonde, her brown curls bobbing over her face, is pink with gratification. Her young class-mistress leans forward, the white veil of novice falling over her black habit.

"Ma Mère Supérieure, pour le mois de S. Joseph, elle se corrige de cette vilaine habitude de mordre ses ongles. Elle a fait de vrais efforts...."

"C'est bien. Faites voir.... Venez, ma petite."

Up the long room marches Bébée, two freshly washed tiny pink hands thrust out proudly for the Superior's inspection.

"Très bien, très bien. Vous ferez bien attention au pouce droit, n'est pas?"

The Superior is quite grave, however, every one laughs, and then the serious part of the proceedings begins.

The very little ones are not nervous. Most of them are good, even the naughty ones only get a very gentle homily from the Superior. Then their class-mistress claps her hands smartly and they get up and file out of the room, it not being considered politic to let *les petites* hear the record of that pen of black sheep, *les moyennes*.

The indictments become more serious. Marie Thérèse, twice impertinent to a mistress, taking no trouble over her lessons, worst of all, taking no trouble to cure that trick of which we have complained so often—sitting with her knees crossed.

"Even in the chapel, Ma Mère Supérieure."

This is very bad! It is unladylike, it is against all rules, it is extremely immodest.... And what an example!

Marie Thérèse, says the Superior decisively, can abandon all hope of obtaining the green ribbon of an *aspirante enfant de Marie* until she has reformed her ways. The mention of a première in literature gains no approving smile from any one and Marie Thérèse sits down in tears.

Gabrielle, Marthe, Sadie—all through the three classes of the *moyenne* division of the school, with very few stainless reports and two or three disastrous ones.

Then *les grandes*. The first of these, in the lowest section, is a name to which the reader, a French woman, always takes exception. She finally compresses her lips and renders it as: "Kevinnie!"

Queenie is always cool and unmoved as she stands up, and Alex always looks at her. At this particular *séance*, the April one, she took her glances more or less surreptitiously, miserably aware that she had not enough self-control to refrain from them and so avoid risking a rebuke later on.

Queenie held no première. She was always last in her form, undistinguished at music, drawing, needlework, anything requiring application or talent alike. But her perfectly serene complacency was more or less justified by the exaggerated applause of her companions at her faultless "conduct" marks and the assurance of her class-mistress, always given readily, that she was "très docile, très appliquée."

Queenie's popularity was independent of anything extraneous to herself.

The Superior leant forward and asked a question in a low voice.

"Non, ma Mère Supérieure, non."

The denial of a possible accusation, of which Alex guessed the purport, was emphatic. She felt glad and relieved, but had no suspicions as to the indictment following on her own name.

"Alexandra Clare," said Mère Alphonsine sonorously, and Alex stood up.

She no longer felt self-conscious over the ordeal, and was indifferent to the habitual litany of complaints as to her unlearnt lessons, disregard of the rule of silence, and frequent bad marks for disorder and unpunctuality. But to the accusations which she knew by heart, and shared with the majority of the *moyenne classe*, came a quite unexpected addition, hissed out with a sort of dramatic horror by Mère Alphonsine:

"Alex recherche Kevinnie sans cesse, ma Mère Supérieure."

Only those familiar with the code of *pensionnaire* discipline in Belgium during the years when Alex Clare and her contemporaries were at school, can gauge the full heinousness of the offence, gravest in the conventual decalogue.

Even Alex, although she had been scolded and punished and made the subject of innumerable homilies, some of them pityingly reproachful, and others explanatorily so, on the same question, felt as though she had never before realized the extent of her own perversion.

She stood up, her hands in the regulation position, pushed under the hideous black-stuff pèlerine that fell from her stiff, hard, white collar to the shapeless waistband of her skirt, the whole uniform carefully designed to conceal and obscure the lines of the figure beneath it.

Overwhelmed with uncomprehending misery and acute shame, she heard two or three of the mistresses add each her quota, for the most part regretfully and with an evident sense of duty overcoming reluctance, to the evidence against her.

"She seeks opportunity to place herself next to Queenie at almost every recreation, ma Mère Supérieure."

"I am afraid that even in the chapel she lets this folly get the better of her—one can see how she lets herself go to distractions all the time...."

So the charges went on.

The summing up of Ma Mère Supérieure was icily condemnatory. She had tried every means with Alex, had spoken to her with kindness and tenderness; in private, had reasoned with her and finally threatened her, and now a public denouncement must be tried, since all these means had proved to be without effect.

Alex was principally conscious of the single, lightning-swift flash of reproach that had shot from the eyes of Queenie Torrance into hers.

How silently and viciously Queenie would resent this public coupling of her immaculate reputation with Alex' idiotic infatuation, only Alex knew.

With the frantic finality of youth, she wondered whether she could go on living. Oh, if only she might die at once, without hearing further blame or reproach, without encountering the ridicule of her companions or the cold withdrawal of Queenie's precariously-held friendship. Alex cried herself sick with terror and shame and utterly ineffectual remorse.

The despair that invades an undeveloped being is the blackest in the world, because of its utter want of perspective.

Alex could see nothing beyond the present. She felt all the weight of an inexpressible guilt upon her, and all the utter isolation of spirit which surrounds the sinner who stands exposed and condemned.

She knew that nobody would take her part. She was young enough to reflect forlornly that an accusation mattered nothing if unjust, since the consciousness of innocence would sustain one, serene and unfaltering, through any ordeal.

But she had no consciousness of innocence. She saw herself eternally different from her companions, eternally destined to lose her way, wickedly and shamefully she supposed, without volition of her own she knew, amongst those standards to which the right thinking conformed, and which she, only, failed to recognize. With sick wistfulness Alex sought Queenie's glance as they came one by one into the refectory, after the *réclame* was over.

Queenie's fair, opaque face was as colourless as ever, her eyes were cast down.

Frantically, Alex willed her to cast one look of pity or forgiveness in her direction, but Queenie passed on to the refectory where the children's mid-day meal was waiting for them without a sign.

Amidst all the blur of emotions, passionate remorse and hopeless loneliness, which made up Alex' schooldays, that Saturday mid-day meal stood out in its black despair.

The choking attempts to swallow a mass of vegetable cooking, made salt and sodden with her own streaming tears, the sobs that strangled her and broke in spite of all her efforts into the decorous silence of the refectory, even the awed and scandalized glances that the younger children cast at her distorted face, remained saliently before her memory for years.

At last the nun in charge rose from her place at the end of the room and came down and told Alex that she might leave the table. The long progress down the endless length of the refectory destroyed the last remnants of Alex' self-control.

The tide of emotional agony that swept over her was to ebb and flow again, and many times again.

But only once or twice was that high-water mark to be reached, that bitter wave to engulf her, and each time add to the undermining of that small stability of spirit with which Alex had been endowed.

She left the misery of that black Saturday behind her, and was left with her childish nerves a little shattered, her childish confidence of outlook rather more overshadowed, her childish strength less steady, and, above all, set fast in her childish mind the ineradicable, unexplained conviction that because she had loved Queenie Torrance and had been punished and rebuked for it, therefore to love was wrong.

III

Queenie Torrance

School days in Belgium went on, through the steamy, rain-sodden days of spring to the end of term and the *grandes vacances* looked forward to with such frantic eagerness even by the children who liked the convent best. Alex was again bitterly conscious of an utter want of conformity setting her apart from her fellow-creatures.

The misery of parting for eight weeks from Queenie Torrance overwhelmed her. Casually, Queenie said:

"I may not come back, next term. I shall be seventeen by then, and I don't see why I should be at school any longer if I can get round father."

"What would you do?"

"Why, come out, of course," said Queenie. "I am quite old enough, and every one says I look older than I am."

She moved her head about slightly so as to get sidelong views of her own reflection in the big window-pane. There were no looking-glasses at the convent.

It was true that, in spite of a skin smooth and unlined as a baby's and the childish, semicircular comb that gathered back the short flaxen ringlets from her rounded, innocent brow, Queenie's slender, but very well-developed figure and the unvarying opaque pallor of her complexion, made her look infinitely nearer maturity than the slim, long-legged American girls, or over-plump, giggling French and Belgian ones. Alex gazed at her with mute, exaggerated despair on her face.

"Your parents will permit that you make your début at once, yes?" queried Marthe Poupard, as one resigned to the incredible folly and weakness of British and American parents.

"I can manage my father," said Queenie gently, and with the perfect conviction of experience in her voice.

As the day of the breaking-up drew nearer, discipline insensibly relaxed, and Queenie suddenly became less averse from responding in some degree to Alex' wistful advances.

On the last day, one of broiling heat, the two spent the afternoon alone together unrebuked, in a corner of the great *verger* where the pupils were scattered in groups, feeling as though the holidays had already begun.

"I shall have the journey with you," said Alex, piteously.

"Madame Hippolyte is taking us over, with one of the lay-sisters," said Queenie, naming the most vigilant of the older French nuns. "So it will be much better if we don't talk together on the boat. You know there will be the three Munroe girls as well, because they are going to spend their holidays in Devonshire or somewhere."

"How do you know it will be Madame Hippolyte?" said Alex disconsolately.

The authority deputed to conduct pupils on the journey to and from Liège was one of the many items in the convent curriculum always shrouded in impenetrable mystery until the actual moment of departure.

"I overheard two of them talking about it, in the linen-room this morning," placidly said Queenie. "I kept behind the door."

Part of her curious attractiveness was, that she never attempted to disguise or deny certain practices which Alex had been taught to consider as dishonourable.

Alex counted this as but one more stone in the edifice erected for the worship of her idol. It was not until she saw Queenie Torrance long after, in other relations and other surroundings, that she dimly realized how much of that streak of extraordinary candour was the direct product of a magnificently justified self-confidence in the potency of her own attraction, needing no enhancement from moral or mental attributes.

"Do you always live in London, Alex?"

"Yes, in Clevedon Square. You know, I told you about it, Queenie."

"Yes, I know, but I only wondered if perhaps you had a house in the country as well."

"No. Father and mother go to Scotland in the summer, and generally they send us to the seaside with Nurse and a governess or some one."

"I see," said Queenie reflectively. She had wondered if perhaps the Clares had a country house to which she, as a favourite school friend, would be asked to stay.

"Father hates the country," said Alex. "We are sure to be in London for a little while in September, before I come back here. Would you—would you—" She gulped and clasped her hands nervously. Certain of Lady Isabel's rules and recommendations rushed to her mind, but she desperately tried to ignore them.

"I suppose you would not come to tea with me one day, if I were allowed to ask you? Oh, if *only* your mother knew my mother!"

Smoothly Queenie took her cue. "Of course, mother won't let me go to tea with any one—unless she knows them herself—but I don't know.... What Club does your father belong to?"

"Two or three, I think," said Alex, surprised. "He often goes to Arthur's or the Turf Club."

"So does father. Perhaps we could manage it that way," said Queenie reflectively.

She had every intention of cultivating her friendship with Alex Clare in London.

"Then you'd like to come, Queenie?" breathed Alex ecstaticly.

"Of course, I would," Queenie told her affectionately. "My dear, you know I have hated all the fuss here, and our never being allowed to speak a word to one another. But what could I do?" She shrugged her shoulders.

Then Queenie had really cared all the time!

Alex in that moment was compensated for all the tears and storms and disgraces of the year. That afternoon spent under the thick, leafy boughs of the old apple-trees with Queenie, enabled Alex to face with some degree of courage the prospect of their approaching separation. She knew that any sign of unhappiness for such a reason would be imputed to her as wrong-doing by the authorities, and as unnatural and heartless indifference to home on the part of her companions.

So Alex, who had no trust in any standards of her own, was ashamed of the tears which she nightly stifled in her hard pillow, and felt them to be one more of those degrading weaknesses with which her Creator had malignantly endowed her in order that she might be as a pariah among her fellows.

She felt no resentment, only blind wonder and fatalistic apathy. Nevertheless, all through Alex' childhood and early girlhood, unhappy though she was, there dwelt within her a curious certainty that, somewhere, happiness awaited her, which she, and she alone, would have full capacity to appreciate.

Side by side with that, was her intense capacity for suffering, but that she was learning to think of as only a cruel, tearing affliction despised alike by God and man.

Of the immense force latent in the power of intense feeling Alex knew nothing, nor did any of the teaching which she received vouchsafe to her any illumination.

She and Queenie and the three Munroe girls made the journey to England with Madame Hippolyte, who showed Alex a marked kindness not usual with her.

At fifteen, wakeful nights and storms of crying leave their traces, and Alex, pale-faced and with encircled eyes, was pitiful in her propitiatory attempts to join in the eager anticipations of holiday enjoyment exchanged between her companions.

Perhaps, thought the French nun, the little black sheep had not a very happy home. A bad report would follow Alex to England she well knew, and it might be that the poor child was dreading its results.

Her manner to Alex grew gentle and compassionate, and Alex noticed it with a relieved, uncomprehending gratitude that held something abject in its surprised, almost incredulous acceptance of any kindness.

Madame Hippolyte, though she sternly rebuked herself for the uncharitable impulse, felt a certain contempt of the way in which her advances were received.

She knew nothing of the self-assertive, arrogant manner that would presently revive, in the childish sense of security in home surroundings, and would yet be merely another manifestation of the unbalanced complexity that was Alex Clare.

But as the crossing came to an end and they found themselves in the train speeding towards London, Alex was silent, her small face white and her eyes tragical.

The American girls made delighted use of the strip of looking-glass in the carriage, and exchanged predictions as to the pleased amazement that would be caused by Sadie's growth, the length of Marie's plait of red hair, and Diana's added inches of skirt.

Queenie Torrance only glanced at her reflection once or twice, though an acute observer might have seen that she was not indifferent to the advantage of facing a looking-glass, after the many weeks in which none had been available. But she was merely completely serene in the immutability of her own attractiveness. Queenie did not need to depend upon her looks, which seldom or never varied from soft, colourless opacity and opulence of contour. The pale, heavy rings of her fair hair always fell back in the same way from her open, rounded forehead, her well-modelled hands, with fingers broad at the base, and pointed, gleaming nails were always cool and white.

The Americans were all three pretty girls, and something of race that showed in Alex' bearing and gestures made her remarkable amongst any assembly of children, but it was at Queenie that every man who passed the little group in the railway carriage glanced a second time.

Good Madame Hippolyte, as serenely unaware of this as only a woman whose life had been passed in a religious Order could be, regarded Queenie as by far the least of the responsibilities on her hands, and did not conceal her satisfaction when Marie and Sadie and Diana were immediately claimed at the terminus by a group of excited, noisy cousins, and hurried away to an enormous waiting carriage-and-pair.

"Et vous?" she demanded, turning to the other two.

"Dad'll come for me," said Queenie confidently, inadvertently uttering a nickname that would not have been permitted to the Clare children, and was, in fact, never in those days heard in the class of society to which they belonged.

Queenie shot an imperceptible glance of confusion at Alex, who was clinging speechlessly to her hand.

Next moment she had recovered herself.

"There's my father!" she cried.

Colonel Torrance was making his way rapidly towards them, a tall, soldierly-looking man, a trifle too conspicuously well groomed, a trifle too upright in his bearing, a trifle too remarkable altogether, with very black moustache and eyebrows and very white hair.

He raised his tall white hat with its black band, at the sight of his daughter, expanded his white waistcoat and grey frock-coat with the *malmaison* buttonhole yet further, and whipped off his pale grey glove to take the limp hand extended to him by Alex, as Queenie self-possessedly introduced her.

Alex hardly heard Colonel Torrance's elaborately courteous allusion to Sir Francis Clare, whom he had had the pleasure of seeing several times at the Club, but she wondered eagerly if that introduction would be considered sufficient to allow of her inviting Queenie to Clevedon Square. She felt as though her spirit were being torn from her body when Queenie said, "Good-bye, Alex, dear. Mind you write. *Au revoir, ma mère.*"

Compliments were exchanged between Madame Hippolyte and Queenie's father, the gentleman flourished his top hat again, and then said to his daughter:

"My dear, I have a hansom waiting; the impudent fellow says his horse won't stand. I trust you have no large amount of luggage."

Queenie shook her head, smiling slightly, and in a moment, the brevity of which seemed incredible to Alex and left her with an instant's absolute suspension of physical faculties, they disappeared among the crowd.

Madame Hippolyte grasped the arm of her distraught-looking pupil.

"But rouse yourself, Alex!" she said vigorously. "Who is to come for you?"

"The carriage," muttered Alex automatically, well aware that neither would Lady Isabel sacrifice an hour of her afternoon to waiting at a crowded London station in July, nor old Nurse permit the other children to do so, had they wished it.

"And where is it, this carriage?" sceptically demanded Madame Hippolyte, harassed and exhausted, and aware that she had yet to find a four-wheeled cab of sufficiently cleanly and sober appearance to satisfy her, in which she might proceed herself to the convent branch-house in the east of London. But presently Alex came partially out of her dream and pointed out the brougham and bay horse and the footman in buff livery at the door.

"But you will not drive alone—in this *quartier*?" cried the nun, in horrified protest at this exhibition of English want of propriety.

Her fears proved groundless.

The neat, black-bonneted head of a maid appeared at the brougham window, and with a sigh of infinite relief Madame Hippolyte bade farewell to the last and most anxiously regarded of her charges.

"How you've grown, Miss Alex!" cried the maid, but her tone was scarcely one of admiration, as she gazed at the stooping shoulders and pale, travel-stained face under the ugly sailor hat of dark blue straw. "We shall have to make you look like yourself, with some of your own clothes, before your mamma sees you," she added kindly.

Alex scarcely answered, and sat squeezing her hands together.

She knew she must come out of this dream of misery that seemed to envelop her, and which was so naughty and undutiful. Of course it was unnatural not to be glad to come home again, and it wasn't as though she had been so very happy at Liège.

It was only Queenie.

No one must know, or she would certainly be blamed and ridiculed for her foolish and headlong fancy.

Alex wondered dimly why she was so constituted as to differ from every one else.

The cab turned into Clevedon Square. Alex looked out of the window.

The big square bore already the look of desertion most associated in her mind with summer in London. Shutters and blinds obscured the windows of the first and second floors of many houses, and against one of the corner houses a ladder was propped and an unwontedly dazzling cream-colour proclaimed fresh paint.

Some of the houses showed striped sun-blinds, and window-boxes of scarlet geraniums. Alex saw that there were flowers in their own balcony as well as an awning.

When the carriage drew up at the front door, she jumped out and replied hastily to the man-servant's respectful greeting, a slight feeling of excitement possessing her for the first time at the prospect of seeing Barbara, and impressing her with her added inches of height.

She ran quickly up the stairs, hoping that Lady Isabel would not chance to come out of the drawing-room as she went past. On the second landing, safely past the double door of the drawing-room, she paused a moment to take breath, and heard a subdued call from overhead.

Barbara was hanging over the banisters with Archie.

"Hallo, Alex!"

Alex went up to the schoolroom landing, and she and Barbara looked curiously at one another, before exchanging a perfunctory kiss.

Alex suddenly felt grubby and rather shabby in her old last year's serge frock, which had been considered good enough for the journey, when she saw Barbara in her clean white muslin, with a very pale blue sash, and her hair tied up with a big pale blue bow.

Barbara's hair had grown, which annoyed Alex. It fell into one long, pale curl down her back, and no longer provoked a contrast with Alex' superior length of shining wave. Deprived of the supervision of Nurse, with her iron insistence on "fifty strokes of the brush every night, and Rowland's Macassor on Saturdays," Alex' hair had somehow lost its shine, and hung limply in a tangled, uneven pigtail.

Alex thought that Barbara eyed her in a rather superior way.

She felt much more enthusiastic in greeting little Archie. He was prettier and pinker and more engaging than ever, and Alex felt glad that he had not yet been sent to school, to have his fair curls cropped, and his little velvet suit exchanged for cricketing flannels.

He pulled Alex into the schoolroom, with the enthusiasm for a new face characteristic of a child to whom shyness is unknown, and Alex received the curt, all-observant greeting which she had learnt to know would always await her from old Nurse.

"So you are back from your foreign parts, are you, Miss Alex?"

Nurse always said "Miss Alex" when addressing her returned charge at first, and as invariably relapsed into her old peremptory form of address before the end of the evening.

"My sakes, child, what have they been doing to you? You look like a scarecrow."

"Has she grown?" asked Barbara jealously. She knew that grown-up people were always, for some mysterious reason, pleased when one had "grown."

"Grown! Yes, and got her back bent like a bow," said Nurse vigorously. "An hour on the backboard's what you'll do every day, and bed at seven o'clock tonight. Have they been giving you enough to eat?"

"Of course," said Alex, tossing her head.

She did not like the convent when she was there, but a contradictory instinct always made her when at home uphold it violently, as a privileged spot to which she alone had access.

"You look half-starved, to me," Nurse said unbelievingly.

Nothing would ever have persuaded her of what was, in fact, the truth, that Alex received more abundant, more wholesome, and infinitely better cooked food in Belgium than in London.

Barbara sat on the end of the sofa, swinging her legs and fidgetting with the tassel of the blind-cord.

"Have you brought back any prizes, Alex?" she enquired negligently.

And Alex replied with an equal air of indifference:

"One for composition, and I've got a certificate of proficiency for music."

This was not at all the way in which she had planned to make her announcements. She had thought that her prizes would impress Barbara very much, and she had foreseen a sort of small ceremony of display when she would bring out the big red-and-gilt book. But Barbara only nodded, and presently said:

"Cedric has got quantities of prizes: the headmaster wrote and told father that he was a 'boy of marked abilities and remarkable power of concentration,' and father is going to give him a whole sovereign, but that's because he made his century."

"When will he be here?"

"Next week. His holidays begin on Tuesday and he's got a whole fortnight longer than we have."

"We?" asked Alex coldly. "How can *you* have holidays? You're not at school."

"I have lessons," cried Barbara angrily. "You know I have, and Ma'moiselle is going to give me a prize for writing, and a prize for history, and a prize for application. So there!"

"Prizes!" said Alex scornfully. "When you're all by yourself! I never heard such nonsense."

She no longer felt wretched and subdued, but full of irritation at Barbara's conceit and absorption in herself.

"It's not nonsense!"

"It is. If you'd been at school you'd know it was."

"One word more of this and you'll go to bed, the pair of you," declared old Nurse, the autocrat whom Alex had for the moment forgotten. "It's argle-bargle the minute you set foot in the place, Miss Alex. Now you just come along and be made fit to be seen before your poor mamma and papa set eyes on you looking like a charity-school child, as hasn't seen a brush or a bit of soap for a month of Sundays."

Useless to protest even at this trenchant description of herself. Useless to attempt resistance during the long process of undressing, dressing again, brushing and combing, inspection of finger-nails and general, dissatisfied scrutiny that ensued. Alex, in a stiff, clean frock, the counterpart, to her secret vexation, of Barbara's, open-work stockings, and new shoes that hurt her feet, was enjoined "to hold back her shoulders and not poke" and dispatched to the drawing-room with Barbara and Archie as soon as the schoolroom tea was over.

She felt as though she had never been away.

No one had asked her anything about the convent, and all through tea Barbara and Archie had talked about the coming holidays, or had made allusions to events of which Alex knew nothing, but which had evidently been absorbing their attention for the last few weeks.

They seemed to Alex futile in the extreme.

Downstairs, Lady Isabel kissed her, and said, "Well, my darling, I'm very glad to have you at home again. Have you been a good girl this term, and brought back a report that will please papa?" and then had turned to speak to some one without waiting for an answer.

Alex sat beside her mother while she talked to the one remaining visitor, and felt discontented and awkward.

Barbara and Archie were looking at pictures together in the corner of the room, very quiet and well behaved. The caller stayed late, and just as she had gone Sir Francis came in from his Club, the faint, familiar smell of tobacco, and Russia leather, and expensive eau-de-Cologne that seemed to pervade him, striking Alex with a fresh sense of recognition as she rose to receive his kiss. He greeted her very kindly, but Alex was quite aware of a dissatisfaction as intense as, though less outspoken than, that of old Nurse as he put up his double eye-glasses and gazed at his eldest daughter.

"We must see if the country or the seaside will bring back some roses to your cheeks," he said in characteristic phraseology.

But when the children were dismissed from the drawing-room, Sir Francis straightened his own broad back, and tapped Alex' rounded shoulder-blades.

"Hold yourself up, my child," he said very decidedly. "I want to see a nice flat, and straight back."

He made no other criticism, and none was needed.

Alex had gauged the extent of his dismay.

IV

Holidays

"Mother, may I ask Queenie Torrance to tea?"

Alex had rehearsed the words so often to herself that they had almost become meaningless.

Her heart beat thickly with the anticipation of a refusal, when at last she found courage and opportunity to utter the little stilted phrase, with a tongue that felt dry and in a voice that broke nervously in her throat.

"What do you say, darling?" absently inquired Lady Isabel; and Alex had to say it again.

"Queenie Torrance?" said Lady Isabel, still vaguely.

"Mother, you remember—I told you about her. She is the only other English girl besides me at the convent, and she knows all about father and you and everything, and her father belongs to the same Club—"

Snobbishness was not in Alex' composition, but she adopted her mother's standards eagerly and instinctively, in the hope of gaining her point.

"But, my darling, what are you talkin' about? You know mother doesn't let you have little girls here unless she knows somethin' about them. Give me the little diamond brooch, Alex; the one in the silver box there."

Lady Isabel, absorbed in the completion of her evening toilette, remained unconscious of the havoc she had wrought. Alex felt rather sick.

The intensity of feeling to which she was a victim, for the most part reacted on her physically, though she was as unconscious of this as was her mother.

But with the cunning borne of urgent desire, Alex knew that persistence, which with Sir Francis would invariably win a courteous rebuke and an immutable refusal, could sometimes bring forth rather querulous concession from Lady Isabel's weakness.

"But, mummy, darling, I do want Queenie to come here and see Barbara and Cedric."

It was not true, but Alex was using the arguments which she felt would be most likely to appeal to her mother.

"She wants to know them so much, and—and I saw her father at the station when we arrived, and he was very polite."

"Who was with you? I don't like your speakin' like that to people whom father and I don't know."

"Oh, it was only a second," said Alex hastily. "Madame Hippolyte was there, and Colonel Torrance just came up to take Queenie away."

"Torrance—Torrance?" said Lady Isabel reflectively. "Who's Torrance?"

The question made Alex' heart sink afresh. It was one which, coming from her parents, she heard applied to new acquaintances, or occasionally to protégés for whom some intimate friends might crave the favour of an invitation to one of the big Clare "crushes" during the season, and the inquiry was seldom one which boded well for the regard in which the newcomer would be held.

"Mother, you'd like her, I think, really and truly you would. She's awfully pretty."

"Alex!"

Lady Isabel for once sounded really angry.

"I'm so sorry; it slipped out—I didn't mean it—I never really say it. I never *do*, mother."

Alex became agitated, trying to fend off the accusation which she foresaw was coming.

"I suppose you learn those horrid slang words from this girl you've taken such a violent fancy to."

"No, no."

"Well, darling, both father and I are very much disgusted with some of the tricks you've picked up at the convent, and you'll have to find some way of curin' yourself before you put up your hair and come out. As for the way you're holdin' yourself, I'm simply shocked at it, and so is your father; I shall see about sendin' you to MacPherson's gymnasium for proper exercises as soon as you get back from the country."

Lady Isabel gazed with dissatisfaction at her daughter.

"You mustn't be a disappointment to us, darling," she said. "You know you'll be coming out in another two years' time, and it's so important—"

She broke off, eyeing Alex anxiously. Already she had forgotten the question of the invitation to Queenie Torrance. Alex, in an agony, rushed recklessly at her point.

"But, mother, you haven't said yet—may I ask Queenie on Saturday? You know we shan't be here after Saturday. May I?"

Lady Isabel moved to the door with more annoyance than she often displayed.

"My dear child, you're old enough to know that these things aren't done, and besides, I've already said no. Father and I dislike these sudden, violent friendships, in any case. Run along upstairs, my darling, and if you and Barbara want a little tea-party on Saturday, you may ask those nice Fitzgerald children. Tell Nurse that I said you might."

Lady Isabel kissed Alex, and went downstairs, the trailing folds of her evening dress carefully held up in one hand as she descended the broad, curving stairs.

From the upper landing Alex watched her for a few moments, her face burning with mortification and the effort to restrain her tears. Then she broke into sobs and ran away upstairs.

Mother had not understood in the very least. She never understood, never would understand.

No one understood.

Alex felt, as so often, that she would barter everything she possessed for the finding of some one who would understand.

In her craving for self-expression, she talked to Barbara about Queenie Torrance, but represented their intercourse as that of an equal friendship, with unbounded affection and confidence on both sides.

Barbara listened believingly enough, and even exhibited signs of a faint jealousy, and gradually Alex' inventions brought her a slight feeling of comfort, as though the ideal friendship which she so readily described to her little sister must have some real existence.

The old sense of supremacy began to assert itself again, and Barbara fell into the old ways of following Alex' lead in everything. She lost her shrinking convent manner, born of the sense of helpless insecurity, and when Cedric's return brought Barbara back to her earliest allegiance— the league which she and Cedric had always formed against Alex' overbearing ways in the nursery—her defection was resented by her sister with no lack of spirit.

"Idiotic little copy-cat! Just because Cedric's come, you pretend you only care for cricket and nonsense like that, as though he wanted to play cricket with a little girl like you."

"He doesn't mind playing cricket with me; he says I can bowl very well for a girl, and it gives him practice. Anyway," said Barbara shrewdly, "he likes talking about it, and how am I to be his pal unless I understand what he means?"

"You're not to say that horrid, vulgar word. You know mother would be very angry."

"I shall say what I like. It's not your business. You're a prig, ever since you went to that hateful convent!"

"You're not to speak to me like that, you're not!" shouted Alex, stamping her foot.

The dispute degenerated into one of the furious quarrels of their nursery days, and Alex, completely mastered by her temper, flew at Barbara, as she had not done since they were seven and ten years old respectively, and hit her and pulled her long curl viciously.

Barbara stood stock-still on the instant. She had infinitely more self-control than Alex, and a strong instinct for being invariably in the right.

But she uttered shriek upon piercing shriek that brought old Nurse, heavy-footed but astonishingly swift, upon the scene, and reduced Alex to dire disgrace for the rest of the day.

She cried again, suffering remorse and shame that seemed almost unbearable, and told herself hopelessly that she could never be good anywhere.

"Such an example to your little sister, who's never given me a moment's trouble all the while you've been away," Nurse declared, at the end of a long monologue during which Alex learnt and implicitly believed that a temper like hers, unbridled at the age of fifteen, must have irrevocably passed beyond one's own control into that of the Devil himself.

"When you remember," Nurse wound up, "how you nearly killed her with your naughty ways and had her on her back for a year, and she with never a word of complaint against you, poor lamb, one would think you'd want to make it up to her, instead of hitting one as never even hits you back. But you've no heart, Alex, as I've always said and always shall say about you."

Heart or no heart, old Nurse thoroughly succeeded in working upon Alex' feelings, and in sobbing abjection she begged Barbara's forgiveness.

Barbara, agreeably conscious of martyrdom, found it easy to grant, with a gentleness that redoubled Alex' shame, and the incident, except for Alex' swollen eyes and subdued tones next day, was closed. Cedric, characteristically, remained oblivious of it throughout.

He had grown into a good-looking boy, not tall for his eleven years, but sturdy and well set up, with steady, straight-gazing eyes behind the spectacles that his short sight still necessitated, to the grief of Lady Isabel. His mind was obsessed by cricket, and from his conversation one might have deduced that no other occupation had filled the summer term. Nevertheless, he brought home a large pile of prizes, and a report that caused Sir Francis to smile his excessively rare smile and utter two words that Cedric never forgot, and never mentioned to any one else: "Well done."

Two days after Cedric's return, Sir Francis and Lady Isabel went away for their annual round of country visits, and old Nurse, with the new, young nurse who devoted her services exclusively to Pamela, and a nursery-maid to wait upon them, went with the children to stay at Fiveapples Farm in Devonshire.

The farm was glorious.

The girls might run about the hay-fields and in the lanes, though Nurse, mindful of Lady Isabel's injunction as to complexion and the danger of freckles, always insisted on hats and gloves; and Cedric, followed everywhere like a little shadow by Archie, rode the farm horses and even went into Exeter to market with Farmer Young on Fridays.

Alex insensibly began to cease her preoccupied outlook for letters from Queenie, and the convent life began to relax its hold on her memory and imagination, as older influences resumed their sway.

Correspondence with Queenie had never been satisfactory.

Although not forbidden, Alex knew that it was considered a foolish and undesirable practice, and that her letters, although, as a matter of fact, generally given to her unopened, were always liable to supervision by the authorities as a matter of course.

Old Nurse might be unable to read, although no one had ever heard her admit as much, but she always slit open any letter that came for Alex or Barbara and made a feint of perusing it; unless the envelope, as rarely happened, bore Lady Isabel's superscription.

"In the absence of your mamma," said old Nurse severely, and she never failed to refuse unhesitatingly any request from Alex to be allowed to go to the post office for the purpose of buying stamps.

Queenie had only written twice. The second letter reached Alex at Fiveapples Farm, when she had nearly given up hope for it.

"DEAR ALEX,

"Thank you very much for your letters. It is nice of you to write to me so often. Please forgive me for not writing oftener to you, but I haven't got much time. It's so hot in London now. You are very lucky to be in the country. I think we shall go soon, but I don't know yet where we shall go.

"Do you know that you are quite near where the Munroes are staying? Diana wrote to me the other day. Perhaps you will see them. Please give them my love. Do you remember how funny Diana was at her singing lessons? I often think of the convent, don't you? Now I must end, Alex, with fond love from your affectionate school friend,

"QUEENIE.

"P.S. I am not going back next term. I am very glad, except for not seeing you. I hope we shall see each other in London."

Alex read and re-read the postscript, and tried not to think that the rest of the letter was disappointing.

"Your great friend doesn't write you nearly such long letters as you write her," observed Barbara, eyeing the four small sheets which Queenie's unformed, curiously immature-looking writing had barely succeeded in covering.

"She hasn't got time," said Alex quickly and defensively.

"More like she's got a sensible governess who doesn't let her waste good pen and paper on such rubbish," old Nurse severely pointed the moral.

"What do girls want to write to one another for?" said Cedric. "They can't Have anything to say."

Barbara, who was secretly curious, seized the opportunity.

"What does she write about, Alex?"

Alex would have liked to tell them to mind their own business, but she knew that any accusation of making mysteries would bring down Nurse's wrath upon her, and as likely as not the confiscation of the letter.

She read it aloud hastily, with a pretence of skipping here and there, leaving out the "dear Alex" at the beginning, and the whole of the last sentence and the postscript.

"I suppose you've left out all the darlings and the loves and kisses," Cedric remarked scornfully, more from conventionality than anything else.

Alex was not averse to having it supposed that Queenie had been more lavish with endearments than she had in reality shown herself.

"Who are the Munroes?" asked Barbara. "Are they nice?"

"The American girls who crossed from Liège with me. I remember now, they were going to spend their holidays with an aunt somewhere in Devonshire."

"Perhaps we shall see them. How old are they?"

"Sadie and Diana are much older than you," Alex told her crushingly. "In fact, they're older than I am. But the little one, Marie, is only twelve."

"Where does the aunt live?"

"How should I know?" said Alex. She reflected bitterly that even if her schoolmates should ever meet her in Devonshire, it would be impossible for her to make any advance to them, with old Nurse, even more strictly mindful of the conventions than Lady Isabel.

But for once it seemed as though fate were on Alex' side.

"I hear," wrote Lady Isabel, in one of her hasty, collective letters, addressed impartially to "My darling Children," "that Mrs. Alfred Cardew, who lives at a very pretty house called Trevose, not more than a few miles from where you are, has her three little nieces with her for the holidays, and that they are at the same convent as Alex. So if you like, darlings, as I know Mrs. Alfred Cardew quite well, you may ask Nurse to let you arrange some little picnic or other and invite the three children."

Alex, taken by surprise, felt doubtful. She did not know whether she wanted to expose herself to the criticisms which she thought, disparagingly gazing round at her brothers and sisters and their autocratic guardian, they would inevitably call forth from strangers. Suppose they came, and Barbara was shy and foolish, and Cedric doggedly bored, and then the Munroes went back to Liège next term and laughed at Alex, and told the other girls what queer relations she had. And again, thought Alex, Nurse would probably think the Americanisms, which had amused Queenie and Alex at the convent, merely vulgar, and Barbara and Cedric would wonder.

"You *are* extraordinary, Alex!" said Barbara petulantly. "You're always talking about your friends at the convent and saying how nice they are, and then when there's a chance of our seeing them too, you don't seem to want to have them."

"Yes, I do," said Alex hastily, and consoled herself with the reflection that very likely the plan would never materialize.

But as luck would have it, Alex, the very next day, saw Sadie Munroe waving to her excitedly from the carriage where she was driving with a very gaily-dressed lady, obviously the aunt.

The following week, a charming note invited Alex, Barbara, Cedric and Archie to lunch and spend the afternoon at Trevose. They should be fetched in the pony-cart, and driven back after tea.

At least, Alex reflected thankfully, old Nurse would not be there to put her to shame.

About Archie, with his clean sailor suit and shining curls, she felt no anxiety. He was always a success.

But she inspected Cedric, and especially Barbara, with anxiety.

The day was a very hot one, and Cedric in cricketing flannels looked sufficiently like every other boy of his age and standing to reassure his critical sister.

But Barbara!

Surely the three pretty, sharp-eyed Americans would despise little, pale, plain Barbara, with her one ridiculous curl of pale hair, and the big, babyish bow of blue ribbon against which Alex had protested so vigorously in her own case that Nurse had finally substituted black.

No amount of protest, however, even had Alex dared to offer it, would have induced Nurse to depart from the rule which decreed that the sisters should be dressed alike, and Barbara's clean cotton frock was the counterpart of Alex'.

Alex thought the similarity ridiculous, and hated the twin Leghorn hats, each with a precisely similar wreath round the crown, of thick, pale blue forget-me-nots, of which the clusters were unrelieved by any blade or hint of green.

Even their brown shoes and stockings and brown gauntlet gloves were alike.

Alex felt disgusted at the aspect which she thought they must present, and was unable to enjoy the four-mile drive in the pony-cart Mrs. Cardew had sent over for them. She could not have told whether she was more apprehensive of the effect Barbara and Cedric might have on the Munroes, or the Munroes on Barbara and Cedric.

"What do you suppose we shall do all the afternoon?" asked Barbara. She was in one of her rare moods of excitement, and her futile chattering and unceasing questions filled Alex with impatience.

The two were on the verge of a quarrel by the time the last hill was reached.

Then came a long, shady avenue, with two pretty little lodges and a wide stone gate, and the groom drove the pony smartly round a triangular gravel sweep which lay before the arched entrance to the big Georgian house.

Sadie, Marie and Diana were sitting on the low stone wall that divided the drive from what looked like a wilderness of pink and red roses, and Alex noticed with relief that they were all three dressed exactly alike in white muslin frocks, although she also saw that in spite of the blazing sun they were without hats or gloves. They jumped off the wall as the pony-cart drew up before the door and greeted the Clare children eagerly, and with no trace of shyness.

V

Other People

It seemed to Alex that the day was going to be a success, and her spirits rose.

She was rather surprised to see that Diana Munroe, who was seventeen, wore her hair in a thick plait twisted round the crown of her head, and asked her almost at once:

"Have you put your hair up, Diana? Are you going to 'come out'?"

"Oh, no. It'll come down again at the end of the holidays, for my last term. Only Aunt Esther likes to see it that way. There's Aunt Esther, at the bottom of the rose garden."

Looking over the terrace wall they saw half-a-dozen grown-up people, men in white flannels, and youthful-looking ladies in thin summer dresses. Alex was rather pleased. She had always been more of a success with her mother's grown-up friends than with her own contemporaries, from the time of her nursery days, when she had been sent for to the drawing-room on the "At Home" afternoons.

But though Mrs. Cardew looked up and waved her hand to the group of children on the terrace, she did not appear to expect them to join the party, and the interval before lunch was spent in the display of white rabbits and guinea-pigs.

At first Alex watched Barbara rather nervously, wondering if she would be shy and foolish, and disgrace her, but Barbara, no longer over-shadowed by an elder sister who outshone her in every way, had acquired a surprising amount of self-assurance. Alex was not even certain that she approved of the ease with which her little sister talked and exclaimed over the pet animals, asking Diana whether she might pick up the guinea-pigs and hold them, without so much as waiting for a lead from Alex.

"Of course, you may!" Diana exclaimed. "Here you are."

She distributed guinea-pigs impartially, and earnestly consulted Cedric as to the bald patch on the Angora rabbit's head.

As they went back towards the house, Sadie Munroe said to him:

"Do you mind not having any other boys here—only girls? I'm afraid it's dull for you, but Aunt Esther's boys will be here after lunch, only they had to go over and play tennis with some people this morning; it was all settled before we knew you were coming."

But Cedric did not seem to mind at all.

At lunch Archie, as Alex had known he would be, was an immediate success.

Even Mr. Cardew, who was bald and looked through Alex and Barbara and Cedric without seeing them when he shook hands with them, patted Archie's curls and said:

"Hullo, Bubbles!"

"Come and sit next to me, you darling," said Mrs. Cardew, "and you shall have two helpings of everything."

It was a very long luncheon-table, and Alex found herself placed between Sadie and a grey-headed gentleman, to whom she talked in a manner which seemed to herself to be very grown-up and efficient.

Barbara was on the same side of the table and invisible to her, but she saw Cedric opposite, quite eagerly talking to Marie Munroe, which rather surprised Alex, who thought that her brother would despise all little girls of twelve.

Quite a number of people whose names Alex did not know asked her about Lady Isabel, and she answered their inquiries readily, pleased to show off her self-possession, and the gulf separating her from the childishness of Barbara, who was giggling almost all through lunch in a manner that would unhesitatingly have been qualified by her parents as ill-bred.

Lunch was nearly over when the two schoolboy sons of the house came rushing in, hot and excited, and demanding a share of dessert and coffee.

"Barbarians," tranquilly said Mrs. Cardew. "Sit down quietly now, Eric and Noel. I hope you said 'How d' you do' to every one."

They had not done so, but both made a sort of circular salutation, and the elder boy dropped into a chair next to Alex, while Eric went to sit beside his mother.

Noel Cardew was fifteen, a straight-featured, good-looking English boy, his fairness burned almost to brick-red, and with a very noticeable cast in one of his light-brown eyes.

Alex looked at him furtively, and wondered what she could talk about.

Noel spared her all trouble.

"Do you ever take photographs?" he inquired earnestly. "I've just got a camera, one of those bran-new sorts, and a tripod, quarter-plate size. I want to do some groups after lunch. I've got a dark-room for developing, the tool-house, you know."

He talked rapidly and eagerly, half turned round in his chair so as almost to face Alex, and she tried to feel flattered by the exclusive monologue.

She knew nothing about photography, but uttered little sympathetic ejaculations, and put one or two timid questions which Noel for the most part hardly seemed to hear.

When Mrs. Cardew at length rose from her place, he turned from Alex at once, in the midst of what he was saying, and demanded vehemently:

"Can't we have a group on the terrace now? Do let me do a group on the terrace—the light will be just right now."

"Dear boy, you really mustn't become a nuisance with that camera of yours—though he's really extraordinarily clever at it," said his mother, in a perfectly audible aside.

"Would it bore you all very much to be victimized? You won't keep us sitting in the glare too long, will you, dear boy?"

Almost every one protested at the suggestion of being photographed, but while a good many of the gentlemen of the party disappeared noiselessly and rapidly before the group could be formed, all the ladies began to straighten their hats, and pull or push at their fringes. Noel kept them waiting in the hot sun for what seemed a long while, and Alex reflected rather gloomily that Mrs. Cardew showed a tolerance of his inconvenient passion for photography that would certainly not have been approved by her own parents.

At last it was over, and Sadie jumped up, crying, "Now we can have some proper games! What shall we play at?"

"Don't get over-heated," her aunt said, smiling and nodding as she moved away.

"Do you like croquet?" Diana asked, and to Alex' disappointment they embarked upon a long, wearisome game. She was not a good player, nor was Barbara, but Cedric surprised them all by the brilliant ease with which he piloted Marie Munroe and himself to victory.

"I say, that's jolly good!" Eric and Noel said, and gazed at their junior with respect.

Alex felt pleased, but rather impatient too, and wished that it were she who was distinguishing herself.

When they played hide-and-seek, however, her opportunity came. She could run faster than any of the other girls at Liège, and when Diana suggested picking up sides, she added good-naturedly:

"Alex runs much faster than any of us—she'd better be captain for one side, and Noel the other."

Noel looked as though his own headship were a matter of course, but Alex felt constrained to say:

"Oh, no, not me—You, Diana."

"Would you rather not? Very well. Cedric, then. Hurry up and choose your sides, boys. You start, Cedric."

"I'll have Marie," said Cedric unhesitatingly, and the little red-haired girl skipped over beside him with undisguised alacrity.

"Noel?"

Noel jerked his head in the direction of Alex.

"You," he said.

She was immensely surprised and flattered, connecting his choice with the same attraction that had made him sit beside her at lunch, and not with her own reported prowess as a runner.

Cedric's reputation for gallantry suffered somewhat in his next selections, which fell with characteristic common sense on Noel's brother Eric, and upon Barbara. Noel took Sadie and Diana, and they drew lots for Archie.

The game proved long and exciting, played all over the terrace and shrubbery.

Alex screamed and laughed with the others, and enjoyed herself, although she found time to wish that Barbara were not so stupid and priggish about keeping on her gloves, because old Nurse had said she must, and to wonder very much why Cedric appeared so pleased with the society of red-haired, chattering Marie, whose side he never left.

Presently, as she was looking for somewhere to hide, Noel Cardew joined her.

"Come on with me—I know a place where they'll never find us," he told her, and led her on tip-toe to where a very small, disused ice-house was half-hidden in a clump of flowering shrubs.

Noel pushed open the door with very little effort, and they crept into the semi-darkness and sat on the floor, pulling the door to behind them. Noel whispered softly:

"Isn't it cool in here? I *am* hot."

"So am I."

Alex was wondering nervously what she could talk about to interest him, and to make him go on liking her. Evidently he did like her, or he would not have sat next her at lunch and told her about his photography, and afterwards have chosen her for his partner at hide-and-seek.

Alex, though she did not know it, possessed a combination that is utterly fatal to any charm: she was unfeignedly astonished that any one should be attracted by her, and at the same time agonizedly anxious to be liked.

She wanted now, wildly and nervously, to maintain the interest which she thought she had excited in her companion.

She found the silence unbearable. Noel would think her dull, or imagine that she was bored.

"Is this where you do your developing?" she asked in an interested voice, although she remembered perfectly that he had said he used a tool-house for his dark-room.

"No—we've got the tool-house for that. Why, there wouldn't be room to stand up in here. Sometimes I get my things developed and printed for me at a shop, you know. Chemists will generally do it for one—though, of course, I prefer doing my own. But there isn't time, except in the holidays, and then one's always running short of some stuff or other. The other day I ruined a simply splendid group—awfully good, it would have been: mother and a whole lot of people out on the steps—like we were today, you know—" He paused for sheer lack of breath.

"I hope the one you took today will be good," said Alex, her heart beating quickly.

"Oh, yes, sure to be, with a day like this. Some fellows say you can get just as much effect on a dull day, using a larger stop, but, of course, that's all nonsense really. I say, I'm not boring you, am I?"

He hardly waited to hear her impassioned negative before going on, still discussing photographic methods.

It was quite true that Alex was not bored, although she was hardly listening to what he said. But his voice went on and on, and it flattered her that he should want to talk to her so exclusively, as though secure of her sympathy.

"... And they say colour-photography will be the next thing. I believe one could get some jolly good effects down here. Young Eric is all for messing about with beastly paints and stuff, but I don't agree with that."

"Oh, no!"

"My plan is to get hold of a real outfit, as soon as they get the thing perfected, and then be one of the pioneers, you know. I say, I hope you don't think this is awful cheek—"

"Oh, no!"

"This isn't a bad place for experiments, I will say. You see, you can get the sea, and quite decent scenery, and any amount of view and stuff. I say, what ages they are finding us," he broke off suddenly.

Alex felt deeply mortified. Evidently Noel was bored, after all. But in another minute he began to talk again.

"I shouldn't be surprised if one of these days I tried my hand at doing sort of book stuff. You know, photographs for illustrations. I believe it's going to pay no end."

"What sort of things?"

"Oh, scenery, you know, and perhaps houses and things. Sure I'm not boring you?"

"No, indeed, I'm very interested."

"It is rather interesting," Noel agreed simply.

"Another thing I'm keen on is swimming. Rather different, you'll say; but then one can't do one thing all the time, and, of course, the swimming is first class at school. I went in for some competition and stuff last term; high diving, you know."

"Oh, did you win?"

"Can't say I did. Young Eric got a cup of sorts, racing, but I just missed the diving. Some day I shall have another try, I daresay. You know, I've got rather a funny theory about swimming. I don't know whether you'll see what I mean at all—in fact, I daresay it'll sound more or less mad, to you—but *I* believe we do it the wrong way."

"Oh," said Alex, wishing at the same time that she could divest herself of the eternal monosyllable. "Do tell me about it."

"Well, it's a bit difficult to explain, but *I* think we're all taught the wrong way to begin with. It doesn't seem to have occurred to any one to look at the way *fishes* swim."

Alex thought that Noel must really be very original and clever, and tried to feel more flattered than ever at being selected as the recipient of his theories.

"I believe the whole thing could be revolutionized and done much better—but I'm afraid I'm always simply chockfull of ideas of that kind."

"But that's so interesting," Alex said, not consciously insincere.

"Don't you have all sorts of ideas like that yourself?" he asked eagerly, filling her with a moment's anticipation that he was about to give the conversation a personal turn. "*I* think it makes life so much more interesting if one goes into things; not just stay on the surface, you know, but go into the *way* things are done."

Alex thought she heard some one coming towards their hiding-place, and wanted to tell Noel to stop talking, or they would be found, but she checked the impulse, fearful lest he should think her unsympathetic.

The dogmatic schoolboy voice went on and on—swimming, photography, cricket, and then photography again. Alex, determined to feel pleased and interested, could only contribute an occasional monosyllable, sometimes only an inarticulate sound, expressive of sympathy.

And at the end of it all, when she was half proud and half irritated at the thought that they must have been sitting there in the semi-darkness for at least an hour, Noel exclaimed:

"I say, they *are* slow finding us. I should think it must be quite tea-time, shouldn't you? How would it be if we came out now?"

"Yes, let's," said Alex, trying to keep the mortification out of her voice.

They emerged into the sunlight again, and Noel pulled out his watch.

"It's only a quarter past four. I thought it would be much later," he remarked candidly. "I wonder where they all are. I expect they'll want to know where we've been hiding, but you won't give it away, will you? It's a jolly good place, and the others don't know about it."

"I won't tell."

Alex revived a little at the idea of being entrusted with a secret.

"Do you often play hide-and-seek?"

"Oh, just to amuse the girls, in the summer holidays. They've spent the last three summers with us, you know. Next year I suppose they'll go to America, lucky kids!"

"I'd love to go to America, wouldn't you?" Alex asked, with considerable over-emphasis.

"Pretty well. I tell you what I'd really like to do—I shall do it one day, too—make a regular tour of England, with a camera. I don't know whether you'll think it's nonsense, of course, but my idea has always been that people go rushing abroad to see other countries before they really know their own. Now, my plan would be that I'd simply start at Land's End, in Cornwall, just taking each principal town as it came on my way, you know, and exploring thoroughly. I shouldn't mind going off the main track, you know, if I heard of any little place that had an old church or castle or something worth looking at. I don't know whether you're at all keen on old buildings?"

"Oh, yes," Alex said doubtfully; "I've seen Liège and Louvain, in Belgium—"

"Ah, but I'm talking about English places," Noel interrupted her inexorably. "Of course the foreign ones are splendid too, and I mean to run over and have a look at them some day, but my theory is that one ought to see something of one's own land first. Now take Devonshire. There are simply millions of old churches in Devonshire, and what I should do, would be to have a note-book with me, and simply jot down my impressions. Then with photographs one might get out quite a sort of record, if you know what I mean—"

Alex was rather glad that her companion should be talking to her so eagerly as they came in sight of a group of people on the terrace.

"Here are the truants," said Mrs. Cardew, laughing, and Diana Munroe exclaimed that Aunt Esther had called them all to tea, and they had given up further hunt for them.

"Noel always finds extraordinary places to hide in," she added rather disparagingly.

It was evident that Noel was not very popular with the American cousins.

"That boy would be very good looking if he had not that terrible cast," Alex overheard one lady say to another, as the visitors were waiting on the steps for the pony-carriage to take them away.

The grey-haired man next to whom Alex had sat at lunch, and who evidently did not know any of the group of children apart, nodded in the direction of little Archie, flushed and excited, trying to climb the terrace wall, surrounded by adoring ladies.

"That's the little chap for my money."

"Isn't he a darling? That's one of Isabel Clare's children—so are the two girls in blue. I couldn't believe anything so tall was really hers."

"Oh, yes—I noticed one of them—rather like her mother?"

Alex felt sure that she ought not to listen, and at the same time kept motionless lest they should notice her and lower their voices.

She felt eagerly anxious to overhear what the grey-haired gentleman might have to say after the very grown-up way in which she had made conversation with him at lunch, and having been a very pretty and much-admired drawing-room child in her nursery days, could not altogether divest herself of the expectation that she must still be found pretty and entertaining.

But the grey-haired gentleman said impartially:

146

"They are neither of them a patch on Lady Isabel, are they?"

"They are at the awkward age," laughed the lady to whom he was talking. "One of them sat next to you at lunch, didn't she?"

"Yes. Not quite so natural as the other children. That little, red-haired American girl, now—a regular child—"

Alex, with a face grown suddenly scarlet, left Barbara, shyly, and Cedric, briefly, to thank their hostess for the pleasant day they had spent.

A new, and far more painful self-consciousness than any she had yet known, hampered her tongue and her movements, until they were safely in the pony-carriage half-way down the drive.

"They are nice, aren't they?" said Barbara. "I'm sure they are nicer than Queenie."

"No, they aren't," Alex contradicted mechanically.

"Well, Marie and Diana are, anyway." She looked slyly at Cedric. "Don't you think so, Cedric?"

"How can I tell whether they are any nicer, as you call it, than another kid whom I've never seen?" inquired Cedric reasonably.

"But didn't you like Marie?"

"She's all right."

Barbara giggled in the way most disliked by her family, the authorities of whom stigmatized the habit as "vulgar," and Cedric said severely:

"I shouldn't think decent girls would want to play with you at all, if you don't leave off that idiotic trick of cackling."

But Barbara, who was not at all easily crushed, continued to giggle silently at intervals.

"Why are you so silly?" Alex asked her crossly, as they were going to bed that night.

She and Barbara shared a room at Fiveapples Farm.

Barbara whined the inevitable contradiction, "I'm not silly," but added immediately, "you wouldn't be so cross, if you knew what I know. I expect you'd laugh too."

"Well, what is it?"

"I shan't tell you."

Alex was not particularly curious, but she had been the nursery autocrat too long to be able to endure resistance to her command.

"Tell me at once, Barbara."

"No, I won't."

"Yes, you will. Well, what is it about?" said Alex, changing her tactics.

"It's about Cedric."

"Is he in a scrape?"

"No, it's just something he did."

"*What?* Did he tell you about it?"

"Oh, no. He doesn't know I know. He'd be furious if he did, I expect."

"Who told you? Does any one else know?"

"Nobody told me. One other person knows," giggled Barbara, jumping up and down in her petticoat.

"Keep still, you'll have the candle over. Who's the other person who knows?"

"Guess."

"Oh, I can't; don't be so silly. I am not going to ask you any more."

"Well," said Barbara in a great hurry, "it's Marie Munroe, then; it's about her."

"What about her? She didn't take any notice of any one except Cedric, and I think it was very rude and stupid of her."

"It was Cedric's doing much more than hers," Barbara said shrewdly. "I think he thinks he is in love with her. I saw them in the shrubbery when we were playing hide-and-seek; and—what do you think, Alex?"

"Well, what?"

"Cedric kissed her—I saw him."

"Then," said Alex, "it was perfectly hateful of him and of Marie and of you."

"Why of *me?*" shrieked Barbara in a high key of indignation. "What have I done, I should like to know?"

"You'd no business to say anything about it. Put out the candle, Barbara, I'm going to get into bed."

In the darkness Alex lay with her mind in a tumult. It seemed to her incredible that her brother, whom she had always supposed to despise every form of sentimentality, as he did any display of feeling on the part of his family, should have wanted to kiss little, red-haired Marie, whom he had only known for one day, and who was by far the least pretty of any of the three Munroe sisters. "And to kiss her in the shrubbery like that!"

Alex felt disgusted and indignant. She thought about it for a long while before she went to sleep, although she would gladly have dismissed the incident from her mind. Most of all, perhaps, she was filled with astonishment. Why should any one want to kiss Marie Munroe?

In the depths of her heart was another wonder which she never formulated even to herself, and of which she would, for very shame, have strenuously denied the existence.

Why had she not the same mysterious attraction as un-beautiful little Marie? Alex knew instinctively that it would never have occurred, say, to Noel Cardew—to ask her if he might kiss her. She did not want him to—would have been shocked and indignant at the mere idea—but, unconsciously, she wished that he had wanted to.

VI
The End of an Era

No salient landmarks ever seemed to Alex to render eventful the two and a half years that elapsed between those summer holidays at Fiveapples Farm and her final departure from the Liège convent to begin her grown-up life at home.

The re-arrangement of the day's routine consequent on the beginning of the winter half-year caused her to miss Queenie less acutely than she had done when she first came home for the holidays, and with Queenie's absence there were fewer revolts against convent law, and less disfavour from the authorities.

She made no other great friends. Marie Munroe showed her a marked friendliness at first, but Alex could not forget that giggling revelation of Barbara's, and shrank from her advances unmistakably. She had very little in common with her French contemporaries, and knew that they thought her English accent and absence of proficiency in needlework, marks of eccentricity and of bad form, so that she became self-conscious and aggressive before them.

She was hardly aware of her own intense loneliness—the poignant realization of it was to come later—but the want of any channel of self-expression for her over-developed emotional capabilities produced in her a species of permanent discontent that reacted on her health and on her spirits, so that she got the reputation, least enviable of any in schoolgirl circles, of being "a tragedy queen."

Her morose pallor, partly the result of an under-vitalized system, and partly of her total lack of any interest in her surroundings, were considered fair game.

"Voyez, Alex! Elle a son air bête aujourd'hui."

"A qui l'enterrement, Alex?"

They were quite good-humoured, and did not mean to hurt her. It was not their fault that such pin-pricks stabbed her and sent her away to cry over her own friendlessness until she felt sick and exhausted.

She did not expend on any one else the extravagant worship bestowed upon Queenie Torrance. For a year she wrote to Queenie throughout the holidays, and received meagre and unsatisfactory replies, and then gradually the correspondence ceased altogether, and Alex only looked forward with an occasional vague curiosity to the possibility of meeting Queenie again in London, on the terms of equality symbolized by their both being "grown-up."

During her last year at school, lack of intimate intercourse with any one, and the languid sentimentality of adolescence, made her take for the first time some interest in religion as understood at the convent. She prolonged her weekly confession, which had hitherto been a matter of routine to be got through as rapidly as possible, in order to obtain the solace of talking about herself, and derived a certain tepid pleasure in minutely following and applying to herself the more anecdotal portions of the New Testament.

For a time, it seemed to her that she had found a refuge.

Then came the affair of the examination. Alex, in her last term, and taking part in the final midsummer*concours*, could not bear the penalty of failure which it seemed to her would be displayed in the mediocrity which had all along been her portion. She had never been admitted to the virtuous society of the *enfants de Marie*, had never taken more than one of the less distinguished prizes at the end of any term, and had no warmly-worded report to display her popularity and the sense of loss that her departure would leave.

Her place in the half-yearly examination was not a good one. She had none of Cedric's power of concentration, and her abilities were not such as to win her any regard in the continental and Catholic system of education of the middle nineties.

She cheated over the examination.

It was quite easy to copy from the girl next her, who happened to be one of the best vehicles for carefully-tabulated and quite unconnected facts, in the school. Alex could read the dates, and the proper names, and all the principal words on her history paper, and transferred them to her own, clothing the dry bones in the imaginative fabric of her own words, for the English girls were allowed to do most of the papers in their own language.

At the end of the morning she was oddly elated, at the sight of her well-filled paper, and felt no qualms at all. In the afternoon she was again next to Marie-Louise, and congratulated herself that the paper should be the literature one. Arithmetic, she knew, was not the strong point of Marie-Louise, and besides, it would be almost impossible to copy the working of problems figure for figure without ultimate detection.

That night, however, when Alex knelt down to say her prayers, she was suddenly overwhelmed by remorse and terror.

Her crime came between her and God.

The vaguely comforting belief that because she was lonely and miserable, He would vouchsafe to her an especial pity, was destroyed. Between God and a sinner, so Alex had been told, lay an impassable gulf that only repentance, confession, atonement and punishment, could bridge—and even then, an indelible entry against one's name testified to eventual exposure and shame at some dreadful, inevitable assizes, when sins hidden and forgotten, large and small, of commission and omission alike, would be made known to all the world, assembled together for the Last Judgment. Faced with this inevitable retribution, Alex felt that no present success was worth it, and wondered whether she could not repair her wickedness as far as possible on the morrow by confession.

But when the morrow had come, the Day of Judgment seemed far removed from the hot July morning, and the breaking-up, when the result of the examinations would be heard, a very present reality indeed.

It was a relief to the hot, tossing sensation of balancing values in her mind, to remember that it was the day of the Catechism examination, which would be viva voce.

She acquitted herself very badly, and the temptation to retrieve her failure in the afternoon was irresistible, when she again found herself placed next to the prodigy Marie-Louise.

The paper was headed "Histoire de l'Église," and immense value was attached to proficiency in the subject, strenuously taught to the convent pupils out of enormous old-fashioned volumes containing much loyal fiction with a modicum of distorted historical fact.

Alex fell.

She could overlook her neighbour's papers so easily, hardly even turning her head, that it only struck her as inconvenient, and did not awake in her any fear of detection, when presently Marie-Louise pulled a piece of blotting-paper towards her so that it covered the page on which she was working.

Alex finished the question to which Marie-Louise had unwittingly supplied her with material for the answer, and looked about her, subconsciously waiting for the removal of the blotting-paper. Her eyes met those of a younger child, seated exactly opposite to her, whose sharp, dark gaze was fixed upon her with a sort of eager, contemptuous horror. In that instant, when it seemed as though her heart had stopped beating, Alex knew herself detected.

The colour rushed from her face and she felt cold and giddy.

Lacking the instinctive guard against self-betrayal which is the hall-mark of the habitual deceiver, her terrified gaze turned straight to Marie-Louise.

The smooth, dark head was bent low, one hand still clutched at the covering blotting-paper, and the ear and piece of cheek which were all that Alex could see, were scarlet.

Marie-Louise knew.

The sharp-eyed child opposite had seen Alex cheat, and had no doubt conveyed a silent telegraphic warning.

It seemed to Alex that the world had stopped. Accusation, disgrace, expulsion, all whirled through her mind and left no permanent image there. Her imagination stopped utterly dead at the horror of it.

She sat perfectly motionless for the remaining hours of the morning, unconscious of the passage of time, only conscious of an increasing sense of physical sickness.

It was an absolute relief to her when the bell rang and she found herself obliged to get up and move across the long class-room with the others to give up her papers.

"Vous êtes malade, Alexandra?"

"J'ai mal-au-coeur," said Alex faintly.

She was sent to the infirmary to lie down, and the old lay-sister in charge of it was so kind to her, and commiserated her wan, forlorn appearance so pityingly, that Alex burst into a flood of tears that relieved the tension of her body, and sent her, quivering, but uncomprehendingly sensible of relief, to rest exhaustedly upon the narrow infirmary bed with little white curtains drawn all round it.

No doubt every one would soon know of her disgrace, and she would be expelled, to the shame and anger of her father and mother, and the downfall of all her boastings to Barbara. No doubt God had abandoned one so unworthy of His forgiveness—but Soeur Clementine was kind, and it seemed, in the incredible comfort of a little human tenderness, that nothing else mattered.

And, after all, that hour's anticipation proved to be the worst that happened to her. She went downstairs for the evening preparation, and Marie-Louise, a trusted *enfant de Marie*, obtained permission to speak to her alone, and solemnly conducted her to the lavatory, as the most private place in the school.

Standing over the sink, with its stiff and solitary tap of cold water, Marie-Louise conducted her inquiry with business-like, passionless directness.

Alex made no attempt either to deny her sin or to palliate it. She was mentally and emotionally far too much exhausted for any effort, and it did not even occur to her that any excuse could avail her anything.

Marie-Louise was not at all unkind.

She knew all about *la charité*, and was agreeably conscious of exercising this reputable virtue to the full, when she informed Alex that no one should ever know of the lapse from her, provided that Alex, making her own explanation to the class-mistress, should withdraw her papers from the examination.

"But what can I say to her?" asked Alex.

"Quant à ça," said Marie-Louise, in the detached tones of one who had accomplished her duty and felt no further interest on the point at issue, "quant à ça, débrouillez-vous avec vôtre conscience."

To this task she left Alex.

And Alex ended by doing nothing at all. Partly from inertia, partly because she knew that Marie-Louise would never ask her what she had done, she shirked the shame and trouble of confession to her class-mistress, and let her papers go in with the others. She knew that she would not get a high place, for her work all through the term had been bad, and would have to be taken into consideration, and over all the remaining papers she muddled hopelessly. Besides, she was leaving for good, and no one would know.

She had lost her self-respect when she first realized that she was cheating, and it was then, as she neared the completion of her seventeenth year, that the belief was ineradicably planted in Alex' soul that she had been born with a natural love of evil, and that goodness was an abstract attitude of mind to which she could never do more than aspire fruitlessly, with no slightest expectation of attainment. She was further conscious of an intense determination to hide the knowledge of her own innate badness from every one.

If she were ever seen in her true colours, no one would love her, and Alex already knew dimly, and with a further sense of having strange, low standards of her own, that she wanted to be loved more than anything in the world.

Far more than she wanted to be good.

The affair of the examination passed, and although Alex did not forget it, she mostly remembered it as merely the culminating scandal of a succession of petty evasions and cowardly deceptions.

She left Liège without regret.

She had hated the physical discomfort of the conventual system, the insufficient hours of sleep, the bitter cold of the Belgian winters and the streaming rain that defiled the summers; she had hated the endless restrictions and the minute system of *surveillance* that was never relaxed; above all, she had hated the sense of her own isolation in a crowd, her own utter absence of attraction for her kind.

It seemed to Alex that when she joined the mysterious ranks of grown-up-people everything would be different. She never doubted that with long dresses and piled-up hair, her whole personality would change, and the meaningless chaos of life reduce itself to some comprehensible solution.

Everything all her life had been tending towards the business of "growing up." Everything that she was taught at home impressed the theory that her "coming out" would usher in the realities of life, and nothing impressed her more with a sense of the tremendous importance of the approaching change than Lady Isabel's greeting, when she came back to Clevedon Square after her final term at Liège.

"We've put off Scotland for a week, darling—your father's been so good about it—so that I may see about your clothes. I've made appointments with Marguerite and the other places for you, so there'll be nothin' to do but try on, but, of course, I shall have to see the things myself before they finish them, and tell them about the colours; they're sure to want to touch everything up with pink or blue, and white is so much prettier for a young girl. White with a tiny little *diamanté* edging, I thought, for one of your evenin' dresses....

"The first thing, of course, is your hair. Louise must go with you to Hugo's, and watch them very carefully while they do it in two or three different styles, then she'll be able to do it for you every evening. I expect she'll have to do it every day to begin with, but you must try and learn. I should like you to be *able* to be independent of a maid in that sort of way—one never knows quite that some time one mightn't find oneself stranded for a day or two....

"I don't think your hair will need waving, Alex, which is such a comfort. So many women have to wear their fringe in curlers every night—thank Heaven, I've never had to. As a matter of fact, they say fringes are goin' out now, but I'm certainly not goin' to let yours grow until we're quite certain about it ... and a bald forehead is always so unbecomin'."

Alex listened with a sense of importance and excitement, but she was also rather bewildered. The contrast between all this preoccupation with her clothes and her appearance, and the austere mental striving after spiritual or moral results which had permeated the convent atmosphere, was too violent.

"You'll be interested in it all, my darling, won't you?" asked Lady Isabel disappointedly. "I couldn't bear to have a daughter who didn't care about her things—some girls are like that—so disappointin'; after one's had all the trouble of their upbringin' and is lookin' forward to a little reward."

Alex could find no words in which to explain what she knew quite well, that she was as full of eager anticipations as Lady Isabel could wish, but was too much bewildered by the novelty of it all, as yet, to give any expression to them.

She became rather boisterous and unconvincing in her endeavours to express, by means which were not spontaneous, the pleasure and excitement expected of her.

151

"You'll learn to move prettily and quietly, darling, and we must see about some dancin' lessons before next year. Dancin' fashions alter so quickly now-a-days," said Lady Isabel, her low, gentle tones a shade lower and more gentle than usual.

"But I shan't go to balls—yet," stammered Alex.

She and Barbara had only been allowed a very few children's parties, and for the last few years she had been considered too old for these. She thought of a ball as a prolonged, glorified party.

"Not until after your presentation, of course, and that won't be till the spring. But there may be one or two affairs in the country at Christmas, if I take you to stay about, as I hope.

"You see, darling, my plan is to let you have the next two months in the country with little Barbara, just as usual—only you must take great care not to let yourself get freckled in the sun—and then, when you come back to town in October, you can have your hair properly put up, and come about with me, so as to get to know people and make a little beginnin' before there's any question of really doing the season properly next summer."

Alex began to feel vastly important. She had never been the centre of so much attention before. Evidently this affair of coming out was the culminating point to which all life had hitherto been tending.

Even Barbara treated her with a rather envious respect now.

Only Cedric remained unimpressed, and treated his eldest sister's marked tendency to assume airs of extreme maturity with silent indifference.

His school career was proceeding more triumphantly than ever, and his "removes" succeeded one another with a rapidity only less startling than his increasing reputation as a cricketer.

He spent most of his holidays with a schoolfellow, and showed himself rather scornful of girls in general and of his sisters in particular, although he played willingly enough with little Pamela, who had grown to an attractive and talkative age.

Barbara asked him once, with the touch of slyness characteristic of her in certain moods, whether he remembered Marie Munroe.

"Red-haired American kid? Oh, yes," said Cedric loftily. "Didn't she have a sister who was bosom friends with Alex at Liège, or some rot of that kind?"

And Alex had felt unaccountably relieved at the implication of the evanescent character of Cedric's whilom admiration.

They spent August and September at the seaside on the Cornish coast.

Alex enjoyed the daily bathing, and scrambling over the rocks barefooted, and the picnic teas in any sheltered cove that old Nurse judged sufficiently protected from the profane gaze of possible trippers. But she had all the time the sense that these hot, leisurely days were only a time of waiting, and even when she enjoyed herself most she was conscious of a gnawing impatience for the next step.

The week in London before Lady Isabel and Sir Francis started for Scotland had rather disappointed Alex, although she did not own it, even to herself.

Perpetual "tryings on" in hot weather had proved a tiring performance, and her feet ached from standing and from the hot pavement, so that she dragged herself rather than walked, or stood on one foot so as to save the other, which had vexed Lady Isabel, and led to a long admonition as to the importance of moving properly and always holding oneself upright.

Moreover, Alex, although she did not give very much thought to her own looks as a rule, had always expected that as soon as she grew up she would almost automatically become very beautiful, and it vexed and surprised her to find that her new frocks, still in a very incompleted stage, did not at once produce any startling change in her appearance. It was also disappointing that her mother and her mother's dressmaker should so often seem to find in her hitherto unsuspected deficiencies.

"Mam'selle won't be able to wear elbow-sleeves just at present, Móddam, I'm afraid—at least, not until we've got rid of that redness."

"Dear me, no! I suppose that comes from keepin' her elbows on a school desk—how very vexin'. Really, the nuns must have been very careless to let you get into the way of it, Alex. And it's made your shoulders round, too."

"Mam'selle *must* keep her shoulders well back if that white chiffon is to look like anything at all," chimed in Madame Marguerite most impressively. "It will simply be ruination to let it drop like that in the front ... takes away all the smartness from it."

Alex straightened herself uneasily.

"It's such a simple little frock, the whole thing is how it's worn...."

Which made Alex feel miserably unequal to the responsibility laid upon her.

"Her neck is very thin," sighed Lady Isabel, and Madame Marguerite, her large head with its weight of elaborate yellow waves well on one side as she gazed at Alex, had looked very disparaging indeed as she said, in tones more consolatory than hopeful:

"Of course, Mam'selle may fill out a bit before next year."

Alex, in her heart, had been thankful when it was all over, and she had gone back to the old blue cotton frocks that were to be worn out at the seaside.

Her only responsibility there was the daily struggle of putting up her hair.

To her disgust, and to Barbara's derision, the hair-dresser had insisted upon a large, bun-like frame, which made her head ache, and, pinned on by her unskilful hands, displayed a strong tendency to slip down the back of her neck. And however much she might brush and pull her hair over it, there always appeared a hiatus sooner or later, through which a large patch of what Barbara jeeringly called "false horsehair," might plainly be seen.

In spite of it all, however, Alex enjoyed those last schoolroom days of hers more than any she had yet known.

Real life was going to begin, and though Alex had no idea as to how the transformation would be effected, she was convinced that everything which she had longed for, and utterly missed, throughout her schooldays, would now be hers.

VII

London Season

Alex' first London season, from the very extravagance of her expectations, was a disappointment to her.

Her own appearance, indeed, in her first ball-dress, surprised and delighted her, and she stood before the great pier glass in the drawing-room, under the chandelier which had been specially lit for the occasion, and gazed at her reflection with incredulous admiration.

Her dress, in the height of the prevailing fashion, had been the subject of Lady Isabel's minute and careful consultations with Madame Marguerite of New Bond Street. Of stiff white satin, the neck was cut into a hard square, and the bodice, as it was still called, unsoftened except for a small draping of pleated white chiffon held on the left shoulder with a cluster of dead-white roses, which were repeated at the side of the broad, white-ribbon belt. The most prominent feature of the dress was the immensity of the sleeves, stiffened within by strips of petersham, and standing well up from the shoulders. Thence, the monstrous, balloon-shaped things narrowed imperceptibly, and were gathered in just below the elbow, leaving no hiatus visible between them and the *mousquetaire* white-kid gloves.

The skirt had no train, but fell into plain, heavy folds, sweeping the ground, and with a slight additional length of "tail," and a considerable additional fulness behind. A white ostrich-feather fan hung by white satin ribbon from her waist.

"It looks charming," said Lady Isabel delightedly. "Better than your presentation frock."

The servants, who had respectfully petitioned through Lady Isabel's maid to be allowed to see Miss Clare in her ball-dress before she started, were grouped in the doorway, the long white streamers of the maids' caps contrasting sharply with their neat black dresses.

Old Nurse, a privileged personage, was right inside the drawing-room, inspecting critically.

"I never thought you'd look so well, Miss Alex," she observed candidly. "They've hid your failings something wonderful, and your hair and complexion was always good, thanks to the care I've took of them—that I will say."

"Don't those shoes pinch, Alex?" asked Barbara, looking on enviously in her plain schoolroom frock and strapped shoes, with her hair still hanging down her back.

Alex did not care whether her pointed, white satin shoes pinched her feet or not. She was too happy in her first triumph.

It was not quite a solitary triumph, for Sir Francis, after a prolonged gazing through his double eye-glasses that made her flush more than ever from nervousness, gave one of his rare smiles of gratification and said:

"Very pretty indeed. I congratulate you on your appearance, my dear child."

But it was to Lady Isabel that he turned next moment, with that sudden softened glance that he never bestowed elsewhere.

"How beautifully you've dressed her, my dear. You will be taken for sisters, now that she is in long dresses."

The compliment was not ill-deserved, and Alex, watching her mother's exquisite flush, felt a vague dissatisfaction with her own immaturity.

She might be pretty, with youthful colouring and smooth skin, but she lacked the poise that added charm to her mother's beauty, and a struggling consciousness of that lack disturbed and vexed her.

"I think she's better without any ornament, don't you, Francis?" asked her mother critically. "Some girls wear pearls, I know, but I never quite like—it not the first year, anyway."

Her opera cloak over her shoulders, its cape-like outline and heavy, turned-back collar of swan-down adding to the already disproportionate width of the upper part of her person, Alex followed Lady Isabel into the carriage.

She wore nothing over her head, for fear of disarranging the light Princess-of-Wales' fringe curling on her forehead.

That first ball remained in her mind as a medley of valse tunes, quadrilles and jigging polkas, blazing lights and red and white flowers everywhere, and a sequence of strange young men brought up in rapid succession by the daughters of her hostess and introduced in an unvarying formula, to which each responded by a bow and a polite request for the pleasure of a dance with her. Alex danced readily enough, but found conversation strangely difficult, expecting she knew not what profundities of intercourse which were never forthcoming. Her chief gratification was that of seeing Lady Isabel's pretty, pleased smile at the sight of her daughter dancing.

"Are you enjoying yourself, darling?" she asked several times, as Alex returned between each dance to the row of gilt chairs against the wall.

Alex said "Yes" sincerely enough, but she was all the time reminded of that strange, disconcerting experience that had been hers a year or two earlier, when she had sought to persuade herself of a great success with the boy Noel Cardew.

She boasted of her enjoyment of the ball to Barbara next day, and said that she had been so busy dancing that she had never gone down to supper at all.

"But that must never happen again," Lady Isabel said, horrified. "Girls do that sort of thing at first, when they're foolish, and then they get over-tired and lose all their looks and have no more good times."

It seemed the omega of disaster.

Nevertheless, there were other balls when Alex did not go down to supper, sometimes because no one had asked her to do so.

She nearly always had partners, for she danced reasonably, though not superlatively, well, and introductions were still the fashion. But the number of her partners depended very largely upon the attentiveness of her hostess or of her hostess's daughters. Young men did not always claim dances from her, although they had been amongst her partners at the ball of the week before. Nor did many of them ask for two or three dances in one evening.

Lady Isabel had said, "Never more than three dances with the same man, Alex, at the very *outside*. It's such bad form to make yourself conspicuous with any one—your father would dislike it very much."

Alex bore the warning carefully in mind, and was naïvely surprised that no occasion for making practical application of it should occur. She was intensely anxious to be liked and admired, and she strangely confounded the two issues in her own mind. Attributes such as her clear skin, her exquisitely-kept hair, or her expensive frocks, she thought would promote interest in her amongst her fellow-creatures, and to the same end she simulated an enthusiasm—which was so entirely foreign to her real feelings that it lacked any semblance of body—for the crazes of her immediate generation, centred in Planchette and in the publication of *Barabbas*. She was full of preconceived ideas as to that which constituted attractiveness, and in her very ardour to realize the conventional ideal of the day failed entirely to attract. In intercourse with other girls, still in their first or second season, she slowly began to suspect the deficiencies in herself.

"I'm engaged for nearly every single valse at the Duchess's ball on Tuesday already!" a very young, childish-looking little creature exclaimed in Alex' hearing.

Alex was astounded. What could the little thing mean?

"Nearly all my last night's partners will be there, and they've all asked me for dances, and some for two or three," said the child with ingenuous pride.

Alex was frankly amazed. Lady Mollie was not particularly pretty, and her conversation was the veriest stream of prattle. Yet she was asked to reserve the favour of her dances three days or four days in advance, and the experience was evidently no new one to her, although she had only come out a few weeks earlier than Alex!

It was the same little Lady Mollie who gave Alex a further shock by demanding of her very seriously:

"Do you know a girl called Miss Torrance, a girl with very fair hair? She says she was at school with you."

"Queenie Torrance? Oh, *yes!*" said Alex, the old fervour rushing to her voice at the sudden memory of Queenie, who had left her letters unanswered—of whom she had heard nothing for two years.

"She's tremendously admired by *some* people," said Lady Mollie, shaking her head with a quaint air of sapience. "I know two or three who rave about her. Mother says she's rather inclined to be fast. I think people don't like her father very much, and he generally takes her about. You don't know them very well, do you?"

Alex hastily disclaimed any intimacy with Queenie's unpopular parent. She felt disloyal to Queenie for the eagerness with which she did so.

Two nights later, at one of the big evening receptions that Alex enjoyed least of any form of entertainment, Miss Torrance's name was again mentioned to her.

She was listening to the conversation of a brilliantly-good-looking young German Jew, whose name of Goldstein, already spoken with bated breath in financial circles, conveyed less to her inexperience than did the dark, glowing eyes, swarthy skin and the Semitic curve of his handsome nose. His voice was very slightly guttural, and he slurred his r's all but imperceptibly as he spoke.

She found that conversation with him was exceedingly easy, and translated the faint hint of servility in his deference, as did most women not of his own race, into sympathy with her utterances.

"You think so, you really think so?" he inquired gently, when she expressed a *banale* admiration for the prettiness of some girl whose entry, preceded by that of an insignificant couple, had made a slight stir round the huge open doorway of the reception-room.

"Yes," said Alex, emboldened by the interested look in the dark eyes which he kept upon her face, as though finding it more worth while to gaze upon her than upon the entering beauty.

"I have seen more beautiful faces than hers, nevertheless," he responded.

The eloquence of his look made Alex feel as though she had received a compliment, and she blushed. As though to cover her shyness, the young Jew went on speaking. "I wonder if you know Miss Torrance—Miss Queenie Torrance?"

She noticed that his throaty voice lingered over the syllables a little.

"She was my great friend at school."

"Indeed! What a delightful friendship for both, if I may say so. I think I may say that I, also, have the privilege of counting myself amongst the friends of Miss Torrance."

"I haven't seen her since she left school," said Alex wistfully. "I should like to see her."

"You spoke of beauty just now," said the young Jew deliberately. "To my mind Miss Torrance was the beauty of the season, when she came out last year."

She felt faintly surprised, but spoke hastily lest he should think her jealous, although he had carefully emphasized the date of Queenie's appearance into society.

"I heard only the other day how much she was admired."

Goldstein's dark face grew darker. "She is very much admired indeed," he said emphatically.

"Perhaps she will be here tonight," Alex suggested, thinking that she would like to see Queenie grown-up.

"She is not coming tonight," said Goldstein with calm assurance. "Are you going to the Duchess's ball on Tuesday? But I need not ask."

Alex felt unreasonably flattered at the homage implied, rather than expressed, in the tone, and replied in the affirmative.

"Then you will see Miss Torrance."

"Oh, I'm glad," said Alex. She felt rather elated at the success which her friend must have undoubtedly met with, to be so much admired, and she remembered with added resentment Lady Isabel's old inquiry: "Torrance—Torrance—who is Torrance?"

"Did you know that the girl I was at Liège with, Queenie Torrance, came out last year, and every one says she's lovely?" she demanded of her mother.

"I'd forgotten you were at school with her. I remember now," said Lady Isabel thoughtfully. "Who says she is lovely?"

"Oh, Lady Mollie and every one. That Mr. Goldstein I was talking to."

"Goldstein!" exclaimed her mother with infinite contempt. She was silent for a little while and then said, "I've heard about the Torrance girl. Men—of a sort—admire her very much indeed, but I should be sorry if you copied her style, Alex."

Alex felt more curious than ever. Blindly though she had adored Queenie, it had not occurred to her that she would be considered very pretty, and she wondered greatly concerning the development of her old playmate.

When she did see Queenie, at the Duchess's ball as Goldstein had predicted, Lady Isabel was not with her. Excess of fatigue had unwillingly constrained her to stay at home, while Sir Francis, bored but courteous, escorted his eldest daughter in her stead.

They arrived late, and stood for a few minutes in the doorway, watching the kaleidoscopic scene of colour and movement in the great illuminated ballroom.

Alex' attention was attracted by a group of men all gathered near the door, and prominent among them Goldstein, his eager, searching gaze fixed upon the broad stairway without, up and down which innumerable figures passed and re-passed. From the sudden lightning flash in his ardent black gaze, not less than from a sort of movement instantly communicated to the whole group, Alex guessed that he had focussed the object of his quest.

The announcement made at the head of the stairs was inaudible amid the crashing of dance music, but Alex recognized the entering couple in a flash.

Colonel Torrance, white-haired, with black moustache and eyebrows, upright and soldierly still, had changed less than Queenie. She looked much taller than Alex had imagined her, and her graceful outline was fuller, but she moved exquisitely.

Her very fair hair, at a time when every woman wore a curled fringe, was combed straight back from her rounded brow, leaving only the merest escaping curls at either temple, and gathered into the ultra-fashionable "jug-handle" knot on the top of her head. She wore a wreath of tiny blue forget-me-nots that deepened the tint of her grey-blue eyes, and the colour was repeated freely in the deep frills and ruchings of her white, *décolletée* dress, of an elaboration that Alex instinctively knew her mother would not have countenanced. Turquoises were twisted round the white, full column of her throat, and clasped her rounded arms.

Alex watched her eagerly.

Every man in the little waiting group was pressing round her, claiming first possession of her attention.

The faint, remotely smiling sweetness of Queenie's heart-shaped mouth recalled to Alex with extraordinary vividness the schoolgirl at the Liège convent.

Goldstein, his eyes flaming, stood demonstratively waiting, with insolent security in his bearing, while she dispensed her favours right and left, always with the same chilly, composed sweetness. The music, which had ceased, broke into the lilt of the *Blue Danube*, and on the instant Goldstein imperiously approached Queenie. She swayed towards him, still smiling slightly, and they drifted into the throng of dancers. Alex turned round with a sort of gasp.

What must it feel like to be the heroine of a ballroom triumph, to know that a dozen men would count the evening worth while for the privilege of dancing once with her, that they would throng in the doorway to watch and wait for her coming?

Some of them remained in the doorway still, watching her dance, the folds of her dress and her great white fan gathered into one hand, her white, heavy eyelids cast down under her pure, open forehead, and Goldstein's arm encircling her waist as he guided her steps skilfully round the crowded room. Alex saw that Sir Francis, his double eyeglass raised, was also watching the couple.

"I wonder who that remarkably pretty woman is, of whom young Goldstein is very obviously enamoured?"

Alex felt oddly that Sir Francis supposed Queenie to be of maturer years than she in reality was.

"It's Queenie Torrance, father. She was at school with me," Alex repeated. "I've not seen her since she grew up—but she's only about a year older than I am."

"Indeed!"

Curiosity as to the unanimity of masculine judgment made Alex appeal to him with a question.

"Do you think she's pretty, father?"

"Exceedingly striking—beautiful, in fact," said Sir Francis.

Queenie was not beautiful, and Alex knew it, but the glamour of her magnetic personality was evidently as potent with older men as with young Goldstein and his contemporaries. Alex felt a curious pang, half of envy and half of wonder.

Sir Francis put down his glasses. "A pity," he said deliberately, "that she is not—altogether—" And raised his grizzled eyebrows.

VIII
Goldstein and Queenie

Queenie Torrance spoke to Alex that night with characteristic suavity, and showed pleasure at meeting her again.

"Those old convent days seem a long way off, don't they?" she asked, smiling a little.

Her glance, sweeping the big ballroom, seemed to appraise its glories and claim them for her own.

It was the glance, rather than the words, to which Alex replied.

"You're having a splendid time, aren't you, Queenie? You like being grown-up?"

"I adore it," said Miss Torrance, her eyes gleaming like stars.

Alex did not wonder at it.

Night after night she watched Queenie Torrance accepting as her right the homage of innumerable men, halving the favour of her dances at crowded balls where "wall-flowers" were too numerous to be rescued from oblivion by the most determined of hostesses, going down to supper on the arm of young Goldstein and lingering with him in prolonged *tête-à-tête*. Goldstein, at the little round table across which he leant, recklessly oblivious of comment, endeavouring, often fruitlessly, throughout a whole evening, to obtain one direct look from those widely-set, downcast eyes under their flaxen lashes.

It was not easy, Alex found, to talk to Queenie. They often met at entertainments, and once or twice in the Park, but Queenie never rode in the mornings, as Alex sometimes did, and Lady Isabel did not allow her daughter to take up the fashionable practice of bicycling in Battersea

Park, at which Queenie Torrance, in the neatest and most daring of rational costumes, was reported to excel. Once Alex, as she had said before in her childish days, asked Lady Isabel:

"Mother, may I ask Queenie Torrance to tea here? We meet everywhere, and it will be so odd if I never ask her to come here. Besides, I should like to have her."

"I'm sorry, Alex, but I'd rather you contented yourself with meetin' her in society—if you do."

"Why?" said Alex unwisely, urged by some mysterious unreason to provoke the answer which she already anticipated with resentment.

"She's not the sort of girl I should care about you being friends with very much," said Lady Isabel without heat. "I hear she's already bein' talked about."

Alex knew what the words meant, uttered by her mother and her mother's circle of intimates.

"Why is she being talked about?" Alex asked rebelliously.

"Any girl who goes in for being fast gets talked about," said Lady Isabel severely. "And it does them no good in the long run either. Men may flirt with girls of that sort, and like to dance with them and pay them attention, but they don't marry them. A man likes his wife to be simple and well-bred and dignified."

"I'm sure heaps of people would like to marry Queenie."

"How do you know?" Lady Isabel asked quickly.

Alex did not reply. She only knew that men looked at Queenie Torrance as they did not look at other women, and, true to the traditions of youth and of the race to which she belonged, the admiration of a man for a woman, to her inexperience spelt a proposal of marriage.

"I don't want to be hard on a girl who is, after all, very young," said Lady Isabel. "And, of course, her father doesn't look after her. She is allowed to go to restaurants with him and every sort of thing.... It's not the girl's fault exactly, though I don't like the way she dresses, and a wreath of artificial flowers, or whatever it is she wears in her hair, is thoroughly bad form. But one can't be too particular, Alex, and I *do* want you to make a success of things, and have the right friends and not the wrong ones."

The wistful anxiety in her mother's voice, no less than in her glance at her daughter, made Alex wonder sensitively if, perhaps, she were secretly somewhat disappointed.

Certainly no overwhelming triumph had attended Alex' social career. She was merely the newly-come-out daughter of a charming and popular mother, less pretty than many of the season's débutantes, alternately embarrassingly self-conscious, or else, when she found herself at her ease, with an unbecomingly dictatorial manner. She had been led to expect, from constant veiled references to the subject, that as soon as she grew up, opportunity would be afforded her to attain the goal of every well-born girl's destiny—that of matrimony. Girls who became engaged to be married in their first season were a success, those who had already twice, or perhaps thrice, been the round of London gaiety with no tangible result of the sort, had almost invariably to give way to a younger sister, in order that she, in her turn, might have "the chances" of which they had failed to profit.

Of young women of twenty-two or twenty-three years old, still going yearly through the season, Lady Isabel merely said matter-of-factly:

"What a pity!"

For the first time, a disquieting twinge seized Alex, lest the same words should apply to her. No one had shown her the faintest inclination to ask her in marriage, or even express any particular admiration for her. She could not imagine any of the men whom she knew falling in love with her.

At balls or dinner-parties, she made conversation with her partners. They never grew to know one another more intimately. Sometimes she had heard girls talk of looking forward to some forthcoming entertainment because they knew that their particular friends would be there.

She herself did not care. She was on the same terms with all of them—polite, impersonal, mutually rather bored and boring.

The nearest approach to intercourse other than merely surface that she attained to, was with Queenie's most openly declared worshipper, Maurice Goldstein. His manner to all women verged upon the effusive, and Alex was secretly faintly ashamed of feeling slightly, but perceptibly, flattered at the deference which he showed her, and even at his favourite mannerism of gazing straight into her eyes as he shook hands with her on meeting or parting.

Although Lady Isabel never invited him to Clevedon Square, and sometimes spoke of him as "that dreadful young Jew who seems to get himself asked everywhere," she did not forbid Alex to dance with him, and he was the only young man of her acquaintance who invariably asked her to keep a second dance for him later in the evening.

She felt greatly curious as to his sentiment for Queenie, partly from youth's love of romance, partly from a desire to find out, if she could, both the cause and the effect of the process known as "falling in love."

If she knew more about it, she felt dimly, perhaps it might happen also to her.

One night, towards the end of the season, at the last big ball she was to attend that year, Alex was taken down to supper by Maurice Goldstein.

She was surprised, and for a moment flattered, for Queenie was also present, although she had apparently vouchsafed him neither word nor look.

Goldstein gave Alex his arm and conducted her ceremoniously downstairs to the supper-room.

It was late in the evening, only four or five couples, or an occasional group of three or four, lingered at the small, round, flower-decked tables.

"Shall we come here?" said Goldstein rather morosely.

He selected a table in a remote corner, and as she took her seat, Alex perceived that they were within sight of the alcove where sat Queenie Torrance with her partner, a young Danish diplomat whom Alex knew only by sight.

"Who is that?" she asked almost involuntarily, as Goldstein's lowering gaze followed the direction of her own.

The young man beside her needed no more to make him launch out into emphatic speech.

Alex was half frightened, as she watched the glow in his eyes and the rapid gesticulations of his hands, as though emotion had startled him into a display of the racial characteristics that he habitually concealed so carefully.

He told her crudely that he adored Queenie, and that it drove him nearly mad to see her in the company of other men.

"But why don't you ask her to marry you?" exclaimed Alex innocently.

Goldstein stared at her.

"I have asked her fourteen times," he said at last with a slight gasp.

"Fourteen times!" Alex was astounded.

According to her preconceived notions a proposal was carefully led up to, uttered at some propitious moment, preferably by moonlight, and then and there either definitely accepted or rejected.

"But I shouldn't have thought you'd even seen her fourteen times," she remarked naïvely.

"I see her every day," Goldstein said gloomily. "It's playing the deuce with my business. You won't give me away, I know—you're her friend, aren't you?—and people are so stupid and conventional, they might talk."

Alex remembered Lady Isabel. Was this what she had meant?

"I can always manage to see her. I know her movements, and when I can meet her, and when I may take her out to lunch or tea—some quiet place, of course."

Alex was puzzled.

"But are you engaged?"

"Yes, a thousand times!" he answered in low, vehement tones, and then appeared to recollect himself. "She has never said no, although I can't induce her to say yes," he admitted; "and I have to see her surrounded and admired everywhere she goes, and have no hold on her whatever. If she would only marry me!" he made a gesture of rather theatrical despair, indicating the far corner where the young Dane still sat, oblivious of everything but Queenie, drooping over the small round table that separated them.

"Cad! he's going to smoke," Goldstein muttered furiously below his breath.

The room had emptied, and Alex saw Queenie deliberately glance over her shoulder, as though to make sure of being unobserved. Her eyes moved unseeingly across Alex and Maurice Goldstein. The rest of the room was empty. With a little half-shrug of her white shoulders she delicately took a cigarette from the case that the diplomat was eagerly proffering.

It was the first time that Alex had seen a woman with a cigarette between her lips. She felt herself colouring hotly, as she watched, with involuntary fascination, Queenie's partner carefully lighting the cigarette for her, his hand very close to her face.

She dared not look at Goldstein. The cheap vulgarity of Queenie's display of modern freedom shocked her sincerely, nor could even her inexperience blind her to the underlying motive governing Queenie's every gesture.

She fumbled hastily for her fan and gloves.

"Shall we come upstairs again?" she asked in a stifled voice.

Goldstein rose without a word.

Alex, venturing to cast one glance at him, saw that his face had grown white.

As he took her back to Lady Isabel, he spoke in a quick, low, dramatic voice between clenched teeth:

"You saw? She knows she is driving me frantic; but after this—it's all over."

Alex was frightened and yet exultant at playing even a secondary rôle in what seemed to her to be a drama of reality.

An hour later, sitting, for the time being partnerless, beside her mother, she saw Queenie re-enter the ballroom, followed by the Dane.

Queenie's widely-set eyes were throwing a glance, innocent, appealing, the length of the long room. At once her eyelids dropped again. But in that instant Maurice Goldstein had left the wall against which he had been leaning, listless and sulky-looking, and was making his way through the lessening crowd.

Alex, wondering, saw him reach the side of the tall, white-clad figure, and claim her from the young diplomat.

He gravely offered Queenie his arm, and Alex saw them no more that night. She herself drove home to Clevedon Square beside Lady Isabel with her mind in a tumult.

She felt that for the first time she had seen love at close quarters, and although a faint but bitter regret that the experience had not been a personal one underlay all her sensations, she was full of excitement.

"No more late nights after this week," said Lady Isabel, her voice sleepy. "A rest will do you good, Alex. You are losing your freshness."

Alex scarcely listened. She stood impatiently while the weary maid, whose duty it was to sit up for her mistress's return, undid the complicated fastenings of her frock, and took the pins out of her hair.

"I'll brush it myself," said Alex hastily. "Good-night, mother."

"Good-night; don't come down till lunch-time, Alex—we are not doing anything."

Alex carried her ball dress carefully over her arm and went up one more flight of stairs to her own room, wrapped in her pink dressing-gown, and with her hair loose on her shoulders.

Sitting on the edge of her bed and gazing at her own reflection in the big, swinging mirror, she made personal application of the small fragment of human drama that she had just witnessed.

What man would speak and think of her as Maurice Goldstein spoke and thought of Queenie Torrance?

When would any man's ardent glance answer hers; any man make his way to her through a crowd in response to the silent summons of her eyes?

She fell into one of the idle, romantic dreams evoked by a highly-strung imagination, untempered by any light of experience. But the hero of the dream was a nebulous, shadowy figure of fiction. No man of flesh and blood held any place in the slender fabric of her fancies.

It occurred to her, more with a sense of disconcertment than of that panic which was to come later, that she did not possess the power of drawing any reality from her communion with others, and that no intimacy other than one of the surface had as yet ever resulted from any intercourse of hers with her fellow-creatures. Her nearest approach to reality had been that one-sided, irrational adoration of her schooldays for Queenie Torrance, that had met with no return, and with so much and such universal condemnation.

Alex did not doubt that the condemnation was justified. The impression left upon her adolescent mind remained ineradicable: it was wrong to attach so much importance to loving; it was *different*, in some mysterious, culpable way, to feel as she did—that nothing mattered except the people one loved, that nothing was so much worth while as the affection and understanding which one knew so well, from oneself, must exist, and for the bestowal of which on one's own lonely, ardent spirit one prayed so passionately; and all these desires, being wrong and unlike other people, must at all costs be concealed and denied. Thus Alex, placing the perverted and yet unescapable interpretation of her disconsolate youth upon such experience of life as had been vouchsafed to her.

Still sitting on the side of the bed and facing the looking-glass, she sought in her own reflection for traces of the spell wielded by Queenie Torrance. She had not yet outgrown the belief that beauty and the power to attract should be synonymous.

Was she as pretty as Queenie?

Her colour was bright and pure, and her hazel eyes reflected the brown lights gleaming in her soft, tumbled hair, that fell no lower than her shoulders. She reflected disconsolately on the undue prominence of the two, white front teeth that the plate which had tormented her childhood had just failed to render level with the others.

Straight brows added to the regularity of her features, only the corners of her mouth habitually drooping very slightly. The angularity which Lady Isabel so regretted was sharply manifested in the exposed collar-bones just above the open dressing-gown, and in the childishly thin arms and wrists. With an odd, detached shrewdness, she appraised the prominent attributes of her own appearance, its ungraceful immaturity.

As she got slowly into bed, she passed other, moral, attributes, in fleeting review.

Alex believed that one might be loved for one's goodness, if not for one's beauty. But she could not suppose herself to be good. The tradition of the nursery black sheep still clung to her.

Should love come to her, she had nothing but the force of the answer within her to bring to it, and that force she had been taught to think of in the light of an affliction to be overcome.

Yet Alex Clare fell asleep smiling a little, nursing the foolish, romantic fancies that usurped the place of realities, and unaware that the temperament which craves to give all, is often that of which least will ever be asked.

IX
Scotland

Queenie's engagement to young Goldstein was formally announced at the beginning of the year following that one in which Alex made her début.

"A most suitable match, I should imagine," was Lady Isabel's emphasized comment.

Alex was romantically delighted, and hoped for an opportunity of obtaining first-hand impressions.

Queenie, however, sent only the most conventional of notes in reply to Alex' eagerly written congratulation, and Alex had only a glimpse of her at the crowded wedding, exquisitely pale and pure under her veil, with Goldstein, his swarthy face radiant and illuminated, at her side.

Remembering the night when the young Jew had spoken to her freely of his adoration for her friend, Alex, with awkward fervour, addressed a few words of ardent congratulation to him.

He showed his remarkably white teeth in a quick smile, brilliant with triumph and happiness, and wrung her hand warmly; but alas! his eyes failed to answer her gaze, and it was obvious that no deeper issues between them held any place in his recollections.

Alex went away vaguely disappointed and humiliated.

She, who so longed for a first place, seemed doomed to relegation to the ranks. Even at home there was no longer any excitement such as that which had surrounded her launch into the great world, and Lady Isabel occasionally betrayed a hint of disappointment that no family council had as yet been required on the subject of Alex' future, such as those which had punctuated the epoch of her own brief girlhood.

Indeed it was rather Barbara who was the centre of attention.

She still suffered from backache and general languor, consequent upon over-rapid growth during the year she had spent on the flat of her back. Old Nurse pitied and was much inclined to spoil her, dosed her religiously with a glass of port at eleven o'clock every morning, and supported her whining assertions that lessons with Mademoiselle made her ill.

"I want to go to school," said Barbara inconsistently. "Alex went to school, so why shouldn't I?"

"Darlin' child, you know very well that your father won't hear of girls goin' to school. A convent is quite different—but I certainly shan't send you to that sort of establishment, after the trick they played me with Alex, sendin' her back round-shouldered, and with her hands all chapped and red and covered with chilblains. *Never* again," said Lady Isabel.

Barbara sulked.

She sulked so long and so effectively that the unfortunate Mademoiselle came of her own accord to implore that Barbara might be released from the schoolroom. She was not learning anything, and her example was making little Pamela naughty and defiant.

"What a plague children are!" Lady Isabel said helplessly.

She consulted her friends, drawing a plaintively humorous picture of the recalcitrant young person, which, to the annoyance of Alex, caused a certain amount of amused sympathy to be expressed in Barbara's favour.

At last some one suggested that she should be sent abroad. Not to a school or a convent, certainly not—every one was unanimous on that point excepting one or two ultra-Catholic old aunts of Sir Francis—but to a charming Marquise, living at Neuilly, and desirous of companionship for her only child, a girl of about the same age as Barbara.

"She will learn to speak French like a native, and have dancing and singing lessons with the Hélène child, and go to all the art galleries and places.... That girl of the Duchess went there to be finished just before she came out, and *loved* it, and she came back so much improved— knowing how to put on her clothes, you know ... just the sort of thing that makes all the difference."

So spoke Lady Isabel's enthusiastic friends.

Barbara was not consulted, but when the plans had been finally settled upon and everything arranged, she was told, in accordance with the usage of her day, that as she was so discontented and troublesome at home, her parents felt obliged, for the sake of the younger children, to send her away from them. Barbara, following her wont, said nothing at all, and did not relax her pouting expression, but once back in the schoolroom again, she jumped up and down on the sofa in a manner denoting extravagant glee.

"I knew they'd have to give in," she chanted. "I knew they would, I knew they would."

For a long while she teased Archie and Pamela by refusing to give them any explanation, and at the same time exciting their curiosity by her continual reference to an approaching triumphant emancipation for her, until Cedric, home for the Easter holidays, and expert in the administrations of schoolboy tortures, ruthlessly made use of them to reduce his sister to her proper position of inferiority.

Barbara was sent to Neuilly early in April, and Alex proceeded to enter upon the second phase of her social career.

It was less of a success than her first season had been.

It was assumed that she had by this time made her own friends, and her mother's contemporaries accordingly took less pains in the matter of introductions on her behalf.

If it be true that nothing succeeds like success, it is truer still that nothing fails so completely as a failure.

When Alex had sat out four or five dances at a ball, partnerless, her conviction of her own social degradation was absolutely overwhelming. Her surroundings only interested her as a background to her own personality, and as she derived no pleasure, but only disappointment and mortification, from the majority of the functions at which she was present, her young, expressive face unconsciously advertised both her vexation and the cause of it.

Her youth and her vanity alike were in rebellion against the truth, which she more than half divined, that she, who so longed to please and to attract, was as utterly devoid of that magnetic charm possessed by other girls in a lesser, and by Queenie Goldstein in supreme, degree, as it was possible for a reasonably pretty and healthy young girl to be.

Neither her health nor her beauty improved, moreover.

Late hours, in her case, uncounteracted by the vivid sparkle of enjoyment, drew unbecoming dark circles beneath her eyes, and the physical fatigue always engendered in her by boredom was most unmistakably manifested in her slouching shoulders and mournful pallor.

"Alex a son air bête aujourd'hui."

Memory mercilessly recalled to her the old gibe of her schoolmates sometimes, as she felt, against her own will, her features stiffening into the stupid "tragedy-queen" look which had met with the mocking of her companions.

"Do try and cheer up, darlin'," Lady Isabel sometimes said, with more impatience than compassion in her voice, as she glanced at her daughter; and the implication that her looks were betraying her feelings made Alex more wretched and self-conscious than ever.

She often saw Queenie Goldstein, as much surrounded as in the days before her marriage, and her excessive *décolletage* now enhanced by the jewels showered upon her by her husband.

Queenie once invited her to a dinner-party at her little house in Curzon Street, but Alex knew that she would not be allowed to go, and showed the invitation with great trepidation to her mother.

"Very impertinent of her! Why, she's never been introduced to me. I shouldn't dream of allowin' any daughter of mine to go and dine with people whom I didn't know personally, even if they were *absolutely* all right."

Lady Isabel, so easy-going and tepidly affectionate towards her children, was adamant where her social creed was concerned.

"In any case, Alex, I've told you before that I don't want you to go on with the acquaintance. That Goldstein woman is gettin' herself talked about, unless I'm very much mistaken."

Again that mysterious accusation! Alex said no more, but wondered naïvely how the phase that had been used in connection with Queenie Torrance could still be applicable to Maurice Goldstein's wife.

Surely married women did not flirt? The term, to Alex, symbolized she knew not what of offensive coquetry, and of general "bad form."

This belief had been inculcated into her as a precept but, nevertheless, she could not divest herself of a secret suspicion that, although Lady Isabel might have rebuked, she would not have been altogether averse from a lapse or two in that direction on the part of her daughter.

But Alex embarked upon no flirtation. The men who danced with her or took her in to dinner never seemed desirous of talking personalities. They made perfunctory remarks about the decorations of the tables, the quality of the floor and the music, and the revival of the Gilbert and Sullivan operas.

The sense that the intercourse between them must be sustained by conversation never left her for an instant.

There had been one occasion when she had actually forgotten to think of herself and of the effect she might be producing, and had joined with real interest in a discussion about books with a man a great deal older than herself, who happened to be placed next to her at a big dinner party. Lady Isabel, opposite, had glanced once or twice at her daughter's unusually animated expression.

"You seemed to be gettin' on very well with the man on your other side—not the one who took you down, but the oldish one," she said afterwards in a pleased voice.

"I never found out his name," said Alex. "He told me he wrote books. It was so interesting; we were talking about poetry a lot of the time."

Her mother's face lost something of its smile. "Oh, my darling!" she exclaimed in sudden flattened tones, "don't go and get a reputation for being *clever*, whatever you do. People do dislike that sort of thing so much in a girl!"

Alex, her solitary triumph killed, knew that there was yet another item to be added to that invisible score of reasons for which one was loved or disliked by one's fellow-creatures.

Without formulating the conviction to herself, she believed implicitly that in the careful simulation of those attributes which she had been told would provoke admiration or affection, lay her only chance of obtaining something of that which she craved.

Dismayed, wearied, and uncheered by success, she continued to act out her little feeble comedies.

At the end of her second season she felt very old, and very much disillusioned. This was not real life as she had thought to find it on leaving schooldays behind her.

There must be something beyond—some happy reality that should reveal the wherefore of all existence, but Alex knew not where to find it.

Morbidity was a word which had no place in the vocabulary of her surroundings, but Lady Isabel said to her rather plaintively, "You must try and look more cheerful, Alex, dear, when I take you about. Your father is quite vexed when he sees such a gloomy face. You enjoy things, don't you?"

And Alex, in her complicated disappointment at disappointing her mother and father, answered hastily in the affirmative.

In the autumn, in Scotland, she met Noel Cardew again.

They were staying at the same house. Alex felt childishly proud of saying, when her hostess brought the young man to her side, with a word of introduction:

"Oh, but we've met before! I know him *quite* well."

She wished that she had spoken less emphatically, at the sight of Noel's politely non-committal smile. It was evident that he had not the faintest recollection of the meeting at his mother's house in Devonshire. She reminded him of it rather shyly.

"Oh, yes, of course. You were at school with my young cousins. I remember you coming over to see us quite well, with your brothers. We all played hunt the slipper or something, didn't we?"

"Hide-and-seek," said Alex literally. She wondered why encounters which remained quite vividly in her own memory should always appear to present themselves so indistinctly and trivially to other people.

"I haven't heard from your cousins for a long while. Are they in America?"

"Diana is in India, of course. She married, you know—a fellow in the Indian Police."

"I remember," said Alex, determined to ignore the tiny prick of jealousy that now habitually assailed her almost every time that she heard of the marriage of another girl.

"Are the other two married?" she made resolute inquiry.

"Oh, no. Why, Marie isn't properly grown-up yet. They are both in America. I've some idea of going over to New York myself next year, and I suppose I shall stay with their people. My uncle's at the Embassy, you know."

"It would be splendid to see New York," said Alex, with the old imitation of enthusiasm.

"I should like the journey as well," young Cardew remarked. "Board ship is an awfully good way of studying human nature, I fancy, and I'm rather keen on that sort of thing. In fact, I've a mad idea of perhaps writing a book one of these days, probably in the form of a novel, because it's only by gilding the pill that you can get the great B.P. to swallow it—but it'll really be a kind of philosophy of life, you know, with a good deal about the different sides of human nature. It may sound rather ambitious, perhaps, but I believe it could be done."

Alex assented eagerly, and wondered what the initials that he had used—"the great B.P."—represented. She glanced at him sideways.

He was even better-looking than he had been as a boy, his sunburn of a deeper tan, and the still noticeable cast in one eye adding a certain character to the straightness of his features. He had grown a little, fair moustache, contrasting pleasantly with his light brown eyes. The boyish immaturity of the loosely knit figure was obscured to her eyes by the excellence of his carriage and his five foot eleven inches of height.

She was inwardly almost incredulously pleased when he chose the place next to hers at breakfast on the following morning, and asked whether she was going out to join the guns at lunch on the moors.

"I think so," said Alex. She would have liked to say, "I hope so," but something within her attached such an exaggerated importance to the words that she found herself unable to utter them.

"Well," said Noel, "I shall look out for you, so mind you come."

Alex's gratification was transparently evident. She was the only girl of the party, which was a small one; and Lady Isabel, declaring herself obliged to write letters, sent her out at lunch-time under the care of her hostess.

They lunched on the moors with the five men, two of whom had only come over for the day.

Noel Cardew at once established himself at Alex' side and began to expatiate upon the day's sport. He talked a great deal, and was as full of theories as in their schoolroom days, and Alex, on her side, listened with the same intense hope that her sympathy might continue to retain him beside her.

She answered him with eager monosyllables and ejaculations expressive of interest. Without analysing her own motives, it seemed to her to be so important that Noel Cardew should continue to address his attention exclusively to her, that she was content entirely to sink her own individuality into that of a sympathetic listener.

When she dressed for dinner that evening and looked at herself in the big mirror, it seemed to her that for the first time her own appearance was entirely satisfactory. She felt self-confident and happy, and after dinner, when the elders of the party sat down to play cards, she declared boldly that she wanted to look at the garden by moonlight.

"Rather," said Noel Cardew.

They went out together through the open French window.

Alex held up her long-tailed white satin with one hand, and walked up and down with him under the glowing red globe of the full moon. Noel talked about his book, taking her interest for granted in a manner that flattered and delighted her.

"I think psychology is simply the most absorbing thing in the world," he declared earnestly. "I hope you don't fight shy of long words, do you?"

Alex uttered a breathless disclaimer.

"I'm glad. So many people seem to think that if any one says anything in words of more than two syllables it's affectation. Oxford and that sort of thing. But, of course, you're not like that, are you?"

He did not wait for an answer this time, but went on talking very eagerly about the scheme that he entertained for obtaining material for his book.

"It might revolutionize the whole standard of moral values in the country," he said very simply. "You know, just put things in a light that hasn't struck home in England yet at all. Of course, on the continent they're far more advanced than we are, on those sort of points. That's why I want to travel, before I start serious work. Of course, I've got a mass of notes already. Just ideas, that have struck me as I go along. I'm afraid I'm fearfully observant, and I generally size up the people I meet, and then make notes about them—or else simply dismiss them from my mind altogether. My idea is rather to classify human nature into various *types*, so that the book can be divided up under different headings, and then have a sort of general summing up at the end. Of course, that's only a rough sketch of the whole plan, but you see what I mean?"

"Yes, I do," said Alex with conviction. "I've always, all my life, thought that *people* mattered much more than anything else, only I've never found anybody else who felt like that too."

"It's rather interesting to look at things the same way, don't you think?" Noel enquired.

"Oh, yes," Alex answered with shy fervour, her heart beating very fast.

She was only anxious to prolong the *tête-à-tête*, and had no idea of suggesting a return to the drawing-room, in spite of the damage that she subconsciously felt the damp ground to be doing to her satin slippers. But presently Lady Isabel called to her from the window, and she came into the lighted room, conscious both of her own glowing face and of a certain kindly, interested look bent upon her by her seniors.

X
Noel

In the ensuing days, Alex met that look very often—a look of pleased, speculative approval, pregnant with unspoken meanings.

Noel sought her company incessantly, and every opportunity was given them of spending time in one another's society. For five glowing, heather-surrounded days and five breathless, moonlit evenings, they became the centre of their tiny world.

Then Lady Isabel said one night to her daughter:

"You've enjoyed this visit, haven't you, darlin'? I'm sorry we're movin' on."

"Oh," said Alex faintly, "are we really leaving tomorrow?"

"Tomorrow morning, by the early train," her mother assented cheerfully.

The true instinct of the feeble, to clutch at an unripe prize lest it be taken from them, made Alex wonder desperately if she could not postpone her departure.

But she dared not make any such suggestion, and Lady Isabel, looking at her dismayed face, laughed a little as though at the unreason of a child. Alex blushed with shame as she thought that her mother might have guessed what was in her mind. That evening, however, Lady Isabel came into her room as she was dressing for dinner.

"I thought you'd like to put *this* over your shoulders, Alex," she said negligently. "It will improve that cream-coloured frock of yours."

It was a painted scarf that she held out, and she stood gazing critically while the maid laid it across Alex' shoulders.

"You look so nice, darling child. Are you ready?"

"Yes, mother."

They went downstairs together.

Alex was acutely conscious of a certain maternal pride and tenderness, such as she had not experienced from Lady Isabel since the first days of her return from Liège, when she had finally left school. She did not let herself speculate to what such unusual emotion might portend.

But at the sight of Noel Cardew, better-looking than ever in evening clothes, a chaotic excitement surged up within her in anticipation of their last evening together.

Almost as she sat down beside him at the dinner-table, she said piteously, "I wish we weren't going away tomorrow."

"You're *not?*"

"Oh, yes. Didn't you know?"

"I hadn't realized it," said Noel, and although she avoided looking at him, she noted with a feeling of triumph the dismay in his voice.

"Oh, I say! What a shame. Must you really go?"

"We're going to pay two more visits and then leave Scotland altogether."

"I shan't stay much longer myself," observed Noel nonchalantly.

Alex was conscious of keeping the words as it were at the back of her mind, with the implication which she attached to them, while the conversation at the small table became general.

As she followed her hostess and Lady Isabel from the room, Noel, holding open the door, said to her in a rapid, anxious tone, very low:

"You'll come out into the garden afterwards, won't you?"

An enigmatic "perhaps" was not in Alex' vocabulary.

She gave him a quick, radiant smile, and nodded emphatically.

It never occurred to her eager prodigality that she ran any risk of cheapening the favours that so few had ever coveted.

In the garden she moved along the gravelled walk beside him, actually breathless from inward excitement.

"There was heaps more I wanted to say to you about the book," Noel remarked disconsolately. "I shan't have any one to exchange ideas with now. They're all so old—and besides, I don't think English people as a rule care much about psychology and that sort of thing. They're so keen on games. So am I, in a way, but I must say it seems to me that the study of human nature is a good deal more worth one's while."

"People are so interesting," said Alex. She was perfectly aware of the futility of her remark as she made it, but in some undercurrent of her consciousness there floated the conviction that one need not put forth any great powers of originality in order to obtain response from Noel Cardew.

"I can be perfectly *natural* with him—we think alike," She defended herself against her own unformulated accusation with inexplicable anger.

166

"I think they're frightfully interesting," said Noel with conviction. "Of course, men are far more interesting than women, if you don't mind my saying so, simply from the psychological point of view. I hope you don't think I'm being rude?"

"Oh, *no*."

"You see, women, as a general rule, are rather shallow, though, of course, there are a great many exceptions. But you know what I mean—as a rule they're rather shallow. That's what I feel about women, they're shallow."

"Perhaps you're right," said Alex, rather discouraged. She would not admit to herself that his sweeping assertion awoke no echo whatever within her.

To her immaturity, the essence of sympathy lay in complete agreement, and abstract questions meant nothing to her when weighed in the balance against her desire to establish, to her own satisfaction at least, the existence of such sympathy between herself and Noel Cardew.

"I've got another mad plan," said Noel slowly. "You'll think I'm always getting insane ideas, and this one rather depends on you."

"Oh, what?"

"I hope you won't mind my suggesting such a thing—" He paused so long that Alex' imagination had time for a hundred foolish, ecstatic promptings, such as her reason knew could not be forthcoming, but for which her whole undisciplined sense of romance was crying.

"Well, look here: what should you think of collaborating with me over the book? I'm sure you could write if you tried, and anyway, you could probably give me sidelights on the feminine part of it. It would be most awfully helpful to me if you would."

"Oh," said Alex uncertainly. She was invaded by unreasoning disappointment. "But how could we do it?"

"Oh, well, notes, you know—just keep notes of anything that struck us particularly, and then put it in together later. We should have to do a good deal of it by correspondence, of course.... I say, are you a conventional person?"

"Not in the least," said Alex hastily.

"I'm glad of that. I'm afraid I'm rather desperately unconventional myself. Of course, in a way it might be rather unconventional, you and me corresponding—but would that matter?"

"Not to me," said Alex resolutely.

"That's splendid. We could do a lot that way, and then I hope, of course, that you'll let me come and see you in London."

"Of course," Alex cried eagerly. "I don't know the exact date when we shall be back, but I could let you know. Have you got the address?"

"Clevedon Square—"

She hastily supplied the number of the house.

"Oh, that's all right. I'm sure to forget it," said Noel easily; "but I shall find you in the books, I suppose."

"Yes," said Alex, feeling suddenly damped.

She herself would have been in no danger of forgetting the number of a house wherein dwelt any one whom she wished to see, but with disastrous and quite unconscious humility, she told herself that it was, of course, not to be expected that any one else should go to lengths equal to her own. In her one-sided experience, Alex had always found herself to be unique.

That Noel Cardew was not in despair at the idea of her departure was evident. But he repeated several times that he wished she were not going so soon, and even asked whether she would stay on if invited to do so.

"I'm sure they'd all love you to," he assured her. "Then Lady Isabel could pay the other visits and call for you on her way back."

"I'm sure I shouldn't be allowed to stay on by myself," said Alex dolefully.

"There you are! Conventionality again. *My* daughters," said Noel instructively, "if I ever have any, shall be brought up quite differently. I've made up my mind to that. I daresay you'll laugh at all these theories of mine, but I've always been keen on ideas, if you remember."

But for once Noel did not receive the habitual ready disclaimer called for by his speech.

His easy allusion to his hypothetical daughters had reduced Alex to utter silence.

Afterwards, alone in the darkness of her own room, she wondered why such a startling sense of protest had revolted within her at his words, but her mind shied away instinctively from the question, and she found herself unable to pursue it.

The next morning, in the unromantic atmosphere induced by an early breakfast, and Sir Francis' anxiety to make sure of catching the connection, politely concealed, but quite evident to the perceptions of his wife and daughter, Noel Cardew and Alex exchanged their brief and entirely public farewell.

"I'll write about the book," was his cheerful parting assurance.

"Don't forget," said Alex.

Lady Isabel was rather humorous on the subject of *fin de siècle* emancipation, amongst the house party in the midst of which she and her daughter found themselves that evening.

"What are boys and girls coming to? I hear young men gaily promisin' to write to Alex on all sorts of subjects, and making private assignations with her," she declared amusedly. "Aren't you and that nice-looking Cardew boy writin' a book in collaboration, or something, darling?"

The slight jest was made popular amongst her seniors, and Alex was kindly rallied about her modern freedom and assumption of privileges undreamed of by the older generation. The inference obviously placed upon her friendship with Noel Cardew was evident, and pleased her starved vanity even more than the agreeable amount of flattery and attention which at last was being bestowed upon her.

It was her first hint of success achieved amid standards which she had been taught to believe were all-prevalent. Brushed lightly by the passing wing of triumph, she became eager and self-confident, even rather over-clamorous in the assertion of her own individuality, as had been the child Alex in the nursery at Clevedon Square.

Lady Isabel did not check her. She made subtle exploitation of Alex' youth and sudden, rather boisterous gaiety, and occasionally laughed a little, and alluded to the collaboration scheme between her and Noel Cardew. "But all the same, darlin' child," she observed to Alex in private, "I can't have you correspondin' with young men all over the country unbeknown to me. Once in a way is all very well, perhaps, but you'll have to let me see the letters, I think."

Alex was only mildly resentful of the injunction. She surmised shrewdly enough that her mother was more anxious to establish the authentic existence of a correspondence between Noel Cardew and herself than to supervise the details of it. She herself waited with frantic, furtive eagerness for his first letter.

It did not reach her until after her return to London. Secretly bitterly disappointed, she read the short, conventional phrases and the subscription:

"I never know how to end up a letter, but hope this will be all right—Yours very sincerely, "NOEL E. CARDEW."

Across the top of the front page was a postscript.

"Next month I shall be in town. Don't forget that I am coming to call upon you. I hope you won't be 'out'!"

Alex, to whom nothing was trivial, saw the proposed call looming enormous upon the horizon of her days.

Every afternoon she either sat beside Lady Isabel in the carriage in an agony, with only one thought in her mind—the expectation of finding Noel's card upon the hall table on their return—or else took her part disjointedly and with obvious absent-mindedness in the entertainment of her mother's visitors.

When, during a crowded At Home afternoon, in the course of which she had necessarily ceased to listen for the sound of the front-door bell, "Mr. Cardew" was at length announced, Alex felt almost unable to turn round and face the entering visitor.

Her own imagination, untempered either by humour or by experience, had led her to picture the next encounter between herself and Noel so frequently, and with such a prodigal folly of romantic detail, that it seemed incredible to her that the reality should take place within a few instants, amidst brief, conventional words and gestures.

Noel did not talk about the book that they were to write together, although he remained beside Alex most of the afternoon. Only just as he was leaving, he asked cheerfully:

168

"You've not forgotten our collaboration, have you, partner? I've heaps of things to discuss with you, only you were so busy this afternoon, looking after all those people."

"We shall be in on Sunday," Alex told him eagerly, "and there won't be such a crowd."

"Oh, good," said Noel. "Perhaps we'll meet in the Park before that, though."

"I hope so," said Alex.

They met in the Park and elsewhere, and Noel, all through the ensuing weeks before Christmas, called often at the house in Clevedon Square.

Lady Isabel twice asked him to dinner, but although he was once placed next her, on neither occasion, to Alex' astonished resentment was he assigned to her as a partner.

Alex, for the first time conscious of being sought after, and receiving with avidity the fragments that fell to her share, forced herself to believe that they would eventually constitute that impossible whole of which she had dreamed wildly and extravagantly all her life.

Into the eager assents which she gave to all Noel's many theories, she read a similarity of outlook, into her almost trembling readiness to fall in with his every suggestion, a community of tastes, and into his interminable expositions of his own views an appeal to her deeper sympathies that surely denoted the consciousness of affinity between them.

She was happy, although principally in a nervous anticipation of happiness to come. She was able, when alone, to imagine that from absolutely impersonal good comradeship, Noel would suddenly plunge into the impassioned declarations of her own fancy, but when she was actually with him, his cool, pleasant, boyish voice dispelled the folly, and her fundamental shyness, that never deserted her save in the realm of her own thoughts, was relieved, with an intense and involuntary relief, that it should be so.

She saw Noel's father and mother again, and was greeted by the latter with a bright and conditional affectionateness that inspected even while it acclaimed.

It was after this that the trend of Noel's thoughts appeared suddenly to change, and he spoke to Alex of the place in Devonshire.

"One's first duty is to the place, of course," he said reflectively, "and I'm not at all sure that I oughtn't to look into the management of an estate, and all that sort of thing, very thoroughly. Some day—a long, long time hence, of course—I shall have to run our own place, and I'm rather keen about the duties of a landlord, and improving the condition of the people. I used to be a Socialist, as you know, but I must say one's ideas alter a bit as one goes on through life, and I've had some talks with the pater lately."

He broke off, and looked rather oddly at Alex for a moment.

"They want me to think of settling down, I believe," he said, almost shyly.

Alex spent that night in feverishly placing possible and impossible interpretations on the words, and on the look he had given her.

The sense of an approaching crisis terrified her so much that she felt she would have given worlds to avoid it.

The following evening it came.

Most conventionally, she met Noel Cardew at an evening reception, and he conducted her rather solemnly to a small conservatory where two chairs were placed, conspicuously enough, beneath a solitary palm.

An orchestra was just audible above the hum and buzz of conversation.

"It's luck getting in here," said Noel. "I wanted to see you very particularly tonight. I must say I never thought I should find myself particularly wanting to see *any* girl—in fact, I'd practically made up my mind never to have anything to do with women—but I see now that two people who had very much the same sort of ideas about life in general could do a tremendous lot for a place, and for the country generally; don't you agree?—and, of course—" He became hopelessly incoherent, "... knowing one another's other's people it all makes such a difference ... I could never understand fellows running after Gaiety girls and marrying them, myself!! After all, one's duty to the estate is ... and then, later on, perhaps, if one thought of Parliament—"

Alex felt that the pounding of her heart was making her physically faint, and she raised her head desperately, in the hope of stopping him. Noel met her eyes courageously.

"I wish you'd let me tell our people that you—that we—we're engaged," he said hoarsely.

His words struck on Alex' ear almost meaninglessly.

Irrationally in love as she was, with Love, she knew only that he was asking something of her—that she had at last an outlet for that which no one had ever yet desired.

Unable to speak, and unconscious of bathos, she vehemently nodded her head.

Noel immediately took both her hands and shook them wildly up and down.

"Thank Heaven, it's over," he cried boyishly. "You can't imagine how I've been funking asking you—I thought you'd say yes, but one feels such an awful fool—and I've never done it before. I say, Alex—I can call you Alex now, can't I—you're like me, aren't you? You don't want sentimentality. If there's one thing I bar," said the newly-accepted lover, "it's sentimentality."

XI
Engagement of Marriage

"I am engaged to be married," Alex repeated to herself, in a vain endeavour to realize the height to which she must have now attained. But that realization, by which she meant tangible certainty, for which she craved, continually eluded her.

The preliminary formalities, indeed, duly took place, from her own avowal before a graciously-maternal Lady Isabel, to Noel's formal interview with Sir Francis in the traditional setting of the library.

After that, however, a freakish fate seemed to take control of all the circumstances connected with Alex' engagement.

Noel Cardew's father became ill, and in the uncertainty consequent upon a state of health which his doctor declared might be almost indefinitely prolonged, there could be no question of immediately announcing the engagement.

"Just as well, perhaps. We're all delighted about it, but they're both young enough to wait a little while," Lady Isabel smilingly made the best of it. "Next year will be quite time enough to settle anything."

Her serenity was the obvious outcome of an extreme contentment.

Alex found herself better able to regard herself in the light of one betrothed in her mother's company than in that of Noel. He treated her almost exactly as he had always done, with cheerful good-fellowship, and only at the very outset of the engagement with any tinge of shyness in his bearing.

"Of course, I ought to have got a ring," he said very seriously, "but I don't believe in taking any chances, and so, just in case there was any hitch, I waited. Besides, I don't know what you like best—you'll have to choose."

Alex smiled at the words. There was a glamour about such a choice, even beyond that with which her own sense of the romantic perforce enveloped it.

She wondered whether she would be allowed to go with Noel to a jeweller's, or whether he would, after all, choose his token alone, and bring it to her, and place it on her finger with one of those low, ardently-spoken sentences which she could hear so clearly in her own mind, and which seemed so strangely and utterly impossible in Noel's real presence.

But the arrival of Noel's ring, after all, took her by surprise.

He had been lunching with them in Clevedon Square, when the jeweller's assistant was announced, just as Lady Isabel was rising from the luncheon-table.

She turned enquiringly.

"Noel?"

"I told him to come here. I thought you wouldn't mind. You see, I want Alex to choose her ring."

"Oh, my dear boy! how very exciting! But may we see too?"

Mrs. Cardew was also present.

"Oh, rather," said Noel heartily. "We shall want your advice."

They all trooped hastily into the library, where the man was waiting, with the very large assortment of gleaming rings ordered for inspection by Noel.

"What beauties!" said Lady Isabel. "But, really, I don't know if I ought to let him."

She glanced at Mrs. Cardew, who said in a very audible voice:

"Of course. He's so happy. It's quite delightful to watch them both."

She was looking hard and appraisingly at the rings as she spoke.

Alex looked at them too, quite unseeing of their glittering magnificence, but acutely conscious that every one was waiting for her first word.

"Oh, how lovely!" she exclaimed faintly.

She chid herself violently for the sick disappointment that invaded her, not, indeed, at the matter, but at the manner of the gift.

And yet she realized dimly, that it was impossible that it should have happened in any other way—that any other way, indeed, would have been as utterly uncharacteristic of Noel Cardew as this was typical.

"Which do you like?" he asked her. "I chose all the most original ones I could see. I always like unconventional designs better than conventional ones, I'm afraid. Where's that long one you showed me this morning?"

"The diamond marquise, sir?" The assistant deferentially produced it, glancing the while at Alex.

"That's it," said Noel eagerly. "Try it on, Alex, won't you?"

He used her name quite freely and without any shyness.

Alex felt more of genuine excitement, and less of wistful bewilderment, than at any moment since Noel had first asked her to marry him, as she shyly held out her left hand and the jeweller slipped the heavy, beautiful ring onto her third finger.

She had long, slim hands, the fingers rather too thin and the knuckles, though small, too prominent for beauty. But, thanks to the tyranny of old Nurse, and to Lady Isabel's insistence upon the use of nightly glycerine-and-honey, they were exquisitely soft and white.

The diamonds gleamed and flashed at her as she moved the ring up and down her finger.

"We can easily make it smaller, to fit your finger," said the jeweller's assistant.

"It really is beautiful. Look, Francis," said Lady Isabel.

Alex' father put up his glasses, and after inspection he also exclaimed:

"Beautiful."

"You've such little fingers, dear, it'll have to be made smaller," said Mrs. Cardew graciously.

"Is it to be that one, then?" Lady Isabel asked.

Alex saw that her mother's pretty, youthful-looking flush of pleasurable excitement had mounted to her face. She herself, conscious of an inexplicable oppression, felt tongue-tied, and unable to do more than repeat foolishly and lifelessly:

"Oh, it's lovely, it's perfectly lovely. It's *too* beautiful."

Noel, however, looked gratified at the words of admiration.

"That's the one *I* like," he said with emphasis. "I knew when I saw them this morning that I liked that one much the best. We'll settle on that one, then, shall we?"

"You silly boy," laughed his mother, "that's for Alex to decide. Perhaps she likes something else better. Try the emerald, Alex?"

"Oh, this is lovely," repeated Alex again, shrinking back a little. Furious with herself, she was yet only desirous that the scene should not be prolonged any longer.

"Come and look at it in the light?" The urgent pressure of Lady Isabel's hand on her arm drew her into the embrasure of the window.

"Alex," said her mother low and swiftly, all the time holding up her hand against the light as though studying the ring. "Alex, you *must* be more gracious. What *is* the matter with you?"

"Nothing," said Alex childishly, feeling inclined to burst into tears.

"Then for Heaven's sake do try and smile and show a *little* enthusiasm," said her mother with unwonted sharpness.

Alex, scarlet, and most visibly discomposed, returned to the group round the library table.

Forcing herself to make some attempt at obeying her mother's behest, she picked up the nearest jewel, two pearls in a prettily-twisted setting, and began to examine it.

"I like that design, too. It's original," said Mrs. Cardew.

"Oh, but pearls are unlucky—she couldn't have pearls," protested Lady Isabel.

"They mean tears, don't they?" Alex contributed to the discussion, for the sake of making her mother see that she was willing to do her best.

"Are you superstitious?" Noel asked rather reproachfully. "I can't say I believe in all that sort of thing myself, you know. In fact I make rather a principle of doing things on a 13th, or walking under ladders, and all the rest of it, just to prove there's nothing in it."

Sir Francis fixed the young man benevolently through his monocle.

"I presume, however, that in this instance you prefer not to tempt the gods," he remarked affably, and Noel, always obviously in awe of his betrothed's father, hastily agreed with him.

"Then it's diamonds, is it?—unless Alex prefers the emerald."

"I like the diamond one best," Noel reiterated. "I really pitched on that one the minute I saw it. I like originality."

"Well, it couldn't be lovelier," said Lady Isabel contentedly.

The jeweller was shown out, leaving the diamond marquise ring, in its little white-velvet case, on the table in front of Alex.

Sir Francis opened the door for his wife and Mrs. Cardew.

"Oh," said Noel urgently. "You *must* stay and see her put it on."

Both ladies laughed at the boyish exclamation, and Alex flushed scarlet once more.

Noel opened the case and looked proudly at his gift.

"You must put it on for her," said his mother, "when it's been made smaller."

The hint was unmistakable.

Noel held out the ring.

"Let's see it on now at once, Alex. It can go back to the shop later."

Alex, in a sort of utter desperation, thrust out her hand, and Noel, politely and carefully avoiding touching it with his own, slipped the heavy hoop over her finger.

"Thank you," she stammered.

There was another laugh.

"Poor dears! Let's leave them in peace," cried Mrs. Cardew mockingly, and rustled to the door again.

"Did you ever see anything so young as they both are?" she murmured sweetly to Lady Isabel, audibly enough for Alex to guess at the words, if she did not actually hear them.

She was thankful that they should no longer be watching her, and turned with something like relief to Noel's gratified, uncritical looks.

It became suddenly much easier to speak unconstrainedly.

Perhaps she was subconsciously aware that of all of them, it was Noel himself who would expect the least of her, because his demands upon her were so infinitesimal.

"It's a beautiful ring; thank you very, very much. I—" She stopped and gulped, then said bravely, "I *love* it."

She emphasized the word almost without knowing it, as though to force from him some response.

Although she had never actually realized it, it was a word which, in point of fact, had never yet passed between them. Noel's fair face coloured at last, as his light eyes met her unconsciously tragical gaze.

"*Alex a son air bête aujourd'hui.*"

With horrid inappropriateness, the hated gibe of her schooldays flashed into Alex' thoughts, stiffening her face into the old lines of morbid, self-conscious misery.

Part of her mind, in unwilling detachment, contemplated ruefully the oddly inadequate spectacle which they must present, staring shamefacedly at one another across the glittering token of their troth.

Frenziedly desirous of breaking the silence, heavy with awkwardness, that hung between them, she began to speak hastily and almost at random.

"Thank you so very much—I've never had such a lovely present—it's lovely; thank you so much."

"I thought you'd like it," muttered Noel, more overcome with confusion, if possible, than was Alex.

"Oh, yes, yes. It's lovely."

"I thought you'd like something rather original, you know, not a conventional one."

"Oh, yes!"

"You're sure you wouldn't rather have one of the others—that emerald one that mother liked?"

"Oh, no."

"I dare say they'd let me change it, the man knows us very well."

"Oh, no, no."

"Well, I, I—I'm awfully glad you like it."

"Yes, I *do* like it. I—I think it's lovely."

"I—I thought you'd like it."

Alex began to feel as though she was in a nightmare, but she was mysteriously unable to put an end to their sorry dialogue.

"It's perfectly lovely, I think. I don't know how to thank you."

Noel swallowed two or three times, visibly and audibly, and then took a couple of determined steps towards her.

"I think you—you'd better let me kiss you," he said hoarsely. "You haven't yet, you know."

Something deep down within Alex was surging up in angry bewilderment, and she was sufficiently aware of a sense of protest to rebut it indignantly and with lightning-swift determination.

It was the humility of love that had prompted her lover to crave that permission which should never have been asked.

So she told herself in the flash of a moment, while she waited for Noel's kiss to lift her once and for all into some far realm of romance where trivial details of manifestation should no longer obscure the true values of life.

Unconsciously, she had shut her eyes, but at an unaccountable pause in the proceedings, she opened them again.

Noel was carefully removing his pince-nez.

"I say," he stammered, "you're—you're sure you don't mind?"

If Alex had followed the impulse of her own feelings, she must have cried out at this juncture:

"Not if you're quick and get it over!"

But instead, she heard herself murmuring feebly:

"Oh, no, not at all."

She hastily raised her face, turning it sideways to Noel, and felt his lips gingerly touching the middle of her cheek. Then she opened her eyes again, and, scrupulously avoiding Noel's embarrassed gaze, saw him diligently polishing his pince-nez before replacing them.

It was the apotheosis of their anti-climax.

Alex possessed neither the light-heartedness which is—mistakenly—generally ascribed to youth, nor the philosophy, to face facts with any determination.

She continued to cram her unwilling mind with illusions which her innermost self perfectly recognized as such.

It was, on the whole, easier to place her own interpretation upon Noel's every act of commission or omission when the shyness subsequent to their first ill-conducted embrace had left him, which it speedily did. Easier still, when intercourse between them was renewed upon much the same terms of impersonal enthusiasm in discussion as in Scotland, and easiest of all when Alex herself, in retrospect, wrenched a sentimental significance out of words or looks that had been meaningless at the time of their occurrence.

When Noel went to Devonshire, whither his father by slow, invalid degrees had at last been allowed to move, he said to Alex in farewell:

"I shall expect to hear from you very often, mind. I always like getting letters, though I'm afraid I'm not much good at writing them. You know what I mean: I can write simply pages if I'm in the mood—just as though I were talking to some one—and other days I can't put pen to paper."

"I don't think I write very good letters myself," said Alex wistfully, in the hope of eliciting reassurance.

"Oh, never mind," said Noel consolingly. "Just write when you feel like it."

Alex, who had composed a score of imaginary love-letters, both on his behalf and her own, tried to compensate herself the following evening for the vague misery that was encompassing her spirit, by writing.

She was alone in her own room, the fire had fallen into red embers, and her surroundings were sufficiently appropriate to render attainable the state of mind which she desired to achieve.

As she involuntarily rehearsed to herself the elements of her own situation, she lulled herself into a species of happiness.

His ring on her finger, his letter on its way to her—she was going to write to the man who had asked her to become his wife.

There was really some one at last, Alex told herself, to whom she had become the centre of the universe, to whom her letters would matter, to whom everything that she might think or feel would be of importance.

She remembered Maurice Goldstein, his knowledge of Queenie's every movement, his triumphant rapture at being allowed to take her out to luncheon or tea. Even now, Alex had seen him follow his wife with his ardent, glowing gaze, as she moved, serene and graceful, round a crowded room on the arm of some other man—and the look had made her heart throb sympathetically, and perhaps not altogether unenviously.

Almost fiercely she told herself that she had Noel's love. She was to him what Queenie was to young Goldstein.

To every rebellious doubt that rose within her, she opposed the soundless, vehement assertions, that the indelible proof of Noel's love lay in the fact that he had asked her to marry him.

Gradually she persuaded herself that only her own self-consciousness, of which she was never more aware than when with Noel, was responsible for that strange lack, which she dared not attempt to define, lest in so doing she should shatter the feeble structure built out of sentimentality and resolute self-blinding.

Partly because she instinctively craved a relief to her own feelings, and partly because she had really almost made herself believe in the truth of her own imaginings, Alex wrote her first love-letter, the shy, yet passionately-worded self-expression of a young and intensely romantic girl, in love with the thought of Love, too ignorant for reserve, and yet too conscious of the novelty of her own experience for absolute spontaneity.

Alex did not sleep after she had written her letter, but she lay in bed in the warm, soft glow of the firelight, and saw the square, white envelope within which she had sealed her letter, leaning against the silver inkstand on her writing-table.

When the maid came to her in the morning, she brought a letter addressed in Noel's unformed hand.

It was quite short, and began:

"DEAREST ALEX (is that right?)"

It told her of the journey to Devonshire, of an improvement in the invalid's state of health, and of Noel's own projected tour of inspection round the estate, which he thought had been neglected by his agent of late.

"But I shall be able to put all that right, I hope, as I'm rather keen about the housing of the poor, and questions of that sort. You might look out for any decent book on social economy, will you, Alex?"

The letter did not extend beyond the bottom of the second page, but Noel was going to write again in a day or two, when there was more to tell her, and with love to every one, he was hers for ever and a day, Noel.

Alex' reply went to Trevose the same day, but the letter she had written in the firelight, she burnt.

XII
Christmas Pantomime

The engagement was not announced, but a good many people knew about it.

Their congratulations pleased Alex, as did her mother's obvious pride and satisfaction.

She liked wearing her diamond ring, although she only did so at home, and she even found pleasure in writing of her new dignities to Barbara at Neuilly.

In such trivial anodynes did Alex seek oblivion for the ever-increasing terror that was gaining upon her.

Noel came back from Devonshire after Christmas—and Lady Isabel sometimes spoke tentatively to Alex of a wedding early in the season.

"Jubilee year would be so charming for your wedding, my darling," she said effusively.

Alex thought of a white satin dress and long train, of orange blossom and a lace veil, of bridesmaids, presents, the exciting music of Mendelssohn's Wedding March, and the glory of a wedding-ring. On any other aspects of the case her mind refused to dwell.

Nevertheless, she made little or no response to her mother's hinted suggestions. Neither Noel nor Alex ever exchanged the slightest reference to their marriage, although Noel often discoursed freely of a Utopian future for the tenantry at Trevose, the basis of which, by implication, was his suzerainty and that of Alex.

"I rather believe in the old-fashioned feudal system, personally. You may say that's just the contrary of my old socialistic ideas, Alex, but then I always think it's a mistake to be absolutely cast-iron in one's convictions. One ought to assimilate new ideas as one goes through life, and, of course, sometimes they're bound to displace preconceived notions. I'm a tremendous believer in *experience*; it teaches one better than anything else. Besides, Emerson says, 'Dare to be inconsistent.' I'm keen on Emerson, you know. Are you?"

"Oh, yes," said Alex enthusiastically, wishing to be sympathetic. "But I only read Emerson a long while ago, when I was at school. Noel, were you happy at school?"

"Oh, yes," said Noel unemotionally. "The great thing at school is to be keen, and get on with the other fellows. They were always very decent to me."

"*I* wasn't very happy," said Alex. She was passionately desirous of sympathy, and was full of youth's mistaken conviction, that unhappiness is provocative of interest.

Noel cheerfully and unconsciously disabused her of the idea.

"Of course, girls don't have nearly such a good time as boys do at school. But don't let's talk about rotten things like being unhappy. I always believe in taking things as they come, don't you? I never look back, personally. I think it's morbid. One ought always to be looking ahead. I tell you what I'll do, Alex—I'll give you a copy of Emerson's *Essays*. You ought to read them."

Noel was very generous, and often made her presents. Alex was disproportionately grateful, but to her extreme, though unavowed relief, he never again claimed such a recognition as that which had followed the bestowal of her engagement-ring.

She drifted on from day to day, scarcely aware of her own unhappiness, but wondering bitterly why this, the supreme initiation, should seem to fail her so utterly, and still hoping against hope that the personal element for which she looked so avidly, might yet enter into her relation with Noel.

One day she told herself, with shock of discovery, that Noel was curiously obtuse. He had taken her with Lady Isabel and his brother Eric to Prince's skating-rink. Alex did not skate, but she enjoyed hearing the band and watching the skaters. Eric Cardew was among the latter, and Alex recognized Queenie Goldstein, in magnificent furs.

"Noel, do you see that very fair girl—the one in blue? She was my great friend at school."

Alex at the same instant saw a look of fleeting, but unmistakable vexation on her mother's face at the description.

"Why, that's Mrs. Goldstein, isn't it?" said Noel, screwing up his eyes in an interested look.

"Yes. I wish I could catch her eye." Alex was reckless of her mother. "I haven't talked to her for such a long while. Do you know her?"

"I've met her once or twice."

"Couldn't you go and speak to her, and bring her over here?" asked Alex wistfully.

Noel looked at her, surprised.

"I don't think I can do that. She wants to skate."

"Of course not," broke in Lady Isabel. "Don't be a little goose, Alex. What do you want her for?"

"Oh, nothing," Alex replied dejectedly, and also very crossly.

She was in the frame of mind that seeks a grievance, and her nerves were far more overstrained than she realized.

She felt a sudden, absolute anger when Noel said didactically:

"I don't think it would be very good manners for me to go and force myself on Mrs. Goldstein's notice. I don't know her at all well, and there are heaps of people who want to talk to her—just look at all those fellows!"

"You might do it just to please me," muttered Alex, less from coquettery than from injured pride.

Noel became rather red, and after a minute he remarked in a severe voice:

"I must say, Alex, I think that's rather a ridiculous thing to say."

Alex was silent, but from that day the spirit of resentment had at last awakened within her.

She became irritable, and although she still strove to persuade herself that her engagement meant the ultimate realization of happiness, she often spoke impatiently to Noel, and no longer sought to conform herself to the type of womanhood which he obviously desired and expected to find her.

The old sense of "waiting for the next thing" was strong upon her, and she spent her days in desultory idleness, since Lady Isabel made fewer engagements for her, and Noel's calls upon her time were far from excessive.

She made the discovery then, less illuminating at the time than when viewed afterwards in retrospect, that she could not bear to read novels.

All of them, sooner or later, seemed to deal with the relations between a man and a woman in love, and Alex found herself reading of emotions and experiences of which her own seemed so feeble a mockery, that she was conscious of a physical pang of sick disappointment.

Was all fiction utterly untrue to life? or was hers the counterfeit, while the printed pages but reproduced something of a reality which was denied to her?

She dared not face the question, and was further perplexed by the axiom mechanically passed on by successive authorities in rebuke of her childhood's passion for reading:

"You can't learn anything about Real Life from story-books."

At all events, Alex found the story-books of no solace to her mental sickness, and turned away from their perusal with a sinking heart.

She seldom quarrelled with Noel because, although he was sometimes unmistakably offended at her petulance, he never lost his temper. On the contrary, he argued with her at such length that Alex, although the arguments left her quite unconvinced of the Tightness of his point of view, often gave in from sheer weariness and the sense of hopeless, exhausting muddle.

She could visualize no possible eventual solution of the intangible problem that somewhere lay heavy, undefined and undefinable, at the back of all her thoughts.

It seemed to her that such a state of affairs had endured for a lifetime, and must extend into eternity, when her relations with Noel entered into the inevitable crisis to which a fortnight's mutual fret and dissatisfaction had been only the prelude.

Sir Francis, graciously benevolent, invited Noel Cardew to make one of an annual gathering that, for the Clare children, amounted to an institution—to view the Christmas pantomime at Drury Lane. For more years than any of them, except Alex, could remember, a box at the pantomime had been the yearly almost the solitary, expression of Sir Francis Clare's recognition of his younger children's existence as beings other than merely ornamental adjuncts to their mother.

Lady Isabel, who detested pantomimes, never joined the party, and Alex could remember still—had, indeed, never altogether lost—the feeling of extreme awe that rendered unnecessary old Nurse's severe injunctions to the children as to the behaviour suitable to so great an occasion.

This year, Barbara was at Neuilly, and it was considered inadvisable to "unsettle" her by a return to London for the Christmas holidays. But Cedric was at home, and Archie and Pamela, as clamorous as they dared to be for their father's treat.

Sir Francis did not sacrifice himself to the extent of foregoing late dinner altogether, but he dined at seven o'clock, and issued what more nearly approached to a royal mandate than an invitation, to Alex, Cedric and Noel to bear him company.

The big cuckoo clock in the hall still showed the hour as short of eight o'clock when Pamela and Archie, the former muffled in a large pink shawl, and both of them prancing with ill-restrained impatience, were at last permitted to dispatch the footman in search of a cab.

The carriage, in the opinion of Sir Francis, would be amply filled by himself, his two daughters and Noel Cardew, and it was part of the procedure that the boys should be allowed to journey to the theatre by themselves in a hansom-cab.

The streets were snowy, and as shafts of light from the street-lamps fell across the crowded pavements and brilliant shop windows, still displaying the Christmas decorations put up a month ago, something of the old childish glamour surrounding the yearly festival came upon Alex.

Pamela, already a modern child in the lack of that self-conscious awe of their father that had kept Alex and Barbara tongue-tied in his presence, nevertheless, had none of the modern child's *blasé* satiety of parties and entertainments of all kinds.

The Drury Lane pantomime was her solitary annual experience of the theatre, and she was proportionately prepared to enjoy herself to the full. When Sir Francis, with kind, unhumorous smile, made time-honoured pretence of having forgotten the tickets, Pamela gave Alex a shock by her cheerful and unhesitating refusal to carry on the dutiful tradition of her elder sisters and conform tacitly to the jest by a display of pretended consternation.

"Oh, no, I know you haven't forgotten them," Pamela cried shrilly. "I saw you look at them just before we started. Besides, you said last year you'd forgotten them, and you had them in your pocket all the time. I remember quite well."

She began to bounce up and down on the seat of the carriage, the accordion-pleated skirts of her new pink frock billowing round her.

"Sit still," said Alex repressively. She reflected that she herself as a little girl, and even Barbara, had been very much nicer than was Pamela.

She wondered what Noel had been like as a little boy, and looked at him almost involuntarily.

His glance met hers, and he smiled slightly. The response touched Alex suddenly and acutely, and she felt a pang of remorse for the intense irritation that his presence had often caused her lately.

When the carriage stopped and he sprang out to offer her his hand in descending, she gave hers to him with a tiny thrill, and her fingers lingered for an instant in his, as though awaiting, almost in spite of herself, an all-but-imperceptible pressure that was not forthcoming.

"It's begun," gasped Pamela in an agony of impatience in the *foyer*.

Sir Francis, always punctilious, placed Alex in the right-hand corner of the box, the two children in the centre, and then, with a slight smile, offered Noel his choice of the remaining chairs.

Alex was conscious of a throb of gratification, perhaps more attributable to vanity than to anything else, when the young man placed himself just behind her own chair.

Sir Francis, the comparative isolation of the engaged couple sufficiently sanctioned by the family party surrounding them, immediately disposed himself behind Cedric at the extreme left of the box.

The curtain went down to the sound of applause almost as they took their places, and the lights were turned up. Alex looked round her.

The huge house was everywhere sprinkled with groups of children—Eton boys in broad, white collars such as Archie wore, little girls in white frocks with wide pink or blue sashes and hair-ribbons.

When the orchestra began a medley of old-fashioned popular airs, *Home, sweet Home, Way down upon the Swanee River, Bluebells of Scotland*, and the like, Alex overwrought, fell an easy victim to the cheap appeal to emotionalism.

In the irrational, passionate desire for reassurance that fell upon her, she leant back until her shoulder almost touched Noel's.

"Look at all those children!" she whispered, hardly knowing what she said.

Noel gazed at the stalls through his pince-nez.

"The place is crammed," he said. "They say it's the best show they've ever had. Of course, I haven't seen it yet, but my own idea about these pantomimes is that they don't stick enough to the original story. Take 'Cinderella,' now, or 'The Babes in the Wood.' The whole thing is simply a mass of interpolations—they never really follow the thread of one idea all the way through. I can't help thinking it would be much better if they did, you know. After all, a pantomime is supposed to be for children, isn't it?"

"Yes."

Alex wondered what reply she had expected from him to her sudden ejaculation, that the actuality should bring such a sense of ironical disappointment.

She leant forward again as the curtain went up.

She was still child enough to enjoy a pantomime for its own sake, but the swing of catchy tunes and sentimental ballads brought with them something more than the easy heartache to which youth falls so ready a victim.

As the crash of the orchestra heralded a big scenic effect of dance and colour, Noel leant a little towards her and began to speak.

"Of course, it's a good show in its way. Look, Alex, you can see the man manipulating the coloured lights, up there. If you lean right back into this corner—there, up there."

His voice was full of interest and almost of eagerness. Alex leant back as he suggested and gazed obediently up at the lime-light operator, although she felt no interest, but rather a faint distaste.

"It's the ingenuity of these things I like," Noel's voice in her ear was explaining. "Of course, the dancing's good, and the comic bits, though I don't know that I care tremendously about that. They're always apt to be rather vulgar, even in front of a lot of ladies and children. Pity, that is. But take the songs, now, Alex; wouldn't you think that it would pay some one to write really *good* libretto, and get it taken on at a place like this and set to decent music? The tunes are good enough, but it's the words that are so poor, I always think."

Alex listened almost without hearing. The time had gone by when she could tell herself, with vehement attempt at self-deception, that such assertions indicated a fundamental resemblance between her tastes and those of Noel Cardew.

She was now only unreasonably angry and disappointed because of her baffled desire for the introduction, however belated, of a personal element into their intercourse.

She actually felt the tears rising to her throat as the evening wore on, and an intolerable fatigue overcame her.

Sitting upright became more and more of an effort, and the box seemed narrow and over-full.

The instinct of self-pity made her attempt to draw Noel's sympathy indirectly.

"Could you move back a little?" she half whispered. "I am getting rather cramped."

"Are you?" returned Noel with surprise, as he pushed his chair back.

But he did not appear to be in the least concerned about the matter. She looked at him once or twice and he met her glance absently. She knew that her face must show signs of the fatigue that she felt, but she knew also that they would not be perceptible to Noel.

For a moment, one of the rebellious gusts of misery of her stormy childhood shook Alex.

Why—why should there be no one to care, no one to whom it mattered that she be weary or out of spirits, no one to perceive, unprompted, when she was tired? She realized what such instinctive protection and care would mean to her, and the almost passionate gratitude with which she could welcome and return such solicitude.

But with Noel, she need not even exercise it. Had she loved him as she had endeavoured to persuade herself that she did, instead of only the figure of Love called by his name, Alex knew that Noel would have passed by all the smaller manifestations of her love unheeding and uncomprehending.

Her gods were mocking her with counterfeit indeed.

"You look tired, Alex," said her father's courteously-displeased voice.

Alex knew that on the rare occasions when he personally supervised a party of pleasure, Sir Francis liked the occasion to be met with due appreciation. She gave a forced smile and sat rather more upright.

"To be sure," her father said seriously, "it is a prolonged entertainment."

178

But Alex knew that neither Cedric, Archie nor Pamela would hear of any curtailment of their enjoyment, and Pamela was already urgently whispering that they *must* stay for the clown—they always did.

Sir Francis yielded graciously, evidently well-pleased, and they remained in the theatre for the final humours of the harlequinade.

Snow was actually falling when at length Sir Francis Clare's carriage was discovered, and Alex, her always low vitality at its lowest, was shivering with mingled cold and fatigue.

"Get in, children," commanded their father. "Noel, my dear boy, we can give you a lift, but pray get in—we must not keep the horses standing. What a terrible night!"

Crouched into a corner of the carriage, with Pamela half asleep on her lap, Alex was conscious of the relief of the darkness and the swift motion of the wheels.

Noel was next her, and in the sudden sense of almost childish terror and loneliness that possessed her, Alex sought instinctive comfort and reassurance in the unavoidable contact. She leant against his shoulder in the shelter of the dark, closely-packed carriage, and was sorry when Clevedon Square was reached at last, and she found herself obliged to descend.

"Good-night—thanks most awfully," said Noel at the door. "Good-night, Alex. I say, I'm afraid you were frightfully jammed up in the corner there—I'm so sorry, but I simply couldn't move."

XIII
Decision

On making up her mind that she must break off her engagement, Alex, unaware, took the bravest decision of her life.

She was being true to an instinctive standard, in which she herself only believed with part of her mind, and which was absolutely unknown to any of those who made up her surroundings.

She hardly knew, however, that she had taken any resolution in her many wakeful nights and discontented days, until the moment when she actually put it into execution. She wrote no eloquent letter, entered into no elaborate explanation such as would have seemed to her, after the manner of her generation, theoretically indispensable to the situation.

She blurted out three bald words which struck upon her own hearing with a sense of extreme shock the moment they were uttered.

"It's no use."

Noel looked hard at her for a moment, and then did not pretend to misunderstand her meaning.

"What, us being engaged?"

His intuitive comprehension, of which Alex had received so little proof ever before, might be unflattering, but it struck her with immense relief.

"Yes."

They gazed at each other in silence for a few moments, and Alex was furious with herself for a phrase sprung from nowhere that reiterated itself in her brain as she looked at Noel's handsome, inexpressive face—"*Fish-like flaccidity....*"

And again and again "*Fish-like flaccidity.*"

They were in the drawing-room at Clevedon Square, and Noel, as though seeking to relieve his obvious embarrassment by moving, got up and walked across the room to the window.

"Of course, I've felt for some time that you weren't very happy about it all, and naturally—if you feel like that...."

All the seething disappointment and wounded vanity and aching loneliness that had tortured her since the very first moments of her engagement to Noel Cardew, rushed back on Alex, but she sought vainly for words in which to convey any part of her feelings to him.

It would be like trying to explain some abstruse principle of science to a little child. The sense of the utter uselessness of any attempt at making clear to him the reasons which were chaotic even to herself, paralysed Alex' utterance.

"I don't think it's any use going on," she repeated feebly.

"You're perfectly free," Noel assured her scrupulously; "and though, of course, I—I—I—you—we—it would be—" He broke off, very red.

Alex wished vaguely that it was possible for them to talk it all out quite frankly and dispassionately with one another, but the hard, crystalline detachment of the generation that was to follow theirs, had as yet no place in the scheme of things known to Noel and Alex.

They made awkward, conventional phrases to one another.

"Naturally," the boy said with an effort, "the whole blame must rest with me."

"Oh, no, I'll tell father and mother that I wanted to—to—break it off."

Alex stopped, conscious that she could not think of anything else to say.

But rather to her surprise, it appeared that Noel had something else to say.

He faced her with hands thrust into his pockets, his hair and little, fair moustache and his brown eyes looking very light indeed contrasted with his flushed face.

"Of course, you're absolutely free, as I said, only I must say, Alex, that you're making rather a mistake. Every one was awfully pleased about it, and we've known each other since we were kids—since *you* were a kid, at any rate—and a broken engagement—well, of course, I don't want to say anything, naturally, but it *does* put a girl in a—a—well, in what's called rather an invidious position. Especially when it isn't as though there was any particular reason for it."

"The principal reason—" Alex began faintly, not altogether certain of what it was that she was about to say.

"You see, I always thought we should hit it off together so well. We always did as kids—when you were a kid, I mean," Noel explained. "We always seemed to like the same things, and have a good deal in common."

"I don't think that you liked any of the things *I* cared about especially," Alex said, with a flash of spirit.

"What does that matter?" Noel demanded naïvely, "so long as one of us likes the things that the other does? It would be exactly the same thing."

Alex had never told herself, and was therefore quite unable to tell Noel, that she had never liked anything particularly, except his liking for her, which she had striven almost frenziedly to gain and retain by means of an artificially-stimulated display of sympathetic interest in his enthusiasms.

"There's another thing—I don't know whether I ought to say it to you, quite—but, of course, after one's—well, married—there's a lot more one has in common, naturally."

"Yes," said Alex forlornly. She quite believed it.

There was an awkward silence.

"Are you angry, Noel?"

She did not think he was at all angry, or very violently moved in any way, but she asked the question from an instinctive desire to hear from him any expression of his real feelings.

He replied stiffly, "Not at all. Of course, it's much better that you should say all this in time ... as I say, I've felt for some time that you weren't particularly cheerful. But I must say, Alex, I'm dashed if I know why."

"I don't know why, exactly—except that I—I don't feel as if we—really—cared enough for one another—"

Alex spoke with a pause between each word, blushing scarlet, as though it really cost her a physical effort to break through the barrier of reserve that she had been taught so relentlessly should always be erected between her own soul and the naked truth of her own sensations and intimate convictions.

Noel blushed too and Alex felt that he was shocked, which increased her own self-contempt almost unbearably.

"Naturally, if I hadn't—" he left a blank to supply the words, "I shouldn't have asked you to be engaged to me. I must say, Alex, I think you're rather exacting, you know."

Alex quivered from head to foot, as though he had insulted her most brutally. She, who had shrunk, with a genuine dread that had surprised herself, from Noel's few, shyly-uttered endearments, and had found so entire a lack of response in herself to his occasionally-attempted displays of tenderness, to be accused of having been exacting!

She did not for an instant realize, what even Noel faintly surmised, that she had indeed been exacting, of a romantic fervour which she was as incapable 'of inspiring as he of bestowing; from which, had it existed, the outward expressions of love would have leapt spontaneously, supremely appropriate, and necessary to them both.

In the mental chaos and muddle of their extreme youth, they looked at one another confused and bewildered, almost like two children suddenly conscious of the magnitude of their own naughtiness.

Noel said, rather proudly, as though one of the children suddenly tried to appear grown-up:

"You must allow me to undertake the distressing task of—breaking it to—*them*."

Alex almost shuddered, so acute was her own apprehension of the disclosure to her father and mother.

"I shall tell mother at once," she said, lacking the courage even to mention Sir Francis.

It was typical of the whole time and circumstances of their brief engagement that both Noel, and, in a lesser degree, Alex, had looked upon the relation into which they had entered as one in which their parents held the stakes and were of primary concern. They themselves were only puppets for whom strings were pulled, so as to cause certain vibrations and reactions over which they had no personal control.

This belief, unformulated by either, and entirely characteristic of a late Victorian generation, was, perhaps, that which they held most in common.

Alex even wondered whether she ought to wait and speak to Lady Isabel before taking the next step which she had in mind, but her desire to try and raise their trivial, shamefaced parting to a higher level by one dramatic touch, was too strong for her.

She slowly pulled the diamond engagement-ring off her finger, and handed it to him.

"Oh, I say," stammered Noel. He looked miserably undecided, and she knew that he was wondering whether he could not ask her to keep it just the same.

But in the end he slipped it into his pocket, after balancing it undecidedly for a moment in the palm of his hand.

She sat on the sofa, her left hand feeling strangely bare, unweighted by the heavy, glittering hoop, and Noel looked out of the window.

"I think I shall go abroad," he announced suddenly, and with mingled relief and mortification, Alex detected the sound of satisfaction latent in his voice. She felt that he thought himself to be doing the proper thing in the circumstances, and the sting inflicted on her pride by his acquiescence in their parting, though she had expected nothing else, gave her the sudden impulse necessary to rise and cross the room until she stood beside him at the window.

"Please forgive me, Noel."

"Oh, there's nothing to forgive," he returned hastily. "Of course, if you feel like that, it's all over."

He looked at her steadily and Alex felt the suspicion rush over her that he was trying obliquely to convey a warning to her that if she dismissed him now, it would be of no use to recall him later.

Alex felt passionately that in the depths of his stubborn vanity lay the truest presentment of himself that Noel would ever show her. If there was another side to his personality—and she was dimly willing to believe it for all her utter ignorance of him—the power to call it forth did not dwell in her.

Her momentary feeling of anger gave way to humiliation, and she half held out her hand.

"Good-bye, Noel," she said humbly.

As though to atone for the lack of feeling in his tone, Noel wrung her hand until it hurt her, as he replied automatically: "Good-bye, Alex."

"I suppose we shall never meet again," thought Alex, with all the finality of youth, and felt dazed as she saw him open the door.

Mechanically, she rang the bell in order that the servants downstairs might know that he was leaving, and come into the hall to find his hat and stick and to open the door for him.

Lady Isabel had instilled into Alex that it was part of her responsibility in grown-up life to ring the bell for departing guests, as unostentatiously as possible, at just the right moment, and every time that she remembered to do it, she always felt rather proud of herself.

This time she thought:

"It's the last time Noel will ever be in this room with me. He is going right out of my life."

She was quite unconsciously trying to awaken in herself an anguish of regret that might yet justify her to herself in recalling her lover.

If he turns round at the door and says, "Alex!" She tried to cheat herself with a hope that was yet not a hope.

Noel turned at the door.

In a solemn, magnanimous voice he said:

"Alex! I don't want you to feel—ever—that you need reproach yourself, whatever any one may say. Remember that, if"—he suddenly looked like a rather frightened little boy—"if there's a great fuss."

Then the door closed very quietly behind him, and Alex heard him go downstairs slowly.

It seemed to her that Noel's farewell had plumbed the final depth of his inadequacy.

Presently she sank into an armchair before the fire, and tried to visualize the effects of her own action.

She was principally conscious of a certain amazement, that a step which seemed likely to have such far-reaching consequences should have been so largely the result of sudden impulse. She had not thought the night before of breaking off her engagement. It had all happened very quickly in a few minutes, when the sense of tension which had hung round her intercourse with Noel had suddenly seemed to reach an unbearable pitch, so that something had snapped. Was this how Important Things happened to one through life?

Alex felt that she could not believe it.

But a broken engagement—could there be anything more important, more desperate? Alex felt with melancholy satisfaction that at least it was real life, as she had always imagined it, full of drama and tragedy. With, of course, a glory of happiness as final climax, that would make up for everything.... More physically tired than she knew, Alex abandoned herself dreamily to the old, idle visions of the wonderful, perfect love that should come to crown her life. There was no faint, latent sense of disloyalty to Noel now, in returning to her old dreams, that had been hers in one form or another ever since her childish ideal of a perfect friend who would always understand, and yet love one just the same.

It was with a violent start that Alex came back to reality again. She had dismissed Noel Cardew, had given him back his beautiful diamond engagement-ring, and now she would have to tell her father and mother, with no better reason to adduce than her own caprice.

She felt sick with fright.

She remembered Sir Francis's silent but unmistakable pride and pleasure in his engaged daughter, and Lady Isabel's additional display of affection, and even of deference to Alex' taste in choosing her frocks and hats, and her own sense of having at last atoned to them both for her unsatisfactory childhood and lack of any conspicuous social success, such as they had coveted for her.

Alex, cowering in her chair now, wondered how she could face them. Her only shred of comfort lay in the remembrance that Lady Isabel had said to her:

"My darlin', I'm so thankful to know you are marrying for love."

Alex, in bitter bewilderment, remembered those words again and again in the days which followed.

No one reproached her, she heard hardly a word of blame, and the most severe censure spoken to her was in her mother's soft voice, far more distressed than angry.

"But, Alex, do you know what people say, about a girl who's behaved as you have? That she's a vulgar *jilt*, neither more nor less. To throw over a young man after being engaged to him for four weeks, with no reason except a capricious fit.... Oh, my darling, *why* couldn't you have asked me first? To go and give him back that lovely ring, and hurt and insult him.... Of course, he'll never come back. Your father says how well he's behaved, poor boy.... Alex, Alex, what shall I do with you?"

Tears were running down her pretty face, so slightly lined even now.

Alex cried too, from pity for her mother and wretched, undefined remorse, and a growing conviction that in acting on her own distorted impulse she had once more involved herself, and, far worse, others, in far-reaching and disastrous consequences.

182

"Thank Heaven, we hadn't announced the engagement, but, of course, it will all get about—things always do. And there's nothing worse for a girl than to get that sort of reputation, especially when she's not—not tremendously sought after, or pretty or anything."

Lady Isabel had never before come so near to an avowal that her eldest daughter's career had proved a disappointment to her, and Alex in the admission, rightly gauged the extent of her mother's dismay.

"Why did you do it, Alex?"

Alex tried haltingly to explain, but she could only say:

"I—I felt I didn't care for him enough."

"But you hadn't had time to find out! You accepted him when he proposed, so you must have been quite ready to like him then, and you'd only been engaged for four weeks. How could you tell—a little thing like you?" wailed Lady Isabel.

"Oh, Alex, if you'd only come to me about it first—I could have explained it all to you—girls often get fancies about being in love."

"I thought you wanted me to marry for love. You said so," sobbed Alex.

"Of course, I don't want you to marry without it. But it's the love that comes *after* marriage that really counts—and a boy you'd known all your life, practically—that we all liked—you could have been ideally happy, Alex." Lady Isabel looked at her almost resentfully.

"I don't know what will happen to you, my darling, I don't indeed. I sometimes think you are just as headstrong and exaggerated as when you were a little girl. And, Alex, I don't like even to say such a thing to you—but—there's never been any one *but* Noel, and I'm afraid this isn't the sort of thing that makes any man.... Nothing puts them off more—and no wonder."

Alex thought momentarily of Queenie, but she knew that was different. In the supreme object of woman, to attract, Queenie stood in a class apart. Nothing that Queenie could ever do would ever rob her of the devotion that was hers, wherever she chose to claim it, by mysterious right of attraction.

From her father, Alex heard very little. She was left, in her abnormal sensitiveness, to measure his disappointment and mortification by his very silence.

Feeling again like the naughty little girl who had been responsible for Barbara's fall from the balusters, and had been sent to Sir Francis for sentence, she listened, in a silence that was broken only by the sobs that she could hardly control, to his few, measured utterances.

"You are old enough to know your own mind." Sir Francis paused, swinging his glasses lightly to and fro in his hand. Then he deliberately put them across his nose and looked at her.

"At least," he added carefully, "I suppose you are. Your mother tells me that you appear to have been—er—rather suddenly overwhelmed by a fear of marrying without love. I don't wish to say, Alex, that such a sentiment was not more or less proper and natural, but to act upon it so hastily, and with such a heartless lack of consideration, appears to me to be the action, my dear child"—Sir Francis paused, and then added calmly—"of a fool. The word is not a pretty one, but I prefer it to the only other alternative that I can see, for describing your conduct."

"Have you anything to say, my dear?"

Alex had nothing to say, and would, in any case, have been rendered by this time powerless of saying it. Sir Francis looked at her with the same grief and mortification on his handsome, severe face that had been there eight years before when the nursery termagant, sobbing and terrified, had stood before him in her short frock and pinafore.

"You could have asked advice," he said gently. "You have parents whose only wish is to see you happy. Why did you not go to your mother?"

Alex tried to say, "Because—" but found that the only reason which presented itself to her mind was her own conviction that Lady Isabel would not have understood, and she dared not speak it aloud.

The Claire axiom, as that of thousands of their class and generation, was that parents by Divine right knew more than their children could ever hope to learn, and that nothing within the ken of these could ever prove beyond their comprehension.

Sir Francis shook his head sadly.

"I will tell you, my poor child, since you will not answer me, why you did not seek your mother's advice. It was because you are weakly impulsive, and by one act of impetuous folly will lay up for yourself years of unavailing remorse and regret."

Alex recognized with something like terror the truth of his description. Weakly impulsive.

She had blindly followed an instinct, and, as usual, all her world had blamed her and she had found herself faced by consequences that appalled her.

Why must one always involve others?

She ceased to see clearly that marriage with Noel Cardew would have meant misery, and blindly accepted the vision thrust upon her by her surroundings. She had hurt and disappointed and shamed them, and they could only see her action as a cruel, capricious impulse.

Alex, weakly impulsive, as Sir Francis had said, and sick with misery at their unspoken blame and silent disappointment, presently lost her always feeble hold of her own convictions, and saw with their eyes.

XIV
Barbara

Alex became more and more unhappy.

It was evident that Lady Isabel felt hardly any pleasure now in taking her daughter about with her, and the consciousness of not being approved rendered Alex more self-conscious and less sure of herself than ever.

It was inevitable that one or two of her mother's more intimate friends should know of her affair with Noel Cardew, and it did not need Lady Isabel's occasional sorrowful comments to persuade Alex that they took the same view of her conduct as did her parents. The sense of being despised overwhelmed her, and she fretted secretly and lost some of her colour, and held herself worse than ever from the lassitude that overwhelmed her physically whenever she was bored or unhappy.

Towards Easter Lady Isabel sent for Barbara to come home from Neuilly.

Alex revived a little at the idea of having Barbara at Clevedon Square again.

She thought it would impress her younger, still schoolgirl sister to see her as a fully-emancipated grown-up person, and she could not help hoping that Barbara, promoted to being a confidante, would thrill at the first-hand story of a real love affair and a broken engagement. Alex was prepared to attribute to Noel a romantic despair that had not been his, at her ruthless dismissal of him, in order to overawe little, seventeen-year-old Barbara.

But behold Barbara, after those months spent in the household of the Marquise de Métrancourt de la Hautefeuille!

No need to tell *her* to keep her shoulders back.

She was not quite so tall as Alex, but her slim figure was exquisitely upright. Encased in French stays that made even Lady Isabel gasp, she wore, with an air, astonishing French clothes that swung gracefully round her as she moved, and her hair, which had developed a surprising ripple, was gathered up at the back of her head with a huge, outstanding bow of smartly-tied ribbon that seemed to form a background for the pale, pointed little face, that was still Barbara's, but had somehow acquired an elusive charm that actually seemed more distinguished than ordinary, healthy English prettiness.

And the self-assurance of the child!

Alex was disgusted at the ease with which Barbara, hitherto shy and tongue-tied in the presence of her parents, chattered lightly to them on the evening of her return, and offered—actually offered unasked!—to sing them some of her new songs. "New songs" indeed, when it was only a year ago that she had written to ask whether she might have a few singing lessons with the Marquise's daughter! But neither Sir Francis nor Lady Isabel rebuked her temerity, and they even exchanged amused, approving glances when the slim, upright figure moved lightly across the room to the big grand piano.

Alex, in her pink evening dress, with her elaborately-coiled hair, felt infinitely childish and awkward as she watched Barbara slip off a new gold bangle from her little white, rounded wrist, and strike a couple of chords with perfect self-assurance.

She was going to play without music! It was absurd; Barbara had never been musical.

Certainly the voice in which she sang a couple of little French *ballades*, was a very tiny one, but there was a tunefulness, above all, a vivacity, about her whole performance which caused even Sir Francis to break into unwonted applause at the finish. Alex applauded too, principally from the desire to prove to herself that it would be impossible for *her* ever to feel jealous of little Barbara.

When they had sent her to bed, Lady Isabel laughed with more animation than she often displayed.

"How the child has developed!"

"Charming, charming!" said Sir Francis. "We must show her something of the world, I think, even if she is rather young."

But it soon became evident, to Alex, at least, that Barbara had not been without glimpses of the world, even at Neuilly. She listened with interest, but very coolly, to Alex' attempted confidences, and finally said, "Well, I can't imagine how you could have borne to give up the diamond ring, and it would have been fun to get married and have a trousseau and a house of your own. But I don't think Noel would make much of a husband."

The calm disparagement in her tone annoyed Alex. It seemed to rob her solitary conquest of any lingering trace of glory.

"I don't think you know very much about it," she said rather scathingly. "You haven't met any men at all, naturally, so how can you judge?"

Barbara laughed.

Something of security that would not even take the trouble to dispute the point, pierced through that cool, self-confident little laugh of hers.

Later on, she told Alex, with rather overdone matter-of-factness, that a young Frenchman, a cousin of Hélène de la Hautefeuille, had fallen very much in love with her at Neuilly.

Alex at first pretended not to believe her, although she felt an uncomfortable inward certainty that Barbara would never waste words on an idle boast that could not be substantiated.

"You need not believe me if you don't want to," said Barbara indifferently.

"But how could you *know*? I thought the Marquise was so particular?"

"So she was. They all are, in France, with *jeunes filles*. It's ridiculous. But, of course, as Hélène was his cousin, they weren't quite so strict, and he used to give her notes and things for me."

"Barbara!"

"You needn't be so shocked, Alex. Of course, *I* never wrote to *him*—that would have been too stupid; but he's very nice, and simply madly in love with me. Hélène said he always admired *le type Anglais*, and that I was his ideal."

Alex was thoroughly angered at the complacency in Barbara's voice.

"You and Hélène are two silly, vulgar, little schoolgirls. I didn't think you could be so—so common, Barbara. What on earth would father and mother say?"

"I daresay they wouldn't mind so very much," said Barbara calmly, "so long as they didn't know about the notes and our having met once or twice in the garden."

"I don't believe it!" exclaimed Alex. "You think it sounds grown-up, and so you're exaggerating the whole thing."

Barbara looked at her sister, with her eyebrows cocked in a provoking, conceited sort of way, not angrily, but rather contemptuously.

"Really, Alex, to hear you make such a fuss about it, any one would think that you'd never set eyes on a man. Of course, that sort of thing happens as soon as one begins to get grown-up. It's part of the fun."

"You know mother would say it was vulgar."

It was almost a relief to see one of Barbara's rare blushes at the word.

"I don't see why it should be more vulgar than you and Noel."

"How can you be so ridiculous! Of course, that was quite different. We were both grown-up, and properly engaged and everything."

"Alex," said Barbara suddenly, "when you were engaged, did he ever kiss you?"

Alex turned nearly as scarlet as her sister had been a moment before.

"Shut up!" she said savagely. A thought struck her. "You don't mean to say you ever let that beastly French boy try to do anything like that?" she demanded.

"No, no," said Barbara hastily; "of course not. But he's not such a boy as all that, you know. He has a moustache, and he's doing his *service militaire* now. Otherwise," said Barbara calmly, "I daresay he would have followed me to England."

"You conceited little idiot! He must have been laughing at you."

Barbara shrugged her shoulders, with a gesture that had certainly not been acquired in Clevedon Square.

"You'll see for yourself presently," she remarked. "He's going to get his *permission* next month, and he's coming to London."

"You don't suppose you'll be able to go sneaking about writing notes and meeting him in corners *here*, do you?" cried Alex, horrified.

Barbara looked at her disdainfully, and gave deft little pulls and pats to the bow on her hair, so that it stood out more than ever.

"What on earth do you take me for, Alex? Of course, I know as well as you do that that sort of thing can't be done in London. It will all be perfectly proper," said Barbara superbly. "I have given him permission to call here."

Alex remained speechless.

She was quite unable to share in the tolerant amusement with which her parents apparently viewed the astonishing emancipation of Barbara, although it was true that Barbara still retained a sufficient sense of decorum to describe M. Achille de Villefranche to them merely as "a cousin of Hélène's, who would like to come and call when he is in London."

Lady Isabel acceded to the proposed visit with gracious amusement, and Alex wondered jealously why her own attempts to prove grown-up and like other girls never seemed to succeed as did Barbara's preposterous, demurely-spoken pretensions—until she remembered with a pang that, after all, *she* had never had to ask whether admiring strangers might call upon her. She knew instinctively that however much Lady Isabel might exact in the way of elaborate chaperonage, she would secretly have welcomed any such proof of her daughter's attraction for members of the opposite sex.

One day Barbara, more boastful or less secretive than usual, showed Alex one of Achille's notes, written to her on the day that she had left Neuilly.

Alex deciphered the pointed writing with some difficulty, and then turned first hot and then cold, as she remembered the few letters she had ever received from Noel Cardew, written during the period of their lawful, sanctioned engagement, when she had so fiercely told herself that, of course, a man was never romantic on paper, and that his very reticence only proved the depth of his feeling.

And all that time Barbara, utterly cold and merely superciliously amused, had been the recipient of this Latin hyperbole, these impassioned poetical flights:

"*Ma petite rose blanche anglaise Ma douce Sainte Barbe.*"

(Good Heavens! he had never seen Barbara in one of her cold furies, when she would sulk in perfect silence for three days on end!) And finally, with humble pleadings that he might be forgiven for such a *débordement*, Achille apostrophized her as "*ma mignonne adorer.*"

Alex could hardly believe that it was really Barbara who had inspired these romantic ebullitions.

"How did you answer him?" she asked breathlessly.

"I didn't answer at all," Barbara coolly replied. "You don't suppose I was so silly as that, do you? Why, girls get into the most awful difficulties by writing letters and signing their names, and then the man won't let them have the letters back afterwards. Achille has never had one single scrap of writing from me."

Alex felt as much rebuked as angered by this display of worldly wisdom. She knew, and was sure that Barbara, pluming herself over her own shrewdness, knew also, that had she herself been

186

able to provoke similar protestations, no considerations of prudence or discretion would have restrained the ardour of her response.

During the Easter holidays Barbara remained in the schoolroom, sometimes playing with Archie and Pamela, but generally engaged on one of the many forms of embroidery which she appeared to have learned at Neuilly, or diligently practising her French songs at the schoolroom piano.

She did not appear to be at all envious of Alex' grown-up privileges, for which Alex felt rather wonderingly grateful to her, until one day when she was out driving with Lady Isabel, when a sudden enlightenment fell upon her.

"What do you think of this ambition of little Barbara's?" her mother asked her, with a trace of hesitation.

"What?" asked Alex stupidly.

"Why, this frantic wish of hers to be presented next May and allowed to make her début. She will be seventeen, after all, and she seems to have set her heart on it."

"Barbara! She wants to be presented and come out in May! Why, it's nearly April now, mother. That would mean in another six weeks."

Alex was stupefied.

"Hasn't she said anything to you?" said Lady Isabel, with a sort of vague, unperceiving wonder. "Funny little thing! I thought she would have been sure to have talked it all over with you. She's been beggin' and implorin' us ever since she got back from Neuilly, and your father is half inclined to say she may."

How like Barbara! Begging and imploring them to let her be presented next May, and all the time saying nothing at all to Alex, and slyly pretending to care nothing for coming out, and listening with deceptive quiet to Alex' little occasional speeches made to mark the difference between twenty and seventeen. No doubt Barbara knew very well that she would get her own way by dint of ardent pleading, and did not want the effect of her arguments and reasonable-sounding representations to be spoilt by Alex' vigorous protest.

For, of course, Alex was indignant. Why should Barbara come out when she was barely seventeen, when her sister had had to wait until the orthodox eighteen?

Alex might not value her privileges highly, but she was far from wishing Barbara to share them.

In the depths of her soul was a lurking consciousness that neither did she want sharp-eyed, critical Barbara to see how poor and dull a figure her sister cut, after the imaginary triumphs of which she had so often boasted.

Lady Isabel might be disappointed, but she never voiced her disappointment or hinted at it, and Alex thought she tried to conceal it from herself. But Barbara would not be disappointed. She might be rather pleased, and make the small, veiled, spiteful comments by which she occasionally, and always unexpectedly, paid one back for past slights or unkindnesses.

Alex felt that she could not bear any further mortifications.

The question of Barbara's coming out was still undecided, principally owing to Alex's strenuous efforts to persuade her mother not to allow it, when M. Achille de Villefranche made the ceremonious visit to Clevedon Square which Barbara had announced.

He came on a Sunday, so soon after three o'clock that Lady Isabel's luncheon guests had barely departed, and sat on the extreme edge of his chair, a slim, beautifully-rolled umbrella between his knees, and his silk hat balanced on the top of it. His tie was tied into an astonishing bow with out-spread ends that irresistibly reminded Alex of Barbara's hair-ribbon.

He spoke excellent English, very rapidly, but occasionally lapsed into still more rapid French, in which he poured forth his enthusiasm for "cette chère île des brouillards," which description of her native land was fortunately uncomprehended by Lady Isabel.

Altogether Achille was so like a Frenchman on the stage that Alex almost expected to see him fall upon his knees in the drawing-room when Barbara demurely obeyed the summons sent up to the schoolroom by her mother, and appeared in her prim, dark-blue schoolroom frock. He certainly sprang to his feet with a sort of bound, but any further intentions were frustrated by his elegant umbrella, which got between his feet and nearly tripped him up, and sent his beautiful top-hat rolling into the furthest corner of the drawing-room.

Alex had to recognize that Achille behaved with great presence of mind, even taken at such a disadvantage. He bowed over Barbara's hand, at the same time kicking his umbrella carelessly aside. He waved a contemptuous hand which made the behaviour of his hat a thing of no account, and he did not even trouble himself to retrieve it until Barbara was seated, when he strolled away to pick it up in a nonchalant manner, talking all the time of other things.

But in spite of the high-handedness of Achille, Alex felt that the whole affair was of the nature of a farce, and was ashamed of herself for deriving unmistakable satisfaction from the conviction that no one could take Barbara's conquest seriously.

Even Sir Francis, who found Achille still discoursing in the drawing-room on his return from the Club at seven o'clock, indulged in a little mild chaffing of his younger daughter when M. de Villefranche amid many bows, had finally taken his leave.

Barbara responded with a sprightly amiability that she had never displayed in her pre-Neuilly days, and which Alex angrily and uncomprehendingly perceived both pleased and amused Sir Francis.

"But I am not sure I approve of your taste in the selection of your admirers, my dear," he said humorously, his right hand lightly swinging his glasses against his left.

"I have never met any Englishmen, you know, father," said Barbara piteously, opening her eyes very wide. "If mother would only let me come out this year and see a few people!"

Alex was aghast at Barbara's duplicity, recognizing perfectly her manoeuvre of implying that only her mother's consent was still required for her début.

"Well, well, well," said Sir Francis, wearing the expression of an indulgent parent; "but surely young ladies are expected to wait till their eighteenth birthday?"

"Oh, but I *should* so like a long frock," sighed Barbara, her head on one side—an admirable rendering of the typical "young lady" known and admired of her father's generation.

Sir Francis laughed, unmistakable yielding foreshadowed in his tone, and in the glance he directed towards his wife.

"'Gad! Isabel, we shall have a regular little society butterfly on our hands; what do you think?"

Lady Isabel, also smiling, nevertheless said almost reluctantly, as though to imply that assent would be in defiance of her better judgment:

"Of course, this year will be exceptionally gay because of the Jubilee. I should rather like her to come out when there is so much going on, but I don't quite know about taking two of them everywhere." She glanced at Alex and sighed almost involuntarily. It was impossible not to remember the tentative plans that they had discussed so short a while ago for a brilliant wedding that should take place, just when all London was busy with festivals in honour of the Queen's Diamond Jubilee. The same recollection shot like a pang through Alex, feeling the pain of her mother's disappointment far more acutely than her own humiliation, and making her speak sharply, and almost unaware of what she said, sooner than endure a moment's silence:

"You can take Barbara instead of me. I hate balls and I'm sick of going to things."

She was horrified at the sound of the words as she spoke them, and at her own roughened, mortified voice.

There was a moment's silence.

"That," said Sir Francis gently and gravely, "is neither a very gracious nor a very dutiful speech, Alex. Your mother has spared herself neither trouble nor fatigue in conducting you to those entertainments organized for your pleasure and advantage, and it is a poor reward for her many sacrifices to be told with a scowling face that you are 'sick of going about.' If those are your sentiments, I shall strongly advise her to consult her own convenience in the future, instead of making everything give way to your pleasures, as she has done for the last two years."

Lady Isabel looked distressed, and said, "It is very difficult to know what you want, Alex. If you'd only say!"

"I don't want anything; I'm quite happy," began Alex, overwhelmed with the sense of her own ingratitude; and by way of proving her words she began to cry hopelessly, although she knew that Sir Francis could not bear tears, and that anything in the nature of a scene made Lady Isabel fed ill.

"Control yourself," said her father.

They all looked at her in silence, and her nervousness made her give a loud sob.

"If you are hysterical, Alex, you had better go to bed."

Alex was only too thankful to obey. Still sobbing, she received the conventional good-night kiss which neither she nor her parents would have dreamed of omitting, however deep their displeasure with her, and left the room reproaching herself bitterly.

They had all been so cheerful before she spoilt it all, Sir Francis in unwontedly good spirits, and both of them pleased at the harmless amusement caused by Barbara's visitor.

"I spoil *everything*," Alex told herself passionately, and longed for some retreat where she might be the solitary victim of her own temperament, and need not bear the double pang of the vexation and grief which she inflicted upon others.

She did not go downstairs to dinner, and soon after eight o'clock Barbara came in and told her that there was supper in the schoolroom for both of them.

"Though after this," said Barbara importantly, "I shall be having dinner properly in the dining-room quite soon. They are going to let me put up my hair, and I *think* they will let me be presented at a late Drawing-room, though they won't promise. It was settled after you went upstairs."

"Are they vexed with me?" asked Alex dejectedly.

"Not particularly. Only disappointed."

Alex would rather have been told that they were angry.

She had not spirit enough left to snub Barbara, discoursing untiringly of all that she meant to do and to wear, until at last her younger sister remarked patronizingly:

"Cheer up, Alex. I believe you're afraid of my cutting you out. But we shall be quite different styles, you know. I can't hope to be a beauty, so I shall go in for being *chic*. Hélène always says it pays in the long run. By the bye, Achille thought you were very pretty."

"How do you know?"

"He told me so."

"Nonsense! How could he? I was in the room the whole time."

"Oh, there are ways and means," retorted Barbara, tossing her head.

Alex would not gratify her by asking further questions. To her habitual fashion of ignoring slights until it became convenient to repay them, however, Barbara added now an impervious armour of self-satisfaction at the prospect of her approaching entry into the world.

She even, three months later, received with no other display of feeling than a rather contemptuous little laugh, the elaborately-worded *lettre de faire part* which announced the approaching marriage of Hélène de Métrancourt de la Hautefeuille to her cousin, Achille Marie de Villefranche.

XV
Diamond Jubilee

All that summer every one spoke of "Jubilee weather," and London grew hotter and sunnier and more crowded day by day.

Alex found herself wishing, fretfully and almost angrily, that she could enjoy it all. But the sensation of loneliness that had always oppressed her, although she did not analyse it, was always most poignant amongst a great number of people, and her listlessness and self-absorption in society at last caused Lady Isabel to ask her gently, but with unmistakable vexation, whether she had rather "leave most of the gaieties to little Barbara, to whom it's all new and amusing."

"Why?" asked Alex, startled.

"My darling, I can see you're not very happy, and I quite understand that, of course, one doesn't get over these things in a minute," said Lady Isabel, with a sigh for the memory of Noel Cardew. "This will be your third season, and I had hoped it would be the best of them all, what with the Jubilee celebrations and everything—but if you're rather out of heart with the gaieties just now, I don't want to force you into them, poor child."

Lady Isabel gazed with wistful, puzzled eyes that held nothing but uncomprehending perplexity at her disappointing eldest daughter. Alex knew that she was wondering silently why that daughter, expensively educated and still more expensively dressed, admittedly pretty and well-bred, should still lack any semblance of attractiveness, should still fail to achieve any semblance of popularity.

Alex herself wondered drearily if she was always destined to find herself out of all harmony with her surroundings. She never questioned but that the fault lay entirely in herself, and a sort of fatalism made her accept it all with apathetic matter-of-factness.

She gave inert acquiescence to Lady Isabel's tentative suggestion that most of the invitations pouring in daily should be accepted on Barbara's behalf only, partly because she hated being taken out with her sister, who was always critical and observant, and partly from sheer desire that Lady Isabel should no longer have the mortification of watching a social progress, the indifference of which Alex regarded with morbid exaggeration.

Barbara, rather to Alex' surprise, although enjoying herself with a sort of quiet determination, proved to be exceedingly shy, but in two months she had achieved several gushing, intimate friendships with girls rather older than herself, which led to her receiving innumerable invitations to tea-parties, a form of entertainment always abhorred by Alex, but from which Barbara generally returned with one or two new acquaintances, who were sure to claim dances from her on meeting her at subsequent balls.

She was not very pretty, and evening dresses, displaying her thin arms and shoulders, took away from the effect of smartness that she had acquired in France, but she danced exceptionally well, and was seldom left partnerless.

Alex often wondered what Barbara, who was notoriously silent and awkward with strangers, could find to talk about to her partners.

It did not occur to her that Barbara made an art of listening to them.

The climax of the season's festivities was reached on the blazing day towards the end of June, when the Jubilee procession wound its way through the flagged and decorated streets, with the small, stout, black-clad figure in the midst of it all, bowing indefatigably to the crowds that thronged streets and windows and balconies and even, when practical roofs.

A window of Sir Francis' Club in Piccadilly was placed by him, with some ceremony, at the disposal of his wife, his eldest son up from Eton, and one daughter, but it was evident that he would regard any further display of family as rather excessive, and Alex herself suggested that she should see it all from a window in Grosvenor Place which had been procured for Pamela and Archie, under the care of old Nurse, and various minor members of the household.

"But that would be so dull!" protested Lady Isabel, shocked.

"Alex can do as she pleases, my dear," said Sir Francis stiffly.

He was not pleased with his eldest daughter, and imagined that her evident shrinking from society arose, not from her acute perception of this fact, but from shame at the recollection of her behaviour towards Noel Cardew, which Sir Francis in his own mind stigmatized as both dishonourable and unladylike. The further reflection he gave to the matter—and reflection with Sir Francis was never anything but deliberate—the more seriously he resented his daughter's lapse from the code of "good form," and the harassed look which she was gradually causing to mar his wife's placid beauty.

He would have liked Alex to be prettily eager for pleasure, as were the young ladies of his day and ideal, and he regarded her obvious discontent and unhappiness as a slur on Lady Isabel's exertions on her behalf.

Very slowly, with the dull implacability of a man slow to assimilate a grievance, and slower still to forgive what he does not understand, Sir Francis was becoming angry with Alex.

"Let her do as she likes, Isabel," he repeated. "If the society we can provide is less amusing than that of children and servants, by all means let her join them."

Lady Isabel did not repeat his words to Alex. She only said:

"Your father says, do as you like, darlin'. We shan't have over-much room, of course, especially as we have asked so many people for lunch afterwards, but if you really cared about comin' with us, I could manage it in a minute—"

She paused, as though for Alex' eager acclamation, but Barbara broke in quickly:

"There won't be *much* room, with all those people coming, will there? And father always says that one grown-up daughter at a time is enough, so if Alex really doesn't want to come it seems a pity...."

So Alex, with an unreasonable sense of injury, that yet was in some distorted way a relief to her, as showing her not to be alone in fault, watched the procession from Grosvenor Place, with Archie flushed and shouting with excitement, and Pamela, in curly, cropped hair and Liberty silk picture frock, such as was just coming into fashion, breaking into shrill cheers of rather spasmodic loyalty, as she fidgeted up and down the length of the bunting-hung balcony.

Alex, on the whole, was sorry when it was all over, and the two children ordered into the carriage by Nurse for the return to Clevedon Square.

She declared that she was going to walk home across the Park, partly because the crowds interested her, partly to assert her independence of old Nurse.

"Then you'll take James with you, in a crowd like this," the old autocrat declared.

"Nonsense, I don't want James. You'll come with me, won't you, Holland?"

"Yes, Miss," said the maid submissively.

Since Barbara's coming out, the sisters had shared a maid of their own, and Holland very much preferred Alex, who cared nothing what happened to her clothes, and read a book all the time that her hair was being dressed, to the exacting and sometimes rather querulous Barbara.

They found the Park comparatively free from people. Every one had gone to find some place of refreshment, or had made a rush to secure places for the return route of the procession from St. Paul's Cathedral.

Flags streamed and waved in the sunshine, and swinging rows of little electric globes hung everywhere, in readiness for the evening's display of illuminations.

Alex suddenly felt very tired and hot, and longed to escape from the glare and the noise.

She wondered whether, if Noel had been with her, she could have taken part in the general sense of holiday and rejoicing, sharing it with him, and whilst her aching loneliness cried, "Yes," some deeper-rooted instinct warned her that a companionship rooted only in proximity brings with it a deeper sense of isolation than any solitude.

Her steps began to flag, and she wished that the way through the Park did not seem so interminable.

"Couldn't we find a cab, Holland? I'm tired."

"It won't be easy, Miss, today," said the maid, a disquieted eye roving over the Park railings to the dusty streets where pedestrians, indeed, thronged endlessly, but few vehicles of any sort were to be discerned.

Alex would have liked to sit down, but none of the benches were unoccupied, and, in any case, she knew that Lady Isabel would be shocked at her doing such a thing, under no better chaperonage than that of a maid.

Quite conscious of her own unreason, she yet said fretfully:

"I really can't get all the way home, unless I can sit down and rest somewhere."

She had only said it to relieve her own sense of fatigue and irritability, and was surprised when Holland replied in a tone of reasonable suggestion:

"There's the convent just close to Bryanston Square, Miss. You can always go in there it's always open."

"What convent?"

Holland named the Order of the house at Liège where Alex had been at school.

She exclaimed at the coincidence.

"I thought their London house was in the East End."

"Yes, Miss," Holland explained, becoming suddenly voluble. "But the Sisters opened a new house last year. I went to the consecration of the chapel. It was a beautiful ceremony, Miss."

"Of course, you're a Catholic, aren't you? I forgot."

"Yes, Miss," said Holland, stiffening. It was evident that the fact to which Alex referred so lightly was of supreme importance to her.

"Well, a church is better than nowhere in this heat," said Miss Clare disconsolately.

Lady Isabel had decreed nearly two years ago that church-going, at all events during the season, was incompatible with late nights, and Alex had acquiesced without much difficulty.

Religion did not interest her, and she had kept up no intercourse with the nuns at Liège since leaving school.

Holland, looking at once shocked and rather excited, pointed out the tall, narrow building, wedged into a line of similar buildings, with a high flight of steps leading to the open door.

"It's always open like that," Holland said. "Any one can go into the chapel."

The open door, indeed, gave straight on to the oak door of the chapel across a narrow entrance lobby.

Alex was instantly conscious of the sharply-defined contrast between the hot glare and incessant roar of multifarious noises outside in the brilliant streets, and the dark, cool hush that pervaded the silent convent chapel.

The sudden sensation of physical relief almost brought tears to her eyes, as she sank thankfully on to a little cushioned *prieu-dieu* drawn up close to the high, carved rood-screen before the chancel steps.

Holland had slid noiselessly to her knees behind one of the humble wooden benches close to the entrance.

There was absolute silence.

As her eyes grew accustomed to the soft gloom, Alex saw that the chapel was a very small one, of an odd oblong shape, with high, carved stalls on either side of it that recalled the big convent chapel at Liège to her mind. The wax candles shed a peculiarly mild glow over the High Altar, which was decked with a mass of white blossom and feathery green, but the rest of the chapel was unlit except by the warm, softened shaft of sunshine that struck through the painted oval windows behind the altar, and lay in deep splashes of colour over the white-embroidered altar-cloth and the red-carpeted altar steps.

The peace and harmony of her surroundings fell on Alex' wearied spirit with an almost poignant realization of their beauty. The impression thus made upon her, striking with utter unexpectedness, struck deep, and to the end of her life the remembrance was to remain with her, of the sudden sense which had come upon her of entering into another world, when she stepped straight from the streets of London into the convent chapel, on Diamond Jubilee Day.

It seemed to her that she had been sitting still there for some time, scarcely conscious of thought or feeling, when the remembrance gradually began to filter through her mind, as it were, of teachings, unheeded at the time, from her schooldays at Liège.

What if the solution to all her troubles lay here, before the small gilt door of the tabernacle?

Alex had never prayed in her life. The mechanical formula extorted from the Clare children by old Nurse had held no meaning for them, least of all to Alex, who was not temperamentally religious, and instinctively disliked anything which was presented to her in the light of an obligation.

Her lack of fundamental religious instruction had remained undiscovered, and consequently unrectified, throughout her schooldays, and she had unconsciously adopted since then the standard typified no less in Sir Francis' courteously blank attitude towards the faith of his fathers, than in Lady Isabel's conventional adherence to the minimum of church-going permitted by the social code.

What if comfort had been waiting for her all the time?

"Come unto Me all ye that labour and are heavy burdened, and I will refresh you."

Alex did not know that she was crying until she found herself wiping away the tears that were blinding her.

The loneliness that encompassed her seemed to her to be suddenly lightened, and she formulated the first vague, stammering prayer of her life.

"Help me ... make me good ... and let there be some one soon who will understand ... some one who will understand and still love me ... who will want me to care too ... If only there was some one for whose sake everything really mattered, I believe I could be good.... Please help me...."

She felt certain that her prayer would be heard and granted.

There was the slightest possible movement beside her, and turning sharply, she saw the tall figure of a woman wearing the habit of the Order, standing over her.

She had not known that this nun was in the chapel.

The tall, commanding presence bent and knelt down on the ground beside her, with a deep inclination of her head towards the High Altar.

"Forgive me for disturbing you, but when you are quite ready to come away, will you come and speak to me for a moment or two before you go?" She paused for a second, but Alex was too much surprised to reply.

"Don't hurry. I shall wait for you outside."

The nun rose slowly, laying her hand for an instant on Alex' shoulder, and moved soundlessly away.

Alex looked at her watch, and was surprised by the lateness of the hour.

She drew down her veil, and gathered up the long, fashionable skirt of her dress, preparatory to leaving the chapel.

In the little lobby outside she looked round curiously. On the instant, some one moved forward out of a shadowy corner.

"Come in here for a moment, won't you? I think it is Miss Clare?"

"Yes."

Alex, faintly uneasy, although she could not have explained why, looked round for her maid. Holland came forward at once.

"Good afternoon, Mary," said the nun, addressing her calmly. "How are you?"

"Very well, thank you, Mother Gertrude. I hadn't hoped to be here again so soon, but Miss Clare was tired, and we were just going past, on the way back after the procession."

"Ah, yes, to be sure," said the nun with the air of recalling an unimportant fact—"the Jubilee procession takes place today. That must make the streets unpleasantly crowded. Won't you rest a little while in the parlour, Miss Clare? Perhaps your maid might find a cab to take you home."

"Will you try, Holland?" said Alex eagerly. She felt unable to walk any more.

This time Holland made no demur at the suggestion, and only glanced a respectful farewell at the nun, who said, with a smile that seemed somehow full of authority: "Good-bye, then, Mary, for the present. I will take care of your young lady whilst you are away. It may take a little while to find a cab on a day like this."

As the maid went out, Mother Gertrude motioned to Alex to precede her down the small, uneven steps leading out of the lobby into a better-lighted passage beyond.

"There are two steps down, that's all. These old houses are dark, and inconveniently built but we are lucky to get anything so central.... Come into the parlour, we shall not be disturbed, and your maid will know where to find us when she returns."

"I had no idea that Holland came here, and—and knew you," said Alex, rather confused.

In the stiff, ugly parlour, furnished with cane-seated chairs and a round table, it was easy to see Mother Gertrude, as she seated herself opposite to Alex in the window.

She was an exceptionally tall, upright woman, a natural dignity of carriage emphasized by the sweeping black folds of veil and habit, her hands demurely hidden under the wide-falling sleeves as she sat with arms lightly crossed. Her strong, handsome face, of a uniform light reddish colour, showed one or two hard lines, noticeably round the closed, determined mouth, and her strongly-marked eyebrows almost met over straight-gazing, very light grey eyes. Even her religious habit could not conceal the lines and contour of a magnificent figure, belonging to a woman in the full maturity of life.

"Are you surprised to find that your maid comes to the convent?" she asked, smiling.

Her voice was deep and of a commanding quality that seemed to match her personality, but her smile was her least attractive feature. It was only a slow widening of her mouth, showing a set of patently porcelain teeth, and deepening the creases on either side of her face. Her eyes remained watchful and unchanged.

"Mary Holland was one of our children when she was quite a little thing, at our Poor-school at Bermondsey. She has always been a good girl, and we take a great interest in her."

"Was that why you knew who I was?" Alex inquired, remembering how the nun had addressed her by-name.

"Yes. I knew that Mary Holland had taken a place with Lady Isabel Clare, and was much interested to hear from her of her 'young lady.' Tell me, were you not at school at our Mother-house in Belgium?"

Alex, unversed in the infinitely far-reaching ramifications of inter-conventual communication, was again surprised.

"Yes, I was there for about five years, but I don't remember—" She hesitated.

"Oh, no, I was never there. I have been Superior in London for more than ten years, but I have heard your name several times, though not since you left school. We like to keep in touch with our children, but you have probably been busy going about with your mother?"

"I didn't even know there was a house of the Order here," Alex admitted.

"It has not been established very long. Our chapel was only consecrated a few months ago. It is very tiny, but perhaps some day you will pay another visit here."

Mother Gertrude was not looking at Alex as she spoke, but down at her own long rosary beads; and the fact somehow made it easier for Alex to reply without embarrassment.

"Yes, I should like to come if I may—and if I can. It felt so—so peaceful."

"Yes," returned the nun, without any show of surprise or indeed, any emotion at all, in her carefully colourless voice. "Yes, it is very peaceful here—a great contrast to the hurry and unrest of the world. And for any one who is tired, or troubled, or perhaps unhappy, and conscious of wrong-doing, there is always comfort to be found here. No one asks any questions, and if, perhaps, a poor soul is too much worn-out with conflict for prayer, why, even that is not necessary."

Alex gazed at her, surprised.

"Do you think that God wants things put into words?" said the nun with her slow smile.

Alex did not know what to reply. She looked silently at the Superior, and felt that those light, penetrating, grey eyes had probed to the depths of her confusion and beyond it, to the scenes of loneliness and bewilderment that had made her weep in the chapel.

"Do a lot of people come here?" she asked involuntarily, from the sense that a wide experience of humanity must have gone to the making of those keen perceptions.

"Yes. Many of them I know, and see here, and anything that passes in this little room is held in sacred confidence. But very often, of course, there are visitors to the chapel of whom we know nothing—just passers-by."

"That was what I was."

The nun looked at her for a moment. "And yet," she said slowly, "something made me want to come and speak to you, even before I caught sight of your maid, and guessed you must be Miss Clare. It is curious that you should have turned out to be one of our children."

Alex thought so too, but the term with its sense of shelter touched her strangely. She was shaken both by physical fatigue and her recent violent crying, and moreover, the forceful, magnetic personality of the Superior was already making its sure impression upon her young, unbalanced susceptibilities.

"May I see you again, next time I come?" she asked rather tremulously.

Mother Gertrude stood up.

"Whenever you like," she said emphatically, her direct gaze adding weight to the deliberately-spoken words. "Come whenever you like. You have been brought here by what looks like a strange chance. Don't neglect the way now that you know it."

She held Alex' hand in hers for a moment, and then took her back to the little lobby.

"Mary has actually got a four-wheeled cab! That is very clever of her. I hope they will not have been anxious about you at home. You must tell them that you were with *friends*, quite safe."

She laid a slight emphasis on the words, smiling a little.

"Good-bye," said Alex; "thank you very much."

"Good-bye," repeated the Nun. "And God bless you, my child."

XVI

Mother Gertrude

Alex felt strangely comforted for some time after that visit to the convent. It seemed to her that in appealing to the God who dwelt in the chapel shrine, she had found a human friend. Secretly she thought very often of the Superior, wondering if Mother Gertrude remembered her and thought of her too. Once or twice when she was out with Holland, or even with her mother, she manoeuvred a little in order to go past the tall, undistinguished-looking building, and look up curiously at its shrouded windows. But she did not actually enter the convent again until three weeks later, after she had said rather defiantly to Lady Isabel:

"Do you mind my going to see the Superior of the convent near Bryanston Square, mother? It's the new house they've opened—a branch of the Liège house, you know."

"If you like," said Lady Isabel indifferently. "What's put it into your head?"

"Holland told me about it. She went there for some ceremony or other when they opened the chapel, and—and she knew I'd been at school at Liège," Alex answered.

She was conscious that the reply was evasive, but she was afraid of admitting that she had already made acquaintance with the Superior, with that innate sense, peculiar to the period in which she lived, that anything undertaken upon the initiative of a child would *ipso facto* be regarded as wrong or dangerous by its parents.

"But mind," added Lady Isabel suspiciously, "I won't have your name used by them. I mean that you are not to promise that you'll patronize all sorts of dowdy, impossible charities."

"Very well, I won't."

Alex was glad to have permission to visit the convent under any conditions, and she secretly resolved that she would make an elastic use of the sanction given her, during the short time that remained before the usual exodus from London.

She felt half afraid that Mother Gertrude might have forgotten her, but the nun greeted her with a warmth that fanned to instant flame the spark of Alex' ready infatuation. She quickly fell into one of the old, enamoured enthusiasms that had cost her so much in her childish days.

Mother Gertrude did not speak of religion to her, or touch upon any religious teaching, but she encouraged Alex to speak much about herself, and to admit that she was very unhappy.

"Have you no one at home?"

"They don't understand me," Alex said with conviction.

"That is hard to bear. And you are very sensitive—and with very great capabilities for either good or evil."

Alex thrilled to the echo of a conviction which she had hardly dared to admit to herself.

"My dear child—do you mind my calling you so?"

"Oh, no—no. I wish you would call me by my name—Alex."

"What," the Superior said, smiling, "as though you were one of my own children, in spite of being a young lady of the world?"

"Oh, yes—if you'll let me," breathed Alex, looking up at the woman who had fascinated her with all the fervour of her ardent, unbalanced temperament in her gaze.

"My poor, lonely little Alex! You shall be my child then." The grave, lingering kiss on her forehead came like a consecration.

Alex went home that day in ecstasy. The whole force of her nature was once more directed into one channel, and she was happy.

One day she told Mother Gertrude, with the complete luxury of unreserve always characteristic of her reckless attachments, the story of her brief engagement to Noel Cardew.

The nun looked strangely at her. "So you had the courage to go against the wishes of your family and break it all off, little Alex?"

It seemed wonderful to Alex that the action which had been so condemned, and which she had long ceased to regard as anything but folly, should be praised as courageous.

"I wasn't happy," she faltered. "I used always to think that love, which one read about, made everything perfect when it came—but from the first moment of our engagement I knew it was all wrong somehow."

"So you knew that?" the Superior said, smilingly. "You have been given very great gifts."

"Me—how?" faltered Alex.

"It is not every one who would have had the courage to withdraw before it was too late."

"You mean, it would have been much worse if I'd actually married him?"

"Much, much worse. A finite human love will never satisfy that restless heart of yours, Alex. Tell me, have you ever found full satisfaction in the love of any creature yet? Hasn't there always been something lacking—something to grieve and disappoint you?"

Alex looked back. She thought of the stormy loves of her childhood; of Queenie, on whom she had lavished such a passion of devotion; of her vain, thwarted longing to bestow all where the merest modicum would have sufficed; lastly, she thought of Noel Cardew.

"Noel did not want all that I could have given him," she faltered. "He never knew the reallest part of me at all."

"And yet he loved you, Alex—he wanted you for his wife. But the closest of human intercourse, the warmest and dearest of human sympathy, will never be enough for a temperament like yours." She spoke with such authority in her voice that Alex was almost frightened.

"Shall I always be lonely, then?" she asked, feeling that whatever the answer she must accept it unquestioningly for truth.

"Until you have learnt the lesson which I think is before you," said the nun slowly.

"I am not lonely now that I have you," Alex asserted, clinging passionately to her hand.

Mother Gertrude did not answer—she never contradicted such assertions—but her steady, light eyes gazed outward with a strange pale flame, as though at some unseen bourne destined both to be her goal and that of Alex.

"No one has ever understood me like you do."

"Poor little child, I think I understand you. You have told me a great deal, and your confidence has meant very much to me. Besides—" The Superior paused. "A nun does not often tell her own story, but I am going to tell you a little of mine. It is not so very unlike your own.

"When I was seventeen I wanted to be a nun. I told my parents so, and they refused their permission. They loved me very, very dearly, and I was the only child. My father told me that it would break his heart if I left them, and my mother was delicate—almost an invalid. I held out for a little time, but their grief nearly broke my heart, and I persuaded myself that it was my duty to listen to them, and to stay at home. So I stifled the voice of God in my heart, and when I was two-and-twenty, a man much older than I was, whom I had known all my life, asked me to marry him." The nun spoke with difficulty. "I have not spoken of this to any human being for over twenty years, but I believe that I am right in telling you a little of what I went through. I will gladly bring myself to speak of it, if it is going to be of any help to you. I hesitated for a long while. He told me that he loved me dearly and I knew it was true. I knew that his wife would have the happiest of homes and the most faithful and devoted of husbands. A hundred times, Alex, I was on the verge of telling him that I would marry him. It would have been the greatest happiness to my father and mother, and it would have done away, once and for all, with that lurking dread of a convent which I knew was always at the back of their minds. They were growing old, too—they had neither of them been young people when I was born—and I knew that a time would come when I should find myself all alone. I had no very great friends, and very few relations—none with whom I could have found a home; and in those days a woman left by herself had very little freedom, very few outlets indeed. I had given up the thought of being a nun altogether. I thought that God had taken away the gift of my vocation because I had wilfully neglected it. Even at my blindest I could never persuade myself that it had never existed—that vocation which I had tried so long to ignore. And then, Alex, God in His great love, again took pity on me, and showed me where my treasure really was. I had tried hard to cling to human love and happiness, to find my comfort there, but—just think of it, Alex—a Divine Love was waiting for me.... It was a very hard struggle, Alex. I knew that he wanted *all* of me, unworthy as I was. And I was so weak and so cowardly and so selfish—that I shrank from giving all. I knew that no half measures would be possible. Like you, I knew that it would have to be, with me, all or none—to whom much is given, from him will much be asked, Alex—and one night I could hold out no longer. I resolved that it should be all. After that, there was no drawing back. I wrote and said that I should never marry—that my mind was made up. Less than a year afterwards I was in the convent. But it was a terrible year. It was not for a long, long while that God let me feel any consolation. Time after time, I felt that He had forsaken me, and I could only cling to the remembrance of the certainty that I had felt at the time, of following His will for me. But He spared me the greatest sacrifice of all, knowing, perhaps, that I should have failed again in courage. My father and mother died within three months of one another that same year, and when my father lay dying, he gave me his blessing and consent, and after he died I went straight to the Mother-house in Paris, where it was then, and a few months after I became an orphan they received me into the novitiate there."

The Superior had flushed very deeply, and her voice was shaken, but there were no tears in her steady eyes. Alex, trembling with passionate sympathy, and with a gratitude so intense as to be almost painful, for the confidence bestowed upon her, asked the inevitable question of youth:

"Have you been happy?—haven't you ever regretted it? Oh, tell me if you are really and truly *happy*."

"Absolutely," said Mother Gertrude unhesitatingly. "But not with happiness such as the world knows. The word has acquired a different meaning. I hardly know how to convey what I mean. 'Grief' and 'Joy' mean something so utterly different to the soul in religious life, and to the soul still in the world. But this much I can say—that I have never known one instant of regret—never anything but the deepest, most intense gratitude that I was given strength to follow my vocation."

There was a long silence, Alex watching the nun's fervent, flame-like gaze, in which her young idolatry detected none of the resolute fanaticism built up in instinctive self-protection from a temperament no less ardent than her own.

"So you have the story of God's great mercy to one poor soul," said the nun at last. "And the story of every vocation is equally wonderful. The more I see of souls, Alex—and a Superior hears many things—the more I marvel at the ways of God's love. As for the paths by which He led me to the shelter of His own house, I shall only know the full wonder of it all when I see Him face to face. I have only given you the barest outlines, but you understand a little?"

"Yes," breathed Alex, her whole being shaken by an emotion to the real danger of which she was entirely blind.

She went home that day in a state of exaltation, and could not have told, had she been obliged to analyse it, how far her uplifted condition was due to the awakening of religious perceptions hitherto undreamed of, to her increasing worship of the woman who had roused those perceptions, or to her exultant sense of having been made the repository of a confidence shared with no other human being. It was small wonder that Lady Isabel traced the rapt look on Alex' face to its source.

"But most girls go through this sort of thing at school," she said hopelessly. "Of course, I know it is only a phase, Alex, whatever you may think now. But *why* can't you be more like other people? Why insist all of a sudden on makin' poor Holland get up early and go out to church with you on Sunday, when I always like the maids to have a rest?"

"Holland doesn't mind," said Alex sulkily. She could not explain to her mother that the Superior had asked a promise of her that she would not again willingly miss going to Mass on Sundays.

"If it was a reasonable hour I shouldn't object so much—I know heaps of very devout Catholics who always do go to Farm Street or somewhere every Sunday, and I wouldn't forbid that, Alex—though *why* you should suddenly get frantic about religion I can't imagine. I suppose it is the influence of that woman you have been seein' at the convent."

Alex grew scarlet, to her own dismay.

"I thought so," said Lady Isabel, looking annoyed. "I don't want to prevent your doing anything that *does* give you pleasure—Heaven knows it's difficult enough to find anything you seem to care about in the very least—but I am not goin' to let you infect Barbara."

"Oh, no!" said Alex, with sincere horror in her voice. The last thing she wanted was to take Barbara to the convent. She instinctively dreaded both her sister's shrewd, cynical judgment, and the misrepresentations that she always somehow contrived to make of all Alex' motives and actions. Alex clung to the thought of her exclusive claim on Mother Gertrude's interest and sympathy as she had never yet clung to any other possession.

"Well, we shall be leavin' town next week, and there'll be an end of it. When I said you might go to the convent, Alex, I never meant you to rush off there three or four times a week, as you know. But if you have taken a fancy to this nun, I suppose nothing will stop you."

Lady Isabel sighed, and Alex, from the glow of contentment that possessed her, felt able to speak more warmly and natural than usual.

"I don't want to do anything to vex you, mother, truly, I don't, but the Superior is very kind to me, and I do like going to see her. You know you always say you want me to do whatever makes me happiest." She spoke urgently and coaxingly, like the impulsive, impetuous child Alex, who had been used to beg for favours and privileges with all the confidence of a favourite.

Lady Isabel sighed again, but her face wore a touched, softened look, and she said resignedly, "So long as you cheer up, and don't vex your father by seeming doleful and uninterested in things.... Of course, girls now-a-days do take up good works and slummin' and all that sort of thing—but not till they are older than you are, darling, and then it's generally because they haven't married—at least," added Lady Isabel hurriedly, "people are sure to say it is that."

"I don't mind if they do," said Alex proudly, her mind full of Mother Gertrude's story.

"Well, I suppose you must do as you like—girls do, now-a-days."

Alex almost instinctively uttered the cry that, with successive generations, has passed from appeal to rebellion, then to assertion, and from the defiance of that assertion to a calm statement of facts. "*It is my life.* Can't I live my own life?"

"A woman who doesn't marry and who has eccentric tastes doesn't have much of a life. I could never bear thinking of it for any of you."

Alex was rather startled at the sadness in her mother's voice.

"But, mother, why? Lots of girls don't marry, and just live at home."

"As long as there is a home. But things alter, Alex. Your father and I, in the nature of things, can't go on livin' for ever, and then this house goes to Cedric. There is no country place, as you know—your great-grandfather sold everything he could lay his hands on, and we none of us have ever had enough ready money to think of buyin' even a small place in the country."

"But I thought we were quite rich."

Lady Isabel flushed delicately.

"We are not exactly poor, but such money as there is mostly came from my father, and there will not be much after my death," she confessed. "Most of it will be money tied up for Archie, poor little boy, because he is the younger son, and your grandfather thought that was the proper way to arrange it. It was all settled when you were quite little children—in fact, before Pamela was born or thought of—and your father naturally wanted all he could hope to leave to go to Cedric, so that he might be able to live on here, whatever happened."

"But what about Barbara and me? Wasn't it rather unfair to want the boys to have everything?"

"Your father said, 'The girls will marry, of course.' There will be a certain sum for each of you on your wedding-day, but there's no question of either of you being able to afford to remain unmarried, and live decently. You won't have enough to make it possible," said Lady Isabel very simply.

"But one of us might want to marry a very poor man."

"A man in your own rank of life, my dear child, could hardly propose to you unless he had enough to support you. Of course, we don't wish either of you to feel that you must marry for money, ever, but at the same time I think you ought to be warned. Girls very often go gaily on, thinkin' it will be time enough to settle later, and then something happens, and they find they have no money of their own, and perhaps no home left. For a few years, perhaps, it's possible to go on paying visits, and staying with other people, but it's never very pleasant to feel one has no alternative, and the sort of environment where a man looks for his wife is in her own sheltered home," said Lady Isabel with emphasis.

Alex felt rather dismayed, though less so than she would have done before her intimacy at the convent had given her glimpses of another possible standard.

She paid one more visit to Mother Gertrude before leaving London.

This time she was kept waiting for a while in the parlour, so that she began to wish that she had not told Holland to call for her in an hour's time. She never dared stay any longer, partly from a vague impression that Mother Gertrude had a good deal to do, and partly from a very distinct certainty that Lady Isabel always noted the length of her visits to the convent, no less than their frequency.

She looked round the ugly room rather disconsolately and fingered the books on the table. They seemed very uninteresting, and were mostly in French. One slim volume, more attractively bound than the others, drew her attention for a moment, and she turned idly to the title-page.

"Notre Mère Fondatrice Esquisse de piété filiale."

Alex smiled at the wording, which she read in the imperfect literal translation of an indifferent French scholar, and turned to the next leaf.

Two photographs facing one another were reproduced on either page.

The first portrait was of a young woman standing by a table in a stiffly artificial attitude, with enormously wide skirts billowing round her, decked with elaborate, and, to Alex' eyes meaningless, trimmings of some dark, narrow ribbon that might have been velvet. She wore long, dangling ear-rings, and her abundant plaits of dark hair were gathered into the nape of her neck, confined by a coarse-fibred net. The face, turned over one shoulder, was heavy rather than handsome, with strongly marked features and big, sombre, dark eyes.

It was with a little thrill approaching to awe that Alex recognized her again on the next page in the veil and habit of the Order.

The girth of the figure had increased, and the face showed traces of having been heavily scored by the passing of some twenty or thirty years, but this time the strong mouth was smiling frankly, and the eyes had lost their brooding look and were directed upwards with an ardent and animated expression. The hands, so plump as to show mere indents in place of knuckles across their remarkable breadth, grasped a small crucifix.

Under the first portrait Alex read the inscription "Angèle Prédoux a dix-huit ans."

Beneath the picture of the nun, Angèle's not very distinguished patronymic had been replaced by the title of "Mère Candide de Sacré Coeur," and still supplemented by the announcement:

"Fondatrice et Supérieure de son Ordre."

Old-fashioned though the dress in the photograph looked to Alex' eyes, she was yet astonished that any woman so nearly of her own time should have founded a religious Order. She had always supposed vaguely that the educational variety of religious Orders which she knew flourished in Europe had taken their existence from the old-established Dominican or Benedictine communities.

But it seemed now that a new foundation might come into being under the auspice of so youthful and plebeian-seeming a pioneer as Angèle Prédoux.

Alex wondered how she had set about it. A grotesque fancy flitted through her mind as to the fashion in which Sir Francis and Lady Isabel might be expected to receive an announcement that Alex or Barbara felt called upon to found a new religious Order.

Alex could not help dismissing the imaginary situation thus conjured up with a slight shudder, and the conviction that Angèle Prédoux, if her position had been in any degree tenable, must have been an orphan.

Wishing all the time that Mother Gertrude would come to her, she glanced through the first few pages of the book.

It somehow slightly amazed her to read of the Founder of a religious Order as a little girl, who had, like herself, passed through the successive phases of babyhood, schooldays and the society of her compeers in the world.

"And to what end," inquired the author of the *esquisse*, when Angèle Prédoux had celebrated her twenty-first birthday at a ball given on her behalf by an adoring grandfather—"to what end?"

Alex repeated the question to herself, and marvelled rather vaguely as various replies floated through her mind. Life all led to something, she supposed, and for the first time it occurred to her that she herself had never aimed at anything save the possession of that which she called happiness. What had been Angèle Prédoux's aim?—what was that of Mother Gertrude? Certainly not human happiness.

Life was disappointing enough, Alex reflected drearily. One was always waiting, always looking forward to the next stage, as though it must reveal the secret solution to the great question of *why*. Alex' thoughts turned to Noel Cardew and the sick misery and disappointment engendered by her engagement.

The door opened and she sprang up.

"Oh, I am so glad you have come at last."

"Were you getting impatient? I'm sorry, but you know our time is not our own."

The nun sat down, and Alex flung, rather than sat herself in her favourite position on the floor, her arms resting on the Superior's knee.

"What is the matter?" asked Mother Gertrude. "What was troubling you just before I came in, Alex?"

"You always know," said Alex, in quick, passionate recognition of an intuition that it had hitherto been her share to exercise on behalf of another, never to receive.

"Your face is not so very difficult to read, and I think I know you pretty well by this time."

"Better than any one," said Alex, in all good faith, and unaware that certain aspects of herself, such as she showed to Barbara, or to her father and mother when they angered or frightened her, had never yet been called forth in the Superior's presence, and probably never would be.

"Well, what was it? Was it our Mother Foundress?"

"How did you know?" gasped Alex, unseeing of the still open book lying on the table.

Mother Gertrude did not refer to it. She passed her hand slowly over the upturned head. Alex had thrown off her hat.

"I was looking at the picture of her. It seemed so difficult to realize that any one who actually formed a new religious Order could live almost now-a-days and be a girl just like myself."

"God bestows His gifts where He pleases! Sometimes the call sounds where one might least expect to hear it—in the midst of the world, and worldly pleasure, sometimes in the midst of the disappointment and grief of the world."

Alex did not speak, but continued to gaze up at the nun. Mother Gertrude went on speaking slowly:

"You see, Alex, sometimes it is necessary for a soul, a loving and undisciplined one especially, to learn the utter worthlessness of human love, in order that it may turn and see the Divine Love waiting for it."

"But all human love isn't worthless," said Alex almost pleadingly, her eyes dilating.

"Surely a finite love is worthless compared to an Infinite," said the nun gently. "We can hardly imagine it, Alex, with our little, limited understanding, but there is a love that satisfies the most exacting of us—asking, indeed *all*, and yet willing to accept so little, and, above all, giving with a completeness to which no human sympathy, however deep and tender, can ever attain."

Alex heard only the ring of utter conviction permeating every word uttered in that deep, ardent voice, and listening to the mystic, heard nothing of the fanatic.

"But not every one," she stammered.

The nun did not pretend to misunderstand her.

"Many are called," she said, "but few are chosen. Do you want me to tell you a little of all that is promised to those who leave all things for His sake?"

"Yes," said Alex, her heart throbbing strangely.

XVII
Lawn-Tennis

Looking back long afterwards, to that last week of the brilliant Jubilee season in London and to the two months that followed, spent in a house near Windsor, taken principally to gratify Cedric's passion for tennis, Alex could never remember whether the first definite suggestion of her entering the religious life had come from herself or from Mother Gertrude.

Neither she nor Barbara had been taken to Cowes that year, and the first fortnight spent at the Windsor house, which stood in a large, rambling garden, full of roses, close to the river, reminded her strangely of the summer holidays they had spent together as children.

Cedric, very sunburnt and sturdy, played tennis with a sort of concentrated, cumulative enthusiasm, took part in innumerable cricket matches—possessing already a very real reputation in Eton circles as a promising slow bowler and a very reliable bat—and occasionally took his sisters on the river. Barbara, on whom late nights in London had told, slept half the morning, and then practised "serves" at tennis assiduously under her brother's coaching, while Pamela, already a hoyden, romped screaming over the lawn, in a fashion that in Alex' and Barbara's nursery days would have met with instant and drastic punishment. But old Nurse was lenient with the last and youngest of her charges, and now-a-days her guardianship was almost a nominal one only.

Alex was preoccupied, aimlessly brooding over one absorbing interest, as in the summer holidays that the Clare children had spent at Fiveapples Farm.

Just as then she had waited and looked and longed for Queenie's letters, so now she waited for those of Mother Gertrude.

Day after sunlit day, she stood at the bottom of the straggling, over-grown paddock that gave on to the dusty high-road, and waited for the afternoon post to be delivered.

She was often disappointed, but never with the sick intensity of dismay that had marked every fresh stage in her realization of Queenie Torrance's indifference to friendship.

Mother Gertrude only wrote when she could find a little spare time, and left by far the greater number of Alex' daily outpourings to her unanswered, but she read them all—she understood, Alex told herself in a passion of pure gratitude—and she thought of her child and prayed daily for her.

Her letters began, "My dearest child," and Alex treasured the words, and the few earnest counsels and exhortations that the letters contained.

It was much easier to carry out those exhortations at Windsor than it had been in London. Alex went almost every day to a small Catholic church, of which Holland had discovered the vicinity, and sometimes spent the whole afternoon in the drowsy heat of the little building, that was almost always empty.

Her thoughts dwelt vaguely on her own future, and on the craving necessity for self-expression, of which Mother Gertrude had made her more intensely aware than she knew. Could it be that her many failures were to prove only the preliminary to an immense success, predestined for her out of Eternity? The allurement of the thought soothed Alex with an infinite sweetness.

When Sir Francis and his wife joined the Windsor party, Lady Isabel exclaimed with satisfaction at her daughters' looks. "Only a fortnight, and it's done such wonders for you both! Barbara was like a little, washed-out rag, and now she's quite blooming. You've got more colour too, Alex, darling, and I'm so thankful to see that you're holdin' yourself rather better. Evidently country air and quiet was what you both needed."

Nevertheless, Lady Isabel lost no time in issuing and accepting various invitations that led to luncheons, tennis-parties and occasional dinners with the innumerable acquaintances whom she immediately discovered to be within walking or driving distance.

It annoyed Alex unreasonably that her liberty should be interfered with thus by entertainments which afforded her no pleasure. She ungraciously conceded her place to Barbara as often as possible, and went off to seek the solitude of the chapel with an inward conviction of her own great unworldliness and spirituality.

Barbara showed plenty of eagerness to avail herself of the opportunities thus passed on to her. She had sedulously cultivated a great enthusiasm for tennis, and by dint of sheer hard practice had actually acquired a certain forceful skill, making up for a natural lack of suppleness that deprived her play of any grace.

Her rather manufactured displays of enjoyment, which had none of the spontaneous vitality of little Pamela's noisy, bounding high spirits, were always in sufficient contrast to Alex' supine self-absorption to render them doubly agreeable to Sir Francis and Lady Isabel.

"I like to take my little daughter about and see her enjoying herself," Sir Francis would say, with more wistfulness than pleasure in his voice sometimes, as though wishing that Barbara's gaiety could have been allied to Alex' prettier face and position as his eldest daughter.

It was only in his two sons—Cedric, with his sort of steady brilliance, and idle, happy-go-lucky Archie, by far the best-looking of the Clare children—that Sir Francis found unalloyed satisfaction.

Pamela was the modern child in embryo, and disconcerted more than she pleased him.

It was principally to gratify Cedric that Lady Isabel arranged a tennis tournament for the end of the summer, on a hot day of late September that was to remain in Alex' memory as a milestone, unrecognized at the time, marking the end of an era.

"Thank Heaven it's fine," piously breathed Barbara at the window in the morning. "I shall wear my white piqué."

Alex shrugged her shoulders.

Neither she nor Barbara would have dreamed of inaugurating a new form of toilette without previous reference to Lady Isabel, and Barbara's small piece of self-assertion was merely designed to emphasize the butterfly rôle which she was embracing with so much determination.

"Of course, you'll wear your piqué. Mother said so," Alex retorted, conscious of childishness. "You've worn a piqué at every tennis party you've been to."

"Well, this is a new piqué," said Barbara, who invariably found a last word for any discussion, and she went downstairs singing in a small, tuneful chirp made carefully careless.

"Who is coming?" Alex inquired, having taken no part whatever in the lengthy discussions as to partners and handicaps which had engrossed Cedric and Barbara for the past ten days.

Cedric looked up, frowning, from the list on which he was still engaged. He did not speak, however; but Barbara said very sweetly, and with an emphasis so nearly imperceptible that only her sister could appreciate it:

"Oh, nobody in whom you're at all specially interested, I'm afraid."

Alex did not miss the implication, and coloured angrily.

"I'm going to play with that artist, the one staying with the Russells. He isn't at all a good player," said Barbara smoothly.

"Then why are you playing with him?"

Barbara smiled rather self-consciously. "It would hardly do to annex the best partners for ourselves, would it?" she inquired. "And we're trying to equalize the setts as far as possible. Cedric has to play with the youngest Russell girl, who's too utterly hopeless."

"I shall take all her balls," said Cedric calmly, "so it'll be all right. She doesn't mind any amount of poaching. We shall lose on her serves, of course, but that may be just as well."

"Why, dear?" innocently inquired Lady Isabel.

"I don't think it looks well to carry off a prize at one's own show," Cedric said candidly.

"I should rather love the Indian bangles," owned Barbara, glancing enviously at the array of silver trifles that constituted the prizes.

"You won't get them, my child—not with McAllister as your partner. You'll see, Lady Essie Cameron will get them, or one of the Nottinghams, if they're in good form."

"Peter Nottingham is playing with you, Alex," Barbara informed her.

"That boy!"

"Nottingham is nearly eighteen, let me tell you," said Cedric in tones of offence, "and plays an extraordinarily good game of tennis. In fact, he'll be about the best man there probably, which is why I've had to give him to you for a partner. As you've not taken the trouble to practise a single stroke the whole summer, I should advise you to keep out of his way, and let him stand up to the net and take every blessed thing he can get.

"It'll be a nice thing for me," said Cedric bitterly, "to have to apologize to Nottingham for making him play with the worst girl there, and that my sister."

"Cedric," said his mother gently, "I'm sure I've seen Alex play very nicely."

Alex was grateful, but she wished that, like Barbara, she had practised her strokes under Cedric's tuition.

It was characteristic of her that when the occasion for excelling had actually come, she should passionately desire to excel, whereas during previous weeks of supine indifference, it had never seemed to her worth while to exert herself in the attainment of proficiency.

After breakfast she went out to the tennis-court, freshly marked and rolled, and wondered if it would be worth while to make Archie send her over some balls, but Cedric hurried up in a business-like way and ordered everybody off the ground while he instructed the garden boy in the science of putting up a new net.

Alex moved disconsolately away, and tried to tell herself that none of these trivial, useless enthusiasms which they regarded so earnestly were of any real importance.

She wandered down to the chapel and sat there, for the most part pondering over her own infinitesimal chances of success in the coming tournament, and thinking how much she would like to astonish and disconcert Barbara and Cedric by a sudden display of skill.

It was true that she had not practised, and was at no time a strong player, but she had sometimes shown an erratic brilliance in a sudden, back-handed stroke and, like all weak people, she had an irrational belief in sudden and improbable accessions of luck.

Needless to say, this belief was not justified.

Peter Nottingham, a tall, shy boy with a smashing service and tremendous length of reach, was intent on nothing but victory, and though he muttered politely, "Not all, 'm sure," at Alex' preliminary, faltering announcement of her own bad play, the very sense of his keenness made her nervous.

She missed every stroke, gave an aimless dash that just succeeded in stopping a ball that would obviously have been "out," and felt her nerve going.

Just as success always led her on to excel, so failure reduced her capabilities to a minimum. Her heart sank.

They lost the first game.

"Will you serve?" enquired Peter Nottingham politely.

"I'd rather you did."

Alex was infinitely relieved that responsibility should momentarily be off her own shoulders, but young Nottingham's swift service was as swiftly returned by Lady Essie Cameron, an excellent player, and one who had no hesitation in smashing the ball on to the farthest corner of the court, where Alex stood, obviously nervous and unready.

She failed to reach it, and could have cried with mortification.

Thanks to Nottingham, however, they won the game.

It was their solitary victory.

Alex served one fault after another, and at last ceased even to murmur perfunctory apologies as she and her partner, whose boyish face expressed scarlet vexation, crossed over the court. She was not clear as to the system on which Cedric had arranged the tournament, but presently she saw that the losing couples would drop out one by one until the champions, having won the greatest number of setts, would finally challenge any remaining couples whom they had not yet encountered.

"I say, I'm afraid this is pretty rotten for you, old chap," she heard Cedric, full of concern, say to her partner.

"Perhaps we may get another look in at the finals," said Peter Nottingham, with gloomy civility.

He and Alex, with several others, sat and watched the progress of the games. It gave Alex a shock of rather unpleasant surprise to see the improvement in Barbara's play.

Her service, an overhand one in which very few girl players were then proficient, gave rise to several compliments. Her partner was the good-looking artist, Ralph McAllister.

"Well played!" he shouted enthusiastically, again and again.

Once or twice, when Barbara missed a stroke, Alex heard him exclaim softly, "Oh, hard luck! Well tried, partner."

Alex, tired and mortified, almost angry, wondered why Fate should have assigned to her as a partner a mannerless young cub like Nottingham, who thought of nothing but the horrid game. It did not occur to her that perhaps McAllister would not have been moved to the same enthusiasm had she, instead of Barbara, been playing with him.

The combination, however, was beaten by Cedric and the youngest of the Russell girls, a pretty, roundabout child, who left all the play to her partner and screamed with excitement and admiration almost every time he hit the ball.

It was quite evident that the final contest lay between them and Lady Essie Cameron, a strapping, muscular Scotch girl, whose partner kept discreetly to the background, and allowed her to stand up to the net and volley every possible ball that came over.

When she and her partner had emerged victorious from every contest, nothing remained but for Cedric and Miss Russell to make good their claim to the second place by conquering the remaining couples.

Alex played worse than ever, and the sett was six games to love. As she went past, Cedric muttered to her low and viciously:

"Are you doing it *on purpose*?"

She knew that he was angry and mortified at his friend Nottingham's disappointment, but his words struck her like a blow.

She stood with her back to every one, gulping hard.

"You didn't have a chance, old man," said a sympathetic youth behind her. "They might have arranged the setts better."

Peter Nottingham growled in reply.

"Who was the girl you were playing with?"

Alex realized that her white frock and plain straw hat were indistinguishable from all the other white frocks and straw hats present, seen from the back.

"Hush," said young Nottingham more cautiously. "That was one of the girls of the house, a Miss Clare."

"Can't play a bit, can she? The other one wasn't bad. Didn't one of them give poor Cardew the chuck or something?"

"Oh, shut up," Nottingham rebuked the indiscreet one. "Much more likely *he* chucked *her*, if you ask me."

Alex could bear the risk of their discovering her proximity no longer, and hastened into the house.

It was the first afternoon since her arrival at Windsor that she had not looked eagerly for the afternoon post.

The letter, a square, bluish envelope of cheap glazed paper, caught her eye almost accidentally on the table in the hall.

She recognized it instantly, and snatching it up, opened and read it standing there, with the scent of a huge bowl of late roses pervading the whole hall, and the distant sound of cries and laughter faintly penetrating to her ears from the tennis-court and garden outside.

Mother Gertrude's writing showed all the disciplined regularity characteristic of a convent, with the conventional French slope and long-tailed letters, the careful making of which Alex herself had had instilled into her in Belgium.

The phraseology of the Superior's letter was conventional, too, and even her most earnest exhortations, when delivered in writing, bore the marks of restraint.

But this letter was different.

Alex knew it at once, even before she had read it to the end of the four closely-covered sheets.

"Sept. 30, 1897.

"MY DEAREST CHILD,

"There are many letters from you waiting to be answered, and I thank you for them all, and for the confidence you bestow upon me, which touches me very deeply.

"Now at last I am able to sit down and feel that I shall have a quiet half-hour in which to talk to my child, although I dare not hope that it will be an uninterrupted one!

"So the life you are leading does not satisfy you, Alex? You tell me that you come in from the gaieties and amusements and little parties, which, after all, are natural to your age and to the position in which God has placed you, full of dissatisfaction and restlessness of mind.

"Alex, my dear child, I am not surprised. You will never find that what the world can offer will satisfy you. Most of us may have known similar moments of fatigue, of disillusionment, but to a heart and mind like yours, above all, it is inconceivable that anything less than Infinity itself should bring any lasting joy. Let me say what I have so often thought, after our conversations together in my little room—there is only one way of peace for such a nature as yours. *Give up all, and you shall find all.*

"I have thought and prayed over this letter, my little Alex, and am not writing lightly. You will forgive me if I am going too far, but I long to see my child at rest, and for such as you there is only one true rest here.

"Human love has failed you, and you are left alone, with all your impulses of sacrifice and devotion to another thrown back upon yourself. But, Alex, there is One to whom all the love and tenderness of which you know yourself capable can be offered—and He *wants* it. Weak though you are, and all-perfect though He is, He wants you.

"I don't think there has been a day since I first heard His call, when I have not marvelled at the wonder of it—at the infinite honour done to me.

"If I have told you more of the secret story of my vocation than to any one else, it has been for a reason which I think you have guessed. I have seen for a long while what it was that God asked of you, Alex, and I believe the time has come when you will see it too. Your last letter, with its cry of loneliness, and the bitter sense of being unwanted, has made me almost sure of it.

"You are not unwanted—you need never be lonely again. '*Leave all things and follow Me!*' If you hear that call, which I believe with all my heart to have sounded for you, can you disobey it? Will you not rather, forsaking all things, follow Him, and in so doing, find all things?"

"I have written a long while, and cannot go on now. God bless you again and again, and help you to be truly generous with Him.

"Write to me as fully as you will, and count upon my poor prayers and my most earnest religious affection. I need not add come and see me again on your return to London. My child will always find the warmest of welcomes! It was not for nothing that you came into the convent chapel to find rest and quiet, that summer day, my Alex!

"Your   devoted   Mother   in   Christ,

"GERTRUDE OF THE HOLY CROSS."

Alex stood almost as though transfixed. The letter hardly came as a surprise. She had long since known subconsciously what was in the Superior's mind, and yet the expression of it produced in her a sort of stupefaction.

Could it be true?

Was there really such a refuge for her, somewhere a need of her, and of that passionate desire for self-devotion that was so essential a part of her?

The thought brought with it a tingling admixture of bitter disappointment and of poignant rapture.

She realized almost despairingly that she could no longer stand in the hall clasping Mother Gertrude's letter unconsciously to her.

Already light, flying feet were approaching from the garden.

"I came to look for you, Alex," said Barbara breathlessly in the doorway. "They're going to give the prizes. What are you doing?"

"I'm coming," said Alex mechanically. She was rather surprised that Barbara should have taken the trouble to come for her.

"Did mother send you?"

"No," said Barbara simply; "but I thought it would look very bad if you kept out of the way of it because you happened to play badly and not win a prize."

So Alex assisted at the prize-giving, and saw Lady Essie accept the jingling, Indian silver bangles that were so much in fashion, with frank pleasure and gratitude, and saw consolation prizes awarded to Cedric and to his partner, who appeared entirely delighted, although she had done nothing at all to deserve distinction.

"You ought to have a prize, you know," she heard Ralph McAllister tell Barbara. "If you'd had a better partner you'd have won easily. You play much better than Lady Essie, really!"

It was not in the least true that Barbara played better than Lady Essie, or nearly so well, but she put on a little, gratified, complacent smile, that apparently satisfied Ralph McAllister quite as well as modest disclaimers.

Alex kept out of her partner's way, and avoided his eye. Not much probability that *he* would address flattering speeches to her!

All the time a subconscious emotion was surging through her at the thought of Mother Gertrude's letter and what it contained.

"The life you are leading does not satisfy you. You will never find that what the world can offer will satisfy you."

It was true enough, Heaven knew, Alex thought drearily, as she addressed perfunctory and obviously absent-minded civilities to her mother's guests.

205

In the sense of depression engendered by the afternoon's failure, no less than by the sight of McAllister's evident delight in Barbara's demure, patently-artificial, alternate coyness and gaiety, Alex realized both her own eternal dissatisfaction with her surroundings and the subtle allurement of a renunciation that should yet promise her all that she most longed for.

XVIII
Crisis

When Alex went back to London in the beginning of October, it was with a sensation as though an enormous gulf of time had been traversed between her visits to the convent in the hot, arid summer days and her return there. For one thing the cold weather had set in early and with unusual severity, and the sight of fires and winter furs seemed to succeed with startling rapidity to the roses and lawn-tennis at Windsor.

In her first greeting with Mother Gertrude, too, Alex was strongly conscious of that indefinable sensation of having made some strange, almost unguessed-at progress in a direction of which she was only now becoming aware. It frightened her when the Superior, gazing at her with those light, steady eyes that now held a depth of undisguised tenderness, spoke firmly, with an implication that could no longer be denied or ignored.

"So the great decision is taken, little Alex. And if peace has not yet come to you, do not feel dismayed. It will come, as surely as I stand here and tell you of it. But there may be—there must be—conflict first."

Whether she spoke of the conflict which Alex foresaw, half with dread and half with exultation, as inevitable between herself and her surroundings, or of some deeper, inward dissension in Alex' own soul, she could not tell.

But there was both joy and a certain excitement in having her destiny so much taken for granted, and the mystical and devotional works to which the Superior gave her free access worked upon her imagination, and dispelled many of her lingering doubts. Those which lay deepest in her soul, she never examined. She was almost, though not quite, unaware of their existence, and to probe deeper into that faint, underlying questioning would have seemed a disloyalty equally to that intangible possession which she had begun to think of as her vocation, and to Mother Gertrude. The sense of closer companionship—of a more intimate spiritual union expressed, though never explicitly so in words, in her relation with the Superior, was unutterably precious to Alex. In the joy that it brought her she read merely another manifestation and the consolation to be found in the way of the Spirit.

A feeling of impending crisis, however, hung over the hurrying days of that brief November, when the convent parlour in the afternoons was illuminated by a single gas-jet that cast strange, clean-cut shadows on the white-washed walls.

Just before Christmas Sir Francis spoke:

"What is this violent attraction that takes you out with your maid in the opposite direction to your mother's expeditions with Barbara?" he suddenly inquired of Alex one evening, very stiffly. She started and coloured, having retained all the childish, uneasy belief that her father lived in an atmosphere far above that into which the sound and sight of his children's daily doings could penetrate to his knowledge without the special intervention of some accredited emissary such as their mother.

As he spoke Lady Isabel looked up, and Barbara left the piano and came slowly down the room.

"*It has come*" flashed through Alex' mind. She only said very lamely:

"I—I don't know what you mean, father." There was all the shifting uneasiness in her manner that Sir Francis most disliked.

"Oh, darling, don't prevaricate," hastily broke in Lady Isabel, with an obvious uneasiness that gave the impression of being rooted in something deeper and of longer standing than the atmosphere of disturbance momentarily created.

"But you did not want me to come with you and Barbara to the Stores this afternoon," said Alex cravenly. The instinct of evading the direct issue was so strongly implanted in her, that she was prepared to have recourse to the feeblest and least convincing of subterfuges in order to gain time.

"Of course, I don't want you to come *anywhere* when it all so obviously bores you," plaintively said Lady Isabel. "I have almost given up trying to take you anywhere, Alex, as you very well know. You evidently prefer to go and sit in a little stuffy back-room somewhere with Heaven knows whom, sooner than remain in the company of your mother and sister."

Alex felt too much dismayed and unwillingly convicted to make any reply, but after a momentary silence Sir Francis spoke ominously.

"Indeed! is that so?"

The suspicion that had laid dormant in Alex for a long time woke to life. Her father's disappointment in her, none the less keenly felt because inarticulate, had become merged into a far greater bitterness: that of his resentment on behalf of his wife. A personal grievance he might overlook, though once perceived he would never forget it, but where Lady Isabel's due was concerned, her husband was capable of implacability.

"And may one inquire whose is the society which you find so preferable to that of your family?" he asked her, with the manifest sarcasm that in him denoted the extreme of anger.

Alex was constitutionally so much terrified of disapproval that it produced in her a veritable physical inability to explain herself. She cast an agonized look around her. Her mother was leaning back, her face strained and tired, and would not meet her eye. Sir Francis, she knew without daring to look at him, was swinging his eye-glasses to and fro, with a measured regularity that indicated his determination to wait inexorably and for any length of time for a reply to his inquiry. Barbara's big, alert eyes moved from one member of the group to another, acute and full of appraisement of them all.

Alex flung a wordless appeal to her sister. Barbara did not fail to receive and understand it, and after a moment she spoke:

"Alex goes to see the Superior of that convent near Bryanston Square. She made friends with her in the summer, didn't you, Alex?"

"Yes," faltered Alex. Some instinct of trying to palliate what she felt would be looked upon as undesirable made her add in feeble extenuation, "It is a house of the same Order as the Liège one where I was at school, you know."

"Your devotion to it was not so marked in those days, if I remember right," said her father in the same, rather elaborately sarcastic strain.

Lady Isabel, no less uneasy under it than was Alex herself, broke in with nervous exasperation in her every intonation:

"Oh, Francis, it is the same old story—one of those foolish infatuations. You know what she has always been like, and how worried I was about that dreadful Torrance girl. It's this nun now, I suppose."

"Who is this woman?"

"How should I know?" helplessly said Lady Isabel. "Alex?"

"The Superior—the Head of the house." Alex stopped. How could one say, "Mother Gertrude of the Holy Cross?" She did not even know what the Superior's name in the world had been, or where she came from.

"Go on," said Sir Francis inexorably.

They were all looking at her, and sheer desperation came to her help.

"Why shouldn't I have friends?... What is all this about?" Alex asked wildly. "It's my own life. I don't want to be undutiful, but why can't I live my own life? Everything I ever do is wrong, and I know you and father are disappointed in me, but I don't know how to be different—I wish I did." She was crying bitterly now. "You wanted me to marry Noel, and I would have if I could, but I knew that it would all have been wrong, and we should have made each other miserable. Only when I did break it off, it all seemed wrong and heartless, and I don't know *what* to do—" She felt herself becoming incoherent, and the tension of the atmosphere grew almost unbearable.

Sir Francis Clare spoke, true to the traditions of his day, viewing with something very much like horror the breaking down of those defences of a conventional reserve that should lay bare the undisciplined emotions of the soul.

"You have said enough, Alex. There are certain things that we do not put into words.... You are unhappy, my child, you have said so yourself, and it has been sufficiently obvious for some time."

"But what is it that you want, Alex? What would make you happy?" her mother broke in, piteously enough.

In the face of their perplexity, Alex lost the last feeble clue to her own complexity. She did not know what she wanted—to make them happy, to be happy herself, to be adored and admired and radiantly successful, never to know loneliness, or misunderstanding again—such thoughts surged chaotically through her mind as she stood there sobbing, and could find no words except the childish foolish formula, "I don't know."

She saw Barbara's eager, protesting gaze flash upon her, and heard her half-stifled exclamation of wondering contempt. Sir Francis turned to his younger daughter, almost as though seeking elucidation from her obvious certainties—her crude assurance with life.

"Oh!" said little Barbara, her hands clenched, "they ask you what you want, what would make you happy—they are practically offering you anything you want in the world—you could choose anything, and you stand there and cry and say you don't know! Oh, Alex—you—*you idiot!*"

"Hush!" said Sir Francis, shocked, and Lady Isabel put out her white hand with its glittering weight of rings and laid it gently on Barbara's shoulder, and she too said, "Hush, darling! why are you so vehement? You're happy, aren't you, Barbara?"

"Of course," said Barbara, wriggling. "Only if you and father asked me what *I* would like, and I had only to say what I wanted, I could think of such millions of things—for us to have a house in the country, and to give a real, proper big ball next year, and for you to let me go to restaurant dinners sometimes, and not only those dull parties and—heaps of things like that. It's such an *opportunity*, and Alex is wasting it all! The only thing she wants is to sit and talk and talk and talk with some dull old nun at that convent!"

Long afterwards Alex was to remember and ponder over again and again that denunciation of Barbara's. It was all fact—was it all true? Was that what she was fighting for—that the goal of her vehement, inchoate rebellion? Had she sought in Mother Gertrude's society the relief of self-expression only, or was her infatuation for the nun the channel through which she hoped to find those abstract possessions of the spirit which might constitute the happiness she craved?

Nothing of all the questionings that were to come later invaded her mind, as she stood sobbing and self-convicted at the crises of her relations with her childhood's home.

"Don't cry so, Alex darlin'." Lady Isabel sank back into her armchair. "Don't cry like that—it's so bad for you and I can't bear it. We only want to know how we can make you happier than you are. It's so dreadful, Alex—you've got everything, I should have thought—a home, and parents who love you—it isn't every girl that has a father like yours, some of them care nothing for their daughters—and you're young and pretty and with good health—you might have such a perfect time, even if you *have* made a mistake, poor little thing, there'll be other people, Alex—you'll know better another time ... only I can't bear it if you lose all your looks by frettin' and refusin' to go anywhere, and every one asks me where my eldest daughter is and why she doesn't make more friends, and enjoy things—" Lady Isabel's voice trailed away. She looked unutterably tired. They had none of them heard so emotional a ring in her voice ever before.

Sir Francis looked down at his wife in silence, and his gaze was as tender as his voice was stern when he finally spoke.

"This cannot go on. You have done everything to please Alex—to try and make her happy, and it has all been of no use. Let her take her own way! We have failed."

"No!" almost shrieked Alex.

"What do you mean? We have your own word for it and your sister's that you are not happy at home, and infinitely prefer the society of some woman of whom we know nothing, in surroundings which I should have thought would have proved highly uncongenial to one of my daughters, brought up among well-bred people. But apparently I am mistaken.

"It is the modern way, I am told. A young girl uses her father's house to shelter and feed her, and seeks her own friends and her own interests the while, with no reference to her parents' wishes.

"But not in this case, Alex. I have your mother and your sisters to consider. Your folly is embittering the home life that might be so happy and pleasant for all of us. Look at your mother!"

Lady Isabel was in tears.

"What shall I do?" said Alex wildly. "Let me go right away and not spoil things any more."

"You have said it," replied Sir Francis gravely, and inclined his head.

"Francis, what are you tellin' her? How can she go away from us? It's her home, until she marries."

Lady Isabel's voice was full of distressed perplexity.

"My dear love, don't don't agitate yourself. This is her home, as you say, and is always open to her. But until she has learnt to be happy there, let her seek these new friends, whom she so infinitely prefers. Let her go to this nun."

Alex, at his words, felt a rush of longing for the tenderness, the grave understanding of Mother Gertrude, the atmosphere of the quiet convent parlour where she had never heard reproach or accusation.

"Oh, yes, let me go there," she sobbed childishly. "I'll try and be good there. I'll come back good, indeed I will."

Barbara's little, cool voice cut across her sobs:

"How can you go there? Will they let you stay? What will every one think?"

"So many girls take up slumming and good works now-a-days," said Lady Isabel wearily. "Every one knows she's been upset and unhappy for a long while. It may be the best plan. My poor darling, when you're tired of it, you can come back, and we'll try again."

There was no reproach at all in her voice now, only exhaustion, and a sort of relief at having reached a conclusion.

"You hear what your mother says. If her angelic love and patience do not touch you, Alex, you must indeed be heartless. Make your arrangements, and remember, my poor child, that as long as her arms remain open to you, I will receive you home again with love and patience and without one word of reproach."

He opened the door for Lady Isabel and followed slowly from the room, his iron-grey head shaking a little.

Alex flung herself down, and Barbara laid her hand half timidly on her sister's, in one of her rare caresses.

"Don't cry, Alex. Are you really going? It's much the best idea, of course, and by the time you come back they may have something else to think about."

She giggled a little, self-consciously, and waited, as though to be questioned.

"I might be engaged to be married, or something like that, and then you'd come back to be my bridesmaid, and no one would think of anything unhappy."

Alex made no answer. Her tears had exhausted her and she felt weak and tired.

"How are you going to settle it all?" pursued Barbara tirelessly. "Hadn't you better write to them and see if they'll have you? Supposing Mother Gertrude said you couldn't go there?"

A pang of terror shot through Alex at the thought.

"Oh, no, no! She won't say she couldn't have me."

She went blindly to the carved writing-table with its heavy gilt and cut-glass appointments, and drew a sheet of paper towards her.

Barbara stood watching her curiously. Feeling as though the power of consecutive thought had almost left her, Alex scrawled a few words and addressed them to the Superior.

"We can send it round by hand," said Barbara coolly. "Then you'll know tonight."

Alex looked utterly bewildered.

"It's quite early—Holland can go in a cab."

Barbara rang the bell importantly and gave her instructions in a small, hard voice.

"It's no use just waiting about for days and days," she said to Alex. "It makes the whole house feel horrid, and father is so grave and sarcastic at meals, and it makes mother ill. You'd much rather be there than here, wouldn't you, Alex?"

Alex thought again of the Superior's welcome, which had never failed her—the Superior who knew nothing of her wicked ingratitude and undutifulness at home, and repeated miserably:

"Yes, yes, I'd much rather be there than here."

The answer to the note came much more quickly than they had expected it. Barbara heard the cab stop in the square outside, and ran down into the hall. She came back in a moment with a small, twisted note.

"What does it say, Alex?"

Alex read the tiny missive, and a great throb of purest relief and comfort went through her.

"I may go at once. She is waiting for me now, this minute, if I like."

"What did I tell you?" cried Barbara triumphantly.

She looked sharply at her sister, who was unconsciously clasping the little note as though she derived positive consolation from the contact. She went to the door.

"Holland! is the cab still there?"

"Yes, Miss Barbara."

"Why don't you go back in it now, Alex?"

"Tonight?"

"Why not? She says she's waiting for you, and it would all be much easier than a lot of good-byes and things, with father and mother."

"I couldn't go without telling them."

"I'll tell them."

Alex felt no strength, only a longing for quiet and for Mother Gertrude.

"Ask if I may," she said faintly.

Barbara darted out of the room.

When she came back, Alex heard her giving orders to Holland to pack a dressing-bag with things for the night.

Then she hurried into the room again.

"They said yes," she announced. "I think they agree with me that it's much the best thing to do it at once. After all, you're only going for a little visit. Mother said I was to give you her love. She's lying down."

"Shall I go in to her?"

"You'd better not. Father's there too. I've told Holland to pack your bag. We can send the other things tomorrow."

"But I shan't want much. It's only for a little while."

"Yes, that's all, isn't it?" said Barbara quickly. "It's only for a little while. Shall I fetch your things, Alex?"

Alex was relieved to be spared the ascent to the top of the house, for which her limbs felt far too weary. She sat and looked round her at the big, double drawing-room, crowded with heavy Victorian furniture, and upholstered in yellow, brocaded satin. She had always thought it a beautiful room, and the recollection of its splendour and of the big, gilt-framed pictures and mirrors that hung round its wall, was mingled with the earliest memories of her nursery days.

"Here you are," said Barbara. "I've brought your fur boa too, because it's sure to be cold. Holland has got your bag."

Without a word Alex rose, and they went down the broad staircase.

"I hope it'll be nice," said Barbara cheerfully.

"It's very brave of you to go, I think, Alex, and you'll write and tell me all about it, and how you like poor people, and all that sort of thing."

Alex realized that her sister was talking for the benefit of the servants.

There was a rush of icy, sleet-laden wind, as the front door was opened.

"Gracious, what a night!"

Barbara retreated to the stairs again.

"Good-bye, Alex. Let me know what things you want sent on."

"Good-bye," said Alex, apathetic from fatigue.

She turned and waved her hand once to Barbara, a slim, alert little figure clinging to the great, carved foot of the balustrade, the lamp-light casting a radiance over her light, puffed-out hair, and gleaming fitfully over the shining steel buckles on her pointed shoes.

Alex hurried through the cold evening to the shelter of the cab.

It jolted slowly through the lighted streets, and she leant back, her eyes closed.

A wave of sick apprehension surged over her every now and then, and she shivered spasmodically under her fur.

"Here we are, Miss. Shall I get out and ring, so that you won't have to wait in this cold?" said the maid compassionately.

From the dark corner of the cab Alex watched the trim, black-clad figure mount the steps.

There was always a long wait before the convent door was opened.

But tonight it was flung back and warm light streamed out.

Alex, cold and frightened, stumbled up the steps in her turn.

It was not the old portress who had thrown back the open door.

The Superior was waiting, her hands outstretched.

"My child, my child, come in! Welcome home."

Book II

XIX
Belgium

"Sister Alexandra, I have put a letter in your cell. And will you go to Mother Gertrude's room after Vespers?"

"Thank you, Sister. I wonder if Mother Gertrude remembers that I have to go down to the children at five o'clock, though?"

"Oh, I dare say not. Perhaps you could get some one to replace you there. Shall I see if Sister Agnes is free?"

"Thank you, I will speak to Mother Gertrude first."

The nuns separated, the lay-sister returning to her eternal task of polishing up the brasses and gilt candlesticks of the chapel perpetually dimmed by the rain and mists of the Belgian climate, and Alexandra Clare, professed religious, wearily mounted the steep, narrow stairs to the tiny cubicle in the large dormitory, designated a "cell." There would just be time to fetch the letter and put it into the deep pocket of her habit before the bell rang for Vespers, otherwise they would have to wait till next morning, for she knew there would be no spare instant for even a momentary return to the cell until she went to bed that night, far too tired for anything but such rest as her pallet-bed could afford. She felt little or no curiosity as to her correspondence.

Nobody wrote to her except Barbara, who had kept her posted in all the general family news with fair regularity for the past nine years.

She recognized without elation the narrow envelope with the thin black edge affected by Barbara ever since she had become the widow of Ralph McAllister, during the course of the war in South Africa. It all seemed to her very remote. The fact that Mother Gertrude had sent for her after Vespers was of far more importance than any news that Barbara might have to give of the outside world that seemed so far away and unreal.

Sister Alexandra had not been very greatly moved by any echoes from without, since the sudden shock of hearing of her mother's death, while she herself was still a novice preparing to take final vows.

Alex still remembered the bewilderment of seeing a black-clad, sobbing, schoolgirl Pamela in the parlour, and the frozen rigidity of grief which had masked her father's anguish.

Barbara and Ralph McAllister had been recalled from their honeymoon—he still rapturous at a marriage which had been deferred for nearly two years owing to Sir Francis' objection to his profession, and Barbara drowned in decorous tears, through which shone all the self-conscious glory of her wedding-ring, and her new position as a married woman. Alex had been thankful when those trying interviews had come to an end—she had been sent to Liège just before her religious profession. It had mitigated the wrench of a separation from her Superior, although the first months spent away from Mother Gertrude had seemed to her unutterably long and dreary. But less than a year later Mother Gertrude had come to the Mother-house as Assistant Superior, and the intercourse between them had been as unbroken as the rule permitted.

It was eight years since Alex had left England, but, except for the extreme cold of the winter, which told upon her health yearly, she had grown to be quite unaware of the surroundings outside. The wave of rather febrile patriotism that rolled over England at the time of the Boer War, left her quite untouched, and no description of Barbara's conveyed anything to her mind of the astoundingly wholesale demolition of old ideals that fell with the death of Victoria, and the succession of Edward VII to the English throne.

For Alex there was no change, except the unseen progress of time itself. She only realized how far apart she had grown from the old life when the news of her father's death reached her in the winter of 1902, and woke in her only a plaintive pity and self-reproachful wonder at her own absence of any acute emotion.

No one came to see her in the parlour after Sir Francis' death. For one thing, she was in Belgium and too far away to be easily visited, and the South African casualties, amongst whom had numbered Barbara's young husband, had familiarized them all with the ideas of death and parting, so that there was little of the consternation and shock that Lady Isabel's death had brought to her children. The house in Clevedon Square knew no more big receptions and elaborate At Home days, but Cedric, already of age, had taken over the headship of the household, and Alex had been conscious of a vague relief that she could still picture the surroundings she remembered as home for the boys and Pamela. Even that picture had become dim and strangely elusive, three years later, at the thought of Cedric's marriage.

Alex had accepted it, however, as she accepted most things now, with a passivity that carried no conviction to her mind. What her outer knowledge told her was true, failed to impress itself in any way upon her imagination, and consequently left her feelings quite untouched. To her inner vision, the life outside remained exactly as she had last seen it, in that summer that she still thought of as "Diamond Jubilee year."

Inside the convent, things had not changed. Looking back, she could remember a faint feeling of amusement when she had returned to the house at Liège at twenty-two years old, believing herself to be immeasurably advanced in years and experience since her schooldays, and had found that scarcely any alteration or modification in the rule-bound convent had taken place. She now sat among the other nuns at the monthly *réclame* and watched the girls rise one by one in their places, their hands concealed under the ugly black-stuff pèlerine, their hair tightly and unbecomingly strained back, their young faces demurely made heavy and impassive, as they listened to the record read aloud just as unrelentingly as ever by old Mère Alphonsine.

Sister Alexandra very rarely contributed any words of praise or blame to the judgment. At first she had been young, and therefore not expected to raise her voice amongst the many dignitaries present, but even now, when by convent standards she had attained to the maturity of middle age, her opinion would have been of little value.

She was seldom sent among the children, although she gave an English lesson to the *moyennes* on two evenings a week. In her first year at Liège, there had been an American girl of fourteen who had taken a sudden rapturous liking to her, which had never proceeded beyond the initial stages, since Alex, without explanation, had merely been told to hand over the charge of the child's English and French lessons hitherto in her hands, and had herself been transferred to other duties. Since then, she had been kept on the Community side of the house, and employed principally by Mother Gertrude to assist with the enormous task of correspondence that fell to the share of the Assistant Superior. She was taught to sew, and a large amount of mending passed through her hands and was badly accomplished, for Lady Isabel Clare's daughter had learned little that could be of use to her in the life she had selected. She was not even sufficiently musical to give lessons in piano or organ playing, nor had she any of the artistic talent that might be utilized for the perpetration of the various pious *objects d'art* that adorned the walls of the parlours or the class-room.

Nevertheless, Sister Alexandra was hard-worked. No one was ever anything else at the convent, where the chanting of the daily Office alone was a very considerable physical strain, both in the raw cold of the early morning and at the dose of the ceaselessly occupied day. Many of the nuns said the Office apart, owing to the numerous duties that called them from the chapel during the hours of praise and supplication, but Sister Alexandra had so few outside calls upon her time that she was one of the most regular in attendance.

At first her health had appeared to improve under the extreme regularity of the life, and later, when her final vows had been made, it was no longer a subject for speculation. She was not ill, and therefore need never reproach herself with being a burden to her Community. Anything else did not matter—one was tired, no doubt—but one had made the sacrifice of one's life.... Thus the conventual creed.

Time had sped by, with strange, monotonous, unperceived rapidity. It was all a matter of waiting for the next thing. At first, Alex Clare had waited eagerly and nervously to be taught some mysterious secret that would enable her to become miraculously happy and good at home in Clevedon Square. Then she had gradually come to see that there would be no return—that her home thenceforward would be with Mother Gertrude, and in the convent. Her novitiate days had come next—strange, trying apprenticeship, that had been lightened and comforted by the woman whose powerful and magnetic personality had never failed to assert itself and its strength.

Belgium, and the anguished waiting and hoping for orders to return to London, and the growing certainty that those orders would not come, had culminated in the rush of relief and joy that heralded Mother Gertrude's unexpected transfer to the Mother-house. After that, her first vows, taken for a term of two years, had inaugurated the long probationary period at the end of which a final and irrevocable pledge would bind her for ever to the way of the chosen few. Those perpetual vows were held out to her as the goal and crown of life itself, and her mind had speculated not at all on what should follow.

She was twenty-six before she was allowed to become a professed religious—according to conventual standards, no longer a very young woman. The delay had inflamed her ardour very much. It was characteristic of Alex to believe implicitly in an overwhelming transformation which should take place within her by virtue of one definite act, so long anticipated as to have acquired the proportions of a miracle.

It sometimes seemed to her that ever since the embracing of those perpetual vows, she had lived on, waiting for the transformation to operate. There was nothing else to wait for. The supreme act in the life of a religious, to the accomplishment of which her whole being had hitherto been tending, impelled at once by precept and by example, had taken place.

The next initiation could only be obtained through death itself, yet Alex was still waiting.

She would tell herself that she was waiting for the children's summer holidays for the beginning of the new term, then for the season of Advent and the Christmas festival, for the long stretch of Lenten weeks, with its additional fastings and fatigue, and still as each year slipped by the sense of unfulfilment remained with her, dormant but occasionally stirring.

In the last four years she had become additionally sensible of a growing exhaustion, that seemed to sap her spirit no less than the strength of her body. She had waited for her weariness to culminate in a breakdown of strength that should send her to the convent infirmary, when the rest that her body craved would be imposed upon her as an obligation, but no such relief came to her.

It sometimes struck her with a feeling of wonder that such utter lassitude of flesh and spirit alike could continue with no apparent and drastic effect upon her powers of following the daily rule. But she had no time in which to think, for the most part, and the example of Mother Gertrude's unflagging energy could always shame her into un-complaint. Her devotion to the elder nun had inevitably increased by the very restrictions that the convent rules placed upon their intercourse.

Even now, after so many years spent beneath the same roof, the thought that she was summoned to a private interview with Mother Gertrude could still make her heart beat faster. Since the days of her novitiate, there had been few such opportunities, and those for the most part hurried and interrupted.

Sister Alexandra went downstairs with a lightened heart.

The bell from the chapel rang out its daily summons, and she mechanically took off her black-stuff apron, folded and put it away, and turned her steps down the long passage.

Her hands were folded under her long sleeves and her head bent beneath her veil, in the attitude prescribed.

Barbara's letter lay in the depths of her pocket, already forgotten.

Her thoughts had flown ahead, and she was hoping that the Superior would allow her to send Sister Agnes in her stead to the children at five o'clock.

In the chapel, she raised her eyes furtively to the big, carved stall on a raised daïs where the Assistant Superior had her place during the frequent absence of the Superior-General.

Mother Gertrude was very often claimed in the parlour or elsewhere, even during the hours of recital of the Office, and Alex was always aware of a faint but perceptible pang of jealousy when this was the case.

Tonight, however, the stately black-robed figure was present. She was always upright and immovable, and her eyes were always downcast to her book.

Alex went through the Psalms, chanted on the accustomed single high note, and was hardly conscious of a word she uttered. Long repetition had very soon dulled her appreciation of the words, and her understanding of even Church Latin had never been more than superficial.

She had come to regard it as part of that pervading and overwhelming fatigue, that she should bring nothing but a faint distaste to her compulsory religious exercises.

Towards the close of Vespers she saw a lay-sister come on tiptoe into the chapel, and kneeling down beside Mother Gertrude's daïs, begin a whispered communication.

Immediately a feverish agony of impatience invaded her.

No doubt some imperative summons to an interview with the parents of a nun or a child, or consultation in the infirmary, where two or three little girls lay with some lingering childish ailment, had come to rob the Superior of her anticipated free time.

Alex, in nervous despair, saw her bend her head in acquiescence.

The lay-sister retired as noiselessly as she had come, and Mother Gertrude closed her book.

The concluding versicles and prayers were spoken kneeling, and Alex was compelled to turn towards the High Altar.

She was quivering from head to foot, and gripped the arms of her stall in order to restrain herself from turning her head. Every nerve was strained in her attempt to hear any movement at the back of the chapel, but she could distinguish nothing.

The few minutes that elapsed before the bell sounded for rising, seemed to her interminable.

She had grown accustomed lately to the grip of these nervous agonies, to which she became a prey for the most trivial of causes.

The modern exploitation of hysteria, however, was still in its embryo stage, half-way between the genteel hysterics of the 'sixties and the suppressed neuroticism of the new century. She did not diagnose her complaint. With the sensation, familiar to her, of blood pumping from her heart to her head, making her face burn, while her hands and feet remained dead and cold, she rose from her knees.

Although she had expected nothing else, a feeling of sick disappointment invaded her as she saw that the Superior's place had been noiselessly vacated.

With leaden feet, she moved out of the chapel and slowly resumed the black apron and the stuff sleeves that protected her habit.

In the absence of any direct order to the contrary, she knew that she must take her accustomed place in the class-room of the *moyennes*, and that the English lesson must proceed as usual.

"A vos places."

She had long ago learnt to speak French fluently, but never without an unmistakable British accent and intonation.

Subconsciously she was always rather relieved, on that account, when the preliminaries were done with, and the lesson could be given, according to the rules, in the English tongue.

"Simone! Begin, please."

Sister Alexandra, seated at the desk, held the book open in front of her, and her eyes rested upon the page, but her mind took in neither the meaning of the printed words nor the sense conveyed by Simone's droning, inexpressive voice.

She wondered whether some one would come to take her place at the desk and tell her that Mother Gertrude was waiting for her downstairs.

A sudden, stealthy opening of the class-room door made her look up with a flash of hope, but it was only a little girl late for her lesson and sidling in, hoping to escape notice.

Alex did not even trouble to give her the accustomed bad mark.

It would have meant opening her desk, and pulling out the mistress's note-book, and looking for a pencil, and she felt too tired. In her earlier days at the convent she would have felt ashamed at the thought of yielding to such slothful unconcern, and would have magnified the omission into a sin, to be confessed with shame to Mother Gertrude.

Now, she was too tired to care, and besides, she never saw Mother Gertrude. Even the poor little half-hour that had been held out to her was not to be hers, after all. She brooded in resentment over the thought.

A titter going round the room roused her.

"What are you saying, Simone?"

Simone stared back at her stupidly, but another keen-faced girl in the front row of desks spoke eagerly:

"She's said nearly all through the lesson, there's nothing left for any one else to say."

"You can repeat it afterwards," said Alex coldly.

She was vexed that her inattention should have been betrayed to the class, and presently she gave her full attention to the recital.

Just as it was over, the young novice, Sister Agnes, came into the room and, approaching the desk, spoke to Alex in a lowered voice:

"Mother Gertrude sent me, Sister. Will you go down to her and wait in her room? She will come in a moment. I am to take the children back to the study-room for you."

"Thank you," said Alex, trembling. The revulsion of feeling was so strong that she felt the chords tightening in her throat, which denoted approaching tears, such as she often shed for no adequate reason. She left the room.

The Assistant Superior's room on the ground floor was vacant.

Alex sat down on the low, rush-bottomed chair drawn close to the Superior's table, and closed her eyes. Now that her agony of suspense was ended, she became even more overwhelmingly conscious of fatigue, and began to wonder, almost against her will, whether Mother Gertrude would not notice it, and perhaps tell her that she was to go to bed after supper and not come to the recital of Office in the chapel.

She wondered whether she looked tired. There were no looking-glasses in the convent, but sometimes she had seen her own reflection in the big, full-length mirror of the sacristy, and she knew that she had lost her colour, and that her face had grown thin, with heavy, black circles underneath her eyes. She knew, too, that her step had lost any elasticity, and that she stooped far more than in the days when Lady Isabel had implored her to "hold up" so that her pretty frocks might be seen to advantage.

Waiting in the small room, with its carefully-closed window, and the big writing-table stacked with papers, and a great crucifix standing upright in the midst of them, she began for the first time to speculate as to the reason of her summons.

It occurred to her, with a slight sense of shock, that such a summons, in the case of nun or novice, had very often been the prelude to an announcement of bad news, such as the death of a relative at home.

Hastily she pulled out Barbara's letter and glanced through it.

There was no hint of approaching disaster in the rather set little phrases, and the four small sheets were mostly concerned with the fact that Barbara was finding it necessary to move into a still smaller house than the one that she and Ralph had taken at Hampstead after their improvident marriage.

Pamela was at Clevedon Square with Cedric and his wife. She was going to heaps of parties, and every one thought her very pretty and amusing.

215

There was no mention of Archie, and Alex hastily ransacked her memory as to his whereabouts. Since the first year of her novitiate in London she had never seen her youngest brother, and although she felt a fleeting sorrow at the thought of harm having befallen him, her tenderness was for the little, curly-haired boy in a sailor suit with whom she had played and quarrelled in the Clevedon Square nursery, and not for the unknown youth of later years.

As she speculated, the well-known tread of the Assistant Superior sounded down the corridors— a hasty, decisive footstep. Alex sprang to her feet as the door opened.

"Oh, what is it?" she cried, at the first sight of the Superior's face.

The strong, lined countenance, suffused with agitation, bore every mark of violent disturbance.

Her deep voice, however, was as well under control as ever, although strong emotion underlay its vibrant quality.

"My little Sister, you have a big sacrifice before you. I cannot pretend to think that it will not cost you dear, as it will me. But we know Who asks it of us."

"What?" gasped Alex again, utterly at a loss, but feeling the blood ebb from her face.

"Our Mother-General has appointed me as Superior to the new house in South America. The boat sails at the end of this week."

XX
Aftermath

Alex could not believe the extent of the calamity that had befallen her, nor did she realize at first that the very mainspring of her life in the convent was attacked.

It astounded her to perceive that to the rest of the community the news brought no overwhelming shock.

Such sudden uprootings and transfers were not uncommon, and the notice given was generally a twenty-four hour one. Mother Gertrude had nearly a week in which to make her few preparations for an exile that almost certainly was for life, and to prepare herself as far as possible for new and heavy responsibilities.

The Superior-General was herself proceeding to South America with the little band of chosen pioneers, representative of almost every European house of the Order, and after inaugurating the establishment of the new venture, was to return to Liège, with one lay-sister only as companion.

In the general concern for her welfare and admiration of her courage in undertaking such a journey on the eve of her sixty-third birthday, it seemed to Alex that all other considerations were overlooked or ignored entirely.

She was aware that the convent spirit of detachment, so much advocated, and the consciousness of that vow of obedience made freely and fully, would alike preclude the possibility of any spoken protest or lamentation over the separation.

The severing of human ties was part and parcel of a nun's sacrifice, and her life was in the hands of her spiritual superiors.

There was no discussion possible.

Mother Gertrude, although the look of strain was deepening round her eyes and mouth, went steadily about her duties and spared herself in nothing.

Her place was to be taken temporarily by a French nun who had been for many years at Liège, and the charge was handed over with the least possible dislocation.

It was on a Tuesday night that Mother Gertrude had been told of the destiny in store for her, and on the following Saturday she was to proceed with her Superior to Paris, and thence to Marseilles to the boat.

Wednesday and Thursday Alex never saw her.

She had expected it, and was, moreover, far too much stunned to realize anything beyond the immediate necessity for taking her habitual place in the Community life without betraying the sense of utter despair that was hovering over her.

On Friday afternoon Mother Gertrude said to her:

"I have not had one spare moment to give you, my poor child. But I think you know everything that I would say to you? Be very, very faithful, Sister, and remember that these separations may be for life, but all Eternity is before us."

Alex could capture nothing of the rapt assurance that lay in the upraised eyes and vibrant voice.

"What shall I do without you?" she asked despairingly, feeling how inadequate the words were to voice her sense of utter deprivation.

The light, watchful eyes of the Superior seemed to pierce through her.

"Don't say that, dear child. You do not depend in any sense upon another creature. I have been nothing to you but a means to an end. It was given to me to help you a little, years ago, to find your holy vocation. You know that human friendships in themselves mean nothing."

Something in Alex seemed to be crying and protesting aloud in heart-broken repudiation of the formula to which her lips had so often subscribed, but her own tacit acquiescence of years rose to rebuke her, and the dread of vexing and alienating the Supervisor at this eleventh hour.

Dumbly she knelt down on the floor beside the Superior's chair.

Mother Gertrude looked at her compassionately enough, but with the strange remoteness induced by the long cultivation of an absolutely impersonal relation towards humanity.

"My poor little Sister, sometimes lately I have wondered whether I have been altogether wise in my treatment of you, and whether I have not allowed you to give way to natural affection too much. Perhaps this break has come in time. You must remember that you have renounced *all* earthly ties, even the holiest and most sacred ones, and therefore you must be ready to make any sacrifice for the sake of your one, supreme Love. There is so much I should like to say to you, but time is getting short now, and there is a great deal to be done. God bless you, my child."

The Superior laid her hand on Sister Alexandra's bent head.

Alex clasped it desperately.

"I shall still be your child always?" she almost wailed, with a weight of things unspoken on her heart, and in a last frantic attempt to carry away one definite assurance.

The slightest possible severity mingled in Mother Gertrude's clear gaze, bent downwards as she rose to her full height, her carriage as upright and as dignified as it had been ten years before.

"No, Sister," she said very distinctly. "You will be the child of whatever Superior God may send you in my place."

"You know that we in the convent have no human ties, only spiritual ones. You will see your Divine Master, and Him only, in the person of your Superior in religion. Remember that, little Sister. You must learn detachment if you are to be truly faithful. That is my last and most earnest counsel to you. I shall pray daily that you may be given strength to follow it."

"Don't go!" gasped Alex, hardly knowing what she said, as she saw the Superior's hand upon the door. "Don't go away like that. Oh, Mother, Mother, how shall I bear it? I've only got you and now you're going away for ever."

She broke into tearless sobs.

"Sister Alexandra! Has it come to this? I am indeed to blame if you are still so undisciplined and so weak as to cling to a mere creature—you that have been chosen by God to love Him, and Him only! I could not have believed it." Mother Gertrude's tone held bitter remorse and shame.

Alex' old, pitiful instinct of propitiating the being she loved best sprang to life within her.

"No, no, I didn't really mean it. I know I mustn't."

The nun gazed at her in compassionate perplexity.

"You are overstrung, and tired; you don't know what you are saying. When you come to yourself, my poor child, you will hardly believe that you could have proved so disloyal, even for a moment."

"Now calm yourself, and do not attempt to join the recreation tonight. You are not fit for it. I will tell our Mother-General that I have told you to go to your cell as soon as supper is over. Goodnight, and again good-bye."

Sheer terror at the bare thought of being left there alone forced Alex to her feet, although she could scarcely stand, and was trembling violently. "You won't forget me?" she entreated almost inaudibly.

217

"I shall always remember you in my prayers, as I do all those who have been under my direction. Indeed, you will have a special place in them," said the Superior gravely, "since I can never forget that, by the grace of God, I was instrumental in bringing you into His holy house. But never forget that *no* human relation, however precious it may be, can have any completeness in itself. It all has to lead on to the one supreme thing, Sister, the 'one thing necessary.'

"Now you must detain me no longer." She freed herself from the convulsive grasp that Alex had unconsciously fastened on to the folds of her habit and moved unhesitatingly to the door.

Alex followed her with eyes that stared blankly from a blanched face. She felt as though she was under a spell and could neither move nor speak. She could not believe that Mother Gertrude would really leave her in that way. The Superior opened the door and passed out, closing it behind her without pausing or looking back.

Alex heard her steps receding, rapid and measured, along the uncarpeted corridor outside.

She stayed on and on in the little cold room, the winter dusk deepening rapidly outside, the silence only broken by the occasional clanging of a bell, to the sound of which she was so much inured that it hardly struck upon her senses. She thought that Mother Gertrude would come back to her.

There must be some other last words between them than those few impersonal counsels of perfection, that repudiated any more intimate link such as Alex' exclusive jealousy, stifled, but never stronger than after those ten years of repression, now claimed with such frantic yearning.

She waited, scarcely moving. She grew colder and colder, but she was unconscious of her icy feet and leaden hands. She was not even aware of consecutive thought.

Her whole body was absorbed in the supreme act of awaiting the Superior's return for the word, the look, that should at least break the dreadful darkness that encompassed her soul at the sudden deprivation of that one outlet which had, unaware, served as a safety-valve for the whole craving dependence of her spirit.

Mother Gertrude did not come back.

Dusk turned rapidly to night, and the distant cries and laughter of the children's evening recreation fell into a quiet that was only shattered by the single note of the deep-toned bell that proclaimed the hour of silence and the final gathering of the Community for the last recital of the Office in the chapel.

There was the flicker of a light along the passage outside, and the door opened at last.

Alex did not move.

She turned anguished eyes, that held scarcely any comprehension in the immensity of their fatigue, towards the entering figure.

It was that of the old Infirmarian, who put down the lighted candle and threw up her hands of dismay as her gaze met that of the younger nun. Mindful of the hour of silence, she asked no question, but she took Alex away to the convent infirmary, and placed her in a bed of which the mattress seemed strangely and wonderfully soft after the *paillasse* in her cell, and gave her a hot, sweet, strongly scented *tisane* and bade her sleep.

"Mais demain?" whispered Alex.

She was thinking of the early departure in the raw morning cold, when the convoy that was leaving for South America would be driven away from the convent. But the Infirmarian shook her head and shuffled slowly away, leaving the room in darkness.

She was old and very tired, and for her there was no *demain*, except the glorious dawn that should herald the day of Eternity.

Alex lay awake in the merciful darkness and envisaged the culmination of long years of stifled repression and self-deception.

She knew now, as she had never let herself know before, what had sustained her through the dragging years after the final objective of her vows had been left behind.

She knew that she had thought herself to be answering to a call of God, when she had been hearing only the voice of Mother Gertrude, and had been craving only for Mother Gertrude's tenderness and approbation.

Physical pangs of terror shot through her and shook her from head to foot as she realized to what she had bound herself, which now presented itself to her overstrung perceptions only in the crudest terms.

To live without earthly affection, to relinquish love as she understood it, in terms of human sympathy, for an ideal to which she knew, with tardy and unerring certainty, that nothing within her would ever conform.

She knew now, with that appalling clear-sightedness to which humanity is mercifully a stranger until or unless the last outposts of sanity are almost reached, that the vocation of which they all spoke so glibly had never been hers.

She had entered a life for which her every instinct declared her to be utterly unfitted, in search of that which her few short years in the outside world had denied her. The convent instinct, engrained in her at last, added to the anguish of startled horror at the wickedness of her own state of mind.

God is not mocked, she thought. Alex had tried to cheat God, and for ten years He had stayed His hand and had allowed her deception to go on.

And now it had all fallen on her—shame and punishment and despair, and nowhere any human help or consolation to turn to. She prayed frenziedly in the darkness, but no comfort came to her. She stifled in the pillow the imploring crying aloud of Mother Gertrude's name that sprang to her lips, but with a pang that sickened her, she recalled the Superior's parting from her that evening, her undeviating fidelity to an austere ideal which should also have been Alex'.

There was nothing anywhere.

And with that final certainty of negation came a rigidity of despair that no terms of time or space could measure.

Alex fell into exhaustion, then into a state of coma that became heavy, dreamless sleep enduring far into the next day. She woke to instant, stabbing recollection. It was a grey, leaden day, with rain lashing the window-panes, and at first Alex thought that it might be still early morning, but there was all the far-away, indescribable stir that tells of a household when the day's work is in full swing, and presently she realized that it must be the middle of the morning.

"They have gone," she thought, but the words conveyed no meaning to her. The Infirmarian came in to her and spoke, and asked whether she felt fit to get up, and although on the day before Alex had so craved for rest, she heard her own voice replying indifferently that she thought she was quite well, and that she was ready to rise at once.

"You are sure you have taken no chill? You must have been there in Mother Gertrude's room for a long time after you were taken faint.... Can you remember?" The nun looked at her, puzzled and anxious.

"Did I faint?"

"I think so, surely. You were almost unconscious when I came in, quite by chance, and found you there, almost frozen, poor little Sister! Now tell me—?" The old Infirmarian put a few stereotyped questions such as she addressed to all those of her patients whose ailments could not be immediately diagnosed at sight.

Alex' matter-of-fact replies, for the most part denials of the suggested ills, left her no wiser. Finally she decided on a *refroidissement*. "Put a piece of flannel over your chest," she said gravely, "and you had, perhaps, better spend recreation indoors until the spell of cold is over."

"Thank you," said Sister Alexandra lifelessly. "What time is it?"

"Nearly eleven. Have you any duties for which you should be replaced this morning?"

"There are a lot of things, I think," said Alex vaguely, "but I can get up."

"Very well," the Infirmarian acquiesced unemotionally. "There is much work to be done, as you say, and we nuns cannot afford to be ill for long."

Alex did not think that she was ill—she was quite able to get up and to dress herself, although her head was aching and her hands shook oddly.

She reflected with dull surprise that all the poignant misery of the days that had gone before seemed to have left her. Evidently this was what people meant by "getting over things." One suffered until one could bear no more, and then it was all numbness and inertia.

She felt a sort of surprised gratitude to God at the cessation of pain, as one who had undergone torture might feel towards the torturers for some brief respite.

Her thankfulness made tears come into her eyes, and she forced them back with a sort of wonder at herself, but that odd disposition to weep still remained with her.

As she went downstairs, rather slowly and cautiously, because her knees were shaking so strangely, she met a very little girl, the pet and baby of the whole establishment, climbing upwards. She was holding up the corners of her diminutive black apron with both hands, and after looking at the nun silently for a moment, she showed her that it contained two tiny, struggling kittens. "Les petits enfants de Minet," she announced gravely, and went on climbing, clasping her burden tenderly.

Alex could never have told what it was that struck her with so unbearable a sense of pathos in the sight of the little childish figure.

Quite suddenly the tears began to pour down her face, and she could neither have checked them nor have assigned any reason for them.

She went on downstairs, wiping the blinding tears from her sight, and amazed at the violence of the uncontrollable sobs that were noiselessly shaking her.

Something had suddenly given way within her and passed far beyond her own control.

It was as though she could never stop crying again.

XXI
Father Farrell

For what seemed a long while afterwards—a period which, indeed, covered three or four weeks—Alex learnt to be intensely and humbly grateful for the convent law that would not allow any form of personalities in intercourse.

She was utterly unable to cease from crying, and in spite of her shame and almost her terror, the tears continued to stream down her face in the chapel, in the refectory, even at the hour of recreation.

Nobody asked her any questions. One or two of the nuns looked at her compassionately, or made some kindly, little, friendly remark; a lay-sister now and then offered her an unexpected piece of help in her work, and the Infirmarian occasionally sent her a cup of *bouillon* for dinner, but it was nobody's business to offer inquiries, and had any one done so, the rule would have compelled Sister Alexandra to reply by a generality and to change the conversation without delay.

Only the Superior was entitled to probe deeper, and at first the Frenchwoman who was temporarily succeeding Mother Gertrude was too much occupied by her new cares to see much of her community individually.

Alex was relieved when the Christmas holidays began, and she had no longer to fear the notice of the sharp-eyed children, but in the reduction of work surrounding the festive season, it became impossible that her breakdown should continue to pass unnoticed. She did not herself know what was the matter, and could scarcely have given a cause for those incessant tears, except that she was unutterably weary and miserable, and that they had passed far beyond her own control.

The idea that that continuous weeping could have any connection with a physical nervous breakdown never occurred to her.

It was with surprise, and very little thought of cause and effect, that she one night noticed her own extraordinary loss of flesh. She had never been anything but thin and slightly built, but now she quite suddenly perceived that her arms and legs in the last two months had taken on an astounding and literal resemblance to long sticks of white wood. All the way up from wrist to armpit, her left hand, with thumb and middle finger joined, could span the circumference of her right arm.

It seemed incredible.

Her mind went back ten years, and she thought of Lady Isabel, and how much she had lamented her daughter's youthful angularity.

"If she could have seen this!" thought Alex. "But, of course, it only mattered for evening dress—she wouldn't have thought it mattered for a nun."

Instantly she began to cry again, although her head throbbed and her eyes burned and smarted. There was no need now to wonder if she looked tired. Accidentally one day, her hand to her face, she had felt the sort of deeply-hollowed pit that now lay underneath each eye, worn into a groove.

She had ceased to wonder whether life would ever offer anything but this mechanical round of blurred pain and misery, these incessant tears, when the Superior sent for her.

"What is the matter with you, Sister? They tell me you are always in tears. Are you ill?"

Alex shook her head dumbly.

"Sister, control yourself. You will be ill if you cry like that. Don't kneel, sit down."

The Superior's tone was very kind, and the note of sympathy shook Alex afresh.

"Tell me what it is. Don't be afraid."

"I want to leave the convent—I want to be released from my vows."

She had never meant to say it—she had never known that such a thought was in her mind, but the moment that the words were uttered, the first sense of relief that she had felt surged within her.

It was the remembrance of that rush of relief that enabled her, sobbing, to repeat the shameful recantation, in the face of the Superior's grave, pitiful urgings and assurance that she did not know what she was saying.

After that—an appalling crisis that left her utterly exhausted and with no vestige of belief left in her own ultimate salvation—everything was changed.

She was treated as an invalid, and sent to lie down instead of joining the community at the hour of recreation, the Superior herself devoted almost an hour to her every day, and nearly all her work was taken away, so that she could walk alone round the big *verger* and the enclosed garden, and read the carefully-selected Lives and Treatises that the Superior chose for her.

Gradually some sort of poise returned to her. She could control her tears, and drink the soups and *tisanes* that were specially prepared and put before her, and as the year advanced, she could feel the first hint of Spring stirring in her exhaustion. She was devoid alike of apprehension and of hope.

No solution appeared to her conceivable, save possibly that of her own death, and she knew that none would be attempted until the return of the Superior-General from South America.

As this delayed, she became more and more convinced, in despite of all reason, of the immutable eternity of the present state of affairs.

It shocked her when one day the Superior said to her:

"You are to go to the Superior of the Jesuits' College in the parlour this afternoon. Do you remember, he preached the sermon for your Profession, and I think he has been here once or twice in the last year or two? He is a very wise and clever and holy man, and ought to help you. Besides, he is of your own nationality."

Alex remembered the tall, good-looking Irishman very well. He had once or twice visited the convent, and had always told amusing stories at recreation, and preached vigorous, inspiring sermons in the chapel, with more than a spice of originality to colour them.

The children adored him.

Alex wondered.

Perhaps Father Farrell, the clever and educated priest, would really see in some new aspect the problem that left her baffled and sick of soul and body.

She went into the parlour that afternoon trembling with mingled dread, and the first faint stirrings of hope that understanding and release from herself and her wickedness might yet be in store for her.

Father Farrell, big and broad-shouldered, with iron-grey, wavy hair and a strong, handsome face, turned from the window as she entered the room.

"Come in, Sister, come in. Sit down, won't you? They tell me ye've not been well—ye don't look it, ye don't look it!"

His voice, too, was big and bluff and hearty, full of decision, the voice of a man accustomed to the command of men.

He pushed a chair forward and motioned her, with a quick, imperious gesture that yet held kindness, to sit down.

He himself stood, towering over her, by the window.

"Well, now, what's all the trouble, Sister?"

There was the suspicion of a brogue in his cultivated tones.

Alex made a tremendous effort. She told herself that he could not help her unless she told him the truth.

She said, as she had said to the French Superior:

"I am very unhappy—I want to be released from my vows as a nun."

The priest gave her one very quick, penetrating look, and his thick eyebrows went up into his hair for an instant, but he did not speak.

"I don't think I have ever had any—any real vocation," said Alex, whitening from the effort of an admission that she knew he must regard as degrading.

"And how long have ye thought ye had no real vocation?"

There was the slightest possible discernible tinge of kindly derision in the inquiry.

It gave the final touch to her disconcertment.

"I don't know."

She felt the folly of her reply even before the priest's laugh, tinged with a sort of vexed contempt, rang through the room.

"Now, me dear child, this is perfect nonsense, let me tell ye. Did ye ever hear the like of such folly? No real vocation, and here ye've been a professed religious for—how long is it?"

"Nearly four years since I was finally professed, but—"

"There's no *but* about it, Sister. A vow made to Our Blessed Lord, I'd have ye know, is not like an old glove, to be thrown away when ye think ye're tired of it. No, no, Sister, that'll not be the way of it. Ye'll get over this, me dear child, with a little faith and perseverance. It's just a temptation, that ye've perhaps been giving way to, owing to fatigue and ill health. Ye feel it's all too hard for ye, is that it?"

"No," said Alex frantically, "that's not it. It's nothing like that. It's that I can't bear this way of living any longer. I want a home, and to be allowed to care for people, and to have friends again—I *can't* live by myself."

She knew that she had voiced the truth as she knew it, and covered her face with her hands in dread lest it might fail to reach his perceptions.

She heard a change in Father Farrell's voice when next he spoke.

"Ye'd better tell me the whole tale, Sister. Who is it ye want to go back to in the world?"

She looked up, bewildered.

"Any one—home. Where I can just be myself again—"

"And how much home have ye got left, after being a nun ten years? Is your mother alive?"

"No."

"Your father?"

"No," faltered Alex.

"They died after ye left home, I daresay?"

"Yes."

"Then, in the name of goodness, who do ye expect is going to make a home for ye? Have ye sisters and brothers?"

"Yes." Alex hesitated, seeing at last whither his inquiries were tending.

"Yes, and I'm thinking they're married and with homes of their own by this time," said the priest shrewdly. "Let me tell ye, ten years sees a good many changes in the world, and it isn't much of a welcome ye'd get by breaking your holy vows and making a great scandal in the Church, and then planting yourself on relations who've lost touch with ye, more or less, and have homes of their own, and a husband or wife, as the case may be, and perhaps little children to care for. A maiden aunt isn't so very much thought of, in the best of circumstances, let me tell ye.

"Now isn't there reason in what I'm saying, Sister?"

Sick conviction shot through her.

"Yes, Father."

"Well, then, ye'll just give up that foolish notion, now."

He looked at her white, desperate face, and began to take long strides up and down the room.

"Have ye confidence in your Superior? Do ye get on with her?" he asked suddenly.

"Our present Superior has only been here a little while—the one before that—"

"I know, I know," he interrupted impatiently. "It's the Superior-General I mean, of course—everything must come to her in the long run, naturally. Have you full confidence in her, now?"

Alex felt as incapable of a negative reply as of an affirmative one. She knew that she did not understand the term "full confidence" as he did, and she temporized weakly.

"But our Mother-General is away in South America—she keeps delaying, and that's one reason why nothing has been settled about me. She hasn't even left America yet."

"I'm well aware of that. Don't waste time playing with me that way, Sister, ye'll get no further. Ye know very well what I mean. Now, tell me now, will it do for ye if I arrange for your transfer to another house—maybe to the one in London, or somewhere in your own country?"

The instinct of the imprisoned creature that sees another form of the same trap offered it under the guise of freedom, made her revolt.

"No," she cried. "No! I want to get right away—I want to stop being a nun."

The priest suddenly hit the table with his clenched fist, making it rock, and making his auditor start painfully.

"That's what you'll never do, not if ye got release from the holy vows ten times over. Once a nun always a nun, Sister, although ye may be false and faithless and go back into the very midst of the world ye've renounced. But ye'll find no comfort there, no blessing, and God'll remember it against ye, Sister. A soul that spurns His choicest graces need expect no mercy, either here or hereafter. I tell ye straight, Sister, that ye'll be deliberately jeopardizing your immortal soul, if ye give in to this wicked folly. Ye've to choose between God and the Devil—between a little while of suffering here, maybe, and then Eternity in which to enjoy the reward of the faithful, or a hideous mockery of freedom here, followed by Hell and its torments for ever and ever. Which is it to be?"

Alex was terrified, but it was the priest's anger that terrified her, not the threats that he uttered. At the back of her mind, lay the dim conviction that no Hell could surpass in intensity of bitterness that which her spirit was traversing on earth.

Father Farrell looked at her frightened, distorted face, and his voice sank into persuasiveness.

"This'll pass, me dear child. Many a poor soul before ye has known what it is to falter by the wayside. But courage, Sister, ye can conquer this weakness with God's help. You're in no trouble about your faith, now are ye?"

Had Alex been able to formulate her thoughts clearly, she might have told him that it had long since become a matter of supreme unimportance to her whether or no she still possessed that which he termed her faith. As a fact, the beliefs which could alone have made the convent life endurable to her, had never struck more than the most shallow of roots into her consciousness. Perhaps the only belief which had any real hold upon her was the one that she had gradually formed upon her experience of the living—that God was a Superior Being who must be propitiated by the sacrifice of all that one held dear, lest He strike it from one.

She looked dimly at Father Farrell, and shook her head, because she was afraid of his anger if she owned to the utter insecurity of her hold upon any religious convictions.

"That's right, that's right," he said hastily. "I felt sure ye were a good child at bottom. Now would ye like to make a good general Confession, and I'll give ye absolution, and ye can start again?"

Some hint of inflexibility in the last words roused Alex to a final, frantic bid for liberty.

"It's no use—it won't do for me to begin again. I can't stay on. If I can't get released from my vows I'll—I'll run away."

Then there was a long silence.

When the priest spoke again, however, his voice held more of meditative speculation than of the anger which she feared.

"Supposing I could arrange it for ye—I don't say I could, mind, but it might be done, if good reasons were shown—what would ye say to another religious order altogether? It may be that this life is unsuited to ye—there have been such cases. I know a holy Carmelite nun who was in quite another order for nearly fifteen years, before she found out where the Lord really wanted her. Are ye one of those, maybe?"

"No," spoke Alex, almost sullenly. The conflict was wearing her out, and she was conscious only of a blind, unreasoning instinct that if she once gave ground, she would find herself for ever bound to the life which had become unendurable to her.

"What d'ye mean, *No?*"

"I want to go away. I want to be released from my vows."

The formula had become almost mechanical now. The Jesuit for the first time dropped the brusqueness of manner habitual to him.

Pacing the length of the big parlour with measured, even strides, his hands clasped behind his shabby cassock, he let his deep, naturally rhetorical voice boom out in full, rolling periods through the room.

"Why did ye come to me at all, Sister? It wasn't for advice, and it wasn't for help. I've offered both, and ye'll take neither. Having put your hand to the plough, you've looked back. Ye say that sooner than remain faithful ye'll run away—ye'll make a scandal and a disgrace for the Community that's sheltered ye, and bring shame and sorrow to the good Mothers here. What did ye expect me to answer to that? If your whole will is turned to evil, it was a farce and a mockery to come to me—I can do nothing.

"But one thing I'll tell ye, Sister. If ye do this thing—if it goes up to Rome, and the vows ye took in full consciousness and free will on the day ye were professed, are dissolved—so far as they ever can be, that is, and let me tell ye that it's neither a quick nor an easy business—if it comes to that, Sister, *there'll be no going back.* No cringing round to the convent afterwards, when ye find there's no place and no welcome for ye in the world, asking to be taken back. They'll not have ye, Sister, and they'll be right. If ye go, it's for ever."

It seemed to Alex that he was purposely seeking to frighten her—that he wanted to add fresh miseries and apprehensions to those already piled upon her, and a faint resentment flicked at her in questioning acceptance of such an assumption.

The shadow of spirit thus restored to her, just enabled her to endure the seemingly endless exposition hurled at her in the priest's powerful voice.

When it was all over, she crawled out of the room like a creature that had been beaten.

Stunned, she only knew that yet another fellow-creature had entered the league of those who were angered against her.

XXII
Rome

The crisis passed, as all such must pass, and Alex found herself in the position openly recognized as that of waiting for the dissolution of her religious vows.

It was as Father Farrell had said, neither a short nor an easy business, nor was she allowed to pass the months of her waiting at the Liège Mother-house.

They sent her to a small house of the Order in Rome, thinking, with the curious convent instinct for misplaced economy, to save the petty cost of incessant passing to and fro of correspondence and documents, between the convent in Belgium and the Papal Secretariat at the Vatican.

Alex went to Italy in a dream. It struck her with a faint sense of irony that she and Barbara, long ago, had entertained an ambition to visit Italy, standing for all that was romantic and picturesque in the South. After all, she was to be the first to realize that girlish dream, the fulfilment of which brought no elation.

At first she lived amongst the nuns, and led their life, but when it became evident beyond question that she was eventually to obtain release from her vows, the Community held no place for her any longer.

Her religious habit was taken away, and a thick, voluminous, black-stuff dress substituted, which the nuns thought light and cool in comparison with their own weighty garments, but of which the hard, stiff cuffs and high collar, unrelieved by any softening of white, made Alex suffer greatly.

The house was too small to admit of a *pensionnat*, but the nuns took in an inconsiderable number of lady boarders, and an occasional pupil. Alex, however, was not suffered to hold any intercourse with these. After her six months spent in Community life a final appeal was made to her, and when it failed of its effect she passed into a kind of moral ostracism.

She had a small bedroom, where her meals were served by the lay-sister who waited on the lady-boarders, and a little *prie-dieu* was put in a remote corner of the chapel for her use, neither to be confounded with the choir-stalls, nor the benches for visitors, nor the seats reserved for the ladies living in the house. The librarian Sister, in charge of the well-filled book-case of the Community-rooms, had instructions to provide her with literature. Beyond that, her existence remained unrecognized.

She often spent hours doing nothing, gazing from the window at the *Corso* far below, so curiously instinct with life after the solitude of the Liège grounds, encompassed by high walls on every side.

She did not read very much.

The books they gave her were all designed to one end—that of making her realize that she was turning her back upon the way of salvation. When she thought about it, Alex believed that this was, in truth, what she was doing, but it hardly seemed to matter.

Her room was fireless, and the old-fashioned house, as most Roman ones, had no form of central heating. She shivered and shivered, and in the early days of February fell ill. One abscess after another formed inside her throat, an unspeakably painful manifestation of general weakness.

One evening she was so ill that there was talk of sending for the chaplain—the doctor had never been suggested—but that same night the worst abscess of all broke inside her throat, and Alex saw that there was no hope of her being about to die.

The bright winter cold seemed to change with incredible rapidity into glowing summer heat, and a modicum of well-being gradually returned to her.

She even crept slowly and listlessly about in the shade of the great Borghese gardens, in the comparative freshness of the Pincio height, and wondered piteously at this strange realization of her girlhood's dream of seeing Italy. She never dared to go into the streets alone, nor would the nuns have permitted it.

Her difficult letters to England had been written.

Cedric had replied with courteous brevity, a letter so much what Sir Francis might have written that Alex was almost startled, and her father's man of business had written her a short, kind little note, rejoicing that the world was again to have the benefit of Miss Clare's society after her temporary retirement.

The only long letter she received was from Barbara.

"*Hampstead,*

"*March* 30, 1908.
"DEAREST ALEX,
"Your letter from Rome was, of course, a great surprise. I had been wondering when I should hear from you again, but I did not at all guess what your news would be when it came, as we had all quite grown to think of you as completely settled in the convent.

"I am afraid that, as you say, there may be complications and difficulties about your vows, as I suppose they are binding to a certain extent, and they are sure not to let you off without a fuss.

"Your letters aren't very explicit, my dear, so I'm still somewhat in the dark as to what you are doing and when you mean to come to London, as I suppose you will eventually do. And why Italy? If you're going to get out of the whole thing altogether, it seems funny that the convent people should trouble to send you to Italy, when you might just as well have come straight to England. However, no doubt you know your own affairs best, Alex, dear, and perhaps you're wise to take advantage of an opportunity that may not come again!

"Travelling has always been my dream, as you know, but except for that time I had at Neuilly, when you came out—Heavens, what ages ago!—and then our honeymoon in Paris, which was so terribly broken into when dear mother died, I've never had any chance at all, and I suppose now I never shall have. Everything is so expensive, and I'm really not a very good traveller unless I can

225

afford to do the thing *comfortably*, otherwise I should simply love to have run over to Rome for Easter and got you to show me all the sights.

"I suppose your time is quite your own now? Of course, when you really do leave the Sisters, I hope you'll come straight to my wee cottage here—at any rate while you look about you and think over future plans.

"Cedric has written to you, I know, and if you feel you'd rather go to Clevedon Square, needless to say, my dear, I shall more than understand. Please yourself *absolutely*.

"But, of course, one's always rather chary of unknown sisters-in-law, and Violet quite rules the roost now-a-days. She and Cedric are a most devoted couple, and all that sort of thing, but as she's got all the money, one rather feels as if it was *her* house. I daresay you know the kind of thing I mean.

"She's quite a dear, in many ways, but I don't go there tremendously.

"Pamela adores her, and lives in her pocket. Pam tells me she hasn't seen you since she was about fifteen—I could hardly believe it. My dear, I don't know what you'll think of her! She's quite appallingly modern, to my mind, and makes me feel about a hundred years old.

"When I think of the way *we* were chaperoned, and sent about everywhere with a maid, and only allowed the dullest of dinner-parties, and tea-parties, and then those stiff, solemn balls! Pamela is for ever being asked to boy-and-girl affairs, and dinner dances and theatre-parties—I must say she's a huge success. Every one raves about her, and she goes in for being tremendously natural and jolly and full of vitality and she's had simply heaps of chances, already, though I daresay some of it has to do with being seen about everywhere with Violet, who simply splashes money out like water. She paid all Archie's debts, poor boy—I will say that for her. The result is that he's quite good and steady now, and every one says he'll make a first-rate Guardsman.

"I'm writing a long screed, Alex, but I really feel you ought to be posted up in all the family news, if you're really going to come and join forces with us again, after all these years. It seems quite funny to think of, so many things have happened since you left home for good—as we thought it was going to be. Do write again and tell me what you think of doing and when you're coming over. My tiny spare-room will be quite ready for you, any time you like.

"Your   loving   sister,

"BARBARA MCALLISTER."

Barbara's letter was astounding.

Even Alex, too jaded for any great poignancy of emotion, felt amazement at her sister's matter-of-fact acceptance of a state of affairs that had been brought about by such moral and physical upheaval.

Had Barbara realized none of it, or was she merely utterly incurious? Alex could only feel thankful that no long, explanatory letter need be written. Perhaps when she got back to England it would be easier to make her explanation to Barbara.

She could hardly imagine that return.

The affair of the release from her vows dragged on with wearisome indefiniteness. Documents and papers were sent for her signature, and there were one or two interviews, painful and humiliating enough.

None of them, however, hurt her as that interview in the parlour at Liège with Father Farrell had done, for to none of them did she bring that faint shred of hope that had underlain her last attempt to make clear the truth as she knew it.

She knew that money had been paid, and Cedric had written a grave and short note, bidding her leave that side of the question to his care, and to that of her father's lawyers.

Then, with dramatic unexpectedness, came the end.

She was told that all the necessary formalities had been complied with, and that her vows were now annulled. It was carefully explained to her that this did not include freedom to marry. The Church would sanction no union of hers.

Alex could have laughed.

She felt as though marriage had been spoken of, for the first time, to an old, old woman, who had never known love, and to whom passion and desire alike had long been as strangers. Why should that, which had never come to her eager, questing youth, be spoken of in connection with the strange, remote self which was all that was left of her now?

She reflected how transitory had been the relations into which she had entered, how little any intimacy of spirit had ever bound her to another human being.

Her first love—Marie-Angèle:

"I love you for your few caresses, I love you for my many tears."

Where was Marie-Angèle now? Alex knew nothing of her. No doubt she had married, had borne children, and somewhere in her native Soissons was gay and prosperous still.

Alex dimly hoped so.

Queenie Torrance.

Her thoughts even now dwelt tenderly for a moment on that fair, irresponsive object of so much devotion. On Queenie as a pale, demure schoolgirl, her fair curls rolled back from her white, open brow, in her black-stuff dress and apron. On Queenie, the blue ribbon for good conduct lying across her gently-curving breast, serenely telling fibs or surreptitiously carrying off the forbidden sweets and dainties procured for her by Alex, or gazing with cold vexation on some extravagant demonstration of affection that had failed to win her approval.

In retrospect Alex could see Queenie again, the white, voluminous ball dresses she had worn, the tiny wreath of blue forget-me-nots, once condemned as "bad form" by Lady Isabel.

On Queenie Goldstein her thoughts dwelt little. She had heard long ago from Barbara of Queenie's divorce, in an action brought by her husband, which had afforded the chief scandal of the year 1899, and then no one had heard or even seen anything of Queenie for a long while, and Barbara had said that she was reported to be abroad with her father.

Five years later Barbara had written excitedly:

"You remember that awful Queenie Goldstein? and how full the papers were of her pictures, when that dreadful divorce case of hers was on, and the five co-respondents and everything? You'll hardly believe it, but she's in London again, having succeeded in marrying an American whom every one says is *the* coming millionaire. I saw her at the theatre myself, in a box, absolutely slung with diamonds. She's taken to making up her face tremendously, but she hasn't altered much, and she's received everywhere. They say her husband simply adores her."

Alex still remembered the rebuke with which Mother Gertrude had handed her that letter, bidding her remind her sister that things of the world, worldly, had no place in the life of a nun.

Nevertheless, although she had put the thought from her, she knew that in her heart she had felt a certain gladness that her erstwhile playmate, given over though she might be to the world, the flesh and the Devil, had yet not found those things that she coveted to have failed her.

Queenie, at least, had known what she wanted, and Alex' thoughts of her held no condemnation.

From Queenie, her mind went to the memory of Noel Cardew, and she was faintly surprised at the unvivid presentment of him which was all that she could evoke.

Noel had held no real place in her life at all.

Nothing that would endure had ever passed between him and her. It was years since she had thought of their ill-starred engagement, and then it had always been in connection with Sir Francis and Lady Isabel—their brief pride and pleasure in it, and the sudden downfall of their hopes.

Of Noel himself she had scarcely a recollection. Perhaps her clearest one was that of the earnest young egoist, only made attractive by a certain simplicity, who had taken her to sit in a disused ice-house one hot summer day, and had talked about photography. Of the later Noel, Alex was astounded to find that she retained no impression at all.

She could not even remember whether it was he or his brother Eric who had married red-haired Marie Munroe in the same year that she herself had taken her first vows as a nun.

Perhaps it was Noel.

At all events, he had probably married long ago, and Alex could believe that some corner of land in Devonshire was the better for the earnest supervision that he would accord to it, both in his own person and in that of the generation that would doubtless succeed him.

Mother Gertrude.

At the last and most worshipped of the shrines before which Alex had offered the sad, futile, unmeasured burnt-offerings of her life, her thoughts lingered least.

It had all been a mistake.

She had given recklessly, foolishly, squandering her all because life had cheated her of any outlet for a force of the strength of which she had had no measure given her, and now she had to pay the bitter penalty for a folly which had not even been met by answering human affection.

She wrote no letter to Mother Gertrude, and received no word from her.

As the days crept on, Alex, without volition of her own, found that her journey to England had been arranged for—that money was to be advanced to her for her expenses, that she was expected to supplement with it her utter penury of worldly possessions. One day she went out, frightened and at a loss, and entered some of the first shops she saw, in a street that led down from the Pincio Gates.

They were not large shops, and she had difficulty in making herself understood, but she purchased a ready-made blue-serge skirt, with a coat that she called a jacket, and an ugly black toque, that most resembled in shape those that she remembered seeing in London ten years earlier. She wore these clothes, with a white cotton blouse that fastened at the back and came high up under her chin, for some days before she left Rome, so as to grow accustomed to them, and to lose the sense of awkwardness that they produced in her.

The heavy boots and a pair of black-cotton gloves that she had brought from Belgium, still served her. The day of her departure was fixed, and she wrote to Barbara, but she knew neither by what route she was going nor how long the journey would take.

Her companions, selected by the Superior of the convent, proved to be an old lady and her daughter who were going to Paris. Evidently they knew her story, for they looked at her with scared, curious faces and spoke to her very little. Both were experienced travellers, and on the long, hot journey in the train, when it seemed as though the seats of the railway carriage were made of molten iron, they extended themselves with cushions and little paper fans, and slept most of the way. At Genoa the daughter, timidly, but with kindness, pressed Alex to eat and drink, and after that she spoke to her once or twice, and gave her a friendly invitation to join them at the small *pension* in Paris to which they were bound, for a night's halt before she proceeded to Boulogne and thence to England. Alex accepted with bewildered thankfulness.

She was weak and exhausted, and the old lady and her daughter were pitiful enough, and saw her into the train next day, and gave her the provision of sandwiches which she had not thought to make for herself.

The train sped through flat, green country, with tall poplars shading the small, narrow French houses that dotted the line on either side. Her eye dilated as she gazed on the sea, when at last Boulogne was reached.

She remembered the same grey expanse of rolling waves tipped with foam on the morning, eight years ago, when the girl Alex Clare had crossed to Belgium, tearful, indeed, and frightened, but believing herself to be making that new beginning which should lead to the eventual goal which life must surely hold in store for her.

Only eight years, and the bitterness of a lifetime's failure encompassed her spirit.

XXIII
N.W.

Alex got off the boat at Folkestone, dazed and bewildered. She had been ill all through the crossing, and her head was still swimming. She grasped her heavy, clumsy suit-case and was thankful to have no luggage, when she saw the seething crowd of passengers, running after uniformed porters in search of heavy baggage that was being flung on to trucks to an accompaniment of noise and shouting that frightened her.

She made her way to the train and into a third-class carriage, too much afraid of its starting without her to dare to go in search of the hot tea which she saw the passengers drinking thankfully. It was a raw, grey day, and Alex, in her thin serge coat and skirt, that had been so much too hot in Italy, shivered violently. Her gloves were nearly thread-bare and her hands felt clammy and stiff. She took off her little black-straw toque and leant her head against the back of the seat, wishing that she could sleep.

It seemed to her that the other people in the carriage were looking at her suspiciously, and she closed her eyes so as not to see them.

After a long while the train started.

Alex tried to make plans. In the shabby purse which she had clasped in her hand all the way, for fear of its being stolen, was a piece of paper with Barbara's address. She would not go to Clevedon Square, for fear of Cedric's unknown wife. Cedric with a wife and child! Alex marvelled, and could not believe that she might soon make the acquaintance of these beings who seemed to her so nearly mythical.

The thought of Barbara as a widow living in a little house of her own in Hampstead, seemed far less unfamiliar. Barbara had always written regularly to Alex, and had twice been to see her when she was in the English house and once in her early days in Belgium.

Barbara had often said in her letters that she was very lonely, and that it was terrible having to live so far out of town because of expenses. Ralph, poor dear, had left her very, very badly off, and there had been very little more for her on the death of Sir Francis. Alex supposed that Downshire Hill must be a very unfashionable address, but she did not connect "N.W." with any particular locality.

She was always very stupid at finding her way about, and, anyhow, her bag was heavy. She decided that she would take a cab.

At Charing Cross it was raining, and the noise was deafening. Alex had meant to send Barbara a telegram from Folkestone, but had not known where to find the telegraph office, and she now realized with a pang of dismay that her sister would not be expecting her.

"How stupid I am, and how badly I manage things," she thought. "I hope she won't be out."

The number of taxis at the station bewildered Alex, who had only seen one or two crawling about the streets in Rome, and had heard of them, besides, as ruinously expensive. She found a four-wheeled cab and put her bag on the floor. The man did not get down from his box to open the door for her, as she expected. He leant down and asked hoarsely.

"Where d'you want to go, Miss?"

"Downshire Hill," said Alex. "No. 101."

"Downshire 'Ill? Where's that?"

"I don't know," said Alex, frightened. She wondered if the man was drunk, and prepared to pull her bag out of the cab again.

"'Alf a minute."

He called out something unintelligible to another driver, and received an answer.

"Downshire 'Ill's N.W.," he then informed her. "Out 'Ampstead w'y."

"Yes," said Alex. "Can't you take me there?"

He looked at her shabby clothes and white, frightened face.

"I'd like to see my fare, first, if *you* please," he said insolently.

Alex was too much afraid of his making a scene to refuse.

"How much will it be?"

"Seven and sixpence, Miss."

She pulled two half-crowns out of her purse. It was all she had left.

"This is all the change I have," she told him in a shaking voice. "They will pay the rest when I get there."

He muttered something dissatisfied, but put the coins into his pocket.

Alex climbed into the cab.

It jolted away very slowly.

The rain was falling fast, and dashing against the windows of the cab. Alex glanced out, but the streets through which they were driving were all unfamiliar to her. It seemed a very long way to Downshire Hill.

She began to wonder very much how Barbara would receive her, and how she could make clear to her the long, restless agony that had led her to obtain release from her vows. Would Barbara understand?

Letters had been very inadequate, and although Barbara had written that Alex had better come to her for a while if she meant to return to England, she had given no hint of any deeper comprehension.

"We must make plans when we meet," she had written at the end of the letter.

Alex wondered with a sense of apprehension what those plans would be. She had for so long become accustomed to being treated as a chattel, without volition of her own, that it did not occur to her that she would have any hand in forming her future life.

Presently she became conscious that the rain had stopped, and that the atmosphere was lighter. She let down the glass of the window nearest her, and saw, with surprise, that there was a rolling expanse of green, with a number of willow-trees, on one side of the road. It did not look like London.

Then the cab turned a corner, and Alex saw "Downshire Hill" on a small board against the wall. This was where Barbara lived, then.

The little houses were small and compact, but of agreeably varying height and shape, with a tiny enclosure of green in front of each, protected by railings and a little gate. No. 101, before which the cab drew up, had a bush that Alex thought must be lilac, and was covered with ivy. There were red blinds to the windows.

She got out, pulling her heavy bag after her, and timidly pushed open the little gate, glancing up at the windows as she did so.

There was no one to be seen.

Still clutching at her suit-case, Alex pulled the bell faintly.

"There's half my fare owing yet," said the cabman gruffly.

Thus reminded, Alex rang again.

An elderly parlour-maid with iron-grey hair and a hard face opened the door.

"Is—is Mrs. MacAllister at home?" faltered Alex.

"I'll inquire," said the maid, with a lightning glance at the suit-case.

She left the door open, and Alex saw a little flight of stairs. A murmured colloquy took place at the top, and then Barbara, slight and severely black-clad, came down.

"Alex, that's not you?"

"Yes. Oh, Barbara!"

"My dear—I've been expecting to hear from you every day! I've been imagining all sorts of awful things. Why didn't you wire? Do come in—you must be dead, and have you been carrying that huge bag?"

"I came from the station in a cab."

"A cab!" echoed Barbara in rather a dismayed voice. "What a long way to come, when you could have done it so easily by the underground railway but I suppose you didn't know?"

"No," repeated Alex blankly. "I didn't know."

"What's he waiting for? Will he carry your trunk upstairs?"

"That is all the luggage I have, and I can carry it up quite well, and it isn't heavy. But I hadn't quite enough money for the fare—he ought to have another half-crown."

"Oh, dear," said Barbara. "Wait a minute, then, Alex."

She disappeared up the stairs, leaving Alex alone with the severe parlour-maid, who still held open the front door.

She leant against the wall in the tiny passage, wondering what she had expected of her actual arrival, that the reality should give her such a sense of misery.

If only she had telegraphed to Barbara from Folkestone!

"Here's two shillings. Ada, have you got a sixpence, by any chance?"

"There's sixpence in the kitchen, 'm," said Ada, and fetched it.

"There!" said Barbara. "Pay him then, please, Ada. Now, Alex, come upstairs and sit down. You look dreadfully ill and worn-out, my dear."

Alex lifted the suit-case again.

230

"Oh, Ada will see to that. Your room is all ready, Alex. It's very small, but then the house is a perfect doll's house, as you see. This is my tiny drawing-room."

"It's very pretty," said Alex, sinking into a chair.

"It's not bad—the things are nice enough. Ralph had some exquisite things—but, of course, the house is too hateful, and I hate living all the way out here. No one ever comes near me. Cedric's wife can't get her chauffeur to bring her—he pretends he doesn't know where it is. The only person who ever comes is Pamela."

"I thought she was to live with you?"

"Pam! Oh, she wouldn't bury herself out here, for long. Pam's very much in request, my dear. She's been paying visits all over the place, and can go on indefinitely, I believe. She makes her headquarters with Cedric and Violet in Clevedon Square, you know, but of course she'll marry. Pam's all right."

"Last time I saw Pam she was in short frocks and a pigtail."

"She's come out in the most extraordinary way. Every one says so. Not exactly pretty, but frightfully taking, and most awfully attractive to men. They say she's so full of life. I must say, when *we* came out, Alex, we didn't have nearly such a good time as she has. Men seem to go down like ninepins before her. She's always bringing them out here to tea, and to look at the view of London from the Heath. One always used to look on Hampstead Heath as a sort of joke—Phil May's drawings, and that kind of thing. I certainly never expected to live here—but lots of artists do, and Ralph had a big studio here. And it's very inexpensive. Besides, if you know you way about, it's quite easy to come in and out from town. Pamela always brings her young men on the top of a 'bus. Girls can do anything now-a-days, of course. Fancy father, if one of *us* had done such a thing!"

"Who looks after her?" asked Alex, rather awe-struck.

"She looks after herself, my dear, and does it uncommonly effectively. She could marry tomorrow if she liked—and marry well, too. Of course, Cedric is her guardian in a sort of way, I suppose, but he lets her do anything she like—only laughs."

"Cedric!" spoke Alex wistfully. "Do you know, I haven't seen Cedric since—I left Clevedon Square."

"My dear, that's ten years, isn't it? Cedric's grown exactly like father. He's got just his way of standing in front of the fire and shaking his spectacles up and down in his hand—you remember father's way? Of course, he's done extraordinarily well—every one says so—and his marriage was an excellent thing, too."

"Is—Violet—nice?"

Barbara laughed rather drily.

"She's got a lot of money, and—yes, I suppose she is nice. Between ourselves, Alex, she's the sort of person who rather aggravates me. She's always so prosperous and happy, as though nothing had ever gone wrong with her, or ever could. She's very generous, I will say that for her—and extraordinarily good-natured. Most people adore her—she's the sort of woman that other women rave about, but I must say most men like her, too. Her people were rather inclined to think she could have done better for herself than Cedric. Of course, he isn't well off, and she's two years older than he is. But it's answered all right, and they were tremendously in love with one another."

"Is she very pretty?"

"She's inclined to be fat, but, of course, she is pretty, in her own style—very. And the little girl is a perfect darling—little Rosemary.

"But, Alex, here am I talking you to death when you must be dying for tea. What sort of a crossing did you have?"

"Not very bad, but I was ill all the way."

"Oh, no wonder you look so washed out," said Barbara, as though relieved, but she went on eyeing her sister uneasily through the rapidly increasing dusk.

When Ada came in with the tea appointments, Barbara told her to bring the lamp.

"Yes'm. And your bag, 'm—may I have the key?"

Alex looked bewildered, then recollected that the maid was offering to unpack for her, and pulled out the key from her purse.

"Isn't there your trunk still to come?" asked Barbara.

"No. You see, I hadn't much to bring—only just one or two things that I got in Rome."

Alex wondered if Barbara understood that until a few months ago she had been a nun, living the life of a nun. She thought of the apprehension with which she had viewed making an explanation to Barbara, and almost smiled. It appeared that no explanation would be required of her.

But presently Barbara said uneasily:

"It seems extraordinary, your having no luggage like this, Alex. I don't know what Ada will think, I'm sure. I told her that you'd been living abroad for a good many years—I thought that was the best thing to say. But I never thought of your having no luggage."

"I hadn't got anything to bring, you see. I must get some things," repeated Alex forlornly.

"You see," said her sister half apologetically, "Ada's been with me ever since I married. She was Ralph's mother's maid, and perfectly devoted to him. I couldn't ever get that sort of servant to live out here, if it wasn't for that—she waits at meals, and maids me, and does everything, except the actual cooking. I know she's rather disagreeable in her manner, but she's a perfect treasure to me."

When Ada had brought in the lamps and filled the little room with cheerful light, drawing the blinds and curtains, Barbara looked again hard at her sister.

"Good heavens, Alex, how thin you are! and you look as though you hadn't slept for a month."

"Oh, but I have," said Alex eagerly, and then stopped.

She did not feel able to explain to Barbara the insatiable powers of sleep which seemed as though they could never be satisfied, after those ten years of unvarying obedience to a merciless five o'clock bell.

"I am glad to hear it," Barbara replied in a dissatisfied voice. "But I never saw any one so changed. Have you been ill?"

"Rather run down," Alex said hurriedly, with the convent instinct of denying physical ills. "I had two or three very troublesome abscesses in my throat, just before Easter, and that left me rather weak."

"My dear, how awful! You never told me. Did you have an operation? Are you scarred?"

"No. They broke of themselves *inside* my throat, luckily."

"Oh—don't!" cried Barbara, and shuddered.

The sisters were very silent during tea. Alex saw her sister looking hard at her hands, and became conscious of contrast. Barbara was thin, but her hands were slender and exceedingly white. She wore, besides her wedding-ring, a sapphire one, which Alex thought must have been her engagement-ring. On her wrist was a tiny gold watch, and a gold curb-chain bracelet. Her own hands, Alex now saw, were more than thin. They were almost emaciated, with knuckles that shone white, and a sharp prominence at each wrist-bone. They were not white, but rough and mottled, with broken skin round each finger-nail. She wondered if her whole person was in as striking a contrast to her sister's. When she had put on the serge skirt and white muslin shirt, the sensation had overwhelmed her, accustomed to the heavy religious habit, of being lightly, almost indecently clad. But Barbara's dress was of soft, silky material, with a low, turned-down collar, such as was just beginning to come into fashion. Her hair was piled into a shining knot of little, sausage-shaped curls, and parted in front. Though she was only twenty-eight, the grey in Barbara's hair was plentiful, but her small face looked youthful enough, and had none of the hard lines and shadows that Alex knew to lie round her own eyes and lips. Her little, slight figure was very erect, and she wore black suède shoes with sparkling buckles. Alex looked down at her own clumsy, ill-made boots, which had already begun to hurt her feet, and instinctively put up her hands to the cheap black toque, that felt heavy on her head.

"Why don't you take off your hat?" Barbara asked her kindly. "I am sure it would rest you."

She was too much used to obedience not to comply instantly, pushing back with both hands the weight of untidy hair that instantly fell over her eyes.

"Oh, Alex! Your hair!"

"It's growing very fast. I—I've not been cutting it lately. There's just enough to put it up, Barbara."

"It's much darker than it used to be, isn't it?"

"Yes, it's nearly black now. Do you remember how light the ends used to be? But I think it lost its colour from being always under the veil, you know. The worst of it is that it's not growing evenly, it's all short lengths."

"Yes. That's very awkward," said Barbara dispassionately. "Especially when it's so straight."

Alex reflected that her sister was just as self-contained as ever.

"Wouldn't you like to come to your room and rest till dinner, Alex?"

Alex got up at once.

"You ought to take Plasmon, or something of that sort, and try to get a little fatter. There's simply nothing of you, Alex—you're all eyes, with rings like saucers round them."

After Barbara had left her in the tiny, pretty bedroom, that Alex thought looked wonderfully luxurious, she went straight to her looking-glass.

"Good heavens, how ugly I am!" she said to herself involuntarily.

Her face was sallow, with sunken cheeks, and the Roman sun had powdered her skin all over with little, pale freckles. Her eyes, as Barbara had said, had rings like saucers round them, and looked oddly large and prominent, from the slight puffiness of the under-lids.

Her teeth had, perhaps, suffered most of all. She had had one or two taken out, and the gaps were visible and unsightly. They had never been very good teeth, and she remembered still all that she had suffered at the hands of an unskilled Brussels dentist in Belgium. For the last few years she had endured intermittent toothache, sooner than submit to further torture, and she saw now that a small black patch was spreading between the two front teeth. Barbara, with the grey mingled freely in her light hair, and her severe widow's weeds, might look more than twenty-eight but Alex, at thirty-one, bore the semblance of a woman of forty.

She hid her face in her disfigured hands.

Presently she saw that there was hot water in a little brass can on the washing-stand, and she thankfully made use of it.

Ada had unpacked everything, and Alex saw the brush and comb that she had hastily purchased, on the dressing-table. Beside them was the packet of hair-pins that she had remembered to get at the last moment, and that was all.

"There ought to be something else, but I've forgotten," thought Alex.

She wondered if Barbara would expect her to dress for dinner. The idea had not occurred to her. She had one other blouse, a much better one, made of black net, so transparent as to show glimpses of her coarse, white-cotton underwear, with its high yoke and long sleeves.

Her hair, of course, was impossible. Even if it had not been so short and of such an intractable, limp straightness. Alex had forgotten how to do it. She remembered with dim surprise that at Clevedon Square Lady Isabel's maid had always done her hair for her.

She brushed it away from her face, and made a small coil on the top of her head, after the fashion which she remembered best, and tried to fasten back the untidy lengths that fell over her ears and forehead.

The hair-pins that she had bought were very long and thick. She wished that they did not show so obviously.

"Alex?" said Barbara's cool voice at her door.

Alex came out, and they went downstairs together, Alex a few steps behind her sister, since the stairs were not broad enough for two to walk abreast. She tried awkwardly not to step on the tail of Barbara's black lace teagown. Ada waited upon them, and although the helpings of food seemed infinitesimal to Alex, everything tasted delicious, and she wondered if Barbara always had three courses as well as a dessert of fruit and coffee, even when she was by herself.

"You don't smoke, I suppose?" Barbara said. "No, of course not how stupid of me! Let's go up to the drawing-room again."

"Barbara, do you smoke?"

"No. Ralph hated women to smoke, and I don't like to see it myself, though pretty nearly every one does it now. Violet smokes *far* too much. I wonder Cedric lets her. But as a matter of fact, he lets her do anything she likes."

"I can't realize Cedric married."

"I know. Look here, Alex, he'll want to see you—and you'll be wanting to talk over plans, won't you?"

"Yes," said Alex nervously. "I—I don't want to have a lot of fuss, you know. Of course I know it's upsetting for everybody—my coming out of the convent after every one thought I was settled. But, oh, Barbara! I *had* to leave!"

"Personally, I can't think why you ever went in," said Barbara impersonally. "Or why you took ten years to find out you weren't suited to the life. That sounds unkind, and I don't mean to be—you know I don't. Of course, you were right to come away. Only I'm afraid they've ruined your health—you're so dreadfully thin, and you look much older than you've any right to, Alex. I believe you ought to go into the country somewhere and have a regular rest-cure. Every one is doing them now. However, we'll see what Cedric and Violet say."

"When shall I see them?" asked Alex nervously.

"Well," said her sister, hesitating, "what about tomorrow? It's better to get it over at once, isn't it? I thought I'd ring them up this evening—I know they're dining at home." She glanced at the clock.

"Look here, Alex, why don't you go to bed? I always go early myself—and you're simply dead tired. Do! Then tomorrow we might go into town and do some shopping. You'll want some things at once, won't you?"

Alex saw that Barbara meant her to assent, and said "Yes" in a dazed way.

She was very glad to go to her room, and the bed seemed extraordinarily comfortable.

Barbara had kissed her and said anxiously, "I do hope you'll feel more like yourself tomorrow, my dear. I hardly feel I know you."

Then she had rustled away, and Alex had heard her go downstairs, perhaps to telephone to Clevedon Square.

Lying in bed in the dark, she thought about her sister.

It seemed incredible to Alex that she could ever have bullied and domineered over Barbara. Yet in their common childhood, this had happened. She could remember stamping her foot at Barbara, and compelling her to follow her sister's lead again and again. And there was the time when she had forced a terrified, reluctant Barbara to play at tight-rope dancing on the stairs, and Barbara had obediently clambered on to the newel-post, and fallen backwards into the hall and hurt her back.

Alex remembered still the agonized days and nights of despairing remorse which had followed, and her own sense of being all but a murderess. She had thought then that she could never, never quarrel and be angry with Barbara again. But she had gone away to school, and Barbara had got well, and in the holidays Alex had been more overbearing than ever in the schoolroom.

And now Barbara seemed so infinitely competent—so remote from the failures and emotional disasters that had wrecked Alex. She made Alex feel like a child in the hands of a serious, rather ironical grown-up person, who did not quite know how to dispose of it.

Alex herself wondered what would happen to her, much as a child might have wondered. But she was tired enough to sleep.

And the next morning Barbara, more competent than ever, came in and suggested that she should have her breakfast in bed, so as to feel rested enough for a morning's shopping in town.

"Though I must say," said Barbara, in a dissatisfied voice, "that you don't look any better than you did last night. I hoped you might look more like yourself, after a night's rest. I really don't think the others will know you."

"Am I going to see them?"

"Oh, I talked to Violet last night on the telephone, and she said I was to give you her love, and she hoped we'd both lunch there tomorrow."

"At Clevedon Square?" asked Alex, beginning to tremble.

"Yes. You don't mind, do you?"

"No, I don't mind."

It was very strange to be in the remembered London streets again, stranger still to be taken to shops by Barbara and authoritatively guided in the choice of a coat and skirt, a hat that should conceal as much as possible of the disastrous *coiffure* underneath, and a pair of black suède walking-shoes, that felt oddly light and soft to her feet.

"There's no hurry about the other things, is there?" said Barbara, more as though stating a fact than asking a question. "Now we'd better take a taxi to Clevedon Square, or we shall be late."

A few minutes later, as the taxi turned into the square, she said, with what Alex recognized in surprise as a kind of nervousness in her voice:

"We thought you'd rather get it all over at once, you know, Alex. Seeing the family, I mean. Pam is staying there anyway, and Violet said Archie was coming to lunch. There'll be nobody else, except, perhaps, one of Violet's brothers. She's always got one or other of them there."

Alex felt sick with dismay. Then some remnant of courage came back to her, and she clenched her hands unseen, and vowed that she would go through with it.

The cab stopped before the familiar steps, and Barbara said, as to a stranger: "Here we are."

XXIV
All of Them

The well-remembered hall and broad staircase swam before Alex' eyes as she followed Barbara upstairs and heard them announced as:

"Mrs. McAllister—and Miss Clare!"

In a dream she entered the room, and was conscious of a dream-like feeling of relief at its totally unfamiliar aspect. All the furniture was different, and there was chintz instead of brocade, everywhere. She would not have known it.

Then she saw, with growing bewilderment, that the room was full of people.

"Alex?" said a soft, unknown voice.

Barbara hovered uneasily beside her, and Alex dimly heard her speaking half-reassuringly and half-apologetically. But Violet Clare had taken her hand, and was guiding her into the inner half of the room, which was empty.

"Don't bother about the others for a minute—Barbara, go and look after them, like a dear—let's make acquaintance in peace, Alex. Do you know who I am?"

"Cedric's wife?"

"Yes, that's it." Then, as Barbara left them, Violet noiselessly stamped her foot. "You poor dear! I don't believe she ever told you there was to be a whole crowd of family here. That's just like poor, dear Barbara! I'm sure she never had one atom of imagination in her life, now had she? The idea of dragging you here the very day after you got back from such a journey." The soft, fluent voice went on, giving her time to recover herself, Alex hardly hearing what was said to her, but with a sensation of adoring gratitude gradually invading her, for this warm, unhesitating welcome and unquestioning sympathy.

She looked dumbly at her sister-in-law.

In Violet she saw the soft, generous contours and opulent prettiness of which she had caught glimpses in the South. The numerous Marchesas who had come to the convent parlour in Rome had had just such brown, liquid eyes, with dark lashes throwing into relief an opaque ivory skin, just such dazzling teeth and such ready, dimpling smiles, and had worn the same wealth of falling laces at *décolleté* throat and white, rounded wrists. Violet was in white, with a single string of wonderful pearls round her soft neck, and her brilliant brown hair was arranged in elaborate waves, with occasional little escaping rings and tendrils.

Alex thought her beautiful, and wondered why Barbara had spoken in deprecation of such sleepy, prosperous prettiness.

She noticed that Violet did not look at her with rather wondering dismay, as her sister had done, and only once said:

"You do look tired, you poor darling! It's that hateful journey. I'm a fearfully bad traveller myself. When we were married, Cedric wanted to go to the south of France for our honeymoon, but I told him nothing would induce me to risk being seasick, and he had to take me to Cornwall instead. Cedric will be here in a minute, and we'll make him come and talk to you quietly out here. You don't want to go in amongst all that rabble, do you?"

"Who is there?" asked Alex faintly.

235

"Pam and the boys—that's my two brothers, you know, whom you needn't bother about the very least bit in the world, and here's Archie," she added, as the door opened again.

Alex would have known Archie in a moment, anywhere, he was so like their mother. Even the first inflection of his voice, as he came towards Violet, reminded her of Lady Isabel.

She had not seen him since his schooldays, and wondered if he would have recognized her without Violet's ready explanation.

"Alex has come, Archie. That goose Barbara went and brought her here without explaining that she's only just got back to England, and is naturally tired to death. I'll leave you to talk, while I see what's happened to Cedric."

"I say!" exclaimed Archie, and stood looking desperately embarrassed. "How are you, Alex, old girl? We meet as strangers, what?"

"I should have known you anywhere, Archie. You're so like Barbara—so like mother."

"They say Pam's exactly like what mother was. Have you seen her?"

"No, not yet. She—Violet—brought me in here."

"I say, she's a ripper, isn't she? Cedric didn't do badly for himself—trust him. Wonder what the beggar'll be up to next? He's done jolly well, all along the line—retrieved the family fortunes, what? It only remains for me to wed an American, and Pamela to bring off her South African millionaire. She's got one after her, did you know?"

He spoke with a certain boyish eagerness that was rather attractive, but his rapid speech and restless manner made Alex wonder if he was nervous.

"Couldn't you ask Pamela to come to me here, so that I could see her without all those people?"

"What people? It's only old Jack Temple, and Carol. Harmless as kittens, what? But I'll get Pam for you in two twos. You watch."

He put his fingers into his mouth and emitted a peculiar low whistle on two prolonged notes. The signal was instantly answered from the other room, but quaveringly, as though the whistler were laughing.

Then in a minute she appeared, very slim and tall, in the opening between the two rooms.

"I like your cheek, Archie!"

"I say, Pam, Alex is here."

"Oh, Alex!"

Pamela, too, looked and sounded rather embarrassed as she came forward and laid a fresh, glowing cheek against her sister's.

"Barbara telephoned last night that you'd come, and seemed awfully seedy," she said in a quick, confused way. "She ought to have made you rest today."

"Oh, no, I'm all right," said Alex awkwardly. "How you've changed, Pamela! I haven't seen you since you were at school."

Looking at her sister, she secretly rather wondered at what Barbara had said of the girl's attractiveness.

Pamela's round face was glowing with health and colour, and she held herself very upright, but Alex thought that her hair looked ugly, plastered exaggeratedly low on her forehead, and she could not see the resemblance to their mother of which Archie had spoken, except in the fairness of colouring which Pamela shared with Barbara and with Archie himself.

"You've changed, too, Alex. You look so frightfully thin, and you've lost all your colour. Have you been ill?"

"No, I've not been ill. Only rather run down. I was ill before Easter—perhaps that's it."

Alex was embarrassed too, a horrible feeling of failure and inadequacy creeping over her, and seeming to hamper her in every word and movement. Pamela's cold, rather wondering scrutiny made her feel terribly unsure of herself. She had often known the sensation before—at school, in her early days at the novitiate, again in Rome, and ever since her arrival in England. It was the helpless insecurity of one utterly at variance with her surroundings.

She was glad when Violet came back and said: "Here's Cedric. Go down to lunch, children—we'll follow you."

Cedric's greeting to his sister was the most affectionate and the least awkward that she had yet received. He kissed her warmly and said, "Well, my dear I'm glad we've got you back in England again. You must come to us, if Barbara will spare you."

236

"Oh, Cedric!"

She looked at him for a moment, emotionally shaken. That Cedric should have grown into a man! She saw in a moment that he was very good-looking, the best-looking of them all, with Sir Francis' pleasantly serious expression and the merest shade of pomposity in his manner. Only the blinking, short-sighted grey eyes behind his spectacles remained of the solemn little brother she had known.

"Come down and have some lunch, dear. What possessed Barbara to bring you here, if you didn't feel up to coming? We could have gone to Hampstead. Violet says she's been most inconsiderate to you."

"Yes, *most*," said Violet herself placidly. "Dear Barbara is always so unimaginative. Of course, it's fearfully trying for Alex, after being away such ages, to have every one thrust upon her like this."

Alex felt a throb of gratitude.

"Barbara thought it had better all be got over at once," she said timidly.

"That's just like her! Barbara is being completely ruined by that parlour-maid of hers—Ada. I always think Ada is responsible for all Barbara's worst inspirations. She rules her with a rod of iron. Shall you hate coming down to lunch, Alex? Those riotous children will be off directly, they're wild about the skating-rink at Olympia. Then we can talk comfortably."

She put her hand caressingly through Alex' arm, as they went downstairs. Alex felt that she could have worshipped her sister-in-law for her easy, pitying tenderness.

The consciousness of it helped her all through the long meal, when the noise of laughter and conversation bewildered her, after so many years of convent refectories and silence, and her solitary dinners in Rome.

Violet had placed her between Cedric and Pamela, and the girl chattered to her intermittently, without appearing to require any answer.

"Are you boys ready?" she cried, just as coffee was brought in. "We can't wait for coffee—come on! My instructor will be engaged."

"How are you going, Pam?" asked Violet.

"Underground. It's the quickest."

"Oh, no, Pam. Take a taxi. Archie, you must!"

Between laughter and admonition, they were dispatched—Pamela, Archie and the two Temple boys, all laughing and talking, and exchanging allusions and references unintelligible to Alex.

The room seemed much quieter and darker when the hall-door had finally slammed behind them. Alex looked round her.

At the head of his own table, Cedric sat reflective. Violet lounged, smoking a cigarette and laughing, where Lady Isabel's place had always been. Opposite Alex, Barbara, in her prim black, was leaning forward and speaking:

"What's the attraction about this roller-skating? Pamela seems to do nothing else, when she isn't dancing."

"Every one's doing it, my dear. I want to take it up myself, so as to reduce my figure, but it's such an impossible place to get at. I've only been to Olympia for the Military Tournaments. But Pam has a perfect passion for getting about by the underground railway. Alex, isn't Pam a refreshing person?"

Alex felt uncertain as to her meaning, and was startled at being addressed. She knew that she coloured and looked confused.

"My dear," said Barbara impressively, "your nerves must simply have gone to pieces. Imagine jumping like that when you're spoken to! Don't you think she ought to do a rest-cure, Violet? There's a place in Belgrave Street."

"No, no," said Violet's kind, soft voice. "She's coming to us. You must let us have her, Barbara, for a good long visit. Mustn't she, Cedric?"

"Of course. You must have your old quarters upstairs, Alex."

The kindness nearly made her cry. She felt as might a child, expecting to be scolded and punished, and unexpectedly met with smiles and re-assurance.

"Come up and see Baby," said Violet. "She's such a little love, and I want her to know her new auntie."

"Violet, we really must talk business some time," said Barbara, hesitating. "There are plans to be settled, you know—what Alex is going to do next."

"She's going to play with Rosemary next. Don't worry, dear—we can talk plans any time. There's really no hurry."

Alex dimly surmised that the words, and the indolent, *dégagée* smile accompanying them, might be characteristic of her new sister-in-law.

Violet took her upstairs.

"The nursery is just the same—we haven't changed a thing," she told her.

Alex gave a cry of recognition at the top of the stairs. "Oh, the little gate that fenced off the landing! It was put up when Cedric was a baby, because he would run out and look through the balusters."

"Was it, really?" cried Violet delightedly. "Cedric didn't know that—he told me that it had always been there. I shall love having you, Alex, you'll be able to tell me such lots of things about Cedric, when he was a little boy, that no one else knows. You see, there's so little difference between him and Barbara, isn't there?"

"I am only three years older than Barbara."

"Then you're the same age—or a little older than I am. I am twenty-nine—two whole years older than Cedric. Isn't it dreadful?"

She laughed gaily as she turned the handle of the nursery door.

"Baby, precious, where are you?"

Alex followed her into the big, sunny room.

A young nurse, in stiff white piqué, sat sewing in the window, and a starched, blue-ribboned baby, with disordered, sunny curls, crawled about the floor at her feet.

When she saw her mother she began to run towards her, with outstretched hands and inarticulate coos of pleasure.

"Come along, then, and see your new Auntie." Violet caught her up and lifted her into her arms. "Isn't she rather a love, Alex? Shall we look after her for a little while, while Nurse goes downstairs?"

Alex nodded. She felt as though she hardly dared speak, for fear of frightening the pretty little laughing child. Besides, the constriction was tightening in her throat.

Violet sank down into a low chair, with Rosemary still in her arms.

"I'll stay with her, Nurse, if you like to go downstairs for half-an-hour."

"Thank you, my lady."

"Sit down and let's be comfy, Alex. Isn't this much nicer than being downstairs?"

Alex looked round the nursery. As Violet had said, it had not been altered. On the mantelpiece she suddenly saw the big white clock, supported by stout Dresden-china cherubs, that had been there ever since she could remember. It was ticking in a sedate, unalterable way.

Something in the sight of the clock, utterly familiar, and yet forgotten altogether during all her years away from Clevedon Square, suddenly caught at Alex. She made an involuntary, choking sound, and to her own dismay, sobs suddenly overpowered her.

"My poor dear!" said Violet compassionately. "Do cry—it'll do you good, and Baby and I won't mind, or ever tell a soul, will we, my Rosemary? I knew you'd feel much better when you'd had it out, and nobody will disturb us here."

Alex had sunk on to the floor, and was leaning her head against Violet's chair.

The soft, murmuring voice went on above her:

"I never heard of such a thing in my life as Barbara's bringing you here today—she never explained when she telephoned that you hadn't been in England for goodness knows how many years, let alone to this house. And, of course, I thought she'd settled it all with you, till I saw your face when she brought you into the drawing-room, all full of tiresome people, and brothers and sisters you hadn't set eyes on for *years*. Then I knew, of course, and I could have smacked her. You poor child!"

"No, no," sobbed Alex incoherently. "It's only just at first, and coming back and finding them all so changed, and not knowing what I am going to do."

"Do! Why, you're coming here. Cedric and Rosemary and I want you, and Barbara doesn't deserve to keep you after the way she's begun. I'll settle it all with her."

"Oh, how _kind_ you are to me!" cried Alex.

Violet bent down and kissed her.

"Kind! Why, aren't I your sister, and Rosemary your one and only niece? Look at her, Alex, and see if she's like any one. Cedric sometimes says she's like your father."

"A little, perhaps. But she's very like you, I think."

"Oh, I never had those great, round, grey eyes! Those are Cedric's. And perhaps yours—they're the same colour. Anyway, I believe she's really very like what you must have been as a baby, Alex!"

It was evident that Violet was paying the highest compliment within her power.

Alex put out her hand timidly to little Rosemary. She was not at all shy, and seemed accustomed to being played with and admired, as she sat on her mother's lap. Alex thought how pretty and happy she and Violet looked together. She was emotionally too much worn-out, and had for too many years felt herself to be completely and for ever outside the pale of warm, human happiness, to feel any pang of envy.

Presently Violet reluctantly gave up Rosemary to the nurse again, and said:

"I'm afraid we ought to go down. I don't like to leave Barbara any longer. She never comes up here—hardly ever. Poor Barbara! I sometimes think it's because she hasn't any babies of her own. Let's come down and find her, Alex."

They found Barbara in the library, earnestly talking to Cedric, who was leaning back, smoking and looking very much bored.

He sprang up when they entered, and from his relieved manner and from Barbara's abrupt silence, Alex conjectured that they had been discussing her own return.

She stood for a moment, forlorn and awkward, till Violet sank on to the big red-leather sofa, and held out her hand in invitation to her.

"Give me a cigarette, Cedric. What have you and Barbara been plotting—like two conspirators?"

Cedric laughed, looking at her with a sort of indulgent pride, but Barbara said with determined rapidity:

"It's all very well, Violet, to laugh, but we've got to talk business. After all, this unexpected step of Alex' has made a lot of difference. One thought of her as absolutely settled—as father did, when he made his will."

"You see, Alex," Cedric told his sister, "the share which should have been yours was divided by father's will between Barbara and Pamela, and there was no mention of you, except just for the fifty pounds a year which my father thought would pay your actual living expenses in the convent. He never thought of your coming away again."

"How could he, after all these years?" ejaculated Barbara.

"I know. But I couldn't have stayed on, Cedric, indeed I couldn't. I know I ought to have found out sooner that I wasn't fitted for the life—but if you knew what it's all been like—"

Her voice broke huskily, and despair overwhelmed her at the thought of trying to explain what they would never understand.

"Poor little thing!" said Violet's compassionate voice. "Of course, you couldn't stay on. They've nearly killed you, as it is—wretched people!"

"No—no. They were kind—"

"The point is, Alex," Barbara broke in, "that you've only got the wretched fifty pounds a year. Of course, I'd be more than glad to let you have what would naturally have been yours—but how on earth I'm to manage it, I don't know. Cedric can tell you what a state poor Ralph left his affairs in—you'd never believe how little I have to live on. Of course, the money from father was a godsend, I don't deny it. But if Cedric thinks it's justice to give it back to you—"

She looked terribly anxious, gazing at her brother.

"No, no, Barbara!" said Alex, horrified. "I don't want the money. Of course, you must keep it—you and Pamela."

"That's all very well, my dear Alex," said Cedric sensibly, "but how do you propose to live? You must look at it from a practical point of view."

"Then you think—" broke from Barbara irrepressibly.

"No, my dear, I don't. One knows very well, as things are—as poor Ralph left things—it would be almost out of the question to expect—"

He looked helplessly at his wife.

"Of course, dear," she said placidly. "But there's Pamela's share."

"Pamela will marry, of course. She's sure to marry, but until then—or at least until she comes of age—I don't think—as her guardian—"

Cedric broke off, looking much harassed.

"If Pam married a rich man—which she probably will," said Violet, with a low laugh.

"We can't take distant possibilities into consideration," Barbara interposed sharply. "We're dealing with actual facts."

Alex looked from one to the other with bewilderment. She hardly understood what they were all discussing. From the natural home of her childhood and girlhood, where she had lived as unthinking of ways and means as every other girl of her class and generation, she had passed into the convent world, where all was communal, and the rights of the individual a thing part shunned, part unknown. She could not, at first, grasp that Cedric and Barbara and Violet, perhaps Pam and Archie, too, were all wondering how she would be able to maintain herself on fifty pounds a year.

"Of course," Barbara was saying, "Alex could come to me for a bit—I'd love to have you, dear—but you saw for yourself what a tiny place mine is—and there's only Ada. I don't quite know what she'd say to having two people instead of one, I must say—"

"We want her, too," Violet exclaimed caressingly. "Let us have her for a little while, Barbara,—while you're preparing Ada's mind for the shock." She broke into her low, gurgling laugh again.

Barbara looked infinitely relieved.

"What do you think, Alex? It isn't that I wouldn't love to have you—but there's no denying that ways and means *do* count, and in a tiny household like mine, every item adds up."

"Oh," said Alex desperately, "I know what you must feel—the difficulty of—of knowing what to do with me. It's always been like that, ever since I was a little girl. I've made a failure of everything. Don't you remember—Barbara, *you* must—old Nurse saying, 'Alex will never stick to anything'? And I never have, I never shall. I can only make dreadful muddles and failures, and upset you all. If only one could wreck one's own life without interfering with other people's!"

There was a silence, which Alex, after her outburst, knew very well was not one of comprehension. Then Cedric said gently:

"You mustn't let yourself exaggerate, my dear. We're very glad to have you with us again, one only can't help wishing it had been rather sooner. But there's no use in crying over spilt milk, and after all, as Violet says, there's no hurry about anything. Come to us and have a good long rest—you look as though you needed it—and get a little flesh on your bones again. We can settle all the rest afterwards."

Alex saw Barbara looking at her with furtive eagerness. She turned to her, with the utter dependence on another's judgment that had become second nature to her.

"When shall I go?"

"My dear!" protested Barbara. "Of course, the longer you can stay with me the better I shall be pleased. It's only that Ada—" She broke off at the sound of Violet's irrepressible laugh.

"You must suit yourself absolutely, of course."

"Supposing you came to us at the end of the week?" Violet suggested. "Say Saturday. Pamela is going away then to pay one or two visits—and I shall have you all to myself."

Alex looked at her wonderingly.

It seemed to her incredible that Violet should actually want her, so engrained was her sense of her own isolation of spirit. That terrible isolation of those who have definitely, and for long past, lost all self-confidence, and which can never be realized or penetrated by those outside.

"That will be delightful," said Violet, seeming to take her acceptance for granted.

Barbara got up, smoothing her skirt gently.

"We really ought to be going, Alex. I said we'd be in to tea, and it takes such ages to get back."

Alex rose submissively. She marvelled at the assurance of Barbara, even at the ease of her conventionally affectionate farewells.

"Well, good-bye, my dear. When are you coming out to the wilds to look me up?"

Then, without giving her sister-in-law time to reply, she added gaily, "You must ring me up and let me know, when you've a spare moment. You know I'm always a fixture. What a blessing the telephone is!"

"Then we'll see you on Saturday, Alex," said her brother. "Good! Take care of yourself, my dear." He looked after her with an expression of concern, as the servant held open the door for her and Barbara and they went into the street. Alex could not believe that this kindly, rather pompous man was her younger brother.

"Cedric has grown very good-looking, but I didn't expect to see him so—so *old*, somehow," she said.

Barbara laughed.

"Time hasn't stood still with any of us, you know. *I* think Violet looks older than he does—she is, of course. She'll be a mountain in a few years' time, if she doesn't take care."

"Oh, Barbara! I think she's so pretty—and sweet."

Barbara shrugged her shoulders very slightly.

"She and I have never made particularly violent friends, though I like her, of course. Pamela adores her—and I must say she's been good to Pam. But her kindness doesn't cost her anything. She's always been rich, and had everything she wanted—she was the only girl, and her people adored her, and now Cedric lets her do everything she likes. She spends any amount of money—look at her clothes, and the way she has little Rosemary always dressed in white."

"Rosemary is lovely. It's so extraordinary to think of Cedric's child!"

Barbara tightened her lips.

"She ought to have been a boy, of course. Cedric pretended not to care, but it must have been a disappointment—and goodness only knows if Violet will ever—"

She stopped, throwing a quick glance out of the corners of her eyes at her sister.

Alex wondered why she did not finish her sentence, and what she had been about to say.

The constraint in her intercourse with Barbara was becoming more and more evident to her perceptions. It was clear that her sister did not intend to ask any questions as to the crisis through which Alex had passed, and when she had once ascertained that Alex had not "seen anybody" whilst in Rome, she did not refer to that either.

Alex wondered if Barbara would tell her anything of Ralph and their married life, but the reserve which had always been characteristic of Barbara since her nursery days, had hardened sensibly, and it was obvious that she wished neither to give nor to receive confidences.

She was quite ready, however, to discuss her brother Cedric and his wife, or the prospects of Pamela and Archie, and Alex listened all the evening to Barbara's incisive little clear tones delivering shrewd comments and judgments. She again suggested that Alex should go to bed early, saying as she kissed her good-night:

"It's quite delightful to have some one to talk to, for me. I generally read or sew all the evening."

"It must be lonely for you, Barbara."

"Oh, I don't mind quiet," she laughed, as though edging away from any hint of emotional topic. "But, of course, it's nice to have some one for a change. Good-night." She turned towards the door of the bedroom. "Oh, Alex! there's just one thing—I know you'd rather I said it. If you wouldn't mind, sometime—any time you think of it—just letting me have the money for those clothes we bought for you today. The bills have come in—I asked for them, as I don't have an account. I knew you'd rather be reminded, knowing what pauper I am. I only wish I hadn't got to worry you. Good-night, my dear. Sleep well."

XXV
Violet

For days and nights to come, the question of the money that Barbara had paid for her clothes weighed upon Alex.

She had no idea how she was to repay her.

The money that had been given her in Rome for her journey to England had only lasted her to Charing Cross, and even her cab fare to Hampstead had been supplemented by Barbara. Alex remembered it with fresh dismay. Even when she had left Downshire Hill and was in Clevedon Square again, the thought lashed her with a secret terror, until one day she said to Cedric:

"What ought I to do, Cedric, to get my fifty pounds a year? Who do I get it from?"

"Don't Pumphrey and Scott send it half yearly? I thought that was the arrangement. You gave them your change of address, I suppose."

"Oh, no," said Alex gently. "I've never written to them, except once, just after father died, to ask them to make the cheques payable to to the Superior."

"What on earth made you do that?"

"They thought it was best. You see, I had no banking account, so the money was paid into the Community's account."

"I see," Cedric remarked drily. "Well, the sooner you write and revoke that arrangement, the better. When did they last send you a cheque? In June?"

"I don't know," Alex was forced to say, feeling all the time that Cedric must be thinking her a helpless, unpractical fool.

"Write and find out. And meanwhile—I say, Alex, have you enough to go on with?"

"I—I haven't any money, Cedric. In Rome they gave me enough for my travelling expenses, but nothing is left of that."

"But what have you done all this time? I suppose you've wanted clothes and things."

"I got some with Barbara, but they aren't paid for. And there are some other things I need—you see, I haven't got anything at all—not even stamps," said Alex forlornly. "Violet said something about taking me to some shops with her, but I suppose all her places are very expensive."

"They are—dashed expensive," Cedric admitted, with a short laugh. "But look here, Alex, will you let me advance you what you want? It couldn't be helped, of course—but the whole arrangement comes rather hard on you, as things are now. You see, poor Barbara is really as badly off as she can be. Ralph was a most awful ass, between ourselves, and muddled away the little he had, and she gets pretty nearly nothing, except a widow's pension, which was very small, and the money father left. If you'll believe me, Ralph didn't even insure his life, before going to South Africa. Of course, he didn't go to fight, but on the staff of one of the big papers, and it was supposed to be a very good thing, and then what did he do but go and get dysentery before he'd been there a fortnight!"

Cedric's voice held all the pitying scorn of the successful.

"Poor Barbara," said Alex.

"That's just what she is. Of course, I think myself that Pamela will make your share over to you again when she marries. *She's* not likely to make a rotten bad match like Barbara—far from it. But until then she can't do anything, you know—at least, not until she's of age, if then."

Cedric stopped, and his right hand tapped with his spectacles on his left hand, in the little, characteristic trick that was so like Sir Francis.

Alex had already heard him make much the same observations, but she realized that Cedric had retained all his old knack of reiteration.

"I see," she said.

"Well, my dear, the long and the short of it is, that you must let me be your banker for the time being. And—and, Alex," said Cedric, with a most unwonted touch of embarrassment breaking into his kind, assured manner, "you needn't mind taking it. There's—there's plenty of money here—there is really—now-a-days."

Alex realized afterwards that it would hardly have occurred to her to *mind* taking the twenty pounds which Cedric offered her with such patent diffidence. She had never known the want of money, either in her Clevedon Square days or during her ten years of convent life. She did not realize its value in the eyes of other people.

The isolation of her point of view on this and other kindred subjects gradually became evident to her. Her scale of relative values had remained that which had been set before her in the early days of her novitiate. That held by her present surroundings differed from it in almost every particular, and more especially in degree of concentration. All Violet's warm, healthy affection for Rosemary did not prevent her intense preoccupation with her own clothes and her own jewels, or her innocently-assured conviction that no one was ever in London during the month of August, and that to be so would constitute a calamity.

All Cedric's pride in' his wife and love for her, in no way lessened his manifest satisfaction at his own success in life and at the renovated fortunes of the house of Clare.

Both he and Violet found their recreation in playing bridge, Cedric at his club and Violet in her own house, or at the houses of what seemed to Alex an infinite succession of elaborately-gowned friends, with all of whom she seemed to be on exactly the same terms of an unintimate affection.

Violet at night, when she dismissed her maid and begged Alex to stay and talk to her until Cedric came upstairs, which he never did until past twelve o'clock, was adorable.

She listened to Alex' incoherent, nervous outpourings, which Alex herself knew to be vain and futile from the very longing which possessed her to make herself clear, and said no word of condemnation or of questioning.

At first the gentle pressure of Violet's soft hand on her hair, and her low, sympathetic, murmuring voice, soothed Alex to a sort of worn-out, tearful gratitude in which she would nightly cry herself to sleep.

It was only as she grew slowly physically stronger that the craving for self-expression, which had tormented her all her life, woke again. Did Violet understand?

She would reiterate her explanations and dissections of her own past misery, with a growing consciousness of morbidity and a positive terror lest Violet should at last repulse, however gently, the endless demand for an understanding that Alex herself perpetually declared to be impossible.

It now seemed to her that nothing mattered so long as Violet understood, and by that understanding restored to Alex in some degree her utterly shattered self-respect and self-confidence. This dependence grew the more intense, as she became more aware how unstable was her foothold in the world of normal life.

With the consciousness of an enormous and grotesque mistake behind her, mingled all the convent tradition of sin and disgrace attached to broken vows and the return to an abjured world. One night she said to Violet:

"I didn't do anything *wrong* in entering the convent. It was a mistake, and I'm bearing the consequence of the mistake. But it seems to me that people find it much easier to overlook a sin than a mistake."

"Well, I'd rather ask a *divorcée* to lunch than a woman who ate peas off her knife," Violet admitted candidly.

"That's what I mean. There's really no place for people who've made bad mistakes—anywhere."

"If you mean yourself, Alex, dear, you know there's always a place for you here. Just as long as you're happy with us. Only I'm sometimes afraid that it's not quite the sort of life—after all you've been through, you poor dear. I know people do come in and out a good deal—and it will be worse than ever when Pam is at home."

"Violet, you're very good to me. You're the only person who has seemed at all to understand."

"My dear, I do understand. Really, I think I do. It's just as you say—you made a mistake when you were very young—*much* too young to be allowed to take such a step, in my opinion—and you're suffering the most bitter consequences. But no one in their senses could blame you, either for going into that wretched place, or—still less—for coming out of it."

"One is always blamed by some one, I think, for every mistake. People would rather forgive one for murder, than for making a fool of oneself."

"Forgiveness," said Violet thoughtfully. "It's rather an overrated virtue, in my opinion. I don't think it ought to be very hard to forgive any one one loved, anything."

"Would *you* forgive anything, Violet?"

"I think so," said Violet, looking rather surprised. "Unless I were deliberately deceived by some one whom I trusted. That's different. Of course, one might perhaps forgive even then in a way— but it wouldn't be the same thing again, ever."

"No," said Alex. "No, of course not. Every one feels the same about deceit."

243

In the depths of her own consciousness, Alex was groping dimly after some other standard—some elusive certainty, that continually evaded her. Were not those things which were hardest to forgive, the most in need of forgiveness?

Alex, with the self-distrust engrained in the unstable, wondered if that question were not born of the fundamental weakness in her own character, which had led her all her life to evade or pervert the truth in a passionate fear lest it should alienate from her the love and confidence that she craved for from others.

Sometimes she thought, "Violet will find me out, and then she will stop being fond of me."

And, knowing that her claim on Violet's compassion was the strongest link that she could forge between them, she would dilate upon the mental and physical misery of the last two years, telling herself all the time that she was trading on her sister's pity.

Her days in Clevedon Square were singularly empty, after Violet had tried the experiment of taking Alex about with her to the houses of one or two old friends, and Alex had come back trembling and nearly crying, and begging never to go again.

Her nerves were still utterly undependable, and her health had suffered no less than her appearance. Violet would have taken her to see a doctor, but Alex dreaded the questions that he would, of necessity, put to her, and Cedric, who distrusted inherently the practice of any science of which he himself knew nothing, declared that rest and good food would be her best physicians.

Sometimes she went to see Barbara at Hampstead, but seldom willingly. One of her visits there was the occasion for a stupid, childish lie, of which the remembrance made her miserable.

Alex, amongst other unpractical disabilities, was as entirely devoid as it is possible to be of any sense of direction. She had never known how to find her way about, and would turn as blindly and instinctively in the wrong direction as a Dartmoor pony turns tail to the wind.

For ten years she had never been outside the walls of the convent alone, and when she had lived in London as a girl, she could not remember ever having been out-of-doors by herself.

Violet, always driven everywhere in her own motor, and accustomed to Pamela's modern resourcefulness and independence, never took so childish an inability into serious consideration.

"Alex, dear, Barbara hoped you'd go down to her this afternoon. Will you do that, or come to Ranelagh? The only thing is, if you wouldn't mind going to Hampstead in a taxi? I shall have to use the Mercédès, and the little car is being cleaned."

"Of course, I shouldn't mind. I'll go to Barbara, I think."

"Just whichever you like best. And you'll be back early, won't you? because we're dining at seven, and you know how ridiculous Cedric is about punctuality and the servants, and all that sort of thing."

After Violet had gone, in all her soft, elaborate laces and flower-wreathed hat, Alex, with every instinct of her convent training set against the extravagance of a taxi, started out on foot, rejoicing that a sunny July day should give her the opportunity of enjoying Pamela's boasted delight, the top of an omnibus.

She took the wrong one, discovered her mistake too late, and spent most of the afternoon in bewilderedly retracing her own footsteps. Finally she found a taxi, and arrived at Downshire Hill very tired, and after five o'clock.

Barbara was shocked, as Alex had known she would be, at the taxi.

"Violet is so inconsiderate. Because she can afford taxis as a matter of course herself, she never thinks that other people can't. I know myself how every shilling mounts up. I'll see you into an omnibus when you go, Alex. It takes just under an hour, and you need only change once."

But that change took place at the junction of four roads, all of them seething with traffic.

And again Alex was hopelessly at sea, and boarded at last an omnibus that conveyed her swiftly in the wrong direction.

She was late for dinner, and when Cedric inquired, with his assumption of the householder whose domestic routine has been flung out of gear, what had delayed her, she stammered and said that Barbara had kept her—she hadn't let her start early enough—had mistaken the time.

It was just such a lie as a child might have told in the fear of ridicule or blame, and she told it badly as a child might have told it, stammering, with a frightened widening of her eyes, so that even easy-going Violet looked momentarily puzzled.

Alex despised and hated herself.

She knew vaguely that her sense of proportion was disorganized. She was a woman of thirty-one, and her faults, her judgments and appreciations, even her mistakes, were those of an ill-regulated, unbalanced child of morbid tendencies.

When Pamela came back to Clevedon Square, Alex was first of all afraid of her, and then became jealous of her.

She was jealous of Pam's self-confidence, of her enormous security in her own popularity and success, jealous even of the innumerable common interests and the mutual love of enjoyment that bound her and Violet together.

She was miserably ashamed of her feelings, and sought to conceal them, none the less as she became aware of a certain shrewdness of judgment underlying all Pamela's breezy vitality and *joie de vivre*. She and her sister had nothing in common.

To Pamela, Alex evidently appeared far removed from herself as a being of another generation, less of a contemporary than pretty, sought-after Violet, or than little Rosemary in her joyous, healthy play. Pamela could accompany Violet everywhere, always radiantly enjoying herself, and receiving endless congratulations, thinly disguised as raillery, on her universal popularity and the charm that she seemed to radiate at will. She could play whole-heartedly with Rosemary, thoroughly enjoying a romp for its own sake, and making even Cedric laugh at her complete *abandon*.

"Don't you like children?" Pamela asked Alex, looking up from the nursery floor where she was playing with her niece.

"Yes, I like them," said Alex sombrely.

She had been reflecting bitterly that she would have known how to play with a baby of her own. But with Pamela and the nurse in the room, she was afraid of picking up Rosemary and making a fuss with her as Pam was doing, afraid with the terrible insecurity of the self-conscious.

And she never would have babies of her own now. The thought had tormented her often of late, watching Violet with her child, and Pamela with her own radiantly-secure future that would hold home and happiness as her rights.

But Alex concealed her thoughts, even, as far as possible, from herself.

The married woman who is denied children may lament her deprivation and receive compassion, but the spinster whose lot forbids her the hope, must either conceal her regrets or know herself to be accounted morbid and indelicate.

"I like babies while they're small," Pam remarked. "Don't I, you little horror of a niece? Other people's, you know. I don't know that I should want any of my own—they're all very well when they're tiny, but I can't bear them at the tell-me-a-story stage. I make it a rule never to tell the children stories at the houses where I stay. I always say, the very first evening, that I don't know any. Then they know what to expect. Some girls let themselves be regularly victimized, if they want to please the children's mother, and get asked again. I must say I do hate that sort of thing myself, and I don't believe it really does any good. Men are generally frightfully bored by the sort of girl who's 'perfectly wonderful with children.' They'd much rather have one who can play tennis, or who's good at bridge."

Pamela laughed comfortably at her own cynicism. "I must say I do think it pays one to be honest in the long run. I always say exactly what I feel myself, and don't care what any one thinks of me."

Alex felt a dull anger at her sister's self-complacent statement of what she knew to be the truth. Pamela could afford to be frank, and her boast seemed to Alex to cast an oblique reflection on herself. She gazed at her without speaking, wretchedly conscious of her own unreason.

"Look at Aunt Alex, Baby!" mischievously exclaimed Pam in a loud whisper. "We're rather afraid of her when she pulls a long face like that, aren't we? Have we been naughty, do you think?"

Alex tried to laugh, contorting her lips stiffly. Pamela jumped up from the floor.

"Really and truly, you know, Alex," she gravely told her sister, "you ought to try and make things less *au grand sérieux*. I think you'd be much happier, if you'd only cultivate a sense of humour—we all think so."

Then she ran out of the room.

245

Alex sat still.

So they all thought that she ought to cultivate a sense of humour. She felt herself to be ridiculous in their eyes, with her eternal air of tragedy, her sombre despair in the midst of their gay, good-humoured conventions, that admitted of everything except of weighty, unseasonable gloom.

Pamela's spontaneous and unwearied high spirits seemed to her to throw her own dejection into greater relief; her own utter social incompetence.

She began to long for the end of July, when the household in Clevedon Square would be dispersed for the remainder of the summer.

Pamela talked incessantly of a yachting invitation which she had received for August, and spoke of the difficulty of "sandwiching in" country-house visits for autumn shooting-parties, and Alex knew that Violet's people were taking a house in Scotland, and wanted her and Cedric and the baby to make it their headquarters. She wondered, with a sense of impending crisis, what would happen to her.

At last Cedric said to her:

"Have you any particular plans for August, Alex? I want to get Violet up north as soon as possible, she's done so much rushing about lately. I wish you could come with us, my dear, but we're going to the Temples'—that's the worst of not having a place of one's own in the country—"

"Oh," said Alex faintly, "don't bother about me, Cedric. I shall find somewhere."

He looked dissatisfied, but said only:

"Well, you'll talk it over with Violet. I know she's been vexed at seeing so little of you lately, but Pamela's an exacting young woman, and chaperoning her is no joke. I wish she'd hurry up and get settled—all this rushing about is too much for Violet."

"I thought she liked it."

"So she does. Anyhow," said Cedric, with an odd, shy laugh, "she'd like anything that pleased somebody else. She's made like that. I've never known her anything but happy—like sunshine."

Then he flung a half-smoked cigarette into the fireplace, looked awkward at his own unusual expression of feeling, and abruptly asked Alex if she'd seen the newspaper.

Alex crept away, wondering why happiness should be accounted a virtue. She loved Violet with a jealous, exclusive affection and admiration, but she thought enviously that she, too, could have been like sunshine if she had received all that Violet received. She, too, would have liked to be always happy.

She had her talk with Violet.

There was the slightest shade of wistfulness in Violet's gentleness.

"I wish we'd made you happier, but I really believe quiet is what you want most, and things aren't ever very quiet here—especially with Pam. I simply love having her, but I'm not sure she is the best person for you, just now."

"I don't feel I know her very well. I mean, I'm not at all at home with her. She makes me realize what a stranger I am to the younger ones, after all these years."

"Poor Alex!"

"You're much more like my sister than she is, and yet a year ago I didn't know you."

"Alex, dear, I'm so glad if I'm a comfort to you—but I wish you wouldn't speak in that bitter way about poor little Pamela. It seems so unnatural."

Violet's whole healthy instinct was always, Alex had already discovered, to tend towards the normal—the outlook of well-balanced sanity. She was instinctively distressed by abnormality of any kind.

"I didn't really mean it," said Alex hurriedly, with the old fatal instinct of propitiation, and read dissent into the silence that received her announcement.

It was the subconscious hope of rectifying herself in Violet's eyes that made her add a moment later:

"Couldn't Barbara have me for a little while when you go up to Scotland? I think she would be quite glad."

"Of course she would. She's often lonely, isn't she? And you think you'd be happy with her?"

"Oh, yes," said Alex eagerly, bent on showing Violet that she had no unnatural aversion from being with her own sister.

But Violet still looked rather troubled.

"You remember that you found it rather difficult there, when you first got back. You said then that Barbara and you had never understood one another even as children."

"Oh, but that will all be different now," said Alex, confused, and knowing that her manner was giving an impression of shiftiness from her very consciousness that she was contradicting herself.

As Pamela's claims and her own ceaseless fear of inadequacy made her increasingly unsure of Violet, Alex became less and less at ease with her.

The old familiar fear of being disbelieved gave uncertainty to every word she uttered and she could not afford to laugh at Pam's merciless amusement in pointing out the number of times that she contradicted herself. Violet always hushed Pamela, but she looked puzzled and rather distressed, and her manner towards Alex was more compassionate than ever.

Alex, with the impetuous unwisdom of the weak, one day forced an issue.

"Violet, do you trust me?"

"My dear child, what *do* you mean? Why shouldn't I trust you? Are you thinking of stealing my pearls?"

But Alex could not smile.

"Do you believe everything that I say?"

Violet looked at her and asked very gently:

"What makes you ask, Alex? You're not unhappy about the nonsense that child Pamela sometimes talks, are you?"

"No, not exactly. It's—it's just everything...." Alex looked miserable, tongue-tied.

"Oh, Alex, do try and take things more lightly. You make yourself so unhappy, poor child, with all this self-torment. Can't you take things as they come, more?"

The counsel found unavailing echo in Alex' own mind. She knew that her mental outlook was wrenched out of all gear, and she knew also, in some dim, undefined way, that a worn-out physical frame was responsible for much of her self-inflicted torment of mind. Sometimes she wondered whether the impending solution to her whole destiny, still hanging over her, would find her on the far side of the abyss which separates the normal from the insane.

The days slipped by, and then, just before the general dispersal, Pamela suddenly announced her engagement to Lord Richard Gunvale, the youngest and by far the wealthiest of her many suitors.

"Oh, Pam, Pam!" cried Violet, laughing, "why couldn't you wait till after we'd left town?"

But every one was delighted, and congratulations and letters and presents and telegrams poured in.

Pamela declared that she would not be married until the winter, and refused to break her yachting engagement. She was more popular than ever now, and every one laughed at her delightful originality and gazed at the magnificence of the emerald and diamond ring on her left hand.

And Alex began to hope faintly that perhaps when Pamela was married, things might be different at Clevedon Square.

Then one night, just before she was to go to Hampstead, she overheard a conversation between Cedric and his wife.

She was on the stairs in the dark, and they were in the lighted hall below, and from the first instant that Cedric spoke, Alex lost all sense of what she was doing, and listened.

"...they're wearing you out, Pam and Alex between them. I won't have any more of it, I tell you."

"No, no, my dear old goose. Of course they're not." Violet's soft laughter came up to Alex' ears with a muffled sound, as though her head were resting against Cedric's shoulder. "Anyhow, it isn't Pam—I'm *delighted* about her, of course. Only Alex—I wish she was happier!"

"And why isn't she? You're a perfect angel to her," said Cedric resentfully.

"I'm so *sorry* for her—only it's difficult sometimes—a feeling like shifting sands. One doesn't know what to be *at* with her. If only she said what she wanted or didn't want, right out, but it's that awful anxiety to please—poor darling."

"She always was like that, from our nursery days. You never could get the rights of a matter out of her—plain black or white—she'd say one thing one day and another the next, always."

"That's what I find so difficult! It's impossible to do anything for a person like that—it's the one thing I *can't* understand."

"Pack her off to Hampstead tomorrow," Cedric observed gruffly. "I *will* not have you bothered."

"Oh, Cedric! I'm not bothered—how can you? She'll be going next week, anyway, poor dear, and it may be easier for her to be herself with Barbara, who's her own sister, after all. But I don't know what about afterwards—when we get back."

"You'll have quite enough to think about with Pam's wedding, without Alex on your hands as well. Violet," said Cedric, with a note in his voice that Alex had never heard there, "when I think of the way you've behaved to all my wretched family—"

Alex did not hear Violet's answer, which was very softly spoken.

She had turned and gone away upstairs in the dark.

XXVI
August

Was it, after all, only for Cedric's sake that Violet had kept her at Clevedon Square—had shown her such heavenly kindness and gentleness?

Alex asked herself the question all night long in utter misery of spirit. She had craved all her life for an exclusive, personal affection, and had been mocked with counterfeit again and again. She knew now that it was only in despair at such cheating of fate that she had flung herself rashly to the opposite end of the scale, and sought to embrace a life that purported detachment from all earthly ties.

"*I will have all or none*" had been the inward cry of her bruised spirit.

Fate had taken her at her word, this time, and she had not been strong enough to endure, and had fled, cowering, from the consequence of her own act.

Tortured, distraught, with self-confidence shattered to the earth, she had turned once again, with hands that trembled as they pleaded, to ask comfort of human love and companionship. Violet had not condemned her, had pitied her, and had shown her untiring sympathy and affection—for love of Cedric.

Alex rose haggard, in the morning. She wanted to be alone. The thought of going to Barbara in Hampstead had become unendurable to her.

It was with a curious sense of inevitability that she found a letter from Barbara asking her if she could put off her visit for the present. The admirable Ada had developed measles.

"Good Lord, can't they send her to a hospital?" exclaimed Cedric, with the irritability of a practical man who finds his well-ordered and practical plans thrown out of gear by some eminently unpractical intervention on the part of Providence.

"I'm sure Barbara never would," said Violet, laughing. "Poor dear, I hope she won't catch it herself. It'll mean having the house disinfected, too—what a nuisance for her. But, Alex, dear, you must come with us! I'll send a wire today—mother will be perfectly delighted."

"Couldn't I stay here?" asked Alex.

Cedric explained that the house would be partially shut up, with only two of the servants left.

"I shouldn't give any trouble—I'd so much rather," Alex urged, unusually persistent.

"My dear, it's out of the question. Not a soul in London—you forget it's August."

"But, Cedric," said Violet, "I don't see why she shouldn't do as she likes. It will be only till Barbara can have her, after all—I suppose Ada will be moved as soon as she's better, and the disinfecting can't take so very long. If she wants to stay here?"

"I do," said Alex, with sudden boldness.

"You don't think you'll be lonely?"

"No, no."

248

"After all," Violet considered, "it will be very good for Ellen and the tweeny to have somebody to wait upon. I never do like leaving them here on enormous board wages, to do nothing at all—though Cedric *will* think it's the proper thing to do, because his father did it."

She laughed, and Cedric said, with an air of concession:

"Well, just till Barbara can take you in, perhaps—if you think London won't be unbearable. But mind you, Alex, the minute you get tired of it, or feel the heat too much for you, you're to make other arrangements."

Alex wondered dully what other arrangements Cedric supposed that she could make. She had no money, and had never even roused herself to write the letter he had recommended, asking to have her half-yearly allowance sent to her own address and not to that of the Superior of the convent.

But on the day before Cedric and Violet, with Violet's maid, and Rosemary, and her nurse, and her pram, all took their departure, Cedric called Alex into the study.

She went to him feeling oddly as though she was the little girl again, who had, on rare occasions, been sent for by Sir Francis, and had found him standing just so, his back to the fireplace, spectacles in hand, speaking in just the same measured, rather regretful tones of kindliness.

"Alex, I've made out two cheques one to cover the servants' board wages, which I thought you would be good enough to give them at the end of the month, and one for your own living expenses. You'd better cash that at once, in case you want any ready money. Have you anywhere to keep it under lock and key?"

Cedric, no more than Sir Francis, trusted to a woman's discretion in matters of money.

"Yes, there's the drawer of the writing-table in my bedroom."

"That will be all right, then. The servants are perfectly trustworthy, no doubt, but loose cash should never be left about in any case—if you want more, write to me. And, Alex, I've seen old Pumphrey—father's man of business. He will see that you get your fifty pounds. Here is the first instalment."

Cedric gravely handed her a third cheque.

"Have you a banking account?"

"I don't think so."

"Then I'll arrange to open one for you at my bank today. You'd better deposit this at once, hadn't you—unless you want anything?"

"No," faltered Alex, not altogether understanding.

"You will have no expenses while you're here, of course," said Cedric, rather embarrassed. Alex looked bewildered. It had never occurred to her to suggest paying for her own keep while she remained alone at Clevedon Square. She gave back to her brother the cheque for twenty-five pounds, and received his assurance that it would be banked in her name that afternoon.

"They will send you a cheque-book, and you can draw out any small sum you may need later on."

"I don't think I shall need any," said Alex, looking at the other two cheques he had given her, made payable to herself, and thinking what a lot of money they represented.

"You will have a thorough rest and change with Barbara," Cedric said, still looking at her rather uneasily. "Then, when we meet again in October, it will be time enough—"

He did not say what for, and Alex remembered the conversation that she had overheard on the stair. With a feeling of cunning, she was conscious of her own determination to take the initiative out of his hands, without his knowledge.

They did not want her, and they would want her less than ever, with all the approaching business connected with Pamela's wedding in December. Barbara did not want her, self-absorbed, and unwearingly considering how to cut down more and yet more expenses.

Alex had made up her mind to go and live alone. She would prove to them that she could do it, though they thought fifty pounds a year was so little money. She thought vaguely that perhaps she could earn something.

But she gave no hint of her plans to any one, knowing that Violet would be remonstrant and Cedric derisive.

Obsessed by this new idea, she said good-bye to them with a sort of furtive eagerness, and found herself alone in the house in Clevedon Square.

At first the quiet and the solitude were pleasant to her. She crept round the big, empty house like a spirit, feeling as though it presented a more familiar aspect with its shrouded furniture and carefully shaded windows, and the absence of most of Violet's expensive silver and china ornaments. The library, which was always kept open for her, was one of the least changed rooms in the house, and she spent hours crouched upon the sofa there, only rousing herself to go to the solitary meals which were punctiliously laid out for her in the big dining-room.

Presently she began to wonder if the elderly upper-housemaid, Ellen, left in charge, resented her being there. She supposed that the presence of some one who never went out, for whom meals had to be provided, who must be called in the morning and supplied with hot water four times a day, would interfere with the liberty of Ellen and the unseen tweeny who, no doubt, cooked for them. They would be glad when she went away. Never mind, she would go very soon. Alex felt that she was only waiting for something to happen which should give her the necessary impetus to carry out her vague design of finding a new, independent foothold for herself.

A drowsy week of very hot weather slipped by, and then one morning Alex received three letters.

Cedric's, short but affectionate, told her that Violet had reached Scotland tired out, and had been ordered by the doctor to undergo something as nearly approaching a rest-cure as possible. She was to stay in bed all the morning, sit in the garden when it was fine, and do nothing. She was to write no letters, but she sent Alex her love and looked forward to hearing from her. Cedric added briefly that Alex was not to be at all anxious. Violet only needed quiet and country air, and no worries. She was looking better already.

Alex put the letter down reflectively. Evidently Cedric did not want his wife disturbed by depressing correspondence, and she did not mean to write to Violet of her new resolution. She even thought that perhaps she would continue to let Violet believe her at Clevedon Square or with Barbara.

Her second letter was from Barbara. It was quite a long letter, and said that Barbara had decided to leave Ada at a convalescent home and take her own much-needed summer holiday abroad. Would Alex join her in a week's time?

"What do you think of some little, cheap seaside hole in Brittany, which we could do for very little? I wish I could have you as my guest, dear, but you'll understand that all the disinfecting of the house has cost money, besides forcing me to go away, which I hadn't meant to do. However, I'm sure I need the change, and I dare say it won't do you any harm either. We ought to do the whole thing for about fifteen pounds each, I think, which, I suppose, will be all right for you? Do ring me up tonight, and let's exchange views. I shan't be free of a suspicion as to these wretched measles till next week, but I don't think really there's much danger, as I've had them already and am not in the least nervous. Ring up between seven and eight tonight. I suppose Violet, as usual, has kept on the telephone, even though they're away themselves?"

Alex knew that she did not want to go abroad with Barbara. She nervously picked up her third letter, which bore a foreign post-mark. When she had read the sheet of thin paper which was all the envelope contained, she sat for a long while staring at it.

The nuns in Rome, with whom she had spent the few weeks previous to her return to England, had sent in their account for her board and lodging, for the few clothes she had purchased, and for the advance made her for her travelling expenses. The sum total, in francs, looked enormous.

At last Alex, trembling, managed to arrive at the approximate amount in English money.

Twenty pounds.

It seemed to her exorbitant, and she realized, with fresh dismay, that she had never taken such a debt into consideration at all. How could she tell Cedric?

She thought how angry he would be at her strange omission in never mentioning it to him before, and how impossible it would be to explain to him that she had, as usual, left all practical issues out of account. Suddenly Alex remembered with enormous relief that twenty-five pounds lay to her credit at the bank. She had received her new cheque-book only two days ago. She would go to the bank today and make them show her how she could send the money to Italy.

Then Cedric and Violet need never know. They need never blame her.

Full of relief, Alex took the cheque-book that morning to the bank. She did not like having to display her ignorance, but she showed the bill to the clerk, who was civil and helpful, and showed her how very simple a matter it was to draw a cheque for twenty pounds odd. When it was done, and safely posted, Alex trembled with thankfulness. It seemed to her that it would have been a terrible thing for Cedric to know of the expenses she had so ignorantly incurred, and of her incredible simplicity in never having realized them before, and she was glad that he need never know how almost the whole of her half-year's allowance of money had vanished so soon after she had received it.

She telephoned to Barbara that night, and said that she could not go abroad with her.

"Oh, very well, my dear, if you think it wiser not. Of course, if you don't *mind* London at this time of year, it's a tremendous economy to stay where you are.... Are the servants looking after you properly?"

"Oh, yes."

"Well, do just as you like, of course. I think I shall get hold of some friend to join forces with me, if you're sure you won't come...."

"Quite sure, Barbara," said Alex tremulously. She felt less afraid of her sister at the other end of the telephone.

She went and saw Barbara off the following week, and Barbara said carelessly:

"Good-bye, Alex. You look a shade better, I think. On the whole you're wiser to stay where you are—I'm sure you need quiet, and when once the rush begins for Pam's wedding, you'll never get a minute's peace. Are you staying on when they get back?"

"I'm not sure," faltered Alex.

"You may be wise. Well, come down to my part of the world if you want economy—and to feel as though you were out of London. Good-bye, dear."

Alex was surprised, and rather consoled, to hear Barbara alluding so lightly to the possibility of her seeking fresh quarters for herself. Perhaps, after all, they all thought it would be the best thing for her to do. Perhaps there was no need to feel guilty and as though her intentions must be concealed.

But Alex, dreading blame or disapproval, or even assurances that the scheme was unpractical and foolish, continued to conceal it.

She wrote and told Violet that she had decided that it would be too expensive to go abroad with Barbara. Might she stay on in Clevedon Square for a little while?

But she had secretly made up her mind to go and look for rooms or a boarding-house in Hampstead, as Barbara had suggested. As usual, it was only by chance that Alex realized the practical difficulties blocking her way.

She had now only five pounds.

On the following Saturday afternoon she found her way out by omnibus to Hampstead. She alighted before the terminus was reached, from a nervous dread of being taken on too far, although the streets in which she found herself were not prepossessing.

For the first time Alex reflected that she had no definite idea as to where she wanted to go in her search for lodgings. She walked timidly along the road, which appeared to be interminably long and full of second-hand furniture shops. Bamboo tables, and armchairs with defective castors, were put out on the pavement in many instances, and there was often a small crowd in front of the window gazing at the cheaply-framed coloured supplements hung up within. The pavements and the road, even the tram-lines, swarmed with untidy, clamouring children.

Alex supposed that she must be in the region vaguely known to her as the slums.

Surely she could not live here?

Then the recollection of her solitary five pounds came to her with a pang of alarm.

Of course, she must live wherever she could do so most cheaply. She had no idea of what it would cost.

It was very hot, and the pavement began to burn her feet. She did not dare to leave the main road, fearing that she should never find her way to the 'bus route again, if once she left it, but she peeped down one or two side-streets. They seemed quieter than Malden Road, but the unpretentious little grey houses did not look as though lodgers were expected in any of them. Alex wondered desperately how she was to find out.

Presently she saw a policeman on the further side of the street.

She went up to him and asked:

"Can you tell me of anywhere near here where they let rooms—somewhere cheap?"

The man looked down at her white, exhausted face, and at the well-cut coat and skirt chosen by Barbara, which yet hung loosely and badly on her stooping, shrunken figure.

"Somebody's poor relation," was his unspoken comment.

"Is it for yourself, Miss? You'd hardly care to be in this neighbourhood, would you?"

"I want to be somewhere near Hampstead—and somewhere very, very cheap," Alex faltered, thinking of her five pounds, which lay at that moment in the purse she was clasping.

"Well, you'll find as cheap here as anywhere, if you don't mind the noise."

"Oh, no," said Alex—who had never slept within the sound of traffic—surprised.

"Then if I was you, Miss, I'd try No. 252 Malden Road—just beyond the *Gipsy Queen*, that is, or else two doors further up. I saw cards up in both windows with 'apartments' inside the last week."

"Thank you," said Alex.

She wished that Malden Road had looked more like Downshire Hill, which had trees and little tiny gardens in front of the houses, which almost all resembled country cottages. But no doubt houses in Downshire Hill did not let rooms, or if so they must be too expensive. Besides, Alex felt almost sure that Barbara would not want her as a very near neighbour.

She was very tired when she reached No. 252, and almost felt that she would take the rooms, whatever they were like, to save herself further search. After all, she could change later on, if she did not like them.

Like all weak people, Alex felt the urgent necessity of acting as quickly as possible on her own impulses.

She looked distastefully at the dingy house, with its paint cracking into hard flakes, and raised the knocker slowly. A jagged end of protruding wire at the side of the door proclaimed that the bell was broken.

Her timid knock was answered by a slatternly-looking young woman wearing an apron, whom Alex took to be the servant.

"Can I see the—the landlady?"

"Is it about a room? I'm Mrs. 'Oxton." She spoke in the harshest possible Cockney, but quite pleasantly.

"Oh," said Alex, still uncertain. "Yes, I want rooms, please."

The woman looked her swiftly up and down. "Only one bed-sittin'-room vacant, Miss, and that's at the top of the 'ouse. Would you care to see that?"

"Yes, please."

Mrs. Hoxton slammed the door and preceded Alex up a narrow staircase, carpeted with oil-cloth. On the third floor she threw open the door of a room considerably smaller than the bath-room at Clevedon Square, containing a low iron bed, and an iron tripod bearing an enamel basin, a chipped pitcher and a very small towel-rail. A looking-glass framed in mottled yellow plush was hung crookedly on the wall, and beneath it stood a wooden kitchen chair. There was a little table with two drawers in it behind the door.

Alex looked round her with bewilderment. A convent cell was no smaller than this, and presented a greater aspect of space from its bareness.

"Is there a sitting-room?" she inquired.

"Not separate to this—no, Miss. Bed-sitting-room, this is called. Small, but then I suppose you'd be out all day."

For a moment Alex wondered why.

"But meals?" she asked feebly.

"Would it be more than just the breakfast and supper, and three meals on Sunday?"

Alex did not know what to answer, and Mrs. Hoxton surveyed her.

"Where are you working, Miss? Anywhere near?"

"I'm not working anywhere—yet."

Mrs. Hoxton's manner changed a little.

"If you want two rooms, Miss, and full board, I could accommodate you downstairs. The price is according, of course—a week in advance, and pay by the week."

Alex followed the woman downstairs again. She was sure that this was not the kind of place where she wanted to live.

Mrs. Hoxton showed her into a larger bedroom on the first floor, just opening the door and giving Alex a glimpse of extreme untidiness and an unmade bed.

"My gentleman got up late today—he don't go to 'is job Saturdays, so I 'aven't put the room to rights yet. But it's a nice room, Miss, and will be vacant on Monday. It goes with the downstairs sitting-room in the front, as a rule, but that's 'ad to be turned into a bedroom just lately. I've been so crowded."

"Will that be empty on Monday, too?" asked Alex, for the sake of answering something.

"Tonight, Miss. I let a coloured gentleman 'ave it—a student, you know; a thing I've never done before, either. Other people don't like it, and it gives a name, like, for not being particular who one takes. So he's going, and I shan't be sorry. I don't 'old with making talk, and it isn't as though the room wouldn't let easy. It's a beautiful room, Miss."

The coloured gentleman's room was tidier than the one upstairs, but a haze of stale tobacco fumes hung round it and obscured Alex' view of a short leather sofa with horsehair breaking from it in patches, a small round table in the middle of the room, and a tightly-closed window looking on to the traffic of Malden Road.

"About terms, Miss," Mrs. Hoxton began suggestively in the passage.

"Oh, I couldn't afford much," Alex began, thinking that it was more difficult than she had supposed to walk out again saying that she did not, after all, want the rooms.

"I'd let you 'ave those two rooms, and full board, for two-ten a week!" cried the landlady.

"Oh, I don't think—"

Mrs. Hoxton shrugged her shoulders, looked at the ceiling and said resignedly:

"Then I suppose we must call it two guineas, though I ought to ask double. But you can come in right away on Monday, Miss, and I think you'll find it all comfortable."

"But—" said Alex faintly.

She felt very tired, and the thought of a further search for lodgings wearied her and almost frightened her. Besides, the policeman had told her that this was a cheap neighbourhood. Perhaps anywhere else they would charge much more. Finally she temporized feebly with the reflection that it need only be for a week—once the step of leaving Clevedon Square had been definitely taken, she could feel herself free to find a more congenial habitation at her leisure, and when she might feel less desperately tired. She sighed, as she followed the line of least resistance.

"Well, I'll come on Monday, then."

"Yes, Miss," the landlady answered promptly. "May I have your name, Miss?—and the first week in advance my rule, as I think I mentioned."

"My name is Miss Clare."

Alex took two sovereigns and two shillings, fumbling, out of her purse and handed them to the woman. It did not occur to her to ask for any form of receipt.

"Will you be wanting anything on Monday, Miss?"

Alex looked uncomprehending, and the woman eyed her with scarcely veiled contempt and added, "Supper, or anything?"

"Oh—yes. I'd better come in time for dinner—for supper, I mean."

"Yes, Miss. Seven o'clock will do you, I suppose?"

Alex thought it sounded very early, but she did not feel that she cared at all, and said that seven would do quite well.

She wondered if there were any questions which she ought to ask, but could think of none, and she was rather afraid of the strident-voiced, hard-faced woman.

But Mrs. Hoxton seemed to be quite satisfied, and pulled open the door as though it was obvious that the interview had come to an end.

"Good afternoon," said Alex.

"Afternoon," answered the landlady, as she slammed the door again, almost before Alex was on the pavement of Malden Road. She went away with a strangely sinking heart. To what had she committed herself?

All the arguments which Alex had been brooding over seemed to crumble away from her now that she had taken definite action.

She repeated to herself again that Violet and Cedric did not want her, that Barbara did not want her, that there was no place for her anywhere, and that it was best for her to make her own arrangements and spare them all the necessity of viewing her in the light of a problem.

But what would Cedric say to Malden Road? Inwardly Alex resolved that he must never come there. If she said "Hampstead" he would think that she was somewhere close to Barbara's pretty little house.

But Barbara?

Alex sank, utterly jaded, into the vacant space in a crowded omnibus. It was full outside, and the atmosphere of heat and humanity inside made her feel giddy. Arguments, self-justification and sick apprehensions, surged in chaotic bewilderment through her mind.

XXVII
The Embezzlement

Alex, full of unreasoning panic, made her move to Malden Road.

She was afraid of the servants in Clevedon Square, all of them new since she had left England, and only told Ellen, with ill-concealed confusion, that she was leaving London for the present. She was unaccountably relieved when Ellen only said, impassively, "Very good, Miss," and packed her slender belongings without comment or question.

Suddenly she remembered the cheque which Cedric had given her for the servants. She looked at it doubtfully. Her own money was already almost exhausted, thanks to that unexpected claim from the convent in Rome, and Alex supposed that the sum still in her purse, amounting to rather less than three pounds, would only last her for about a fortnight in Malden Road. She decided, with no sense of doubt, that she had better keep Cedric's cheque. It was only a little sum to him, and he would send money for the servants. He had said that he was ready to advance money to his sister. Characteristically, Alex dismissed the matter from her mind as unimportant. She had never learnt any accepted code in dealings with money, and her own instinct led her to believe it an unessential question. She judged only from her own feelings, which would have remained quite unstirred by any emotions but those the most matter-of-fact at any claim, direct or indirect, justifiable or not, upon her purse.

She had never learnt the rudiments of pride, or of straight-dealing in questions of finance. But in Malden Road Alex was, after all, to learn many things.

There were material considerations equally unknown to Clevedon Square and to the austere but systematic doling-out of convent necessities, which were brought home to her with a startled sense of dismay from her first evening at 252. She had never thought of bringing soap with her, or boxes of matches, yet these commodities did not appear as a matter of course, as they had always done elsewhere. There was gas in both the rooms, but there were no candles. There was no hot water.

"You can boil your own kettle on the gas-ring on the landing," Mrs. Hoxton said indifferently, and left her new lodger to the realization that the purchase of a kettle had never occurred to her at all.

Buying the kettle, and a supply of candles and matches and soap, left her with only just enough money in hand for her second week's rent, and when she wanted notepaper and ink and stamps to write to Barbara, Alex decided that she must appropriate Cedric's cheque for the servants' wages to her own uses. She felt hardly any qualms.

This wasn't like that bill from Rome, which she would have been afraid to let him see. He would have talked about the dishonesty of convents, and asked why she had not told him sooner of their charges against her, and have looked at her with that almost incredulous expression of amazed disgust had she admitted her entire oblivion of the whole consideration.

But this cheque for the servants.

It would enable her to pay her own expenses until she could get the work which she still vaguely anticipated, and the sum meant nothing to Cedric. She would write and tell him that she had cashed the money, sure that he would not mind, in fulfilment of his many requests to her to look upon him as her banker.

But she did not write, though she cashed the cheque. The days slipped by in a sort of monotonous discomfort, but it was very hot, and she learnt to find her way to Hampstead Heath, where she could sit for hours, not reading, for she had no books, but brooding in a sort of despairing resignation over the past and the nightmare-seeming present. The conviction remained with her ineradicably that the whole thing was a dream—that she would wake up again to the London of the middle 'nineties and find herself a young girl again, healthy and eager, and troubling Lady Isabel, and, more remotely, Sir Francis, with her modern exigencies and demands to live her own life, the war-cry of those clamorous 'eighties and 'nineties, of which the young new century had so easily reaped the harvest. She could not bring herself to believe that her own life had been lived, and that only this was left.

Alex sometimes felt that she was not alive at all—that she was only a shade moving amongst the living, unable to get into real communication with any of them.

She did not think of the future. There was no future for her. There was only an irrevocable past and a sordid, yet dream-like present, that clung round her spirit as a damp mist might have clung round her person, intangible and yet penetrating and all-pervading, hampering and stifling her.

The modicum of physical strength which she had regained in Clevedon Square was ebbing imperceptibly from her. It was difficult to sleep very well in Malden Road, where the trams and the omnibuses passed in incessant, jerking succession, and the children screamed in the road late at nights and incredibly early in the mornings. The food was neither good nor well prepared, but Alex ate little in the heat, and reflected that it was an economy not to be hungry.

The need for economy was being gradually borne in upon her, as her small stock of money diminished and there came nothing to replace it. Presently she exerted herself to find a registry office, where she gave her name and address, and was contemptuously and suspiciously eyed by an old lady with dyed red hair who sat at a writing-table, and asked her a fee of half-a-crown for entering her name in a ledger.

"No diplomas and no certificate won't take you far in teaching now-a-days," she said unpleasantly. "Languages?"

"French quite well and a little Italian. Enough to give conversation lessons," Alex faltered.

"No demand for 'em whatever. I'll let you know, but don't expect anything to turn up, especially at this time of year, with every one out of town."

But by a miraculous stroke of fortune something did turn up. The woman from the registry office sent Alex a laconic postcard, giving her the address of "a lady singer in Camden Town" who was willing to pay two shillings an hour in return for sufficient instruction in Italian to enable her to sing Italian songs.

Elated, Alex looked out the conversation manual of her convent days, and at three o'clock set out to find the address in Camden Town.

She discovered it with difficulty, and arrived late. The appointed hour had been half-past three.

Shown into a small sitting-room, crowded with furniture and plastered with signed photographs, she sank, breathless and heated, into a chair, and waited.

The lady singer, when she came, was irate at the delay. Her manner frightened Alex, who acquiesced in bewildered humiliation to a stipulation that only half-fees must be charged for the curtailed hour. She gave her lesson badly, imparting information with a hesitation that even to her own ears sounded as though she were uncertain of her facts. However, her pupil ungraciously drew out a shilling from a small chain-purse and gave it to Alex when she left, and she bade her come again in three days' time.

The lessons went on for three weeks. They tired Alex strangely, but she felt glad that she could earn money, however little; and although the shillings went almost at once in small necessities which she had somehow never foreseen, it was not until the middle of September that she began once more to reach the end of her resources.

Just as she had decided that it would be necessary for her to write to Cedric, she received a letter from him, forwarded from her bank.

Alex turned white as she read it.

"MY DEAR ALEX,

"I am altogether at a loss to understand why Ellen (the upper-housemaid at home) writes to Violet on Friday last, Sept. 12, that you have left Clevedon Square, and that she and the other servant have not yet received the money for their board and wages. This last I take to be an oversight on your part, but you will doubtless put it right at once, since you will remember that I handed you a cheque for that purpose just before leaving London. As to your own movements, I need hardly say, my dear Alex, that I do not claim to have any sort of authority over them of whatever kind, but both Violet and I cannot help feeling that it would have been more friendly, to say the least of it, had you given us some hint as to your intentions. Knowing that Barbara is already abroad, and Pamela with her friends yachting, I can only hope that you have received some unforeseen invitation which appealed to you more than the prospect of solitude in Clevedon Square. It would have been desirable had you left your address with the servants, but I presume the matter escaped your memory, as they appear to be completely in the dark as to your movements.

"Violet is looking quite herself again, and sends many affectionate messages. She will doubtless write to you on receipt of a few lines giving her your address. I am compelled to send this letter through the care of Messrs. Williams, which you will agree with me is an unnecessarily elaborate method of communication.

"Your   affectionate   brother,

"CEDRIC CLARE."

Alex was carried back through the years to the sense of remorse and bewilderment with which she had listened to the measured, irrefutable condemnations, expressed with the same unerring precision, of Sir Francis Clare. She realized herself again, sick with crying and cold with terror, standing shaking before his relentless justice, knowing herself to be again, for ever and hopelessly, in the wrong. She would never be anything else.

She knew it now.

Her sense of honour, of truth and justice, was perverted—in direct disaccord with that of the world. What would her brother say to her misuse of the money that he had entrusted to her? Alex knew now, with sudden, terrifying certainty how he would view the transaction which had seemed to her so simple an expedient. She knew that even were she able to make the almost incredible plea of a sudden temptation, a desperate need of money, that had led her voluntarily to commit an act of dishonesty, it would stand her in better stead than a mere statement of the terrible truth—that no voice within her had told her of dishonour, that she had—outrageous paradox!—committed an act of dishonesty in good faith.

To Cedric, the lack in her would seem so utterly perverted, so incomprehensible, that there would appear to be no possibility of that forgiveness which, as a Christian, he could consciously have extended to any wilful breaking of the law. But there would be no question of forgiveness for this. It was not the money, Alex knew that. It was her own extraordinary moral deficiency that put her outside the pale.

Perhaps, thought Alex drearily, this was how criminals always felt. They did the things for which they were punished because of some flaw in their mental outlook—they didn't see that the things mattered, until it was too late. They had to be saved from themselves by punishment or removal, or sometimes by death; and for the protection of the rest of the community, too, it was necessary to penalize those who could not or would not conform to the standard. Alex saw it all.

But dimly, involuntarily almost, an echo from her childhood's days came back to her, vaguely formulated into words:

"*Always take the part of the people in the wrong—they need it most.*"

The only conviction to which she could lay claim was somehow embodied in that sentiment.

XXVIII
Cedric

She wrote to Cedric, the sense of having put herself irrevocably in the wrong by her own act making her explanation into an utterly bald, lifeless statement of fact. She felt entirely unable to enter into any analysis of her folly, and besides, it would have been of no use. Facts were facts. She had taken Cedric's money, which he had given her for one purpose, and used it for another. There had not even been any violent struggle with temptation to palliate the act.

Alex felt a sort of dazed stupefaction at herself.

She was bad, she told herself, bad all through, and this was how bad people felt. Sick with disappointment, and utterly unavailing remorse, knowing all the time that there was no strength in them ever to resist any temptation, however base.

She wondered if there was a hell, as the convent teaching had so definitely told her. If so, Alex shudderingly contemplated her doom. But she prayed desperately that there might be nothing after death but utter oblivion. It was then that the thought of death first came to her, not with the wild, impotent longing of her days of struggle, but with an insidious suggestion of rest and escape.

She played with the idea, but for the most part her faculties were absorbed in the increasing strain of waiting for Cedric's reply to her confession.

It came in the shape of a telegram.

"Shall be in London Wednesday 24th. Will you lunch Clevedon Square 1.30. Reply paid."

Alex felt an unreasonable relief, both at the postponement of an immediate crisis, and at the reflection that, at all events, Cedric did not mean to come to Malden Road. She did not want him to see those strange, sordid surroundings to which she had fled from the shelter of her old home.

Alex telegraphed an affirmative reply to her brother, and waited in growing apathy for the interview, which she could now only dread in theory. Her sense of feeling seemed numbed at last.

Something of the old terror, however, revived when she confronted Cedric again in the library. He greeted her with a sort of kindly seriousness, under which she wonderingly detected a certain nervousness. During lunch they spoke of Violet, of the shooting that Cedric had been enjoying in Scotland. The slight shade of pomposity which recalled Sir Francis was always discernible in all Cedric's kindly courtesy as host. After lunch he rather ceremoniously ushered his sister into the library again.

"Sit down, my dear you look tired. You don't smoke, I know. D'you mind if I—?"

He drew at his pipe once or twice, then carefully rammed the tobacco more tightly into the bowl with a nicotine-stained finger. Still gazing at the wedged black mass, he said in a voice of careful unconcern:

"About this move of yours, Alex. Violet and I couldn't altogether understand—That's really what brought me down, and the question of that cheque I gave you for the servants. I couldn't quite make out your letter—"

He paused, as though to give her an opportunity for speech, still looking away from her. But Alex remained silent, in a sort of paralysis.

"Suppose we take one question at a time," suggested Cedric pleasantly. "The cheque affair is, of course, a very small one, and quite easily cleared up. One only has to be scrupulous in money matters because they *are* money matters—you know father's way of thinking, and I must say I entirely share it."

There was no need to tell Alex so.

"Have you got the cheque with you, Alex?"

"No," said Alex at last. "Didn't you understand my letter, then?"

Cedric's spectacles began to tap slowly against the back of his left hand, held in the loose grasp of his right.

"You—er—cashed that cheque?"

"Yes."

Alex felt as though she were being put to the torture of the Inquisition, but was utterly unable to do more than reply in monosyllables to Cedric's level, judicial questions.

"May I ask to what purpose you applied the money?"

"Cedric, it's not fair!" broke from Alex. "I've written and told you what I did—I needed money, and I—I thought you wouldn't mind. I used it for myself—and I meant to write and tell you—"

"You thought I wouldn't mind!" repeated Cedric in tones of stupefaction.

"You said you would advance me money—I knew you could write another cheque for the servants' wages. I—I didn't think of your minding."

"Mind!" said Cedric again, with reiteration worthy of his nursery days. "My dear girl, you don't suppose it's the money I mind, do you?"

"No, no—I ought to have asked you first—but I didn't think—it seemed a natural thing to do—"

"Good Lord, Alex!" cried Cedric, more moved than she had ever seen him. "Do you understand what you're saying? A natural thing to do to *embezzle money*?"

Tears of terror and of utter bewilderment seized on Alex' enfeebled powers, and deprived her of utterance.

Cedric began to pace the library, speaking rapidly and without looking at her.

"If you'd only written and told me what you'd done at once—though Heaven knows that would have been bad enough but to do a thing like that and then let it rest! Didn't you know that it *must* be found out sooner or later?"

He cast a fleeting glance at Alex, who sat with the tears pouring down her quivering face, but she said nothing. It was of no use to explain to Cedric that she had never thought of not being found out. She had meant no concealment. She had thought her action so simple a one that it had hardly needed explanation or justification. It had merely been not worth while to write.

Cedric's voice went on, gradually gaining in power as the agitation that had shaken him subsided under his own fluency.

"You know that it's a prosecutable offence, Alex? Of course, there's no question of such a thing, but to trade on that certainty—"

Alex made an inarticulate sound.

"Violet says of course you didn't know what you were doing. That wretched place—that convent—has played havoc with you altogether. When I think of those people—!" Cedric's face darkened. "But hang it, Alex, you were brought up like the rest of us. And on a question of honour—think of father!"

Alex had stopped crying. She was about to make her last stand, with the last strength that in her lay.

"Cedric—listen to me. You must! You don't understand. I didn't look at it from your point of view—I didn't see it like that. There's something wrong with me—there must be—but it didn't seem to me to matter. I know you won't believe me—but I thought the money was quite a little, unimportant thing, and that you'd understand, and say I'd done right to take it for granted that I might have it."

"But it's *not* the money!" groaned Cedric. "Though what on earth you wanted it for, when you had no expenses and your allowance just paid in—But that's not the point. Can't you see, Alex? It's not this wretched cheque in itself; it's the principle of the thing."

Alex gazed at him quite hopelessly. The flickering spark of spirit died out and left her soul in darkness.

Cedric faced her.

"I couldn't believe that your letter really meant what it seemed to mean," he said slowly; "but if it does—as on your own showing it does—then I understand your leaving us, needless to say. Where are you living—what is this place, Malden Road?"

Characteristically, he drew out her letter, and referred to the address carefully.

"Where is Malden Road?"

"In Hampstead—near Barbara."

"Are you in rooms?"

"Yes."

"How did you find them? Who recommended them?"

She made no answer, and Cedric gazed at her with an expression of half-angry, half-compassionate perplexity.

"You are entitled to keep your own counsel, of course, and to make your own arrangements, but I must say, Alex, that the thought of you disturbs me very much. Your whole position is unusual—and your attitude makes it almost impossible to—" He broke off. "Violet begged me—quite unnecessarily, but you know what she is—not to let you feel as though there were any estrangement—to say that whatever arrangement you preferred should be made. Of course, Pamela's marriage will add to your resources—you understand that? She is marrying an extremely wealthy man, and I shall have not the slightest hesitation in allowing her to make over her share of father's money to you as soon as it can be arranged. She wishes it herself."

He paused, as though for some expression of gratitude from Alex, but she made none. Pam had everything, and now she was to have the credit and pleasure of a generosity which would cost her nothing as well. Alex maintained a bitter silence.

"The obvious course is for you to join Barbara, paying your half of expenses, as you will now be enabled to do."

"Barbara doesn't want me."

"It is the natural arrangement," repeated Cedric inflexibly. "And I must add, Alex, that you seem to me to be terribly unfitted to manage your own life in any way. If what you have told me is the case, I can only infer that your moral sense is completely perverted. I couldn't have believed it of one of us—of one of my father's children."

Alex knew that the bed-rock of Cedric's character was reached. She had come to the point where, for Cedric, right and wrong began and ended—honour.

They would never get any nearer to one another now. The fundamental principle which governed life for Cedric was deficient in Alex.

She got up slowly and began to pull on her shabby gloves.

"Will you forgive me, Cedric?" she half sobbed.

"It isn't a question of forgiveness. Of course I will. But if you'd only asked me for that wretched money, Alex! What you did was to embezzle—it neither more nor less. Oh, good Lord!"

He looked at her with fresh despair and then rang the bell.

"You're going to have a taxi," he told her authoritatively. "You're not fit to go any other way. Alex, my dear, I'd give my right hand for this not to have happened—for Heaven's sake come to me if you want anything. How much shall I give you now?"

He unlocked the writing-table drawer agitatedly. Alex thought to herself hysterically, "He thinks I may *steal* money, perhaps, from somebody else, if I want it, and *perhaps I should*." And with a sense of degradation that made her feel physically sick, she put into her purse the gold and the pile of silver that he pushed into her hand.

Cedric straightened himself, and taking off his glasses, wiped them carefully.

"Write to me, Alex, and let me know What you want to do. Barbara will be back soon—you *must* go to her—at any rate for a time—till after Pamela's wedding. You know that's fixed for December now? And, my dear, for Heaven's sake let's forget this ghastly business. No one on this earth but you and I and Violet need ever know of it."

"No," said Alex.

She looked at him with despair invading her whole being.

"Good-bye, Cedric. You've been very, very kind to me."

"The taxi is at the door, sir."

"Thank you."

Cedric took his sister into the hall, and she gave a curious, fleeting glance round her at the familiar surroundings, and at the broad staircase where the Clare children had run up and down and played and quarrelled together, in that other existence.

"Good-bye, dear. Write your plans, and come and see us as soon as we get back. It won't be more than a week or two now."

Cedric put her into the waiting taxi, and stood on the steps looking after her as the cab turned out of Clevedon Square. And Alex, crouched into a corner of the swiftly-moving taxi, knew herself capable of any treachery, any moral infamy to which she might be tempted, since Cedric had been right when he said that her sense of honour, of fundamental rectitude, was completely perverted.

XXIX
Forgiveness

The weather broke suddenly, and it became cold and rainy. For two or three days Alex sat in her sitting-room at Malden Road and heard the trams and the omnibuses clash past, and the children screaming to one another in the street. She could hardly have said when she had first realized that it was impossible for her to go on living. But the determination, now that it was there, full-grown, had brought with it a sense of utter finality.

For two or three days she felt stunned, and yet driven by a desperate feeling that it was necessary for her to think, to make a plan. But she could not think.

Then one evening Mrs. Hoxton, the landlady, said to her curiously:

"Wouldn't you like a fire, tonight?" She seldom said "Miss" in speaking to Alex. "It's so chilly, all of a sudden, and you look ill, really, now, you do."

Alex felt rather surprised. Perhaps she was ill, which would account for the impossibility of consecutive thought. A fire would be very nice. She shivered involuntarily, looking at her little empty grate crammed with cut paper. She remembered that there was no need to consider expense any more.

"Yes, I'd like a fire, please," she said gently. And that evening she sat close to the pleasant blaze, flickering on the wall, and dimly recalling to her the nursery at Clevedon Square in the old days, and the power of thought came back to her.

It was as though the warmth and companionship of the flames had suddenly unsealed something frozen up within her, and she became more herself than she had been for many months. With the horrible, pressing dread of an unbearable present and an unimaginable future lifted from her heart, Alex felt a pervading lucidity of thought, to which she had for years been a stranger, take possession of her. She knew suddenly that she was, for a little while, to regain faculties that had been atrophied within her since the far, free days of her girlhood. She began to reflect.

Why had life, to which she had looked forward so eagerly, with such confident anticipation of some wonderful happiness, which should be in proportion to the immense capacity for realizing it which she knew to exist within her, have proved to be only a succession of defeats, of receding hopes and of unfulfilled desires?

Alex did not question that the fault lay with herself. From her baby days, under the unvarnished plain speaking of old Nurse, she had known herself to be the black sheep of every flock. And she had not sinned splendidly, dramatically, either. Her sins had been those of petty meanness, of shirking and evading, of small self-indulgences and childish tyranny at the expense of others, of vulgar lies and half-truths.

Those sins which find little or no place in the decalogue, and which stand lowest in the scale by which the opinion of others is meted out to us.

Those are the things which are not forgiven. That was it, Alex told herself, with a feeling of having suddenly struck the keynote. Forgiveness.

Forgiveness was the key to everything. Alex, in the sudden surety of vision that had come to her, did not doubt that her own interpretation of the word was the right one. Forgiveness meant understanding—not condemnation and subsequent pardon. It did not mean the bewildered, scandalized, and yet regretful oblivion to which Cedric would consign her memory and that of her many failings, it did not mean Barbara's detached, indifferent kindness, carefully measured in terms of material resources, nor Pamela's and Archie's good-natured patronage, half-stifled in mirth, of which the very object was the gulf that separated them from their sister. It did not even mean Violet's soft pity and unresentful acceptance of facts that amazed her. Looking further back, Alex knew that it did not mean either the serious, perplexed pardon that Sir Francis had tendered to his troublesome daughter, or Lady Isabel's half-complaining, half-affectionate remonstrances.

It did not in any way occur to her to blame them for a lack of which she had all her life been subconsciously aware in all their forbearance. She told herself, with a fresh sense of enlightenment, that they had not understood because it was in none of them to have yielded to those temptations which had beset and mastered her so easily. Measuring her frailty by their own strength, they had only seen her utter failure in resistance, and been shamed and grieved by it. Alex knew that in herself was another standard of forgiveness; she could never condemn, for the simple reason that she herself had failed, in every sense of the word. Unresentfully, she was able to sum it all up, as it were, when she told herself, "People who would have resisted temptation themselves, can't understand those who fall—so they can't really forgive. But the bad ones, who know that they have given way all along the line, know that any temptation would have been too strong for them—it's only chance whether it comes their way or not—so they can understand."

She felt oddly contented, as at having reached a solution.

Later on, her thoughts turned to the past again, and to the childish days when she had been the leading spirit in the Clevedon Square nursery. But the memory of that past, incredible, security and assurance, made her begin to cry, and she wiped away blinding tears and told herself that she must not give way to them. She did not at first quite know why she must reserve the tiny modicum of strength still left her, but presently she realized that the end which had become inevitable could not be reached without decisive action of her own.

Alex' logic was elementary, and its directness left her no loophole for doubt.

She could endure the plane of existence on which she found herself no longer. If she fled in search of other conditions, it was with full certainty that these could not be less tolerable than those from which she was flying, and at the back of her mind was a strange, growing hope that perhaps that forgiveness of which her mind was full, might be found beyond the veil.

"After all," thought Alex, "it's even chances. If religion is all true, then I *must* go to hell, whether I kill myself or not, and if it isn't, then perhaps I shall just go out and know nothing more—ever—or perhaps it will be really a new beginning, and there will be somebody or something who will forgive me, and let me start over again."

She began to feel rather excited, as though she were about to try an experiment that might best be described as a gamble.

Mrs. Hoxton, coming in with the small supper-tray, looked at her sharply two or three times, and when she had gone away again, Alex, turning to the glass, saw that her eyes were shining and looking enormously large and wide-pupilled.

"I believe I am happy tonight," she thought wonderingly.

While she ate her supper she tried to make a plan, but the excitement within her was growing steadily, and she could only think out eager self-justification for her own decision.

"It won't hurt any one else—nobody will mind. In fact, when they've got over the first shock, it will be a relief to them all. They've been very kind—Violet and Cedric—Violet most of all—but they haven't understood. They'd have understood better if I'd been a bad woman—lived with wicked men, or things like that. I suppose I should have done that too, if it had come my way—but then I never had the temptation. I had only little, mean, horrible temptations—and I didn't resist any of them. The other sort of sin would have made me happier—it would have meant a sort of success in a way—but I have been a failure at everything—always."

Her heart hammering against her side, Alex resolved that in this, her last disgrace, she would not fail.

Making no preparations, no written farewells, she rose presently and went to her room, where she put on her thickest coat and tied a woollen scarf over her head.

Then she went out.

It had stopped raining, and the air was soft and moist. It was a starless night, and when Alex got to the Heath and away from the lighted streets, it was very dark. Underneath her sense of adventure she was conscious of terror—sheer physical terror—and also of the deeper dread that her resolution might fail her.

"I mustn't—I mustn't," she kept on muttering to herself.

Then, as though reassuring somebody else, "But it's only like going for a journey—to a quite new place where everything may be different and much, much better ... or else to sleep, and never any waking up to misery again.... Just one dreadful minute or two, perhaps, and then it will all be over ... only a question of a little physical courage ... not to struggle ... like taking gas ... much easier if one doesn't struggle...."

She was struck by a sudden thought and said aloud, triumphantly, as though she were defeating by her inspiration some one who was urging difficulties upon her:

"I won't give myself any chances. I'll put big stones in my pocket and tie my scarf over my mouth. That'll make it quicker, too."

When she came to the part of the Heath where the water lay, Alex began to stoop down and hunt for stones. She pounced on each one that seemed larger than its fellows with a sense of pride at her own success, and put them into the pockets of her coat. The moon appeared palely through clouds and then disappeared again, but not before she had taken her bearings.

She was on one of the many wide bridges that span the long pools dotted over the Heath—pools shelving at the sides with an effect of shallowness and deepening suddenly in the middle. Alex threw an indifferent glance at the dark water, and only felt annoyance that so few stones should be loose upon the pathway, and none of them very large ones. When her pockets were filled, she did not think the weight very noticeable.

Then came another evanescent gleam of moonlight, and Alex, still with that sharpening of all her perceptions, noticed that there was a man's figure at the far end of the bridge. He appeared to be stationary, leaning on the parapet and gazing down at the almost invisible pond.

She was conscious of vexation. His presence would surely interfere with her scheme.

For a moment she wondered, detachedly enough, whether she should go away and come back the following evening. But the next instant she recoiled from the thought, as though seeing in it the promptings of her own weakness.

"I am not frightened tonight—at least, hardly at all. If I wait I may never feel like this again. I shall make a failure of it all, and that would be worse than anything. I must do it tonight, while I'm not frightened."

She was not cold. Walking in her heavy coat had warmed her, and the evening was mild as well as damp. So she waited quietly in the shadow, hoping that the man would presently move away.

The thought crossed her mind, with a certain humour, that the situation held possibilities of romance.

"If it were in a book, he would save me at the last minute and fall in love with me and it would all end happily. Or he would see me now, and perhaps speak to me, and he would understand all I told him, and persuade me not to. Anyhow, it would all come right."

She smiled in the darkness.

"But that won't happen to *me*. There never was any one—and nobody would love me now, especially when they knew all about me." She remembered the haggard, distorted countenance that the looking-glass had shown her—the great, starting eyes with discoloured circles beneath them, and the blackened, prominent teeth, more salient than ever from the thinness of her face.

She could almost have laughed, without any conscious bitterness, at the idea of any romance in connection with her present self.

And yet the girl, Alex Clare, could have loved—had looked forward to love and to happiness as her rights, just as Pamela Clare did now.

But Pamela was different. Every one was—No!

It was Alex that was different—that had always been different.

She began to feel less warm, and shivered a little as she waited.

It occurred to her, not with any sense of fear, but with vexation, that her purpose would be far more difficult of achievement if she waited until she was physically chilled.

She looked up at the bridge again, and the figure was still there, at the furthest end. Alex measured the length of the bridge with her eyes.

It was doubtful if he would see her from the furthest end of it, but she reflected matter-of-factly:

"If I jump there will be the noise of a splash—and he might do something—he would try to save me, I suppose—or run for help. It wouldn't be safe. If he would *only* go."

She became irritated. With a sense of despair she determined to circumvent the motionless, watchful figure.

Moving very quietly and almost soundlessly over the soft muddy ground, Alex made her way from the path to the bank, and further and further down it till only a short declivity of shelving mud lay between her and the water.

She could feel the brambles catching in her thick coat as though pulling her back, but she went on, cautiously and steadily. Once or twice she pushed at the low, tangled bushes that impeded her progress, and paused aghast at the rustling that ensued. But from the bridge above her there came no sound.

Within a few steps of the dark water, her feet already sinking ankle-deep into the wet, spongy ground, she stopped.

She realized with wondering joy that, after all, she was not very much afraid. It was as though the self-confidence which had for so long deserted her had come back now to carry her through the last need.

She felt proud, because she knew that for this once she was not going to fail.

She talked to herself in a whisper:

"This one time—just a few minutes when it may be very bad—but remember that it can't last long, and then it'll all be over. And perhaps there'll never be anything more afterwards—like being always asleep, and no one need be vexed or disappointed any more. But perhaps—"

She paused on the thought, and her heart began to beat faster with a hopeful excitement such as she had not known for a very long while.

"Perhaps it will be much better than one imagines possible. Perhaps there'll be real forgiveness and understanding—and then my having done this won't matter. Anyway, I shall know very soon, if only I'm brave just for a few minutes."

She drew a long breath, then, instinctively stretching her arms straight out before her so as to balance herself, she began to move forward.

The first unmistakable touch of the water round her feet made her gasp and stifle a scream, but she waded on, encouraging herself in a low murmur, as though speaking to a child:

"It's only like going into the sea when one's bathing—pretend it's that, then you won't be frightened. Just straight on—it will be over quite soon—"

She was moving, slowly, but without pause, her hands held out in front of her, the ground still beneath her slipping feet, which felt oddly weighted. Once she began to pull the woollen scarf over her mouth, but with the sense of breathlessness came the beginning of panic, and she tore it away again.

"Go on—coward—coward," she urged herself. "Remember what it would mean to make another muddle of this, and to fail."

The cold invaded her body and her teeth began to chatter.

For an instant she stood, surrounded by the silent water, cold and terror and the weight of her now sodden clothing paralysing her, so that she could move neither backwards to the shore nor forward into the blackness in front of her.

"I must," muttered Alex, and wrenched one foot desperately out of the mud below. With the forward movement, she lost her balance, and her hands clutched instinctively at the water's level. Then the clogging bottom of the pond sheered away suddenly from beneath her, and there was only water, dark and icy and rushing, above and below and all round her.

XXX
Epitaph

They sat round, afterwards, in the Clevedon Square drawing-room—all the people who had helped misguided, erring Alex, according to their lights, or again, according to their limitations, and who had failed her so completely in the ultimate essential.

Pamela and her lover whispered together in the window.

"After all, you know," hesitated the girl, "she had nothing much to live for, poor Alex. She'd got out of touch with all of us—and she had no one of her very own."

"Not like us."

His hand closed for an instant over hers.

"There was no reason why she should not have come to us if—if she was in money difficulties," reiterated Cedric uneasily. He consciously refrained from adding "again."

Violet was crying softly, lying back in the depths of a great arm-chair.

"Poor Alex! I never guessed Malden Road was like that. Why *did* she go there? Oh, poor Alex!"

"You were nicer to her than any of us, Violet," said Archie gruffly. "She was awfully fond of you, wasn't she, and of the little kid?"

Barbara, hard and self-contained, gazed round the familiar room. For a moment it seemed to her that they were all children again, sent down from the nursery by old Nurse, on Lady Isabel's "At Home" afternoon.

Her eyes met those of Cedric, who had taken up his stand against the mantelpiece, in his hand his glasses, which he was shaking with little, judicial jerks.

"Oh, Cedric," said Barbara with a sudden catch in her voice.

"Don't you remember—Alex was such a *pretty* little girl!"

London,   1917.
Bristol, 1918.

The Diary of a Provincial Lady

November 7th.—Plant the indoor bulbs. Just as I am in the middle of them, Lady Boxe calls. I say, untruthfully, how nice to see her, and beg her to sit down while I just finish the bulbs. Lady B. makes determined attempt to sit down in armchair where I have already placed two bulb-bowls and the bag of charcoal, is headed off just in time, and takes the sofa.

Do I know, she asks, how very late it is for indoor bulbs? September, really, or even October, is the time. Do I know that the only really reliable firm for hyacinths is Somebody of Haarlem? Cannot catch the name of the firm, which is Dutch, but reply Yes, I do know, but think it my duty to buy Empire products. Feel at the time, and still think, that this is an excellent reply. Unfortunately Vicky comes into the drawing-room later and says: "O Mummie, are those the bulbs we got at Woolworths?"

Lady B. stays to tea. (*Mem.*: Bread-and-butter too thick. Speak to Ethel.) We talk some more about bulbs, the Dutch School of Painting, our Vicar's wife, sciatica, and *All Quiet on the Western Front*.

(Query: Is it possible to cultivate the art of conversation when living in the country all the year round?)

Lady B. enquires after the children. Tell her that Robin—whom I refer to in a detached way as "the boy" so that she shan't think I am foolish about him—is getting on fairly well at school, and that Mademoiselle says Vicky is starting a cold.

Do I realise, says Lady B., that the Cold Habit is entirely unnecessary, and can be avoided by giving the child a nasal douche of salt-and-water every morning before breakfast? Think of several rather tart and witty rejoinders to this, but unfortunately not until Lady B.'s Bentley has taken her away.

Finish the bulbs and put them in the cellar. Feel that after all cellar is probably draughty, change my mind, and take them all up to the attic.

Cook says something is wrong with the range.

November 8th.—Robert has looked at the range and says nothing wrong whatever. Makes unoriginal suggestion about pulling out dampers. Cook very angry, and will probably give notice. Try to propitiate her by saying that we are going to Bournemouth for Robin's half-term, and that will give the household a rest. Cook replies austerely that they will take the opportunity to do some extra cleaning. Wish I could believe this was true.

Preparations for Bournemouth rather marred by discovering that Robert, in bringing down the suit-cases from the attic, has broken three of the bulb-bowls. Says he understood that I had put them in the cellar, and so wasn't expecting them.

November 11th.—Bournemouth. Find that history, as usual, repeats itself. Same hotel, same frenzied scurry round the school to find Robin, same collection of parents, most of them also staying at the hotel. Discover strong tendency to exchange with fellow-parents exactly the same remarks as last year, and the year before that. Speak of this to Robert, who returns no answer. Perhaps he is afraid of repeating himself? This suggests Query: Does Robert, perhaps, take in what I say even when he makes no reply?

Find Robin looking thin, and speak to Matron who says brightly, Oh no, she thinks on the whole he's put *on* weight this term, and then begins to talk about the New Buildings. (Query: Why do all schools have to run up New Buildings about once in every six months?)

Take Robin out. He eats several meals, and a good many sweets. He produces a friend, and we take both to Corfe Castle. The boys climb, Robert smokes in silence, and I sit about on stones. Overhear a woman remark, as she gazes up at half a tower, that has withstood several centuries, that This looks *fragile*—which strikes me as a singular choice of adjective. Same woman, climbing over a block of solid masonry, points out that This has evidently fallen off somewhere.

Take the boys back to the hotel for dinner. Robin says, whilst the friend is out of hearing: "It's been nice for us, taking out Williams, hasn't it?" Hastily express appreciation of this privilege.

Robert takes the boys back after dinner, and I sit in hotel lounge with several other mothers and we all talk about our boys in tones of disparagement, and about one another's boys with great enthusiasm.

Am asked what I think of *Harriet Hume* but am unable to say, as I have not read it. Have a depressed feeling that this is going to be another case of *Orlando* about which was perfectly able to talk most intelligently until I read it, and found myself unfortunately unable to understand any of it.

Robert comes up very late and says he must have dropped asleep over the *Times*. (Query: Why come to Bournemouth to do this?)

Postcard by the last post from Lady B. to ask if I have remembered that there is a Committee Meeting of the Women's Institute on the 14th. Should not dream of answering this.

November 12th.—Home yesterday and am struck, as so often before, by immense accumulation of domestic disasters that always await one after any absence. Trouble with kitchen range has resulted in no hot water, also Cook says the mutton has *gone*, and will I speak to the butcher, there being no excuse weather like this. Vicky's cold, unlike the mutton, hasn't gone. Mademoiselle says, "Ah, cette petite! Elle ne sera peut-être pas longtemps pour ce bas monde, madame." Hope that this is only her Latin way of dramatising the situation.

Robert reads the *Times* after dinner, and goes to sleep.

November 13th.—Interesting, but disconcerting, train of thought started by prolonged discussion with Vicky as to the existence or otherwise of a locality which she refers to throughout as H.E.L. Am determined to be a modern parent, and assure her that there is not, never has been, and never could be, such a place. Vicky maintains that there *is*, and refers me to the Bible. I become more modern than ever, and tell her that theories of eternal punishment were invented to frighten people. Vicky replies indignantly that they don't frighten her in the least, she *likes* to think about H.E.L. Feel that deadlock has been reached, and can only leave her to her singular method of enjoying herself.

(Query: Are modern children going to revolt against being modern, and if so, what form will reaction of modern parents take?)

Much worried by letter from the Bank to say that my account is overdrawn to the extent of Eight Pounds, four shillings, and fourpence. Cannot understand this, as was convinced that I still had credit balance of Two Pounds, seven shillings, and sixpence. Annoyed to find that my accounts, contents of cash-box, and counterfoils in cheque-book, do not tally. (*Mem.*: Find envelope on which I jotted down Bournemouth expenses, also little piece of paper (probably last leaf of grocer's book) with note about cash payment to sweep. This may clear things up.)

Take a look at bulb-bowls on returning suit-case to attic, and am inclined to think it looks as though the cat had been up here. If so, this will be the last straw. Shall tell Lady Boxe that I sent all my bulbs to a sick friend in a nursing-home.

November 14th.—Arrival of Book of the Month choice, and am disappointed. History of a place I am not interested in, by an author I do not like. Put it back into its wrapper again and make fresh choice from Recommended List. Find, on reading small literary bulletin enclosed with book, that exactly this course of procedure has been anticipated, and that it is described as being "the mistake of a lifetime". Am much annoyed, although not so much at having made (possibly) mistake of a lifetime, as at depressing thought of our all being so much alike that intelligent writers can apparently predict our behaviour with perfect accuracy.

Decide not to mention any of this to Lady B., always so tiresomely superior about Book of the Month as it is, taking up attitude that she does not require to be told what to read. (Should like to think of good repartee to this.)

Letter by second post from my dear old school-friend Cissie Crabbe, asking if she may come here for two nights or so on her way to Norwich. (Query: Why Norwich? Am surprised to realise that anybody ever goes to, lives at, or comes from, Norwich, but quite see that this is unreasonable of me. Remind myself how very little one knows of the England one lives in, which vaguely suggests a quotation. This, however, does not materialise.)

Many years since we last met, writes Cissie, and she expects we have both *changed* a good deal. P.S. Do I remember the dear old pond, and the day of the Spanish Arrowroot. Can recall, after some thought, dear old *pond*, at bottom of Cissie's father's garden, but am completely baffled by Spanish Arrowroot. (Query: Could this be one of the Sherlock Holmes stories? Sounds like it.)

Reply that we shall be delighted to see her, and what a lot we shall have to talk about, after all these years! (This, I find on reflection, is not true, but cannot re-write letter on that account.) Ignore Spanish Arrowroot altogether.

Robert, when I tell him about dear old school-friend's impending arrival, does not seem pleased. Asks what we are expected to *do* with her. I suggest showing her the garden, and remember too late that this is hardly the right time of the year. At any rate, I say, it will be nice to talk over old times—(which reminds me of the Spanish Arrowroot reference still unfathomed).

Speak to Ethel about the spare room, and am much annoyed to find that one blue candlestick has been broken, and the bedside rug has gone to the cleaners, and cannot be retrieved in time. Take away bedside rug from Robert's dressing-room, and put it in spare room instead, hoping he will not notice its absence.

November 15th.—Robert does notice absence of rug, and says he must have it back again. Return it to dressing-room and take small and inferior dyed mat from the night-nursery to put in spare room. Mademoiselle is hurt about this and says to Vicky, who repeats it to me, that in this country she finds herself treated like a worm.

November 17th.—Dear old school-friend Cissie Crabbe due by the three o'clock train. On telling Robert this, he says it is most inconvenient to meet her, owing to Vestry Meeting, but eventually agrees to abandon Vestry Meeting. Am touched. Unfortunately, just after he has started, telegram arrives to say that dear old school-friend has missed the connection and will not arrive until seven o'clock. This means putting off dinner till eight, which Cook won't like. Cannot send message to kitchen by Ethel, as it is her afternoon out, so am obliged to tell Cook myself. She is not pleased. Robert returns from station, not pleased either. Mademoiselle, quite inexplicably, says, "Il ne manquait que ca!" (This comment wholly unjustifiable, as non-appearance of Cissie Crabbe cannot concern her in any way. Have often thought that the French are tactless.)

Ethel returns, ten minutes late, and says Shall she light fire in spare room? I say No, it is not cold enough—but really mean that Cissie is no longer, in my opinion, deserving of luxuries. Subsequently feel this to be unworthy attitude, and light fire myself. It smokes.

Robert calls up to know What is that Smoke? I call down that It is Nothing. Robert comes up and opens the window and shuts the door and says It will Go all right Now. Do not like to point out that the open window will make the room cold.

Play Ludo with Vicky in drawing-room.

Robert reads the *Times* and goes to sleep, but wakes in time to make second expedition to the station. Thankful to say that this time he returns with Cissie Crabbe, who has put on weight, and says several times that she supposes we have both *changed* a good deal, which I consider unnecessary.

Take her upstairs—spare room like an icehouse, owing to open window, and fire still smoking, though less—She says room is delightful, and I leave her, begging her to ask for anything she wants—(*Mem.*: tell Ethel she *must* answer spare room bell if it rings—Hope it won't.)

Ask Robert while dressing for dinner what he thinks of Cissie. He says he has not known her long enough to judge. Ask if he thinks her good-looking. He says he has not thought about it. Ask what they talked about on the way from the station. He says he does not remember.

November 19th.—Last two days very, very trying, owing to quite unexpected discovery that Cissie Crabbe is strictly on a diet. This causes Robert to take a dislike to her. Utter impossibility of obtaining lentils or lemons at short notice makes housekeeping unduly difficult. Mademoiselle in the middle of lunch insists on discussing diet question, and several times exclaims: "Ah, mon doux St. Joseph!" which I consider profane, and beg her never to repeat.

Consult Cissie about the bulbs, which look very much as if the mice had been at them. She says: Unlimited Watering, and tells me about her own bulbs at Norwich. Am discouraged.

Administer Unlimited Water to the bulbs (some of which goes through the attic floor on to the landing below), and move half of them down to the cellar, as Cissie Crabbe says attic is airless.

Our Vicar's wife calls this afternoon. Says she once knew someone who had relations living near Norwich, but cannot remember their name. Cissie Crabbe replies that very likely if we knew their name we might find she'd heard of them, or even *met* them. We agree that the world is a small place. Talk about the Riviera, the new waist-line, choir-practice, the servant question, and Ramsay MacDonald.

November 22nd.—Cissie Crabbe leaves. Begs me in the kindest way to stay with her in Norwich (where she has already told me that she lives in a bed-sitting-room with two cats, and cooks her own lentils on a gas-ring). I say Yes, I should love to. We part effusively.

Spend entire morning writing the letters I have had to leave unanswered during Cissie's visit.

Invitation from Lady Boxe to us to dine and meet distinguished literary friends staying with her, one of whom is the author of *Symphony in Three Sexes*. Hesitate to write back and say that I have never heard of *Symphony in Three Sexes*, so merely accept. Ask for *Symphony in Three Sexes* at the library, although doubtfully. Doubt more than justified by tone in which Mr. Jones replies that it is not in stock, and never has been.

Ask Robert whether he thinks I had better wear my Blue or my Black-and-gold at Lady B.'s. He says that either will do. Ask if he can remember which one I wore last time. He cannot. Mademoiselle says it was the Blue, and offers to make slight alterations to Black-and-gold which will, she says, render it unrecognisable. I accept, and she cuts large pieces out of the back of it. I say: "Pas trop décolletée," and she replies intelligently: "Je comprends, Madame ne desire pas se voir nue au salon."

(Query: Have not the French sometimes a very strange way of expressing themselves, and will this react unfavourably on Vicky?)

Tell Robert about the distinguished literary friends, but do not mention *Symphony in Three Sexes*. He makes no answer.

Have absolutely decided that if Lady B. should introduce us to distinguished literary friends, or anyone else, as Our Agent, and Our Agent's Wife, I shall at once leave the house.

Tell Robert this. He says nothing. (*Mem.*: Put evening shoes out of window to see if fresh air will remove smell of petrol.)

November 25th.—Go and get hair cut and have manicure in the morning, in honour of Lady B.'s dinner party. Should like new pair of evening stockings, but depressing communication from Bank, still maintaining that I am overdrawn, prevents this, also rather unpleasantly worded letter from Messrs. Frippy and Coleman requesting payment of overdue account by return of post. Think better not to mention this to Robert, as bill for coke arrived yesterday, also reminder that Rates are much overdue, therefore write civilly to Messrs. F. and C. to the effect that cheque follows in a few days. (Hope they may think I have temporarily mislaid cheque-book.)

Black-and-gold as rearranged by Mademoiselle very satisfactory, but am obliged to do my hair five times owing to wave having been badly set. Robert unfortunately comes in just as I am using bran-new and expensive lip-stick, and objects strongly to result.

(Query: If Robert could be induced to go to London rather oftener, would he perhaps take broader view of these things?)

Am convinced we are going to be late, as Robert has trouble in getting car to start, but he refuses to be agitated. Am bound to add that subsequent events justify this attitude, as we arrive before anybody else, also before Lady B. is down. Count at least a dozen Roman hyacinths growing in bowls all over the drawing-room. (Probably grown by one of the gardeners, whatever Lady B. may say. Resolve not to comment on them in any way, but am conscious that this is slightly ungenerous.)

Lady B. comes down wearing silver lace frock that nearly touches the floor all round, and has new waist-line. This may or not be becoming, but has effect of making everybody else's frock look out-of-date.

Nine other people present besides ourselves, most of them staying in house. Nobody is introduced. Decide that a lady in what looks like blue tapestry is probably responsible for *Symphony in Three Sexes*.

Just as dinner is announced Lady B. murmurs to me: "I've put you next to Sir William. He's interested in *water-supplies*, you know, and I thought you'd like to talk to him about local conditions."

Find, to my surprise, that Sir W. and I embark almost at once on the subject of Birth Control. Why or how this topic presents itself cannot say at all, but greatly prefer it to water-supplies. On the other side of the table, Robert is sitting next to *Symphony in Three Sexes*. Hope he is enjoying himself.

Conversation becomes general. Everybody (except Robert) talks about books. We all say (a) that we have read *The Good Companions*, (b) that it is a very *long* book, (c) that it was chosen by the Book of the Month Club in America and must be having immense sales, and (d) that American sales are What Really Count. We then turn to *High Wind in Jamaica* and say (a) that it is quite a short book, (b) that we hated—or, alternatively, adored—it, and (c) that it Really*Is* exactly *Like* Children. A small minority here surges into being, and maintains No, they Cannot Believe that any children in the World wouldn't ever have *noticed* that John wasn't there any more. They can swallow everything else, they say, but not *that*. Discussion very active indeed. I talk to pale young man with horn-rimmed glasses, sitting at my left-hand, about Jamaica, where neither of us has ever been. This leads—but cannot say how—to stag-hunting, and eventually to homeopathy. (*Mem.*: Interesting, if time permitted, to trace train of thought leading on from one topic to another. Second, and most disquieting idea: perhaps no such train of thought exists.) Just as we reach interchange of opinions about growing cucumbers under glass, Lady B. gets up.

Go into the drawing-room, and all exclaim how nice it is to see the fire. Room very cold. (Query: Is this good for the bulbs?) Lady in blue tapestry takes down her hair, which she says she is growing, and puts it up again. We all begin to talk about hair. Depressed to find that everybody in the world, except apparently myself, has grown, or is growing, long hair again. Lady B. says that Nowadays, there Isn't a Shingled Head to be seen *anywhere*, either in London, Paris, or New York. Nonsense.

Discover, in the course of the evening, that the blue tapestry has nothing whatever to do with literature, but is a Government Sanitary Inspector, and that *Symphony in Three Sexes* was written by pale young man with glasses. Lady B. says, Did I get him on to the subject of *perversion*, as he is always so amusing about it? I reply evasively.

Men come in, and all herded into billiard room (just as drawing-room seems to be getting slightly warmer) where Lady B. inaugurates unpleasant game of skill with billiard balls, involving possession of a Straight Eye, which most of us do not possess. Robert does well at this. Am thrilled, and feel it to be more satisfactory way of acquiring distinction than even authorship of *Symphony in Three Sexes*.

Congratulate Robert on the way home, but he makes no reply.

November 26th.—Robert says at breakfast that he thinks we are no longer young enough for late nights.

Frippy and Coleman regret that they can no longer allow account to stand over, but must request favour of a cheque by return, or will be compelled, with utmost regret, to take Further Steps. Have written to Bank to transfer Six Pounds, thirteen shillings, and tenpence from Deposit Account to Current. (This leaves Three Pounds, seven shillings, and twopence, to keep Deposit Account open.) Decide to put off paying milk book till next month, and to let cleaners have something on account instead of full settlement. This enables me to send F. and C. cheque, post-dated Dec. 1st, when allowance becomes due. Financial instability very trying.

November 28th.—Receipt from F. and C. assuring me of attention to my future wishes—but evidently far from realising magnitude of effort involved in setting myself straight with them.

December 1st.—Cable from dear Rose saying she lands at Tilbury on 10th. Cable back welcome, and will meet her Tilbury, 10th. Tell Vicky that her godmother, my dearest friend, is returning home after three years in America. Vicky says: "Oh, will she have a present for me?" Am disgusted with her mercenary attitude and complain to Mademoiselle, who replies: "Si la Sainte Vierge revenait sur la terre, madame, ce serait notre petite Vicky." Do not at all agree with this. Moreover, in other moods Mademoiselle first person to refer to Vicky as "ce petit demon enrage".

(Query: Are the Latin races always as sincere as one would wish them to be?)

December 3rd.—Radio from dear Rose, landing Plymouth 8th after all. Send return message, renewed welcomes, and will meet her Plymouth.

Robert adopts unsympathetic attitude and says This is Waste of Time and Money. Do not know if he means cables, or journey to meet ship, but feel sure better not to enquire. Shall go to Plymouth on 7th. (*Mem.*: Pay grocer's book before I go, and tell him last lot of gingernuts were soft. Find out first if Ethel kept tin properly shut.)

December 8th.—Plymouth. Arrived last night, terrific storm, ship delayed. Much distressed at thought of Rose, probably suffering severe sea-sickness. Wind howls round hotel, which shakes, rain lashes against window-pane all night. Do not like my room and have unpleasant idea that someone may have committed a murder in it. Mysterious door in corner which I feel conceals a corpse. Remember all the stories I have read to this effect, and cannot, sleep. Finally open mysterious door and find large cupboard, but no corpse. Go back to bed again.

Storm worse than ever in the morning, am still more distressed at thought of Rose, who will probably have to be carried off ship in state of collapse.

Go round to Shipping Office and am told to be on docks at ten o'clock. Having had previous experience of this, take fur coat, camp-stool, and copy of *American Tragedy* as being longest book I can find, and camp myself on docks. Rain stops. Other people turn up and look enviously at camp-stool. Very old lady in black totters up and down till I feel guilty, and offer to give up camp-stool to her. She replies: "Thank you, thank you, but my Daimler is outside, and I can sit in that when I wish to do so."

Return to *American Tragedy* feeling discouraged.

Find *American Tragedy* a little oppressive, but read on and on for about two hours when policeman informs me that tender is about to start for ship, if I wish to go on board. Remove self, camp-stool, and *American Tragedy* to tender. Read for forty minutes. (Mem.: Ask Rose if American life is really like that.)

Very, very unpleasant half-hour follows. Camp-stool shows tendency to slide about all over the place, and am obliged to abandon *American Tragedy* for the time being.

Numbers of men of seafaring aspect walk about and look at me. One of them asks Am I a good sailor? No, I am not. Presently ship appears, apparently suddenly rising up from the middle of the waves, and ropes are dangled in every direction. Just as I catch sight of Rose, tender is carried away from ship's side by colossal waves.

Consoled by reflection that Rose is evidently not going to require carrying on shore, but presently begin to feel that boot, as they say, may be on the other leg.

More waves, more ropes, and tremendous general activity.

I return to camp-stool, but have no strength left to cope with *American Tragedy*. A man in oilskins tells me I am In the Way there, Miss.

Remove myself, camp-stool, and *American Tragedy* to another corner. A man in sea-boots says that If I stay there, I may get Badly Knocked About.

Renewed déménagement of self, camp-stool, *American Tragedy*. Am slightly comforted by having been called "Miss".

Catch glimpse of Rose from strange angles as tender heaves up and down. Gangway eventually materialises, and self, camp-stool, and *American Tragedy* achieve the ship. Realise too late that camp-stool and *American Tragedy* might equally well have remained where they were.

Dear Rose most appreciative of effort involved by coming to meet her, but declares herself perfectly good sailor, and slept all through last night's storm. Try hard not to feel unjustly injured about this.

December 9th.—Rose staying here two days before going on to London. Says All American houses are Always Warm, which annoys Robert. He says in return that All American houses are Grossly Overheated and Entirely Airless. Impossible not to feel that this would carry more weight if Robert had ever been to America. Rose also very insistent about efficiency of American Telephone Service, and inclined to ask for glasses of cold water at breakfast time—which Robert does not approve of.

Otherwise dear Rose entirely unchanged and offers to put me up in her West-End flat as often as I like to come to London. Accept gratefully. (*N.B.* How very different to old school-friend Cissie Crabbe, with bed-sitting-room and gas-ring in Norwich! But should not like to think myself in any way a snob.)

On Rose's advice, bring bulb-bowls up from cellar and put them in drawing-room. Several of them perfectly visible, but somehow do not look entirely healthy. Rose thinks too much watering. If so, Cissie Crabbe entirely to blame. (*Mem.*: Either move bulb-bowls upstairs, or tell Ethel to show Lady Boxe into morning-room, if she calls. Cannot possibly enter into further discussion with her concerning bulbs.)

COOK.

December 10th.—Robert, this morning, complains of insufficient breakfast. Cannot feel that porridge, scrambled eggs, toast, marmalade, scones, brown bread, and coffee give adequate grounds for this, but admit that porridge is slightly burnt. How impossible ever to encounter burnt porridge without vivid recollections of Jane Eyre at Lowood School, say I parenthetically! This literary allusion not a success. Robert suggests ringing for Cook, and have greatest difficulty in persuading him that this course utterly disastrous.

Eventually go myself to kitchen, in ordinary course of events, and approach subject of burnt porridge circuitously and with utmost care. Cook replies, as I expected, with expressions of astonishment and incredulity, coupled with assurances that kitchen range is again at fault. She also says that new double-saucepan, fish-kettle, and nursery tea-cups are urgently required. Make enquiries regarding recently purchased nursery tea-set and am shown one handle without cup, saucer in three pieces, and cup from which large semicircle has apparently been bitten. Feel that Mademoiselle will be hurt if I pursue enquiries further. (Note: Extreme sensibility of the French sometimes makes them difficult to deal with.)

Read Life and Letters of distinguished woman recently dead, and am struck, as so often, by difference between her correspondence and that of less distinguished women. Immense and affectionate letters from celebrities on every other page, epigrammatic notes from literary and political acquaintances, poetical assurances of affection and admiration from husband, and even infant children. Try to imagine Robert writing in similar strain in the (improbable) event of my attaining celebrity, but fail. Dear Vicky equally unlikely to commit her feelings (if any) to paper.

Robin's letter arrives by second post, and am delighted to have it as ever, but cannot feel that laconic information about boy—unknown to me—called Baggs, having been swished, and Mr. Gompshaw, visiting master, being kept away by Sore Throat—is on anything like equal footing with lengthy and picturesque epistles received almost daily by subject of biography, whenever absent from home.

Remainder of mail consists of one bill from chemist—(*Mem.*: Ask Mademoiselle why *two* tubes of Gibbs' Toothpaste within ten days)—illiterate postcard from piano-tuner, announcing visit to-morrow, and circular concerning True Temperance.

Inequalities of Fate very curious. Should like, on this account, to believe in Reincarnation. Spend some time picturing to myself completely renovated state of affairs, with, amongst other improvements, total reversal of relative positions of Lady B. and myself.

272

(Query: Is thought on abstract questions ever a waste of time?)

December 11th.—Robert, still harping on topic of yesterday's breakfast, says suddenly Why Not a Ham? to which I reply austerely that a ham is on order, but will not appear until arrival of R.'s brother William and his wife, for Christmas visit. Robert, with every manifestation of horror, says Are William and Angela coming to us for *Christmas?* This attitude absurd, as invitation was given months ago, at Robert's own suggestion.

(Query here becomes unavoidable: Does not a misplaced optimism exist, common to all mankind, leading on to false conviction that social engagements, if dated sufficiently far ahead, will never really materialise?)

Vicky and Mademoiselle return from walk with small white-and-yellow kitten, alleged by them homeless and starving. Vicky fetches milk, and becomes excited. Agree that kitten shall stay "for to-night" but feel that this is weak.

(*Mem.*: Remind Vicky to-morrow that Daddy does not like cats.) Mademoiselle becomes very French, on subject of cats generally, and am obliged to check her. She is *blessée*, and all three retire to schoolroom.

MADEMOISELLE.

December 12th.—Robert says out of the question to keep stray kitten. Existing kitchen cat more than enough. Gradually modifies this attitude under Vicky's pleadings. All now depends on whether kitten is male or female. Vicky and Mademoiselle declare this is known to them, and kitten already christened Napoleon. Find myself unable to enter into discussion on the point in French. The gardener takes opposite view to Vicky's and Mademoiselle's. They thereupon re-christen the kitten, seen playing with an old tennis ball, as Helen Wills.

Robert's attention, perhaps fortunately, diverted by mysterious trouble with the water-supply. He says The Ram has Stopped. (This sounds to me Biblical.)

Give Mademoiselle a hint that H. Wills should not be encouraged to put in injudicious appearances downstairs.

December 13th.—Ram resumes activities. Helen Wills still with us.

December 16th.—Very stormy weather, floods out and many trees prostrated at inconvenient angles. Call from Lady Boxe, who says that she is off to the South of France next week, as she Must have Sunshine. She asks Why I do not go there too, and likens me to piece of chewed string, which I feel to be entirely inappropriate and rather offensive figure of speech, though perhaps kindly meant.

Why not just pop into the train, enquires Lady B., pop across France, and pop out into Blue Sky, Blue Sea, and Summer Sun? Could make perfectly comprehensive reply to this, but do not do so, question of expense having evidently not crossed Lady B.'s horizon. (*Mem.*: Interesting subject for debate at Women's Institute, perhaps: That Imagination is incompatible with Inherited Wealth. On second thoughts, though, fear this has a socialistic trend.)

Reply to Lady B. with insincere professions of liking England very much even in the Winter. She begs me not to let myself become parochially-minded.

Departure of Lady B. with many final appeals to me to reconsider South of France. Make civil pretence, which deceives neither of us, of wavering, and promise to ring her up in the event of a change of mind.

(Query: Cannot many of our moral lapses from Truth be frequently charged upon the tactless persistence of others?)

December 17th, London.—Come up to dear Rose's fiat for two days' Christmas shopping, after prolonged discussion with Robert, who maintains that All can equally well be done by Post.

Take early train so as to get in extra afternoon. Have with me Robert's old leather suit-case, own ditto in fibre, large quantity of chrysanthemums done up in brown paper for .Rose, small packet of sandwiches, handbag, fur coat in case weather turns cold, book for journey, and illustrated paper kindly presented by Mademoiselle at the station. (Query: suggests itself: Could not some of these things have been dispensed with, and if so which?)

Bestow belongings in the rack, and open illustrated paper with sensation of leisured opulence, derived from unwonted absence of all domestic duties.

Unknown lady enters carriage at first stop, and takes seat opposite. She has expensive-looking luggage in moderate quantity, and small red morocco jewel-case, also bran-new copy, without library label, of *Life of Sir Edward Marshall-Hall.* Am reminded of Lady B. and have recrudescence of Inferiority Complex.

Remaining seats occupied by elderly gentleman wearing spats, nondescript female in a Burberry, and young man strongly resembling an Arthur Watts drawing. He looks at a copy of *Punch*, and I spend much time in wondering if it contains an Arthur Watts drawing and if he is struck by resemblance, and if so what his reactions are, whether of pain or gratification.

Roused from these unprofitable, but sympathetic, considerations by agitation on the part of elderly gentleman, who says that, upon his soul, he is being dripped upon. Everybody looks at ceiling, and Burberry female makes a vague reference to unspecified "pipes" which she declares often "go like that". Someone else madly suggests turning off the' heat. Elderly gentleman refuses all explanations and declares that *It comes from the rack.* We all look with horror at Rose's chrysanthemums, from which large drips of water descend regularly. Am overcome with shame, remove chrysanthemums, apologise to elderly gentleman, and sit down again opposite to superior unknown, who has remained glued to *Sir E. Marshall-Hall* throughout, and reminds me of Lady B. more than ever.

(*Mem.*: Speak to Mademoiselle about officiousness of thrusting flowers into water unasked, just before wrapping up.)

Immerse myself in illustrated weekly. Am informed by it that Lord Toto Finch (inset) is responsible for camera-study (herewith) of the Loveliest Legs in Los Angeles, belonging to well-known English Society girl, near relation (by the way) of famous racing peer, father of well-known Smart Set twins (portrait overleaf).

(Query: Is our popular Press going to the dogs?)

Turn attention to short story, but give it up on being directed, just as I become interested, to page XLVIIb, which I am quite unable to locate. Become involved instead with suggestions for Christmas Gifts. I want my gifts, the writer assures me, to be individual and yet appropriate—beautiful, and yet enduring. Then why not Enamel dressing-table set, at £94 16s. 4d. or Set of crystal-ware, exact replica of early English cut-glass, at moderate price of £34 17s. 9d.?

Why not, indeed?

Am touched to discover further on, however, explicit reference to Giver with Restricted Means—though even here, am compelled to differ from author's definition of restricted means. Let originality of thought, she says, add character to trifling offering. Would not many of my friends welcome suggestion of a course of treatment—(six for 5 guineas)—at Madame Dolly Varden's Beauty Parlour in Piccadilly to be placed to my account?

Cannot visualise myself making this offer to our Vicar's wife, still less her reception of it, and decide to confine myself to one-and-sixpenny calendar with picture of sunset on Scaw Fell, as usual.

(Indulge, on the other hand, in a few moments' idle phantasy, in which I suggest to Lady B. that she should accept from me as a graceful and appropriate Christmas gift, a course of Reducing Exercises accompanied by Soothing and Wrinkle-eradicating Face Massage.)

This imaginative exercise brought to a conclusion by arrival.

Obliged to take taxi from station, mainly owing to chrysanthemums (which would not combine well with two suit-cases and fur coat on moving stairway, which I distrust and dislike anyhow, and am only too apt to make conspicuous failure of Stepping Off with Right Foot foremost)— but also partly owing to fashionable locality of Rose's flat, miles removed from any Underground.

Kindest welcome from dear Rose, who is most appreciative of chrysanthemums. Refrain from mentioning unfortunate incident with elderly gentleman in train.

December 19th.—Find Christmas shopping very exhausting. Am paralysed in the Army and Navy Stores on discovering that List of Xmas Presents is lost, but eventually run it to earth in Children's Books Department. While there choose book for dear Robin, and wish for the hundredth time that Vicky had been less definite about wanting Toy Greenhouse and *nothing else*. This apparently unprocurable. (*Mem.:* Take early opportunity of looking up story of the Roc's Egg to tell Vicky.)

Rose says "Try Selfridge's." I protest, but eventually go there, find admirable—though expensive—Toy Greenhouse, and unpatriotically purchase it at once. Decide not to tell Robert this.

Choose appropriate offerings for Rose, Mademoiselle, William, and Angela—(who will be staying with us, so gifts must be above calendar-mark)—and lesser trifles for everyone else. Unable to decide between almost invisibly small diary, and really handsome card, for Cissie Crabbe, but eventually settle on diary, as it will fit into ordinary-sized envelope.

December 20th.—Rose takes me to see St. John Ervine's play, and am much amused. Overhear one lady in stalls ask another: Why don't *you* write a play, dear? Well, says the friend, it's so difficult, what with one thing and another, to find *time*. Am staggered. (Query: Could I write a play myself? Could we *all* write plays, if only we had the time? Reflect that St. J. E. lives in the same county as myself, but feel that this does not constitute sound excuse for writing to ask him how he finds the time to write plays.)

December 22nd.—Return home. One bulb in partial flower, but not satisfactory.

December 23rd.—Meet Robin at the Junction. He has lost his ticket, parcel of sandwiches, and handkerchief, but produces large wooden packing-case, into which little shelf has been wedged. Understand that this represents result of Carpentry Class—expensive "extra" at school—and is a Christmas present. Will no doubt appear on bill in due course.

Robin says essential to get gramophone record called "Is Izzy Azzy Wozz?" (*N.B.* Am often struck by disquieting thought that the dear children are entirely devoid of any artistic feeling whatever, in art, literature, or music. This conviction intensified after hearing "Is Izzy Azzy Wozz?" rendered fourteen times running on the gramophone, after I have succeeded in obtaining record.)

Much touched at enthusiastic greeting between Robin and Vicky. Mademoiselle says, "Ah, c'est gentil!" and produces a handkerchief, which I think exaggerated, especially as in half-an-hour's time she comes to me with complaint that R. and V. have gone up into the rafters and are shaking down plaster from nursery ceiling. Remonstrate with them from below. They sing "Is Izzy Azzy Wozz?" Am distressed at this, as providing fresh confirmation of painful conviction that neither has any ear for music, nor ever will have.

Arrival of William and Angela, at half-past three. Should like to hurry up tea, but feel that servants would be annoyed, so instead offer to show them their rooms, which they know perfectly well already. We exchange news about relations. Robin and Vicky appear, still singing "Is Izzy Azzy Wozz?" Angela says that they have grown. Can see by her expression that she thinks them odious, and very badly brought-up. She tells me about the children in the last house she stayed at. All appear to have been miracles of cleanliness, intelligence, and charm. A. also adds, most unnecessarily, that they are musical, and play the piano nicely.

(*Mem.*: A meal the most satisfactory way of entertaining any guest. Should much like to abridge the interval between tea and dinner—or else to introduce supplementary collation in between.)

At dinner we talk again about relations, and ask one another if anything is ever heard of poor Frederick, nowadays, and how Mollie's marriage is turning out, and whether Grandmama is thinking of going to the East Coast again this summer. Am annoyed because Robert and William sit on in the dining-room until nearly ten o'clock, which makes the servants late.

THE RECTOR.

December 24th.—Take entire family to children's party at neighbouring Rectory. Robin says Damn three times in the Rector's hearing, an expression never used by him before or since, but apparently reserved for this unsuitable occasion. Party otherwise highly successful, except that I again meet recent arrival at the Grange, on whom I have not yet called. She is a Mrs. Somers, and is said to keep Bees. Find myself next to her at tea, but cannot think of anything to say about Bees, except Does she *like* them, which sounds like a bad riddle, so leave it unsaid and talk about Preparatory Schools instead. (Am interested to note that no two parents ever seem to have heard of one another's Preparatory Schools. Query: Can this indicate an undue number of these establishments throughout the country?)

After dinner, get presents ready for children's stockings. William unfortunately steps on small glass article of doll's furniture intended for Vicky, but handsomely offers a shilling in compensation, which I refuse. Much time taken up in discussing this. At eleven P.M. children still wide awake. Angela suggests Bridge and asks Who is that Mrs. Somers we met at the Rectory, who seems to be interested in Bees? (A. evidently more skilled than myself in social amenities, but do not make this comment aloud.)

Xmas Day.—Festive, but exhausting, Christmas. Robin and Vicky delighted with everything, and spend much of the day eating. Vicky presents' her Aunt Angela with small square of canvas on which blue donkey is worked in cross-stitch. Do not know whether to apologise for this or not, but eventually decide better to say nothing, and hint to Mademoiselle that other design might have been preferable.

The children perhaps rather too much *en évidence*, as Angela, towards tea-time, begins to tell me that the little Maitlands have such a delightful nursery, and always spend entire day in it except when out for long walks with governess and dogs.

William asks if that Mrs. Somers is one of the *Dorsetshire* lot—a woman who knows about Bees.

Make a note that I really must call on Mrs. S. early next week. Read up something about Bees before going.

Turkey and plum-pudding cold in the evening, to give servants a rest. Angela looks at bulbs, and says What made me think they would be in flower for Christmas? Do not reply to this, but suggest early bed for us all.

December 27th.—Departure of William and Angela. Slight shock administered at eleventh hour by Angela, who asks if I realise that *she* was winner of first prize in last week's *Time and Tide* Competition, under the pseudonym of *Intelligensia*. Had naturally no idea of this, but congratulate her, without mentioning that I entered for same competition myself, without success.

(Query: Are Competition Editors always sound on questions of literary merit? Judgement possibly becomes warped through overwork.)

Another children's party this afternoon, too large and elaborate. Mothers stand about it in black hats and talk to one another about gardens, books, and difficulty of getting servants to stay in the country. Tea handed about the hall in a detached way, while children are herded into another room. Vicky and Robin behave well, and I compliment them on the way home, but am informed later by Mademoiselle that she has found large collection of chocolate biscuits in pocket of Vicky's party-frock.

(*Mem.*: Would it be advisable to point out to Vicky that this constitutes failure in intelligence, as well as in manners, hygiene, and common honesty?)

January 1st, 1930.—We give a children's party ourselves. Very, very exhausting performance, greatly complicated by stormy weather, which keeps half the guests away, and causes grave fears as to arrival of the conjurer.

Decide to have children's tea in the dining-room, grown-ups in the study, and clear the drawing-room for games and conjurer. Minor articles of drawing-room furniture moved up to my bedroom, where I continually knock myself against them. Bulb-bowls greatly in everybody's way and are put on window-ledges in passage, at which Mademoiselle says: "Tiens! ça fait un drôle d'effet, ces malheureux petits brins de verdure!" Do not like this description at all.

The children from neighbouring Rectory arrive too early, and are shown into completely empty drawing-room. Entrance of Vicky, in new green party-frock, with four balloons, saves situation.

(Query: What is the reason that clerical households are always unpunctual, invariably arriving either first, or last, at any gathering to which bidden?)

Am struck at variety of behaviour amongst mothers, some so helpful in organising games and making suggestions, others merely sitting about. (*N.B.* For sake of honesty, should rather say *standing* about, as supply of chairs fails early.) Resolve always to send Robin and Vicky to parties without me, if possible, as children without parents infinitely preferable from point of view of hostess. Find it difficult to get "Oranges and Lemons" going, whilst at same time appearing to give intelligent attention to remarks from visiting mother concerning Exhibition of Italian Pictures at Burlington House. Find myself telling her how marvellous I think them, although in actual fact have not yet seen them at all. Realise that this mis-statement should be corrected at once, but omit to do so, and later find myself involved in entirely unintentional web of falsehood. Should like to work out how far morally to blame for this state of things, but have not time.

Tea goes off well. Mademoiselle presides in dining-room, I in study. Robert and solitary elderly father—(looks more like a grandfather)—stand in doorway and talk about big-game shooting and the last General Election, in intervals of handing tea.

Conjurer arrives late, but is a success with children. Ends up with presents from a bran-tub, in which more bran is spilt on carpet, children's clothes, and house generally, than could ever have been got into tub originally. Think this odd, but have noticed similar phenomenon before.

Guests depart between seven and half-past, and Helen Wills and the dog are let out by Robin, having been shut up on account of crackers, which they dislike.

Robert and I spend evening helping servants to restore order, and trying to remember where ash-trays, clock, ornaments, and ink were put for safety.

January 3rd.—Hounds meet in the village. Robert agrees to take Vicky on the pony. Robin, Mademoiselle, and I walk to the Post Office to see the start, and Robin talks about Oliver Twist, making no reference whatever to hunt from start to finish, and viewing horses, hounds, and huntsmen with equal detachment. Am impressed at his non-suggestibility, but feel that some deep Freudian significance may lie behind it all. Feel also that Robert would take very different view of it.

Meet quantities of hunting neighbours, who say to Robin, "Aren't you riding too?" which strikes one as lacking in intelligence, and ask me if we have lost many trees lately, but do not wait for answer, as what they really want to talk about is the number of trees they have lost themselves.

Mademoiselle looks at hounds and says, "Ah, ces bons chiens!" also admires horses, "quelles bêtes superbes"—but prudently keeps well away from all, in which I follow her example.

Vicky looks nice on pony, and I receive compliments about her, which I accept in an off-hand manner, tinged with incredulity, in order to show that I am a modern mother and should scorn to be foolish about my children.

Hunt moves off, Mademoiselle remarking, "Voilà bien le sport anglais!" Robin says: "Now can we go home?" and eats milk-chocolate. We return to the house and I write order to the Stores, post-card to the butcher, two letters about Women's Institutes, one about Girl Guides, note to the dentist asking for appointment next week, and make memorandum in engagement-book that I *must* call on Mrs. Somers at the Grange.

Am horrified and incredulous at discovery that these occupations have filled the entire morning. Robert and Vicky return late, Vicky plastered with mud from head to foot but unharmed. Mademoiselle removes her, and says no more about *le sport anglais.*

January 4th.—A beautiful day, very mild, makes me feel that with any reasonable luck Mrs. Somers will be out, and I therefore call at the Grange. She is, on the contrary, in. Find her in the drawing-room, wearing printed velvet frock that I immediately think would look nice on *me.* No sign anywhere of Bees, but am getting ready to enquire about them intelligently when Mrs. Somers suddenly says that her Mother is here, and knows my old school-friend Cissie Crabbe, who says that I am so *amusing.* The Mother comes in—very elegant Marcel wave—(cannot imagine where she got it, unless she has this moment come from London)—and general air of knowing how to dress in the country. She is introduced to me—name sounds exactly like Eggchalk but do not think this possible—and says she knows my old school-friend Miss Crabbe, at Norwich, and has heard all about how very, very amusing I am. Become completely paralysed and can think of nothing whatever to say except that it has been very stormy lately. Leave as soon as possible.

January 5th.—Rose, in the kindest way, offers to take me as her guest to special dinner of famous Literary Club if I will come up to London for the night. Celebrated editor of literary weekly paper in the chair, spectacularly successful author of famous play as guest of honour. Principal authors, poets, and artists from—says Rose—all over the world, expected to be present. Spend much of the evening talking to Robert about this. Put it to him: (a) That no expense is involved beyond 3rd class return ticket to London; (b) that in another twelve years Vicky will be coming out, and it is therefore incumbent on me to Keep in Touch with People; (c) that this is an opportunity that will never occur again; (d) that it isn't as if I were asking him to come too. Robert says nothing to (a) or (b) and only "I should hope not" to (c), but appears slightly moved by (d). Finally says he supposes I must do as I like, and very likely I shall meet some old friends of my Bohemian days when living with Rose in Hampstead.

Am touched by this, and experience passing wonder if Robert can be feeling slightly jealous. This fugitive idea dispelled by his immediately beginning to speak about failure of hot water this morning.

January 7th.—Rose takes me to Literary Club dinner. I wear my Blue. Am much struck by various young men who have defiantly put on flannel shirts and no ties, and brushed their hair up on end. They are mostly accompanied by red-headed young women who wear printed crêpe frocks and beads. Otherwise, everyone in evening dress. Am introduced to distinguished Editor, who turns out to be female and delightful. Should like to ask her once and for all why prizes in her paper's weekly competition are so often divided, but feel this would be unsuitable and put Rose to shame.

Am placed at dinner next to celebrated best-seller, who tells me in the kindest way how to evade paying super-tax. Am easily able to conceal from him the fact that I am not at present in a position to require this information. Very distinguished artist sits opposite, and becomes more and more convivial as evening advances. This encourages me to remind him that we have met before—which we have, in old Hampstead days. He declares enthusiastically that he remembers me perfectly—which we both know to be entirely untrue—and adds wildly that he has followed my work ever since. Feel it better to let this pass unchallenged. Later on, distinguished artist is found to have come out without any money, and all in his immediate neighbourhood are required to lend him amount demanded by head-waiter.

Feel distinctly thankful that Robert is not with me, and am moreover morally certain that distinguished artist will remember nothing whatever in the morning, and will therefore be unable to refund my three-and-sixpence.

Rose handsomely pays for my dinner as well as her own.

(This suggests *Mem.*: That English cooking, never unduly attractive, becomes positively nauseating on any public occasion, such as a banquet. Am seriously distressed at probable reactions of foreign visitors to this evening's fish, let alone other items.)

Young gentleman is introduced to me by Rose—(she saying in rapid murmur that he is part-author of a one-act play that has been acted three times by a Repertory company in Jugo-Slavia.) It turns out later that he has met Lady Boxe, who struck him, he adds immediately, as a poisonous woman. We then get on well together. (Query: Is not a common hate one of the strongest links in human nature? Answer, most regrettably, in the affirmative.)

Very, very distinguished Novelist approaches me (having evidently mistaken me for someone else), and talks amiably. She says that she can only write between twelve at night and four in the morning, and not always then. When she cannot write, she plays the organ. Should much like to ask whether she is married—but get no opportunity of asking that or anything else. She tells me about her sales. She tells me about her last book. She tells me about her new one. She says that there are many people here to whom she *must* speak, and pursues well-known Poet—who does not, however, allow her to catch up with him. Can understand this.

"VERY, VERY DISTINGUISHED NOVELIST."

Speeches are made. Am struck, as so often, by the eloquence and profundity of other people, and reflect how sorry I should be to have to make a speech myself, although so often kept awake at night composing wholly admirable addresses to the servants, Lady B., Mademoiselle, and others—which, however, never get delivered.

Move about after dinner, and meet acquaintance whose name I have forgotten, but connect with literature. I ask if he has published anything lately. He says that his work is not, and never can be, for publication. Thought passes through my mind to the effect that this attitude might with advantage be adopted by many others. Do not say so, however, and we talk instead about Rebecca West, the progress of aviation, and the case for and against stag-hunting.

Rose, who has been discussing psychiatry as practised in the U.S.A. with Danish journalist, says Am I ready to go? Distinguished artist who sat opposite me at dinner offers to drive us both home, but his friends intervene. Moreover, acquaintance whose name I have forgotten takes me aside, and assures me that D.A. is quite unfit to take anybody home, and will himself require an escort. Rose and I depart by nearest Tube, as being wiser, if less exalted, procedure.

Sit up till one o'clock discussing our fellow-creatures, with special reference to those seen and heard this evening. Rose says I ought to come to London more often, and suggests that outlook requires broadening.

January 9th.—Came home yesterday. Robin and Mademoiselle no longer on speaking terms, owing to involved affair centering round a broken window-pane. Vicky, startlingly, tells me in private that she has learnt a new Bad Word, but does not mean to use it. Not now, anyway, she disquietingly adds.

Cook says she hopes I enjoyed my holiday, and it is very quiet in the country. I leave the kitchen before she has time to say more, but am only too well aware that this is not the last of it.

Write grateful letter to Rose, at the same time explaining difficulty of broadening my outlook by further time spent away from home, just at present.

January 14th.—I have occasion to observe, not for the first time, how extraordinarily plain a cold can make one look, affecting hair, complexion, and features generally, besides nose and upper lip. Cook assures me that colds always run through the house and that she herself has been suffering from sore throat for weeks, but is never one to make a fuss. (Query: Is this meant to imply that similar fortitude should be, but is not, displayed by me?) Mademoiselle says

280

she *hopes* children will not catch my cold, but that both sneezed this morning. I run short of handkerchiefs.

January 16th.—We all run short of handkerchiefs.

January 17th.—Mademoiselle suggests butter-muslin. There is none in the house. I say that I will go out and buy some. Mademoiselle says, "No, the fresh air gives pneumonia." Feel that I ought to combat this un-British attitude, but lack energy, especially when she adds that she will go herself—"Madame, j'y cours." She puts on black kid gloves, buttoned boots with pointed tips and high heels, hat with little feather in it, black jacket and several silk neckties, and goes, leaving me to amuse Robin and Vicky, both in bed. Twenty minutes after she has started, I remember it is early-closing day.

Go up to night-nursery and offer to read Lamb's *Tales from Shakespeare*. Vicky says she prefers *Pip, Squeak, and Wilfred*. Robin says that he would like *Gulliver's Travels*. Compromise on Grimm's Fairy Tales, although slightly uneasy as to their being in accordance with best modern ideals. Both children take immense interest in story of highly undesirable person who wins fortune, fame, and beautiful Princess by means of lies, violence, and treachery. Feel sure that this must have disastrous effect on both in years to come.

Our Vicar's wife calls before Mademoiselle returns. Go down to her, sneezing, and suggest that she had better not stay. She says, much better not, and she won't keep me a minute. Tells me long story about the Vicar having a stye on one eye. I retaliate with Cook's sore throat. This leads to draughts, the, heating apparatus in church, and news of Lady Boxe in South of France: The Vicar's wife has had a picture postcard from her (which she produces from bag), with small cross marking bedroom window of hotel. She says, It's rather interesting, isn't it? to which I reply Yes, it is, very, which is not in the least true. (*N.B.* Truth-telling in everyday life extraordinarily difficult. Is this personal, and highly deplorable, idiosyncrasy, or do others suffer in the same way? Have momentary impulse to put this to our, Vicar's wife, but decide better not.)

How, she says, are the dear children, and how is my husband? I reply suitably, and she tells me about cinnamon, Viapex, gargling with glycerine of thymnol, blackcurrant tea, onion broth, friar's balsam, linseed poultices, and thermogene wool. I sneeze and say Thank you—thank you very much, a good many times.. She goes, but turns back at the door to tell me about wool next the skin, nasal douching, and hot milk last thing at night. I say Thank you, again.

On returning to night-nursery, find that Robin has unscrewed top of hot-water bottle in Vicky's bed, which apparently contained several hundred gallons of tepid water, now distributed through and through pillows, pyjamas, sheets, blankets, and mattresses of both. I ring for Ethel—who helps me to reorganise entire situation and says It's like a hospital, isn't it, trays up and down stairs all day long, and all this extra work.

January 20th.—Take Robin, now completely restored, back to school. I ask the Headmaster what he thinks of his progress. The Headmaster answers that the New Buildings will be finished before Easter, and that their numbers are increasing so rapidly that he will probably add on a New Wing next term, and perhaps I saw a letter of his in the *Times* replying to Dr. Cyril Norwood? Make mental note to the effect that Headmasters are a race apart, and that if parents would remember this, much time could be saved.

Robin and I say good-bye with hideous brightness, and I cry all the way back to the station.

January 22nd.—Robert startles me at breakfast by asking if my cold—which he has hitherto ignored—is better. I reply that it has gone. Then why, he asks, do I look like that? Refrain from asking like what, as I know only too well. Feel that life is wholly unendurable, and decide madly to get a new hat.

Customary painful situation between Bank and myself necessitates expedient, also customary, of pawning great-aunt's diamond ring, which I do, under usual conditions, and am greeted as old friend by Plymouth pawnbroker, who says facetiously, And what name will it be *this* time?

Visit four linen-drapers and try on several dozen hats. Look worse and worse in each one, as hair gets wilder and wilder, and expression paler and more harassed. Decide to get myself shampooed and waved before doing any more, in hopes of improving the position.

Hairdresser's assistant says, It's a pity my hair is losing all its colour, and have I ever thought of having it touched up? After long discussion, I do have it touched up, and emerge with mahogany-coloured head. Hairdresser's assistant says this will wear off "in a few days". I am very angry, but all to no purpose. Return home in old hat, showing as little hair as possible, and keep it on till dressing time—but cannot hope to conceal my shame at dinner.

January 23rd.—Mary Kellway telegraphs she is motoring past here this morning, can I give her lunch? Telegraph Yes, delighted, and rush to kitchen. Cook unhelpful and suggests cold beef and beetroot. I say Yes, excellent, unless perhaps roast chicken and bread sauce even better? Cook talks about the oven. Compromise in the end on cutlets and mashed potatoes, as, very luckily, this is the day butcher calls.

Always delighted to see dear Mary—so clever and amusing, and able to write stories, which actually get published and paid for—but very uneasy about colour of my hair, which is not wearing off in the least. Think seriously of keeping a hat on all through lunch, but this, on the whole, would look even more unnatural. Besides, could not hope that it would pass without observation from Vicky, let alone Robert.

Later.—Worst fears realised, as to hair. Dear Mary, always so observant, gazes at it in nerve-shattering silence but says nothing, till I am driven to make half-hearted explanation. Her only comment is that she cannot imagine why anybody should deliberately make themselves look ten years older than they need. Feel that, if she wishes to discourage further experiments on my part, this observation could scarcely be improved upon. Change the subject, and talk about the children. Mary most sympathetic, and goes so far as to say that my children have brains, which encourages me to tell anecdotes about them until I see Robert looking at me, just as I get to Robin's precocious taste for really good literature. By curious coincidence second post brings letter from Robin, saying that he wishes to collect cigarette-cards and will I send him all the types of National Beauty, Curious Beaks, and Famous Footballers, that I can find. Make no comment on this singular request aloud.

Mary stays to tea and we talk about H. G. Wells, Women's Institutes, infectious illness, and *Journey's End.* Mary says she cannot go and see this latter because she always cries at the theatre. I say, Then once more will make no difference. Discussion becomes involved, and we drop it. Vicky comes in and immediately offers to recite. Can see that Mary (who has three children of her own) does not in the least want to hear her, but she feigns enthusiasm politely. Vicky recites: "Maître Corbeau sur un arbre perché"—(*N.B.* Suggest to Mademoiselle that Vicky's repertory should be enlarged. Feel sure that I have heard Maitre Corbeau, alternately with La Cigale et la Fourmi, some eight hundred times within the last six months.)

After Mary has gone, Robert looks at me and suddenly remarks: "Now *that's* what I call an attractive woman." Am gratified at his appreciation of talented friend, but should like to be a little clearer regarding exact significance of emphasis on the word *that.* Robert, however, says no more, and opportunity is lost as Ethel comes in to say Cook is sorry she's run right out of milk, but if I will come to the store-cupboard she thinks there's a tin of Ideal, and she'll make do with that.

January 25th.—Attend a Committee Meeting in the village to discuss how to raise funds for Village Hall. Am asked to take the chair. Begin by saying that I know how much we all have this excellent object at heart, and that I feel sure there swill be no lack of suggestions as to best method of obtaining requisite sum of money. Pause for suggestions, which is met with death-like silence. I say, There are so many ways to choose from—implication being that I attribute silence to plethora of ideas, rather than to absence of them. (*Note*: Curious and rather depressing, to see how frequently the pursuit of Good Works leads to apparently unavoidable duplicity.) Silence continues, and I say Well, twice, and Come, come, once. (Sudden impulse to exclaim, "I lift up my finger and I say Tweet, Tweet," is fortunately overcome.) At last: extract a suggestion of a concert from Mrs. L. (whose son plays the violin) and a whist-drive from Miss P. (who won Ladies' First Prize at the last one). Florrie P. suggests a dance and is at once reminded that it will be Lent. She says that Lent isn't what it was. Her mother says the Vicar is one that holds with Lent, and always has been. Someone else says That reminds her, has anyone heard that old Mr. Small passed away last night? We all agree that eighty-six is a great age. Mrs. L. says that on her mother's side of the family, there is an aunt of ninety-eight. Still with us, she adds. The aunt's husband, on the other hand, was gathered just before his sixtieth birthday. Everyone says, You can't ever *tell*, not really. There is a suitable pause before we go back to Lent and the Vicar. General opinion that a concert isn't like a dance, and needn't—says Mrs. L.—interfere.

On this understanding, we proceed. Various familiar items—piano solo, recitation, duet, and violin solo from Master L.—are all agreed upon. Someone says that Mrs. F. and Miss H. might do a dialogue, and has to be reminded that they are no longer on speaking terms, owing to strange behaviour of Miss H. about her bantams. Ah, says Mrs. S., it wasn't only *bantams* was at the bottom of it, there's two sides to every question. (There are at least twenty to this one, by the time we've done with it.)

THE VICAR'S WIFE.

Sudden appearance of our Vicar's wife, who says apologetically that she made a mistake in the time. I beg her to take the chair. She refuses. I insist. She says No, no, positively not, and takes it.

We begin all over again, but general attitude towards Lent much less elastic.

Meeting ends at about five o'clock. Our Vicar's wife walks 'home with me, and tells me that I look tired. I ask her to come in and have tea. No, she says, no, it's too kind of me, but she must go on to the far end of the parish. She remains standing at the gate telling me about old Small—eighty-six a great age—till quarter-to-six, when she departs, saying that she cannot *think* why I am looking so tired.

February 11th.—Robin writes again about cigarette-cards. I send him all those I have collected, and Vicky produces two which she has obtained from the garden-boy. Find that this quest grows upon one, and am apt now, when in Plymouth or any other town, to scan gutters, pavements, and tram-floors in search of Curious Beaks, Famous Football Players, and the like. Have even gone so far as to implore perfect stranger, sitting opposite me in train, *not* to throw cigarette-card out of the window, but give it to me instead. Perfect stranger does so with an air of courteous astonishment, and as he asks for no explanation, am obliged to leave him under the impression that I have merely been trying to force him into conversation with me.

(*Note:* Could not short article, suitable for *Time and Tide*, be worked up on some such lines as: Lengths to which Mother-love may legitimately go? On second thoughts abandon the idea, as being faintly reminiscent of *démodé* enquiry: Do Shrimps make Good Mothers?)

Hear that Lady Boxe has returned from South of France and is entertaining house-party. She sends telephone message by the butler, asking me to tea to-morrow. I accept. (Why?)

February 12th.—Insufferable behaviour of Lady B. Find large party, all of whom are directed at front door to go to the Hard Courts, where, under inadequate shelter, in Arctic temperature, all are compelled to watch young men in white flannels keeping themselves warm by banging a little ball against a wall. Lady B. wears an emerald-green leather coat with fur collar and cuffs. I, having walked down, have on ordinary coat and skirt, and freeze rapidly. Find myself next unknown lady who talks wistfully about the tropics. Can well understand this. On other side elderly gentleman, who says conversationally that this Naval Disarmament is All his Eye. This contribution made to contemporary thought, he says no more. Past five o'clock before we are allowed to go in to tea, by which time am only too well aware that my face is blue and my hands purple. Lady B. asks me at tea how the children are, and adds, to the table at large, that I am "A Perfect Mother". Am naturally avoided, conversationally, after this, by everybody at the tea-table. Later on, Lady B. tells us about South of France. She quotes repartees made by herself in French, and then translates them.

LADY B.

(Unavoidable Query presents itself here: Would a verdict of Justifiable Homicide delivered against their mother affect future careers of children unfavourably?)

Discuss foreign travel with unknown, but charming, lady in black. We are delighted with one another—or so I confidently imagine—arid she begs me to go and see her if I am ever in her neighbourhood. I say that I will—but am well aware that courage will fail me when it comes to the point. Pleasant sense of mutual sympathy suddenly and painfully shattered by my admitting—in reply to direct enquiry—that I am *not* a gardener—which the lady in black is, to an extent that apparently amounts to monomania. She remains charming, but quite ceases to be delighted with me, and I feel discouraged.

(*N.B. Must* try to remember that Social Success is seldom the portion of those who habitually live in the provinces. No doubt they serve some other purpose in the vast field of Creation—but have not yet discovered what.)

Lady B. asks if I have seen the new play at the Royalty. I say No. She says Have I been to the Italian Art Exhibition? I have not. She enquires what I think of *Her Privates We*—which I haven't yet read—and I at once give her a long and spirited account of my reactions to it. Feel after this that I had better go, before I am driven to further excesses.

Shall she, says Lady B., ring for my car? Refrain from replying that no amount of ringing will bring my car to the door all by itself, and say instead that I walked. Lady B. exclaims that this is Impossible, and that I am Too Marvellous, Altogether. Take my leave before she can add that I am such a Perfect Countrywoman, which I feel is coming next.

Get home—still chilled to the bone owing to enforced detention at Hard Court—and tell Robert what I think of Lady B. He makes no answer, but I feel he agrees.

Mademoiselle says: "Tiens! Madame a mauvaise mine. On dirait un cadavre..."

Feel that this is kindly meant, but do not care about the picture that it conjures up.

Say good-night to Vicky, looking angelic in bed, and ask what she is thinking about, lying there. She disconcertingly replies with briskness: "Oh, Kangaroos and things."

(*Note:* The workings of the infant mind very, very difficult to follow, sometimes. Mothers by no means infallible.)

February 14th.—Have won first prize in *Time and Tide* competition, but again divided. Am very angry indeed, and write excellent letter to the Editor under false name, protesting against this iniquitous custom. After it has gone, become seriously uneasy under the fear that the use of a false name is illegal. Look through *Whitaker*, but can find nothing but Stamp Duties and Concealment of Illegitimate Births, so abandon it in disgust.

Write to Angela—under my own name—to enquire kindly if *she* went in for the competition. Hope she did, and that she will have the decency to say so.

February 16th.—Informed by Ethel, as she calls me in the morning, that Helen Wills has had six kittens, of which five survive.

Cannot imagine how I shall break this news to Robert. Reflect—not for the first time—that the workings of Nature are most singular.

Angela writes that she *didn't* go in for competition, thinking the subject puerile, but that she solved "Merope's" Crossword puzzle in fifteen minutes.

(*N.B.* This last statement almost certainly inaccurate.)

February 21st.—Remove bulb-bowls, with what is left of bulbs, to greenhouse. Tell Robert that I hope to do better another year. He replies, Another year, better not waste my money. This reply depresses me, moreover weather continues Arctic, and have by no means recovered from effects of Lady B.'s so-called hospitality.

Vicky and Mademoiselle spend much time in boot-cupboard, where Helen Wills is established with five kittens. Robert still unaware of what has happened, but cannot hope this ignorance will continue. Must, however, choose suitable moment for revelation—which is unlikely to occur today owing to bath-water having been cold again this morning.

Lady B. calls in the afternoon—not, as might have been expected, to see if I am in bed with pneumonia, but to ask if I will help at a Bazaar early in May. Further enquiry reveals that it is in aid of the Party Funds. I say What Party? (Am well aware of Lady B.'s political views, but resent having it taken for granted that mine are the same—which they are not.)

Lady B. says she is Surprised. Later on she says Look at the Russians, and even, Look at the Pope. I find myself telling her to Look at Unemployment—none of which gets us any further. Am relieved when tea comes in, and still more so when Lady B. says she really mustn't wait, as she has to call on such a number of Tenants. She asks after Robert, and I think seriously of replying that he is out receiving the Oath of Allegiance from all the vassals on the estate, but decide that this would be undignified.

Escort Lady B. to the hall-door. She tells me that the oak dresser would look better on the other side of the hall, and that it is a mistake to put mahogany and walnut in the same room. Her last word is that she will Write, about the bazaar. Relieve my feelings by waving small red flag belonging to Vicky, which is lying on the hall-stand, and saying *A la lanterne*! as chauffeur drives off. Rather unfortunately, Ethel chooses this moment to walk through the hall. She says nothing, but looks astonished.

February 22nd.—Gloom prevails, owing to Helen Wills having elected, with incredible idiocy, to introduce progeny, one by one, to Robert's notice at late hour last night, when he was making final round of the house.

Send Mademoiselle and Vicky on errand to the village whilst massacre of the innocents takes place in pail of water in backyard. Small ginger is allowed to survive. Spend much time in thinking out plausible story to account to Vicky for disappearance of all the rest. Mademoiselle, when informed privately of what has happened, tells me to leave Vicky to her—which I gladly agree to do—and adds that "les hommes manquent de coeur". Feel that this is leading us in the direction of a story which I have heard before, and do not wish to hear again, regarding *un mariage échoué* arranged years ago for Mademoiselle by her parents, in which negotiations broke down owing to mercenary attitude of *le futur*. Break in with hasty enquiry regarding water-tightness or otherwise of Vicky's boots.

(Query: Does incessant pressure of domestic cares vitiate capacity for human sympathy? Fear that it does, but find myself unable to attempt reformation in this direction at present.)

Receive long, and in parts illegible, letter from Cissie Crabbe, bearing on the back of the envelope extraordinary enquiry: Do you know of a really *good* hotel Manageress? Combat strong inclination to reply on a postcard: No, but can recommend thoroughly reliable Dentist. Dear Cissie, one remembers from old schooldays, has very little sense of humour.

February 24th.—Robert and I lunch with our Member and his wife. I sit next elderly gentleman who talks about stag-hunting and tells me that there is Nothing Cruel about it. The Stag *likes* it, and it is an honest, healthy, thoroughly*English* form of sport. I say Yes, as anything else would be waste of breath, and turn to Damage done by recent storms, New arrivals in the neighbourhood, and Golf-links at Budleigh Salterton. Find that we get back to stag-hunting again in next to no time, and remain there for the rest of lunch.

"CAN HEAR ROBERT'S NEIGHBOUR . . . TELLING HIM ABOUT HER CHILBLAINS."

Can hear Robert's neighbour, sitting opposite in cochineal three-piece suit, telling him about her Chilblains. Robert civil, but does not appear unduly concerned. (Perhaps three-piece cochineal thinks that he is one of those people who feel more than they can express?) She goes on to past appendicitis, present sciatica, and threat of colitis in the near future. Robert still unmoved.

Ladies retire to the drawing-room and gather round quite inadequate fire. Coffee. I perform my usual sleight-of-hand, transferring large piece of candy-sugar from saucer to handbag, for Vicky's benefit. (Query: Why do people living in same neighbourhood as myself obtain without difficulty minor luxuries that I am totally unable to procure? Reply to this, if pursued to logical conclusion, appears to point to inadequate housekeeping on my part.)

Entrance of males. I hear my neighbour at lunch beginning all over again about stag-hunting, this time addressed to his hostess, who is well-known supporter of the R.S.P.C.A.

Our Member talks to me about Football. I say that I think well of the French, and that Béhotéguy plays a good game. (*N.B.* This solitary piece of knowledge always coming in useful, but *must* try and find out name of at least one British player, so as to vary it.)

As we take our leave with customary graceful speeches, clasp of handbag unfortunately gives way, and piece of candy-sugar falls, with incredible noise and violence, on to the parquet, and is pursued with officious zeal and determination by all present except myself.

Very, very difficult moment...

Robert, on the whole, takes this well, merely enquiring on the way home if I suppose that we shall ever be asked inside the house again.

February 28th.—Notice, and am gratified by, appearance of large clump of crocuses near the front gate. Should like to make whimsical and charming reference to these, and try to fancy myself as "Elizabeth of the German Garden", but am interrupted by Cook, saying that the Fish is here, but he's only brought cod and haddock, and the haddock doesn't smell any too fresh, so what about cod?

Have often noticed that Life is like that.

March 1st.—The Kellways lunch with us, before going on all together to wedding of Rosemary H., daughter of mutual friend and neighbour. Fire refuses to burn up, and am still struggling with it when they arrive, with small boy, Vicky's contemporary—all three frozen with cold. I say, Do come and get warm! and they accept this, alas meaningless, offer with enthusiasm. Vicky rushes in, and am struck, as usual, by the complete and utter straightness of her hair in comparison with that of practically every other child in the world. (Little Kellway has natural wave.)

Chickens over-done, and potatoes underdone. Meringues quite a success, especially with the children, though leading to brisk *sotto-voce* encounter between Vicky and Mademoiselle on question of second helping. This ends by an appeal from Mademoiselle for "un bon mouvement" on Vicky's part—which she facilitates by summarily removing her plate, spoon, and fork. Everybody ignores this drama, with the exception of the infant Kellway, who looks amused, and unblenchingly attacks a second meringue.

Start directly after lunch, Robert and Mary's husband appearing in a highly unnatural state of shiny smartness with a top-hat apiece. Effect of this splendour greatly mitigated, when they don the top-hats, by screams of unaffected amusement from both children. We drive off, leaving them leaning against Mademoiselle, apparently helpless with mirth.

(Query: Is not the inferiority complex, about which so much is written and spoken, nowadays shifting from the child to the parent?)

Mary wears blue with admirable diamond ornament, and looks nice. I wear red, and think regretfully of great-aunt's diamond ring, still reposing in back street of Plymouth, under care of old friend the pawnbroker. (*Note:* Financial situation very low indeed, and must positively take steps to send assortment of old clothes to second-hand dealer for disposal. Am struck by false air of opulence with which I don fur coat, white gloves, and new shoes—one very painful—and get into the car. Irony of life thus exemplified.)

Charming wedding, Rosemary H. looks lovely, bridesmaids highly picturesque. One of them has bright red hair, and am completely paralysed by devastating enquiry from Mary's husband, who hisses at me through his teeth: *Is that the colour yours was when you dyed it?*

Crowds of people at the reception. Know most of them, but am startled by strange lady in pink, wearing eye-glasses, who says that I don't remember her—which is only too true—but that she has played tennis at my house. How, she says, are those sweet twins? Find myself telling her that they are very well indeed, before I know where I am. Can only trust never to set eyes on her again.

Exchange talk with Mrs. Somers, recent arrival to the neighbourhood, who apologises profusely for never having returned my call. Am in doubt whether to say that I haven't noticed the omission, or that I hope she will repair it as quickly as possible. Either sounds uncivil.

Speak to old Lady Dufford, who reminds me that the last time we met was at the Jones wedding. *That*, she says, came to grief within a year. She also asks if I have heard about the Greens, who have separated, and poor Winifred R., who has had to go back to her parents because He drinks. Am not surprised when she concludes with observation that it is rather *heartrending* to see the two young things setting out together.

Large car belonging to bridegroom draws up at hall-door, and old Lady D. further wags her head at me and says Ah, in *our* day it would have been a carriage and pair—to which I offer no assent, thinking it very unnecessary reminder of the flight of Time—and in any event, am Lady D.'s junior by a good many years.

Melancholy engendered by the whole of this conversation is lightened by glass of champagne. I ask Robert, sentimentally, if this makes him think of *our* wedding. He looks surprised and says No, not particularly, why should it? As I cannot at the moment think of any particular reply to this, the question drops.

VICKY.

Departure of the bridal couple is followed by general exodus, and I take the Kellways home to tea.

Remove shoes with great thankfulness.

March 3rd.—Vicky, after Halma, enquires abruptly whether, if she died, I should cry? I reply in the affirmative. But, she says, should I cry really *hard*. Should I roar and scream? Decline to commit myself to any such extravagant demonstrations, at which Vicky displays a tendency to hurt astonishment. I speak to Mademoiselle and say that I hope she will discourage anything in Vicky that seems to verge upon the morbid. Mademoiselle requires a translation of the last word, and, after some consideration, I suggest dénaturé, at which she screams dramatically and crosses herself, and assures me that if I knew what I was saying, I should "en reculer d'effroi".

We decide to abandon the subject.

Our Vicar's wife calls for me at seven o'clock, and we go to a neighbouring Women's Institute at which I have, rather rashly, promised to speak. On the way there, our Vicar's wife tells me that the secretary of the Institute is liable to have a heart attack at any minute and must on no account exert herself, or be allowed to get over-excited. Even a violent fit of laughing, she adds impressively, might carry her off in a moment.

Hastily revise my speech, and remove from it two funny stories. After this it is a shock to find that the programme for the evening includes dancing and a game of General Post. I ask our Vicar's wife what would happen if the secretary *did* get a heart attack, and she replies mysteriously, Oh, she always carries Drops in her handbag. The thing to do is to keep an eye on her handbag. This I do nervously throughout the evening, but fortunately no crisis supervenes.

I speak, am thanked, and asked if I will judge a Darning Competition. This I do, in spite of inward misgivings that few people are less qualified to give any opinion about darning than I am. I am thanked again and given tea and a doughnut. We all play General Post and get very heated. Signal success of the evening when two stout and elderly members collide in the middle of the room, and both fall heavily to the floor together. This, if anything, will surely bring on a heart attack, and am prepared to make a rush at the handbag, but nothing happens. We all sing the National Anthem, and our Vicar's wife says she does hope the lights of her two-seater are in order, and drives me home. We are relieved, and surprised, to find that the lights, all except the rear one, are in order, although rather faint.

I beg our Vicar's wife to come in; she says, No, No, it is far too late, really, and comes. Robert and Helen Wills both asleep in the drawing-room. Our Vicar's wife says she must not stay a moment, and we talk about Countrywomen, Stanley Baldwin, Hotels at Madeira (where none of us have ever been), and other unrelated topics. Ethel brings in cocoa, but can tell from the way she puts down the tray that she thinks it an unreasonable requirement, and will quite likely give notice to-morrow.

At eleven our Vicar's wife says that she *does* hope the lights of the two-seater are still in order, and gets as far as the hall-door. There we talk about forthcoming village concert, parrot-disease, and the Bishop of the diocese.

Her car refuses to start, and Robert and I push it down the drive. After a good deal of jerking and grinding, engine starts, the hand of our Vicar's wife waves at us through the hole in the talc, and car disappears down the lane.

Robert inhospitably says, let us put out the lights and fasten up the hall-door and go up to bed immediately, in case she comes back for anything. We do so, only delayed by Helen Wills, whom Robert tries vainly to expel into the night. She retires under the piano, behind the bookcase, and finally disappears altogether.

March 4th.—Ethel, as I anticipated, gives notice. Cook says this is so unsettling, she thinks she had better go too. Despair invades me. Write five letters to Registry Offices.

March 7th.—No hope.

March 8th.—Cook relents, so far as to say that she will stay until I am suited. Feel inclined to answer that, in, that case, she had better make up her mind to a lifetime spent together—but naturally refrain. Spend exhausting day in Plymouth chasing mythical house-parlourmaids. Meet Lady B., who says the servant difficulty, in reality, is non-existent. She has No trouble. It is a question of knowing how to treat them. Firmness, she says, but at the same time one must be human. Am I human? she asks. Do I understand that they want occasional diversion, just as I do myself? I lose my head and reply No, that it is my custom to keep my servants chained up in the cellar when their work is done. This flight of satire rather spoilt by Lady B. laughing heartily, and saying that I am always so amusing. Well, she adds, we shall no doubt see one another at lunch-time at the Duke of Cornwall Hotel, where alone it is possible to get a decent meal. I reply with ready cordiality that no doubt we shall, and go and partake of my usual lunch of baked beans and a glass of water in small and obscure café.

Unavoidable Query, of painfully searching character, here presents itself: If Lady B. had invited me as her guest to lunch at the D. of C. Hotel, should I have accepted? Am conscious of being heartily tired of baked beans and water, which in any case do not really serve to support one through long day of shopping and servant-hunting. Moreover, am always ready to See Life, in hotels or anywhere else. On the other hand, am aware that self-respect would suffer severely through accepting five-shillings-worth of luncheon from Lady B. Ponder this problem of psychology in train on the way home, but reach no definite conclusion.

Day a complete failure as regards house-parlourmaid, but expedition not wasted, having found two cigarette-cards on pavement, both quite clean Curious Beaks.

March 9th.—Cannot hear of a house-parlourmaid. Ethel, on the other hand, can hear of at least a hundred situations, and opulent motor-cars constantly dash up to front door, containing applicants for her services. Cook more and more unsettled. If this goes on, shall go to London and stay with Rose, in order to visit Agencies.

Meet Barbara, wearing new tweed, in village this morning—nice bright girl, but long to suggest she should have adenoids removed. She says, Will I be an Angel and look in on her mother, now practically an invalid? I reply warmly Of course I will, not really meaning it, but remember that we are now in Lent and suddenly decide to go at once. Admire the new tweed. Barbara says It *is* rather nice, isn't it, and adds—a little strangely—that it came out of John Barker's Sale Catalogue, under four guineas, and only needed letting out at the waist and taking in a bit on the shoulders. Especially, she adds elliptically, now that skirts are longer again.

Barbara goes to Evening Service, and I go to look in on her mother, whom I find in shawls, sitting in an armchair reading—rather ostentatiously—enormous *Life of Lord Beaconsfield*. I ask how she is, and she shakes her head and enquires if I should ever guess that her pet name amongst her friends once used to be Butterfly? (This kind of question always so difficult, as either affirmative or negative reply apt to sound unsympathetic. Feel it would hardly do to suggest that Chrysalis, in view of the shawls, would now be more appropriate.) However, says Mrs. Blenkinsop with a sad smile, it is never her way to dwell upon herself and her own troubles. She just sits there, day after day, always ready to sympathise in the little joys and troubles of others, and I would hardly believe how unfailingly these are brought to her. People say, she adds deprecatingly, that just her Smile does them good. She does not know, she says, what they mean. (Neither do I.)

After this, there is a pause, and I feel that Mrs. B. is waiting for me to pour out my little joys and troubles. Perhaps she hopes that Robert has been unfaithful to me, or that I have fallen in love with the Vicar.

MRS. BLENKINSOP.

Am unable to rise to the occasion, so begin instead to talk about Barbara's new tweed. Mrs. Blenkinsop at once replies that, for her part, she has never given up all those little feminine touches that make All the Difference. A ribbon here, a flower there. This leads to a story about what was once said to her by a friend, beginning "It's so wonderful, dear Mrs. Blenkinsop, to see the trouble you always take on behalf of others", and ending with Mrs. B.'s own reply, to the effect that she is only A Useless Old Woman, but that she has many, many friends, and that this must be because her motto has always been: Look Out and Not In: Look Up and not Down: Lend a Hand.

Conversation again languishes, and I have recourse to *Lord Beaconsfield*. What, I ask, does Mrs. B. feel about him? She feels, Mrs. B. replies, that he was a most Remarkable Personality. People have often said to Mrs. B., Ah, how lonely it must be for you, alone here, when dear Barbara is out enjoying herself with other young things. But Mrs. B.'s reply to this is No, no. She is never alone when she has Her Books. Books, to her, are *Friends*. Give her Shakespeare or Jane Austen, Meredith or Hardy, and she is Lost—lost in a world of her own. She sleeps so little that most of her nights are spent in reading. Have I any idea, asks Mrs. B., what it is like to hear every hour, every half-hour, chiming out all through the night? I have no idea whatever, since am invariably obliged to struggle with overwhelming sleepiness from nine o'clock onwards, but do not like to tell her this, so take my departure. Mrs. B.'s parting observation is an expression of thanks to me for coming to enquire after an old woman, and she is as well as she can hope to be, at sixty-six years old—she *should* say, sixty-six years *young*, all her friends tell her.

Reach home totally unbenefited by this visit, and with strange tendency to snap at everybody I meet.

March 10th.—Still no house-parlourmaid, and write to ask Rose if I can go to her for a week. Also write to old Aunt Gertrude in Shropshire to enquire if I may send Vicky and Mademoiselle there on a visit, as this will make less work in house while we are short-handed. Do not, however, give Aunt Gertrude this reason for sending them. Ask Robert if he will be terribly lonely, and he says Oh no, he hopes I shall enjoy myself in London. Spend a great deal of eloquence explaining that I am *not* going to London to enjoy myself, but experience sudden fear that I am resembling Mrs. Blenkinsop, and stop abruptly.

Robert says nothing.

March 11th.—Rose wires that she will be delighted to put me up. Cook, very unpleasantly, says, "I'm sure I hope you'll enjoy your holiday, mum." Am precluded from making the kind of reply I should *like* to make, owing to grave fears that she should also give notice. Tell her instead that I hope to "get settled" with a house-parlourmaid before my return. Cook looks utterly incredulous and says she is sure she hopes so too, because really, things have been so unsettled lately. Pretend not to hear this and leave the kitchen.

Look through my clothes and find that I have nothing whatever to wear in London. Read in *Daily Mirror* that all evening dresses are worn long, and realise with horror that not one of mine comes even half-way down my legs.

March 12th.—Collect major portion of my wardrobe and dispatch to address mentioned in advertisement pages of *Time and Tide* as prepared to pay Highest Prices for Outworn Garments, cheque by return. Have gloomy foreboding that six penny stamps by return will more adequately represent value of my contribution, and am thereby impelled to add Robert's old shooting-coat, mackintosh dating from 1907, and least reputable woollen sweater. Customary struggle ensues between frank and straightforward course of telling Robert What I have done, and less straightforward, but more practical, decision to keep complete silence on the point and let him make discovery for himself after parcel has left the house. Conscience, as usual, is defeated, but nevertheless unsilenced.

(Query: Would it not indicate greater strength of character, even if lesser delicacy of feeling, not to spend so much time on regretting errors of judgement and of behaviour? Reply almost certainly in the affirmative. Brilliant, but nebulous, outline of powerful Article for *Time and Tide* here suggests itself: *Is Ruthlessness more Profitable than Repentance?* Failing article—for which time at the moment is lacking, owing to departure of house-parlourmaid and necessity of learning "Wreck of the Hesperus" to recite at Village Concert—would this make suitable subject for Debate at Women's Institute? Feel doubtful as to whether our Vicar's wife would not think subject-matter trenching upon ground more properly belonging to our Vicar.)

Resign from Book of the Month Club, owing to wide and ever-increasing divergence of opinion between us as to merits or demerits of recently published fiction. Write them long and eloquent letter about this, but remember after it is posted that I still owe them twelve shillings and sixpence for Maurois's *Byron*.

March 13th.—Vicky and Mademoiselle leave, in order to pay visit to Aunt Gertrude. Mademoiselle becomes sentimental and says, "Ah, déjà je languis pour notre re-tour!" As total extent of her absence at this stage is about half-an-hour, and they have three weeks before them, feel that this is not a spirit to be encouraged. See them into the train, when Mademoiselle at once produces eau-de-Cologne in case either, or both, should be ill, and come home again. House resembles the tomb, and the gardener says that Miss Vicky seems such a little bit of a thing to be sent right away like that, and it isn't as if she could write and *tell* me how she was getting on, either.

Go to bed feeling like a murderess.

March 14th.—Rather inadequate Postal Order arrives, together with white tennis coat trimmed with rabbit, which—says accompanying letter—is returned as being unsaleable. Should like to know *why*. Toy with idea of writing to *Time and Tide*'s Editor, enquiring if every advertisement is subjected to personal scrutiny before insertion, but decide that this, in the event of a reply, might involve me in difficult explanations and diminish my *prestige* as occasional recipient of First Prize (divided) in Weekly Competition.

(*Mem.*: See whether tennis coat could be dyed and transformed into evening cloak.)

Am unfortunately found at home by callers, Mr. and Mrs. White, who are starting a Chicken-farm in the neighbourhood, and appear to have got married on the expectation of making a fortune out of it. We talk about chickens, houses, scenery, and the train-service between here and London. I ask if they play tennis, and politely suggest that both are probably brilliant performers. Mr. White staggers me by replying Oh, he wouldn't say *that*, exactly—meaning that he would, if it didn't seem like boasting. He enquires about Tournaments. Mrs. White is reminded of Tournaments in which they have, or have not, come out victors in the past. They refer to their handicap. Resolve never to ask the Whites to play on our extremely inferior court.

Later on talk about politicians. Mr. White says that in *his* opinion Lloyd George is clever, but Nothing Else. That's *all*, says Mr. White impressively. Just Clever. I refer to Coalition Government and Insurance Act, but Mr. White repeats firmly that both were brought about by mere Cleverness. He adds that Baldwin is a thoroughly *honest* man, and that Ramsay MacDonald is *weak*. Mrs. White supports him with an irrelevant statement to the effect that the Labour Party must be hand in glove with Russia, otherwise how would the Bolshevists dare to go on like that?

She also suddenly adds that Prohibition and the Jews and Everything are really the thin end of the wedge, don't I think so? I say Yes, I do, as the quickest way of ending the conversation, and ask if she plays the piano, to which she says No, but the Ukelele a little bit, and we talk about local shops and the delivery of a Sunday paper.

(*N.B.* Amenities of conversation afford very, very curious study sometimes, especially in the country.)

The Whites take their departure. Hope never to set eyes on either of them again.

March 15th.—Robert discovers absence of mackintosh dating from 1907. Says that he would "rather have lost a hundred pounds"—which I know to be untrue. Unsuccessful evening follows. Cannot make up my mind whether to tell him at once about shooting-coat and sweater, and get it all over in one, or leave him to find out for himself when present painful impression has had time to die away. Ray of light pierces impenetrable gloom when Robert is driven to enquire if I can tell him "a word for *calmer* in seven letters" and I, after some thought, suggest "*serener*"—which he says will do, and returns to *Times* Crossword Puzzle. Later he asks for famous mountain in Greece, but does not accept my too-hasty offer of Mount Atlas, nor listen to interesting explanation as to associative links between Greece, Hercules, and Atlas, which I proffer. After going into it at some length, I perceive that Robert is not attending, and retire to bed.

March 17th.—Travel up to London with Barbara Blenkinsop—(wearing new tweed)—who says she is going to spend a fortnight with old school-friend at Streatham and is looking forward to the Italian Art Exhibition. I say that I am, too, and ask after Mrs. B. Barbara says that she is Wonderful. We discuss Girl Guides, and exchange surmises as to reason why Mrs. T. at the Post Office is no longer on speaking terms with Mrs. L. at the shop. Later on, conversation takes a more intellectual turn, and we agree that the Parish Magazine needs Brightening Up. I suggest a crossword puzzle, and Barbara says a Children's Page. Paddington is reached just as we decide that it would be hopeless to try and get a contribution to the Parish Magazine from anyone really *good*, such as Shaw, Bennett, or Galsworthy.

I ask Barbara to tea at my club one day next week, she accepts, and we part.

Met by Rose, who has a new hat, and says that *no one* is wearing a brim, which discourages me—partly because I have nothing *but* brims, and partly because I know only too well that I shall look my worst without one. Confide this fear to Rose, who says, Why not go to well-known Beauty Culture Establishment, and have course of treatment there? I look at myself in the glass, see much room for improvement, and agree to this, only stipulating that all shall be kept secret as the grave, as could not tolerate the idea of Lady B.'s comments, should she ever come to hear of it. Make appointment by telephone. In the meantime, says Rose, what about the Italian Art Exhibition? She herself has already been four times. I say Yes, yes—it is one of the things I have come to London *for*, but should prefer to go earlier in the day. Then, says Rose, the first thing tomorrow morning? To this I reply, with every sign of reluctance, that to-morrow morning*must* be devoted to Registry Offices. Well, says Rose, when *shall* we go? Let us, I urge, settle that a little later on, when I know better what I am doing. Can see that Rose thinks anything but well of me, but she is too tactful to say more. Quite realise that I shall have to go to the Italian Exhibition sooner or later, and am indeed quite determined to do so, but feel certain that I shall understand nothing about it when I do get there, and shall find myself involved in terrible difficulties when asked my impressions afterwards.

Rose's cook, as usual, produces marvellous dinner, and I remember with shame and compassion that Robert, at home, is sitting down to minced beef and macaroni cheese, followed by walnuts.

Rose says that she is taking me to dinner to-morrow, with distinguished woman-writer who has marvellous collection of Jade, to meet still more distinguished Professor (female) and others. Decide to go and buy an evening dress to-morrow, regardless of overdraft.

March 18th.—Very successful day, although Italian Art Exhibition still unvisited. (Mem.: Positively *must* go there before meeting Barbara for tea at my club.)

Visit several Registry Offices, and am told that maids do not like the country—which I know already—and that the wages I am offering are low. Come away from there depressed, and decide to cheer myself up by purchasing evening dress—which I cannot afford—with present-day waist—which does not suit me. Select the Brompton Road, as likely to contain what I want, and crawl up it, scrutinising windows. Come face-to-face with Barbara Blenkinsop, who says,*How* extraordinary we should meet here, to which I reply that that is so often the way, when one comes to London. She is, she tells me, just on her way to the Italian Exhibition...I at once say Good-bye, and plunge into elegant establishment with expensive-looking garments in the window.

Try on five dresses, but find judgement of their merits very difficult, as hair gets wilder and wilder, and nose more devoid of powder. Am also worried by extraordinary and tactless tendency of saleswoman to emphasise the fact that all the colours I like are very trying by daylight, but will be less so at night. Finally settle on silver tissue with large bow, stipulate for its immediate delivery, am told that this is impossible, reluctantly agree to carry it away with me in cardboard box, and go away wondering if it wouldn't have been better to choose the black chiffon instead.

Hope that Beauty Parlour experiment may enhance self-respect, at present at rather low ebb, but am cheered by going into Fuller's and sending boxes of chocolates to Robin and Vicky respectively. Add peppermint creams for Mademoiselle by an afterthought, as otherwise she may find herself *blessée*. Lunch on oxtail soup, lobster mayonnaise, and cup of coffee, as being menu furthest removed from that obtainable at home.

Beauty Parlour follows. Feel that a good deal could be written on this experience, and even contemplate—in connection with recent observations exchanged between Barbara B. and myself—brightening the pages of our Parish Magazine with result of my reflections, but on second thoughts abandon this, as unlikely to appeal to the Editor (Our Vicar).

Am received by utterly terrifying person with dazzling complexion, indigo-blue hair, and orange nails, presiding over reception room downstairs, but eventually passed on to extremely pretty little creature with auburn bob and charming smile. Am reassured. Am taken to discreet curtained cubicle and put into long chair. Subsequent operations, which take hours and hours, appear to consist of the removal of hundreds of layers of dirt from my face. (These discreetly explained away by charming operator as the result of "acidity".) She also plucks away portions of my eyebrows. Very, very painful operation.

Eventually emerge more or less unrecognisable, and greatly improved. Lose my head, and buy Foundation Cream, rouge, powder, lip-stick. Foresee grave difficulty in reconciling Robert to the use of these appliances, but decide not to think about this for the present.

Go back to Rose's flat in time to dress for dinner. She tells me that she spent the afternoon at the Italian Exhibition.

March 19th.—Rose takes me to dine with talented group of her friends, connected with Feminist Movement. I wear new frock, and for once in my life am satisfied with my appearance (but still regret great-aunt's diamond ring, now brightening pawnbroker's establishment back-street Plymouth). Am, however, compelled to make strong act of will in order to banish all recollection of bills that will subsequently come in from Beauty Parlour and dressmaker. Am able to succeed in this largely owing to charms of distinguished Feminists, all as kind as possible. Well-known Professor—(concerning whom I have previously consulted Rose as to the desirability of reading up something about Molecules or other kindred topic, for conversational purposes)—completely overcomes me by producing, with a charming smile, two cigarette-cards, as she has heard that I collect them for Robin. After this, throw all idea of Molecules to the winds, and am happier for the rest of the evening in consequence.

Editor of well-known literary weekly also present, and actually remembers that we met before at Literary Club dinner. I discover, towards the end of the dinner, that she has not visited the Italian Exhibition—and give Rose a look that I hope she takes to heart.

Cocktails, and wholly admirable dinner, further brighten the evening. I sit next Editor, and she rather rashly encourages me to give my opinion of her paper. I do so freely, thanks to cocktail and Editor's charming manners, which combine to produce in me the illusion that my words are witty, valuable, and thoroughly well worth listening to. (Am but too well aware that later in the night I shall wake up in cold sweat, and view this scene in retrospect with very different feelings as to my own part in it.)

Rose and I take our leave just before midnight, sharing taxi with very well-known woman dramatist. (Should much like Lady B. to know this, and have every intention of making casual mention to her of it at earliest possible opportunity.)

Offices, less

March 20th.—More Registry Offices, less success than ever.

Barbara Blenkinsop comes to tea with me at my club, and says that Streatham is very gay, and that her friends took her to a dance last night and a Mr. Crosbie Carruthers drove her home afterwards in his car. We then talk about clothes—dresses all worn long in the evening—this graceful, but not hygienic—women will never again submit to long skirts in the day-time—most people growing their hair—but eventually Barbara reverts to Mr. C. C. and asks if I think a girl makes herself cheap by allowing a man friend to take her out to dinner in Soho? I say No, not at all, and inwardly decide that Vicky would look nice as bridesmaid in blue taffetas, with little wreath of Banksia roses.

A letter from dear Robin, forwarded from home, arrives to-night. He says, wouldn't a motor tour in the Easter holidays be great fun, and a boy at school called Briggs is going on one. (Briggs is the only son of millionaire parents, owning two Rolls-Royces and any number of chauffeurs.) Feel that it would be unendurable to refuse this trustful request, and decide that I can probably persuade Robert into letting me drive the children to the far side of the county in the old Standard. Can call this modest expedition a motor tour if we stay the night at a pub. and return the next day.

At the same time realise that, financial situation being what it is, and moreover time rapidly approaching when great-aunt's diamond ring must either be redeemed, or relinquished for ever, there is nothing for it but to approach Bank on subject of an overdraft.

Am never much exhilarated at this prospect, and do not in the least find that it becomes less unpleasant with repetition, but rather the contrary. Experience customary difficulty in getting to the point, and Bank Manager and I discuss weather, political situation, and probable Starters for the Grand National with passionate suavity for some time. Inevitable pause occurs, and we look at one another across immense expanse of pink blotting-paper. Irrelevant impulse rises in me to ask if he has other supply, for use, in writing-table drawer, or if fresh pad is brought in whenever a client calls. (Strange divagations of the human brain under the stress of extreme nervousness presents itself here as interesting topic for speculation. Should like to hear opinion of Professor met last night on this point. Subject far preferable to Molecules.)

Long, and rather painful, conversation follows. Bank Manager kind, but if he says the word "security" once, he certainly says it twenty times. Am, myself, equally insistent with "temporary accommodation only", which I think sounds thoroughly businesslike, and at the same time optimistic as to speedy repayment. Just as I think we are over the worst, Bank Manager reduces me to spiritual pulp by suggesting that we should see how the Account Stands at the Moment. Am naturally compelled to agree to this with air of well-bred and detached amusement, but am in reality well aware that the Account Stands—or, more accurately, totters—on a Debit Balance of Thirteen Pounds, two shillings, and tenpence. Large sheet of paper, bearing this impressive statement, is presently brought in and laid before us.

Negotiations resumed.

Eventually emerge into the street with purpose accomplished, but feeling completely unstrung for the day. Rose is kindness personified, produces Bovril and an excellent lunch, and agrees with me that it is All Nonsense to say that Wealth wouldn't mean Happiness, because we know quite well that it *would*.

March 21st.—Express to Rose serious fear that I shall lose my reason if no house-parlourmaid materialises. Rose, as usual, sympathetic, but can suggest nothing that I have not already tried. We go to a Sale in order to cheer ourselves up, and I buy yellow linen tennis-frock—£1 9s. 6d.— on strength of newly-arranged overdraft, but subsequently suffer from the conviction that I am taking the bread out of the mouths of Robin and Vicky.

Rather painful moment occurs when I suggest the Italian Exhibition to Rose, who replies—after a peculiar silence—that it is now *over*. Can think of nothing whatever to say, and do not care for dear Rose's expression, so begin at once to discuss new novels with as much intelligence as I can muster.

March 22nd.—Completely amazed by laconic postcard from Robert to say that local Registry Office can supply us with house-parlour*man*, and if I am experiencing difficulty in finding anyone, had we not better engage him? I telegraph back Yes, and then feel that I have made a mistake, but Rose says No, and refuses to let me rush out and telegraph again, for which, on subsequent calmer reflection, I feel grateful to her—and am sure that Robert would be still more so, owing to well-authenticated masculine dislike of telegrams.

Spend the evening writing immense letter to Robert enclosing list of duties of house-parlourman. (Jib at thought of being called by him in the mornings with early tea, and consult Rose, who says boldly, Think of waiters in Foreign Hotels!—which I do, and am reminded at once of many embarrassing episodes which I would rather forget.) Also send detailed instructions to Robert regarding the announcement of this innovation to Cook. Rose again takes up modern and fearless attitude, and says that Cook, mark her words, will be delighted.

I spend much of the night thinking over the whole question of running the house successfully, and tell myself—not by any means for the first time—that my abilities are very, very deficient in this direction. Just as the realisation of this threatens to overwhelm me altogether, I fall asleep.

HOWARD FITZSIMMONS.

March 25th.—Return home, to Robert, Helen Wills, and new house-parlourman, who is—I now learn for the first time—named Fitzsimmons. I tell Robert that it is impossible that he should be called this. Robert replies, Why not? Can only say that if Robert cannot see this for himself, explanation will be useless. Then, says Robert, no doubt we can call him by his first name. This, on investigation, turns out to be Howard. Find myself quite unable to cope with any of it, and the whole situation is met by my never calling the house-parlourman anything at all except "you" and speaking of him to Robert as "Howard Fitzsimmons", in inverted commas as though intending to be funny. Very unsatisfactory solution.

Try to tell Robert all about London—(with exception of Italian Exhibition, which I do not mention)—but Aladdin lamp flares up, which interferes, and have also to deal with correspondence concerning Women's Institute Monthly Meeting, replacement of broken bedroom tumblers—attributed to Ethel—disappearance of one pyjama-jacket and two table-napkins in the wash, and instructions to Howard Fitzs. concerning his duties. (*Mem.:* Must certainly make it crystal-clear that acceptable formula, when receiving an order, is not "Right-oh!" Cannot, at the moment, think how to word this, but must work it out, and then deliver with firmness and precision.)

Robert very kind about London, but perhaps rather more interested in my having met Barbara Blenkinsop—which, after all, I can do almost any day in the village—than in my views on *Nine till Six* (the best play I have seen for ages) or remarkable increase of traffic in recent years. Tell Robert by degrees about my new clothes. He asks when I expect to wear them, and I reply that one never knows—which is only too true—and conversation closes.

Write long letter to Angela, for the express purpose of referring casually to Rose's distinguished friends, met in London.

March 27th.—Angela replies to my letter, but says little about distinguished society in which I have been moving, and asks for full account of my impressions of Italian Exhibition. She and William, she says, went up on purpose to see it, and visited it three times. Can only say—but do not, of course, do so—that William must have been dragged there by the hair of his head.

March 28th.—Read admirable, but profoundly discouraging, article in *Time and Tide* relating to Bernard Shaw's women, but applying to most of us. Realise—not for the first time—that intelligent women can perhaps best perform their duty towards their own sex by devastating process of telling them the truth about themselves. At the same time, cannot feel that I shall really enjoy hearing it. Ultimate paragraph of article, moreover, continues to haunt me most unpleasantly with reference to own undoubted vulnerability where Robin and Vicky are concerned. Have very often wondered if Mothers are not rather A Mistake altogether, and now definitely come to the conclusion that they *are*.

Interesting speculation as to how they might best be replaced interrupted by necessity of seeing that Fitzs. is turning out spare-bedroom according to instructions. Am unspeakably disgusted at finding him sitting in spare-room armchair, with feet on the window-sill. He says that he is "not feeling very well". Am much more taken aback than he is, and lose my head to the extent of replying: "Then go and be it in your own room." Realise afterwards that this might have been better worded.

April 2nd.—Barbara calls. Can she, she says, speak to me in *confidence?* I assure her that she can, and at once put Helen Wills and kitten out of the window in order to establish confidential atmosphere. Sit, seething with excitement, in the hope that I am at least going to be told that Barbara is engaged. Try to keep this out of sight, and to maintain expression of earnest and sympathetic attention only, whilst Barbara says that it is sometimes very difficult to know which way Duty lies, that she has always thought a true woman's highest vocation is home-making, and that the love of a Good Man is the crown of life. I say Yes, Yes, to all of this. (Discover, on thinking it over, that I do not agree with any of it, and am shocked at my own extraordinary duplicity.)

Barbara at length admits that Crosbie has asked her to marry him—he did it, she says, at the Zoo—and go out with him as his wife to the Himalayas. This, says Barbara, is where all becomes difficult. She may be old-fashioned—no doubt she is—but can she leave her mother alone? No, she cannot. Can she, on the other hand, give up dear Crosbie, who has never loved a girl before, and says that he never will again? No, she cannot.

"HE DID IT, SHE SAYS, AT THE ZOO."

Barbara weeps. I kiss her. Howard Fitzsimmons selects this moment to walk in with the tea, at which I sit down again in confusion and begin to talk about the Vicarage daffodils being earlier than ours, just as Barbara launches into the verdict in the Podmore Case. We gyrate uneasily in and out of these topics while Howard Fitzsimmons completes his preparations for tea. Atmosphere ruined, and destruction completed by my own necessary enquiries as to Barbara's wishes in the matter of milk, sugar, bread-and-butter, and so on. (*Mem.*: Must speak to Cook about sending in minute segment of sponge-cake, remains of one which, to my certain recollection, made its first appearance more than ten days ago. Also, why perpetual and unappetising procession of small rock-cakes?)

Robert comes in, he talks of swine-fever, all further confidences become impossible. Barbara takes her leave immediately after tea, only asking if I could look in on her mother and have a Little Talk? I reluctantly agree to do so, and she mounts her bicycle and rides off. Robert says, That girl holds herself well, but it's a pity she has those ankles.

April 4th.—Go to see old Mrs. Blenkinsop. She is, as usual, swathed in shawls, but has exchanged *Lord Beaconsfield* for *Froude and Carlyle*. She says that I am very good to come and see a poor old woman, and that she often wonders how it is that so many of the younger generation seem to find their way to her by instinct. Is it, she suggests, because her *heart* has somehow kept young, in spite of her grey hair and wrinkles, ha-ha-ha, and so she has always been able to find the Silver Lining, she is thankful to say. I circuitously approach the topic of Barbara. Mrs. B. at once says that the young are very hard and selfish. This is natural, perhaps, but it saddens her. Not on her own account—no, no, no—but because she cannot bear to think of what Barbara will have to suffer from remorse when it is Too Late.

Feel a strong inclination to point out that this is *not* finding the Silver Lining, but refrain. Long monologue from old Mrs. B. follows. Main points that emerge are: (a) That Mrs. B. has not got very many more years to spend amongst us; (b) that all her life has been given up to others, but that she deserves no credit for this, as it is just the way she is made; (c) that all she wants is to see her Barbara happy, and it matters nothing at all that she herself should be left alone and helpless in her old age, and no one is to give a thought to that for a moment. Finally, that it has never been her way to think of herself or of her own feelings. People have often said to her that they believe she *has* no self—simply, none at all.

Pause, which I do not attempt to fill, ensues.

We return to Barbara, and Mrs. B. says it is very natural that a girl should be wrapped up in her own little concerns. I feel that we are getting no further, and boldly introduce the name of Crosbie Carruthers. Terrific effect on Mrs. B., who puts her hand on her heart, leans back, and begins to gasp and turn blue. She is sorry, she pants, to be so foolish, but it is now many nights since she has had any sleep at all, and the strain is beginning to tell. I must forgive her. I hastily do forgive her, and depart.

Very, very unsatisfactory interview.

Am told, on my way home, by Mrs. S. of the *Cross and Keys*, that a gentleman is staying there who is said to be engaged to Miss Blenkinsop, but the old lady won't hear of it, and he seems such a nice gentleman too, though perhaps not quite as young as some, and do I think the Himalayas would be All Right if there was a baby coming along? Exchange speculations and comments with Mrs. S. for some time before recollecting that the whole thing is supposed to be private, and that in any case gossip is undesirable.

Am met at home by Mademoiselle with intelligent enquiry as to the prospects of Miss Blenkinsop's immediate marriage, and the attitude adopted by old Mrs. B. "Le coeur d'une mère," says Mademoiselle sentimentally. Even the infant Vicky suddenly demands if that gentleman at the *Cross and Keys* is really Miss Blenkinsop's True Love? At this, Mademoiselle screams, "Ah, mon Dieu, ces enfants anglais!" and is much upset at impropriety of Vicky's language.

Even Robert enquires What All This Is, about Barbara Blenkinsop? I explain, and he returns—very, very briefly—that old Mrs. Blenkinsop ought to be Shot—which gets us no further, but meets with my entire approval.

April 10th.—Entire parish now seething with the *affaire* Blenkinsop. Old Mrs. B. falls ill, and retires to bed. Barbara bicycles madly up and down between her mother and the garden of the *Cross and Keys*, where C. C. spends much time reading copies of *The Times of India* and smoking small cigars. We are all asked by Barbara What she Ought to Do, and all give different advice. Deadlock appears to have been reached, when C. C. suddenly announces that he is summoned to London and must have an answer One Way or the Other immediately.

Old Mrs. B.—who has been getting better and taking Port—instantly gets worse again and says that she will not long stand in the way of dear Barbara's happiness.

Period of fearful stress sets in, and Barbara and C. C. say Good-bye in the front sitting-room of the *Cross and Keys*. They have, says Barbara in tears, parted For Ever, and Life is Over, and will I take the Guides' Meeting for her to-night—which I agree to do.

April 12th.—Return of Robin for the holidays. He has a cold, and, as usual, is short of handkerchiefs. I write to the Matron about this, but have no slightest hope of receiving either handkerchiefs or rational explanation of their disappearance. Robin mentions that he has invited "a boy" to come and stay for a week. I ask, Is he very nice and a great friend of yours? Oh no, says Robin, he is one of the most unpopular boys in the school. And after a moment he adds, *That's why*. Am touched, and think that this denotes a generous spirit, but am also undeniably rather apprehensive as to possible characteristics of future guest. I repeat the story to Mademoiselle, who—as usual, when I praise Robin—at once remarks: "Madame, notre petite Vicky n'a pas de défauts"—which is neither true nor relevant.

Receive a letter from Mary K. with postscript: Is it true that Barbara Blenkinsop is engaged to be married? and am also asked the same question by Lady B., who looks in on her way to some ducal function on the other side of the county. Have no time in which to enjoy being in the superior position of bestowing information, as Lady B. at once adds that *she* always advises girls to marry, no matter what the man is like, as any husband is better than none, and there are not nearly enough to go round.

I immediately refer to Rose's collection of distinguished Feminists, giving her to understand that I know them all well and intimately, and have frequently discussed the subject with them. Lady B. waves her hand—(in elegant white kid, new, not cleaned)—and declares That may be all very well, but if they could have got *husbands* they wouldn't be Feminists. I instantly assert that all have had husbands, and some two or three. This may or may not be true, but have seldom known stronger homicidal impulse. Final straw is added when Lady B. amiably observes that *I*, at least, have nothing to complain of, as she always thinks Robert such a safe, respectable husband for *any* woman. Give her briefly to understand that Robert is in reality a compound of Don Juan, the Marquis de Sade, and Dr. Crippen, but that we do not care to let it be known locally. Cannot say whether she is or is not impressed by this, as she declares herself obliged to go, because ducal function "cannot begin without her". All I can think of is to retort that Duchesses—(of whom, in actual fact, I do not know any)—always remind me of Alice in Wonderland, as do white kid gloves of the White Rabbit. Lady B. replies that I am always so well-read, and car moves off leaving her with, as usual, the last word.

Evolve in my own mind merry fantasy in which members of the Royal Family visit the neighbourhood and honour Robert and myself by becoming our guests at luncheon. (Cannot quite fit Howard Fitzs. into this scheme, but gloss over that aspect of the case.) Robert has just been raised to the peerage, and I am, with a slight and gracious inclination of the head, taking precedence of Lady B. at large dinner party, when Vicky comes in to say that the Scissor-Grinder is at the door, and if we haven't anything to grind, he'll be pleased to attend to the clocks or rivet any china.

Am disconcerted at finding itinerant gipsy, of particularly low appearance, encamped at back door, with collection of domestic articles strewn all round him and his machine. Still more disconcerted at appearance of Mademoiselle, in fits of loud and regrettable Gallic merriment, bearing extremely unsuitable fragments of bedroom ware in either hand...She, Vicky, and the Scissor-Grinder join in unseemly mirth, and I leave them to it, thankful that at least Lady B. is by now well on her way and cannot descend upon the scene. Am seriously exercised in my mind as to probable standard of humour with which Vicky will grow up.

Look for Robin and eventually find him with the cat, shut up into totally unventilated linen-cupboard, eating cheese which he says he found on the back stairs.

(Undoubtedly, a certain irony can be found in the fact that I have recently been appointed to new Guardians Committee, and am expected to visit Workhouse, etc., with particular reference to children's quarters, in order that I may offer valuable suggestions on questions of hygiene and general welfare of inmates...Can only hope that fellow-members of the Committee will never be inspired to submit my own domestic arrangements to similar inspection.)

Write letters. Much interrupted by Helen Wills, wanting to be let out, kitten, wanting to be let in, and dear Robin, who climbs all over all the furniture, apparently unconscious that he is doing so, and tells me at the same time, loudly and in full, the story of *The Swiss Family Robinson*.

April 14th.—Cook electrifies me by asking me if I have heard that Miss Barbara Blenkinsop's engagement is on again, it's all over the village. The gentleman, she says, came down by the 8.45 last night, and is at the *Cross and Keys*. As it is exactly 9.15 A.M. when she tells me this, I ask how she knows? Cook merely repeats that It is All Over the Village, and that Miss Barbara will quite as like as not be married by special licence, and old Mrs. B. is in such a way as never was. Am disconcerted to find that Cook and I have been talking our heads off for the better part of forty minutes before I remember that gossip is both undignified and undesirable.

Just as I am putting on my hat to go down to the Blenkinsops' our Vicar's wife rushes in. All is true, she says, *and more.* Crosbie Carruthers, in altogether desperate state, has threatened suicide, and written terrific farewell letter to Barbara, who has cried herself—as our Vicar's wife rather strangely expresses it—to the merest *pulp*, and begged him to Come At Once. A Blenkinsop Family Council has been summoned—old Mrs. B. has had Attacks—(nobody quite knows what of)—but has finally been persuaded to reconsider entire problem. Our Vicar has been called in to give impartial advice and consolation to all parties. He is there now. Surely, I urge, he will use all his influence on behalf of C. C. and Barbara? Our Vicar's wife, agitated, says Yes, Yes,—he is all in favour of young folk living their own lives, whilst at the same time he feels that a mother's claims are sacred, and although he realises the full beauty of self-sacrifice, yet on the other hand no one knows better than he does that the devotion of a Good Man is not to be lightly relinquished.

Feel that if this is to be our Vicar's only contribution towards the solution of the problem, he might just as well have stayed at home—but naturally do not impart this opinion to his wife. We decide to walk down to the village, and do so. The gardener stops me on the way, and says he thought I might like to know that Miss Barbara's young gentleman has turned up again, and wants to marry her before he sails next month, and old Mrs. Blenkinsop is taking on so, they think she'll have a stroke.

Similar information also reaches us from six different quarters in the village. No less than three motor-cars and two bicycles are to be seen outside old Mrs. B.'s cottage, but no one emerges, and I am obliged to suggest that our Vicar's wife should come home with me to lunch. This she does, after many demurs, and gets cottage-pie—(too much onion)—rice-shape, and stewed prunes. Should have sent to the farm for cream, if I had known.

COUSIN MAUD.

300

April 15th.—Old Mrs. Blenkinsop reported to have Come Round. Elderly unmarried female Blenkinsop, referred to as Cousin Maud, has suddenly materialised, and offered to live with her—Our Vicar has come out boldly in support of this scheme—and Crosbie Carruthers has given Barbara engagement ring with three stones, said to be rare Indian Topazes, and has gone up to town to Make Arrangements. Immediate announcement in the *Morning Post* expected.

April 18th.—Receive visit from Barbara, who begs that I will escort her to London for quiet and immediate wedding. Am obliged to refuse, owing to bad colds of Robin and Vicky, general instability of domestic staff, and customary unsatisfactory financial situation. Offer then passed on to our Vicar's wife, who at once accepts it. I undertake, however, at Barbara's urgent request, to look in as often as possible on her mother. Will I, adds Barbara, make it clear that she is not losing a Daughter, but only gaining a Son, and two years will soon be over, and at the end of that time dear Crosbie will bring her home to England. I recklessly commit myself to doing anything and everything, and write to the Army and Navy Stores for a luncheon-basket, to give as wedding-present to Barbara. The Girl Guides present her with a sugar-castor and a waste-paper basket embossed with raffia flowers. Lady B. sends a chafing-dish with a card bearing illegible and far-fetched joke connected with Indian curries. We all agree that this is not in the least amusing. Mademoiselle causes Vicky to present Barbara with small tray-cloth, on which two hearts are worked in cross-stitch.

April 19th.—Both children simultaneously develop incredibly low complaint known as "pink-eye" that everyone unites in telling me is peculiar to the more saliently neglected and underfed section of the juvenile population in the East End of London.

Vicky has a high temperature and is put to bed, while Robin remains on his feet, but is not allowed out of doors until present cold winds are over. I leave Vicky to Mademoiselle and *Les Mémoires d'un Ane* in the night-nursery, and undertake to amuse Robin downstairs. He says that he has a Splendid Idea. This turns out to be that I should play the piano, whilst he simultaneously sets off the gramophone, the musical-box, and the chiming clock.

I protest.

Robin implores, and says It will be just like an Orchestra. (Shade of Dame Ethel Smyth, whose Reminiscences I have just been reading!) I weakly yield, and attack, *con spirito*, "The Broadway Melody" in the key of C Major. Robin, in great excitement, starts the clock, puts "Mucking About the Garden" on the gramophone, and winds up the musical-box, which tinkles out the Waltz from *Floradora* in a tinny sort of way, and no recognisable key. Robin springs about and cheers. I watch him sympathetically and keep down, at his request, the loud pedal.

The door is flung open by Howard Fitzs., and Lady B. enters, wearing bran-new green Kasha with squirrel collar, and hat to match, and accompanied by military-looking friend.

Have no wish to record subsequent few minutes, in which I endeavour to combine graceful greetings to Lady B. and the military friend, with simple and yet dignified explanation of singular state of affairs presented to them, and unobtrusive directions to Robin to switch off musical-box and gramophone and betake himself and his pink-eye upstairs. Clock has mercifully ceased to chime, and Robin struggles gallantly with musical-box, but "Mucking About the Garden" continues to ring brazenly through the room for what seems about an hour and a half...(Should not have minded quite so much if it had been "Classical Memories", which I also possess, or even a Layton and Johnstone duet.)

Robin goes upstairs, but not until after Lady B. has closely scrutinised him, and observed that He looks like Measles, to her. Military friend tactfully pretends absorption in the nearest bookcase until this is over, when he emerges with breezy observation concerning *Bulldog Drummond*.

Lady B. at once informs him that he must not say that kind of thing to *me*, as I am so Very Literary. After this, the military friend looks at me with unconcealed horror, and does not attempt to speak to me again. On the whole, am much relieved when the call is over.

Go upstairs and see Vicky, who seems worse, and telephone for the doctor. Mademoiselle begins lugubrious story, which is evidently destined to end disastrously, about a family in her native town mysteriously afflicted by Smallpox—(of which all the preliminary symptoms were identical with those of Vicky's present disorder)—afterwards traced to unconsidered purchase by *le papa* of Eastern rugs, sold by itinerant vendor on the quay at Marseilles. Cut her short after the death of the six-months-old baby, as I perceive that all the other five children are going to follow suit, as slowly and agonisingly as possible.

April 20th.—Vicky develops unmistakable measles, and doctor says that Robin may follow suit any day. Infection must have been picked up at Aunt Gertrude's, and shall write and tell her so. Extraordinary and nightmare-like state of affairs sets in, and I alternate between making lemonade for Vicky and telling her the story of *Frederick and the Picnic* upstairs, and bathing Robin's pink-eye with boracic lotion and reading *The Coral Island* to him downstairs.

Mademoiselle is *dévouée* in the extreme, and utterly refuses to let anyone but herself sleep in Vicky's room, but find it difficult to understand exactly on what principle it is that she persists in wearing a *peignoir* and *pantoufles* day and night alike. She is also unwearied in recommending very strange *tisanes*, which she proposes to brew herself from herbs—fortunately unobtainable—in the garden.

Robert, in this crisis, is less helpful than I could wish, and takes up characteristically masculine attitude that We are All Making a Great Fuss about Very Little, and the whole thing has been got up for the express purpose of putting him to inconvenience—(which, however, it does not do, as he stays out all day, and insists on having dinner exactly the same as usual every evening).

Vicky incredibly and alarmingly good, Robin almost equally so in patches, but renders himself unpopular with Fitzs. by leaving smears of Plasticine, pools of paint-water, and even blots of ink on much of the furniture. Find it very difficult to combine daily close inspection of him, with a view to discovering the beginning of measles, with light-hearted optimism that I feel to be right and rational attitude of mind.

Weather very cold and rainy, and none of the fires will burn up. Cannot say why this is, but it adds considerably to condition of gloom and exhaustion which I feel to be gaining upon me hourly.

April 25th.—Vicky recovering slowly, Robin showing no signs of measles. Am myself victim of curious and unpleasant form of chill, no doubt due to over-fatigue.

Howard Fitzsimmons gives notice, to the relief of everyone, and I obtain service of superior temporary house-parlourmaid at cost of enormous weekly sum.

April 27th.—Persistence of chill compels me to retire to bed for half a day, and Robert suggests gloomily that I have caught the measles. I demonstrate that this is impossible, and after lunch get up and play cricket with Robin on the lawn. After tea, keep Vicky company. She insists upon playing at the Labours of Hercules, and we give energetic representations of slaughtering the Hydra, cleaning out the Augean Stables, and so on. Am divided between gratification at Vicky's classical turn of mind and strong disinclination for so much exertion.

May 7th.—Resume Diary after long and deplorable interlude, vanquished chill having suddenly reappeared with immense force and fury, and revealed itself as measles. Robin, on same day, begins to cough, and expensive hospital nurse materialises and takes complete charge. She proves kind and efficient, and brings me messages from the children, and realistic drawing from Robin entitled "Ill person being eaten up by jerms".

(Query: Is dear Robin perhaps future Heath Robinson or Arthur Watts?)

Soon after this all becomes incoherent and muddled. Chief recollection is of hearing the doctor say that of course my Age is against me, which hurts my feelings and makes me feel like old Mrs. Blenkinsop. After a few days, however, I get the better of my age, and am given champagne, grapes, and Valentine's Meat Juice.

Should like to ask what all this is going to cost, but feel it would be ungracious.

The children, to my astonishment, are up and about again, and allowed to come and see me. They play at Panthers on the bed, until removed by Nurse. Robin reads aloud to me, article on Lord Chesterfield from pages of *Time and Tide*, which has struck him because he, like the writer, finds it difficult to accept a compliment gracefully. What do *I* do, he enquires, when I receive so many compliments all at once that I am overwhelmed? Am obliged to admit that I have not yet found myself in this predicament, at which Robin looks surprised, and slightly disappointed.

Robert, the nurse, and I decide in conclave that the children shall be sent to Bude for a fortnight with Nurse, and Mademoiselle given a holiday in which to recover from her exertions. I am to join the Bude party when doctor permits.

Robert goes to make this announcement to the nursery, and comes back with fatal news that Mademoiselle is *blessée*, and that the more he asks her to explain, the more monosyllabic she becomes. Am not allowed either to see her or to write explanatory and soothing note and am far from reassured by Vicky's report that Mademoiselle, bathing her, has wept, and said that in England there are hearts of stone.

May 12th.—Further interlude, this time owing to trouble with the eyes. (No doubt concomitant of my Age, once again.) The children and hospital nurse depart on the 9th, and I am left to gloomy period of total inactivity and lack of occupation. Get up after a time and prowl about in kind of semi-ecclesiastical darkness, further intensified by enormous pair of tinted spectacles. One and only comfort is that I cannot see myself in the glass. Two days ago, decide to make great effort and come down for tea, but nearly relapse and go straight back to bed again at sight of colossal demand for the Rates, confronting me on hall-stand without so much as an envelope between us.

(*Mem.*: This sort of thing so very unlike picturesque convalescence in a novel, when heroine is gladdened by sight of spring flowers, sunshine, and what not. No mention ever made of Rates, or anything like them.)

Miss the children very much and my chief companion is kitchen cat, a hard-bitten animal with only three and a half legs and a reputation for catching and eating a nightly average of three rabbits. We get on well together until I have recourse to the piano, when he invariably yowls and asks to be let out. On the whole, am obliged to admit that he is probably right, for I have forgotten all I ever knew, and am reduced to playing popular music by ear, which I do badly.

Dear Barbara sends me a book of Loopy Limericks, and Robert assures me that I shall enjoy them later on. Personally, feel doubtful of surviving many more days of this kind.

May 13th.—Regrettable, but undeniable ray of amusement lightens general murk on hearing report, through Robert, that Cousin Maud Blenkinsop possesses a baby Austin, and has been seen running it all round the parish with old Mrs. B., shawls and all, beside her. (It is many years since Mrs. B. gave us all to understand that if she so much as walked across the room unaided, she would certainly fall down dead.)

Cousin Maud, adds Robert thoughtfully, is not *his* idea of a good driver. He says no more, but I at once have dramatic visions of old Mrs. B. flying over the nearest hedge, shawls waving in every direction, while Cousin Maud and the baby Austin charge a steam-roller in a narrow lane. Am sorry to record that this leads to hearty laughter on my part, after which I feel better than for weeks past.

The doctor comes to see me, says that he *thinks* my eyelashes will grow again—(should have preferred something much more emphatic, but am too much afraid of further reference to my age to insist)—and agrees to my joining children at Bude next week. He also, reluctantly, and with an air of suspicion, says that I may use my eyes for an hour every day, unless pain ensues.

May 15th.—Our Vicar's wife, hearing that I am no longer in quarantine, comes to enliven me. Greet her with an enthusiasm to which she must, I fear, be unaccustomed, as it appears to startle her. Endeavour to explain it (perhaps a little tactlessly) by saying that I have been alone so long...Robert out all day...children at Bude...and end up with quotation to the effect that I never hear the sweet music of speech, and start at the sound of my own. Can see by the way our Vicar's wife receives this that she does not recognise it as a quotation, and believes the measles to have affected my brain. (Query: Perhaps she is right?) More normal atmosphere established by a plea from our Vicar's wife that kitchen cat may be put out of the room. It is, she knows, very foolish of her, but the presence of a cat makes her feel faint. Her grandmother was exactly the same. Put a cat into the same room as her grandmother, hidden under the sofa if you liked, and in two minutes the grandmother would say: "I believe there's a cat in this room," and at once turn queer. I hastily put kitchen cat out of the window, and we agree that heredity is very odd.

And now, says our Vicar's wife, how am I? Before I can reply, she does so for me, and says that she knows just how I feel. Weak as a rat, legs like cotton-wool, no spine whatever, and head like a boiled owl. Am depressed by this diagnosis, and begin to feel that it must be correct. However, she adds, all will be different after a blow in the wind at Bude, and meanwhile, she must tell me all the news.

She does so.

Incredible number of births, marriages, and deaths appear to have taken place in the parish in the last four weeks; also Mrs. W. has dismissed her cook and cannot get another one, our Vicar has written a letter about Drains to the local paper and it has been put in, and Lady B. has been seen in a new car. To this our Vicar's wife adds rhetorically: Why not an aeroplane, she would like to know? (Why not, indeed?)

Finally a Committee Meeting has been held—at which, she interpolates hastily I was much missed—and a Garden Fête arranged, in aid of funds for Village Hall. It would be so nice, she adds optimistically, if the Fête could be held *here*. I agree that it would, and stifle a misgiving that Robert may not agree. In any case, he knows, and I know, and our Vicar's wife knows, that Fete will have to take place here, as there isn't anywhere else.

Tea is brought in—superior temporary's afternoon out, and Cook has, as usual, carried out favourite labour-saving device of three sponge-cakes and one bun jostling one another on the same plate—and we talk about Barbara and Crosbie Carruthers, beekeeping, modern youth, and difficulty of removing oil-stains from carpets. Have I, asks our Vicar's wife, read *A Brass Hat in No Man's Land*? No, I have not. Then, she says, *don't*, on any account. There are so many sad and shocking things in life as it *is*, that writers should confine themselves to the bright, the happy, and the beautiful. This the author of *A Brass Hat* has entirely failed to do. It subsequently turns out that our Vicar's wife has not read the book herself, but that our Vicar has skimmed it, and declared it to be very painful and unnecessary. (*Mem.*: Put *Brass Hat* down for *Times* Book Club list, if not already there.)

Our Vicar's wife suddenly discovers that it is six o'clock, exclaims that she is shocked, and attempts *fausse sortie*, only to return with urgent recommendation to me to try Valentine's Meat Juice, which once practically, under Providence, saved our Vicar's uncle's life. Story of the uncle's illness, convalescence, recovery, and subsequent death at the age of eighty-one, follows. Am unable to resist telling her, in return, about wonderful effect of Bemax on Mary Kell-way's youngest, and this leads—curiously enough—to the novels of Anthony Trollope, death of the Begum of Bhopal, and scenery in the Lake Country.

At twenty minutes to seven, our Vicar's wife is again shocked, and rushes out of the house. She meets Robert on the doorstep and stops to tell him that I am as thin as a rake, and a very bad colour, and the eyes, after measles, often give rise to serious trouble. Robert, so far as I can hear, makes no answer to any of it, and our Vicar's wife finally departs.

(Query here suggests itself: Is not silence frequently more efficacious than the utmost eloquence? Answer probably yes. Must try to remember this more often than I do.)

Second post brings a long letter from Mademoiselle, recuperating with friends at Clacton-on-Sea, written, apparently, with a pin point dipped in violet ink on thinnest imaginable paper, and crossed in every direction. Decipher portions of it with great difficulty, but am relieved to find that I am still "Bien-chère Madame" and that recent mysterious affront has been condoned.

(*Mem.*: If Cook sends up jelly even once again, as being suitable diet for convalescence, shall send it straight back to the kitchen.)

May 16th.—But for disappointing children, should be much tempted to abandon scheme for my complete restoration to health at Bude. Weather icy cold, self feeble and more than inclined to feverishness, and Mademoiselle, who was to have come with me, and helped with children, now writes that she is *désolée*, but has developed *une angine*. Do not know what this is, and have alarming thoughts about Angina Pectoris, but dictionary reassures me. I say to Robert: "After all, shouldn't I get well just as quickly at home?" He replies briefly: "Better go," and I perceive that his mind is made up. After a moment he suggests—but without real conviction—that I might like to invite our Vicar's wife to come with me. I reply with a look only, and suggestion falls to the ground.

A letter from Lady B. saying that she has only just heard about measles—(Why only just, when news has been all over parish for weeks?) and is so sorry, especially as measles are no joke at my age—(Can she be in league with Doctor, who also used identical objectionable expression?).—She cannot come herself to enquire, as with so many visitors always coming and going it wouldn't be wise, but if I want anything from the House, I am to telephone without hesitation. She has given "her people" orders that anything I ask for is to be sent up. Have a very good mind to telephone and ask for a pound of tea and Lady B.'s pearl necklace—(Could Cleopatra be quoted as precedent here?)—and see what happens.

Further demand for the Rates arrives, and Cook sends up jelly once more for lunch. I offer it to Helen Wills, who gives one heave, and turns away. Feel that this would more than justify me in sending down entire dish untouched, but Cook will certainly give notice if I do, and cannot face possibility. Interesting to note that although by this time all Cook's jellies take away at sight what appetite measles have left me, am more wholly revolted by emerald green variety than by yellow or red. Should like to work out possible Freudian significance of this, but find myself unable to concentrate.

Go to sleep in the afternoon, and awake sufficiently restored to do what I have long contemplated and Go Through my clothes. Result so depressing that I wish I had never done it. Have nothing fit to wear, and if I had, should look like a scarecrow in it at present. Send off parcel with knitted red cardigan, two evening dresses (much too short for present mode), three out-of-date hats, and tweed skirt that bags at the knees, to Mary Kellway's Jumble Sale, where she declares that *anything* will be welcome. Make out a list of all the new clothes I require, get pleasantly excited about them, am again confronted with the Rates, and put the list in the fire.

May 17th.—Robert drives me to North Road station to catch train for Bude. Temperature has fallen again, and I ask Robert if it is below zero. He replies briefly and untruthfully that the day will get warmer as it goes on, and no doubt Bude will be one blaze of sunshine. We arrive early and sit on a bench on the platform next to a young woman with a cough, who takes one look at me and then says: "Dreadful, isn't it?" Cannot help feeling that she has summarised the whole situation quite admirably. Robert hands me my ticket—he has handsomely offered to make it first-class and I have refused—and gazes at me with rather strange expression. At last he says: "You don't think you're going there to*die*, do you?" Now that he suggests it, realise that I *do* feel very like that, but summon up smile that I feel to be unconvincing and make sprightly reference to Bishop, whose name I forget, coming to lay his bones at place the name of which I cannot remember. All of it appears to be Greek to Robert, and I leave him still trying to unravel it. Journey ensues and proves chilly and exhausting. Rain lashes at the windows, and every time carriage door opens—which is often—gust of icy wind, mysteriously blowing in two opposite directions at once, goes up my legs and down back of my neck. Have not told children by what train I am arriving, so no one meets me, not even bus on which I had counted. Am, however, secretly thankful, as this gives me an excuse for taking a taxi. Reach lodgings at rather uninspiring hour of 2.45, too early for tea or bed, which constitute present summit of my ambitions. Uproarious welcome from children, both in blooming health and riotous spirits, makes up for everything.

May 19th.—Recovery definitely in sight, although almost certainly retarded by landlady's inspiration of sending up a nice jelly for supper on evening of arrival. Rooms reasonably comfortable—(except for extreme cold, which is, says landlady, quite unheard-of at this or any other time of year)—all is linoleum, pink and gold china, and enlarged photographs of females in lace collars and males with long moustaches and bow ties. Robin, Vicky, and the hospital nurse—retained at vast expense as a temporary substitute for Mademoiselle—have apparently braved the weather and spent much time on the Breakwater. Vicky has also made friends with a little dog, whose name she alleges to be "Baby", a gentleman who sells papers, another gentleman who drives about in a Sunbeam, and the head waiter from the Hotel. I tell her about Mademoiselle's illness, and after a silence she says "Oh!" in tones of brassy indifference, and resumes topic of little dog "Baby". Robin, from whom I cannot help hoping better things, makes no comment except "Is she?" and immediately adds a request for a banana.

(*Mem.*: Would it not be possible to write more domesticated and less foreign version of *High Wind in Jamaica*, featuring extraordinary callousness of infancy?) Can distinctly recollect heated correspondence in *Time and Tide* regarding *vraisemblance* or otherwise of Jamaica children, and now range myself, decidedly and for ever, on the side of the author. Can quite believe that dear Vicky would murder any number of sailors, if necessary.

May 23rd.—Sudden warm afternoon, children take off their shoes and dash into pools, landlady says that it's often like this On the. *last* day of a visit to the sea, she's noticed, and I take brisk walk over the cliffs, wearing thick tweed coat, and really begin to feel quite warm at the end of an hour. Pack suit-case after children are in bed, register resolution never to let stewed prunes and custard form part of any meal ever again as long as I live, and thankfully write postcard to Robert, announcing time of our arrival at home to-morrow.

May 28th.—Mademoiselle returns, and is greeted with enthusiasm—to my great relief. (Robin and Vicky perhaps less like Jamaica children than I had feared.) She has on new black and white check skirt, white blouse with frills, black kid gloves, embroidered in white on the backs, and black straw hat almost entirely covered in purple violets, and informs me that the whole outfit was made by herself at a total cost of one pound, nine shillings, and fourpence-halfpenny. The French undoubtedly thrifty, and gifted in using a needle, but cannot altogether stifle conviction that a shade less economy might have produced better results.

She presents me, in the kindest way, with a present in the shape of two blue glass flower-vases, of spiral construction, and adorned with gilt knobs at many unexpected points. Vicky receives a large artificial-silk red rose, which she fortunately appears to admire, and Robin a small affair in wire that is intended, says Mademoiselle, to extract the stones out of cherries.

(*Mem.*: Interesting to ascertain number of these ingenious contrivances sold in a year.)

Am privately rather overcome by Mademoiselle's generosity, and wish that we could reach the level of the French in what they themselves describe as *petits soins*. Place the glass vases in conspicuous position on dining-room mantelpiece, and am fortunately just in time to stem comment which I see rising to Robert's lips when he sits down to midday meal and perceives them.

After lunch, Robin is motored back to school by his father, and I examine Vicky's summer wardrobe with Mademoiselle, and find that she has outgrown everything she has in the world.

May 30th.—Arrival of *Time and Tide*, find that I have been awarded half of second prize for charming little effort that in my opinion deserves better. Robert's attempt receives an honourable mention. Recognise pseudonym of first-prize winner as being that adopted by Mary Kellway. Should like to think that generous satisfaction envelops me, at dear friend's success, but am not sure. This week's competition announces itself as a Triolet—literary form that I cannot endure, and rules of which I am totally unable to master.

Receive telephone invitation to lunch with the Frobishers on Sunday. I accept, less because I want to see them than because a change from domestic roast beef and gooseberry-tart always pleasant; moreover, absence makes work lighter for the servants. (*Mem.*: Candid and intelligent self-examination as to motive, etc., often leads to very distressing revelations.)

Constrained by conscience, and recollection of promise to Barbara, to go and call on old Mrs. Blenkinsop. Receive many kind enquiries in village as to my complete recovery from measles, but observe singular tendency on part of everybody else to treat this very serious affliction as a joke.

Find old Mrs. B.'s cottage in unheard-of condition of hygienic ventilation, no doubt attributable to Cousin Maud. Windows all wide open, and casement curtains flapping in every direction, very cold east wind more than noticeable. Mrs. B.—(surely fewer shawls than formerly?)—sitting quite close to open window, and not far from equally open door, seems to have turned curious shade of pale-blue, and shows tendency to shiver. Room smells strongly of furniture polish and black-lead. Fireplace, indeed, exhibits recent handsome application of the latter, and has evidently not held fire for days past. Old Mrs. B. more silent than of old, and makes no reference to silver linings and the like. (Can spirit of optimism have been blown away by living in continual severe draught?) Cousin Maud comes in almost immediately. Have met her once before, and say so, but she makes it clear that this encounter left no impression, and has entirely escaped her memory. Am convinced that Cousin Maud is one of those people who pride themselves on always speaking the truth. She is wearing brick-red sweater—feel sure she knitted it herself—tweed skirt, longer at the back than in front—and large row of pearl beads. Has very hearty and emphatic manner, and uses many slang expressions.

I ask for news of Barbara, and Mrs. B.—(voice a mere bleat, by comparison with Cousin Maud's)—says that the dear child will be coming down once more before she sails, and that continued partings are the lot of the Aged, and to be expected. I begin to hope that she is approaching her old form, but all is stopped by Cousin Maud, who shouts out that we're not to talk Rot, and it's a jolly good thing Barbara has got Off the Hooks at last, poor old girl. We then talk about golf handicaps, Roedean—Cousin Maud's dear old school—and the baby Austin. More accurate statement would perhaps be that Cousin Maud talks, and we listen. No sign of *Life of Disraeli*, or any other literary activities, such as old Mrs. B. used to be surrounded by, and do not like to enquire what she now does with her time. Disquieting suspicion that this is probably settled for her, without reference to her wishes.

Take my leave feeling depressed. Old Mrs. B. rolls her eyes at me as I say goodbye, and mutters something about not being here much longer, but this is drowned by hearty laughter from Cousin Maud, who declares that she is Nothing but an Old Humbug and will See Us All Out.

Am escorted to the front gate by Cousin Maud, who tells me what a topping thing it is for old Mrs. B. to be taken out of herself a bit, and asks if it isn't good to be Alive on a bracing day like this? Should like to reply that it would be far better for some of us to be dead, in my opinion, but spirit for this repartee fails me, and I weakly reply that I know what she means. I go away before she has time to slap me on the back, which I feel certain will be the next thing.

Had had in mind amiable scheme for writing to Barbara to-night to tell her that old Mrs. B. is quite wonderful, and showing no signs of depression, but this cannot now be done, and after much thought, do not write at all, but instead spend the evening trying to reconcile grave discrepancy between account-book, counterfoils of cheque-book, and rather unsympathetically worded communication from the Bank.

June 1st.—Sunday lunch with the Frobishers, and four guests staying in the house with them—introduced as, apparently, Colonel and Mrs. Brightpie—(which seems impossible)—Sir William Reddieor Ready, or Reddy, or perhaps even Reddeigh—and My sister Violet. Latter quite astonishingly pretty, and wearing admirable flowered tussore that I, as usual, mentally try upon myself, only to realise that it would undoubtedly suggest melancholy saying concerning mutton dressed as lamb.

The Colonel sits next to me at lunch, and we talk about fishing, which I have never attempted, and look upon as cruelty to animals, but this, with undoubted hypocrisy and moral cowardice, I conceal. Robert has My sister Violet, and I hear him at intervals telling her about the pigs, which seems odd, but she looks pleased, so perhaps is interested.

Conversation suddenly becomes general, as topic of present-day Dentistry is introduced by Lady F. We all, except Robert, who eats bread, have much to say.

(*Mem.*: Remember to direct conversation into similar channel, when customary periodical deathly silence descends upon guests at my own table.)

Weather is wet and cold, and had confidently hoped to escape tour of the garden, but this is not to be, and directly lunch is over we rush out into the damp. Boughs drip on to our heads and water squelches beneath our feet, but rhododendrons and lupins undoubtedly very magnificent, and references to Ruth Draper not more numerous than usual. I find myself walking with Mrs. Brightpie (?), who evidently knows all that can be known about a garden. Fortunately she is prepared to originate all the comments herself, and I need only say, "Yes, isn't that an attractive variety?" and so on. She enquires once if I have *ever* succeeded in making the dear blue Grandiflora Magnifica Superbiensis—(or something like that)—feel really happy and at home in this climate? to which I am able to reply with absolute truth by a simple negative, at which I fancy she looks rather relieved. Is her own life perhaps one long struggle to acclimatise the G. M. S.? and what would she have replied if I had said that, in *my* garden, the dear thing grew like a weed?

(*Mem.*: Must beware of growing tendency to indulge in similar idle speculations, which lead nowhere, and probably often give me the appearance of being absentminded in the society of my fellow-creatures.)

After prolonged inspection, we retrace steps, and this time find myself with Sir William R. and Lady F. talking about grass. Realise with horror that we are now making our way towards the *stables*. Nothing whatever to be done about it, except keep as far away from the horses as possible, and refrain from any comment whatever, in hopes of concealing that I know nothing about horses except that they frighten me. Robert, I notice, looks sorry for me, and places himself between me and terrifying-looking animal that glares out at me from loose-box and curls up its lip. Feel grateful to him, and eventually leave stables with shattered nerves and soaking wet shoes. Exchange customary graceful farewells with host and hostess, saying how much I have enjoyed coming.

(Query here suggests itself, as often before: Is it utterly impossible to combine the amenities of civilisation with even the minimum of honesty required to satisfy the voice of conscience? Answer still in abeyance at present.)

Robert goes to Evening Service, and I play Halma with Vicky. She says that she wants to go to school, and produces string of excellent reasons why she should do so. I say that I will think it over, but am aware, by previous experience, that Vicky has almost miraculous aptitude for getting her own way, and will probably succeed in this instance as in others.

Rather depressing Sunday supper—cold beef, baked potatoes, salad, and depleted cold tart—after which I write to Rose, the Cleaners, the Army and Navy Stores, and the County Secretary of the Women's Institute, and Robert goes to sleep over the *Sunday Pictorial.*

June 3rd.—Astounding and enchanting change in the weather, which becomes warm. I carry chair, writing-materials, rug, and cushion into the garden, but am called in to have a look at the Pantry Sink, please, as it seems to have blocked itself up. Attempted return to garden frustrated by arrival of note from the village concerning Garden Fete arrangements, which requires immediate answer, necessity for speaking to the butcher on the telephone, and sudden realisation that Laundry List hasn't yet been made out, and the Van will be here at eleven. When it does come, I have to speak about the tablecloths, which leads—do not know how—to long conversation about the Derby, the Van speaking highly of an outsider—*Trews*—whilst I uphold the chances of *Silver Flare*—(mainly because I like the name).

Shortly after this, Mrs. S. arrives from the village, to collect jumble for Garden Fête, which takes time. After lunch, sky clouds over, and Mademoiselle and Vicky kindly help me to carry chair, writing-materials, rug, and cushion into the house again.

Robert receives letter by second post announcing death of his godfather, aged ninety-seven, and decides to go to the funeral on 5th June.

(*Mem.*: Curious, but authenticated fact, that a funeral is the only gathering to which the majority of men ever go willingly. Should like to think out why this should be so, but must instead unearth top-hat and other accoutrements of woe and try if open air will remove smell of naphthaline.)

June 7th.—Receive letter—(Why, in Heaven's name, not telegram?)—from Robert, to announce that godfather has left him Five Hundred Pounds. This strikes me as so utterly incredible and magnificent that I shed tears of pure relief and satisfaction. Mademoiselle comes in, in the midst of them, and on receiving explanation kisses me on both cheeks and exclaims: "Ah, je m'en doutais! Voilá bien ce bon Saint Antoine!" Can only draw conclusion that she has, most touchingly, been petitioning Heaven on our behalf, and very nearly weep again at the thought. Spend joyful evening making out lists of bills to be paid, jewellery to be redeemed, friends to be benefited, and purchases to be made, out of legacy, and am only slightly disconcerted on finding that net total of lists, when added together, comes to exactly one thousand three hundred and twenty pounds.

June 9th.—Return, yesterday, of Robert, and have every reason to believe that, though neither talkative nor exuberant, he fully appreciates newly achieved stability of financial position. He warmly concurs in my suggestion that great-aunt's diamond ring should be retrieved from Plymouth pawnbroker's in time to figure at our next excitement, which is the Garden Fete, and I accordingly hasten to Plymouth by earliest available bus.

Not only do I return with ring—(pawnbroker, after a glance at the calendar, congratulates me on being just in time)—but have also purchased new hat for myself, many yards of material for Vicky's frocks, a Hornby train for Robin, several gramophone records, and a small mauve bag for Mademoiselle. All give the utmost satisfaction, and I furthermore arrange to have hot lobster and fruit salad for dinner—these, however, not a great success with Robert, unfortunately, and he suggests—though kindly—that I was perhaps thinking more of my own tastes than of his, when devising this form of celebration. Must regretfully acknowledge truth in this. Discussion of godfather's legacy fills the evening happily, and I say that we ought to give a Party, and suggest combining it with Garden Fete. Robert replies, however,—and on further reflection find that I agree with him—that this would not conduce to the success of either entertainment, and scheme is abandoned. He also begs me to get Garden Fête over before I begin to think of anything else, and I agree to do so.

June 12th.—Nothing is spoken of but weather, at the moment propitious—but who can say whether similar conditions will prevail on 17th?—relative merits of having the Tea laid under the oak trees or near the tennis-court, outside price that can be reasonably asked for articles on Jumble Stall, desirability of having Ice-cream combined with Lemonade Stall, and the like. Date fortunately coincides with Robin's half-term, and I feel that he must and shall come home for the occasion. Expense, as I point out to Robert, now nothing to us. He yields. I become reckless, have thoughts of a House-party, and invite Rose to come down from London. She accepts.

Dear old school-friend Cissie Crabbe, by strange coincidence, writes that she will be on her way to Land's End on 16th June; may she stay for two nights? Yes, she may. Robert does not seem pleased when I explain that he will have to vacate his dressing-room for Cissie Crabbe, as Rose will be occupying spare bedroom, and Robin at home. This will complete House-party.

June 17th.—Entire household rises practically at dawn, in order to take part in active preparations for Garden Fete. Mademoiselle reported to have refused breakfast in order to put final stitches in embroidered pink satin boot-bag for Fancy Stall, which she has, to my certain knowledge, been working at for the past six weeks. At ten o'clock our Vicar's wife dashes in to ask what I think of the weather, and to say that she cannot stop a moment. At eleven she is still here, and has been joined by several stall-holders, and tiresome local couple called White, who want to know if there will be a Tennis Tournament, and if not, is there not still time to organise one? I reply curtly in the negative to both suggestions and they depart, looking huffed. Our Vicar's wife says that this may have lost us their patronage at the Fete altogether, and that Mrs. White's mother, who is staying with them, is said to be rich, and might easily have been worth a couple of pounds to us.

Diversion fortunately occasioned by unexpected arrival of solid and respectable-looking claret-coloured motor-car, from which Barbara and Crosbie Carruthers emerge. Barbara is excited; C. C. remains calm but looks benevolent. Our Vicar's wife screams, and throws a pair of scissors wildly into the air. (They are eventually found in Bran Tub containing Twopenny Dips, and are the cause of much trouble, as small child who fishes them out maintains them to be *bona fide* dip and refuses to give them up.)

Barbara looks blooming, and says how wonderful it is to see the dear old place quite unchanged. Cannot whole-heartedly agree with this, as it is not three months since she was here last, but fortunately she requires no answer, and says that she and C. C. are looking up old friends and will return for the Opening of the Fete this afternoon.

Robert goes to meet old school-friend Cissie Crabbe at station, and Rose and I to help price garments at Jumble Stall. (Find that my views are not always similar to those of other members of Committee. Why, for instance, only three-and-sixpence for grey georgette only sacrificed reluctantly at eleventh hour from my wardrobe?)

Arrival of Cissie Crabbe (wearing curious wool hat which I at once feel would look better on Jumble Stall) is followed by cold lunch. Have made special point of remembering nuts and banana sandwiches for Cissie, but have difficulty in preventing Robin and Vicky—to whom I have omitted to give explanation—making it obvious that they would prefer this diet to cold lamb and salad. Just as tinned pineapple and junket stage is passed, Robin informs me that there are people beginning to arrive, and we all disperse in desperate haste and excitement, to reappear in best clothes. I wear red foulard and new red hat, but find—as usual—that every petticoat I have in the world is either rather too long or much too short. Mademoiselle comes to the rescue and puts safety-pins in shoulder-straps, one of which becomes unfastened later and causes me great suffering. Rose, also as usual, looks nicer than anybody else in delightful green delaine. Cissie Crabbe also has reasonably attractive dress, but detracts from effect with numerous scarab rings, cameo brooches, tulle scarves, enamel buckles, and barbaric necklaces. Moreover, she clings (I think mistakenly) to little wool hat, which looks odd. Robin and Vicky both present enchanting appearance, although Mary's three little Kellways, all alike in pale rose tussore, undeniably decorative. (Natural wave in hair of all three, which seems to me unjust, but nothing can be done until Vicky reaches age suitable for Permanent Waving.)

CISSIE CRABBE.

Lady Frobisher arrives—ten minutes too early—to open Fete, and is walked about by Robert until our Vicar says, Well, he thinks perhaps that we are now all gathered together...(Have profane impulse to add "*In the sight of God*", but naturally stifle it.) Lady F. is poised gracefully on little bank under the chestnut tree, our Vicar beside her, Robert and myself modestly retiring a few paces behind, our Vicar's wife kindly, but mistakenly, trying to induce various unsuitable people to mount bank—which she humorously refers to as the Platform—when all is thrown into confusion by sensational arrival of colossal Bentley containing Lady B.—in sapphire-blue and pearls—with escort of fashionable creatures, male and female, apparently dressed for Ascot.

LADY FROBISHER.

"Go on, go on!" says Lady B., waving hand in white kid glove, and dropping small jewelled bag, lace parasol, and embroidered handkerchief as she does so. Great confusion while these articles are picked up and restored, but at last we do go on, and Lady F. says what a pleasure it is to her to be here to-day, what a desirable asset a Village Hall is, and much else to the same effect. Our Vicar thanks her for coming here to-day—so many claims upon her time—Robert seconds him with almost incredible brevity—someone else thanks Robert and myself for throwing open these magnificent grounds—(tennis-court, three flower borders, and microscopic shrubbery)—I look at Robert, who shakes his head, thus obliging me to make necessary reply myself, and our Vicar's wife, with undeniable presence of mind, darts forward and reminds Lady F. that she has forgotten to declare the Fete open. This is at once done and we disperse to stalls and sideshows.

Am stopped by Lady B., who asks reproachfully, Didn't I know that she would have been perfectly ready to open the Fete herself, if I had asked her? Another time, she says, I am not to hesitate for a *moment*. She then spends ninepence on a lavender bag, and drives off again with expensive-looking friends. This behaviour provides topic of excited conversation for us all, throughout the whole of the afternoon.

Everyone else buys nobly, unsuitable articles are raffled—(raffling illegal, winner to pay sixpence)—guesses are made as to contents of sealed boxes, number of currants in large cake, weight of bilious-looking ham, and so on. Band arrives, is established on lawn, and plays selections from *The Geisha*. Mademoiselle's boot-bag bought by elegant purchaser in grey flannels, who turns out, on closer inspection, to be Howard Fitzsimmons. Just as I recover from this, Robin, in wild excitement, informs me that he has won a Goat in a raffle. (Goat has fearful local reputation, and is of immense age and savageness.) Have no time to do more than say how *nice* this is, and he had better run and tell Daddy, before old Mrs. B., Barbara, C. C., and Cousin Maud all turn up together. (Can baby Austin *possibly* have accommodated them all?) Old Mrs. B. rather less subdued than at our last meeting, and goes so far as to say that she has very little money to spend, but that she always thinks a smile and a kind word are better than gold, with which I inwardly disagree.

Am definitely glad to perceive that C. C. has taken up cast-iron attitude of unfriendliness towards Cousin Maud, and contradicts her whenever she speaks. Sports, tea, and dancing on the tennis-lawn all successful—(except possibly from point of view of future tennis-parties)—and even Robin and Vicky do not dream of eating final ice cream cornets, and retiring to bed, until ten o'clock.

Robert, Rose, Cissie Crabbe, Helen Wills, and myself all sit in the drawing-room in pleasant state of exhaustion, and congratulate ourselves and one another. Robert has information, no doubt reliable, but source remains mysterious, to the effect that we have Cleared Three Figures. All, for the moment, is *couleur-de-rose*.

June 23rd.—Tennis-party at wealthy and elaborate house, to which Robert and I now bidden for the first time. (Also, probably, the last.) Immense opulence of host and hostess at once discernible in fabulous display of deck-chairs, all of complete stability and miraculous cleanliness. Am introduced to youngish lady in yellow, and serious young man with horn-rimmed spectacles. Lady in yellow says at once that she is sure I have a lovely garden. (Why?) Elderly, but efficient-looking, partner is assigned to me, and we play against the horn-rimmed spectacles and agile young creature in expensive crepe-de-chine. Realise at once that all three play very much better tennis than I do. Still worse, realise that *they* realise this. Just as we begin, my partner observes gravely that he ought to tell me he is a left-handed player. Cannot imagine what he expects me to do about it, lose my head, and reply madly that That is Splendid.

Game proceeds, I serve several double-faults, and elderly partner becomes graver and graver. At beginning of each game he looks at me and repeats score with fearful distinctness, which, as it is never in our favour, entirely unnerves me. At "Six-*one*" we leave the court and silently seek chairs as far removed from one another as possible. Find myself in vicinity of Our Member, and we talk about the Mace, peeresses in the House of Lords—on which we differ—winter sports, and Alsatian dogs.

Robert plays tennis, and does well.

Later on, am again bidden to the court and, to my unspeakable horror, told to play once more with elderly and efficient partner.

I apologise to him for this misfortune, and he enquires in return, with extreme pessimism. Fifty years from now, what will it matter if we *have* lost this game? Neighbouring lady—probably his wife?—looks agitated at this, and supplements it by incoherent assurances about its being a great pleasure, in any case. Am well aware that she is lying, but intention evidently very kind, for which I feel grateful. Play worse than ever, and am not unprepared for subsequent enquiry from hostess as to whether I think I have *really* quite got over the measles, as she has heard that it often takes a full year. I reply, humorously, that, so far as tennis goes, it will take far more than a full year. Perceive by expression of civil perplexity on face of hostess that she has entirely failed to grasp this rather subtle witticism, and wish that I hadn't made it. Am still thinking about this failure, when I notice that conversation has, mysteriously, switched on to the United States of Ameerca, about which we are all very emphatic. Americans, we say, undoubtedly *hospitable*—but what about the War Debt? What about Prohibition? What about Sinclair Lewis? Aimée MacPherson, and Co-education? By the time we have done with them, it transpires that none of is have ever been to America, but all hold definite views, which fortunately coincide with the views of everybody else.

(Query: Could not interesting little experiment he tried, by possessor of unusual amount of moral courage, in the shape of suddenly producing perfectly brand-new opinion: for example, to the effect that Americans have better manners than we have, or that their divorce laws are a great improvement upon our own? Should much like to see effect of these, or similar, psychological bombs, but should definitely wish Robert to he absent from the scene.)

Announcement of tea breaks off these intelligent speculations.

Am struck, as usual, by infinite superiority of other people's food to my own.

Conversation turns upon Lady B. and everyone says she is really very kindhearted, and follows this up by anecdotes illustrating all her less attractive qualities. Youngish lady in yellow declares that she met Lady B. last week in London, face three inches thick in new sunburn-tan. Can quite believe it. Feel much more at home after this, and conscious of new bond of union cementing entire party. Sidelight thus thrown upon human nature regrettable, but not to be denied. Even tennis improves after this, entirely owing to my having told funny story relating to Lady B.'s singular behaviour in regard to local Jumble Sale, which meets with success. Serve fewer double-faults, but still cannot quite escape conviction that whoever plays with me invariably loses the set—which I cannot believe to be mere coincidence.

Suggest to Robert, on the way home, that I had better give up tennis altogether, to which, after long silence—during which I hope he is perhaps evolving short speech that shall be at once complimentary and yet convincing—he replies that he does not know what I could take up instead. As I do not know either, the subject is dropped, and we return home in silence.

June 27th.—Cook says that unless I am willing to let her have the Sweep, she cannot possibly be responsible for the stove. I say that of course she can have the Sweep. If not, Cook returns, totally disregarding this, she really can't say what won't happen. I reiterate my complete readiness to send the Sweep a summons on the instant, and Cook continues to look away from me and to repeat that unless I *will* agree to having the Sweep in, there's no knowing.

This dialogue—cannot say why—upsets me for the remainder of the day.

June 30th.—The Sweep comes, and devastates the entire day. Bath-water and meals are alike cold, and soot appears quite irrelevantly in portions of the house totally removed from sphere of Sweep's activities. Am called upon in the middle of the day to produce twelve-and-sixpence in cash, which I cannot do. Appeal to everybody in the house, and find that nobody else can, either. Finally Cook announces that the Joint has just come and can oblige at the back door, if I don't mind its going down in the hook. I do not, and the Sweep is accordingly paid and disappears on a motor-bicycle.

July 3rd.—Breakfast enlivened by letter from dear Rose written at, apparently, earthly paradise of blue sea and red rocks, on South Coast of France. She says that she is having complete rest, and enjoying congenial society of charming group of friends, and makes unprecedented suggestion that I should join her for a fortnight. I am moved to exclaim—perhaps rather thoughtlessly—that the most wonderful thing in the world must be to be a childless widow—but this is met by unsympathetic silence from Robert, which recalls me to myself, and impels me to say that that isn't in the least what I meant.

(*Mem.*: Should often be very, very sorry to explain exactly what it is that I *do* mean, and am in fact conscious of deliberately avoiding self-analysis on many occasions. Do not propose, however, to go into this now or at any other time.)

I tell Robert that if it wasn't for the expense, and not having any clothes, and the servants, and leaving Vicky, I should think seriously of Rose's suggestion. Why, I enquire rhetorically, should Lady B. have a monopoly of the South of France? Robert replies, Well—and pauses for such a long while that I get agitated, and have mentally gone through the Divorce Court with him, before he ends up by saying Well, again, and picking up the *Western Morning News*. Feel—but do not say—that this, as contribution to discussion, is inadequate. Am prepared, however, to continue it single-handed sooner than allow subject to drop altogether. Do so, but am interrupted first by entrance of Helen Wills through the window—(Robert says, Dam' that cat, I shall have it drowned, but only absent-mindedly)—and then by spirit-lamp, which is discovered to be extinct, and to require new wick. Robert strongly in favour of ringing immediately, but I discourage this, and undertake to speak about it instead, and tie knot in pocket-handkerchief. (Unfortunately overcharged memory fails later when in kitchen, and find myself unable to recollect whether marmalade has run to sugar through remaining too long in jar, or merely porridge lumpier than usual—but this a digression.)

I read Rose's letter all over again, and feel that I have here opportunity of a lifetime. Suddenly hear myself exclaiming passionately that Travel broadens the Mind, and am immediately reminded of our Vicar's wife, who frequently makes similar remark before taking our Vicar to spend fortnight's holiday in North Wales.

Robert finally says Well, again—this time tone of voice slightly more lenient—and then asks if it is quite impossible for his bottle of Eno's to be left undisturbed on bathroom shelf?

I at once and severely condemn Mademoiselle as undoubted culprit, although guiltily aware that original suggestion probably emanated from myself. And what, I add, about the South of France? Robert looks astounded, and soon afterwards leaves the dining-room without having spoken.

I deal with my correspondence, omitting Rose's letter. Remainder boils down to rather uninspiring collection of Accounts Rendered, offensive little pamphlet that makes searching enquiry into the state of my gums, postcard from County Secretary of Women's Institutes with notice of meeting that I am expected to attend, and warmly worded personal communication addressed me by name from unknown Titled Gentleman, which ends up with a request for five shillings if I cannot spare more, in aid of charity in which he is interested. Whole question of South of France is shelved until evening, when I seek Mademoiselle in schoolroom, after Vicky has gone to bed. Am horrified to see that supper, awaiting her on the table, consists of cheese, pickles, and slice of jam roly-poly, grouped on single plate—(Would not this suggest to the artistic mind a Still-life Study in Modern Art?)—flanked by colossal jug of cold water. Is this, I ask, what Mademoiselle *likes*? She assures me that it is and adds, austerely, that food is of no importance to her. She could go without anything for days and days, without noticing it. From her early childhood, she has always been the same.

(Query unavoidably suggests itself here: Does Mademoiselle really expect me to believe her, and if so, what can be her opinion of my mental capacity?)

We discuss Vicky: tendency to argumentativeness, I hint. "C'est un petit coeur d 'or," returns Mademoiselle immediately. I agree, in modified terms, and Mademoiselle at once points out dear Vicky's undeniable obstinacy and self-will, and goes so far as to say: "Plus tard, ce sera un esprit fort...elle ira loin, cette petite."

I bring up the subject of the South of France. Mademoiselle more than sympathetic, assures me that I must, at all costs, go, adding—a little unnecessarily—that I have grown many, many years older in the last few months, and that to live as I do, without any distractions, only leads to madness in the end.

Feel that she could hardly have worded this more trenchantly, and am a good deal impressed.

(Query: Would Robert see the force of these representations, or not? Robert apt to take rather prejudiced view of all that is not purely English.)

Return to drawing-room and find Robert asleep behind the *Times*. Read Rose's letter all over again, and am moved to make list of clothes that I should require if I joined her, estimate of expenses—financial situation, though not scintillating, still considerably brighter than usual, owing to recent legacy—and even Notes, on back of envelope, of instructions to be given to Mademoiselle, Cook, and the tradespeople, before leaving.

July 6th.—Decide definitely on joining Rose at Ste. Agathe, and write and tell her so. Die now cast, and Rubicon crossed—or rather will be, on achieving further side of the Channel. Robert, on the whole, takes lenient view of entire project, and says he supposes that nothing else will satisfy me, and better not count on really hot weather promised by Rose but take good supply of woollen underwear. Mademoiselle is sympathetic, but theatrical, and exclaims: "C'est la Ste. Vierge qui a tout arrange!" which sounds like a travel agency, and shocks me.

Go to Women's Institute Meeting and tell our Secretary that I am afraid I shall have to miss our next Committee Meeting. She immediately replies that the date can easily be altered. I protest, but am defeated by small calendar, which she at once produces, and begs me to select my own date, and says that It will be All the Same to the eleven other members of the Committee.

(Have occasional misgivings at recollection of rousing speeches made by various speakers from our National Federation, to the effect that all W.I. members enjoy equal responsibilities and equal privileges...Can only hope that none of them will ever have occasion to enter more fully into the inner workings of our Monthly Committee Meetings.)

July 12th.—Pay farewell calls, and receive much good advice. Our Vicar says that it is madness to drink water anywhere in France, unless previously boiled and filtered; our Vicar's wife shares Robert's distrust as to climate, and advises Jaeger next the skin, and also offers loan of small travelling medicine-chest for emergencies. Discussion follows as to whether Bisulphate of Quinine is, or is not, dutiable article, and is finally brought to inconclusive conclusion by our Vicar's pronouncing definitely that, in *any* case, Honesty is the Best Policy.

Old Mrs. Blenkinsop—whom I reluctantly visit whenever I get a letter from Barbara saying how grateful she is for my kindness—adopts quavering and enfeebled manner, and hopes she may be here to welcome me home again on my return, but implies that this is not really to be anticipated. I say Come, come, and begin well-turned sentence as to Mrs. B.'s wonderful vitality, when Cousin Maud bounces in, and inspiration fails me on the spot. What Ho! says Cousin Maud—(or at least, produces the effect of having said it, though possibly slang slightly more up-to-date than this—but not much)—What is all this about our cutting a dash on the Lido or somewhere, and leaving our home to take care of itself? Talk about the Emancipation of Females, says Cousin Maud. Should like to reply that no one, except herself, ever *does* talk about it—but feel this might reasonably be construed as uncivil, and do not want to upset unfortunate old Mrs. B., whom I now regard as a victim pure and simple. Ignore Cousin Maud, and ask old Mrs. B. what books she would advise me to take. Amount of luggage strictly limited, both as to weight and size, but could manage two very long ones, if in pocket editions, and another to be carried in coat-pocket for journey.

Old Mrs. B.—probably still intent on thought of approaching dissolution—suddenly says that there is nothing like the Bible—suggestion which I feel might more properly have been left to our Vicar. Naturally, give her to understand that I agree, but do not commit myself further.

Cousin Maud, in a positive way that annoys me, recommends No book At All, especially when crossing the sea. It is well known, she affirms, that any attempt to fix the eyes on printed page while ship is moving induces sea-sickness quicker than anything else. Better repeat poetry, or the multiplication-table, as this serves to distract the mind. Have no assurance that the multiplication-table is at my command, but do not reveal this to Cousin Maud.

Old Mrs. B., abandoning Scriptural attitude, now says, Give her Shakespeare. Everything is to be found in Shakespeare. Look at *King Lear*, she says. Cousin Maud assents with customary energy—but should be prepared to take considerable bet that she has never read a word of *King Lear* since it was—presumably—stuffed down her throat at dear old Roedean, in intervals of cricket and hockey.

We touch on literature in general—old Mrs. B. observes that much that is published nowadays seems to her unnecessary, and why so much Sex in everything?—Cousin Maud says that books collect dust, anyway, and whisks away inoffensive copy of *Time and Tide* with which old Mrs. B. is evidently solacing herself in intervals of being hustled in and out of baby Austin—and I take my leave. Am embraced by old Mrs. B. (who shows tendency to have one of her old-time Attacks, but is briskly headed off it by Cousin Maud) and slapped on the back by Cousin Maud in familiar and extremely offensive manner.

Walk home, and am overtaken by well-known blue Bentley, from which Lady B. waves elegantly, and commands chauffeur to stop. He does so, and Lady B. says, Get in, Get in, never mind muddy boots—which makes me feel like a plough-boy. Good works, she supposes, have been taking me plodding round the village as usual? The way I go on, day after day, is too marvellous. Reply with utmost distinctness that I am just on the point of starting for the South of France, where I am joining party of distinguished friends. (This not entirely untrue, since dear Rose has promised introduction to many interesting acquaintances, including Viscountess.)

Really, says Lady B. But why not go at the right time of year? Or why not go all the way by sea?—yachting too marvellous. Or why not, again, make it Scotland, instead of France?

Do not reply to any of all this, and request to be put down at the corner. This is done, and Lady B. waves directions to chauffeur to drive on, but subsequently stops him again, and leans out to say that she can find out all about quite inexpensive *pensions* for me if I like. I do *not* like, and we part finally.

Find myself indulging in rather melodramatic fantasy of Bentley crashing into enormous motor-bus and being splintered to atoms. Permit chauffeur to escape unharmed, but fate of Lady B. left uncertain, owing to ineradicable impression of earliest childhood to the effect that It is Wicked to wish for the Death of Another. Do not consider, however, that severe injuries, with possible disfigurement, come under this law—but entire topic unprofitable, and had better be dismissed.

July 14th.—Question of books to be taken abroad undecided till late hour last night. Robert says, Why take any? and Vicky proffers *Les Malheurs de Sophie*, which she puts into the very bottom of my suit-case, whence it is extracted with some difficulty by Mademoiselle later. Finally decide on *Little Dorrit* and *The Daisy Chain*, with *Jane Eyre* in coat-pocket. Should prefer to be the kind of person who is inseparable from volume of Keats, or even Jane Austen, but cannot compass this.

July 15th.—*Mem.*: Remind Robert before starting that Gladys's wages due on Saturday. Speak about having my room turned out. Speak about laundry. Speak to Mademoiselle about Vicky's teeth, glycothymoline, Helen Wills *not* on bed, and lining of tussore coat. Write butcher. Wash hair.

July 17th.—Robert sees me off by early train for London, after scrambled and agitating departure, exclusively concerned with frantic endeavours to induce suit-case to shut. This is at last accomplished, but leaves me with conviction that it will be at least equally difficult to induce it to open again. Vicky bids me cheerful, but affectionate, good-bye and then shatters me at eleventh hour by enquiring trustfully if I shall be home in time to read to her after tea? As entire extent of absence has already been explained to her in full, this enquiry merely senseless—but serves to unnerve me badly, especially as Mademoiselle ejaculates: "Ah! la pauvre chère mignonne!" into the blue.

(*Mem.*: The French very often carried away by emotionalism to wholly preposterous lengths.)

Cook, Gladys, and the gardener stand at hall-door and hope that I shall enjoy my holiday, and Cook adds a rider to the effect that It seems to be blowing up for a gale, and for her part, she has always had a Norror of death by drowning. On this, we drive away.

THE GARDENER.

Arrive at station too early—as usual—and I fill in time by asking Robert if he will telegraph if anything happens to the children, as I could be back again in twenty-four hours. He only enquires in return whether I have my passport? Am perfectly aware that passport is in my small purple dressing-case, where I put it a week ago, and have looked at it two or three times every day ever since—last time just before leaving my room forty-five minutes ago. Am nevertheless mysteriously impelled to open hand-bag, take out key, unlock small purple dressing-case, and verify presence of passport all over again.

(Query: Is not behaviour of this kind well known in therapeutic circles as symptomatic of mental derangement? Vague but disquieting association here with singular behaviour of Dr. Johnson in London streets—but too painful to be pursued to a finish.)

Arrival of train, and I say good-bye to Robert, and madly enquire if he would rather I gave up going at all? He rightly ignores this altogether.

(Query: Would not extremely distressing situation arise if similar impulsive offer were one day to be accepted? This gives rise to unavoidable speculation in regard to sincerity of such offers, and here again, issue too painful to be frankly faced, and am obliged to shelve train of thought altogether.)

Turn my attention to fellow-travellerdistrustful-looking woman with grey hair—who at once informs me that door of lavatory—opening out of compartment—has defective lock, and will not stay shut. I say Oh, in tone of sympathetic concern, and shut door. It remains shut. We watch it anxiously, and it flies open again. Later on, fellow-traveller makes fresh attempt, with similar result. Much of the journey spent in this exercise. I observe thoughtfully that Hope springs eternal in the human breast, and fellow-traveller looks more distrustful than ever. She finally says in despairing tones that Really, it isn't what she calls very nice, and lapses into depressed silence. Door remains triumphantly open.

Drive from Waterloo to Victoria, take out passport in taxi in order to Have It Ready, then decide safer to put it back again in dressing-case, which I do. (Dr. Johnson recrudesces faintly, but is at once dismissed.) Observe with horror that trees in Grosvenor Gardens are swaying with extreme violence in stiff gale of wind.

Change English money into French at Victoria Station, where superior young gentleman in little kiosk refuses to let me have anything smaller than one-hundredfranc notes. I ask what use that will be when it comes to porters, but superior young gentleman remains adamant. Infinitely competent person in blue and gold, labelled Dean & Dawson, comes to my rescue, miraculously provides me with change, says Have I booked a seat, pilots me to it, and tells me that he represents the best-known Travel Agency in London. I assure him warmly that I shall never patronise any other—which is true—and we part with mutual esteem. I make note on half of torn luggage-label to the effect that it would be merest honesty to write and congratulate D. & D. on admirable employe—but feel that I shall probably never do it.

Journey to Folkestone entirely occupied in looking out of train window and seeing quite large trees bowed to earth by force of wind. Cook's words recur most unpleasantly. Also recall various forms of advice received, and find it difficult to decide between going instantly to the Ladies' Saloon, taking off my hat, and lying down Perfectly Flat—(Mademoiselle's suggestion)—or Keeping in the Fresh Air at All Costs and Thinking about Other Things—(course advocated on a postcard by Aunt Gertrude). Choice taken out of my hands by discovery that Ladies' Saloon is entirely filled, within five minutes of going on board, by other people, who have all taken off their hats and are lying down Perfectly Flat.

"SCHOOLMASTER AND HIS WIFE . . . TALK TO ONE ANOTHER
ACROSS ME."

Return to deck, sit on suit-case, and decide to Think about Other Things. Schoolmaster and his wife, who are going to Boulogne for a holiday, talk to one another across me about University Extension Course, and appear to be superior to the elements. I take out *Jane Eyre* from coatpocket—partly in faint hope of impressing them, and partly to distract my mind—but remember Cousin Maud, and am forced to conclusion that she may have been right. Perhaps advice equally correct in respect of repeating poetry? Can think of nothing whatever, except extraordinary damp chill which appears to be creeping over me. Schoolmaster suddenly says to me: "Quite all *right*, aren't you?" To which I reply, Oh yes, and he laughs in a bright and scholastic way, and talks about the Matterhorn. Although unaware of any conscious recollection of it, find myself inwardly repeating curious and ingenious example of alliterative verse, committed to memory in my schooldays. (*Note:* Can dimly understand why the dying revert to impressions of early infancy.)

Just as I get to:

"Cossack Commanders cannonading come
Dealing destruction's devastating doom—"

elements overcome me altogether. Have dim remembrance of hearing schoolmaster exclaim in authoritative tones to everybody within earshot: "Make way for this lady—she is *Ill*"—which injunction he repeats every time I am compelled to leave suitcase. Throughout intervals, I continue to grapple, more or less deliriously, with alliterative poem, and do not give up altogether until

"Reason returns, religious rights redound"

is reached. This I consider creditable.

Attain Boulogne at last, discover reserved seat in train, am told by several officials whom I question that we do, or alternatively, do not, change when we reach Paris, give up the elucidation of the point for the moment, and demand—and obtain small glass of brandy, which restores me.

July 18th, at Ste. Agathe.—Vicissitudes of travel very strange, and am struck—as often—by enormous dissimilarity between journeys undertaken in real life, and as reported in fiction. Can remember very few novels in which train journey of any kind does not involve either (a) Hectic encounter with member of opposite sex, leading to tense emotional issue; (6) discovery of murdered body in hideously battered condition, under circumstances which utterly defy detection; (c) elopement between two people each of whom is married to somebody else, culminating in severe disillusionment, or lofty renunciation.

Nothing of all this enlivens my own peregrinations, but on the other hand, the night not without incident.

Second-class carriage full, and am not fortunate enough to obtain corner-seat. American young gentleman sits opposite, and elderly French couple, with talkative friend wearing blue béret, who trims his nails with a pocket-knife and tells us about the state of the wine-trade.

I have dusty and elderly mother in black on one side, and her two sons—names turn out to be Guguste and Dédé—on the other. (Dédé looks about fifteen, but wears socks, which I think a mistake, but must beware of insularity.)

Towards eleven o'clock we all subside into silence, except the blue béret, who is now launched on tennis-champions, and has much to say about all of them. American young gentleman looks uneasy at mention of any of his compatriots, but evidently does not understand enough French to follow blue béret's remarks—which is as well.

Just as we all—except indefatigable béret, now eating small sausage-rolls—drop one by one into slumber, train stops at station and fragments of altercation break out in corridor concerning admission, or otherwise, of someone evidently accompanied by large dog. This is opposed by masculine voice repeating steadily, at short intervals: "Un chien n'est pas une personne," and heavily backed by assenting chorus, repeating after him: "Mais non, un chien n'est pas une personne."

To this I fall asleep, but wake a long time afterwards, to sounds of appealing enquiry, floating in from corridor: "Mais voyons—N'est-ce pas qu'un chien n'est pas une personne?"

ELDERLY FRENCH COUPLE WITH TALKATIVE FRIEND.

The point still unsettled when I sleep again, and in the morning no more is heard, and I speculate in vain as to whether owner of the *chien* remained with him on the station, or is having *tête-à-tête* journey with him in separate carriage altogether. Wash inadequately, in extremely dirty accommodation provided, after waiting some time in lengthy queue. Make distressing discovery that there is no way of obtaining breakfast until train halts at Avignon. Break this information later to American young gentleman, who falls into deep distress and says that he does not know the French for grapefruit. Neither do I, but am able to inform him decisively that he will not require it.

Train is late, and does not reach Avignon till nearly ten. American young gentleman has a severe panic, and assures me that if he leaves the train it will start without him. This happened once before at Davenport, Iowa. In order to avoid similar calamity, on this occasion, I offer to procure him a cup of coffee and two rolls, and successfully do so—but attend first to my own requirements. We all brighten after this, and Guguste announces his intention of shaving. His mother screams, and says, "Mais c'est fou"—with which I privately agree—and everybody else remonstrates with Guguste (except Dédé, who is wrapped in gloom), and points out that the train is rocking, and he will cut himself. The blue béret goes so far as to predict that he will decapitate himself, at which everybody screams.

319

Guguste remains adamant, and produces shaving apparatus and a little mug, which is given to Dédé to hold. We sit around in great suspense, and Guguste is supported by one elbow by his mother, while he conducts operations to a conclusion which produces no perceptible change whatever in his appearance.

After this excitement, we all suffer from reaction, and sink into hot and dusty silence. Scenery gets rocky and sandy, with heat-haze shimmering over all, and occasional glimpses of bright blue-and-green sea.

At intervals train stops, and ejects various people. We lose the elderly French couple—who leave a Thermos behind them and have to be screamed at by Guguste from the window—and then the blue béret, eloquent to the last, and turning round on the platform to bow as train moves off again. Guguste, Deck, and the mother remain with me to the end, as they are going on as far as Antibes. American young gentleman gets out when I do, but lose sight of him altogether in excitement of meeting Rose, charming in yellow embroidered linen. She says that she is glad to see me, and adds that I look a Rag—which is true, as I discover on reaching hotel and looking-glass—but kindly omits to add that I have smuts on my face, and that petticoat has mysteriously descended two and a half inches below my dress, imparting final touch of degradation to general appearance.

She recommends bath and bed, and I agree to both, but refuse proffered cup of tea, feeling this would be altogether too reminiscent of English countryside, and quite out of place. I ask, insanely, if letters from home are awaiting me—which, unless they were written before I left, they could not possibly be. Rose enquires after Robert and the children, and when I reply that I feel I ought not really to have come away without them, she again recommends bed. Feel that she is right, and go there.

ROSE.

May 23rd.—Cannot avoid contrasting deliriously rapid flight of time when on a holiday, with very much slower passage of days and even hours, in other and more familiar surroundings.

(*Mem.*: This disposes once and for all of fallacy that days seem long when spent in complete idleness. They seem, on the contrary, very much longer when filled with ceaseless activities.)

Rose—always so gifted in discovering attractive and interesting friends—is established in circle of gifted—and in some cases actually celebrated—personalities. We all meet daily on rocks, and bathe in sea. Temperature and surroundings very, very different to those of English Channel or Atlantic Ocean, and consequently find myself emboldened to the extent of quite active swimming. Cannot, however, compete with Viscountess, who dives, or her friend, who has unique and very striking method of doing back-fall into the water. Am, indeed, led away by spirit of emulation into attempting dive on one solitary occasion, and am convinced that I have plumbed the depths of the Mediterranean—have doubts, in fact, of ever leaving it again—but on enquiring of extremely kind spectator—(famous Headmistress)—How I went In, she replies gently: About level with the Water, she thinks—and we say no more about it.

July 25th.—Vicky writes affectionately, but briefly—Mademoiselle at greater length, and quite illegibly, but evidently full of hopes that I am enjoying myself. Am touched, and send each a picture-postcard. Robin's letter, written from school, arrives later, and contains customary allusions to boys unknown to me, also information that he has asked two of them to come and stay with him in the holidays, and has accepted invitation to spend a week with another. Postscript adds straightforward enquiry, Have I bought any chocolate yet?

I do so forthwith.

July 26th.—Observe in the glass that I look ten years younger than on arrival here, and am gratified. This, moreover, in spite of what I cannot help viewing as perilous adventure recently experienced in (temporarily) choppy sea, agitated by *vent d'est*, in which no one but Rose's Viscountess attempts to swim. She indicates immense and distant rock, and announces her intention of swimming to it. I say that I will go too. Long before we are half-way there, I know that I shall never reach it, and hope that Robert's second wife will be kind to the children. Viscountess, swimming calmly, says, Am I all right? I reply, Oh quite, and am immediately submerged.

(Query: Is this a Judgement?)

Continue to swim. Rock moves further and further away. I reflect that there will be something distinguished about the headlines announcing my demise in such exalted company, and mentally frame one or two that I think would look well in local paper. Am just turning my attention to paragraph in our Parish Magazine when I hit a small rock, and am immediately submerged again. Mysteriously rise again from the foam—though not in the least, as I know too well, like Venus.

Death by drowning said to be preceded by mental panorama of entire past life. Distressing reflection which very nearly causes me to sink again. Even one recollection from my past, if injudiciously selected, disconcerts me in the extreme, and cannot at all contemplate entire series.. Suddenly perceive that space between myself and rock has actually diminished. Viscountess— who has kept near me and worn slightly anxious expression throughout—achieves it safely, and presently find myself grasping at sharp projections with tips of my fingers and bleeding profusely at the knees. Perceive that I have been, as they say, Spared.

(*Mem.*: Must try and discover for what purpose, if any.)

Am determined to take this colossal achievement as a matter of course, and merely make literary reference to Byron swimming the Hellespont—which would sound better if said in less of a hurry, and when not obliged to gasp, and spit out several gallons of water.

Minor, but nerve-racking, little problem here suggests itself: What substitute for a pocket-handkerchief exists when sea-bathing? Can conceive of no occasion—except possibly funeral of nearest and dearest—when this homely little article more frequently and urgently required. Answer, when it comes, anything but satisfactory.

I say that I am cold—which is true—and shall go back across the rocks. Viscountess, with remarkable tact, does not attempt to dissuade me, and I go.

July 27th.—End of holiday quite definitely in sight, and everyone very kindly says, Why not stay on? I refer, in return, to Robert and the children—and add, though not aloud, the servants, the laundry, the Women's Institute, repainting the outside of bath, and the state of my overdraft. Everyone expresses civil regret at my departure, and I go so far as to declare recklessly that I shall be coming back next year—which I well know to be unlikely in the extreme.

Spend last evening sending picture-postcards to everyone to whom I have been intending to send them ever since I started.

July 29th, London.—Return journey accomplished under greatly improved conditions, travelling first-class in company with one of Rose's most distinguished friends. (Should much like to run across Lady B. by chance in Paris or elsewhere, but no such gratifying coincidence supervenes. Shall take care, however, to let her know circles in which I have been moving.)

Crossing as tempestuous as ever, and again have recourse to "An Austrian Army" with same lack of success as before. Boat late, train even more so, last available train for west of England has left Paddington long before I reach Victoria, and am obliged to stay night in London. Put through long-distance call to tell Robert this, but line is, as usual, in a bad way, and all I can hear is "What?" As Robert, on his side, can apparently hear even less, we do not get far. I find that I have no money, in spite of having borrowed from Rose—expenditure, as invariably happens, has exceeded estimate—but confide all to Secretary of my club, who agrees to trust me, but adds, rather disconcertingly—"as it's for one night only".

July 30th.—Readjustment sometimes rather difficult, after absence of unusual length and character.

July 31st.—The beginning of the holidays signalled, as usual, by the making of appointments with dentist and doctor. Photographs taken at Ste. Agathe arrive, and I am—perhaps naturally—much more interested in them than anybody else appears to be. (Bathing dress shows up as being even more becoming than I thought it was, though hair, on the other hand, not at its best—probably owing to salt water.) Notice, regretfully, how much more time I spend in studying views of myself, than on admirable group of delightful friends, or even beauties of Nature, as exemplified in camera studies of sea and sky.

Presents for Vicky, Mademoiselle, and our Vicar's wife all meet with acclamation, and am gratified. Blue flowered chintz frock, however, bought at Ste. Agathe for sixty-three francs, no longer becoming to me, as sunburn fades and original sallowness returns to view. Even Mademoiselle, usually so sympathetic in regard to clothes, eyes chintz frock doubtfully, and says, "Tiens! On dirait un bal masqué." As she knows, and I know, that the neighbourhood never has, and never will, run to *bals masqués*, this equals unqualified condemnation of blue chintz, and I remove it in silence to furthest corner of the wardrobe.

Helen Wills, says Cook, about to produce more kittens. Cannot say if Robert does, or does not, know this.

Spend much time in writing to, and hearing from, unknown mothers whose sons have been invited here by Robin, and one grandmother, with whose descendant Robin is to spend a week. Curious impossibility of combining dates and trains convenient to us all, renders this whole question harassing in the extreme. Grandmother, especially, sends unlimited letters and telegrams, to all of which I feel bound to reply—mostly with civil assurances of gratitude for her kindness in having Robin to stay. Very, very difficult to think of new ways of wording this—moreover, must reserve something for letter I shall have to write when visit is safely over.

August 1st:—Return of Robin, who has grown, and looks pale. He has also purchased large bottle of brilliantine, and applied it to his hair, which smells like inferior chemist's shop. Do not like to be unsympathetic about this, so merely remain silent while Vicky exclaims rapturously that it is *lovely*—which is also Robin's own opinion. They get excited and scream, and I suggest the garden. Robin says that he is hungry, having had no lunch. Practically—he adds conscientiously. "Practically" turns out to be packet of sandwiches, two bottles of atrocious liquid called Cherry Ciderette, slab of milk chocolate, two bananas purchased on journey, and small sample tin of cheese biscuits, swopped by boy called Sherlock, for Robin's last year's copy of *Pop's Annual*.

ROBIN.

Customary rather touching display of affection between Robin and Vicky much to the fore, and am sorry to feel that repeated experience of holidays has taught me not to count for one moment upon its lasting more than twenty-four hours—if that.

(Query: Does motherhood lead to cynicism? This contrary to every convention of art, literature, or morality, but cannot altogether escape conviction that answer may be in the affirmative.)

In spite of this, however, cannot remain quite unmoved on hearing Vicky inform Cook that when she marries, her husband will be *exactly* like Robin. Cook replies indulgently, That's right, but come out of that sauce-boat, there's a good girl, and what about Master Robin's wife? To which Robin rejoins, he doesn't suppose he'll be *able* to get a wife exactly like Vicky, as she's so good, there couldn't be another one.

August 2nd.—Noteworthy what astonishing difference made in entire household by presence of one additional child. Robert finds one marble—which he unfortunately steps upon—mysterious little empty box with hole in bottom, and half of torn sponge on the stairs, and says, This house is a perfect Shambles—which I think excessive. Mademoiselle refers to sounds emitted by Robin, Vicky, the dog, and Helen Wills—all, apparently, gone mad together in the hay-loft—as "tohu-bohu". Very expressive word.

Meal-times, especially lunch, very, very far from peaceful. From time to time remember, with pained astonishment, theories subscribed to in pre-motherhood days, as to inadvisability of continually saying Don't, incessant fault-finding, and so on. Should now be sorry indeed to count number of times that I find myself forced to administer these and similar checks to the dear children. Am often reminded of enthusiastic accounts given me by Angela of other families, and admirable discipline obtaining there without effort on either side. Should like—or far more probably should *not* like—to hear what dear Angela says about *our* house, when visiting mutual friends or relations.

Rose writes cheerfully, still in South of France—sky still blue, rocks red, and bathing as perfect as ever. Experience curious illusion of receiving communication from another world, visited many aeons ago, and dimly remembered. Weather abominable, and customary difficulty

324

experienced of finding indoor occupation for children that shall be varied, engrossing, and reasonably quiet. Cannot imagine what will happen if these conditions still prevail when visiting school-fellow—Henry by name—arrives. I ask Robin what his friend's tastes are, and he says, Oh, anything. I enquire if he likes cricket, and Robin replies, Yes, he expects so. Does he care for reading? Robin says that he does not know. I give it up, and write to Army and Navy Stores for large tin of Picnic Biscuits.

Messrs. R. Sydenham, and two unknown firms from places in Holland, send me little books relating to indoor bulbs. R. Sydenham particularly optimistic, and, though admitting that failures have been known, pointing out that all, without exception, have been owing to neglect of directions on page twenty-two. Immerse myself in page twenty-two, and see that there is nothing for it but to get R. Sydenham's Special Mixture for growing R. Sydenham's Special Bulbs.

Mention this to Robert, who does not encourage scheme in any way, and refers to last November. Cannot at the moment think of really good answer, but shall probably do so in church on Sunday, or in other surroundings equally inappropriate for delivering it.

August 3rd.—Difference of opinion arises between Robin and his father as to the nature and venue of former's evening meal, Robin making sweeping assertions to the effect that All Boys of his Age have Proper Late Dinner downstairs, and Robert replying curtly More Fools their Parents, which I privately think unsuitable language for use before children. Final and unsatisfactory compromise results in Robin's coming nightly to the dining-room and partaking of soup, followed by interval, and ending with dessert, during the whole of which Robert maintains disapproving silence and I talk to both at once on entirely different subjects.

(Life of a wife and mother sometimes very wearing.)

Moreover, Vicky offended at not being included in what she evidently looks upon as nightly banquet of Lucullan magnificence, and covertly supported in this rebellious attitude by Mademoiselle. Am quite struck by extraordinary persistence with which Vicky, day after day, enquires *Why* she can't stay up to dinner too? and equally phenomenal number of times that I reply with unvarying formula that Six years old is too young, darling.

Weather cold and disagreeable, and I complain. Robert asserts that it is really quite warm, only I don't take enough exercise. Have often noticed curious and prevalent masculine delusion, to the effect that sympathy should never, on any account, be offered when minor ills of life are in question.

Days punctuated by recurrent question as to whether grass is, or is not, too wet to be sat upon by children, and whether they shall, or shall not, wear their woollen pullovers. To all enquiries as to whether they are cold, they invariably reply, with aggrieved expressions, that they are *Boiling*. Should like scientific or psychological explanation of this singular state of affairs, and mentally reserve the question for bringing forward on next occasion of finding myself in intellectual society. This, however, seems at the moment remote in the extreme.

Cook says that unless help is provided in the kitchen they cannot possibly manage all the work. I think this unreasonable, and quite unnecessary expense. Am also aware that there is no help to be obtained at this time of the year. Am disgusted at hearing myself reply in hypocritically pleasant tone of voice that, Very well, I will see what can be done. Servants, in truth, make cowards of us all.

August 7th.—Local Flower Show takes place. We walk about in Burberrys, on wet grass, and say that it might have been much worse, and look at the day they had last week at West Warmington! Am forcibly reminded of what I have heard of Ruth Draper's admirable sketch of country Bazaar, but try hard not to think about this. Our Vicar's wife takes me to look at the school-children's needlework, laid out in tent amidst onions, begonias, and other vegetable products. Just as I am admiring pink cotton camisole embroidered with mauve pansies, strange boy approaches me and says, If I please, the little girl isn't very well, and can't be got out of the swing-boat, and will I come, please. I go, our Vicar's wife following, and saying—absurdly— that it must be the heat, and those swingboats have always seemed to her very dangerous, ever since there was a fearful accident at her old home, when the whole thing broke down, and seven people were killed and a good many of the spectators injured. A relief, after this, to find Vicky merely green in the face, still clinging obstinately to the ropes and disregarding two men below saying Come along out of it, missie, and Now then, my dear, and Mademoiselle in terrific state of agitation, clasping her hands and pacing backwards and forwards, uttering many Gallic ejaculations and adjurations to the saints. Robin has removed himself to furthest corner of the ground, and is feigning interest in immense carthorse tied up in red ribbons.

(*N.B.* Dear Robin perhaps not so utterly unlike his father as one is sometimes tempted to suppose.)

I tell Vicky, very, very shortly, that unless she descends instantly, she will go to bed early every night for a week. Unfortunately, tremendous outburst of "Land of Hope and Glory" from brass band compels me to say this in undignified bellow, and to repeat it three times before it has any effect, by which time quite large crowd has gathered round. General outburst of applause when at last swing-boat is brought to a standstill, and Vicky—mottled to the last degree—is lifted out by man in check coat and tweed cap, who says *Here* we are, Amy Johnson! to fresh applause.

Vicky removed by Mademoiselle, not a moment too soon. Our Vicar's wife says that children are all alike, and it may be a touch of ptomaine poisoning, one never knows, and why not come and help her judge decorated perambulators?

Meet several acquaintances and newly-arrived Miss Pankerton, who has bought small house in village, and on whom I have not yet called. She wears pince-nez and is said to have been at Oxford. All I can get out of her is that the whole thing reminds her of Dostoeffsky.

Feel that I neither know nor care what she means. Am convinced, however, that I have not heard the last of either Miss P. or Dostoeffsky, as she assures me that she is the most unconventional person in the whole world, and never stands on ceremony. If she meets an affinity, she adds, she knows it directly, and then nothing can stop her. She just follows the impulse of the moment, and may as like as not stroll in for breakfast, or be strolled in upon for after-dinner coffee.

Am quite unable to contemplate Robert's reaction to Miss P. and Dostoeffsky at breakfast, and bring the conversation to an end as quickly as possible.

Find Robert, our Vicar, and neighbouring squire, looking at horses. Our Vicar and neighbouring squire talk about the weather, but do not say anything new. Robert says nothing.

Get home towards eight o'clock, strangely exhausted, and am discouraged at meeting both maids just on their way to the Flower-Show Dance. Cook says encouragingly that the potatoes are in the oven, and everything else on the table, and she only hopes Pussy hasn't found her way in, on account of the butter. Eventually do the washing-up, while Mademoiselle puts children to bed, and I afterwards go up and read *Tanglewood Tales* aloud.

(Query, mainly rhetorical: Why are nonprofessional women, if married and with children, so frequently referred to as "leisured"? Answer comes there none.)

MISS PANKERTON.

August 8th.—Frightful afternoon, entirely filled by call from Miss Pankerton, wearing hand-woven blue jumper, wider in front than at the back, very short skirt, and wholly incredible small black béret. She smokes cigarettes in immense holder, and sits astride the arm of the sofa.

(*N.B.* Arm of the sofa not at all calculated to bear any such strain, and creaks several times most alarmingly. Must remember to see if anything can be done about it, and in any case manoeuvre Miss P. into sitting elsewhere on subsequent visits, if any.)

Conversation very, very literary and academic, my own part in it being mostly confined to saying that I haven't yet read it, and, It's down on my library list, but hasn't come, so far. After what feels like some hours of this, Miss P. becomes personal, and says that I strike her as being a woman whose life has never known fulfilment. Have often thought exactly the same thing myself, but this does not prevent my feeling entirely furious with Miss P. for saying so. She either does not perceive, or is indifferent to, my fury, as she goes on to ask accusingly whether I realise that I have no *right* to let myself become a domestic beast of burden, with no interests beyond the nursery and the kitchen. What, for instance, she demands rousingly, have I read within the last two years? To this I reply weakly that I have read *Gentlemen Prefer Blondes*, which is the only thing I seem able to remember, when Robert and the tea enter simultaneously. Curious and difficult interlude follows, in the course of which Miss P. talks about the N.U.E.C.—(Cannot imagine what this is, but pretend to know all about it)—and the situation in India, and Robert either says nothing at all, or contradicts her very briefly and forcibly. Miss P. finally departs, saying that she is determined to scrape all the barnacles off me before she has done with me, and that I shall soon be seeing her again.

August 9th.—The child Henry deposited by expensive-looking parents in enormous red car, who dash away immediately, after one contemptuous look at house, garden, self, and children. (Can understand this, in a way, as they arrive sooner than expected, and Robin, Vicky, and I are all equally untidy owing to prolonged game of Wild Beasts in the garden.)

Henry unspeakably immaculate in grey flannel and red tie—but all is discarded when parents have departed, and he rapidly assumes disreputable appearance and loud, screeching tones of complete at-homeness. Robert, for reasons unknown, appears unable to remember his name, and calls him Francis. (Should like to trace connection of ideas, if any, but am baffled.)

Both boys come down to dinner, and Henry astonishes us by pouring out steady stream of information concerning speedboats, aeroplanes, and submarines, from start to finish. Most informative. Am quite relieved, after boys have gone to bed, to find him looking infantile in blue-striped pyjamas, and asking to have door left open so that he can see light in passage outside.

I go down to Robert and ask—not very straightforwardly, since I know the answer only too well—if he would not like to take Mademoiselle, me, and the children to spend long day at the sea next week. We might invite one or two people to join us and have a picnic, say I with false optimism. Robert looks horrified and says, Surely that isn't necessary? but after some discussion, yields, on condition that weather is favourable.

(Should not be surprised to learn that he has been praying for rain ever since.)

August 10th.—See Miss Pankerton through Post Office window and have serious thoughts of asking if I may just get under the counter for a moment, or retire into back premises altogether, but am restrained by presence of children, and also interesting story, embarked upon by Postmistress, concerning extraordinary decision of Bench, last Monday week, as to Separation Order applied for by Mrs. W. of the *Queen's Head*. Just as we get to its being well known that Mr. W. once threw hand-painted plate with view of Teignmouth right across the bedroom—absolutely right across it, from end to end, says Postmistress impressively—we are invaded by Miss P., accompanied by two sheep-dogs and some leggy little boys.

Little boys turn out to be nephews, paying a visit, and are told to go and make friends with Robin, Henry, and Vicky—at which all exchange looks of blackest hatred, with regrettable exception of Vicky, who smirks at the tallest nephew, who takes no notice. Miss P. pounces on Henry and says to me Is this my boy, his eyes are so exactly like mine she'd have known him anywhere. Nobody contradicts her, although I do not feel pleased, as Henry, in my opinion, entirely undistinguished-looking child.

Postmistress—perhaps diplomatically—intervenes with, Did I say a two-shilling book, she has them, but I usually take the three-shilling, if I'll excuse her. I do excuse her, and explain that I only have two shillings with me, and she says that doesn't matter at all and Harold will take the other shilling when he calls for the letters. I agree to all, and turn cast-iron deafness to Miss P. in background exclaiming that this is Pure Hardy.

We all surge out of Post Office together, and youngest Pankerton nephew suddenly remarks that at *his* home the water once came through the bathroom floor into the dining-room. Vicky says Oh, and all then become silent again until Miss P. tells another nephew not to twist the sheep-dog's tail like that, and the nephew, looking astonished, says in return, Why not? to which Miss P. rejoins, Noel, that will *Do*.

Mem.: Amenities of conversation sometimes very curious, especially where society of children is involved. Have sometimes wondered at what stage of development the idea of continuity in talk begins to seem desirable—but here, again, disquieting reflection follows that perhaps this stage is never reached at all. Debate for an instant whether to put the point to Miss Pankerton, but decide better not, and in any case, she turns out to be talking about H. G. Wells, and do not like to interrupt. Just as she is telling me that it is quite absurd to compare Wells with Shaw—(which I have never thought of doing)—a Pankerton nephew and Henry begin to kick one another on the shins, and have to be told that that is Quite Enough. The Pankerton nephew is agitated and says, Tell him my name *isn't* Noah, it's Noel. This misunderstanding cleared up, but the nephew remains Noah to his contemporaries, and is evidently destined to do so for years to come, and Henry receives much applause as originator of brilliant witticism.

Do not feel that Miss P. views any of it as being in the least amusing, and in order to create a diversion, rush into an invitation to them all to join projected picnic to the sea next week.

(Query: Would it not be instructive to examine closely exact motives governing suggestions and invitations that bear outward appearance of spontaneity? Answer: Instructive undoubtedly, but probably in many cases painful, and—on second thoughts—shall embark on no such exercise.)

We part with Pankertons at the crossroads, but not before Miss P. has accepted invitation to picnic, and added that her brother will be staying with her then, and a dear friend who Writes, and that she hopes that will not be too large a party. I say No, not at all, and feel that this settles the question of buying another half-dozen picnic plates and enamel mugs, and better throw in a new Thermos as well, otherwise not a hope of things going round. That, says Miss P., will be delightful, and shall they bring their own sandwiches?—at which I exclaim in horror, and she says Really? and I say Really, with equal emphasis but quite different inflection, and we part.

Robin says he does not know why I asked them to the picnic, and I stifle impulse to reply that neither do I, and Henry tells me all about hydraulic lifts.

Send children upstairs to wash for lunch, and call out several times that they must hurry up or they will be late, but am annoyed when gong, eventually, is sounded by Gladys nearly ten minutes after appointed hour. Cannot decide whether I shall, or shall not, speak about this, and am preoccupied all through roast lamb and mint sauce, but forget about it when fruit-salad is reached, as Cook has disastrously omitted banana and put in loganberries.

August 13th.—I tell Cook about the picnic lunch—for about ten people, say I—which sounds less than if I just said "ten" straight out—but she is not taken in by this, and at once declares that there isn't anything to make sandwiches of, that she can see, and butcher won't be calling till the day after tomorrow, and then it'll be scrag-end for Irish stew. I perceive that the moment has come for taking up absolutely firm stand with Cook, and surprise us both by suddenly saying Nonsense, she must order chicken from farm, and have it cold for sandwiches. It won't go round, Cook protests—but feebly—and I pursue advantage and advocate supplementary potted meat and hard-boiled eggs. Cook utterly vanquished, and I leave kitchen triumphant, but am met in the passage outside by Vicky, who asks in clarion tones (easily audible in kitchen and beyond) if I know that I threw cigarette-end into drawing-room grate, and that it has lit the fire all by itself?

August 15th.—Picnic takes place under singular and rather disastrous conditions, day not beginning well owing to Robin and Henry having strange overnight inspiration about sleeping out in summer-house, which is prepared for them with much elaboration by Mademoiselle and myself—even to crowning touch from Mademoiselle of small vase of flowers on table. At 2 A.M. they decide that they wish to come in, and do so through study window left open for them. Henry involves himself in several blankets, which he tries to carry upstairs, and trips and falls down, and Robin knocks over hall-stool, and treads on Helen Wills.

Robert and myself are roused, and Robert is not pleased. Mademoiselle appears on landing in *peignoir* and with head swathed in little grey shawl, but screams at the sight of Robert in pyjamas, and rushes away again. (The French undoubtedly very curious mixture of modesty and the reverse.)

Henry and Robin show tendency to become explanatory, but are discouraged, and put into beds. Just as I return down passage to my room, sounds indicate that Vicky has now awakened, and is automatically opening campaign by saying Can't I come too? Instinct—unclassified, but evidently stronger than maternal one—bids me leave Mademoiselle to deal with this, which I unhesitatingly do.

JAHSPER.

Get into bed again, feeling that the day has not opened very well, but sleep off and on until Gladys calls me—ten minutes late—but do not say anything about her unpunctuality, as Robert does not appear to have noticed it.

Sky is grey, but not necessarily threatening, and glass has not fallen unreasonably. All is in readiness when Miss Pankerton (wearing Burberry, green knitted cap, and immense yellow gloves) appears in large Ford car which brims over with nephews, sheep-dogs, and a couple of men. Latter resolve themselves into the Pankerton brother—who turns out to be from Vancouver—and the friend who Writes—very tall and pale, and is addressed by Miss P. in a proprietary manner as "Jahsper".

(Something tells me that Robert and Jahsper are not going to care about one another.)

After customary preliminaries about weather, much time is spent in discussing arrangements in cars. All the children show tendency to wish to sit with their own relations rather than anybody else, except Henry, who says simply that the hired car looks much the best, and may he sit in front with the driver, please. All is greatly complicated by presence of the sheep-dogs, and Robert offers to shut them into an outhouse for the day, but Miss Pankerton replies that this would break their hearts, bless them, and they can just pop down anywhere amongst the baskets. (In actual fact, both eventually pop down on Mademoiselle's feet, and she looks despairing, and presently ask if I have by any chance a little bottle of eau-de-Cologne with me—which I naturally haven't.)

Picnic baskets, as usual, weigh incredible amount, and Thermos flasks stick up at inconvenient angles and run into our legs. (I quote "John Gilpin", rather aptly, but nobody pays any attention.)

When we have driven about ten miles, rain begins, and goes on and on. Cars are stopped, and we find that two schools of thought exist, one—of which Miss P. is leader—declaring that we are Running out of It, and the other—headed by the Vancouver brother and heavily backed by

Robert—that we are Running into It. Miss P.—as might have been expected—wins, and we proceed; but Run into It more and more. By the time destination is reached, we have Run into It to an extent that makes me wonder if we shall ever Run out of It.

Lunch has to be eaten in three bathing huts, hired by Robert, and the children become hilarious and fidgety. Miss P. talks about Companionate Marriage to Robert, who makes no answer, and Jahsper asks me what I think of James Elroy Flecker. As I cannot remember exact form of J. E. F.'s activities, I merely reply that in many ways he was very wonderful—which no doubt he was—and Jahsper seems satisfied, and eats tomato sandwiches. The children ask riddles—mostly very old and foolish ones—and Miss P. looks annoyed, and says See if it has stopped raining—which it hasn't. I feel that she and the children must, at all costs, be kept apart, and tell Robert in urgent whisper that, rain or no rain, they must go out.

They do.

Miss Pankerton becomes expansive, and suddenly remarks to Jahsper that *Now* he can see what she meant, about positively Victorian survivals still to be found in English family life. At this, Vancouver brother looks aghast—as well he may—and dashes out into the wet. Jahsper says Yerse, Yerse, and sighs, and I at once institute vigorous search for missing plate, which creates a diversion.

Subsequently the children bathe, get wetter than ever, drip all over the place, and are dried—Mademoiselle predicts death from pneumonia for all—and we seek the cars once more. One sheep-dog is missing, but eventually recovered in soaking condition, and is gathered on to united laps of Vicky, Henry, and a nephew. I lack energy to protest, and we drive away.

Beg Miss P., Jahsper, brother, nephews, sheep-dogs, and all, to come in and get dry and have tea, but they have the decency to refuse, and I make no further effort, but watch them depart with untold thankfulness.

(Should be sorry to think impulses of hospitality almost entirely dependent on convenience, but cannot altogether escape suspicion that this is so.)

Robert extremely forbearing on the whole, and says nothing worse than Well!—but this very expressively.

August 16th.—Robert, at breakfast, suddenly enquires if that nasty-looking fellow does anything for a living? Instinct at once tells me that he means Jahsper, but am unable to give him any information, except that Jahsper writes, which Robert does not appear to think is to his credit. He goes so far as to say that he hopes yesterday's rain may put an end to him altogether—but whether this means to his presence in the neighbourhood, or to his existence on this planet, am by no means certain, and prefer not to enquire. Ask Robert instead if he did not think, yesterday, about Miss Edgeworth, Rosamond, and the Party of Pleasure, but this wakens no response, and conversation—such as it is—descends once more to level of slight bitterness about the coffee, and utter inability to get really satisfactory bacon locally. This is only brought to a close by abrupt entrance of Robin, who remarks without preliminary: "Isn't Helen Wills going to have kittens almost at once? Cook thinks so."

Can only hope that Robin does not catch exact wording of short ejaculation with which his father receives this.

August 18th.—Pouring rain, and I agree to let all three children dress up, and give them handsome selection from my wardrobe for the purpose. This ensures me brief half-hour uninterrupted at writing-table, where I deal with baker—brown bread far from satisfactory—Rose—on a picture-postcard of Backs at Cambridge, which mysteriously appears amongst stationery—Robin's Headmaster's wife—mostly about stockings, but Boxing may be substituted for Dancing, in future—and Lady Frobisher, who would be so delighted if Robert and I would come over for tea whilst there is still something to be seen in the garden. (Do not like to write back and say that I would far rather come when there is nothing to be seen in the garden, and we might enjoy excellent tea in peace—so, as usual, sacrifice truth to demands of civilisation.)

Just as I decide to tackle large square envelope of thin blue paper, with curious purple lining designed to defeat anyone endeavouring to read letter within—which would anyhow be impossible, as Barbara Carruthers always most illegible—front door bell rings.

Thoughts immediately fly to Lady B., and I rapidly rehearse references that I intend to make to recent stay in South of France—(shall not specify length of visit)—and cordial relations there established with distinguished society, and Rose's Viscountess in particular. Have also sufficient presence of mind to make use of pocket comb, mirror, and small powder-puff kept for emergencies in drawer of writing-table. (Discover, much later, that I have overdone powder-puff very considerably, and reflect, not for the first time, that we are spared much by inability—so misguidedly deplored by Scottish poet—to see ourselves as others see us.)

Door opens, and Miss Pankerton is shown in, followed—it seems to me reluctantly—by Jahsper. Miss P. has on military-looking cape, and béret as before, which strikes me as odd combination, and anyhow cape looks to me as though it might drip rain-drops on furniture, and I beg her to take it off. This she does with rather spacious gesture—(Can she have been seeing *The Three Musketeers* at local cinema?)—and unfortunately one end of it, apparently heavily weighted, hits Jahsper in the eye. Miss P. is very breezy and off-hand about this, but Jahsper, evidently in severe pain, falls into deep dejection, and continues to hold large yellow crêpe-de-chine handkerchief to injured eye for some time. Am distracted by wondering whether I ought to ask him if he would like to bathe it—which would involve taking him up to bathroom, probably untidy—and trying to listen intelligently to Miss P., who is talking about Proust.

This leads, by process that I do not follow, to a discussion on Christian names, and Miss P. says that All Flower Names are Absurd. Am horrified to hear myself replying, senselessly, that I think Rose is a pretty name, as one of my greatest friends is called Rose—to which Miss P. rightly answers that that, really, has nothing to do with it, and Jahsper, still dabbing at injured eye, contributes austere statement to the effect that only the Russians really understand Beauty in Nomenclature. Am again horrified at hearing myself interject "*Ivan Ivanovitch*" in entirely detached and irrelevant manner, and really begin to wonder if mental weakness is overtaking me. Moreover, am certain that I have given Miss P. direct lead in the direction of Dostoeffsky, about whom I do not wish to hear, and am altogether unable to converse.

Entire situation is, however, revolutionised by totally unexpected entrance of Robin—staggering beneath my fur coat and last summer's red crinoline straw hat—Henry, draped in blue kimono, several scarfs belonging to Mademoiselle, old pair of fur gloves, with scarlet school-cap inappropriately crowning all—and Vicky, wearing nothing whatever but small pair of green silk knickerbockers and large and unfamiliar black felt hat put on at rakish angle.

Completely stunned silence overtakes us all, until Vicky, advancing with perfect aplomb, graciously says, "How do you do?" and shakes hands with Jahsper and Miss P. in turn, and I succeed in surpassing already well-established record for utter futility,, by remarking that They have been Dressing Up.

Atmosphere becomes very, very strained indeed, only Vicky embarking on sprightly reminiscences of recent picnic, which meet with no response. Final depths of unsuccess are plumbed, when it transpires that Vicky's black sombrero, picked up in the hall, is in reality the property of Jahsper. I apologise profusely, the children giggle, Miss P. raises her eyebrows to quite unnatural heights, and gets up and looks at the book-shelves in a remote and superior way, and Jahsper says, Oh, never mind, it really is of no consequence, at the same time receiving hat with profound solicitude, and dusting it with two fingers.

Greatest possible relief when Miss P. declares that they must go, otherwise they will miss the Brahms Concerto on the wireless. I hastily agree that this would never do, and tell Robin to open the door. Just as we all cross the hall, Gladys is inspired to sound the gong for tea, and I am compelled to say, Won't they stay and have some? but Miss P. says she never takes anything at all between lunch and dinner, thanks, and Jahsper pretends he hasn't heard me and makes no reply whatever.

They march out into pouring rain, Miss P. once more giving martial fling to military cape—(at which Jahsper flinches, and removes himself some yards away from her)—and entirely disdaining small and elegant umbrella beneath which Jahsper and his black felt take refuge. Robin enquires, in tones of marked distaste, if I *like* those people? but I feel it better to ignore this, and recommend getting washed for tea. Customary discussion follows as to whether washing is, or is not, necessary.

(*Mem.*: Have sometimes considered—though idly—writing letter to the *Times* to find out if any recorded instances exist of parents and children whose views on this subject coincide. Topic of far wider appeal than many of those so exhaustively dealt with.)

August 25th.—Am displeased by Messrs. R. Sydenham, who have besought me, in urgently worded little booklet, to Order Bulbs Early, and when I do so—at no little inconvenience, owing to customary pressure of holidays—reply on a postcard that order will be forwarded "when ready". Have serious thoughts of cancelling the whole thing—six selected, twelve paper-whites, a dozen early assorteds, and a half bushel of Fibre, Moss, and Charcoal. Cannot very well do this, however, owing to quite recent purchase of coloured bowls from Woolworth's, as being desirable additions to existing collection of odd pots, dented enamel basins, large red glass jam-dish, and dear grandmamma's disused willow-pattern foot-bath.

Departure of the boy Henry—who says that he has enjoyed himself, which I hope is true—accompanied by Robin, who is to be met and extracted from train at Salisbury by uncle of boy with whom he is to stay.

(Query: How is it that others are so frequently able to obtain services of this nature from their relations? Feel no conviction that either William or Angela would react favourably, if called upon to meet unknown children at Salisbury or anywhere else.)

Vicky, Mademoiselle, and I wave goodbye from hall door—rain pouring down as usual—and Vicky seems a thought depressed at remaining behind. This tendency greatly enhanced by Mademoiselle's exclamation, on retiring into the house once more—"On dirait un tombeau!"

Second post brings letter from Barbara in the Himalayas, which gives me severe shock of realising that I haven't yet read her last one, owing to lack of time and general impression that it is illegibly scrawled and full of allusions to native servants. Remorsefully open this one, perceive with relief that it is quite short and contains nothing that looks like native servants, but very interesting piece of information, rather circuitously worded by dear Barbara, but still quite beyond misunderstanding. I tell Mademoiselle, who says "Ah, comme c'est touchant!" and at once wipes her eyes—display which I think excessive.

Robert, to whom I also impart news, goes to the other extreme, and makes no comment except "I daresay". On the other hand, our Vicar's wife calls, for the express purpose of asking whether I think it will be a boy or a girl, and of suggesting that we should at once go together and congratulate old Mrs. Blenkinsop. I remind her that Barbara stipulates in letter for secrecy, and our Vicar's wife says, Of course, of course—it had slipped her memory for the moment—but surely old Mrs. B. must know all about it? However, she concedes that dear Barbara may perhaps not wish her mother to know that we know, just yet, and concludes with involved quotation from Thomas a Kempis about exercise of discretion. We then discuss educational facilities in the Himalayas, the Carruthers nose—which neither of us cares about—and the desirability or otherwise of having twins. Our Vicar's wife refuses tea, talks about books—she likes to have something *solid* in hand, always—is reminded of Miss Pinkerton, about whom she is doubtful, but admits that it is early days to judge—again refuses tea, and assures me that she must go. She eventually stays to tea, and walks up and down the lawn with me afterwards, telling me of Lady B.'s outrageous behaviour in connection with purchase of proposed site for the Village Hall. This, as usual, serves to unite us in warm friendship, and we part cordially.

August 28th.—Picnic, and Cook forgets to put in the sugar. Postcard from Robin's hostess says that he has arrived, but adds nothing as to his behaviour, or impression that he is making, which makes me feel anxious.

August 31st.—Read *The Edwardians* which everybody else has read months ago—and am delighted and amused. Remember that V. Sackville-West and I once attended dancing classes together at the Albert Hall, many years ago, but feel that if I do mention this, everybody will think I am boasting—which indeed I should be—so better forget about it again, and in any case, dancing never my strongest point, and performance at Albert Hall extremely mediocre and may well be left in oblivion. Short letter from Robin which I am very glad to get, but which refers to nothing whatever except animals at home, and project for going out in a boat and diving from it on some unspecified future occasion. Reply to all, and am too modern to beg tiresomely for information concerning himself.

September 1st.—Postcard from the station announces arrival of parcel, that I at once identify as bulbs, with accompanying Fibre, Moss, and Charcoal mixture. Suggest that Robert should fetch them this afternoon, but he is unenthusiastic, and says tomorrow, when he will be meeting Robin and school-friend, will do quite well.

(*Mem.*: Very marked difference between the sexes is male tendency to procrastinate doing practically everything in the world except sitting down to meals and going up to bed. Should like to purchase little painted motto: *Do it now*, so often on sale at inferior stationers' shops, and present it to Robert, but on second thoughts quite see that this would not conduce to domestic harmony, and abandon scheme at once.)

Think seriously about bulbs, and spread sheets of newspaper on attic floor to receive them and bowls. Resolve also to keep careful record of all operations, with eventual results, for future guidance. Look out notebook for the purpose, and find small green booklet, with mysterious references of which I can make neither head nor tail, in own handwriting on two first pages. Spend some time in trying to decide what I could have meant by: Kp. p. in sh. twice p. w. *without* fail or: Tell H. *not* 12" by 8" Washable f.c. to be g'd, but eventually give it up, and tear out two first pages of little green book, and write BULBS and to-morrow's date in capital letters.

September 2nd.—Robert brings home Robin, and friend called Micky Thompson, from station, but has unfortunately forgotten to call for the bulbs. Micky Thompson is attractive and shows enchanting dimple whenever he smiles, which is often.

(*Mem.*: Theory that mothers think their own children superior to any others Absolute Nonsense. Can see only too plainly that Micky easily surpasses Robin and Vicky in looks, charm, and good manners—and am very much annoyed about it.)

September 4th.—Micky Thompson continues to show himself as charming child, with cheerful disposition, good manners, and excellent health. Enquiry reveals that he is an orphan, which does not surprise me in the least. Have often noticed that absence of parental solicitude usually very beneficial to offspring. Bulbs still at station.

September 10th.—Unbroken succession of picnics, bathing expeditions, and drives to Plymouth Cafe in search of ices. Mademoiselle continually predicts catastrophes to digestions, lungs, or even brains—but none materialise.

September 11th.—Departure of Micky Thompson, but am less concerned with this than with Robert's return from station, this time accompanied by bulbs and half-bushel of Fibre, Moss, and Charcoal. Devote entire afternoon to planting these, with much advice from Vicky and Robin, and enter full details of transaction in little green book. Prepare to carry all, with utmost care, into furthest and darkest recess of attic, when Vicky suddenly announces that Helen Wills is there already, with six bran-new kittens.

Great excitement follows, which I am obliged to suggest had better be modified before Daddy enquires into its cause. Children agree to this, but feel very little confidence in their discretion. Am obliged to leave bulbs in secondary corner of attic, owing to humane scruples about disturbing H. Wills and family.

September 20th.—Letter from County Secretary of adjoining County, telling me that she knows how busy I am—which I'm certain she doesn't—but Women's Institutes of Chick, Little March, and Crimpington find themselves in terrible difficulty owing to uncertainty about next month's speaker. Involved fragments about son coming, or not coming, home on leave from Patagonia, and daughter ill—but not dangerously—at Bromley, Kent—follow. President is away—(further fragment, about President being obliged to visit aged relative while aged relative's maid is on holiday)—and County Secretary does not know what to do. What she does do, however, is to suggest that I should be prepared to come and speak at all three Institute meetings, if—as she rather strangely puts it—the worst comes to the worst. Separate half-sheet of paper gives details about dates, times, and bus between Chick and Little March, leading on to doctor's sister's two-seater, at cross-roads between Little March and Crimpington Hill. At Crimpington, County Secretary concludes triumphantly, I shall be put up for the night by Lady Magdalen Crimp—always so kind, and such a friend to the Movement—at Crimpington Hall. P.S. Travel talks always popular, but anything I like will be delightful. Chick very keen about Folk Lore, Little March more on the Handicraft side. *But anything I like.* P.P.S. Would I be so kind as to judge Recitation Competition at Crimpington?

I think this over for some time, and decide to write and say that I will do it, as Robin will have returned to school next week, and should like to distract my mind. Tell Mademoiselle casually that I may be going on a short tour, speaking, and she is suitably impressed. Vicky enquires:

"Like a menagerie, mummie?" which seems to me very extraordinary simile, though innocently meant. I reply, "No, not in the least like a menagerie," and Mademoiselle adds, officiously, "More like a mission." Am by no means at one with her here, but have no time to go further into the subject, as Gladys summons me to prolonged discussion with the Laundry—represented by man in white coat at the back gate—concerning cotton sheet, said to be one of a pair, but which has been returned in solitary widowhood. The Laundry has much to say about this, and presently Cook, gardener, Mademoiselle, Vicky, and unidentified boy apparently attached to Laundry, have all gathered round. Everyone except boy supports Gladys by saying "That's right" to everything she asserts, and I eventually leave them to it. Evidently all takes time, as it is not till forty minutes later that I see gardener slowly returning to his work, and hear van driving away.

Go up to attic and inspect bulb-bowls, but nothing to be seen. Cannot decide whether they require water or not, but think perhaps better be on the safe side, so give them some. Make note in little green book to this effect, as am determined to keep full record of entire procedure.

September 22nd.—Invitation from Lady B.—note delivered by hand, wait reply—to Robert and myself to come and dine tonight. Reads more like a Royal Command, and no suggestion that short notice may be inconvenient. Robert out, and I act with promptitude and firmness on own responsibility, and reply that we are already engaged for dinner.

(Query: Will this suggest convivial evening at neighbouring Rectory, or rissoles and cocoa with old Mrs. Blenkinsop and Cousin Maud? Can conceive of no other alternatives.)

Telephone rings in a peremptory manner just as I am reading aloud enchanting book, *The Exciting Family* by M. D. Hillyard—(surely occasional contributor to *Time and Tide*?)—and I rush to dining-room to deal with it. (*N.B.* Must really overcome foolish and immature tendency to feel that any telephone-call may be prelude to (a) announcement of a fortune or, alternatively, (6) news of immense and impressive calamity.)

On snatching up receiver, unmistakable tones of Lady B. are heard—at once suggesting perhaps rather ill-natured, but not unjustifiable, comparison with a pea-hen. What, she enquires, is all this nonsense? Of course we must dine to-night—she won't hear of a refusal. Besides, what else can we possibly be doing, unless it's Meetings, and if so, we can cut them for once.

Am at once invaded by host of improbable inspirations: e.g. that the Lord-Lieutenant of the County and his wife are dining here informally, or that Rose's Viscountess is staying with us and refuses either to be left alone or to be taken to Lady B.'s—(which I know she would at once suggest)—or even that, really, Robert and I have had so many late nights recently that we cannot face another one—but do not go so far as to proffer any of them aloud. Am disgusted, instead, to hear myself saying weakly that Robin goes back to school day after tomorrow, and we do not like to go out on one of his last few evenings at home. (This may be true so far as I am concerned, but can imagine no suggestion less likely to be endorsed by Robert, and trust that he may never come to hear of it.) In any case, it instantly revives long-standing determination of Lady B.'s to establish me with reputation for being a Perfect Mother, and she at once takes advantage of it.

I return to *The Exciting Family* in a state of great inward fury.

September 24th.—Frightful welter of packing, putting away, and earnest consultations of School List. Robin gives everybody serious injunctions about not touching anything *whatever* in his bedroom—which looks like inferior pawnbroking establishment at stocktaking time—and we all more or less commit ourselves to leaving it alone till Christmas holidays—which is completely out of the question.

He is taken away by Robert in the car, looking forlorn and infantile, and Vicky roars. I beseech her to desist at once, but am rebuked by Mademoiselle, who says, "Ah, elle a tant de coeur!" in tone which implies that she cannot say as much for myself.

October 1.—Tell Robert about proposed short tour to Chick, Little March, and Crimpington, on behalf of W. Is. He says little, but that little not very enthusiastic. I spend many hours—or so it seems—looking out Notes for Talks, and trying to remember anecdotes that shall be at once funny and suitable. (This combination rather unusual.)

Pack small bag, search frantically all over writing-table, bedroom, and drawing-room for W.I. Badge—which is at last discovered by Mademoiselle in remote corner of drawer devoted to stockings—and take my departure. Robert drives me to station, and I beg that he will keep an eye on the bulbs whilst I am away.

October 2nd.—Bus from Chick conveys me to Little March, after successful meeting last night, at which I discourse on Amateur Theatricals, am applauded, thanked by President in the chair—name inaudible—applauded once more, and taken home by Assistant Secretary, who is putting me up for the night. We talk about the Movement—Annual Meeting at Blackpool perhaps a mistake, why not Bristol or Plymouth?—difficulty of thinking out new Programmes for monthly meetings, and really magnificent performance of Chick at recent Folk-dancing Rally, at which Institute members called upon to go through "Gathering Peas-cods" no less than three times—two of Chick's best performers, says Assistant Secretary proudly, being grandmothers. I express astonished admiration, and we go on to Village Halls, Sir Oswald Mosley, and methods of removing ink-stains from linen. Just as Assistant Secretary—who is unmarried and lives in nice little cottage—has escorted me to charming little bedroom, she remembers that I am eventually going on to Crimpington, and embarks on interesting scandal about two members of Institute there, and unaccountable disappearance of one member's name from Committee. This keeps us up till eleven o'clock, when she begs me to say nothing whatever about her having mentioned the affair, which was all told her in strictest confidence, and we part.

Reach Little March, via the bus—which is old, and rattles—in time for lunch. Doctor's sister meets me—elderly lady with dog—and talks about hunting. Meeting takes place at three o'clock, in g delightful Hut, and am impressed by business-like and efficient atmosphere. Doctor's sister, in the chair, introduces me—unluckily my name eludes her at eleventh hour, but I hastily supply it and she says, "Of course, of course"—and I launch out into A Visit to Switzerland. As soon as I have finished, elderly member surges up from front row and says that this has been particularly interesting to *her*, as she once lived in Switzerland for nearly fourteen years and knows every inch of it from end to end. (My own experience confined to six weeks round and about Lucerne, ten years ago.)

We drink cups of tea, eat excellent buns, sing several Community Songs, and Meeting comes to an end. Doctor's sister's two-seater, now altogether home-like, receives me once again, and I congratulate her on Institute. She smiles and talks about hunting.

Evening passes off quietly, doctor comes in—elderly man with two dogs—he also talks about hunting, and we all separate for bed at ten o'clock.

October 3rd.—Part early from doctor, sister, dogs, and two-seater, and proceed by train to Crimpington, as Meeting does not take place till afternoon, and have no wish to arrive earlier than I need. Curious cross-country journey with many stops, and one change involving long and draughty wait that I enliven by cup of Bovril.

Superb car meets me, with superb chauffeur who despises me and my bag at sight, but is obliged to drive us both to Crimping-ton Hall. Butler receives me, and I am conducted through immense and chilly hall with stone flags to equally immense and chilly drawing-room, where he leaves me. Very small fire is lurking behind steel bars at far end of room, and I make my way to it past little gilt tables, large chairs, and sofas, cabinets apparently lined with china cups and lustre tea-pots, and massive writing-tables entirely furnished with hundreds of photographs in silver frames. Butler suddenly reappears with the *Times*, which he hands to me on small salver. Have already read it from end to end in the train, but feel obliged to open it and begin all over again. He looks doubtfully at the fire, and I hope he is going to put on more coal, but instead he goes away, and is presently replaced by Lady Magdalen Crimp, who is about ninety-five and stone-deaf. She wears black, and large fur cape—as well she may. She produces trumpet, and I talk down it, and she smiles and nods, and has evidently not heard one word—which is just as well, as none of them worth hearing. After some time she suggests my room, and we creep along slowly for about quarter of a mile, till first floor is reached, and vast bedroom with old-fashioned four-poster in the middle of it. Here she leaves me, and I wash, from little brass jug of tepid water, and note—by no means for the first time—that the use of powder, when temperature has sunk below a certain level, merely casts extraordinary azure shade over nose and chin.

Faint hope of finding fire in dining-room is extinguished on entering it, when I am at once struck by its resemblance to a mausoleum. Lady M. and I sit down at mahogany circular table, she says Do I mind a Cold Lunch? I shake my head, as being preferable to screaming "No" down trumpet—though equally far from the truth—and we eat rabbit-cream, coffee-shape, and Marie biscuits.

Conversation spasmodic and unsatisfactory, and I am reduced to looking at portraits on wall, of gentlemen in wigs and ladies with bosoms, also objectionable study of dead bird, dripping blood, lying amongst oranges and other vegetable matter. (Should like to know what dear Rose, with her appreciation of Art, would say to this.) Later we adjourn to drawing-room—fire now a mere ember—and Lady M. explains that she is not going to the Meeting, but Vice-President will look after me, and she hopes I shall enjoy Recitation Competition—some of our members really very clever, and one in particular, so amusing in dialect. I nod and smile, and continue to shiver, and presently car fetches me away to village. Meeting is held in reading-room, which seems to me perfect paradise of warmth, and I place myself as close as possible to large oil-stove. Vice-President—very large and expansive in blue—conducts everything successfully, and I deliver homily about What Our Children Read, which is kindly received. After tea—delightfully hot, in fact scalds me, but I welcome it—Recitation Competition takes place and have to rivet my attention on successive members, who mount a little platform and declaim in turns. We begin with not very successful rendering of verses hitherto unknown to me, entitled "Our Institute", and which turn out to be original composition of reciter. This followed by "Gunga Din" and very rousing poem about Keeping the Old Flag Flying. Elderly member then announces "The Mine" and is very dramatic and impressive, but not wholly intelligible, which I put down to Dialect. Finally award first place to "The Old Flag", and second to "The Mine", and present prizes. Am unfortunately inspired to observe that dialect poems are always so interesting, and it then turns out that "The Mine" wasn't in dialect at all. However, too late to do anything about it.

Meeting is prolonged, for which I am thankful, but finally can no longer defer returning to arctic regions of Crimpington Hall. Lady M. and I spend evening cowering over grate, and exchanging isolated remarks, and many nods and smiles, across ear-trumpet. Finally I get into enormous four-poster, covered by very inadequate supply of blankets, and clutching insufficiently heated hot-water bottle.

October 5th.—Develop really severe cold twenty-four hours after reaching home. Robert says that all Institutes are probably full of germs—which is both unjust and ridiculous.

October 13th.—Continued cold and cough keep me in house, and make me unpopular with Robert, Cook, and Gladys—the latter of whom both catch my complaint. Mademoiselle keeps Vicky away, but is sympathetic, and brings Vicky to gesticulate dramatically at me from outside the drawing-room window, as though I had the plague. Gradually this state of affairs subsides, my daily quota of pocket-handkerchiefs returns to the normal, and Vapex, cinnamon, camphorated oil, and jar of cold cream all go back to medicine-cupboard in bathroom once more. Unknown benefactor sends me copy of new Literary Review, which seems to be full of personal remarks from well-known writers about other well-known writers. This perhaps more amusing to themselves than to average reader. Moreover, competitions most alarmingly literary, and I return with immense relief to old friend *Time and Tide*.

October 17th.—Surprising invitation to evening party—Dancing, 9.30—at Lady B.'s. Cannot possibly refuse, as Robert has been told to make himself useful there in various ways; moreover, entire neighbourhood is evidently being polished off, and see no object in raising question as to whether we have, or have not, received invitation. Decide to get new dress, but must have it made locally, owing to rather sharply worded enquiry from London shop which has the privilege of serving me, as to whether I have not overlooked overdue portion of account? (Far from overlooking it, have actually been kept awake by it at night.) Proceed to Plymouth, and get very attractive black taffeta, with little pink and blue posies scattered over it. Mademoiselle removes, and washes, Honiton lace from old purple velvet every-night tea-gown, and assures me that it will be *gentil á croquer* on new taffeta. Also buy new pair black evening-shoes, but shall wear them every evening for at least an hour in order to ensure reasonable comfort at party.

Am able to congratulate myself that great-aunt's diamond ring, for once, is at home when needed.

Robert rather shatteringly remarks that he believes the dancing is only for the *young* people, and I heatedly enquire how line of demarcation is to be laid down? Should certainly not dream of accepting ruling from Lady B. on any such delicate question. Robert merely repeats that only the young will be *expected* to dance, and we drop the subject, and I enquire into nature of refreshments to be expected at party, as half-past nine seems to me singularly inhospitable hour, involving no regular meal whatever. Robert begs that I will order dinner at home exactly as usual, and make it as substantial as possible, so as to give him every chance of keeping awake at party, and I agree that this would indeed appear desirable.

October 9th.—Rumour that Lady B.'s party is to be in Fancy Dress throws entire neighbourhood into consternation. Our Vicar's wife comes down on gardener's wife's bicycle—borrowed, she says, for greater speed and urgency—and explains that, in her position, she does not think that fancy dress would do at all—unless perhaps *poudré*, which, she asserts, is different, but takes ages to brush out afterwards. She asks what I am going to do, but am quite unable to enlighten her, as black taffeta already completed. Mademoiselle, at this, intervenes, and declares that black taffeta can be transformed by a touch into Dresden China Shepherdess *à ravir*. Am obliged to beg her not to be ridiculous, nor attempt to make me so, and she then insanely suggests turning black taffeta into costume for (a) Mary Queen of Scots, (b) Mme. de Pompadour, (c) Cleopatra. I desire her to take Vicky for a walk; she is *blessée*, and much time is spent in restoring her to calm.

Our Vicar's wife—who has meantime been walking up and down drawing-room in state of stress and agitation—says What about asking somebody else? What about the Kellways? Why not ring them up?

We immediately do so, and are lightheartedly told by Mary Kellway that it *is* Fancy Dress, and she is going to wear her Russian Peasant costume—absolutely genuine, brought by sailor cousin from Moscow long years ago—but if in difficulties, can she lend me anything? Reply incoherently to this kind offer, as our Vicar's wife, now in uncontrollable agitation, makes it impossible for me to collect my thoughts. Chaos prevails, when Robert enters, is frenziedly appealed to by our Vicar's wife, and says Oh, didn't he say so? one or two people *have* had "Fancy Dress" put on invitation cards, as Lady B.'s own house-party intends to dress up, but no such suggestion has been made to majority of guests.

Our Vicar's wife and I agree at some length that, really, nobody in this world *but* Lady B. would behave like this, and we have very good minds not to go near her party. Robert and I then arrange to take our Vicar and his wife with us in car to party, she is grateful, and goes.

October 23rd.—Party takes place. Black taffeta and Honiton lace look charming and am not dissatisfied with general appearance, after extracting two quite unmistakable grey hairs. Vicky goes so far, as to say that I look Lovely, but enquires shortly afterwards why old people so often wear black—which discourages me.

Received by Lady B. in magnificent Eastern costume, with pearls dripping all over her, and surrounded by bevy of equally bejewelled friends. She smiles graciously and shakes hands without looking at any of us, and strange fancy crosses my mind that it would be agreeable to bestow on her sudden sharp shaking, and thus compel her to recognise existence of at least one of guests invited to her house. Am obliged, however, to curb this unhallowed impulse, and proceed quietly into vast drawing-room, at one end of which band is performing briskly on platform.

Our Vicar's wife—violet net and garnets—recognises friends, and takes our Vicar away to speak to them. Robert is imperatively summoned by Lady B.—(Is she going to order him to take charge of cloak room, or what?)—and I am greeted by an unpleasant-looking Hamlet, who suddenly turns out to be Miss Pankerton. Why, she asks accusingly, am I not in fancy dress? It would do me all the good in the world to give myself over to the Carnival spirit. It is what I *need*. I make enquiry for Jahsper—should never be surprised to hear that he has come as Ophelia—but Miss P. replies that Jahsper is in Bloomsbury again. Bloomsbury can do nothing without Jahsper. I say, No, I suppose not, in order to avoid hearing any more about either Jahsper or Bloomsbury, and talk to Mary Kellway—who looks nice in Russian Peasant costume—and eventually dance with her husband. We see many of our neighbours, most of them not in fancy dress, and am astounded at unexpected sight of Blenkinsops' Cousin Maud, bounding round the room with short, stout partner, identified by Mary's husband as great hunting man.

Lady B.'s house-party, all in expensive disguises and looking highly superior, dance languidly with one another, and no introductions take place.

It later becomes part of Robert's duty to tell everyone that supper is ready, and we all flock to buffet in dining-room, and are given excellent sandwiches and unidentified form of cup. Lady B.'s expensive-looking house-party nowhere to be seen, and Robert tells me in gloomy aside that he thinks they are in the library, having champagne. I express charitable—and improbable— hope that it may poison them, to which Robert merely replies, Hush, not so loud—but should not be surprised to know that he agrees with me.

Final, and most unexpected, incident of the evening is when I come upon old Mrs. Blenkinsop, all over black jet and wearing martyred expression, sitting in large armchair underneath platform, and exactly below energetic saxophone. She evidently has not the least idea how to account for her presence there, and saxophone prevents conversation, but can distinguish something about Maud, and not getting between young things and their pleasure, and reference to old Mrs. B. not having very much longer to spend amongst us. I smile and nod my head, then feel that this may look unsympathetic, so frown and shake it, and am invited to dance by male Frobisher—who talks about old furniture and birds. House-party reappear, carrying balloons, which they distribute like buns at a School-feast, and party proceeds until midnight.

Band then bursts into Auld Lang Syne and Lady B. screams Come along, Come along, and all are directed to forma circle. Singular mêlée ensues, and I see old Mrs. Blenkinsop swept from armchair and clutching our Vicar with one hand and unknown young gentleman with the other. Our Vicar's wife is holding hands with Miss Pankerton—whom she cannot endure—and looks distraught, and Robert is seized upon by massive stranger in scarlet, and Cousin Maud. Am horrified to realise that I am myself on one side clasping hand of particularly offensive young male specimen of house-party, and on the other that of Lady B. We all shuffle round to well-known strains, and sing For *Ole* Lang Syne, For *Ole*Lang Syne, over and over again, since no one appears to know any other words, and relief is general when this exercise is brought to a close.

Lady B., evidently fearing that we shall none of us know when she has had enough of us, then directs band to play National Anthem, which is done, and she receives our thanks and farewells.

Go home, and on looking at myself in the glass am much struck with undeniable fact that at the end of a party I do not look nearly as nice as I did at the beginning. Should like to think that this applies to every woman, but am not sure—and anyway, this thought ungenerous—like so many others.

Robert says, Why don't I get into Bed? I say, Because I am writing my Diary. Robert replies, kindly, but quite definitely, that In his opinion, That is Waste of Time.

I get into bed, and am confronted by Query: Can Robert be right?

Can only leave reply to Posterity.

The Provincial Lady Goes Further

June 9th.--Life takes on entirely new aspect, owing to astonishing and unprecedented success of minute and unpretentious literary effort, published last December, and--incredibly--written by myself. Reactions of family and friends to this unforeseen state of affairs most interesting and varied.

Dear Vicky and Robin more than appreciative although not allowed to read book, and compare me variously to Shakespeare, Dickens, author of the Dr. Dolittle books, and writer referred to by Vicky as Lambs' Tails.

Mademoiselle--who has read book--only says *Ah, je m'en doutais bien*! which makes me uneasy, although cannot exactly say why.

Robert says very little indeed, but sits with copy of book for several evenings, and turns over a page quite often. Eventually he shuts it and says Yes. I ask what he thinks of it, and after a long silence he says that It is Funny--but does not look amused. Later he refers to financial situation-- as well he may, since it has been exceedingly grave for some time past--and we agree that this ought to Make a Difference.

Conversation is then diverted to merits or demerits of the Dole--about which Robert feels strongly, and I try to be intelligent but do not bring it off--and difficulty of obtaining satisfactory raspberries from old and inferior canes.

June 12th.--Letter from Angela arrives, expressing rather needless astonishment at recent literary success. Also note from Aunt Gertrude, who says that she has not read my book and does not as a rule care about modern fiction, as *nothing* is left to the imagination. Personally, am of opinion that this, in Aunt Gertrude's case, is fortunate--but do not, of course, write back and say so.

Cissie Crabbe, on postcard picturing San Francisco--but bearing Norwich postmark as usual-- says that a friend has lent her copy of book and she is looking forward to reading it. Most unlike dear Rose, who unhesitatingly spends seven-and-sixpence on acquiring it, in spite of free copy presented to her by myself on day of publication.

Customary communication from Bank, drawing my attention to a state of affairs which is only too well known to me already, enables me to write back in quite unwonted strain of optimism, assuring them that large cheque from publishers is hourly expected. Follow this letter up by much less confidently worded epistle to gentleman who has recently become privileged to act as my Literary Agent, enquiring when I may expect money from publishers, and how much.

Cook sends in a message to say that there has been a misfortune with the chops, and shall she make do with a tin of sardines? Am obliged to agree to this, as only alternative is eggs, which will be required for breakfast. (*Mem.*: Enquire into nature of alleged misfortune in the morning.) (*Second, and more straightforward, Mem.*: Try not to lie awake cold with apprehension at having to make this enquiry, but remind myself that it is well known that all servants despise mistresses who are afraid of them, and therefore it is better policy to be firm.)

June 14th.--Note curious and rather disturbing tendency of everybody in the neighbourhood to suspect me of Putting Them into a Book. Our Vicar's Wife particularly eloquent about this, and assures me that she recognised every single character in previous literary effort. She adds that she has never had time to write a book herself, but has often thought that she would like to do so. Little things, she says--one here, another there--quaint sayings such as she hears every day of her life as she pops round the parish--Cranford, she adds in conclusion. I say Yes indeed, being unable to think of anything else, and we part.

Later on, our Vicar tells me that he, likewise, has never had time to write a book, but that if he did so, and put down some of his personal experiences, no one would ever believe them to be true. Truth, says our Vicar, is stranger than fiction.

Very singular speculations thus given rise to, as to nature of incredible experiences undergone by our Vicar. Can he have been involved in long-ago *crime passionnel*, or taken part in a duel in distant student days when sent to acquire German at Heidelberg? Imagination, always so far in advance of reason, or even propriety, carries me to further lengths, and obliges me to go upstairs and count laundry in order to change current of ideas.

Vicky meets me on the stairs and says with no preliminary Please can she go to school. Am unable to say either Yes or No at this short notice, and merely look at her in silence. She adds a brief statement to the effect that Robin went to school when he was her age, and then continues on her way downstairs, singing something of which the words are inaudible, and the tune unrecognisable, but which I have inward conviction that I should think entirely unsuitable.

Am much exercised regarding question of school, and feel that as convinced feminist it is my duty to take seriously into consideration argument quoted above.

June 15th.--Cheque arrives from publishers, via Literary Agent, who says that further instalment will follow in December. Wildest hopes exceeded, and I write acknowledgment to Literary Agent in terms of hysterical gratification that I am subsequently obliged to modify, as being undignified. Robert and I spend pleasant evening discussing relative merits of Rolls-Royce, electric light, and journey to the South of Spain--this last suggestion not favoured by Robert--but eventually decide to pay bills and Do Something about the Mortgage. Robert handsomely adds that I had better spend some of the money on myself, and what about a pearl necklace? I say Yes, to show that I am touched by his thoughtfulness, but do not commit myself to pearl necklace. Should like to suggest very small flat in London, but violent and inexplicable inhibition intervenes, and find myself quite unable to utter the words. Go to bed with flat still unmentioned, but register cast-iron resolution, whilst brushing my hair, to make early appointment in London for new permanent wave.

Also think over question of school for Vicky very seriously, and find myself coming to at least three definite conclusions, all diametrically opposed to one another.

June 16th.--Singular letter from entire stranger enquires whether I am aware that the doors of every decent home will henceforward be shut to me? Publications such as mine, he says, are harmful to art and morality alike. Should like to have this elucidated further, but signature illegible, and address highly improbable, so nothing can be done. Have recourse to waste-paper basket in absence of fires, but afterwards feel that servants or children may decipher fragments, so remove them again and ignite small private bonfire, with great difficulty, on garden path.

(*N.B.* Marked difference between real life and fiction again exemplified here. Quite massive documents, in books, invariably catch fire on slightest provocation, and are instantly reduced to ashes.)

Question of school for Vicky recrudesces with immense violence, and Mademoiselle weeps on the sofa and says that she will neither eat nor drink until this is decided. I say that I think this resolution unreasonable, and suggest Horlick's Malted Milk, to which Mademoiselle replies *Ah, ça, jamais!* and we get no further. Vicky remains unmoved throughout, and spends much time with Cook and Helen Wills. I appeal to Robert, who eventually--after long silence--says, Do as I think best.

Write and put case before Rose, as being Vicky's godmother and person of impartial views. Extreme tension meanwhile prevails in the house, and Mademoiselle continues to refuse food. Cook says darkly that it's well known as foreigners have no powers of resistance, and go to pieces-like all in a moment. Mademoiselle does not, however, go to pieces, but instead writes phenomenal number of letters, all in purple ink, which runs all over the paper whenever she cries.

I walk to the village for no other purpose than to get out of the house, which now appears to me intolerable, and am asked at the Post Office if it's really true that Miss Vicky is to be sent away, she seems such a baby. Make evasive and unhappy reply, and buy stamps. Take the longest way home, and meet three people, one of whom asks compassionately how the foreign lady is. Both the other two content themselves with being sorry to hear that we're losing Miss Vicky.

VICKY IN THE HALL

Crawl indoors, enveloped in guilt, and am severely startled by seeing Vicky, whom I have been thinking of as a moribund exile, looking blooming, lying flat on her back in the hall eating peppermints. She says in a detached way that she needs a new sponge, and we separate without further conversation.

June 17th.--Mademoiselle shows signs of recovery, and drinks cup of tea at eleven o'clock, but relapses again later, and has une crise de nerfs. I suggest bed, and escort her there. Just as I think she can safely be left, swathed in little shawls and eiderdown quilt, she recalls me and enquires feebly if I think her health would stand life in a convent? Refuse--though I hope kindly--to discuss the question, and leave the room.

Second post brings letter from secretary of Literary Club, met once in London, informing me that I am now a member, and thoughtfully enclosing Banker's Order in order to facilitate payment of subscription, also information concerning International Congress to be held shortly in Brussels, and which she feels certain that I shall wish to attend. Decide that I *would* like to attend it, but am in some doubt as to whether Robert can be persuaded that my presence is essential to welfare of Literature. Should like to embark on immediate discussion, but all is overshadowed at lunch by devastating announcement that the Ram is not Working, and there is no water in the house. Lunch immediately assumes character of a passover, and Robert refuses cheese and departs with the gardener in order to bring Ram back to its duty--which they accomplish in about two and a half hours.

June 18th.--Dear Rose, always so definite, writes advocating school for Vicky. Co-educational, she says firmly, and Dalcroze Eurythmics. Robert, on being told this, says violently that no child of his shall be brought up amongst natives of any description. Am quite unable either to move him from this attitude, or to make him see that it is irrelevant to educational scheme at present under discussion.

Rose sends addresses of two schools, declares that she knows all about both, and invites me to go and stay with her in London and inspect them. I explain to Robert that this can be combined with new permanent wave, but Robert evidently not in a receptive mood, and remains immersed in *The Times*.

Post also brings officious communication from old Mrs. Blenkinsopp's Cousin Maud, saying that if I'm looking for a school for my brat, she could put in a word at dear old Roedean. Shall take no notice of this whatever.

June 20th.--Take bold step of writing to secretary of Literary Society to say that I will accompany its members to Brussels, and assist at Conference. Am so well aware that I shall regret this letter within an hour of writing it, that I send Vicky to village with instructions to post it instead of leaving it in box in hall as usual.

(*Query:* Does this denote extreme strength of mind or the reverse? *Answer* immediately presents itself, but see no reason for committing it to paper.)

Mademoiselle reappears in family circle, and has apparently decided that half-mourning is suitable to present crisis, as she wears black dress from which original green accessories have been removed, and fragments of mauve tulle wound round head and neck. Robert, meeting her on stairs, says kindly Mew, maln'zelle? which Mademoiselle receives with very long and involved reply, to which Robert merely returns Oh wee, and leaves her. Mademoiselle, later, tells Vicky, who repeats it to me, that it is not always education, nor even intelligence, that makes a gentleman.

Go through the linen in the afternoon, and find entirely unaccountable deficit of face-towels, but table-napkins, on the other hand, as numerous as they ever were. Blankets, as usual, require washing, but cannot be spared for the purpose, and new sheets are urgently required. Add this item to rapidly lengthening list for London. Just as I am going downstairs again, heavily speckled with fluff off blankets and reeking of camphor, enormous motor-car draws up in perfect silence at open front-door, and completely unknown woman--wearing bran-new hat about the size of a saucer with little plume over one eye--descends from it. I go forward with graceful cordiality and say, Come in, come in, which she does, and we sit and look at one another in drawing-room for ten minutes, and talk about wireless, the neighbourhood--which she evidently doesn't know--the situation in Germany, and old furniture. She turns out to be Mrs. Callington-Clay, recently come to live in house at least twenty miles away.

(Cannot imagine what can ever have induced me to call upon her, but can distinctly remember doing so, and immense relief at finding her out when I did.)

An old friend of mine, says Mrs. Callington Clay, is a neighbour of hers. Do I remember Pamela Pringle? Am obliged to say that I do not. Then perhaps I knew her as Pamela Templer-Tate? I say No again, and repress inclination to add rather tartly that I have never heard of her in my life. Mrs. C.-C. is undefeated and brazenly suggests Pamela Stevenson--whom I once more repudiate. Then, Mrs. C.-C. declares, I *must* recollect Pamela Warburton. Am by this time dazed, but admit that I did once, about twenty-three years ago, meet extraordinarily pretty girl called Pamela Warburton, at a picnic on the river. Very well then, says Mrs. C.-C., there I am! Pamela Warburton married man called Stevenson, ran away from him with man called Templer-Tate, but this, says Mrs. C.-C., a failure, and divorce ensued. She is now married to Pringle--very rich. Something in the City--Templer-Tate children live with them, but *not* Stevenson child. Beautiful old place near Somersetshire border, and Mrs. C.-C. hopes that I will call. Am still too much stunned at extraordinary activity of my contemporary to do more than say Yes, I will, and express feeble and quite insincere hope that she is as pretty as she used to be at eighteen--which is a manifest absurdity.

Finally, Mrs. C.-C. says that she enjoyed my book, and I say that that was very kind, and she asks if it takes long to write a book, and I reply Oh no, and then think it sounds conceited and wish that I had said Oh yes instead, and she departs.

Look at myself in the glass, and indulge in painful, and quite involuntary, exercise of the imagination, in which I rehearse probable description of myself that Mrs. C.-C. will give her husband on her return home. Emerge from this flight of fancy in wholly devitalised condition. Should be sorry indeed to connect this in any way with singular career of Pamela Pringle, as outlined this afternoon. At the same time, cannot deny that our paths in life have evidently diverged widely since distant occasion of river-picnic. Can conceive of no circumstances in which I should part from two husbands in succession, but am curiously depressed at unescapable conviction that my opportunities for doing so have been practically non-existent.

Write to Rose, and say that I will come and stay with her next week and inspect possible schools for Vicky, but cannot promise to patronise any of them.

June 21st.--Post agreeably diversified by most unusual preponderance of receipts over bills.

I pack for London, and explain to Robert that I am going on to Brussels for Literary Conference of international importance. He does not seem to take it in, and I explain all over again. Am sorry to realise that explanation gradually degenerates into something resembling rather a whining apology than a straightforward statement of rational intentions.

Mademoiselle appears soon after breakfast and says, coldly and elaborately, that she would Like to Speak to me when I can spare ten minutes. I say that I can spare them at once, but she replies No, no, it is not her intention to *déranger la matinée*, and she would prefer to wait, and in consequence I spend extremely unpleasant morning anticipating interview, and am quite unable to give my mind to anything at all.

(*Mem.*: This attitude positively childish, but cannot rid myself of overwhelming sensation of guilt.)

Interview with Mademoiselle takes place after lunch, and is fully as unpleasant as I anticipated.

(*Mem.*: Generalisation, so frequently heard, to the effect that things are never as bad as one expects them to be, once more proved untrue up to the hilt.)

Main conclusions to emerge from this highly distressing conference are: (a) That Mademoiselle is *pas du tout susceptible, tout au contraire*; (b) that she is profoundly *blessée*, and *froissée*, and *agacée*, and (c) that she could endure every humiliation and privation heaped upon her, if at least her supper might be brought up punctually.

This sudden introduction of entirely new element in the whole situation overcomes me completely, and we both weep.

I say, between sobs, that we both wish nothing except what is best for Vicky, and Mademoiselle replies with an offer to cut herself into a thousand pieces, and we agree to postpone further discussion for the moment.

The French not only extraordinarily exhausting to themselves and others in times of stress, but also possess very marked talent for transferring their own capacity for emotion to those with whom they are dealing.

Interesting speculation rises in my mind as to Robert's probable reactions to recent conversation with Mademoiselle, had he been present at it, but am too much exhausted to pursue subject further.

June 23rd.--Find myself in London with greatest possible relief. Rose takes one look at me, and then enquires if we have had a death in the house. I explain atmospheric conditions recently prevailing there, and she assures me that she quite understands, and the sooner I get my new permanent wave the better. Following this advice, I make early appointment.

We go to see Charles Laughton in *Payment Deferred*, and am confirmed in previous opinion that he is the most intelligent actor I have ever seen in my life. Rose says, On the *English* stage, in a cosmopolitan manner, and I say Yes, yes, very thoughtfully, and hope she does not realise that my acquaintance with any other stage is confined to performance of *La Grande Duchesse* at Boulogne, witnessed in childhood, and one sight of the Guitrys in Paris, about eleven years ago.

June 24th.--Rose takes me to visit school, which she says she is pretty certain I shall not like. Then why, I ask, go there? She replies that it is better to leave no stone unturned, and anyhow it will give me some idea of the kind of thing.

(On thinking over this reply, it seems wholly inadequate, but at the time am taken in by it.)

We go by train to large and airy red-brick establishment standing on a hill and surrounded by yellow-ochre gravel which I do not like. The Principal--colouring runs to puce and canary, and cannot avoid drawing inward parallel between her and the house--receives us in large and icy drawing-room, and is bright. I catch Rose's eye and perceive that she is unfavourably impressed, as I am myself, and that we both know that This will Never Do--nevertheless we are obliged to waste entire morning inspecting class-rooms--very light and cold--dormitories--hideously tidy, and red blankets like an institution--and gymnasium with dangerous-looking apparatus.

Children all look healthy, except one with a bandage on leg, which Principal dismisses lightly, when I enquire, as boils--and adds that child was born in India. (This event must have taken place at least ten years ago, and cannot possibly have any bearing on the case.)

Rose, behind Principal's back, forms long sentence silently with her lips, of which I do not understand one word, and then shakes her head violently. I shake mine in reply, and we are shown Chapel--chilly and unpleasant building--and Sick-room, where forlorn-looking child with inadequate little red cardigan on over school uniform is sitting in a depressed way over deadly-looking jigsaw puzzle of extreme antiquity.

The Principal says Hallo, darling, unconvincingly, and darling replies with a petrified stare, and we go out again.

I say Poor little thing! and Principal replies, more brightly than ever, that Our children love the sick-room, they have such a good time there. (This obviously untrue--and if not, reflects extremely poorly on degree of enjoyment prevalent out of the sick-room.)

Principal, who has referred to Vicky throughout as "your daughter" in highly impersonal manner, now presses on us terrific collection of documents, which she calls All Particulars, I say that I Will Write, and we return to station.

I tell Rose that really, if that is her idea of the kind of place I want--but she is apologetic, and says the next one will be quite different, and she *does*, really, know exactly what I want. I accept this statement, and we entertain ourselves on journey back to London by telling one another how much we disliked the Principal, her establishment, and everything connected with it.

I even go so far as to suggest writing to parents of bandaged child with boils, but as I do not know either her name or theirs, this goes no further.

(Am occasionally made uneasy at recollection of pious axiom dating back to early childhood, to the effect that every idle word spoken will one day have to be accounted for. If this is indeed fact, can foresee a thoroughly well-filled Eternity for a good many of us.)

June 25th.--Undergo permanent wave, with customary interludes of feeling that nothing on earth can be worth it, and eventual conviction that it *was*.

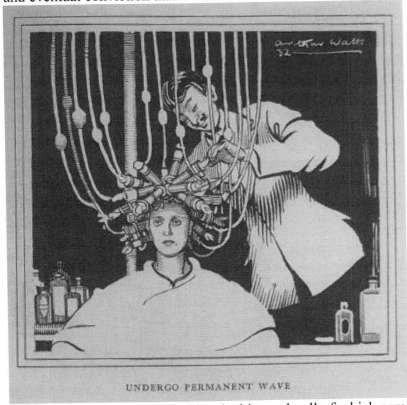

UNDERGO PERMANENT WAVE

The hairdresser tells me that he has done five heads this week, all of which came up beautifully. He also assures me that I shall *not* be left alone whilst the heating is on, and adds gravely that no client ever is left alone at that stage--which has a sinister sound, and terrifies me. However, I emerge safely, and my head is also declared to have come up beautifully--which it has.

I go back to Rose's flat, and display waves, and am told that I look fifteen years younger--which leaves me wondering what on earth I could have looked like before, and how long I have been looking it.

Rose and I go shopping, and look in every shop to see if my recent publication is in window, which it never is except once. Rose suggests that whenever we do not see book, we ought to go in and ask for it, with expressions of astonishment, and I agree that certainly we ought. We leave it at that.

June 26th.--Inspect another school, and think well of Headmistress, also of delightful old house and grounds. Education, however, appears to be altogether given over to Handicrafts--green raffia mats and mauve paper boxes--and Self-expression--table manners of some of the pupils far from satisfactory. Decide, once more, that this does not meet requirements, and go away again.

Rose takes me to a party, and introduces me to several writers, one male and eight females. I wear new mauve frock, purchased that afternoon, and thanks to that and permanent wave, look nice, but must remember to have evening shoes re-covered, as worn gold brocade quite unsuitable.

Tall female novelist tells me that she is a friend of a friend of a friend of mine--which reminds me of popular song--and turns out to be referring to young gentleman known to me as Jahsper, once inflicted upon us by Miss Pankerton. Avoid tall female novelist with horror and dismay for the remainder of the evening.

June 28th.--Letter reaches me forwarded from home, written by contemporary of twenty-three years ago, then Pamela Warburton and now Pamela Pringle. She has heard so much of me from Mrs. Callington-Clay (who has only met me once herself and cannot possibly have anything whatever to say about me, except that I exist) and would so much like to meet me again. Do I remember picnic on the river in dear old days now so long ago? Much, writes Pamela Pringle--as well she may--has happened since then, and perhaps I have heard that after many troubles, she has at last found Peace, she trusts lasting. (Uncharitable reflection crosses my mind that P. P., judging from outline of her career given by Mrs. Callington-Clay, had better not count too much upon this, if by Peace she means matrimonial stability.)

Will I, pathetically adds Pamela, come and see her soon, for the sake of old times?

Write and reply that I will do so on my return--though less for the sake of old times than from lively curiosity, but naturally say nothing about this (extremely inferior) motive.

Go to large establishment which is having a Sale, in order to buy sheets. Find, to my horror, that I return having not only bought sheets, but blue lace tea-gown, six pads of writing-paper, ruled, small hair-slide, remnant of red brocade, and reversible black-and-white bath-mat, with slight flaw in it.

Cannot imagine how any of it happened.

Rose and I go to French film called *Le Million*, and are much amused. Coming out we meet Canadian, evidently old friend of Rose's, who asks us both to dine and go to theatre on following night, and says he will bring another man. We accept, I again congratulate myself on new and successful permanent wave.

Conscience compels me to hint to Rose that I have really come to London in order to look for schools, and she says Yes, yes, there is one more on her list that she is certain I shall like, and we will go there this afternoon.

I ask Rose for explanation of Canadian friend, and she replies that they met when she was travelling in Italy, which seems to me ridiculous. She adds further that he is very nice, and has a mother in Ontario. Am reminded of Ollendorf, but do not say so.

After lunch--cutlets excellent, and quite unlike very uninspiring dish bearing similar name which appears at frequent intervals at home--go by Green Line bus to Mickleham, near Leatherhead. Perfect school is discovered, Principal instantly enquires Vicky's name and refers to her by it afterwards, house, garden and children alike charming, no bandages to be seen anywhere, and Handicrafts evidently occupy only rational amount of attention. Favourite periodical *Time and Tide* lies on table, and Rose, at an early stage, nods at me with extreme vehemence behind Principal's back. I nod in return, but feel they will think better of me if I go away without committing myself. This I succeed in doing, and after short conversation concerning fees, which are not unreasonable, we take our departure. Rose enthusiastic, I say that I must consult Robert,--but this is mostly *pour la forme*, and we feel that Vicky's fate is decided.

June 29th.--Colossal success of evening's entertainment offered by Rose's Canadian. He brings with him delightful American friend, we dine at exotic and expensive restaurant, filled with literary and theatrical celebrities, and go to a revue. American friend says that he understands I have written a book, but does not seem to think any the worse of me for this, and later asks to be told name of book, which he writes down in a business-like way on programme, and puts into his pocket.

They take us to the Berkeley, where we remain until two o'clock in the morning, and are finally escorted to Rose's flat. Have I, asks the American, also got a flat? I say No, unfortunately I have not, and we all agree that this is a frightful state of things and should be remedied immediately. Quite earnest discussion ensues on the pavement, with taxi waiting at great expense.

At last we separate, and I tell Rose that this has been the most wonderful evening I have known for years, and she says that champagne often does that, and we go to our respective rooms.

Query presents itself here: Are the effects of alcohol always wholly to be regretted, or do they not sometimes serve useful purpose of promoting self-confidence? *Answer*, to-night, undoubtedly Yes, but am not prepared to make prediction as to to-morrow's reactions.

June 30th.--Realise with astonishment that Literary Conference in Brussels is practically due to begin, and that much has yet to be done with regard to packing, passport, taking of tickets and changing money. Much of this accomplished, with help of Rose, and I write long letter to Robert telling him where to telegraph in case anything happens to either of the children.

Decide to travel in grey-and-white check silk.

Ring up Secretary of Literary Club in order to find out further details, and am told by slightly reproachful subordinate that Conference started this morning, and everybody else crossed yesterday. Am stunned by this, but Rose, as usual, is bracing, and says What does it Matter, and on second thoughts, agree with her that it doesn't. We spend agreeable evening, mostly talking about ourselves, and Rose says Why go to Belgium at all? but at this I jib, and say that Plans are Plans, and anyhow, I want to see the country. We leave it at that.

July 2nd.--Cannot decide whether it is going to be hot or cold, but finally decide Hot, and put on grey-and-white check silk in which I think I look nice, with small black hat. Sky immediately clouds over and everything becomes chilly. Finish packing, weather now definitely cold, and am constrained to unpack blue coat and skirt, with Shetland jumper, and put it on in place of grey-and-white check, which I reluctantly deposit in suit-case, where it will get crushed. Black hat now becomes unsuitable, and I spend much time trying on remaining hats in wardrobe, to the total of three.

Suddenly discover that it is late--boat-train starts in an hour--and take taxi to station. Frightful conviction that I shall miss it causes me to sit on extreme edge of seat in taxi, leaning well forward, in extraordinarily uncomfortable position that subsequently leads to acute muscular discomfort. However, either this, or other cause unspecified, leads to Victoria being reached with rather more than twenty minutes to spare.

A porter finds me a seat, and I ask if there will be food on the train. He disquietingly replies: Food, *if at all*, will be on the boat. Decide to get some fruit, and find my way to immense glass emporium, where I am confronted by English Peaches, One shilling apiece, Strawberries in baskets, and inferior peaches, of unspecified nationality, at tenpence. Am horrified, in the midst of all this, to hear myself asking for two bananas in a bag, please. Should not be in the least surprised if the man refused to supply them. He does not, however, do so, and I return to the train, bananas and all.

Embarkation safely accomplished. Crossing more successful than usual, and only once have recourse to old remedy of reciting *An Austrian army awfully arrayed*.

LITERARY CLUB MEMBERS

Reach Brussels, and am at Hotel Britannia by eight o'clock. All is red plush, irrelevant gilt mouldings, and Literary Club members. I look at them, and they at me, with horror and distrust. (*Query:* Is not this reaction peculiar to the English, and does patriotism forbid conviction that it is by no means to be admired? Americans totally different, and, am inclined to think, much nicer in consequence.)

Find myself at last face to face with dear old friend, Emma Hay, author of many successful plays. Dear old friend is wearing emerald green, which would be trying to almost anyone, and astonishing quantity of rings, brooches and necklaces. She says, Fancy seeing me here! and have I broken away at last? I say, No, certainly not, and suggest dinner. Am introduced by Emma to any number of literary lights, most of whom seem to be delegates from the Balkans.

(*N.B.* Should be very, very sorry if suddenly called upon to give details as to situation, and component parts, of the Balkans.)

Perceive, without surprise, that the Balkans are as ignorant of my claims to distinction as I of theirs, and we exchange amiable conversation about Belgium,--King Albert popular, Queen Elizabeth shingled, and dresses well--and ask one another if we know Mr. Galsworthy, which none of us do.

July 3rd.--Literary Conference takes place in the morning. The Balkans very eloquent. They speak in French, and are translated by inferior interpreters into English. Am sorry to find attention wandering on several occasions to entirely unrelated topics, such as Companionate Marriage, absence of radiators in Church at home, and difficulty in procuring ice. Make notes on back of visiting-card, in order to try and feel presence at Conference in any way justified. Find these again later, and discover that they refer to purchase of picture-postcards for Robin and Vicky, memorandum that blue evening dress requires a stitch before it can be worn again, and necessity for finding out whereabouts of Messrs. Thos. Cook & Son, in case I run short of money--which I am almost certain to do.

Emma introduces Italian delegate, who bows and kisses my hand. Feel certain that Robert would not care for this Continental custom. Conference continues. I sit next to (moderately) celebrated poet, who pays no attention to me, or anybody else. Dear Emma, always so energetic, takes advantage of break in Conference to introduce more Balkans, both to me and to adjacent poet. The latter remains torpid throughout, and elderly Balkan, who has mistakenly endeavoured to rouse him to conversation, retires with embittered ejaculation: *Ne vous réveillez pas, monsieur.*

Close of Conference, and general conversation, Emma performing many introductions, including me and Italian delegate once more. Italian delegate remains apparently unaware that he has ever set eyes on me before, and can only conclude that appearance and personality alike have failed to make slightest impression.

Find myself wondering why I came to Belgium at all. Should like to feel that it was in the interests of literature, but am doubtful, and entirely disinclined to probe further. Feminine human nature sometimes very discouraging subject for speculation.

Afternoon devoted to sight-seeing. We visit admirable Town Hall, are received by Mayor, who makes speech, first in English, and then all over again in French, other speeches are made in return, and energetic Belgian gentleman takes us all over Brussels on foot. Find myself sympathising with small and heated delegate,--country unknown, but accent very odd--who says to me dejectedly, as we pace the cobbles: *C'est un tour de la Belgique à pied, hein*?

July 5th.--Extreme exhaustion overwhelms me, consequent on excessive sight-seeing. I ask Emma if she would think it unsporting if I evaded charabanc expedition to Malines this afternoon, and she looks pained and astonished and says Shall she be quite honest? I lack courage to say how much I should prefer her not to be honest at all, and Emma assures me that it is my duty, in the interests of literature and internationalism alike, to go to Malines. She adds that there will be tea in the Town Hall--which I know means more speeches--and that afterwards we shall hear a Carillon Concert.

Shall she, Emma adds, wear her green velvet, which will be too hot, or her Rumanian peasant costume, which is too tight, but may please our Rumanian delegates? I advocate sacrificing our Rumanian delegates without hesitation.

Large motor-bus is a great relief after so much walking, and I take my seat beside an unknown French lady with golden hair and a bust, but am beckoned away by Emma, who explains in agitation that the French lady has come to Belgium entirely in order to see something of a Polish friend, because otherwise she never gets away from her husband. Am conscious of being distinctly shocked by this, but do not say so in case Emma should think me provincial. Yield my place to the Polish friend, who seems to me to be in need of soap and water and a shave, but perhaps this mere insular prejudice, and go and sit next to an American young gentleman, who remains indifferent to my presence.

(*Query:* Does this complaisancy on my part amount to countenancing very singular relation which obviously obtains between my fellow-littérateurs? If so, have not the moral courage to do anything about it.)

Nothing of moment passes during drive, except that the French lady takes off her hat and lays her head on her neighbour's shoulder, and that I hear Belgian delegate enquiring of extremely young and pretty Englishwoman: What is the English for Autobus, to which she naïvely returns that: It is Charabanc.

Arrival at Town Hall, reception, speeches and tea take place exactly as anticipated, and we proceed in groups, and on foot, to the Carillon Concert. American neighbour deserts me--have felt certain all along that he always meant to do so at earliest possible opportunity--and I accommodate my pace to that of extremely elderly Belgian, who says that it is certainly not for us to emulate *les jeunes* on a hot day like this, and do I realise that for *nous autres* there is always danger of an apoplexy? Make no reply to this whatever, but inwardly indulge in cynical reflections about extremely poor reward afforded in this life to attempted acts of good nature.

July 6th.--Final Conference in the morning, at which much of importance is doubtless settled, but cannot follow owing to reading letters from home, which have just arrived. Robert says that he hopes I am enjoying myself, and we have had one and a quarter inches of rain since Thursday, and bill for roof-repairs has come in and is even more than he expected. Robin and Vicky write briefly, but affectionately, information in each case being mainly concerned with food, and--in Robin's case--progress of Stamp Collection, which now, he says, must be worth 10d. or 11d. altogether.

Inspection of Antwerp Harbour by motor-launch takes place in the afternoon, and the majority of us sit with our backs to the rails and look at one another. Conversation in my immediate vicinity concerns President Hoover, the novels of J. B. Priestley and *Lady Chatterley's Lover*, which everyone except myself seems to have read and admired. I ask unknown lady on my right if it can be got from the Times Book Club, and she says No, only in Paris, and advises me to go there before I return home. Cannot, however, feel that grave additional expense thus incurred would be justified, and in any case could not possibly explain *détour* satisfactorily to Robert.

Disembark from motor-launch chilled and exhausted, and with conviction that my face has turned pale-green. Inspection in pocket-mirror more than confirms this intuition. Just as I am powdering with energy, rather than success, Emma--vitality evidently unimpaired either by society of fellow-writers or by motor-launch approaches with Italian delegate, and again introduces us.

All is brought to a close by State Banquet this evening, for which everyone--rather strangely--has to pay quite a large number of francs. Incredible number of speeches delivered: ingenious system prevails by which bulb of crimson light is flashed on as soon as any speech has exceeded two and a half minutes. Unfortunately this has no effect whatever on many of our speakers, who disregard it completely. Dear Emma not amongst these, and makes admirably concise remarks which are met with much applause. I sit next to unknown Dutchman--who asks if I prefer to speak English, French, Dutch or German--and very small and dusty Oriental, who complains of the heat.

We rise at eleven o'clock, and dancing is suggested. Just as I move quietly away in search of cloak, taxi and bed, Emma appears and says This will never do, and I must come and dance. I refuse weakly, and she says Why not? to which the only rational reply would be that I have splitting headache, and am not interested in my colleagues nor they in me. Do not, needless to say, indulge in any such candour, and result is that I am thrust by Emma upon American young gentleman for a foxtrot. I say that I dance very badly, and he says that no one can ever keep step with him. Both statements turn out to be perfectly true, and I go back to Hotel dejected, and remind myself that It is Useless to struggle against Middle-age.

July 8th.--Embark for England, not without thankfulness. Am surprised to discover that I have a sore throat, undoubted result of persistent endeavour to out-screech fellow-members of Literary Club for about a week on end.

Emma travels with me, and says that she is camping in Wales all next month, and will I join her? Nothing but a tent, and she lives on bananas and milk chocolate. Associations with the last words lead me to reply absently that the children would like it, at which Emma seems hurt and enquires whether I intend to spend my life between the nursery and the kitchen? The only possible answer to this is that I like it, and discussion becomes animated and rather painful. Emma, on board, avoids me, and I am thrown into society of insufferable male novelist, who is interested in Sex. He has an immense amount to say about it, and we sit on deck for what seems like hours and hours. He says at last that he hopes he is not boring me, and I hear myself, to my incredulous horror, saying pleasantly No, not at all--at which he naturally goes on.

EMMA IN WALES

Become gradually paralysed, and unable to think of anything in the world except how I can get away, but nothing presents itself. At last I mutter something about being cold--which I am--and he at once suggests walking round and round the deck, while he tells me about extraordinarily distressing marriage customs prevalent amongst obscure tribes of another hemisphere. Find myself wondering feebly whether, if I suddenly jumped overboard, he would stop talking. Am almost on the verge of trying this experiment when Emma surges up out of deck-chair and enveloping rugs, and says Oh there I am, she has been looking for me everywhere.

Sink down beside her with profound gratitude, and male novelist departs, assuring me that he will remember to send me list of books on return to London. Can remember nothing whatever of any books discussed between us, but am absolutely convinced that they will be quite unsuitable for inclusion in respectable book-shelves.

Emma is kind, says that she didn't mean a single word she said--(have quite forgotten by this time what she did say, but do not tell her so)--and assures me that what I need is a good night's rest. She then tells me all about a new Trilogy that she is planning to write and which ought to be published by 1938, and also about her views on Bertrand Russell, the works of Stravinsky, and Relativity. At one o'clock in the morning we seek our cabin, last thing I hear being Emma's positive assurance that I need not be afraid of America's influence on the English stage...

July 9th.--London regained, though not before I have endured further spate of conversation from several lights of literature.

(*Query:* Does not very intimate connection exist between literary ability and quite inordinate powers of talk? And if so, is it not the duty of public-spirited persons to make this clear, once for all? *Further Query:* How?)

Part from everybody with immeasurable relief, and wholly disingenuous expressions of regret.

Find Rose in great excitement, saying that she has found the Very Thing. I reply firmly If Bertrand Russell for Vicky, then *No*, to which Rose rejoins that she does not know what I am talking about, but she has found me a flat. Logical and straightforward reply to this would be that I am not looking for a flat, and cannot afford one. This, however, eludes me altogether, and I accompany Rose, via bus No. 19, to Doughty Street, where Rose informs me that Charles Dickens once lived. She adds impressively that she *thinks*, but is not sure, that Someone-or-other was born at a house in Theobald's Road, close by. Brisk discussion as to relative merits of pronouncing this as "Theobald" or "Tibbald" brings us to the door of the flat, where ground-floor tenant hands us keys. Entirely admirable first-floor flat is revealed, unfurnished, and including a bedroom, sitting-room, bathroom and kitchen. To the last, I say that I would rather go out for all my meals than do any cooking at all. Then, Rose replies with presence of mind, use it as a box-room. We make intelligent notes of questions to be referred to agents--Rose scores highest for sound common-sense enquiries as to Power being Laid On and Rates included in Rent--and find soon afterwards that I am committed to a three-year tenancy, with power to sub-let, and a choice of wall-papers, cost not to exceed two shillings a yard. From September quarter, says the agent, and suggests a deposit of say two pounds, which Rose and I muster with great difficulty, mostly in florins.

Go away feeling completely dazed, and quite unable to imagine how I shall explain any of it to Robert. This feeling recrudesces violently in the middle of the night, and in fact keeps me awake for nearly an hour, and is coupled with extremely agitating medley of quite unanswerable questions, such as What I am to Do about a Telephone, and who will look after the flat when I am not in it, and what about having the windows cleaned? After this painful interlude I go to sleep again, and eventually wake up calm, and only slightly apprehensive. This, however, may be the result of mental exhaustion.

July 11th.--Return home, and am greeted with customary accumulation of unexpected happenings, such as mysterious stain on ceiling of spare bedroom, enormous bruise received by Vicky in unspecified activity connected with gardener's bicycle, and letters which ought to have been answered days ago and were never forwarded. Am struck by the fact that tea is very nasty, with inferior bought cake bearing mauve decorations, and no jam. Realisation that I shall have to speak to cook about this in the morning shatters me completely, and by the time I go to bed, Rose, London and Doughty Street have receded into practically forgotten past.

Robert comes to bed soon after one--am perfectly aware that he has been asleep downstairs--and I begin to tell him about the flat. He says that it is very late, and that he supposes the washerwoman puts his pyjamas through the mangle, as the buttons are always broken. I brush this aside and revert to the flat, but without success. I then ask in desperation if Robert would like to hear about Vicky's school; he replies Not now, and we subside into silence.

July 12th.--Cook gives notice.

July 14th.--Pamela Warburton--now Pamela Pringle--and I meet once again, since I take the trouble to motor into the next county in response to an invitation to tea.

Enormous house, with enormous gardens--which I trust not to be asked to inspect--and am shown into room with blue ceiling and quantities of little dogs, all barking. Pamela surges up in a pair of blue satin pyjamas and an immense cigarette-holder, and astonishes me by looking extremely young and handsome. Am particularly struck by becoming effect of brilliant coral lip-stick, and insane thoughts flit through my mind of appearing in Church next Sunday similarly adorned, and watching the effect upon our Vicar. This flight of fancy routed by Pamela's greetings, and introduction to what seems like a small regiment of men, oldest and baldest of whom turns out to be Pringle. Pamela then tells them that she and I were at school together--which is entirely untrue--and that I haven't changed in the least--which I should like to believe, and can't--and offers me a cocktail, which I recklessly accept in order to show how modern I am. Do not, however, enjoy it in the least, and cannot see that it increases my conversational powers. Am moreover thrown on my beam-ends at the very start by unknown young man who asks if I am not the Colonel's wife? Repudiate this on the spot with startled negative, and then wonder if I have not laid foundations of a scandal, and try to put it right by feeble addition to the effect that I do not even know the Colonel, and am married to somebody quite different. Unknown young man looks incredulous, and at once begins to talk about interior decoration, the Spanish Royal Family, and modern lighting. I respond faintly, and try to remember if Pamela P. always had auburn hair. Should moreover very much like to know how she has collected her men, and totally eliminated customary accompanying wives.

Later on, have an opportunity of enquiring into these phenomena, as P. P. takes me to see children. Do not like to ask much about them, for fear of becoming involved in very, very intricate questions concerning P.'s matrimonial extravagances.

Nurseries are entirely decorated in white, and furnished exactly like illustrated articles in *Good Housekeeping*, even to coloured frieze all round the walls. Express admiration, but am inwardly depressed, at contrast with extraordinarily inferior school-room at home. Hear myself agreeing quite firmly with P. P. that it is most important to Train the Eye from the very beginning--and try not to remember large screen covered with scraps from illustrated papers; extremely hideous Brussels carpet descended from dear Grandmamma, and still more hideous oil-painting of quite unidentified peasant carrying improbable-looking jar--all of which form habitual surroundings of Robin and Vicky.

P. P. calls children, and they appear, looking, if possible, even more expensive and hygienic than their nursery. Should be sorry to think that I pounce with satisfaction on the fact that all of them wear spectacles, and one a plate, but cannot quite escape suspicion that this is so. All have dark hair, perfectly straight, and am more doubtful than ever about P.'s auburn waves.

We all exchange handshakes, I say that I have a little boy and a little girl at home--which information children rightly receive with brassy indifference--Pamela shows me adjoining suite of night-nurseries, tiled bathroom and kitchen, and says how handy it is to have a nursery wing quite apart from the rest of the house, and I reply Yes indeed, as if I had always found it so, and say good-bye to the little Spectacles with relief.

Pamela, on the way downstairs, is gushing, and hopes that she is going to see a great deal of me, now that we are neighbours. Forty-one miles does not, in my opinion, constitute being neighbours, but I make appropriate response, and Pamela says that some day we must have a long, long talk. Cannot help hoping this means that she is going to tell me the story of Stevenson, Templer-Tate and Co.

(*N.B.* Singular and regrettable fact that I should not care twopence about the confidences of P. P. except for the fact that they are obviously bound to contain references to scandalous and deplorable occurrences, which would surely be better left in oblivion?)

Drive forty-one miles home again, thinking about a new cook--practically no ray of hope anywhere on horizon here--decision about Vicky's school, Mademoiselle's probable reactions to final announcement on the point, and problem in regard to furnishing of Doughty Street flat.

July 17th.--Am obliged to take high line with Robert and compel him to listen to me whilst I tell him about the flat. He eventually gives me his attention, and I pour out torrents of eloquence, which grow more and more feeble as I perceive their effect upon Robert. Finally he says, kindly but gloomily, that he does not know what can have possessed me--neither do I, by this time--but that he supposes I had to do *something*, and there is a good deal too much furniture here, so some of it can go to Doughty Street.

At this I revive, and we go into furniture in detail, and eventually discover that the only things we can possibly do without are large green glass vase from drawing-room, small maple-wood table with one leg missing, framed engraving of the Prince Consort from bathroom landing, and strip of carpet believed--without certainty--to be put away in attic. This necessitates complete readjustment of furniture question on entirely new basis. I become excited, and Robert says Well, it's my own money, after all, and Why not leave it alone for the present, and we can talk about it again later? Am obliged to conform to this last suggestion, as he follows it up by immediately leaving the room.

Write several letters to Registry Offices, and put advertisement in local *Gazette*, regarding cook. Advertisement takes much time and thought, owing to feeling that it is better to be honest and let them know the worst at once, and equally strong feeling that situation must be made to sound as attractive as possible. Finally put in "good outings" and leave out "oil lamps only" but revert to candour with "quiet country place" and "four in family".

Am struck, not for the first time, with absolutely unprecedented display of talent and industry shown by departing cook, who sends up hitherto undreamed-of triumphs of cookery, evidently determined to show us what we are losing.

July 19th.--Receive two replies to *Gazette* advertisement, one from illiterate person who hopes we do not want dinner in the night--(*Query:* Why should we?)--and another in superior, but unpleasant, handwriting demanding kitchen-maid, colossal wages and improbable concessions as to times off. Reason tells me to leave both unanswered; nevertheless find myself sending long and detailed replies and even--in case of superior scribe--suggesting interview.

Question of Vicky's school recrudesces, demanding and receiving definite decisions. Am confronted with the horrid necessity of breaking this to Mademoiselle. Decide to do so immediately after breakfast, but find myself inventing urgent errands in quite other parts of the house, which occupy me until Mademoiselle safely started for walk with Vicky.

(*Query:* Does not moral cowardice often lead to very marked degree of self-deception? *Answer:* Most undoubtedly yes.)

Decide to speak to Mademoiselle after lunch. At lunch, however, she seems depressed, and says that the weather *lui Porte sur les nerfs*, and I feel better perhaps leave it till after tea. Cannot decide if this is true consideration, or merely further cowardice. Weather gets steadily worse as day goes on, and is probably going to *porter sur les nerfs* of Mademoiselle worse than ever, but register cast-iron resolution not to let this interfere with speaking to her after Vicky has gone to bed.

Robin's Headmaster's wife writes that boys are all being sent home a week earlier, owing to case of jaundice, which is--she adds--*not* catching. Can see neither sense nor logic in this, but am delighted at having Robin home almost at once. This satisfaction, most regrettably, quite unshared by Robert. Vicky, however, makes up for it by noisy and prolonged display of enthusiasm. Mademoiselle, as usual, is touched by this, exclaims *Ah, quel bon petit coeur!* and reduces me once more to despair at thought of the blow in store for her. Find myself desperately delaying Vicky's bed-time, in prolonging game of Ludo to quite inordinate lengths.

THE SOCKS LADY

Just as good-night is being said by Vicky, I am informed that a lady is the back door, and would like to speak to me, please. The lady turns out to be in charge of battered perambulator, filled with apparently hundreds of green cardboard boxes, all--she alleges--containing garments knitted by herself. She offers to display them; I say No, thank you, not to-day, and she immediately does so. They all strike me as frightful in the extreme.

Painful monologue ensues, which includes statements about husband having been a Colonel in the Army, former visits to Court, and staff of ten indoor servants. Am entirely unable to believe any of it, but do not like to say so, or even to interrupt so much fluency. Much relieved when Robert appears, and gets rid of perambulator, boxes and all, apparently by power of the human eye alone, in something under three minutes.

(He admits, later, to having parted with half a crown at back gate, but this I think touching, and much to his credit.)

Robert, after dinner, is unwontedly talkative--about hay--and do not like to discourage him, so bed-time is reached with Mademoiselle still unaware of impending doom.

July 21st.--Interview two cooks, results wholly unfavourable. Return home in deep depression, and Mademoiselle offers to make me a tisane--but substitutes tea at my urgent request--and shows so much kindness that I once more postpone painful task of enlightening her as to immediate future.

July 22nd.--Return of Robin, who is facetious about jaundice case--supposed to be a friend of his--and looks well. He eats enormous tea and complains of starvation at school. Mademoiselle says *Le pauvre gosse!* and produces packet of Menier chocolate, which Robin accepts with gratitude--but am only too well aware that this alliance is of highly ephemeral character.

I tell Robin about Doughty Street flat and he is most interested and sympathetic, and offers to make me a box for shoes, or a hanging bookshelf, whichever I prefer. We then adjourn to garden and all play cricket, Mademoiselle's plea for *une balle de caoutchouc* being, rightly, ignored by all. Robin kindly allows me to keep wicket, as being post which I regard as least dangerous, and Vicky is left to bowl, which she does very slowly, and with many wides. Helen Wills puts in customary appearance, but abandons us on receiving cricket-ball on front paws. After what feels like several hours of this, Robert appears, and game at once takes on entirely different--and much brisker--aspect. Mademoiselle immediately says firmly *Moi, je ne joue plus* and walks indoors. Cannot feel that this is altogether a sporting spirit, but have private inner conviction that nothing but moral cowardice prevents my following her example. However, I remain at my post--analogy with Casabianca indicated here--and go so far as to stop a couple of balls and miss one or two catches, after which I am told to bat, and succeed in scoring two before Robin bowls me.

Cricket decidedly not my game, but this reflection closely followed by unavoidable enquiry: What is? Answer comes there none.

July 23rd.--Take the bull by the horns, although belatedly, and seek Mademoiselle at two o'clock in the afternoon--Vicky resting, and Robin reading *Sherlock Holmes* on front stairs, which he prefers to more orthodox sitting-rooms--May I, say I feebly, sit down for a moment?

Mademoiselle at once advances her own armchair and says *Ah, ça me fait du bien de recevoir madame dans mon petit domaine*--which makes me feel worse than ever.

Extremely painful half-hour follows. We go over ground that we have traversed many times before, and reach conclusions only to unreach them again, and the whole ends, as usual, in floods of tears and mutual professions of esteem. Emerge from it all with only two solid facts to hold on to--that Mademoiselle is to return to her native land at an early date, and that Vicky goes to school at Mickleham in September.

(*N.B.* When announcing this to Vicky, must put it to her in such a way: that she is neither indecently joyful at emancipation, nor stonily indifferent to Mademoiselle's departure. Can foresee difficult situation arising here, and say so to Robert, who tells me not to cross my bridges before I get to them--which I consider aggravating.)

Spend a great deal of time writing to Principal of Vicky's school, to dentist for appointments, and to Army and Navy Stores for groceries. Am quite unable to say why this should leave me entirely exhausted in mind and body--but it does.

July 25th.--Go to Exeter in order to interview yet another cook, and spend exactly two hours and twenty minute in Registry Office waiting for her to turn up--which she never does. At intervals, I ask offenive-looking woman in orange *béret*, who sits at desk, What she thinks can have Happened, and she replies that she couldn't say, she's sure, and such a thing has never happened in the office before, never--which makes me feel that it is all my fault.

Harassed-looking lady in transparent pink mackintosh trails in, and asks for a cook-general, but is curtly dismissed by orange *béret* with assurance that cooks-general for the country are not to be found. If they were, adds the orange *béret* cynically, her fortune would have been made long ago. The pink mackintosh, like Queen Victoria, is not amused, and goes out again. She is succeeded by a long interval, during which the orange *béret* leaves the room and returns with a cup of tea, and I look--for the fourteenth time--at only available literature, which consists of ridiculous little periodical called "Do the Dead Speak?" and disembowelled copy of the *Sphere* for February 1929.

Orange *béret* drinks tea, and has long and entirely mysterious conversation conducted in whispers with client who looks like a charwoman.

Paralysis gradually invades me, and feel that I shall never move again--but eventually, of course, do so, and find that I have very nearly missed bus home again. Evolve scheme for selling house and going to live in hotel, preferably in South of France, and thus disposing for ever of servant question. Am aware that this is not wholly practicable idea, and would almost certainly lead to very serious trouble with Robert.

(*Query:* Is not theory mistaken, which attributes idle and profitless day-dreaming to youth? Should be much more inclined to add it to many other unsuitable and unprofitable weaknesses of middle-age.)

Spend the evening with children, who are extraordinarily energetic, and seem surprised when I refuse invitation to play tip-and-run, but agree, very agreeably, to sit still instead and listen to *Vice Versa* for third time of reading.

July 26th.--Spirited discussion at breakfast concerning annual problem of a summer holiday. I hold out for Brittany, and produce little leaflet obtained from Exeter Travel Agency, recklessly promising unlimited sunshine, bathing and extreme cheapness of living. Am supported by Robin--who adds a stipulation that he is not to be asked to eat frogs. Mademoiselle groans, and says that the crossing will assuredly be fatal to us all and this year is one notable for *naufrages*. At this stage Vicky confuses the issue by urging travel by air, and further assures us that in France all the little boys have their hair cut exactly like convicts. Mademoiselle becomes *froissée*, and says *Ah non, par exemple, je ne m' offense pas, moi, mais ça tout de même*--and makes a long speech, the outcome of which is that Vicky has neither heart nor common sense, at which Vicky howls, and Robert says My God and cuts ham.

Discussion then starts again on a fresh basis, with Vicky outside the door where she can be heard shrieking at intervals--but this mechanical, rather than indicative of serious distress--and Mademoiselle showing a tendency to fold her lips tightly and repeat that nobody is to pay any attention to her wishes about anything whatever.

I begin all over again about Brittany, heavily backed by Robin, who says It is well known that all foreigners live on snails. (At this I look apprehensively at Mademoiselle, but fortunately she has not heard.)

Robert's sole contribution to discussion is that England is quite good enough for him.

(Could easily remind Robert of many occasions, connected with Labour Government activities in particular, when England has been far from good enough for him--but refrain.)

Would it not, I urge, be an excellent plan to shut up the house for a month, and have thorough change, beneficial to mind and body alike? (Should also, in this way, gain additional time in which to install new cook, but do not put forward this rather prosaic consideration.)

Just as I think my eloquence is making headway, Robert pushes back his chair and says Well, all this is great waste of time, and he wants to get the calf off to market--which he proceeds to do.

Mademoiselle then begs for ten minutes' Serious Conversation--which I accord with outward calm and inward trepidation. The upshot of the ten minutes--which expand to seventy by the time we have done with them--is that the entire situation is more than Mademoiselle's nerves can endure, and unless she has a complete change of environment immediately, she will *succomber*.

I agree that this must at all costs be avoided, and beg her to make whatever arrangements suit her best. Mademoiselle weeps, and is still weeping when Gladys comes in to clear the breakfast things. (Cannot refrain from gloomy wonder as to nature of comments that this prolonged *tête-à-tête* will give rise to in kitchen.)

Entire morning seems to pass in these painful activities, without any definite result, except that Mademoiselle does not appear at lunch, and both children behave extraordinarily badly.

(*Mem.:* A mother's influence, if any, almost always entirely disastrous. Children invariably far worse under maternal supervision than any other.)

Resume Brittany theme with Robert once more in the evening, and suggest--stimulated by unsuccessful lunch this morning--that a Holiday Tutor might be engaged. He could, I say, swim with Robin, which would save me many qualms, and take children on expeditions. Am I, asks Robert, prepared to pay ten guineas a week for these services? Reply to this being self-evident, I do not make it, and write a letter to well-known scholastic agency.

July 29th.--Brittany practically settled, small place near Dinard selected, passports frantically looked for, discovered in improbable places, such as linen cupboard, and--in Robert's case--acting as wedge to insecurely poised chest of drawers in dressing-room--and brought up to date at considerable expense.

I hold long conversations with Travel Agency regarding hotel accommodation and registration of luggage, and also interview two holiday tutors, between whom and myself instant and violent antipathy springs up at first sight.

One of these suggests that seven and a half guineas weekly would be suitable remuneration, and informs me that he must have his evenings to himself, and the other one assures me that he is a good disciplinarian but insists upon having a Free Hand. I reply curtly that this is not what I require, and we part.

July 30th.--Wholly frightful day, entirely given up to saying good-bye to Mademoiselle. She gives us all presents, small frame composed entirely of mussel shells covered with gilt paint falling to Robert's share, and pink wool bed-socks, with four-leaved clover worked on each, to mine. We present her in return with blue leather hand-bag--into inner pocket of which I have inserted cheque--travelling clock, and small rolled-gold brooch representing crossed tennis racquets, with artificial pearl for ball--(individual effort of Robin and Vicky). All ends in emotional crescendo, culminating in floods of tears from Mademoiselle, who says nothing except *Mais voyons! Il faut se calmer*, and then weeps harder than ever. Should like to see some of this feeling displayed by children, but they remain stolid, and I explain to Mademoiselle that the reserve of the British is well known, and denotes no lack of heart, but rather the contrary.

(On thinking this over, am pretty sure that it is not in the least true--but am absolutely clear that if occasion arose again, should deliberately say the same thing.)

August 4th.--Travel to Salisbury, for express purpose of interviewing Holiday Tutor, who has himself journeyed from Reading. Terrific expenditure of time and money involved in all this makes me feel that he must at all costs be engaged--but am aware that this is irrational, and make many resolutions against foolish impetuosity.

We meet in uninspiring waiting-room, untenanted by anybody else, and I restrain myself with great difficulty from saying "Doctor Livingstone, I presume?" which would probably make him doubtful of my sanity.

Tutor looks about eighteen, but assures me that he is nearly thirty, and has been master at Prep. School in Huntingdonshire for years and years.

(*N.B.* Huntingdon most improbable-sounding, but am nearly sure that it does exist. *Mem.*: Look it up in Vicky's atlas on return home.)

Conversation leads to mutual esteem. I am gratified by the facts that he neither interrupts me every time I speak, nor assures me that he knows more about Robin than I do--(*Query:* Can he really be a schoolmaster?)--and we part cordially, with graceful assurances on my part that "I will write". Just as he departs I remember that small, but embarrassing, issue still has to be faced, and recall him in order to enquire what I owe him for to-day's expenses? He says Oh, nothing worth talking about, and then mentions a sum which appalls me. Pay it, however, without blenching, although well aware it will mean that I shall have to forgo tea in the train, owing to customary miscalculation as to amount of cash required for the day.

Consult Robert on my return; he says Do as I think best, and adds irrelevant statement about grass needing cutting, and I write to Huntingdonshire forthwith, and engage tutor to accompany us to Brittany.

Painful, and indeed despairing, reflections ensue as to relative difficulties of obtaining a tutor and a cook.

August 6th.--Mademoiselle departs, with one large trunk and eight pieces of hand luggage, including depressed-looking bouquet of marigolds, spontaneously offered by Robin. (*N.B.* Have always said, and shall continue to say, that fundamentally Robin has nicer nature than dear Vicky.) We exchange embraces; she promises to come and stay with us next summer, and says *Allons, du courage, n'est-ce pas?* and weeps again. Robert says that she will miss her train, and they depart for the station, Mademoiselle waving her handkerchief to the last, and hanging across the door at distinctly dangerous angle.

Vicky says cheerfully How soon will the Tutor arrive? and Robin picks up Helen Wills and offers to take her to see if there are any greengages--(which there cannot possibly be, as he ate the last ones, totally unripe, yesterday).

Second post brings me letter from Emma Hay, recalling Belgium--where, says Emma, I was the greatest success, underlined--which statement is not only untrue, but actually an insult to such intelligence as I may possess. She hears that I have taken a flat in London--(How?)--and is more than delighted, and there are many, many admirers of my work who will want to meet me the moment I arrive.

Am distressed at realising that although I know every word of dear Emma's letter to be entirely untrue, yet nevertheless cannot help being slightly gratified by it. Vagaries of human vanity very very curious. Cannot make up my mind in what strain to reply to Emma, so decide to postpone doing so at all for the present.

Children unusually hilarious all the evening, and am forced to conclude that loss of Mademoiselle leaves them entirely indifferent.

Read *Hatter's Castle* after they have gone to bed, and am rapidly reduced to utmost depths of gloom. Mentally compose rather eloquent letter to Book Society explaining that most of us would rather be exhilarated than depressed, although at the same time handsomely admitting that book is, as they themselves claim, undoubtedly powerful. But remember *Juan in America*-- earlier choice much approved by myself--and decide to forbear. Also Robert says Do I know that it struck half-past ten five minutes ago? which I know means that he wants to put out Helen Wills, bolt front door and extinguish lights. I accordingly abandon all thoughts of eloquent letters to unknown *littérateurs* and go to bed.

August 7th.--Holiday Tutor arrives, and I immediately turn over both children to him, and immerse myself in preparations for journey, now imminent, to Brittany. At the same time, view of garden from behind bedroom window curtains permits me to ascertain that all three are amicably playing tip-and-run on lawn. This looks like auspicious beginning, and am relieved.

August 8th.--Final, and exhaustive, preparations for journey. Eleventh hour salvation descends in shape of temporary cook, offered me through telephone by Mary Kellaway, who solemnly engages to send her over one day before our return. Maids dismissed on holiday, gardener and wife solemnly adjured to Keep an Eye on the house and feed Helen Wills, and I ask tutor to sit on Robin's suitcase so that I can shut it, then forget having done so and go to store-cupboard for soap--French trains and hotels equally deficient in this commodity--and return hours later to find him still sitting there, exactly like Casabianca. Apologise profusely, am told that it does not matter, and suitcase is successfully dealt with.

Weather gets worse and worse, Shipping Forecast reduces us all to despair--(except Vicky, who says she does so hope we shall be wrecked)--and gale rises hourly. I tell Casabianca that I hope he's a good sailor; he says No, very bad indeed, and Robert suddenly announces that he can see no sense whatever in leaving home at all.

August 10th.--St. Briac achieved, at immense cost of nervous wear and tear. Casabianca invaluable in every respect, but am--rather unjustly--indignant when he informs me that he has slept all night long. History of my own night very different to this, and have further had to cope with Vicky, who does not close an eye after four A.M. and is brisk and conversational, and Robin, who becomes extremely ill from five onwards.

Land at St. Malo, in severe gale and torrents of rain, and Vicky and Robin express astonishment at hearing French spoken all round them, and Robert says that the climate reminds him of England. Casabianca says nothing, but gives valuable help with luggage and later on tells us, very nicely, that we have lost one suitcase. This causes delay, also a great deal of conversation between taxi-driver who is to take us to St. Briac, porter and unidentified friend of taxi-driver's who enters passionately into the whole affair and says fervently *Ah, grâce a Dieu!* when suitcase eventually reappears. Entire incident affords taxi-driver fund for conversation all the way to St. Briac, and he talks to us over his shoulder at frequent intervals. Robert does not seem to appreciate this, and can only hope that taxi-driver is no physiognomist, as if so, his feelings will inevitably be hurt.

We pass through several villages, and I say This must be it, to each, and nobody takes any notice except Casabianca, who is polite and simulates interest, until we finally whisk into a little *place* and stop in front of cheerful-looking Hotel with awning and little green tables outside--all dripping wet. Am concerned to notice no sign of sea anywhere, but shelve this question temporarily, in order to deal with luggage, allotment of bedrooms--(mistake has occurred here, and Madame shows cast-iron determination to treat Casabianca and myself as husband and wife)--and immediate *cafés complets* for all. These arrive, and we consume them in the hall under close and unwavering inspection of about fifteen other visitors, all British and all objectionable-looking.

Inspection of rooms ensues; Robin says When can we bathe--at which, in view of temperature, I feel myself growing rigid with apprehension--and general process of unpacking and settling in follows. Robert, during this, disappears completely, and is only recovered hours later, when he announces that The Sea is about Twenty Minutes' Walk.

General feeling prevails that I am to blame, about this, but nothing can be done, and Casabianca, after thoughtful silence, remarks that Anyway the walk will warm us. Cannot make up my mind whether this is, or is not, high example of tact. Subsequent experience, however, proves that it is totally untrue, as we all--excepting children--arrive at large and windy beach in varying degrees of chilliness. Sea is extremely green, with large and agitated waves, blown about by brisk East wind. Incredible and stupefying reflection that in less than quarter of an hour we shall be in the water--and am definitely aware that I would give quite considerable sum of money to be allowed to remain in my clothes, and on dry land. Have strong suspicion that similar frame of mind prevails elsewhere, but all cram ourselves into two bathing-huts with false assumption of joviality, and presently emerge, inadequately clad in bathing-suits.

(*N.B.* Never select blue bathing-cap again. This may be all right when circulation normal, but otherwise, effect repellent in the extreme.)

Children dash in boldly, closely followed by Holiday Tutor--to whom I mentally assign high marks for this proof of devotion to duty, as he is pea-green with cold, and obviously shivering--Robert remains on edge of sea, looking entirely superior, and I crawl with excessive reluctance into several inches of water and there become completely paralysed. Shrieks from children, who say that It is Glorious, put an end to this state of affairs, and eventually we all swim about, and tell one another that really it isn't so very cold *in* the water, but better not stay in too long on the first day.

Regain bathing-huts thankfully and am further cheered by arrival of ancient man with *eau chaude pour les pieds.*

Remainder of day devoted to excellent meals, exploring of St. Briac between terrific downpours of rain, and purchase of biscuits, stamps, writing-pad, peaches--(very inexpensive and excellent)--and Tauchnitz volume of *Sherlock Holmes* for Robin, and *Robinson Crusoe* for Vicky.

Children eventually disposed of in bed, and Robert and Casabianca discuss appearance of our fellow-visitors with gloom and disapproval, and join in condemning me for suggesting that we should enter into conversation with all or any of them. Cannot at all admire this extremely British frame of mind, and tell them so, but go up to bed immediately before they have time to answer.

August 13th.--Opinion that St. Briac is doing us all good, definitely gaining ground. Bathing becomes less agonising, and children talk French freely with Hotel chambermaids, who are all charming. Continental breakfast unhappily not a success with Robert, who refers daily to bacon in rather embittered way, but has nothing but praise for *langoustes* and *entrecôtes* which constitute customary luncheon menu.

CONTINENTAL BREAKFAST UNHAPPILY NOT A SUCCESS
WITH ROBERT

Casabianca proves admirable disciplinarian, after fearful contest with Robin concerning length of latter's stay in water. During this episode, I remain in bathing-hut, dripping wet and with one eye glued to small wooden slats through which I can see progress of affairs. Just as I am debating whether to interfere or not, Robin is vanquished, and marched out of sea with appalling calm by Casabianca. Remainder of the day wrapped in gloom, but reconciliation takes place at night, and Casabianca assures me that all will henceforward be well. (*N.B.* The young often very optimistic.)

August 15th.--I enter into conversation with two of fellow-guests at hotel, one of whom is invariably referred to by Robert as "the retired Rag-picker" owing to unfortunate appearance, suggestive of general decay. He tells me about his wife, dead years ago--(am not surprised at this)--who was, he says, a genius in her own way. Cannot find out what way was. He also adds that he himself has written books. I ask what about, and he says Psychology, but adds no more. We talk about weather--bad here, but worse in England--Wolverhampton, which he once went through and where I have never been at all--and humane slaughter, of which both of us declare ourselves to be in favour. Conversation then becomes languid, and shows a tendency to revert to weather, but am rescued by Casabianca, who says he thinks I am wanted--which sounds like the police, but is not.

Casabianca inclined to look superior, and suggest that really, the way people force their acquaintance upon one when abroad--but I decline to respond to this and tell him in return that there will be a dance at the hotel to-night and that I intend to go to it. He looks horror-stricken, and says no more.

Small problem of conduct arises here, as had no previous intention whatever of patronising dance, where I know well that Robert will flatly refuse to escort me--but do not see now how I can possibly get out of it. (*Query:* Would it be possible to compel Casabianca to act as my partner, however much against his inclination? This solution possibly undignified, but not without rather diverting aspect.)

Look for Vicky in *place*, where she habitually spends much time, playing with mongrel French dogs in gutter. Elderly English spinster--sandy-haired, and name probably Vi--tells me excitedly that some of the dogs have not been behaving quite decently, and it isn't very nice for my little girl to be with them. I reply curtly that Dogs will be Dogs, and think--too late--of many much better answers. Dogs all seem to me to be entirely respectable and well-conducted and see no reason whatever for interfering with any of them. Instead, go with Robin to grocery across the street, where we buy peaches, biscuits and bunches of small black grapes. It pours with rain, Vicky and dogs disperse, and we return indoors to play General Information in obscure corner of dining-room.

Casabianca proves distressingly competent at this, and defeats everybody, Robert included, with enquiry: "What is Wallis's line?" which eventually turns out to be connected with distinction--entirely unintelligible to me--between one form of animal life and another. Should like to send him to explain it to Vi, and see what she says--but do not, naturally, suggest this.

Children ask excessively ancient riddles, and supply the answers themselves, and Robert concentrates on arithmetical problems. Receive these in silence, and try and think of any field of knowledge in which I can hope to distinguish myself--but without success. Finally, Robin challenges me with what are Seven times Nine? to which I return brisk, but, as it turns out, incorrect, reply. Casabianca takes early opportunity of referring, though kindly, to this, and eventually suggests that half an hour's arithmetic daily would make my accounts much simpler. I accept his offer, although inwardly aware that only drastic reduction of expenditure, and improbable increase of income, could really simplify accounts--but quite agree that counting on fingers is entirely undesirable procedure, at any time of life, but more especially when early youth is past.

Bathing takes place as usual, but additional excitement is provided by sudden dramatic appearance of unknown French youth who asks us all in turns if we are doctors, as a German gentleman is having a fit in a bathing-hut. Casabianca immediately dashes into the sea--which--he declares--an English doctor has just entered. (*Query:* Is this second sight, or what?) Robin and Vicky enquire with one voice if they can go and see the German gentleman having a fit, and are with great difficulty withheld from making one dash for his bathing-cabin, already surrounded by large and excited collection.

Opinions fly about to the effect that the German gentleman is unconscious--that he has come round--that he is already dead--that he has been murdered. At this, several people scream, and a French lady says *Il ne manquait que cela!* which makes me wonder what the rest of her stay at St. Briac can possibly have been like.

Ask Robert if he does not think he ought to go and help, but he says What for? and walks away.

Casabianca returns, dripping, from the sea, followed by equally dripping stranger, presumably the doctor, and I hastily remove children from spectacle probably to be seen when bathing-hut opens; the last thing I hear being assurance from total stranger to Casabianca that he is tout *à fait aimable*.

Entire episode ends in anti-climax when Casabianca shortly afterwards returns, and informs us that The Doctor Said it was Indigestion, and the German gentleman is now walking home with his wife--who is, he adds impressively, a Norwegian. This, for reasons which continue to defy analysis, seems to add weight and respectability to whole affair.

We return to hotel, again caught in heavy shower, are besought by Robin and Vicky to stop and eat ices at revolting English tea-shop, which they patriotically prefer to infinitely superior French establishments, and weakly yield. Wind whistles through cotton frock--already wet through--that I have mistakenly put on, and Casabianca, after gazing at me thoughtfully for some moments, murmurs that I look Pale--which I think really means, Pale Mauve.

On reaching hotel, defy question of expense, and take hot bath, at cost of four francs, *prix spécial*.

Children, with much slamming of doors, and a great deal of conversation, eventually get to bed, and I say to Robert that we *might* look in at the dance after dinner--which seems easier than saying that I should like to go to it.

Robert's reply much what I expected. Eventually find myself crawling into dance-room, sideways, and sitting in severe draught, watching *le tango*, which nobody dances at all well. Casabianca, evidently feeling it his duty, reluctantly suggests that we should dance the next foxtrot--which we do, and it turns out to be Lucky Spot dance and we very nearly--but not quite--win bottle of champagne. This, though cannot say why, has extraordinarily encouraging effect, and we thereupon dance quite gaily until midnight.

August 18th.--Singular encounter takes place between Casabianca and particularly rigid and unapproachable elderly fellow-countryman in hotel, who habitually walks about in lounge wearing canary-yellow cardigan, and eyes us all with impartial dislike. Am therefore horrified when he enquires, apparently of universe at large: "What's afoot?" and Casabianca informatively replies: "Twelve inches one foot"--evidently supposing himself to be addressing customary collection of small and unintelligent schoolboys. Canary-yellow cardigan is naturally infuriated, and says that he did not get up early in the morning in order to put conundrums, or listen to their idiotic solutions--and unpleasant situation threatens.

Further discussion is, however, averted by Vicky, who falls into large open space which has suddenly appeared in floor, and becomes entangled with pipes that I hope are Gas, but much fear may be Drains. She is rescued, amongst loud cries of *Ah, pauvre petite!* and *Oh, là là!* and Casabianca removes her and says austerely that People should look where they are going. Should like to retort that People should think what they are saying--but unfortunately this only occurs to me too late.

Robert, on being told of this incident, laughs whole-heartedly for the first time since coming to St. Briac, and I reflect--as so frequently before--that masculine sense of humour is odd.

Discover that Robin is wearing last available pair of shorts, and that these are badly torn, which necessitates visit to Dinard to take white shorts to cleaners and buy material with which to patch grey ones. No one shows any eagerness to escort me on this expedition and I finally depart alone.

French gentleman with moustache occupies one side of bus and I the other, and we look at one another. Extraordinary and quite unheralded idea springs into my mind to the effect that it is definitely agreeable to find myself travelling anywhere, for any purpose, without dear Robert or either of the children. Am extremely aghast at this unnatural outbreak and try to ignore it.

(*Query:* Does not modern psychology teach that definite danger attaches to deliberate stifling of any impulse, however unhallowed? Answer probably Yes. Cannot, however, ignore the fact that even more definite danger probably attached to encouragement of unhallowed impulse. Can only conclude that peril lies in more or less every direction.)

The moustache and I look out of our respective windows, but from time to time turn round. This exercise not without a certain fascination. Should be very sorry indeed to recall in any detail peculiar fantasies that pass through my mind before Dinard is reached.

Bus stops opposite Casino, the moustache and I rise simultaneously--unfortunately bus gives a last jerk and I sit violently down again--and all is over. Final death-blow to non-existent romance is given when Robin's white shorts, now in last stages of dirt and disreputability, slide out of inadequate paper wrappings and are collected from floor by bus-conductor and returned to me.

Dinard extremely cold, and full of very unengaging trippers, most of whom have undoubtedly come from Lancashire. I deal with cleaners, packet of Lux, chocolate for children, and purchase rose-coloured bathing-cloak for myself, less because I think it suitable or becoming than because I hope it may conduce to slight degree of warmth.

Am moved by obscure feelings of remorse--(what about, in Heaven's name?)--to buy Robert a present, but can see nothing that he would not dislike immeasurably. Finally in desperation select small lump of lead, roughly shaped to resemble Napoleonic outline, and which I try to think may pass as rather unusual antique.

Do not like to omit Casabianca from this universal distribution, so purchase Tauchnitz edition of my own literary effort, but think afterwards that this is both tactless and egotistical, and wish I hadn't done it. Drink chocolate in crowded *pâtisserie*, all by myself, and surrounded by screeching strangers; am sure that French cakes used to be nicer in far-away youthful days, and feel melancholy and middle-aged. Sight of myself in glass when I powder my nose does nothing whatever to dispel any of it.

August 19th.--Robert asks if Napoleonic figure is meant for a paper-weight? I am inwardly surprised and relieved at this extremely ingenious idea, and at once say Yes, certainly. Can see by Robert's expression that he feels doubtful, but firmly change subject immediately.

Day unmarked by any particularly sensational development except that waves are even larger than usual, and twice succeed in knocking me off my feet, the last time just as I am assuring Vicky that she is perfectly safe with *me*. Robert retrieves us both from extremest depths of the ocean, and Vicky roars. Two small artificial curls--Scylla and Charybdis--always worn under bathing-cap in order that my own hair may be kept dry--are unfortunately swept away, together with bathing-cap, in this disaster, and seen no more. Bathing-cap retrieved by Casabianca, but do not like to enquire whether he cannot also pursue Scylla and Charybdis, and am accordingly obliged to return to shore without them.

(Interesting, although unprofitable, speculation comes into being here: Would not conflict between chivalry and common sense have arisen if Casabianca *had* sighted elusive side-curls, Scylla and Charybdis? What, moreover, would have been acceptable formula for returning them to me? Should much like to put this problem to him, but decide not to do so, at any rate for the present.)

August 21st.--End of stay at St. Briac approaches, and I begin to feel sentimental, but this weakness unshared by anybody else.

Loss of Scylla and Charybdis very inconvenient indeed.

August 23rd.--Am put to shame by Vicky whilst sitting outside drinking coffee on the *place* with Robert and Casabianca, fellow-guests surrounding us on every side. She bawls from an upper window that she is just going to bed, but has not kissed Casabianca good-night and would like to do so. I crane my head upwards at very uncomfortable angle and sign to her to desist, upon which she obligingly yells that To-morrow morning will *do*, and everybody looks at us. Casabianca remains unperturbed, and merely says chillingly that he Hopes she will Wash her Face first. On thinking this over, it strikes me as surely unsurpassed effort as deterrent to undesired advances, and can only trust that Vicky will not brazenly persist in path of amorous indiscretion in spite of it.

(*N.B.* Am often a prey to serious anxiety as to dear Vicky's future career. Question suggests itself: Is Success in Life incompatible with High Moral Ideals? Answer, whatever it is, more or less distressing. Can only trust that delightful scholastic establishment at Mickleham will be able to deal adequately with this problem.)

Robert shows marked tendency to say that Decent English Food again will come as a great relief, and is more cheerful than I have seen him since we left home. Take advantage of this to suggest that he and I should visit Casino at Dinard and play roulette, which may improve immediate finances, now very low, and in fact have twice had to borrow from Casabianca, without saying anything about it to Robert.

AT THE CASINO

Casino agreed upon, and we put on best clothes--which have hitherto remained folded in suitcase and extremely inadequate shelves of small wardrobe that always refuses to open.

Bus takes us to Dinard at breakneck speed, and deposits us at Casino. All is electric light, advertisement--(*Byrrh*)--and vacancy, and bartender tells us that no one will think of arriving before eleven o'clock. We have a drink each, for want of anything better to do, and sit on green velvet sofa and read advertisements. Robert asks What is *Gala des Tou-tous?* and seems disappointed when I say that I think it is little dogs. Should like--or perhaps not--to know what he thought it was.

We continue to sit on green velvet sofa, and bar-tender looks sorry for us, and turns on more electric light. This obliges us, morally, to have another drink each, which we do. I develop severe pain behind the eyes--(*Query:* Wood-alcohol, or excess of electric light?)--and feel slightly sick. Also *Byrrh* now wavering rather oddly on wall.

Robert says Well, as though he were going to make a suggestion, but evidently thinks better of it again, and nothing transpires. After what seems like several hours of this, three men with black faces and musical instruments come in, and small, shrouded heap in far corner of *salle* reveals itself as a piano.

Bar-tender, surprisingly, has yet further resources at his command in regard to electric light, and we are flooded with still greater illumination. Scene still further enlivened by arrival of very old gentleman in crumpled dress-clothes, stout woman in a green beaded dress that suggests Kensington High Street, and very young girl with cropped hair and scarlet arms. They stand in the very middle of the *salle* and look bewildered, and I feel that Robert and I are old *habitués*.

Robert says dashingly What About Another Drink? and I say No, better not, and then have one, and feel worse than ever. Look at Robert to see if he has noticed anything, and am struck by curious air about him, as of having been boiled and glazed. Cannot make up my mind whether this is, or is not, illusion produced by my own state, and feel better not to enquire, but devote entire attention to focussing *Byrrh* in spot where first sighted, instead of pursuing it all over walls and ceiling.

By the time this more or less accomplished, quite a number of people arrived, though all presenting slightly lost and *dégommé* appearance.

Robert stares at unpleasant-looking elderly man with red hair, and says Good Heavens, if that isn't old Pinkie Morrison, whom he last met in Shanghai Bar in nineteen-hundred-and-twelve. I say, Is he a friend? and Robert replies No, he never could stand the fellow, and old Pinkie Morrison is allowed to lapse once more.

Am feeling extremely ill, and obliged to say so, and Robert suggests tour of the rooms, which we accomplish in silence. Decide, by mutual consent, that we do not want to play roulette, or anything else, but would prefer to go back to bed, and Robert says he thought at the time that those drinks had something fishy about them.

I am reminded, by no means for the first time, of Edgeworthian classic, *Rosamond and the Party of Pleasure*--but literary allusions never a great success with Robert at any time, and feel sure that this is no moment for taking undue risks.

We return to St. Briac and make no further reference to evening's outing, except that Robert enquires, just as I am dropping off to sleep, whether it seems quite worth while, having spent seventy francs or so just for the sake of being poisoned and seeing a foul sight like old Pinkie Morrison? This question entirely rhetorical, and make no attempt to reply to it.

August 24th.--Much struck with extreme tact and good feeling of Casabianca at breakfast, who, after one look at Robert and myself, refrains from pressing the point as to How We enjoyed the Casino last night?

August 27th.--Last Day now definitely upon us, and much discussion as to how we are to spend it. Robert suggests Packing--but this not intended to be taken seriously--and Casabianca assures us that extremely interesting and instructive Ruins lie at a distance of less than forty kilometres, should we care to visit them. Am sorry to say that none of us *do* care to visit them, though I endeavour to palliate this by feeble and unconvincing reference to unfavourable weather.

I say what about Saint Cast, which is reputed to have admirable water-chute? or swimming-baths at Dinard? Children become uncontrollably agitated here, and say Oh, *please* can we bathe in the morning, and then come back to hotel for lunch, and bathe again in the afternoon and have tea at English Tea-Rooms? As this programme is precisely the one that we have been following daily ever since we arrived, nothing could be easier, and we agree. I make mental note to the effect that the young are definitely dependent on routine, and have dim idea of evolving interesting little article on the question, to be handsomely paid for by daily Press--but nothing comes of it.

Packing takes place, and Casabianca reminds me--kindly, but with an air of having expected rather better staff-work--that Robin's shorts are still at cleaners in Dinard. I say O Hell, and then weakly add -p to the end of it, and hope he hasn't noticed, and he offers to go into Dinard and fetch them. I say No, no, really, I shouldn't dream of troubling him, and he goes, but unfortunately brings back wrong parcel, from which we extract gigantic pair of white flannel trousers that have nothing to do with any of us.

French chambermaid, Germaine, who has followed entire affair from the start, says *Mon Dieu! alors c'est tout à recommencer?* which has a despairing ring, and makes me feel hopeless, but Casabianca again comes to the rescue and assures me that he can Telephone.

(*N.B.* Casabianca's weekly remuneration entirely inadequate and have desperate thoughts of doubling it on the spot, but financial considerations render this impossible, and perhaps better concentrate on repaying him four hundred francs borrowed on various occasions since arrival here.)

We go to bathe as usual, and I am accosted by strange woman in yellow pyjamas--cannot imagine how she can survive the cold--who says she met me in South Audley Street some years ago, don't I remember? Have no association whatever with South Audley Street, except choosing dinner-service there with Robert in distant days of wedding presents--(dinner service now no longer with us, and replaced by vastly inferior copy of Wedgwood). However, I say Yes, yes, of course, and yellow pyjamas at once introduces My boy at Dartmouth--very lank and mottled, and does not look me in the eye--My Sister who Has a Villa Out Here, and My Sister's Youngest Girl--Cheltenham College. Feel that I ought to do something on my side, but look round in vain, Robert, children and Casabianca all having departed, with superhuman rapidity, to extremely distant rock.

The sister with the villa says that she has read my book--ha-ha-ha--and how *do* I think of it all? I look blankly at her and say that I don't know, and feel that I am being inadequate. Everybody else evidently thinks so too, and rather distressing silence ensues, ice-cold wind--cannot say why, or from whence--suddenly rising with great violence and blowing us all to pieces.

I say Well, more feebly than ever, and yellow pyjamas says O dear, this weather, really--and supposes that we shall all meet down here to-morrow, and I say Yes, of course, before I remember that we cross to-night--but feel quite unable to reopen discussion, and retire to bathing-cabin.

Robert enquires later who that woman was? and I say that I cannot remember, but think her name was something like Busvine. After some thought, Robert says Was it Morton? to which I reply No, more like Chamberlain.

Hours later, remember that it was Heywood.

August 28th.--Depart from St. Briac by bus at seven o'clock, amidst much agitation. Entire personnel of hotel assembles to see us off, and Vicky kisses everybody. Robin confines himself to shaking hands quite suddenly with elderly Englishman in plus-fours--with whom he has never before exchanged a word--and elderly Englishman says that Now, doors will no longer slam on his landing every evening, he supposes. (*N.B.* Disquieting thought: does this consideration perhaps account for the enthusiasm with which we are all being despatched on our way?)

Robert counts luggage, once in French and three times in English, and I hear Casabianca--who has never of his own free will exchanged a syllable with any of his fellow-guests--replying to the retired Rag-picker's hopes of meeting again some day, with civil assent. Am slightly surprised at this.

(*Query:* Why should display of duplicity in others wear more serious aspect than similar lapse in oneself? *Answer* comes there none.)

Bus removes us from St. Briac, and we reach Dinard, and are there told that boat is *not* sailing to-night, and that we can (a) Sleep at St. Malo, (b) Remain at Dinard or (c) Return to St. Briac. All agree that this last would be intolerable anti-climax and not to be thought of, and that accommodation must be sought at Dinard.

Robert says that this is going to run us in for another ten pounds at least--which it does.

September 1st.--Home once more, and customary vicissitudes thick as leaves in Vallombrosa.

Temporary cook duly arrived, and is reasonably amiable--though soup a disappointment and strong tincture of Worcester Sauce bodes ill for general standard of cooking--but tells me that Everything was left in sad muddle, saucepans not even clean, and before she can do anything whatever will require three pudding basins, new frying-pan, fish-kettle and colander, in addition to egg-whisk, kitchen forks, and complete restocking of store-cupboard.

St. Briac hundreds of miles away already, and feel that twenty years have been added to my age and appearance since reaching home. Robert, on the other hand, looks happier.

Weather cold, and it rains in torrents. Casabianca ingenious in finding occupations for children and is also firm about proposed arithmetic lesson for myself, which takes place after lunch. Seven times table unfortunately presents difficulty that appears, so far, to be insuperable.

September 3rd.--Ask Robert if he remembers my bridesmaid, Felicity Fairmead, and he says Was that the little one with fair hair? and I say No, the very tall one with dark hair, and he says Oh yes--which does not at all convince me. Upshot of this conversation, rather strangely, is that I ask Felicity to stay, as she has been ill, and is ordered rest in the country. She replies gratefully, spare room is Turned Out--(paper lining drawer of dressing-table has to be renewed owing to last guest having omitted to screw up lip-stick securely--this probably dear Angela, but cannot be sure--and mysterious crack discovered in looking-glass, attributed--almost certainly unjustly--to Helen Wills).

I tell Casabianca at lunch that Miss Fairmead is very Musical--which is true, but has nothing to do with approaching visit, and in any case does not concern him--and he replies suitably, and shortly afterwards suggests that we should go through the Rule of Three. We do go through it, and come out the other end in more or less shattered condition. Moreover, am still definitely defeated by Seven times Eight.

September 5th.--I go up to London--Robert says, rather unnecessarily, that he supposes money is no object nowadays?--to see about the Flat. This comprises very exhausting, but interesting, sessions at furniture-shop, where I lose my head to the tune of about fifty pounds, and realise too late that dear Robert's attitude perhaps not altogether without justification.

Rose unfortunately out of town, so have to sleep at Club, and again feel guilty regarding expenditure, so dine on sausage-and-mash at Lyons establishment opposite to pallid young man who reads book mysteriously shrouded in holland cover. Feel that I must discover what this is at all costs, and conjectures waver between *The Well of Loneliness* and *The Colonel's Daughter*, until title can be spelt out upside down, when it turns out to be *Gulliver's Travels*. Distressing side-light thrown here on human nature by undeniable fact that I am distinctly disappointed by this discovery, although cannot imagine why.

In street outside I meet Viscountess once known to me in South of France, but feel doubtful if she will remember me so absorb myself passionately in shop-front, which I presently discover to be entirely filled with very peculiar appliances. Turn away again, and confront Viscountess, who remembers me perfectly, and is charming about small literary effort, which she definitely commits herself to having read. I walk with her to Ashley Gardens and tell her about the flat, which she says is the Very Thing--but does not add what for.

I say it is too late for me to come up with her, and she says Oh no, and we find lift out of order-- which morally compels me to accept her invitation, as otherwise it would look as if I didn't think her worth five flights of stairs.

Am shown into beautiful flat--first-floor Doughty Street would easily fit, lock, stock and barrel, into dining-room--and Viscountess says that the housekeeper is out, but would I like anything? I say a glass of water, please, and she is enthusiastic about the excellence of this idea, and goes out, returning, after prolonged absence, with large jug containing about an inch of water, and two odd tumblers, on a tray. I meditate writing a short article on How the Rich Live, but naturally say nothing of this aloud, and Viscountess explains that she does not know where drinking-water in the flat is obtainable, so took what was left from dinner. I make civil pretence of thinking this entirely admirable arrangement, and drink about five drops--which is all that either of us can get after equitable division of supplies. We talk about Rose, St. John Ervine and the South of France, and I add a few words about Belgium, but lay no stress on literary society encountered there.

Finally go, at eleven o'clock, and man outside Victoria Station says Good-night, girlie, but cannot view this as tribute to lingering remnant of youthful attractions as (a) it is practically pitch-dark, (b) he sounds as though he were drunk.

Return to Club bedroom and drink entire contents of water bottle.

September 6th.--Housekeeper from flat above mine in Doughty Street comes to my rescue, offers to obtain charwoman, stain floors, receive furniture and do everything else. Accept all gratefully, and take my departure with keys of flat--which makes me feel, quite unreasonably, exactly like a burglar. Should like to analyse this rather curious complex, and consider doing so in train, but all eludes me, and read *Grand Hotel* instead.

September 7th.--Felicity arrives, looking ill. (*Query:* Why is this by no means unbecoming to her, whereas my own afflictions invariably entail mud-coloured complexion, immense accumulation of already only-too-visible lines on face, and complete limpness of hair?) She is, as usual, charming to the children--does not tell them they have grown, or ask Robin how he likes school, and scores immediate success with both.

I ask what she likes for dinner--(should be indeed out of countenance if she suggested anything except chicken, sardines or tinned corn, which so far as I know is all we have in the house)--and she says An Egg. And what about breakfast to-morrow morning? She says An Egg again, and adds in a desperate way that an egg is all she wants for any meal, ever.

Send Vicky to the farm with a message about quantity of eggs to be supplied daily for the present.

Felicity lies down to rest, and I sit on windowsill and talk to her. We remind one another of extraordinary, and now practically incredible, incidents in bygone schooldays, and laugh a good deal, and I feel temporarily younger and better-looking.

Remember with relief that Felicity is amongst the few of my friends that Robert *does* like, and evening passes agreeably with wireless and conversation. Suggest a picnic for to-morrow--at which Robert says firmly that he is obliged to spend entire day in Plymouth--and tie knot in handkerchief to remind myself that cook must be told jam sandwiches, not cucumber. Take Felicity to her room, and hope that she has enough blankets--if not, nothing can be easier than to produce others without any trouble whatever--Well, in that case, says Felicity, perhaps--Go to linen-cupboard and can find nothing there whatever except immense quantities of embroidered tea-cloths, unhealthy-looking pillow oozing feathers, and torn roller-towel. Go to Robin's bed, but find him wide-awake, and quite impervious to suggestion that he does not *really* want more than one blanket on his bed, so have recourse to Vicky, who is asleep. Remove blanket, find it is the only one and replace it, and finally take blanket off my own bed, and put in on Felicity's, where it does not fit, and has to be tucked in till mattress resembles a valley between two hills. Express hope--which sounds ironical--that she may sleep well, and leave her.

September 8th.--Our Vicar's Wife calls in the middle of the morning, in deep distress because no one can be found to act as producer in forthcoming Drama Competition. Will I be an angel? I say firmly No, not on this occasion, and am not sure that Our Vicar's Wife does not, on the whole, look faintly relieved. But what, I ask, about herself? No--Our Vicar has put his foot down. Mothers' Union, Women's Institute, G.F.S. and Choir Outings by all means--but one evening in the week must and shall be kept clear. Our Vicar's Wife, says Our Vicar, is destroying herself, and this he cannot allow. Quite feel that the case, put like this, is unanswerable.

Our Vicar's Wife then says that she knows the very person--excellent actress, experienced producer, willing to come without fee. Unfortunately, is now living at Melbourne, Australia. Later on she also remembers other, equally talented, acquaintances, one of whom can now never leave home on account of invalid husband, the other of whom died just eleven months ago.

I feel that we are getting no further, but Our Vicar's Wife says that it has been a great relief to talk it all over, and perhaps after all she can persuade Our Vicar to let her take it on, and we thereupon part affectionately.

September 10th.--Picnic, put off on several occasions owing to weather, now takes place, but is--like so many entertainments--rather qualified success, partly owing to extremely mountainous character of spot selected. Felicity shows gallant determination to make the best of this, and only begs to be allowed to take her own time, to which we all agree, and divide rugs, baskets, cushions, thermos flasks and cameras amongst ourselves. Ascent appears to me to take hours, moreover am agitated about Felicity, who seems to be turning a rather sinister pale blue colour. Children full of zeal and activity, and dash on ahead, leaving trail of things dropped on the way. Casabianca, practically invisible beneath two rugs, mackintosh and heaviest basket, recalls them, at which Robin looks murderous, and Vicky feigns complete deafness, and disappears over the horizon.

Question as to whether we shall sit in the sun or out of the sun arises, and gives rise to much amiable unselfishness, but is finally settled by abrupt disappearance of sun behind heavy clouds, where it remains. Felicity sits down and pants, but is less blue. I point out scenery, which constitutes only possible excuse for having brought her to such heights, and she is appreciative. Discover that sugar has been left behind. Children suggest having tea at once, but are told that it is only four o'clock, and they had better explore first. This results in Robin's climbing a tree, and taking *Pickwick Papers* out of his pocket to read, and Vicky lying flat on her back in the path, and chewing blades of grass. Customary caution as to unhygienic properties peculiar to blades of grass ensues, and I wonder--not for the first time--why parents continue to repeat admonitions to which children never have paid, and never will pay, slightest attention. Am inspired by this reflection to observe suddenly to Felicity that, anyway, I'm glad my children aren't *prigs*--at which she looks startled, and says, Certainly not--far from it--but perceive that she has not in any way followed my train of thought--which is in no way surprising.

We talk about Italy, the Book Society--*Red Ike* a fearful mistake, but *The Forge* good--and how can Mr. Hugh Walpole find time for all that reading, and write his own books as well--and then again revert to far-distant schooldays, and ask one another what became of that girl with the eyes, who had a father in Patagonia, and if anybody ever heard any more of the black satin woman who taught dancing the last year we were there?

Casabianca, who alone has obeyed injunction to explore, returns, followed by unknown black-and-white dog, between whom and Vicky boisterous and ecstatic friendship instantly springs into being--and I unpack baskets, main contents of which appear to be bottles of lemonade--at which Felicity again reverts to paleblueness--and pink sugar-biscuits. Can only hope that children enjoy their meal.

Customary feelings of chill, cramp and general discomfort invade me--feel certain that they have long ago invaded Felicity, although she makes no complaint--and picnic is declared to be at an end. Black-and-white dog remains glued to Vicky's heels, is sternly dealt with by Casabianca, and finally disappears into the bracken, but at intervals during descent of hill, makes dramatic reappearances, leaping up in attitudes reminiscent of ballet-dancing. Owners of dog discovered at foot of hill, large gentleman in brown boots, and very thin woman with spats and eye-glasses. Vicky is demonstrative with dog, the large gentleman looks touched, and the eye-glasses beg my pardon, but if my little girl has really taken a fancy to the doggie, why, they are looking for a home for him--just off to Zanzibar--otherwise, he will have to be destroyed. I say Thank you, thank you, we really couldn't think of such a thing, and Vicky screams and ejaculates.

The upshot of it all is that we *do* think of such a thing--Casabianca lets me down badly, and backs up Vicky--the large gentleman says Dog may not be one of these pedigree animals--which I can see for myself he isn't--but has no vice, and thoroughly good-natured and affectionate--and Felicity, at whom I look, nods twice--am reminded of Lord Burleigh, but do not know why--and mutters *Oui, oui, pourquoi pas?*--which she appears to think will be unintelligible to anyone except herself and me.

Final result is that Vicky, Robin and dog occupy most of the car on the way home, and I try and make up my mind how dog can best be introduced to Robert and Cook.

September 11th.--Decision reached--but cannot say how--that dog is to be kept, and that his name is to be Kolynos.

September 12th.--All is overshadowed by National Crisis, and terrific pronouncements regarding income-tax and need for economy. Our Vicar goes so far as to talk about the Pound from the pulpit, and Robert is asked by Felicity to explain the whole thing to her after dinner--which he very wisely refuses to do.

We lunch with the Frobishers, who are depressed, and say that the wages of everyone on the Estate will have to be reduced by ten per cent. (*Query:* Why are they to be sympathised with on this account? Am much sorrier for their employés.)

Young Frobisher, who is down from Oxford, says that he has seen it coming for a long while now. (Should like to know why, in that case, he did not warn the neighbourhood.) He undertakes to make all clear--this, once more, at Felicity's request--and involved monologue follows, in which the Pound, as usual, figures extensively. Am absolutely no wiser at the end of it all than I was at the beginning and feel rather inclined to say so, but Lady F. offers me coffee, and asks after children--whom she refers to as "the boy and that dear little Virginia"--and we sink into domesticities and leave the Pound to others. Result is that it overshadows the entire evening and is talked about by Felicity and Robert all the way home in very learned but despondent strain.

(*N.B.* A very long while since I have heard Robert so eloquent, and am impressed by the fact that it takes a National Crisis to rouse him, and begin to wish that own conversational energies had not been dissipated for years on such utterly unworthy topics as usually call them forth. Can see dim outline of rather powerful article here, or possibly viers fibres more suitable form--but nothing can be done to-night.) Suggest hot milk to Felicity, who looks cold, take infinite trouble to procure this, but saucepan boils over and all is wasted.

September 13th.--Curious and regrettable conviction comes over me that Sunday in the country is entirely intolerable. Cannot, however, do anything about it.

Kolynos chases Helen Wills up small oak-tree, and eats arm and one ear off teddy-bear owned by Vicky. This not a success, and Robert says tersely that if the dog is going to do *that* kind of thing--and then leaves the sentence unfinished, which alarms us all much more than anything he could have said.

ROBIN SINGING IN CHURCH

Am absent-minded in Church, but recalled by Robin singing hymn, entirely out of tune, and half a bar in advance of everybody else. Do not like to check evident zeal, and feel that this should come within Casabianca's province, but he takes no notice. (*Query:* Perhaps he, like Robin, has no ear for music? He invariably whistles out of tune.)

Return to roast beef--underdone--and plates not hot. I say boldly that I think roast beef every Sunday is a mistake--why not chicken, or even mutton? but at this everyone looks aghast, and Robert asks What next, in Heaven's name? so feel it better to abandon subject, and talk about the Pound, now familiar topic in every circle.

General stupor descends upon Robert soon after lunch, and he retires to study with *Blackwood's Magazine.* Robin reads *Punch*; Vicky, amidst customary protests, disappears for customary rest; and Casabianca is nowhere to be seen. Have strong suspicion that he has followed Vicky's example.

369

I tell Felicity that I *must* write some letters, and she rejoins that so must she, and we talk until twenty minutes to four, and then say that it doesn't really matter, as letters wouldn't have gone till Monday anyhow. (This argument specious at the moment, but has very little substance when looked at in cold blood.)

Chilly supper--only redeeming feature, baked potatoes--concludes evening, together with more talk of the Pound, about which Robert and Casabianca become, later on, technical and masculine, and Felicity and I prove unable to stay the course, and have recourse to piano instead. Final peak of desolation is attained when Felicity, going to bed, wishes to know why I have so completely given up my music, and whether it isn't a Great Pity?

Point out to her that all wives and mothers always *do* give up their music, to which she agrees sadly, and we part without enthusiasm.

Should be very sorry to put on record train of thought aroused in me by proceedings of entire day.

September 15th.--End of holidays, as usual, suddenly reveal themselves as being much nearer than anyone had supposed, and Cash's Initials assume extraordinary prominence in scheme of daily life, together with School Lists, new boots for Robin, new everything for Vicky, and tooth-paste for both.

This all dealt with, more or less, after driving Felicity to station, where we all part from her with regret. Train moves out of station just as I realise that egg sandwiches promised her for journey have been forgotten. Am overcome with utterly futile shame and despair, but can do nothing. Children sympathetic, until distracted by man on wheels--Stop me and Buy One--which they do, to the extent of fourpence. Should be prepared to take my oath that far more than fourpenny-worth of ice-cream will subsequently be found in car and on their clothes.

Extraordinarily crowded morning concluded with visit to dentist, who says that Vicky is Coming Along Nicely, and that Robin can be Polished Off Now, and offers, on behalf of myself, to have a look round, to which I agree, with unsatisfactory results. Look at this! says dentist unreasonably. *Look* at it! Waving in the Wind! Object strongly to this expression, which I consider gross exaggeration, but cannot deny that tooth in question is not all it should be. Much probing and tapping follows, and operator finally puts it to me--on the whole very kindly and with consideration--that this is a Question of Extraction. I resign myself to extraction accordingly, and appoint a date after the children have gone to school.

(Have often wondered to what extent mothers, if left to themselves, would carry universal instinct for putting off everything in the world until after children have gone to school? Feel certain that this law would, if it were possible, embrace everything in life, death itself included.)

It is too late to go home to lunch, and we eat fried fish, chipped potatoes, galantine and banana splits in familiar café.

September 20th.--Suggest to Robert that the moment has now come for making use of Doughty Street flat. I can take Vicky to London, escort her from thence to Mickleham, and then settle down in flat. Settle down what to? says Robert. Writing, I suggest weakly, and seeing Literary Agent. Robert looks unconvinced, but resigned. I make arrangements accordingly.

Aunt Gertrude writes to say that sending a little thing of Vicky's age right away from home is not only unnatural, but absolutely wrong. Have I, she wants to know, any idea of what a childless home will be like? Decide to leave this letter unanswered, but am disgusted to find that I mentally compose at least twelve different replies in the course of the day, each one more sarcastic than the last. Do not commit any of them to paper, but am just as much distracted by them as if I had--and have moments, moreover, of regretting that Aunt Gertrude will never know all the things I *might* have said.

Vicky, whom I observe anxiously, remains unmoved and cheerful, and refers constantly and pleasantly to this being her Last Evening at home. Moreover, pillow remains bone-dry, and she goes peacefully to sleep rather earlier than usual.

September 22nd.--Robin is taken away by car, and Casabianca escorts Vicky and myself to London, and parts from us at Paddington. I make graceful speech, which I have prepared beforehand, about our gratitude, and hope that he will return to us at Christmas. (Am half inclined to add, if state of the Pound permits--but do not like to.) He says, Not at all, to the first part, and Nothing that he would like better, to the second, and makes a speech on his own

370

account. Vicky embraces him with ardour and at some length, and he departs, and Vicky immediately says Now am I going to school? Nothing is left but to drive with her to Waterloo and thence to Mickleham, where Vicky is charmingly received by Principal, and made over to care of most engaging young creature of seventeen, introduced as Jane. Fearful inclination to tears comes over me, but Principal is tact personified, and provides tea at exactly right moment. She promises, unprompted, to telephone in the morning, and write long letter next day, and Vicky is called to say good-bye, which she does most affectionately, and with undiminished radiance.

September 25th.--Doughty Street.--Quite incredibly, find myself more or less established, and startlingly independent. Flat--once I have bought electric fire, and had it installed by talkative young man with red hair--very comfortable; except for absence of really restful arm-chair, and unfamiliarity of geyser-bath, of which I am terrified. Bathroom is situated on stairs, which are in continual use, and am therefore unable to take bath with door wide open, as I should like to do. Compromise with open window, through which blacks come in, and smell of gas and immense quantities of steam, go out. Remainder of steam has strange property of gathering itself on to the ceiling and there collecting, whence it descends upon my head and shoulders in extraordinarily cold drops. Feel sure that there is scientific, and doubtless interesting, explanation of this minor chemical phenomenon, but cannot at the moment work it out. (*N.B.* Keep discussion of this problem for suitable occasion, preferably when seated next to distinguished scientist at dinner-party. In the meantime, cower beneath bath towel in farthest corner of bathroom--which is saying very little--but am quite unable to dodge unwanted shower-bath.)

Housekeeper from flat above extremely kind and helpful, and tells me all about arrangements for window-cleaning, collecting of laundry and delivery of milk.

Excellent reports reach me of Vicky at Mickleham--Robin writes--as usual--about unknown boy called Felton who has brought back a new pencil-box this term, and other, equally unknown, boy whose parents have become possessed of house in the New Forest--and Robert sends laconic, but cheerful, account of preparations for Harvest Home supper. Less satisfactory communication arrives from Bank, rather ungenerously pointing out extremely small and recent overdraft. This almost incredible, in view of recent unexpected literary gains, and had felt joyfully certain of never again finding myself in this painful position--but now perceive this to have been wholly unjustifiable optimism. (Material for short philosophic treatise on vanity of human hopes surely indicated here? but on second thoughts, too reminiscent of Mr. Fairchild, so shall leave it alone.)

Write quantities of letters, and am agreeably surprised at immense advantage to be derived from doing so without any interruptions.

September 27th.--Rose telephones to ask if I would like to come to literary evening party, to be given by distinguished novelist whose books are well known to me, and who lives in Bloomsbury. I say Yes, if she is sure it will be All Right. Rose replies Why not, and then adds--distinct afterthought--that I am myself a Literary Asset to society, nowadays. Pause that ensues in conversation makes it painfully evident that both of us know the last statement to be untrue, and I shortly afterwards ring off.

I consider the question of what to wear, and decide that black is dowdy, but green brocade with Ciro pearls will be more or less all right, and shall have to have old white satin shoes recovered to match.

September 28th.--Literary party, to which Rose takes me as promised. Take endless trouble with appearance, and am convinced, before leaving flat, that this has reached very high level indeed, thanks to expensive shampoo-and-set, and moderate use of cosmetics. Am obliged to add, however, that on reaching party and seeing everybody else, at once realise that I am older, less well dressed, and immeasurably plainer than any other woman in the room. (Have frequently observed similar reactions in myself before.)

Rose introduces me to hostess--she looks much as I expected, but photographs which have appeared in Press evidently, and naturally, slightly idealised. Hostess says how glad she is that I was able to come--(*Query:* Why?)--and is then claimed by other arrivals, to whom she says exactly the same thing, with precisely similar intonation. (*Note:* Society of fellow-creatures promotes cynicism. Should it be avoided on this account? If so, what becomes of Doughty Street flat?)

THE PARTY IN BLOOMSBURY

Rose says Do I see that man over there? Yes, I do. He has written a book that will, says Rose impressively, undoubtedly be seized before publication and burnt. I enquire how she knows, but she is claimed by an acquaintance and I am left to gaze at the man in silent astonishment and awe. Just as I reach the conclusion that he cannot possibly be more than eighteen years old, I hear a scream--this method of attracting attention absolutely unavoidable, owing to number of people all talking at once--and am confronted by Emma I lay in rose-coloured fishnet, gold lace, jewelled turban and necklace of large barbaric pebbles.

Who, shrieks Emma, would have dreamt of this? and do I see that man over there? He has just finished a book that is to be seized and burnt before publication. A genius, of course, she adds casually, but far in advance of his time. I say Yes, I suppose so, and ask to be told who else is here, and Emma gives me rapid outline of many rather lurid careers, leading me to conclusion that literary ability and domestic success not usually compatible. (*Query:* Will this invalidate my chances?)

Dear Emma then exclaims that It is Too Bad I should be so utterly Out of It--which I think might have been better worded--and introduces a man to me, who in his turn introduces his wife, very fair and pretty. (Have unworthy spasm of resentment at sight of so much attractiveness, but stifle instantly.) Man offers to get me a drink, I accept, he offers to get his wife one, she agrees, and he struggles away through dense crowd. Wife points out to me young gentleman who has written a book that is to be seized, etc., etc. Am disgusted to hear myself saying in reply Oh really, in tone of intelligent astonishment.

Man returns with two glasses of yellow liquid--mine tastes very nasty, and wife leaves hers unfinished after one sip--and we talk about Income Tax, the Pound, France, and John van Druten, of whom we think well. Rose emerges temporarily from press of distinguished talkers, asks Am I all right, and is submerged again before I can do more than nod. (Implied lie here.) Man and his wife, who do not know anyone present, remain firmly glued to my side, and I to theirs for precisely similar reason. Conversation flags, and my throat feels extremely sore. Impossibility of keeping the Pound out of the conversation more and more apparent, and character of the observations that we make about it distinguished neither for originality nor for sound constructive quality.

Emma recrudesces later, in order to tell me that James--(totally unknown to me) has at last chucked Sylvia--(of whom I have never heard)--and is definitely living with Naomi--(again a complete blank)--who will have to earn enough for both, and for her three children--but James' children by Susan are being looked after by dear Arthur. I say, without conviction, that this at least is a comfort, and Emma--turban now definitely over right eyebrow--vanishes again.

Original couple introduced by Emma still my sole hope of companionship, and am morally certain that I am theirs. Nevertheless am quite unable to contemplate resuming analysis of the Pound, which I see looming ahead, and am seriously thinking of saying that there is a man here whose book is to be seized prior to publication, when Rose intervenes, and proposes departure. Our hostess quite undiscoverable, Emma offers officious and extremely scandalous explanation of this disappearance, and Rose and I are put into taxi by elderly man, unknown to me, but whom I take to be friend of Rose's, until she tells me subsequently that she has never set eyes on him in her life before. I suggest that he may be man-servant hired for the occasion, but Rose says No, more likely a distinguished dramatist from the suburbs.

October 1st.--Direct result of literary party is that I am rung up on telephone by Emma, who says that she did not see anything like enough of me and we must have a long talk, what about dinner together next week in Soho where she knows of a cheap place? (This, surely, rather odd form of invitation?) Am also rung up by Viscountess's secretary, which makes me feel important, and asked to lunch at extremely expensive and fashionable French restaurant. Accept graciously, and spend some time wondering whether circumstances would justify purchase of new hat for the occasion. Effect of new hat on *morale* very beneficial, as a rule.

Also receive letter--mauve envelope with silver cipher staggers me from the start--which turns out to be from Pamela Pringle, who is mine affectionately as ever, and is so delighted to think of my being in London, and *must* talk over dear old days, so will I ring her up immediately and suggest something? I do ring her up--although not immediately--and am told that she can just fit me in between massage at four and Bridge at six, if I will come round to her flat in Sloane Street like an angel. This I am willing to do, but make mental reservation to the effect that dear old days had better remain in oblivion until P. P. herself introduces them into conversation, which I feel certain she will do sooner or later.

Proceed in due course to flat in Sloane Street--entrance impressive, with platoons of hall-porters, one of whom takes me up in lift and leaves me in front of bright purple door with antique knocker representing mermaid, which I think unsuitable for London, although perhaps applicable to Pamela's career. Interior of flat entirely furnished with looking-glass tables, black pouffes, and acutely angular blocks of green wood. Am over-awed, and wonder what Our Vicar's Wife would feel about it all--but imagination jibs.

Pamela receives me in small room--more looking-glass, but fewer pouffes, and angular blocks are red with blue zigzags--and startles me by kissing me with utmost effusion. This very kind, and only wish I had been expecting it, as could then have responded better and with less appearance of astonishment amounting to alarm. She invites me to sit on a pouffe and smoke a Russian cigarette, and I do both, and ask after her children. Oh, says Pamela, the *children!* and begins to cry, but leaves off before I have had time to feel sorry for her, and bursts into long and complicated speech. Life, declares Pamela, is very, *very* difficult, and she is perfectly certain that I feel, as she does, that nothing in the world matters except Love. Stifle strong inclination to reply that banking account, sound teeth and adequate servants matter a great deal more, and say Yes Yes, and look as intelligently sympathetic as possible.

Pamela then rushes into impassioned speech, and says that It is not her fault that men have always gone mad about her, and no doubt I remember that it has always been the same, ever since she was a mere tot--(do not remember anything of the kind, and if I did, should certainly not say so)--and that after all, divorce is not looked upon as it used to be, and it's always the woman that has to pay the penalty, don't I agree? Feel it unnecessary to make any very definite reply to this, and am in any case not clear as to whether I do agree or not, so again have recourse to air of intelligent understanding, and inarticulate, but I hope expressive, sound. Pamela apparently completely satisfied with this, as she goes on to further revelations to which I listen with eyes nearly dropping out of my head with excitement. Stevenson, Templer-Tate, Pringle, are all referred to, as well as others whose names have not actually been borne by Pamela--but this, according to her own account, her fault rather than theirs. Feel I ought to say something, so enquire tentatively if her first marriage was a happy one--which sounds better than asking if *any* of her marriages were happy ones. *Happy?* says Pamela. Good Heavens, what am I talking about? Conclude from this, that it was *not* a happy one. Then what, I suggest, about Templer-Tate? That, Pamela replies sombrely, was Hell. (Should like to enquire for whom, but do not, naturally, do so.) Next branch of the subject is presumably Pringle, and here I again hesitate, but Pamela takes initiative and long and frightful story is poured out.

Waddell--such is Pringle's Christian name, which rouses in me interesting train of speculative thought as to mentality of his parents--Waddell does not understand his wife. Never has understood her, never possibly could understand her. She is sensitive, affectionate, intelligent in her own way though of course not *clever*, says Pamela--and really, although she says so herself, remarkably easy to get on with. A Strong Man could have done anything in the world with her. She is like that. The ivy type. Clinging. I nod, to show agreement. Further conversation reveals that she has clung in the wrong directions, and that this has been, and is being, resented by Pringle. Painful domestic imbroglio is unfolded. I say weakly that I am sorry to hear this--which is not true, as I am thoroughly enjoying myself--and ask what about the children? This brings us back to the beginning again, and we traverse much ground that has been gone over before. Bridge at six is apparently forgotten, and feel that it might sound unsympathetic to refer to it, especially when Pamela assures me that she very, very often thinks of Ending it All. Am not sure if she means life altogether, or only life with Pringle--or perhaps just present rather irregular course of conduct?

Telephone-calls five times interrupt us, when Pamela is effusive and excitable to five unknown conversationalists and undertakes to meet someone on Friday at three, to go and see someone else who is being too, too ill in a Nursing Home, and to help somebody else to meet a woman who knows someone who is connected with films.

Finally, take my leave, after being once more embraced by Pamela, and am shot down in lift--full of looking-glass, and am much struck with the inadequacy of my appearance in these surroundings, and feel certain that lift-attendant is also struck by it, although aware that his opinion ought to be matter of complete indifference to me.

Temperature of Sloane Street seems icy after interior of flat, and cold wind causes my nose to turn scarlet and my eyes to water. Fate selects this moment for the emergence of Lady B.--sable furs up to her eyebrows and paint and powder unimpaired--from Truslove and Hanson, to waiting car and chauffeur. She sees me and screams--at which passers-by look at us, astonished--and says Good gracious her, what next? She would as soon have expected to see the geraniums from the garden uprooting themselves from the soil and coming to London. (Can this be subtle allusion to effect of the wind upon my complexion?) I say stiffly that I am staying at My Flat for a week or two. Where? demands Lady B. sceptically--to which I reply, Doughty Street, and she shakes her head and says that conveys *nothing*. Should like to refer her sharply to *Life of Charles Dickens*, but before I have time to do so she asks what on earth I am doing in Sloane Street, of all places--I say, spending an hour or two with my old friend Pamela Pringle--(for which I shall later despise myself, as should never have dreamt of referring to her as anything of the kind to anybody else). Oh, *that* woman, says Lady B., and offers to give me a lift to Brondesbury or wherever-it-is, as her chauffeur is quite brilliant at knowing his way *anywhere*. Thank her curtly and refuse. We part, and I wait for a 19 bus and wish I'd told Lady B. that I *must* hurry, or should arrive late for dinner at Apsley House.

October 3rd.--Observe in myself tendency to go further and further in search of suitable cheap restaurants for meals--this not so much from economic considerations, as on extremely unworthy grounds that walking in the streets amuses me. (Cannot for one instant contemplate even remote possibility of Lady B.'s ever coming to hear of this, and do not even feel disposed to discuss it with Robert. Am, moreover, perfectly well aware that I have come to London to Write, and not to amuse myself.)

THE BLOOMSBURY TEA SHOP

Determination to curb this spirit causes me to lunch at small establishment in Theobald's Road, completely filled by hatless young women with cigarettes, one old lady with revolting little dog that growls at everyone, and small, pale youth who eats custard, and reads mysterious periodical entitled *Helping Hands*.

Solitary waitress looks harassed, and tells me--unsolicited--that she has only a small portion of The Cold left. I say Very Well, and The Cold, after long interval, appears, and turns out to be pork. Should like to ask for a potato, but waitress avoids me, and I go without.

Hatless young women all drink coffee in immense quantities, and I feel this is literary, and should like to do the same, but for cast-iron conviction that coffee will be nasty. Am also quite unattracted by custard, and finally ask for A Bun, please, and waitress--more harassed than ever--enquires in return if I mind the one in the window? I recklessly say No, if it hasn't been there too long, and waitress says Oh, not very, and seems relieved.

Singular conversation between hatless young women engages my attention, and distracts me from rather severe struggle with the bun. My neighbours discuss Life, and the youngest of them remarks that Perversion has practically gone out altogether now. The others seem to view this as pessimistic, and assure her encouragingly that, so far, nothing else has been found to take its place. One of them adjures her to Look at Sprott and Nash--which sounds like suburban grocers, but is, I think, mutual friends. Everybody says Oh, of course, to Sprott and Nash, and seems relieved. Someone tells a story about a very old man, which I try without success to overhear, and someone else remarks disapprovingly that *he* can't know much about it, really, as he's well over seventy and it only came into fashion a year or two ago. Conversation then becomes inconsequent, and veers about between *Cavalcade*, methods of hair-dressing, dog-breeding, and man called William--but with tendency to revert at intervals to Sprott and Nash.

Finish bun with great difficulty, pay tenpence for entire meal, leave twopence for waitress, and take my departure. Decide quite definitely that this, even in the cause of economy, wasn't worth it. Remember with immense satisfaction that I lunch to-morrow at Boulestin's with charming Viscountess, and indulge in reflections concerning strange contrasts offered by Life: cold pork and stale bun in Theobald's Road on Tuesday, and lobster and *poire Hélène*--(I hope)--at

Boulestin's on Wednesday. Hope and believe with all my heart that similar startling, dissimilarity will be observable in nature of company and conversation.

Decide to spend afternoon in writing and devote much time to sharpening pencils, looking for india-rubber--finally discovered inside small cavity of gramophone, intended for gramophone needles. This starts train of thought concerning whereabouts of gramophone needles, am impelled to search for them, and am eventually dumbfounded at finding them in a match-box, on shelf of kitchen cupboard. (Vague, but unpleasant, flight of fancy here, beginning with Vicky searching for biscuits in insufficient light, and ending in Coroner's Court and vote of severe censure passed--rightly--by Jury.)

(*Query:* Does not imagination, although in many ways a Blessing, sometimes carry its possessor too far? *Answer*emphatically Yes.) Bell rings, and I open door to exhausted-seeming woman, who says she isn't going to disturb me--which she has already done--but do I know about the new electric cleaner? I feel sorry for her, and feel that if I turn her away she will very likely break down altogether, so hear about new electric cleaner, and engage, reluctantly, to let it come and demonstrate its powers to-morrow morning. Woman says that I shall never regret it--which is untrue, as I am regretting it already--and passes out of my life.

Second interruption takes place when man--says he is Unemployed--comes to the door with a Poem, which he says he is selling. I buy the Poem for two shillings, which I know is weak, and say that he really must not send anyone else as I cannot afford it. He assures me that he never will, and goes.

Bell rings again, and fails to leave off. I am filled with horror, and look up at it--inaccessible position, and nothing to be seen except two mysterious little jam-jars and some wires. Climb on a chair to investigate, then fear electrocution and climb down again without having done anything. Housekeeper from upstairs rushes down, and unknown females from basement rush up, and we all look at the ceiling and say Better fetch a Man. This is eventually done, and I meditate ironical article on Feminism, while bell rings on madly. Man, however, arrives, says Ah, yes, he thought as much, and at once reduces bell to order, apparently by sheer power of masculinity.

Am annoyed, and cannot settle down to anything.

October 7th.--Extraordinary behaviour of dear Rose, with whom I am engaged--and have been for days past--to go and have supper tonight. Just as I am trying to decide whether bus to Portland Street or tube to Oxford Circus will be preferable, I am called up on telephone by Rose's married niece, who lives in Hertfordshire, and is young and modern, to say that speaker for her Women's Institute to-night has failed, and that Rose, on being appealed to, has at once suggested my name and expressed complete willingness to dispense with my society for the evening. Utter impossibility of pleading previous engagement is obvious; I contemplate for an instant saying that I have influenza, but remember in time that niece, very intelligently, started the conversation by asking how I was, and that I replied Splendid, thanks--and there is nothing for it but to agree.

(*Query:* Should much like to know if it was for this that I left Devonshire.)

Think out several short, but sharply worded, letters to Rose, but time fails; I can only put brush and comb, slippers, sponge, three books, pyjamas and hot-water bottle into case--discover later that I have forgotten powder-puff, and am very angry, but to no avail--and repair by train to Hertfordshire.

Spend most of journey in remembering all that I know of Rose's niece, which is that she is well under thirty, pretty, talented, tremendous social success, amazingly good at games, dancing, and--I think--everything else in the world, and married to brilliantly clever young man who is said to have Made Himself a Name, though cannot at the moment recollect how.

Have strong impulse to turn straight round and go home again, sooner than confront so much efficiency, but non-stop train renders this course impracticable.

Niece meets me--clothes immensely superior to anything that I ever have had, or shall have--is charming, expresses gratitude, and asks what I am going to speak about. I reply, Amateur Theatricals. Excellent, of course, she says unconvincingly, and adds that the Institute has a large Dramatic Society already, that they are regularly produced by well-known professional actor, husband of Vice-President, and were very well placed in recent village-drama competition, open to all England.

At this I naturally wilt altogether, and say Then perhaps better talk about books or something--which sounds weak, even as I say it, and am convinced that niece feels the same, though she remains imperturbably charming. She drives competently through the night, negotiates awkward entrance to garage equally well, extracts my bag and says that It is Heavy--which is undeniable, and is owing to books, but cannot say so, as it would look as though I thought her house likely to be inadequately supplied--and conducts me into perfectly delightful, entirely modern, house, which I feel certain--rightly, I discover later--has every newest labour-saving device ever invented.

Bathroom especially--(all appears to be solid marble, black-and-white tiles, and dazzling polish)--impresses me immeasurably. Think regretfully, but with undiminished affection, of extremely inferior edition at home--paint peeling in several directions, brass taps turning green at intervals until treated by housemaid, and irregular collection of home-made brackets on walls, bearing terrific accumulation of half-empty bottles, tins of talcum powder and packets of Lux.

Niece shows me her children--charming small boy, angelic baby--both, needless to say, have curls. She asks civilly about Robin and Vicky, and I can think of nothing whatever to the credit of either, so merely reply that they are at school.

N.B. Victorian theory as to maternal pride now utterly discredited. Affection, yes. Pride, no.

We have dinner--niece has changed into blue frock which suits her and is, of course, exactly right for the occasion. I do the best I can with old red dress and small red cap that succeeds in being thoroughly unbecoming without looking in the least up to date, and endeavour to make wretched little compact from bag do duty for missing powder-puff. Results not good.

We have a meal, am introduced to husband--also young--and we talk about Rose, mutual friends, *Time and Tide* and Electrolux cleaners.

Evening at Institute reasonably successful--am much impressed by further display of efficiency from niece, as President--I speak about Books, and obtain laughs by introduction of three entirely irrelevant anecdotes, am introduced to felt hat and fur coat, felt hat and blue jumper, felt hat and tweeds, and so on. Names of all alike remain impenetrably mysterious, as mine no doubt to them.

(Flight of fancy here as to whether this deplorable, but customary, state of affairs is in reality unavoidable? Theory exists that it has been completely overcome in America, where introductions always entirely audible and frequently accompanied by short biographical sketch. Should like to go to America.)

Niece asks kindly if I am tired. I say No not at all, which is a lie, and she presently takes me home and I go to bed. Spare-room admirable in every respect, but no waste-paper basket. This solitary flaw in general perfection a positive relief.

October 8th.--All endeavours to communicate with Rose by telephone foiled, as her housekeeper invariably answers, and says that she is Out. Can quite understand this. Resolve that dignified course is to take no further steps, and leave any advances to Rose.

This resolution sets up serious conflict later in day, when I lunch with Viscountess, originally met as Rose's friend, as she does nothing but talk of her with great enthusiasm, and I am torn between natural inclination to respond and sense of definite grievance at Rose's present behaviour.

Lunch otherwise highly successful. Have *not* bought new hat, which is as well, as Viscountess removes hers at an early stage, and is evidently quite indifferent to millinery.

October 10th.--Am exercised over minor domestic problem, of peculiarly prosaic description, centering round collection of Dust-bins in small, so-called back garden of Doughty Street flat. All these dust-bins invariably brim-full, and am convinced that contents of alien waste-paper baskets contribute constantly to mine, as have no recollection at all of banana-skin, broken blue-and-white saucer, torn fragments of *Police-Court Gazette*, or small, rusty tin kettle riddled with holes.

Contemplate these phenomena with great dislike, but cannot bring myself to remove them, so poke my contribution down with handle of feather-duster, and retire.

October 13th.--Call upon Rose, in rather unusual frame of mind which suddenly descends upon me after lunch--cannot at all say why--impelling me to demand explanation of strange behaviour last week.

Rose at home, and says How nice to see me, which takes the wind out of my sails, but I rally, and say firmly that That is All Very Well, but what about that evening at the Women's Institute? At this Rose, though holding her ground, blanches perceptibly, and tells me to sit down quietly and explain what I mean. Am very angry at *quietly*, which sounds as if I usually smashed up all the furniture, and reply--rather scathingly--that I will do my best not to rouse the neighbourhood. Unfortunately, rather unguarded movement of annoyance results in upsetting of small table, idiotically loaded with weighty books, insecurely fastened box of cigarettes, and two ash-trays. We collect them again in silence--cigarettes particularly elusive, and roll to immense distances underneath sofa and behind electric fire--and finally achieve an arm-chair apiece, and glare at one another across expanse of Persian rug.

Am astonished that Rose is able to look me in the face at all, and say so, and long and painful conversation ensues, revealing curious inability on both our parts to keep to main issue. Should be sorry to recall in any detail exact number and nature of utterly irrelevant observations exchanged, but have distinct recollection that Rose asserts at various times that: (a) If I had been properly psycho-analysed years ago, I should realise that my mind has never really come to maturity at all. (b) It is perfectly ridiculous to wear shoes with such high heels. (c) Robert is a perfect *saint* and has a lot to put up with. (d) No one in the world can be readier than Rose is to admit that I can Write, but to talk about The Piano is absurd.

Cannot deny that in return I inform her, in the course of the evening, that: (a) Her best friend could never call Rose tidy--look at the room now! (b) There is a great difference between being merely impulsive, and being utterly and grossly inconsiderate. (c) Having been to America does not, in itself, constitute any claim to infallibility on every question under the sun. (d) Naturally, what's past is past, and I don't want to remind her about the time she lost her temper over those idiotic iris-roots.

Cannot say at what stage I am reduced to tears, but this unfortunately happens, and I explain that it is entirely due to rage, and nothing else. Rose suddenly says that there is nothing like coffee, and rings the bell. Retire to the bathroom in great disorder, mop myself up--tears highly unbecoming, and should much like to know how film-stars do it, usual explanation of Glycerine seems to me quite inadequate--Return to sitting-room and find that Rose, with extraordinary presence of mind, has put on the gramophone. Listen in silence to Rhapsody in Blue, and feel better.

Admirable coffee is brought in, drink some, and feel better still. Am once more enabled to meet Rose's eye, which now indicates contrition, and we simultaneously say that this is Perfectly Impossible, and Don't let's quarrel, whatever we do. All is harmony in a moment, and I kiss Rose, and she says that the whole thing was her fault, from start to finish, and I say No, it was mine *absolutely*, and we both say that we didn't really mean anything we said.

(Cold-blooded and slightly cynical idea crosses my mind later that entire evening has been complete waste of nervous energy, if neither of us meant any of the things we said--but refuse to dwell on this aspect of the case.)

Eventually go home feeling extraordinarily tired. Find letter from Vicky, with small drawing of an elephant, that I think distinctly clever and modernistic, until I read letter and learn that it is A Table, laid for Dinner, also communication from Literary Agent saying how much he looks forward to seeing my new manuscript. (Can only hope that he enjoys the pleasures of anticipation as much as he says, since they are, at present rate of progress, likely to be prolonged.)

Am also confronted by purple envelope and silver cypher, now becoming familiar, and scrawled invitation from Pamela Pringle to lunch at her flat, and meet half a dozen dear friends who simply adore my writing. Am sceptical about this, but shall accept, from degraded motives of curiosity to see the dear friends, and still more degraded motives of economy, leading me to accept a free meal from whatever quarter offered.

October 16th.--Find myself in very singular position as regards the Bank, where distinctly unsympathetic attitude prevails in regard to quite small overdraft. Am interviewed by the

Manager, who says he very much regrets that my account at present appears to be absolutely *Stationary*. I say with some warmth that he cannot regret it nearly as much as I do myself, and dead-lock appears to have been reached. Manager--cannot imagine why he thinks it a good idea--suddenly opens a large file, and reads me out extract from correspondence with very unendearing personality referred to as his Director, instructing him to bring pressure to bear upon this client--(me). I say Well, that's all right, he *has*brought pressure to bear, so he needn't worry--but perfect understanding fails to establish itself, and we part in gloom.

Idle fantasy of suddenly acquiring several hundreds of thousands of pounds by means of Irish Sweep ticket nearly causes me to be run over by inferior-looking lorry with coal.

October 18th.--Go to Woolworth's to buy paper handkerchiefs--cold definitely impending--and hear excellent sixpenny record, entitled "Around the Corner and Under the Tree", which I buy. Tune completely engaging, and words definitely vulgar, but not without cheap appeal. Something tells me that sooner or later I shall be explaining purchase away by saying that I got it to amuse the children.

(*Note:* Self-knowledge possibly beneficial, but almost always unpleasant to a degree.)

Determine to stifle impending cold, if only till after Pamela's luncheon-party to-morrow, and take infinite trouble to collect jug, boiling water, small bottle of Friar's Balsam and large bath-towel. All is ruined by one careless movement, which tips jug, Friar's Balsam and hot water down front of my pyjamas. Am definitely scalded--skin breaks in one place and turns scarlet over area of at least six inches--try to show presence of mind and remember that Butter is The Thing, remember that there is no butter in the flat--frantic and irrelevant quotation here, *It was the Best butter*--remember vaseline, use it recklessly, and retire to bed in considerable pain and with cold unalleviated.

October 19th.--Vagaries of Fate very curious and inexplicable. Why should severe cold in the head assail me exactly when due to lunch with Pamela Pringle in character of reasonably successful authoress, in order to meet unknown gathering of smart Society Women? Answer remains impenetrably mysterious.

Take endless trouble with appearance, decide to wear my Blue, then take it all off again and revert to my Check, but find that this makes me look like a Swiss nursery governess, and return once more to Blue. Regret, not for the first time, that Fur Coat, which constitutes my highest claim to distinction of appearance, will necessarily have to be discarded in hall.

Sloane Street achieved, as usual, via bus No. 19, and I again confront splendours of Pamela's purple front door. Am shown into empty drawing-room, where I meditate in silence on unpleasant, but all-too-applicable, maxim that It is Provincial to Arrive too Early. Presently strange woman in black, with colossal emerald brooch pinned in expensive-looking frills of lace, is shown in, and says How d'y do, very amiably, and we talk about the weather, Gandhi and French poodles. (Why? There are none in the room, and can trace no association of ideas whatsoever.)

Two more strange women in black appear, and I feel that my Blue is becoming conspicuous. All appear to know one another well, and to have met last week at lunch, yesterday evening at Bridge, and this morning at an Art Exhibition: No one makes any reference to Pamela, and grave and unreasonable panic suddenly assails me that I am in wrong flat altogether. Look madly round to see if I can recognise any of the furniture, and woman with osprey and rope of pearls enquires if I am missing that *precious* horse. I say No, not really--which is purest truth--and wonder if she has gone off her head. Subsequent conversation reveals that horse was made of soapstone.

(*Query:* What is soapstone? Association here with Lord Darling, but cannot work out in full.)

More and more anxious about non-appearance of Pamela P., especially when three more guests arrive--black two-piece, black coat-and-skirt, and black crêpe-de-chine with orange-varnished nails. (My Blue now definitely revealed as inferior imitation of Joseph's coat, no less, and of very nearly equal antiquity.)

They all call one another by Christian names, and have much to say about mutual friends, none of whom I have ever heard of before. Someone called Goo-goo has had influenza, and while this is being discussed, I am impelled to violent sneezing fit. Everybody looks at me in horror, and conversation suffers severe check.

(*Note:* Optimistic conviction that two handkerchiefs will last out through one luncheon party utterly unjustified in present circumstances. Never forget this again.)

Door flies open and Pamela Pringle, of whom I have now given up all hope, rushes in, kisses everybody, falls over little dog--which has mysteriously appeared out of the blue and vanishes again after being fallen over--and says Oh do we all know one another, and isn't she a *fearfully* bad hostess but she simply could *not* get away from Amédé, who really is a Pet. (Just as I have decided that Amédé is another little dog, it turns out that he is a Hairdresser.)

Lunch is announced, and we all show customary reluctance to walking out of the room in simple and straightforward fashion, and cluster round the threshold with self-depreciating expressions until herded out by Pamela. I find myself sitting next to her--quite undeserved position of distinction, and probably intended for somebody else--with extraordinarily elegant black crêpe-de-chine on other side.

Black crepe-de-chine says that she adored my book, and so did her husband, and her sister-in-law, who is Clever and never says *Anything* unless she really Means It, thought it quite marvellous. Having got this off her chest, she immediately begins to talk about recent visit of her own to Paris, and am forced to the conclusion that her standards of sincerity must fall definitely below those of unknown sister-in-law.

Try to pretend that I know Paris as well as she does, but can see that she is not in the least taken in by this.

Pamela says Oh, *did* she see Georges in Paris, and what are the new models like? but crêpe-de-chine shakes her head and says Not out yet, and Georges never will show any Spring things before December, at very earliest--which to me sounds reasonable, but everybody else appears to feel injured about it, and Pamela announces that she sometimes thinks seriously about letting Gaston make for her instead of Georges--which causes frightful sensation. Try my best to look as much startled and horrified as everybody else, which is easy as am certain that I am about to sneeze again--which I do.

(Both handkerchiefs now definitely soaked through and through, and sore will be out on upper lip before day is over.)

Conversation veers about between Paris, weight-reduction--(quite unnecessary, none of them can possibly weigh more than seven stone, if that)--and annexation by someone called Diana of second husband of someone else called Tetsie, which everyone agrees was *utterly* justified, but no reason definitely given for this, except that Tetsie is a perfect *darling*, we all know, but no one on earth could possibly call her smartly turned-out.

(Feel that Tetsie and I would have at least one thing in common, which is more than I can say about anybody else in the room--but this frame of mind verging on the sardonic, and not to be encouraged.)

Pamela turns to me just as we embark on entirely admirable *coupe Jacques*, and talks about books, none of which have been published for more than five minutes and none of which, in consequence, I have as yet read--but feel that I am expected to be on my own ground here, and must--like Mrs. Dombey--make an effort, which I do by the help of remembering Literary Criticisms in *Time and Tide*'s issue of yesterday.

Interesting little problem hovers on threshold of consciousness here: How on earth do Pamela and her friends achieve conversation about books which I am perfectly certain they have none of them read? Answer, at the moment, baffles me completely.

Return to drawing-room ensues; I sneeze again, but discover that extreme left-hand corner of second pocket handkerchief is still comparatively dry, which affords temporary, but distinct, consolation.

On the whole, am definitely relieved when emerald-brooch owner says that It is too, too sad, but she must fly, as she really is responsible for the whole thing, and it can't begin without her--which might mean a new Permanent Wave, or a command performance at Buckingham Palace, but shall never now know which, as she departs without further explanation.

Make very inferior exit of my own, being quite unable to think of any reason for going except that I have been wanting to almost ever since I arrived,--which cannot, naturally, be produced. Pamela declares that having me has been Quite Wonderful, and we part.

Go straight home and to bed, and Housekeeper from upstairs most kindly brings me hot tea and cinnamon, which are far too welcome for me to make enquiry that conscience prompts, as to their rightful ownership.

October 23rd.--Telephone bell rings at extraordinary hour of eleven-eighteen P.M., and extremely agitated voice says Oh is that me, to which I return affirmative answer and rather curt rider to the effect that I have been in bed for some little while. Voice then reveals itself as belonging to Pamela P.--which doesn't surprise me in the least--who is, she says, in great, great trouble, which she cannot possibly explain. (Should much like to ask whether it was worth while getting me out of bed in order to hear that no explanation is available.) But, Pamela asks, will I, whatever happens, *swear* that she has spent the evening with me, in my flat? If I will not do this, then it is--once more--perfectly impossible to say what will happen. But Pamela knows that I will--I always was a darling--and I couldn't refuse such a tiny, tiny thing, which is simply a question of life and death.

Am utterly stunned by all this, and try to gain time by enquiring weakly if Pamela can by any chance tell me where she really *has* spent the evening? Realise as soon as I have spoken that this is not a tactful question, and am not surprised when muffled scream vibrates down receiver into my ear. Well, never mind *that*, then, I say, but just give me some idea as to who is likely to ask me what Pamela's movements have been, and why. Oh, replies Pamela, she is the most absolutely misunderstood woman on earth, and don't I feel that men are simply brutes? There isn't one of them--not one--whom one can trust to be really tolerant and broad-minded and understanding. They only want One Thing.

Feel quite unable to cope with this over telephone wire, and am, moreover, getting cold, and find attention straying towards possibility of reaching switch of electric fire with one hand whilst holding receiver with the other. Flexibility of the human frame very remarkable, but cannot altogether achieve this and very nearly overbalance, but recover in time to hear Pamela saying that if I will do this one thing for her, she will never, never forget it. There isn't anyone else, she adds, whom she *could* ask. (Am not at all sure if this is any compliment.) Very well, I reply, if asked, I am prepared to say that Pamela spent the evening with me here, but I hope that no one *will* ask and Pamela must distinctly understand that this is the first and last time I shall ever do anything of the kind. Pamela begins to be effusive, but austere voice from the unseen says that Three Minutes is Up, will we have another Three, to which we both say No simultaneously, and silence abruptly supervenes.

Crawl into bed again feeling exactly as if I had been lashed to an iceberg and then dragged at the cart's tail. Very singular and unpleasant sensation. Spend disturbed and uncomfortable night, evolving distressing chain of circumstances by which I may yet find myself at the Old Bailey committing perjury and--still worse--being found out--and, alternatively, imagining that I hear rings and knocks at front door, heralding arrival of Pamela P.'s husband bent on extracting information concerning his wife's whereabouts.

Wake up, after uneasy dozings, with bad headache, impaired complexion and strong sensation of guilt. Latter affects me to such a degree that am quite startled and conscience-stricken at receiving innocent and childlike letters from Robin and Vicky, and am inclined to write back and say that they ought not to associate with me--but breakfast restores balance, and I resolve to relegate entire episode to oblivion. (*Mem.:* Vanity of human resolutions exemplified here, as I find myself going over and over telephone conversation all day long, and continually inventing admirable exhortations from myself to Pamela P.)

Robert writes briefly, but adds P.S. Isn't it time that I thought about coming home again? which I think means that he is missing me, and feel slightly exhilarated.

October 25th.--Am taken out to lunch by Literary Agent, which makes me feel important, and celebrated writers are pointed out to me--mostly very disappointing, but must on no account judge by appearances. Literary Agent says Oh, by the way, he has a small cheque for me at the office, shall he send it along? Try to emulate this casualness, and reply Yes, he may as well, and shortly afterwards rush home and write to inform Bank Manager that, reference our recent conversation, he may shortly expect to receive a Remittance--which I think sounds well, and commits me to nothing definite.

October 27th.--Am chilled by reply from Bank Manager, who has merely Received my letter and Noted Contents. This lack of *abandon* very discouraging, moreover very different degree of eloquence prevails when subject under discussion is deficit, instead of credit, and have serious thoughts of writing to point this out.

Receive curious and unexpected tribute from total stranger in the middle of Piccadilly Circus, where I have negotiated crossing with success, but pause on refuge, when voice says in my ear that owner has been following me ever since we left the pavement--which does, indeed, seem like hours ago--and would like to do so until Haymarket is safely reached. Look round at battered-looking lady carrying three parcels, two library books, small umbrella and one glove, and say Yes, yes, certainly, at the same time wondering if she realises extraordinarily insecure foundations on which she has built so much trust. Shortly afterwards I plunge, Look Right, Look Left, and execute other manoeuvres, and find myself safe on opposite side. Battered-looking lady has, rather to my horror, disappeared completely, and I see her no more. Must add this to life's many other unsolved mysteries.

THE BATTERED LADY (p. 164)

Meanwhile, select new coat and skirt--off the peg, but excellent fit, with attractive black suede belt--try on at least eighteen hats--very, very aggravating assistant who tells me that I look Marvellous in each, which we both know very well that I don't--and finally select one with a brim--which is not, says the assistant, being worn at all now, but after all, there's no telling when they may come in again--and send Robert small jar of *pâté de foie gras* from Jackson's in Piccadilly.

October 31st.--Letters again give me serious cause for reflection. Robert definitely commits himself to wishing that I would come home again, and says--rather touchingly--that he finds one can see the house from a hill near Plymouth, and he would like me to have a look at it. Shall never wholly understand advantages to be derived from seeing any place from immense distance instead of close at hand, as could so easily be done from the tennis lawn without any exertion at all--but quite realise that masculine point of view on this question, as on so many others, differs from my own, and am deeply gratified by dear Robert's thought of me.

Our Vicar's Wife sends post card of Lincoln Cathedral, and hopes on the back of it that I have not forgotten our Monthly Meeting on Thursday week, and it seems a long time since I left home, but she hopes I am enjoying myself and has no time for more as post just going, and if I am anywhere near St. Paul's Churchyard, I might just pop into a little bookseller's at the corner of a little courtyard somewhere quite near the Cathedral, and see if they are doing anything about

Our Vicar's little pamphlet, of which they had several copies in the summer. But I am not to take *any* trouble about this, on any account. Also, across the top of post card, could I just look in at John Barker's, when I happen to be anywhere near, and ask the price of filet lace there? But not to put myself out, in any way. Robert, she adds across top of address, seems *very lonely*, underlined, also three exclamation marks, which presumably denote astonishment. Why?

November 2nd.--Regretfully observe in myself cynical absence of surprise when interesting invitations pour in on me just as I definitely decide to leave London and return home. Shall not, however, permit anything to interfere with date appointed and undertaking already given by Robert on half-sheet of note-paper, to meet 4.1 8 train at local station next Tuesday.

Buy two dust-sheets--yellow-and-white check, very cheap--with which to swathe furniture of fiat during my absence. Shopman looks doubtful and says Will two be all I require, and I say Yes, I have plenty of others. Absolute and gratuitous lie, which covers me with shame when I think of it afterwards.

November 3rd.--Further telephone communication from Pamela P., but this time of a less sensational character, as she merely says that the fog makes her feel too, too suicidal, and she's had a fearful run of bad luck at Bridge and lost twenty-three pounds in two afternoons, and don't I feel that when things have got to *that* stage there's nothing for it but a complete change? To this I return with great conviction Oh, absolutely *nothing*, and mentally frame witty addition to the effect that after finding myself unplaced in annual whist-drive in our village, I always make a point of dashing over the Somerset border. This quip, however, joins so many others in limbo of the unspoken.

I ask Pamela where she is going for complete change and she astonishes me by replying Oh, the Bahamas. That is, if Waddell agrees, but so far he is being difficult, and urging the Pyrenees. I say weakly Well, wouldn't the Pyrenees be very nice in their own way?--but Pamela, to this, exclaims My dear! in shocked accents, and evidently thinks less than nothing of the Pyrenees. The fact is, she adds, that she has a *very* great friend in the Bahamas, and he terribly wants her to come out there, and really things are so dreadfully complicated in London that she sometimes feels the only thing to do is to GO. (This I can well believe, but still think the Bahamas excessive.) Meanwhile, however, have I a free afternoon because Pamela has heard of a really marvellous clairvoyante, and she wants someone she can really *trust* to go there with her, only not one word about it to Waddell, ever. Should like to reply to this that I now take it for granted that any activity of Pamela's is subject to similar condition--but instead say that I should like to come to marvellous clairvoyante, and am prepared to consult her on my own account. All is accordingly arranged, including invitation from myself to Pamela to lunch with me at my Club beforehand, which she effusively agrees to do.

Spend the rest of the afternoon wishing that I hadn't asked her.

November 6th.--Altogether unprecedented afternoon, with Pamela Pringle. Lunch at my Club not an unmitigated success, as it turns out that Pamela is slimming and can eat nothing that is on menu and drink only orangeade, but she is amiable whilst I deal with chicken casserole and pineapple flan, and tells me about a really wonderful man--(who knows about wild beasts)--who has adored her for years and years, absolutely without a thought of self. Exactly like something in a book, says Pamela. She had a letter from him this morning, and do I think it's fair to go on writing to him? If there is one thing that Pamela never has been, never possibly could be, it is the kind of woman who Leads a Man On. Lead, kindly Light, I say absently, and then feel I have been profane as well as unsympathetic, but Pamela evidently not hurt by this as she pays no attention to it whatever and goes on to tell me about brilliant man-friend in the Diplomatic Service, who telephoned from The Hague this morning and is coming over next week by air apparently entirely in order that he may take Pamela out to dine and dance at the Berkeley.

Anti-climax supervenes here whilst I pay for lunch and conduct Pamela to small and crowded dressing-room, where she applies orange lipstick and leaves her rings on wash-stand and has to go back for them after taxi has been called and is waiting outside.

Just as I think we are off page-boy dashes up and says Is it Mrs. Pringle, she is wanted on the telephone, and Pamela again rushes. Ten minutes later she returns and says Will I forgive her, she gave this number as a very great friend wanted to ring her up at lunch-time, and in Sloane Street flat the telephone is often so difficult, not that there's anything to conceal, but people get such queer ideas, and Pamela has a perfect horror of things being misunderstood. I say that I can quite believe it, then think this sounds unkind, but on the whole do not regret having said it.

Obscure street in Soho is reached, taxi dismissed after receiving vast sum from Pamela, who insists on paying, and we ascend extraordinarily dirty stairs to second floor, where strong smell of gas prevails. Pamela says Do I think it's all right? I reply with more spirit than sincerity, that of course it is, and we enter and are received by anaemic-looking young man with curls, who takes one look at us and immediately vanishes behind green plush curtain, but reappears, and says that Madame Inez is quite ready but can only receive one client at a time. Am not surprised when Pamela compels me to go first, but give her a look which I hope she understands is not one of admiration.

Interview with unpleasant-looking sibyl follows. She gazes into large glass ball and says that I have known grief--(should like to ask her who hasn't)--and that I am a wife and a mother. Juxtaposition of these statements no doubt unintentional. Long and apparently inspired monologue follows, but little of practical value emerges except that: (a) There is trouble in the near future. (If another change of cook, this is definitely unnerving.) (b) I have a child whose name will one day be famous. (Reference here almost certainly to dear Vicky.) (c) In three years' time I am to cut loose from my moorings, break new ground and throw my cap over the windmill.

THE VISIT TO THE FORTUNE TELLER

None of it sounds to me probable, and I thank her and make way for Pamela. Lengthy wait ensues, and I distinctly hear Pamela scream at least three times from behind curtain. Finally she emerges in great agitation, throws pound notes about, and tells me to Come away quickly--which we both do, like murderers, and hurl ourselves into first available taxi quite breathless.

Pamela shows disposition to clutch me and weep, and says that Madame Inez has told her she is a reincarnation of Helen of Troy and that there will never be peace in her life. (Could have told her the last part myself, without requiring fee for doing so.) She also adds that Madame Inez predicts that Love will shortly enter into her life on hitherto unprecedented scale, and alter it completely--at which I am aghast, and suggest that we should both go and have tea somewhere at once.

We do so, and it further transpires that Pamela did not like what Madame Inez told her about the past. This I can well believe.

We part in Sloane Street, and I go back to fiat and spend much time packing.

November 7th.--Doughty Street left behind, yellow-and-white dust-sheets amply sufficing for entire flat, and Robert meets me at station. He seems pleased to see me but says little until seated in drawing-room after dinner, when he suddenly remarks that He has Missed Me. Am astonished and delighted, and should like him to enlarge on theme, but this he does not do, and we revert to wireless and *The Times.*

* * * * *

April 13th.--Immense and inexplicable lapse of time since diary last received my attention, but on reviewing past five months, can trace no unusual activities, excepting arrears of calls--worked off between January and March on fine afternoons, when there appears to be reasonable chance of finding everybody out--and unsuccessful endeavour to learn cooking by correspondence in twelve lessons.

Financial situation definitely tense, and inopportune arrival of Rates casts a gloom, but Robert points out that they are not due until May 28th, and am unreasonably relieved. *Query:* Why? *Reply* suggests, not for the first time, analogy with Mr. Micawber.

April 15th.--Felicity Fairmead writes that she *could* come for a few days' visit, if we can have her, and may she let me know exact train later, and it will be either the 18th or the 19th, but, if inconvenient, she could make it the 27th, only in that case, she would have to come by Southern Railway and *not* G.W.R. I write back five pages to say that this would be delightful, only not the 27th, as Robert has to take the car to Crediton that day, and any train that suits her best, of course, but Southern easiest for us.

Have foreboding that this is only the beginning of lengthy correspondence and number of extremely involved arrangements. This fear confirmed by telegram received at midday from Felicity: Cancel letter posted yesterday could after all come on twenty-first if convenient writing suggestions to-night.

Say nothing to Robert about this, but unfortunately fresh telegram arrives over the telephone, and is taken down by him, to the effect that Felicity is So sorry but plans altered Writing.

Robert makes no comment, but goes off at seven o'clock to a British Legion Meeting, and does not return till midnight. Casablanca and I have dinner *tête-à-tête*, and talk about dog-breeding, the novels of E. F. Benson, and the Church of England, about which he holds to my mind optimistic views. Just as we retire to the drawing-room and wireless, Robin appears in pyjamas, and says that he has distinctly heard a burglar outside his window.

I give him an orange--but avoid Casabianca's eye, which is disapproving--and after short sessions by the fire, Robin departs and no more is heard about burglar. Drawing-room, in the most extraordinary way, smells of orange for the rest of the evening to uttermost corners of the room.

April 19th.--Felicity not yet here, but correspondence continues briskly, and have given up telling Robert anything about which train he will be required to meet.

Receive agreeable letter from well-known woman writer, personally unknown to me, who says that We have Many Friends in Common, and will I come over to lunch next week and bring anyone I like with me? Am flattered, and accept for self and Felicity. (*Mem.*: Notify Felicity on post card of privilege in store for her, as this may help her to decide plans.) Further correspondence consists of Account Rendered from Messrs. Frippy and Coleman, very curtly worded, and far more elaborate epistle, which fears that it has escaped my memory, and ventures to draw my attention to enclosed, also typewritten notice concerning approaching Jumble Sale-- (about which I know a good deal already, having contributed two hats, three suspender-belts, disintegrating fire-guard, and a foot-stool with Moth)--and request for reference of last cook but two.

Weather very cold and rainy, and daily discussion takes place between Casabianca and children as to desirability or otherwise of A Walk. Compromise finally reached with Robin and Vicky each wheeling a bicycle uphill, and riding it down, whilst Casabianca, shrouded in mackintosh to the eyebrows, walks gloomily in the rear, in unrelieved solitude. Am distressed at viewing this unnatural state of affairs from the window, and meditate appeal to Robin's better feelings, if any, but shall waste no eloquence upon Vicky.

Stray number of weekly Illustrated Paper appears in hall--cannot say why or how--and Robert asks where this rag came from? and then spends an hour after lunch glued to its pages. Paper subsequently reaches the hands of Vicky, who says Oh, look at that picture of a naked lady, and screams with laughter. Ascertain later that this description, not wholly libellous, applies to full-page photograph of Pamela Pringle--wearing enormous feathered headdress, jewelled breast-plates, one garter, and a short gauze skirt--representing Chastity at recent Pageant of Virtue through the Ages organised by Society women for the benefit of Zenana Mission.

PAMELA PRINGLE AS "CHASTITY"

I ask Robert, with satirical intent, if he would like me to take in Illustrated Weekly regularly, to which he disconcerts me by replying Yes, but not that one. He wants the one that Marsh writes in. Marsh? I say. Yes, Marsh. Marsh is a sound fellow, and knows about books. That, says Robert, should appeal to me. I agree that it does, but cannot, for the moment, trace Marsh. Quite brisk discussion ensues, Robert affirming that I know all about Marsh--everyone does--fellow who writes regularly once a week about books. Illumination suddenly descends upon me, and I exclaim, Oh, Richard King! Robert signifies assent, and adds that he knew very well that I knew about the fellow, everyone does--and goes into the garden.

(*Mem.*: Wifely intuition very peculiar and interesting, and apparently subject to laws at present quite unapprehended by finite mind. Material here for very deep, possibly scientific, article. Should like to make preliminary notes, but laundry calls, and concentrate instead on total omission of everything except thirty-four handkerchiefs and one face-towel from clothes-basket. Decide to postpone article until after the holidays.)

Ethel's afternoon out, and customary fatality of callers ensues, who are shown in by Cook with unsuitable formula: Someone to see you, 'm. Someone turns out to be unknown Mrs. Poppington, returning call with quite unholy promptitude, and newly grown-up daughter, referred to as My Girl. Mrs. Poppington sits on window-seat--from which I hastily remove Teddy-bear, plasticine, and two pieces of bitten chocolate--and My Girl leans back in arm-chair and reads *Punch* from start to finish of visit.

Mrs. P. and I talk about servants, cold East Winds and clipped yew hedges. She also says hopefully that she thinks I know Yorkshire, but to this I have to reply that I don't, which leads us nowhere. Am unfortunately inspired to add feebly--Except, of course, the Brontes--at which Mrs. P. looks alarmed, and at once takes her leave. My Girl throws *Punch* away disdainfully, and we exchange good-byes, Mrs. P. saying fondly that she is sure she does not know what I must think of My Girl's manners. Could easily inform her, and am much tempted to do so, but My Girl at once starts engine of car, and drives herself and parent away.

April 21st.--Final spate of letters, two post cards, and a telegram, herald arrival of Felicity--not, however, by train that she has indicated, and minus luggage, for which Robert is obliged to return to station later. Am gratified to observe that in spite of this, Robert appears pleased to see her, and make mental note to the effect that a Breath of Air from the Great World is of advantage to those living in the country.

April 22nd.--Singular reaction of Felicity to announcement that I am taking her to lunch with novelist, famous in two continents for numerous and brilliant contributions to literature. It is very kind of me, says Felicity, in very unconvincing accents, but should I mind if she stayed at home with the children? I should, I reply, mind very much indeed. At this we glare at one another for some moments in silence, after which Felicity--spirit evidently quailing--mutters successively that: (a) She has no clothes. (b) She won't know what to talk about. (c) She doesn't want to be put into a book.

I treat (a) and (b) with silent contempt, and tell her that (c) is quite out of the question, to which she retorts sharply that she doesn't know what I mean.

Dead-lock is again reached.

Discussion finally closed by my declaring that Casabianca and the children are going to Plymouth to see the dentist, and that Robert will be out, and I have told the maids that there will he no dining-room lunch. Felicity submits, I at once offer to relinquish expedition altogether, she protests violently, and we separate to go and dress.

Query, at this point, suggests itself: Why does my wardrobe never contain anything except heavy garments suitable for arctic regions, or else extraordinarily flimsy ones suggestive of the tropics? Golden mean apparently non-existent.

Am obliged to do the best I can with brown tweed coat and skirt, yellow wool jumper--sleeves extremely uncomfortable underneath coat sleeves--yellow handkerchief tied in artistic sailor's knot at throat, and brown straw hat with ciré ribbon, that looks too summery for remainder of outfit. Felicity achieves better results with charming black-and-white check, short pony-skin jacket, and becoming black felt hat.

Car, which has been washed for the occasion, is obligingly brought to the door by Casabianca, who informs me that he does not think the self-starter is working, but she will probably go on a slope, only he doesn't advise me to try and wind her, as she kicked badly just now. General impression diffused by this speech is to the effect that we are dealing with a dangerous wild beast rather than a decrepit motor-car.

I say Thank you to Casabianca, Good-bye to the children, start the car, and immediately stop the engine. Not a very good beginning, is it? says Felicity, quite unnecessarily.

STARTING THE CAR

Casabianca, Robin and Vicky, with better feeling, push car vigorously, and eventually get it into the lane, when engine starts again. Quarter of a mile further on, Felicity informs me that she thinks one of the children is hanging on to the back of the car. I stop, investigate, and discover Robin, to whom I speak severely. He looks abashed. I relent, and say, Well, never mind this time, at which he recovers immediately, and waves us off with many smiles from the top of a hedge.

Conversation is brisk for the first ten miles. Felicity enquires after That odious woman--cannot remember her name--but she wore a ridiculous cape, and read books, from which description I immediately, and correctly, deduce Miss Pankerton, and reply that I have not, Thank Heaven, come across her for weeks. We also discuss summer clothes, Felicity's married sister's children, Lady B.--now yachting in the Mediterranean--and distant days when Felicity and I were at school together.

Pause presently ensues, and Felicity--in totally different voice--wishes to know if we are nearly there? We are; I stop the car before the turning so that we can powder our noses, and we attain small and beautiful Queen Anne house in silence.

Am by this time almost as paralysed as Felicity, and cannot understand why I ever undertook expedition at all. Leave car in most remote corner of exquisite courtyard--where it presents peculiarly sordid and degraded appearance--and permit elegant parlourmaid--mauve-and-white dress and mob cap--to conduct us through panelled hall to sitting-room evidently designed and furnished entirely regardless of cost.

Madam is in the garden, says parlourmaid, and departs in search of her. Felicity says to me, in French--(Why not English?)--*Dites que je ne suis pas* literary *du tout*, and I nod violently just as celebrated hostess makes her appearance.

She is kind and voluble; Felicity and I gradually recover; someone in a blue dress and pince-nez appears, and is introduced as My Friend Miss Postman who Lives with Me; someone else materialises as My Cousin Miss Crump, and we all go in to lunch. I sit next to hostess, who talks competently about modern poetry, and receives brief and evasive replies from myself. Felicity has My Friend Miss Postman, whom I hear opening the conversation rather unfortunately with amiable remark that she has so much enjoyed Felicity's book. Should like to hear with exactly what energetic turn of phrase Felicity disclaims having had anything to do with any book ever, but cannot achieve this, being under necessity of myself saying something reasonably convincing about Masefield, about whose work I can remember nothing at all.

Hostess then talks about her own books, My Friend Miss Postman supplies intelligent and laudatory comments, seconded by myself, and Felicity and the cousin remain silent, but wear interested expressions.

This carries us on safely to coffee in the *loggia*, where Felicity suddenly blossoms into brilliancy owing to knowing names, both Latin and English, of every shrub and plant within sight.

She is then taken round the garden at great length by our hostess, with whom she talks gardening. Miss P. and I follow, but ignore flora, and Miss P. tells me that Carina--(reference, evidently, to hostess, whose name is Charlotte Volley)--is Perfectly Wonderful. Her Work is Wonderful, and so are her Methods, her Personality, her Vitality and her Charm.

I say Yes, a great many times, and feel that I can quite understand why Carina has Miss P. to live with her. (Am only too certain that neither Felicity nor dear Rose would dream of presenting me to visitors in similar light, should occasion for doing so ever arise.)

Carina and herself, continues Miss P., have been friends for many years now. She has nursed Carina through illness--Carina is not at all strong--and never, never rests. If only she would sometimes *spare* herself, says Miss P. despairingly--but, no, she has to be Giving Out all the time. People make demands upon her. If it isn't one, it's another.

At this, I feel guilty, and suggest departure. Miss P. protests, but faintly, and is evidently in favour of scheme. Carina is approached, but says, No, no, we must stay to tea, we are expected. Miss P. murmurs energetically, and is told, No, no, *that* doesn't matter, and Felicity and I feign absorption in small and unpleasant-looking yellow plant at our feet. Later, Miss P. admits to me that Carina ought to relax *absolutely* for at least an hour every afternoon, but that it is terribly, terribly difficult to get her to do it. To-day's failure evidently lies at our door, and Miss P. remains dejected, and faintly resentful, until we finally depart.

Carina is cordial to the last, sees us into car, has to be told that *that* door won't open, will she try the other side, does so, shuts it briskly, and says that we must come again *soon*. Final view of her is with her arm round Miss P.'s shoulder, waving vigorously. What, I immediately enquire, did Felicity think of her? to which Felicity replies with some bitterness that it is not a very good moment for her to give an opinion, as Carina has just energetically slammed door of the car upon her foot.

Condolences follow, and we discuss Carina, Miss P., cousin, house, garden, food and conversation, all the way home. Should be quite prepared to do so all over again for benefit of Robert in the evening, but he shows no interest, after enquiring whether there wasn't a man anywhere about the place, and being told Only the Gardener.

April 23rd.--Felicity and I fetch as many of Carina's works as we can collect from Boots', and read them industriously. Great excitement on discovering that one of them--the best known--is dedicated to Carina's Beloved Friend, D. P., whom we immediately identify as Miss Postman, Felicity maintaining that D. stands for Daisy, whilst I hold out for Doris. Discussion closes with ribald reference to *Well of Loneliness*.

April 26th.--Felicity, after altering her mind three times, departs, to stay with married sister in Somersetshire. Robin and Vicky lament and I say that we shall all miss her, and she replies that she has loved being here, and it is the only house she knows where the bath towels are really *large*. Am gratified by this compliment, and subsequently repeat it to Robert, adding that it proves I *can't* be such a bad housekeeper. Robert looks indulgent, but asks what about that time we ran out of flour just before a Bank Holiday week-end? To which I make no reply--being unable to think of a good one.

Telephone message from Lady Frobisher, inviting us to dinner on Saturday next, as the dear Blamingtons will be with her for the weekend. I say The Blamingtons? in enquiring tones, and she says Yes, yes, *he* knew me very well indeed eighteen years ago, and admired me tremendously. (This seems to me to constitute excellent reason why we should not meet again, merely in order to be confronted with deplorable alterations wrought by the passage of eighteen years.)

Lady F., however, says that she has promised to produce me--and Robert, too, of course, she adds hastily--and we *must* come. The Blaming-tons are wildly excited. (Have idle and frivolous vision of the Blamingtons standing screaming and dancing at her elbow, waiting to hear decision.)

But, says Lady F., in *those* days--reference as to period preceding the Stone Age at least-- in *those* days, I probably knew him as Bill Ransom? He has only this moment come into the title. I say Oh! *Bill Ransom*, and lapse into shattered silence, while Lady F. goes on to tell me what an extraordinarily pretty, intelligent, attractive and wealthy woman Bill has married, and how successful the marriage is. (Am by no means disposed to credit this offhand.)

Conversation closes with renewed assurances from Lady F. of the Blamingtons' and her own cast-iron determination that they shall not leave the neighbourhood without scene of reunion between Bill and myself, and my own enfeebled assent to this preposterous scheme.

Spend at least ten minutes sitting by the telephone, still grasping receiver, wondering what Bill and I are going to think of one another, when compelled to meet, and why on earth I ever agreed to anything so senseless.

Tell Robert about invitation, and he says Good, the Frobishers have excellent claret, but remains totally unmoved at prospect of the Blamingtons. This--perhaps unjustly--annoys me, and I answer sharply that Bill Ransom once liked me very much indeed, to which Robert absently replies that he daresays, and turns on the wireless. I raise my voice, in order to dominate Happy Returns to Patricia Trabbs of Streatham, and screech that Bill several times asked me to marry him, and Robert nods, and walks out through the window into the garden.

Helen Wills and children rush in at the door, draught causes large vase to blow over, and inundate entire room with floods of water, and incredibly numerous fragments of ribes-flower, and all is merged into frantic moppings and sweepings, and adjurations to children not to cut themselves with broken glass. Happy Families follows, immediately succeeded by Vicky's bath, and supper for both, and far-distant indiscretions of self and Bill Ransom return to oblivion, but recrudesce much later, when children have gone to bed, Casabianca is muttering quietly to himself over cross-word puzzle, and Robert absorbed in *Times*.

Take up a book and read several pages, but presently discover that I have no idea what it is all about, and begin all over again, with similar result. Casabianca suddenly remarks that he would so much like to know what I think of that book, to which I hastily reply Oh! very good indeed, and he says he thought so too, and I offer help with cross-word puzzle in order to stem further discussion.

Spend much time in arranging how I can best get in to hairdresser's for shampoo-and-set before Saturday, and also consider purchase of new frock, but am aware that financial situation offers no justification whatever for this.

Much later on, Robert enquires whether I am ill, and on receiving negative reply, urges that I should try and get to sleep. As I have been doing this, without success, for some time, answer appears to me to be unnecessary.

(*Mem.:* Self-control very, very desirable quality, especially where imagination involved, and must certainly endeavour to cultivate.)

April 30th.--Incredible quantity of household requirements immediately springs into life on my announcing intention of going into Plymouth in order to visit hairdresser. Even Casabianca suddenly says Would it be troubling me too much to ask me to get a postal-order for three shillings and tenpence-halfpenny? Reply tartly that he will find an equally acceptable one at village Post Office, and then wish I hadn't when he meekly begs my pardon and says that, Yes, of course he can.

(*N.B.* This turning of the cheek has effect, as usual, of making me much crosser than before. Feel that doubt is being cast on Scriptural advice, and dismiss subject immediately.)

Bus takes me to Plymouth, where I struggle with Haberdashery--wholly uncongenial form of shopping, and extraordinarily exhausting--socks for Vicky, pants for Robin, short scrubbing-brush demanded by Cook, but cannot imagine what she means to do with it, or why it has to be short--also colossal list of obscure groceries declared to be unobtainable anywhere nearer than Plymouth. None of these are ever in stock at counters where I ask for them, and have to be procured either Upstairs or in the Basement, and am reminded of comic song prevalent in days of youth: The Other Department, If you please, Straight On and Up the Stairs. Quote it to grey-headed shopman, in whom I think it may rouse memories, but he only replies Just so, moddam, and we part without further advances on either side.

Rather tedious encounter follows with young gentleman presiding over Pickles, who endeavours to persuade me that I want particularly expensive brand of chutney instead of that which I have asked for, and which he cannot supply. Am well aware that I ought to cut him short with curt assurance that No Substitute will Do, but find myself mysteriously unable to do anything of the kind, and we continue to argue round and round in a circle, although without acrimony on either side. Curious and unsatisfactory conclusion is reached by my abandoning Chutney *motif* altogether, and buying small and unknown brand of cheese in a little jar. Young gentleman then becomes conversational in lighter vein, and tells me of his preference in films, and we agree that No-one has ever come near Dear Old Charlie. Nor ever will, says the young gentleman conclusively, as he ties string into elegant bow, which will give way the moment I get into street. I say No indeed, we exchange mutual expressions of gratitude, and I perceive that I am going to be late for appointment with hairdresser.

Collect number of small parcels--including particularly degraded-looking paper-bag containing Chips for which Robin and Vicky have implored--sling them from every available finger until I look like inferior Christmas-tree, thrust library-books under one arm--(they slip continually, and have to be pushed into safety from behind by means of ungraceful acrobatics)--and emerge into street. Unendearing glimpse of myself as I pass looking-glass reveals that my hat has apparently engulfed the whole of my head and half of my face as well. (Disquieting query here: Is this perhaps all for the best?) Also that blue coat with fur collar, reasonably becoming when I left home, has now assumed aspect of something out of a second-hand clothes-shop. Encourage myself with visions of unsurpassed brilliance that is to be mine after shampoo-and-set, careful dressing to-night, and liberal application of face-powder, and--if necessary--rouge.

Just as I have, mentally, seen exquisite Paris-model gown that exactly fits me, for sale in draper's window at improbable price of forty-nine shillings and sixpence, am recalled to reality by loud and cordial greetings of Our Vicar's Wife, who plunges through traffic at great risk to life in order to say what a coincidence this is, considering that we met yesterday, and are sure to be meeting to-morrow. She also invites me to come and help her choose white linen buttons for pillow-cases--but this evidently leading direct to Haberdashery once more, and I refuse--I hope with convincing appearance of regret.

Am subsequently dealt with by hairdresser--who says that I am the only lady he knows that still wears a bob--and once more achieve bus, where I meet Miss S. of the Post Office, who has also been shopping. We agree that a day's shopping is tiring--One's Feet, says Miss S.--and that the bus hours are inconvenient. Still, we can't hope for everything in this world, and Miss S. admits that she is looking forward to a Nice Cup of Tea and perhaps a Lay-Down, when she gets home. Reflect, not for the first time, that there are advantages in being a spinster. Should be sorry to say exactly how long it is since I last had a Lay-Down myself, without being disturbed at least fourteen times in the course of it.

Spend much time, on reaching home, in unpacking and distributing household requirements, folding up and putting away paper and string, and condoling with Vicky, who alleges that Casabianca had made her walk miles and *miles*, and she has a pain in her wrist. Do not attempt to connect these two statements, but suggest the sofa and *Dr. Dolittle*, to which Vicky agrees with air of exhaustion, which is greatly intensified every time she catches my eye.

Later on, Casabianca turns up--looking pale-green with cold and making straight for the fire--and announces that he and the children have had a Splendid Walk and are all the better for it. Since I know, and Vicky knows, that this is being said for the express benefit of Vicky, we receive it rather tepidly, and conversation lapses while I pursue elusive sum of ten shillings and threepence through shopping accounts. Robin comes in by the window--I say, too late, Oh, your*boots*!--and Robert, unfortunately choosing this moment to appear, enquires whether there isn't a schoolroom in the house?

Atmosphere by this time is quite unfavourable to festivity, and I go up to dress for the Frobishers--or, more accurately, for the Blamingtons--feeling limp.

Hot bath restores me slightly--but relapse occurs when entirely vital shoulder-strap gives way and needle and thread become necessary.

Put on my Green, dislike it very much indeed, and once more survey contents of wardrobe, as though expecting to find miraculous addition to already perfectly well-known contents.

Needless to say, this does not happen, and after some contemplation of my Black--which looks rusty and entirely out of date--and my Blue--which is a candidate for the next Jumble sale--I return to the looking-glass still in my Green, and gaze at myself earnestly.

(*Query:* Does this denote irrational hope of sudden and complete transformation in personal appearance? If so, can only wonder that so much faith should meet with so little reward.)

Jewel-case unfortunately rather low at present--(have every hope of restoring at least part of the contents next month, if American sales satisfactory)--but great-aunt's diamond ring fortunately still with us, and I put it on fourth finger of left hand, and hope that Bill will think Robert gave it to me. Exact motive governing this wish far too complicated to be analysed, but shelve entire question by saying to myself that Anyway, Robert certainly *would* have given it to me if he could have afforded it.

Evening cloak is smarter than musquash coat; put it on. Robert says Am I off my head and do I want to arrive frozen? Brief discussion follows, but I know he is right and I am wrong, and eventually compromise by putting on fur coat, and carrying cloak, to make decent appearance with on arrival in hall.

Fausse sortie ensues--as it so frequently does in domestic surroundings--and am twice recalled on the very verge of departure, once by Ethel, with superfluous observation that she supposes she had better not lock up at ten o'clock, and once by Robin, who takes me aside and says that he is very sorry, he has broken his bedroom window. It was, he says, entirely an accident, as he was only kicking his football about. I point out briefly, but kindly, that accidents of this nature are avoidable, and we part affectionately. Robert, at the wheel, looks patient, and I feel perfectly convinced that entire evening is going to be a failure.

Nobody in drawing-room when we arrive, and butler looks disapprovingly round, as though afraid that Lady F. or Sir William may be quietly hiding under some of the furniture, but this proving groundless, he says that he will Inform Her Ladyship, and leaves us. I immediately look in the glass, which turns out to be an ancient Italian treasure, and shows me a pale yellow reflection, with one eye much higher than the other. Before I have in any way recovered, Lady F. is in the room, so is Sir William, and so are the Blamingtons. Have not the slightest idea what happens next, but can see that Bill, except that he has grown bald, is unaltered, and has kept his figure, and that I do not like the look of his wife, who has lovely hair, a Paris frock, and is elaborately made-up.

We all talk a great deal about the weather, which is--as usual--cold, and I hear myself assuring Sir W. that our rhododendrons are not yet showing a single bud. Sir W. expresses astonishment--which would be even greater if he realised that we only have one rhododendron in the world, and that I haven't set eyes on it for weeks owing to pressure of indoor occupations--and we go in to dinner. I am placed between Sir W. and Bill, and Bill looks at me and says Well, well, and we talk about Hampstead, and mutual friends, of whom Bill says Do you ever see anything of them nowadays? to which I am invariably obliged to reply No, we haven't met for years. Bill makes the best of this by observing civilly that I am lucky to live in such a lovely part of the world, and he supposes we have a very charming house, to which I reply captiously No, quite ordinary, and we both laugh.

Conversation after this much easier, and I learn that Bill has two children, a boy and a girl. I say that I have the same, and, before I can stop myself, have added that this is really a most extraordinary coincidence. Wish I hadn't been so emphatic about it, and hastily begin to talk about aviation to Sir William. He has a great deal to say about this, and I ejaculate Yes at intervals, and ascertain that Bill's wife is telling Robert that the policy of the Labour party is suicidal, to which he assents heartily, and that Lady F. and Bill are exchanging views about Norway.

Shortly after this, conversation becomes general, party-politics predominating--everyone except myself apparently holding Conservative views, and taking it for granted that none other exist in civilised circles--and I lapse into silence.

(*Query:* Would not a greater degree of moral courage lead me to straightforward and open declaration of precise attitude held by myself in regard to the Conservative and other parties? *Answer:* Indubitably, yes--but results of such candour not improbably disastrous, and would assuredly add little to social amenities of present occasion.)

Entirely admirable dinner brought to a close with South African pears, and Lady F. says Shall we have coffee in the drawing-room?--entirely rhetorical question, as decision naturally rests with herself.

Customary quarter of an hour follows, during which I look at Bill's wife, and like her less than ever, especially when she and Lady F. discuss hairdressers, and topic of Permanent Waves being introduced--(probably on purpose)--by Bill's wife, she says that her own is Perfectly Natural, which I feel certain, to my disgust, is the truth.

It transpires that she knows Pamela Pringle, and later on she tells Bill that Pamela P. is a great friend of mine, and adds Fancy! which I consider offensive, *whatever* it means.

Bridge follows--I play with Sir William, and do well, but as Robert loses heavily, exchequer will not materially benefit--and evening draws to a close.

Hold short conversation with Bill in the hall whilst Robert is getting the car. He says that Sevenoaks is all on our way to London whenever we motor up--which we never do, and it wouldn't be even if we did--and it would be very nice if we'd stay a night or two. I say Yes, we'd love that, and we agree that It's a Promise, and both know very well that it isn't, and Robert reappears and everybody says good-bye.

Experience extraordinary medley of sensations as we drive away, and journey is accomplished practically in silence.

May 1st.--I ask Robert if he thought Lady Blamington good-looking, and he replies that he wouldn't say *that* exactly. What would he say, then? Well, he would say striking, perhaps. He adds that he'll eat his hat if they have a penny less than twenty-thousand a year between them, and old Frobisher says that their place in Kent is a show place. I ask what he thought of Bill, and Robert says Oh, he seemed all right. Make final enquiry as to what *I* looked like last night, and whether Robert thinks that eighteen years makes much difference in one's appearance?

Robert, perhaps rightly, ignores the last half of this, and replies to the former--after some thought--that I looked just as usual, but he doesn't care much about that green dress. Am sufficiently unwise to press for further information, at which Robert looks worried, but finally admits that, to his mind, the green dress makes me look Tawdry.

Am completely disintegrated by this adjective, which recurs to me in the midst of whatever I am doing, for the whole of the remainder of the day.

Activities mainly concerned with school-clothes, of which vast quantities are required by both children, Robin owing to school exigencies, and Vicky to inordinately rapid growth. Effect on domestic finances utterly disastrous in either case. Robin's trunk is brought down from the attic, and Vicky's suitcase extracted from beneath bed. Casabianca and the gardener are obliged to deal with Casabianca's trunk, which is of immense size and weight, and sticks on attic staircase.

(*Query, of entirely private nature:* Why cannot Casabianca travel about with reasonable luggage like anybody else? Is he concealing murdered body or other incriminating evidence from which he dares not be parted? *Answer:* Can obviously never be known.)

Second post brings unexpected and most surprising letter from Mademoiselle, announcing that she is in England and cannot wait to embrace us once again--may she have one sight of Vicky--*ce petit ange*--and Robin--*ce gentil gosse*--before they return to school? She will willingly, in order to obtain this privilege, *courir nu-pieds* from Essex to Devonshire. Despatch immediate telegram inviting her for two nights, and debate desirability of adding that proposed barefooted Marathon wholly unnecessary--but difficulty of including this in twelve words deters me, moreover French sense of humour always incalculable to a degree. Announce impending visit to children, who receive it much as I expected. Robin says Oh, and continues to decipher "John Brown's Body" very slowly on the piano with one finger--which he has done almost hourly every day these holidays--and Vicky looks blank and eats unholy-looking mauve lozenge alleged to be a present from Cook.

(*Mem.:* Speak to Cook, tactfully and at the same time decisively. Must think this well out beforehand.)

Robert's reaction to approaching union with devoted friend and guardian of Vicky's infancy lacking in any enthusiasm whatever.

May 3rd.--Mademoiselle arrives by earlier train than was expected, and is deposited at front door, in the middle of lunch, by taxi, together with rattan basket, secured by cord, small attaché case, large leather hat-box, plaid travelling rug, parcel wrapped in American oilcloth, and two hand-bags.

We all rush out (excepting Helen Wills, who is subsequently found to have eaten the butter off dish on sideboard) and much excitement follows. If Mademoiselle says *Ah, mais ce qu'ils ont grandis!* once, she says it thirty-five times. To me she exclaims that I have *bonne mine*, and do not look a day over twenty, which is manifestly absurd. Robert shakes hands with her--at which she cries *Ah! quelle bonne poignée de main anglaise!* and introduction of Casabianca is effected, but this less successful, and rather distant bows are exchanged, and I suggest adjournment to din in groom.

Lunch resumed--roast lamb and mint sauce recalled for Mademoiselle's benefit, and am relieved at respectable appearance they still present, which could never have been the case with either cottage pie or Irish stew--and news is exchanged. Mademoiselle has, it appears, accepted another post--doctor's household in *les environs de Londres*, which I think means Putney--but has touchingly stipulated for two days in which to visit us before embarking on new duties.

I say how glad I am, and she says, once more, that the children have grown, and throws up both hands towards the ceiling and tosses her head.

Suggestion, from Robert, that Robin and Vicky should take their oranges into the garden, is adopted, and Casabianca escorts them from the room.

Mademoiselle immediately enquires *Qu'est-ce que c'est que ce petit jeune homme?* in tones perfectly, and I think designedly, audible from the hall where Vicky and Casabianca can be heard in brisk dispute over a question of goloshes. I reply, in rebukefully lowered voice, with short outline of Casabianca's position in household--which is, to my certain knowledge, perfectly well known to Mademoiselle already. She slightingly replies *Tiens, c'est drôle*--words and intonation both, in my opinion, entirely unnecessary. The whole of this dialogue rouses in me grave apprehension as to success or otherwise of next forty-eight hours.

Mademoiselle goes to unpack, escorted by Vicky--should like to think this move wholly inspired by grateful affection, but am more than doubtful--Casabianca walks Robin up and down the lawn, obviously for purpose of admonishment--probably justifiable, but faint feeling of indignation assails me at the sight--and I stand idle just outside hall-door until Robert goes past me with a wheelbarrow and looks astonished, when I remember that I must (a) Write letters, (b) Telephone to the Bread, which ought to be here and isn't, (c) Go on sorting school clothes, (d) Put Cash's initials on Vicky's new stockings, (e) See about sending nursery chintzes to the cleaners.

Curious and unprofitable reflection crosses my mind that if I were the heroine of a novel, recent encounter between Bill and myself would lead to further developments of tense and emotional description, culminating either in renunciation, or--if novel a modern one--complete flight of cap over windmill.

Real life, as usual, totally removed from literary conventions, and nothing remains but to hasten indoors and deal with accumulated household duties.

Arrival of second post, later on, gives rise to faint recrudescence of romantic speculations, when letter in unknown, but educated, handwriting, bearing London postmark, is handed to me. Have mentally taken journey to Paris, met Bill by appointment, and said good-bye to him for ever--and also, alternatively, gone with him to the South Sea Islands, been divorced by Robert, and heard of the deaths of both children--before opening letter. It turns out to be from unknown gentleman of high military rank, who asks me whether I am interested in the New Economy, as he is selling off mild-cured hams very cheaply indeed.

May 5th.--Fears relating to perfect harmony between Mademoiselle and Casabianca appear to have been well founded, and am relieved that entire party disperses to-morrow. Children, as usual on last day of holidays, extremely exuberant, but am aware, from previous experience, that fearful reaction will set in at eleventh hour.

Decide on picnic, said to be in Mademoiselle's honour, and Robert tells me privately that he thinks Casabianca had better be left behind. Am entirely of opinion that he is right, and spend some time in evolving graceful and kindhearted little formula with which to announce this arrangement, but all ends in failure.

Casabianca says Oh no, it is very kind of me, but he would quite enjoy a picnic, and does not want an afternoon to himself. He has no letters to write--very kind of me to think of such a thing. Nor does he care about a quiet day in the garden, kind though it is of me. Final desperate suggestion that he would perhaps appreciate vague and general asset of A Free Day, he receives with renewed reference to my extreme kindness, and incontrovertible statement that he wouldn't know what to do with a free day if he had it.

Retire defeated, and tell Robert that Casabianca *wants* to come to the picnic--which Robert appears to think unnatural in the extreme. Towards three o'clock it leaves off raining, and we start, customary collection of rugs, mackintoshes, baskets and thermos flasks in back of car.

Mademoiselle says *Ah, combien ça me rappelle le passé que nous ne reverrons plus!* and rolls her eyes in the direction of Casabianca, and I remember with some thankfulness that his knowledge of French is definitely limited. Something tells me, however, that he has correctly interpreted meaning of Mademoiselle's glance.

Rain begins again, and by the time we reach appointed beauty-spot is falling very briskly indeed. Robert, who has left home under strong compulsion from Vicky, is now determined to see the thing through, and announces that he shall walk the dog to the top of the hill, and that the children had better come too. Mademoiselle, shrouded in large plaid cape, exerts herself in quite unprecedented manner, and offers to go with them, which shames me into doing likewise, sorely against my inclination. We all get very wet indeed, and Vicky falls into mysterious gap in a hedge and comes out dripping and with black smears that turn out to be tar all over her.

Mon Dieu, says Mademoiselle, *il n'y a done plus personne pour s'occuper de cette malheureuse petite?* Should like to remind her of many, many similar misfortunes which have befallen Vicky under Mademoiselle's own supervision--but do not, naturally, do so.

TENSION AT THE PICNIC

Situation, already slightly tense, greatly aggravated by Casabianca, who selects this ill-judged moment for rebuking Vicky at great length, at which Mademoiselle exclaims passionately *Ah ma bonne Sainte Vierge, ayez pitié de nous!* which strikes us all into a deathly silence.

Rain comes down in torrents, and I suggest tea in the car, but this is abandoned when it becomes evident that we are too tightly packed to be able to open baskets, let alone spread out their contents. Why not tea in the dining-room at home? is Robert's contribution towards solving difficulty, backed quietly, but persistently, by Casabianca. This has immediate effect of causing Mademoiselle to advocate *un goûter en plein air*, as though we were at Fontainebleau, or any other improbable spot, in blazing sunshine.

Robin suddenly and brilliantly announces that we are quite near Bull Alley Manor, which is empty, and that the gardener will allow us to have a picnic in the hen-house. Everybody says The Hen-house? except Vicky, who screams and looks enchanted, and Mademoiselle, who also screams, and refers to *punaises*, which she declares will abound. Robin explains that he means a summer-house on the Bull Alley tennis-ground, which has a wire-netting and *looks* like a hen-house, but he doesn't think it really is. He adds triumphantly that it has a bench that we can sit on. Robert puts in a final plea for the dining-room at home, but without conviction, and we drive ten miles to Bull Alley Manor, where picnic takes place under Robin's auspices, all of us sitting in a row on long wooden seat, exactly like old-fashioned school feast. I say that it reminds me of *The Daisy Chain*, but nobody knows what I mean, and reference is allowed to drop while we eat potted-meat sandwiches and drink lemonade, which is full of pips.

Return home at half-past six, feeling extraordinarily exhausted. Find letter from Literary Agent, suggesting that the moment has now come when fresh masterpiece from my pen may definitely be expected, and may he hope to receive my new manuscript quite shortly? Idle fancy, probably born of extreme fatigue, crosses my mind as to results of a perfectly candid reply--to the effect that literary projects entirely swamped by hourly activities concerned with children, housekeeping, sewing, letter-writing, Women's Institute Meetings, and absolute necessity of getting eight hours' sleep every night.

Decide that another visit to Doughty Street is imperative, and say to Robert, feebly and untruthfully, that I am sure he would not mind my spending a week or two in London, to get some writing done. To this Mademoiselle, officiously and unnecessarily, adds that, naturally, *madame désire se distraire de temps en temps*--which is not in the least what I want to convey.

Robert says nothing, but raises one eyebrow.

May 6th.--Customary heart-rending half-hour in which Robin and Vicky appear to realise for the first time since last holidays that they must return to school. Robin says nothing whatever, but turns gradually *eau-de-nil*, and Vicky proclaims that she feels almost certain she will not be able to survive the first night away from home. I tell myself firmly that, as a modern mother, I must be Bracing, but very inconvenient lump in my throat renders this difficult, and I suggest instead that they should go and say good-bye to the gardener.

Luggage, which has theoretically been kept within very decent limits, fills the hall and overflows outside front door, and Casabianca's trunk threatens to take entire car all to itself. Mademoiselle eyes it disparagingly and says *Ciel! on dirait tout un déménagement*, but relents at the moment of farewell, and gives Casabianca her hand remarking *Sans rancune, hein?* which he fortunately does not understand, and can therefore not reply to, except by rather chilly bow, elegantly executed from the waist. Mademoiselle then without warning bursts into tears, kisses children and myself, says *On se reverra au Paradis, au moins*--which is on the whole optimistic--and is driven by Robert to the station.

Hired car removes Casabianca, after customary exchange of compliments between us, and extraordinarily candid display of utter indifference from both Robin and Vicky, and I take them to the Junction, when unknown parent of unknown schoolfellow of Robin's takes charge of him with six other boys, who all look to me exactly alike.

Vicky weeps, and I give her an ice and then escort her to station all over again, and put her in charge of the guard to whom she immediately says Can she go in the Van with him? He agrees, and they disappear hand-in-hand.

Drive home again, and avoid the nursery for the rest of the day. *May 10th.*--Decide that a return to Doughty Street flat is imperative, and try to make clear to Robert that this course really represents Economy in the Long Run. Mentally assemble superb array of evidence to this effect, but it unfortunately eludes me when trying to put it into words and all becomes feeble and incoherent. Also observe in myself tendency to repeat over and over again rather unmeaning formula: It Isn't as if It was going to be For Long, although perfectly well aware that Robert heard me the first time, and was unimpressed. Discussion closes with my fetching A.B.C. out of the dining-room, and discovering that it dates from 1929.

May 17th.--Return to Doughty Street flat, and experience immense and unreasonable astonishment at finding it almost exactly as I left it, yellow-and-white check dust-sheets and all. Am completely entranced, and spend entire afternoon and evening arranging two vases of flowers, unpacking suit-case and buying tea and biscuits in Gray's Inn Road where I narrowly escape extinction under a tram.

Perceive that Everybody in the World except myself is wearing long skirts, a tiny hat on extreme back of head, and vermilion lip-stick. Look at myself in the glass and resolve instantly to visit Hairdresser, Beauty Parlour, and section of large Store entitled Inexpensive Small Ladies, before doing anything else at all.

Ring up Rose, who says Oh, am I back?--which I obviously must be--and charmingly suggests dinner next week--two friends whom she wants me to meet--and a luncheon party at which I must come and help her. Am flattered, and say Yes, yes, how? to which Rose strangely replies, By leaving rather early, if I don't mind, as this may break up the party.

Note: Extraordinary revelations undoubtedly hidden below much so-called hospitality, if inner thoughts of many hostesses were to be revealed. This thought remains persistently with me, in spite of explanation from Rose that she has appointment miles away at three o'clock, on day of luncheon, and is afraid of not getting there punctually. Agree, but without enthusiasm, to leave at half-past two in the hopes of inducing fellow-guests to do likewise.

Rose also enquires, with some unnecessary mirth, whether I am going to Do Anything about my little friend Pamela Pringle, to which I reply Not that I know of, and say Good-night and ring off. Completely incredible coincidence ensues, and am rung up five minutes later by P. P. who alleges that she "had a feeling" I should be in London again. Become utterly helpless in the face of this prescience, and agree in enthusiastic terms to come to a cocktail party at Pamela's flat, meet her for a long talk at her Club, and go with her to the Royal Academy one morning. Entire prospect fills me with utter dismay, and go to bed in completely dazed condition.

Pamela rings up again just before midnight, and hopes so, so much she hasn't disturbed me or anything like that, but she forgot to say--she knows so well that I shan't misunderstand--there's nothing in it at all--only if a letter comes for her addressed to my flat, will I just keep it till we meet? Quite likely it won't come at all, but *if* it does, will I just do that and not say anything about it, as people are so terribly apt to misunderstand the simplest thing? Am I sure I don't mind? As by this time I mind nothing at all except being kept out of my bed any longer, I agree to everything, say that I understand absolutely, and am effusively thanked by Pamela and rung off.

May 21st.--Attend Pamela Pringle's cocktail party after much heart-searching as to suitable clothes for the occasion. Consult Felicity--on a postcard--who replies--on a postcard--that she hasn't the least idea, also Emma Hay (this solely because I happen to meet her in King's Road, Chelsea, not because I have remotest intention of taking her advice). Emma says lightly Oh, pyjamas are the thing, she supposes, and I look at her and am filled with horror at implied suggestion that she herself ever appears anywhere in anything of the kind. But, says Emma, waving aside question which she evidently considers insignificant, Will I come with her next week to really delightful evening party in Bloomsbury, where every single Worth While Person in London is to be assembled? Suggest in reply, with humorous intention, that the British Museum has, no doubt, been reserved to accommodate them all, but Emma not in the least amused, and merely replies No, a basement flat in Little James Street, if I know where that is. As it is within two minutes' walk of my own door, I do, and agree to be picked up by Emma and go on with her to the party.

She tells me that all London is talking about her slashing attack on G. B. Stern's new novel, and what did I feel? I ask where the slashing attack is to be found, and Emma exclaims Do I really mean that I haven't seen this month's *Hampstead Clarionet?* and I reply with great presence of mind but total disregard for truth, that they've probably Sold Out, at which Emma, though obviously astounded, agrees that that must be it, and we part amiably.

Question of clothes remains unsolved until eleventh hour, when I decide on black crêpe-de-chine and new hat that I think becoming.

Bus No. 19, as usual, takes me to Sloane Street, and I reach flat door at half-past six, and am taken up in lift, hall-porter--one of many--informing me on the way that I am the First. At this I beg to be taken down again and allowed to wait in the hall, but he replies, not unreasonably, that *Someone* has got to be first, miss. Revive at being called miss, and allow myself to be put down in front of P. P.'s door, where porter rings the bell as if he didn't altogether trust me to do it for myself--in which he is right--and I subsequently crawl, rather than walk, into Pamela's drawing-room. Severe shock ensues when Pamela--wearing pale pink flowered chiffon--reveals herself in perfectly bran-new incarnation as purest platinum blonde. Recover from this with what I consider well-bred presence of mind, but am shattered anew by passionate enquiry from Pamela as to whether I like it. Reply, quite truthfully, that she looks lovely, and all is harmony. I apologise for arriving early, and Pamela assures me that she is only too glad, and adds that she wouldn't have been here herself as early as this if her bedroom clock hadn't been an hour fast, and she wants to hear all my news. She then tells me all hers, which is mainly concerned with utterly unaccountable attitude of Waddell, who goes into a fit if any man under ninety so much as *looks* at Pamela. (Am appalled at cataclysmic nature of Waddell's entire existence, if this is indeed the case.)

Previous experience of Pamela's parties leads me to enquire if Waddell is to be present this afternoon, at which she looks astonished and says Oh Yes, she supposes so, he is quite a good host in his own way, and anyway she is sure he would adore to see me.

(Waddell and I have met exactly once before, on which occasion we did not speak, and am morally certain that he would not know me again if he saw me.)

Bell rings, and influx of very young gentlemen supervenes, and are all greeted by Pamela and introduced to me as Tim and Nicky and the Twins. I remain anonymous throughout, but Pamela lavishly announces that I am very, very clever and literary--with customary result of sending all the very young gentlemen into the furthermost corner of the room, from whence they occasionally look over their shoulders at me with expressions of acute horror.

They are followed by Waddell--escorting, to my immense relief, Rose's Viscountess, whom I greet as an old friend, at which she seems faintly surprised, although in quite a kind way--and elderly American with a bald head. He sits next me, and wants to know about Flag-days, and--after drinking something out of a little glass handed me in a detached way by one of the very young gentlemen--I suddenly find myself extraordinarily eloquent and informative on the subject.

Elderly American encourages me by looking at me thoughtfully and attentively while I speak-- (difference in this respect between Americans and ourselves is marked, and greatly to the advantage of the former)--and saying at intervals that what I am telling him Means Quite a Lot to him--which is more than it does to me. Long before I think I have exhausted the subject, Pamela removes the American by perfectly simple and direct method of telling him to come and talk to her, which he obediently does--but bows at me rather apologetically first.

THE POLITE AMERICAN

Waddell immediately refills my glass, although without speaking a word, and Rose's Viscountess talks to me about *Time and Tide*. We spend a pleasant five minutes, and at the end of them I have promised to go and see her, and we have exchanged Christian names. Can this goodwill be due to alcohol? Have a dim idea that this question had better not be propounded at the moment.

Room is by this time entirely filled with men, cigarette smoke and conversation. Have twice said No, really, not any more thank you, to Waddell, and he has twice ignored it altogether, and continued to pour things into my glass, and I to drink them. Result is a very strange mixture of exhilaration, utter recklessness and rather sentimental melancholy. Am also definitely feeling giddy and aware that this will be much worse as soon as I attempt to stand up.

Unknown man, very attractive, sitting near me, tells me of very singular misfortune that has that day befallen him. He has, to his infinite distress, dealt severe blow with a walking-stick to strange woman, totally unknown to him, outside the Athenaeum. I say Really, in concerned tones, Was that just an accident? Oh, yes, purest accident. He was showing a friend how to play a stroke at golf, and failed to perceive woman immediately behind him. This unhappily resulted in the breaking of her spectacles, and gathering of a large crowd, and moral obligation on his own part to drive her immense distance in a taxi to see (a) a doctor, (b) an oculist, (c) her husband, who turns out to live at Richmond. I sympathise passionately, and suggest that he will probably have to keep both woman and her husband for the rest of their lives, which, he says, had already occurred to him.

This dismays us both almost equally, and we each drink another cocktail.

Pamela--had already wondered why she had left attractive unknown to me so long--now breaks up this agreeable conversation, by saying that Waddell will never, never, forgive anybody else for monopolising me, and I simply must do my best to put him into a really *good* mood, as Pamela has got to tell him about her dressmaker's bill presently, so will I be an angel--? She then removes delightful stranger, and I am left in a dazed condition. Have dim idea that Waddell is reluctantly compelled by Pamela to join me, and that we repeatedly assure one another that there are No Good Plays Running Nowadays. Effect of this eclectic pronouncement rather neutralised later, when it turns out that Waddell never patronises anything except talkies, and that I haven't set foot inside a London theatre for eight-and-a-half months.

Later still it dawns on me that I am almost the last person left at the party, except for Waddell, who has turned on the wireless and is listening to Vaudeville, and Pamela, who is on the sofa having her palm read by one young man, while two others hang over the back of it and listen attentively.

I murmur a very general and unobtrusive good-bye, and go away. Am not certain, but think that hall-porter eyes me compassionately, but we content ourselves with exchange of rather grave smiles--no words.

Am obliged to return to Doughty Street in a taxi, owing to very serious fear that I no longer have perfect control over my legs.

Go instantly to bed on reaching flat, and room whirls round and round in distressing fashion for some time before I go to sleep.

May 25th.--Life one round of gaiety, and feel extremely guilty on receiving a letter from Our Vicar's Wife, saying that she is certain I am working hard at a New Book, and she should so like to hear what it's all about and what its name is. If I will tell her this, she will speak to the girl at Boots', as every little helps. She herself is extremely busy, and the garden is looking nice, but everything very late this year. P.S. Have I heard that old Mrs. Blenkinsopp is going to Bournemouth?

Make up my mind to write really long and interesting reply to this, but when I sit down to do so find that I am quite unable to write anything at all, except items that would appear either indiscreet, boastful or scandalous. Decide to wait until after Emma Hay's party in Little James Street, as this will give me something to write about.

(*Mem.:* Self-deception almost certainly involved here, as reflection makes it perfectly evident that Our Vicar's Wife is unlikely in the extreme to be either amused or edified by the antics of any acquaintances brought to my notice via Emma.)

Go down to Mickleham by bus--which takes an hour and a half--to see Vicky, who is very lively and affectionate, and looks particularly well, but declares herself to be overworked. I ask What at? and she says Oh, Eurhythmics. It subsequently appears that these take place one afternoon in every week, for one hour. She also says that she likes all her other lessons and is doing very well at them, and this is subsequently confirmed by higher authorities. Again patronise bus route--an hour and three-quarters, this time--and return to London, feeling exactly as if I had had a night journey to Scotland, travelling third-class and sitting bolt upright all the way.

May 26th.--Emma--in green sacque that looks exactly like *démodé* window-curtain, sandals and varnished toe-nails--calls for me at flat, and we go across to Little James Street. I ask whom I am going to meet and Emma replies, with customary spaciousness, Everyone, absolutely Everyone, but does not commit herself to names, or even numbers.

Exterior of Little James Street makes me wonder as to its capacities for dealing with Everyone, and this lack of confidence increases as Emma conducts me into extremely small house and down narrow flight of stone stairs, the whole culminating in long, thin room with black walls and yellow ceiling, apparently no furniture whatever, and curious, but no doubt interesting, collection of people all standing screaming at one another.

Emma looks delighted and says Didn't she tell me it would be a crush, that man over there is living with a negress now, and if she gets a chance she will bring him up to me.

(Should very much like to know with what object, since it will obviously be impossible for me to ask him the only thing I shall really be thinking about.)

Abstracted-looking man with a beard catches sight of Emma, and says Darling, in an absentminded manner, and then immediately moves away, followed, with some determination, by Emma.

Am struck by presence of many pairs of horn-rimmed spectacles, and marked absence of evening dress, also by very odd fact that almost everybody in the room has either abnormally straight or abnormally frizzy hair. Conversation in my vicinity is mainly concerned with astonishing picture on the wall, which I think represents Adam and Eve at very early stage indeed, but am by no means certain, and comments overheard do not enlighten me in the least. Am moreover seriously exercised in my mind as to exact meaning of *tempo, brio, appassionata* and *coloratura* as applied to art.

Strange man enters into conversation with me, but gives it up in disgust when I mention Adam and Eve, and am left with the impression--do not exactly know why--that picture in reality represents Sappho on the Isle of Lesbos.

(*Query:* Who was Sappho, and what was Isle of Lesbos?)

Emma presently reappears, leading reluctant-looking lady with red hair, and informs her in my presence that I am a country mouse--which infuriates me--and adds that we ought to get on well together, as we have identical inferiority complexes. Red-haired lady and I look at one another with mutual hatred, and separate as soon as possible, having merely exchanged brief comment on Adam and Eve picture, which she seems to think has something to do with the 'nineties and the *Yellow Book*.

Make one or two abortive efforts to find out if we have a host or hostess, and if so what they look like, and other more vigorous efforts to discover a chair, but all to no avail, and finally decide that as I am not enjoying myself, and am also becoming exhausted, I had better leave. Emma makes attempt that we both know to be half-hearted to dissuade me, and I rightly disregard it altogether, and prepare to walk out, Emma at the last moment shattering my nerve finally by asking what I think of that wonderful satirical study on the wall, epitomising the whole of the modern attitude towards Sex?

June 1st.--Life full of contrasts, as usual, and after recent orgy of Society, spend most of the day in washing white gloves and silk stockings, and drying them in front of electric fire. Effect of this on gloves not good, and remember too late that writer of Woman's Page in illustrated daily paper has always deprecated this practice.

Pay a call on Robert's Aunt Mary, who lives near Battersea Bridge, and we talk about relations. She says How do I think William and Angela are getting on? which sounds like preliminary to a scandal and excites me pleasurably, but it turns out to refer to recent venture in Beekeeping, no reference whatever to domestic situation, and William and Angela evidently giving no grounds for agitation at present.

Aunt Mary asks about children, says that school is a great mistake for girls, and that she does so hope Robin is good at games--which he isn't--and do I find that it answers to have A Man in the house? Misunderstanding occurs here, as I take this to mean Robert, but presently realise that it is Casabianca.

Tea and seed-cake appear, we partake, and Aunt Mary hopes that my writing does not interfere with home life and its many duties, and I hope so too, but in spite of this joint aspiration, impression prevails that we are mutually dissatisfied with one another. We part, and I go away feeling that I have been a failure. Wish I could believe that Aunt Mary was similarly downcast on her own account, but have noticed that this is seldom the case with older generation. Find extraordinary little envelope waiting for me at flat, containing printed assurance that I shall certainly be interested in recent curiosities of literature acquired by total stranger living in Northern manufacturing town, all or any of which he is prepared to send me under plain sealed cover. Details follow, and range from illustrated History of Flagellation to Unexpurgated Erotica.

Toy for some time with the idea that it is my duty to communicate with Scotland Yard, but officials there probably overworked already, and would be far more grateful for being left in peace, so take no action beyond consigning envelope and contents to the dust-bin.

June 9th.--Am rung up on the telephone by Editor of Time and Tide and told that We are Giving a Party on June 16th, at newest Park Lane Hotel. (Query: Is this the Editorial We, or does she conceivably mean she and I?--because if so, must at once disabuse her, owing to present financial state of affairs.) Will I serve on the Committee? Yes, I will. Who else is on it? Oh, says the Editor, Ellen Wilkinson is on it, only she won't be able to attend any of the meetings. I make civil pretence of thinking this a businesslike and helpful arrangement, and ask Who Else? Our Miss Lewis, says the Editor, and rings off before I can make further enquiries. Get into immediate touch with Our Miss Lewis, who turns out to be young, and full of activity. I make several suggestions, mostly to the effect that she should do a great deal of hard work, she accedes delightfully, and I am left with nothing to do except persuade highly distinguished Professor to take the Chair at Debate which is to be a feature of the party.

June 11th.--Distinguished Professor proves far less amenable than I had expected, and am obliged to call in Editorial assistance. Am informed by a side-wind that Distinguished Professor has said she Hates me, which seems to me neither dignified nor academic method of expressing herself--besides being definitely un-Christian.

Apart from this, preparations go on successfully, and I get myself a new frock for the occasion.

June 16th.--Reach Hotel at 4 o'clock, marvellous weather, frock very successful, and all is *couleur-de-rose*. Am met by official, to whom I murmur *Time and Tide*? and he commands minor official, at his elbow, to show Madam the Spanish Grill. (Extraordinary and unsuitable association at once springs to mind here, with Tortures of the Inquisition.) The Spanish Grill is surrounded by members of the *Time and Tide* Staff--Editor materialises, admirably dressed in black, and chills me to the heart by saying that as I happen to be here early I had better help her receive arrivals already beginning. (This does not strike me as a happy way of expressing herself.) Someone produces small label, bearing name by which I am--presumably--known to readers of *Time and Tide*, and this I pin to my frock, and feel exactly like one of the lesser exhibits at Madame Tussaud's.

Distinguished Professor, who does not greet me with any cordiality, is unnecessarily insistent on seeing that I do my duty, and places me firmly in receiving line. Several hundred millions then invade the Hotel, and are shaken hands with by Editor and myself. Official announcer does marvels in catching all their names and repeating them in superb shout. After every tenth name he diversifies things by adding, three semi-tones lower, *The Editor receiving*, which sounds like a Greek chorus, and is impressive.

Delightful interlude when I recognise dear Rose, with charming and beautifully dressed doctor friend from America, also Rose's niece--no reference made by either of us to Women's Institutes--the Principal from Mickleham Hall, of whom I hastily enquire as to Vicky's welfare and am told that she is quite well, and Very Good which is a relief,--and dear Angela, who is unfortunately just in time to catch this maternal reference, and looks superior. Regrettable, but undoubtedly human, aspiration crosses my mind that it would be agreeable to be seen by Lady B. in all this distinguished society, but she puts in no appearance, and have very little doubt that next time we meet I shall be riding a bicycle strung with parcels on way to the village, or at some similar disadvantage.

Soon after five o'clock I am told that We might go and have some tea now--which I do, and talk to many very agreeable strangers. Someone asks me Is Francis Iles here? and I have to reply that I do not know, and unknown woman suddenly joins in and assures me that Francis Iles is really Mr. Aldous Huxley, she happens to know. Am much impressed, and repeat this to several people, by way of showing that I possess inside information, but am disconcerted by unknown gentleman who tells me, in rather grave and censorious accents, that I am completely mistaken, as he happens to know that Francis Iles is in reality Miss Edith Sitwell. Give the whole thing up after this, and am presently told to take my seat on platform for Debate.

Quite abominable device has been instituted by which names of speakers are put into a hat, and drawn out haphazard, which means that none of us know when we are to speak except one gentleman who has--with admirable presence of mind--arranged to have a train to catch, so that he gets called upon at once.

Chairman does her duties admirably--justifies my insistence over and over again--speeches are excellent, and audience most appreciative.

Chairman--can she be doing it on purpose, from motives of revenge?--draws my name late in the day, and find myself obliged to follow after admirable and experienced speakers, who have already said everything that can possibly be said. Have serious thoughts of simulating a faint, but conscience intervenes, and I rise. Special Providence mercifully arranges that exactly as I do so I should meet the eye of American publisher, whom I know well and like. He looks encouraging--and I mysteriously find myself able to utter. Great relief when this is over.

Short speech from *Time and Tide*'s Editor brings down the house, and Debate is brought to a close by the Chairman.

Party definitely a success, and am impressed by high standard of charm, good looks, intelligence, and excellent manners of *Time and Tide* readers. Unknown and delightful lady approaches me, and says, without preliminary of any kind: How is Robert? which pleases me immensely, and propose to send him a post card about it to-night.

Am less delighted by another complete stranger, who eyes me rather coldly and observes that I am What She Calls Screamingly Funny. Cannot make up my mind if she is referring to my hat, my appearance generally, or my contributions to *Time and Tide*. Can only hope the latter.

Am offered a lift home in a taxi by extremely well-known novelist, which gratifies me, and hope secretly that as many people as possible see me go away with him, and know who he is--which they probably do--and who I am--which they probably don't.

Spend entire evening in ringing up everybody I can think of, to ask how they enjoyed the Party.

June 18th.--Heat-wave continues, and everyone says How lovely it must be in the country, but personally think it is lovely in London, and am more than content.

Write eloquent letter to Robert suggesting that he should come up too, and go with me to Robin's School Sports on June 25th and that we should take Vicky. Have hardly any hope that he will agree to any of this.

Rose's Viscountess--henceforth Anne to me--rings up, and says that she has delightful scheme by which Rose is to motor me on Sunday to place--indistinguishable on telephone--in Buckinghamshire, where delightful Hotel, with remarkably beautiful garden, exists, and where we are to meet Anne and collection of interesting literary friends for lunch. Adds flatteringly that it will be so delightful to meet me again--had meant to say this myself about her, but must now abandon it, being unable to think out paraphrase in time. Reply that I shall look forward to Sunday, and we ring off.

Debate question of clothes--wardrobe, as usual, is deficient--and finally decide on green coat and skirt if weather cool, and new flowered tussore if hot.

(Problem here concerned with head-gear, as hat suitable for flowered tussore too large and floppy for motoring, and all other smaller hats--amounting to two, and one cap--entirely wrong colour to go with tussore.)

Literary Agent takes me out to lunch--is very nice--suggests that a little work on my-part would be desirable. I agree and sit and write all the evening vigorously.

June 19th.--Really very singular day, not calculated to rank amongst more successful experiences of life. Am called for by dear Rose in car, and told to hold map open on my knee, which I do, but in spite of this we get lost several times and Rose shows tendency to drive round and round various villages called Chalfont. After saying repeatedly that I expect the others will be late too, and that Anyway we have time in hand, I judge it better to introduce variations to the effect that We can't be far off now, and What about asking? Rose reluctantly agrees, and we ask three people, two of whom are strangers in the district, and the third is sorry but could not say at all, it might be ahead of us, or on the other hand we might be coming away from it. At this Rose mutters expletives and I feel it best to be silent.

Presently three Boy Scouts are sighted, and Rose stops again and interrogates them. They prove very willing and produce a map, and giggle a good deal, and I decide that one of them is rather like Robin, and forget to listen to what they say. Rose, however, dashes on again, and I think with relief that we are now doing well, when violent exclamation breaks from her that We have passed that self-same church tower three times already. Am filled with horror--mostly at my own inferior powers of observation, as had no idea whatever that I had ever set eyes on church tower in my life before--and suggest madly that we ought to turn to the right, I think. Rose--she must indeed be desperate--follows this advice and in about three minutes we miraculously reach our destination, and find that it is two o'clock. Dining-room is discovered--entire party half-way through lunch, and obviously not in the least pleased to see us--which is perfectly natural, as eruptions of this kind destructive to continuity of conversation, always so difficult of achievement in any case. Everyone says we must be Starving, and egg-dish is recalled--eggs disagree with me and am obliged to say No and my neighbour enquires Oh, why? which is ridiculous, and great waste of time--and we speed through cold chicken and strawberries and then adjourn to garden, of which there are acres and acres, and everybody very enthusiastic except myself. Just as I select comfortable chair next to Anne--whom I have, after all, come to see--perfectly unknown couple surge up out of the blue, and are introduced as General and Mrs. St. Something--cannot catch what--and General immediately says Wouldn't I like to go round the garden? Have not strength of mind enough to reply baldly No I wouldn't, and he conducts me up and down steps and in and out of paths and at intervals we say Just look at those lupins! and That's a good splash of colour--but mostly he tells me about Lord Rothermere. Try not to betray that I have never yet been able to distinguish between Lord R. and Lord Beaverbrook. General St. ? evidently thinks ill of both, and I make assenting sounds and am inwardly perfectly certain that Anne's party is being amused at my progress. Can hear them in shrieks of laughter in different parts of garden, which I now perceive to be the size of Hampton Court, more or less.

Rose suddenly appears round a yew hedge, and I give her a look that I hope she appreciates, and we gradually work our way back via more lupins, to deck-chairs. Anne still sitting there, looking extraordinarily amused. General St. Something instantly says that his wife would so like to have a talk with me about books, she materialises at his elbow, and at once declares that she must show me the garden. I demur, on the ground of having seen it already, and she assures me breezily that it will well bear seeing twice, or even more often, and that she herself could never get tired of that Blaze of Colour.

We accordingly pursue blaze of colour, while Mrs. St. ? talks to me about poetry, which she likes and I don't, Siamese cats, that both of us like, and the lace-making industry.

Garden now definitely acquires dimensions of the Zoo at least, and I give up all hope of ever being allowed to sit down again. Can see Anne talking to Rose in the distance, and both appear to be convulsed with mirth.

Distant clock strikes four--should not have been surprised if it had been eight--and I break in on serious revelations about lack of rear-lights on bicycles in country districts, and say that I am perfectly certain I ought to be going. Civil regrets are exchanged--entirely hypocritical on my part, and probably on hers as well--and we walk about quarter of a mile and find Rose. Mrs. St. Something disappears (probably going round the garden again) and I am very angry indeed and say that I have never had such a day in all my life. Everybody else laughs heartily, and appears to feel that afternoon has been highly successful and Rose hysterically thanks Anne for inviting us. Make no pretence whatever of seconding this. Drive home is very much shorter than drive out, and I do not attempt to make myself either useful or agreeable in any way.

June 23rd.--Am pleased and astonished at being taken at my word by Robert, who appears at the flat, and undertakes to conduct me, and Vicky, to half-term Sports at Robin's school. In the meantime, he wants a hair-cut. I say that there is a place quite near Southampton Row, at which Robert looks appalled, and informs me that there is *No* place nearer than Bond Street. He accordingly departs to Bond Street, after telling me to meet him at twelve at his Club in St. James's. Am secretly much impressed by nonchalance with which Robert resumes these urban habits, although to my certain knowledge he has not been near Club in St. James's for years.

Reflection here on curious dissimilarity between the sexes as exemplified by self and Robert: in his place, should be definitely afraid of not being recognised by hall-porter of Club, and quite possibly challenged as to my right to be there at all. Robert, am perfectly well aware, will on the contrary ignore hall-porter from start to finish with probable result that h.-p. will crawl before him, metaphorically if not literally.

I CALL FOR ROBERT AT HIS CLUB

This rather interesting abstract speculation recurs to me with some violence when I actually do go to Club, and enter imposing-looking hall, presided over by still more imposing porter in uniform, to whom I am led up by compassionate-looking page, who evidently realises my state of inferiority. Am made no better by two elderly gentlemen talking together in a corner, both of whom look at me with deeply suspicious faces and evidently think I have designs on something or other--either the Club statuary, which is looming above me, or perhaps themselves? Page is despatched to look for Robert--feel as if my only friend had been taken from me--and I wait, in state of completely suspended animation, for what seems like a long week-end. This comes to an end at last, and am moved to greet Robert by extraordinary and totally unsuitable quotation: *Time and the hour runs through the roughest day*--which I hear myself delivering, in an inward voice, exactly as if I were talking in my sleep. Robert--on the whole wisely--takes not the faintest notice, beyond looking at me with rather an astonished expression, and receives his hat and coat, which page-boy presents as if they were Coronation robes and sceptre at the very least. We walk out of Club, and I resume customary control of my senses.

Day is one of blazing sunlight, streets thronged with people, and we walk along Piccadilly and Robert says Let's lunch at Simpson's in the Strand, to which I agree, and add Wouldn't it be heavenly if we were rich? Conversation then ensues on more or less accustomed lines, and we talk about school-bills, inelastic spirit shown by the Bank, probabilities that new house-parlourmaid will be giving notice within the next few weeks, and unlikelihood of our having any strawberries worth mentioning in the garden this year. Robert's contribution mostly consists of ejaculations about the traffic--he doesn't know what the streets are coming to, but it can't go on like this--and a curt assurance to the effect that we shall all be in the workhouse together before so very long. After this we reach Simpson's in the Strand, and Robert says that we may as well have a drink--which we do, and feel better.

Am impressed by Simpson's, where I have never been before, and lunch is agreeable. In the middle of it perceive Pamela Pringle, wearing little black-and-white hat exactly like old-fashioned pill-box, and not much larger, and extraordinarily effective black frock--also what looks like, and probably is, a collection of at least nine real-diamond bracelets. She is, needless to say, escorted by young gentleman, who looks totally unsuited to his present surroundings, as he has side-whiskers, a pale green face, and general aspect that reminds me immediately of recent popular song entitled: "My Canary has Circles under His Eyes".

Pamela deeply absorbed in conversation, but presently catches sight of me, and smiles--smile a very sad one, which is evidently tone of the interview--and then sees Robert, at which she looks more animated, and eventually gets up and comes towards us, leaving Canary with Circles under His Eyes throwing bits of bread about the table in highly morose and despairing fashion.

Robert is introduced; Pamela opens her eyes very widely and says she has heard so very much about him--(who from? Not me)--and they shake hands. Can see from Robert's expression exactly what he thinks of Pamela's finger-nails, which are vermilion. P. P. says that we must come and see her--can we dine together tonight, Waddell will be at home and one or two people are looking in afterwards?--No, we are very sorry, but this is impossible. Then Pamela will ring up this dear thing--evidently myself, but do not care about the description--and meanwhile she simply must go back. The boy she is lunching with is Hipps, the artist. Robert looks perfectly blank and I--not at all straightforwardly--assume an interested expression and say Oh really, as if I knew all about Hipps, and Pamela adds that the poor darling is all decadent and nervy, and she thought this place would do him good, but really he's in such a state that Paris is the only possible thing for him. She gives Robert her left hand, throws me a kiss with the other, and rejoins the Canary--whose face is now buried in his arms. Robert says Good God and asks why that woman doesn't wash that stuff off those nails. This question obviously rhetorical, and do not attempt any reply, but enquire if he thought Pamela pretty. Robert, rather strangely, makes sound which resembles Tchah! from which I deduce a negative, and am not as much distressed as I ought to be at this obvious injustice to P. P.'s face and figure. Robert follows this by further observation, this time concerning the Canary with Circles under His Eyes, which would undoubtedly lead to libel action, if not to charge of using obscene language in public, if overheard, and I say Hush, and make enquiries as to the well-being of Our Vicar and Our Vicar's Wife, in order to change the subject.

That reminds Robert: there is to be a concert in the Village next month for most deserving local object, and he has been asked to promise my services as performer, which he has done. Definite conviction here that reference ought to be made to Married Women's Property Act or something like that, but exact phraseology eludes me, and Robert seems so confident that heart fails me, and I weakly agree to do what I can. (This, if taken literally, will amount to extraordinarily little, as have long ceased to play piano seriously, have never at any time been able to sing, and have completely forgotten few and amateurish recitations that have occasionally been forced upon me on local platforms.)

Plans for the afternoon discussed: Robert wishes to visit Royal Academy, and adds that he need not go and see his Aunt Mary as I went there the other day--which seems to me illogical, and altogether unjust--and that we will get stalls for to-night if I will say what play I want to see. After some thought, select *Musical Chairs*, mainly because James Agate has written well of it in the Press, and Robert says Good, he likes a musical show, and I have to explain that I don't think it is a musical show, at all, and we begin all over again, and finally select a revue. Debate question of Royal Academy, but have no inclination whatever to go there, and have just said so, as nicely as I can, when Pamela again appears beside us, puts her hand on Robert's shoulder--at which he looks startled and winces slightly--and announces that we *must* come to Hipps' picture-show this afternoon--it is in the Cygnet Galleries in Fitzroy Square, and if no one turns up it will break the poor pet's heart, and as far as she can see, no one but herself has ever heard of it, and we simply must go there, and help her out. She will meet us there at five.

Before we have recovered ourselves in any way, we are more or less committed to the Cygnet Galleries at five, Pamela has told us that she adores us both--but looks exclusively at Robert as she says it--and has left us again. Shortly afterwards, observe her paying bill for herself and the Canary, who is now drinking old brandy in reckless quantities.

Robert again makes use of expletives, and we leave Simpson's and go our several ways, but with tacit agreement to obey Pamela's behest. I fill in the interval with prosaic purchases of soap, which I see in mountainous heaps at much reduced prices, filling an entire shop-window, sweets to take down to Robin on Saturday, and quarter-pound of tea in order that Robert may have usual early-morning cup before coming out--unwillingly--to breakfast at Lyons'.

Am obliged to return to Doughty Street, and get small jug in which to collect milk from dairy in Gray's Inn Road, pack suitcase now in order to save time in the morning, and finally proceed to Fitzroy Square, where Cygnet Galleries are discovered, after some search, in small adjoining street which is not in Fitzroy Square at all.

Robert and the Canary are already together, in what I think really frightful juxtaposition, and very, very wild collection of pictures hangs against the walls. Robert and I walk round and round, resentfully watched by the Canary, who never stirs, and Pamela Pringle fails to materialise.

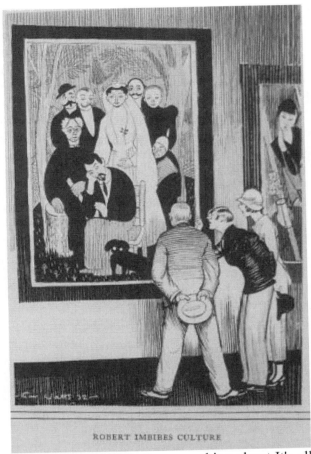

ROBERT IMBIBES CULTURE

Can think of nothing whatever to say, but mutter something about It's all being Very Interesting, from time to time, and at last come to a halt before altogether astonishing group that I think looks like a wedding--which is a clearer impression than I have managed to get of any of the other pictures. Am just wondering whether it is safe to take this for granted, when the Canary joins us, and am again stricken into silence. Robert, however, suddenly enquires If that is the League of Nations, to which the Canary, in a very hollow voice, says that he knows nothing whatever about the League of Nations, and I experience strong impulse to reply that we know nothing whatever about pictures, and that the sooner we part for ever, the better for us all.

This, however, is impossible, and feel bound to await Pamela, so go round the room all over again, as slowly as possible, only avoiding the wedding-group, to which no further reference is made by any of us. After some time of this, invisible telephone-bell rings, and the Canary--very curious writhing movement, as he walks--goes away to deal with it, and Robert says For God's sake let's get out of this. I ask Does he mean now this minute, and he replies Yes, before that morbid young owl comes back, and we snatch up our various possessions and rush out. The Canary, rather unfortunately, proves to be on the landing half-way downstairs, leaning against a wall and holding telephone receiver to his ear. He gives us a look of undying hatred as we go past, and the last we hear of him is his voice, repeating desperately down the telephone that Pamela *can't* do a thing like that, and fail him utterly--she absolutely can't. (Personally, am entirely convinced that she can, and no doubt will.)

Robert and I look at one another, and he says in a strange voice that he must have a drink, after that, and we accordingly go in search of it.

June 25th.--Vicky arrives by green bus from Mickleham, carrying circular hat-box of astonishing size and weight, with defective handle, so that every time I pick it up, it falls down again, which necessitates a taxi. She is in great excitement, and has to be calmed with milk and two buns before we proceed to station, meet Robert, and get into the train.

Arrival, lunch at Hotel, and walk up to School follow normal lines, and in due course Robin appears and is received by Vicky with terrific demonstrations of affection and enthusiasm, to which he responds handsomely. (Reflect, as often before, that Fashion in this respect has greatly altered. Brothers and sisters now almost universally deeply attached to one another, and quite prepared to admit it. *0 temporal 0 mores!*) We are conducted to the playing-fields, where hurdles and other appliances of sports are ready, and where rows and rows of chairs await us.

Parents, most of whom I have seen before and have no particular wish ever to see again, are all over the place, and am once more struck by tendency displayed by all Englishwomen to cling to most unbecoming outfit of limp coat and skirt and felt hat even when blazing summer day demands cooler, and infinitely more becoming, *ensemble* of silk frock and shady hat.

Crowds of little boys all look angelic in running shorts and singlets, and am able to reflect that even if Robin's hair *is* perfectly straight, at least he doesn't wear spectacles.

Headmaster speaks a few words to me--mostly about the weather, and new wing that he proposes, as usual, to put up very shortly--I accost Robin's Form-master and demand to be told How the Boy is Getting On, and Form-master looks highly astonished at my audacity, and replies in a very off-hand way that Robin will never be a cricketer, but his football is coming on, and he has the makings of a swimmer. He then turns his back on me, but I persist, and go so far as to say that I should like to hear something about Robin's Work.

Form-master appears to be altogether overcome by this unreasonable requirement, and there is a perceptible silence, during which he evidently meditates flight. Do my best to hold him by the Power of the Human Eye, about which I have read much, not altogether believingly. However, on this occasion, it does its job, and Form-master grudgingly utters five words or so, to the effect that we needn't worry about Robin's Common-entrance exam. in two years' time. Having so far committed himself he pretends to see a small boy in imminent danger on a hurdle and dashes across the grass at uttermost speed to save him, and for the remainder of the day, whenever he finds himself within yards of me, moves rapidly in opposite direction.

Sports take place, and are a great success. Robin murmurs to me that he thinks, he isn't at all sure, but he *thinks*, he may have a chance in the High Jump. I reply, with complete untruth, that I shan't mind a bit if he doesn't win and he mustn't be disappointed--and then suffer agonies when event actually takes place and he and another boy out-jump everybody else and are at last declared to have tied. (Vicky has to be rebuked by Robert for saying that this is Unjust and Robin jumped by far the best--which is not only an unsporting attitude, but entirely unsupported by fact.) Later in the afternoon Robin comes in a good second in Hurdling, and Vicky is invited to take part in a three-legged race, which she does with boundless enthusiasm and no skill at all.

Tea and ices follow--boys disappear, and are said to be changing--and I exchange remarks with various parents, mostly about the weather being glorious, the sports well organised, and the boys a healthy-looking lot.

Trophies are distributed--inclination to tears, of which I am violently ashamed, assails me when Robin goes up to receive two little silver cups--various people cheer various other people, and we depart for the Hotel, with Robin. Evening entirely satisfactory, and comes to an end at nine o'clock, with bed for Vicky and Robin's return to school.

June 27th.--Return to London, departure of Vicky by green bus and under care of the conductor, and of Robert from Paddington. I have assured him that I shall be home in a very few days now, and he has again reminded me about the concert, and we part. Am rung up by Pamela in the afternoon, to ask if I can bring Robert to tea, and have great satisfaction in informing her that he has returned to Devonshire. Pamela then completely takes the wind out of my sails by saying that she will be motoring through Devonshire quite soon, and would simply love to look us up. A really very interesting man who Rows will be with her, and she thinks that we should like to know him. Social exigencies compel me to reply that of course we should, and I hope she will bring her rowing friend to lunch or tea whenever she is in the neighbourhood.

After this, permit myself to enquire why P. P. never turned up at Cygnet Galleries on recent painful occasion; to which she answers, in voice of extreme distress, that I simply can't imagine how complicated life is, and men give one no peace at all, and it's so difficult when one friend hates another friend and threatens to shoot him if Pamela goes out with him again.

Am obliged to admit that attitude of this kind does probably lead to very involved situations, and Pamela says that I am so sweet and understanding, always, and I must give that angel Robert her love--and rings off.

June 29th.--Am filled with frantic desire to make the most of few remaining days in London, and recklessly buy two pairs of silk stockings, for no other reason than that they catch my eye when on my way to purchase sponge-bag and tooth-paste for Vicky.

(*Query:* Does sponge-bag exist anywhere in civilised world which is positively water-proof and will not sooner or later exude large, damp patches from sponge that apparently went into it perfectly dry? Secondary, but still important, *Query:* Is it possible to reconcile hostile attitude invariably exhibited by all children towards process of teeth-cleaning with phenomenal rapidity with which they demolish tube after tube of tooth-paste?)

Proceed later to small and newly established Registry Office, which has been recommended to me by Felicity, and am interviewed by lady in white satin blouse, who tells me that maids for the country are almost impossible to find--which I know very well already--but that she will do what she can for me, and I mustn't mind if it's only an inexperienced girl. I agree not to mind, provided the inexperienced girl is willing to learn, and not expensive, and white-satin blouse says Oh dear yes, to the first part, and Oh dear no, to the second, and then turns out to have twenty-five shillings a week in mind, at which I protest, and we are obliged to begin all over again, on totally different basis. She finally dismisses me, with pessimistic hopes that I may hear from her in the next few days, and demand for a booking-fee, which I pay.

Return to Doughty Street, where I am rung up by quite important daily paper and asked If I would care to write an Article about Modern Freedom in Marriage. First impulse is to reply that they must have made a mistake, and think me more celebrated than I am--but curb this, and ask how long article would have to be--really meaning what is the shortest they will take--and how much they are prepared to pay? They--represented by brisk and rather unpleasant voice--suggest fifteen hundred words, and a surprisingly handsome fee. Very well then, I will do it--how soon do they want it? Voice replies that early next week will be quite all right, and we exchange good-byes. Am highly exhilarated, decide to give a dinner-party, pay several bills, get presents for the children, take them abroad in the summer holidays, send Robert a cheque towards pacifying the Bank, and buy myself a hat. Realise, however, that article is not yet written, far less paid for, and that the sooner I collect my ideas about Modern Freedom in Marriage, the better.

Just as I have got ready to do so, interruption comes in the person of Housekeeper from upstairs, who Thinks that I would like to see the laundry-book. I do see it, realise with slight shock that it has been going on briskly for some weeks unperceived by myself, and produce the necessary sum. Almost immediately afterwards a Man comes to the door, and tells me that I have no doubt often been distressed by the dirty and unhygienic condition of my telephone. Do not like to say that I have never thought about it, so permit him to come in, shake his head at the telephone, and say Look at that, now, and embark on long and alarming monologue about Germs. By the time he has finished, realise that I am lucky to be alive at all in midst of numerous and insidious perils, and agree to telephone's being officially disinfected at stated intervals. Form, as usual, has to be filled up, Man then delivers parting speech to the effect that he is very glad I've decided to do this--there's so many ladies don't realise, and if they knew what they was exposing themselves to, they'd be the first to shudder at it--which sounds like White Slave Traffic, but is, I think, still Germs. I say Well, Good-morning, and he replies rebukefully--and correctly--Good afternoon, which I feel bound to accept by repeating it after him, and he goes downstairs.

I return to Modern Freedom in Marriage and get ready to deal with it by sharpening a pencil and breaking the lead three times. Extremely violent knock at flat door causes me to drop it altogether--(fourth and absolutely final break)--and admit very powerful-looking window-cleaner with pair of steps, mop, bucket and other appliances, all of which he hurls into the room with great *abandon*. I say Will he begin with the bedroom, and he replies that it's all one to him, and is temporarily lost to sight in next room, but can be heard singing: *I Don't Know Why I Love*

You Like I Do. (Remaining lines of this idyll evidently unknown to him as he repeats this one over and over again, but must in justice add that he sings rather well.)

Settle down in earnest to Modern Freedom in Marriage. Draw a windmill on blotting-paper. Tell myself that a really striking opening sentence is important. Nothing else matters. Really striking sentence is certainly hovering somewhere about, although at the moment elusive. (*Query:* Something about double standard of morality? Or is this unoriginal? Thread temporarily lost, owing to absorption in shading really admirable little sketch of Cottage Loaf drawn from Memory...)

Frightful crash from bedroom, and abrupt cessation of not Knowing Why He Loves Me Like He Does, recalls window-cleaner with great suddenness to my mind, and I open door that separates us and perceive that he has put very stalwart arm clean through windowpane and is bleeding vigorously, although, with great good feeling, entirely avoiding carpet or furniture.

Look at him in some dismay, and enquire--not intelligently--if he is hurt, and he answers No, the cords were wore clean through, it happens sometimes with them old-fashioned sashes. Rather singular duet follows, in which I urge him to come and wash his arm in the kitchen, and he completely ignores the suggestion and continues to repeat that the cords were wore clean through. After a good deal of this, I yield temporarily, look at the cords and agree that they do seem to be wore clean through, and finally hypnotise window-cleaner--still talking about the cords--into following me to the sink, where he holds his arm under cold water and informs me that the liability of his company is strictly limited, so far as the householder is concerned, and in my case the trouble was due to them cords being practically wore right through.

I enquire if his arm hurts him--at which he looks blankly astonished--inspect the cut, produce iodine and apply it, and finally return to Modern Freedom in Marriage, distinctly shattered, whilst window-cleaner resumes work, but this time without song.

Literary inspiration more and more evasive every moment, and can think of nothing whatever about Modern Freedom except that it doesn't exist in the provinces. Ideas as to Marriage not lacking, but these would certainly not be printed by any newspaper on earth, and should myself be deeply averse from recording them in any way.

Telephone rings and I instantly decide that: (a) Robert has died suddenly. (b) Literary Agent has effected a sale of my film-rights, recent publication, for sum running into five figures, pounds not dollars. (c) Robin has met with serious accident at school. (d) Pamela Pringle wishes me once more to cover her tracks whilst engaged in pursuing illicit amour of one kind or another.

(*Note:* Swiftness of human (female) imagination surpasses that of comet's trail across the heavens quite easily. Could not this idea be embodied in short poem? Am convinced, at the moment, that some such form of expression would prove infinitely easier than projected article about Modern Freedom, etc.)

I say Yes? into the telephone--entire flight of fancy has taken place between two rings--and unknown contralto voice says that I shan't remember her--which is true--but that she is Helen de Liman de la Pelouse and we met at Pamela Pringle's at lunch one day last October. To this I naturally have to reply Oh yes, yes--indeed we did--as if it all came back to me--which it does, in a way, only cannot possibly remember anything except collection of women all very much better dressed and more socially competent than myself, and am perfectly certain that H. de L. de la P. was never introduced by name at all. (Would probably have taken too long, in crowded rush of modern life.)

Will I forgive last-minute invitation and come and dine to-night and meet one or two people, all interested in Books, and H. de la P.'s cousin, noted literary critic whom I may like to know? Disturbing implication here that literary critics allow their judgment to be influenced by considerations other than aesthetic and academic ones--but cannot unravel at the moment, and merely accept with pleasure and say What time and Where? Address in large and expensive Square is offered me, time quarter to nine if that isn't too late? (*Query:* What would happen, if I said Yes, it is too late? Would entire scheme be reorganised?)

Am recalled from this rather idle speculation by window-cleaner--whose very existence I have completely forgotten--taking his departure noisily, but with quite unresentful salutation, and warning--evidently kindly intended--that them cords are wore through and need seeing to. I make a note on the blotting-paper to this effect, and am again confronted with perfectly blank sheet of paper waiting to receive masterpiece of prose concerning Modern Freedom in Marriage. Decide that this is definitely not the moment to deal with it, and concentrate instead on urgent and personal questions concerned with to-night's festivity. Have practically no alternative as to frock--recently acquired silver brocade--and hair has fortunately been shampoo'd and set within the last three days so still looks its best--evening cloak looks well when on, and as it will remain either in hall or hostess's bedroom, condition of the lining need concern no one but myself and servant in attendance--who will be obliged to keep any views on the subject concealed. Shoes will have to be reclaimed immediately from the cleaners, but this easily done. More serious consideration is that of taxi-fare, absolutely necessitated by situation of large and expensive Square, widely removed from bus or tube routes. Am averse from cashing cheque, for very sound reason that balance is at lowest possible ebb and recent passages between Bank and myself give me no reason to suppose that they will view even minor overdraft with indulgence-- and am only too well aware that shopping expedition and laundry-book between them have left me with exactly fivepence in hand.

Have recourse, not for the first time, to perhaps rather infantile, but by no means unsuccessful, stratagem of unearthing small hoards of coins distributed by myself, in more affluent moments, amongst all the hand-bags I possess in the world.

Two sixpences, some halfpence, one florin and a half-crown are thus brought to light, and will see me handsomely through the evening, and breakfast at Lyons' next morning into the bargain.

Am unreasonably elated by this and go so far as to tell myself that very likely I shall collect some ideas for Modern Freedom article in general conversation to-night and needn't bother about it just now.

Rose comes in unexpectedly, and is immediately followed by Felicity Fairmead, but they do not like one another and atmosphere lacks *entrain* altogether. Make rather spasmodic conversation about the children, *The Miracle*--which we all three of us remember perfectly well in the old days at Olympia, but all declare severally that we were more or less children at the time and too young to appreciate it--and State of Affairs in America, which we agree is far worse than it is here. This is openly regretted by Rose (because she knows New York well and enjoyed being there) and by me (because I have recently met distinguished American publisher and liked him very much) and rejoiced in by Felicity (because she thinks Prohibition is absurd). Feminine mentality rather curiously and perhaps not altogether creditably illustrated here. Have often wondered on exactly what grounds I am a Feminist, and am sorry to say that no adequate reply whatever presents itself. Make note to think entire question out dispassionately when time permits--if it ever does.

Rose and Felicity both refuse my offer of tea and mixed biscuits--just as well, as am nearly sure there is no milk--and show strong inclination to look at one another expectantly in hopes of an immediate departure. Rose gives in first, and goes, and directly she has left Felicity asks me what on earth I see in her, but does not press for an answer. We talk about clothes, mutual friends, and utter impossibility of keeping out of debt. Felicity--who is, and always has been, completely unworldly, generous and utterly childlike--looks at me with enormous brown eyes, and says solemnly that nothing in this world--NOTHING--matters except Money, and on this she takes her departure. I empty cigarette ash out of all the ash-trays--Felicity doesn't smoke at all and Rose and I only had one cigarette each, but results out of all proportion--and go through customary far-sighted procedure of turning down bed, drawing curtains and filling kettle for hot-water bottle, before grappling with geyser, of which I am still mortally terrified, and getting ready for party. During these operations I several times encounter sheet of paper destined to record my views about Modern Freedom in Marriage, but do nothing whatever about it, except decide again how I shall spend the money.

Am firmly resolved against arriving too early, and do not telephone for taxi until half-past eight, then find number engaged, and operator--in case of difficulty dial 0--entirely deaf to any appeal. Accordingly rush out into the street--arrangement of hair suffers rather severely--find that I have forgotten keys and have to go back again--make a second attack on telephone, this time with success, rearrange coiffure and observe with horror that three short minutes in the open air are enough to remove every trace of powder from me, repair this, and depart at last.

After all this, am, as usual, first person to arrive. Highly finished product of modern civilisation, in white satin with no back and very little front, greets me, and I perceive her to be extremely beautiful, and possessed of superb diamonds and pearls. Evidently Helen de Liman de la Pelouse. This conjecture confirmed when she tells me, in really very effective drawl, that we sat opposite to one another at Pamela Pringle's luncheon party, and may she introduce her husband? Husband is apparently Jewish--why de Liman de la Pelouse?--and looks at me in a rather lifeless and exhausted way and then gives me a glass of sherry, evidently in the hope of keeping me quiet. H. de L. de la P. talks about the weather--May very wet, June very hot, English climate very uncertain--and husband presently joins in and says all the same things in slightly different words. We then all three look at one another in despair, until I am suddenly inspired to remark that I have just paid a most interesting visit to the studio of a rather interesting young man whose work I find interesting, called Hipps. (Should be hard put to it to say whether construction of this sentence, or implication that it conveys, is the more entirely alien to my better principles.) Experiment proves immediately successful, host and hostess become animated, and H. de L. de la P. says that Hipps is quite the most mordant of the younger set of young present-day satirists, don't I think, and that last thing of his definitely had *patine*. I recklessly agree, but am saved from further perjury by arrival of more guests. All are unknown to me, and fill me with terror, but pretty and harmless creature in black comes and stands next me, and we talk about *1066 and All That* and I say that if I'd known in time that the authors were schoolmasters I should have sent my son to them at all costs, and she says Oh, have I children?--but does not, as I faintly hope, express any surprise at their being old enough to go to school at all--and I say Yes, two, and then change the subject rather curtly for fear of becoming involved in purely domestic conversation.

Find myself at dinner between elderly man with quantities of hair, and much younger man who looks nice and smiles at me. Make frantic endeavours, without success, to read names on little cards in front of them, and wish violently that I ever had sufficient presence of mind to listen to people's names when introduced--which I never do.

Try the elderly man with Hipps. He does not respond. Switch over to thinking he knows a friend of mine, Mrs. Pringle? No, he doesn't think so. Silence follows, and I feel it is his turn to say something, but as he doesn't, and as my other neighbour is talking hard to pretty woman in black, I launch into Trade Depression and Slump in America, and make a good deal of use of all the more intelligent things said by Rose and Felicity this afternoon. Elderly neighbour still remains torpid except for rather caustic observation concerning Mr. Hoover. Do not feel competent to defend Mr. Hoover, otherwise should certainly do so, as by this time am filled with desire to contradict everything elderly neighbour may ever say. He gives me, however, very little opportunity for doing so, as he utters hardly at all and absorbs himself in perfectly admirable lobster *Thermidor*. Final effort on my part is to tell him the incident of the window-cleaner, which I embroider very considerably in rather unsuccessful endeavour to make it amusing, and this at last unseals his lips and he talks quite long and eloquently about Employers' Liability, which he views as an outrage. Consume lobster silently, in my turn, and disagree with him root and branch, but feel that it would be waste of time to say so and accordingly confine myself to invaluable phrase: I See What He Means.

We abandon mutual entertainment with great relief shortly afterwards, and my other neighbour talks to me about books, says that he has read mine and proves it by a quotation, and I decide that he must be distinguished critic spoken of by H. de L. de la P. Tell him the story of window-cleaner, introducing several quite new variations, and he is most encouraging, laughs heartily, and makes me feel that I am a witty and successful *raconteuse*--which in saner moments I know very well that I am not.

(*Query:* Has this anything to do with the champagne? *Answer*, almost certainly, Yes, everything.)

Amusing neighbour and myself continue to address one another exclusively--fleeting wonder as to what young creature in black feels about me--and am sorry when obliged to ascend to drawing-room for customary withdrawal. Have a feeling that H. de L. de la P.--who eyes me anxiously--is thinking that I am Rather A Mistake amongst people who all know one another very well indeed. Try to tell myself that this is imagination, and all will be easier when drinking coffee, which will not only give me occupation--always a help--but clear my head, which seems to be buzzing slightly.

H. de L. de la P. refers to Pamela--everybody in the room evidently an intimate friend of Pamela's, and general galvanisation ensues. *Isn't* she adorable? says very smart black-and-white woman, and Doesn't that new platinum hair suit her too divinely? asks somebody else, and we all cry Yes, quite hysterically, to both. H. de L. de la P. then points me out and proclaims--having evidently found a *raison d' etre* for me at last--that I have known Pamela for years and years-- longer than any of them. I instantly become focus of attention, and everyone questions me excitedly.

Do I know what became of the *second* husband?--Templer-Something was his name. No explanation ever forthcoming of his disappearance, and immediate replacement by somebody else. Have I any idea of Pamela's real age? Of course she looks too, too marvellous, but it is an absolute fact that her eldest child can't possibly be less than fifteen, and it was the child of the second marriage, *not* the first.

Do I know anything about that Pole who used to follow her about everywhere, and was supposed to have been shot by his wife in Paris on account of P. P.?

Is it true that Pringle--unfortunate man--isn't going to stand it any longer and has threatened to take Pamela out to Alaska to live?

And is she--poor darling--still going about with the second husband of that woman she's such friends with?

Supply as many answers as I can think of to all this, and am not perturbed as to their effect, feeling perfectly certain that whatever I say Pamela's dear friends have every intention of believing, and repeating, whatever they think most sensational and nothing else.

This conviction intensified when they, in their turn, overwhelm me with information.

Do I realise, says phenomenally slim creature with shaven eyebrows, that Pamela will really get herself into difficulties one of these days, if she isn't more careful? That, says the eyebrows-- impressively, but surely inaccurately--is Pamela's trouble. She isn't *careful*. Look at the way she behaved with that South American millionaire at Le Touquet!

Look, says somebody else, at her affair with the Prince. Reckless--no other word for it.

Finally H. de L. de la P.--who has been quietly applying lip-stick throughout the conversation-- begs us all to Look at the *type* of man that falls for Pamela. She knows that Pamela is attractive, of course--sex-appeal, and all that--but after all, that can't go on for ever, and then what will be left? Nothing whatever. Pamela's men aren't the kind to go on being devoted. They simply have this brief flare-up, and then drift off to something younger and newer. Every time. Always.

Everybody except myself agrees, and several people look rather relieved about it. Conversation closes, as men are heard upon the stairs, with H. de L. de la P. assuring us all that Pamela is one of her very dearest friends, and she simply adores her--which is supported by assurances of similar devotion from everyone else. Remain for some time afterwards in rather stunned condition, thinking about Friendship, and replying quite mechanically, and no doubt unintelligently, to thin man who stands near me--(wish he would sit, am getting crick in my neck)--and talks about a drawing in *Punch* of which he thought very highly, but cannot remember if it was Raven Hill or Bernard Partridge, nor what it was about, except that it had something to do with Geneva.

Evening provides no further sensation, and am exceedingly sleepy long before somebody in emeralds and platinum makes a move. Pleasant man who sat next me at dinner has hoped, in agreeable accents, that we shall meet again--I have echoed the hope, but am aware that it has no foundation in probability--and H. de L. de la P. has said, at parting, that she is so glad I have had an opportunity of meeting her cousin, very well known critic. Do not like to tell her that I have never identified this distinguished *littérateur* at all, and leave the house still uninformed as to whether he was, or was not, either of my neighbours at dinner. Shall probably now never know.

July 1st.--Once more prepare to leave London, and am haunted by words of out-of-date song once popular: *How're you Going to Keep' em Down on the Farm, Now that they've seen Paree?* Answer comes there none.

Day filled with various activities, including packing, which I dislike beyond anything on earth and do very badly--write civil letter to H. de L. de la P. to say that I enjoyed her dinner-party, and ring up Rose in order to exchange good-byes. Rose, as usual, is out--extraordinary gadabout dear Rose is--and I leave rather resentful message with housekeeper, and return to uncongenial task of folding garments in sheets of tissue paper that are always either much too large or a great deal too small.

Suitcase is reluctant to close, I struggle for some time and get very hot, success at last, and am then confronted by neatly folded dressing-gown which I have omitted to put in.

Telephone rings and turns out to be Emma Hay, who is very very excited about satire which she says she has just written and which will set the whole of London talking. If I care to come round at once, says Emma, she is reading it aloud to a few Really Important People, and inviting free discussion and criticism afterwards.

I express necessary regrets, and explain that I am returning to the country in a few hours' time. What, shrieks Emma, *leaving London?* Am I mad? Do I intend to spend the whole of the rest of my life pottering about the kitchen, and seeing that Robert gets his meals punctually, and that the children don't bring muddy boots into the house? Reply quite curtly and sharply: Yes, I Do, and ring off--which seems to me, on the whole, the quickest and most rational method of dealing with Emma.

July 4th.--Return home has much to recommend it, country looks lovely, everything more or less in bloom, except strawberries, which have unaccountably failed, Robert gives me interesting information regarding recent sale of heifer, and suspected case of sclerosis of the liver amongst neighbouring poultry, and Helen Wills claws at me demonstratively under the table as I sit down to dinner. Even slight *faux pas* on my own part, when I exclaim joyfully that the children will be home in a very short time now, fails to create really serious disturbance of harmonious domestic atmosphere.

Shall certainly not, in view of all this, permit spirits to be daunted by rather large pile of letters almost all concerned with Accounts Rendered, that I find on my writing-table. Could have dispensed, however, with the Milk-book, the Baker's Bill, and the Grocer's Total for the Month, all of them handed to me by Cook with rider to the effect that There was twelve-and-sixpence had to be given to the sweep, and twopence to pay on a letter last Monday week, and she hopes she did right in taking it in.

Robert enquires very amiably what I have been writing lately, and I say lightly, Oh, an article on Modern Freedom in Marriage, and then remember that I haven't done a word of it, and ask Robert to give me some ideas. He does so, and they are mostly to the effect that People talk a great deal of Rubbish nowadays, and that Divorce may be All Very Well in America, and the Trouble with most women is that they haven't got nearly Enough to Do. At this I thank Robert very much and say that will do splendidly--which is true in the spirit, though not the letter--but he appears to be completely wound up and unable to stop, and goes on for quite a long time, telling me to Look at Russia, and wishing to know How I should like to see the children whisked off to Siberia--which I think forceful but irrelevant.

Become surprisingly sleepy at ten o'clock--although this never happened to me in London--and go up to bed.

Extraordinary and wholly undesirable tendency displays itself to sit upon window-seat and think about Myself--but am well aware that this kind of thing never a real success, and that it will be the part of wisdom to get up briskly instead and look for shoe-trees to insert in evening-shoes-- which I accordingly do; and shortly afterwards find myself in bed and ready to go to sleep.

July 8th.--Short, but rather poignant article on Day-Dreaming which appears in to-day's *Time and Tide* over signature of L. A. G. Strong, strangely bears out entry in my diary previous to this one. Am particularly struck--not altogether agreeably, either--by Mr. Strong's assertion that: "Day-dreaming is only harmful when it constitutes a mental rebellion against the circumstances of our life, which does not tend to any effort to improve them".

This phrase, quite definitely, exactly epitomises mental exercise in which a large proportion of my life is passed. Have serious thoughts of writing to Mr. Strong, and asking him what, if anything, can be done about it--but morning passes in telephone conversation with the Fishmiddle-cut too expensive, what about a nice sole?--post card to Cissie Crabbe, in return for view of Scarborough with detached enquiry on the back as to How I am and How the children are--other post cards to tradespeople, cheque to the laundry, cheque to Registry Office, and cheque to local newsagent--and Mr. Strong is superseded. Nevertheless am haunted for remainder of the day by recollection surging up at unexpected moments, of the harmfulness of daydreams. Foresee plainly that this will continue to happen to me at intervals throughout the rest of life.

Just before lunch Our Vicar's Wife calls, and says that It's too bad to disturb me, and she has only just popped in for one moment and has to nip off to the school at once, but she did so want to talk to me about the concert, and hear all about London. Rather tedious and unnecessary argument follows as to whether she will or will not stay to lunch, and ends--as I always knew it would--in my ringing bell and saying Please lay an extra place for lunch, at the same time trying to send silent telepathic message to Cook that meat-pie alone will now not be enough, and she must do something with eggs or cheese as first course.

(Cook's interpretation of this subsequently turns out to be sardines, faintly grilled, lying on toast, which I think a mistake, but shall probably not say so, as intentions good.)

Our Vicar's Wife and I then plunge into the concert, now only separated from us by twenty-four hours. What, says Our Vicar's Wife hopefully, am I giving them? Well--how would it be if I gave them "John Gilpin"? (Know it already and shall not have to learn anything new.) Splendid, perfectly splendid, Our Vicar's Wife asserts in rather unconvinced accents. The only thing is, Didn't I give it to them at Christmas, and two years ago at the Church Organ Fête, and, unless she is mistaken, the winter before that again when we got up that entertainment for St. Dunstan's?

If this is indeed fact, obviously scheme requires revision. What about "An Austrian Army"? "An Austrian Army?" says Our Vicar's Wife. Is that the League of Nations?

(Extraordinary frequency with which the unfamiliar is always labelled the League of Nations appalls me.)

I explain that it is very, very interesting example of Alliterative Poetry, and add thoughtfully: "Apt Alliteration's Artful Aid", at which Our Vicar's Wife looks astounded, and mutters something to the effect that I mustn't be too clever for the rest of the world.

Conversation temporarily checked, and I feel discouraged, and am relieved when gong rings. This, however, produces sudden spate of protests from Our Vicar's Wife, who says she really must be off, she couldn't dream of staying to lunch, and what can she have been thinking of all this time?

Entrance of Robert--whose impassive expression on being unexpectedly confronted with a guest I admire--gives fresh turn to entire situation, and we all find ourselves in dining-room quite automatically.

Conversation circles round the concert, recent arrivals at neighbouring bungalow, on whom we all say that we must call, and distressing affair in the village which has unhappily ended by Mrs. A. of Jubilee Cottages being summonsed for assault by her neighbour Mrs. H. Am whole-heartedly thrilled by this, and pump Our Vicar's Wife for details, which she gives spasmodically, but has to switch off into French, or remarks about the weather, whenever parlour-maid is in the room.

Cook omits to provide coffee--in spite of definite instructions always to do so when we have a guest--and have to do the best I can with cigarettes, although perfectly well aware that Our Vicar's Wife does not smoke, and never has smoked.

Concert appears on the *tapis* once more, and Robert is induced to promise that he will announce the items. Our Vicar's Wife, rather nicely, says that everyone would love it if dear little Vicky could dance for us, and I reply that she will still be away at school, and Our Vicar's Wife replies that she knows *that*, she only meant how nice it would be if she *hadn't* been away at school, and could have danced for us. Am ungrateful enough to reflect that this is as singularly pointless an observation as ever I heard.

What, asks Our Vicar's Wife, am I doing this afternoon? Why not come with her and call on the new people at the bungalow and get it over? In this cordial frame of mind we accordingly set out, and I drive Standard car, Our Vicar's Wife observing--rather unnecessarily--that it really is *wonderful* how that car goes on and on and on.

THE GARDENING FAMILY

Conversation continues, covering much ground that has been traversed before, and only diversified by hopes from me that the bungalow inhabitants may all be out, and modification from Our Vicar's Wife to the effect that she is hoping to get them to take tickets for the concert.

Aspirations as to absence of new arrivals dashed on the instant of drawing up at their gate, as girl in cretonne overall, older woman--probably mother--with spectacles, and man in tweeds, are all gardening like mad at the top of the steps. They all raise themselves from stooping postures, and all wipe their hands on their clothes--freakish resemblance here to not very well co-ordinated revue chorus--and make polite pretence of being delighted to see us. Talk passionately about rock-gardens for some time, then are invited to come indoors, which we do, but cretonne overall and man in tweeds--turns out to be visiting uncle--sensibly remain behind and pursue their gardening activities.

We talk about the concert--two one-and-sixpenny tickets disposed of successfully--hostess reveals that she thinks sparrows have been building in one of the water-pipes, and I say Yes, they do do that, and Our Vicar's Wife backs me up, and shortly afterwards we take our leave.

On passing through village, Our Vicar's Wife says that we may just as well look in on Miss Pankerton, as she wants to speak to her about the concert. I protest, but to no avail, and we walk up Miss P.'s garden-path and hear her practising the violin indoors, and presently she puts her head out of ground-floor window and shrieks--still practising--that we are to walk straight in, which we do, upon which she throws violin rather recklessly on to the sofa--which is already piled with books, music, newspapers, appliances for raffia-work, garden-hat, hammer, chisel, sample tin of biscuits, and several baskets--and shakes us by both hands. She also tells me that she sees I have taken her advice, and released a good many of my inhibitions in that book of mine. Should like to deny violently having ever taken any advice of Miss P.'s at all, or even noticed that she'd given it, but she goes on to say that I ought to pay more attention to Style--and I diverge into wondering inwardly whether she means prose, or clothes.

(If the latter, this is incredible audacity, as Miss P.'s own costume--on broiling summer's day--consists of brick-red cloth dress, peppered with glass knobs, and surmounted by abominable little brick-red three-tiered cape, closely fastened under her chin.)

Our Vicar's Wife again launches out into the concert--has Miss P. an *encore* ready? Yes, she has. Two, if necessary. She supposes genially that I am giving a reading of some little thing of my own--I reply curtly that I am not, and shouldn't dream of such a thing--and Our Vicar's Wife, definitely tactful, interrupts by saying that She Hears Miss P. is off to London directly the concert is over. If this is really so, and it isn't giving her any trouble, could she and would she just look in at Harrods', where they are having a sale, and find out what about tinned apricots?

416

Any reduction on a quantity, and how about carriage? And while she's in that neighbourhood--but not if it puts her out in any way--could she just look in at that little shop in the Fulham Road--the name has escaped Our Vicar's 'Wife for the moment--but it's really quite unmistakable--where they sell bicycle-parts? Our Vicar has lost a nut, quite a small nut, but rather vital, and it simply can't be replaced. Fulham Road the last hope.

Miss P.--I think courageously--undertakes it all, and writes down her London address, and Our Vicar's Wife writes down everything she can remember about Our Vicar's quite small nut, and adds on the same piece of paper the word "haddock".

But this, she adds, is only if Miss P. really *has* got time, and doesn't mind bringing it down with her, as otherwise it won't be fresh, only it does make a change and is so very difficult to get down here unless one is a regular customer.

At this point I intervene, and firmly suggest driving Our Vicar's Wife home, as feel certain that, if I don't, she will ask Miss P. to bring her a live crocodile from the Zoo, or something equally difficult of achievement.

We separate, with light-hearted anticipations of meeting again at the concert.

July 10th.--Concert permeates the entire day, and I spend at least an hour looking through *A Thousand and One Gems* and *The Drawing-room Reciter* in order to discover something that I once knew and can recapture without too much difficulty. Finally decide on narrative poem about Dick Turpin, unearthed in *Drawing-room Reciter*, and popular in far-away schooldays. Walk about the house with book in my hand most of the morning, and ask Robert to Hear Me after lunch, which he does, and only has to prompt three times. He handsomely offers to Hear Me again after tea, and to prompt if necessary during performance, and I feel that difficulty has been overcome.

Everything subject to interruption: small children arrive to ask if I can possibly lend them Anything Chinese, and am able to produce two paper fans--obviously made in Birmingham--one cotton kimono--eight-and-eleven at Messrs. Frippy and Coleman's--and large nautilus shell, always said to have been picked up by remote naval ancestor on the shore at Hawaii.

They express themselves perfectly satisfied, I offer them toffee, which they accept, and they depart with newspaper parcel. Later on message comes from the Rectory, to say that my contribution to Refreshments has not arrived, am covered with shame, and sacrifice new ginger-cake just made for to-day's tea.

Concert, in common with every other social activity in the village, starts at 7.30, and as Robert has promised to Take the Door and I am required to help with arranging the platform, we forgo dinner altogether, and eat fried fish at tea, and Robert drinks a whisky-and-soda.

Rumour has spread that Our Member and his wife are to appear at concert, but on my hoping this is true, since both are agreeable people, Robert shakes his head and says there's nothing in it. Everyone else, he admits, will be there, but *not* Our Member and his wife. I resign myself, and we both join in hoping that we shan't have to sit next Miss Pankerton. This hope realised, as Robert is put at the very end of front row of chairs, in order that he may get off and on platform frequently, and I am next him and have Our Vicar's Wife on my other side.

I ask for Our Vicar, and am told that his hay-fever has come on worse than ever, and he has been persuaded to stay at home. Regretful reference is made to this by Robert from the platform, and concert begins, as customary, with piano duet between Miss F. from the shop, and Miss W. of the smithy.

Have stipulated that Dick Turpin is to come on very early, so as to get it over, and am asked by Our Vicar's Wife if I am nervous. I say Yes, I am, and she is sympathetic, and tells me that the audience will be indulgent. They are, and Dick Turpin is safely accomplished with only one prompt from Robert--unfortunately delivered rather loudly just as I am purposely making what I hope is pregnant and dramatic pause--and I sit down again and prepare to enjoy myself.

Miss Pankerton follows me, is accompanied by pale young man who loses his place twice, and finally drops his music on the ground, picks it up again and readjusts it, while Miss P. glares at him and goes on vigorously with *Une Fête à Trianon* and leaves him to find his own way home as best he can. This he never quite succeeds in doing until final chord is reached, when he joins in again with an air of great triumph, and we all applaud heartily.

Miss P. bows, and at once launches into *encore*--which means that everybody else will have to be asked for an *encore* too, otherwise there will be feelings--and eventually sits down again and we go on to Sketch by the school-children, in which paper fans and cotton kimonos are in evidence.

The children look nice, and are delighted with themselves, and everybody else is delighted too, and Sketch brings down the house, at which Miss Pankerton looks superior and begins to tell me about Classical Mime by children that she once organised in large hall--seats two thousand people--near Birmingham, but I remain unresponsive, and only observe in reply that Jimmie H. of the mill is a duck, isn't he?

At this Miss P.'s eyebrows disappear into her hair, and she tells me about children she has seen in Italy who are pure Murillo types--but Our Butcher's Son here mounts the platform, in comic checks, bowler and walking-stick, and all is lost in storms of applause.

Presently Robert announces an Interval, and we all turn round in our seats and scan the room and talk to the people behind us, and someone brings forward a rumour that they've taken Close on Three Pounds at the Door, and we all agree that, considering the hot weather, it's wonderful.

IMPORTED TALENT GRACES THE PROGRAMME

Shortly afterwards Robert again ascends platform, and concert is resumed. Imported talent graces last half of the programme, in the shape of tall young gentleman who is said to be a friend of the Post Office, and who sings a doubtful comic song which is greeted with shrieks of appreciation. Our Vicar's Wife and I look at one another, and she shakes her head with a resigned expression, and whispers that it can't be helped, and she hopes the *encore* won't be any worse. It *is* worse, but not very much, and achieves enormous popular success.

By eleven o'clock all is over, someone has started God Save the King much too high, and we have all loyally endeavoured to make ourselves heard on notes that we just can't reach--Miss Pankerton has boldly attempted something that is evidently meant to be seconds, but results not happy--and we walk out into the night.

Robert drives me home. I say Weren't the children sweet? and Really, it was rather fun, wasn't it? and Robert changes gear, but makes no specific reply. Turn into our own lane, and I experience customary wonder whether house has been burnt to the ground in our absence, followed by customary reflection that anyway, the children are away at school--and then get severe shock as I see the house blazing with light from top to bottom.

Robert ejaculates, and puts his foot on the accelerator, and we dash in at gate, and nearly run into enormous blue car drawn up at front door.

I rush into the hall, and at the same moment Pamela Pringle rushes out of the drawing-room, wearing evening dress and grey fur coat with enormous collar, and throws herself on my neck. Am enabled, by mysterious process quite inexplicable to myself, to see through the back of my head that Robert has recoiled on threshold and retired with car to the garage.

Pamela P. explains that she is staying the night at well-known hotel, about forty miles away, and that when she found how near I was, she simply had to look me up, and she had simply no idea that I ever went out at night. I say that I never do, and urge her into the drawing-room, and there undergo second severe shock as I perceive it to be apparently perfectly filled with strange men. Pamela does not introduce any of them, beyond saying that it was Johnnie's car they came in, and Plum drove it. Waddell is not included in the party, nor anybody else that I ever saw in my life, and all seem to be well under thirty, except very tall man with bald head who is referred to as Alphonse Daudet, and elderly-looking one with moustache, who I think looks Retired, probably India.

I say weakly that they must have something to drink, and look at the bell--perfectly well aware that maids have gone to bed long ago--but Robert, to my great relief, materialises and performs minor miracle by producing entirely adequate quantities of whisky-and-soda, and sherry and biscuits for Pamela and myself. After this we all seem to know one another very well indeed, and Plum goes to the piano and plays waltz tunes popular in Edwardian days. (Pamela asks at intervals What that one was called? although to my certain knowledge she must remember them just as well as I do myself.)

Towards one o'clock Pamela, who has been getting more and more affectionate towards everybody in the room, suddenly asks where the darling children are sleeping, as she would love a peep at them. Forbear to answer that if they had been at home at all, they couldn't possibly have been sleeping through conversational and musical orgy of Pamela and friends, and merely reply that both are at school. What, shrieks Pamela, that tiny weeny little dot of a Vicky at school? Am I utterly unnatural? I say Yes, I am, as quickest means of closing futile discussion, and everybody accepts it without demur, and we talk instead about Auteuil, Helen de Liman de la Pelouse--(about whom I could say a great deal more than I do)--and Pamela's imminent return home to country house where Waddell and three children await her.

Prospect of this seems to fill her with gloom, and she tells me, aside, that 'Waddell doesn't quite realise her present whereabouts, but supposes her to be crossing from Ireland to-night, and I must remember this, if he says anything about it next time we meet.

Just as it seems probable that *séance* is to continue for the rest of the night, Alphonse Daudet rises without any warning at all, says to Robert that, for his part, he's not much good at late nights, and walks out of the room. We all drift after him, Pamela announces that she is going to drive, and everybody simultaneously exclaims No, No, and Robert says that there is a leak in the radiator, and fetches water from the bathroom.

(Should have preferred him to bring it in comparatively new green enamel jug, instead of incredibly ancient and battered brass can.)

Pamela throws herself into my arms, and murmurs something of which I hear nothing at all except Remember!--like Bishop Juxon and then gets into the car, and is obliterated by Plum on one side and elderly Indian on the other.

Just as they start, Helen Wills dashes out of adjacent bushes, and is nearly run over, but this tragedy averted, and car departs.

Echoes reach us for quite twenty minutes, of lively conversation, outbreaks of song and peals of laughter, as car flies down the lane and out of sight. Robert says that they've turned the wrong way, but does not seem to be in the least distressed about it, and predicts coldly that they will all end up in local police station.

I go upstairs, all desire for sleep having completely left me, and find several drawers in dressing-table wide open, powder all over the place like snow on Mont Blanc, unknown little pad of rouge on pillow, and face-towel handsomely streaked with lip-stick.

Bathroom is likewise in great disorder, and when Robert eventually appears he brings with him small, silver-mounted comb which he alleges that he found, quite incomprehensibly, on lowest step of remote flight of stairs leading to attics. I say satirically that I hope they all felt quite at home, Robert snorts in reply, and conversation closes.

July 13th.--Life resumes its ordinary course, and next excitement will doubtless be return of Robin and Vicky from school. Am already deeply immersed in preparations for this, and Cook says that extra help will be required. I reply that I think we shall be away at the sea for at least a month--(which is not perfectly true, as much depends on financial state)--and she listens to me in silence, and repeats that help will be wanted anyway, as children make such a difference. As usual, Cook gets the last word, and I prepare to enter upon familiar and exhausting campaign in search of Extra Help.

This takes up terrific amount of time and energy, and find it wisest to resign all pretensions to literature at the moment, and adopt role of pure domesticity. Interesting psychological reaction to this--(must remember to bring it forward in discussion with dear Rose, always so intelligent)--is that I tell Robert that next year I should like to Go to America. Robert makes little or no reply, except for rather eloquent look, but nevertheless I continue to think of going to America, and taking diary with me.

The Provincial Lady in America

July 7th.—Incredulous astonishment on receiving by second post—usually wholly confined to local bills and circulars concerning neighbouring Garden Fêtes—courteous and charming letter from publishers in America. They are glad to say that they feel able to meet me on every point concerning my forthcoming visit to the United States, and enclose contract for my approval and signature.

Am completely thrown on my beam-ends by this, but remember that visit to America *was* once mooted and that I light-heartedly reeled off stipulations as to financial requirements, substantial advances, and so on, with no faintest expectation that anybody would ever pay the slightest attention to me. This now revealed as complete fallacy. Read contract about fourteen times running, and eyes—figuratively speaking—nearly drop out of my head with astonishment. Can I possibly be worth all this?

Probably not, but should like to see America, and in any case am apparently committed to going there whether I want to or not.

Long and involved train of thought follows, beginning with necessity for breaking this news to Robert at the most auspicious moment possible, and going on to requirements of wardrobe, now at lowest possible ebb, and speculating as to whether, if I leave immediately after children's summer holidays, and return just before Christmas ones, it would not be advisable to embark upon Christmas shopping instantly.

All is interrupted by telephone ring—just as well, as I am rapidly becoming agitated—and voice says that it is Sorry to Disturb Me but is just Testing the Bell. I say Oh, all right, and decide to show publishers' letter to Robert after tea.

Am absent-minded all through tea as a result, and give Robert sugar, which he doesn't take. He says Am I asleep or what, and I decide to postpone announcement until evening.

It rains, and presently Florence appears and says If I please, the water's coming in on the landing through the ceiling, and I say she had better go at once and find Robert—it occurs to me too late that this attitude is far from consistent with feminist views so often proclaimed by myself—and meanwhile put small basin, really Vicky's sponge-bowl, on stairs to catch water, which drips in steadily.

Return to writing-table and decide to make list of clothes required for American trip, but find myself instead making list of all the things I shall have to do before starting, beginning with passport requirements and ending with ordering China tea from the Stores, 7 lbs. cheaper than smaller quantity.

Just as I am bringing this exercise to a close Robert comes in, and shortly afterwards I hear him stumble over sponge-bowl, on stairs, about which nobody has warned him. This definitely precludes breaking American news to him for the present.

He spends the evening up a ladder, looking at gutters, and I write to American publishers but decide not to post letter for a day or two.

July 8th.—Robert still unaware of impending announcement.

July 10th.—Telegram—reply prepaid—arrives from American publishers' representative in London, enquiring what I have decided, and this is unfortunately taken down over the telephone by Robert. Full explanations ensue, are not wholly satisfactory, and am left with extraordinary sensations of guilt and duplicity which I do not attempt to analyse.

Woman called Mrs. Tressider, whom I once met when staying with Rose, writes that she will be motoring in this direction with The Boy and will call in on us about tea-time to-morrow. *(Query:* Why not go out? *Answer*: *(a)* The laws of civilisation forbid. *(b)* Such a course might lead to trouble with dear Rose. *(c)* Cannot think of anywhere to go.)

Write, on the contrary, amiable letter to Mrs. T. saying that I look forward to seeing her and The Boy. Try to remember if I know anything whatever about the latter, but nothing materialises, not even approximate age. *Mem.:* Order extra milk for tea in case he turns out to be very young—but this not probable, from what I remember of Mrs. T.'s appearance.

Go with Robert in the afternoon to neighbouring Agricultural Show, and see a good many iron implements, also a bath standing all by itself outside a tent and looking odd, and a number of animals, mostly very large. Meet the Frobishers, who say There are more people here than there were last year, to which I agree—remember too late that I didn't come at all last year. Subsequently meet the Palmers, who say Not so many people as there were last year, and I again agree. Am slightly appalled on reflection, and wonder what would happen in the event of Frobishers and Palmers comparing notes as to their respective conversations with me—but this is unlikely in the extreme. (*Query:* Are the promptings of conscience regulated in proportion to the chances of discovery in wrongdoing? *Answer:* Obviously of a cynical nature.)

We continue to look at machinery, and Robert becomes enthusiastic over extraordinary-looking implement with teeth, and does not consider quarter of an hour too long in which to stand looking at it in silence. Feel that personally I have taken in the whole of its charms in something under six seconds—but do not, of course, say so. Fall instead into reverie about America, imagination runs away with me, and I die and am buried at sea before Robert says Well, if I've had enough of the caterpillar—(caterpillar?)—What about some tea?

We accordingly repair to tea-tent—very hot and crowded, and benches show tendency to tip people off whenever other people get up. I drink strong tea and eat chudleighs, and cake with cherries in it. Small girl opposite, wedged in between enormous grandfather and grandfather's elderly friend, spills her tea, it runs down the table, which is on a slope, and invades Robert's flannel trousers. He is not pleased, but says that It doesn't Matter, and we leave tent.

Meet contingent from our own village, exchange amiable observations, and Miss S. of the Post-Office draws me aside to ask if it is true that I am going to America? I admit that it is, and we agree that America is A Long Way Off; with rider from Miss S. to the effect that she has a brother in Canada, he's been there for years and has a Canadian wife whom Miss S. has never seen, and further addition that things seem to be in a bad way there, altogether.

This interchange probably overheard by Robert, as he later in the evening says to me rather suddenly that he supposes this American business is really settled? I reply weakly that I suppose it is, and immediately add, more weakly still, that I can cancel the whole thing if he wants me to. To this Robert makes no reply whatever, and takes up *The Times*.

I listen for some time to unsympathetic female voice from the wireless, singing song that I consider definitely repellent about a forest, and address picture-postcards to Robin and Vicky at school, switch off wireless just as unsympathetic female branches off into something about wild violets, write list of clothes that I shall require for America, and presently discover that I have missed the nine o'clock news altogether. Robert also discovers this, and is again not pleased.

Go up to bed feeling discouraged and notice a smell in the bathroom, but decide to say nothing about it till morning. Robert, coming up hours later, wakes me in order to enquire whether I noticed anything when I was having my bath? Am obliged to admit that I did, and he says this means taking up the whole of the flooring, and he'll take any bet it's a dead rat. Do not take up this challenge as *(a)* he is probably right, *(b)* I am completely sodden with sleep.

July 11th.—Car of extremely antiquated appearance rattles up to the door, and efficient-looking woman in grey trousers and a jumper gets out, evidently Mrs. Tressider. The Boy is shortly afterwards revealed, cowering amongst suit-cases, large kettle, portions of a camp-bed, folding rubber bath and case of groceries, in back of car. He looks pale and hunted, and is said to be fourteen, but seems to me more like ten. (Extra milk, however, almost certainly superfluous. *Mem.:* tell Cook to use up for pudding to-night.)

Mrs. T. very brisk and talkative, says that she and The Boy are on their way to Wales, where they propose to camp. I hint that the holidays have begun early and Mrs. T. shakes her head at me, frowns, hisses, and then says in a loud voice and with an unnatural smile that The Boy hasn't been very strong and was kept at home last term but will be going back next, and what he'd love better than anything would be a ramble round my lovely garden.

Am well aware that this exercise cannot possibly take more than four and a half minutes, but naturally agree, and The Boy disappears, looking depressed, in the direction of the pigsty.

Mrs. T. then tells me that he had a nervous breakdown not long ago, and that the school mismanaged him, and the doctor did him no good, and she is taking the whole thing into her own hands and letting him Run Wild for a time. (Should much like to enquire how she thinks he is to run wild on back seat of car, buried under a mountain of luggage.)

She then admires the house, of which she hasn't seen more than the hall door, says that I am marvellous—(very likely I am, but not for any reasons known to Mrs. T.)—and asks if it is true that I am off to America? Before I know where I am, we are discussing this quite violently still standing in the hall. Suggestion that Mrs. T. would like to go upstairs and take her hat off goes unheeded, so does appearance of Florence with kettle on her way to the dining-room. I keep my eye fixed on Mrs. T. and say Yes, Yes, but am well aware that Florence has seen grey trousers and is startled by them, and will quite likely give notice to-morrow morning.

Mrs. T. tells me about America—she knows New York well, and has visited Chicago, and once spoke to a Women's Luncheon Club in Boston, and came home *via* San Francisco and the Coast—and is still telling me about it when I begin, in despair of ever moving her from the hall, to walk upstairs. She follows in a sleep-walking kind of way, still talking, and am reminded of Lady Macbeth, acted by Women's Institute last winter.

Just as we reach top landing, Robert appears in shirt-sleeves, at bathroom door, and says that *half* a dead rat has been found, and the other half can't be far off. Have only too much reason to think that this is probably true. Robert then sees Mrs. T., is introduced, but—rightly—does not shake hands, and we talk about dead rat until gong sounds for tea.

The Boy reappears—inclination to creep sideways, rather than walk, into the room—and Mrs. T. asks Has he been galloping about all over the place, and The Boy smiles feebly but says nothing, which I think means that he is avoiding the lie direct.

Mrs. T. reverts to America, and tells me that I must let my flat whilst I am away, and she knows the very person, a perfectly charming girl, who has just been turned out of Taviton Street. I say: Turned out of Taviton Street? and have vision of perfectly charming girl being led away by the police to the accompaniment of stones and brickbats flung by the more exclusive inhabitants of Taviton Street, but it turns out that no scandal is implied, lease of perfectly charming girl's flat in Taviton Street having merely come to an end in the ordinary way. She has, Mrs. T. says, absolutely *nowhere* to go. Robert suggests a Y.W.C.A. and I say what about the Salvation Army, but these pleasantries not a success, and Mrs. T. becomes earnest, and says that Caroline Concannon would be the *Ideal* tenant. Literary, intelligent, easy to get on with, absolutely independent, and has a job in Fleet Street. Conceive violent prejudice against C. C. on the spot, and say hastily that flat won't be available till I sail, probably not before the 1st October. Mrs. T. then extracts from me, cannot imagine how, that flat contains two rooms, one with sofa-bed, that I am not in the least likely to be there during the summer holidays, that it would Help with the Rent if I had a tenant during August and September, and finally that there is no sound reason why C. Concannon should not move in on the spot, provided I will post the keys to her at once and write full particulars. Robert tries to back me up by saying that the post has gone, but Mrs. T. is indomitable and declares that she will catch it in the first town she comes to. She will also write to C. C. herself, and tell her what an Opportunity it all is. She then springs from the tea-table in search of writing materials, and Robert looks at me compassionately and walks out into the garden, followed at a distance by The Boy, who chews leaves as he goes, as if he hadn't had enough tea.

Feel worried about this, and suggest to Mrs. T. that Fabian doesn't look very strong, but she laughs heartily and replies that The. Boy is one of the wiry sort, and it's against all her principles to worry. Should like to reply that I wish she would apply this rule to her concern about my flat—but do not do so. Instead, am compelled by Mrs. T. to write long letter to her friend, offering her every encouragement to become my tenant in Doughty Street.

This, when accomplished, is triumphantly put into her bag by Mrs. T. with the assurance that she is pretty certain it is going to be absolutely All Right. Feel no confidence that her definition of all-rightness will coincide with mine.

We then sit in the garden and she tells me about education, a new cure for hay-fever, automatic gear-changing, and books that she has been reading. She also asks about the children, and I say that they are at school, and she hopes that the schools are run on New Thought lines—but to this I can only give a doubtful affirmative in Vicky's case and a definite negative in Robin's. Mrs. T. shakes her head, smiles and says something of which I only hear the word Pity. Feel sure that it will be of no use to pursue this line any further, and begin firmly to tell Mrs. T. about recent letter from Rose,—but in no time we are back at education again, and benefits that The Boy has derived from being driven about the country *tête-à-tête* with his parent. (Can only think that his previous state must have been deplorable indeed, if this constitutes an improvement.)

Time goes on, Mrs. T. still talking, Robert looks over box-hedge once and round may-tree twice, but disappears again without taking action. The Boy remains invisible.

Gradually find that I am saying Yes and I See at recurrent intervals, and that features are slowly becoming petrified into a glare. Mrs. T. fortunately appears to notice nothing, and goes on talking. I feel that I am probably going to yawn, and pinch myself hard, at the same time clenching my teeth and assuming expression of preternatural alertness that I know to be wholly unconvincing. Mrs. T. still talking. We reach Caroline Concannon again, and Mrs. T. tells me how wonderfully fortunate I shall be if what she refers to—inaccurately—as "our scheme" materialises. Decide inwardly that I shall probably murder Caroline C. within a week of meeting her, if she has anything like the number of virtues and graces attributed to her by Mrs. T.

Just as I am repeating to myself familiar lines, frequently recurred to in similar situations, to the effect that Time and the hour runs through the roughest day, all is brought to an end by Mrs. T., who leaps to her feet—movements surely extraordinarily sudden and energetic for a woman of her age?—and declares that they really must be getting on.

The Boy is retrieved, Robert makes final appearance round may-tree, and we exchange farewells. (Mine much more cordial than is either necessary or advisable, entirely owing to extreme relief at approaching departure).

Mrs. T. wrings my hand and Robert's, smiles and nods a good deal, says more about Caroline Concannon and the flat, and gets into driving seat. The Boy is already crouching amongst luggage at the back, and car drives noisily away.

Robert and I look at one another, but are too much exhausted to speak.

July 17th.—Decide that I must go to London, interview Caroline Concannon, and collect Robin and Vicky on their way home from school. I tell Robert this, and he says in a resigned voice that he supposes this American plan is going to Upset Everything—which seems to me both unjust and unreasonable. I explain at some length that Caroline C. has been foisted on me by Mrs. Tressider, that I have been in vigorous correspondence with her for days about the flat, and should like to bring the whole thing to an end, and that an escort for Vicky from London to Devonshire would have to be provided in any case, so it might just as well be me as anybody else. To all of this Robert merely replies, after some thought, that he always knew this American scheme would mean turning everything upside down, and he supposes we shall just have to put up with it.

Am quite unable to see that Robert has anything whatever to put up with at present, but realise that to say so will be of no avail, and go instead to the kitchen, where Cook begs my pardon, but it's all over the place that I'm off to America, and she doesn't know what to answer when people ask her about it. Nothing for it, evidently, but to tell Cook the truth, which I do, and am very angry with myself for apologetic note that I hear in my voice, and distinct sensation of guilt that invades me.

Cook does nothing to improve this attitude by looking cynically amused when I mutter something about my publisher having wished me to visit New York, and I leave the kitchen soon afterwards. Directly I get into the hall, remember that I never said anything about eggs recently put into pickle and that this has got to be done. Return to kitchen, Cook is in fits of laughter talking to Florence, who is doing nothing at the sink.

I say Oh, Cook—which is weak in itself, as an opening—deliver vacillating statement about eggs, and go away again quickly. Am utterly dissatisfied with my own conduct in this entire episode, and try to make up for it—but without success—by sharply worded postcard to the newsagent, who never remembers to send *The Field* until it is a fortnight old.

July 20th. Doughty Street.—Am taken to the station and seen off by Robert, who refrains from further reference to America, and regain Doughty Street flat, now swathed in dust-sheets. Remove these, go out into Gray's Inn Road and buy flowers, which I arrange in sitting-room, also cigarettes, and then telephone to Miss Caroline Concannon in Fleet Street office. Fleet Street office replies austerely that if I will wait a minute I shall be Put Through, and a good deal of buzzing goes on. Draw small unicorn on blotting-pad while I wait. Another voice says Do I want Miss Concannon? Yes, I do. Then just one minute, please. At least three minutes elapse, and I draw rather good near-Elizabethan cottage, with shading. Resentfully leave this unfinished when C. Concannon at last attains the telephone and speaks to me. Voice sounds young and cheerful, nicer than I expected. We refer to Mrs. Tressider, and recent correspondence, and agree that an early interview is desirable. Shall she, says Caroline C., come round at once in her tiny car? Nothing could be easier. Am much impressed *(a)* at her having a tiny car, *(b)* at her being able to drive it in London, *(c)* at the ease with which she can leave Fleet Street office to get on without her services.

Look round flat, which has suddenly assumed entirely degraded appearance, feel certain that she will despise both me and it, and hastily powder my nose and apply lipstick. Fleeting fancy crosses my mind that it would look rather dashing, and perhaps impress C. C., if I put on last year's beach-pyjamas—red linen, with coffee-coloured top—but courage fails me, and I remain as I am, in blue delaine, thirty-five shillings off the peg from Exeter High Street establishment.

Car is audible outside, I look from behind curtains and see smallest baby Austin in the world—(I should imagine)—draw up with terrific *verve* outside the door. Incredibly slim and smart young creature steps out—black-and-white frock with frills, tiny little white hat well over one ear, and perfectly scarlet mouth. She is unfortunately inspired to look up at window just as I crane my neck from behind curtain, and am convinced that she has seen me perfectly well, and is— rightly—disgusted at exhibition of vulgar and undignified curiosity.

Bell rings—very autocratic touch, surely?—I open the door and Miss C. comes in. Should be very sorry to think that I am dismayed solely because she is younger, smarter and better-looking than I am myself.

Agreeable conversation ensues, C. C. proves easy and ready to talk, we meet on the subject of Mrs. Tressider—boy looks browbeaten, Mrs. T. altogether too breezy and bracing—and further discover that we both know, and rather admire, Pamela Pringle. What, I ask, is the latest about Pamela, of whom I have heard nothing for ages? Oh, don't I know? says Miss C. Not about the Stock-Exchange man, and how he put Pamela on to a perfectly good thing, and it went up and up, and Pamela sold out and went to Antibes on the proceeds, and had a most thrilling affair with a gigolo, and the Stock Exchange nearly went mad? At this I naturally scream for details, which C. C. gives me with immense enthusiasm.

We remain utterly absorbed for some time, until at last I remember that the flat still has to be inspected, and offer to show Miss C. round. (This a complete farce, as she could perfectly well show herself, in something under five minutes.)

She says How lovely to everything, but pauses in the bathroom, and I feel convinced that she has a prejudice against the geyser. (It would be even stronger if she knew as much about this one as I do.) Silence continues until I become unnerved, and decide that I must offer to take something off the rent. Just as I am getting ready to say so, C. C. suddenly utters: to the effect that she would like me to call her Caroline.

Am surprised, relieved and rather gratified, and at once agree. Request, moreover, seems to imply that we are to see something of one another in the future, which I take it means that she is prepared to rent the flat. Further conversation reveals that this is so, and that she is to move in next week, on the understanding that I may claim use of sofa-bed in sitting-room if I wish to do so. C. C. handsomely offers to let me have the bedroom, and take sofa herself, I say No, No, and we part with mutual esteem and liking.

Am much relieved, and feel that the least I can do is to write and thank Mrs. Tressider, to whom the whole thing is owing, but unaccountable reluctance invades me, and day comes to an end without my having done so.

July 22nd.—Ring up dear Rose and consult her about clothes for America. She says at once that she knows the very person. A young man who will one day be a second Molyneux. I mustn't dream of going to anybody else. She will send me the address on a postcard. She also knows of a woman who makes hats, a remedy for seasickness and a new kind of hair-slide. I say Yes, and Thank you very much, to everything, and engage to meet Rose for lunch to-morrow at place in Charlotte Street where she says elliptically that you can eat on the pavement.

Just as I have hung up receiver, telephone bell rings again and I find myself listening to Mrs. Tressider. She has, she says, left The Boy in Wales with his father—(never knew he had one, and am startled)—and dashed up on business for one night, but is dashing back again to-morrow. She just wanted to say how glad she was that Caroline and I have settled about the flat. She always knew it was the ideal arrangement for us both.

Experience instant desire to cancel deal with Caroline C. on the spot, but do not give way to it, and conversation ends harmoniously, with promise from myself to let Mrs. T. know when and in what ship I am sailing, as she thinks she may be able to Do Something about it.

July 24th.—Arrival of Robin at Charing Cross, where I go to meet him and see customary collection of waiting parents, and think how depressing they all look, and feel certain they think exactly the same about me. Train is late, as usual, and I talk to pale mother in beige coat and skirt and agree that the boys all come back looking very well, and that schools nowadays are quite different, and children really adore being there. After that she tells me that her Peter hates games and is no good at lessons, and I say that my Robin has never really settled down at school at all, and we agree that boys are much more difficult than girls. (Shall not, however, be surprised, if I find occasion to reverse this dictum after a few days of dear Vicky's society at home.)

Train comes in, and parents, including myself, hurry madly up and down platform amongst shoals of little boys in red caps. Finally discover Robin, who has grown enormously, and is struggling under immensely heavy bag.

We get into a taxi, and dash to Poland Street, where Green Line bus deposits Vicky with suitcase—handle broken, and it has to be dragged bulging hat, box, untidy-looking brown-paper parcel, two books—*Mickey Mouse Annual* and *David Copperfield,* which I think odd mixture—and half-eaten packet of milk chocolate.

She screams and is excited, and says she is hungry, and Robin supports her with assertion that he is absolutely starving, and we leave luggage at depot and go and eat ices at establishment in Oxford Street.

Remainder of the day divided between shopping, eating and making as much use as possible of Underground moving stairway, for which R. and V. have a passion.

July 25th.—Telephone appeal from Caroline Concannon saying can she move into Doughty Street flat immediately, as this is the best day for the van. Am alarmed by the sound of the van, and ask if she has realised that the flat is furnished already, and there isn't much room to spare. Yes, she knows all that, and it's only one or two odds and ends, and if she may come round with a tape-measure, she can soon tell. Feel that this is reasonable and must be acceded to, and suggest to the children that they should play quietly with bricks in the bedroom. They agree to this very readily, and shortly afterwards I hear them playing, not quietly at all, with a cricket-ball in the kitchen.

Caroline Concannon arrives soon afterwards—velocity of tiny car, in relation to its size, quite overwhelming—and rushes into the flat. No sign of tape-measure, but the van, she says, will be here directly. This proves to be only too true, and the van shortly afterwards appears, and unloads a small black wardrobe, a quantity of pictures—some of these very, very modern indeed and experience fleeting hope that the children will not insist on detailed examination, but this probably old-fashioned and not to be encouraged—two chairs, at least seventeen cushions, little raffia footstool that I do not care about, plush dog with green eyes that I care about still less,—two packing-cases, probably china?—a purple quilt which is obviously rolled round a large number of miscellaneous objects, and a portmanteau that C. C. says is full of books. I ask What about her clothes, and she says, Oh, those will all come later with the luggage.

Am rather stunned by this, and take no action at all. C. C. is active and rushes about, and shortly afterwards Robin and Vicky emerge from the kitchen and become active too. Small man materialises and staggers up and down stairs, carrying things, and appeals to me—as well he may—about where they are to go. I say Here, and What about *that* corner, as hopefully as possible, and presently find that all my own belongings are huddled together in the middle of the sitting-room, like survivors of a wreck clinging to a raft, while all C. C.'s goods and chattels are lined in rows against the walls.

C. C.—must remember to call her Caroline—is apologetic, and offers rather recklessly to take all her things away again, if I like, but this is surely purely rhetorical, and I take little notice of it. At twelve o'clock she suddenly suggests that the children would like an ice, and rushes them away, and I am left feeling partly relieved at getting rid of them and partly agitated because it is getting so near lunch-time.

Make a few tentative efforts about furniture and succeed in clearing a gangway down the middle of sitting-room—this a definite improvement—but find increasing tendency to move everything that seems to be occupying too much space, into kitchen. Caroline has evidently had same inspiration, as I find small armchair there, unknown to me hitherto, standing on its head, two waste-paper baskets (something tells me these are likely to be very much used in the near future), large saucepan, Oriental-looking drapery that might be a bed-spread, and folded oak table that will not, to my certain knowledge, fit into any single room when extended.

Telephone bell interrupts me—just as well, as I am growing rather agitated—and Rose's voice enquires if I have done anything yet about my clothes for America. Well, no, not so far, but I am really going to see about it in a day or two. Rose is, not unjustifiably, cynical about this, and says that she will herself make an appointment for me to-morrow afternoon. Can see no way of getting out of this, as Felicity Fairmead has offered to take children for the day, so as to set me free, and therefore can only acquiesce. Unescapable conviction comes over me that I shan't be able to find a complete set of undergarments that match, for when I have to be tried on but perhaps this will only take place at a later stage? Must remember to bear the question in mind when dealing with laundry, but am aware that I have been defeated on the point before, and almost certainly shall be again.

Caroline Concannon returns with children, we all go out together and have inexpensive lunch of fried fish, chipped potatoes and meringues at adjacent Lyons, after which there seems to be a general feeling that C. C. is one of ourselves, and both the children address her by her Christian name.

Am much struck by all of this, and decide that the Modern Girl has been maligned. Possible material here for interesting little article on Preconceived Opinions in regard to Unfamiliar Types? Have vague idea of making a few notes on these lines, but this finally resolves itself into a list of minor articles required by Robin and Vicky, headed, as usual, by Tooth-Paste.

(Query: Do all schools possess a number of pupils whose parents are unable or unwilling to supply them with tooth-paste, and are they accordingly invited to share that of the better-equipped? Can think of no other explanation for the permanently depleted state of tubes belonging to Robin and Vicky.)

August 15th.—Holidays rush by, with customary dizzying speed and extremely unusual number of fine days. We go for picnics—sugar is forgotten once, and salt twice—drive immense distances in order to bathe for ten minutes in sea which always turns out cold—and Robin takes up tennis. Felicity Fairmead comes to stay, is as popular as ever with children, and more so than ever with Robert as she has begun to play the piano again, and does so whenever we ask her. This leads to successful musical evenings, except when I undertake to sing solo part of "Alouette" and break down rather badly. Make up for it—or so I think—by restrained, but at the same time moving, interpretation of "In the Gloaming". Felicity, however, says that it reminds her of her great-grandmother, and Robert enquires if that is What's-his-name's Funeral March? and I decide to sing no more for the present.

Caroline Concannon also honours us by week-end visit, and proves incredibly lively. Am led to ask myself at exactly what stage youth, in my own case, gave way to middle-age, and become melancholy and introspective. C. C., however, insists on playing singles with me at eleven o'clock in the morning, and showers extravagant praise on what she rightly describes as my *one* shot, and soon afterwards she suggests that we should all go in the car to the nearest confectioner's and get ices. Children are naturally enthusiastic, and I find myself agreeing to everything, including bathing-picnic in the afternoon.

This leads to complete neglect of household duties hitherto viewed as unescapable, also to piles of unanswered letters, unmended clothes and total absence of fresh flowers indoors, but no cataclysmic results ensue, and am forced to the conclusion that I have possibly exaggerated the importance of these claims on my time hitherto.

Ask C. C. about the flat and she is airy, and says Oh, she hopes I won't think it too frightfully untidy—(am perfectly certain that I shall)—and she had a new washer put on the kitchen tap the other day, which she evidently thinks constitutes conclusive evidence as to her being solid and reliable tenant. She also adds that there is now a kitten in Doughty Street, practically next door, and that the chandelier needs cleaning but can only be done by A Man. Am struck, not for the first time, by the number of contingencies, most of a purely domestic character, that can apparently only be dealt with by A Man.

August 31st.—Imperatively worded postcard from Mrs. Tressider informs me that I am to write instantly to offices of the Holland-Amerika Line, and book passage in s.s. *Rotterdam,* sailing September 30th. If I do this, says postcard, very illegibly indeed, I shall be privileged to travel with perfectly delightful American, wife of well-known financier, and great friend of Mrs. T.'s. Details will follow, but there is not a moment to be lost. Am infected by this spirit of urgency, write madly to the Holland-Amerika Line, and then wonder—too late—whether I really want to thrust my companionship on perfectly delightful unknown American and—still more—whether she will see any reason to thank me for having done so. Letter, however, arrives from shipping offices, enclosing enormous plan, entirely unintelligible to me, over which Robert spends a good deal of time with his spectacles on, and quantities of information from which I extract tonnage of ship—which leaves me cold—and price of single fare, which is less than I expected, and reassures me. Robert says that he supposes this will do as well as anything else—not at all enthusiastically—and Vicky quite irrationally says that I *must* go in that ship and no other. (Disquieting thought: Will Vicky grow up into a second Mrs. T.? Should not be in the very least surprised if she did.)

Second postcard from Mrs. T. arrives: She has seen her American friend—(How?)—and the friend is absolutely delighted at the idea of travelling with me, and will do everything she can to help me. Idle impulse assails me to write back on another postcard and say that it would really help me more than anything if she would pay my passage for me—but this, naturally, dismissed at once. Further inspection of postcard, which is extensively blotted, reveals something written in extreme right-hand corner, of which I am unable to make out a word. Robert is appealed to, and says that he thinks it has something to do with luggage, but am quite unable to subscribe to this, and refer to Our Vicar's Wife, who has called in about morris-dancing. She says Yes, yes, where are her glasses, and takes a good many things out of her bag and puts them all back again and finally discovers glasses in a little case in her bicycle basket, and studies postcard from a distance of at least a yard away.

Result of it all is that It Might be Anything, and Our Vicar's Wife always has said, and always will say, that plain sewing is a great deal more important than all this higher education. As for Our Vicar, says Our Vicar's Wife, he makes an absolute point of seeing that the Infant School is taught its multiplication-table in the good old-fashioned way.

We all agree that this is indeed essential, and conversation drifts off to Harvest Festival, drought in Cheshire—Our Vicar's married sister in despair about her french beans—tennis at Wimbledon, and increasing rarity of the buzzard-hawk.

Hours later, Robin picks up Mrs. T.'s postcard, and reads the whole of it from end to end, including postscript, to the effect that I must be prepared to pay duty on every single thing I take to America, especially anything new in the way of clothes. Am so much impressed by dear Robin's skill that I quite forget to point out utter undesirability of reading postcards addressed to other people till long after he has gone to bed.

Am much disturbed at the idea of paying duty on all my clothes, and lie awake for some time wondering if I can possibly evade obligations already incurred towards Rose's friend—the coming Molyneux—but decide that this cannot honourably be done.

Sept. 1st.—Call upon aged neighbour, Mrs. Blenkinsop, to meet married daughter Barbara Carruthers, newly returned from India with baby. Find large party assembled, eight females and one very young man—said to be nephew of local doctor—who never speaks at all but hands tea about very politely and offers me dish containing swiss-roll no less than five times.

Barbara proves to have altered little, is eloquent about India, and talks a good deal about *tiffin,* also Hot Weather and Going up to the Hills. We are all impressed, and enquire after husband. He is, says Barbara, well, but he works too hard. Far too hard. She thinks that he will kill himself, and is always telling him so.

Temporary gloom cast by the thought of Crosbie Carruthers killing himself is dissipated by the baby, who crawls about on the floor, and is said to be like his father. At this, however, old Mrs. Blenkinsop suddenly rebels, and announces that dear Baby is the image of herself as a tiny, and demands the immediate production of her portrait at four years old to prove her words. Portrait is produced, turns out to be a silhouette, showing pitch-black little profile with ringlets and necklace, on white background, and we all say Yes, we quite see what she means.

Baby very soon afterwards begins to cry—can this be cause and effect?—and is taken away by Barbara.

Mrs. B. tells us that it is a great joy to have them with her, she has given up the whole of the top floor to them, and it means engaging an extra girl, and of course dear Baby's routine has to come before everything, so that her little house is upside-down—but that, after all, is nothing. She is old, her life is over, nothing now matters to her, except the welfare and happiness of her loved ones.

Everybody rather dejected at these sentiments, and I seek to make a diversion by referring to approaching departure for America.

Several pieces of information are then offered to me:

The Americans are very hospitable.

The Americans are so hospitable that they work one to death. (Analogy here with Barbara's husband?)

The Americans like the English.

The Americans do not like the English at all.

It is not safe to go out anywhere in Chicago without a revolver. (To this I might well reply that, so far as I am concerned, it would be even less safe to go out with one.)

Whatever happens I must visit Hollywood, eat waffles, see a baseball match, lunch at a Women's Club, go up to the top of the Woolworth Building, and get invited to the house of a millionaire so as to see what it's like.

All alcohol in America is wood-alcohol and if I touch it I shall die, or become blind or go raving mad.

It is quite impossible to refuse to drink alcohol in America, because the Americans are so hospitable.

Decide after this to go home, and consult Robert as to advisability of cancelling proposed visit to America altogether.

Sept. 7th.—Instructions from America reach me to the effect that I am to stay at Essex House, in New York. Why Essex? Should much have preferred distinctive American name, such as Alabama or Connecticut House. Am consoled by enclosure, which gives photograph of superb skyscraper, and informs me that, if I choose, I shall be able to dine in the Persian Coffee Shop, under the direction of a French chef, graduate of the Escoffier School.

The English Molyneux sends home my clothes in instalments, am delighted with flowered red silk which is—I hope—to give me self-confidence in mounting any platform on which I may have the misfortune to find myself—also evening dress, more or less devoid of back, in very attractive pale brocade. Show red silk to Our Vicar's Wife, who says Marvellous, dear, but do not produce backless evening frock.

Sept. 20th.—Letter arrives from complete stranger—signature seems to be Ella B. Chickhyde, which I think odd—informing me that she is so disappointed that the sailing of the *Rotterdam* has been cancelled, and we must sail instead by the *Statendam,* on October 7th, unless we like to make a dash for the *previous* boat, which means going on board the day after to-morrow, and will I be so kind as to telegraph? Am thrown into confusion by the whole thing, and feel that Robert will think it is all my fault—which he does, and says that Women Never Stick to Anything for Five Minutes Together—which is wholly unjust, but makes me feel guilty all the same. He also clears up identity of Ella B. Chickhyde, by saying that she must be the friend of that woman who came in a car on her way to Wales, and talked. This at once recalls Mrs. Tressider, and I telegraph to Ella B. Chickhyde to say that I hope to sail on the *Statendam.*

Last day of the holidays then takes its usual course. I pack frantically in the intervals of reading *Vice Versa* aloud, playing Corinthian Bagatelle, sanctioning an expedition to the village to buy sweets, and helping Vicky over her holiday task, about which she has suddenly become acutely anxious, after weeks of brassy indifference.

Sept. 21st.—Take children to London, and general dispersal ensues. Vicky drops large glass bottle of sweets on platform at Waterloo, with resultant breakage, amiable porter rushes up and tells her not to cry, as he can arrange it all. This he does by laboriously separating broken glass from sweets, with coal-black hands, and placing salvage in a piece of newspaper. Present him with a florin, and am not sufficiently strong-minded to prevent Vicky from going off with newspaper parcel bulging in coat pocket.

Robin and I proceed to Charing Cross—he breaks lengthy silence by saying that to *him* it only seems one second ago that I was meeting him here, instead of seeing him off—and this moves me so much that I am quite unable to answer, and we walk down Platform Six—Special School-train—without exchanging a syllable. The place is, as usual, crowded with parents and boys, including minute creature who can scarcely be seen under grey wide-awake hat, and who I suggest must be a new boy. Robin, however, says Oh no, that's *quite* an old boy, and seems slightly amused.

Parting, thanks to this blunder on my part, is slightly less painful than usual, and I immediately go and have my hair washed and set, in order to distract my thoughts, before proceeding to Doughty Street. Caroline awaits me there, together with lavish display of flowers that she has arranged in my honour, which touches me, and entirely compensates for strange disorder that prevails all over flat. Moreover, C. C. extraordinarily sweet-tempered and acquiesces with apologies when I suggest the removal of tiny green hat, two glass vases and a saucepan, from the bathroom.

Sept. 25th.—Attend dinner-party of most distinguished people, given by celebrated young publisher connected with New York house. Evening is preceded by prolonged mental conflict on my part, concerning—as usual—clothes. Caroline C. urges me to put on new backless garment, destined for America, but superstitious feeling that this may be unlucky assails me, and I hover frantically between very old blue and comparatively new black-and-white stripes. Caroline is sympathetic throughout, but at seven o'clock suddenly screams that she is due at a sherry party and must rush, she'd forgotten all about it.

(Extraordinary difference between this generation and my own impresses me immensely. Should never, at C. C.'s age—or probably any other—have forgotten even a tea-party, let alone a sherry one. This no time, however, for indulging in philosophical retrospective studies.)

Baby Austin, as usual, is at the door; C. C. leaps into it and vanishes, at terrific pace, into Guilford Street, leaving me to get into black-and-white stripes, discover that black evening shoes have been left at home, remember with relief that grey brocade ones are here and available, and grey silk stockings that have to be mended, but fortunately above the knee. Result of it all is that I am late, which I try to feel is modern, but really only consider bad-mannered.

Party is assembled when I arrive, am delighted to see Distinguished Artist, well known to me in Hampstead days, whom I at once perceive to have been celebrating the occasion almost before it has begun—also famous man of letters next whom I am allowed to sit at dinner, and actor with Whom I have—in common with about ninety-nine per cent of the feminine population—been in love for years. (This state of affairs made much worse long before the end of the evening.)

Party is successful from start to finish, everybody wishes me a pleasant trip to America, I am profoundly touched and feel rather inclined to burst into tears—hope this has nothing to do with the champagne—but fortunately remember in time that a' scarlet nose and patchy face can be becoming to no one. (Marked discrepancy here between convention so prevalent in fiction, and state of affairs common to everyday life.)

Am escorted home at one o'clock by Distinguished Artist and extraordinarily pretty girl called Dinah; and retire to sofa-bed in sitting-room, taking every precaution not to wake Caroline C., innocently slumbering in bedroom.

Just as I have dropped asleep, hall-door bangs, and I hear feet rushing up the stairs, and wonder if it can be burglars, but decide that only very amateurish ones, with whom I could probably deal, would make so much noise. Point is settled by sudden appearance of light under bedroom door, and stifled, but merry rendering of "Stormy Weather" which indicates that C. C. has this moment returned from belated revels no doubt connected with sherry party. Am impressed by this fresh evidence of the gay life lived by the young to-day, and go to sleep again.

Oct. 1st.—Return home yesterday coincides with strong tendency to feel that I can't possibly go to America at all, and that most likely I shall never come back alive if I do, and anyway everything here will go to rack and ruin without me. Say something of these premonitions to Robert, who replies that *(a)* It would be great waste of money to cancel my passage now—*(b)* I shall be quite all right if I remember to look where I'm going when I cross the streets—and*(c)* he dares say Cook and Florence will manage very well. I ask wildly if he will cable to me if anything goes wrong with the children, and he says Certainly and enquires what arrangements I have made about the servants' wages? Remainder of the evening passes in domestic discussion, interrupted by telephone call from Robert's brother William, who says that he wishes to see me off at Southampton. Am much gratified by this, and think it tactful not to enquire why dear William's wife Angela has not associated herself with the scheme.

Oct. 7th.—Long and agitating day, of which the close finds me on board s.s.*Statendam,* but cannot yet feel wholly certain how this result has been achieved, owing to confusion of mind consequent on packing, unpacking—for purpose of retrieving clothes-brush and cheque-book, accidentally put in twenty-four hours too early—consulting numbers of Lists and Notes, and conveying self and luggage—six pieces all told, which I think moderate—to boat-train at Waterloo.

Caroline Concannon has handsomely offered to go with me to Southampton, and I have accepted, and Felicity Fairmead puts in unexpected and gratifying appearance at Waterloo. I say, Isn't she astonished to find me travelling first-class? and she replies No, not in the least, which surprises me a good deal, but decide that it's a compliment in its way.

Caroline C. and I have carriage to ourselves, but label on window announces that H. Press is to occupy Corner Seat, window side, facing engine. We decide that H. P. is evidently fussy, probably very old, and—says Caroline with an air of authority—most likely an invalid. The least we can do, she says, is to put all hand-luggage up on the rack and leave one side of carriage entirely free, so that he can put his feet up. Felicity says, Suppose he is lifted in on a wheel-chair? but this we disregard, as being mere conjecture. All, however, is wasted, as H. Press fails to materialise, and train, to unbounded concern of us all three, goes off without him.

Robert and William meet us at Southampton, having motored from Devonshire and Wiltshire respectively, and take us on board tender, where we all sit in a draught, on very hard seats. Robert shows me letters he has brought me from home—one from Our Vicar's Wife, full of good wishes very kindly expressed, and will I, if absolutely convenient, send photograph of Falls of Niagara, so helpful in talking to school-children about wonders of Nature—the rest mostly bills. I tell Robert madly that I shall pay them all from America—which I know very well that I shan't—and we exchange comments, generally unfavourable, about fellow-passengers. Tender gets off at last—draught more pervasive than ever. Small steamers rise up at intervals, and Caroline says excitedly: There she is! to each of them. Enormous ship with four funnels comes into view, and I say: There she is! but am, as usual, wrong, and *Statendam* only reached hours later, when we are all overawed by her size, except Robert.

On board Robert takes charge of everything—just as well, as I am completely dazed—conducts us to Cabin 89, miraculously produces my luggage, tells me to have dinner and unpack the moment the tender goes off—(this advice surely strikes rather sinister note?)—and shows me where dining-saloon is, just as though he'd been there every day for years.

He then returns me to cabin, where William is quietly telling Caroline the story of his life, rings for steward and commands him to bring a bottle of champagne, and my health is drunk.

Am touched and impressed, and wonder wildly if it would be of any use to beg Robert to change all his plans and come with me to America after all? Unable to put this to the test, as bell rings loudly and dramatically, tender is said to be just off, and farewells become imminent. Robert, William and Caroline are urged by various officials to Mind their Heads, please, and Step this way—I exchange frantic farewells with all three, feel certain that I shall never see any of them again, and am left in floods of tears in what seems for the moment to be complete and utter solitude, but afterwards turns out to be large crowd of complete strangers, stewards in white jackets and colossal palms in pots.

Can see nothing for it but to follow Robert's advice and go to dining-saloon, which I do, and find myself seated next to large and elderly American lady who works her way steadily through eight-course dinner and tells me that she is on a very strict diet. She also says that her cabin is a perfectly terrible one, and she knew the moment she set foot on the ship that she was going to dislike everything on board. She is, she says, like that. She always knows within the first two minutes whether she is going to like or dislike her surroundings. Am I, she enquires, the same? Should like to reply that it never takes me more than one minute to know exactly what I feel, not only about my surroundings, but about those with whom I have to share them. However, she waits for no answer, so this *mot*, as so many others, remains unuttered.

Friend of Mrs. Tressider, whom I have forgotten all about, comes up half-way through dinner, introduces herself as Ella Wheelwright—Chickhyde evidently a mistake—and seems nice. She introduces married sister and husband, from Chicago, and tells me that literary American, who says he has met me in London, is also on board. Would I like to sit at their table for meals? I am, however, to be perfectly honest about this. Am perfectly honest and say Yes, I should, but wonder vaguely what would happen if perfect honesty had compelled me to say No?

Elderly American lady seems faintly hurt at prospect of my desertion, and says resentfully how nice it is for me to have found friends, and would I like to come and look at her cabin? Question of perfect honesty not having here been raised, I do so, and can see nothing wrong with it whatever. Just as I am leaving it-which I do as soon as civility permits—see that name on door is H. Press. Must remember to send Felicity and Caroline postcards about this.

Oct. 9th.—Interior of my own cabin becomes extremely familiar, owing to rough weather and consequent collapse. Feel that I shall probably not live to see America, let alone England again.

Oct. 11th.—Emerge gradually from very, very painful state of affairs. New remedy for sea-sickness provided by Rose may or may not be responsible for my being still alive, but that is definitely the utmost that can be said for it.

Remain flat on my back, and wish that I could either read or go to sleep, but both equally impossible. Try to recall poetry, by way of passing the time, and find myself involved in melancholy quotations: *Sorrow's crown of sorrow is remembering happier things* alternating with *A few more years shall roll.* Look at snapshots of Robert and the children, but this also a failure, as I begin to cry and wonder why I ever left them. Have died and been buried at sea several times before evening and—alternatively—have heard of fatal accident to Robin, dangerous illness of Vicky, and suicide of Robert, all owing to my desertion. Endless day closes in profound gloom and renewed nausea.

Oct. 12th.—Situation improved, I get up and sit on deck, eat raw apple for lunch, and begin to feel that I may, after all, live to see America. Devote a good deal of thought, and still more admiration, to Christopher Columbus who doubtless performed similar transit to mine, under infinitely more trying conditions.

Ella Wheelwright comes and speaks to me—she looks blooming in almond-green dress with cape, very smart—and is compassionate. We talk about Mrs. Tressider—a sweet thing, says Ella W., and I immediately acquiesce, though description not in the least applicable to my way of thinking—and agree that The Boy does not look strong. (Perceive that this is apparently the only comment that ever occurs to anybody in connection with The Boy, and wonder if he is destined to go through life with this negative reputation and no other.)

Just as I think it must be tea-time, discover that all ship clocks differ from my watch, and am informed by deck steward that The Time Goes Back an Hour every night. Pretend that I knew this all along, and had merely forgotten it, but am in reality astonished, and wish that Robert was here to explain.

Day crawls by slowly, but not too unpleasantly, and is enlivened by literary American, met once before in London, who tells me all about English authors in New York, and gives me to understand that if popular, they get invited to cocktail parties two or three times daily, and if unpopular, are obliged to leave the country.

Oct. 14th.—America achieved. Statue of Liberty, admirably lit up, greets me at about seven o'clock this evening, entrance to harbour is incredibly beautiful, and skyscrapers prove to be just as impressive as their reputation, and much more decorative.

Just as I am admiring everything from top deck two unknown young women suddenly materialise—(risen from the ocean, like Venus?)—also young man with camera, and I am approached and asked if I will at once give my views on The United States, the American Woman and Modern American Novels. Young man says that he wishes to take my photograph, which makes me feel like a film star—appearance, unfortunately, does nothing to support this illusion—and this is duly accomplished, whilst I stand in *dégagé* attitude, half-way down companion-ladder on which I have never before set foot throughout the voyage.

Exchange farewells with fellow-passengers—literary American, now known to me as Arthur, is kindness itself and invites me on behalf of his family to come and visit them in Chicago, and see World Fair—Ella Wheelwright also kind, and gives me her card, but obviously much preoccupied with question of Customs—as well she may be, as she informs me that she has declared two hundred dollars' worth of purchases made in Europe, and has another five hundred dollars' worth undeclared.

American publisher has come to meet me and is on the Dock, I am delighted to see him, and we sit on a bench for about two hours, surrounded by luggage, none of which seems to be mine Eventually, however, it appears—which slightly surprises me—publisher supports me through Customs inspection, and finally escorts me personally to Essex House, where I am rung up five times before an hour has elapsed, with hospitable greetings and invitations. (Nothing from Ella Wheelwright, and cannot help wondering if she has perhaps been arrested?)

Am much impressed by all of it, including marvellous view from bedroom on sixteenth story, but still unable to contemplate photographs of children with complete calm.

Oct. 16th.—Come to the conclusion that everything I have ever heard or read about American Hospitality is an understatement. Telephone bell rings incessantly from nine o'clock onwards, invitations pour in, and complete strangers ring up to say that they liked my book, and would be glad to give a party for me at any hour of the day or night. Am plunged by all this into a state of bewilderment, but feel definitely that it will be a satisfaction to let a number of people at home hear about it all, and realise estimation in which professional writers are held in America.

(Second thought obtrudes itself here, to the effect that, if I know anything of my neighbours, they will receive any such information with perfect calm and probably say Yes, they've always heard that Americans were Like That.)

Am interviewed by reporters on five different occasions—one young gentleman evidently very tired, and droops on a sofa without saying much, which paralyses me, and results in long stretches of deathly silence. Finally he utters, to the effect that John Drinkwater was difficult to interview. Experience forlorn gleam of gratification at being bracketed with so distinguished a writer, but this instantly extinguished, as reporter adds that in the end J. D. talked for one hour and fifteen minutes. Am quite unable to emulate this achievement, and interview ends in gloom. Representative of an evening paper immediately appears, but is a great improvement on his colleague, and restores me to equanimity.

Three women reporters follow—am much struck by the fact that they are all good-looking and dress nicely—they all ask me what I think of the American Woman, whether I read James Branch Cabell—which I don't—and what I feel about the Problem of the Leisured Woman. Answer them all as eloquently as possible, and make mental note to the effect that I have evidently never taken the subject of Women seriously enough, the only problem about them in England being why there are so many.

Lunch with distinguished publisher and his highly decorative wife and two little boys. Am not in the least surprised to find that they live in a flat with black-velvet sofas, concealed lighting, and three diagonal glass tables for sole furniture. It turns out, however, that this is *not* a typical American home, and that they find it nearly as remarkable as I do myself. We have lunch, the two little boys behave like angels—reputation of American children' evidently libellous, and must remember to say so when I get home—and we talk about interior decoration dining-room has different-coloured paint on each one of its four walls—books and sea voyages. Elder of the two little boys suddenly breaks into this and remarks that he just loves English sausages—oh boy!—which I accept as a compliment to myself, and he then relapses into silence. Am much impressed by this display of social competence, and feel doubtful whether Robin or Vicky could ever have equalled it.

Afternoon is spent, once more, in interviews, and am taken out to supper-party by Ella Wheelwright, who again appears in clothes that I have never seen before. At supper I sit next elderly gentleman wearing collar exactly like Mr. Gladstone's. He is slightly morose, tells me that times are not at all what they were—which I know already—and that there is No Society left in New York. This seems to me uncivil, as well as ungrateful, and I decline to assent. Elderly Gentleman is, however, entirely indifferent as to whether I agree with him or not, and merely goes on to say that no club would dream of admitting Jews to its membership. (This, if true, reflects no credit on clubs.) It also appears that, in his own house, cocktails, wireless, gramophones and modern young people are—like Jews—never admitted. Should like to think of something really startling to reply to all this, but he would almost certainly take no notice, even if I did, and I content myself with saying that that is Very Interesting—which is not, unfortunately, altogether true.

Ella Wheelwright offers to drive me home, which she does with great competence, though once shouted at by a policeman who tells her: Put your lights on, sister!

Ella is kind, and asks me to tell her all about my home, but follows this up by immediately telling me all about hers instead. She also invites me to two luncheons, one tea, and to spend Sunday with her on Long Island.

Return to my room, which is now becoming familiar, and write long letter to Robert, which makes me feel homesick all over again.

October 17th.—Conference at publisher's office concerning my future movements, in which I take passive, rather than active part. Head of well-known lecture agency is present, and tells me about several excellent speaking-engagements that he might have got for me if: *(a)* He had had longer notice, *(b)* All the Clubs in America hadn't been affected by the depression, and *(c)* I could arrange to postpone my sailing for another three months.

Since *(a)* and *(b)* cannot now be remedied, and I entirely refuse to consider *(c),* deadlock appears to have been reached, but agent suddenly relents and admits that he *can,* by dint of superhuman exertions, get me one or two bookings in various places that none of them seem to be less than eighteen hours' journey apart. I agree to everything, only stipulating for Chicago where I wish to visit literary friend Arthur and his family, and to inspect the World Fair.

Social whirl, to which I am by now becoming accustomed, follows, and I am put into the hands of extraordinarily kind and competent guardian angel, picturesquely named Ramona Herdman. She takes me to the Vanderbilt Hotel for so-called tea, which consists of very strong cocktails and interesting sandwiches. I meet Miss Isabel Paterson, famous literary critic, by whom I am completely fascinated, but also awe-stricken in the extreme, as she has terrific reputation and is alarmingly clever in conversation.

She demolishes one or two English novelists, in whose success I have always hitherto believed implicitly, but is kind about my own literary efforts, and goes so far as to hope that we shall meet again. I tell her that I am going to Chicago and other places, and may be lecturing, and she looks at the floor and says, Yes, Clubwomen, large women with marcelled hair, wearing reception gowns.

Am appalled by this thumbnail sketch, and seriously contemplate cancelling tour altogether.

Ella Wheelwright joins us. She now has on a black ensemble, and hair done in quite a new way—and we talk about books. I say that I have enjoyed nothing so much as *Flush,* but Miss Paterson again disconcerts me by muttering that to write a whole book about a dog is Simply Morbid.

Am eventually taken to Essex House by Ella W., who asks, very kindly, if there is anything she can do for me. Yes, there is. She can tell me where I can go to get my hair shampooed and set, and whether it will be much more expensive than it is at home. In reply, Ella tells me that her own hair waves naturally. It doesn't curl—that isn't what she means at all but it just waves. In damp weather, it just goes into natural waves. It always has done this, ever since she was a child. But she has it set once a month, because it looks nicer. Hairdresser always tells her that it's lovely hair to do anything with, because the wave is really natural.

She then says Good-night and leaves me, and I decide to have my own inferior hair, which does *not* wave naturally, washed and set in the Hotel Beauty-parlour.

Oct. 23rd.—Extraordinary week-end with Ella Wheelwright on Long Island, at superb country-house which she refers to as her cottage. She drives me out from New York very kindly, but should enjoy it a great deal more if she would look in front of her, instead of at me, whilst negotiating colossal and unceasing stream of traffic. This, she says gaily, is what she has been looking forward to—a really undisturbed *tête-à-tête* in which to hear all about my reactions to America and the American Woman. I say, What about the American Man? but this not a success, Ella evidently feeling that reactions, if any, on this subject are of no importance whatever to anybody.

She then tells me that she spent a month last year in London, staying at the Savoy, and gives me her opinion of England, which is, on the whole, favourable. I say at intervals that I see what she means, and utter other non-committal phrases whenever it occurs to me that if I don't say something she will guess that I am not really listening.

We gradually leave New York behind and creep into comparative country—bright golden trees, excite my admiration, together with occasional scarlet ones—Ella still talking—have not the least idea what about, but continue to ejaculate from time to time. Presently country mansion is reached, three large cars already standing in front of door, and I suggest that other visitors have arrived. But Ella says Oh no, one is her *other* car, and the remaining two belong to Charlie. Decide that Charlie must be her husband, and wonder whether she has any children, but none have ever been mentioned, and do not like to ask.

House is attractive—furniture and decorations very elaborate—am particularly struck by enormous pile of amber beads coiled carelessly on one corner of old oak refectory table, just where they catch the light—and I am taken up winding staircase, carpeted in rose colour.

(Evidently no children, or else they use a separate staircase.)

Ella's bedroom perfectly marvellous. Terrific expanse of looking-glass, and sofa has eighteen pillows, each one different shade of purple. Should like to count number of jars and bottles—all with mauve enamel tops—in bathroom, but this would take far too long, and feel it necessary, moreover, to concentrate on personal appearance, very far from satisfactory. Am aware that I cannot hope to compete with Ella, who is looking wonderful in white wool outfit obviously made for her in Paris, but make what efforts I can with powder and lipstick, try to forget that I am wearing my Blue, which never has suited me and utterly refuses to wear out. Decide to take off my hat, but am dissatisfied with my hair when I have done so, and put it on again and go downstairs. Complete house-party is then revealed to me, sitting on silk cushions outside French windows, the whole thing being entirely reminiscent of illustrations to society story in American magazine. I am introduced, everyone is very polite, and complete silence envelops the entire party.

Young man in white sweater at last rises to the occasion and asks me what I think of *Anthony Adverse*. Am obliged to reply that I haven't read it, which gets us no further. I then admire the trees, which are beautiful, and everybody looks relieved and admires them too, and silence again ensues.

Ella, with great presence of mind, says that it is time for cocktails, these are brought, and I obediently drink mine and wonder what Our Vicar's Wife would say if she could see me now. This leads, by natural transition, to thoughts of television, and I ask my neighbour—grey flannels and flaming red hair—whether he thinks that this will ever become part of everyday life. He looks surprised—as well he may—but replies civilly that he doubts it very much. This he follows up by enquiring whether I have yet read *Anthony Adverse*.

Charlie materialises—imagine him to be Ella's husband, but am never actually told so—and we all go in to lunch, which is excellent.

(Standard of American cooking very, very high indeed. Reflect sentimentally that Robert is, in all probability, only having roast beef and Yorkshire pudding, then remember difference in time between here and England, and realise that beef and Yorkshire pudding are either in the past or the future, although cannot be quite sure which.)

Tennis is suggested for the afternoon, and Ella tells me that she can easily find me a pair of shoes. As I am far from sharing this confidence—every other woman in the room looks like size

5, whereas I take 6½—and think my Blue very ill-adapted to the tennis-court, I say that I would rather look on, and this I do. They all play extremely well, and look incredibly handsome, well dressed, and athletic. I decide, not for the first time, that Americans are a great deal more decorative than Europeans.

Just as inferiority complex threatens to overwhelm me altogether, I am joined by Ella, who says that she is taking me to a tea-party. Tea-parties are A Feature of Life on Long Island, and it is essential, says Ella, that I should attend one.

Everybody else turns out to be coming also, a complete platoon of cars is marshalled and we drive off, about two people to every car, and cover total distance of rather less than five hundred yards.

Am by this time becoming accustomed to American version of a tea-party, and encounter cocktails and sandwiches with equanimity, but am much struck by scale on which the entertainment is conducted; large room being entirely filled by people, including young gentleman who is playing the piano violently and has extremely pretty girl on either side of him, each with an arm round his waist.

It now becomes necessary to screech at really terrific pitch, and this everyone does. Cannot feel that *Anthony Adverse* motif, which still recurs, has gained by this, nor do my own replies to questions concerning the length of my stay, my reactions to America, and opinion of the American Woman. Ella, who has heroically introduced everybody within sight, smiles and waves at me encouragingly, but is now too firmly wedged in to move, and I sit on a sofa, next to slim woman in scarlet, and she screams into my ear, and tells me that she is a Southerner, and really lives in the South.

Am obliged to give up all hope of hearing everything she says, but can catch quite a lot of it, and am interested. She was, she tells me, the mascot of the baseball team at her College. Whenever a match took place, she was carried on to the field by two members of the team. (Frightful vision assails me of similar extravagance taking place on village football ground at home, and results, especially as to mud and bruises, that would certainly ensue.) On one occasion, yells my neighbour, the opposing team objected to her presence—(am not surprised) but her Boys held firm. Either, said her Boys, they had their mascot on the field, or else the whole match must be called off.

Cannot, unfortunately, hear the end of the story, but feel certain that it was favourable to the mascot and her Boys. Experience temporary difficulty in thinking out reasonably polite answer to such a singular statement, and finally say that it must have been rather fun, which is weak, and totally untrue, at least as far as the teams were concerned—but as all is lost in surrounding noise, it matters little. People walk in and out, and scream at one another—should be interested to identify my host and hostess, but see no hope of this whatever. Ella presently works her way up to me and makes signs that she is ready to leave, and we struggle slowly into the air again.

Remaining members of Ella's house-party, whom I am now rather disposed to cling to, as being old and familiar friends, all gradually reassemble, and we return to Ella's house, where I discover that recent vocal efforts have made my throat extremely sore.

October 25th.—English mail awaits me on return to New York Hotel and is handed to me by reception-clerk with agreeable comment to the effect that the Old Country hasn't forgotten me *this* time. Feel that I can't possibly wait to read mail till I get upstairs, but equally impossible to do so in entrance-hall, and am prepared to make a rush for the elevator when firm-looking elderly woman in black comes up and addresses me by name. Says that she is very glad indeed to know me. Her name is Katherine Ellen Blatt, which may not mean anything to me, but stands for quite a lot to a section of the American public.

I try to look intelligent, and wonder whether to ask for further details or not, but something tells me that I am going to hear them anyway, so may as well make up my mind to it. Invite Miss Blatt to sit down and wait for me one moment whilst I go up and take off my hat—by which I really mean tear open letters from Robert and the children—but she says, No, she'd just love to come right upstairs with me. This she proceeds to do, and tells me on the way up that she writes articles for the women's magazines and that she makes quite a feature of describing English visitors to America, especially those with literary interests. The moment she heard that I was in New York she felt that she just had to come around right away and have a look at me (idea crosses my mind of replying that A Cat may look at a King, but this colloquialism probably unappreciated, and in any case Miss B. gives me no time).

Bed still unmade, which annoys me, especially as Miss B. scrutinises entire room through a pince-nez and asks, What made me come here, as this is a place entirely frequented by professional people? She herself could, if I wish it, arrange to have me transferred immediately to a women's club, where there is a lovely group of highly intelligent cultivated women, to which she is proud to say that she belongs. Can only hope that my face doesn't reflect acute horror that invades me at the idea of joining any group of women amongst whom is to be numbered Miss Blatt.

Incredibly tedious half-hour ensues. Miss B. has a great deal to say, and fortunately seems to expect very little answer, as my mind is entirely fixed on letters lying unopened in my handbag. She tells me, amongst other things, that Noel Coward, Somerset Maugham—whom she calls "Willie", which I think profane—the Duchess of Atholl, Sir Gerald du Maurier and Miss Amy Johnson are all very dear friends of hers, and she would never dream of letting a year pass without going to England and paying each of them a visit. I say rather curtly that I don't know any of them, and add that I don't really feel I ought to take up any more of Miss Blatt's time. That, declares Miss Blatt, doesn't matter at all. I'm not to let that worry me for a moment. To hear about dear old London is just everything to her, and she is just crazy to be told whether I know her close friends, Ellen Wilkinson, Nancy Astor and Ramsay MacDonald. Frantic impulse assails me and I say, No, but that the Prince of Wales is a great friend of mine. Is that so? returns Miss Blatt quite unmoved. She herself met him for the first time last summer at Ascot and they had quite a talk. (If this really true, can only feel perfectly convinced that any talk there was emanated entirely from Miss B.)

Just as I feel that the limits of sanity have been reached, telephone bell rings and I answer it and take complicated message from Lecture Agent about Buffalo, which at first I think to be Natural History, but afterwards realise is a town.

Continuity of atmosphere is now destroyed and I remain standing and inform Miss Blatt that I am afraid that I shall have to go out. She offers to take me up-town, and I thank her and say No. Then, she says, it won't be any trouble to take me down-town. This time I say No without thanking her.

We spend about ten minutes saying good-bye. Miss Blatt assures me that she will get in touch with me again within a day or two, and meanwhile will send me some of her articles to read, and I finally shut the door on her and sit down on the bed, after locking the door for fear she should come back again.

Tear open letters from Robert and the children, read them three times at least, become homesick and rather agitated, and then read them all over again. Robert says that he will be glad when I get home again—(am strongly tempted to book my passage for to-morrow)—and adds details about the garden. Our Vicar, he adds, preached quite a good sermon on Sunday last, and Cook's sponge-cake is improving. Vicky's letter very affectionate, with rows of kisses and large drawing of a horse with short legs and only one visible ear. The Literary Society at school, writes Vicky, is reading Masefield, and this she enjoys very much. Am a good deal impressed and try to remember what I know of Masefield's work and how much of it is suitable for nine years old.

Robin's letter, very long and beautifully written, contains urgent request for any American slang expressions that I may meet with, but it must be *new* slang. Not, he explicitly states, words like Jake and Oke, which everybody knows already. He also hopes that I am enjoying myself and have seen some gangsters. A boy called Saunders is now reading a P. G. Wodehouse book called *Love Among the Chickens*. A boy called Badger has had his front tooth knocked out. There isn't, says Robin in conclusion, much to write about, and he sends Best Love.

Receive also charming letter from Caroline Concannon, who says, gratifyingly, that she misses me, and adds in a vague way that everything is ALL RIGHT in the flat. Remaining correspondence mostly bills, but am quite unable to pay any attention to them for more reasons than one, and merely put them all together in an elastic band and endorse the top one "Bills", which makes me feel business-like and practically produces illusion of having paid them already.

Extraordinary feeling of exhaustion comes over me, due partly to emotion and partly to visit of Miss Katherine Ellen Blatt, and I decide to go out and look at shop-windows on Fifth Avenue, which I do, and enjoy enormously.

Later in the day am conducted to a Tea—cocktails and sandwiches as usual. Meet distinguished author and critic, Mr. Alexander Woollcott, who is amusing and talks to me very kindly. In the middle of it telephone bell rings and he conducts conversation with—presumably—an Editor, in which he says, No, no, he must positively decline to undertake any more work. The terms, he admits, are wonderful, but it simply can't be done. No, he can't possibly reconsider his decision. He has had to refuse several other offers of the same kind already. He can undertake nothing more. On this he rings off and resumes conversation just as if nothing has happened. Am completely lost in awe and admiration.

Oct. 26th.—Telephone message reaches me just as I am contemplating familiar problem of packing more into suit-cases, hat-box and attaché-case than they can possibly contain. Will I at once get into touch with Mrs. Margery Brown, who has received a letter about me from Mrs. Tressider in England? Conviction comes over me in a rush that I cannot, and will not, do anything of the kind, and I go on packing.

Telephone bell rings—undoubtedly Mrs. Margery Brown—and I contemplate leaving it unanswered, but am mysteriously unable to do so. Decide to pretend that I am my Secretary and say that I've gone out. Do so, but find myself involved in hideous and unconvincing muddle, in which all pronouns become badly mixed up. Discover, moreover, after some moments, that I am not talking to Mrs. Margery Brown at all, but to unknown American lady who repeats patiently that an old friend wishes to come round and see me. Name of old friend is unintelligible to me throughout, but finally I give way and say Very well, I shall be here for another hour before starting for Chicago.

(Am not, in actual point of fact, departing for Chicago until to-eight. *Query:* Would it not, when time permits, be advisable to concentrate very seriously on increasing tendency to distort the truth to my own convenience? *Ans.:* Advisable, perhaps, but definitely unnerving, and investigation probably better postponed until safely returned to home surroundings. Cannot wholly escape the suspicion that moral standards are largely dependent upon geographical surroundings.)

Return to suit-cases, and decide that if bottle of witch-hazel is rolled in paper it can perfectly well be placed inside bedroom slipper, and that it will make all the difference if I remove bulky evening wrap from its present corner of suit-case, and bestow it in the bottom of hat-box. Result of these manoeuvres not all I hope, as situation of best hat now becomes precarious, and I also suddenly discover that I have forgotten to pack photographs of Robin and Vicky, small red travelling clock, and pair of black shoes that are inclined to be too tight and that I never by any chance wear.

Despair invades me and I am definitely relieved when knock at the door interrupts me. I open it and am greeted by a scream:—*Ah, madame, quelle émotion!*—and recognise Mademoiselle. She screams again, throws herself into my arms, says *Mon Dieu, je vais me trouver mal, alors?* and sinks on to the bed, but does not cease to talk. She is, she tells me, with *une famille très américaine—assez comme-il-faut*—(which I think an ungenerous description)—and has promised to remain with them in New York for six months, at the end of which they are going to Paris, where she originally met them. Are they nice, and is Mademoiselle happy? I enquire. To this Mademoiselle can only throw up her hands, gaze at the ceiling, and exclaim that *le bonheur* is *bien peu de chose*—with which I am unable to agree. She further adds that never, for one moment, day or night, does she cease to think of *ce cher petit chez-nous du Devonshire* and *cet amour de Vicky.*

(If this is literally true, Mademoiselle cannot possibly be doing her duty by her present employers. Can also remember distinctly many occasions on which Mademoiselle, in Devonshire, wept and threw herself about in despair, owing to alleged dullness of the English countryside, insults heaped upon her by the English people, and general *manque de coeur et de délicatesse* of my own family, particularly Vicky.)

All, however, is now forgotten, and we indulge in immense and retrospective conversation in which Mademoiselle goes so far as to refer sentimentally to *ces bons jeux de cricket dans le jardin*. Do not, naturally, remind her of the number of times in which *ces bons jeux* were brought to an abrupt end by Mademoiselle herself flinging down her bat and walking away saying *Moi, je ne joue plus*, owing to having been bowled out by Robin.

She inspects photographs of the children and praises their looks extravagantly, but on seeing Robert's only observes resentfully *Tiens! on dirait qu'il vieilli!* She then looks piercingly at me, and I feel that only politeness keeps her from saying exactly the same thing about me, so turn the conversation by explaining that I am packing to go to Chicago.

Packing! exclaims Mademoiselle. *Ah, quelle horreur! Quelle façon de faire les choses!* At this she throws off black kid gloves, small fur jacket, three scarves, large amethyst brooch, and mauve wool cardigan, and announces her intention of packing for me. This she does with extreme competence and unlimited use of tissue paper, but exclaims rather frequently that my folding of clothes is enough to *briser le coeur*.

I beg her to stay and have lunch with me, and she says *Mais non, mais non, c'est trop*, but is finally persuaded, on condition that she may take down her hair and put it up again before going downstairs. To this I naturally agree, and Mademoiselle combs her hair and declares that it reminds her of *le bon temps passé*.

Find it impossible to extract from her any coherent impressions of America as she only replies to enquiries by shaking her head and saying *Ah, l'Amérique, l'Amérique! C'est toujours le dollarrr, n'est-ce pas?* Decide, however, that Mademoiselle has on the whole met with a good deal of kindness, and is in receipt of an enormous salary.

We lunch together in Persian Coffee Shop, Mademoiselle talking with much animation, and later she takes her departure on the understanding that we are to meet again before I sail.

Send hurried postcards of Tallest Building in New York to Robin and Vicky respectively, tip everybody in Hotel who appears to expect it, and prepare myself for night journey to Chicago.

Oct. 27th.—Remember, not without bitterness, that everybody in England has told me that I shall find American trains much too hot, Our Vicar's Wife—who has never been to America—going so far as to say that a temperature of 100 degrees is quite usual. Find myself, on the contrary, distinctly cold, and am not in the least surprised to see snow on the ground as we approach Chicago.

Postcards of the World Fair on sale in train, mostly coloured very bright blue and very bright yellow. I buy one of the Hall of Science—suitable for Robert—Observation Tower—likely to appeal to Robin—Prehistoric Animals—Vicky—and Streets of Paris, which has a sound of frivolity that I think will please Caroline Concannon Rose and Felicity get Avenue of Flags and Belgian Village respectively, because I have nothing else left. Inscribe various rather illegible messages on all these, mostly to the effect that I am enjoying myself, that I miss them all very much, and that I haven't time to write more just now, but will do so later.

Breakfast is a success—expensive, but good—and I succeed in attaining a moderate cleanliness of appearance before train gets in. Customary struggle with suit-case ensues—pyjamas and sponge-bag shut in after prolonged efforts, and this achievement immediately followed by discovery that I have forgotten to put in brush and comb. At this, coloured porter comes to my rescue, and shortly afterwards Chicago is reached.

Literary friend Arthur has not only gratifyingly turned up to meet me, but has brought with him very pretty younger sister, visiting friend from New York (male) and exclusive-looking dachshund, referred to as Vicki Baum.

Moreover, representative from publishers puts in an appearance—hat worn at a very dashing angle—know him only as Pete and cannot imagine how I shall effect introductions, but this fortunately turns out to be unnecessary.

Am rather moved at finding that both literary friend and Pete now appear to me in the light of old and dear friends, such is my satisfaction at seeing faces that are not those of complete strangers.

Someone unknown takes a photograph, just as we leave station—this, says Arthur impressively, hasn't happened since the visit of Queen Marie of Roumania—and we drive off.

Chicago strikes me as full of beautiful buildings, and cannot imagine why nobody ever says anything about this aspect of it. Do not like to ask anything about gangsters, and see no signs of their activities, but hope these may be revealed later, otherwise children will be seriously disappointed. The lake, which looks to me exactly like the sea, excites my admiration, and building in which Arthur's family lives turns out to be right in front of it.

They receive me in kindest possible manner—I immediately fall in love with Arthur's mother—and suggest, with the utmost tact, that I should like a bath at once. (After one look in the glass, can well understand why this thought occurred to them.)

Perceive myself to be incredibly dirty, dishevelled and out of repair generally, and do what I can, in enormous bedroom and bathroom, to rectify this. Hair, however, not improved by my making a mistake amongst unaccustomed number of bath-taps, and giving myself quite involuntary shower.

October 30th.—Feel quite convinced that I have known Arthur, his family, his New York friend and his dog all my life. They treat me with incredible kindness and hospitality, and introduce me to all their friends.

Some of the friends—but not all—raise the Problem of the American Woman. Find myself as far as ever from having thought out intelligent answer to this, and have serious thoughts of writing dear Rose, and asking her to cable reply, if Problem is to pursue me wherever I go in the United States.

Enormous cocktail-party is given by Arthur's mother, entirely in honour of New York friend—whom I now freely address as Billy—and myself. Bond of union immediately established between us, as we realise joint responsibility of proving ourselves worthy of all this attention.

Am introduced to hundreds of people—quite as many men as women, which impresses me, and which I feel vaguely should go at least half-way towards solving American Woman Problem, if only I could make the connection—but clarity of thought distinctly impaired, probably by cocktails.

Attractive woman in blue tells me that she knows a friend of mine: Mrs. Tressider? I instinctively reply. Yes, Mrs. Tressider. And The Boy too. He doesn't look strong. I assert—without the slightest justification—that he is much stronger than he was, and begin to talk about the Fair. Am told in return that I *must* visit the Hall of Science, go up the Observation Tower, and inspect the Belgian Village.

Complete stranger tells me that I am dining at her apartment to-morrow, another lady adds that she is looking forward to seeing me on Sunday at her home in the country, an elderly gentleman remarks that he is so glad he is to have the pleasure of giving me lunch and taking me round the Fair, and another complete, and charming, stranger informs me that Arthur and I are to have tea at her house when we visit Chicago University.

Am beginning to feel slightly dazed—cocktails have undoubtedly contributed to this—but gratified beyond description at so much attention and kindness, and have hazy idea of writing letter home to explain that I am evidently of much greater importance than any of us have ever realised.

Am brought slightly down to earth again by remembrance that I am not in Chicago entirely for purpose of enjoyment, and that to-morrow Pete is escorting me to important department store, where I am to sign books and deliver short speech.

Decide that I must learn this by heart overnight, but am taken to a symphony concert, come back very late, and go to bed instead.

October 31st.—Am called for in the morning by Pete—hat still at very daring angle—and we walk through the streets. He tells me candidly that he does not like authors; I say that I don't either, and we get on extremely well.

Department store is the most impressive thing I have ever seen in my life, and the largest. We inspect various departments, including Modern Furniture, which consists of a number of rooms containing perfectly square sofas, coloured glass animals, cocktail appliances and steel chairs. Am a good deal impressed, and think that it is all a great improvement on older style, but at the same time cannot possibly conceive of Robert reading *The Times* seated on oblong black-and-green divan with small glass-topped table projecting from the wall beside him, and statuette of naked angular woman with large elbows exactly opposite.

Moreover, no provision made anywhere for housing children, and do not like to enquire what, if anything, is ever done for them.

Admirable young gentleman who shows us round says that the Modern Kitchen will be of special interest to me, and ushers us into it. Pete, at this stage, looks slightly sardonic, and I perceive that he is as well aware as I am myself that the Modern Kitchen is completely wasted on me. Further reflection also occurs to me that if Pete were acquainted with Cook he would realise even better than he does why I feel that the Modern Kitchen is not destined to hold any significant place in my life.

Pete informs me that he is anxious to introduce me to charming and capable woman, friend of his, who runs the book department of the Store. He tells me her name, and I immediately forget it again. Later on, short exercise in Pelmanism enables me to connect wave in her hair with first name, which is Marcella. Remaining and more important half continues elusive, and I therefore call her nothing. Am impressed by her office, which is entirely plastered with photographs, mostly inscribed, of celebrities. She asks if I know various of these. I have to reply each time that I don't, and begin to feel inferior. (Recollection here of Katherine Ellen Blatt, intimate personal friend of every celebrity that ever lived.) Become absent-minded, and hear myself, on-being asked if I haven't met George Bernard Shaw, replying No, but I know who he is. This reply not a success, and Marcella ceases to probe into the state of my literary connections.

Soon afterwards I am escorted back to book department—should like to linger amongst First Editions, or even New Juveniles, but this is not encouraged—and young subordinate of Marcella's announces that Quite a nice lot of people are waiting. Last week, she adds, they had Hervey Allen. Foresee exactly what she is going to say next, which is What do I think of *Anthony Adverse,* and pretend to be absorbed in small half-sheet of paper on which I have written rather illegible Notes.

Quite a nice lot of people turns out to mean between four and five hundred ladies, with a sprinkling of men, all gathered round a little dais with a table behind which I am told to take up my stand. Feel a great deal more inclined to crawl underneath it and stay there, but quite realise that this is, naturally, out of the question.

Marcella says a few words—I remind myself that nothing in the world can last for ever, and anyway they need none of them ever meet me again after this afternoon—and plunge forthwith into speech.

Funny story goes well—put in another one which I have just thought of, and which isn't so good—but that goes well too. Begin to think that I really am a speaker after all, and wonder why nobody at home has ever said anything about it, and how I am ever to make them believe it, without sounding conceited.

Sit down amidst applause and try to look modest, until I suddenly catch sight of literary friend Arthur and his friend Billy, who have evidently been listening. Am rather agitated at this, and feel that instead of looking modest I merely look foolish.

At this point Pete, who hasn't even pretended to listen to me, for which I am grateful rather than otherwise, reappears from some quite other department where he has sensibly been spending his time, and says that I had better autograph a few books, as People will Like It.

His idea of a few books runs into hundreds, and I sit and sign them and feel very important indeed. Streams of ladies walk past and we exchange a few words. Most of them ask How does one write a book? and several tell me that they heard something a few weeks ago which definitely *ought* to go into a book. This is usually a witticism perpetrated by dear little grandchild, aged six last July, but is sometimes merely a Funny Story already known to me, and—probably—to everybody else in the civilised world. I say Thank you, Thank you very much, and continue to sign my name. Idle fancy crosses my mind that it would be fun if I was J. P. Morgan, and all this was cheques.

After a time Marcella retrieves me, and says that she has not forgotten I am an Englishwoman, and will want my Tea. Am not fond of tea at the best of times, and seldom take it, but cannot of course say so, and only refer to Arthur and his friend Billy, who may be waiting for me. No, not at all, says Marcella. They are buying tortoises. Tortoises? Yes, tiny little tortoises. There is, asserts Marcella, a display of them downstairs, with different flowers hand-painted on their shells. She takes advantage of the stunned condition into which this plunges me to take me back to her office, where we have tea—English note struck by the fact that it is pitch-black, and we have lemon instead of milk—and Pete rejoins us, and confirms rumour as to floral tortoises being on sale, only he refers to them as turtles. Later on, am privileged to view them, and they crawl about in a little basin filled with water and broken shells, and display unnatural-looking bunches of roses and forget-me-nots on their backs.

Sign more books after tea, and am then taken away by friend Arthur, who says that his mother is waiting for me at the English-. Speaking Union. (Why not at home, which I should much prefer?) However, the English-Speaking Union is very pleasant. I meet a number of people, they ask what I think of America, and if I am going to California, and I say in return that I look forward to visiting the Fair and we part amicably.

Interesting and unexpected encounter with one lady, dressed in black and green, who says that when in New York she met my children's late French governess. I scream with excitement, and black-and-green lady looks rather pitying, and says Oh yes, the world is quite a small place. I say contentiously No, no, not as small as all that, and Mademoiselle and I met in New York, and I do so hope she is happy and with nice people. She is, replies black-and-green lady severely, with perfectly delightful people—Southerners—one of our very oldest Southern families. They all speak with a real Southern accent. Stop myself just in time from saying that Mademoiselle will probably correct that, and ask instead if the children are fond of her. Black-and-green lady only repeats, in reply, that her friends belong to the oldest Southern family in the South, practically, and moves off looking as though she rather disapproves of me.

This encounter, for reason which I cannot identify, has rather thrown me off my balance, and I shortly afterwards ask Arthur if we cannot go home. He says Yes, in the most amiable way, and takes me away in a taxi with his very pretty sister. Enquire of her where and how I can possibly get my hair washed, and she at once undertakes to make all necessary arrangements, and says that the place that does *her* hair can very well do mine. (As she is a particularly charming blonde, at least ten years' younger than I am, the results will probably be entirely different, but keep this pessimistic reflection to myself.)

Literary friend Arthur, with great good-feeling, says that he knows there are some letters waiting for me, which I shall wish to read in peace, and that he is sure I should like to rest before dinner-party, to which he is taking me at eight o'clock. (Should like to refer Katherine Ellen Blatt to dear Arthur, for lessons in *savoir-faire*.)

Letters await me in my room, but exercise great self-control by tearing off my hat, throwing my coat on the floor, and dashing gloves and bag into different corners of the room before I sit down to read them.

Only one is from England: Our Vicar's Wife writes passionate enquiry as to whether I am going anywhere near Arizona, as boy in whom she and Our Vicar took great interest in their *first* parish—North London, five-and-twenty years ago—is supposed to have gone there and done very well. Will I make enquiries—name was Sydney Cripps, and has one front tooth missing, knocked out at cricket, has written to Our Vicar from time to time, but last occasion nearly twelve years ago—Time, adds Our Vicar's Wife, passes. All is well at home—very strange not to see me about—Women's Institute Committee met last week, how difficult it is to please everybody.

Can believe from experience that this is, indeed, so.

November 1st.—Visit the World Fair in company with Arthur and his family. Buildings all very modern and austere, except for colouring, which is inclined to be violent, but aspect as a whole is effective and impressive, and much to be preferred to customary imitations of ancient Greece. Individual exhibits admirably displayed, and total area of space covered must be enormous, whether lake—of which I see large bits here and there—is included or not. Private cars not admitted—which I think sensible—but rickshaws available, drawn by University students—to whom, everybody says, It's Interesting to Talk—and small motor-buses go quietly round and round the Fair.

Arthur and I patronise rickshaws—I take a good look at my University Student, and decide that conversation would probably benefit neither of us—and visit various buildings. Hall of Science not amongst our successes, unfortunately, as the sight of whole skeletons, portions of the human frame executed in plaster, and realistic maps of sinews and blood-vessels, all ranged against the wall in glass show-cases, merely causes me to hurry past with my eyes shut. Arthur is sympathetic, and tells me that there *is* an exhibit of Live Babies in Incubators to be seen, but cannot decide whether he means that this would be better than scientific, wonders at present surrounding us, or worse.

Resume rickshaws, and visit Jade Chinese Temple, which is lovely, Prehistoric Animals-unpleasant impression of primitive man's existence derived from these, but should like to have seen a brontosaurus in the flesh nevertheless—and Belgian Village, said to be replica of fifteenth century. (If not fifteenth, then sixteenth. Cannot be sure.)

Here Arthur and I descend, and walk up and down stone steps and cobbled streets, and watch incredibly clean-looking peasants in picturesque costumes dancing hand in hand and every now and then stamping. Have always hitherto associated this with Russians, but evidently wrong.

Just as old Flemish Clock on old Flemish Town Hall clangs out old Flemish Air, and Arthur and I tell one another that this is beautifully done, rather brassy voice from concealed loudspeaker is inspired to enquire: Oh boy! What about that new tooth-paste? Old Flemish atmosphere goes completely to bits, and Arthur and I, in disgust, retire to Club, where we meet his family, and have most excellent lunch.

Everyone asks what I want to see next, and Arthur's mother says that she has a few friends coming to dinner, but is thrown into consternation by Arthur's father, who says that he has invited two South Americans to come in afterwards. Everyone says South Americans? as if they were pterodactyls at the very least, and antecedents are enquired into, but nothing whatever transpires except that they are South Americans and that nobody knows anything about them, not even their names.

Return to Fair after lunch—new rickshaw student, less forbidding-looking than the last, and I say feebly that It is very hot for November, and he replies that he can tell by my accent that I come from England and he supposes it's always foggy there, and I say No, not always, and nothing further passes between us. Am evidently not gifted, where interesting students from American Colleges are concerned, and decide to do nothing more in this line. More exhibits follow—mostly very good—and Arthur says that he thinks we ought to see the North American Indians.

He accordingly pays large sum of money which admits us into special enclosures where authentic Red Indians are stamping about—(stamping definitely discredited henceforward as a Russian monopoly)—and uttering sounds exclusively on two notes, all of which, so far as I can tell, consist of Wah Wah! and nothing else. Listen to this for nearly forty minutes but am not enthusiastic. Neither is Arthur, and we shortly afterwards go home.

Write postcards to Rose, the children, and Robert, and after some thought send one to Cook, although entirely uncertain as to whether this will gratify her or not. Am surprised, and rather disturbed, to find that wording of Cook's postcard takes more thought than that on all the others put together.

Small dinner takes place later on, and consists of about sixteen people, including a lady whose novel won the Pulitzer Prize, a lady who writes poetry—very, very well known, though not, unhappily, to me—a young gentleman who has something to do with Films, an older one who is connected with Museums, and delightful woman in green who says that she knows Devonshire and has stayed with the Frobishers. Did she, I rashly enquire, enjoy it? Well, she replies tolerantly, Devonshire is a lovely part of the world, but she is afraid Sir William Frobisher dislikes Americans. I protest, and she then adds, conclusively, that Sir W. told her *himself* how much he disliked Americans. Feel that it would indeed be idle to try and get round this, so begin to talk at once about the Fair.

Dinner marvellous, as usual—company very agreeable—and my neighbour—Museums—offers to conduct me to see Chicago Historical Museum at ten o'clock next morning.

Just as dinner is over, two extremely elegant young gentlemen, with waists and superbly smooth *coiffures,* come in and bow gracefully to our hostess. New York friend, Billy, hisses at me: *"The South Americans",* and I nod assent, and wonder how on earth they are going to be introduced, when nobody knows their names. This, however, is achieved by hostess who simply asks them what they are called, and then introduces everybody else.

Am told afterwards that neither of them speaks much English, and that Arthur's father asked them questions all the evening. No one tells me whether they answered them or not, and I remain mildly curious on the point.

November 4th.—Singular and interesting opportunity is offered me to contrast Sunday spent on Long Island and Sunday spent in equivalent country district outside Chicago, called Lake Forest, where I am invited to lunch and spend the afternoon. Enquire of Arthur quite early if this is to be a large party. He supposes About Thirty. Decide at once to put on the Coming Molyneux's best effort—white daisies on blue silk. But, says Arthur, country clothes. Decide to substitute wool coat and skirt, with red beret. And, says Arthur, he is taking me on to dinner with very, very rich acquaintance, also at Lake Forest. I revert, mentally, to blue silk and daisies, and say that I suppose it won't matter if we're not in evening dress? Oh, replies Arthur, we've got to take evening clothes with us, and change there. Our hostess won't hear of anything else. I take a violent dislike to her on the spot, and say that I'm not sure I want to go at all. At this Arthur is gloomy, but firm. *He* doesn't want to go either, and neither does Billy, but we can't get out of it now. We must simply pack our evening clothes in bags and *go.* Have not sufficient moral courage to rebel any further, and instead consider the question of packing up my evening clothes. Suit-case is too large, and attaché-case too small, but finally decide on the latter, which will probably mean ruin to evening frock.

November 5th.—Literary friend Arthur, still plunged in gloom, takes Billy and me by car to Lake Forest, about thirty miles from Chicago. We talk about grandmothers—do not know why or how this comes to pass—and then about Scotland. Scenery very beautiful, but climate bad. Arthur once went to Holyrood, but saw no bloodstains. Billy has a relation who married the owner of a Castle in Rossunshire and they live there and have pipers every evening. I counter this by saying that I have a friend, married to a distinguished historian or something, at Edinburgh University. Wish I hadn't said "or something" as this casts an air of spuriousness over the whole story. Try to improve on it by adding firmly that they live in Wardie Avenue, Edinburgh—but this is received in silence.

(*Query:* Why are facts invariably received so much less sympathetically than fictions? Had I only said that distinguished historian and his wife lived in a cellar of Edinburgh Castle and sold Edinburgh rock, reactions of Arthur and Billy probably much more enthusiastic.)

Arrive at about one o'clock. House, explains Arthur, belongs to great friends of his—charming people—Mrs. F. writes novels—sister won Pulitzer Prize with another novel. At this I interject Yes, yes, I met her the other day—and feel like a dear old friend of the family.

House, says Arthur all over again—at which I perceive that I must have interrupted him before he'd finished, and suddenly remember that Robert has occasionally complained of this—House belongs to Mr. and Mrs. F. and has been left entirely unaltered since it was first built in 1874, furniture and all. It is, in fact, practically a Museum Piece.

Discover this to be indeed no overunstatement, and am enchanted with house, which is completely Victorian, and has fretwork brackets in every available corner, and a great deal of furniture. Am kindly welcomed, and taken upstairs to leave my coat and take off my hat. Spend the time instead in looking at gilt clock under glass shade, wool-and-bead mats, and coloured pictures of little girls in pinafores playing with large white kittens. Have to be retrieved by hostess's daughter, who explains that she thought I might have lost my way. I apologise and hope that I'm not late for lunch.

This fear turns out later to be entirely groundless, as luncheon party—about thirty-five people—assembles by degrees on porch, and drinks cocktails, and nobody sits down to lunch until three o'clock. Have pleasant neighbours on either side, and slightly tiresome one opposite, who insists on talking across the table and telling me that I must go to the South, whatever I do. She herself comes of a Southern family, and has never lost her Southern accent, as I have no doubt noticed. Am aware that she intends me to assent to this, but do not do so, and conversation turns to *Anthony Adverse* as usual—and the popularity of ice-cream in America. Lunch over at about four o'clock—can understand why tea, as a meal, does not exist in the U.S.A.—and we return to the porch, and everyone says that this is the Indian Summer.

Find myself sitting with elderly man, who civilly remarks that he wants to hear about the book I have written. Am aware that this cannot possibly be true, but take it in the spirit in which it is meant, and discuss instead the British Museum—which he knows much better than I do—trout-fishing—about which neither of us knows anything whatever—and the state of the dollar.

Soon afterwards Arthur, with fearful recrudescence of despair, tells me that there is nothing for it, as we've got another forty miles to drive, but to say good-bye and go. We may not *want* to, but we simply haven't any choice, he says.

After this we linger for about thirty-five minutes longer, repeating how sorry we are that we've got to go, and hearing how very sorry everybody else is as well. Eventually find ourselves in car again, suit-cases with evening clothes occupying quite a lot of space, and again causing Arthur to lament pertinacity of hostess who declined to receive us in ordinary day clothes.

Fog comes on—is this a peculiarity of Indian Summer?—chauffeur takes two or three wrong turnings, but says that he knows where we shall Come Out—and Billy goes quietly to sleep. Arthur and I talk in subdued voices for several minutes, but get louder and louder as we become more interested, and Billy wakes up and denies that he has ever closed an eye at all.

Silence then descends upon us all, and I lapse into thoughts of Robert, the children, and immense width and depth of the Atlantic Ocean. Have, as usual, killed and buried us all, myself included, several times over before we arrive.

Just as we get out of car—Billy falls over one of the suit-cases and says Damn—Arthur mutters that I *must* remember to look at the pictures. Wonderful collection, and hostess likes them to be admired. This throws me off my balance completely, and I follow very superb and monumental butler with my eyes fixed on every picture I see, in series of immense rooms through which we are led. Result of this is that I practically collide with hostess, advancing gracefully to receive us, and that my rejoinders to her cries of welcome are totally lacking in *empressement*, as I am still wondering how soon I ought to say anything about the pictures, and what means I can adopt to sound as if I really knew something about them. Hostess recalls me to myself by enquiring passionately if we have brought evening things, as she has rooms all ready for us to change in.

Am struck by this preoccupation with evening clothes, and interesting little speculation presents itself, as to whether she suffers from obsession on the point, and if so Could psychoanalysis be of any help? Treatment undoubtedly very expensive, but need not, in this case, be considered.

Just as I have mentally consigned her to luxurious nursing home, with two specialists and a trained nurse, hostess again refers to our evening clothes, and says that we had better come up and see the rooms in which we are to dress. Follow her upstairs—more pictures all the way up, and in corridor of vast length—I hear Arthur referring to "that marvellous Toulouse-Lautrec" and look madly about, but cannot guess which one he means, as all alike look to me marvellous, except occasional still-life which I always detest—and shortly afterwards I am parted from Arthur and Billy, and shown into complete *suite*, with bedroom, bathroom and sitting-room. Hostess says solicitously: Can I manage?

Yes, on the whole I think I can.

(Wonder what she would feel about extremely shabby bedroom at home, total absence of either private bathroom or Toulouse-Lautrec, and sitting-room downstairs in which Robert, children, cat, dog and myself all congregate together round indifferent wood fire. This vision, however, once more conducive to home-sickness, and hastily put it aside and look at all the books in the five bookcases to see what I can read in the bath.)

Am surprised and gratified to find that I have remembered to pack everything I want, and perform satisfactory toilette, twice interrupted by offers of assistance from lady's maid, who looks astonished when I refuse them. Look at myself in three different mirrors, decide—rather ungenerously—that I am better-looking than my hostess, and on this reassuring reflection proceed downstairs.

November 5th (continued).—Decide that I am, beyond a doubt, making acquaintance with Millionaire Life in America, and that I must take mental notes of everything I see and eat, for benefit of Robert and the Women's Institute. Hostess, waiting in the drawing-room, has now gone into mauve chiffon, triple necklace of large uncut amethysts, and at least sixteen amethyst bracelets. Do not think much of mauve chiffon, but am definitely envious of uncut amethysts, and think to myself that they would look well on me.

Hostess is vivacious—talks to me in a sparkling manner about World Fair, the South—which I must, at all costs, visit—and California, which is, she says, overrated. But not, I urge, the climate? Oh yes, the climate too. Am disillusioned by this, and think of saying that even Wealth cannot purchase Ideal Climatic Conditions, but this far too reminiscent of the *Fairchild Family,* and is instantly dismissed.

Arthur and Billy come down, and I experience renewed tendency to cling to their society in the midst of so much that is unfamiliar, and reflect that I shall never again blame dear Robin for invariably electing to sit next to his own relations at parties. Guests arrive—agreeable man with bald head comes and talks to me, and says that he has been looking forward to meeting me again, and I try, I hope successfully, to conceal fact that I had no idea that we had ever met before.

Dinner follows—table is made of looking-glass, floor has looking-glass let into it and so has ceiling. This arrangement impressive in the extreme, though no doubt more agreeable to some of us than to others. Try to imagine Robert, Our Vicar and even old Mrs. Blenkinsop in these surroundings, and fail completely.

After dinner return to quite another drawing-room, and sit next to yellow-satin lady with iron-grey hair, who cross-questions me rather severely on my impressions of America, and tells me that I don't really like Chicago, as English people never do, but that I shall adore Boston. Am just preparing to contradict her when she spills her coffee all over me. We all scream, and I get to my feet, dripping coffee over no-doubt-invaluable Persian rug, and iron-grey lady, with more presence of mind than regard for truth, exclaims that I must have done it with my elbow and what a pity it is! Cannot, in the stress of the moment, think of any form of words combining both perfect candour and absolute courtesy in which to tell her that she is not speaking the truth and that her own clumsiness is entirely responsible for disaster. Iron-grey woman takes the initiative and calls for cold water—hot water no good at all, the colder the better, for coffee.

(Query: Why does she know so much about it? Is it an old habit of hers to spill coffee? Probably.)

Extensive sponging follows, and everybody except myself says that It ought to be All Right now—which I know very well only means that they are all thoroughly tired of the subject and wish to stop talking about it.

Sit down again at furthest possible distance from iron-grey woman—who is now informing us that if my frock had been velvet she would have advised steaming, *not* sponging—and realise that, besides having ruined my frock, I am also running grave risk of rheumatic fever, owing to general dampness.

Remainder of the evening, so far as I am concerned, lacks *entrain.*

November 6th.—Chicago visit draws to a close, and Pete, after a last solemn warning to me about the importance of visiting book-stores in all the towns I go to, returns to New York, but tells me that we shall meet again somewhere or other very soon. Hope that this is meant as a pleasant augury, rather than a threat, but am by no means certain.

November 7th.—Wake up in middle of the night and remember that I never asked Robert to water indoor bulbs, planted by me in September and left, as usual, in attic. Decide to send him a cable in the morning. Doze again, but wake once more with strong conviction that cable would not be a success as: *(a)* It might give Robert a shock. *(b)* He would think it extravagant. Decide to write letter about bulbs instead.

Final spate of social activities marks the day, and includes further visit to World Fair, when I talk a great deal about buying presents for everybody at home, but in the long run only buy Indian silver bracelet with turquoise for Caroline C. (Will take up no extra room in flat, and am hoping she will wear it, rather than leave it about.)

Telegram is brought me in the course of the afternoon, am seized by insane conviction that it must be from Robert to say he *has* watered the bulbs, but this stretching long arm of coincidence altogether too far, and decide instead that Robin has been mortally injured at football. Turns out to be communication of enormous length inviting me to Lecture in New York some weeks hence followed by lunch at which many distinguished writers hope to be present which will mean many important contacts also publicity Stop Very cordially Katherine Ellen Blatt. Read all this through at least four times before any of it really sinks in, and then send back brief, but I hope civil, refusal.

Eat final dinner with Arthur and his family—tell them how much I hope they will all come and stay with Robert and myself next summer—and part from them with extreme regret.

Just as I am leaving, another telegram arrives: Please reconsider decision cannot take no for an answer literary luncheon really important function will receive wide press publicity letter follows Stop Very sincerely Katherine Ellen Blatt.

Am a good deal stunned by this and decide to wait a little before answering.

Arthur sees me off at station, and I board immense train on which I appear to be the only passenger. Procedure ensues with which I am rapidly becoming familiar, including unsatisfactory wash in small Toilet Compartment which only provides revolting little machine that oozes powder instead of decent soap. Reflect how much Robert would dislike this. Thought of Robert is, as usual, too much for me, and I retire to sleeping accommodation behind customary green curtains, and prepare to sink into a sentimental reverie, but discover that I am sitting on green paper bag into which porter has put my hat. Revulsion of feeling follows, and I give way to anger instead of sorrow.

November 8th.—Consider in some detail American preference for travelling at night, and decide that I do not, on the whole, share it. Meals undoubtedly excellent, but other arrangements poor, and arrival in small hours of the morning utterly uncongenial.

Cleveland reached at 8 A.M.—eyes still bunged with sleep and spirits at a very low ebb—and am met by extremely blue-eyed Miss V. from book-store who says that she has Heard About me from Pete. She gets into a car with me but does not say where she is taking me, and talks instead about Winchester—which she says she has never seen—American novels, and the Chicago World Fair. (Can foresee that long before the end of tour I shall have said all I have to say about World Fair, and shall find myself trying to invent brand-new details.)

Drive through a great many streets, and past large numbers of superb shop-fronts, and presently Miss V. says in a reverent voice, *There* is Hallé Brothers, and I say Where, and have a vague idea that she is referring to local Siamese Twins, but this turns out complete mistake and Hallé Brothers revealed as enormous department store, in which Miss V. is in charge of book department. Moreover Mrs. Hallé, it now appears, is to be my hostess in Cleveland and we have practically reached her house.

At this I look frantically in my hand-bag, discover that I have left lipstick in the train, do what I can with powder-compact, but results on pale-green complexion not at all satisfactory, and realise, not for the first time, that accidental sitting on my hat in the train did it no good.

Mrs. Hallé, however, receives me kindly in spite of these misfortunes, shows me very nice bedroom which she says belongs to her daughter Katherine, now in Europe, and says that breakfast will be ready when I am. Spend some time walking round Katherine's bedroom, and am deeply impressed by her collection of books, which comprises practically everything that I have always meant to read. Decide that Katherine must be wholly given over to learning, but reverse this opinion on going into Katherine's bathroom and finding it filled with coloured glass bottles, pots, and jars of the most exotic description. Evidently other and more frivolous preoccupations as well.

This conjecture confirmed when I meet Katherine's sister Jane at breakfast—very pretty and well dressed, and can probably do everything in the world well. Distinct tendency comes over me to fall into rather melancholy retrospect concerning my own youth, utterly denuded of any of the opportunities afforded to present generation. Remind myself in time, however, that this reflection is as wholly un-original as any in the world, and that I myself invariably dislike and despise those who give vent to it.

Excellent coffee and bacon help further to restore me, and I decide that almost every sorrow can probably be assuaged by a respectable meal. (*Mem.:*Try to remember this and act upon it next time life appears to be wholly intolerable.)

Programme for the day is then unfolded, and comprises—to my surprise—inspection of three schools. The blue-eyed Miss V. has said that I am interested in education. Think this over, decide that I ought to be interested in education, and that therefore I probably am, and accept with what is invariably referred to by dear Vicky as *alacricity*.

Morning is accordingly spent in visiting schools, of which I like two and am staggered by the third, which is said to be on totally New Age lines, and designed in order to enable the very young—ages two to nine—to develop their own life-pattern without interference.

We get various glimpses of the life-patterns, many of which seem to me to be rather lacking in coherence, and are shown round by very earnest lady with projecting teeth, wearing a cretonne smock.

She says that the Little Ones are never interfered with, and that punishments are unknown. Even supervision is made as unobtrusive as possible. This she demonstrates by conducting us to landing on the staircase, where large window overlooks playground. Here, she says, teachers and parents can watch the little people at play. Play very often a great revelation of character.

Can see no reason in the world why little people should not look up from play and plainly perceive the noses of their parents and guardians earnestly pressed to the window above them—but do not, naturally, say so.

We then inspect Art—angular drawings of crooked houses and deformed people and animals, painted in pale splotches of red and green and yellow—Handwork—paper boxes with defective corners, and blue paper mats—and Carpentry—a great many pieces of wood and some sawdust.

Just as we leave Bathrooms—each child, says the cretonne smock passionately, has its own little tooth-brush in its own little mug—on our way downstairs to Gymnasium, Miss V. draws my attention to a door with a little grille in it, through which we both peer in some astonishment.

Infant child aged about three is revealed, sitting in solitude on tiny little chair in front of tiny little table gazing thoughtfully at a dinner-plate. What, I ask the cretonne smock, is this? She looks distressed and replies Oh, that's the Food Problem.

We all three contemplate this distressing enigma in silence, and the Food Problem gazes back at us with intelligent interest and evident gratification, and we shortly afterwards retire.

Should be very sorry indeed to see New Age methods adopted at eminently sane and straightforward establishment where Vicky is—I hope—at present receiving education.

November 9th.—Life in Cleveland agreeable, but rushed. Book-store talk takes place as ordained by Pete, and is principally remarkable because Lowell Thomas, celebrated American writer, precedes me and gives very amusing lecture. Entire book department turned upside-down searching for green ink, as it is, says Miss V., well known that Lowell T. never will autograph his books in any other colour. Am frightfully impressed by this, and join in green-ink hunt. It is finally run to earth, and I suggest gumming on small label with L. T.'s name and telling him that it has been waiting ever since his last visit. Am unfortunately never informed whether this ingenious, though perhaps not very straightforward, scheme is actually adopted.

Shake hands with Lowell Thomas afterwards, and like the look of him, and buy two of his books, which are all about Arabia, and will do for Robert. He autographs them in green ink, and I seriously contemplate telling Miss V. that it will be utterly impossible for me to sign a single volume of my own unless I can do so with an old-fashioned goose-quill and blue blotting-paper.

Rather amusing incident then ensues, on my preferring modest request that I may be allowed to Wash My Hands. Will I, says Miss V., anxiously, be *very careful indeed?* No later than last year, celebrated Winner of Pulitzer Prize succeeded in locking the door in such a way that it was totally impossible to unlock it again, and there she was, says Miss V. agitatedly, unable to make anybody hear, and meanwhile everybody was looking for her all over the store, and couldn't imagine what had happened, and eventually A Man had to break down the door.

Am horrified by this tragedy, and promise to exercise every care, but feel that Miss V. is still reluctant to let me embark on so perilous an enterprise. Moreover, am stopped no less than three time's, on my way down small and obscure passage, and told by various young employees to be very careful indeed, last year Pulitzer Prize-winner was locked in there for hours and hours and couldn't be got out, man had to be sent for, door eventually broken down. Am reminded of the Mistletoe Bough and wonder if this distressing modern version has ever been immortalised in literature, and if not how it could be done.

Various minor inspirations flit across my mind, but must be dealt with later, and I concentrate on warnings received, and succeed in locking and unlocking door with complete success.

Pulitzer Prize-winner either remarkably unfortunate, or else strangely deficient in elementary manual dexterity. Am taken home in car by Mrs. Hallé—who tells me on the way the whole story of Pulitzer Prize-winner and her misfortune all over again—and am tactfully invited to rest before dinner.

(Rumour that American hostesses give one no time to breathe definitely unjust.)

November 10th.—Bid reluctant farewell to Cleveland. Last day is spent in visiting book store, signing name—which I shall soon be able to do in my sleep—and being taken by the Hallé family to see film: *Private Life of Henry VIII.* Charles Laughton is, as usual, marvellous, but film itself seems to me overrated. Tell Mrs. H. that I would leave home any day for C. Laughton, at which she looks surprised, and I feel bound to add that I don't really mean it literally. She then takes me to the station and we part amicably with mutual hopes of again meeting, in England or elsewhere.

Just as I am preparing to board train, Miss V. arrives with English mail for me, which she has received at eleventh hour and is kindly determined that I shall have without delay. Am extremely grateful, and settle down to unwonted luxury of immediate and uninterrupted reading.

Robert, Vicky and Robin all well: Robert much occupied with British Legion concert, which he says was well attended, but accompanist suddenly overcome by influenza and great difficulty in finding a substitute. Miss Pankerton played Violin Solo, and this, says Robert, was much too long. Can well believe it. Nothing whatever in garden, but one indoor bulb shows signs of life. Am not at all exhilarated at this, and feel sure that bulbs would have done better under my own eye. Early Romans should certainly be well above ground by now.

Only remaining news is that Lady B. has offered to organise Historical Pageant in the village next summer, featuring herself as Mary Queen of Scots, and everybody else as morris-dancers, jesters, knights and peasantry. Robert and Our Vicar dead against this, and Our Vicar's Wife said to have threatened to resign the living. Living not hers to resign, actually, but am in complete sympathy with general attitude implied, and think seriously of cabling to say so.

In any case, Why Mary Queen of Scots? No possible connection with remote village in Devonshire. Can only suppose that Lady B. can think of no better way of displaying her pearls.

Surprised to find that dear Rose has actually remembered my existence—no doubt helped by extraordinarily interesting series of postcards sent at intervals ever since I left—and has written short letter to say that she hopes I am having a very interesting time, and she envies me for being in America, London is very cold and foggy. Brief references follow to concert, lecture on child-guidance, and several new plays recently attended by Rose, and she closes with best love and is mine ever. *P.S.* Agatha is engaged to Betty's brother, followed by three marks of exclamation.

Have never, to my certain knowledge, heard of Agatha, Betty or the brother in my life.

Large envelope addressed by Caroline Concannon comes next, and discloses number of smaller envelopes, all evidently containing bills, also card of invitation to a Public Dinner, price one guinea, postcard from Cissie Crabbe—saying that it is a Long While since she had news of me—and a letter from C. C. herself.

This proves to be agreeably scandalous, and relates astonishing behaviour of various prominent people. C. C. also adds that she thinks it will amuse me to hear that a great friend of hers is divorcing his wife and twelve co-respondents will be cited, there could have been many more, but only twelve names have come out. Am disturbed by Caroline's idea of what is likely to amuse me, but after a while feel that perhaps she has not wholly misjudged me after all.

Forgive her everything when final page of letter reveals that she has been to visit both Robin and Vicky at school, and gives full and satisfactory account of each, even entering into details regarding Robin's purchases at penny-in-the-slot machines on pier, and Vicky's plate.

Letter concludes, as usual, with sweeping and optimistic assertion that Everything in Doughty Street is Absolutely All Right, the carpets want cleaning rather badly, and Caroline will try and get them done before I get back, also the chandelier, absolutely pitch-black.

Caroline Concannon is followed by Felicity—blue envelope and rather spidery handwriting—who hopes that I am making some money. She herself is overdrawn at the Bank and can't make it out, she *knows* she has spent far less than usual in the last six months, but it's always the way. Felicity further hopes that I have good news of the children, and it will be nice to know I'm safely home again, and ends with renewed reference to finance, which is evidently an overwhelming preoccupation. Feel sorry for Felicity, and decide to send her another postcard, this time from Toronto.

Remaining correspondence includes earnest letter of explanation—now some weeks out of date—from laundry concerning pair of Boy's Pants—about which I remember nothing whatever—begging letter from a Society which says that it was established while King William IV. was still on the throne—and completely illegible letter from Mary Kellway.

Make really earnest effort to decipher this, as dear Mary always so amusing and original—but can make out nothing whatever beyond my own name—which I naturally know already—and statement that Mary's husband has been busy with what looks like—but of course cannot be—pencils and geranium-tops—and that the three children have gone either to bed, to the bad, to board or to live at place which might be either Brighton, Ilford or Egypt.

Feel that this had better be kept until time permits of my deciphering it, and that all comment should be reserved until I can feel really convinced of exact nature of items enumerated. In the meanwhile, dear Mary has received no postcards at all, and decide that this omission must be repaired at earliest opportunity.

November 11th.—Reach Toronto at preposterous hour of 5.55 A.M. and decide against night-travelling once and for ever, day having actually started with Customs inspection considerably before dawn. Decide to try and see what I can of Canada and glue my face to the window, but nothing visible for a long while. Am finally rewarded by superb sunrise, but eyelids feel curiously stiff and intelligence at lowest possible ebb. Involve myself in rather profound train of thought regarding dependence of artistic perception upon physical conditions, but discover in the midst of it that I am having a nightmare about the children both being drowned, and have dropped two books and one glove.

Coloured porter appears with clothes-brush, and is evidently convinced that I cannot possibly present myself to Canadian inspection without previously submitting to his ministrations. As I feel that he is probably right, I stand up and am rather half-heartedly dealt with, and then immediately sit down again, no doubt in original collection of dust, and weakly present porter with ten cents, at which he merely looks disgusted and says nothing.

Train stops, and I get out of it, and find myself—as so often before—surrounded by luggage on strange and ice-cold platform, only too well aware that I probably look even more *dégommée* than I feel.

Canadian host and hostess, with great good-feeling, have both turned out to meet me, and am much impressed at seeing that neither cold nor early rising have impaired complexion of my hostess. Find myself muttering quotation—

Alike   to   her   was   time   or   tide,
November's snow, or July's pride—

but Canadian host, Mr. Lee, says Did I speak? and I have to say No, no, nothing at all, and remind myself that talking aloud to oneself is well-known preliminary to complete mental breakdown. Make really desperate effort, decide that I *am* awake and that the day has begun—began, in fact, several hours ago—and that if only I am given a cup of very strong coffee quite soon, I shall very likely find myself restored to normal degree of alertness.

Mr. Lee looks kind; Mrs. Lee—evidently several years younger—is cheerful and good-looking, and leads the way to small car waiting outside station.

This appears to me to be completely filled already by elderly lady in black, large dog and little girl with pigtails. These, I am told, are the near neighbours of the Lees. Should like to ask why this compels them to turn out at four o'clock in the morning in order to meet complete stranger, but do not, naturally, do so.

Explanation is presently proffered, to the effect that the Falls of Niagara are only eighty miles away, and I am to visit them at once, and the little girl—Minnie—has never seen them either, so it seemed a good opportunity. Minnie, at this, jumps up and down on the seat and has to be told to Hush, dear. Her mother adds that Minnie is very highly strung. She always has been, and her mother is afraid she always will be. The doctor has said that she has, at nine years old, the brain of a child of fifteen. I look at Minnie, who at once assumes an interesting expression and puts her head on one side, at which I immediately look away again, and feel that I am not going to like Minnie. (This impression definitely gains ground as day goes on.) Mrs. Lee, on the other hand, earns gratitude almost amounting to affection by saying that I must have breakfast and a bath before anything else, and that both these objectives can be attained on the way to Niagara.

I ask what about my luggage? and am told that a friend of some cousins living near Hamilton has arranged to call for it later and convey it to Mr. Lee's house. Am impressed, and decide that mutual readiness to oblige must be a feature of Canadian life. Make mental note to develop this theme when talking to Women's Institute at home.

At this point Minnie's mother suddenly asks What we are all here for, if not to help one another, and adds that, for her part, her motto has always been: Lend a Hand. Revulsion of feeling at once overtakes me, and I abandon all idea of impressing the Women's Institute with the desirability of mutual good-will.

Car takes us at great speed along admirable roads—very tight squeeze on back seat, and Minnie kicks me twice on the shins and puts her elbow into my face once—and we reach house standing amongst trees.

Is this, I civilly enquire of Mrs. Lee, her home? Oh dear no. The Lees live right on the other side of Toronto. This is Dr. MacAfie's place, where we are all having breakfast. And a bath, adds Mrs. L., looking at me compassionately. Dr. MacAfie and his wife both turn out to be Scotch. They receive us kindly, and Mrs. L. at once advocates the bathroom for me.

Bath is a success, and I come down very hungry, convinced that it must be nearer lunch-time than breakfast-time. Clock, however, declares it to be just half-past seven. Find myself counting up number of hours that must elapse before I can hope to find myself in bed and asleep. Results of this calculation very discouraging.

Breakfast, which is excellent, restores me, and we talk about America—the States very unlike Canada—the Dominions—life in Canada very like life in the Old Country—snow very early this year and my impressions of Chicago World Fair.

Minnie interrupts a good deal, and says Need she eat bacon, and If she went on a big ship to England she knows she'd be very sick. At this everybody laughs—mine very perfunctory indeed—and her mother says that really, the things that child says...and it's always been like that, ever since she was a tiny tot. Anecdotes of Minnie's infant witticisms follow, and I inwardly think of all the much more brilliant remarks made by Robin and Vicky. Should much like an opportunity for retailing these, and do my best to find one, but Minnie's mother gives me no opening whatever.

Expedition to Niagara ensues, and I am told on the way that it is important for me to see the Falls from the *Canadian* side, as this is greatly superior to the *American* side. Can understand this, in a way, as representing viewpoint of my present hosts, but hope that inhabitants of Buffalo, where I go next, will not prove equally patriotic and again conduct me immense distances to view phenomenon all over again.

Am, however, greatly impressed by Falls, and say so freely. Mr. Lee tells me that I really ought to see them by night, when lit up by electricity, and Mrs. Lee says No, that vulgarises them completely, and I reply Yes to both of them, and Minnie's mother asks What Minnie thinks of Niagara, to which Minnie squeaks out that she wants her dinner right away this minute, and we accordingly proceed to the Hotel.

Buy a great many postcards. Minnie watches this transaction closely, and says that she collects postcards. At this I very weakly present her with one of mine, and her mother says that I am really much too kind—with which I inwardly agree. This opinion intensified on return journey, when Minnie decides to sit on my lap, and asks me long series of complicated questions, such as Would I rather be an alligator who didn't eat people, or a man who had to make his living by stealing, or a tiny midget in a circus? Reply to these and similar conundrums more or less in my sleep, and dimly hear Minnie's mother telling me that Minnie looks upon her as being just a great, big, elder sister, and always tells her everything just as it pops into her little head, and don't I feel that it's most important to have the complete confidence of one's children?

Can only think, at the moment, that it's most important to have a proper amount of sleep.

Mr. Lee's house is eventually attained, and proves to be outside Toronto. Minnie and her parent are dropped at their own door, and say that they will be popping in quite soon, and I get out of car and discover that I am alarmingly stiff, very cold, and utterly exhausted.

Am obliged to confess this state of affairs to Mrs. Lee, who is very kind, and advises bed. Can only apologise, and do as she suggests.

November 12th.—Spend comparatively quiet day, and feel better. Host and hostess agree that I must remain indoors, and as it snows violently I thankfully do so, and write very much overdue letters.

Quiet afternoon and evening of conversation. Mr. Lee wants to know about the Royal Family—of which, unfortunately, I can tell him little except what he can read for himself in the papers—and Mrs. Lee asks if I play much Bridge. She doesn't, she adds hastily, mean on Sundays. Am obliged to reply that I play very little on any day of the week, but try to improve this answer by adding that my husband is very good at cards. Then, says Mrs. Lee, do I garden? No—unfortunately not. Mrs. Lee seems disappointed, but supposes indulgently that writing a book takes up quite a lot of time, and I admit that it does, and we leave it at that.

Am rather disposed, after this effort, to sit and ponder on extreme difficulty of ever achieving continuity of conversation when in the society of complete strangers. Idle fancy crosses my mind that Mr. Alexander Woollcott would make nothing of it at all, and probably conduct whole conversation all by himself with complete success. Wonder—still more idly—if I shall send him a postcard about it, and whether he would like one of Niagara.

November 12th. (continued).—Main purpose of Canadian visit—which is small lecture—safely accomplished. Audience kind, rather than enthusiastic. Mrs. Lee says that she could tell I was nervous. Cannot imagine more thoroughly discouraging comment than this.

Mr. Lee very kindly takes me to visit tallest building in the British Empire, which turns out to be a Bank. We inspect Board-rooms, offices, and finally vaults, situated in basement and behind enormous steel doors, said to weigh incredible number of tons and only to be opened by two people working in conjunction. I ask to go inside, and am aghast when I do so by alarming notice on the wall which tells me that if I get shut into the vaults by accident I am not to be alarmed, as there is a supply of air for several hours. Do not at all like the word "several", which is far from being sufficiently specific, and have horrid visions of being shut into the vaults and spending my time there in trying to guess exactly when "several" may be supposed to be drawing to an end. Enquire whether anyone has ever been locked into the vaults, and if they came out mad, but Mr. Lee only replies No one that he has ever heard of, and appears quite unmoved by the idea.

Have often associated banking with callousness, and now perceive how right I was.

Evening is passed agreeably with the Lees until 9 o'clock, when Minnie and parent descend upon us and we all talk about Minnie for about half an hour. Take cast-iron resolution before I sleep never to make either of the dear children subjects of long conversations with strangers.

(Mem.: To let Robert know of this resolution, as feel sure he would approve of it.)

November 13th.—Five o'clock train is selected to take me to Buffalo, and am surprised and relieved to find that I have not got to travel all night, but shall arrive in four and a half hours. Luncheon-party is kindly given in my honour by the Lees—Minnie not present, but is again quoted extensively by her mother—and I am asked more than once for opinion on relative merits of Canada and the United States. Can quite see that this is very delicate ground, and have no intention whatever of committing myself to definite statement on the point. Talk instead about English novelists—Kipling evidently very popular, and Hugh Walpole looked upon as interesting new discovery—and I am told by several people that I ought to go to Quebec.

As it is now impossible for me to do so, this leads to very little, beyond repeated assurances from myself that I should *like* to go to Quebec, and am exceedingly sorry not to be going there. One well-informed lady tells me that Harold Nicolson went there and liked it very much. Everybody receives this in respectful silence, and I feel that Harold Nicolson has completely deflated whatever wind there may ever have been in my sails.

Morale is restored later by my host, who takes me aside and says that I have been Just a breath of fresh air from the Old Country, and that I must come again next year. Am touched, and recklessly say that I will. Everyone says good-bye very kindly, and gentleman hitherto unknown—tells me that he will drive me to the station, as he has to go in that direction later. Minnie's mother heaps coals of fire on my head by telling me that she has a little present for my children, and is going just across the street to get it. This she does, and present turns out to be a Service revolver, which she thinks my boy may like. Can reply with perfect truth that I feel sure of it, and am fortunately not asked for my own reaction; or Robert's.

Revolver, of which I am secretly a good deal afraid, is wedged with the utmost difficulty into the least crowded corner of my attaché-case, and I take my departure.

Rather strange sequel follows a good deal later, when I am having dinner on train and am called out to speak to Customs official. Cannot imagine what he wants me for, and alarming visions of

Sing-Sing assail me instantly. Go so far as to decide that I shall try and brief Mr. Clarence Darrow for the defence—but this probably because he is the only American barrister whose name I can remember.

Customs awaits me in the corridor, and looks very grave. Is mine, he enquires, the brown attaché-case under the fur coat in the parlour-car? Yes, it is. Then why, may he ask, do I find it necessary to travel with a revolver? Freakish impulse momentarily assails me, and I nearly—but not quite—reply that I have to do so for the protection of my virtue. Realise in time that this flippancy would be quite out of place, and might very likely land me in serious trouble, so take wiser and more straightforward course of telling Customs the whole story of the Service revolver.

He receives it sympathetically, and tells me that he is a family man himself. (Association here with Dickens—"I'm a mother myself, Mr. Copperfull"—but Customs perhaps not literary, or may prefer Mark Twain, so keep it to myself.)

Conversation follows, in which I learn names and ages of the whole family of Customs, and in return show him small snapshot of Robin and Vicky with dog Kolynos, playing in the garden. Customs says That's a fine dog, and asks what breed, but says nothing about R. and V. Am slightly disappointed, but have noticed similar indifference to the children of others on the part of parents before.

November 13th (continued).—Train, in the most singular way, arrives at Buffalo ahead of time. Large and very handsome station receives me, and I walk about vast hall, which I seem to have entirely to myself. Red-capped porter, who is looking after my luggage, seems prepared to remain by it for ever in a fatalistic kind of way, and receives with indifference my announcement that Someone will be here to meet me by and by.

Can only hope I am speaking the truth, but feel doubtful as time goes on. Presently, however, tall lady in furs appears, and looks all round her, and I say "Dr. Livingstone, I presume?" but not aloud—and approach her. Am I, I ask, speaking to Mrs. Walker? Lady, in a most uncertain voice, replies No, no—not Mrs. *Walker*. We gaze at one another helplessly and she adds, in a still more uncertain voice: Mrs. Luella White Clarkson. To this I can think of no better reply than Oh, and we walk away from one another in silence, only, however, to meet again repeatedly in our respective perambulations. (Should much like to know what peculiar law governs this state of affairs. Station is perfectly enormous, and practically empty, and neither Mrs. L. W. C. nor myself has the slightest wish ever again to come face to face with one another, yet we seem perfectly unable to avoid doing so. Eventually take to turning my back whenever I see her approaching, and walking smartly in the opposite direction.)

Mental comparison of American and English railway stations follows, and am obliged to admit that America wins hands down. Have never in my life discovered English station that was warm, clean or quiet, or at which waiting entailed anything but complete physical misery. Compose long letter to Sir Felix Pole on the subject, and have just been publicly thanked by the Lord Mayor of London for ensuing reformations, when I perceive Red-cap making signs. Mrs. Walker—small lady in black, very smart, and no resemblance whatever to Mrs. L. W. C.—has appeared. She apologises very nicely for being late, and I apologise—I hope also very nicely—for the train's having been to early—and we get into her motor which is, as usual, very large and magnificent. (Remarkable contrast between cars to which I am by now becoming accustomed and ancient Standard so frequently pushed up the hills at home—but have little doubt that I shall be delighted to find myself in old Standard once more.)

Have I, Mrs. Walker instantly enquires, visited the Falls of Niagara? Am obliged to admit, feeling apologetic, that I have. Thank God for that, she surprisingly returns. We then embark on conversation, and I tell her about Canada, and make rather good story out of preposterous child Minnie. Mrs. Walker is appreciative, and we get on well.

Buffalo is under snow, and bitterly cold. House, however, delightfully warm, as usual. Mrs. Walker hopes that I won't mind a small room: I perceive that the whole of drawing-room, dining-room and Robert's study could easily be fitted inside it, and that it has a bath-room opening out of one end and a sitting-room the other, and say, Oh no, not in the least.

She then leaves me to rest.

November 14th.—Clothes having emerged more crumpled than ever from repeated packings, I ask if they could be ironed, and this is forthwith done by competent maid, who tells me what I know only too well already, that best black-and-white evening dress has at one time been badly stained by coffee, and will never really look the same again.

Mrs. Walker takes me for a drive, and we see as much of Buffalo as is compatible with its being almost altogether under snow, and she asks me rather wistfully if I can tell her anything about celebrated English woman pianist who once stayed with her for a fortnight and was charming, but has never answered any letters since. Am disgusted with the ingratitude of my distinguished countrywoman, and invent explanations about her having been ill, and probably forbidden by the doctor to attend to any correspondence whatever.

Mrs. Walker receives this without demur, but wears faintly cynical expression, and am by no means convinced that she has been taken in by it, especially as she tells me later on that when in London a year ago she rang up distinguished pianist, who had apparently great difficulty in remembering who she was. Feel extremely ashamed of this depth of ingratitude, contrast it with extraordinary kindness and hospitality proffered to English visitors by American hosts, and hope that someone occasionally returns some of it.

Become apprehensive towards afternoon, when Mrs. W. tells me that the Club at which I am to lecture has heard all the best-known European speakers, at one time or another, and is composed of highly cultivated members.

Revise my lecture frantically, perceive that it is totally lacking in cultivation, or even ordinary evidences of intelligence, and ask Mrs. W. whether she doesn't think the Club would like a reading instead. Have no real hope that this will succeed, nor does it. Nothing for it but to put on my newly ironed blue, powder my nose, and go.

Mrs. W. is considerate, and does not attempt conversation on the way, except when she once says that she hopes I can eat oysters. Feel it highly improbable that I shall be able to eat anything again, and hear myself muttering for sole reply: *"Who knows but the world may end to-night?"*

World, needless to say, does not end, and I have to pull myself together, meet a great many Club members—alert expressions and very expensive clothes—and subsequently mount small platform on which stand two chairs, table and reading-desk.

Elderly lady in grey takes the chair—reminds me of Robert's Aunt Eleanor, but cannot say why—and says that she is not going to speak for more than a few moments. Everyone, she knows, is looking forward to hearing something far more interesting than any words of *hers* can be. At this she glances benevolently towards me, and I smile modestly, and wish I could drop down in a fit and be taken away on the spot. Instead, I have presently to get on to my feet and adjust small sheet of notes—now definitely looking crumpled and dirty—on to reading-desk.

Head, as usual, gets very hot, and feet very cold, and am badly thrown off my balance by very ancient lady who sits in the front row and holds her hand to her ear throughout, as if unable to hear a word I utter. This, however, evidently not the case, as she comes up afterwards and tells me that she was one of the Club's original members, and has never missed a single lecture. Offer her my congratulations on this achievement, and then wish I hadn't, as it sounds conceited, and add that I hope she has found it worth the trouble. She replies rather doubtfully Yes—on the whole, Yes—and refers to André Maurois. *His* lecture was positively brilliant. I reply, truthfully, that I feel sure it was, and we part. Aunt Eleanor and I exchange polite speeches—I meet various ladies, one of whom tells me that she knows a great friend of mine. Rose, I suggest? No, not Rose. Dear Katherine Ellen Blatt, who is at present in New York, but hopes to be in Boston when I am. She has, says the lady, a perfectly lovely personality. And she has been saying the most wonderful things about *me.* Try to look more grateful than I really feel, over this.

(Query: Does not public life, even on a small scale, distinctly lead in the direction of duplicity? *Answer:* Unfortunately, Yes.)

Aunt Eleanor now approaches and says—as usual—that she knows an Englishwoman can't do without her tea, and that some is now awaiting me. Am touched by this evidence of thoughtfulness, and drink tea—which is much too strong—and eat cinnamon toast, to which I am by no means accustomed, and which reminds me very painfully of nauseous drug frequently administered to Vicky by Mademoiselle.

Conversation with Aunt Eleanor ensues. She does not, herself, write books, she says, but those who do have always had a strange fascination for her. She has often *thought* of writing a book—many of her friends have implored her to do so, in fact—but no, she finds it impossible to begin. And yet, there are many things in her life about which whole, entire novels might well be written. Everybody devotes a moment of rather awed silence to conjecturing the nature of Aunt Eleanor's singular experiences, and anti-climax is felt to have ensued when small lady in rather frilly frock suddenly announces in a pipy voice that she has a boy cousin, living in Oklahoma, who once wrote something for the *New Yorker,* but they didn't ever publish it.

This more or less breaks u the party, and Mrs. Walker drives me home again, and says in a rather exhausted way that she thanks Heaven that's over.

We talk about Aunt Eleanor—she has been twice married, one husband died and the other one left her, but no divorce—and she has two daughters but neither of them live at home. Can quite understand it, and say so. Mrs. Walker assents mildly, which encourages me to add that I didn't take to Aunt Eleanor much. No, says Mrs. Walker thoughtfully, she doesn't really think that Aunt E. and I would ever get on together very well.

Am quite surprised and hurt at this, and realise that, though I am quite prepared to dislike Aunt Eleanor, I find it both unjust and astonishing that she should be equally repelled by me. Rather interesting side-light on human nature thrown here, and have dim idea of going into the whole thing later, preferably with Rose—always so well informed—or dear Mary Kellway, full of intelligence, even though unable to write legibly—but this probably owing to stress of life in country parish, so much more crowded with activities than any other known form of existence.

Dinner-party closes the day, and I put on backless evening dress, add coatee, take coatee off again, look at myself with mirror and hand-glass in conjunction, resume coatee, and retain it for the rest of the evening.

November 15th.—Weather gets colder and colder as I approach Boston, and this rouses prejudice in me, together with repeated assurances from everybody I meet to the effect that Boston is the most English town in America, and I shall simply adore it. Feel quite unlike adoration as train takes me through snowy country, and affords glimpses of towns that appear to be entirely composed of Gasoline Stations and Motion-Picture Theatres. Towards nine-o'clock in the morning I have an excellent breakfast—food in America definitely a very bright spot—and return to railway carriage, where I see familiar figure, hat still worn at very dashing angle, and recognise Pete. Feel as if I had met my oldest friend, in the middle of a crowd of strangers, and we greet one another cordially. Pete tells me that I seem to be standing up to it pretty well—which I take to be a compliment to my powers of endurance—and unfolds terrific programme of the activities he has planned for me in Boston.

Assent to everything, but add that the thing I want to do most of all is to visit the Alcott House at Concord, Mass. At this Pete looks astounded, and replies that this is, he supposes, merely a personal fancy, and so far as he knows no time for anything of that kind has been allowed in the schedule. Am obliged to agree that it probably hasn't, but repeat that I really want to do that more than anything else in America. (Much later on, compose eloquent and convincing speech, to the effect that I have worked very hard and done all that was required of me, and that I am fully entitled to gratify my own wishes for one afternoon at least. Am quite clear that if I had only said all this at the time, Pete would have been left without a leg to stand upon. Unfortunately, however, I do not do so.)

Boston is reached—step out of the train into the iciest cold that it has ever been my lot to encounter—and am immediately photographed by unknown man carrying camera and unpleasant little light-bulb which he flashes unexpectedly into my eyes. No one makes the slightest comment on this proceeding, and am convinced that he has mistaken me for somebody quite different.

Two young creatures from the *Boston Transcript* meet me, and enquire, more or less instantly, what I feel about the Problem of the American Woman, but Pete, with great good-feeling, suggests that we should discuss it all in taxi on our way to Hotel, which we do. One of them then hands me a cable—(announcing death of Robin or Vicky?)—and says it arrived this morning.

455

Cable says, in effect, that I must at all costs get into touch with Caroline Concannon's dear friend and cousin Mona, who lives in Pinckney Street, would love to meet me, has been written to, everything all right at flat, love from Caroline.

Am quite prepared to get into touch with dear friend and cousin, but say nothing to Pete about it, for fear of similar disconcerting reaction to that produced by suggestion of visiting Alcott House.

Am conducted to nice little Hotel in Charles Street, and told once by Pete, and twice by each of the *Boston Transcript* young ladies, that r am within a stone's-throw of the Common Chief association with the Common is *An Old-Fashioned Girl,* in which heroine goes tobogganing, but do not refer to this, and merely reply that That is very nice. So it may be, but not at the moment when Common, besides being deep in snow, is quite evidently being searched from end to end by ice-laden north-east wind.

Pete, with firmness to which I am by now accustomed, says that he will leave me to unpack but come and fetch me again in an hour's time, to visit customary book-shops.

Telephone bell in sitting-room soon afterwards rings, and it appears that dear Rose—like Caroline Concannon—has a friend in Boston, and that the friend is downstairs and proposes to come up right away and see me. I say Yes, yes, and I shall be delighted, and hastily shut suit-cases which I have this moment opened, and look at myself in the glass instead.

Results of this inspection are far from encouraging, but nothing can be done about it now, and can only concentrate on trying to remember everything that Rose has ever told me about her Boston friend called, I believe, Fanny Mason. Sum-total of my recollections is that the friend is very literary, and has written a good deal, and travelled all over the world, and is very critical.

Am rather inclined to become agitated by all this, but friend appears, and has the good-feeling to keep these disquieting attributes well out of sight, and concentrate on welcoming me very kindly to Boston—(exactly like England and all English people always love it on that account)—and enquiring affectionately about Rose. (Am disgusted to learn from what she says that dear Rose has written to her far more recently, as well as at much greater length, than to myself. Shall have a good deal to say to Rose when we meet again.)

Friend then announces that she has A Girl downstairs. The Girl has brought a car, and is going to show me Boston this morning, take me to lunch at a Women's Club, and to a tea later. This more than kind, but also definitely disconcerting in view of arrangements made by Pete, and I say Oh, Miss Mason—and then stop, rather like heroine of a Victorian novel.

Miss M. at once returns that I must not dream of calling her anything but Fanny. She has heard of me for years and years, and we are already old friends. This naturally calls for thanks and acknowledgments on my part, and I then explain that publishers' representative is in Boston, and calling for me in an hour's time, which I'm afraid means that I cannot take advantage of kind offer.

Miss M.—Fanny—undefeated, and says it is Important that I should see Boston, no one who has not done so can be said to know anything whatever about America, and The Girl is waiting for me downstairs. Suggest—mostly in order to gain time—that The Girl should be invited to come up, and this is done by telephone.

She turns out to be very youthful and good-looking blonde, introduced to me as "Leslie"—(first names evidently the fashion in Boston)—and says she is prepared to take me anywhere in the world, more or less, at any moment.

Explain all over again about Pete and the booksellers. Fanny remains adamant, but Leslie says reasonably: What about tomorrow instead, and I advance cherished scheme for visiting Alcott House. This, it appears, is fraught with difficulties, as Alcott House is impenetrably shut at this time of year. Feel that if Pete comes to hear of this, my last hope is gone. Leslie looks rather sorry for me, and says perhaps something could be arranged, but anyway I had better come out now and see Boston. Fanny is also urgent on this point, and I foresee deadlock, when telephone rings and Pete is announced, and is told to come upstairs.

Brilliant idea then strikes me; I introduce everybody, and tell Pete that there has been rather a clash of arrangements, but that doubtless he and Miss Mason can easily settle it between themselves. Will they, in the meanwhile, excuse me, as I positively must see about my unpacking? Retreat firmly into the bedroom to do so, but spend some of the time with ear glued to the wall, trying to ascertain whether Pete and Miss M.—both evidently very strong personalities—are going to fly at one another's throats or not. Voices are certainly definitely raised, usually both at once, but nothing more formidable happens, and I hope that physical violence may be averted.

Decide that on the whole I am inclined to back Pete, as possessing rock-like quality of immovability once his mind is made up—doubtless very useful asset in dealing with authors, publishers and so on.

Subsequent events prove that I am right, and Pete walks me to book-shop, with laconic announcement to Leslie and Miss M.—Fanny—that I shall beat their disposal by 12.30.

November 16th.—Most extraordinary revolution in everybody's outlook—excepting my own—by communication from Mr. Alexander Woollcott. He has, it appears, read in a paper *(Boston Transcript?)* that my whole object in coming to America was to visit the Alcott House, and of this he approves to such an extent that he is prepared to Mention It in a Radio Talk, if I will immediately inform him of my reactions to the expedition.

Entire *volte-face* now takes place in attitude of Pete, Fanny and everybody else. If Alexander Woollcott thinks I ought to visit Alcott House, it apparently becomes essential that I should do so and Heaven and earth must, if necessary, be moved in order to enable me to. Am much impressed by the remarkable difference between enterprise that I merely want to undertake for my own satisfaction, and the same thing when it is advocated by Mr. A. W.

Result of it all is that the members of the Alcott-Pratt family are approached, they respond with the greatest kindness, and offer to open the house especially for my benefit. Fanny says that Leslie will drive me out to Concord on Sunday afternoon, and she will herself accompany us, not in order to view Alcott House—she does not want to see it, which rather shocks me—but to visit a relation of her own living there. Pete does not associate himself personally with the expedition, as he will by that time have gone to New York, Charleston, Oshkosh or some other distant spot—but it evidently meets with his warmest approval, and his last word to me is an injunction to take paper and pencil with me and send account of my impressions red-hot to Mr. Alexander Woollcott.

November 18th.—Go to see football game, Harvard v. Army. Am given to understand—and can readily believe—that this is a privilege for which Presidents, Crowned Heads and Archbishops would one and all give ten years of life at the very least. It has only been obtained for me by the very greatest exertions on the part of everybody.

Fanny says that I shall be frozen—(can well believe it) but that it will be worth it, and Leslie thinks I may find it rather difficult to follow—but it will be worth it—and they both agree that there is always a risk of pneumonia in this kind of weather. Wonder if they are going to add that it will still be worth it, because if so, shall disagree with them forcibly—but they heap coals of fire on my head for this unworthy thought by offering to lend me rugs, furs, mufflers and overshoes. Escort has been provided for me in the person of an admirer of Fanny's—name unknown to me from first to last—and we set out together at one o'clock. Harvard stadium is enormous—no roof, which I think a mistake—and we sit in open air, and might be comfortable if temperature would only rise above zero. Fanny's admirer is extremely kind to me, and can only hope he isn't thinking all the time how much pleasanter it would be if he were only escorting Fanny instead.

(Reminiscence here of once-popular song: *I am dancing with tears in my eyes 'Cos the girl in my arms isn't you.* Have always felt this attitude rather hard on girl actually being danced with at the moment of singing.)

Ask questions that I hope sound fairly intelligent, and listen attentively to the answers. Escort in return then paralyses me by putting to me various technical points in regard to what he calls the English Game. Try frantically to recall everything that I can ever remember having heard from Robin, but am only able to recollect that he once said Soccer was absolutely lousy and that I rebuked him for it. Translate this painful reminiscence into civilised version to the effect that Rugger is more popular than Soccer with Our Schoolboys.

Presently a mule appears and is ridden round the field by a member of one team or the other—am not sure which—and I observe, idiotically, that It's like a Rodeo—and immediately perceive that it isn't in the least, and wish I hadn't spoken. Fortunately a number of young gentlemen in white suddenly emerge on to the ground, turn beautiful back somersaults in perfect unison, and cheer madly through a megaphone. Am deeply impressed, and assure Fanny's admirer that we have, nothing in the least like that at Wembley, Twickenham, nor, so far as I know, anywhere else. He agrees, very solemnly, that the cheers are a Great Feature of the Game.

Soon afterwards we really get started, and I watch my first game of American football. Players all extensively padded and vast numbers of substitute-players wait about in order to rush in and replace them when necessary. Altogether phenomenal number of these exchanges takes place, but as no stretchers visible, conclude that most of the injuries received fall short of being mortal.

Fanny's admirer gives me explanations about what is taking place from time to time, but is apt to break off in the middle of a phrase when excitement overcomes him. Other interruptions are occasioned by organised yellings and roarings, conducted from the field, in which the spectators join.

At about four o'clock it is said to be obvious that Harvard hasn't got a chance, and soon afterwards the Army is declared to have won.

Escort and I look at each other and say Well, and Wasn't it marvellous? and then stand up, and I discover that I am quite unable to feel my feet at all, and that all circulation in the rest of my body has apparently stopped altogether—probably frozen.

We totter as best we can through the crowd—escort evidently just as cold as I am, judging by the colour of his face and hands—and over bridge, past buildings that I am told are all part of the College, and to flat with attractive view across the river. As I have not been warned by anybody that this is in store, I remain unaware throughout why I am being entertained there, or by whom. Hot tea, for once, is extraordinarily welcome, and so is superb log-fire; and I talk to unknown, but agreeable, American about President Roosevelt, the state of the dollar—we both take a gloomy view of this—and extreme beauty of American foliage in the woods of Maine—where I have never set foot, but about which I have heard a good deal.

November 19th.—Expedition to Concord—now smiled upon by all, owing to intervention of dear Alexander W.—takes place, and definitely ranks in my own estimation higher than anything else I have done in America.

All is snow, silence and loveliness, with frame-houses standing amongst trees, and no signs of either picture-houses, gasoline-stations, or hot-dog stalls. Can think of nothing but *Little Women,* and visualise scene after scene from well-remembered and beloved book. Fanny, sympathetic, but insensible to appeal of *Little Women,* is taken on to see her relations, and I remain with Mrs. Pratt, surviving relative of Miss Alcott, and another elderly lady, both kind and charming and prepared to show me everything there is to see.

Could willingly remain there for hours and hours.

Time, however, rushes by with its usual speed when I am absorbed and happy, and I am obliged to make my farewells, collect postcards and pictures with which I have most kindly been presented, and book given me for Vicky which I shall, I know, be seriously tempted to keep for myself.

Can think of nothing but the March family for the remainder of the day, and am much annoyed at being reminded by Fanny and Leslie that whatever happens, I must send my impressions to Mr. Alexander Woollcott without delay.

November 20th.—Just as day of my departure from Boston arrives, weather relents and suddenly becomes quite mild. I go and call on Caroline Concannon's friend, and am much taken with her. She has no party, which is a great relief, and we talk about England and C. C. Very amusing and good company, says the friend, and I agree, and add that Caroline is looking after my flat during my absence. Slight misgiving crosses my mind as to the literal accuracy of this statement, but this perhaps ungenerous, and make amends by saying that she is Very Good with Children—which is perfectly true.

Walk back across Common, and see very pretty brick houses, Queen Anne style. Old mauve glass in many window-panes, but notice cynically that these always appear in ground-floor windows, where they can be most easily admired by the passers-by.

Decide that this is certainly a good moment for taking Rose's advice to buy myself a Foundation Garment in America, as they understand these things, says Rose, much better than we do in England. I accordingly enter a shop and find elderly saleswoman, who disconcerts me by saying in a sinister way that I certainly can't wear the ordinary suspender-belt, that's very evident. She supplies me with one that is, I suppose, removed from the ordinary, and her last word is an injunction to me not to forget that whatever I do, I mustn't wear an ordinary belt. It'll be the complete ruin of my figure if I do. Depart, in some dejection.

Shock awaits me on return to Hotel when I discover that Miss Katherine Ellen Blatt has just arrived, and has sent up a note to my room to say so. It will, she writes, be so delightful to meet again, she revelled in our last delightful talk and is longing for another. Entertain myself for some little while in composing imaginary replies to this, but candour, as usual, is obliged to give, way to civility, and I write very brief reply suggesting that K. E. B. and I should meet in the hall for a moment before my train leaves when she, Fanny Mason—whom she doubtless knows already—and Leslie will all be privileged to see one another.

Customary preoccupation with my appearance follows, and I go in search of hotel Beauty-parlour. Intelligent young operator deals with me, and says that one of her fellow-workers is also British and would be very happy to meet me. My English accent, she adds thoughtfully, is a prettier one than hers. This definitely no overstatement, as fellow-worker turns out to be from Huddersfield and talks with strong North-country accent.

On return to ground floor—hair at least clean and wavy—Miss Blatt materialises. She greets me as an old and dear friend and tells me that one or two perfectly lovely women of her acquaintance are just crazy to meet me, and are coming to a Tea in the hotel this very afternoon in order that they may have the pleasure of doing so.

I thank her, express gratification and regret, and explain firmly that I am going on to Washington this afternoon. Oh, returns Miss Blatt very blithely indeed, I don't have to give that a thought. She has taken it up with my publishers by telephone, and they quite agree with her that the contacts she has arranged for me are very, very important, and I can easily make the ten-thirty train instead of the six, and reach Washington in plenty of time.

All presence of mind deserts me, and I say Yes, and Very Well, to everything, and soon afterwards find myself suggesting that Miss Blatt should lunch at my table.

(Query: Why? Answer: comes there none.)

Lunch proves definitely informative: Miss Blatt tells me about dear Beverley Nichols, who has just sent her a copy of his new book, and dear Anne Parrish, who hasn't yet sent a copy of hers, but is certainly going to do so. I say Yes, and How Splendid, and wonder what Miss Blatt can be like when she is all by herself, with no celebrities within miles, and no telephone. Strange idea crosses my mind that in such circumstances she would probably hardly exist as a personality at all, and might actually dissolve into nothingness. Something almost metaphysical in this train of thought, and am rather impressed by it myself, but cannot, naturally, ask Miss Blatt to share in my admiration.

Talk to her instead about murder stories, which I like, and instance Mrs. Belloc Lowndes as a favourite of mine. Miss Blatt says No, murder stories make no appeal to her whatever, but Mrs. Belloc Lowndes—Marie—is one of her very dearest friends. So is another Marie—Queen of Roumania. So, oddly enough, is Marie Tempest.

On this note we part, before K. E. B. has time to think of anybody else whose name happens to be Marie.

Am obliged to extract red frock from suit-case, in which I have already carefully folded it—but perhaps not as carefully as I hoped, as it comes out distinctly creased—and put it on in honour of Miss Blatt's tea. This duly takes place, and is handsomely attended, Miss B. no doubt as well known in Boston as in New York, London, Paris and Hong Kong. Am gratified at seeing Caroline C.'s charming friend, and should like to talk to her, but am given no opportunity.

Very large lady in black pins me into a corner, tells me to sit down, and takes her seat beside me on small sofa. She then tells me all about a local literary society, of which she is herself the foundress and the president, called the Little Thinkers. (Can only hope that in original days when name of club was chosen, this may have been less ironical than it is now.) President—hope with all my heart that she hasn't guessed my thoughts—adds that they chose to call themselves Little Thinkers because it indicates modesty. They are none of them, she explains, really Deep and Profound—not like Darwin or Huxley—(I make effort—not good—to look surprised and incredulous at this). But they all like to *think,* and to ask themselves questions. They read, if she may say so, very deeply. And they meet and Discuss Things every Tuesday afternoon. Had I

459

been staying here rather longer, says President, the Little Thinkers would have been only too pleased to invite me as Guest of Honour to one of their meetings, and perhaps I would have given them a short talk on the Real Meaning of Life.

Should like to reply flippantly: Perhaps and Perhaps Not—but President of the Little Thinkers evidently no good subject for wit of this description, so express instead respectful regret that time will not allow me to avail myself of the suggested privilege.

Moment, it now seems to me, has definitely arrived for both the President of the L. T.s and myself to move gracefully away from one another and each talk to somebody else. This turns out to be not easy of accomplishment, as President is between me and the rest of the world, and seems not to know how to get away, though am morally convinced that she would give quite a lot to be able to do so. We continue to look at one another and to say the same things over and over again in slightly different words, and I see Katherine Ellen Blatt eyeing me rather severely from the far end of the room, and evidently feeling—with justice—that I am not doing my fair share towards making a success of the party.

At last become desperate, say Well, in a frantic way, and rise to my feet. President of the L. T.s immediately leaps to hers—looking unspeakably relieved—and we exchange apologetic smiles and turn our backs on one another.

(*Mem.:* Surely very interesting statistics might be collected with regard to the number of such social problems and varying degrees of difficulty with which these can, or cannot, be solved? Would willingly contribute small *exposé* of my own, to any such symposium. *Query:* Approach Lord Beaverbrook on the point, or not? Sunday papers frequently very dull, and topics raised by correspondents often tedious to the last degree.)

Catch the eye of Caroline C.'s friend, Mona, and am delighted and prepare to go and talk to her, but Miss Blatt immediately stops me and says that I must meet a very old friend of hers, Mr. Joseph Ross, who has lived for fifty-three years in America.

Take this to imply that he once lived somewhere else, and after a few words have no difficulty in guessing that this was Scotland. Refer to it rather timidly—who knows what reasons Mr. J. R. may have had for leaving his native land?—but he tells me rather disconcertingly that he goes home once in every two years, and merely lives in America because the climate suits him. I say Yes, it's very dry, and we both look out of the window, and Mr. Joseph Ross—rather to my relief—is taken away from me by a strange lady, who smiles at me winningly and says that I mustn't mind, as millions of people are just waiting for a chance to talk to me, and it isn't fair of Uncle Joe to monopolise me. Am struck by this flattering, if inaccurate, way of putting it, and look nervously round for the millions, but can see no sign of any of them.

Make another effort to reach Caroline's friend, and this time am successful. She smiles, and looks very pretty, and says that Caroline never writes to her but she sometimes gets news through Jane and Maurice. Do I know Jane and Maurice and the twins?

Am obliged to disclaim any knowledge of any of them, but add madly that I do so wish I *did*. Friend receives this better than it deserves, and we are just going happily into the question of mutual acquaintances when the President of the Little Thinkers recrudesces, and says that She wants to have me meet one of their very brightest members, Mrs. Helen Dowling Dean. Mrs. Helen Dowling Dean is a Southerner by birth and has a perfectly wonderful Southern accent.

Caroline's friend melts away and Mrs. Helen Dowling Dean and I confront one another, and she tells me that Boston is a very English town, and that she herself comes from the South and that people tell her she has never lost her Southern accent. She is—as usual—extremely agreeable to look at, and I reflect dejectedly that all the women in America are either quite young and lovely, or else quite old and picturesque. Ordinary female middle-age, so prevalent in European countries, apparently nonexistent over here. (Katherine Ellen Blatt an exception to this rule, but probably much older than she looks. Or perhaps much younger? Impossible to say.)

Party draws to a close—discover that, as usual, I have a sore throat from trying to scream as loud as everybody else is screaming—and Fanny Mason kindly extracts me from saying good-bye and takes me up to my room—which I shall have to leave only too soon for the station.

Take the opportunity of writing letters to Robert and to each of the children. Am obliged to print in large letters for Vicky, and this takes time, as does endeavour to be reasonably legible for

Robin's benefit. Robert's letter comes last, and is definitely a scrawl. (Wish I had judged Mary Kellway rather less severely.)

Am seen off at station by Fanny, Leslie, Katherine Ellen Blatt, and three unidentified men—probably admirers of Fanny and Leslie. One of them, quite gratuitously and much to my surprise and gratification, presents me with large and handsome book, called *American Procession,* for the journey.

Train departs—extraordinary and unpleasant jerk that I have noticed before in American trains, and which I think reflects ill on their engine-drivers—and I look at *American Procession,* which is full of photographs and extremely interesting. Am, however, depressed to realise that I can quite well remember most of the incidents depicted, and that fashions which now appear wholly preposterous were worn by myself in youth and even early middle life.

Retire to bed, under the usual difficulties, behind curtain—always so reminiscent of film stories—though nothing could be less like heroines there depicted than I am myself.

November 21st.—Immense relief to find Washington very much warmer than Boston, even at crack of dawn. Nobody meets me, at which I am slightly relieved owing to rather disastrous effect of curtailed sleep on complexion and appearance generally, and I proceed by taxi to Hotel indicated by Pete. General impression as I go that Washington is very clean and pretty, with numbers of dazzlingly white buildings. Am rather disposed to feel certain that every house I see in turn must be the White House. Hotel is colossal building of about thirty-five stories, with three wings, and complete platoon of negro porters in pale-blue uniforms standing at the entrance. Find myself at once thinking of *Uncle Tom's Cabin,* and look compassionately at porters, but am bound to say they all seem perfectly cheerful and prosperous.

Rather disconcerting reception at the desk in office follows. The clerk is extremely sorry, but the hotel is absolutely full up. Not a bedroom anywhere. We look at one another rather blankly, and I feebly mention name of extremely distinguished publishing firm by which I have been directed to came here and not elsewhere. That don't make a mite of difference, says the clerk, shaking his head. He's just as sorry as he can be, but not a bed is available. Very well. I resign myself. But as I am a complete stranger, perhaps he will very kindly tell me where I can go next? Oh yes, says the clerk, looking infinitely relieved, he can easily do that. The Woodman-Park Hotel will be tickled to death to have me go there. He will phone up right away and make the reservation for me, if I like. Accept this gratefully, and in a moment all is settled, and blue-uniformed darkie has put me and my luggage into another taxi, after I have gratefully thanked hotel-clerk and he has assured me that I am very welcome. (This perhaps slightly ironical in the circumstances—but evidently not intended to be so.)

Woodman-Park Hotel also turns out to be enormous, and reflection assails me that if I am also told here that Every room is full up, I shall definitely be justified in coming to the conclusion that there is something about my appearance which suggests undesirability. Am, however, spared this humiliation. Woodman-Park—negroes this time in crushed-strawberry colour—receives me with affability, and accommodates me with room on the fifteenth floor.

I unpack—dresses creased as usual, and I reflect for the thousandth time that I shall never make a good packer, and that continual practice is, if anything, making me worse—and go down to breakfast. Excellent coffee starts, not for the first time, rather melancholy train of thought concerning Cook, and her utter inability to produce even moderately drinkable coffee. Shall make a point of telling her how much I have enjoyed *all* coffee in America.

(Query: Is this a cast-iron resolution, to be put into effect directly I get home in whatever mood I may happen to find Cook—or is it merely one of those rhetorical flashes, never destined to be translated into action? *Answer,* all too probably: The latter.)

Reflect with satisfaction that I can actually claim friendship with official in the State Department, met several times in London, and whom I now propose to ring up on the telephone as soon as the day is respectably advanced. Recollect that I liked him very much, and hope that this may still hold good after lapse of five years, and may also extend to newly acquired wife, whom I have never met, and that neither of them will take a dislike to me.

(Query: Has rebuff at first Hotel visited slightly unnerved me? If so, morale will doubtless be restored by breakfast. Order more coffee and a fresh supply of toast on the strength of this thought.)

Greatly surprised as I leave dining-room to find myself presented with small card on which is printed name hitherto totally unknown to me: General Clarence Dove. I say to the waiter—not very intelligently—What is this? and he refrains from saying, as he well might, that It's a visiting-card, and replies instead that It's the gentleman at the table near the door.

At this I naturally look at the table near the door, and elderly gentleman with bald head and rather morose expression makes half-hearted movement towards getting up, and bows. I bow in return, and once more scrutinise card, but it still looks exactly the same, and I am still equally unable to wake any association in connection with General Clarence Dove. Feel constrained to take one or two steps towards him, which courtesy he handsomely returns by standing up altogether and throwing his table-napkin on the floor.

Cannot help wishing the waiter would put things on a more solid basis by introducing us, but this feeling probably only a manifestation of British snobbishness, and nothing of the kind occurs. Elderly gentleman, however, rises to the occasion more or less, and tells me that he has been written to by Mrs. Wheelwright, of Long Island, and told to look out for me, and that I am writing a book about America. He has therefore ventured to make himself known to me.

Express my gratification, and beg him to go on with his breakfast. This he refuses to do, and says—obviously untruly—that he has finished, but that we could perhaps take a little turn together in the sunshine. This hope rather optimistic, as sunshine though present turns out to be of poor quality, and we hastily retire to spacious hall, furnished with alternate armchairs and ashtrays on stands. Central heating, undeniably, far more satisfactory than sunshine, at this time of year, but doubtful if this thought would appeal to General Clarence Dove—aspect rather forbidding—so keep it to myself.

Just as I am preparing to make agreeable speech anent the beauties of Washington, the General utters.

He hears, he says, that I am writing a book about America. Now, he may be old-fashioned, but personally he finds this rather difficult to understand.

I say, No, no, in great agitation, and explain that I am *not* writing a book about America, that I shouldn't ever dream of doing such a thing, after a six months' visit, and that on the contrary—

A book about America, says the General, without paying the slightest attention to my eloquence, is not a thing to be undertaken in that spirit at all. Far too many British and other writers have made this mistake. They come over—whether invited or not—and are received by many of the best people in America, and what do they do in return? I again break in and say that I know, and I have often thought what a pity it is, and the last thing I should ever dream of doing would be to—

Besides, interrupts the General, quite unmoved, America is a large country. A very large country indeed. To write a book about it would be a very considerable task. What people don't seem to understand is that no person can call themselves qualified to write a book about it after a mere superficial visit lasting less than two months.

Am by now almost frantic, and reiterate in a subdued shriek that I agree with every word the General is saying, and have always thought exactly the same thing—but all is in vain. He continues to look straight in front of him, and to assure me that there can be no greater mistake than to come over to a country like America, spend five minutes there, and then rush home and write a book about it. Far too many people have done this already.

Can see by now that it is completely useless to try and persuade General Clarence Dove that I am not amongst these, and have no intention of ever being so—and I therefore remain silent whilst he says the same things all over again about five times more.

After this he gets up, assures me that it has been a pleasure to meet me, and that he will certainly read my book about America when it comes out, and we part—never, I hope, to meet again.

Am completely shattered by this extraordinary encounter for several hours afterwards, but eventually summon up enough strength to ring up Department of State—which makes me feel important—and get into touch with friend James. He responds most agreeably, sounds flatteringly pleased at my arrival, and invites me to lunch with himself and his wife and his baby. Baby?

Oh yes, he has a daughter aged two months. Very intelligent. I say, quite truthfully, that I should love to see her, and feel that she will be a much pleasanter companion than General Clarence Dove—and much more on my own conversational level into the bargain.

James later fetches me by car, and we drive to his apartment situated in street rather strangely named O. Street. I tell him that he hasn't altered in the very least—he says the same, though probably with less truth, about me, and enquires after Robert, the children, Kolynos the dog—now, unfortunately, no longer with us—and Helen Wills the cat. I then meet his wife, Elizabeth—very pretty and attractive—and his child, Katherine—not yet pretty, but I like her and am gratified because she doesn't cry when I pick her up—and we have peaceful and pleasant lunch.

Conversation runs on personal and domestic lines, and proves thoroughly congenial, after recent long spell of social and literary exertions. Moreover, *Anthony Adverse* motif entirely absent, which is a relief.

Reluctantly leave this agreeable atmosphere in order to present myself at Department Store, in accordance with explicit instructions received from Pete.

Arrange, however, to go with James next day and be shown house of George Washington.

Store is, as usual, large and important, and I enter it with some trepidation, and very nearly walk straight out again on catching sight of large and flattering photograph of myself, taken at least three years ago, propped up in prominent position. Printed notice below says that I am Speaking at Four O'clock this afternoon.

Memory transports me to village at home, and comparative frequency with which I Speak, alternately with Our Vicar's Wife, at Women's Institute, Mothers' Union, and the like organisations, and total absence of excitement with which both of us are alike hailed. Fantastic wonder crosses my mind as to whether photograph, exhibited beforehand, say in Post Office window, would be advisable, but on further reflection decide against this.

(Photograph was taken in Bond Street, head and shoulders only, and can distinctly recollect that Vicky, on seeing it, enquired in horrified tones if I was *all* naked?)

Enquire for book department, am told to my confusion that I am in it, and realise with horror that I am, but have been completely lost in idiotic and unprofitable reverie. Make no attempt to explain myself, but simply ask for Mrs. Roberta Martin, head of department. She appears—looks about twenty-five but is presumably more—and welcomes me very kindly.

Would I like tea *before* I speak, or *after?*

She asks this so nicely that I am impelled to candour, and say that I wouldn't really like tea at all, but could we have a cup of coffee together afterwards?

We could, and do.

Find ourselves talking about boys. Mrs. R. M. says she has a son of fourteen, which I find quite incredible, and very nearly tell her so, but am restrained by sudden obscure association with extraordinary behaviour of General Clarence Dove.

Boys a great responsibility, we agree, but very nice. Her Sidney and my Robin have points in common. Did Sidney like parties in early childhood? No, not at all. Wild horses wouldn't drag him to one. Am relieved to hear it, especially when his mother adds that It All Came Later.

Have vision of Robin, a year or two hence, clamouring for social life. (Probably finding it very difficult to get, now I come to think of it, as neighbourhood anything but populous.)

Time, with all this, passes very agreeably, and Mrs. Roberta Martin and I part with mutual esteem and liking.

Take a look round various departments as I go out, and see several things I should like to buy, but am already doubtful if funds are going to hold out till return to New York, so restrict myself to small sponge, pad of note-paper, and necklace of steel beads that I think may appeal to Mademoiselle and go with her Grey.

November 22nd.—Home of George Washington inspected, and am much moved by its beauty. Enquire where historical cherry-tree can be seen, but James replies—surely rather cynically?—that cherry-tree episode now practically discredited altogether. Find this hard to believe.

(*Mem.:* Say nothing about it at home. Story of George W. and cherry-tree not infrequently useful as illustration when pointing out to dear Vicky the desirability of strict truthfulness. Moreover, entire story always most popular when playing charades.)

On leaving George Washington, we proceed to home of General Robert E. Lee, but unfortunately arrive there too late and have to content ourselves with pressing our noses against the windows. Subsequently miss the way, in terrific maze of avenues that surround the house, find gate at last and discover that it is locked, have visions of staying there all night, but subsequently unfastened gate is reached, and we safely emerge.

James shows me the Lincoln Memorial, and I definitely think it the most beautiful thing, without exception, that I have seen in America.

Tour is concluded by a drive through Washington, and I see the outside of a good many Embassies, and am reluctantly obliged to conclude that the British one is far indeed from being the most beautiful amongst them. Decide that the Japanese one is the prettiest.

Evening spent with James and Elizabeth. Katherine still engaging, but slightly inclined to scream when left alone in bed-room. (Am forcibly reminded of dear Robin's very early days.)

Leave early, as I fancy James and Elizabeth both kept thoroughly short of sleep by infant Katherine. Cannot, however, deter James from driving me back to Hotel. Am greatly impressed with this chivalrous, and universal, American custom.

James and I part at the door, strawberry-clad negro porters spring to attention as I enter, and I perceive, to my horror, that General Clarence Dove is sitting in the hall, doing nothing whatever, directly between me and elevator. Turn at once to the newspaper-stand and earnestly inspect motion-picture magazines—in which I am not in the least interested—cigars, cigarettes and picture-postcards. Take a long time choosing six of these, and paying for them. Cannot, however, stand there all night, and am at last compelled to turn round. General Clarence Dove still immovable. Decide to bow as I go past, but without slackening speed, and this proves successful, and I go up to bed without hearing more of my book about America.

November 23rd.—Am introduced by James to important Head of Department, Miss Bassell, who kindly takes me to the White House, where I am shown State Rooms and other items of interest.

Portraits of Presidents' Wives in long rows present rather discouraging spectacle. Prefer not to dwell on these, but concentrate instead on trying to remember Who was Dolly Madison? Decide—tentatively—that she must have been an American equivalent of Nell Gwyn, but am not sufficiently sure about it to say anything to Miss B. In any case, have no idea which, if any, of America's Presidents would best bear comparison with King Charles II.

Lunch-party brings my stay in Washington to a close, and James and Elizabeth—kind-hearted and charming to the last—take me and my luggage to the station. Am relieved to find that both look rested, and are able to assure me that dear little Katherine allowed them several hours of uninterrupted sleep.

Say good-bye to them with regret, and promise that I will come and stay with them in their first Consulate, but add proviso—perhaps rather ungraciously?—that it must be in a warm climate.

Find myself wondering as train moves out what dear Robert will say to the number of future invitations that I have both given and accepted?

November 25th.—Philadelphia reached yesterday, and discover in myself slight and irrational tendency to repeat under my breath: "I'm off to Philadelphia in the morning". Do not know, or care, where this quotation comes from.

Unknown hostess called Mrs. Elliot receives me, and I join enormous house-party consisting of all her relations. Do not succeed, from one end of visit to the other, in discovering the name of any single one of them.

Mrs. E. says she likes *The Wide Wide World*. Am pleased at this, and we talk about it at immense length, and I tell her that a Life of Susan Warner exists, which she seems to think impossible, as she has never heard of it. Promise to send her a copy from England, and am more convinced than ever—if possible—that we are none of us prophets in our own country.

(Mem.: Make note of Mrs. Elliot's address. Also send postcard to favourite second-hand bookseller to obtain copy of *Susan Warner* for me. Shall look extremely foolish if it isn't forthcoming, after all I've said. But must not meet trouble half-way.)

Lecture—given, unfortunately, by myself—takes place in the evening at large Club. Everyone very kind, and many intelligent questions asked, which I do my best to answer. Secretary forgets to give me my fee, and lack courage to ask for it, but it subsequently arrives by special delivery, just as I am going to bed.

November 27th.—Unexpected arrival of guardian angel Ramona Herdman from New York. Am delighted to see her, and still more so when she gives me collection of letters from England. As usual, am on my way to book-store where I have to make short speech, and am unable to read letters in any but the most cursory way—but ascertain that no calamity has befallen anybody, that Robert will be glad to hear when he is to meet me at Southampton, and that Caroline Concannon has written a book, and it has instantly been accepted by highly superior publishing-house. Am not in the least surprised at this last piece of information. C. C. exactly the kind of young person to romp straight to success. Shall probably yet see small blue oval announcement on the walls of 57 Doughty Street, to the effect that they once sheltered the celebrated writer, Caroline Concannon. Feel that the least I can do is to cable my congratulations, and this I do, at some expense.

Miss Ramona Herdman and I then proceed to book-store, where we meet head of department, Mrs. Kooker. Talk about Vera Brittain—*Testament of Youth* selling superbly, says Mrs. K.—also new film, *Little Women,* which everyone says I *must* see in New York—(had always meant to, anyway)—and recent adoption by American women of tomato-juice as a substitute for cocktails. Conversation then returns to literature, and Mrs. Kooker tells me that Christmas sales will soon be coming on, but that Thanksgiving interferes with them rather badly. Try and look as if I thoroughly understood and sympathised with this, but have to give it up when she naively enquires whether Thanksgiving has similar disastrous effect on trade in England? Explain, as delicately as I can, that England has never, so far as I know, returned any particular thanks for occasion thus commemorated in the United States, and after a moment Mrs. K. sees this, and is amused.

Customary talk takes place—shall soon be able to say it in my sleep—and various listeners come up and speak to me kindly afterwards. Completely unknown lady in brown tells me that we met years ago, and she remembers me so well, and is so glad to see me again. Respond to this as best I can, and say—with only too much truth—that the exact whereabouts of our last encounter has, temporarily, escaped me. What! cries the lady reproachfully, have I forgotten dear old Scarborough?

As I have never in my life set foot in dear old Scarborough, this proves very, very difficult to answer. Do not, in fact, attempt to do so, but merely shake hands with her again and turn attention to someone who is telling me that she has a dear little granddaughter, aged five, who says most amusing things. If only, grandmother adds wistfully, she could *remember* them, she would tell them to me, and then I should be able to put them into a book.

Express regrets—unfortunately civil, rather than sincere—at having to forgo this privilege, and we separate. Miss Herdman—has mysteriously produced a friend and a motor-car—tells me that I am going with her to tea at the house of a distinguished critic. Alexander Woollcott? I say hopefully, and she looks rather shocked and replies No, no, don't I remember that A. W. lives in unique apartment in New York, overlooking the East River? There are, she adds curtly, other distinguished critics besides Alexander Woollcott, in America. Have not the courage,\ after this *gaffe,* to enquire further as to my present destination.

Tea-party, however, turns out pleasantly—which is, I feel, more than I deserve—and I enjoy myself, except when kind elderly lady—mother of hostess—suddenly exclaims that We mustn't forget we have an Englishwoman as our guest, and immediately flings open two windows. Ice-cold wind blows in, and several people look at me—as well they may—with dislike and resentment.

Should like to tell them that nobody is more resentful of this hygienic outburst than I am myself—but cannot, of course, do so. Remind myself instead that a number of English people have been known to visit the States, only to die there of pneumonia.

Am subsequently driven back to Mrs. Elliot's by R. Herdman and friend, Miss H. informing me on the way that a speaking engagement has been made for me at the Colony Club in New York. At this the friend suddenly interposes, and observes morosely that the Colony Club is easily the most difficult audience in the world. They look at their wrist-watches all the time.

Can quite see what fun this must be for the speaker, and tell Miss H. that I do not think I can possibly go to the Colony Club at all but she takes no notice.

November 28th. New York.—Return to New York, in company with Miss Herdman, and arrive at Essex House once more. Feel that this is the first step towards home, and am quite touched and delighted when clerk at bureau greets me as an old *habituée*. Feel, however, that he is disappointed in me when I am obliged to admit, in reply to enquiry, that I did *not* get to Hollywood—and was not, in fact, invited to go there. Try to make up for this by saying that I visited World Fair at Chicago extensively—but can see that this is not at all the same thing.

Letters await me, and include one from Mademoiselle, written as usual in purple ink on thin paper, but crossed on top of front page in green—association here with Lowell Thomas—who says that she is all impatience to see me once more, it seems an affair of centuries since we met in *"ce brouhaha de New-York",* and she kisses my hand with the respectful affection.

(The French given to hyperbolical statements. No such performance has ever been given by Mademoiselle, or been permitted by myself to take place. Am inclined to wonder whether dear Vicky's occasional lapses from veracity may not be attributed to early influence of devoted, but not flawless, Mademoiselle?)

Just as I come to this conclusion, discover that Mademoiselle has most touchingly sent me six American Beauty roses, and immediately reverse decision as to her effect on Vicky's morals. This possibly illogical, but definitely understandable from feminine point of view.

Ring up Mademoiselle—who screeches a good deal and is difficult to hear, except for *Mon Dieu!* which occurs often thank her for letter and roses, and ask if she can come and see a film with me to-morrow afternoon. Anything she likes, but not *Henry VIII. Mais non, mais non,* Mademoiselle shrieks, and adds something that sounds like *"ce maudit roi",* which I am afraid refers to the Reformation, but do not enter on controversial discussion and merely suggest *Little Women* instead.

Ah, cries Mademoiselle, *voilà une bonne idée! Cette chère vie de famille—ce gentil roman de la jeunesse—cette drôle de Jo—coeur d'or—tête de linotte*—and much else that I do not attempt to disentangle.

Agree to everything, suggest lunch first but this, Mademoiselle replies, duty will not permit—appoint meeting-place and ring off.

Immediate and urgent preoccupation, as usual, is my hair, and retire at once to hotel Beauty-parlour, where I am received with gratifying assurances that I have been missed, and competently dealt with.

Just as I get upstairs again telephone bell rings once more, and publishers demand—I think unreasonably—immediate decision as to which boat I mean to sail in, and when. Keep my head as far as possible, turn up various papers on which I feel sure I have noted steamship sailings—(but which all turn out to be memos about buying presents for the maids at home, pictures of America for the Women's Institute, and evening stockings for myself)—and finally plump for the *Berengaria.*

Publishers, with common sense rather than tenderness, at once reply that they suppose I had better go tourist class, as purposes of publicity have now been achieved, and it will be much cheaper.

Assent to this, ring off, and excitedly compose cable to Robert.

November 29th.—Gratifying recrudescence of more or less all the people met on first arrival in New York, who ring up and ask me to lunch or dine before I sail.

Ella Wheelwright sends round note by hand, lavishly invites me to lunch once, and dine twice, and further adds that she is coming to see me off when I sail. Am touched and impressed, and accept lunch, and one dinner, and break it to her that she will have to see me off—if at all—tourist section. Morning filled by visit to publishers' office, where I am kindly received, and told that I have Laid Some Very Useful Foundations, which makes me feel like a Distinguished Personage at the opening of a new Town Hall.

Lecture-agent, whom I also visit, is likewise kind, but perhaps less enthusiastic, and hints that it might be an advantage if I had more than two lectures in my repertoire. Am bound to admit that this seems reasonable. He further outlines, in a light-hearted way, scheme by which I am to undertake lengthy lecture-tour next winter, extending—as far as I can make out—from New York to the furthermost point in the Rockies, and including a good deal of travelling by air.

Return modified assent to all of it, graciously accept cheque due to me, and depart.

Lunch all by myself in a Childs', and find it restful, after immense quantities of conversation indulged in of late. Service almost incredibly prompt and efficient, and find myself wondering how Americans can endure more leisurely methods so invariably prevalent in almost every country in Europe.

Soon afterwards meet Mademoiselle, and am touched—but embarrassed by her excessive demonstrations of welcome. Have brought her small present from Chicago World Fair, but decide not to bestow it until moment immediately preceding separation, as cannot feel at all sure what form her gratitude might take.

We enter picture-house, where I have already reserved seats—Mademoiselle exclaims a good deal over this, and says that everything in America is *un prix fou*—and Mademoiselle takes off her hat, which is large, and balances it on her knee. Ask her if this is all right, or if she hadn't better put it under the seat, and she first nods her head and then shakes it, but leaves hat where it is.

Comic film precedes *Little Women* and is concerned with the misadventure of a house-painter. Am irresistibly reminded of comic song of my youth: "When Father papered the parlour, You couldn't see Pa for paste". Am unfortunately inspired to ask Mademoiselle if she remembers it too. *Comment?* says Mademoiselle a good many times.

Explain that it doesn't matter, I will tell her about it later, it is of no importance. Mademoiselle, however, declines to be put off and I make insane excursion into French: *Quand mon père—*? and am then defeated. *Mais oui,* says Mademoiselle, *quand votre père—*? Cannot think how to say "papered the parlour" in French, and make various efforts which are not a success.

We compromise at last on Mademoiselle's suggestion that *mon père* was perhaps *avec le journal dans le parloir?* which I know is incorrect, but have not the energy to improve upon.

Comic film, by this time, is fortunately over, and we prepare for *Little Women.*

Well-remembered house at Concord is thrown on the screen, snow falling on the ground, and I dissolve, without the slightest hesitation, into floods of tears. Film continues unutterably moving throughout, and is beautifully acted and produced. Mademoiselle weeps beside me—can hear most people round us doing the same—and we spend entirely blissful afternoon.

Performances of Beth, Mrs. March and Professor Bhaer seem to me artistically flawless, and Mademoiselle, between sobs, agrees with me, but immediately adds that Amy and Jo were equally good, if not better.

Repair emotional disorder as best we can, and go and drink strong coffee in near-by drug-store, when Mademoiselle's hat is discovered to be in sad state of disrepair, and she says Yes, it fell off her knee unperceived, and she thinks several people must have walked upon it. I suggest, diffidently, that we should go together and get a new one, but she says No, no, all can be put right by herself in an hour's work, and she has a small piece of black velvet and two or three artificial *bleuets* from her hat of the summer before last with which to construct what will practically amount to a new hat.

The French, undoubtedly, superior to almost every other nationality in the world in thrift, ingenuity and ability with a needle.

Talk about the children—Vicky, says Mademoiselle emotionally, remains superior to any other child she has ever met, or can ever hope to meet, for intelligence, heart and beauty. (Can remember many occasions when Mademoiselle's estimate of Vicky was far indeed from being equally complimentary.) Mademoiselle also tells me about her present pupils, with moderate enthusiasm, and speaks well of her employers—principally on the grounds that they never interfere with her, pay her an enormous salary, and are taking her back to Paris next year.

She enquires about my lecture-tour, listens sympathetically to all that I have to say, and we finally part affectionately, with an assurance from Mademoiselle that she will come and see me off on s.s. *Berengaria, Même,* she adds, *si ça doit me colter la vie.*

Feel confident that no such sacrifice will, however, be required, but slight misgiving crosses my mind, as I walk back towards Central Park, as to the reactions of Mademoiselle and Ella Wheelwright to one another, should they both carry out proposed amiable design of seeing me off.

Cheque received from lecture-bureau, and recollection of dinner engagement at Ella's apartment, encourage me to look in at shop-windows and consider the question of new evening dress, of which I am badly in need, owing to deplorable effects of repeated and unskilful packings and unpackings. Crawl along Fifth Avenue, where shops all look expensive and intimidating, but definitely alluring.

Venture into one of them, and am considerably dashed by the assistant, who can produce nothing but bottle-green or plum colour—which are, she informs me, the only shades that will be worn *at all* this year. As I look perfectly frightful in either, can see nothing for it but to walk out again.

Am then suddenly accosted in the street by young and pretty woman with very slim legs and large fur-collar to her coat. She says How delightful it is to meet again, and I at once agree, and try in vain to remember whether I knew her in Cleveland, Chicago, Buffalo or Boston. No success, but am moved to ask her advice as to purchase of frocks.

Oh, she replies amiably, I must come *at once* to her place—she is, as it happens, on her way there now.

We proceed to her place, which turns out a great success. No prevalence of either bottle-green or plum-colour is noticeable, and I try on and purchase black evening frock with frills and silver girdle. Unknown friend is charming, buys an evening wrap and two scarves on her own account, and declares her intention of coming to see me off on the *Berengaria*.

We then part cordially, and I go back to Essex House, still—and probably for ever—unaware of her identity. Find five telephone messages waiting for me, and am rather discouraged—probably owing to fatigue—but ring up all of them conscientiously, and find that senders are mostly out. Rush of American life undoubtedly exemplified here. Am full of admiration for so much energy and vitality, but cannot possibly attempt to emulate it, and in fact go quietly to sleep for an hour before dressing for Ella's dinner-party.

This takes place in superb apartment on Park Avenue. Ella is in bottle-green—(Fifth Avenue saleswoman evidently quite right)—neck very high in front, but back and shoulders uncovered. She says that she is dying to hear about my trip. She knows that I just loved Boston, and thought myself back in England all the time I was there. She also knows that I didn't much care about Chicago, and found it very Middle-West. Just as I am preparing to contradict her, she begins to tell us all about a trip of her own to Arizona, and I get no opportunity of rectifying her entirely mistaken convictions about me and America.

Sit next man who is good-looking—though bald—and he tells me very nicely that he hears I am a great friend of Miss Blatt's. As I know only too well that he must have received this information from Miss Blatt and none other, do not like to say that he has been misinformed. We accordingly talk about Miss Blatt with earnestness and cordiality for some little while. (Sheer waste of time, no less.)

Leave early, as packing looms ahead of me and have still immense arrears of sleep to make up. Good-looking man—name is Julius van Adams—offers to drive me back, he has his own car waiting at the door. He does so, and we become absorbed in conversation—Miss Blatt now definitely forgotten—and drive five times round Central Park.

Part cordially outside Essex House in the small hours of the morning.

November 30th.—Final stages of American visit fly past with inconceivable rapidity. Consignment of books for the voyage is sent me, very, very kindly, by publishers, and proves perfectly impossible to pack, and I decide to carry them. Everyone whom I consult says Yes, they'll be all right in a strap. Make many resolutions about purchasing a strap.

Packing, even apart from books, presents many difficulties, and I spend much time on all-fours in hotel bedroom, amongst my belongings. Results not very satisfactory.

In the midst of it all am startled—but gratified—by sudden telephone enquiry from publishers: Have I seen anything of the Night Life of New York? Alternative replies to this question flash rapidly through my mind If the Night Life of New York consists in returning at late hours by taxi, through crowded streets, from prolonged dinner-parties, then Yes. If something more specific, then No. Have not yet decided which line to adopt when all is taken out of my hands. Publishers' representative, speaking through the telephone, says with great decision that I cannot possibly be said to have seen New York unless I have visited a night-club and been to Harlem. He has, in fact, arranged that I should do both. When, I ask weakly. He says, To-night, and adds—belatedly and without much sense—If that suits me. As I know, and he knows, that my engagements are entirely in the hands of himself and his firm, I accept this as a mere gesture of courtesy, and simply enquire what kind of clothes I am to wear.

(Note: Shampoo-and-set before to-night, and make every effort to get in a facial as well—if time permits, which it almost certainly won't.)

Later: I become part of the Night Life of New York, and am left more or less stunned by the experience, which begins at seven o'clock when Miss Ramona Herdman comes to fetch me. She is accompanied by second charming young woman—Helen Something—and three men, all tall. (Should like to congratulate her on this achievement but do not, of course, do so.)

Doubt crosses my mind as to whether I shall ever find anything to talk about to five complete strangers, but decide that I shall only impair my morale if I begin to think about that now, and fortunately they suggest cocktails; and these have their customary effect. (Make mental note to the effect that the influence of cocktails on modern life cannot be exaggerated.) Am unable to remember the names of any of the men but quite feel that I know them well, and am gratified when one of them—possessor of phenomenal eyelashes—tells me that we have met before. Name turns out to be Eugene, and I gradually identify his two friends as Charlie and Taylor, but uncertainty prevails throughout as to which is Charlie and which is Taylor.

Consultation takes place—in which I take no active part—as to where we are to dine, Miss Herdman evidently feeling responsible as to impressions that I may derive of New York's Night Life. Decision finally reached that we shall patronise a *Speak-easy de luxe.* Am much impressed by this extraordinary contradiction in terms.

Speak-easy is only two blocks away, we walk there, and I am escorted by Taylor—who may be Charlie but I think not—and he astounds me by enquiring if from my Hotel I can hear the lions roaring in Central Park? No, I can't. I can hear cars going by, and horns blowing, and even whistles—but no lions. Taylor evidently disappointed but suggests, as an alternative, that perhaps I have at least, in the very early mornings, heard the ducks quacking in Central Park? Am obliged to repudiate the ducks also, and can see that Taylor thinks the worse of me. He asserts, rather severely, that he himself has frequently heard both lions and ducks—I make mental resolution to avoid walking through Central Park until I know more about the whereabouts and habits of the lions—and we temporarily cease to converse.

Speak-easy de luxe turns out to be everything that its name implies—all scarlet upholstery, chromium-plating and terrible noise—and we are privileged to meet, and talk with, the proprietor. He says he comes from Tipperary—(I have to stifle immediately impulse to say that It's a long, long way to Tipperary)—and we talk about Ireland, London night-clubs and the Empire State Building. Charlie is suddenly inspired to say—without foundation—that I want to know what will happen to the speak-easy when Prohibition is repealed? To this the proprietor replies—probably with perfect truth—that he is, he supposes, asked that question something like one million times every evening—and shortly afterwards he leaves us.

Dinner is excellent, we dance at intervals, and Eugene talks to me about books and says he is a publisher.

We then depart in a taxi for night-club, and I admire—not for the first time—the amount of accommodation available in American taxis. We all talk, and discuss English food, of which Ramona and her friend Helen speak more kindly than it deserves—probably out of consideration for my feelings. Eugene and Charlie preserve silence—no doubt for the same reason—but Taylor, evidently a strong-minded person, says that he has suffered a good deal from English cabbage. Savouries, on the other hand, are excellent. They are eaten, he surprisingly adds, with a special little knife and fork, usually of gold. Can only suppose that Taylor, when in England, moves exclusively in ducal circles, and hastily resolve never in any circumstances to ask him to my own house where savouries, if any, are eaten with perfectly ordinary electro-plate.

Night-club is reached—name over the door in electric light is simply but inappropriately—*Paradise.* It is, or seems to me, about the size of the Albert Hall, and is completely packed with people all screaming at the tops of their voices, orchestra playing jazz, and extremely pretty girls with practically no clothes on at all, prancing on a large stage.

We sit down at a table, and Charlie immediately tells me that the conductor of the band is Paul Whiteman, and that he lost 75 lbs. last year and his wife wrote a book. I scream back Really? and decide that conversationally I can do no more, as surrounding noise is too overwhelming.

Various young women come on and perform unnatural contortions with their bodies, and I indulge in reflections on the march of civilisation, but am roused from this by Taylor, who roars into my ear that the conductor of the orchestra is Whiteman and he has recently lost 75 lbs. in weight. Content myself this time with nodding in reply.

Noise continues deafening, and am moved by the sight of three exhausted-looking women in black velvet, huddled round a microphone on platform and presumably singing into it—but no sound audible above surrounding din. They are soon afterwards eclipsed by further instalment of entirely undressed *houris,* each waving wholly inadequate feather-fan.

Just as I am deciding that no one over the age of twenty-five should be expected to derive satisfaction from watching this display, Taylor again becomes my informant. The proprietors of this place, he bellows, are giving the selfsame show, absolutely free, to four hundred little newsboys on Thanksgiving Day. Nothing, I reply sardonically, could possibly be healthier or more beneficial to the young—but this sarcasm entirely wasted as it is inaudible, and shortly afterwards we leave. Air of Broadway feels like purity itself, after the atmosphere prevalent inside *Paradise,* which might far more suitably be labelled exactly the opposite.

Now, I enquire, are we going to Harlem? Everyone says Oh no, it's no use going to Harlem before one o'clock in the morning at the very earliest. We are going to another night-club on Broadway. This one is called *Montmartre,* and is comparatively small and quiet.

This actually proves to be the case, and am almost prepared to wager that not more than three hundred people are sitting round the dance-floor screaming at one another. Orchestra is very good indeed—coloured female pianist superlatively so—and two young gentlemen, acclaimed as "The Twins" and looking about fifteen years of age, are dancing admirably. We watch this for some time, and reward it with well-deserved applause. Conversation is comparatively audible, and on the whole I can hear quite a number of the things we are supposed to be talking about. These comprise Mae West, the World Fair in Chicago, film called *Three Little Pigs,* and the difference in programmes between the American Radio and the British Broadcasting Corporation.

Charlie tells me that he has not read my book—which doesn't surprise me—and adds that he will certainly do so at once—which we both know to be a polite gesture and not to be taken seriously.

Conviction gradually invades me that I am growing sleepy and that in another minute I shan't be able to help yawning. Pinch myself under the table and look round at Helen and Ramona, but both seem to be perfectly fresh and alert. Involuntary and most unwelcome reflection crosses my mind that *age will tell.* Yawn becomes very imminent indeed and I set my teeth, pinch harder than ever, and open my eyes as widely as possible. Should be sorry indeed to see what I look like, at this juncture, but am fortunately spared the sight. Taylor is now talking to me—I think about a near relation of his own married to a near relation of an English Duke—but all reaches me through a haze, and I dimly hear myself saying automatically at short intervals that I quite agree with him, and he is perfectly right.

Situation saved by orchestra, which breaks into the "Blue Danube", and Eugene, who invites me to dance. This I gladly do and am restored once more to wakefulness. This is still further intensified by cup of black coffee which I drink immediately after sitting down again, and yawn is temporarily defeated.

Eugene talks about publishing, and I listen with interest, except for tendency to look at his enormous eyelashes and wonder if he has any sisters, and if theirs are equally good.

Presently Ramona announces that it is two o'clock, and what about Harlem? We all agree that Harlem is the next step, and once more emerge into the night.

By the time we are all in a taxi, general feeling has established itself that we are all old friends, and know one another very well indeed. I look out at the streets, marvellously lighted, and remember that I must get Christmas presents for the maids at home. Decide on two pairs of silk stockings for Florence, who is young, but Cook presents more difficult problem. Cannot believe that silk stockings would be really acceptable, and in any case feel doubtful of obtaining requisite size. What about hand-bag? Not very original, and could be equally well obtained in England. Book out of the question, as Cook has often remarked, in my hearing, that reading is a sad waste of time.

At this juncture Taylor suddenly remarks that he sees I am extremely observant, I take mental notes of my surroundings all the time, and he has little doubt that I am, at this very moment, contrasting the night life of America with the night life to which I am accustomed in London and Paris. I say Yes, yes, and try not to remember that the night life to which I am accustomed begins with letting out the cat at half-past ten and winding the cuckoo-clock, and ends with going straight to bed and to sleep until eight o'clock next morning.

Slight pause follows Taylor's remark, and I try to look as observant and intelligent as I can, but am relieved when taxi stops, and we get out at the Cotton Club, Harlem.

Coloured girls, all extremely nude, are dancing remarkably well on stage, coloured orchestra is playing—we all say that Of course they understand Rhythm as nobody else in the world does—and the usual necessity prevails of screaming very loudly in order to be heard above all the other people who are screaming very loudly.

(*Query:* Is the effect of this perpetual shrieking repaid by the value of the remarks we exchange? *Answer:* Definitely, No.)

Coloured dancers, after final terrific jerkings, retire, and spectators rise up from their tables and dance to the tune of "Stormy Weather", and we all say things about Rhythm all over again.

Sleep shortly afterwards threatens once more to overwhelm me, and I drink more black coffee.

At half-past three Ramona suggests that perhaps we have now explored the night life of New York sufficiently, I agree that we have, and the party breaks up. I say that I have enjoyed my evening—which is perfectly true—and thank them all very much.

Take one look at myself in the glass on reaching my room again, and decide that gay life is far from becoming to me, at any rate at four o'clock in the morning.

Last thought before dropping to sleep is that any roaring that may be indulged in by the lions of Central Park under my window will probably pass unnoticed by me, after hearing the orgy of noise apparently inseparable from the night life of New York.

December 1st.—Attend final lunch-party, given by Ella Wheelwright, and at which she tells me that I shall meet Mr. Allen. Experience strong inclination to scream and say that I can't, I'm the only person in America who hasn't read his book—but Ella says No, no—she doesn't mean Hervey Allen at all, she means Frederick Lewis Allen, who did *American Procession.* This, naturally, is a very different thing, and I meet Mr. Allen and his wife with perfect calm, and like them both very much. Also meet English Colonel Roddie, author of *Peace Patrol,* which I haven't read, but undertake to buy for Robert's Christmas present, as I think it sounds as though he might like it.

Female guests consist of two princesses—one young and the other elderly, both American, and both wearing enormous pearls. Am reminded of Lady B. and experience uncharitable wish that she could be here, as pearls far larger than hers, and reinforced with colossal diamonds and sapphires into the bargain. Wish also that convention and good manners alike did not forbid my frankly asking the nearest princess to let me have a good look at her black pearl ring, diamond bracelet and wrist-watch set in rubies and emeralds.

Remaining lady strikes happy medium between dazzling display of princesses, and my own total absence of anything except old-fashioned gold wedding-ring—not even platinum—and modest diamond ring inherited from Aunt Julia—and tells me that she is the wife of a stockbroker. I ought, she thinks, to see the New York Exchange, and it will be a pleasure to take me all over it. Thank her very much, and explain that I am sailing at four o'clock to-morrow. She says: We could go in the morning. Again thank her very much, but my packing is not finished, and am afraid it will be impossible. Then, she says indomitably, what about this afternoon? It could, she is sure, be managed. Thank her more than ever, and again decline, this time without giving any specific reason for doing so.

She is unresentful, and continues to talk to me very nicely after we have left the dining-room. Ella and the two princesses ignore us both, and talk to one another about Paris, the Riviera and clothes.

Ella, however, just before I take my leave, undergoes a slight change of heart—presumably—and reminds me that she has promised to come and see me off, and will lunch with me at the Essex and take me to the docks. She unexpectedly adds that she is sending me round a book for the voyage—*Anthony Adverse.* Am horrified, but not in the least surprised, to hear myself thanking her effusively, and saying how very much I shall look forward to reading it.

Stockbroking lady offers me a lift in her car, and we depart together. She again makes earnest endeavour on behalf of the Stock Exchange, but I am unable to meet her in any way, though grateful for evidently kind intention.

Fulfil absolutely final engagement, which is at Colony Club, where I naturally remember recent information received, that the members do nothing but look at their wrist-watches. This, fortunately for me, turns out to be libellous, at least so far as present audience is concerned. All behave with the utmost decorum, and I deliver lecture, and conclude by reading short extract from my own published work.

Solitary *contretemps* of the afternoon occurs here, when I hear lady in front row enquire of her neighbour: What is she going to read? Neighbour replies in lugubrious accents that she doesn't know, but it will be *funny.* Feel that after this no wit of mine, however brilliant, could be expected to succeed.

Day concludes with publisher calling for me in order to take me to a party held at Englewood, New Jersey. He drives his own car, with the result that we lose the way and arrive very late. Host says, Didn't we get the little map that he sent out with the invitation? Yes, my publisher says, he got it all right, but unfortunately left it at home. Feel that this is exactly the kind of thing I might have done myself.

Pleasant evening follows, but am by now far too much excited by the thought of sailing for home to-morrow to give my mind to anything else.

December 2nd.—Send purely gratuitous cable to Robert at dawn saying that I am Just Off—which I shan't be till four o'clock this afternoon—and then address myself once more to packing, with which I am still struggling when Ella Wheelwright is announced. She is, she says, too early, but she thought she might be able to help me.

This she does by sitting on bed and explaining to me that dark-red varnish doesn't really suit her nails. Coral, yes, rose-pink, yes. But not dark-red. Then why, I naturally enquire—with my head more or less in a suit-case—does she put it on? Why? Ella repeats in astonishment. Because she has to, of course. It's the only colour that anyone is wearing now, so naturally she has no alternative. But it's too bad, because the colour really doesn't suit her at all, and in fact she dislikes it.

I make sounds that I hope may pass as sympathetic—though cannot really feel that Ella has made out a very good case for herself as a victim of unkind Fate—and go on packing and—still more—unpacking.

Impossibility of fitting in present for Our Vicar's Wife, besides dressing-slippers and travelling-clock of my own, overcomes me altogether, and I call on Ella for help. This she reluctantly gives, but tells me at the same time that her dress wasn't meant for a strain of any kind, and may very likely split under the arms if she tries to lift anything.

This catastrophe is fortunately spared us, and boxes are at last closed and taken downstairs, hand-luggage remaining in mountainous-looking pile, surmounted by tower of books. Ella looks at these with distaste, and says that what I need is a Strap, and then immediately presents me with *Anthony Adverse.* Should feel much more grateful if she had only brought me a strap instead.

We go down to lunch in Persian Coffee Shop, and talk about Mrs. Tressider, to whom Ella sends rather vague messages, of which only one seems to me at all coherent—to the effect that she hopes The Boy is stronger than he was. I promise, to deliver it, and even go so far as to suggest that I should write and let Ella know what I think of The Boy next time I see him. She very sensibly replies that I really needn't trouble to do that, and I dismiss entire scheme forthwith. Discover after lunch that rain is pouring down in torrents, and facetiously remark that I may as well get used to it again, as I shall probably find the same state of affairs on reaching England. Ella makes chilly reply to the effect that the British climate always seems to her to be thoroughly maligned, especially by the English—which makes me feel that I have been unpatriotic. She then adds that she only hopes this doesn't, mean that the *Berengaria* is in for a rough crossing.

Go upstairs to collect my belongings in mood of the deepest dejection. Books still as unmanageable as ever, and I eventually take nine of them, and Ella two, and carry them downstairs.

Achieve the docks by car, Ella driving. She reiterates that I ought to have got a strap—especially when we find that long walk awaits us before we actually reach gangway of the *Berengaria.*

Hand-luggage proves too much for me altogether, and I twice drop various small articles, and complete avalanche of literature. Ella—who is comparatively lightly laden—walks on well ahead of me and has sufficient presence of mind not to look behind her—which is on the whole a relief to me.

Berengaria looks colossal, and thronged with people. Steward, who has been viewing my progress with—or without—the books, compassionately, detaches himself from the crowd and comes to my assistance. He will, he says, take me—and books—to my cabin.

Ella and I then follow him for miles and miles, and Ella says thoughtfully that I should be a long way from the deck if there was a fire.

Cabin is filled, in the most gratifying way, with flowers and telegrams. Also several parcels which undoubtedly contain more books. Steward leaves us, and Ella sits on the edge of the bunk and says that when she took her last trip to Europe her stateroom was exactly like a florist's shop. Even the stewardess said she'd never seen anything like it, in fifteen years' experience.

Then, I reply with spirit, she couldn't ever have seen a film star travelling. Film stars, to my certain knowledge, have to engage, one, if not two, extra cabins solely to accommodate flowers, fruit, literature and other gifts bestowed upon them. This remark not a success with Ella—never thought it would be—and she says very soon afterwards that perhaps I should like to unpack and get straight, and she had better leave me.

Escort her on deck—lose the way several times and thoughts again revert to probable unpleasant situation in the event of a fire—and we part.

Ella's last word to me is an assurance that she will be longing to hear of my safe arrival, and everyone always laughs at her because she gets such quantities of night letters and cables from abroad, but how can she help it, if she has so many friends? Mine to her is—naturally—an expression of gratitude for all her kindness. We exchange final reference to Mrs. Tressider, responsible for bringing us together—she is to be given Ella's love—The Boy should be outgrowing early delicacy by this time—and I lean over the side and watch Ella, elegant to the last in hitherto unknown grey squirrel coat, take her departure.

Look at fellow-travellers surrounding me, and wonder if I am going to like any of them—outlook not optimistic, and doubtless they feel the same about me. Suddenly perceive familiar figure—Mademoiselle is making her way towards me. She mutters *Dieu! quelle canaille!*—which I think is an unnecessarily strong way of expressing herself—and I remove myself and her to adjacent saloon, where we sit in armchairs and Mademoiselle presents me with a small chrysanthemum in a pot.

She is in very depressed frame of mind, sheds tears, and tells me that many a fine ship has been *englouti par les vagues* and that it breaks her heart to think of my two unhappy little children left without their mother. I beg Mademoiselle to take a more hopeful outlook, but at this she shows symptoms of being offended, so hastily add that I have often known similar misgivings myself—which is true. *Ah,* replies Mademoiselle lugubriously, *les pressentiments, les pressentiments!* and we are again plunged in gloom.

Suggest taking her to see my cabin, as affording possible distraction, and we accordingly proceed there, though not by any means without difficulty.

Mademoiselle, at sight of telegrams, again says *Mon Dieu!* and begs me to open them at once, in case of bad news. I do so, and am able to assure her that they contain only amiable wishes for a good journey from kind American friends. Mademoiselle—evidently in overwrought condition altogether—does not receive this as I had hoped, but breaks into floods of tears and says that she is suffering from *mal du pays* and *la nostalgie.*

Mistake this for neuralgia, and suggest aspirin, and this error fortunately restores Mademoiselle to comparative cheerfulness. Does not weep again until we exchange final and affectionate farewells on deck, just as gang-plank is about to be removed. *Vite!* shrieks Mademoiselle, dashing down it, and achieving the dock in great disarray.

473

I wave good-bye to her, and *Berengaria* moves off. Dramatic moment of bidding Farewell to America is then entirely ruined for me by unknown Englishwoman who asks me severely if that was a friend of mine?

Yes, it was.

Very well. It reminds her of an extraordinary occasion when her son was seeing her off from Southampton. He remained too long in the cabin—very devoted son, anxious to see that all was comfortable for his mother—and when he went up on deck, what do I think had happened?

Can naturally guess this without the slightest difficulty, but feel that it would spoil the story if I do, so only say What? in anxious tone of voice, as though I had no idea at all. The ship, says unknown Englishwoman impressively, had moved several yards away from the dock. And what do I suppose her son did then?

He swam, I suggest.

Not at all. He jumped. Put one hand on the rail, and simply leapt. And he just made it. One inch less, and he would have been in the water. But as it was, he just landed on the dock. It was a most frightful thing to do, and upset her for the whole voyage. She couldn't get over it at all. Feel rather inclined to suggest that she hasn't really got over it yet, if she is compelled to tell the story to complete stranger—but have no wish to be unsympathetic, so reply instead that I am glad it all ended well. Yes, says Englishwoman rather resentfully—but it upset her for the rest of the voyage.

Can see no particular reason why this conversation should ever end, and less reason still why it should go on, so feel it better to smile and walk away, which I do. Stewardess comes to my cabin later, and is very nice and offers to bring vases for flowers. Some of them, she thinks, had better go on my table in dining-saloon.

I thank her and agree, and look at letters, telegrams and books. Am gratified to discover note from Mr. Alexander Woollcott, no less. He has, it appears, two very distinguished friends also travelling on the *Berengaria,* and they will undoubtedly come and introduce themselves to me, and make my acquaintance. This will, writes Mr. W. gracefully, be to the great pleasure and advantage of all of us.

Am touched, but know well that none of it will happen, *(a)* because the distinguished friends are travelling first-class and I am not, and *(b)* because I shall all too certainly be laid low directly the ship gets into the open sea, and both unwilling and unable to make acquaintance with anybody.

Unpack a few necessities—am forcibly reminded of similar activities on s.s.*Statendam* and realise afresh that I really am on my way home and need not become agitated at mere sight of children's photographs—and go in search of dining-saloon.

Find myself at a table with three Canadian young gentlemen who all look to me exactly alike—certainly brothers, and quite possibly triplets—and comparatively old acquaintance whose son performed athletic feat at Southampton Docks.

Enormous mountain of flowers decorates the middle of the table—everybody says Where do these come from? and I admit ownership and am evidently thought the better of thenceforward:

Much greater triumph, however, awaits me when table-steward, after taking a good look at me, suddenly proclaims that he and I were on board s.s. *Mentor* together in 1922. Overlook possibly scandalous interpretation to which his words may lend themselves, and admit to s.s. *Mentor.* Table-steward, in those days, was with the Blue Funnel line. He had the pleasure, he says, of waiting upon my husband and myself at the Captain's table. He remembers us perfectly, and I have changed very little.

At this my prestige quite obviously goes up by leaps and bounds, and English fellow-traveller—name turns out to be Mrs. Smiley—and Canadian triplets all gaze at me with awe-stricken expressions.

Behaviour of table-steward does nothing towards diminishing this, as he makes a point of handing everything to me first, and every now and then breaks off in the performance of his duties to embark on agreeable reminiscences of our earlier acquaintance.

Am grateful for so much attention, but feel very doubtful if I shall be able to live up to it all through voyage.

December 4th.—Flowers have to be removed from cabin, and books remain unread, but stewardess is kindness itself and begs me not to think of moving.

I do not think of moving.

December 5th.—Stewardess tells me that storm has been frightful, and surpassed any in her experience. Am faintly gratified at this—Why?—and try not to think that she probably says exactly the same thing more or less every voyage to every sea-sick passenger.

Practically all her ladies, she adds impressively, have been laid low, and one of the stewardesses. And this reminds her: the table-steward who looks after me in the dining-saloon has enquired many times how I am getting on, and if there is anything I feel able to take, later on, I have only to let him know.

Am touched by this, and decide that I could manage a baked potato and a dry biscuit. These are at once provided, and do me a great deal of good. The stewardess encourages me, says that the sea is now perfectly calm, and that I shall feel better well wrapped up on deck.

Feel that she is probably right, and follow her advice. Am quite surprised to see numbers of healthy-looking people tramping about vigorously, and others—less active, but still robust— sitting in chairs with rugs round their legs. Take up this attitude myself, but turn my back to the Atlantic Ocean, which does not seem to me quite to deserve eulogies bestowed upon it by stewardess. Canadian triplets presently go past—all three wearing black bérets—and stop and ask how I am. They have, they say, missed me in the dining-room. I enquire How they are getting on with Mrs. Smiley? and they look at one another with rather hunted expressions, and one of them says Oh, she talks a good deal.

Can well believe it.

Alarming thought occurs to me that she may be occupying the chair next mine, but inspection of card on the back of it reveals that this is not so, and that I am to be privileged to sit next to Mr. H. Cyril de Mullins Green. Am, most unjustly, at once conscious of being strongly prejudiced against him. Quote Shakespeare to myself in a very literary way—What's in a Name?—and soon afterwards doze.

Day passes with extreme slowness, but not unpleasantly. Decide that I positively must write and thank some of the people who so kindly sent me flowers and books for journey, but am quite unable to rouse myself to the extent of fetching writing materials from cabin. Take another excursion into the realms of literature and quote to myself from Mrs. Gamp: "Rouge yourself, Mr. Chuffey"—but all to no avail.

Later in the afternoon Mr. H. Cyril de Mullins Green materialises as pale young man with horn-rimmed glasses and enormous shock of black hair. He tells me—in rather resentful tone of voice—that he knows my name, and adds that *he writes himself* Feel inclined to reply that I Thought as Much—but do not do so. Enquire instead—though not without misgivings as to tactfulness of the question—with whom the works of Mr. H. C. de M. G. are published? He mentions a firm of which I have never heard, and I reply Oh really? as if I had known all about them for years, and the conversation drops. Remain on deck for dinner, but have quite a good one nevertheless, and immediately afterwards go down below.

December 6th.—Receive cable from Robert, saying All Well and he will meet me at Southampton. This has definitely bracing effect, and complete recovery sets in.

Mrs. Smiley, in my absence, has acquired complete domination over Canadian triplets, and monopolises conversation at meals. She appears only moderately gratified by my restoration to health, and says that she herself has kept her feet throughout. She has, also, won a great deal at Bridge, played deck tennis and organised a treasure-hunt which was a great success. To this neither I nor the Canadians have anything to counter, but after a time the youngest-looking of the triplets mutters rather defiantly that they have walked four miles every day, going round and round the deck. I applaud this achievement warmly, and Mrs. Smiley says that Those calculations are often defective, which silences us all once mire.

Learn that concert has been arranged for the evening-Mrs. Smiley has taken very active part in organising this and is to play several accompaniments—and H. Cyril de Mullins G. tells me later that he hopes it won't give great offence if he keeps away, but he cannot endure amateur performances of any sort or kind. As for music, anything other than Bach is pure torture to him. I suggest that in that case he must suffer quite a lot in the dining-saloon, where music quite other than Bach is played regularly, and he asks in a pained way whether I haven't noticed that he very seldom comes to the dining-saloon at all? He cannot, as a rule, endure the sight of his fellow-creatures eating. It revolts him. For his own part, he very seldom eats anything at all. No breakfast, an apple for lunch, and a little red wine, fish and fruit in the evening is all that he ever requires. I say, rather enviously, How cheap! and suggest that this must make housekeeping easy for his mother, but H. C. de M. G. shudders a good deal and replies that he hasn't lived with his parents for years and years and thinks family life extremely *bourgeois.* As it seems obvious that Cyril and I differ on almost every point of importance, I decide that we might as well drop the conversation, and open new novel by L. A. G. Strong that I want to read.

Modern fiction! says Cyril explosively. How utterly lousy it all is! He will, he admits, give me Shaw—(for whom I haven't asked)—but there are no writers living to-day. Not one. I say Come, Come, what about ourselves? but Mr. de M. G. evidently quite impervious to this witty shaft and embarks on very long monologue, in the course of which he demolishes many worldwide reputations. Am extremely thankful when we are interrupted by Mrs. Smiley, at the sight of whom C. de M. G. at once gets on to his feet and walks away. (Deduce from this that they have met before.)

Mrs. Smiley has come, she tells me, in order to find out if I will give a little Reading from Something of my Own at to-night's concert. No, I am very sorry, but I cannot do anything of the kind. Now *why?* Mrs. S. argumentatively enquires. No one will be critical, in fact as likely as not they won't listen, but it will *give pleasure.* Do I not believe in brightening this sad old world when I get the chance? For Mrs. Smiley's own part, she never grudges a little trouble if it means happiness for others. Naturally, getting up an entertainment of this kind means hard work, and probably no thanks at the end of it—but she feels it's a duty. That's all. Just simply a duty. I remain unresponsive, and Mrs. S. shakes her head and leaves me.

(If I see or hear any more of Mrs. S. shall almost certainly feel it my duty, if not my pleasure, to kick her overboard at earliest possible opportunity.)

Concert duly takes place, in large saloon, and everyone—presumably with the exception of Cyril—attends it. Various ladies sing ballads, mostly about gardens or little boys with sticky fingers—a gentleman plays a concertina solo, not well, and another gentleman does conjuring tricks. Grand *finale* is a topical song, said to have been written by Mrs. Smiley, into which references to all her fellow-passengers are introduced not without ingenuity. Should much like to know how she has found out so much about them all in the time.

Appeal is then made—by Mrs. Smiley—for Naval Charity to which we are all asked to subscribe—Mrs. Smiley springs round the room with a tambourine, and we all drop coins into it—and we disperse.

Obtain glimpse, as I pass smoking-saloon, of Mr. H. Cyril de Mullins Green drinking what looks like brandy-and-soda, and telling elderly gentleman—who has, I think, reached senility—that English Drama has been dead—absolutely *dead*—ever since the Reformation.

December 7th.—Pack for—I hope—the last time, and spend most of the day listening to various reports that We shan't be in before midnight, We shall get in by four o'clock this afternoon, and We can't get in to-day at all.

Finally notice appears on a board outside dining-saloon, informing us that we shall get to Southampton at nine P.M. and that dinner will be served at six—(which seems to me utterly unreasonable).—Luggage to be ready and outside cabins at four o'clock. (More unreasonable still.) Every possible preparation is completed long before three o'clock, and I feel quite unable to settle down to anything at all, and am reduced to watching Mrs. Smiley play table-tennis with one of the Canadian triplets, and beat him into a cocked hat.

Dinner takes place at six o'clock—am far too much excited to eat any—and from thence onward I roam uneasily about from one side of ship to the other, and think that every boat I see is tender from Southampton conveying Robert to meet me.

Am told at last by deck-steward—evidently feeling sorry for me—that tender is the *other* side, and I rush there accordingly, and hang over the side and wave passionately to familiar figure in blue suit. Familiar figure turns out to be that of complete stranger.

Scan everybody else in advancing tender, and decide that I have at last sighted Robert—raincoat and felt hat—but nerve has been rather shattered and am doubtful about waving. This just as well, as raincoat is afterwards claimed by unknown lady in tweed coat and skirt, who screams: Is that you, Dad? and is in return hailed with: Hello, Mum, old girl! how are you!

I decide that Robert has *(a)* had a stroke from excitement, *(b)* been summoned to the death-bed of one of the children, *(c)* missed the tender.

Remove myself from the rail in dejection, and immediately come face to face with Robert, who has mysteriously boarded the ship unperceived. Am completely overcome, and disgrace myself by bursting into tears.

Robert pats me very kindly and strolls away and looks at entirely strange pile of luggage whilst I recover myself. Recovery is accelerated by Mrs. Smiley, who comes up and asks me If that is my husband? to which I reply curtly that it is, and turn my back on her.

Robert and I sit down on sofa outside the dining-saloon, and much talk follows, only interrupted by old friend the table-steward, who hurries out and greets Robert with great enthusiasm, and says that he will personally see my luggage through the Customs.

This he eventually does, with the result that we get through with quite unnatural rapidity, and have a choice of seats in boat-train. Say good-bye to old friend cordially, and with suitable recognition of his services.

Robert tells me that He is Glad to See Me Again, and that the place has been very quiet. I tell him in return that I never mean to leave home again as long as I live, and ask if there are any letters from the children?

There is one from each, and I am delighted. Furthermore, says Robert, Our Vicar's Wife sent her love, and hopes that we will both come to tea on Thursday, five o'clock, *not* earlier because of the Choir Practice.

Agree with the utmost enthusiasm that this will be delightful, and feel that I am indeed Home again.

The Provincial Lady in Russia

Tourists in all the Intourist hotels in all the principal towns of Soviet Russia exchange the same fragments of conversation.

"Have you done Moscow yet?"

"No, I'm going there to-morrow night. I came in by Odessa. I've done Kharkov and Rostov and Kiev."

"Ah, then you're going out by sea from Leningrad. Unless you're flying from Moscow?"

"No, I shall be going by sea. Have you done Odessa and the south?"

"No, I've done the Caucasus. You should do the Caucasus. What is Odessa like?"

"Odessa is delightful. The hotel at Rostov was good except for the cockroaches. The food was bad at Kharkov.'

"Ah, there was a Frenchman here yesterday who had just come from Kharkov, and *he* said the food wasn't good."

And at this gratifying coincidence everybody looks pleased.

Sometimes it is a little like the survivors of a shipwreck meeting on a fragment of desert island.

"Are you still all right for soap?"

"Yes, I shall just last out till Kiev. What about you?"

"Oh, I'm all right. I brought a great deal. But my ink is pretty low."

"There's an American lady who can let you have ink. She gave me some in Leningrad and she's coming on here. She had safety-pins too."

"How marvelous! Perhaps she'd like some soda-mints or aspirins. I have heaps of those."

"I dare say. Or Keatings. Or perhaps you could lend her a book."

People part at Moscow and meet again, sometimes most unwillingly, at Yalta. They ask one another how they have been getting on, and if they met the French astronomer and the English journalist and the noisy young Finns with the portable gramophone. Those who met at Leningrad, and were in the same train coming from Moscow, and parted gracefully at Tillls only to be once more confronted with one another at Gorki, are bound by some unwritten law to sit at the same table for meals. At first, I often wondered whether they really like to do this, or if they just feel obliged to do it for old sake's sake. Later on I fall under the same spell, and the question is answered.

In Moscow I meet Peter—but not as one meets stray French astronomers and English journalists and gramophone-playing Finns. It is a meeting that was arranged—incredibly, as it now seems—in Bloomsbury, some four months ago. I have had the name of his hotel and the dates when he expects to be there in my diary ever since I left England.

His dates have been altered—so have mine—all knowledge of him is denied at the Metropole Hotel, where he ought to be—and Intourist tells me: (1) That there are no letters for me and no messages, (2) That if there were I couldn't have them because it is a Day of Rest.

It is anything but a Day of Rest for me, whatever it may be for Moscow.

I have traveled all night, and walked about looking for Peter half the day, and I have not yet got used to having my luncheon between three and five o'clock in the afternoon, and the hotel to which I have been sent is on one side of the Red Square—which no trams traverse—and everything else in Moscow is on the other side.

All the same, the Red Square is very beautiful, and they are quite right to allow no trams there. In the evening I walk across it once more, and admire the huge walls and towers of the Kremlin and the long row of fir-trees against the gray stone and the pure, beautiful lines of the Lenin Mausoleum, perfectly placed before the great fort, and the strange, Byzantine domes and whorls and minarets of the ancient Basil Cathedral.

Sentinels with fixed bayonets guard the Mausoleum, and there are long, long queues of people— they must number hundreds—waiting to pass inside. From the top of the Kremlin flutters the red flag, and from somewhere beneath it a light strikes upward, so that the brave scarlet color shows as plainly against the clear evening sky as it did in the morning sunlight.

One walks across the Red Square more safely than anywhere else in Moscow. Not as regards one's feminine virtue (*that*, I think, would be safe anywhere in Russia, were I a quarter of my present age and as alluring as Venus), but simply as regards life and limb.

Everywhere else the traffic is shattering, and the comrades, running for their lives in every direction—as well they may—are a menace. So are the trams, which bucket along on uneven rails and draw up with a slow jerk which gives a misleading impression altogether. One feels that here are deliberate, rather uncertain trams, that may very likely require a good strong push from somebody before starting at all.

And on the contrary, hardly have they stopped and hardly have hundreds of Comrades fought their way out of them than a bell clangs and they start off again, leaving hundreds more biting and kicking and pushing their way inside, hanging on the step and very often being violently shoved off it again.

The tram-question—one of the less picturesque and endearing characteristics of the new regime—is complicated in Moscow by the reconstructions that are going on everywhere. Whole streets are lying more or less inside-out, caverns yawn in the middle of roads, scaffolding suddenly blocks up pavements, and irrelevant-seeming pyramids of earth and loose stones and rubble rise up in quite unexpected places.

The trams do their gallant best, and often remind me of the story of Jules Verne in which the driver of a passenger-train negotiated a precipice by previously going full steam ahead and causing the train to jump the chasm. The trams too do something like that, but even so they have to make colossal detours, and every few days their route is, without any warning, altered, because the old route has become impassable.

In Leningrad there were hardly any cars. In Moscow there are a great many, and they all go hell-for-leather and make a point of sounding their horns only at the very last minute when the lives of the walking comrades positively hang by a thread.

In Moscow, as in Leningrad, people throng the streets. They keep on walking; they are like Felix the Cat. The Intourist guides, as usual, point out how purposeful they all are, how they walk with an object. One guide, more honest or less well-trained than the others, tells me that the housing shortage is very acute, and so perhaps it is more agreeable to spend one's free time in the street rather than in the home. A kind of Scylla or Charybdis.

These grim impressions dawn upon me little by little as I cross the Red Square, for perhaps the fourth time in twenty-four hours, to make another assault on the Metropole and Peter.

To my own unbounded astonishment, I am successful. There is a note from Peter. It has, I have no doubt, been there all along. It says that he is at the National Hotel. Have I got to cross the Red Square all over again? It is very beautiful, but I don't seem to care about crossing it again just yet.

I haven't got to. The National Hotel is only a few hundred yards from the Metropole.

If Peter and I were in London I should not run, like an excited hare, up four flights of stairs to his bedroom. Old friends as we are, I shouldn't scream aloud with joy at the sight of him, nor he at the sight of me. In Moscow, however, we do all these things. We behave, in a word, almost like two foreigners.

And we talk and we talk and we talk.

Our impressions of Soviet Russia, most fortunately, coincide. We have had identical experiences with fleas, guides, indiscreet indulgence in Russian bread, and the non-arrival of letters from home.

We offer each other soap, biscuits, Bromo, and soda-mints. It is almost like two Eastern potentates exchanging gifts, especially when Peter generously says that I shall have his clothes-brush when he leaves—I forgot to pack mine—and I, in return, gracefully offer to wash his pocket handkerchiefs when I do my own. And I stay and have supper with him—at about eleven p.m.—and at one o'clock in the morning cross the Red Square once more.

My bedroom window overlooks the river. I am pleased about it until I notice that a particularly zealous form of reconstruction is taking place on the bank, and that Comrades in vast numbers are operating a huge drill. They are a night-shift, and a kind of *mieux de fa mort* overtakes them at two in the morning, when they evolve a special series of noises, indicative of terrific energy. Then it all dies away and the next shift doesn't begin till seven o'clock.

479

II

Peter is under the auspices of an organization which takes an interest in literary tourists and the organization is very kind to him, and gives him theater tickets and special facilities and a guide all to himself. These benefits he shares with me.

I am secretly terrified of the guide, who is youngish and very tough and has a swivel eye. She has lived in the United States and says that she once hiked from Denver, Colorado, to California. It can't have been half as exhausting as hiking from one end of Moscow to the other, which is our daily achievement.

We visit museums and picture galleries and crèches and factories and schools and clinics. We see, at a rough estimate, a hundred thousand busts of Lenin and ninety thousand pictures of Stalin.

The guide has a curious habit of leading us briskly along over the cobbles, round such bits of reconstruction as lie in our way, for some time, and then abruptly stopping while she asks a passer-by the way to wherever she is taking us. This always turns out to be in some quite opposite direction to the one in which we are going. All is *à refaire*, and we turn round and begin all over again.

The result, not unnaturally, is that we always arrive late for our appointments.

"The Little Monster has no sense of time," says Peter—this being the endearing *sobriquet* by which he refers to the guide.

"And she evidently hasn't any bump of locality at all. Some people haven't," I say—having the best of reasons for knowing what I'm talking about.

Peter only replies, not unjustifiably, that to have no sense of time and no sense of direction seems to him a poor equipment with which to set up as a guide.

Sometimes we board a tram together. It is invariably bunged to the roof with pale, grimy, heavily built comrades, too tightly jammed together for strap-hanging to be necessary, or even possible. No one sits down. There are people sitting when one gets in, but I think it is because they have got wedged there and can't move.

On one occasion the Little Monster, startlingly and suddenly, says in my ear:

"A pregnant woman may go in the front part of the tram, where there is more room. It is a law."

I wonder whether she thinks I am going to make a fraudulent attempt to take advantage of this concession. But I don't. I remain where I am, leaning heavily on the shoulder of a man in a blouse, with somebody's portfolio digging into the small of my back, and an enormous female Comrade grasping my elbow with one hand and wiping the sweat off her face with the other.

I often think of the Black Hole of Calcutta.

The tram jerks and jolts and stops, and more people get in, and the Little Monster—who isn't more than five feet high—disappears from view altogether. This time I think of the House of Stone, in *The Four Feathers* and how those who fell down there never got up again. A mind well-stored with literary references is said to be a great comfort to the possessor. I think my references must be of the wrong kind.

Peter, who is a large young man and stands like the Rock of Gibraltar in the tram, is much more of a comfort to me than any number of literary references. He always knows when to get out, which I never do, and the guide seldom.

Getting out of the tram is a very tense and difficult business. Every inch of the way has to be fought for, and there is always a sporting chance that the tram will start again before the people in front of one will let one go through, or the people behind one have ceased to try to push past. I carry a bruise on one ankle for days, where one of the more impetuous Comrades gave me a vigorous kick, in order that I should get out of his way.

I ask Peter if he knew about the pregnant women going in the front of the tram, and he says Yes, but he doesn't see how they're to get there. Neither do I unless they confide their pretty secret to the conductor and he or she passes it on to all the comrades in the tram, and a way is cleared. (Like Charlotte Bronte when she went to a party, and everybody stood up and made way for her.)

"We might ask the Little Monster," Peter suggests. Any delicacy which either of us has ever possessed at home has long since left us. There are no inhibitions in Russia.

It is in a spirit of simple *camaraderie* that he and I and the Little Monster go together to a clinic for the welfare of mothers and babies—actually a most excellent institution, admirably organized—and are given much full and intelligent physiological information, with Lenin—aged three—looking benevolently down on us from the wall.

As there is practically no wall in Moscow from which I have *not* seen Lenin looking down—either as an infant or as an elderly man exhorting the workers (there is no intervening stage), I have ceased to notice him consciously; but on this occasion I prefer him to the other pictures with which the walls are covered.

I prefer him to the unwholesome-looking red and blue maps of the human organism. I prefer him to the things in bottles on a shelf. I prefer him, a thousand times, to the masterpiece which the woman doctor who is showing us round, has kept to the last.

"This tumor is one of the largest we have ever..." I say it is interesting—which I suppose it is, if I could bring myself to look at it, which I can't—and Peter says nothing. I think he is stunned. He is looking with a fixed, unnatural intensity at an artificial tomato, carrot, apple, and beetroot in a little case. Necessary items in the diet of infants, says the notice.

I think perhaps if one had seen all this—not the tumor, which *can't* be essential to anybody's education except a medical student's—but all the maps and photographs and measurements and the instructions—at a much earlier age, before one had grown squeamish and when one's curiosity was young and strong, it might have been a very good thing.

It *does* give vital information, and it does give it in a scientific, impersonal way, and it does stress the importance of bodily hygiene.

"Are school-children ever brought here to be taught physiological and biological facts?"

"Yes, often. They come in groups."

The last piece of information is superfluous. The Comrades, especially the school-children, go everywhere in groups. They are taught from the very beginning to lead the collective life.

Peter and I agree that the mother-and-babies Welfare Clinic is one of the best things we have seen in the Soviet Union, and that we approve of the visits there of the school-children—with a mental reservation excluding the tumor.

From the Clinic the Little Monster takes us—going first in the wrong direction but afterward recovering herself—to the Court of Marriages and Divorces. It consists of a desk in a little room, with a middle-aged woman in charge, and two plants that look like india-rubber-plants in pots in the doorway, each tied up with a pale, frail bow of papery white ribbon—like the ghosts of dead bridal decorations.

There are, as usual, Comrades sitting about and waiting, and the guide says that they have come either to register their marriage or to get a divorce. They all look to me equally unexhilarated, and nearly all of them are holding small children.

A young Russian is at the desk, and has said something, and it has been written down in a ledger, and he has, in his Russian way, settled down on to a hard-looking stool as if for life.

"He has just got a divorce," says the guide, and she asks him a great many questions about his private affairs and translates his answers. (I am, and always have been, thoroughly aghast at the way in which private individuals in Russia are turned inside-out for the benefit of tourists; but I am bound to say that they never seem to raise any objection.)

It seems that the young Russian is not pleased with his wife. She reproaches him, rather strangely, with spending his money on amusements and on presents for her. It makes her, she complains, into a slave. They quarrel. He has, without telling her anything about it, got a divorce. When she reproaches him this evening because he wishes to take her out to a cinema or a café, he will simply confront her with the *fait accompli*.

"It is very simple," says the Little Monster, looking unspeakably superior. She knows that in capitalist countries nothing, least of all divorce, is as simple as that.

"Are marriages equally simple?"

"Yes, they are. This couple with the two children have come to register their marriage."

The husband with the divorce smiles at us very amiably and makes way for the couple with the two children. Some people might think that it is a little late in the day for them to come and register their marriage. But the guide, after the usual questions and answers, is able to explain it all.

481

They have been eight years together. If they should get tired of each other and decide to separate it will be very much simpler to make arrangements for the welfare of the children if the marriage has been registered. So here they are.

The whole thing—barring the questions of the guide and her translations of the replies to us—takes about five minutes. We have witnessed a wedding in Moscow.

I wonder, sentimentally, whether the woman—who is sufficiently middle-aged to remember the old days—gives a thought to a new dress and music and flowers and a wedding party.

I don't suppose she does. I see her grasp one child by the hand, and the husband takes the other, and they depart, without so much as a vestige of Mendelssohn's Wedding March to encourage them.

Peter, who collects information much more assiduously than I do, asks intelligent questions, and enters the answers in a little book, and the woman at the desk—I suppose she is the Registrar—is very obliging and only breaks off once or twice to divorce or marry a few people who drift in and out.

As I return to my hotel—by way of the Kremlin, the fir trees, the Mausoleum, and the Basil Cathedral—I reflect that Moscow, whether through its fault or my own, has a most depressing effect on me. I think it's partly the number of Comrades who walk the streets and throng the trams and stand in queues outside the shops and the cinemas, all looking rather drab and unwashed and solemn. And one has caught such depressing glimpses, through unshaded windows, of dormitories with beds packed like sardines. Besides, it is never exhilarating to see such quantities of wholesale destruction going on as is necessitated by the Soviet determination to make a completely new city of Moscow.

I quite see that wonders have been achieved in a very short time. I haven't any doubt that the condition of the workers before the Revolution was abominable beyond description. I haven't really any serious doubts that they are working toward a better state of things than they have ever known.

But I have a bourgeois longing to see gaily dressed shop windows, and perhaps gaily dressed people in the streets as well, and to see more individualism and less collectivism—and, in a word, there seems to me to be a total absence of *fun* in Moscow.

Beauty, there is. In some of the buildings that have survived, in the Ballet, in the Gallery of Western Art, in many of the theater productions. "Romeo and Juliet" was a beautiful production. So was "Eugene Onegin" at the Opera.

Probably I have come to Moscow in quite the wrong spirit. I am making the mistake of comparing its newly begun institutions—of which, God wot, I have seen plenty of examples—with similar institutions in England and in America. Absurd and unreasonable.

The Soviet institutions—clinics, welfare centers, schools, crèches, hospitals—are all working under difficulties and are all hampered by lack of experience and lack of appliances. (They handicap themselves still further by a cast-iron determination to accept no outside criticism whatever and by assuming that perfection has already been achieved, which is far from being the case.)

A recollection—inaccurate, as usual—comes to my mind of some uncivil aphorism of Dr. Johnson's about women writing books or pursuing any other intellectual avocation.

"It is like a dog that walks upon its hind legs, sir. We do not ask whether the thing be well or ill done. The wonder is that it should be done at all." I am sure that I had better remember about Dr. Johnson and the dog when I try to collect my impressions of Soviet Russia.

III

At eleven o'clock at night an American acquaintance of Peter's appears and suggests taking us to pay a call on a man who writes books—a Russian. He has said that he will be at home between twelve and one.

He isn't, and we all settle down in his kitchen—situated on the staircase, and which he shares with five other families in the same building—and wait for his arrival.

At a quarter to one he comes, bringing three friends—a woman and two men.

We all sit in the bed-sitting room and talk. There ought to be a samovar, but there isn't. Only a wireless. I think my ideas are out of date.

The conversation is about the law concerning abortion (naturally, for it is the most popular topic in Russia), the new Metro, a poet who has annoyed the Government by one of his poems and has been sent as a punishment to work at the construction of a new bridge across the Neva—where he will surely be of no use whatever—and the state of literature in England.

I do not join in this intelligently. For one thing, I am getting sleepy, and for another, nobody in Russia has ever heard of me as a writer—and wouldn't be interested if he had—as none of my works is political or sociological—so nobody refers to me. Just as I am thinking that with any luck nobody will notice it if I do go to sleep, my host abruptly inquires of me which writer of fiction is leading the younger school in England now? Which indeed?

I *must* think of a name, and I must try to think of one that will convey something to my hearers into the bargain.

I hope to combine a modicum of truth with a certain amount of diplomacy by saying: "Dreiser."

"Theodore Dreiser?"

"Theodore Dreiser," I repeat firmly, and I really think I have displayed great presence of mind, considering that I am more than half asleep.

"I meant," says my host, "which of the *moderns*. Theodore Dreiser is the literature of the grandmothers, yes?"

Not of any of the grandmothers I know, he isn't. But I don't say so. Theodore Dreiser and I retire together into the ranks of the grandmothers and are disinterred no more.

Only just before we go away, at three o'clock, the only other woman present asks me rather sharply if I have any silk stockings, aspirins, lip-sticks, cotton frocks, or nail-scissors to sell.

I suppose she thinks it's all I'm fit for—and I am disposed to agree with her, and make a rendezvous for next day, for her to come to my hotel and inspect my belongings.

Shortly afterward I say good-night to Peter at his door and continue on my way—Red Square, Kremlin, Mausoleum, fir trees, Basil Cathedral, Old Uncle Tom Cobley and all, Old Uncle Tom Cobley and all.

IV

The Russian lady keeps her word. She much more than keeps it. She not only comes and buys everything that I want to sell, but swoops down on a large number of things that I *don't* want to sell, and says she'll take them as well. She opens my wardrobe and takes down my frocks, she lifts up the pillow on my bed by a sort of unerring instinct—like a water-diviner—and discloses my pajamas, and she looks inside my sponge-bag. (What can she possibly suppose that I am hiding inside my sponge-bag?)

"Look, I take this ink-bottle off of you as well, and if you have a fountain-pen I take that, and I take for my husband the blue frame (he will not want the photograph; besides it is your children, you will like to keep it) and for myself I take those things what I have already bought, and the red jumper, the pajamas, the two frocks. Have you any boiled sweets?"

No, I haven't any boiled sweets. And nothing will induce me to part with the safety ink-bottle or the blue frame or my only two frocks.

It takes a long while to convince the Russian lady that I really mean this, and I have eventually to concede the red jumper and the pajamas. She still looks so fixedly at the ink-bottle that I become unnerved, and distract her by an offer of meat-juice tablets—for her husband—and handkerchiefs and safety-pins for herself.

She buys them all and pays me in roubles on the spot. When I put the money away in my bag she says she will buy the bag, and when I hastily thrust the bag into my suitcase she says she will buy the suitcase.

I get her out of the room at last by giving her a lip-stick as a sort of bonus, like a pound of tea for a cash sale.

When, in the passage outside, I refer to our morning's work she says, "Hush Not so loud," and I realize that the whole transaction has been an illicit one and that Comrade Stalin would disapprove. We might perhaps even find ourselves, like the ill-conducted poet, constructing a new bridge across the Neva.

All the same, if I'd known what a shortage there is of pretty, brightly colored odds and ends in the Soviet Republic, I think I should have brought a great many more of them with me—and not only for the sake of turning a doubtfully honest rouble out of them either.

V

One morning Peter and I go to Kolominsky escorted by the Little Monster. She says it is an ancient monastery, and when we get there it *looks* like an ancient monastery but she recants and says it was a Palace of Ivan the Terrible. I don't know which she means. Prefer to think of it as a monastery.

Much the most peaceful spot I have seen in Russia—no Comrades, no reconstruction, not even a picture of Lenin with outstretched arm and clenched fist.

Just as I am sitting on a stone wall under the lime trees and looking down at the fields and the river, the guide tells me that on this exact spot Ivan the Terrible used to watch the peasants being flogged.

It is a great pity she cannot let well alone. However, it is to-day that we hear her, for the first and last time, make a joke. On the way back to the tram, passing through a tiny village, we see a little calf lying on the roadside, with a small pig nuzzling affectionately against it, both of them fast asleep in the sunshine.

Even the swivel eye of the Little Monster softens as she gazes down at them and she says:

"Look! In a Socialist state—no prejudice!"

For the moment, as we all three laugh, she seems quite human.

It doesn't last. She becomes as hortatory and tiresome as ever long before the tram has lurched back into Moscow with us, and makes us get off at the wrong stop, so that we have to walk several additional miles to Peter's hotel.

"It still seems odd to be lunching at four o'clock."

"Yes, doesn't it? Shall you have Bortsch again to-day?"

"Yes, I like it."

"How fortunate you are. But their fish is better than their meat, and the ice cream is good."

"Excellent. Much, much better than the *compote*."

"Oh, the *compote*!"

We do not describe the *compote* to each other. It is not necessary, as we have met it, both here and in Leningrad, at every meal. We know all about the rather tough, acid little fruits in the top of the glass dish and the sliced apple below and the two rather consoling little bits of tinned apricot at the very bottom. Curious, how very much one seems to think and talk about one's food in Moscow.

Also one's drink. The mineral water is good but expensive. The ordinary, plain water—what, in any other country, would be the drinking-water—arrives on the table boiled. And very well-advised too. But either the boiling or its own natural properties have turned it pale yellow and given it a strange smell and a very peculiar taste. The remaining alternative, since neither of us drinks wine, and the beer—which is excellent—is a ruinous price—is tea in a glass.

Meals, it is scarcely necessary to say, take a very long time in Russia. Hours elapse between the moment of sitting down, and detaching from its book the coupon that represents food, and the moment when the waiter comes to take one's order. Hours more between each course. (The coupon entitles one to three courses. I have never tried to ask for a second helping, but I don't think the coupon would run to it.)

The tea comes at the very end, and is always much too hot to drink, and so necessitates another long wait.

Sometimes Peter and I talk like the thoughtful and intelligent people we really are, and discuss Socialism, and Communism, and tell each other that we *really* ought to have seen Russia *before* the Revolution in order to judge of the vast improvement effected. (When Peter says this to me it is very reasonable. When I say it to him it is simply idiotic, as before the Revolution he was an infant in the nursery.)

Sometimes we discuss our neighbors.

"I saw that man over there when I was in Batum. He speaks Dutch."

"Does he? Yes, he looks as though he might. There are some Germans at my hotel. They've made friends with Mrs. Pansy Baker and she went with them to see an abortion clinic—and a boot-factory."

"What fun. Have you seen a single pretty woman yet in Russia?"

"No. Have you?"

"No."

Once, when a blonde with black eyelashes and a tightly fitting white frock comes in and sits down all by herself at the table next to ours, Peter hisses at me through his teeth:

"If ever there was one, I'll take my oath that's one of what we know there aren't any of in Russia!"

I understand him perfectly.

In Russia now, we have repeatedly been told, there are no prostitutes.

They have all been collected and placed in a sort of Home of Rest, like aged horses in England.

It is, I believe, possible to go and visit them. I suppose if we ever do, they will be expected to answer any indiscreet question that any of us may, through the guide, elect to ask them.

I think, on the whole, I won't visit the prostitutes.

Sometimes Peter and I just talk about England, and Hartland Quay, and the Fourth of June at Eaton, and people we both know in London or Devonshire. It feels like looking back into another life, and on those occasions—which are generally in the small hours of the morning after a gruelling day of trams, comrades, museums, clinics, and factories—I go past the Kremlin, the fir trees, and the Mausoleum without so much as noticing them. I go on down the hill, and past the reconstruction on the river-bank, where the drill is hard at it, and into my hotel.

The dining room is brightly lit and full of people, and a little orchestra is playing "*Sous les Toits de Paris*"—as it does nightly.

I look in as I go by.

Mrs. Pansy Baker, the American communist, it at a table with her Germans, talking to them very earnestly. She is saying: "I have had a sad life."

I think this must be the beginning of a reference to Mr. Baker. Very likely he too has had a sad life.

In my bedroom is one cockroach. I don't like it at all. But it is headed toward the door, which I civilly hold open for it, and out it goes. A lull in the reconstruction work has set in, and I think what a good moment this will be in which to go to sleep.

The orchestra, now playing something very odd that I keep on thinking I know but can't identify, is nothing. Sometimes I win this nightly race with the reconstruction, sometimes I don't.

To-night it has only *reculé pour mieux sauter*, And they have got quite a new tool to work with—something like a hammer, dropping slowly down a flight of steps, over and over again, one step at a time. At last it drops once too often, and they don't pick it up again.

We are back once more at "*Sous les Toits de Paris.*" Sur les lits de Moscou...

THEY ALSO SERVE: THE PROVINCIAL LADY IN LENINGRAD
Published in Harpers Magazine, February 1937

There is no unemployment in the Soviet Union: everybody can, and indeed must, work; and so far as I know, everybody does. As a kind of offset to this universal activity, everybody—when not working—sits about and waits.

At the Leningrad Hotel I also sit about and wait. I wait for the Intourist Bureau to telephone the people to whom I have brought letters of introduction. I wait for the lift, which has just taken three Comrades upstairs, to come down again—which it never does. I wait for my ten o'clock supper—ordered at nine, and brought—with any luck—at about eleven. I sit in the hall and wait, for nothing in particular. I am becoming Russianized.

A very old man comes in, wearing a fur cap and a coat. (*Ancien régime*, like a picture in an old nurserybook.) He sits down on a fraction of a bench which is already occupied by two French ladies, a girl in a blouse and skirt, and a Comrade smoking a cigarette.

There are never enough seats to go round in the hotel. Most of the people who come in and wait have to wait on their feet, leaning against walls. They do it fatalistically, obviously inured. The enormous shabby portfolios they all carry—like degraded music-cases—lie at their feet.

What, I wonder, are all these cases? They can't *all* be carrying important secret documents for the Government. Yet all the Comrades have portfolios, except the very old man who has a newspaper parcel instead, from which protrudes the tail of a fish. Perhaps the Comrades who are less *ancien régime*carry their fish in portfolios? The old man, I am sorry to say, spits.

I turn my attention elsewhere. An English tourist has come into the office, and I know by the brisk and businesslike way in which he begins that he is newly arrived and has no experience of Russian methods—unlike me. (At this I feel elderly and superior, and think of Julia Mills amid the Desert of Sahara.)

"There's a man I want to get hold of as soon as possible," says the Englishman blithely. "I haven't got his address, but you'll find him in the telephone book. Harrison, the name is."

"Harrison?"

"Harrison."

"You do not know where he lives?"

"I'm afraid not."

"Not in which street is his apartment?"

"No. But he'll be in the telephone book."

"Perhaps you know where is his office?"

"No, but—"

"Not in which street is his office?"

"I only know that his name is Harrison, and he's in Leningrad, and you'll find him in the telephone book."

"Ah, But you have not his address."

"It'll be in the telephone book."

"Ah."

There is a long silence. At this stage—for I have heard this dialogue before, and have often taken part in it myself—some English tourists, and most American ones, look round for the telephone book and swoop down upon it. This Englishman, however, is of inferior mettle. Or perhaps he has Russian blood in him.

He waits.

Presently Intourist utters once more:

"He has a telephone number?"

"Yes. He'll be in the book."

"Ah, It is at his house or at his office, the telephone?"

"His office, I think."

"And the name it is *Harrison?*"

"Harrison."

Faint demonstrations of searching for the book.

"The book it is not here. I will send."

A young blonde, who has, to my certain knowledge, been standing waiting for the better part of an hour, is sent to fetch the book. Perhaps it is for that and nothing else that she has been waiting? Intourist waits, the Englishman waits, we all wait.

The French ladies on the bench have begun to mutter to one another, low and venomously.

"Mais voilè—elle n'a pas de cceur. Tout simplement. Elle manque de coeur."

"Ça, par exemple—non!"

"Moi, je vous dis que si."

"Moi, je vous dis que non."

Deadlock.

The very old man has now, I think, fallen into a coma. What an abominable thing it is to keep him waiting all this time! He is a hard-working peasant, and his haughty employer, the Grand Duke, is upstairs drinking champagne—

What am I thinking of? The poor Grand Duke is, if fortunate, giving dancing lessons somewhere on the Riviera. The old man is a worker, a Comrade—he is quite all right.

Still I don't think they need keep him waiting such a very long while.

Presently the blonde returns with the telephone book, and Intourist begins to turn over the leaves, and to say once more:

"Harrison?"

"Harrison."

"Ah, Harrison," Along pause.

"No. He is not here,"

"But I think he must be. I say, would you mind if I had a look?"

The Englishman has a look, and runs Harrison to ground in a moment.

"Here he is! A. M. Harrison—that's the man."

"Ah? He is in the book?"

Intourist is only mildly surprised, and not in the least interested. The blonde, in a thoughtful way, says into space:

"Harrison."

The voices of the French ladies surge upward once more.

"Ah! son mari! Comme je le plains!"

"Et moi, non. Au contraire."

I should like to know more of the ménage under discussion—they can't *both* be right—but they shrug their shoulders simultaneously, glare, and say nothing more.

The Harrison quest goes on. I say to myself, we are progressing slowly, ma'am. If I knew as many quotations from Shakespeare or Plato, or even Karl Marx, as I do from Dickens, I should hold a very different, and much more splendid, place in the ranks of the literary.

"You want that I should telephone to him, yes?"

"Please. If you will."

Intourist will.

But not at once.

"It is his apartment or his office?"

"Well, I don't really know—but whichever number is in the book will find him, I expect."

"I will try," says Intourist pessimistically.

They know, and I know, that their pessimism is justified. The Englishman, as yet, does not know.

He waits—I suppose hopefully—and the telephone is brought into action.

It is customary—necessary, for all I know to the contrary—to shriek, rather than speak into it, and the first fifteen "Allo's" meet with no acknowledgment. Then something happens. The Exchange has replied.

The two French ladies, tired of looking angrily at each other, turn their heads; the blonde lifts hers from its apathetic angle; only the old man is unmoved. (Disgraceful, that he should have been ignored so long. I believe no one has so much as asked him what he wants. Hotel servants the same all the world over, Comrades or no Comrades.)

"Shall I—?" says the Englishman, ready to leap at the receiver.

"The number is bee-zy,"

"Busy?"

"It is bee-zy, If you will wait a little I will try once more."

We all settle down again.

A woman with a baby—and a portfolio—comes into the hotel with a businesslike air, and goes up and speaks to the porter in Russian.

He nods.

Like Jove, I think, and ought to be pleased to find that I am moving a step away from Dickens and toward the classics; but on the other hand I like Dickens, and I don't even know the classics.

The woman with the baby sits down, in the absence of any unoccupied chair, on a marble step leading to the barber's shop, and waits.

I wonder what amount of information Jove can have conveyed to her in that single nod, for her to know—as she presumably does—that it is going to be worth her while to sit down and wait.

Presently the French ladies get up. They both say "*Eh bien!*" and the one who *didn't* pity the husband adds: "*A quelque chose, malheur est bon*" in a philosophical way.

They move toward the lift, their mysterious allusions for ever unexplained.

Not that they leave us immediately. Far from it. They have to wait for the lift. Then they have to wait because the lift can take only four people, and there are already three inside it and they decline—fiercely—to go separately.

"Mais passez donc—"

"Non, non, non. Allez, je vous en prie."

"Mais non, mais non. Allez, vous—"

"Da tout."

A solitary Ukranian, who has been waiting—probably for the lift—for hours, is encouraged by the liftman to take advantage of this indecision and fill the vacant place.

He does so, and the French ladies are left, shrugging their shoulders again. One of them says that it is *"fantastique."*

The bench on which the old man of the *ancien régime* is sitting has now two vacant places, which are at once filled by four people. They take advantage of the old man's state of suspended animation to shove him and his fish to the extremest edge of the seat. I think that presently he will fall off.

The Englishman is still seeking his Harrison.

"I should think you might give them another ring now."

"I will try."

The effort is made.

"There is no reply from that number."

"No reply?"

"No. I think it is his office. It does not answer,"

"But there must be somebody there."

"There is nobody there. To-day it is the day of rest. The offices are all shut."

The Englishman is staggered. I can positively *see* the thoughts flying through his mind.

Tuesday, the day of rest? By Jove, yes! there are no Sundays in Russia now, but they have a holiday every sixth day. Then why on earth couldn't they say so sooner? Of course the offices *would* be shut. Good God, what a country!

"I suppose I'd better try again to-morrow morning," he says angrily. "Unless you could ask the Exchange if they know the number of his private house?"

"You want to ask the telephone number of his house?"

"If they can give it to you."

"Ah. I can ask them, if you wish,"

He does wish.

A little boy with a shaven head and bare feet and carrying a small attaché-case, comes in and adds to the congestion.

The lift returns and the two French ladies, after a few passes as to which of them shall enter it first, get inside. Then they wait again while the lift-man looks for a singleton passenger. He may not take more than four people at a time, but is determined not to take less.

The Englishman is now leaning against the wall with his arms folded. Russia is growing on him, I can see it plainly.

"They ring his apartment," says Intourist. "They say there is no reply."

"He must be away."

"He is bee-zy, Or perhaps he is seek."

These are the favorite alternatives of Intourist when a telephone connection is unobtainable. They do not say that the number is engaged or the telephone out of order. They make the less impersonal suggestion that the owner of the required number is either busy—too busy presumably to answer his telephone calls—or that he is ill.

The Englishman says that he supposes he must wait till to-morrow. Already he seems to me to be wilting slightly.

As he moves away from the Intourist Bureau he stops and reads a notice informing him that excursions will start punctually at ten o'clock each morning and tourists must on no account be late. I wonder if he believes it?

Perhaps I have been here long enough, and ought to give up my chair to one of the numerous Comrades who are standing about doing nothing. I am not really waiting for anything in particular—only just waiting. But I should like to see somebody pay a little attention to the ancient in the fur cap. He has been waiting longer than anybody else and has probably got rooted to his minute fragment of the bench by this time.

Comrades come and Comrades go, the blonde in the office folds her arms on a table and lays her head upon them, the Englishman buys a copy of the *Moscow Daily News* and reads about abortion—at least I suppose he does, as the papers devote much more space to that than to any other subject—and the Comrade with the cigarette gets up and is followed by the Comrade in the blouse and skirt, who has been sitting next him all the time but with whom he has never exchanged word or look. But they go away arm-in-arm and are, no doubt, husband and wife in the sight of Stalin.

Other people drift in, and take their places, and wait. The old man comes out of his coma. He is going to demand attention, to insist upon doing whatever it is that he has come to do, and for which he has waited so interminably. Not at all. He picks up his fish, rises very slowly to his feet, and walks out again into the street. He came, apparently, for the express purpose of sitting and waiting, and for nothing else. How little he knows that he has supplied me with the title for this article.

TO SPEAK MY MIND ABOUT RUSSIA: THE PROVINCIAL LADY IN ODESSA
Published in Harpers Magazine, March 1937

As my Russian visit draws to an end, I feel that the time has come for me to speak my mind about the Soviet Republic.

But to whom? My fellow-travelers all have opinions of their own which they regard, rightly or wrongly, as being of more value than mine. Most of them are pessimistic and declare that they don't ever want to come back again, and that the Crimea was lovely but the plugs in the hotels wouldn't pull, and Moscow was interesting but very depressing.

Some, on the other hand—like Mrs. Pansy Baker, the American communist—are wholly enthusiastic. (There is no *juste milieu* where the Soviet is concerned.) How splendid it all is, they cry, and how fine to see everybody busy, happy, and cared for. As for the institutions—the crèches, the schools, the public parks, and the prisons—all, without any qualification whatsoever, are perfect. Russia has nothing left to learn.

It would be idle to argue with them. For the matter of that, it is almost always idle to argue with anybody.

In Russia it is not only idle but practically impossible. One had thought of Russia, in one's out-of-date bourgeois way, as a country of tremendous discussions—of long evenings spent in splendid talk round the samovar—of abstract questions thrashed out between earnest thinkers. All that must have gone out with the Grand Dukes, the beautiful women, the borzois, the sables, and the diamonds.

The Comrades do not discuss; they assert. They contradict. They admit of no criticism whatever. Nothing could be more difficult or, probably, more unprofitable, than to speak one's mind in Russia concerning one's impressions of Russia. But all the same, I shall try. After all, it's my turn. For weeks and weeks I have followed meekly in the wake of pert and rather aggressive young women, who have told me how vastly superior everything in the U.S.S.R. is to everything in my own Capitalistic country (where they have never set foot).

And although several of the guides have been neither pert nor aggressive, but very obliging and friendly, even they have smiled rather pityingly at any comment other than one of unqualified approval.

In fact, the U.S.S.R., like the Pope, is infallible, and whereas the Pope's claim has at least the dignity of some two thousand years of experience behind it, that of the U.S.S.R. has not.

I shall speak my mind before I leave the country. I am resolved upon it. And I shall have to do it fairly soon too. Odessa is my last stopping-place. A Russian boat is to take me to Constantinople in a week's time.

There is a very intelligent Russian in the hotel. He is a doctor and has lived for several years in the United States. I shall speak my mind to the Russian doctor.

We often sit at the same table for breakfast. Surely he would welcome an impartial discussion of the state of his country from an intelligent visitor?

"I shall be leaving next week, I am going to Turkey and then back to England. Everything I have seen in Russia has been most interesting."

This is not perhaps literally true—but then, so very few statements ever are. After the first fifty, for instance, none of the pictures of Lenin and Stalin was in the least interesting. But it will do, I think, to start the impartial discussion.

"You find Soviet Russia interesting? Yes, that is what everybody says,"

Well, it wasn't a very original opening. I see that now, and wish that I had thought of something new and brilliant instead.

"But," says the Russian doctor, "it is quite impossible for you to form any correct opinion of the country unless you knew it before the Revolution."

Then I've been wasting the whole of my time?

"No one can judge of the New Russia who did not know intimately, over a period of many years and from the inside, the Old Russia."

The only reply I can think of to this is Good God! and I do not make it aloud. But really, if I left home and children and country and spent months of discomfort in places I haven't liked, only to learn at the end of it all that none of my collected impressions are of any value whatever, it does seem rather discouraging. The Russian doctor is either unaware of or indifferent to the blow that he has dealt.

"Many people make that mistake," he remarks somberly. "They think that because they have visited with an interpreter a few museums, schools, hospitals they know something about this country. They do not. They know *nothing*."

In that case I ought to get a refund from Intourist. They sent me out here on entirely false pretenses.

"Another thing," continues the doctor, evidently warming to his work, "not only is it impossible to know anything about Soviet Russia without a profound knowledge of Russia under the Tzars; it is also *absolutely*impossible to judge of it in any way correctly at the present date. For that you would have to come again, say in twenty years' time."

How unreasonable he is. If I come to Russia again in twenty years—which God forbid—it will be in a bath-chair.

"So it would really take a whole lifetime," I dejectedly suggest, "to understand exactly what is happening in the Soviet?"

"More than a lifetime. Two or three generations."

I give up, altogether, the idea of speaking my mind about the U.S.S.R. to the Russian doctor. I must find somebody else.

II

I am inspired to choose one of the Odessa Intourist guides. She has a more pliable outlook than most of them and is married to an Austrian husband. She has been abroad, to France and Austria and America.

"Did you like America?"

"Yeah, America was fine."

"Perhaps some day you will go back there. Would you like to go back?"

"Perhaps. But it is not a free country,"

"Not a free country?"

"The workers there are slaves. The women are slaves," says the guide firmly.

"I really don't think they are. American women always seem to me to have a great deal of liberty."

"No. They have no liberty. They cannot do the work that the men do."

"But I don't think they want to."

"In the Socialist state a woman is the equal of a man in every way. She can become a mechanic, an engineer, a bricklayer, a mason. If she is expecting a child she does no work for two months before and one month after it is born, and she gets her money just the same while she is nursing the child—"

I know all this. I have heard it, and more than once, from every guide in every town that I have visited. The treatment of the expectant mother is the *cheval-de-bataille* of the whole Soviet system—and a very respectable *cheval*, too—but it cannot, surely, be the answer to every question, the triumphant last word in every discussion?

"I think the care that the Government takes of mothers and children in Russia is most excellent—but on the other hand, there is not very much individual freedom for women in the upbringing of their children. It is all really in the hands of the State."

"The children are very happy. You have seen the crèches, the little beds for them to sleep on in the daytime, yes? Each child has its own toothbrush."

"I know. But the mothers don't see very much of them, do they, if they only have them home at night?"

"In the daytime they are at work. They have the right to work."

"Supposing they didn't want to work, and would look after their children at home?"

"Some of the women become Stakhanovite workers. Then they have privileges given to them—an extra room or a wireless or perhaps a car. We have many like that."

Yes, I know that too. In every factory there is a board bearing photographs of the Stakhanovite workers—who are usually distinguished for their capability rather than for their looks.

I cannot help feeling that the guide is not keeping to the point of the discussion—or even trying to do so.

"The experiment that is being tried over here is most interesting, but it seems to me to allow very little scope for individuality. Isn't that one of the drawbacks to the Communist system?"

"There are no drawbacks to the Communist system."

One looks at her in mingled admiration and despair. Admiration because she has been drilled into such blind and stubborn loyalty to her employers, and despair because it is so obviously impossible to conduct any discussion on such a basis.

I make one more effort.

"But surely there must be a few drawbacks to every system, to begin with, until it has been perfected. For instance, the complete lack of privacy must be trying, such a number of people all living in one or two rooms. Even in the hospitals. I suppose there's no such thing as a private ward."

"Here in Odessa, on the way to the sea, the houses that used to belong to rich people have all been converted into sanatoria for the workers. Those who need it are sent out here for a month, two months, as they require, by their trades unions."

"I know. I've seen them."

"There are beautiful gardens to those houses. They can sit there. And they can go and bathe in the sea."

"That's splendid. Do the workers who need a holiday choose where they go or is it settled for them?"

"They are told by the Government where to go for their holidays."

"That's what I meant. There isn't a great deal of freedom. Don't some of them feel they'd rather decide those things for themselves?"

"Sometimes the doctor orders special treatment. We have near here very celebrated mud-baths that cure all kinds of rheumatism."

It is like a conversation from an old-fashioned travel book:

"'Where is the band-box containing hats of which I asked you to take care, you good-for-nothing fellow?'

"'Sir, if you and your lady will rest awhile at the Inn, there is a fine view of Mont Blanc to be obtained from the parlor window.'"

Nothing is to be gained by going on talking with the guide. I shall have to speak my mind elsewhere.

But how difficult it is! Russians do not want one to speak one's mind. It is true that they like to talk, but they do not in the least like to listen. Least of all, do they like to listen to criticism of any kind. Well, perhaps they have their reasons for that. Only once do I go so far as to ask the lady who shows us round a Palace of the Pioneers in Rostov whether she would not like to visit some similar institutions in England or in America.

"Have you such things in England and America?"

"Yes, certainly. They are not called Palaces of the Pioneers, but we have technical schools and kindergartens and clubs for children and young people."

(The Palace of the Pioneers partakes of the nature of all these institutions, and has a really excellent marionette-show in a special little theater, into the bargain.)

"If you visited some of these places in other countries you could compare them with your own. It would be very interesting."

"No," says the Comrade, employing the simple form of flat contradiction favored by so many of the Comrades. "No, it would not be interesting. We do not wish to see how things are done in capitalist countries. When the foundation is wrong the building cannot be right. We know that our way is better."

I should like to tell her the story of the two Army chaplains, of whom the Church of England padre said to his Roman Catholic colleague:

"After all, you and I are both serving the same God," and met with the reply:

"Yes, indeed. You in your way, and I in His."

But if I did tell her she wouldn't think it funny, nor would she see its application to the official attitude of the U.S.S.R.

One can only congratulate the Government on the thoroughness with which it has seen to it that everyone coming into contact with foreign visitors upholds the theory that Soviet Russia has attained to earthly perfection within the past twenty years and has no longer anything to learn.

I wish one could talk to the old people or the people living in remote villages or the few remaining White Russians who still stay on and contrive somehow to live.

Stories filter through, from time to time...of people who try to get away and can't, of people who live hunted lives, in cellars, of people who are serving long terms of forced labor, as prisoners...Nobody really knows the truth.

It is evident that enormous progress is being made all over the country in civilization, and that the coming generation is to have a fair chance of acquiring health, and education and a limited amount of culture. (Limited, because everything is forbidden that is not directly in sympathy with Communist ideals, and because no society from which individualism is excluded can ever hope to produce creative artists.)

Perhaps it is inevitable that a country which has fought its way from centuries of tyranny and ignorance through bloody civil war, into the throes of a colossal rebirth should meet criticism with this blind, aggressive self-assertion. All the same, it is very far from prejudicing one in favor of the Soviet system to find so many of its exponents without humor, without manners, and without imagination.

III

I am leaving Russia. I sail from Odessa for Istanbul to-night. I have still not spoken my mind.

In defiance of repeated instructions from Intourist—and also from many of my fellow-travelers—to the effect that "tips are neither expected nor required in the Soviet Union," I have tipped several of the hotel servants, and they have accepted my offerings without the slightest demur.

I have said good-by to Intourist, and they to me, without very much abandon on either side.

I have packed. I have spent hours and hours debating within myself the best means of taking out of Russia a thirty-thousand-word manuscript containing my impressions of my travels. Sometimes I think that the general atmosphere of intrigue and mystery, so characteristic of the country, has quite gone to my head, and that there is in reality no reason at all why I shouldn't pack the manuscript in the ordinary way, among spongebags and pajamas. At other times— mostly in the middle of the night, when judgments always tend to become melodramatic—I see the Customs officials seizing the manuscript, and the police seizing me, and each of us being taken away in different directions. And I wonder how I shall be able to explain the position to my publishers.

I have asked advice twice—which is a grave mistake because each adviser says something quite different. Both, however, are agreed that the Customs officials are a great deal more interested in books, papers, manuscripts, and films than in any other form of contraband. This interest is manifested not only when one enters the country but, even more actively, when one leaves it.

Finally, I am decided by the frightful story of an American journalist in the Odessa Hotel who tells me that he once wrote half a novel while he was in Russia and put it in his suitcase to take to America, only to have to part with it at the Customs.

"They said they'd have to look through it," he disconsolately remarks. "That was eighteen months ago, and I guess they're still looking."

"Was it about Russia?"

"No. It was about night life in New York."

"Did you tell them that?"

"Sure I did. But they couldn't any of them read English, so they took it away to find someone who could."

I think of my own manuscript, entirely written in pencil, and feel that it may well take a very long while indeed before any persons are found who can read it. And when they do, they almost certainly won't like it.

"If you've written anything at all that you want to take home with you," says the American journalist significantly, "just carry it under your coat or somewhere. You'll find it saves a very great deal of time."

I think he is right.

He is less right when he adds: "It's only for a few minutes after all."

In my experience of Russia nothing is ever done there in the space of a few minutes.

With an agreeable feeling that I am being like someone in a novel all about international gangs, I lock the door of my bedroom and proceed to wedge the manuscript against my spine, under my elastic belt.

It is agony. I shall never endure it for five minutes, let alone five hours. I remove the hard cover of the manuscript, find quite another part of my spine, and try again. Bad, but endurable.

If I put on my loose coat now I shall be much too hot, but I defy anybody to notice anything abnormal in my back view.

Besides, I shall face them all the time, and look them straight in the eyes with that directness of gaze which is well known to be the outward sign of utter rectitude of spirit.

The least agreeable of the guides has been given the task of seeing off the departing tourists. There are only six of us: two Swedish astronomers, who came to see the eclipse of the sun, an elderly English couple, a young American college boy, and myself.

We drive down to the docks. I see the last of the beautiful crescent of houses above the sea-front, the last of the two-hundred steps down to the Black Sea, the last of Karl Marx preening himself on the pedestal originally occupied by the (probably better-looking) statue of the Empress Catherine, the last of the town that I have liked best of all those I have visited in the U.S.S.R.

I have no regrets. If I had any I shouldn't be in a position to indulge in them, partly because I am preoccupied by the displeasing thought that if I get much hotter most of my manuscript will probably become blurred and undecipherable, and partly because I feel ill.

Either the black bread, the salad-grown in a drain?—or the drinking-water has chosen this inconvenient moment for taking its toll of me.

If I faint—and I feel as though, between the heat, my coat, and my indisposition, I certainly shall—someone will have the brilliant idea of loosening my clothes, and the manuscript will fall out, and I shall come to under a strong police guard...

I do not faint. Instead, I get out of the car with everybody else, and we all go into a shed on the docks and the inevitable wait begins, and goes on, and goes on, and goes on.

A great number of rather *dégommés*-looking Comrades are scattered about the long shed, all engaged in their usual occupation of waiting. Their luggage includes bedding, little hand-carts, bundles of wraps (one of which startles me by suddenly turning out to be an old woman), bags, boxes, and the customary mysterious portfolios.

Some of the Comrades eat dried fish. Some of them sleep. Almost all of them cough and spit.

"I wonder what we're waiting for," says the elderly Englishwoman.

She can't have been very long in Russia.

But the guide—as usual—has her answer.

"They are not yet ready," she says.

"The Customs officers?"

"They are busy."

As there are none of them in sight, the guide can't possibly know if they're busy or not. She just says it automatically. I admire the spirit of the elderly Englishwoman who replies at once that they ought to be busy over our luggage, not over anything else.

The guide, for once, has nothing to say, and we all continue to await the pleasure of the Customs officials.

(By this time most of my penciled records *must* have come off on my back.)

A little baby, swaddled to the eyebrows in shawls, screams and howls from behind its mullings—as well it may. Nobody unwraps it or takes much notice.

Nobody seems to be taking much notice of anything. We are all sunk in fatalistic apathy. It is an atmosphere that seems very characteristic of a Russian gathering. Even when the officials at last crawl in, one at a time, from an inner office, nobody is in the least excited.

One or two of the people nearest the counter heave their luggage on to it and then turn aside in a dejected way, as though knowing that nothing is really going to happen yet, and ashamed of their own misguided impetuosity.

Only the elderly English couple, stalwart and determined, march up with their solid, respectable-looking suitcases and take up their stand in front of the counter. The guards at Waterloo probably looked like that, only with better effect; for the French are more impressionable than the Soviet Comrades, by a very long way.

The college boy is consulting the guide about his films and his photographs. He has been consulting everybody about them throughout the last two days. His predicament is very far from being peculiar to himself.

He has been in Russia four weeks and has taken a great many snapshots. Belatedly, he has discovered that no undeveloped films will be allowed to leave the country. Very well—he will have them developed and printed in Moscow. He does and is asked to pay a sum in roubles that would handsomely buy up films, photographs, camera, and all, twice over. We have all heard of this outrage and we have all assured him, with varying degrees of sympathy, that the same thing has happened to other tourists in the U.S.S.R. before now.

He seems unable to believe it. I watch him walking agitatedly to and fro, until a new wave of nausea comes over me and I clutch the sides of my bench and pass into a brief, unpleasant coma. When I emerge, wet through and with the manuscript surely in worse case than ever, the college boy and his films are being dealt with by the officials. Strip after strip of negatives is being unrolled, held up to the light, and scrutinized. The inspection requires the full attention of all the Customs officials—not one is left to attend to anybody else.

The Comrades, seeming neither surprised nor resentful, continue to cough, spit, sleep, or eat fish. The crying baby, still muffled, is being carried up and down by a young man with a beard, who holds a book in one hand and reads as he walks. (Culture)

The tourists mutter a little among themselves at the new delay, but are, I think, supported by the hope of some dramatic discovery, such as that the films include a snapshot of the interior of the Kremlin (where nobody, except officials is now allowed to set foot) or a complete set of naval and military plans of the utmost importance.

Nothing of the kind happens.

However, the last roll of all, which the American youth has not had the sense to slip into his pocket, has not been developed. It is, says the young man, nothing. Just some pictures of the scenery in the Crimea.

Officials of any other nation might be expected to take one of two courses: either to accept this statement and pass the films or to reject it and confiscate them.

In Russia, the situation apparently calls for the formation of a kind of minor parliament. The original officials send for more and higher officials, who come out of the main office one by one, mostly in shirtsleeves, and gather solemnly round the little red cylinder lying on the counter.

The Intourist guide hovers about, talking a great deal and looking anxious.

"If you like, they will keep and have develop' and send after you."

"That'll be very expensive, won't it?"

The guide shrugs her shoulders. We all know that it will be very expensive—and very uncertain into the bargain.

494

"Better let them go," advises the Englishwoman.

Her husband supports her, though he adds sternly that the *principle* of the thing is all wrong from start to finish.

The college boy, muttering that it's disgraceful, decides to let the films go. Twelve views of the Crimea scenery are lost for ever to the United States of America.

Nobody else's luggage yields anything sensational.

IV

Mine is the last to be examined, owing to the qualms of sickness which keep on breaking over me and preventing me from moving.

Perhaps I am, after all, starting one of the illnesses against which I was solemnly inoculated before leaving England. I suppose inoculations wear off after a time?

If it's smallpox they won't let me leave the country.

Say nothing about it.

I would rather die at sea than in Russia.

"What is this?"

"A book."

"It is a book you got in Russia?"

Obviously, it is a book I got in Russia. It is a large album with Russian text, containing some beautiful reproductions of the pictures in the gallery of Western Art at Moscow.

As it is large and heavy I have packed it in the bottom of my suitcase, and from thence it is extracted—with a bad effect on all the layers of things above it.

The conscientious Customs official looks through every single page of it. I do not know what he expects to find hidden between them. Perhaps he just likes pictures.

My other books get off lightly—so do my clothes. My letter-case is turned inside out, my very small diary severely scrutinized, upside down.

I am asked to open my hand-bag.

What shall I do if they suggest searching me?

They do not.

They repack my suitcase, quite obligingly, and shut it up again—the heavy Russian album is now on the top of my clothes instead of underneath them—and I have passed the Customs.

"Can I go through to the boat now?"

"You must wait a little," says the guide kindly. "You are tired, yes?"

I am, in my own opinion, at the point of death—but I do not say so.

"It's rather hot in here."

"There are many people."

The Comrades certainly do look numerous as they crowd round the long, dirty wooden counter on which their belongings are now being opened and examined.

The guide keeps on looking at me—no doubt I am pale green by now—and I feel I ought to distract her attention.

Would this be a good opportunity for speaking my mind, for the first and last time, in the Soviet Republic? It must be now or never.

Quite suddenly a crisis supervenes between the Customs officials and a middle-aged and rather battered-looking Comrade. He shouts, and they shout, he tries to get out at the far door that leads to where the boat is lying, and is prevented.

"What is the matter?"

"His passport is not in order. He cannot leave."

"Poor man!"

"He is upset because his family, they will have to go."

"Without him?"

"He cannot go. His passport is not in order."

"But they'll stay behind with him, won't they?"

"No, they will have to go. It is all arranged."

How very dreadful this is...The unfortunate Comrade with the defective passport is now in tears on our side of the counter and his family on the other—two women, a little boy, a baby, and the grandmother whom I mistook for a bundle.

495

They say good-by, in a very spectacular way, across the counter, though I think there is really no reason why they should not all be on the same side.

"When will he be able to join them?"

"I cannot say."

"I think it would be far better if they all waited together till his papers have been put in order."

"No," says the guide. "They cannot. They have given up their room. There is nowhere for them to be now except the ship."

And I realize that what she says is quite true.

The Swedish astronomers look disturbed, and say "Poor things!" and the college boy gives it as his considered opinion that Russia is *not* a free country, no, sir, it is *not*.

The unfortunate family are saying good-by again, and the baby is being handed to and fro across the counter repeatedly. It makes me, if possible, feel dizzier than before and I can watch them no longer.

The far door has been opened. I go out—manuscript and all—along the dock and up the gangway and onto the waiting boat.

I am off the soil of Soviet Russia.

In the very next berth to ours lies the *Jan Rudzutak*, in which I sailed from London Docks to Leningrad months and months ago.

Time and the hour, I think sententiously, ride through the roughest day. And on the whole, I have found it a fairly rough day.

But it ends on a note of unforeseen brightness.

The Comrade whom I left in such trouble among the officials is, at the eleventh hour, after all allowed to sail. He is hustled up the gangway and into the steerage and all his family receive him with cries and screams, and the baby is again bandied about from hand to hand.

"But how did he get through if his passport wasn't in order?"

"Definitely, by bribery," says the English traveler.

He brings forward no particular evidence to support this statement, and I shall never know whether it is really true or not. But I think that most probably it is.

So I go down to my dirty little cabin and retrieve my manuscript and find it less damaged than I expected, and ask a steward if I can have a little brandy to restore me (but none comes), and have every intention of going on deck to see the last of Soviet Russia, but find, after all, that I can't stir and must remain, ignominiously prone, until I feel better.

The ship has begun to move. The journey away from Russia has started.

In a few minutes I think I shall be asleep, although a Russian loud-speaker is blaring jazz somewhere on deck, and a group of Comrades, apparently exactly outside the porthole, is discussing the Government's new suggestion of making abortion illegal—just as it is in capitalist countries.

I wish I *had* spoken my mind, just once, in the U.S.S.R. Even though I know that nobody would have paid any attention to it, and even though it occurs to me to wonder whether I am absolutely certain of what my mind really is, concerning the new Russia.

———————

The Provincial Lady in Wartime

September 1st, 1939.—Enquire of Robert whether he does not think that, in view of times in which we live, diary of daily events might be of ultimate historical value to posterity. He replies that It Depends.

Explain that I do not mean events of national importance, which may safely be left to the Press, but only chronicle of ordinary English citizen's reactions to war which now appears inevitable.

Robert's only reply—if reply it can be called—is to enquire whether I am really quite certain that Cook takes a medium size in gas-masks. Personally, he should have thought a large, if not out-size, was indicated. Am forced to realise that Cook's gas-mask is intrinsically of greater importance than problematical contribution to literature by myself, but am all the same slightly aggrieved. Better nature fortunately prevails, and I suggest that Cook had better be asked to clear up the point once and for all. Inclination on the part of Robert to ring the bell has to be checked, and I go instead to kitchen passage door and ask if Cook will please come here for a moment.

She does come, and Robert selects frightful-looking appliances, each with a snout projecting below a little talc window, from pile which has stood in corner of the study for some days.

Cook shows a slight inclination towards coyness when Robert adjusts one on her head with stout crosspiece, and replies from within, when questioned, that It'll do nicely, sir, thank you. (Voice sounds very hollow and sepulchral.)

Robert still dissatisfied and tells me that Cook's nose is in quite the wrong place, and he always thought it would be, and that what she needs is a large size. Cook is accordingly extracted from the medium-size, and emerges looking heated, and much inclined to say that she'd rather make do with this one if it's all the same to us, and get back to her fish-cakes before they're spoilt. This total misapprehension as to the importance of the situation is rather sharply dealt with by Robert, as A.R.P. Organiser for the district, and he again inducts Cook into a gas-mask and this time declares the results to be much more satisfactory.

Cook (evidently thinks Robert most unreasonable) asserts that she's sure it'll do beautifully—this surely very curious adverb to select?—and departs with a look implying that she has been caused to waste a good deal of valuable time.

Cook's gas-mask is put into cardboard box and marked with her name, and a similar provision made for everybody in the house, after which Robert remarks, rather strangely, that *that's* a good job done.

Telephone bell rings, Vicky can be heard rushing to answer it, and shortly afterwards appears, looking delighted, to say that that was Mr. Humphrey Holloway, the billeting officer, to say that we may expect three evacuated children and one teacher from East Poplar at eleven o'clock to-night.

Have been expecting this, in a way, for days and days, and am fully prepared to take it with absolute calm, and am therefore not pleased when Vicky adopts an *air capable* and says: It'll be all right, I'm not to throw a fit, she can easily get everything ready. (Dear Vicky in many ways a great comfort, and her position as House prefect at school much to her credit, but cannot agree to be treated as though already in advanced stage of senile decay.)

I answer repressively that she can help me to get the beds made up, and we proceed to top-floor attics, hitherto occupied by Robin, who has now, says Vicky, himself been evacuated to erstwhile spare bedroom.

Make up four beds, already erected by Robin and the gardener in corners, as though about to play Puss-in-the-Corner, and collect as many mats from different parts of the house as can be spared, and at least two that can't. Vicky undertakes to put flowers in each room before nightfall, and informs me that picture of Infant Samuel on the wall is *definitely* old-fashioned and must go. Feel sentimental about this and inclined to be slightly hurt, until she suddenly rather touchingly adds that, as a matter of fact, she thinks she would like to have it in her own room—to which we accordingly remove it.

Robin returns from mysterious errand to the village, for which he has borrowed the car, looks all round the rooms rather vaguely and says: Everything seems splendid—which I think is overestimating the amenities provided, which consist mainly of very old nursery screen with pictures pasted on it, green rush-bottomed chairs, patchwork quilts and painted white furniture. He removes his trouser-press with an air of deep concern and announces, as he goes, that the evacuated children can read all his books if they want to. Look round at volumes of Aldous Huxley, André Maurois, Neo-Georgian Poets, the *New Yorker* and a number of Greek textbooks, and remove them all.

Inspection of the schoolroom—also to be devoted to evacuated children—follows, and I am informed by Vicky that they may use the rocking-horse, the doll's house and all the toys, but that she has locked the bookcases. Am quite unable to decide whether I should, or should not, attempt interference here.

(Remembrance awakens, quite involuntarily, of outmoded educational methods adopted by Mr. Fairchild. But results, on the whole, not what one would wish to see, and dismiss the recollection at once.)

Vicky asks whether she hadn't better tell Cook, Winnie and May about the arrival of what she calls "The little evacuments", and I say Certainly, and am extremely relieved at not having to do it myself. Call after her that she is to say they will want a hot meal on arrival but that if Cook will leave the things out, I will get it ready myself and nobody is to sit up.

Reply reaches me later to the effect that Cook will be sitting up in *any* case, to listen-in to any announcements that may be on the wireless.

Announcement, actually, is made at six o'clock of general mobilisation in England and France.

I say, Well, it's a relief it's come at last, Robin delivers a short speech about the Balkan States and their political significance, which is not, he thinks, sufficiently appreciated by the Government—and Vicky declares that if there's a war, she ought to become a V.A.D. and not go back to school.

Robert says nothing.

Very shortly afterwards he becomes extremely active over the necessity of conforming to the black-out regulations, and tells me that from henceforward no chink of light must be allowed to show from any window whatever.

He then instructs us all to turn on every light in the house and draw all the blinds and curtains while he makes a tour of inspection outside. We all obey in frenzied haste, as though a fleet of enemy aircraft had already been sighted making straight for this house and no other, and then have to wait some fifteen minutes before Robert comes in again and says that practically every curtain in the place will have to be lined with black and that sheets of brown paper must be nailed up over several of the windows. Undertake to do all before nightfall to-morrow, and make a note to get in supply of candles, matches, and at least two electric torches.

Telephone rings again after dinner, and conviction overwhelms me that I am to receive information of world-shaking importance, probably under oath of secrecy. Call turns out to be, once more, from Mr. Holloway, to say that evacuees are not expected before midnight. Return to paper-games with Robin and Vicky.

Telephone immediately rings again.

Aunt Blanche, speaking from London, wishes to know if we should care to take her as paying guest for the duration of the war. It isn't, she says frenziedly, that she would *mind* being bombed, or is in the least afraid of anything that Hitler—who is, she feels perfectly certain, simply the Devil in disguise—may do to her, but the friend with whom she shares a flat has joined up as an Ambulance driver and says that she will be doing twenty-four-hour shifts, and sleeping on a camp bed in the Adelphi, and that as the lease of their flat will be up on September 25th, they had better give it up. The friend, to Aunt Blanche's certain knowledge, will never see sixty-five again, and Aunt Blanche has protested strongly against the whole scheme—but to no avail. Pussy—Mrs. Winter-Gammon—has bought a pair of slacks and been given an armlet, and may be called up at any moment.

I express whole-hearted condemnation of Mrs. Winter-Gammon—whom I have never liked—and put my hand over the mouthpiece of the telephone to hiss at Robert that it's Aunt Blanche, and she wants to come as P.G., and Robert looks rather gloomy but finally nods—like Jove—and I tell Aunt Blanche how delighted we shall all be to have her here as long as she likes.

Aunt Blanche thanks us all—sounding tearful—and repeats again that it isn't *air-raids* she minds—not for one minute—and enquires if Robin is nineteen yet—which he won't be for nearly a year. She then gives me quantities of information about relations and acquaintances.

William is an A.R.P. Warden and Angela is acting as his skeleton staff—which Aunt Blanche thinks has a very odd sound. Emma Hay is said to be looking for a job as Organiser, but what she wants to organise is not known. Old Uncle A. has refused to leave London and has offered his services to the War Office, but in view of his age—eighty-two—is afraid that he may not be sent on active service.

She asks what is happening to Caroline Concannon, that nice Rose and poor Cissie Crabbe.

Rose is still in London, I tell her, and will no doubt instantly find Hospital work—Caroline married years ago and went to Kenya and is tiresome about never answering letters—and Cissie Crabbe I haven't seen or heard of for ages.

Very likely not, replies Aunt Blanche in a lugubrious voice, but at a time like this one is bound to recollect old ties. Can only return a respectful assent to this, but do not really see the force of it.

Aunt Blanche then tells me about old Mrs. Winter-Gammon all over again, and I make much the same comments as before, and she further reverts to her attitude about air-raids. Perceive that this conversation is likely to go on all night unless steps are taken to check Aunt Blanche decisively, and I therefore tell her that we are expecting a party of evacuees at any moment—(can distinctly hear Vicky exclaiming loudly: Not till midnight—exclamation no doubt equally audible to Aunt Blanche)—and that I *must* ring off.

Of course, of course, cries Aunt Blanche, but she just felt she *had* to have news of all of us, because at a time like this—

Can see nothing for it but to replace receiver sharply, hoping she may think we have been cut off by exchange.

Return to paper-games and am in the midst of searching my mind for famous Admiral whose name begins with D—nothing but Nelson occurs to me—when I perceive that Robin is smoking a pipe.

Am most anxious to let dear Robin develop along his own lines without undue interference, but am inwardly shattered by this unexpected sight, and by rather green tinge all over his face. Do not say anything, but all hope of discovering Admiral whose name begins with D has now left me, as mind definitely—though temporarily, I hope—refuses to function.

Shortly afterwards pipe goes out, but Robin—greener than ever—re-lights it firmly. Vicky says Isn't it marvellous, he got it in the village this afternoon—at which Robin looks at me with rather apologetic smile, and I feel the least I can do is to smile back again. Am rather better after this.

Vicky embarks on prolonged discussion as to desirability or otherwise of her sitting up till twelve to receive little evacuments, when front-door bell peals violently, and everyone except Robert says: Here they are!

Winnie can be heard flying along kitchen passage at quite unprecedented speed, never before noticeable when answering any bell whatever, and almost instantly appears to say that Robert is Wanted, please—which sounds like a warrant for his arrest, or something equally dramatic.

Vicky at once says that it's quite impossible for her to go to bed till she knows what it is.

Robin re-lights pipe, which has gone out for the seventh time.

Suspense is shortly afterwards relieved when Robert reappears in drawing-room and says that a crack of light is distinctly visible through the pantry window and a special constable has called to say that it must immediately be extinguished.

Vicky asks in awed tones how he knew about it and is told briefly that he was making his rounds, and we are all a good deal impressed by so much promptitude and efficiency. Later on, Robert tells me privately that special constable was only young Leslie Oakford from the Home Farm, and that he has been told not to make so much noise another time. Can see that Robert is in slight state of conflict between patriotic desire to obey all regulations, and private inner conviction that young Leslie is making a nuisance of himself. Am glad to note that patriotism prevails, and pantry light is replaced by sinister-looking blue bulb and heavily draped shade.

Telephone rings once more—Humphrey Holloway thinks, apologetically, that we may like to know that evacuated children now not expected at all, but may be replaced next Monday by three young babies and one mother. Can only say Very well, and ask what has happened. Humphrey Holloway doesn't know. He adds that all is very difficult, and one hundred and forty children evacuated to Bude are said to have arrived at very small, remote moorland village instead. On the other hand, Miss Pankerton—who asked for six boys—has got them, and is reported to be very happy. (Can only hope the six boys are, too.) Lady B.—whose house could very well take in three dozen—has announced that she is turning it into a Convalescent Home for Officers, and can therefore receive no evacuees at all. Am indignant at this, and say so, but H. H. evidently too weary for anything but complete resignation, and simply replies that many of the teachers are more difficult than the children, and that the mothers are the worst of all.

(Mental note here, to the effect that no more unpopular section of the community exists, anywhere, than mothers as a whole.)

Robert, when told that evacuees are *not* coming to-night, says Thank God and we prepare to go upstairs when Vicky makes dramatic appearance in vest and pants and announces that there is No Blind in the W.C. Robert points out, shortly and sharply, that no necessity exists for turning on the light at all; Vicky disagrees and is disposed to argue the point, and I beg her to retire to bed instantly.

Impression prevails as of having lived through at least two European wars since morning, but this view certainly exaggerated and will doubtless disperse after sleep.

September 3rd, 1939.—England at war with Germany. Announcement is made by Prime Minister over the radio at eleven-fifteen and is heard by us in village church, where wireless has been placed on the pulpit.

Everyone takes it very quietly and general feeling summed up by old Mrs. S. at the Post Office who says to me, after mentioning that her two sons have both been called up: Well, we've got to *show* 'Itler, haven't we? Agree, emphatically, that we have.

September 7th.—Discuss entire situation as it affects ourselves with Robert, the children and Cook.

Robert says: Better shut up the house as we shan't be able to afford to live anywhere, after the war—but is brought round to less drastic views and agrees to shutting up drawing-room and two bedrooms only. He also advocates letting one maid go—which is as well since both have instantly informed me that they feel it their duty to leave and look for war work.

Cook displays unexpectedly sporting spirit, pats me on the shoulder with quite unprecedented familiarity, and assures me that I'm not to worry—she'll see me through, whatever happens. Am extremely touched and inclined to shed tears. Will Cook agree to let Aunt Blanche take over the housekeeping, if Robert is away all day, the children at school, and I am doing war work in London and coming down here one week out of four? (This course indicated by absolute necessity of earning some money if possible, and inability to remain out of touch with current happenings in London.)

Yes, Cook declares stoutly, she will agree to anything and she quite understands how I'm situated. (Hope that some time or other she may make this equally clear to me.) We evolve hurried scheme for establishment of Aunt Blanche, from whom nothing as to date of arrival has as yet been heard, and for weekly Help for the Rough from the village.

Cook also asserts that May can do as she likes, but Winnie is a silly girl who doesn't know what's good for her, and she thinks she can talk her round all right. She *does* talk her round, and Winnie announces a change of mind and says she'll be glad to stay on, please. Should much like to know how Cook accomplished this, but can probably never hope to do so.

Spend most of the day listening to News from the wireless and shutting up the drawing-room and two bedrooms, which involves moving most of the smaller furniture into the middle of the room and draping everything with dust-sheets.

Robin—still dealing with pipe, which goes out oftener than ever—has much to say about enlisting, and Vicky equally urgent—with less foundation—on undesirability of her returning to school. School, however, telegraphs to say that reopening will take place as usual, on appointed date.

September 8th.—Am awakened at 1.10 A.M. by telephone. Imagination, as usual, runs riot and while springing out of bed, into dressing-gown and downstairs, has had ample time to present air-raid, assembly of household in the cellar, incendiary bombs, house in flames and all buried beneath the ruins. Collide with Robert on the landing—he says briefly that It's probably an A.R.P. call and dashes down, and I hear him snatch up receiver.

Reach the telephone myself in time to hear him say Yes, he'll come at once. He'll get out the car. He'll be at the station in twenty minutes' time.

What station?

Robert hangs up the receiver and informs me that that was the station-master. An old lady has arrived from London, the train having taken twelve hours to do the journey—usually accomplished in five and says that we are expecting her, she sent a telegram. She is, the station-master thinks, a bit upset.

I ask in a dazed way if it's an evacuee, and Robert says No, it's Aunt Blanche, and the telegram must, like the train, have been delayed.

Am torn between compassion for Aunt Blanche—stationmaster's description almost certainly an understatement—and undoubted dismay at unpropitious hour of her arrival. Can see nothing for it but to assure Robert—untruthfully—that I can Easily Manage, and will have everything ready by the time he's back from station. This is accomplished without awakening household, and make mental note to the effect that air-raid warning itself will probably leave Cook and Winnie quite impervious and serenely wrapped in slumber.

Proceed to make up bed in North Room, recently swathed by my own hands in dust-sheets and now rapidly disinterred, put in hot-water bottle, and make tea and cut bread-and-butter. *(N.B.:* State of kitchen, as to cleanliness and tidiness, gratifying. Larder less good, and why four half-loaves of stale bread standing uncovered on shelf? Also note that cat, Thompson, evidently goes to bed nightly on scullery shelf. Hope that Robert, who to my certain knowledge puts Thompson out every night, will never discover this.)

Have agreeable sense of having dealt promptly and efficiently with war emergency—this leads to speculation as to which Ministerial Department will put me in charge of its workings, and idle vision of taking office as Cabinet Minister and Robert's astonishment at appointment. Memory, for no known reason, at this point recalls the fact that Aunt Blanche will want hot water to wash in and that I have forgotten to provide any. Hasten to repair omission boiler fire, as I expected, practically extinct and I stoke it up and put on another kettle and fetch can from bathroom. (Brass cans all in need of polish, and enamel ones all chipped. Am discouraged.)

Long wait ensues, and drink tea prepared for Aunt Blanche myself, and put on yet another kettle. Decide that I shall have time to dress, go upstairs, and immediately hear car approaching and dash down again. Car fails to materialise and make second excursion, which results in unpleasant discovery in front of the mirror that my hair is on end and my face pale blue with cold. Do the best I can to repair ravages of the night, though not to much avail, and put on clothes.

On reaching dining-room, find that electric kettle has boiled over and has flooded the carpet. Abandon all idea of Ministerial appointment and devote myself to swabbing up hot water, in the midst of which car returns. Opening of front door reveals that both headlights have turned blue and it minute ray of pallid light only. This effect achieved by Robert unknown to me, and am much impressed.

Aunt Blanche is in tears, and has brought three suit-cases, one bundle of rugs, a small wooden box, a portable typewriter, a hat-box and a trunk. She is in deep distress and says that she would have spent the night in the station willingly, but the station-master wouldn't let her. Station-master equally adamant at her suggestion of walking to the Hotel—other end of the town—and assured her it was full of the Militia. Further offer from Aunt Blanche of walking about the streets till breakfast-time also repudiated and telephone call accomplished by strong-minded station-master without further attention to her protests.

I tell Aunt Blanche five separate times how glad I am to have her, and that we are not in the least disturbed by nocturnal arrival, and finally lead her into the dining-room where she is restored by tea and bread-and-butter. Journey, she asserts, was terrible—train crowded, but everyone good-tempered—no food, but what can you expect in wartime?—and she hopes I won't think she has brought too much luggage. No, not at all—because she *has* two *large* trunks, but they are waiting at the station.

Take Aunt Blanche to the North Room, on entering which she again cries a good deal but says it is only because I am so kind and I mustn't think her in any way unnerved because that's the last thing she ever is—and get to bed at 3.15.

Hot-water bottle cold as a stone and cannot imagine why I didn't refill it, but not worth going down again. Later on decide that it *is* worth going down again, but don't do so. Remainder of the night passed in similar vacillations.

September 12th.—Aunt Blanche settling down, and national calamity evidently bringing out best in many of us, Cook included, but exception must be made in regard to Lady Boxe, who keeps large ambulance permanently stationed in drive and says that house is to be a Hospital (Officers only) and is therefore not available for evacuees. No officers materialise, but Lady B. reported to have been seen in full Red Cross uniform with snow-white veil floating in the breeze behind her. (Undoubtedly very trying colour next to any but a youthful face; but am not proud of this reflection and keep it to myself.)

Everybody else in neighbourhood has received evacuees, most of whom arrive without a word of warning and prove to be of age and sex diametrically opposite to those expected.

Rectory turns its dining-room into a dormitory and Our Vicar's Wife struggles gallantly with two mothers and three children under five, one of whom is thought to be suffering from fits. Both her maids have declared that they must find war work and immediately departed in search of it. I send Vicky up to see what she can do, and she is proved to be helpful, practical, and able to keep a firm hand over the under-fives.

Am full of admiration for Our Vicar's Wife and very sorry for her, but feel she is at least better off than Lady Frobisher, who rings up to ask me if I know how one gets rid of *lice?* Refer her to the chemist, who tells me later that if he has been asked that question once in the last week, he's been asked it twenty times.

Elderly neighbours, Major and Mrs. Bergery, recent arrivals at small house in the village, are given two evacuated teachers and appear in consequence to be deeply depressed. The teachers sit about and drink cups of tea and assert that the organisation at the *London* end was wonderful, but at *this* end there isn't any organisation at all. Moreover, they are here to teach—which they do for about four hours in the day—but not for anything else. Mrs. Bergery suggests that they should collect all the evacuated children in the village and play with them, but this not well received.

Our Vicar, appealed to by the Major, calls on the teachers and effects a slight improvement. They offer, although without much enthusiasm, to organise an hour of Recreative Education five days a week. He supposes, says Our Vicar, that this means play, and closes with the suggestion at once.

Light relief is afforded by Miss Pankerton, who is, we all agree, having the time of her life. Miss P.—who has, for no known reason, sprung into long blue trousers and leather jerkin—strides about the village marshalling six pallid and wizened little boys from Bethnal Green in front of her. Extraordinary legend is current that she has taught them to sing "Under a spreading chestnut-tree, the village smithy stands", and that they roar it in chorus with great docility in her presence, but have a version of their own which she has accidentally overheard from the bathroom and that this runs:

Under	*a*		*spreading*		*chestnut-tree*
Stands		*the*		*bloody*	*A.R.P.*

So says the —ing B.B.C.

Aunt Blanche, in telling me this, adds that: "It's really wonderful, considering the eldest is only seven years old." Surely a comment of rather singular leniency?

Our own evacuees make extraordinarily brief appearance, coming—as usual—on day and at hour when least expected, and consisting of menacing-looking woman with twins of three and baby said to be eighteen months old but looking more like ten weeks. Mother comes into the open from the very beginning, saying that she doesn't fancy the country, and it will upset the children, and none of it is what she's accustomed to. Do my best for them with cups of tea, cakes, toys for the children and flowers in bedroom. Only the cups of tea afford even moderate satisfaction, and mother leaves the house at dawn next day to find Humphrey Holloway and inform him that he is to telegraph to Dad to come and fetch them away immediately—which he does twenty-four hours later. Feel much cast-down, and apologise to H. H., who informs me in reply that evacuees from all parts of the country are hastening back to danger zone as rapidly as possible, as being infinitely preferable to rural hospitality. Where this *isn't* happening, adds Humphrey in tones of deepest gloom, it is the country hostesses who are proving inadequate and clamouring for the removal of their guests.

Cannot believe this to be an accurate summary of the situation, and feel that Humphrey is unduly pessimistic owing to overwork as Billeting Officer. He admits this may be so, and further says that, now he comes to think of it, some of the families in village are quite pleased with the London children. Adds—as usual—that the *real* difficulty is the mothers.

Are we, I ask, to have other evacuees in place of departed failures? Try to sound as though I hope we are—but am only too well aware that effort is poor and could convince nobody. H. H. says that he will see what he can do, which I think equal,

as a reply, to anything ever perpetrated by Roman oracle.

September 13th.—Question of evacuees solved by Aunt Blanche, who proposes that we should receive two children of Coventry clergyman and his wife, personally known to her, and their nurse. Children are charming, says Aunt Blanche—girls aged six and four—and nurse young Irishwoman about whom she knows nothing but that she is *not* a Romanist and is called Doreen Fitzgerald. Send cordial invitation to all three.

September 17th.—Installation of Doreen Fitzgerald, Marigold and Margery. Children pretty and apparently good. D. Fitzgerald has bright red hair but plain face and to all suggestions simply replies: Certainly I shall.

House and bedrooms once more reorganised, schoolroom temporarily reverts to being a nursery again—am inwardly delighted by this but refrain from saying so—and D. Fitzgerald, asked if she will look after rooms herself, again repeats: Certainly I shall. Effect of this is one of slight patronage, combined with willing spirit.

Weather continues lovely, garden all Michaelmas daisies, dahlias and nasturtiums—autumn roses a failure, but cannot expect everything—and Aunt Blanche and I walk about under the apple-trees and round the tennis-court and ask one another who could ever believe that England is at war? Answer is, alas, only too evident—but neither of us makes it aloud.

Petrol rationing, which was to have started yesterday, postponed for a week. *(Query:* Is this an ingenious device for giving the whole country agreeable surprise, thereby improving public morale?) Robin and Vicky immediately point out that it is Vicky's last day at home, and ask if they couldn't go to a film and have tea at the café? Agree to this at once and am much moved by their delighted expressions of gratitude.

Long talk with Aunt Blanche occupies most of the afternoon. She has much to say about Pussy—old Mrs. Winter-Gammon. Pussy, declares Aunt Blanche, has behaved neither wisely, considerately nor even with common decency. She may look many years younger than her age, but sixty-six is sixty-six and is *not* the proper time of life for driving a heavy ambulance. Pussy might easily be a grandmother. She *isn't* a grandmother, as it happens, because Providence has—wisely, thinks Aunt Blanche—withheld from her the blessing of children, but so far as age goes, she could very well be a grandmother ten times over.

Where, I enquire, are Mrs. Winter-Gammon and the ambulance in action?

Nowhere, cries Aunt Blanche. Mrs. W.-G. has pranced off in this irresponsible way to an A.R.P. Station in the Adelphi—extraordinary place, all underground, somewhere underneath the Savoy—and so far has done nothing whatever except Stand By with crowds and crowds of others. She is on a twenty-four-hour shift and supposed to sleep on a camp-bed in a Women's Rest-room without any ventilation whatever in a pandemonium of noise. Suggest that if this goes on long enough old Mrs. W.-G. will almost certainly become a nervous wreck before very long and be sent home incapacitated.

Aunt Blanche answers, rather curtly, that I don't know Pussy and that in any case the flat has now been given up and she herself has no intention of resuming life with Pussy. She has had more to put up with than people realise and it has now come to the parting of the ways. Opening here afforded leads me to discussion of plans with Aunt Blanche. Can she, and will she, remain on here in charge of household if I go to London and take up a job, preferably in the nature of speaking or writing, so that I can return home for, say, one week in every four? Cook—really pivot on whom the whole thing turns has already expressed approval of the scheme.

Aunt Blanche—usually perhaps inclined to err on the side of indecisiveness—rises to the occasion magnificently and declares firmly that Of Course she will. She adds, in apt imitation of D. Fitzgerald, Certainly I shall—and we both laugh. Am startle d beyond measure when she adds that it doesn't seem *right*that my abilities should be wasted down here, when they might be made use of in wider spheres by the Government. Can only hope that Government will take view similar to Aunt Blanche's.

Practical discussion follows, and I explain that dear Rose has asked me on a postcard, days ago, if I know anyone who might take over tiny two-roomed furnished flat in Buckingham Street, Strand, belonging to unknown cousin of her own, gone with R.N.V.R. to East Africa. Have informed her, by telephone, that I might consider doing so myself, and will make definite pronouncement shortly.

Go! says Aunt Blanche dramatically. This is no time for making two bites at a cherry, and she herself will remain at the helm here and regard the welfare of Robert and the evacuated children as her form of national service. It seems to her more suited to the elderly, she adds rather caustically, than jumping into a pair of trousers and muddling about in an ambulance.

Think better to ignore this reference and content myself with thanking Aunt Blanche warmly. Suggest writing to Rose at once, securing flat, but Aunt Blanche boldly advocates a trunk call and says that this is a case of Vital Importance and in no way contrary to the spirit of national economy or Government's request to refrain from unnecessary telephoning.

Hours later, Aunt Blanche startles Marigold, Margery and myself—engaged in peacefully playing game of Happy Families—by emitting a scream and asking: Did I say *Buckingham* Street?

Yes, I did.

Then, I shall be positively next door to Adelphi, underworld, A.R.P. Station, ambulance and Pussy. Within one minute's walk. But, what is far more important, I shall be able to see there delightful young friend, also standing by, to whom Aunt Blanche is devoted and of whom I must have heard her speak. Serena Thingamy.

Acknowledge Serena Thingamy—have never been told surname—but attention distracted by infant Margery who has remained glued to Happy Families throughout and now asks with brassy determination for Master Bones the Butcher's Son. Produce Master Potts by mistake, am rebuked gravely by Margery and screamed at by Marigold, and at the same time informed by Aunt Blanche that she can never remember the girl's name but I *must* know whom she means—dear little Serena Fiddlededee. Agree that I do, promise to go down into the underworld in search of her, and give full attention to collecting remaining unit of Mr. Bun the Baker's family.

Robin and Vicky come back after dark—I have several times visualised fearful car smash, and even gone so far as to compose inscription on tombstone—and declare that driving without any lights is absolutely *marvellous* and that film—*Beau Geste*—was super.

September 18th.—Departure of Vicky in the company of athletic-looking science mistress who meets her at Exeter station. Robin and I see them off, with customary sense of desolation, and console ourselves with cocoa and buns in the town. Robin then says he will meet me later, as he wishes to make enquiries about being placed on the Reserve of the Devon Regiment.

Am torn between pride, tenderness, incredulity and horror, but can only acquiesce.

September 20th.—Robin informed by military authorities that he is to return to school for the present.

September 21st.—Am struck, not for the first time, by extraordinary way in which final arrangements never *are* final, but continue to lead on to still further activities until parallel with eternity suggests itself, and brain in danger of reeling.

Spend much time in consulting lists with which writing-desk is littered and trying to decipher mysterious abbreviations such as Sp. W. about T-cloths and Wind cl. in s. room, and give Aunt Blanche many directions as to care of evacuees and Robert's taste in breakfast dishes. No cereal on any account, and eggs not to be poached more than twice a week. Evacuees, on the other hand, require cereals every day and are said by Doreen Fitzgerald not to like bacon. Just as well, replies Aunt Blanche, as this is shortly to be rationed. This takes me into conversational byway concerning food shortage in Berlin, and our pity for the German people with whom, Aunt Blanche and I declare, we have no quarrel whatever, and who must on no account be identified with Nazi Party, let alone with Nazi Government. The whole thing, says Aunt Blanche, will be brought to an end by German revolution. I entirely agree, but ask when, to which she replies with a long story about Hitler's astrologer. Hitler's astrologer—a woman—has predicted every event in his career with astounding accuracy, and the Führer has consulted her regularly. Recently, however, she has—with some lack of discretion—informed him that his downfall, if not his assassination, is now a matter of months, and as a result, astrology has been forbidden in Germany. The astrologer is said to have disappeared.

Express suitable sentiments in return, and turn on wireless for the Four. O'clock News. Am, I hope, duly appreciative of B.B.C. Home Service, but struck by something a little unnatural in almost total omission of any reference in their bulletins to any reverses presumably suffered by the Allies. Ministry of Information probably responsible for this, and cannot help wondering what its functions *really* are. Shall perhaps discover this if proffered services, recently placed at Ministry's disposal by myself, should be accepted.

Say as much to Aunt Blanche, who replies—a little extravagantly—that she only wishes they would put me in charge of the whole thing. Am quite unable to echo this aspiration and in any case am aware that it will not be realised.

Pay parting call on Our Vicar's Wife, and find her very pale but full of determination land not to be daunted by the fact that she has no maids at all. Members of the Women's Institute have, she says, come to the rescue and several of them taking it in turns to come up and Give a Hand in the Mornings, which is, we agree, what is really needed everywhere. They have also formed a Mending Pool—which is, Our Vicar's Wife says, wartime expression denoting ordinary old-fashioned working-party.

Doubt has been cast on the possibility of continuing W.I. Monthly Meetings but this dispersed by announcement, said to have come from the Lord Privy Seal, no less, that they are to be continued. Mrs. F. from the mill—our secretary has undertaken to inform all members that the Lord Privy Seal says that we are to go on with our meetings just the same and so it will be all right.

Enquire after Rectory evacuees—can see two of them chasing the cat in garden—and Our Vicar's Wife says Oh, well, there they are, poor little things, and one mother has written to her husband to come and fetch her and the child away but he hasn't done so, for which Our Vicar's Wife doesn't blame him—and the other mother seems to be settling down and has offered to do the washing-up. The child who had fits is very well-behaved and the other two will, suggests Our Vicar's Wife optimistically, come into line presently. She then tells me how they went out and picked up fir-cones and were unfortunately inspired to throw them down lavatory pan to see if they floated, with subsequent jamming of the drain.

Still, everything is all right and both she and Our Vicar quite feel that nothing at all matters except total destruction of Hitlerism. Applaud her heartily and offer to try to find maid in London and send her down. Meanwhile, has she tried Labour Exchange? She has, but results not good. Only one candidate available for interview, who said that she had hitherto looked after dogs. Particularly sick dogs, with mange. Further enquiries as to her ability to cook only elicited information that she used to cook for the dogs—and Our Vicar's Wife compelled to dismiss application as unsuitable.

Conversation is interrupted by fearful outburst of screams from infant evacuees in garden between whom mysterious feud has suddenly leapt into being, impelling them to fly at one another's throats. Our Vicar's Wife taps on window-pane sharply—to no effect whatever—but assures me that It's Always Happening, and they'll settle down presently, and the mothers will be sure to come out and separate them in a minute.

One of them does so, slaps both combatants heartily, and then leads them, bellowing, indoors.

Can see that Our Vicar's Wife—usually% so ready with enlightened theories on upbringing of children, of whom she has none of her own—is so worn-out as to let anybody do anything, and am heartily sorry for her.

Tell her so—she smiles wanly, but repeats that she will put up with anything so long as Hitler *goes*—and we part affectionately.

Meet several people in the village, and exchange comments on such topics as food-rationing, possible shortage of sugar, and inability ever to go anywhere on proposed petrol allowance. Extraordinary and characteristically English tendency on the part of everybody to go into fits of laughter and say Well, we're all in the same boat, aren't we, and we've got to *show* 'Itler he can't go on like that, haven't we?

Agree that we have, and that we will.

On reaching home Winnie informs me that Mr. Humphrey Holloway is in the drawing-room and wishes to speak to me. Tell her to bring in an extra cup for tea and ask Cook for some chocolate biscuits.

Find H. H.—middle-aged bachelor who has recently bought small bungalow on the Common—exchanging views about Stalin with Aunt Blanche. Neither thinks well of him. Ask Aunt Blanche if she has heard the Four O'clock News—Yes, she has, and there was nothing. Nothing turns out to be that Hitler, speaking yesterday in Danzig, has declared that Great Britain is responsible for the war, and that Mr. Chamberlain, speaking to-day in Parliament, has reaffirmed British determination to redeem Europe from perpetual fear of Nazi aggression. Thank Heaven for that, says Aunt Blanche piously, we've got to fight it out to a finish now, and would Mr. Holloway very kindly pass her the brown bread-and-butter.

It turns out that H. H. has heard I am going up to London to-morrow and would I care to go up with him in his car, as he wishes to offer his services to the Government, but has been three times rejected for the Army owing to myopia and hay-fever. The roads, he asserts, will very likely be blocked with military transport, especially in Salisbury neighbourhood, but he proposes—if I agree—to start at seven o'clock in the morning.

Accept gratefully, and enquire in general terms how local evacuees are getting on? Better, returns H. H. guardedly, than in some parts of the country, from all he hears. Recent warning broadcast from B.B.C. regarding probability of London children gathering and eating deadly nightshade from the hedges, though doubtless well-intended, has had disastrous effect on numerous London parents, who have hurriedly reclaimed their offspring from this perilous possibility.

Point out that real deadly nightshade is exceedingly rare in any hedge, but Aunt Blanche says compassionately that probably the B.B.C. doesn't know this, error on the subject being extremely common. Am rather taken aback at this attitude towards the B.B.C. and can see that H. H. is too, but Aunt Blanche quite unmoved and merely asks whether the blackberry jelly is homemade. Adds that she will willingly help to make more if Marigold, Margery and Doreen Fitzgerald will pick the blackberries.

Accept this gratefully and hope it is not unpatriotic to couple it with a plea that Aunt Blanche will neither make, nor allow Cook to make, any marrow jam—as can perfectly remember its extreme and universal unpopularity in 1916, '17 and '18.

Robin, due to return to school to-morrow, comes in late and embarks on discussion with H. H. concerning probability or otherwise of repeal of the arms embargo in the U.S.A. This becomes so absorbing that when H. H. takes his leave, Robin offers to accompany him in order to continue it, and does so.

Aunt Blanche says that Robin is a very dear boy and it seems only yesterday that he was running about in his little yellow smock and look at him now! My own thoughts have been following very similar lines, but quite realise that morale—so important to us all at present juncture—will be impaired if I dwell upon them for even two minutes. Suggest instead that Children's Hour now considerably overdue, and we might play Ludo with little evacuees, to which Aunt Blanche at once assents, but adds that she can play just as well while going on with her knitting.

Towards seven o'clock Robert returns from A.R.P. office—large, ice-cold room kindly lent by Guild of Congregational Ladies—is informed of suggestion that H. H. should motor me to London, to which he replies with a reminder that I must take my gas-mask, and, after a long silence, tells me that he has a new helper in the office who is driving him mad. She is, he tells me in reply to urgent questioning, a Mrs. Wimbush, and she has a swivel eye.

As Robert adds nothing to this, feel constrained to ask What Else?

Elicit by degrees that Mrs. Wimbush is giving her services voluntarily, that she types quickly and accurately, is thoroughly efficient, never makes a mistake, arrives with the utmost punctuality, and always knows where to find everything.

Nevertheless, Robert finds her intolerable.

Am very sorry for him and say that I can quite understand it—which I can—and refer to Dr. Fell. Evening spent in remembering quantities of things that I meant to tell Cook, Winnie, Aunt Blanche and the gardener about proper conduct of the house in my absence.

Also write long letter to mother of Marigold and Margery, begging her to come down and see them when she can, and assuring her of the well-being of both. (Just as I finish this, Robin informs me that Marigold was sick in the bathroom after her supper, but decide not to reopen letter on that account.) Make all farewells overnight and assert that I shall leave the house noiselessly without disturbing anyone at dawn.

September 22nd.—Ideal of noiseless departure not wholly realised (never really thought it would be); as Robert appears in dressing-gown and pyjamas to carry my suit-case downstairs for me, Cook, from behind partially closed kitchen-passage door, thrusts a cup of tea into my hand, and dog Benjy, evidently under impression that I am about to take him for an early walk, capers joyfully round and round, barking.

Moreover, Humphrey Holloway, on stroke of seven precisely, drives up to hall door by no means inaudibly.

Say goodbye to Robert—promise to let him hear the minute I know about my job—snatch up gas-mask in horrible little cardboard container, and go. Have extraordinarily strong premonition that I shall never see home again. (Have often had this before.) Humphrey H. and I exchange good-mornings, he asks, in reference to my luggage, if that is All, and we drive away.

Incredibly lovely September morning, with white mists curling above the meadows and cobwebs glittering in the hedges, and am reminded of Pip's departure from the village early in the morning in *Great Expectations*. Ask H. H. if he knows it and he says Yes, quite well but adds that he doesn't remember a word of it. Subject is allowed to drop. Roads are empty, car flies along and we reach Mere at hour which admits of breakfast and purchase of newspapers. Am, as usual, unable to resist remarkable little column entitled *Inside Information* in *Daily Sketch,* which has hitherto proved uncannily correct in every forecast made. Should much like to know how this is achieved.

Likewise buy and read *The Times,* excellent in its own way but, as H. H. and I agree, quite a different cup of tea. Resume car again and drive off with equal speed. H. H. makes no idle conversation, which is all to the good, and am forced to the conclusion that men, in this respect, far better than women. When he eventually breaks silence, it is to suggest that we should drive round by Stonehenge and have a look at it. The sight of Stonehenge, thinks H. H., will help us to realise the insignificance of our own troubles.

Am delighted to look at Stonehenge and theoretically believe H. H. to be right, but am practically certain, from past experience, that neither Stonehenge nor any other monument, however large and ancient, will really cause actual present difficulties to vanish into instant nothingness. *(Note:* Theory one thing, real life quite another. Do not say anything of this aloud.)

Overtake the military, soon afterwards, sitting in heaps on large Army lorries and all looking very youthful. They wave, and laugh, and sing "We'll Hang Out the Washing on the Siegfried Line" and "South of the Border".

Wave back again, and am dreadfully reminded of 1914. In order to dispel this, owing to importance of keeping morale in good repair, talk to Humphrey H. about—as usual—evacuees, and we exchange anecdotes.

H. H. tells me of rich woman who is reported to have said that the secret of the whole thing is to Keep the Classes Separate and that High School children must never, on any account, be asked to sit down to meals with Secondary School children. Am appalled and agree heartily with his assertion that if we get a Bolshevik régime over here, it will be no more than some of us deserve.

I then tell H. H. about builder in South Wales who received three London school children and complained that two cried every night and the third was a young tough who knocked everything about, and all must be removed or his wife would have immediate nervous breakdown. Weeping infants accordingly handed over to elderly widow, and tough sent off in deep disgrace to share billet of teacher. Two days later—it may have been more, but two days sounds well—widow appears before billeting officer, with all three evacuees, and declares her intention of keeping the lot. The tough, in tears, is behind her pushing juniors in a little go-cart. No further complaints heard from either side.

H. H. seems touched, and says with great emphasis that that's exactly what he means. (This passes muster at the time, but on thinking it over, can see no real justification for the assertion.)

Interchange of stories interrupted by roarings overhead, and I look up with some horror at wingless machine, flying low and presenting appearance as of giant species of unwholesome-looking insect. H. H.—association of ideas quite unmistakable—abruptly observes that he hopes I have remembered to bring my gas-mask. Everyone up here, he asserts, will be wearing them.

Does he mean *wearing* them, I ask, or only just wearing them?

He means just wearing them, slung over one shoulder. Sure enough shortly afterwards pass group of school children picking blackberries in the hedges, each one with little square box—looking exactly like picnic lunch—hanging down behind.

After this, gas-masks absolutely universal and perceive that my own cardboard container, slung on string, is quite *démodé* and must be supplied with more decorative case. Great variety of colour and material evidently obtainable, from white waterproof to gay red and blue checks.

Traffic still very scarce, even when proceeding up Putney Hill, and H. H. says he's never seen anything like it and won't mind driving into London at all, although he usually stops just outside, but this is all as simple as possible.

Very soon afterwards he dashes briskly down one-way street and is turned back by the police into Trafalgar Square, round which we drive three times before H. H. gets into right line of traffic for the Strand. He also makes abortive effort to shoot direct down Buckingham Street—likewise one-way—but am able to head him off in time.

Strand has very little traffic, but men along edges of pavement are energetically hawking gas-mask cases, and also small and inferior-looking document, evidently of facetious nature, purporting to be Last Will and Testament of Adolf Hitler.

Am reminded of cheap and vulgar conundrum, brought home by Robin, as to What Hitler said when he fell through the bed. Reply is: At last I'm in Poland. Dismiss immediately passing fancy of repeating this to Humphrey Holloway, and instead make him civil speech of gratitude for having brought me to my door. In return he extracts my suit-case and gas-mask, from car, declares that it has been a pleasure, and drives off.

September 23rd.—Installed in Buckingham Street top-floor flat, very nicely furnished and Rose's cousin's taste in pictures—reproductions of Frith's Derby Day, Ramsgate Sands and Paddington Station—delight me and provide ideal escape from present-day surroundings. Foresee that much time will be spent sitting at writing-table looking at them, instead of writing. *(Query:* Should this be viewed as sheer waste of time, or reasonable relaxation? *Answer:* Reminiscent of Robert—can only be that It Depends.)

This thought takes me straight to telephone, so as to put through trunk call home. Operator tells me austerely that full fee of half a crown will be charged for three minutes, and I cancel call. Ring up Rose instead, at cost of twopence only, and arrange to meet her for lunch on Wednesday.

Is she, I enquire, very busy?

No, not at present. But she is Standing By.

Gather from tone in which she says this that it will be useless to ask if she can think of anything for me to do, so ring off.

Ministry of Information will no doubt be in better position to suggest employment.

Meanwhile, am under oath to Aunt Blanche to go down to Adelphi underworld and look up Serena Fiddlededee, and also—has said Aunt Blanche—let her know if Pussy Winter-Gammon has come to her senses yet. Just as I am departing on this errand, occupier of ground-floor offices emerges and informs me that he is owner of the house, and has never really approved of the subletting of top flat. Still, there it is, it's done now. But he thinks it right that I should be in possession of following facts:

This house is three hundred years old and will burn like tinder if—am not sure he didn't say *when*—incendiary bomb falls on the roof.

It is well within official danger zone.

The basement is quite as unsafe as the rest of the house.

The stairs are extremely steep, narrow and winding, and anyone running down them in a hurry in the night would have to do so in pitch darkness and would almost certainly end up with a broken neck at the bottom.

If I choose to sleep in the house, I shall be quite alone there. (Can well understand this, after all he has been saying about its disadvantages.)

Rather more hopeful note is struck when he continues to the effect that there *is* an air-raid shelter within two minutes' walk, and it will accommodate a hundred and fifty people.

I undertake to make myself instantly familiar with its whereabouts, and to go there without fail in the event of an air-raid alarm.

Conversation concludes with the owner's assurance that whatever I do is done on my own responsibility, in which I acquiesce, and my departure into Buckingham Street.

Spirits rather dashed until I glance up and see entire sky peppered with huge silver balloons, which look lovely. Cannot imagine why they have never been thought of before and used for purely decorative purposes.

Find entrance to Adelphi underground organisation strongly guarded by two pallid-looking A.R.P. officials to whom I show pass, furnished by Aunt Blanche, *via*—presumably—Miss Serena Fiddlededee. Perceive that I am getting into the habit of thinking of her by this name and must take firm hold of myself if I am not to make use of it when we meet face to face.

Descend lower and lower down concrete-paved slope—classical parallel here with Proserpina's excursion into Kingdom of Pluto—and emerge under huge vaults full of ambulances ranged in rows, with large cars sandwiched between.

Trousered women are standing and walking about in every direction, and great number of men with armlets. Irrelevant reflection here to the effect that this preponderance of masculine society, so invaluable at any social gathering, is never to be seen on ordinary occasions.

Rather disquieting notice written in red chalk on matchboard partitions, indicates directions to be taken by Decontaminated Women, Walking Cases, Stretcher-bearers and others—but am presently relieved by perceiving arrow with inscription: To No. 1 Canteen—where I accordingly proceed. Canteen is large room, insufficiently lit, with several long fables, a counter with urns and plates, kitchen behind, and at least one hundred and fifty people standing and sitting about, all looking exactly like the people already seen outside.

Wireless is blaring out rather inferior witticisms, gramophone emitting raucous rendering of "We'll Hang Out the Washing on the Siegfried Line" and very vocal game of darts proceeding merrily. Am temporarily stunned, but understand that everybody is only Standing By. Now I come to think of it, am doing so myself.

Atmosphere thick with cigarette smoke and no apparent ventilation anywhere. Noise indescribable. Remember with some horror that Aunt Blanche said everybody was doing twenty-four-hour shifts and sleeping on camp-beds on the premises. Am deeply impressed by this devotion to duty and ask myself if I could possibly do as much. Answer probably No.

Very pretty girl with dark curls—in slacks, like everybody else—screams into my ear, in order to make herself heard: Am I looking for anyone? Should like to ask for Serena, whom I have always thought charming, but impossible to shriek back: Have you anybody here called Serena Fiddlededee?—name still a complete blank. Am consequently obliged to enquire for my only other acquaintance in the underworld, old Mrs. Winter-Gammon—not charming at all.

Very pretty girl giggles and says Oh, do I mean Granny Bo-Peep? which immediately strikes me as most brilliant nickname ever invented and entirely suited to Mrs. Winter-Gammon. She is at once pointed out, buying Gold Flake cigarettes at Canteen counter, and I look at her with considerable disfavour. Cannot possibly be less than sixty-six, but has put herself into diminutive pair of blue trousers, short-sleeved wool jumper, and wears her hair, which is snow-white, in roguish mop of curls bolt upright all over her head. Old Mrs. W.-G. stands about five foot high, and is very slim and active, and now chatting away merrily to about a dozen ambulance men.

Pretty girl informs me very gloomily that Granny Bo-Peep is the Sunbeam of the Adelphi.

Am filled with horror and say that I made a mistake, I don't really want to see her after all. Mrs. W.-G. has, however, seen me and withdrawal becomes impossible. She positively dances up to me, and carols out her astonishment and delight at my presence. Am disgusted at hearing myself replying with cordiality amounting to enthusiasm.

She enquires affectionately after Aunt Blanche, and I say that she sent her love—cannot be *absolutely* certain that she didn't really say something of the kind—and Mrs. W.-G. smiles indulgently and says Poor dear old Blanche, she'll be better and happier out of it all in the country, and offers to show me round.

We proceed to inspect ambulances—ready day and night—motor cars, all numbered and marked Stretcher Parties—Red Cross Station—fully equipped and seems thoroughly well organised, which is more than can be said for Women's Rest-room, packed with uncomfortable-looking little camp-beds of varying designs, tin helmets slung on hooks round matchboarded walls, two upright wooden chairs and large printed sheet giving Instructions in the event of an Air-raid Warning. Several women—still in trousers and jumpers—huddle exhaustedly on the camp-beds, and atmosphere blue with cigarette smoke.

Noise is, if possible, greater in Rest-room than anywhere else in the building as it is situated between Canteen and ambulance station, where every now and then all engines are started up and run for five minutes. Canteen wireless and gramophone both clearly audible, also rather amateurish rendering of "South of the Border" on unlocated, but not distant, piano.

Screech out enquiry as to whether anyone can ever manage to sleep in here, and Mrs. W.-G. replies Yes, indeed, it is a comfort to have Winston in the Cabinet. This takes me outside the door, and am able to repeat enquiry which is, this time, audible.

Mrs. W.-G.—very sunny—assures me that the young ones sleep through everything. As for old campaigners like herself, what does it matter? She went through the last war practically side by side with Our Boys behind the lines, as near to the trenches as she could get. Lord Kitchener on more than one occasion said to her: Mrs. Winter-Gammon, if only the regulations allowed me to do so, *you* are the person whom I should recommend for the Victoria Cross. That, of course, says Mrs. W.-G. modestly, was nonsense—(should think so indeed) but Lord K. had ridiculous weakness for her. Personally, she never could understand what people meant by calling him a woman-hater. Still, there it was. She supposes that she *was* rather a privileged person in the war.

Have strong inclination to ask if she means the Crimean War, but enquire instead what work she is engaged on here and now. Well, at the moment, she is Standing By, affirms Mrs. W.-G. lighting cigarette and sticking it into one corner of her mouth at rakish angle. She will, when the emergency arises, drive a car. She had originally volunteered to drive an ambulance but proved—hee-hee-hee—to be too tiny. Her feet wouldn't reach the pedals and her hands wouldn't turn the wheel.

Am obliged, on Mrs. W.-G.'s displayal of what look to me like four particularly frail claws, to admit the justice of this.

She adds that, in the meantime, she doesn't mind what she does. She just gives a hand here, there and everywhere, and tries to jolly everybody along. People sometimes say to her that she will destroy herself, she gives out so much all the time—but to this her only reply is: What does it matter if she does? Why, just nothing at all!

Am wholly in agreement, and much inclined to say so. Ruffianly-looking man in red singlet, khaki shorts and armlet goes by and Mrs. W.-G. calls out merrily: Hoo-hoo! to which he makes no reply whatever, and she tells me that he is one of the demolition squad and a dear boy, a very special friend of hers, and she loves pulling his leg.

Am unsympathetically silent, but old Mrs. W.-G. at once heaps coals of fire on my head by offering me coffee and a cigarette from the Canteen, and we sit down at comparatively empty table to strains of "The Siegfried Line" from gramophone and "In the Shadows" from the wireless. Coffee is unexpectedly good and serves to support me through merry chatter of Granny Bo-Peep, who has more to say of her own war service, past and present.

Coma comes on, partly due to airless and smoke-laden atmosphere, partly to mental exhaustion, and am by no means clear whether Mrs. W.-G.'s reminiscences are not now taking us back to Peninsular War or possibly even Wars of the Roses.

Am sharply roused by series of shrill blasts from powerful whistle: Mrs. W.-G. leaps up like a (small) chamois and says, It's a mock Air-raid alarm, only for practice—I'm not to be frightened—which I wasn't, and shouldn't dream of being, and anyhow shouldn't show it if I was—and she must be off to her post. She then scampers away, tossing her curls as she goes, darts out at one door and darts in again at another—curls now extinguished under tin-hat—pulling on leather jacket as she runs. Quantities of other people all do the same, though with less celerity.

Can hear engines, presumably of ambulances, being started and temporarily displacing gramophone and wireless.

Spirited game of darts going on in one corner amongst group already pointed out to me by old Mrs. W.-G. as those dear, jolly boys of the Demolition Squad, comes to an abrupt end, and only Canteen workers remain, conversing earnestly behind plates of buns, bananas and chocolate biscuits. Can plainly hear one of them telling another that practically every organisation in London is turning voluntary workers away by the hundred, as there is nothing for them to do. *At present,* she adds darkly. Friend returns that it is the same story all over the country. Land Army alone has had to choke off several thousand applicants—and as for civil aviation—

Before I can learn what is happening about civil aviation—but am prepared to bet that it's being told to Stand By—I am accosted by Aunt Blanche's friend, Serena Fiddlededee. She is young and rather pretty, with enormous round eyes, and looks as if she might—at outside estimate—weigh seven and a half stone. Trousers brown, which is a relief after so much navy blue, jumper scarlet and leather jacket orange. General effect gay and decorative. Quite idle fancy flits through my mind of adopting similar attire and achieving similar result whilst at the selfsame moment the voice of common sense informs me that a considerable number of years separates me from Serena and the wearing of bright colours alike. (Opening here for interesting speculation: Do not all women think of themselves as still looking exactly as they did at twenty-five, whilst perfectly aware that as many years again have passed over their heads?)

Serena astonishes me by expressing delight at seeing me, and asks eagerly if I have come to join up. Can only say that I have and I haven't. Am more than anxious to take up work for King and Country but admit that, so far, every attempt to do so has been met with discouragement.

Serena says Yes, yes-.—she knows it's like that—and she herself wouldn't be here now if she hadn't dashed round to the Commandant two days before war was declared at all and offered to scrub all the floors with disinfectant. After that, they said she might drive one of the cars.

And has she?

Serena sighs, and rolls her enormous eyes, and admits that she was once sent to fetch the Commandant's laundry from Streatham. All the other drivers were most fearfully jealous, because none of *them* have done anything at all except Stand By.

I enquire why Serena isn't taking part in the mock air-raid, and she says negligently that she's off duty just now but hasn't yet summoned up energy to go all the way to Belsize Park where she inconveniently lives. She adds that she is rather sorry, in a way, to miss the test, because the last one they had was quite exciting. A girl called Moffat or Muffet was the first driver in the line and had, Serena thinks, only just passed her "L" test and God alone knows how she'd done that. And instead of driving up the ramp, round the corner and out into the Adelphi, she'd shot straight forward, missed the Commandant by millimetres, knocked down part of the structure of Gentlemen and reversed onto the bumpers of the car behind. You could, avers Serena, absolutely *see* the battle-bowlers rising from the heads of the four stretcher-bearers inside the car. Moffat or Muffet, shortly after this dramatic performance, was sacked.

Serena then offers me coffee and a cigarette. I reply, though gratefully, that I have already had both and she assures me that this war is really being won on coffee and cigarettes, by women in trousers. Speaking of trousers, have I seen Granny Bo-Peep. Yes, I have. Serena goes off into fits of laughter, and says Really, this war is terribly funny *in its own way,* isn't it? Reply that I see what she means—which I do—and that, so far, it's quite unlike any other war. One keeps on wondering when something is going to happen. Yes, agrees Serena mournfully, and when one says that, everybody looks horrified and asks if one wants to be bombed by the Germans and see the Nelson Column go crashing into Trafalgar Square. They never, says Serena in a rather resentful tone, suggest the Albert Hall crashing into Kensington, which for her part could view with equanimity.

We then refer to Aunt Blanche—how she stood Granny Bo-Peep as long as she did is a mystery to Serena—the evacuees at home—how lucky I am to have really nice ones. No lice?

interpolates Serena, sounding astonished. Certainly no lice. They're not in the *least* like that. Charming children, very well brought-up—sometimes I am inclined to think, better brought-up than Robin and Vicky—to which Serena civilly ejaculates Impossible!

Canteen comes under discussion—very well run and no skin on the cocoa, which Serena thinks is *the* test. Open day and night because workers are on twenty-four-hour shift. Enquire of Serena whether she ever gets any sleep in the Rest-room, and she replies rather doubtfully that she thinks she does, sometimes. On the whole most of her sleeping is done at home. She has four Jewish Refugees in her flat—very, very nice ones, but too many of them—and they cook her the most excellent Viennese dishes. Originally she had only one refugee, but gradually a mother, a cousin, and a little boy have joined the party, Serena doesn't know how. They all fit into one bedroom and the kitchen and she herself has remaining bedroom and sitting-room, only she's never there.

Suggest that she should make use of Buckingham Street flat whenever convenient, and she accepts and says may she go there immediately and have a bath?

Certainly.

We proceed at once to Rest-room for Serena to collect her things, and she shows me horrible-looking little canvas affair about three inches off the floor, swung on poles like inferior sort of hammock. Is that her bed?

Yes, says Serena, and she has shown it to a doctor friend who has condemned it at sight, with rather strangely-worded observation that any bed of that shape is always more or less fatal in the long run, as it throws the kidneys on the bum.

Conduct Serena to top-story flat, present her with spare latchkey and beg her to come in when she likes and rest on properly constructed divan, which presumably is not open to similar objection.

Am touched when she assures me that I am an angel and have probably saved her life.

Wish I could remember whether I have ever heard her surname, and if so, what it is.

September 23rd.—Postcard from Our Vicar who writes because he feels he ought, in view of recent conversation, to let me know that he has had a letter from a friend in Northumberland on whom two evacuated teachers are billeted, both of whom are *very nice indeed.* Make beds, and play with children, and have offered to dig potatoes. It is a satisfaction, adds Our Vicar across one corner, to know that we were mistaken in saying that everyone complained of the teachers. There are evidently exceptions.

Think well of Our Vicar for this, and wonder if anyone will ever say that mothers, in some cases, are also satisfactory inmates.

Should doubt it.

Spend large part of the day asking practically everybody I can think of, by telephone or letter, if they can suggest a war job for me.

Most of them reply that they are engaged in similar quest on their own account.

Go out into Trafalgar Square and see gigantic poster on Nelson's plinth asking me what form MY service is taking.

Other hoardings of London give equally prominent display to such announcements as that 300,000 Nurses are wanted, 41,000 Ambulance Drivers, and 500,000 Air-raid Wardens. Get into touch with Organisations requiring these numerous volunteers, and am told that queue five and a half miles long is already besieging their doors.

Ring up influential man at B.B.C.—name given me by Sir W. Frobisher as being dear old friend of his—and influential man tells me in tones of horror that they have a list of really *first-class* writers and speakers whom they can call upon at any moment—which, I gather, they have no intention of doing—and really couldn't possibly make any use of me whatever. At the same time, of course, I can always feel I'm Standing By.

I say Yes, indeed, and ring off.

Solitary ray of light comes from Serena Fiddlededee whom I hear in bathroom—on door of which she has pinned paper marked ENGAGED—at unnatural hour of 2 p.m. and who emerges in order to say that *until* I start work at the Ministry of Information, she thinks the Adelphi Canteen might be glad of occasional help, if voluntary, and given on night-shift.

Pass over reference to Ministry of Information and at once agree to go and offer assistance at Canteen. Serena declares herself delighted, and offers to introduce me there to-night.

Meanwhile, why not go and see Brigadier Pinflitton, said to be important person in A.R.P. circles? Serena knows him well, and will ring up and say that I am coming and that he will do well to make sure of my assistance before I am snapped up elsewhere.

I beg Serena to modify this last improbable adjuration, but admit that I should be glad of introduction to Brigadier P. if there is the slightest chance of his being able to tell me of something I can do. What does Serena think?

Serena thinks there's almost certain to be a fire-engine or something that I could drive, or perhaps I might decontaminate someone—which leads her on to an enquiry about my gas-mask. How, she wishes to know, do I get on inside it? Serena herself always feels as if she must faint after wearing it for two seconds. She thinks one ought to practise sitting in it in the evenings sometimes.

Rather unalluring picture is conjured up by this, but admit that Serena may be right, and I suggest supper together one evening, followed by sessions in our respective gas-masks.

We can, I say, listen to Sir Walford Davies.

Serena says That would be lovely, and offers to obtain black paper for windows of flat, and put it up for me with drawing-pins.

Meanwhile she will do what she can about Brigadier Pinflitton, but wiser to write than to ring up as he is deaf as a post.

September 25th.—No summons from Brigadier Pinflitton, the Ministry of Information, the B.B.C. or anybody else.

Letter from Felicity Fairmead enquiring if she could come and help me, as she is willing to do anything and is certain that I must be fearfully busy.

Reply-paid telegram from Rose asking if I know any influential person on the British Medical Council to whom she could apply for post.

Letter from dear Robin, expressing concern lest I should be over-working, and anxiety to know exactly what form my exertions on behalf of the nation are taking.

Tremendous scene of reunion—not of my seeking—takes place in underworld between myself and Granny Bo-Peep, cantering up at midnight for cup of coffee and cigarettes. What, she cries, am I here again? Now, that's what she calls setting a *real* example.

Everyone within hearing looks at me with loathing and I explain that I am doing nothing whatever.

Old Mrs. W.-G., unmoved, goes on to say that seeing me here reminds her of coffee-stall run by herself at the Front in nineteen-fourteen. The boys loved it, she herself loved it, Lord Roberts loved it. Ah, well, Mrs. W.-G. is an old woman now and has to content herself with trotting about in the background doing what she can to cheer up the rest of the world.

Am sorry to say that Demolition Squad, Stretcher-bearers and Ambulance men evince greatest partiality for Mrs. W.-G. and gather round her in groups.

They are, says Serena, a low lot—the other night two of them had a fight and an ambulance man who went to separate them emerged bitten to the bone.

Should be delighted to hear further revelations, but supper rush begins and feel that I had better withdraw.

September 27th.—Day pursues usual routine, so unthinkable a month ago, now so familiar, and continually recalling early Novels of the Future by H. G. Wells—now definitely established as minor prophet. Have very often wondered why all prophecies so invariably of a disturbing nature, predicting unpleasant state of affairs all round. Prophets apparently quite insensible to any brighter aspects of the future.

Ring up five more influential friends between nine and twelve to ask if they know of any national work I can undertake. One proves to be on duty as L.C.C. ambulance driver—at which I am very angry and wonder how on earth she managed to get the job—two more reply that I am the tenth person at least to ask this and that they don't know of anything whatever for me, and the remaining two assure me that I must just *wait*, and in time I shall be told what to do.

Ask myself rhetorically whether it was for this that I left home?

Conscience officiously replies that I left home partly because I had no wish to spend the whole of the war in doing domestic work, partly because I felt too cut-off owing to distance between Devonshire and London, and partly from dim idea that London will be more central if I wish to reach Robin or Vicky in any emergency.

Meet Rose for luncheon. She says that she has offered her services to every hospital in London without success. The Hospitals, says Rose gloomily, are all fully staffed, and the beds are all empty, and nobody is allowed to go in however ill they are, and the medical staff goes to bed at ten o'clock every night and isn't called till eleven next morning because they haven't anything to do. The nurses, owing to similar inactivity, are all quarrelling amongst themselves and throwing the splints at one another's heads.

I express concern but no surprise, having heard much the same thing repeatedly in the course of the last three weeks. Tell Rose in return that I am fully expecting to be offered employment of great national importance by the Government at any moment. Can see by Rose's expression that she is not in the least taken in by this. She enquires rather sceptically if I have yet applied for work as voluntary helper on night-shift at Serena's canteen, and I reply with quiet dignity that I shall do so directly I can get anybody to attend to me.

Rose, at this, laughs heartily, and I feel strongly impelled to ask whether the war has made her hysterical—but restrain myself. We drink quantities of coffee, and Rose tells me what she thinks about the Balkans, Stalin's attitude, the chances of an air-raid over London within the week, and the probable duration of the war. In reply I give her my considered opinion regarding the impregnability or otherwise of the Siegfried Line, the neutrality of America, Hitler's intentions with regard to Rumania, and the effect of the petrol rationing on this country as a whole.

We then separate with mutual assurances of letting one another know if we Hear of Anything. In the meanwhile, says Rose rather doubtfully, do I remember the Blowfields? Sir Archibald Blowfield is something in the Ministry of Information, and it might be worth while ringing them up.

I do ring them up in the course of the afternoon, and Lady Blowfield—voice sounds melancholy over the telephone—replies that of course she remembers me well, we met at Valescure in the dear old days. Have never set foot in Valescure in my life, but allow this to pass, arid explain that my services as lecturer, writer, or even shorthand typist, are entirely at the disposal of my country if only somebody will be good enough to utilise them.

Lady Blowfield emits a laugh—saddest sound I think I have ever heard—and replies that thousands and thousands of highly-qualified applicants are waiting in a queue outside her husband's office. In *time,* no doubt, they will be needed, but at present there is Nothing, Nothing, Nothing! Unspeakably hollow effect of these last words sends my morale practically down to zero, but I rally and thank her very much. (What for?)

Have I tried the Land Army? enquires Lady Blowfield.

No, I haven't. If the plough, boots, smock and breeches are indicated, something tells me that I should be of very little use to the Land Army.

Well, says Lady Blowfield with a heavy sigh, she's terribly, terribly sorry. There seems nothing for anybody to do, really, except wait for the bombs to rain down upon their heads.

Decline absolutely to subscribe to this view, and enquire after Sir Archibald.

Oh, Archibald is killing himself. Slowly but surely. He works eighteen hours a day, Sundays and all, and neither eats nor sleeps.

Then why, I urge, not let me come and help him, and set him free for an occasional meal at least? But to this Lady Blowfield replies that I don't understand at all. There will be work for us all eventually—provided we are not Wiped Out instantly—but for the moment we must *wait.* I enquire rather peevishly how long, and she returns that the war, whatever some people may say, is quite likely to go on for years and years. Archibald, personally, has estimated the probable duration at exactly twenty-two years and six months. Feel that if I listen to Lady Blowfield for another moment I shall probably shoot myself, and ring off.

Just as I am preparing to listen to the Budget announcement on the Six O'clock News, telephone rings and I feel convinced that I am to be sent for by someone at a moment's notice, to do something, somewhere, and dash to the receiver.

514

Call turns out to be from old friend Cissie Crabbe, asking if I can find her a war job. Am horrified at hearing myself replying that in time, no doubt, we shall all be needed, but for the moment there is nothing to do but *wait*.

Budget announcement follows and is all that one could have foreseen, and more. Evolve hasty scheme for learning to cook and turning home into a boarding-house after the war, as the only possible hope of remaining there at all.

September 28th.—Go through now habitual performance of pinning up brown paper over the windows and drawing curtains before departing to underworld. Night is as light as possible, and in any case only two minutes' walk.

Just as I arrive, Serena emerges in trousers, little suède jacket and tin hat, beneath which her eyes look positively gigantic. She tells me she is off duty for an hour, and suggests that we should go and drink coffee somewhere.

We creep along the street, feeling for edges of the pavement with our feet, and eventually reach a Lyons Corner House, entrance to which is superbly buttressed by mountainous stacks of sandbags with tiny little aperture dramatically marked "In" and "Out" on piece of unpainted wood. Serena points cut that this makes it all look much more war-like than if "In" and "Out" had been printed in the ordinary way on cardboard.

She then takes off her tin hat, shows me her new gas-mask container—very elegant little vermilion affair with white spots, in waterproof—and utters to the effect that, for her part, she has worked it all out whilst Standing By and finds that her income tax will *definitely* be in excess of her income, which simplifies the whole thing. Ask if she minds, and Serena says No, not in the least, and orders coffee.

She tells me that ever since I last saw her she has been, as usual, sitting about in the underworld, but that this afternoon everybody was told to attend a lecture on the treatment of Shock. The first shock that Serena herself anticipates is the one we shall all experience when we get something to do. Tell her of my conversation over the telephone with Lady Blowfield and Serena says Pah! to the idea of a twenty-two-years war and informs me that she was taken out two days ago to have a drink by a very nice man in the Air Force, and he said Six months at the very outside—and he ought to know.

We talk about the Canteen—am definitely of opinion that I shall never willingly eat sausage-and-mashed again as long as I live—the income tax once more—the pronouncement of the cleaner of the Canteen that the chief trouble with Hitler is that he's such a *fidget*—and the balloon barrage, which, Serena assures me in the tone of one giving inside information, is all to come down in November. (When I indignantly ask why, she is unable to substantiate the statement in any way.)

We smoke cigarettes, order more coffee, and I admit to Serena that I don't think I've ever really understood about the balloons. Serena offers to explain—which I think patronising but submit to—and I own to rather fantastic idea as to each balloon containing an observer, more or less resembling the look-out in crow's-nest of old-fashioned sailing vessel. This subsequently discarded on being told, probably by Serena herself, that invisible network of wires connect the balloons to one another, all wires being electrified and dealing instant death to approaching enemy aircraft.

Serena now throws over electrified-wire theory completely, and says Oh, no, it isn't like that at all. Each balloon is attached to a huge lorry below, in which sits a Man, perpetually on guard. She has actually seen one of the lorries, in front of the Admiralty, with the Man inside sitting reading a newspaper, and another man close by to keep him company, cooking something on a little oil-stove.

Shortly afterwards Serena declares that she *must* go—positively *must*.

She then remains where she is for twenty minutes more, and when she does go, leaves her gas-mask behind her and we have to go back for it. The waiter who produces it congratulates Serena on having her name inside the case. Not a day, he says in an offhand manner, passes without half-a-dozen gas-masks being left behind by their owners and half of them have no name, and the other half just have "Bert" or "Mum" or "Our Stanley", which, he says, doesn't take you anywhere at all.

He is thanked by Serena, whom I then escort to entrance of underworld, where she trails away swinging her tin helmet and assuring me that she will probably get the sack for being late if anybody sees her.

September 30th.—Am invited by Serena to have tea at her flat, Jewish refugees said to be spending day with relations at Bromley. Not, says Serena, that she wants to get rid of them—she likes them—but their absence does make more room in the flat.

On arrival it turns out that oldest of the refugees has changed his mind about Bromley and remained behind. He says he has a letter to write.

Serena introduces me—refugee speaks no English and I no German and we content ourselves with handshakes, bows, smiles and more handshakes. He looks patriarchal and dignified, sitting over electric fire in large great-coat.

Serena says he feels the cold. They all the cold. She can't bear to contemplate what it will be like for them when the cold really begins—which it hasn't done at all so far—and she has already piled upon their beds all the blankets she possesses. On going to buy others at large Store, she is told that all blankets have been, are being, and will be, bought by the Government and that if by any extraordinary chance one or two *do* get through, they will cost five times more than ever before.

Beg her not to be taken in by this for one moment and quote case of Robert's aunt, elderly maiden lady living in Chester, who has, since outbreak of war, purchased set of silver dessert-knives, large chiming clock, bolt of white muslin, new rabbit-skin neck-tie and twenty-four lead pencils—none of which she required—solely because she has been told in shops that these will in future be unobtainable. Serena looks impressed and refugee and I shake hands once more.

Serena takes me to her sitting-room, squeezes past two colossal trunks in very small hall, which Serena explains as being luggage of her refugees. The rest of it is in the kitchen and under the beds, except largest trunk of all which couldn't be got beyond ground floor and has had to be left with hall-porter.

Four O'clock News on wireless follows. Listeners once more informed of perfect unanimity on all points between French and English Governments. Make idle suggestion to Serena that it would be much more interesting if we were suddenly to be told that there had been several sharp divergences of opinion. And probably much truer too, says Serena cynically, and anyway, if they always agree so perfectly, why meet at all? She calls it waste of time and money.

Am rather scandalised at this, and say so, and Serena immediately declares that she didn't mean a word of it, and produces tea and admirable cakes made by Austrian refugee. Conversation takes the form—extraordinarily prevalent in all circles nowadays—of exchanging rather singular pieces of information, never obtained by direct means but always heard of through friends of friends.

Roughly tabulated, Serena's news is to following effect:

The whole of the B.B.C. is really functioning from a place in the Cotswolds, and Broadcasting House is full of nothing but sandbags.

A Home for Prostitutes has been evacuated from a danger zone outside London to Aldershot.

(At this I protest, and Serena admits that it was related by young naval officer who has reputation as a wit.)

A large number of war casualties have already reached London, having come up the Thames in barges, and are installed in blocks of empty flats by the river—but nobody knows they're there.

Hitler and Ribbentrop are no longer on speaking terms.

Hitler and Ribbentrop have made it up again.

The Russians are going to turn dog on the Nazis at any moment.

In return for all this, I am in a position to inform Serena:

That the War Office is going to Carnarvon Castle.

A letter has been received in London from a German living in Berlin, with a private message under the stamp saying that a revolution is expected to break out at any minute.

President Roosevelt has been flown over the Siegfried Line and flown back to Washington again, in the strictest secrecy.

The deb. at the canteen, on being offered a marshmallow out of a paper bag, has said: What *is* a marshmallow? (Probably related to a High Court Judge.)

The Russians are determined to assassinate Stalin at the first opportunity.

A woman fainted in the middle of Regent Street yesterday and two stretcher-bearers came to the rescue and put her on the stretcher, then dropped it and fractured both her arms. Serena assures me that in the event of her being injured in any air-raid she has quite decided to emulate Sir Philip Sidney and give everybody else precedence.

Talking of that, would it be a good idea to practise wearing our gas-masks?

Agree, though rather reluctantly, and we accordingly put them on and sit opposite one another in respective armchairs, exchanging sepulchral-sounding remarks from behind talc-and-rubber snouts.

Serena says she wishes to time herself, as she doesn't think she will be able to breathe for more than four minutes at the very most.

Explain that this is all nerves. Gas-masks may be rather warm—(am streaming from every pore)—and perhaps rather uncomfortable, and certainly unbecoming—but any sensible person can breathe inside them for hours.

Serena says I shall be sorry when she goes off into a dead faint.

The door opens suddenly and remaining Austrian refugees, returned early from Bromley, walk in and, at sight presented by Serena and myself, are startled nearly out of their senses and enquire in great agitation What is happening.

Remove gas-mask quickly—Serena hasn't fainted at all but is crimson in the face, and hair very untidy—and we all bow and shake hands.

Letter-writing refugee joins us—shakes hands again—and we talk agreeably round tea-table till the letter-motif recurs—they all say they have letters to write, and—presumably final—handshaking closes séance.

Just as I prepare to leave, Serena's bell rings and she says It's J. L. and I'm to wait, because she wants me to meet him.

J. L. turns out to be rather distinguished-looking man, face perfectly familiar to me from *Radio Times* and other periodicals as he is well-known writer and broadcaster. (Wish I hadn't been so obliging about gas-mask, as hair certainly more untidy than Serena's and have not had the sense to powder my nose.)

J. L. is civility itself and pretends to have heard of me often—am perfectly certain he hasn't—and even makes rather indefinite reference to my Work, which he qualifies as well known, but wisely gives conversation another turn immediately without committing himself further.

Serena produces sherry and enquires what J. L. is doing.

Well, J. L. is writing a book.

He is, as a matter of fact, going on with identical book—merely a novel—that he was writing before war began. It isn't that he *wants* to do it, or that he thinks anybody else wants him to do it. But he is over military age, and the fourteen different organisations to whom he has offered his services have replied, without exception, that they have far more people already than they know what to do with.

He adds pathetically that authors, no doubt, are very useless people.

Not more so than anybody else, Serena replies. Why can't they be used for propaganda?

J. L. and I—with one voice—assure her that every author in the United Kingdom has had exactly this idea, and has laid it before the Ministry of Information, and has been told in return to Stand By for the present.

In the case of Sir Hugh Walpole, to J. L.'s certain knowledge, a Form was returned on which he was required to state all particulars of his qualifications, where educated, and to which periodicals he has contributed, also names of any books he may ever have had published.

Serena enquires witheringly if they didn't want to know whether the books had been published at Sir H. W.'s own expense, and we all agree that if this is official reaction to Sir H.'s offer, the rest of us need not trouble to make any.

Try to console J. L. with assurance that there is to be a boom in books, as nobody will be able to do anything amusing in the evenings, what with black-out, petrol restrictions, and limitations of theatre and cinema openings, so they will have to fall back on reading.

Realise too late that this not very happily expressed.

J. L. says Yes indeed, and tells me that he finds poetry more helpful than anything else. The Elizabethans for choice. Don't I agree?

Reply at once that I am less familiar with the Elizabethan poets than I should like to be, and hope he may think this means that I know plenty of others. (Am quite unable to recall any poetry at all at the moment, except "How they Brought the Good News from Ghent" and cannot imagine why in the world I should have thought of that.)

Ah, says J. L. very thoughtfully, there is a lot to be said for prose. He personally finds that the Greeks provide him with escapist literature. Plato.

Should not at all wish him to know that *The Fairchild Family* performs the same service for me—but remember with shame that E. M. Forster, in admirable wireless talk, has told us *not* to be ashamed of our taste in reading.

Should like to know if he would apply this to *The Fairchild Family* and can only hope that he would.

Refer to Dickens—compromise here between truth and desire to sound reasonably cultured—but J. L. looks distressed, says Ah yes—really? and changes conversation at once.

Can see that I have dished myself with him for good.

Talk about black-out—Serena alleges that anonymous friend of hers goes out in the dark with extra layer of chalk-white powder on her nose, so as to be seen, and resembles Dong with the Luminous Nose.

J. L. not in the least amused and merely replies that there are little disks on sale, covered with luminous paint, or that pedestrians are now allowed electric torch if pointed downwards, and shrouded in tissue-paper. Serena makes fresh start, and enquires whether he doesn't know Sir Archibald and Lady Blowfield—acquaintances of mine.

He does know them—had hoped that Sir A. could offer him war work—but that neither here nor there. Lady Blowfield is a charming woman.

I say Yes, isn't she—which is quite contrary to my real opinion. Moreover, am only distressed at this lapse from truth because aware that Serena will recognise it as such. Spiritual and moral degradation well within sight, but cannot dwell on this now. *(Query:* Is it in any way true that war very often brings out the best in civil population? *Answer:* So far as I am concerned, Not at all.)

Suggestion from Serena that Sir Archibald and Lady Blowfield both take rather pessimistic view of international situation causes J. L. to state it as his considered opinion that no one, be he whom he may, *no one,* is in a position at this moment to predict with certainty what the Future may hold.

Do not like to point out to him that no one ever has been, and shortly afterwards J. L. departs, telling Serena that he will ring her up when he knows any more. (Any more what?)

October 1st.—Am at last introduced by Serena Fiddlededee to underworld Commandant. She is dark, rather good-looking young woman wearing out-size in slacks and leather jacket, using immensely long black cigarette-holder, and writing at wooden trestle-table piled with papers.

Serena—voice sunk to quite unnaturally timid murmur—explains that I am very anxious to make myself of use in any way whatever, while waiting to be summoned by Ministry of Information.

The Commandant—who has evidently heard this kind of thing before—utters short incredulous ejaculation, in which I very nearly join, knowing even better than she does herself how thoroughly well justified it is.

Serena—voice meeker than ever—whispers that I can drive a car if necessary, and have passed my First Aid examination—(hope she isn't going to mention date of this achievement which would take us a long way back indeed)—and am also well used to Home Nursing. Moreover, I can write shorthand and use a typewriter.

Commandant goes on writing rapidly and utters without looking up for a moment—which I think highly offensive. Utterance is to the effect that there are no paid jobs going.

Oh, says Serena, sounding shocked, we never thought of anything like *that.* This is to be voluntary work, and anything in the world, and at any hour.

Commandant—still writing—strikes a bell sharply.

It has been said that the Canteen wants an extra hand, suggests Serena, now almost inaudible. She knows that I should be perfectly willing to work all through the night, or perhaps all day on

Sundays, so as to relieve others. And, naturally, voluntary work. To this Commandant—gaze glued to her rapidly-moving pen—mutters something to the effect that voluntary work is all very well—

Have seldom met more un-endearing personality.

Bell is answered by charming-looking elderly lady wearing overall, and armlet badge inscribed *Messenger,* which seems to me unsuitable.

Commandant—tones very peremptory indeed—orders her to Bring the Canteen Time-Sheet. Grey-haired messenger flies away like the wind. Cannot possibly have gone more than five yards from the door before the bell is again struck, and on her reappearance Commandant says sharply that she has just asked for Canteen Time-Sheet. Why hasn't it come?

Obvious reply is that it hasn't come because only a pair of wings could have brought it in the time—but no one says this, and Messenger again departs and can be heard covering the ground at race-track speed.

Commandant continues to write—says Damn once, under her breath, as though attacked by sudden doubt whether war will stop exactly as and when she has ordained—and drops cigarette-ash all over the table.

Serena looks at me and profanely winks enormous eye.

Bell is once more banged—am prepared to wager it will be broken before week is out at this rate. It is this time answered by smart-looking person in blue trousers and singlet and admirable make-up. Looks about twenty-five, but has prematurely grey hair, and am conscious that this gives me distinct satisfaction.

(Not very commendable reaction.)

Am overcome with astonishment when she enquires of Commandant in brusque, official tones: Isn't it time you had some lunch, darling?

Commandant for the first time raises her eyes and answers No, darling, she can't possibly bother with lunch, but she wants a staff car instantly, to go out to Wimbledon for her. It's urgent.

Serena looks hopeful but remains modestly silent while Commandant and Darling rustle through quantities of lists and swear vigorously, saying that it's a most extraordinary thing, the Time-Sheets ought to be always available at a second's notice, and they never *are.*

Darling eventually turns to Serena, just as previous—and infinitely preferable—Messenger returns breathless, and asks curtly, Who is on the Staff Car? Serena indicates that she is herself scheduled for it, is asked why she didn't say so, and commanded to get car out instantly and dash to Wimbledon.

Am deeply impressed by this call to action, but disappointed when Commandant instructs her to go *straight* to No. 478 Mottisfont Road, Wimbledon, and ask for clean handkerchief, which Commandant forgot to bring this morning.

She is to come *straight* back, as quickly as possible, *with* the handkerchief. Has she, adds Commandant suspiciously, quite understood?

Serena replies that she has. Tell myself that in her place I should reply No, it's all too complicated for me to grasp—but judging from lifelong experience, this is a complete fallacy and should in reality say nothing of the kind but merely wish, long afterwards, that I had.

Departure of Serena, in search, no doubt, of tin helmet and gas-mask, and am left, together with elderly Messenger, to be ignored by Commandant whilst she and Darling embark on earnest argument concerning Commandant's next meal, which turns out to be lunch, although time now five o'clock in the afternoon.

She must, says Darling, absolutely *must* have something. She has been here since nine o'clock and during that time what has she had? One cup of coffee and a tomato. It isn't enough on which to do a heavy day's work.

Commandant—writing again resumed and eyes again on paper—asserts that it's all she wants. She hasn't time for more. Does Darling realise that there's a *war* on, and not a minute to spare?

Yes, argues Darling, but she could eat something without leaving her desk for a second. Will she try some soup?

No.

Then a cup of tea and some buns?

No, no, no. *Nothing.*

She *must* take some black coffee. Absolutely and definitely must. Oh, very well, cries Commandant—at the same time striking table quite violently with her hand, which produces confusion among the papers. (Can foresee fresh trouble with mislaid Time-Sheets in immediate future.) Very well—black coffee, and she'll have it here. Instantly.

Darling dashes from the room throwing murderous look at elderly Messenger who has temporarily obstructed the dash.

Commandant writes more frenziedly than ever and snaps out single word *What,* which sounds like a bark, and is evidently addressed to Messenger, who respectfully lays Canteen Time-Sheet on table. This not a success, as Commandant snatches it up again and cries *Not* on the table, my God, *not* on the table! and scans it at red-hot speed.

She then writes again, as though nothing had happened.

Decide that if I am to be here indefinitely I may as well sit down, and do so.

Elderly Messenger gives me terrified, but I think admiring, look. Evidently this display of initiative quite unusual, and am, in fact, rather struck by it myself.

Darling reappears with a tray. Black coffee has materialised and is flanked by large plate of scrambled eggs on toast, two rock-buns and a banana.

All are placed at Commandant's elbow and she wields a fork with one hand and continues to write with the other.

Have sudden impulse to quote to her historical anecdote of British Sovereign remarking to celebrated historian: Scribble, scribble, scribble, Mr. Gibbon.

Do not, naturally, give way to it.

Darling asks me coldly If I want anything, and on my replying that I have offered my services to Canteen tells me to go *at once* to Mrs. Peacock. Decide to assume that this means I am to be permitted to serve my country, if only with coffee and eggs, so depart, and Elderly Messenger creeps out with me.

I ask if she will be kind enough to take me to Mrs. Peacock and she says Of course, and we proceed quietly—no rushing or dashing. *(Query:* Will not this dilatory spirit lose us the war? *Answer:* Undoubtedly, Nonsense!) Make note not to let myself be affected by aura of agitation surrounding Commandant and friend.

Messenger takes me past cars, ambulances, Rest-room, from which unholy din of feminine voices proceeds, and gives me information.

A Society Deb. is working in the Canteen. She is the only one in the whole place. A reporter came to interview her once and she was photographed kneeling on one knee beside an ambulance wheel, holding tools and things Photograph published in several papers and underneath it was printed: Débutante Jennifer Jamfather Stands By on Home Front.

Reach Mrs. Peacock, who is behind Canteen counter, sitting on a box, and looks kind but harassed.

She has a bad leg. Not a permanent bad leg but it gets in the way, and she will be glad of extra help.

Feel much encouraged by this. Nobody else has made faintest suggestion of being glad of extra help—on the contrary.

Raise my voice so as to be audible above gramophone ("Little Sir Echo") and wireless (...And so, bairns, we bid Goodbye to Bonnie Scotland)—roarings and bellowings of Darts Finals being played in a corner, and clatter of dishes from the kitchen—and announce that I am Come to Help—which I think sounds as if I were one of the Ministering Children Forty Years After.

Mrs. Peacock, evidently too dejected even to summon up customary formula that there is nothing for me to do except Stand By as she is turning helpers away by the hundred every hour, smiles rather wanly and says I am very kind.

What, I enquire, can I do?

At the moment nothing. (Can this be a recrudescence of Stand By theme?)

The five o'clock rush is over, and the seven o'clock rush hasn't begun. Mrs. Peacock is taking the opportunity of sitting for a moment. She heroically makes rather half-hearted attempt at offering me half packing-case, which I at once decline, and ask about her leg.

Mrs. P. displays it, swathed in bandages beneath her stocking, and tells me how her husband had two boxes of sand, shovel and bucket prepared for emergency use—(this evidently euphemism for incendiary bombs)—and gave full instructions to household as to use of them, demonstrating in back garden. Mrs. P. herself took part in this, she adds impressively. I say Yes, yes, to encourage her, and she goes on. Telephone call then obliged her to leave the scene—interpolation here about nature of the call involving explanation as to young married niece—husband a sailor, dear little baby with beautiful big blue eyes—from whom call emanated.

Ninth pip-pip-pip compelled Mrs. P. to ring off and, in retracing her steps, she crossed first-floor landing on which husband, without a word of warning, had meanwhile caused boxes of sand, shovel and bucket to be ranged, with a view to permanent instalment there. Mrs. P.—not expecting any of them—unfortunately caught her foot in the shovel, crashed into the sand-boxes, and was cut to the bone by edge of the bucket.

She concludes by telling me that it really was a lesson. Am not clear of what nature, or to whom, but sympathise very much and say I shall hope to save her as much as possible.

Hope this proceeds from unmixed benevolence, but am inclined to think it is largely actuated by desire to establish myself definitely as canteen worker—in which it meets with success.

Return to Buckingham Street flat again coincides with exit of owner, who at once enquires whether I have ascertained whereabouts of nearest air-raid shelter.

Well, yes, I have in a way. That is to say, the A.R.P. establishment in Adelphi is within three minutes' walk, and I could go there. Owner returns severely that that is Not Good Enough. He must beg of me to take this question seriously, and pace the distance between bedroom and shelter and find out how long it would take to get there in the event of an emergency. Moreover, he declares there is a shelter nearer than the Adelphi, and proceeds to indicate it.

Undertake, reluctantly, to conduct a brief rehearsal of my own exodus under stimulus of air-raid alarm, and subsequently do so.

This takes the form of rather interesting little experiment in which I lay out warm clothes, heavy coat, *Our Mutual Friend*—Shakespeare much more impressive but cannot rise to it—small bottle of boiled sweets—sugar said to increase energy and restore impaired morale—and electric torch. Undress and get into bed, then sound imaginary tocsin, look at my watch, and leap up.

Dressing is accomplished without mishap and proceed downstairs and into street with *Our Mutual Friend,* boiled sweets and electric torch. Am shocked to find myself strongly inclined to run like a lamplighter, in spite of repeated instructions issued to the contrary. If this is the case when no raid at all is taking place, ask myself what it would be like with bombers overhead—and do not care to contemplate reply.

Street seems very dark, and am twice in collision with other pedestrians. Reaction to this is merry laughter on both sides. (Effect of black-out on national hilarity quite excellent.)

Turn briskly down side street and up to entrance of air-raid shelter, which turns out to be locked. Masculine voice enquires where I think I am going, and I say, Is it the police? No, it is the Air-raid Warden. Explain entire situation; he commends my forethought and says that on the first sound of siren alarm He Will be There. Assure him in return that in that case we shall meet, as I shall also Be There, with equal celerity, and we part—cannot say whether temporarily or for ever.

Wrist-watch, in pocket of coat, reveals that entire performance has occupied four and a half minutes only.

Am much impressed, and walk back reflecting on my own efficiency and wondering how best to ensure that it shall be appreciated by Robert, to whom I propose to write spirited account.

Return to fiat reveals that I have left all the electric lights burning—though behind blue shades—and forgotten gas-mask, still lying in readiness on table.

Decide to put off writing account to Robert.

Undress and get into bed again, leaving clothes and other properties ready as before—gas-mask in prominent position on shoes—but realise that if I have to go through whole performance all over again to-night, shall be very angry indeed.

October 2nd.—No alarm takes place. Wake at two o'clock and hear something which I think may be a warbling note from a siren—which we have been told to expect—but if so, warbler very poor and indeterminate performer, and come to the conclusion that it is not worth my attention and go to sleep again.

Post—now very late every day—does not arrive until after breakfast.

Short note from Robert informs me that all is well, he does not care about the way the Russians are behaving—(he never has)—his A.R.P. office has more volunteers than he knows what to do with—and young Cramp from the garage, who offered to learn method of dealing with unexploded bombs, has withdrawn after ten minutes' instruction on the grounds that he thinks it seems rather dangerous.

Robert hopes I am enjoying the black-out—which I think is satirical—and has not forwarded joint letter received from Robin as there is nothing much in it. (Could willingly strangle him for this.)

Vicky's letter, addressed to me, makes some amends, as she writes ecstatically about heavenly new dormitory, divine concert and utterly twee air-raid shelter newly constructed (towards which parents will no doubt be asked to contribute). Vicky's only complaint is to the effect that no air-raid has yet occurred, which is very dull.

Also receive immensely long and chatty letter from Aunt Blanche. Marigold and Margery are well, Doreen Fitzgerald and Cook have failed to reach identity of views regarding question of the children's supper but this has now been adjusted by Aunt Blanche and I am not to worry, and Robert seems quite all right, though not saying much.

Our Vicar's Wife has been to tea—worn to a thread and looking like death—but has declared that she is getting on splendidly and the evacuees are settling down, and a nephew of a friend of hers, in the Militia, has told his mother, who has written it to his aunt, who has passed it on to Our Vicar's Wife, that all Berlin is seething with discontent, and a revolution in Germany is scheduled for the first Monday in November.

Is this, asks Aunt Blanche rhetorically, what the Press calls Wishful Thinking?

She concludes with affectionate enquiries as to my well-being, begs me to go and see old Uncle A. when I have time, and is longing to hear what post I have been offered by the Ministry of Information. *P.S.:* What about the Sweep? Cook has been asking.

Have never yet either left home, or got back to it, without being told that Cook is asking about the Sweep.

Large proportion of mail consists of letters, full of eloquence, from tradespeople who say that they are now faced with a difficult situation which will, however, be improved on receipt of my esteemed cheque.

Irresistible conviction comes over me that my situation is even more difficult than theirs, and, moreover, no cheques are in the least likely to come and improve it.

Turn, in hopes of consolation, to remainder of mail and am confronted with Felicity Fairmead's writing—very spidery—on envelope, and typewritten letter within, which she has forgotten to sign. Tells me that she is using typewriter with a view to training for war work, and adds candidly that she can't help hoping war may be over before she finds it. This, says Felicity, is awful, she knows very well, but she can't help it. She is deeply ashamed of her utter uselessness, as she is doing nothing whatever except staying as Paying Guest in the country with delicate friend whose husband is in France, and who has three small children, also delicate, and one maid who isn't any use, so that Felicity and friend make the beds, look after the children, do most of the cooking and keep the garden in order. Both feel how wrong it is not to be doing real work for the country, and this has driven Felicity to the typewriter and friend to the knitting of socks and Balaclava helmets.

Felicity concludes with wistful supposition that I am doing something splendid.

Should be very sorry to enlighten her on this point, and shall feel constrained to leave letter unanswered until reality of my position corresponds rather more to Felicity's ideas.

Meanwhile, have serious thoughts of sending copies of her letter to numerous domestic helpers of my acquaintance who have seen fit to leave their posts at a moment's notice in order to seek more spectacular jobs elsewhere.

Remaining item in the post is letter-card—which I have customary difficulty in tearing open and only succeed at the expense of one corner—and proves to be from Barbara Carruthers *née* Blenkinsop, now living in Midlands. She informs me that this war is upsetting her very much: it really is dreadful for *her,* she says, because she has children, and situation may get very difficult later on and they may have to do without things and she has always taken so much trouble to see that they have *everything*. They are at present in Westmorland, but this is a considerable expense and moreover petrol regulations make it impossible to go and see them, and train-service—about which Barbara is indignant and says it is *very* hard on her—most unsatisfactory. How long do I think war is going on? She had arranged for her elder boys to go to excellent Preparatory School near London this autumn, but school has moved to Wales, which isn't at all the same thing, and Barbara does feel it's rather too bad. And what do I think about food shortage? It is*most* unfair if her children are to be rationed, and she would even be prepared to pay extra for them to have additional supplies. She concludes by sending me her love and enquiring casually whether Robin has been sent to France yet, or is he just too young?

Am so disgusted at Barbara's whole attitude that I dramatically tear up letter into fragments and cast it from me, but realise later that it should have been kept in order that I might send suitable reply.

Draft this in my own mind several times in course of the day, until positively vitriolic indictment is evolved which will undoubtedly never see the light of day, and would probably land me in the Old Bailey on a charge of defamatory libel if it did.

Purchase overall for use in Canteen, debate the question of trousers and decide that I must be strong-minded enough to remain in customary clothing which is perfectly adequate to work behind the counter. Find myself almost immediately afterwards trying on very nice pair of navy-blue slacks, thinking that I look well in them and buying them.

Am prepared to take any bet that I shall wear them every time I go on duty.

As this is not to happen till nine o'clock to-night, determine to look up the Weatherbys, who might possibly be able to suggest whole-time National Service job—and old Uncle A. about whom Aunt Blanche evidently feels anxious.

Ring up Uncle A.—his housekeeper says he will be delighted to see me at tea-time—and also Mrs. Weatherby, living in Chelsea, who invites me to lunch and says her husband, distinguished Civil Servant, will be in and would much like to meet me. Imagination instantly suggests that he has heard of me (in what connection cannot possibly conceive), and, on learning that he is to be privileged to see me at his table, will at once realise that Civil Service would be the better for my assistance in some highly authoritative capacity.

Spend hours wondering what clothes would make me look most efficient, but am quite clear *not* slacks for the Civil Service. Finally decide on black coat and skirt, white blouse with frill of austere, *not* frilly, type, and cone-shaped black hat. Find that I look like inferior witch in third-rate pantomime in the latter, and take it off again. Only alternative is powder-blue with rainbow-like swathings, quite out of the question. Feel myself obliged to go out and buy small black hat, with brim like a jockey-cap and red edging. Have no idea whether this is in accordance with Civil Service tastes or not, but feel that I look nice in it.

Walk to Chelsea, and on looking into small mirror in handbag realise that I don't after all. Can do nothing about it, and simply ask hall-porter for Mrs. Weatherby, and am taken up in lift to sixth-floor flat, very modern and austere, colouring entirely neutral and statuette—to me wholly revolting—of misshapen green cat occupying top of bookcase, dominating whole of the room.

Hostess comes in—cannot remember if we are on Christian-name terms or not, but inclined to think not and do not risk it—greets me very kindly and again repeats that her husband wishes to meet me.

(Civil Service appointment definitely in sight, and decide to offer Serena job as my private secretary.)

Discuss view of the river from window—Mrs. Weatherby says block of flats would be an excellent target from the air, at which we both laugh agreeably—extraordinary behaviour of the Ministry of Information, and delightful autumnal colouring in neighbourhood of Bovey Tracy, which Mrs. Weatherby says she knows well.

Entrance of Mr. Weatherby puts an end to this interchange, and we are introduced. Mr. W. very tall and cadaverous, and has a beard, which makes me think of Agrippa.

He says that he has been wishing to meet me, but does not add why. Produces sherry and we talk about black-out, President Roosevelt—I say that his behaviour throughout entire crisis has been magnificent and moves me beyond measure—Mrs. Weatherby agrees, but Agrippa seems surprised and I feel would like to contradict me but politeness forbids—and we pass on to cocker spaniels, do not know how or why.

Admirable parlourmaid—uniform, demeanour and manner all equally superior to those of Winnie, or even departed May—announces that Luncheon is served, madam, and just as I prepare to swallow remainder of sherry rapidly, pallid elderly gentleman crawls in, leaning on stick and awakening in me instant conviction that he is not long for this world.

Impression turns out to be not without foundation as it transpires that he is Agrippa's uncle, and has recently undergone major operation at London Nursing Home but was desired to leave it at five minutes' notice in order that bed should be available if and when required. Uncle asserts that he met this—as well he might—with protests but was unfortunately too feeble to enforce them and accordingly found himself, so he declares, on the pavement while still unable to stand. From this fearful plight he has been retrieved by Agrippa, and given hospitality of which he cannot speak gratefully enough.

Story concludes with examples of other, similar cases, of which we all seem to know several, and Mrs. Weatherby's solemn assurance that all the beds of all the Hospitals and Nursing Homes in England are standing empty, and that no civilian person is to be allowed to be ill until the war is over.

Agrippa's uncle shakes his head, and looks worse than ever, and soon after he has pecked at chicken soufflé, waved away sweet omelette and turned his head from the sight of Camembert cheese, he is compelled by united efforts of the Weatherbys to drink a glass of excellent port and retire from the room.

They tell me how very ill he has been—can well believe it—and that there was another patient even more ill, in room next to his at Nursing Home, who was likewise desired to leave. She, however, defeated the authorities by dying before they had time to get her packing done.

Find myself exclaiming "Well done!" in enthusiastic tone before I have time to stop myself, and am shocked. So, I think, are the Weatherbys—rightly.

Agrippa changes the conversation and asks my opinion about the value of the natural resources of Moravia. Fortunately answers his own question, at considerable length.

Cannot see that any of this, however interesting, is leading in the direction of war work for me.

On returning to drawing-room and superb coffee which recalls Cook's efforts at home rather sadly to my mind—I myself turn conversation forcibly into desired channel.

What an extraordinary thing it is, I say, that so many intelligent and experienced people are not, so far as one can tell, being utilised by the Government in any way!

Mrs. Weatherby replies that she thinks most people who are *really* trained for anything worth while have found no difficulty whatever in getting jobs, and Agrippa declares that it is largely a question of Standing By, and will continue to be so for many months to come.

Does he, then, think that this will be a long war?

Agrippa, assuming expression of preternatural discretion, replies that he must not, naturally, commit himself. Government officials, nowadays, have to be exceedingly careful in what they say as I shall, he has no doubt, readily understand.

Mrs. Weatherby strikes in to the effect that it is difficult to see how the war can be a very *short* one, and yet it seems unlikely to be a very *long* one.

I enquire whether she thinks it is going to be a middling one, and then feel I have spoken flippantly and that both disapprove of me.

Should like to leave at once, but custom and decency alike forbid as have only this moment finished coffee.

Ask whether anything has been heard of Pamela Pringle, known to all three of us, at which Agrippa's face lights up in the most extraordinary way and he exclaims that she is, poor dear, quite an invalid but as charming as ever.

Mrs. Weatherby—face not lighting up at all but, on the contrary, resembling a thunder-cloud—explains that Pamela, since war started, has developed unspecified form of Heart and retired to large house near the New Forest where she lies on the sofa, in *eau-de-nil* velvet wrapper, and has all her friends down to stay in turns.

Her husband has a job with the Army and is said to be in Morocco, and she has despatched the children to relations in America, saying that this is a terrible sacrifice, but done for their own sakes.

Can only reply, although I hope indulgently, that it all sounds to me exactly like dear Pamela. This comment more of a success with Mrs. W. than with Agrippa, who stands up—looks as if he might touch the ceiling—and says that he must get back to work.

Have abandoned all serious hope of his offering me a post of national importance, or even of no importance at all, but put out timid feeler to the effect that he must be very busy just now.

Yes, yes, he is. He won't get back before eight o'clock to-night, if then. At one time it was eleven o'clock, but things are for the moment a little easier, though no doubt this is only temporary. *(Query:* Why is it that all those occupied in serving the country are completely overwhelmed by pressure of work but do not apparently dream of utilising assistance pressed upon them by hundreds of willing helpers? *Answer* comes there none.)

Agrippa and I exchange unenthusiastic farewells, but he sticks to his guns to the last and says that he has always wanted to meet me. Does not, naturally, add whether the achievement of this ambition has proved disappointing or the reverse.

Linger on for a few moments in frail and unworthy hope that Mrs. Weatherby may say something more, preferably scandalous, about Pamela Pringle, but she only refers, rather bleakly, to Agrippa's uncle and his low state of health and asserts that she does not know what the British Medical Association can be thinking about.

Agree that I don't either—which is true not only now but at all times—and take my leave. Tell her how much I have liked seeing them both, and am conscious of departing from spirit of truth in saying so, but cannot, obviously, inform her that the only parts of the entertainment I have really enjoyed are her excellent lunch and hearing about Pamela.

Go out in search of bus—all very few and far between now—and contemplate visit to hairdresser's, but conscience officiously points out that visits to hairdresser constitute an unnecessary expense and could very well be replaced by ordinary shampoo in bedroom basin at flat. Inner prompting—probably the Devil—urges that Trade must be Kept Going and that it is my duty to help on the commercial life of the nation.

Debate this earnestly, find that bus has passed the spot at which I intended to get out, make undecided effort to stop it, then change my mind and sit down again and am urged by conductor to Make up My Mind. I shall have to move a lot faster than that, he jocosely remarks, when them aeroplanes are overhead. Much amusement is occasioned to passengers in general, and we all part in high spirits.

Am much too early for Uncle A. and walk about the streets—admire balloons which look perfectly entrancing—think about income-tax, so rightly described as crushing, and decide not to be crushed at all but readjust ideas about what constitutes reasonable standard of living, and learn to cook for self and family—and look at innumerable posters announcing contents of evening papers.

Lowest level seems to me to be reached by one which features *exposé,* doubtless apocryphal, of Hitler's sex life—but am not pleased with another which enquires—idiotically—Why Not Send Eden to Russia?

Could suggest hundreds of reasons why not, and none in favour.

Remaining posters all display ingenious statements, implying that tremendous advance has been made somewhere by Allies, none of whom have suffered any casualties at all, with enormous losses to enemy.

Evolve magnificent piece of rhetoric, designed to make clear once and for all what does, and what does not, constitute good propaganda, and this takes me to Mansions in Kensington at the very top of which dwell Uncle A. and housekeeper, whose peculiar name is Mrs. Mouse.

Sensation quite distinctly resembling small trickle of ice-cold water running down spine assails me, at the thought that rhetoric on propaganda will all be wasted, since no Government Department wishes for my assistance—but must banish this discouraging reflection and remind myself that at least I am to be allowed a few hours' work in Canteen.

Hall-porter—old friend—is unfortunately inspired to greet me with expressions of surprise and disappointment that I am not in uniform. Most ladies are, nowadays, he says. His circle of acquaintances evidently more fortunate than mine. Reply that I have been trying to join something—but can see he doesn't believe it.

We go up very slowly and jerkily in aged Victorian lift—pitch dark and smells of horse-hair—and porter informs me that nearly all the flats are empty, but he doubts whether 'Itler himself could move the old gentleman. Adds conversationally that, in his view, it is a *funny* war. Very funny indeed. He supposes we might say that it hasn't hardly begun yet, has it? Agree, though reluctantly, that we might.

Still, says the hall-porter as lift comes to an abrupt stop, we couldn't very well have allowed 'im to carry on as he was doing, could we, and will I please mind the step.

I do mind the step—which is about three feet higher than the landing—and ring Uncle A.'s bell.

Can distinctly see Mrs. Mouse applying one eye to ground-glass panel at top of door before she opens it and welcomes my arrival. In reply to enquiry she tells me that Uncle A. is remarkably well and has been all along, and that you'd never give him seventy, let alone eighty-one. She adds philosophically that nothing isn't going to make him stir and she supposes, with hearty laughter, that he'll never be satisfied until he's had the both of them smothered in poison gas, set fire to, blown sky-high and buried under the whole of the buildings.

Point out that this is surely excessive and enquire whether they have a shelter in the basement. Oh yes, replies Mrs. M., but she had the work of the world to get him down there when the early-morning alarm was given, at the very beginning of the war, as he refused to move until fully dressed and with his teeth in. The only thing that has disturbed him at all, she adds, is the thought that he is taking no active part in the war.

She then conducts me down familiar narrow passage carpeted in red, with chocolate-and-gilt wallpaper, and into rather musty but agreeable drawing-room crammed with large pieces of furniture, potted palm, family portraits in gilt frames, glass-fronted cupboards, china, books, hundreds of newspapers and old copies of *Blackwood's Magazine,* and grand piano on which nobody has played for about twenty-seven years.

Uncle A. rises alertly from mahogany kneehole writing-table—very upright and distinguished-looking typical Diplomatic Service—(quite misleading, Uncle A. retired stockbroker)—and receives me most affectionately.

He tells me that I look tired—so I probably do, compared with Uncle A. himself—commands Mrs. M. to bring tea, and wheels up an armchair for me in front of magnificent old-fashioned coal fire. Can only accept it gratefully and gaze in admiration at Uncle A.'s slim figure, abundant white hair and general appearance of jauntiness.

He enquires after Robert, the children and his sister—whom he refers to as poor dear old Blanche—(about fifteen years his junior)—and tells me that he has offered his services to the War Office and has had a very civil letter in acknowledgment, but they have not, as yet, actually found a niche for him. No doubt, however, of their doing so in time.

The Government is, in Uncle A.'s opinion, underrating the German strength, and as he himself knew Germany well in his student days at Heidelberg, he is writing a letter to *The Times* in order to make the position better understood.

He asks about evacuees—has heard all about them from Blanche—and tells me about his great-niece in Shropshire. She is sitting in her manor-house waiting for seven evacuated children whom she has been told to expect; beds are already made, everything waiting, but children haven't turned up. I suggest that this is reminiscent of Snow White and seven little dwarfs, only no little dwarfs.

Uncle A. appears to be immeasurably amused and repeats at intervals: Snow White and no little dwarfs. Capital, capital!

Tea is brought in by Mrs. M., and Uncle A. declines my offer of pouring out and does it himself, and plies me with hot scones, apricot jam and home-made gingerbread. All is the work of Mrs. M. and I tell Uncle A. that she is a treasure, at which he looks rather surprised and says she's a good gel enough and does what she's told.

Can only remember, in awe-stricken silence, that Mrs. M. has been in Uncle A.'s service for the past forty-six years.

Take my leave very soon afterwards and make a point of stating that I have presently to go on duty at A.R.P. Canteen, to which Uncle A. replies solicitously that I mustn't go overdoing it.

He then escorts me to the lift, commands the hall-porter to look after me and call a cab should I require one, and remains waving a hand while lift, in a series of irregular leaps, bears me downstairs.

No cab is required—hall-porter does not so much as refer to it—and take a bus back to the Strand.

Bathroom has now familiar notice pinned on door—"Occupied"—which I assume to be Serena, especially on finding large bunch of pink gladioli in sitting-room, one empty sherry-glass, and several biscuit crumbs on rug. Moreover, black-out has been achieved and customary sheets of paper pinned up, and also customary number of drawing-pins strewn over the floor.

Serena emerges from bathroom, very pink, and says she hopes it's All Right, and I say it is, and thank her for gladioli, to which she replies candidly that flowers are so cheap nowadays they're being practically *given* away.

She asks what I have been doing, and I relate my experiences—Serena carries sympathy so far as to declare that Mr. Weatherby ought to be taken out and shot and that Mrs. W. doesn't sound much of a one either, but Uncle A. too adorable for words.

She then reveals that she came round on purpose to suggest we should have supper at Canteen together before going on duty.

Am delighted to agree, and change into trousers and overall. Greatly relieved when Serena ecstatically admires both.

Extraordinary thought that she is still only known to me as Serena Fiddlededee.

1.30 A.M.—Return from Canteen after evening of activity which has given me agreeable illusion that I am now wholly indispensable to the Allies in the conduct of the war.

Canteen responsibilities, so far as I am concerned, involve much skipping about with orders, memorising prices of different brands of cigarettes—which mostly have tiresome halfpenny tacked on to round sum, making calculation difficult—and fetching of fried eggs, rashers, sausages-and-mashed and Welsh rarebits from kitchen.

Mrs. Peacock—leg still giving trouble—very kind, and fellow workers pleasant; old Mrs. Winter-Gammon only to be seen in the distance, and Serena not at all.

Am much struck by continuous pandemonium of noise in Canteen, but become more accustomed to it every moment, and feel that air-raid warning, by comparison, would pass over my head quite unnoticed.

October 3rd.—Old Mrs. Winter-Gammon develops tendency, rapidly becoming fixed habit, of propping herself against Canteen counter, smoking cigarettes and chattering merrily. She asserts that she can do without sleep, without rest, without food and without fresh air. Am reluctantly forced to the conclusion that she can.

Conversation of Mrs. W.-G. is wholly addressed to me, since Mrs. Peacock—leg in no way improved—remains glued to her box from which she can manipulate Cash-register—and leaves Débutante to do one end of the counter, Colonial young creature with blue eyes in the middle, and myself at the other end.

Custom goes entirely to Débutante, who is prettyish, and talks out of one corner of tightly-shut mouth in quite unintelligible mutter, and Colonial, who is amusing. Am consequently left to company of Granny Bo-Peep.

She says roguishly that we old ones must be content to put up with one another and before I have time to think out civil formula in which to tell her that I disagree, goes on to add that, really, it's quite ridiculous the way all the boys come flocking round her. They like, she thinks, being mothered—and yet, at the same time, she somehow finds she can keep them laughing. It isn't that she's specially witty, whatever some of her clever men friends—such as W. B. Yeats, Rudyard Kipling and Lord Oxford and Asquith—may have said in the past. It's just that she was born, she supposes, under a dancing star. Like Beatrice.

(If Granny Bo-Peep thinks that I am going to ask her who Beatrice was, she is under a mistake. Would willingly submit to torture rather than do so, even if I didn't know, which I do.)

She has the audacity to ask, after suitable pause, if I know my Shakespeare.

Reply No, not particularly, very curtly, and take an order for two Welsh rarebits and one Bacon-and-sausage to the kitchen. Have barely returned before Granny Bo-Peep is informing me that her quotation was from that lovely comedy *Much Ado About Nothing*. Do I know *Much Ado About Nothing?*

Yes, I do—and take another order for Sausages-and-mashed. Recollection comes before me, quite unnecessarily, of slight confusion which has always been liable to occur in my mind, as to which of Shakespeare's comedies is called *As You Like It* and which *Much Ado About Nothing*. Should be delighted to tell old Mrs. W.-G. that she has made a mistake, but am not sufficiently positive myself.

Moreover, she gives me no opportunity.

Have I heard, she wants to know, from poor Blanche? I ask Why poor? and try to smile pleasantly so as to show that I am not being disagreeable—which I am. Well, says Granny Bo-Peep indulgently, she always thinks that poor Blanche—perfect dear though she is—is a wee bit lacking in *fun*. Granny Bo-Peep herself has such a keen sense of the ridiculous that it has enabled her to bear all her troubles where others, less fortunately endowed, would almost certainly have gone to pieces. Many, many years ago her doctor—one of the best-known men in Harley Street—said to her: Mrs. Winter-Gammon, by rights you ought not to be alive to-day. You ought to be dead. Your health, your sorrows, your life of hard work for others, all should have killed you long, long ago. What has kept you alive? Nothing but your wonderful spirits.

And I am not, says Mrs. W.-G., to think for one instant that she is telling me this in a boastful spirit. Far from it. Her vitality, her gaiety, her youthfulness and her great sense of humour have all been bestowed upon her from Above. She has had nothing to do but rejoice in the possession of these attributes and do her best to make others rejoice in them too.

Could well reply to this that if she has succeeded with others no better than she has with me, all has been wasted—but do not do so.

Shortly afterwards Commandant comes in, at which Mrs. Peacock rises from her box, blue-eyed young Colonial drops a Beans-on-Toast on the floor, and Society Deb. pays no attention whatever.

Granny Bo-Peep nods at me very brightly, lights her fourteenth cigarette and retires to trestle-table on which she perches swinging her legs, and is instantly surrounded—to my fury—by crowd of men, all obviously delighted with her company.

Commandant asks what we have for supper—averting eyes from me as she speaks—and on being handed list goes through items in tones of utmost contempt.

She then orders two tomatoes on toast. Friend—known to me only as Darling—materialises behind her, and cries out that Surely, surely, darling, she's going to have more than *that*. She must. She isn't going to be allowed to make her supper on tomatoes—it isn't *enough*.

Commandant makes slight snarling sound but no other answer, and I retire to kitchen with order, leaving Darling still expostulating.

Previously ordered Sausages-and-mashed, Welsh rarebit, Bacon-and-sausages are now ready, and I distribute them, nearly falling over distressed young Colonial who is scraping up baked beans off the floor. She asks madly what she is to do with them and I reply briefly: Dustbin.

Commandant asks me sharply where her tomatoes are and I reply, I hope equally sharply, In the frying-pan. She instantly takes the wind out of my sails by replying that she didn't say she wanted them fried. She wants the *bread* fried, and the tomatoes uncooked. Darling breaks out into fresh objections and I revise order given to kitchen.

Cook is not pleased.

Previous orders now paid for over counter, and Mrs. Peacock, who has conducted cash transactions with perfect accuracy hitherto, asserts that nine-pence from half a crown leaves one and sixpence change. Ambulance driver to whom she hands this sum naturally demands an explanation, and the whole affair comes to the notice of the Commandant, who addresses a withering rebuke to poor Mrs. P. Am very sorry for her indeed and should like to help her if I could, but this a vain aspiration at the moment and can only seek to distract attention of Commandant by thrusting at her plate of fried bread and un-fried tomatoes. She takes no notice whatever and finishes what she has to say, and Darling makes imperative signs to me that I am guilty of *lèse-majesté* in interrupting. Compose short but very pungent little essay on Women in Authority. *(Query:* Could not leaflets be dropped by our own Air Force, in their spare moments, on Women's Organisations all over the British Isles?)

Sound like a sharp bark recalls me, and is nothing less than Commandant asking if *that* is her supper.

Yes, it is.

Then will I take it back at once and have it put into the oven. It's stone cold.

Debate flinging the whole thing at her head, which I should enjoy doing, but instincts of civilisation unfortunately prevail and I decide—probable rationalising process here—that it will impress her more to display perfect good-breeding.

Accordingly reply Certainly in tones of icy composure—but am not sure they don't sound as though I were consciously trying to be refined, and wish I'd let it alone. Moreover Commandant, obviously not in the least ashamed of herself, merely tells me to be quick about it, please, in insufferably authoritative manner.

Cook angrier than ever.

Very pretty girl with curls all over her head and waist measurement apparently eighteen-inch, comes and leans up against the counter and asks me to advise her in choice between Milk Chocolate Bar and Plain Chocolate Biscuit.

Deb. addresses something to her which sounds like Hay-o Mule! and which I realise, minutes later, may have been Hallo, Muriel. Am much flattered when Muriel merely shakes her curls in reply and continues to talk to me. Am unfortunately compelled to leave her, still undecided, in order to collect Commandant's supper once more.

Cook hands it to me with curtly expressed, but evidently heart-felt, hope that it may choke her. Pretend I haven't heard, but find myself exchanging very eloquent look with Cook all the same.

Plate, I am glad to say unpleasantly hot, is snatched from me by Darling and passed on to Commandant, who in her turn snatches it and goes off without so much as a Thank you.

Rumour spreads all round the underworld—cannot say why or from where—that the German bombers are going to raid London to-night. They are, it is said, *expected.* Think this sounds very odd, and quite as though we had invited them. Nobody seems seriously depressed, and Society Deb. is more nearly enthusiastic than I have ever heard her and remarks Ra way baw way, out of one corner of her mouth. Cannot interpret this, and make very little attempt to do so. Have probably not missed much.

Night wears on; Mrs. Peacock looks pale green and evidently almost incapable of stirring from packing-case at all, but leg is not this time to blame, all is due to Commandant, and Mrs. P.'s failure in assessing change correctly. Feel very sorry for her indeed.

Customary pandemonium of noise fills the Canteen: We Hang up our Washing on the Siegfried Line and bellow aloud requests that our friends should Wish us Luck when they Wave us Good-bye: old Mrs. Winter-Gammon sits surrounded by a crowd of ambulance men, stretcher-bearers and demolition workers talk far into the night, and sound of voices from Women's Rest-room goes on steadily and ceaselessly.

I become involved with sandwich-cutting and think I am doing well until austere woman who came on duty at midnight confronts me with a desiccated-looking slice of bread and asks coldly if I cut that?

Yes, I did.

Do I realise that one of those long loaves ought to cut up into thirty-two slices, and that, at the rate I'm doing it, not more than twenty-four could possibly be achieved?

Can only apologise and undertake—rashly, as I subsequently discover—to do better in future.

A lull occurs between twelve and one, and Mrs. Peacock—greener than ever—asks Do I think I can manage, if she goes home now? Her leg is paining her. Assure her that I can, but austere woman intervenes and declares that both of us can go. *She* is here now, and will see to everything.

Take her at her word and depart with Mrs. P.

Street pitch-dark but very quiet, peaceful and refreshing after the underworld. Starlight night, and am meditating a reference to Mars—hope it *is* Mars—when Mrs. Peacock abruptly enquires if I can tell her a book to read. She has an idea—cannot say why, or whence derived—that I know something about books.

Find myself denying it as though confronted with highly scandalous accusation, and am further confounded by finding myself unable to think of any book whatever except *Grimm's Fairy*

Tales, which is obviously absurd. What, I enquire in order to gain time, does Mrs. Peacock like in the way of books?

In times such as these, she replies very apologetically indeed, she thinks a novel is practically the only thing. Not a detective novel, not a novel about politics, nor about the unemployed, nothing to do with sex, and above all not a novel about life under Nazi régime in Germany.

Inspiration immediately descends upon me and I tell her without hesitation to read a delightful novel called *The Priory* by Dorothy Whipple, which answers all requirements, and has a happy ending into the bargain.

Mrs. Peacock says it seems too good to be true, and she can hardly believe that *any* modern novel is as nice as all that, but I assure her that it is and that it is many years since I have enjoyed anything so much.

Mrs. P. thanks me again and again, I offer to help her to find her bus in the Strand—leg evidently giving out altogether in a few minutes—beg her to take my arm, which she does, and I immediately lead her straight into a pile of sandbags.

Heroic pretence from Mrs. P. that she doesn't really mind—she likes it—if anything, the jar will have *improved* the state of her leg. Say Good-night to her before she can perjure herself any further and help her into bus which may or may not be the one she wants.

Return to Buckingham Street and find it is nearly two o'clock. Decide that I must get to bed quickly—but find myself instead mysteriously impelled to wash stockings, write to Vicky, tidy up writing-desk, and cut stems and change water of Serena's gladioli.

Finally retire to bed with *The Daisy Chain* wishing we were all back in the England of the 'fifties.

October 4th.—Serena tells me that Brigadier Pinflitton is very sorry, he doesn't think the War Office likely to require my services. But she is to tell me that, in time, all will find jobs.

If I hear this even once again, from any source whatever, I cannot answer for consequences.

Serena, who brings me this exhilarating message, asks me to walk round the Embankment Gardens with her, as she has got leave to come out for an hour's fresh air on the distinct understanding that in the event of an air-raid warning she instantly flies back to her post.

We admire the flowers, which are lovely, and are gratified by the arrival of a balloon in the middle of the gardens, with customary Man and Lorry attached.

Serena informs me that Hitler's peace proposals—referred to on posters as "peace offensive"—will be refused, and we both approve of this course and say that any other would be unthinkable and express our further conviction that Hitler is in fearful jam, and knows it, and is heading for a catastrophe. He will, predicts Serena, go right off his head before so very long.

Then we shall be left, I point out, with Goering, Ribbentrop and Hess.

Serena brushes them aside, asserting that Goering, though *bad,* is at least a soldier and knows the rules—more or less—that Ribbentrop will be assassinated quite soon—and that Hess is a man of straw.

Hope she knows what she is talking about.

We also discuss the underworld, and Serena declares that Granny Bo-Peep has offered to get up a concert on the premises and sing at it herself. She does not see how this is to be prevented.

Tells me that girl with curls—Muriel—is rather sweet and owns a Chow puppy whose photograph she has shown Serena, and the Chow looks *exactly* like Muriel and has curls too.

The Commandant, thinks Serena, will—like Hitler—have a breakdown quite soon. She and Darling had a quarrel at six o'clock this morning because Darling brought her a plate of minced ham and the Commandant refused to touch it on the grounds of having No Time.

Darling reported to have left the premises in a black fury.

We then go back to flat and I offer Serena tea, which she accepts, and biscuits. Reflection occurs to me—promoted by contrast between Serena and the Commandant—that Golden Mean not yet achieved between refusal to touch food at all, and inability to refrain from practically unbroken succession of odd cups of tea, coffee, and biscuits all day and all night.

Just as I am preparing to expound this further, telephone bell rings. Call is from Lady Blowfield: If I am not *terribly* busy will I forgive short notice and lunch with her to-morrow to meet exceedingly interesting man—Russian by birth, married a Roumanian but this a failure and subsequently married a Frenchwoman, who has now divorced him. Speaks every language *well,* and is absolutely certain to have inside information about the European situation. Works as a free-lance journalist. Naturally accept with alacrity and express gratitude for this exceptional opportunity.

Am I, solicitously adds Lady Blowfield, keeping fairly well? Voice sounds so anxious that I don't care to say in return that I've never been better in my life, so reply Oh yes, I'm fairly all right, in tone which suggests that I haven't slept or eaten for a week—which isn't the case at all.

(Note: Adaptability to another's point of view is one thing, and rank deceit quite another. Should not care to say under which heading my present behaviour must be listed.)

Lady Blowfield says Ah! compassionately, down the telephone, and I feel the least I can do is ask after her and Sir Archibald, although knowing beforehand that she will give no good account of either.

Archie, poor dear, is fearfully over-worked and she is very, very anxious about him, and wishes he would come into the country for a week-end, but this is impossible. He has begged her to go without him, but she has refused because she *knows* that if she once leaves London, there will be an air-raid and the whole transport system of the country will be disorganised, communications will be cut off everywhere, petrol will be unobtainable, and the Government—if still in existence at all—flung into utter disarray.

Can only feel that if all this is to be the direct result of Lady Blowfield's going into Surrey for a week-end she had undoubtedly better remain where she is.

She further tells me—I think—that Turkey's attitude is still in doubt and that neither she nor Archie care for the look of things in the Kremlin, but much is lost owing to impatient mutterings of Serena who urges me to ring off, and says Surely that's *enough,* and How much longer am I going on saying the same things over and over again?

Thank Lady Blowfield about three more times for the invitation, repeat that I shall look forward to seeing her and meeting cosmopolitan friend—she reiterates all his qualifications as an authority on international politics, and conversation finally closes.

Apologise to Serena, who says It doesn't matter a bit, only she particularly wants to talk to me and hasn't much time. (Thought she had been talking to me ever since she arrived, but evidently mistaken.)

Do I remember, says Serena, meeting J. L. at her flat?

Certainly. He said Plato provided him with escape literature.

Serena exclaims in tones of horror that he isn't *really* like that. He's quite nice. Not a great sense of humour, perhaps, but a *kind* man, and not in the least conceited.

Agree that this is all to the good.

Do I think it would be a good plan to marry him?

Look at Serena in surprise. She is wearing expression of abject wretchedness and seems unable to meet my eye.

Reply, without much originality, that a good deal depends on what she herself feels about it.

Oh, says Serena, she doesn't know. She hasn't the slightest idea. That's why she wants my advice. Everyone seems to be getting married: haven't I noticed the announcements in *The Times* lately?

Yes, I have, and they have forcibly recalled 1914 and the three succeeding years to my mind. Reflections thus engendered have not been wholly encouraging. Still, the present question, I still feel, hinges on what Serena herself feels about J. L.

Serena says dispassionately that she likes him, she admires his work, she finds it very easy to get on with him, and she doesn't suppose they would make more of a hash of things than most people.

If that, I say, is all, better leave it alone.

Serena looks slightly relieved and thanks me.

I venture to ask her whether she has quite discounted the possibility of falling in love, and Serena replies sadly that she has. She used to fall in love quite often when she was younger, but it always ended in disappointment, and anyway the *technique* of the whole thing has changed, and people never get married now just *because* they've fallen in love. It's an absolutely understood thing.

Then why, I ask, *do* they get married?

531

Mostly, replies Serena, because they want to make a change.

I assure her, with the greatest emphasis, that this is an inadequate reason for getting married. Serena is most grateful and affectionate, promises to do nothing in a hurry, and says that I have helped her enormously—which I know to be quite untrue.

Just as she is leaving, association of ideas with announcement in *The Times* leads me to admit that she is still only known to me as Serena Fiddlededee, owing to Aunt Blanche's extraordinary habit of always referring to her thus. Serena screams with laughter, asserts that nowadays one has to know a person *frightfully* well before learning their surname, and that hers is Brown with no E.

October 5th.—Lunch with Lady Blowfield and am privileged to meet cosmopolitan friend.

He turns out to be very wild-looking young man, hair all over the place and large eyes, and evidently unversed in uses of nailbrush. Has curious habit of speaking in two or three languages more or less at once, which is very impressive as he is evidently thoroughly at home in all—but cannot attempt to follow all he says.

Sir Archibald not present. He is, says Lady Blowfield, more occupied than ever owing to Hitler's iniquitous peace proposals. (Should like to ask what, exactly, he is doing about them, but difficult, if not impossible, to word this civilly.)

Young cosmopolitan—introduced as Monsieur Gitnik—asserts in French, that *Ce fou d'Itlère fera un dernier attentat, mais il n'y a que lui qui s'imagine que cela va réussir.* Reply *En effet,* in what I hope is excellent French, and Monsieur Gitnik turns to me instantly and makes me a long speech in what I think must be Russian.

Look him straight in the eye and say very rapidly *Da, da, da!* which is the only Russian word I know, and am shattered when he exclaims delightedly, Ah, you speak Russian?

Can only admit that I do not, and he looks disappointed and Lady Blowfield enquires whether he can tell us what is going to happen next.

Yes, he can.

Hitler is going to make a speech to the Reich at midday tomorrow. (Newspapers have already revealed this, as has also the wireless.) He will outline peace proposals—so called. These will prove to be of such a character that neither France nor England will entertain them for a moment. *Monsieur Chamberlain prendra la parole et enverra promener Monsieur Itlère, Monsieur Daladier en fera autant, et zut! la lutte s'engagera, pour de bon cette fois-ci.*

Poor de *ploo* bong? says Lady Blowfield uneasily.

Gitnik makes very rapid reply—perhaps in Hungarian, perhaps in Polish or possibly in both— which is evidently not of a reassuring character, as he ends up by stating, in English, that people in this country have not yet realised that we are wholly vulnerable not only from the North and the East, but from the South and the West as *well.*

And what, asks Lady Blowfield faintly, about the air?

London, asserts Gitnik authoritatively, has air defences. Of that there need be no doubt at all. The provinces, on the other hand, could be attacked with the utmost ease and probably will be. It is being openly stated in Istanbul, Athens and New Mexico that a seventy-hour bombardment of Liverpool is the first item on the Nazi programme.

Lady Blowfield moans, but says nothing.

Remaining guests arrive: turn out to be Mr. and Mrs. Weatherby, whom I am not particularly pleased to meet again, but feel obliged to assume expression as of one receiving an agreeable surprise.

Gitnik immediately addresses them in Italian, to which they competently reply in French, whereupon he at once reverts to English. Weatherbys quite unperturbed, and shortly afterwards enquire whether he can tell us anything about America's attitude.

Yes, as usual, he can.

America will, for the present, keep out of the conflict. Her sympathies, however, are with the Allies. There will undoubtedly be much discussion over this business of the embargo on the sale of arms. It has been said in Rome—and Gitnik must beg of us to let this go no further—that the embargo will probably be lifted early next year.

At this Lady Blowfield looks impressed, but the Weatherbys are left cold—for which I admire them—and conviction gains strength in my own mind that Monsieur Gitnik resembles fourteenth-rate crystal-gazer, probably with business premises in mews off Tottenham Court Road.

Luncheon extremely welcome, and make determined effort to abandon the sphere of European unrest and talk about rock-gardens instead. This a dead failure.

Excellent omelette, chicken-casserole and accompaniments are silently consumed while Monsieur Gitnik, in reply to leading question from hostess—(evidently determined to Draw him Out, which is not really necessary)—tells us that if ever he goes to Russia again, he has been warned that he will be thrown into prison because he Knows Too Much. Similar fate awaits him in Germany, Esthonia and the Near East generally, for the same reason.

Mrs. Weatherby—my opinion of her going up every moment by leaps and bounds—declares gaily that this reminds her of a play, once very popular, called *The Man Who Knew Too Much*. Or does she mean *The Man Who Stayed At Home*?

Mr. Weatherby thinks that she does. So do I. Lady Blowfield says sadly that it matters little now, it all seems so very far away.

Gitnik crumbles bread all over the table and says something in unknown tongue, to which nobody makes any immediate reply, but Lady Blowfield's dog emits short, piercing howl.

This leads the conversation in the direction of dogs, and I find myself giving rather maudlin account of the charms of Robert's Benjy, wholly adorable puppy resembling small, square woolly bear. Mrs. Weatherby is sympathetic, Mr. W. looks rather remote but concedes, in a detached way, that Pekinese dogs are sometimes more intelligent than they are given credit for being, and Lady Blowfield strokes her dog and says that he is to be evacuated to her sister's house in Hampshire next week.

Gitnik firmly recalls us to wider issues by announcing that he has received a rather curious little communication from a correspondent whose name and nationality, as we shall of course understand, he cannot disclose, and who is writing from a neutral country that must on no account be mentioned by name.

He is, however, prepared to let us see the communication if we should care to do so.

Oui, oui, replies Lady Bloomfield in great agitation—evidently under the impression that this cryptic answer will wholly defeat the butler, now handing coffee and cigarettes.

(Take a good look at butler, to see what he thinks of it all, but he remains impassive.)

Coffee is finished hastily—regret this, as should much have preferred to linger—and we retreat to drawing-room and Gitnik produces from a pocket-book several newspaper cuttings—which he replaces—envelope with a foreign stamp but only looks like ordinary French one—and postcard of which he displays one side on which is written: *"Je crois que Monsieur Hitler a les jitters".*

The rest of the card, says. Gitnik, tells nothing—nothing at all. But that one phrase—coming as it does from a man who is probably better informed on the whole situation than almost anybody in Europe—that one phrase seems to him quite startlingly significant. *Non é vero?*

Everybody looks very serious, and Lady Blowfield shakes her head several times and only hopes that it's true. We all agree that we only hope it's true, and postcard is carefully replaced in pocket-book again by Monsieur Gitnik.

Shortly afterwards he evidently feels that he has shot his bolt and departs, asserting that the Ministry of Information has sent for him, but that they will not like what he feels himself obliged to say to them.

Lady Blowfield—rather wistful tone, as though not absolutely certain of her ground—enquires whether we don't think that that really is a most interesting man, and I find myself unable to emulate the Weatherbys, who maintain a brassy silence, but make indeterminate sounds as though agreeing with her.

Take my departure at the same moment as Weatherbys, and once outside the front door Mr. W. pronounces that the wretched fellow is a complete fraud, and knows, if anything, rather less than anybody else.

Mrs. W. and I join in, and I feel more drawn towards them than I should ever have believed possible. Am sorry to note that abuse and condemnation of a common acquaintance often constitutes very strong bond of union between otherwise uncongenial spirits.

Part from them at Hyde Park Corner: Mr. W. must on no account be late—Home Office awaits him—and springs into a taxi, Mrs. W. elects to walk across the park and view dahlias, and I proceed by bus to large Oxford Street shop, where I find myself the only customer, and buy two pairs of lisle stockings to be despatched to Vicky at school.

October 6th.—Wireless reports Hitler's speech to the Reich, setting forth utterly ridiculous peace proposals. Nobody in the least interested, and wireless is switched off half-way through by Serena who says that Even the Londonderry Air, of which the B.B.C. seems so fond, would be more amusing.

Agree with her in principle, and express the hope that Mr. Chamberlain will be in no hurry to reply to Adolf's nonsense. Serena thinks that he won't, and that it'll be quite fun to see what America says as their newspapers always express themselves so candidly, and asks me to serve her with a cup of coffee, a packet of cigarettes and two apples.

We then discuss at great length rumour that W.V.S. is to be disbanded and started again on quite a new basis, with blue uniforms.

Mrs. Peacock asks if I would like to take over Cash Register, and I agree to do so subject to instruction, and feel important.

She also suggests that I should take duty on Sunday for an hour or two, as this always a difficult day on which to get help, and I light-heartedly say Yes, yes, any time she likes—I live just over the way and nothing can be easier than to step across. She can put me down for whatever hour is most difficult to fill. She immediately puts me down for 6 A.M.

October 8th.—Inclined to wish I hadn't been so obliging. Six A.M. very un-inspiring hour indeed.

Granny Bo-Peep enters Canteen at half-past seven—looks as fresh as a daisy—and tells me roguishly that my eyes are full of sleepy-dust and she thinks the sand-man isn't far away, and orders breakfast—a pot of tea, buttered toast and scrambled eggs.

Colonial fellow-worker hands them to her and ejaculates—to my great annoyance—that she thinks Mrs. Winter-Gammon is just wonderful. Always cheerful, always on her feet, always thinking of others.

Granny Bo-Peep—must have preternaturally acute hearing—manages to intercept this and enquires what nonsense is that? What is there wonderful about a good-for-nothing old lady doing her bit, as the boys in brave little Belgium used to call it? Why, she's *proud* to do what she can, and if the aeroplanes do come and a bomb drops on her—why, it just isn't going to matter. Should like, for the first time in our association, to tell old Mrs. W.-G. that I entirely agree with her. Young Colonial—evidently nicer nature than mine—expresses suitable horror at suggested calamity, and Mrs. W.-G. is thereby encouraged to ruffle up her curls with one claw and embark on story concerning one of the stretcher-bearers who has—she alleges—attached himself to her and follows her about everywhere like a shadow. Why, she just can't imagine. (Neither can I.)

Order for Two Sausages from elderly and exhausted-looking Special Constable who has been on duty in the street all night takes me to the kitchen, where Cook expresses horror and incredulity at message and says I must have made a mistake, as nobody could order *just* sausages. He must have meant with fried bread, or mashed, or even tomatoes.

Special Constable says No, he didn't. He *said* sausages and he *meant* sausages.

Can only report this adamant spirit to Cook, who seems unable to credit it even now, and takes surreptitious look through the hatch at Special Constable, now leaning limply against the counter. He shakes his head at my suggestions of coffee, bread-and-butter or a nice cup of tea, and removes his sausages to corner of table, and Cook says it beats her how anybody can eat a sausage all on its own, let alone two of them, but she supposes it'll take all sorts to win this war.

Lull has set in and sit down on Mrs. Peacock's box and think of nineteen hundred and fourteen and myself as a V.A.D. and tell myself solemnly that a quarter of a century makes a *difference* to one in many ways.

This leads on to thoughts of Robin and Vicky and I have mentally put one into khaki and the other into blue slacks, suède jacket and tin hat, when Granny Bo-Peep's voice breaks in with the assertion that she knows *just* what I'm thinking about: she can read it in my face. I'm thinking about my children.

Have scarcely ever been so near committing murder in my life.

Young Colonial—could wish she had either more discrimination or less kindliness—is encouraging old Mrs. W.-G.—who isn't in the least in need of encouraging—by respectful questions as to her own family circle, and Mrs. W.-G. replies that she is alone, except for the many, many dear friends who are good enough to say that she means something in their lives. She has never had children, which she implies is an error on the part of Providence as she knows she *ought* to have been the mother of sons. She has a natural affinity with boys and they with her.

When she was living with her dear Edgar in his East End parish, many years ago, she invariably asked him to let her teach the boys. Not the girls. The boys. Just the boys. And Edgar used to reply: These boys are the Roughest of the Rough. They are beyond a gentlewoman's control. But Mrs. W.-G. would simply repeat: Give me the boys, Edgar. And Edgar—her beloved could never hold out against her—eventually gave her the boys. And what was the result?

The result was that the boys—though still the Roughest of the Rough—became tamed. A lady's influence, was the verdict of Edgar, in less than a month. One dear lad—a scallywag from the dockside if ever there was one, says Mrs. W.-G. musingly—once made use of Bad Language in her presence. And the other poor lads almost tore him to pieces, dear fellows. Chivalry. Just chivalry. The Beloved always said that she seemed to call it out.

She herself—ha-ha-ha—thinks it was because she was such A Tiny—it made them feel protective. Little Mother Sunshine they sometimes called her—but that might have been because in those days her curlywig was gold, not silver.

Even the young Colonial is looking rather stunned by this time, and only ejaculates very feebly when Mrs. W.-G. stops for breath. As for myself, a kind of coma has overtaken me and I find myself singing in an undertone "South of the Border, down Mexico Way"—to distant gramophone accompaniment.

Am relieved at Cash Register what seems like weeks later—but is really only two hours—and retire to Buckingham Street.

Curious sense of unreality pervades everything—cannot decide if this is due to extraordinary and unnatural way in which the war is being conducted, without any of the developments we were all led to expect, or to lack of sleep, or merely to prolonged dose of old Mrs. Winter-Gammon's conversation.

Debate the question lying in hot bath, wake up with fearful start although am practically positive that I haven't been asleep, and think how easily I might have drowned—recollections of George Joseph Smith and Brides in the Bath follow—crawl into bed and immediately become mentally alert and completely wide awake.

This state of things endures until I get up and dress and make myself tea and hot buttered toast.

Timid tap at flat door interrupts me, and, to my great surprise, find Muriel—curls and all—outside. She explains that Serena has said that I have a bathroom and that I am very kind and that there is no doubt whatever of my allowing her to have a bath. Is this all right?

Am touched and flattered by this trusting spirit, and assure her that it is.

(Query: Are my services to the Empire in the present world-war to take the form of supplying hot baths to those engaged in more responsible activities?*Answer:* At present, apparently, yes.)

Muriel comes out from bathroom more decorative than ever—curls evidently natural ones—and we have agreeable chat concerning all our fellow workers, about whom our opinions tally. She then drifts quietly out again, saying that she is going to have a really *marvellous* time this afternoon, because she and a friend of hers have been saving up all their petrol and they are actually going to drive out to Richmond Park. Remembrance assails me, after she has gone, that Serena has said that Muriel's parents own a Rolls-Royce and are fabulously wealthy. Have dim idea of writing short, yet brilliant, article on New Values in War-Time—but nothing comes of it.

Instead, write a letter to Robert—not short, but not brilliant either. Also instructions to Aunt Blanche about letting Cook have the Sweep, if that's what she wants, and suggesting blackberry jelly if sugar will run to it, and not allowing her, on any account, to make pounds and pounds of marrow jam which she is certain to suggest and which everybody hates and refuses to touch.

P.S.: I have seen Mrs. Winter-Gammon quite a lot, and she seems very energetic indeed and has sent Aunt Blanche her love. Can quite understand why Aunt Blanche has said that she will not agree to share a flat with her again when the war is over. Mrs. W.-G. has dynamic personality and is inclined to have a devitalising effect on her surroundings.

Re-read postscript and am not at all sure that it wouldn't have been better to say in plain English that old Mrs. W.-G. is more aggravating than ever, and Aunt Blanche is well out of sharing a flat with her.

Ring up Rose later on and enquire whether she has yet got a job.

No, nothing like that. Rose has sent in her name and qualifications to the British Medical Association, and has twice been round to see them, and she has received and filled in several forms, and has also had a letter asking if she is prepared to serve with His Majesty's Forces abroad with the rank of Major, and has humorously replied Yes, certainly, if H.M. Forces don't mind about her being a woman, and there the question, at present, remains.

All Rose's medical colleagues are equally unoccupied and she adds that the position of the Harley Street obstetricians is particularly painful, as all their prospective patients have evacuated themselves from London and the prospect of their talents being utilised by the Services is naturally non-existent.

What, asks Rose, about myself?

Make the best show I can with the Canteen—position on Cash Register obviously quite a responsible one in its way—but Rose simply replies that it's too frightful the way we're all hanging about wasting our time and doing nothing whatever.

Retire from this conversation deeply depressed.

October 9th.—Mrs. Peacock electrifies entire Canteen by saying that she has met a man who says that the British Government is going to accept Hitler's peace terms.

Can only reply that he must be the only man in England to have adopted this view—and this is supported by everyone within hearing, Serena going so far as to assert that man must be a Nazi propaganda-agent as nobody else could have thought of anything so absurd.

Mrs. P. looks rather crushed, but is not at all resentful, only declaring that man is *not* a Nazi propaganda-agent, but she thinks perhaps he just said it so as to be unlike anybody else—in which he has succeeded.

Man forthwith dismissed from the conversation by everybody.

No further incident marks the day until supper-time, when customary uproar of radio, gramophone, darts contest and newly imported piano (situated just outside Women's Rest-room) has reached its climax.

Ginger-headed stretcher-bearer then comes up to order two fried eggs, two rashers, one sausage-roll and a suet dumpling, and asks me if I've heard the latest.

Prepare to be told that Dr. Goebbels has been executed at the behest of his Führer at the very least, but news turns out to be less sensational. It is to the effect that the underworld has now been issued with shrouds, to be kept in the back of each car. Am dreadfully inclined to laugh at this, but stretcher-bearer is gloom personified, and I feel that my reaction is most unsuitable and immediately stifle it.

Stretcher-bearer then reveals that his chief feeling at this innovation is one of resentment. He was, he declares, in the last war, and nobody had shrouds*then,* but he supposes that this is to be a regular Gentleman's Business.

Condole with him as best I can, and he takes his supper and walks away with it, still muttering very angrily about shrouds.

October 10th.—Letter received from extremely distinguished woman, retired from important Civil Service post less than a year ago, and with whom I am only in a position to claim acquaintance at all because she is friend of Rose's. She enquires—very dignified phraseology—if I can by any chance tell her of suitable war work.

Can understand use of the word suitable when she adds, though without apparent rancour, entire story of recent attempts to serve her country through the medium of local A.R.P. where she lives. She has filled up numbers of forms, and been twice interviewed by very refined young person of about nineteen, and finally summoned to nearest Council Offices for work alleged to be in need of experienced assistance.

Work takes the form of sitting in very chilly entrance-hall of Council Offices directing enquirers to go Upstairs and to the Right for information about Fuel Control, and Downstairs and Straight Through for Food Regulations.

Adds—language still entirely moderate—that she can only suppose the hall-porter employed by Council Offices has just been called up.

Am shocked and regretful, but in no position to offer any constructive suggestion.

Letter also reaches me from Cook—first time we have ever corresponded—saying that Winnie's mother has sent a message that Winnie's young sister came back from school with earache which has now gone to her foot and they think it may be rheumatic fever and can Winnie be spared for a bit to help. Cook adds that she supposes the girl had better go, and adds *P.S.:* The Butcher has took Winnie and dropped her the best part of the way. *P.P.S.:* Madam, what about the Sweep?

Am incredibly disturbed by this communication on several counts. Winnie's absence more than inconvenient, and Cook herself will be the first person to complain of it bitterly. Have no security that Winnie's mother's idea of "a bit" will correspond with mine.

Cannot understand why no letter from Aunt Blanche. Can Cook have made entire arrangement without reference to her? Allusion to Sweep also utterly distracting. Why so soon again? Or, alternatively, did Aunt Blanche omit to summon him at Cook's original request, made almost immediately after my departure? If so, for what reason, and why have I been told nothing?

Can think of nothing else throughout very unsatisfactory breakfast, prepared by myself, in which electric toaster alternately burns the bread or produces no impression on it whatever except for three pitch-black perpendicular lines.

Tell myself that I am being foolish, and that all will be cleared up in the course of a post or two, and settle down resolutely to Inside Information column of favourite daily paper, which I read through five times only to find myself pursuing long, imaginary conversation with Cook at the end of it all.

Decide that the only thing to do is to telephone to Aunt Blanche this morning and clear up entire situation.

Resume Inside Information.

Decide that telephoning is not only expensive, but often unsatisfactory as well, and letter will serve the purpose better.

Begin Inside Information all over again.

Imaginary conversation resumed, this time with Aunt Blanche.

Decide to telephone, and immediately afterwards decide not to telephone.

Telephone bell rings and strong intuitional flash comes over me that decision has been taken out of my hands. (Just as well.)

Yes?

Am I Covent Garden? says masculine voice.

No, I am not.

Masculine voice ejaculates—tone expressive of annoyance, rather than regret for having disturbed me—and conversation closes.

Mysterious unseen compulsion causes me to dial TRU and ask for home number.

Die now cast.

After customary buzzing and clicking, Robert's voice says Yes? and is told by Exchange to go ahead.

We do go ahead and I say Is he all right? to which he replies, sounding rather surprised, that he's quite all right. Are the children, Aunt Blanche and the maids all right? What about Winnie?

Robert says, rather vaguely, that he believes Winnie has gone home for a day or two, but they seem to be Managing, and do I want anything special?

Answer in the weakest possible way that I only wanted to know if they were All Right, and Robert again reiterates that they are and that he will be writing to-night, but this A.R.P. business takes up a lot of time. He hopes the Canteen work is proving interesting and not too tiring, and he thinks that Hitler is beginning to find out that he's been playing a mug's game.

So do I, and am just about to elaborate this theme when I remember the Sweep and enquire if I can speak to Aunt Blanche.

Robert replies that he thinks she's in the bath.

Telephone pips three times, and he adds that, if that's all, perhaps we'd better ring off.

Entire transaction strikes me as having been unsatisfactory in the extreme.

October 11th.—Nothing from Aunt Blanche except uninformative picture postcard of Loch in Scotland—in which I take no interest whatever—with communication to the effect that the trees are turning colour and looking lovely and she has scarcely ever before seen so *many* holly-berries out *so early*. The children brought in some beautiful branches of beech-leaves on Sunday and Aunt Blanche hopes to put them in glycerine so that they will last in the house for *months*. The news seems to her good *on the whole*. The Russians evidently *not* anxious for war, and Hitler, did he but know it, *up a gum-tree*. Much love.

Spend much time debating question as to whether I had not better go home for the week-end.

October 12th.—Decide finally to ask Mrs. Peacock whether I can be spared for ten days in order to go home on urgent private affairs. Am unreasonably reluctant to make this suggestion in spite of telling myself what is undoubtedly the fact: that Canteen will easily survive my absence without disaster.

Mrs. Peacock proves sympathetic but tells me that application for leave will have to be made direct to Commandant. Can see she expects me to receive this announcement with dismay, so compel myself to reply Certainly, with absolute composure.

(Do not believe that she is taken in for one second.)

Debate inwardly whether better to tackle Commandant instantly, before having time to dwell on it, or wait a little and get up more spirit. Can see, however, that latter idea is simply craven desire to postpone the interview and must not on any account be entertained seriously.

Serena enters Canteen just as I am preparing to brace myself and exclaims that I look very green in the face, do I feel ill?

Certainly not. I am perfectly well. Does Serena know if Commandant is in her office, as I wish to speak to her.

Oh, says Serena, that accounts for my looks. Yes, she is.

I say Good, in very resolute tone, and go off. Fragmentary quotations from Charge of the Light Brigade come into my mind, entirely of their own accord.

Serena runs after me and says she'll come too, and is it anything very awful?

Not at all. It is simply that I feel my presence to be temporarily required at home, and am proposing to go down there for ten days. This scheme to be subjected to Commandant's approval as a mere matter of courtesy.

At this Serena laughs so much that I find myself laughing also, though perhaps less whole-heartedly, and I enquire whether Serena supposes Commandant will make a fuss? Serena replies, cryptically, that it won't exactly be a *fuss,* but she's sure to be utterly odious—which is precisely what I anticipate myself.

Temporary respite follows, as Serena, after pressing her nose against glass panel of office window, reports Commandant to be engaged in tearing two little Red Cross nurses limb from limb.

Cannot feel that this bodes well for me, but remind myself vigorously that I am old enough to be Commandant's mother and that, if necessary, shall have no hesitation in telling her so.

(Query: Would it impress her if I did? *Answer:* No.)

Office door flies open and Red Cross nurse comes out, but leaves fellow victim within.

Serena and I, with one voice, enquire what is happening, and are told in reply that Her Highness is gone off of the deep end, that's what. Long and very involved story follows of which nothing is clear to me except that Red Cross nurse declares that she isn't going to be told by anyone that she doesn't know her job, and have we any of us ever heard of Lord Horder?

Yes, we not unnaturally have.

Then who was it, do we suppose, who told her himself that he never wished to see better work in the ward than what hers was?

Office door, just as she is about to reply to this rhetorical question, flies open once more and second white veil emerges, which throws first one into still more agitation and they walk away arm-in-arm, but original informant suddenly turns her head over her shoulder and finishes up reference to Lord Horder with very distinctly-enunciated monosyllable: E.

Serena and I giggle and Commandant, from within the office, calls out to someone unseen to shut that door *at once,* there's far too much noise going on and is this a girls' school, or an Organisation of national importance?

Should like to reply that it's neither.

Rather draughty pause ensues, and I ask Serena if she knows how the underworld manages to be chilly and stuffy at one and the same time—but she doesn't.

Suggests that I had better knock at the door, which I do, and get no reply.

Harder, says Serena.

I make fresh attempt, again unsuccessful, and am again urged to violence by Serena. Third effort is much harder than I meant it to be and sounds like onslaught from a battering-ram. It produces a very angry command to Come In! and I do so.

Commandant is, as usual, smoking and writing her head off at one and the same time, and continues her activities without so much as a glance in my direction.

I contemplate the back of her head—coat collar wants brushing—and reflect that I could *(a)* throw something at her—nearest available missile is cardboard gas-mask container, which I don't think heavy enough; *(b)* walk out again; *(c)* tell her clearly and coldly that I have No Time to Waste.

Am bracing myself for rather modified form of *(c)* when she snaps out enquiry as to what I want. I want to leave London for a week or ten days.

Commandant snaps again. This time it is Why.

Because my presence is required in my own house in Devonshire.

Devonshire? replies Commandant in offensively incredulous manner. What do I mean by Devonshire?

Cannot exactly explain why, but at this precise moment am suddenly possessed by spirit of defiance and hear myself replying in superbly detached tones that I am not here to waste either her time or my own and should be much obliged if she would merely note that I shall not be giving my services at Canteen for the next ten days.

Am by no means certain that thunderbolt from Heaven will not strike me where I stand, but it is withheld, and sensation of great exhilaration descends upon me instead.

Commandant looks at me—first time she has ever done so in the whole of our association—and says in tones of ice that I *am* wasting her time, as the Canteen Time-Sheet is entirely in the hands of Mrs. Peacock and I ought to have made my application for leave through her.

She then slams rubber stamp violently onto inoffensive piece of paper and turns her back again.

I rejoin Serena, to whom I give full account of entire episode—probably too full, as Serena—after highly commending me—says that I couldn't have made half such a long speech in the time. Realise that I couldn't, and that imagination has led me astray, and withdraw about half of what I have told her, but the other half accurate and much applauded by Serena and subsequently by Mrs. Peacock.

Mrs. P. also says that Of course I must go home, and Devonshire sounds lovely, and she wishes she lived there herself. Do I know Ilfracombe? Yes, quite well. Does Mrs. Peacock? No, but she's always heard that it's lovely. I agree that it is, and conversation turns to macaroni-and-tomato, again on the menu to-night, bacon now off, and necessity of holding back the brown bread as it will be wanted for to-morrow's breakfast.

Serena orders coffee and stands drinking it, and says that there is to be a lecture on Fractures at midnight. I ask why midnight, and she replies vaguely, Oh, because they think it'll be dark then.

Am unable to follow this, and do not attempt to do so.

News percolates through Canteen—cannot at all say how—that I am going to Devonshire for ten days and fellow workers tell me how fortunate I am, and enquire whether I know Moretonhampstead, Plymouth Hoe, and the road between Axminster and Charmouth.

Old Granny Bo-Peep appears as usual—have strong suspicion that she never leaves the underworld at all, but stays there all day and all night—and romps up to me with customary air of roguish enjoyment.

What is this, she asks, that a little bird has just told her? That one of our very latest recruits is looking back from the plough already? But that's only her fun—she's delighted, really, to hear that I'm to have a nice holiday in the country. All the way down to Devon, too! Right away from the war, and hard work, and a lovely rest amongst the birds and the flowers.

Explain without any enthusiasm that my presence is required at home and that I am obliged to take long and probably crowded journey in order to look into various domestic problems, put them in order, and then return to London as soon as I possibly can.

Old Mrs. W.-G. says she quite understands, in highly incredulous tones, and proceeds to a long speech concerning her own ability to work for days and nights at a stretch without ever requiring any rest at all. As for taking a holiday—well, such a thing never occurs to her. It just simply doesn't ever cross her mind. It isn't that she's exactly stronger than anybody else—on the contrary, she's always been supposed to be rather fragile—but while there's work to be done, she just has to do it, and the thought of rest never occurs to her.

Beloved Edgar used to say to her: One day you'll break down. You *must* break down. You cannot possibly go on like this and *not* break down. But she only laughed and went on just the same. She's always been like that, and she hopes she always will be.

Feel sure that hope will probably be realised

Evening proceeds as usual. Mock air-raid alarm is given at ten o'clock, and have the gratification of seeing Serena race for her tin hat and fly back with it on her head, looking very *affairée* indeed.

Canteen workers, who are not expected to take any part in manoeuvres, remain at their posts and seize opportunity to drink coffee, clear the table, and tell one another that we are all to be disbanded quite soon and placed under the Home Office—that we are all to be given the sack—that we are all to be put into blue dungarees at a cost of eleven shillings per head—and similar pieces of intelligence.

Stretcher-bearers presently reappear and story goes round that imaginary casualty having been placed on stretcher and left there with feet higher than his head, has been taken off to First Aid Post in a dead faint and hasn't come round yet.

Rather sharp words pass between one of the cooks and young Canteen voluntary helper in flowered cretonne overall, who declares that her orders are not receiving proper attention. Cook asserts that *all* orders are taken in rotation and Flowered Cretonne replies No, hers aren't. Deadlock appears to have been reached and they glare at one another through the hatch.

Two more cooks in background of kitchen come nearer in support of colleague, or else in hopes of excitement, but Cretonne Overall contents. herself with repeating that she must say it seems rather extraordinary, and then retiring to tea-urn, which I think feeble.

She asks for a cup of tea—very strong and plenty of sugar—which I give her and tells me that she doesn't think this place is properly run, just look how the floor wants sweeping, and I am impelled to point out that there is nothing to prevent her from taking a broom and putting this right at once.

Cretonne Overall gives me a look of concentrated hatred, snatches up her cup of tea and walks away with it to furthest table in the room. Can see her throwing occasional glances of acute dislike in my direction throughout remainder of the night.

Serena returns—tells me that the feature of the practice has been piled-up bodies and that these have amused themselves by hooking their legs and arms together quite inextricably and giving the first-aid men a good deal of trouble, but everyone has seen the funny side of it and it's been a very merry evening altogether.

Better, she adds gloomily, than the concert which we are promised for next week is likely to be.

She then drinks two cups of coffee, eats half a bar of chocolate and a banana, and announces that she is going to bed.

Presently my relief arrives: tiny little creature with bobbed brown hair, who has taken duty from 10 P.M. to 10 A.M. every night since war started. I express admiration at her self-sacrifice, and she says No, it's nothing, because she isn't a voluntary worker at all—she gets paid.

As this no doubt means that she is working part of the day as well, can only feel that grounds for admiration are, if anything, redoubled and tell her so, but produce no effect whatever, as she merely replies that there's nothing to praise her for, she gets paid.

She adds, however, that it is a satisfaction to her to be doing something Against that Man. She said to Dad at the very beginning: Dad, I want to do something *against* him. So she took this job, and she put herself down at the Hospital for blood-transfusion, and they've took some from her already and will be wanting more later. In this way, she repeats, she can feel she's doing something *Against Him*—which is what she wants.

Am much struck by contrast between her appearance—tiny little thing, with very pretty smile—and extreme ferocity of her sentiments.

We exchange Good-nights and I collect my coat from Women's Rest-room where it hangs on a peg, in the midst of camp-beds.

On one of them, under mountain of coverings, huge mop of curls is just visible—no doubt belonging to Muriel.

Serena is sitting bolt-upright on adjacent bed, legs straight out in front of her in surely very uncomfortable position, writing letters. This seems to me most unnatural hour at which to conduct her correspondence, which apparently consists largely of picture postcards.

Wireless outside is emitting jazz with tremendous violence, engines are running, and a group of persons with surely very loud voices are exchanging views about the Archbishop of York. They are of opinion, after listening to His Grace's broadcast the other night, that Where a Man like that is wanted is In the Cabinet.

Agree with them, and should like to go out and say so, adding suggestion that he would make first-class Prime Minister—but Serena intervenes with plaintive observation that, as they all agree with one another and keep on saying That's Right, she can't imagine why they *must* go on discussing it instead of letting her get a little sleep.

At this I feel the moment has come for speech which I have long wished to deliver, and I suggest to Serena that she has undertaken a form of war service which is undoubtedly going to result in her speedy collapse from want of sleep, fresh air, and properly-regulated existence generally. Wouldn't it be advisable to do something more rational?

There *isn't* anything, says Serena positively. Nobody wants anybody to do anything, and yet if they do nothing they go mad.

Can see that it will take very little to send Serena into floods of tears, and have no wish to achieve this result, or to emulate Darling's methods with Commandant, so simply tell her that I suppose she knows her own business best—(not that I do, for one minute)—and depart from the underworld.

October 13th.—Countryside bears out all that Aunt Blanche has written of its peaceful appearance, autumn colouring, and profusion of scarlet berries prematurely decorating the holly-trees.

Train very crowded and arrives thirty-five minutes late, and I note that my feelings entirely resemble those of excited small child returning home for the holidays. Robert has said that he cannot meet me owing to A.R.P. duties but is there at the station, and seems pleased by my return, though saying nothing openly to that effect.

We drive home—everything looks lovely and young colt in Home Farm field has miraculously turned into quite tall black horse. Tell Robert that I feel as if I had been away for years, and he replies that it is two and a half weeks since I left.

I ask after the evacuees, the puppy, Aunt Blanche, Cook and the garden and tell Robert about Serena, the Canteen, the Blowfields and their cosmopolitan friend—Robert of opinion that he ought to be interned at once—and unresponsive attitude of the Ministry of Information.

What does Robert think about Finland? Envoy now in Moscow. Robert, in reply, tells me what he thinks, not about Finland, but about Stalin. Am interested, but not in any way surprised, having heard it all before a great many times.

As we drive in at the gate Marigold and Margery dart round the house—and I have brief, extraordinary hallucination of having returned to childish days of Robin and Vicky. Cannot possibly afford to dwell on this illusion for even one second, and get out of the car with such haste that suit-case falls with me and most of its contents are scattered on the gravel, owing to defective lock.

Robert not very pleased.

Marigold and Margery look pink and cheerful, Miss Doreen Fitzgerald comes up from garden, knitting, and says I'm Very Welcome, certainly I am. (Should never be surprised if she offered to show me my room.)

Winnie appears at hall door, at which I exclaim, Oh, are you back, Winnie? and then feel it would be no more than I deserve if she answered No, she's in Moscow with the Finnish Envoy at the Kremlin—but this flight of satire fortunately does not occur to her, and she smiles very cheerfully and says, Yes, Mum thought it might be a long job with Bessie, and if she found she couldn't manage, she'd send for Winnie again later on.

Can think of no more unsatisfactory arrangement, from domestic point of view, but hear myself assuring Winnie cordially that that'll be quite all right.

We all collect various properties from the gravel, and Benjy achieves *succès fou* with evacuees and myself by snatching up bedroom slipper and prancing away with it under remotest of the lilac bushes, from whence he looks out at us with small growls, whilst shaking slipper between his teeth.

Marigold and Margery scream with laughter and applaud him heartily under pretence of rescuing slipper, and Aunt Blanche comes downstairs and picks up my sponge and then greets me most affectionately.

Am still pursuing scattered belongings, rolled to distant points of the compass, when small car dashes in at the gate and I have only time to tell Aunt Blanche to get rid of them *whoever* it is, and hasten into the house.

(They cannot possibly have failed to see me, but could they perhaps think, owing to unfamiliar London clothes, that I am newly-arrived visitor with eccentric preference for unpacking just outside the hall door? Can only hope so, without very much confidence.)

Hasten upstairs—rapturously delighted at familiar bedroom once more—and am moved at finding particularly undesirable green glass vase with knobs, that I have never liked, placed on dressing-table and containing two yellow dahlias, one branch of pallid Michaelmas daisies, and some belated sprigs of catmint—undoubted effort of Marigold and Margery.

Snatch off hat and coat—can hear Aunt Blanche under the window haranguing unknown arrivals—and resort to looking-glass, brush and comb, lipstick and powder-puff, but find myself breaking off all operations to straighten favourite Cézanne reproduction hanging on the wall, and also restoring small clock to *left*-hand corner of table where I left it, and from which it has been moved to the right.

(*Query:* Does this denote unusually orderly mind and therefore rank as an asset, or is it merely quality vulgarly—and often inaccurately—known to my youth as old-maidishness?)

Sounds of car driving away again—look out of the window, but am none the wiser except for seeing number on the rear-plate, which conveys nothing, and Benjy now openly chewing up slipper-remains.

Ejaculate infatuatedly that he is a little lamb, and go downstairs to tea.

This laid in dining-room and strikes me as being astonishingly profuse, and am rendered speechless when Aunt Blanche says Dear, dear, they've forgotten the honey, and despatches Marigold to fetch it. She also apologises for scarcity of butter—can only say that it hadn't struck me, as there must be about a quarter of a pound per head in the dish—but adds that at least we can have as much clotted cream as we like, and we shall have to make the best of that.

We do.

She asks after Serena Fiddlededee—am able to respond enthusiastically and say we've made great friends and that Serena is so amusing—and then mentions Pussy Winter-Gammon. Totally different atmosphere at once becomes noticeable, and although I only reply that she seems to be very well indeed and full of energy, Aunt Blanche makes deprecatory sort of sound with her tongue, frowns heavily and exclaims that Pussy—not that she wants to say anything against her—really is a perfect fool, and enough to try the patience of a saint. What on earth she wants to behave in that senseless way for, at her time of life, Aunt Blanche doesn't pretend to understand, but there it is—Pussy Winter-Gammon always has been inclined to be thoroughly tiresome. Aunt Blanche is, if I know what she means, devoted to Pussy but, at the same time, able to recognise her faults.

Can foresee that Aunt Blanche and I are going to spend hours discussing old Mrs. W.-G. and her faults.

I enquire what the car was, and am told It was Nothing Whatever, only a man and his wife who suggested that we should like to give them photographs from which they propose to evolve exquisitely-finished miniatures, painted on ivorine, suitably framed, to be purchased by us for the sum of five guineas each.

Ask how Aunt Blanche got rid of them and she seems reluctant to reply, but at last admits that she told them that we ourselves didn't want any miniatures at the moment but that they might go on down the road, turn to the left, and call on Lady Boxe.

The butler, adds Aunt Blanche hurriedly, will certainly know how to get rid of them.

Cannot pretend to receive the announcement of this unscrupulous proceeding with anything but delighted amusement.

It also leads to my asking for news of Lady B.'s present activities and hearing that she still talks of a Red Cross Hospital—officers only—but that it has not so far materialised. Lady B.'s Bentley, however, displays a Priority label on wind-screen, and she has organised First Aid classes for the village.

At this I exclaim indignantly that we all attended First Aid classes all last winter, under conditions of the utmost discomfort, sitting on tiny chairs in front of minute desks in the Infant School, as being only available premises. What in the name of common sense do we want *more* First Aid for?

Aunt Blanche shakes her head and says Yes, she knows all that, but there it is. People are interested in seeing the inside of a large house, and they get coffee and biscuits, and there you are.

I tell Aunt Blanche that, if it wasn't for Stalin and his general behaviour, I should almost certainly become a Communist to-morrow. Not a Bolshevik, surely? says Aunt Blanche. Yes, a Bolshevik—at least to the extent of beheading quite a number of the idle rich.

On thinking this over, perceive that the number really boils down to one—and realise that my political proclivities are of a biassed and personal character, and not worth a moment's consideration. *(Note:* Say no more about them.)

Tea is succeeded by Happy Families with infant evacuees Marigold and Margery, again recalling nursery days now long past of Robin and Vicky.

Both are eventually despatched to bed, and I see that the moment has come for visiting Cook in the kitchen. Remind myself how splendidly she behaved at outbreak of war, and that Aunt Blanche has said she thinks things *are* all right, but am nevertheless apprehensive.

Have hardly set foot in the kitchen before realising—do not know how or why—that apprehensions are about to be justified. Start off nevertheless with *faux air* of confident cheerfulness, and tell Cook that I'm glad to be home again, glad to see that Winnie's back at work, glad to see how well the children look, very glad indeed to see that she herself doesn't look too tired. Cannot think of anything else to be glad about, and come to a stop.

Cook, in very sinister tones, hopes that I've enjoyed my holiday.

Well, it hasn't been exactly a *holiday.*

(Should like to tell her that T have been engaged, day and night, on activities of national importance but this totally unsupported by facts, and do not care to mention Canteen which would not impress Cook, who knows the extent of my domestic capabilities, in the very least.)

Instead, ask weakly if everything has been All Right?

Cook says Yes'm, in tones which mean No'm, and at once adds that she's been on the go from morning till night, and of course the nursery makes a great deal of extra work and that girl Winnie has no head at all. She's not a *bad* girl, in her way, but she hasn't a head. She never will have, in Cook's opinion.

I express concern at this deficiency, and also regret that Winnie, with or without head, should have had to be away.

As to that, replies Cook austerely, it may or may not have been necessary. All*she* knows is that she had to be up and on her hands and knees at half-past five every morning, to see to that there blessed kitchen range.

(If this was really so, can only say that Cook has created a precedent, as no servant in this house has ever, in any circumstances, dreamed of coming downstairs before a quarter to seven at the very earliest—Cook herself included.)

The range, continues Cook, has been more trying than she cares to say. She does, however, say—and again describes herself at half-past five every morning, on her hands and knees.

(Cannot see that this extraordinary position could have been in any way necessary, or even desirable.)

There is, in Cook's opinion, Something Wrong with the Range. Make almost automatic reply to this well-worn domestic plaint, to the effect that it must be the flues, but Cook repudiates the flues altogether and thinks it's something more like the whole range *gone,* if I know what she means.

I do know what she means, only too well, and assure her that a new cooking-stove is quite out of the question at present and that I regret it as much as she does. Cook obviously doesn't believe me and we part in gloom and constraint.

Am once again overcome by the wide divergence between fiction and fact, and think of faithful servant Hannah in the March family and how definite resemblance between her behaviour and Cook's was quite discernible at outbreak of war, but is now no longer noticeable in any way. All would be much easier if Cook's conduct rather more consistent, and would remain preferably on Hannah-level, or else definitely below it—but *not* veering from one to the other.

Make these observations in condensed form to Robert and he asks Who is Hannah? and looks appalled when I say that Hannah is character from the classics. Very shortly afterwards he goes into the study and I have recourse to Aunt Blanche.

She is equally unresponsive about Hannah, but says Oh yes, she knows *Little Women* well, only she can't remember anybody called Hannah, and am I sure I don't mean Aunt March? And anyway, books are no guide to real life.

Abandon all literary by-paths and come into the open with straightforward enquiry as to the best way of dealing with Cook.

Give her a week's holiday, advises Aunt Blanche instantly. A week will make all the difference. She and I and Winnie can manage the cooking between us, and perhaps Doreen Fitzgerald would lend a hand.

Later on I decide to adopt this scheme, with modifications—eliminating all assistance from Aunt Blanche, Winnie and Doreen Fitzgerald and sending for Mrs. Vallence—once kitchen-maid to Lady Frobisher—from the village.

October 15th.—We plough the fields and scatter, at Harvest Home service, and church is smothered in flowers, pumpkins, potatoes, apples and marrows. The infant Margery pulls my skirt—which is all she can reach—and mutters long, hissing communication of which I hear not one word and whisper back in dismay: Does she want to be taken out?

She shakes her head.

I nod mine in return, to imply that I quite understand whatever it was she meant to convey, and hope she will be satisfied—but she isn't, and hisses again.

This time it is borne in on me that she is saying it was she who placed the largest marrow— which is much bigger than she is herself—in position near the organ-pipes, and I nod very vigorously indeed, and gaze admiringly at the marrow.

Margery remains with her eyes glued to it throughout the service.

Note that no single member of the congregation is carrying gas-mask, and ask Robert afterwards if he thinks the omission matters, and he says No.

Our Vicar is encouraging from the pulpit—sensation pervades entire church when one R.A.F. uniform and one military one walk in and we recognise, respectively, eldest son of the butcher and favourite nephew of Mrs. Vallence—and strange couple in hiker's attire appear in pew belonging to aged Farmer (who has been bed-ridden for years and never comes to church)—and are viewed with most un-Christian disfavour by everybody. (Presumable exception must here be made, however, in favour of Our Vicar.)

Exchange customary greetings outside with neighbours, take automatic glance—as usual—at corner beneath yew-tree where I wish to be deposited in due course and register hope that Nazi bombs may not render this impracticable—and glean the following items of information:

Johnnie Lamb from Water Lane Cottages, has *gone.*

(Sounds very final indeed, but really means training-camp near Salisbury.)

Most of the other boys haven't yet Gone, but are anxious to Go, and expect to do so at any minute.

Bill Chuff, who was in the last war, got himself taken at once and is said by his wife to be guarding the Power Station at Devonport. (Can only say, but do not of course do so, that Bill Chuff will have to alter his ways quite a lot if he is to be a success at the Power Station at Devonport. Should be interested to hear what Our Vicar, who has spent hours in spiritual wrestling with Bill Chuff in the past fifteen years, thinks of this appointment.)

An aeroplane was seen over the mill, flying very low, three days ago, and had a foreign look about it—but it didn't *do* anything, so may have been Belgian. Cannot attempt to analyse the component parts of this statement and simply reply, Very Likely.

Lady B. has sent up to say that she will employ any girl who has passed her First Aid Examination, in future Red Cross Hospital, and has met with hardly any response as a rumour has gone round that she intends to make everybody else scrub the floors and do the cooking while she manages all the nursing.

Am quite prepared to believe this, and manage to convey as much without saying it in so many words.

Gratified at finding myself viewed as a great authority on war situation, and having many enquiries addressed to me.

What is going to happen about Finland, and do I think that Russia is playing a Double Game? (To this I reply, Triple, at the very least.)

Can I perhaps say where the British Army is, exactly?

If I can't, it doesn't matter, but it would be a Comfort to know whether it has really moved up to the Front yet, or not. The Ministry of Information doesn't *tell* one much, does it?

No, it doesn't.

Then what, in my opinion, is it *for?*

To this, can only return an evasive reply.

The village of Mandeville Fitzwarren, into which Mrs. Greenslade's Ivy married last year, hasn't had a single gas-mask issued to it yet, and is much disturbed, because this looks as though it was quite Out of the World, which isn't the case at all.

Promise to lay the case of Mandeville Fitzwarren before Robert in his official A.R.P. capacity without delay.

(M. F. is minute cluster of six cottages, a farm, inn and post-office, in very remote valley concealed in a labyrinth of tiny lanes and utterly invisible from anywhere at all, including the sky.)

Final enquiry is whether Master Robin is nineteen yet, and when I reply that he isn't, everybody expresses satisfaction and hopes It'll be Over before he's finished his schooling.

Am rather overcome and walk to the car, where all emotion is abruptly dispersed by astonishing sight of cat Thompson sitting inside it, looking out of the window.

Evacuees Marigold and Margery, who are gazing at him with admiration, explain that he followed them all the way from home and they didn't know what else to do with him, so shut him into the car. Accordingly drive back with Thompson sitting on my knee and giving me sharp, severe scratch when Robert sounds horn at the corner.

Peaceful afternoon ensues, write quantity of letters, and Aunt Blanche says it is a great relief not to have to read the newspapers, and immerses herself in *Journals of Miss Weeton* instead and says they are so restful.

Tell her that I have read them all through three times already and find them entrancing, but not a bit restful. Doesn't Aunt Barton's behaviour drive her to a frenzy, and what about Brother Tom's?

Aunt Blanche only replies, in thoroughly abstracted tones, that poor little Miss Pedder has just caught fire and is in a fearful blaze, and will I please not interrupt her till she sees what happens next.

Can only leave Aunt Blanche to enjoy her own idea of restful literature.

Finish letters—can do nothing about Cook owing to nationwide convention that employers do not Speak on a Sunday in any circumstance whatever—decide that this will be a good moment to examine my wardrobe—am much discouraged by the result—ask Robert if he would like a walk and he says No, not now, this is his one opportunity of going through his accounts.

As Robert is leaning back in study armchair in front of the fire, with *Blackwood's Magazine* on his knees, I think it tactful to withdraw.

Reflect on the number of times I have told myself that even *one* hour of leisure would enable me to mend arrears of shoulder-straps and stockings, wash gloves, and write long letter to Robert's mother in South of France, and then instantly retire to drawing-room fire and armchair opposite to Aunt Blanche's, and am only roused by ringing of gong for tea.

Evening is spent in playing Spillikins with evacuees, both of whom are highly skilled performers, and leave Aunt Blanche and myself standing at the post.

Eleven o'clock has struck and I am half-way to bed before I remember Mandeville Fitzwarren and go down again and lay before Robert eloquent exposition of the plight of its inhabitants.

Robert not at all sympathetic—he has had several letters from Mandeville Fitzwarren, and has personally addressed a Meeting of its fourteen parishioners, and assured them that they have not been forgotten. In the meantime, he declares, nobody is, in the least likely to come and bomb them from the air, and they need not think it. It's all conceit.

This closes the discussion.

October 16th.—Very exhausting debate between myself and Cook.

I tell her—pleasant tone, bright expression, firmness mingled with benevolence—that she has thoroughly earned a rest and that I should like her to take at least a week's holiday whilst I am at home. Wednesday, I should suggest, would be a good day for her to go.

Cook immediately assumes an air of profound offence and says Oh no'm, that isn't at all necessary. *She* doesn't want any holiday.

Yes, I say, she does. It will do her good.

Cook shakes her head and gives superior smile, quite devoid of mirth.

Yes, Cook, really.

No'm. It's very kind of me, but she couldn't think of such a thing.

But we could manage, I urge—at which Cook looks highly incredulous and rather resentful—and I should *like* her to have a holiday, and I feel sure she *needs* a holiday.

Cook returns, unreasonably, that she is too tired for a holiday to do her any good. She wouldn't enjoy it.

In another moment we are back at the stove *motif* again, and I am once more forced to hear of Cook's suspicion that something is wrong with it, that she thinks the whole range is going, if it hasn't actually gone, and of her extraordinary and unnatural activities, on her hands and knees, at half-past five in the morning.

I tell Cook—not without defiance—that A Man will come and look at the range whilst she is away. She says a *man* won't be able to do nothing. The Sweep, last time he saw it, said he couldn't understand how it was still holding together. In his opinion it wouldn't take more than a touch to send the whole thing to pieces, it was in such a way.

Sweep has evidently been very eloquent indeed, as Cook continues to quote him at immense length.

(*Note:* Make enquiries as to whether any other Sweep lives within a ten-mile radius, and if so, employ him for the future.)

Find myself edging nearer and nearer to the door, while at the same time continuing to look intelligently and responsively at Cook, but no break occurs in her discourse to enable me to disappear altogether.

After what seems like hours, Cook pauses for a moment and I again reiterate my intention of sending her for a holiday, to which she again replies that this is not necessary, nor even possible. Should like to ask whether Cook has ever heard of Mr. Bultitude who said that Everything would go to rack and ruin without him and was informed in return, not unreasonably, that he couldn't be as important as all that.

Instead, tell her that I shall expect her to be ready on Wednesday, and that Mrs. Vallence from the village is coming in to lend a hand.

Have just time to see, quite unwillingly, Cook assume an expression of horrified incredulity, before going out of the kitchen as quickly as I can.

Meet Aunt Blanche in the hall, and she asks if I am feeling ill as I am such a queer colour. Admit to feeling Upset, if not actually ill, after discussion in the kitchen and Aunt Blanche at once replies that she knows exactly what I mean, and it always does make a wreck of one, but I shall find that everything will go simply perfectly for at least a fortnight now. This is always the result of Speaking.

Feel that Aunt Blanche is right, and rally.

Serena very kindly takes the trouble to write and say that I am missed in the underworld, that they have had another lecture on the treatment of shock, and everybody says the air-raids are to begin on Sunday next. *P.S.:* She was taken out to dinner last night by J.L. and things are getting rather difficult, as she still *can't* make up her mind. When I come back she would like my advice. (This leads to long train of thought as to the advisability or otherwise of *(a)*asking and *(b)* giving, advice. Reach the conclusion that both are undesirable. Am convinced that nothing I can say will in reality alter the course of Serena's existence, and that she probably knows this as well as I do, but wants to talk to somebody. Can quite understand this, and am more than ready to oblige her.)

Also receive official-looking envelope—no stamp—and decide that the Ministry of Information has at last awakened to a sense of its own folly in failing to utilise my services for the nation, and has written to say so. Have already mentally explained situation to Robert, left Aunt Blanche to deal with Cook, packed up and gone to London by 11.40—if still running—before I have so much as slit open the envelope. It turns out to be strongly-worded appeal on behalf of no-doubt excellent charity, in no way connected with the war.

Robert departs for his A.R.P. office in small official two-seater, and tells me not to forget, if I want to take the car out, that I have barely three gallons of petrol and am not entitled to have my next supply until the twenty-third of the month.

I remind him in return about Mandeville Fitzwarren, and he assures me that he has not forgotten it at all and it's as safe as the Bank of England.

Go up and make the beds.

Doreen Fitzgerald, who is helping me, asserts that it is unlucky to turn the mattress on a Monday, and we accordingly leave it unturned. Learn subsequently from Aunt Blanche that D.F. holds similar views concerning Sundays, Fridays and the thirteenth of every month.

Learn from wireless News at one o'clock that Finnish-Soviet negotiations have been suspended, and am not in any way cheered by Aunt Blanche, who says that it is only a question of time, now, before every country in Europe is dragged into war.

Lunch follows, and we make every effort not to talk of world situation in front of the children, but are only moderately successful, and Marigold—eating apple-tart—suddenly enquires in most intelligent tones whether I think the Germans will actually *land* in England, or only drop bombs on it from aeroplanes?

Instantly decide to take both Marigold and Margery out in car, petrol or no petrol, and have tea at small newly-opened establishment in neighbouring market town, by way of distracting their thoughts.

Both are upstairs, having official rest—(can hear Margery singing "South of the Border" very loudly and Marigold kicking the foot of the bed untiringly)—when Winnie opens drawing-room door and announces Lady B. with what seems like deliberate unexpectedness.

Lady B., whom I have not seen for months, has on admirable black two-piece garment, huge mink collar, perfectly brand-new pair of white gloves, exquisite shoes and stockings and tiny little black-white-red-blue-orange hat, intrinsically hideous but producing effect of extreme smartness and elegance.

Am instantly aware that my hair is out of curl, that I have not powdered my nose for hours, that my shoes—blue suède—bear no relation whatever to my dress—grey tweed—and that Aunt Blanche, who has said earlier in the day that she can't possibly go about for another minute in her old mauve wool cardigan, has continued to do so. Lady B. is doubtless as well aware as I am myself of these deficiencies, but both of us naturally ignore them, and assume appearance of delight in our reunion.

Aunt Blanche is introduced; Lady B. looks over the top of her head and says Don't let me disturb you, in very patronising tones indeed, and sits down without waiting to be asked.

What a world, she says, we're living in! All in it together. (Can see that this seems to her very odd.) We shall all alike suffer, all alike have to play our part—rich *and* poor.

Aunt Blanche, with great spirit, at once retorts that it won't be rich and poor at all, but poor and poor, with the new income-tax, and Lady B.—evidently a good deal startled—admits that Aunt

Blanche is *too* right. She herself is seriously considering closing the London house, selling the villa in the South of France, making over the place in Scotland to the younger generation, and living quite, quite quietly on a crust in one half of the house at home.

Enquire whether she has taken any steps as yet towards accomplishing all this, and she says No, she is expecting a number of wounded officers at any moment, and has had to get the house ready for them. Besides, it would in any case be unpatriotic to dismiss members of the staff and cause unemployment, so Lady B. is keeping them all on except the second footman, who has been called up, and to whom she has said: Henry, you must *go*. The country has called for you, and I should be the very last person in the world not to wish you to go and fight. Leave your address and I will arrange to send you some cigarettes.

Henry, says Lady B., had tears in his eyes as he thanked her.

She then asks very solicitously what I have been doing to cause myself to look like a scarecrow, and she has heard that I am taking in evacuees, and where *have* I managed to squeeze them in, it's too clever of me for words.

Wonder whether to reply that I have set apart two *suites* for the evacuees and still have the whole of the West Wing empty, but decide on the truth as being simpler and more convincing, and merely inform Lady B. that as my own children are away, it is all very easy.

Lady B. at once supposes that My Girl, who must be quite grown-up by now, is working somewhere.

No, she's still at school, and will be for another two and a half years at least.

Lady B. says Really! in tones of astonishment. And what about My Boy? In France?

Not at all. In the Sixth at Rugby.

Ah, Rugby! says Lady B.

Am perfectly certain that in another second she is going to tell me about her nephews at Eton, and accordingly head her off by enquiring what she thinks about the probable duration of the war.

Lady B. shakes her head and is of opinion that we are not being told *everything,* by any means.

At the same time, she was at the War Office the other day (should like to know why, and how) and was told in strict confidence—

At this point Lady B. looks round the room, as though expecting to see a number of the Gestapo hiding behind the curtains, and begs me to shut the window, if I don't mind One never can be absolutely certain, and she has to be so particularly careful, because of being related to Lord Gort. (First I've ever heard of it.)

Shut the window—nothing to be seen outside except one blackbird on the lawn—and Aunt Blanche opens the door and then shuts it again.

Have often wondered what exact procedure would be if, on opening a door, Cook or Winnie should be discovered immediately outside it. Prefer not to pursue the thought.

Well, says Lady B., she knows that what she is going to say will *never* go beyond these four walls. At this she fixes her eyes on Aunt Blanche, who turns pale and murmurs Certainly not, and is evidently filled with apprehension.

Does Aunt Blanche, enquires Lady B., happen to know Violetta, Duchess of Tittington?

No.

Then do I know Violetta, Duchess of Tittington?

Am likewise obliged to disclaim Violetta, Duchess of Tittington—but dishonestly do so in rather considering tones, as though doubtful whether thinking of Violetta or of some other Duchess of my acquaintance.

Violetta, it seems, is a dear friend of Lady B's. She is naturally in close touch with the Cabinet, the House of Lords, the Speaker of the House of Commons, the War Office and Admiralty House. And from one or all of these sources, Violetta has deduced that a *lull* is expected shortly. It will last until the spring, and is all in favour of the Allies.

Will this lull, asks Aunt Blanche agitatedly, extend to the air? She is not, she adds hastily, in the least afraid of bombs or gas or anything of that kind—not at all—but it is very unsettling not to *know*. And, of course, we've all been expecting air-raids ever since the very beginning, and can't quite understand why they haven't happened.

Oh, they'll happen! declares Lady B. very authoritatively.

They'll *happen* all right—(surely rather curious form of qualification?)—and they'll be quite unpleasant. Aunt Blanche must be prepared for that. But at the same time she must remember that our defences are very good, and there's the balloon barrage to reckon with. The Duke, Violetta's husband, has pronounced that not more than one in fifteen of the enemy bombers will get through.

And will the raids all be over London? further enquires Aunt Blanche.

Try to convey to her in a single look that Lady B. is by no means infallible, and that I should be much obliged if Aunt Blanche wouldn't encourage her to believe that she is, and also that if we are to take evacuees out in the car, it is time this call came to an end—but message evidently beyond the compass of a single look, or of Aunt Blanche's powers of reception, and she continues to gaze earnestly at Lady B. through large pair of spectacles, reminding me of anxious, but intelligent, white owl.

Lady B. is grave, but not despairing, about London.

It will be the main objective, but a direct hit on any one particular building from the air is practically impossible. Aunt Blanche may take that as a fact.

Am instantly filled with a desire to repudiate it altogether, as a fact, and inform Lady B. that the river is unfortunately visible from the air at almost any height.

Completely defeated by Lady B., who adopts an attitude of deep concern and begs to be told instantly from what source I have heard this, as it is *exactly* the kind of inaccurate and mischievous rumour that the Government are most anxious to track down and expose.

As I have this moment evolved it, I find myself at a loss, and answer that I can't remember where I heard it.

I *must* remember, says Lady B. A great many utterly false statements of the kind are being circulated all over the country by Nazi propaganda agents, and the Authorities are determined to put an end to it. They are simply designed to impair the morale of the nation.

Can only assure her that I am practically certain it didn't emanate from a Nazi propaganda agent—but Lady B. is still far from satisfied, and begs me to be very much more careful, and, above all, to communicate with her direct, the moment I meet with any kind of subversive rumour.

Should not dream of doing anything of the kind.

Aunt Blanche—do not care at all for the tone that she is taking—begs Lady B. for inside information in regard to the naval situation, and is told that this is Well in Hand. Lady B. was dining with the First Lord of the Admiralty only a few nights ago and he told her—but this must on no account go further—that the British Navy was doing wonders.

It always does, says Aunt Blanche firmly—at which she goes up in my estimation and I look at her approvingly, but she ignores me and continues to fix her eyes immovably on Lady B.

Tell myself, by no means for the first time, that Time and the Hour run through the Roughest Day.

Lady B. asks what I have been doing in London and doesn't wait for an answer, but adds that she is very glad to see me back again, as really there is plenty to do in one's own home nowadays, and no need to go out hunting for war jobs when there are plenty of *young* people ready and willing to undertake them.

Should like to inform Lady B. that I have been urgently invited to work for the Ministry of Information, but Aunt Blanche intervenes and states—intentions very kind but wish she had let it alone—that I am making myself *most* useful taking night duty at a W.V.S. Canteen.

The one in Berkeley Square?

No, not the one in Berkeley Square. In the Adelphi.

Lady B. loses all interest on learning of this inferior locality, and takes her leave almost at once.

She looks round the study and tells me that I am quite right to have shut up the drawing-room—she herself is thinking of only using three or four of the downstairs rooms—and asks why I don't put down *parquet* flooring, as continual sweeping always does wear any carpet into holes, and professes to admire three very inferior chrysanthemums in pots, standing in the corner.

Do I know La Garonne? A lovely pink one, and always looks so well massed in the corners of a room or at the foot of the staircase.

(Should be very sorry to try to mass even two chrysanthemums in pots at the foot of my own staircase, as they would prevent anybody from either going up or down.)

Express civil interest in La Garonne and ring the bell for Winnie, who doesn't answer it. Have to escort Lady B. to hall door and waiting Bentley myself, and there bid her goodbye. Her last word is to the effect that if things get *too* difficult, I am to ring her up as, in times like these, we must all do what we can for one another.

She then steps into Bentley, is respectfully shrouded in large fur rug by chauffeur, and driven away.

Return to study fire and inform Aunt Blanche that, much as I dislike everything I have ever heard or read about Stalin and his régime, there are times when I should feel quite prepared to join Communist party. Aunt Blanche only answers, with great common sense, that she does not think I had better say anything of that kind in front of Robert, and what about telling Marigold and Margery to get ready for their drive?

Follow her advice and very successful expedition ensues, with much running downhill with car in neutral gear, in the hope that this saves petrol, and tea at rather affected little hostelry recently opened under the name of Betty's Buttery.

Return before black-out and listen to the Six O'clock News. German aircraft have made daylight raid over Firth of Forth and have been driven off, and aerial battle has been watched from the streets by the inhabitants of Edinburgh.

Aunt Blanche waxes very indignant over this, saying that her sister-in-law *deliberately* went up North in search of safety and now she has had all this excitement and seen the whole thing. She is unable to get over this for the rest of the evening, and says angrily at intervals that it's all so exactly *like* Eleanor.

Evening passes uneventfully. Robert returns, says that he's already heard the News, seems unwilling to enter into any discussion of it, and immerses himself in *Times* crossword puzzle.

Aunt Blanche not deterred by this from telling him all about air-raid over Firth of Forth with special emphasis on the fact of her sister-in-law Eleanor having been there and, as she rather strangely expresses it, had all the fun for nothing.

Robert makes indeterminate sound, but utters no definite comment.

Later on, however, he suggests that Vicky's school, on the East Coast, may have heard something of raid and that, if so, she will be delighted.

October 18th.—Long letter from Vicky informs us that school *did* receive air-raid warning, interrupting a lacrosse match, and that everybody had to go into the shelter. The weather has been foul, and a most divine concert has taken place, with a divine man playing the violin marvellously. Vicky is trying a new way of doing her hair, curled under, and some of her friends say it's like Elizabeth Bergner and others say it's simply frightful. Tons of love and Vicky is frightfully sorry for sending such a deadly letter but it's been a frightfully dull term and nothing ever seems to happen.

Robert, at this, enquires caustically what the young want nowadays? Nothing ever satisfies them.

October 19th.—Cook, steeped in gloom, is driven by myself to distant crossroads where she is met by an uncle, driving a large car full of milkcans. Her suit-case is wedged amongst the milk-cans, and she tells me in sepulchral tones that if she's wanted back in a hurry I can always ring up the next farm—name of Blore—and they'll always run across with a message and she can be got as far as the cross-roads if not all the way, as uncle has plenty of petrol.

Take my leave of her, reflecting how much more fortunately situated uncle is than I am myself.

Mrs. Vallence is in the kitchen on my return and instantly informs me that she isn't going to say a word. Not a single word. But it'll take her all her time, and a bit over, just to get things cleaned up.

I give a fresh turn to the conversation by suggesting that I am anxious to learn as much as I can in the way of cooking, and should be glad of anything that Mrs. Vallence can teach me, and we come to an amicable agreement regarding my presence in the kitchen at stated hours of the day.

Indulge in long and quite unprofitable fantasy of myself preparing and cooking very superior meals for (equally superior) succession of Paying Guests, at the end of the war. Just as I have achieved a really remarkable dinner of which the principal features are lobster *à l'Américaine* and grapes in spun sugar, Winnie comes in to say that the grocer has called for orders please'm and Mrs. Vallence says to say that we're all right except for a packet of cornflour and half-a-dozen of eggs for the cakes if that'll be all right.

I give my sanction to the packet of cornflour and half-dozen of eggs and remind myself that there is indeed a wide difference between fact and fancy.

This borne in on me even more sharply at a later hour when Mrs. Vallence informs me that gardener has sent in two lovely rabbits and they'll come in handy for to-morrow's lunch and give me an opportunity of seeing how they ought to be got ready, which is a thing many ladies never have any idea of whatever.

Do not care to reply that I should be more than content to remain with the majority in this respect.

October 21st.—Aunt Blanche tells me very seriously to have nothing to do with rabbits. Breakfast scones if I like, mayonnaise sauce and an occasional sweet if I really feel I must, but *not* rabbits. They can, and should, be left to professional cooks.

Could say a great deal in reply, to the effect that professional cooks are anything but numerous and that those there are will very shortly be beyond my means—but remember in time that argument with the elderly, more especially when a relative, is of little avail and go to the kitchen without further discussion.

Quite soon afterwards am wishing from the bottom of my heart that I had taken Aunt Blanche's advice.

This gives place, after gory and unpleasant interlude, to rather more self-respecting frame of mind, and Mrs. V. tells me approvingly that I have now done The Worst Job in all Cooking.

Am thankful to hear it.

Rabbit-stew a success, but make my own lunch off scrambled eggs.

October 24th.—Obliged to ring up Cook's uncle's neighbour and ask him to convey a message to the effect that petrol will be insufficient to enable me to go and meet her either at station or bus stop. Can the uncle convey her to the door, or must conveyance be hired?

Aunt Blanche says that Robert has plenty of A.R.P. petrol, she supposes, but Robert frowns severely on this, and says with austerity that he hasn't plenty at all—only just enough to enable him to perform his duties.

Aunt Blanche inclined to be hurt at Robert's tone of voice and, quite unjustly, becomes hurt with me as well, and when I protest says that she doesn't know what I mean, there's nothing the matter at all, and she's not the kind of person to take offence at nothing, and never has been. I ought to know her better than that, after all these years.

Assure her in return that of course I do, but this not a success either and I go off to discuss Irish stew and boiled apple pudding with Mrs. Vallence in kitchen, leaving Aunt Blanche looking injured over the laundry book. She is no better when I return, and tells me that practically not a single table-napkin is fit to be seen and most of them are One Large Darn.

Receive distinct impression that Aunt Blanche feels that I am solely to blame for this, and cannot altogether escape uneasy feeling that perhaps I am.

(*Query:* Why? Is not this distressing example of suggestibility amounting to weak-mindedness? *Answer:* Do not care to contemplate it.)

Can see that it will be useless to ask Aunt Blanche if she would like to accompany me to village, and accordingly go there without her but with Marigold dashing ahead on Fairy bicycle and Margery pedalling very slowly on minute tricycle.

Expedition fraught with difficulty owing to anxiety about Marigold, always just ahead of me whisking round corners from which I feel certain that farm lorry is about to appear, and necessity of keeping an eye on Margery, continually dropping behind and evidently in utmost distress every time the lane slopes either up or down. Suggestion that she might like to push tricycle for a bit only meets with head-shakes accompanied by heavy breathing.

Am relieved and astonished when village is achieved without calamity and bicycle and tricycle are left outside Post Office whilst M. and M. watch large, mottled-looking horse being shod at the forge.

Mrs. S. at the Post Office—having evidently been glued to the window before recalled to the counter—observes that they look just like Princess Elizabeth and Princess Margaret, don't they?

Can see no resemblance whatever, but reply amiably and untruthfully that perhaps they do, a little.

Long and enthralling conversation ensues, in the course of which I learn that Our Vicar's Wife has Got Help at last—which sounds spiritual, but really means that she has found A Girl from neighbouring parish who isn't, according to Mrs. S., not anyways what you'd call trained, but is thought not to mind being *told.* We agree that this is better than nothing, and Mrs. S. adds darkly that we shall be seeing a bit of a change in the Girls, unless she's very much mistaken, with the gentry shutting up their houses all over the place, like, and there's a many Girls will find out that they didn't know which way their bread was buttered, before so very long.

I point out in return that nobody's bread is likely to be buttered at all, once rationing begins, and Mrs. S. appears delighted with this witticism and laughs heartily. She adds encouragingly that Marge is now a very different thing from what it was in the last war.

Hope with all my heart that she may be right.

A three-shilling book of stamps, then says Mrs. S.—making no effort to produce it—and can I tell her what Russia is going to do?

No, not definitely at the moment.

Well, says Mrs. S., Hitler, if he'd asked *her,* wouldn't never have got himself into this mess. For it *is* a mess, and if he doesn't know it now, he soon will.

Can see that if Mrs. S. and I are to cover the whole range of European politics it will take most of the day, and again recall her to my requirements.

We discuss the Women's Institute—speakers very difficult to get, and Mrs. S. utterly scouts my suggestion that members should try and entertain one another, asserting that none of our members would care to put themselves forward, she's quite sure, and there'd only be remarks passed if they did—and rumour to the effect that a neighbouring Village Hall has been Taken Away from the W.I. by the A.R.P. The W.I. has pleaded to be allowed to hold its Monthly Meetings there and has finally been told that it may do so, on the sole condition that in the event of an air-raid alarm the members will instantly all vacate the Hall and go out into the street.

It is not known whether conditions have been agreed to or not, but Mrs. S. would like to know if I can tell her, once and for all, whether we are to expect any air-raids or not, and if so, will they be likely to come over the Village?

Can only say to this that I Hope Not, and again ask for stamps which Mrs. S. produces from a drawer, and tells me that she's sorry for Finland and is afraid they're in for trouble and that'll be three shillings.

Horse at the forge still being shod, and evacuees Marigold and Margery still rooted to the ground looking at it. Am about to join them when smart blow on the shoulder causes me to turn round, very angry, and confront Miss Pankerton.

Miss P. is in khaki—cannot imagine any colour less suited to her—and looks very martial indeed except for pince-nez, quite out-of-place but no doubt inevitable.

She has come to meet her six young toughs, she says, now due out of school. Regular East End scallywags, they are, but Miss P. has made them toe the line and has no trouble with them now. I shall see in a few minutes.

And what, asks Miss P., am I doing? A woman of my intelligence ought to be at the very heart of things at a time like this.

Fleeting, but extraordinarily powerful, feeling comes over me that I have often thought this myself, but that this does not in any way interfere with instant desire to contradict Miss P. flatly.

Compromise—as usual—by telling her that I am not really doing very much, I have two very nice evacuated children and their nurse in the house and am a good deal in London, where I work at a Canteen.

But, replies Miss P.—in voice that cannot fail to reach Mrs. S. again at Post Office window, which she has now opened—but this is pure *Nonsense.* I ought to be doing something of *real* importance. One of the very first things she thought of, when war broke out, was me. Now, she said to herself, that unfortunate woman will have her chance at last. She can stop frittering her time and her talents away, and Find Herself at last. It is *not,* whatever I may say, too late.

Can only gaze at Miss Pankerton with horror, but she quite misunderstands the look and begs me, most energetically, to pull myself together at once. Whitehall is Crying Out for executives.

I inform Miss P. that if so, cries have entirely failed to reach me, or anybody else that I've met. On the contrary, everybody is asking to be given a job and nobody is getting one.

I have, says Miss P., gone to the wrong people.

No, I reply, I haven't.

Deadlock has evidently been reached and Miss P. and I glare at one another in the middle of the street, no doubt affording interesting material for conjecture to large number of our neighbours.

Situation is relieved by general influx of children coming out of school. Miss P.'s toughs materialise and turn out to be six pallid and undersized little boys, all apparently well under nine years old.

Am rather relieved to see that they look cheerful, and not as though bullied by Miss P., who presently marshals them all into a procession and walks off with them.

Parting observation to me is a suggestion that I ought to join the W.A.A.C.S. and that Miss P. could probably arrange it for me, at which I thank her coldly and say I shouldn't think of such a thing. Miss P.—quite undaunted—calls back over her shoulder that perhaps I'm right, it isn't altogether in my line, and I'd better go to the Ministry of Information, they've got a scheme for making use of the Intellectuals.

Should like to yell back in reply that I am not an Intellectual and don't wish to be thought one— but this proceeding undignified and moreover only very powerful screech indeed could reach Miss Pankerton, now half-way up the hill, with toughs capering along beside her looking like so many white mice.

Turn to collect Marigold and Margery—both have disappeared and are subsequently retrieved from perfectly harmless-seeming lane from which they have mysteriously collected tar all over their shoes.

Make every effort to remove this with handfuls of grass—have no expectations of succeeding, nor do I—and say It's lucky it didn't get onto their coats, and proceed homewards. Find tar on both coats on arriving, also on Marigold's jumper and Margery's socks.

Apologise to Doreen Fitzgerald, tell her I'm afraid she may find it rather difficult to remove, and she answers bitterly Certainly I will, and I feel that relations between us have not been improved.

Situation with regard to Aunt Blanche is fortunately easier and at lunch we talk quite pleasantly about Serena—whom Aunt Blanche still refers to as Serena Fiddlededee—and National Registration Cards.

Do I know, enquires Aunt Blanche, that if one loses one's Identity Card, one is issued with a *bright scarlet* one?

Like the Scarlet Woman? I ask.

Yes, exactly like that, or else the Scarlet Letter—Aunt Blanche isn't sure which, or whether both are the same, but anyway it's a scarlet card, and even if lost Identity Card reappears, the scarlet one cannot be replaced, but remains for ever.

Can only reply, after a long silence, that it sounds perfectly terrible, and Aunt Blanche says Oh yes, it is.

Conversation only revives when infant Margery abruptly informs us that she made two of the beds unaided this morning.

Commend her highly for this and she looks gratified, but have inward misgiving that her parents, if they hear of her domestic activities, may think that I have made her into a household drudge.

Offer her and Marigold the use of gramophone and all the records for the whole afternoon.

Aunt Blanche, later, tells me that she does not think this was at all a good idea.

Second pest brings me letter from Serena. I am much missed at the Canteen, and Mrs. Peacock has said that mine is a *bright* face, and she hopes soon to see it back again. (Serena, to this, adds three exclamation marks—whether denoting admiration or astonishment, am by no means certain. Do not, in any case, care for Mrs. P.'s choice of descriptive adjective.)

The underworld, Serena informs me, is a seething mass of intrigue and Darling and the Commandant have made up their quarrel and are never out of one another's pockets for a single instant, but on the other hand Mrs. Nettleship (First Aid) and Miss Carloe-Hill (Ambulance

Driver) have had the most tremendous row and are not speaking to one another, and everybody is taking sides and threatening to resign as a protest.

Serena herself hasn't slept for nights and nights because there's been a ping-pong craze and people play it all night long, just outside the Rest-room, and J. L. has taken her out to dinner and to a dreadful film, all full of Nazi atrocities, and this has ensured still further wakefulness.

Serena ends by begging me in most affectionate terms to come back, as she misses me dreadfully, and it's all awful. Have I read a book called *The Confidential Agent?* It's fearfully good, but dreadfully upsetting, and perhaps I'd better not.

(If *The Confidential Agent* had not been on my library list already—which it is—should instantly have put it there.)

Am asked by Aunt Blanche, rather apologetically, if that is a letter from Serena Fiddlededee? She didn't, needless to say, *look* at the envelope, nor has she, of course, the slightest wish to know anything about my private correspondence—but she couldn't help *seeing* that I had a letter from Serena.

Have too often said exactly-the same thing myself to entertain slightest doubts as to Aunt Blanche's veracity, and offer to show her Serena's letter at once as there is nothing private about it.

No, no, she didn't mean that, Aunt Blanche assures me—at the same time putting on her spectacles with one hand and taking the letter with the other. When she comes to J. L. Aunt Blanche emits rather inarticulate exclamation and at once enquires if I don't think it would be a very good thing?

Well, no, on the whole I don't. It doesn't seem to me that Serena cares two straws about him.

Aunt Blanche moans, and says it seems a very great pity, then cheers up again and declares that when J. L. gets into uniform and is sent out to fight, it will probably make all the difference, and Serena will find out that she *does* care about him, and one can only hope it won't then be too late.

Perceive that Aunt Blanche and I hold fundamentally divergent views on what does or does not constitute a successful love-affair, and abandon the topic.

Evening closes in with return of Cook, who looks restored and tells me that she enjoyed her holiday and spent most of it in helping her uncle's second wife to make marrow jam.

Enquire of Robert whether he thinks he can spare me if I return to London on Thursday.

He replies that he supposes he can, and asks what I think I shall do, up there?

Write articles about London in War-Time, I suggest, and help at W.V.S. Canteen. Should like to add, Get Important job at Ministry of Information—but recollections of Miss Pankerton forbid.

Robert seems unenthusiastic, but agrees that he is not likely to be much at home and that Aunt Blanche can manage the house all right. He incomprehensibly adds: Who is this Birdie that she is always talking about?

Can only enquire in return: What birdie?

Some name of that kind, Robert says. And a double-barrelled surname. Not unlike Gammon-and-Spinach, and yet *not* quite that. Instantly recognise old Granny Bo-peep and suggest that he means Pussy Winter-Gammon, to which Robert replies Yes, that's what he said, isn't it?

Explain old Mrs. W.-G. to him in full and Robert, after a long silence, remarks that it sounds to him as though what she needed was the lethal chamber.

October 26th.—Robert leaves me at the station on his way to A.R.P. office, with parting information that he thinks—he is not certain at all but he *thinks*—that the gas-masks for the inhabitants of Mandeville Fitzwarren are now available for distribution.

Train comes in late, and is very crowded. Take up commanding position at extreme edge of platform and decide to remain there firmly and on no account join travellers hurrying madly from one end of train to the other. Am obliged to revise entire scheme of action when I find myself opposite coach consisting entirely of first-class carriages. Third-class, by the time I reach it, completely filled by other people and their luggage. Get in as best I can and am looked at with resentment amounting to hatred by four strangers comfortably installed in corner seats.

Retire at once behind illustrated daily paper and absorb stream of Inside Information from column which I now regard as being practically omniscient. Can only suppose that its special correspondent spends his days and nights concealed in, alternately, Hitler's waste-paper basket and Stalin's ink-pot.

Realise too late that I have placed bag in rack, sandwiched amongst much other luggage, and that it contains library book on which I am relying to pass the journey.

Shall be more unpopular than ever if I now get up and try to disentangle bag.

Postpone things as long as possible by reading illustrated paper all over again, and also printed notice—inconsiderately pasted over looking-glass—telling me how I am to conduct myself in the event of an air-raid.

Suggestion that we should all lie down on floor of the carriage rouses in me no enthusiasm, and I look at all my fellow travellers in turn and, if possible, care about the idea even less than before.

Following on this I urge myself to Make an Effort, Mrs. Dombey, and actually do so, to the extent of getting up and attacking suit-case. Prolonged struggle results in, no doubt, fearful though unseen havoc amongst folded articles in case and extraction of long novel about Victorian England.

Sit down again feeling, and doubtless looking, as though all my clothes had been twisted round back to front, and find that somebody has opened a window with the result that several pieces of my hair blow intermittently into my eyes and over my nose.

This happens to nobody else in the carriage.

Am not in the least interested by long novel about Victorian England and think the author would have known more about it after a course of Charlotte M. Yonge. Sleep supervenes and am awakened by complete stranger patting me sharply on the knee and asking Do I want Reading?

No, it is very kind of her, but I do not.

Complete stranger gets out and I take the occasion of replacing book in suit-case and observing in pocket-mirror that sleep, theoretically so beneficial, has appalling effect on the appearance of anybody over thirty years of age.

Do my best to repair its ravages.

Reappearance of fellow traveller, carrying cup of tea, reminds me that luncheon car is no longer available and I effect purchase of ham roll through the window.

Step back again into cup of tea, which has been idiotically placed on the floor.

Apologies naturally ensue. I blame myself entirely and say that I am dreadfully sorry—which indeed I am—unknown lady declares heroically that it doesn't really matter, she'd had all she wanted (this can't possibly be true)—and I tell her that I will get her another cup of tea.

No, really.

Yes, yes, I insist.

Train starts just as she makes up her mind to accept, and I spend remainder of the journey thinking remorsefully how thirsty she must be.

We exchange no further words, but part at Paddington, where I murmur wholly inarticulate farewell and she smiles at me reproachfully in return.

Flat has been adorned with flowers, presumably by Serena, and this makes up for revolting little pile of correspondence, consisting entirely of very small bills, uninteresting advertisements, and circular letters asking me to subscribe to numerous deserving causes.

Spend entire evening in doing, so far as I can see, nothing in particular and eventually ring up Rose to see if she has got a job yet.

Am not in the least surprised to hear that she hasn't.

She says that if it wasn't for the black-out she would invite me to come and have supper with her, and I reply that if it wasn't for the black-out I should simply love to come. This seems to be as near as we get to any immediate rendezvous, and I ring off rather dejectedly.

Go out to Chinese basement restaurant across the street and restore my morale with exotic dish composed of rice, onions and unidentifiable odds and ends.

October 29th.—Have occasion to remark, as often before in life, that quite a short absence from any given activity almost invariably results in finding it all quite different on return. Canteen no exception to this rule.

Mrs. Peacock has completely disappeared—nothing to do with leg, which I fear at first may have taken a turn for the worse—and is said to have transferred her services to another branch— professional cashier has taken over cash-register and sits entrenched with it behind a high wooden barricade as though expecting robbery with violence at any minute—and two enormous new urns are installed at one end of counter, rather disquietingly labelled Danger. Enquire humorously of lady in charge whether they are filled with explosives and she looks perfectly blank and replies in a strong Scottish accent that One wad be the hot milk like, and the other the coffee,

Serena is not on duty when I arrive, and telephone-call to her flat has only produced very long and painstaking statement in indifferent English from one of her Refugees, of which I understand scarcely a word, except that Serena is The Angel of Hampstead, is it not? Agree that it is, and exchange cordial farewells, with the Refugee, who says something that I think refers to the goodness of my heart. (Undeserved.)

Canteen gramophone has altered its repertoire—this a distinct relief—and now we have "Love Never Grows Old" and "Run, rabbit, run". Final chorus to the latter—Run, Hitler, run—I think a great mistake and quote to myself Dr. Dunstan from *The Human Boy*: "It ill becomes us, sir, to jest at a fallen potentate—and still less before he has fallen".

Helpers behind the counter now number two very young and rather pretty sisters, who say that they wish to be called Patricia and Juanita. Tendency on the part of all the male *clientèle,* to be served by them and nobody else, and they hold immense conversations, in undertones, with youths in leather jackets and brightly-coloured ties.

This leaves Red Cross workers, female ambulance drivers, elderly special constables and stretcher-bearers, to me.

One of these—grey-headed man in spectacles—comes up and scrutinises the menu at great length and then enquires What there is to-night? Suppose his sight has been dimmed by time, and offer to read him the list. He looks offended and says No, no, he has read it. Retrieve this error by asserting that I only made the suggestion because the menu seemed to be so illegibly written.

Instant judgment follows, as Scottish lady leans down from elevation beside the urns and says severely that *she* wrote out those cards and took particular pains to see that they were *not* illegible.

Decide to abandon the whole question without attempting any explanations whatever.

Brisk interlude follows, time goes by before I know it, and at eleven o'clock Serena suddenly materialises and asks for coffee—as usual—and says that she is so glad I've come back. Can't I take my supper now and come and join her?

Yes, I can. Am entitled to free meal and, after much consideration, select sardines, bread-and-butter, tea and two buns. Inform Serena, on principle, that I do not approve of feminine habit of eating unsuitable food at unseasonable hours whilst working and that I had a proper dinner before I came out.

Serena begs me not to be so grown-up and asks what the meal was. Am obliged to turn the conversation rather quickly, as have just remembered that it was taken in a hurry at a milk-bar and consisted of soup and tinned-salmon sandwich.

What, I ask, has Serena been doing?

Serena groans and says Oh, on Sunday morning there was an air-raid alarm and she was all ready for anything, and started up her car, and then the whole thing petered out. She popped up into the street and saw the Embankment Gardens balloon getting ready to defend England, but as soon as the All Clear was given, it came down again, which Serena thinks denotes slackness on the part of somebody.

She has also been seeing J. L. and would like to talk to me some time, and could she bring him to the flat for a drink one evening?

Yes, certainly—to-morrow if she likes.

Serena sighs, and looks distressed, and says That would be great fun. J. L. wants cheering-up—in fact, he's utterly wretched. He has finished his novel, and it is all about a woman whose husband is a political prisoner in a Concentration Camp and she can't get news of him and she goes on the streets and one of her children is an epileptic and the other one joins a gang and goes to the bad, and in the end this woman gets shot and the children are just left starving in a cellar. J. L. thinks that it is the very best piece of work he's ever done, and his publishers say Yes, it is, but they don't feel sure that anybody is going to want to read it just now, let alone buy it.

They have gone so far as to suggest that what people want is something more like P. G. Wodehouse, and J. L. is greatly upset, not because he does not admire P. G. Wodehouse, but because he feels himself to be so entirely incapable of emulating him.

Serena, rather fortunately, does not enquire whether my views on topical fiction coincide with those of J. L. or those of his publishers, and we proceed to the discussion of wider issues.

What does Serena think of the news?

Well, she doesn't think we're being *told* much. It's all very well to say our aircraft is always flying about all over Germany and the Siegfried Line, but do we really *always* return intact without a single casualty? Nor does she understand about Russia.

Russia, according to the news, can't do anything at all. They have masses of oil and masses of grain and probably masses of ammunition as well, but no Russian transport is apparently capable of moving a yard without instantly breaking down, all Russian ports are stiff with ice throughout three-quarters of the year, and no Russian engineers, telephone-operators, engine-drivers, miners or business executives are able at any time to take any constructive action whatsoever.

Serena cannot help feeling that if Russia had signed a pact with us, instead of with Germany, this would all be described quite differently.

She also complains that Nazi aircraft has so far directed all its activities towards the North. Scotland, in the opinion of Serena, always has been rather inclined to think itself the hub of the universe, and this will absolutely clinch it. The Scots will now suppose that the enemy share their own opinion, that Edinburgh is more important than London.

As for the Ministry of Information, Serena is *sorry* for it. Definitely and absolutely sorry. Look at the things that people have said about it in Parliament, and outside Parliament for that matter, and all the things in the papers! They may have made their mistakes, Serena admits, but the really fatal blunder was to call them Ministry of Information in a war where the one thing that nobody is allowed to have is any information.

Have they, she adds, done anything about me yet?

Nothing whatever.

I am proposing to go there, however, on the strength of a letter of introduction from Uncle A. who stood godfather, some thirty years ago, to the Head of one of the Departments.

He is not, as yet, aware of the privilege in store for him.

Serena hopes that I shall be able to find him, but has heard that the Ministry—situated in London University buildings—is much larger than the British Museum and far less well sign-posted. Moreover, if one asks for anybody, one is always told, firstly, that he has never been there at all; secondly, that he isn't in the department over which he is supposed to be reigning; thirdly, that the department itself is not to be found because it has moved to quite another part of the building and nobody knows where it is, and fourthly, that he left the Ministry altogether ten days ago.

Can quite see that I shall be well advised to allow plenty of time for the projected visit.

Serena's fellow worker, Muriel, appears and asks whether we have heard that the Ritz Hotel has outdistanced all other hotels, which merely advertise Air-Raid Shelter, by featuring elegant announcement outside its portals: *Abri du Ritz.*

Shall look at it next time I am waiting for a bus in Piccadilly, which is the only occasion on which I am in the least likely to find myself even outside entrance to the Ritz, let alone inside it.

Finish supper and return to my own side of the counter.

Inhabitants of the underworld invariably take on second lease of life towards midnight, and come in search of eggs and bacon—bacon now Off; shepherd's pie all finished; and toad-in-the-hole just crossed off the list. Do the best we can with scrambled eggs, sausages and ham—which also runs low before the night is out.

Scottish tea-dispenser presently gets down from high seat which enables her to deal with urns, and commands, rather than requests me, to take her place.

Do so quite successfully for an hour, when hot-milk tap, for no reason known to me, turns on but declines to turn off and floods the floor, also my own shoes and stockings.

Succeed in turning it off again after some damage and much expenditure of milk.

Professional cashier says Dear, dear, it does seem a waste of milk, doesn't it? and Patricia suggests without enthusiasm that it really ought to be mopped up.

557

Am in full agreement with both, but feel unreasonably annoyed with them and go home, after mopping-up, inclined to tell myself that I have evidently outlived such powers of usefulness as were ever mine This conviction continues during process of undressing and increases by leaps and bounds when bath-water turns out cold.

(*Note:* Minor calamities of life apt to assume importance in inverse ratio to advancing hours of the night. *Query:* Will the black-out in any way affect this state of affairs?)

Kettle in no hurry to boil water for bottle, and go to bed eventually feeling chilly and dejected.

October 31st.—Visit the Ministry of Information, and find vast area of Hall where I am eyed with disfavour by Minor Official in uniform who wishes to know what I want.

I want Mr. Molesworth, and have had enough presence of mind to arrange appointment with him by telephone.

Minor Official repeats *Molesworth?* in tones of utter incredulity, and fantastic wonder crosses my mind as to what he would say if I suddenly replied, Oh no, I didn't mean Molesworth at all. I just said that for fun. What I *really* meant all the time was Fisher.

Realise instantly that this would serve no good purpose, and reiterate Molesworth. At this Minor Official shakes his head very slowly, looks at a book, and shakes his head again.

But I have, I urge, an appointment.

This evidently necessitates calling in a second opinion, and somebody standing by a lift is asked if he knows anything about Molesworth.

Molesworth? No. Wait a minute. *Molesworth?* Yes.

Where can he be found?

Second Opinion hasn't the least idea. He *was* up on the sixth floor, last week, but that's all been changed now. Miss Hogg may know.

Miss Hogg—evidently less elusive than some of her collaborators—is telephoned to. Reply, received after a long wait, is inaudible to me but Minor Official reports that I had better try the third floor; he can't say for certain, but Mr. M. *was* there at one time, and Miss Hogg hasn't heard of his having moved.

Start off hopefully for lift, am directed to go right across the hall and into quite another part of the building, and take the lift there. Final inspiration of Minor Official is to ask whether I know the number of Mr. M.'s Room—which of course I don't.

Walk along lengthy passages for what seems like some time, and meet with kindness, but no definite information, from several blonde young lovelies who mostly—rather mistakenly—favour scarlet jumpers.

Compare myself mentally with Saracen lady, said to have travelled to England in search of her lover with no vocabulary except two words, *London* and *Gilbert.* (London in those days probably much smaller than Ministry of Information in these.)

Astonishment temporarily surpasses relief when I am at last definitely instructed by young red-headed thing—fortunately *not* in scarlet—to Room 568. Safeguards herself by adding that Mr. M. *was* there an hour ago, but of course he may have been moved since then.

He hasn't.

His name is on a card over the door.

Shall be surprised if I do not hear myself calling him Gilbert.

Am horrified to find myself quarter of an hour after appointed time, and feel it is only what I deserve when Mr. M. keeps me waiting for twenty minutes.

Eventually meet him face to face across his own writing-table and he is kindness and civility personified, tells me that he hasn't seen Uncle A. since early childhood but still has silver mug bestowed at his christening, and has always heard that the old gentleman is wonderful.

Yes indeed. Wonderful.

Cannot avoid the conclusion that contemplating the wonderfulness of Uncle A. will get us no further in regard to winning the war, and suggest, I hope diffidently, that I should much like to do something in this direction.

Mr. M. tells me that *this* war is quite unlike that of 1914. (Not where Ministries are concerned it isn't—but do not tell him this.)

In 1914, he says instructively, a tremendous Machinery had to be set in motion, and this was done with the help of unlimited expenditure and numerous experiments. *This* time it is all different. The Machinery is expected to be, at the very beginning, all that it was at the very end last time. And expenditure is not unlimited at all. Far from it.

I say No, I suppose not—as though having given the question a good deal of thought.

Mr. M. then successively talks about the French, the Turks, the Russians, and recent reconnaissance flights over Germany.

I suggest that I mustn't take up any more of his time. I really only wanted to see if I could do some kind of work.

He appreciates my offer, replies Mr. M., and tells me about Hore-Belisha and the House of Commons.

I offer him in return my opinion of Winston Churchill—favourable—and of Sir Samuel Hoare—not so good.

We find ourselves—I cannot say how—talking of the self-government of India.

A man with a beard and an appearance of exhaustion comes in, apologises, is begged not to go away, and we are introduced—his name inaudible to me, as doubtless mine to him.

He tells me almost at once that *this* war is quite unlike that of 1914. Tremendous Machinery set in motion...expenditure...experiment...*This* time, Machinery expected to begin at stage previously reached in 1918...

Try to look as though I haven't heard all this before, express concern at state of affairs depicted, and explain that I am anxious to place my services—etc.

Ah, says the beard, it is being found very difficult—very, very difficult indeed—to make use of all those whom the Ministry would *like* to make use of. Later on, no doubt, the right field of activity will present itself—much, much later on.

Does he, then, think that the war is going to be a lengthy affair?

It would, says Mr. M. gravely, be merely wishful thinking to take too optimistic a view. The probabilities are that nothing much will happen for some months—perhaps even longer. But let us not look further ahead than the winter.

The long, cold, dark, dreary, interminable winter lies ahead of us—petrol will be less, travelling more restricted, the black-out more complete and the shortage of certain foodstuffs more noticeable. People will be *tired* of the war. Their morale will tend to sink lower and lower.

Quote to myself:

| *The* | *North* | *wind* | *doth* | *blow* |
| *And* | *we* | *shall* | *have* | *snow,* |

And what will Robin do then, poor thing?
but feel that it would be quite out of place to say this aloud.

I ask instead whether there is anything I can do, to alleviate the melancholy state of things that evidently lies ahead.

All of us can do something, replies Mr. M. There are, for instance, a number of quite false rumours going about. These can be tracked to their source—(how?)—discredited and contradicted.

The man with the beard breaks in, to tell me that in the last war there were innumerable alarms concerning spies in our midst.

(As it is quite evident, notwithstanding the beard, that he was still in his cradle at the time of the last war, whilst I had left mine some twenty years earlier, this information would really come better from me to him.)

The Government wishes to sift these rumours, one and all—(they will have their hands full if they undertake anything of the kind)—and it is possible to assist them in this respect. Could I, for instance, tell him what is being said in the extreme North of England where I live?

Actually, it is in the extreme *West* that I live.

Of course, of course. Mr. M. knew it perfectly well—nothing he knows better—extraordinary slip of the tongue only. What exactly, then, is being said in the extreme West?

Complete blank comes over me. Can remember nothing but that we have all told ourselves that even if butter *is* rationed we can get plenty of clotted cream, and that we really needn't bother to take our gas-masks wherever we go.

Can only summon to my help very feeble statement to the effect that our morale seems to be in very good repair and that our evacuees seem to be settling down—at which he looks disappointed, as well he may.

Can see that my chances of getting a job—never very good—are now practically moribund.

Raise the subject again, although not confidently, and Mr. M. tells me—evidently in order to get rid of me—that I had better see Captain Skein-Tring. He is—or *was,* two days ago—in Room 4978, on the fourth floor, in the other building. Do I think I can find my way there?

Know perfectly well that I can't, and say so frankly, and Mr. M. sighs but handsomely offers to escort me himself, and does so.

On the way, we talk about the Papal Encyclical, Uncle A. again, and the B.B.C. Mr. M. is pained about most of the programmes and thinks they are too*bright* and why so much cinema organ? I defend the B.B.C. and tell him I like most of the popular music, but not the talks to housewives.

Mr. M. sighs heavily and no point of agreement is found, until we find a joint admiration for L. A. G. Strong's short stories.

Just as this desirable stage is reached, we meet with a pallid young man carrying hundreds of files, to whom Mr. M. says compassionately, Hallo, Basil, moving again?

Basil says Yes, wearily, and toils on, and Mr. M. explains that Poor Basil has been moved three times within the last ten days.

Just as he disappears from view Mr. M. recalls him, to ask if he knows whether Captain Skein-Tring is still in Propaganda, 4978. Basil looks utterly bewildered and replies that he has never heard of anybody called Skein-Tring. Anyhow, the Propaganda people have all been transferred now, and the department has been taken over by the people from National Economy.

Mr. M. groans, but pushes valiantly on, and this bulldog spirit is rewarded by totally unexpected appearance—evidently the very last thing he has expected—of Captain S.-T.'s name on the door of Room 4978. He accordingly takes me in and introduces me, assures me that I shall be absolutely all right with Jerry, hopes—I think untruthfully—that we may meet again, and goes.

Jerry—looks about my own age, wears rather defiant aspect and spectacles with preternaturally convex lenses—favours direct method of approach and says instantly that he understands that I write.

Yes, I do.

Then the one thing that those whom he designates as "All You People" have got to realise is that we must all go on *exactly as usual.* If we are novelists, we must go on writing novels; if poets, write poetry just as before; if our line happens to be light journalism, then let it still be light journalism. But keep away from war topics. Not a word about war.

And what about lecturing, I enquire?

Lecture by all means, replies Jerry benevolently.

Read up something about the past—not history, better keep away from history—but what about such things as Conchology, Philately, the position of Woman in the Ice Age, and so on. Anything, in fact, which may suggest itself to us that has no bearing whatever on the present international situation.

I feel obliged to point out to Jerry that the present international situation is what most people, at the moment, wish to know about.

Jerry taps on his writing-desk very imperatively indeed and tells me that All You People are the same. All anxious to do something about the war. Well, we mustn't. We must keep right out of it. Forget about it. Go on writing just as though it didn't exist.

Cannot, at this, do less than point out to Jerry that most of us are writing with a view to earning our living and those of our dependents, and this is difficult enough already without deliberately avoiding the only topic which is likely, at the present juncture, to lead to selling our works.

It won't do, says Jerry, shaking his head, it won't do at all. Authors, poets, artists—(can see that the word he really has in mind is riff-raff)—and All You People must really come into line and be content to carry on exactly as usual. Otherwise, simply doing more harm than good.

Am by this time more than convinced that Jerry has no work of national significance to offer me, and that I had better take my leave. Final flicker of spirit leads me to ask whether he realises that it is very difficult indeed to find a market for any writings just now, and Jerry replies offhandedly that, of course, the paper shortage *is* very severe and will get much worse—much, much worse.

At the same time it is quite on the cards that people will take to reading when they find there's absolutely nothing else to do. Old ladies, for instance, or women who are too idle and incompetent to do any war work. They may quite likely take to reading light novels in the long evenings, so as to help kill time. So long as I remember to carry on just exactly as I should if we weren't at war at all, Jerry feels sure that I shall be quite all right.

Can only get up and say Goodbye without informing him that I differ from this conclusion root and branch, and Jerry shakes hands with me with the utmost heartiness, driving ring inherited from great-aunt Julia into my finger with extremely painful violence.

Goodbye, he says, he is only too glad to have been of any help to me, and if I want advice on any other point I am not to hesitate for one moment to come and see him again.

Walk out completely dazed, with result that I pay no heed to my direction and find myself almost at once on ground floor, opposite entrance, without the slightest idea of how I got there.

(Note: Promptings of the unconscious, when it comes to questions of direction, incomparably superior to those of the conscious mind. Have serious thoughts of working this up into interesting article for any publication specialising in Psychology Made Easy.)

Rain pours down; I have no umbrella and am reluctantly compelled to seek shelter in a tea-shop where I ask for coffee and get some with skin on it. Tell myself in a fury that this could never happen in America, or any other country except England.

In spite of this, am deeply dejected at the thought that the chances of my serving my country are apparently non-existent.

November 2nd.—Tremendous outbreak of knitting overtakes the underworld—cannot say why or how. Society Deb. works exclusively in Air-Force blue, and Muriel—who alone can understand her muttered utterances—reports that Jennifer has never done any knitting before and isn't really any good at it, but her maid undoes it all when she has a night at home and knits it up again before Jennifer wakes.

Muriel is herself at work on a Balaclava helmet, elderly Messenger very busy with navy-blue which it is thought will turn into socks sooner or later, and everybody compares stitches, needles and patterns. Mrs. Peacock (reappeared, leg now well again but she still has tendency to retire to upturned box as often as possible) knits very rapidly and continuously but says nothing, until she privately reveals to me that she is merely engaged on shawl for prospective grandchild but does not like to talk about it as it seems unpatriotic.

Am sympathetic about grandchild, but inwardly rather overcome as Mrs. P. is obviously contemporary of my own and have not hitherto viewed myself as potential grandmother, but quite see that better accustom myself to this idea as soon as possible.

(Have not yet succeeded in doing so, all the same.)

Serena, also knitting—stout khaki muffler, which she says is all she can manage, and even so, broader at one end than at the other—comes and leans against Canteen counter at slack moments and tells me that she doesn't know what to do about J. L. If his novel had been accepted by publishers, she declares, it would all be quite easy because she wouldn't mind hurting his feelings, but with publishers proving discouraging and poor J. L. in deepest depression, it is, says Serena, practically impossible to say No.

Is she, then, engaged to him?

Oh *no,* says Serena, looking horrified.

But is she going to marry him?

Serena doesn't know. Probably *not.*

Remind myself that standards have changed and that I must be modern-minded, and enquire boldly whether Serena is considering having An Affair with J. L.

Serena looks unspeakably shocked and assures me that she isn't like that *at all.* She is very old-fashioned, and so are all her friends, and nowadays it's a wedding ring or nothing.

Am completely taken aback and realise that I have, once again, entirely failed to keep abreast of the times.

Apologise to Serena, who replies that of course it's all right and she knows that in post-last-war and pre-this-war days, people had some rather odd ideas, but they all went out with the nineteen-twenties.

Can see that, if not literally a grandmother, am definitely so in spiritual sense.

Serena then presents further, and totally unrelated, problem for my consideration. It appears that Commandant of Stretcher-party has recently resigned position in order to take up service abroad and those to whom he has given series of excellent and practical lectures have made him presentation of fountain-pen and pencil in red morocco case.

Farewell speeches have been exchanged, and red morocco case appreciatively acknowledged.

Now, however, Stretcher-party Commandant has suddenly reappeared, having been medically rejected for service abroad, and Serena feels that morocco case is probably a source of embarrassment to him.

Can make no constructive comments about this whatever, and simply tell her that next move—if any—rests entirely with Commandant of Stretcher-party.

Interruption occurs in the person of old Mrs. Winter-Gammon who comes up and asks me what I can suggest for an old lady's supper.

Steak-pudding, sausages-and-mashed or spaghetti? Mrs. W.-G. shakes her curls and screws up her eyes and says gaily, No, no, no—it's very naughty of her to say so, but none of it sounds attractive. She will have a teeny drop of soup and some brown bread-and-butter.

Collect this slender meal and place it before her, and she says that will last her until breakfast-time next morning. Her dear Edgar used to get quite worried sometimes, and tell her that she didn't eat more than a sparrow, but to this she had only one answer: Dearest one, you forget how tiny I am. I don't need more than a sparrow would. All I ask is that what I *do* have shall be daintily cooked and served. A vase of flowers on the table, a fringed doily or two, and I'm every bit as happy with a crust of bread and an apple as I could be with a banquet. In fact, happier.

Cannot think of any reply whatever to all this and merely look blankly at Granny Bo-peep, who smiles roguishly and informs me that she believes I'm only half-awake. (Feel that she might just as well have said half-witted.)

Can quite understand why Serena, who has also listened to Mrs. W.-G., now abruptly declares that she wants cold beef, pickles and toasted cheese for *her* supper.

Mrs. W.-G.—still immovable at counter—asks how I found Devonshire, and what poor Blanche is doing, and whether my husband doesn't miss me dreadfully. She herself, so long as beloved Edgar was with her, was always beside him. He often said that she knew more about his work than he did himself. That, of course, was nonsense—her talents, if she had any at all, were just the little humble domestic ones. She made their home as cosy as she could—a touch here, another one there—a few little artistic contrivances—and above all, a smile. Whatever happened, she was determined that Edgar should always see a smiling face. With that end in view, Mrs. W.-G. used to have a small mirror hanging up over her desk so that every time she raised her eyes she could see herself and make sure that the smile was *there*. If it wasn't, she just said to herself, Now, Pussy, what are you about? and went on looking, until the smile *was* there.

Am suddenly inspired to enquire of old Mrs. W.-G. what first occasioned her to share a flat with Aunt Blanche. Can never remember receiving any explanation on the point from Aunt Blanche herself, and am totally at a loss to understand why anyone should ever have wished to pursue joint existence with Granny Bo-Peep and her smile.

Ah, says Mrs. W.-G., a dear mutual friend—now Passed On—came to her, some years ago, and suggested the whole idea. Poor Blanche, in the opinion of the mutual friend, needed Taking Out of Herself. *Why* the friend thought that Mrs. W.-G. was the right person to accomplish this, she cannot pretend to guess—but so it was. And somehow or other—and it's no use my asking Mrs. W.-G. to explain, because she just doesn't know how it's done herself—but *somehow* or other, dear old Blanche did seem to grow brighter and to realise something of the sheer *fun* of thinking about other people, instead of about one's own little troubles. She must just have caught it, like the measles, cries Granny Bo-Peep merrily. People have always told her that she has such an infectious chuckle, and she simply can't help seeing the funny side of things. So she can only suppose that Blanche—bless her—somehow took the infection.

Then came the war, and Mrs. W.-G. instantly decided that she was nothing but a worthless old woman and must go and offer her services, and the Commandant to whom she offered them—not this one, but quite another one, now doing something entirely different in another part of England altogether—simply replied: Pussy, I only wish I was as plucky, as efficient, as cheery, and as magnificent as you are. Will you drive an ambulance?

I will, replied Mrs. W.-G., drive anything, anywhere and at any time whatsoever.

Feel that any comment I could make on this would only be in the nature of an anti-climax and am immensely relieved when Scottish voice in my ear asks would I not take over the tea-pot for a wee while?

I would, and I do.

Mysterious behaviour of tea, which is alternately black as ink and strong as death, or revoltingly pallid and with tea-leaves floating about unsymmetrically on the surface of the cup. Can see that more intelligent management of hot-water supply would remedy both states of affairs, but all experiments produce unsatisfactory results and am again compelled to recognise my own inefficiency, so unlike general competence of Granny Bo-Peep.

Dispense tea briskly for nearly an hour, discuss menu with cashier—rather good-looking Jewess—who agrees with me that it lacks variety.

Why not, I ask, have kippers, always popular? Or fish-cakes? Jewess agrees to kippers but says a fish-cake isn't a thing to eat out.

Spend some minutes in wondering what she means, until it is borne in on me that she, probably rightly, feels it desirable to have some personal knowledge as to the ingredients of fish-cakes before embarking on them.

Cannot think why imagination passes from fish-cakes to Belgrave Square ballroom somewhere about the year 1912, and myself in the company of young Guardsman—lost sight of for many years, and in any case, no longer either young or in the Guards. Realise very slowly that gramophone record of "Merry Widow" waltz is now roaring through the Canteen, and accounts for all.

Am struck by paradoxical thought that youth is by no means the happiest time of life, but that most of the rest of life is tinged by regret for its passing, and wonder what old age will feel like, in this respect. (Shall no doubt discover very shortly.)

Girl with lovely red hair—name unknown—comes up for customary meal of hot milk and one digestive biscuit and tells me that I look very profound.

I say Yes, *I am* very profound, and was thinking about Time.

Am rather astonished and greatly impressed when she calmly returns that she often thinks about Time herself, and has read through the whole of J. W. Dunne's book.

Did she understand it?

Well, the first two and a half pages she understood perfectly. The whole thing seemed to her so simple that she was unable to suppose that even a baby wouldn't understand it.

Then, all of a sudden, she found she wasn't understanding it any more. Complete impossibility of knowing at what page, paragraph, or even sentence, this inability first overtook her. It just was *like* that. At one minute she was understanding it all perfectly—at the next, all was incomprehensible.

Can only inform her that my own experiences with J. W. D. have been identical, except that I think I only understood the first two, *not* two and a half pages.

Decide—as often before—that one of these days I shall tackle Time and J. W. D. all over again.

In the meanwhile, fresh vogue for tea has overtaken denizens of the underworld, and I deal with it accordingly.

Nine O'clock News comes and goes unheard by me, and probably by most other people owing to surrounding din. Serena drifts up later and informs us that Lord Nuffield has been appointed Director General of Maintenance in Air Ministry. Have idle thoughts of asking him whether he would like capable, willing and efficient secretary, and am just receiving urgent pre-paid telegram from him begging me to accept the post at once when I discover that the milk has given out and supply ought to have been renewed from the kitchen ten minutes ago.

Go back to flat soon afterwards, write letter to Robert and tell him that nothing has as yet materialised from Ministry of Information—which I prefer to saying that repeated applications have proved quite unavailing—but that I am still serving at Canteen, and that everybody seems fairly hopeful.

Reflect, whilst going to bed, that I am thoroughly tired of all my clothes and cannot afford new ones.

November 4th.—Am rung up, rather to my astonishment, by Literary Agent, wishing to know What I Am Doing.

Well, I am in touch with the Ministry of Information, and also doing voluntary work at a Canteen every night. At the same time, if he wishes to suggest that I should use my pen for the benefit of the country...

No, he hasn't anything of that kind to suggest. On the contrary. The best thing I can do is just carry on exactly as usual, and no doubt I am at work on a new novel at this very moment.

I urge that it's very difficult to give one's mind to a new novel under present conditions, and Literary Agent agrees that doubtless this is so, but it is my plain duty to make the attempt. He has said the same thing to *all* his authors.

Reflection occurs to me later, though not, unfortunately, at moment of conversation, that if all of them take his advice the literary market will be completely swamped with novels in quite a short time, and authors' chances of making a living, already very precarious, will cease to exist at all.

Spend some time at writing-desk, under hazy impression that I am thinking out a new novel. Discover at the end of two hours that I have achieved rather spirited little drawing on cover of telephone-book of man in a fez—slightly less good representation of rustic cottage, Tudor style, front elevation, on envelope of Aunt Blanche's last letter—also written two cheques meeting long-overdue accounts—smoked (apparently) several cigarettes, of which I have no recollection whatever, and carefully cut out newspaper advertisement of Fleecy-lined Coats with Becoming Hoods—which I have no intention whatever of purchasing.

New novel remains wholly elusive.

Telephone rings again: on raising receiver become aware of tremendous pandemonium of sound which tells me instantly that this must be the Adelphi underworld.

It is.

May Serena bring round J. L. for a drink at about 6.30 this evening? He would like to talk about his new novel. Reply mirthlessly that perhaps he would also like to hear about mine—but this cynical reference wasted, as Serena only replies What? and adds Blast this place, it's like a rookery, only worse.

Tell her that it doesn't matter, and I can tell her later, and she suggests that if I scream straight into the mouthpiece very loud, she'll probably be able to hear—but I again assure her that this would be wasted energy.

We end conversation—if conversation it can be called—with reciprocal assurances that we shall look forward to meeting at my flat, 6.30. P.M., with J. L. in Serena's train.

Go to wine merchant at corner of the street and tell him that I require an Amontillado—which is the only name I know in the sherry world—and that I hope he has some in stock.

Well—Amontillado is now very, very difficult to obtain—(knew perfectly well he was going to say this)—but he *thinks* he can supply me. That is, if I do not require it in any very great quantity.

Had actually only considered purchasing a single bottle but have not now got the face to say so, and reply that two bottles will satisfy me *for the moment.* (Distinct implication here that I shall be back in about an hour's time for several more.)

Ah, then in *that* case—says wine merchant with quite unabated suavity of manner, for which I think highly of him.

We hold very brief discussion as to the degree of dryness required in sherry, in which I hope I produce an effect of knowing the subject *à fond*—and I pay for my two bottles and am told that they will be delivered within a few moments at my door—which in fact they are.

Proceed to purchase of small cheese biscuits, and hope that Serena will think I have done her credit.

Canteen duty follows—very uneventful interlude. Serena not on duty, and Granny Bo-Peep visible only in the distance where she is—apparently—relating the story of her life to group of Decontamination men who seem, unaccountably, to find it interesting.

Mrs. Peacock tells me that Old Moore predicted the war and said that it would come to an end in 1940. Did he, whilst about it, say in what month? Mrs. Peacock thinks he said November, but is not sure, and I suggest that he was mixing it up with the Great War, at which she seems hurt.

Shift comes to an end at six o'clock, and I leave underworld thinking how best to arrange seating for three people in flat sitting-room, which is scarcely large enough to contain two with any comfort, when folding-table is extended to receive Amontillado and glasses.

Find flat door wide open, curtains drawn—(no brown paper)—lamp and fire burning merrily, and Serena entertaining J. L., Muriel and unknown young man of film-star appearance. Table has been set up, Amontillado opened, and agreeable haze of cigarette-smoke fills the air.

Serena says It's lovely that I've come at last, and she hopes it's all right, she thought I should wish them to have a drink, and couldn't she pour one out for me?

Agree that she could, and congratulate myself inwardly on having dealt with lipstick, powder and pocket comb on the stairs.

Ensuing party proves gay and amusing, and I enter into conversation with film-star young man, who tells me that he has been reading J. L.'s novel in typescript and thinks it very good. Have I seen it?

No, I've only heard about it from Serena. What is it called? It is called *Poached Eggs to the Marble Arch.*

At this I bend my head appreciatively as if to say that's exactly the sort of name I should have *expected* from a really good modern novelist, and then have the wind taken out of my sails when young film-star observes thoughtfully that he thinks it's an utterly vague and off-putting title. But, he adds candidly, he isn't absolutely sure he's got it right. It might be *Poached Eggs ON the Marble Arch,* or even *Poached Eggs AT the Marble Arch.*

Conversation then becomes general, and Serena and Muriel talk about their war service and I say nothing about mine—not from modesty but because Canteen work very unimpressive—and film-star young man reveals that he has just joined the Air Force Reserve, and isn't a film-star at all but a psychiatrist, and that ever since war started he has had no patients at all as most of the ones he had before were children who have been sent away from London.

Enquire at once whether he knows Rose, in very similar position to his own, and he says he knows her well by name. This does not, really, get us very much further.

J. L. looks, as before, intelligent and melancholy and latter expression seems to be merely deepened by Amontillado. Curiously opposite effect is produced on myself and I become unusually articulate and—I think—very witty about the Ministry of Information.

This conviction deepened every moment by shrieks of laughter from Serena and Muriel, definite appearance of amusement on face which still seems to me that of a film-star, and even faint smiles from J. L.

Am regretful when S. and M. declare that duty now calls them to the Adelphi. (It must, to be accurate, have been calling for rather more than an hour, as both were due there at seven o'clock.)

They take some time to make their farewells, and are escorted away by pseudo film-star, who thanks me very earnestly for having invited him. Do not, naturally, point out to him that I didn't do so and have, in fact, no idea who did.

J. L. to my astonishment enquires whether I am, by any possible chance, free for dinner this evening?

Am entirely free, and say so instantly, and J. L. invites me to come and dine somewhere with him at once and go on afterwards to Arts Club of which he is a member, and listen to Ridgeway's Late Joys. They sing Victorian songs and the audience joins in the choruses.

Am entranced at this prospect and only hope that effect of Amontillado will not have worn off by the time we get there, as should certainly join in choruses, Victorian or otherwise, far better if still under its influence.

J. L. and I depart forthwith into the black-out, and are compelled to cling to one another as we go, and even so do not escape minor collisions with sandbags and kindly expressed, but firm, rebuke from the police for displaying electric-torch beams too freely.

J. L. takes me to nice little restaurant and orders excellent dinner, and then talks to me about Serena.

He is, he admits, practically in despair about Serena. She has charm, she has intelligence, she has brains, she has looks—but would marriage with her be a hundred per cent success?

Can only tell him that I really have no idea, and that very few marriages *are* a hundred per cent success, but that on the other hand most people would think even seventy-five per cent quite handsome. Is he, if I may ask, engaged to Serena?

Oh dear, no.

Has he—if he doesn't mind my asking—asked Serena to be engaged to him?

Well, yes and no.

Can only look at him in despair, and reflect with no originality whatever that Things have Changed in the last twenty years.

J. L. continues to maunder, but breaks off to ask what I would like to drink, and to hold quite animated discussion about Alsatian wine with the wine-waiter—then relapses into distress and refers to Serena as being at once the Worst and the Best Thing in his life.

Can see that nothing I say will make the slightest impression on him and that I may just as well save myself exertion of thinking by merely looking interested and sympathetic.

This succeeds well until J. L. suddenly bends forward and enquires earnestly whether I don't feel that Serena is too highly-strung to be the ideal wife for a writer. I inform him in return, without hesitation, that the point seems to me quite insignificant and that what really disturbs me is the conviction that writers are too egotistical to make ideal husbands for anybody.

J. L. instantly agrees with me but is evidently quite fatalistic about it and has no intention whatever of reforming.

Can only suggest to him that perhaps we had better start for Late Joys or we shall be late.

He agrees amiably and cheers up more and more as evening progresses—just as well, as I am perfectly enraptured by beautifully-produced performance of the Joys and too much absorbed to pay any attention to him even if suicidal tendencies should develop.

Instead, however, J. L. joins in chorus to "See me Dance the Polka" and "Her Golden Hair was Hanging Down her Back" in unexpectedly powerful baritone, and we drink beer and become gayer and gayer until reluctantly compelled to leave theatre.

November 9th.—Bomb Explosion in Munich Beer-hall reported, apparently timed to coincide with speech by Hitler and to destroy him and numerous Nazi leaders seated immediately beneath spot where bomb was placed. Hitler said to have finished speech twenty minutes earlier than usual, and left Hall just—(from his point of view)—in time.

Hear all this from wireless at 8 A.M. and rush out into the Strand where posters tell me that Hess was amongst those killed, and I buy three newspapers and see that Hess is only *reported* killed. Can only say that instincts of Christianity and civilisation alike are severely tried, and am by no means prepared to state that they emerge victorious.

Have invited Lady Blowfield to lunch at Club as small return for past hospitality and also with faint hope of her eventually inducing Sir Archibald to suggest war job for me, and proceed there by bus, which fails to materialise for at least twenty minutes and is then boarded by about five hundred more people than it can possibly accommodate.

Situation very reminiscent of 1914 and succeeding years.

Hess resurrected on posters.

Reach Club just before one, am told by hall-porter that my guest has not yet arrived and go to upstairs drawing-room, which is filled with very, very old ladies in purple wool cardigans, and exceedingly young ones in slacks. No golden mean achieved between youth and age, excepting myself.

Small room off drawing-room contains wireless, to which I hasten, and find fearfully distraught-looking member—grey hair all over the place and spectacles on the floor—who glances at me and tells me imperatively to Hush!

I do Hush, to the extent of not daring even to sit down on a chair, and One O'clock News repeats the information that Hitler left Munich Beer-hall exactly fifteen minutes before bomb exploded.

At this, grey-haired member astounds me by wringing her hands—have never seen this done before in real earnest—and emits a sort of frantic wail to the effect that it's dreadful—dreadful! That he should just have missed it by quarter of an hour! Why, oh, why couldn't they have timed it better?

Moral conflict assails me once more at this, since I am undeniably in sympathy with her, but at the same time rather shattered by her unusual outspokenness. No comment fortunately necessary, or even possible, as she desperately increases volume of wireless to bellowing-point, then extinguishes it with equal lack of moderation.

Can see that she is in totally irresponsible frame of mind and feel very sorry for her.

Try to convey this by a look when News is over, and am only to successful as she at once pours out a torrent of rather disconnected phrases, and ends up by asking what my views are.

There will, I assure her, be a revolution in Germany very soon.

She receives this not-very-novel theory with starting eyes and enquires further whether It will come from the top, or from the bottom.

Both, I reply without hesitation, and leave the room before she has time to say more.

Lady Blowfield awaits me—hat with a black feather, very *good*-looking fur cape, and customary air of permanent anxiety—and we exchange greetings and references—moderate at least in tone—to Munich explosion, Hess being authoritatively declared alive and unhurt on the strength of responsible newspapers seen by Lady Blowfield.

Offer her sherry which she declines—am rather sorry, as I should have liked some myself but feel it now quite out of the question—and we proceed to dining-room.

Has she, I ask, any news about the war other than that which is officially handed out to all of us?

Lady Blowfield at once replies that Gitnik, whom I shall remember meeting, has flown to Paris and that therefore she has not seen him. He is, I shall naturally understand, her chief authority on world affairs—but failing him, Archibald has a certain amount of inside information—in a comparatively small way—and he has said that, in his opinion, the war will begin very soon now.

Am much dejected by this implication, although I—like everybody else—have frequently said myself that It hasn't yet Started.

Has Sir Archibald given any intimation of the place or time selected for the opening of hostilities?

Lady Blowfield shakes her head and says that Holland is in great danger, so is Belgium, so are Finland and Sweden. At the same time it is perfectly certain that Hitler's *real* objective is England, and he is likely to launch a tremendous air-attack against not only London, but the whole of the country. It is nonsense—wishful thinking, in fact—to suggest that winter will make any difference. Weather will have nothing to do with it. Modern aircraft can afford to ignore *all* weather conditions.

Has Lady Blowfield any information at all as to when this attack may be expected?

Lady Blowfield—not unreasonably—says that it won't be *expected* at all.

Conversation, to my relief, is here interrupted by prosaic enquiry from waitress as to our requirements and I urge grapefruit and braised chicken on Lady Blowfield and again suggest drink. Would willingly stand her entire bottle of anything at all, in the hope of cheering her up. She rejects all intoxicants, however, and sips cold water.

What, she wishes to know, am I doing with my time? Am I writing anything? Archibald, no later than the day before yesterday, wished to know whether I was writing anything in particular, and whether I realised how useful I could be in placing before the public points which it was desirable for them to know.

Feel more hopeful at this, and ask what points?

There is, replies Lady Blowfield, the question of Root Vegetables. English housewives do not make the best use of these, in cooking. An attractive pamphlet on the subject of Root Vegetables might do a lot just now.

Can only suppose that I look as unenthusiastic as I feel, since she adds, with rather disappointed expression, that if I don't care about *that,* there is a real need, at the moment, for literature that shall be informative, helpful, and at the same time amusing, about National Economy. How to avoid waste in the small household, for instance.

Tell her that if I knew how to avoid waste in the small household, I should find myself in a very different position financially from that in which I am at present, and Lady Blowfield then shifts her ground completely and suggests that I should Read It Up.

She will send me one or two little booklets, if I like. I have the honesty to admit in reply that I have, in the past, obtained numbers of little booklets, mostly at Women's Institutes, and have even read some of them, but cannot feel that the contents have ever altered the course of my days.

Ah, says Lady Blowfield darkly, perhaps not *now*, but when the war is over—though heaven alone knows when that may be—*then* I shall realise how difficult mere *existence* is going to be, and that all life will have to be reorganised into something very, very different from anything we have ever known before. Have frequently thought and said the same thing myself, but am nevertheless depressed when I hear it from Lady Blowfield. (This quite unreasonable, especially as I hold definite opinion that entire readjustment of present social system is desirable from every point of view.)

Shall we, I next suggest with an air of originality, try and forget about the war and talk about something entirely different? Lady Blowfield, though seeming astonished, agrees and at once asks me if by any chance I know of a really good kitchen-maid—she believes they are easier to find now—as hers is leaving to be married.

(If this is part of Lady Blowfield's idea of preparing for entirely reorganised scheme of life, can only say that it fails to coincide with mine.)

Am compelled to admit that I am a broken reed indeed as regards kitchen-maids, and enquire whether Lady Blowfield has seen *George and Margaret.*

No, she says, who are George and Margaret? Do I mean Daisy Herrick-Delaney and poor dear Lord George?

Explain what I do mean.

She has *not* seen *George and Margaret* and does not sound, even after I have assured her that it is very amusing, as if she either wished or intended to do so.

Fortunately recollect at this stage that the Blowfields are friends of Robert's married sister in Kenya—whom I have only met twice and scarcely know—and we discuss her and her children—whom I have never met at all—for the remainder of luncheon.

Coffee subsequently served in library is excellent and Lady Blowfield compliments me on it, and says how rare it is to find good coffee, and I agree whole-heartedly and feel that some sort of *rapprochement* may yet take place between us.

If so, however, it must be deferred to another occasion, as Lady Blowfield looks at her watch, screams faintly, and asserts that her Committee will be expecting her at this very moment and she must Fly.

She does fly—though not rapidly—and I retire to Silence Room with every intention of writing out brief, but at the same time complete, synopsis of new novel.

Two members are already seated in Silence Room, hissing quietly at one another, but lapse into frustrated silence at my entrance.

Sit down at writing-table with my back to them but can feel waves of resentment still emanating towards me.

Tell myself quite firmly that this is Great Nonsense, and that anyway they can perfectly well go and talk somewhere which *isn't* a Silence Room, and that I really must give my mind to proposed synopsis.

Do so, for what seems like three weeks.

Customary pen-and-ink drawings result and lead me to wonder, without much conviction, whether I have perhaps mistaken my vocation and should have done better as black-and-white artist. Brief dream ensues of myself in trousers, smock and large black bow, figuring in Bohemian life on the *rive gauche* at the age of twenty-two. Have just been escorted by group of enthusiastic fellow students to see several of my own works of art exhibited at the Salon, when recollections of Robert and the children—cannot say why or how—suddenly come before me, and I realise that all are quite unsuitable figures in scene that Fancy has depicted.

Revert once more to synopsis.

Cannot imagine why concentration should prove next door to impossible, until instinct tells me that psychic atmosphere is again distinctly hostile, and that the hissing members are probably wishing I would drop down dead.

Look cautiously round for them, and see that one is sleeping heavily and the other has completely disappeared.

(How? Have not heard door either open or shut. Have evidently concentrated better than I supposed. But *on what?* Answer comes there none.)

Inspiration, without a word of warning, descends upon me and I evolve short and rather flippant topical article which may reasonably be expected to bring me in a small sum of money, fortunately payable in guineas, *not* pounds.

Am highly elated—frame of mind which will undoubtedly undergo total eclipse on re-reading article in type—and return to Buckingham Street. Remember quite a long while afterwards that projected synopsis is still non-existent.

Find flat occupied, on my arrival, by Serena—face a curious shade of green—who says that she feels rather like death and has leave of absence for an hour in order to get into the fresh air. This she has evidently elected to do by putting on electric fire, shutting the window, boiling the kettle and drinking quantities of very strong tea.

Commiserate with her, and suggest that conditions under which she is serving the country are both very strenuous and extremely unhygienic and that she may shortly be expected to break down under them.

Serena says Yes, she quite agrees.

Then what about trying something else?

Yes, replies Serena, but *what?* Everybody she knows, practically, is trying to Get Into Something, and everybody is being told that, whilst everybody is urgently needed, nobody can be given any work at the moment. Quite highly qualified persons are, she asserts, begging and imploring to be allowed to scrub floors and wash dishes without pay, but nobody will have them. Am obliged to admit that this is only too true.

And there is another thing, says Serena. The moment—the very moment—that she leaves her A.R.P., there will be an air-raid over London. Then she will have had all these weeks and weeks of waiting about for nothing, and will just have to cower in a basement like everybody else while old Granny Bo-Peep is getting all the bombs.

Assure Serena that while I know what she means—which I do—it seems to me an absolute certainty that Granny Bo-Peep will succeed in getting well into the middle of whatever calamity may occur, and in getting out of it again with unimpaired spirits and increased prestige.

I therefore suggest that Serena may put her out of her calculations altogether.

Serena—surely rather exasperatingly?—declares that she wasn't really thinking what she was saying, and Granny Bo-Peep doesn't come into it at all.

Then what does?

Serena's only reply is to weep.

Am very sorry for her, tell her so, give her a kiss, suggest brandy, all to no avail. Remember Spartan theory many times met with both in literature and in life, that hysterical tendencies can be instantly checked by short, sharp word of command or, in extreme cases, severe slap. Do not feel inclined for second alternative, but apply the first—with the sole result that Serena cries much harder than before.

Spartan theory definitely discredited.

Electric bell is heard from below, and Serena says Oh, good heavens, is someone coming! and rushes into the bedroom.

Someone turns out to be The Times Book Club, usually content to leave books in hall but opportunely inspired on this occasion to come up the stairs and demand threepence.

This I bestow on him and we exchange brief phrases about the weather—wet—the war—not yet really begun—and Hitler's recent escape from assassination—better luck next time. (This last contribution from Times Book Club, but endorsed by myself.)

Times Book Club clatters away again, and I look at what he has brought—murder story by Nicholas Blake, which I am delighted to see, and historical novel by author unknown but well spoken of in reviews.

Serena emerges again—nose powdered until analogy with Monte Rosa in a snowstorm is irresistibly suggested, but naturally keep it to myself—and says she is very sorry indeed, she's quite all right now and she can't imagine what made her so idiotic.

Could it, I hint, by any possible chance be over-fatigue and lack of adequate sleep and fresh air? Serena says that has nothing to do with it, and I think it inadvisable to dispute the point.

She again consults me about J. L. (who has so recently consulted me about her) and I again find it wiser to remain silent while she explains how difficult it all is and admits to conviction that whatever they decide, both are certain to be wretched.

She then becomes much more cheerful, tells me how kind and helpful I have been, and takes affectionate farewell.

Indulge in philosophical reflections on general feminine inability to endure prolonged strain without emotional collapse.

November 11th.—Armistice Day, giving rise to a good many thoughts regarding both past and present. Future, to my mind, better left to itself, but this view evidently not universally held, as letters pour out from daily and weekly Press full of suggestions as to eventual peace terms and reorganisation of the world in general.

Telephone to Robert, who says nothing in particular but seems pleased to hear my voice.

Interesting, but rather academic, letter from Robin full of references to New Ideology but omitting any reply to really very urgent enquiry from myself regarding new winter vests.

November 12th.—Take afternoon duty instead of evening at Canteen and learn that Society Deb. has developed signs of approaching nervous breakdown and been taken away by her mother.

Girl with curls—Muriel—has disappeared, unnoticed by anybody at all, until she is required to take a car to Liverpool Street station, when hue and cry begins and Serena finally admits that Muriel has a fearful cold and went home to bed three days ago without notifying anybody at all.

Defence offered by Serena is to the effect that Muriel thought, as she wasn't doing anything, she could easily go and come back again unperceived.

Various members of personnel are likewise wilting, and Serena looks greener than ever.

Commandant can be heard raging at Darling behind closed door of office, and is said to have uttered to the effect that if there's any more of this rank insubordination she is going to hand in her resignation. In fact she would do so at once, if she didn't happen to realise, as nobody else appears to do, that England Is At War.

Have serious thoughts of asking her whether she hasn't heard anybody say that It Hasn't yet Started? If not, this establishes a record.

Afternoon very slack and principal activities consist in recommending the bread-and-butter and toast, which can honestly be done, to all enquirers—saying as little as possible about the buns—and discouraging all approaches to jam tarts.

Mrs. Peacock offers me half-seat on her box, which I accept, and we look at new copy of very modern illustrated weekly, full of excellent photographs. Also read with passionate interest Correspondence Column almost entirely devoted to discussion of recent issue which apparently featured pictures considered by two-thirds of its readers to be highly improper, and by the remainder, artistic in the extreme.

Mrs. P. and I are at one in our regret that neither of us saw this deplorable contribution, and go so far as to wonder if it is too late to get hold of a copy.

Not, says Mrs. P., that she *likes* that kind of thing—very far from it—but one can't help wondering how far the Press will go nowadays, and she hadn't realised that there was anything left which would shock anybody.

Am less pessimistic than she is about this, but acknowledge that, although not particularly interested on my own account, I feel that one might as well see what is being put before the younger generation.

Having delivered ourselves of these creditable sentiments, Mrs. P. and I look at one another, both begin to laugh, and admit candidly distressing fact that both of us are definitely curious.

Mrs. P. then recklessly advocates two cups of tea, which we forthwith obtain and prepare to drink whilst seated on upended sugar-box, but intense activity at counter instantly surges into being and requirements of hitherto non-existent clients rise rapidly to peak height.

By the time these have been dealt with, and used cups, plates and saucers collected and delivered to kitchen, cups of tea have grown cold and all desire for refreshment passed, and Mrs. P. says That's life all over, isn't it?

Return to Buckingham Street and find telephone message kindly taken down by caretaker, asking if I can lunch with Mr. Pearman to-morrow at one o'clock, and the house is No. 501 Sloane Street and can be found in the telephone book under name of Zonal.

Am utterly bewildered by entire transaction, having never, to my certain knowledge, heard either of Mr. Pearman or anyone called Zonal in my life, and Sloane Street address—Cadwallader House—conveying nothing whatever to me.

Enquire further details of caretaker.

She says apologetically that the line was very bad—she thinks the war has made a difference—and she asked for the name three times, but didn't like to go on.

Then she isn't quite certain that it *was* Pearman?

Well, no, she isn't. It *sounded* like that, the first time, but after that she didn't feel so sure, but she didn't like to go on bothering the lady.

Then was Mr. Pearman a lady? I enquire,

This perhaps not very intelligently worded but entirely comprehensible to caretaker, who replies at once that he was, and said that I should know who it was.

Adopt new line of enquiry and suggest that *Zonal* not very probable in spite of being in telephone book.

But at this caretaker takes up definite stand. Zonal, Z for zebra, and she particularly asked to have it spelt because it seemed so funny but it's in the book all right—Brigadier A. B. Zonal—and Cadwallader House is that new block of flats up at the end.

Decide that the only thing to do is ring up Cadwallader House and ask for either Pearman or Zonal.

Line proves to be engaged.

I say that The Stars in their Courses are Fighting against Me, and caretaker, whom I have forgotten, looks extremely startled and suggests that perhaps I could ring up again later—which seems reasonable and obvious solution.

Make fresh attempt, am told that I am speaking to the hall-porter and enquire if there is anyone in the house of the name of Pearman—or, I add weakly, anything *like* that.

Will I spell the name?

I do.

No, the hall-porter is very sorry, but he doesn't know of anybody of that name. I don't mean old Mrs. Wain, by any chance, do I?

Decline old Mrs. Wain, and suggest Zonal, of whom I am unable to give any other particulars than that he is a Brigadier.

Brigadier Zonal, says the porter, lives on the second floor, and his niece and her friend are staying there. The niece is Miss Armitage, and the other lady is Miss Fairmead.

Everything, I tell the porter, is explained. It *is* Miss Fairmead, of course, and would he ask her to speak to me? Porter—evidently man of imperturbable calm—replies Very good, madam, and I assure the caretaker—still hovering—that the name may have *sounded* like Mr. Pearman but was in reality Miss Fairmead. She replies that she *did* think of its being that at one time, but it didn't seem likely, somehow.

Consider this highly debatable point, but decide to let it drop and thank her instead for her trouble. (Trouble, actually, has been entirely mine.)

Explanation with Felicity Fairmead ensues. She is in London for two nights only, staying with Veronica Armitage, whom I don't know, in her turn staying with her uncle Brigadier Zonal, who has kindly offered hospitality to Felicity as well.

She and Veronica are leaving London the day after to-morrow, will I come and lunch to-morrow and meet Veronica? Also, naturally, the uncle—who will be my host.

Agree to all and say how glad I am to think of seeing Felicity, and should like to meet Veronica, of whom I have heard much. And, of course, the uncle.

November 13th.—Lunch—at Brigadier Zonal's expense—with Felicity, who is looking particularly nice in dark red with hair very well set. Veronica turns out pretty, with attractive manners, but is shrouded in blue woollen hood, attributable to violent neuralgia from which she is only just recovering.

Uncle not present after all, detained at War Office on urgent business.

571

Felicity asks respectfully after my war work—am obliged to disclaim anything of national significance—and immediately adds solicitous enquiry as to the state of my overdraft.

Can only reply that it is much what it always was—certainly no better—and my one idea is to economise in every possible way, and what about Felicity herself?

Nothing, declares Felicity, is paying any dividends at all. The last one she received was about twenty-five pounds less than it should have been and she paid it into the Bank and it was completely and immediately swallowed up by her overdraft. It just didn't exist any more. And the extraordinary thing is, she adds thoughtfully, that although this invariably happens whenever she pays anything into her Bank, the overdraft *never* gets any smaller. On the contrary.

She has asked her brother to explain this to her, and he has done so, but Felicity has failed to understand the explanation.

Perhaps, I suggest, the brother wasn't very clear?

Oh yes he was, absolutely. *He* knows a great deal about finance. It was just that Felicity hasn't got that kind of a mind.

Sympathise with her once more, admit—what she has known perfectly well ever since long-ago schooldays—that I haven't got that kind of mind either, and enquire what Veronica feels about it all.

Veronica thinks it's dreadful, and most depressing, and wouldn't it cheer us both up to go out shopping?

Personally, she has always found that shopping, even on a tiny scale, does one a great deal of good. She also feels that Trade ought to be encouraged.

Felicity and I readily agree to encourage Trade on a tiny scale. It is, I feel, imperative that I should get myself some stockings, and send Vicky a cake, and Felicity is prepared to encourage Trade to the extent of envelopes and a hair-net.

Veronica, in the absence of the uncle, presides over a most excellent lunch, concluding with coffee, chocolates and cigarettes, and gratifies me by taking it for granted that we are on Christian-name terms.

Felicity looks at me across the table and enquires with her eyebrows What I think of Veronica? to which I reply, like Lord Burleigh, with a nod.

We discuss air-raids—Germany does not mean to attack London for fear of reprisals—she *does* mean to attack London but not till the spring—she hasn't yet decided whether to attack London or not. This war, in Felicity's brother's opinion, is just as beastly as the last one but will be shorter.

Enquire of Veronica what the uncle thinks, and she answers that, being in the War Office, he practically never tells one anything at all. Whether from discretion, or because he doesn't know, Veronica isn't sure—but inclines to the latter theory.

Shortly afterwards Felicity puts on her hat and extremely well-cut coat—which has the effect of making me feel that mine isn't cut at all but just hangs on me—and we say goodbye to Veronica and her blue hood.

Agreeable hour is spent in Harrods Stores, and I get Vicky's cake but substitute black felt hat and a check scarf for stockings. Felicity, who has recently had every opportunity of inspecting woollen hoods at close quarters, becomes passionately absorbed in specimens on counter and wishes to know if I think crochet or knitted would suit Veronica best. Do not hesitate to tell her that to me they look exactly alike and that, anyway, Veronica has a very nice one already.

Felicity agrees, but continues to inspect hoods none the less, and finally embarks on discussion with amiable shop-girl as to relative merits of knitting and crochet. She eventually admits that she is thinking of making a hood herself as friend with whom she is living as P.G. in the country does a great deal of knitting and Felicity does not like to be behindhand. Anyway, she adds, she isn't of any *use* to anybody, or doing anything to win the war.

Point out to her that very few of us *are* of any use, unless we can have babies or cook, and that none of us—so far as I can see—are doing anything to win the war. I also explain how different it will all be with Vicky's generation, and how competent they all are, able to cook and do housework and make their own clothes. Felicity and I then find ourselves, cannot say how, sitting on green sofa in large paved black-and-white hall in the middle of Harrods, exchanging the most extraordinary reminiscences.

Felicity reminds me that she was never, in early youth, allowed to travel by herself, that she shared a lady's-maid with her sister, that she was never taught cooking, and never mended her own clothes.

Inform her in return that my mother's maid always used to do my hair for me, that I was considered industrious if I practised the piano for an hour in the morning, that nobody expected me to lift a finger on behalf of anybody else, except to write an occasional note of invitation, and that I had no idea how to make a bed or boil an egg until long after my twenty-first year.

We look at one another in the deepest dismay at these revelations of our past incompetence, and I say that it's no wonder the world is in the mess it's in to-day.

Felicity goes yet further, and tells me that, in a Revolution, our heads would be the first to go—and quite right too. But at this I jib and say that, although perhaps not really important assets to the community, we are, at least, able and willing to mend our ways and have in fact been learning to do so for years and years and years.

Felicity shakes her head and asserts that it's different for me, I've had two children and I write books. She herself is nothing but a cumberer of the ground and often contemplates her own utter uselessness without seeing any way of putting it right. She isn't intellectual, she isn't mechanically-minded, she isn't artistic, she isn't domesticated, she isn't particularly practical and she isn't even strong.

Can see, by Felicity's enormous eyes and distressed expression, that she would, in the event of the Revolution she predicts, betake herself to the scaffold almost as a matter of course.

Can only assure her, with the most absolute truth, that she possesses the inestimable advantages of being sympathetic, lovable and kind, and what the devil does she want more? Her friends, I add very crossly, would hate to do without her, and are nothing if not grateful for the way in which she always cheers them up.

Felicity looks at me rather timidly—cannot imagine why—and suggests that I am tired and would it be too early for a cup of tea?

It wouldn't, and we go in search of one.

Realise quite suddenly, and for no reason whatever, that I have lost my gas-mask, in neat new leather case.

Had I, I agitatedly ask Felicity, got it on when I arrived at Cadwallader House?

Felicity is nearly certain I had. But she couldn't swear. In fact, she thinks she is really thinking of someone else. Can I remember if I had it on when I left home?

I am nearly certain I hadn't. But I couldn't swear either. Indeed, now I come to think of it, I am, after all, nearly certain I last saw it lying on my bed, with my National Registration Card.

Then is my National Registration Card lost too?

If it's on the bed in my flat, it isn't, and if it's not, then it is. Agitated interval follows.

Felicity telephones to Cadwallader House—negative result—then to Buckingham Street caretaker, who goes up to look in bedroom but finds nothing, and I return to green sofa in black-and-white hall where places so recently occupied by Felicity and self are now taken up by three exquisite young creatures with lovely faces and no hats, smoking cigarettes and muttering to one another. They look at me witheringly when I enquire whether a gas-mask has been left there, and assure me that it hasn't, and as it is obviously inconceivable that they should be sitting on it unaware, can only apologise and retreat to enquire my way to Lost Property Office.

Am very kindly received, asked for all particulars and to give my name and address, and assured that I shall be notified if and when my gas-mask appears.

Felicity points out that loss of National Registration Card is much more serious and will necessitate a personal application to Caxton Hall, and even then I shall only get a temporary one issued. Can I remember when I saw mine last?

On my bed, with my gas-mask.

It couldn't have been, says Felicity, because caretaker says there's nothing there except a handkerchief and the laundry.

Then it must have got underneath the laundry.

Neither of us really believes this consoling theory, but it serves to buoy me up till I get home and find—exactly as I really expected—that nothing is underneath the laundry except the bed.

573

Extensive search follows and I find myself hunting madly in quite impossible spots, such as small enamelled box on mantelpiece, and biscuit-tin which to my certain knowledge has never contained anything except biscuits.

Serena walks in whilst this is going on and expresses great dismay and commiseration, and offers to go at once to the underworld where she feels certain I must have left both gas-mask and National Registration Card.

Tell her that I never took either of them there in my life. It is well known that gas-mask is *not* obligatory within seven minutes' walk of home, and National Registration Card has lived in my bag.

Then have I, asks Serena with air of one inspired, *have* I looked in my bag?

Beg Serena, if she has nothing more helpful than this to suggest, to leave me to my search.

November 14th.—Visit Caxton Hall, and am by no means sure that I ought not to do so in sackcloth with rope round my neck and ashes on my head.

Am not, however, the only delinquent. Elderly man stands beside me at counter where exhausted-looking official receives me, and tells a long story about having left card in pocket of his overcoat at his Club. He then turned his back for the space of five minutes and overcoat was instantly stolen.

Official begs him to fill in a form and warns him that he must pay a shilling for new Registration Card.

Elderly gentleman appalls me by replying that he cannot possibly do that. He hasn't got a shilling.

Official, unmoved, says he needn't pay it *yet*. It will do when he actually receives the new card. It will perhaps then, he adds kindly, be more convenient.

The only reply of elderly gentleman is to tell the story of his loss all over again—overcoat, card in pocket, Club, and theft during the five minutes in which his back was turned. Official listens with patience, although no enthusiasm, and I am assailed by ardent desire to enquire *(a)* name of Club, *(b)* how he can afford to pay his subscription to it if he hasn't got a shilling.

Endeavour to make my own story as brief as possible by way of contrast—can this be example of psychological phenomenon frequently referred to by dear Rose as compensating?—but find it difficult to make a good showing when I am obliged to admit that I have no idea either when or where National Registration Card was lost.

Nothing for it, says official, but to fill up a form and pay the sum of one shilling.

I do so; at the same time listen to quavering of very old person in bonnet and veil who succeeds me.

She relates, in very aggrieved tones, that she was paying a visit in Scotland when National Registration took place and her host and hostess registered her without her knowledge or permission. This resulted in her being issued with a ration book. She does not wish for a ration book. She didn't ask for one, and won't have one.

Should like to hear much more of this, but official removes completed form, issues me with receipt for my shilling and informs me that I shall be communicated with in due course.

Can see no possible excuse for lingering and am obliged to leave Caxton Hall without learning what can be done for aged complainant. Reflect as I go upon extraordinary tolerance of British bureaucrats in general and recall everything I have heard or read as to their counterparts in Germany. This very nearly results in my being run over by bus in Victoria Street, and I am retrieved into safety by passer-by on the pavement, who reveals himself as Humphrey Holloway looking entirely unfamiliar in London clothes.

Look at him in idiotic astonishment, but eventually pull myself together and say that I'm delighted to meet him, and is he up here for long?

No, he doesn't think so. He has come up in order to find Something to Do as his services as Billeting Officer are now at an end.

Do not like to tell him how extremely slender I consider his chances of succeeding in this quest. Instead, I ask for news of Devonshire.

H. H. tells me that he saw Robert at church on Sunday and that he seemed all right.

Was Aunt Blanche there as well?

Yes, she was all right too.

And Marigold and Margery?

Both seemed to be quite all right.

Am rather discouraged by these laconic announcements and try to lure H. H. into details Did Robert say anything about his A.R.P. work?

He said that the woman who is helping him—H. H. can't remember her name—is a damned nuisance. Also that there's a village that hasn't got its gas-masks yet, but Robert thinks it will really have them before Christmas, with luck.

Not Mandeville Fitzwarren? I say, appalled.

H. H. thinks that was the name.

Can only reply that I hope the enemy won't find out about this before Christmas comes.

And what about Our Vicar and his wife and their evacuees?

They are, replies H. H., settling down very nicely. At least the evacuees are. Our Vicar's Wife thought to be over-working, and looks very pale. She always seems, adds H. H., to be here, there and everywhere. Parents of the evacuees all came down to see them the other day, and this necessitated fresh exertions from Our Vicar's Wife, but was said to have been successful on the whole.

Lady B. still has no patients to justify either Red Cross uniform or permanently-installed ambulance, and Miss Pankerton has organised a Keep Fit class in village every other evening, which is, says H. H. in tone of surprise, being well attended. He thinks that Aunt Blanche is one of the most regular members, together with Marigold and Margery. Do not inform him in return that Aunt Blanche has already told me by letter that Marigold, Margery and Doreen Fitzgerald attend classes but has made no mention of her own activities.

H. H. then enquires very civilly if the Ministry of Information keeps me very busy and I am obliged, in common honesty, to reply that it doesn't. Not, at all events, at present. H. H. says Ah, very non-committally, and adds that it's, in many ways, a very extraordinary war.

I agree that it is and we part, but not until I have recklessly suggested that he should come and meet one or two friends for a glass of sherry to-morrow, and he has accepted.

November 16th.—Ask Serena, across Canteen counter, whether she would like to come and help me entertain Humphrey Holloway over a glass of sherry to-morrow evening. She astonishingly replies that drink is the only thing—absolutely the *only* thing—at a time like this, and if I would like to bring him to her flat, where there's more room, she will ask one or two other people and we can provide the sherry between us. Then, I say—in rather stupefied accents—it will be a sherry-party.

Well, says Serena recklessly, why not? If we ask people by telephone at the last minute it won't be like a *real* sherry-party and anyway not many of them will come, because of the black-out. Besides, one of her Refugees is perfectly wonderful with sandwiches, as she once worked in a Legation, and it seems waste not to make the most of this talent.

I suggest that this had better be Serena's party, and that I should be invited as guest, with Humphrey Holloway in attendance, but Serena is firm: it must be a joint party and I am to invite everybody I can think of and tell them that she lives, fortunately, only one minute from a bus-stop. She particularly wishes to have Uncle A. and is certain—so am I—that the blackout will not deter him for a moment.

We can get everything ready to-morrow, when she will be off duty, says Serena—looking wild—and I must take the evening off from the Canteen.

Mrs. Peacock, who has been following the conversation rather wistfully, backs this up—and is instantly pressed by Serena to come too.

Mrs. Peacock would love it—she hasn't been to a party for years and years—at least, not since this war started, which *feels* to her like years and years. Would it be possible for her husband to come too? She doesn't like to trespass on Serena's kindness but she and the husband practically never set eyes on one another nowadays, what with A.R.P. and Red Cross and one thing and another, and she isn't *absolutely* certain of her leg now, and is glad of an arm—(very peculiar wording here, but meaning crystal-clear to an intelligent listener)—and finally, the husband has heard so much about Serena and myself that he is longing to meet us.

Cannot help feeling that much of this eloquence is really superfluous as Serena at once exclaims in enchanted accents that she is only too delighted to think of *anybody* bringing *any* man, as parties are usually nothing but a pack of women. Point out to her later this not at all happily expressed and she agrees, but maintains that it's true.

Later in the evening Serena again approaches me and mutters that, if we count Uncle A. and J. L., she thinks we shall run to half-a-dozen men at the very least.

Tell her in return that I don't see why I shouldn't ask my Literary Agent, and that if she doesn't mind the Weatherbys, Mr. W. will be another man.

Serena agrees to the Weatherbys with enthusiasm—although entirely, I feel, on the grounds of Agrippa's masculinity.

Remain on duty till 12.30, and have brief passage of arms with Red Cross nurse who complains that I have *not* given her two-pennyworth of marmalade. Explain that the amount of marmalade bestowed upon her in return for her twopence is decided by a higher authority than my own, then think this sounds ecclesiastical and slightly profane and add that I only mean the head cook, at which the Red Cross nurse looks astounded and simply reiterates that two-pennyworth of marmalade should reach to the *rim* of the jar, and not just below it. Can see by her expression that she means to contest the point from now until the Day of Judgment if necessary, and that I shall save much wear and tear by yielding at once. Do so, and feel that I am wholly lacking in strength of mind—but not the first time that this has been borne in on me, and cannot permit it to overshadow evening's activities.

Mock air-raid takes place at midnight, just as I am preparing to leave, and I decide to stay on and witness it, which I do, and am privileged to see Commandant racing up and down, smoking like a volcano, and directing all operations with great efficiency but, as usual, extreme high-handedness.

Stand at entrance to the underworld, with very heavy coat on over trousers and overall, and embark on abstract speculation as to women's fitness or otherwise for positions of authority and think how much better I myself should cope with it than the majority, combining common sense with civility, and have just got to rather impressive quotation—*Suaviter in modo fortiter in re*—when ambulance-man roars at me to Move out of the way or I shall get run over, and stretcher-bearing party at the same moment urges me to Keep that Gangway clear for Gawd's sake.

I go home shortly afterwards.

Gas-mask still missing, have only got temporary Registration Card, and find I have neglected to get new battery for electric torch.

Go to bed to the reflection that if Hitler should select to-night for long-awaited major attack on London by air, my chances of survival are not good. Decide that in the circumstances I shall feel justified in awaiting the end in comparative comfort of my bed.

November 17th.—Last night *not* selected by Hitler.

Serena appears at what seems to me like dawn and discusses proposed party for to-night with enthusiasm. She is going home to get some sleep and talk to Refugee sandwich-expert, and get out the sherry. Will I collect flowers, cigarettes and more sherry, and lend her all the ash-trays I have?

Agree to everything and point out that we must also expend some time in inviting guests, which Serena admits she has forgotten. Shall she, she asks madly, ring some of them up at once?

No, eight o'clock in the morning not at all a good time, and I propose to take her out for some breakfast instead. Lyons' coffee much better than mine. (Serena agrees to this more heartily than I think necessary.)

Proceed to Lyons and am a good deal struck by extraordinary colour of Serena's face, reminding me of nothing so much as the sea at Brighton. Implore her to spend the morning in sleep and leave all preparations to me, and once again suggest that she might employ her time to more purpose than in sitting about in the underworld, where she is wrecking her health and at present doing nothing particularly useful.

Serena only says that the war has got to be won *somehow,* by someone.

Can think of several answers but make none of them, as Serena, for twopence, would have hysterics in the Strand.

We separate after breakfast and I make a great number of telephone calls, on behalf of myself and Serena, inviting our friends and acquaintances to drink sherry—not a party—and eat sandwiches—Refugee, ex-Legation, a genius with sandwiches—in Hampstead—flat one minute's walk from bus-stop.

Humphrey Holloway accepts change of *locale* without a murmur, Rose declares that she will be delighted to come—she has, ha-ha-ha, nothing whatever to do and sees no prospect of getting anything.

The Weatherbys also thank me, thank Serena, whom they don't yet know, and will turn up if Mr. W. can possibly leave his office in time. He hopes to be able to—believes that he will—but after all, anything may happen, at any moment, anywhere—and if it does, I shall of course understand that he will be Tied. Absolutely Tied.

Reply that I do, and refuse to dwell on foolish and flippant fancy of Agrippa, fastened up by stout cords, dealing with national emergency from his office desk.

Ring up Uncle A's flat, answered by Mrs. Mouse, and request her to take a message to Uncle A. which I give her in full, and beg her to ascertain reply whilst I hold on. Within about two seconds Uncle A. has arrived at the telephone in person and embarked on long and sprightly conversation in the course of which he assures me that nothing could give him greater pleasure than to accept my young friend's very civil invitation, and I am to present his compliments and assure her that he will not fail to put in an appearance. Frail attempt to give Uncle A. precise instructions as to how he is to find the scene of the entertainment in the blackout proves a failure, as he simply tells me that he will be able to manage very well indeed between the public conveyance (bus from Kensington High Street?) and Shanks' mare.

He further adds recommendation to me to be very careful, as the streets nowadays are—no doubt properly—uncommonly dark, and says that he looks forward to meeting me and my young friend. Affairs in Germany, in Uncle A.'s opinion, are rapidly approaching a crisis and that unhappy fellow is in what is vulgarly known—(though surely only to Uncle A.?)—as The Mulligatawny. Express my gratification in words that I hope are suitable, and Uncle A. rings off.

Later in the morning case arrives—which I have great difficulty in opening, owing to absence of any tools except small hammer, and have to ask if caretaker's husband will very kindly Step Up—and proves to contain half-dozen bottles of sherry with affectionately-inscribed card from Uncle A.

Am deeply touched and ring up again, but Mrs. M. replies that Uncle A. has gone out for his walk and announced his intentions of lunching at the Club and playing Bridge afterwards.

Lady Blowfield, also invited, is grateful, but dejected as ever and feels quite unequal to Society at present. Assure her that this *isn't* Society, or anything in the least like it, but she remains unconvinced and only repeats that, what with one thing and another, neither she nor Archie can bear the thought of being anywhere but at home just now, waiting for whatever Fate may send. (Implication here that Fate is preparing something that will be unpleasant at best, and fatal at worst. Probably bombs.)

Assure Lady Blowfield untruthfully that I know exactly what she means, but am very sorry not to be seeing her and, naturally, Sir Archibald. *How* kind I am, returns Lady Blowfield—voice indicates that she is evidently nearly in tears—she can only hope that in happier times, if such are one day vouchsafed to this disordered world, we may achieve another meeting.

Tell her that I hope so too, and am rather shocked at hearing myself adopt most aggressively cheerful accents. Cannot suppose that these will really encourage Lady Blowfield to brighter frame of mind, but rather the contrary.

Final invitation is to Literary Agent, who much regrets that he is already engaged and would like to know how my new novel is getting on.

Well, it isn't very far on *yet,* I reply—as though another week would see it half-way to completion at least.

No? repeats Literary Agent, in tone of distressed surprise. Still, no doubt I realise that now—if ever—is the time when books are going to be *read,* and of course, whilst there are so few places of entertainment open, and people go out so little in the evenings, they will really be almost *forced* to take to books.

Am left wondering how many more people are going to dangle this encouraging reflection before me, and why they should suppose it to be a source of inspiration.

577

Review my wardrobe and can see nothing I should wish to wear for sherry-party. Decide that my Blue is less unbearable than my Black, but that both are out-of-date, unbecoming and in need of pressing, and that I shall wear no hat at all as none of mine are endurable and can never now afford to buy others. Ring at the bell interrupts very gloomy train of thought—Lady Blowfield outdone—and am startled at seeing familiar, but for an instant unrecognisable, figure at the door. Turns out to be old school-friend Cissie Crabbe, now presenting martial, and yet at the same time rather bulging, figure in khaki uniform.

Cissie assures me that she couldn't pass the door without looking in on me, but that she hasn't a moment to call her own, and that she expects to be sent Behind the Line any time now. Can only congratulate her, and say that I wish I was making myself equally useful. Suggestion from Cissie that I can sign on for four years or the duration, if I like, is allowed to pass unheeded.

Enquire what she has done with her cats, which are the only items I can ever remember in her life, and Cissie says that one Dear old Pussy passed away just after Munich—as though he knew—another one has been evacuated to the Isle of Wight, which Cissie feels to be far safer than Norwich for her—and the third one, a very, very individual temperament indeed and could never have survived for even a day if separated from Cissie—had to be Put to Sleep.

Consecrate a moment of reverent silence to this announcement, and then Cissie says that she can't possibly stop, but she felt she had to get a glimpse of me, she never forgets dear old days in the Fifth Form and do I remember reciting "The Assyrian Came Down like a Wolf on the Fold" and breaking down in the third verse?

No, I don't, but feel it would be unsympathetic to say so crudely, and merely reply that we've all *changed* a good deal since then, with which contribution to original contemporary thought we exchange farewells.

Watch Cissie walking at unnaturally smart pace towards the Strand and decide once and for all that women, especially when over forty, do not look their best in uniform.

Remainder of the morning goes in the purchase of cigarettes—very expensive—and flowers—so cheap that I ask for explanation and shopman informs me gloomily that nobody is buying them at all and he would be glad to *give* away carnations, roses and gardenias. He does not, however, offer to do so, and I content myself with chrysanthemums and anemones, for which I pay.

Pause in front of alluring window of small dress-shop has perfectly fatal result, as I am completely carried away by navy-blue siren suit, with zip fastener—persuade myself that it is not only practical, warm and inexpensive—which it is—but indispensable as well, and go straight in and buy it for Serena's party.

Cannot regret this outburst when I put it on again before the glass in flat, and find the result becoming. Moreover, telephone call from Serena ensues later, for the express purpose of asking *(a)* How many men have I raked up? she's only got four, and five women not counting ourselves and the Refugees, and *(b)* What do I mean to Wear?

On hearing of siren-suit she shrieks and says she's got one *too,* and it was meant to surprise me, and we shall both look too marvellous.

Hope she may be right.

Do the best I can with my appearance, but am obliged to rely on final half-hour before Serena's mirror as I start early for Hampstead, heavily laden with flowers and cigarettes. Am half-way to Charing Cross before I remember Uncle A.'s case of sherry, when nothing is left for it but to take a taxi, go back and collect case, and start out all over again. Appearance by now much disordered but am delighted at having excellent excuse for taxi, and only regret that no such consideration will obtain on return journey.

Youngest and most elegant of Serena's Refugees opens the door to me—she is now disguised in charming pink check, frills and pleated apron, exactly like stage soubrette, and equally well made-up—we shake hands and she says Please!—takes all the packages from me, and when I thank her says Please! again—case of sherry is deposited by taxi-driver, to whom soubrette repeats Please, please! with very engaging smiles—and she then shows me into Serena's sitting-room, on the threshold of which we finally exchange Thank you and Please!

Serena is clad in claret-coloured siren-suit and delighted with herself—quite justifiably—and we compliment one another.

Strenuous half-hour follows, in the course of which Serena moves small bowl of anemones from window-sill to bookcase and back again not less than five several times.

Sherry is decanted—Serena has difficulties with corkscrew and begs soubrette to fetch her the scissors, but soubrette rightly declines, and takes corkscrew and all the bottles away, and presently returns two of them, uncorked, and says that her grandfather will open the others as required.

Is the oldest Refugee her grandfather, I enquire.

Serena—looks rather worried—says that they all seem to be related but she doesn't quite know how, anyway it's perfectly all *right*.

Accept this without hesitation and presently Serena's Refugees come in more or less *en bloc* and we all shake hands, Serena pours out sherry and we drink one another's healths, and glasses are then rushed away by the soubrette, washed and returned.

Serena puts on Six O'clock News—nothing sensational has transpired and we assure one another that, what with one thing and another, the Hitler régime is on the verge of a smash, but, says Serena in tones of preternatural wisdom, we must beware at all costs of wishful thinking. The German Reich *will* collapse, but not immediately, and anything may happen meanwhile. We have got to be prepared.

Assure her that I am prepared—except for loss of gas-mask, which has not yet been replaced— and that, so far as I know, the whole of the British Empire has been prepared for weeks and weeks, and hasn't had its morale in the least impaired by curious and unprecedented nature of Hitler's War of Nerves.

Serena, rather absent-mindedly, says Rule, Britannia, moves small pink crystal ash-tray from one table to another, and studies the effect with her head on one side.

Diversion is occasioned by the soubrette, who comes in bearing succession of plates with sandwiches, tiny little sausages on sticks, and exotic and unfamiliar looking odds-and-ends at which Serena and I simultaneously shriek with excitement.

Very shortly afterwards Serena's guests begin to arrive—J. L. amongst the earliest, and my opinion of him goes up when I see him in earnest discussion with grandfather-presumptive Refugee, I think about the Nature of Eternity, to which both have evidently given a good deal of thought.

Mrs. Peacock comes, as expected, with Mr. Peacock, who is pale and wears pince-nez and is immediately introduced by Serena to pretty A.R.P. worker, Muriel, with whom she thinks he may like to talk about air-raids. They at once begin to discuss Radio-stars Flotsam and Jetsam, and are evidently witty on the subject as both go into fits of laughter.

Party is now going with a swing and second glass of sherry causes me, as usual, to think myself really excellent conversationalist and my neighbours almost equally well worth hearing.

This agreeable frame of mind probably all to the good, as severe shock is inflicted by totally unexpected vision of old Mrs. Winter-Gammon, in rakish-looking toque and small fur cape over bottle-green wool.

Shall never believe that Serena really invited her.

She waves small claw at me from a distance and is presently to be seen perched on arm of large chair—toes unable to touch the floor—in animated conversation with three men at once.

Am much annoyed and only slightly restored when Rose arrives, looking very distinguished as usual, and informs me—quite pale with astonishment—that she thinks she has got a very interesting job, with a reasonable salary attached, at Children's Clinic in the North of England. Congratulate her warmly and introduce Mr. Weatherby, whom I very nearly—but not quite— refer to as Tall Agrippa. Hope this *rapprochement* will prove a success as I hear them shortly afterwards talking about Queen Wilhelmina of Holland, and both sound full of approval.

Uncle A.—more like distinguished diplomat than ever—arrives early and stays late, and assures me that he has little or no difficulty in finding his way about in black-out. He takes optimistic view of international situation, says that it will take probably years to establish satisfactory peace terms but he has no doubt that eventually—say in ten or fifteen years' time—we shall see a very different Europe—free, he trusts and believes, from bloodshed and tyranny. Am glad to see that Uncle A. has every intention of assisting personally at this world-wide regeneration and feel confident that his expectation of doing so will be realised.

He seems much taken with Serena, and they sit in a corner and embark on long *tête-à-tête,* while J. L. and I hand round Serena's refreshments. (J. L. inclined to be rather dejected, and when I refer to Plato—which I do solely with a view to encouraging him—he only says in reply that he has, of late, been reading Tolstoy. In the French translation, of course, he adds. Look him straight in the eye and answer, Of course; but he is evidently not taken in by this for one instant.) Humphrey Holloway—original *raison d'être* for entire gathering—never turns up at all, but telephones to say that he is very sorry he can't manage it.

Am quite unable to feel particularly regretful about this—but find myself wishing several times that Robert could be here, or even Aunt Blanche.

Similar idea, to my great fury, has evidently come over Granny Bo-Peep, and she communicates it to me very shrilly above general noise, which has now reached riotous dimensions.

What a pity that dear, good man of mine isn't here! she cries—she knows very well that I should feel much happier if he were. She can read it in my face. (At this I instinctively do something with my face designed to make it look quite different, and have no doubt that I succeed—but probably at cost of appearance, as Mrs. W.-G. sympathetically enquires whether I bit on a tooth.) And poor dear Blanche! *What* a lot of good it would do dear old Blanche to be taken out of herself, and made to meet people. Mrs. W.-G. doesn't want to say anything about herself—(since when?)—but friends have told her over and over again: Pussy—you *are* the party. Where you are, with your wonderful vitality and your ridiculous trick of making people laugh, and that absurd way you have of getting on with everybody—*there* is the party. How well she remembers her great friend, the late Bishop of London, saying those very words to her—and she at once told him he mustn't talk nonsense. She could say anything she liked to the Bishop—anything. He always declared that she was as good as a glass of champagne.

Think this Episcopal pronouncement quite unsuitable, and have serious thoughts of saying so—but Mrs. W.-G. gives me no time.

She has heard, she says, that dear Blanche's eldest brother is here and wishes to meet him. Is that him over there, talking to Serena?

It is, and can plainly see that if I do not perform introduction instantly, Mrs. W.-G. will do it for herself.

Can only conform to her wishes, and she supplants Serena at Uncle A.'s side.

Serena makes long, hissing speech in an undertone of which I can only make out that she thinks the party is going well, and is her face purple, she *feels* as though it were, and whatever happens I'm not to go.

Had had no thought of going.

Everybody talks about the war, and general opinion is that it can't last long—Rose goes so far as to say Over by February, but J. L. tells her that the whole thing is going to be held up till the spring begins—at which I murmur to myself: Air-raid by air-raid the spring begins, and hopes that nobody hears me—and then, says J. L., although short, it will be appalling. Hitler is a desperate man, and will launch a fearful attack in every direction at once. His main objective will be London.

J. L. states this so authoritatively that general impression prevails that he has received his information direct from Berlin, and must know what he is talking about.

Mrs. Weatherby alone rallies very slightly and points out that an air-raid over London would be followed instantly by reprisals, and she doubts whether the morale of the German people would survive it. She believes them to be on the brink of revolution already, and the Czechs and the Austrians are actually *over* the brink.

She adds that she wouldn't break up the party for anything—none of us are to stir—but she must go.

She does go, and we all do stir, and party is broken up—but can quite feel that it has been a success.

Serena, the Refugees and I, see everybody off into depths of blackness unlit by single gleam of light anywhere at all, and Serena says they'll be lucky if they don't all end up with broken legs, and if they do, heaven knows where they'll go as no patients allowed in any of the Hospitals.

One of her Refugees informs her, surprisingly, that the blackout is nothing—nothing at all. Vienna has always been as dark as this, every night, for years—darker, if anything.

Serena and I and the Refugees finish such sandwiches as are left, she presses cigarettes on them and in return they carry away all the plates and glasses and insist that they will wash them and put them away—please—and Serena and I are not to do anything but rest ourselves—please, please.

Thank you, thank you.

Please.

November 21st.—Am startled as never before on receiving notification that my services as a writer are required, and may even take me abroad.

Am unable to judge whether activities will permit of my continuing a diary but prefer to suppose that they will be of too important a nature.

Ask myself whether war, as term has hitherto been understood, can be going to begin at last. Reply, of sorts, supplied by Sir Auckland Geddes over the wireless.

Sir A. G. finds himself obliged to condemn the now general practice of running out into the street in order to view aircraft activities when engaged with the enemy overhead.

Can only hope that Hitler may come to hear of this remarkable reaction to his efforts, on the part of the British.

Printed in Great Britain
by Amazon.co.uk, Ltd.,
Marston Gate.